THE REAL ALE PUB GUIDE

2010

Edited by Nicolas Andrews
with the Real Ale Research Team

foulsham

LONDON • NEW YORK • TORONTO • SYDNEY

foulsham

The Oriel, Thames Valley Court, 183–187 Bath Road, Slough,
Berkshire SL1 4AA, England

Foulsham books can be found in all good bookshops and direct from
www.foulsham.com

ISBN: 978-0-572-03525-9

Copyright © 2010 W. Foulsham & Co. Ltd

Back cover photograph: The Royal Standard, Wooburn Common, Bucks

A CIP record for this book is available from the British Library

Printed in Great Britain by J F Print Ltd, Sparkford, Somerset

CONTENTS

CONTENTS

YOUR 2010 PUB GUIDE

These are truly the best of times, and the worst of times. Over the years I have used this introduction as a chance to accentuate the positive and to celebrate all that is rosy on the real ale scene. I'm a glass half-full kind of guy who would much rather dwell on the many success stories up and down the country. I am, however, writing this in late summer 2009 and, though it may just be possible to detect some green shoots of recovery in the economy at large, the pub and brewing industries have been hit very hard over the past 12 months and, according to many indicators, it seems that things can only get harder.

At least five pubs are currently closing across Britain every day and, if the Beer and Pub Association is to be believed, this will accelerate to account for one in eight, or 12.5 per cent, of the 54,000 establishments still open by 2012. That's about 6,480 more pubs predicted to close their doors to you and to me within the next two or three years. While there are undoubtedly a fair few mediocre street-corner boozers that will not be widely missed, there are also many small towns and villages up and down the land in great danger of losing if not their heart and soul then certainly a focal point, a place that always has and always should play a key part in fostering the community spirit.

Many drinkers, myself included, applauded the introduction of the smoking ban. The absence of smoke-filled rooms and nicotine-stained wallpaper greatly enhances my pub-going experience. But inevitably it has made the pub less attractive to some and, overall, has done the hard-pressed landlord few favours. Not nearly as few as the level of tax and excise duty now being applied to each pint, however.

The average price of a pint of real ale increased by 12p at the last budget and there are plans for more price rises. In many parts of the country the £3 pint is now commonplace. As a result of the rise in VAT set for January 1, the Campaign for Real Ale predicts that beer price inflation could well exceed 10 per cent during 2010 and that, by the 2012 Olympics, the £5 pint will not be unknown.

With increased competition from supermarkets and falling beer sales generally, landlords and licensees have little option but to pass on the increased prices that they are being forced to pay. But this is a vicious circle. The higher the price they charge, the greater the number of drinkers who will decide that they just cannot justify a couple of swift ones down the pub. So, inevitably, more pubs will close and then more consumers as well as more industry workers will suffer.

How, though, do we square all this doom and gloom with other figures that point to a booming real ale industry? For, truly, in many ways the cask-conditioned ale lover has never had it so good. Every year I highlight the number of new microbreweries that have opened. Even as pubs are shutting at a record rate, new craft brewers are taking up their malt shovels as never before.

More than 200 have risen to the challenge over the past four years and there could well be 700 British breweries producing real ale by the start of 2010, twice as many as when Camra was set up in the early 1970s and more than at any time since the Second World War. At the same time, Camra membership has passed the 100,000 mark. Its research also suggests that women are drinking real ale in record numbers and that, while overall beer sales are undoubtedly declining, sales of real ale are actually up 10 per cent year on year. Fewer pubs, more drinkers staying at home and yet more real ale being drunk?

The explanation is a victory for quality over quantity. Real ale, often produced locally by real brewers passionate about a real, living product, is being drunk as never before in pubs where the landlord or licensee really knows how to care for and serve the result. It is real ale, as opposed to mass-produced keg beer or imported lager, that can and will keep the British pub alive.

And that is where we come in. There is obviously still a huge potential market for good beer to be drunk in good places, which is why you have bought this book. We are grateful for your support as we continue our mission to search out and highlight as many of these pubs as possible and we urge you to go that extra mile to visit them.

A few that we have previously championed have closed in the past 12 months and a few more will no doubt have followed them by the time you read this. But there is another more virtuous circle which says that the pubs worth writing about are the ones worth supporting and they will, if we all do so, continue to survive and flourish.

For almost 40 years the real ale cause has made impressive progress. There is a danger that all the good work could be undone if the affordable pint becomes a thing of the past. But if enough of us keep campaigning, and we all keep drinking in and supporting the many wonderful real ale pubs of Britain, then they will remain a source of pleasure for millions of people for many years to come.

Use the questionnaire at the back of the book to tell us about your recommendations and updates and send it to us, or simply send an e-mail to realale@foulsham.com.

WHAT IS REAL ALE?

Real ale is different from other beers because, when it is put into a bottle or cask, the yeast present is still alive and the fermentation process continues all the way until it is poured into a glass. That bottle or cask conditioning makes it a fresher, more natural and more interesting drink.

It was the Romans who brought beer to Britain, though it probably had its origins in Mesopotamia perhaps 10,000 years ago. The first brewer probably stumbled across the secret by accident, perhaps as a result of airborne wild yeast infecting food, but from there it spread to Greece, Egypt and eventually to Rome.

Beer and brewing continued to thrive in Britain long after the Romans had gone, and more than 40 breweries were listed in the Domesday Book of 1086. Hops, which impart flavour and aroma, and act as a preservative, were introduced from Scandinavia in the middle of the tenth century, but they were not widely used until the fifteenth century, when they were grown here, primarily in Kent.

Many of the early brewers were monks, and it was in monasteries that brewing techniques were improved and refined, particularly with the introduction of better varieties of barley. During the Reformation, however, and Henry VIII's break with Rome, the monasteries were shut down and the noble art passed into the hands of farmers and owners of estates, who installed private brewhouses to supply beer for farm workers and staff.

Commercial breweries began to appear during the latter part of the sixteenth century, growing steadily in number until, by the 1870s, 30,000 were registered in Britain. This was a golden age, with beer drinking per head of the population at its all-time peak.

One hundred years ago, a brewery was to be found serving almost every local community, but as the market became increasingly competitive and preservation techniques and transport improved, the vast majority went out of business, were bought up or simply faded away. Only about 40 of the independent breweries that were in operation at the turn of the last century still brew today. Of these, Shepherd Neame Ltd at Faversham in Kent is believed to be the oldest.

Britain's oldest surviving brewpub is believed to be the Blue Anchor at Helston in Cornwall. It first became a pub around the middle of the sixteenth century, although it seems certain that monks were already brewing beer on the premises long before then.

The title of the oldest pub in Britain is disputed, but it probably belongs to the Trip to Jerusalem in Nottingham, part of which is cut into the rock of the castle and dates from 1189.

HOW TO USE THIS BOOK

The Real Ale Pub Guide is a celebration of the art of brewing in Britain. Our concern is not with the mass-produced market leaders but with the smaller, independent makers of what we consider to be the real, real ales. For this reason, we do not tell you about the multi national brewers and their products, good or bad. Nor do we tell you about the pubs whose reputation owes more to their location, their cooking or their range of malt whiskies, although we may mention this in passing. This is a book about beer aimed squarely at those who love drinking it, who want to know more about it and who want to know where to find it at its best.

The entries are arranged alphabetically by county, taking into account the boundary changes that came into force in England in 1996. Unitary authorities have been placed in their most logical county. For some border towns and villages, the postal address is in one county while the actual pub is over the boundary. We have tried to place all the entries in the counties to which they actually belong, but be prepared for some county-hopping along borders.

Each county contains details first of the breweries (including brewpubs and micro-breweries linked or attached to pubs) within it and then of the pubs themselves, organised alphabetically by town or village. We list as many beers brewed as possible but an increasing number of occasional, seasonal and celebration ales make this an inexact science. You may find a beer not listed here – well, rejoice at the diversity!

We have attempted to give as full an address as possible for pubs and a telephone number in almost every case. An increasing number have websites, although these may not be too rigorously maintained. Brief directions may also be found within the entry itself but, if you do get lost, a call ahead should keep the inconvenience to a minimum.

London is treated slightly differently from the rest of the book. There are more pubs in the capital than anywhere else in the country and a large number of them sell real ale, albeit of varying quality. There are also many pub chains and tied houses owned by the region's brewers, many of which are hard to separate. With this in mind, full entries in London are only given to pubs that we feel offer a selection of good quality, interesting beers. Chains and tied houses are still listed at the end of each postal area and these are well worth a look, too.

Our primary aim is to make this guide as useful as possible to people looking for a place to drink good real ale. The criterion for an entry, therefore, is that a selection of real ales is always available, whether the pub is a freehouse, a tied house or belongs to a chain.

Where possible, we have sought to include the licensee's name for we believe that the character and quality of a pub owes much to the person who runs it.

Because we believe the beers are the most important thing, we have sought to give an indication of the names and numbers of ales that you are likely to find when you walk through the door. Of course, availability varies and, on some days, the choice will be wider than on others. Nevertheless, a pub that says it has 12 beers on tap should come reasonably close to doing just that. If you discover this is not the case, then we want to know.

There is a short description of the type of pub to be found with each entry. If they specialise in a certain type of food, or have accommodation or other features, we have sought to tell you. However, as this is not the purpose of our guide, we have kept the details to a minimum.

Opening hours are another feature that will vary. An increasing number of pubs are opening for longer and later than was the case just a few years ago. The relaxation of the laws in 2005 means that some pubs now open even later than advertised, particularly at weekends.

It would be impossible to include an entry for every real ale pub in the country. Similarly, there are many pubs about which we have heard favourable reports but which we have so far been unable to verify for ourselves. Perhaps, if you get there first, you can let us know what you find by returning one of the questionnaires at the back of the book. If you find a pub that does not live up to your expectations or you know of an absent pub that should be included, we would love to hear from you. Please send us your completed questionnaire to the address provided, or e-mail **realale@ foulsham.com** with your comments. Many thanks.

Nicolas Andrews

TWELVE OF THE BEST

While we sincerely hope that every pub featured in this guide will satisfy those who go looking for something a little bit special in their pint glass. We also recognise that taste is a personal thing and so seek to celebrate the diversity of beers produced by the nation's independent regional and micro-brewers. Some pubs, though, are extra special: centres of real ale excellence about which we might all agree.

In 2004 we introduced a section highlighting a dozen pubs that we believe are well worth travelling that extra mile to visit. We have tried to spread our selection around Britain and we know that there are many other equally deserving candidates. Next year, we will highlight 12 more. Each of the pubs chosen is marked in the book with a star. We should be delighted to hear your views and your nominations for 2010 but, in the meantime (and in no particular order), we give you *The Real Ale Pub Guide* Twelve of the Best 2010.

Punch Bowl Inn, Crosthwaite, Cumbria
Award winning Lake District hotel and restaurant that thankfully appreciates the importance of its real ale too. Up to four beers come from Barngates brewery in Ambleside. See page 80.

Black Horse, Amberley, Gloucestershire
Worth an entry for its village setting and spectacular views. Then add the five real ales, a couple of them from the local Stroud brewery. This pub has had its up and downs in recent years but is thriving again. See page 154.

Rose and Crown, Halstead, Kent
Welcoming, unpretentious, the quintessential village freehouse serving local Kentish ales and many more plus a popular Sunday roast. See page 224.

The Rake, Borough Market, London SE1
Very small pub with a big (very big) appetite for interesting beer. Two or three ever-changing real ales on tap plus dozens more from all corners of the globe in bottles. See page 288.

The Talbot, Knightwick, Worcestershire
Set alongside the river Teme and home to the Teme Valley Brewery, which produces beer using hops grown on the farm next door. Good locally-sourced food and comfortable accommodation. See page 508.

Kelham Island Tavern, Sheffield, Yorkshire
This pub has won so many awards recently that it really ought to have one from us as well. At least nine constantly-rotating real ales always available, many of which come from local microbreweries. See page 543.

Stein Inn, Skye, Scotland
Is there a better pub view anywhere in Britain? And with tip-top local ales and guests to enjoy while you appreciate it. Plus good food and accommodation. Best of all you can arrive by yacht. See page 569.

The Crown Inn, Stockport, Greater Manchester
Pre-Victorian freehouse located under the railway viaduct and a recent finalist in the CAMRA national pub of the year competition. Sixteen handpumps, with beers changing daily. See page 320.

The Ship Inn, Low Newton, Northumberland
Seaside inn owned by the National Trust and run by a mother and daughter team who produce their own beer in a microbrewery on the premises. Popular with coastal walkers. See page 360.

Goose and Cuckoo, Upper Llanover, Gwent, Wales
Charming, isolated country freehouse with four rotating, well kept and keenly priced real ales. Meet ducks, geese and goats as well as walkers and cyclists. See page 600.

The Crown at Pantygelli, Pantygelli, Gwent, Wales
Two Welsh entries for the first time this year. Located on the old Hereford road just outside Abergavenny with excellent ales from the Wye Valley Brewery. Good food as well. See page 599.

And finally,

The Isles of Scilly
This year's award for the best 'town' goes to a group of islands 28 miles off Cornwall. Fine real ales are available on all five inhabited islands, which is in itself no small achievement. The local Ales of Scilly brewery supplies many of them with others from the Cornish mainland and The Turk's Head on St Agnes stands out as one of the very finest pubs anywhere in the South West. See pages 212–213.

Eyemouth

M8 LOTHIAN

Penicuik
Peebles· ·Galashiels
Duns
Berwick upon Tweed
·Kelso
BORDERS ·Jedburgh
Alnwick
·Moffat Hawick

LLOWAY
Langholm
NORTHUMBERLAND
Anann
lbeattie ·Carlisle Newcastle upon Tyne

·Maryport
M6
TYNE & WEAR ·
Sunderland
DURHAM Durham ·Hartlepool
haven CUMBRIA ·Appleby A1(M) ·Middlesborough
CLEVELAND ·Whitby
Windermere · ·Kendal
Richmond ·Northallerton
NORTH YORKSHIRE ·Scarborough

Morecambe· M6 Malton· ·Bridlington
Lancaster
LANCASHIRE Harrogate· York· HUMBERSIDE ·Hornsea
Blackpool· Burnley Bradford Leeds Selby
Preston· Halifax WEST M62 ·Withernsea
Southport· M6 YORKSHIRE M62
GREATER M6 M1 Barnsley ·Scunthorpe ·Grimsby
MERSEYSIDE MANCHESTER SOUTH M18 M180
Liverpool· Manchester YORKSHIRE ·Rotherham ·Gainsborough ·Mablethorpe
olwyn Bay M53 M56 Sheffield
bigh· Flint CHESHIRE Lincoln Horncastle
WYD Wrexham· Chester M6 DERBY NOTTINGHAM LINCOLN
Crewe Stoke Nottingham Sleaford Boston· Skegness
·Bala Llangollen on Trent Derby M1 ·Grantham ·Hunstanton
Llanfyllin STAFFORD
llau Telford M6 Tamworth Spalding NORFO
SHROPSHIRE WEST LEICESTER King's Lynn Swaffha
Newtown Wolverhampton· MIDLANDS Leicester ·Peterborough
·Llanidloes M69 ·
POWYS Birmingham M6 Coventry Corby CAMBRIDGE Ely Bury
Knighton ·Ludlow ·Rugby Newmarket St Edmunds SUFFO
Kington HEREFORD Warwick ·Northampton Cambridge
Hereford· & Worcester NORTHAMPTON ·Bedford
Brecon WORCESTER WARWICK Milton. BEDFORD ·Letchworth Braintree
Ross on Wye· M50 ·Tewkesbury Banbury Keynes M11
Monmouth· ·Gloucester BUCKINGHAMSHIRE HERTFORD ESSEX
MID GLOUCESTER Oxford Aylesbury M1 ·Chelmsfor
GLAMORGAN GWENT Stroud A1
·Newport AVON OXFORDSHIRE M25 Watford ·Epping Southend on S
OUTH ·Cardiff Swindon Henley M40 GREATER M25
MORGAN ·Bristol BERKSHIRE Windsor LONDON ·Dartford
M5 M4 Reading M4 Wimbledon M20
inehead ·Weston Chippenham Newbury M3 SURREY Sevenoaks M26 Canterb
Super Mare WILTSHIRE Basingstoke Guildford M23 KENT
Warminster HAMPSHIRE ·East Grinstead M2
SOMERSET Winchester WEST EAST
SUSSEX

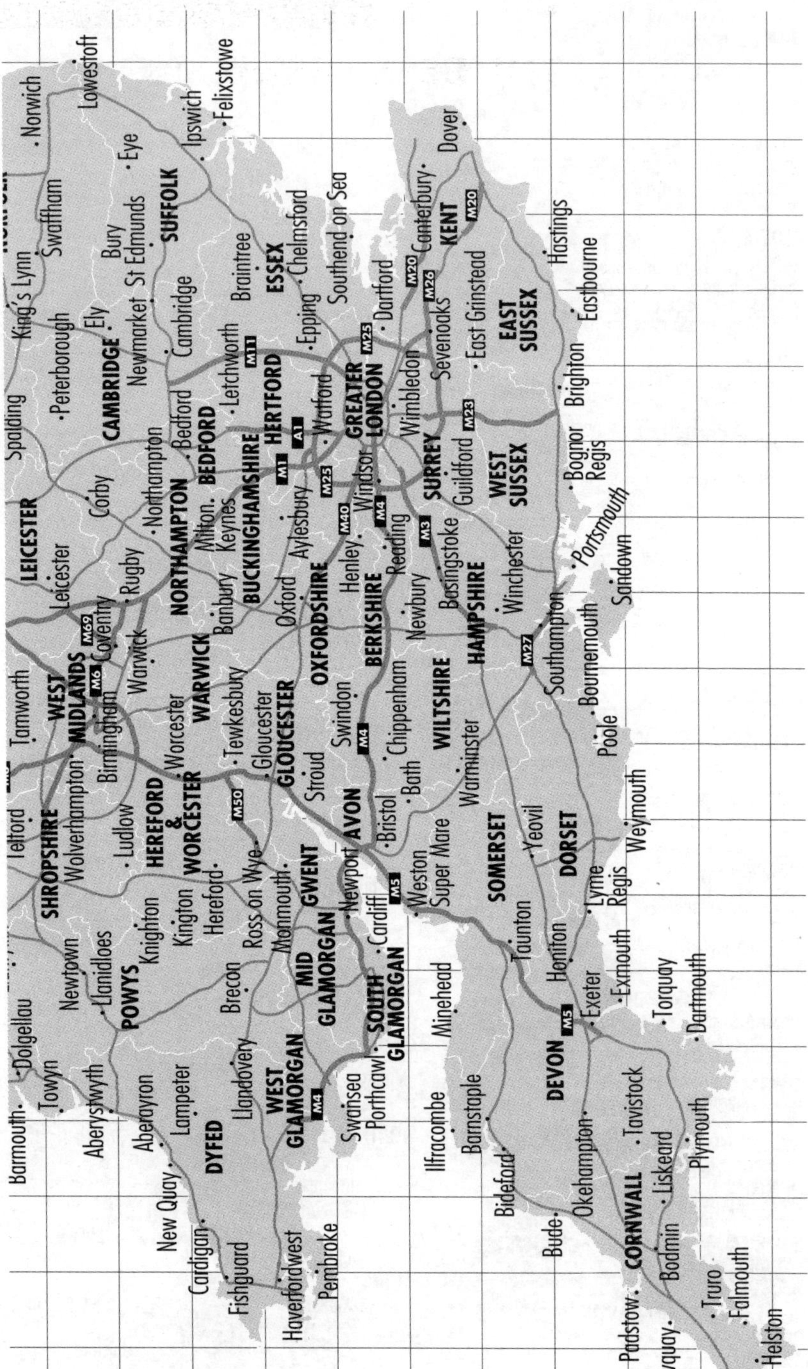
Norwich
Lowestoft
Felixstowe
Ipswich
Eye
SUFFOLK
Swaffham
King's Lynn
Bury St Edmunds
Newmarket
Ely
Cambridge
Braintree
ESSEX
Chelmsford
Southend on Sea
Epping
Dover
Canterbury
KENT
M20
Dartford
M26
Sevenoaks
East Grinstead
Hastings
Eastbourne
EAST SUSSEX
Brighton
Peterborough
CAMBRIDGE
Spalding
Letchworth
M11
Watford
HERTFORD
A1
GREATER LONDON
M25
Wimbledon
M23
Bognor Regis
WEST SUSSEX
Guildford
SURREY
Windsor
M1
Bedford
BEDFORD
Northampton
Corby
LEICESTER
Leicester
Rugby
NORTHAMPTON
Milton Keynes
BUCKINGHAMSHIRE
Aylesbury
M40
Henley
Reading
M4
M3
Basingstoke
Winchester
Portsmouth
Sandown
Southampton
M27
HAMPSHIRE
Newbury
BERKSHIRE
Oxford
OXFORDSHIRE
Banbury
Coventry
M69
Warwick
WARWICK
WEST MIDLANDS
M6
Tamworth
Birmingham
Wolverhampton
Telford
SHROPSHIRE
Worcester
Tewkesbury
Gloucester
GLOUCESTER
Swindon
Chippenham
WILTSHIRE
Warminster
Bournemouth
Poole
Weymouth
DORSET
Yeovil
SOMERSET
Stroud
Bath
Bristol
AVON
Weston Super Mare
M5
Lyme Regis
M50
HEREFORD & WORCESTER
Ludlow
Hereford
Ross on Wye
Monmouth
GWENT
Newport
Cardiff
SOUTH GLAMORGAN
MID GLAMORGAN
Kington
Knighton
Llanidloes
Newtown
POWYS
Brecon
Taunton
Honiton
Exeter
Exmouth
Torquay
Dartmouth
Minehead
DEVON
Dolgellau
Towyn
Barmouth
Aberystwyth
Aberayron
Lampeter
Llandovery
WEST GLAMORGAN
Swansea
Porthcawl
Ilfracombe
Barnstaple
Tavistock
Okehampton
Plymouth
Liskeard
DYFED
New Quay
Cardigan
Fishguard
Haverfordwest
Pembroke
Bideford
Bude
CORNWALL
Bodmin
Padstow
Truro
Falmouth
Newquay
Helston
St Ives
Penzance

THE BEER GUIDE

THE BREWERIES

B & T BREWERY LTD
The Brewery, Shefford SG17 5DZ
☎ *(01462) 815080*
www.banksandtaylor.com

TWO BREWERS' BITTER 3.6% ABV
Hoppy, amber beer.
SHEFFORD BITTER 3.8% ABV
Golden and hoppy with dry hop finish.
SHEFFORD DARK MILD 3.8% ABV
Rich, mellow, dry and hoppy. Roast malt taste.
GOALDEN HATTER 4.0% ABV
Pale, hoppy, dry-tasting bitter.
GOLDEN FOX 4.1% ABV
Pearl pale malt, golden beer with fruity overtones.
BLACK DRAGON MILD 4.3% ABV
Strong dark mild with pronounced roast flavour.
DRAGONSLAYER 4.5% ABV
Light-coloured, with subtle malt and hops.
EDWIN TAYLOR'S EXTRA STOUT 4.5% ABV
Strong roast malt flavour.
SHEFFORD PALE ALE 4.5% ABV
Hoppy with balancing malt and dry finish.
SHEFFORD OLD DARK 5.0% ABV
Deep red, sweet caramel and malt flavour.
SHEFFORD OLD STRONG 5.0% ABV
Hoppy with bitter malty flavour.
Plus monthly specials and celebratory brews.

POTTON BREWING COMPANY
10 Shannon Place, Potton, Sandy SG19 2SP
☎ *(01767) 261042*
www.potton-brewery.co.uk

SHANNON IPA 3.6% ABV
Traditional, hoppy IPA.
JOHN CUNNINGHAM NIGHT FIGHTER 4.0% ABV
Dark, malty bitter with light hop character.
POTTON GOLD 4.1% ABV
Golden colour with floral hop character.
SHAMBLES 4.3% ABV
Hoppy bitterness with balancing sweetness.
THE VILLAGE BIKE 4.3% ABV
Complex hoppy brew.
Plus seasonal and occasional brews.

WELLS AND YOUNG'S BREWING CO. LTD
Havelock Street, Bedford MK40 4LU
☎ *(01234) 279298*
www.wellsandyoungs.co.uk

WELLS EAGLE IPA 3.6% ABV
Balanced, dry, full-flavoured IPA.
YOUNG'S BITTER 3.7% ABV
Golden, light, fruity aroma.
WELLS JOHN BULL BITTER 4.1% ABV
Distinctive hop bitter with citrus overtones.
YOUNG'S SPECIAL PREMIUM ALE 4.5% ABV
Amber-coloured, malty and fruit-flavoured bitter.
YOUNG'S WAGGLE DANCE 5.0% ABV
Balanced, golden coloured.
BOMBARDIER 5.2% ABV
Hoppy, well-balanced with dry finish.
Seasonals including:
SUMMER SOLSTICE 4.1% ABV
Full flavoured, refreshingly malty with distinctive bitterness.
BANANA BREAD BEER 5.2% ABV
Dark, golden and intense with banana flavour.

THE PUBS

ASTWICK

Tudor Oaks Lodge
Taylors Road, Astwick, Nr Hitchin, Hertfordshire SG5 4AZ
☎ *(01462) 834133* Mr EA Welek
www.tudoroakslodge.co.uk

Freehouse serving up to seven real ales from a constantly changing range that features micro-breweries from around the country. Also real cider.

Just over the Bedfordshire border, despite the Hertfordshire postal address. A 15th-century coaching inn with 14 en-suite bedrooms, an oak-beamed bar and restaurant. Set around a central courtyard. Food available 12–2pm and 6.30–10pm. Children allowed, outside seating, large car park. Situated off the A1, one mile north of junction 10.

OPEN *All day, every day.*

BEDFORD

The Castle
17 Newnham Street, Bedford MK40 3JR
☎ *(01234) 353295* Avtar and Joanne Sahota

A Wells and Young's tenancy, with Eagle and Bombardier plus four guests that might include Greene King Old Speckled Hen, Marston's Pedigree, Young's Special, Brains Bitter, St Austell Tribute, Adnams Broadside and Badger Tanglefoot.

Traditional two-bar pub on the edge of the town centre, but with a country pub atmosphere. Food available at lunchtimes and evenings. Garden. Car park. Accommodation available in a cottage behind the pub. Well-behaved children welcome.

OPEN *12–3pm and 5.30–11pm Mon–Thurs and Sun; all day Fri–Sat.*

De Pary's Hotel
45 De Pary's Avenue, Bedford MK40 2UA
☎ *(01234) 352121* Sonia Pollard
www.hotelsinbedford.co.uk

Charles Wells Eagle plus guests such as Fuller's London Pride and something from Potton, Nethergate or Crouch Vale breweries. The selection changes weekly.

A 25-bedroom, privately owned hotel with bar, 100-seater restaurant and function room. Food available at lunchtimes and evenings Mon–Sat, and all day Sun. Large, attractive award-winning garden with children's play area. Beer festivals and family fun days. Situated near the park.

OPEN *11am–11pm (10.30pm Sun).*

The Embankment Hotel

The Embankment, Bedford MK40 3PD
☎ *(01234) 261332* Declan Clancy
www.hotelsinbedford.co.uk

 Freehouse with Charles Wells Eagle and Bombardier plus two guests that change every week.

A 19th-century hotel beside the River Ouse. Twenty en-suite bedrooms and an 80-seater restaurant. Food served 11–2.30pm Mon–Sat and 12–10pm Sun. Car park at rear, children welcome. Tables and chairs outside for riverside drinking. Five minutes from the town centre.

🍺 *11am–11pm (10.30pm Sun).*

The Wellington Arms

40–2 Wellington Street, Bedford MK40 2JX
☎ *(01234) 308033*
Royston Beer and Lesley Griffin
www.wellingtonarms.co.uk

 Award-winning B&T tied house with 14 hand pumps. Two Brewers (the house brew) plus Adnams Bitter and at least nine guests. Always a mild and usually a stout and/or porter. Six Belgian, one German and one Czech beer on draught, as well as perry and Weston's cider, plus over 100 foreign bottled beers.

T raditional one-bar, street-corner local with wooden floors. Regular local and regional CAMRA Pub of the Year including 2008. Large collection of real ale memorabilia, including bottles and pump clips. Filled rolls available at lunchtime (not Sun). Outside drinking area. Small car park. Live music most Tuesdays. No children. Near the prison, on the A6 coming south as it enters the one-way system from the bypass.

🍺 *12–11pm (10.30pm Sun).*

The Brown Bear

29 Hitchin Street, Biggleswade SG18 8BE
☎ *(01767) 316161* David Carter

 At least four hand pumps serving a range that might include Shepherd Neame Spitfire, Timothy Taylor Landlord and Fuller's London Pride.

F ormer freehouse sold by its previous owners to Enterprise Inns and scaling down the real ale emphasis as a result. A two-bar, open-plan town-centre pub with eating area. Bar snacks available at lunchtime and evenings. On the main street, off the market square.

🍺 *12–3pm and 5–11pm Mon–Fri; 11am–11pm Sat; 7–10.30pm Sun (closed lunchtime).*

The Wheatsheaf

5 Lawrence Road, Biggleswade SG18 0LS
☎ *(01767) 222220* Mr R Stimson

A Greene King tied house serving IPA and XX Dark Mild. Cask Marque award winner.

S imple, unspoilt one-bar pub dating from 1873. No food. Pub games, Sky TV plus racing channel and Setanta Sports. Beer garden. Smoking facilities with touch heaters. Cycle park, but no car park. Barbecues on Sundays in summer. Near railway station. From town centre take second left near the library, then first right near ambulance station.

🍺 *11am–4pm and 7–11pm Mon–Thurs; all day Fri–Sun.*

The Plough

Kimbolton Road, Bolnhurst, Bedford MK44 2EX
☎ *(01234) 376274* Mr and Mrs Martin, Jayne Lee and Michael Moscrop

 Freehouse with Bateman XB plus two guests, one from the local Potton brewery changed seasonally and another changed weekly, perhaps Caledonian Deuchars IPA or Adnams Bitter.

A ttractive pub that was built as a farmhouse in 1480. Modern British food using fresh, quality ingredients served lunchtimes Tues–Sat and evenings Tues–Sun. Large garden and car park. Children welcome. On the B660 from Kimbolton to Bedford.

🍺 *12–3pm and 6–11pm (closed Sun evening and all day Mon).*

The Cock

23 High Street, Broom SG18 9NA
☎ *(01767) 314411* Gerry Lant

Greene King tied house serving IPA, Abbot and Ruddles County.

A 300-year-old Grade II listed village pub with real fire and beers served direct from the barrels in the cellar. Food available at lunchtimes and evenings (except Sun evening). Children welcome (family room available). Dogs allowed. Car park. Garden, plus adjacent caravan and campsite. Just off the A1 at Biggleswade roundabout.

🍺 *12–3pm and 6–11pm (10.30pm Sun).*

The White Horse

The Village Green, Broom SG18 9NN
☎ *(01767) 313425* Dean Hankins
www.whitehorsebroom.co.uk

Greene King house serving IPA and Abbot plus two guests, perhaps Adnams Broadside, Charles Wells Bombardier, Everards Tiger or Brains SA.

A 17th-century Grade II listed family-run village pub. Beams and open fires. Food served 12–2pm Mon–Sat and 7–9pm Weds–Sat plus Sunday lunches 1–3pm. Children welcome in the dining room and beer garden. Car parking. Space for 20 caravans at the bottom of the garden.

🍺 *12–3pm every day; 5.30–11pm Mon–Fri, 6–11pm Sat and 7–10.30pm Sun.*

CAMPTON
The White Hart
Mill Lane, Campton, Nr Shefford SG17 5NX
☎ *(01462) 812657* Jerry Cannon

Genuine freehouse with up to six real ales. Theakston Best and Mild and beers from Everards, Fuller's, Bateman and Hook Norton are regulars and rotate weekly.

Grade II listed, 300-year-old village freehouse with three bar areas. Run by the same family for nearly 40 years. Traditional brick and beam interior including inglenook fireplaces, decorated with rural artefacts and antiquities. No pool table, no juke box. No food except when pre-booked for functions. Children welcome. Large garden with patio, petanque area and children's play area. Large heated and lit smoking area. Pub games also popular. Large car park. Off the A507, just outside Shefford.

OPEN *7–11pm Mon–Thurs (closed lunchtimes); 5–11pm Fri–Sat; 12–4pm and 7–11pm Sun.*

CLOPHILL
The Stone Jug
Back Street, Clophill MK45 4BY
☎ *(01525) 860526* Joyce and Vikki Stevens

B&T Shefford, Fuller's London Pride and Young's Bitter are regulars, plus two guests, changed twice weekly, from breweries across Britain.

Traditional, backstreet country freehouse, built around 1600 as three cottages and converted into a pub in the 19th century. One large bar area, front patio and small garden at back. Crib, darts and dominoes. Food available 12–2pm Tues–Sat. Separate room available for children. Good walking (on the Greensand Ridge) nearby. Local CAMRA Pub of the Year in 2006. Between Luton and Bedford, off the A6.

OPEN *12–3pm and 6–11pm Mon–Thurs; 12–11pm Fri–Sat; 12–10.30pm Sun.*

DUNSTABLE
The Globe
43 Winfield St, Dunstable LU6 1LS
☎ *(01582) 512300* Melvyn Hall
www.globe-pub.co.uk

B&T tied house with 13 hand pumps, of which five feature brewery regulars. Six constantly rotating guests plus two strong ciders. Foreign beers also on tap, plus a large selection of bottled Belgian beers.

A traditional, friendly backstreet pub, reopened in October 2005 after extensive refurbishment. Local CAMRA Most Improved Pub in 2006 and Pub of the Year in 2007 and 2008. No music, no fruit machines, no pool table, no TVs. Also no food except snacks and pickled eggs. Darts, cribbage, dominoes. Dog-friendly. Patio garden for outside drinking. Regular beer festivals in March and October, with around 50 beers plus ciders. Check website for current and forthcoming beers, plus details of festivals and events.

OPEN *12–11pm (10.30pm Sun).*

The Victoria
69 West Street, Dunstable LU6 1ST
☎ *(01582) 662682* Dave and Val Hobbs

Victoria Bitter, from Tring Brewery, is always on offer, plus three guests from independent breweries such as Fuller's, Wells and Young's, Mauldons, Cottage, York, Archers, Everards and Adnams.

Traditional, friendly single-bar freehouse next to the police station just outside the town centre. Bar food is served 12–7pm Mon–Fri, 11.30am–4pm Sat and 12.30–4.30pm Sun. Four beer festivals a year held in the barn at the rear of the pub. Function room. Heated beer garden where barbecues are held in summer.

OPEN *All day, every day (until midnight).*

EVERSHOLT
Green Man
Church End, Eversholt MK17 9DU
☎ *(01525) 280293*

Theakston Best plus a rotating guest from a range of independent breweries.

Early Victorian building opposite the church. Food available at lunchtimes and evenings (bar snacks all day). Garden with children's play area, patio and aviary. Occasional music. Free Wi-Fi access. Car park. Two miles from Woburn Abbey and safari park.

OPEN *12–11pm (10.30pm Sun).*

EVERTON
The Thornton Arms
1 Potton Road, Everton, Sandy SG19 2LD
☎ *(01767) 681149* Michael Hall
www.the-thornton-arms.co.uk

Freehouse with three real ales, two rotated weekly. Greene King IPA, Fuller's London Pride and Theakston Best feature regularly.

Friendly, traditional 19th-century pub with lounge, sports bar and great atmosphere. Food is served lunchtimes and evenings, including Sunday roasts. There is a clean, bright restaurant with two aspect windows. Monthly steak night. Children allowed until 9pm. Beer garden. Live music. Sunday quiz nights. Darts, skittles, pool and cribbage. In the centre of the village, at the top of the hill.

OPEN *12–2.30pm and 6–11pm Mon–Fri; 12–11pm Sat; 12–10.30pm Sun.*

FLITTON
The White Hart
Brook Lane, Flitton MK45 5EJ
☎ *(01525) 862022*
Steve Plant and Sheral Wilson
www.whitehartflitton.co.uk

Freehouse serving London Pride and Adnams Bitter plus a guest changed fortnightly.

Refurbished 200-year-old pub plus restaurant with 38 covers and extensive wine list. Separate bar. Extensive garden and patio area. Alfresco dining, jazz and BBQs on selected Sundays in summer. Food served Mon evening, Tues–Fri lunch and evening, 12–5pm Sat–Sun. Car park. Children welcome. Next to Grey's Mausoleum, within two miles of Wrest Park. Can accommodate small meetings and cater for christenings, weddings, birthdays etc. Wi-Fi access. Take J12 from the M1; pub is next to the church.

OPEN *6–11pm Mon; 12–3pm and 6–11pm Tues–Fri; 12–12 Sat; 12–6pm Sun.*

GREAT BARFORD
Anchor Inn
High Street, Great Barford MK44 3LF
☎ *(01234) 870364* Neal and Charlotte Lloyd

Wells and Young's tied house featuring Charles Wells Eagle IPA and at least two guests. Cask Marque holder.

Village pub and restaurant located beside the River Ouse. Food available 12–2.30pm and 6.30–9pm. Large garden and car park.

OPEN *12–3pm and 6–11pm Mon–Fri; 12–11pm Sat; 12–4pm and 6.30–10.30pm Sun.*

The Golden Cross
2–4 Bedford Road, Great Barford MK44 3JD
☎ *(01234) 870439/871727* KP Li

Freehouse with four real ales, including Charles Wells Eagle IPA and Everards Tiger.

Traditional, 150-year-old village pub on the main road with an unconventional twist as the rear lounge bar houses a Chinese restaurant. Only Chinese food available (not Mon or Tues lunchtimes). Children allowed in restaurant. Outside seating and car park.

OPEN *12–2.30pm and 5.30–11pm Mon–Fri; 12–11pm Sat; 12–10.30pm Sun.*

HARROLD
The Magpie
54 High Street, Harrold, Bedford MK43 7DA
☎ *(01234) 721391*
Terry Churchman and Tanya Paston

Wells and Young's house with Charles Wells Eagle IPA and Bombardier plus something from Young's usually available.

A friendly village pub with one main bar and sports bar, and seating areas to front and rear. Oak beams and real fire. Darts, pool. Live music monthly. Children welcome. Quiz night Tuesday.

OPEN *11am–11pm Mon, Wed, Thurs and Sat; 3pm–11pm Tues and Fri; 12–10.30pm Sun.*

HENLOW
The Engineers Arms
68 High Street, Henlow SG16 6AA
☎ *(01462) 812284*
Kevin Machin and Clarie Sturgeon
www.engineersarms.co.uk

Everards Tiger and Timothy Taylor Landlord always available plus an ever-changing range of guests. Up to ten real ales on offer at any one time (28 per week) and the selection changes daily. Breweries such as Cottage, Potton, Buntingford and Church End are among the favourites.

Established in 1830 and bought from Charles Wells in 1993. A popular, award-winning, two-bar village freehouse with a real fire and pleasant beer terrace. Full of sport memorabilia and breweriana. Sky TV in a separate room. Fresh rolls and traditional hot pies available at weekends. Children welcome in separate room and garden. Live music weekly plus regular beer festivals and brewery tours. Bedfordshire CAMRA Pub of the Year five times in the past six years. In Henlow village, not Henlow Camp. Off the A507 Hitchin to Bedford road (from A1 junction 10, M1 junction 13).

OPEN *12–12 (1am Fri–Sat).*

KENSWORTH
The Farmer's Boy
216 Common Road, Kensworth LU6 2PJ
☎ *(01582) 872207*
Anthony Badger and Lisa Clarke

Tied to Fuller's, with London Pride and ESB plus a weekly guest such as Wychwood Hobgoblin, Gale's HSB or Butcombe Bitter.

Built in 1860, this was formerly two cottages and features leaded light windows. Traditional bar, beer garden and children's area with play equipment. Food served 12–2.30pm and 7–9.15pm Mon–Thurs; 12–5pm and 7–9.15pm Fri–Sat; 12–6pm (roasts until 3pm) Sun. Featured in the *Good Food Guide*. Parking for 40 cars. From M1 J9, follow signs for Whipsnade Zoo.

OPEN *12–2.30pm and 5–11pm Mon–Thurs; 12–12 Fri–Sat; 12–11pm Sun.*

LEIGHTON BUZZARD
The Crown
72 North Street, Leighton Buzzard LU7 1EN
☎ *(01525) 217770* David Maslen

Mad Monk from the local Digfield brewery and Jack O'Legs from the local Tring brewery plus up to two guests from independent or micro-brewers.

Traditional-style pub in a modern building on the outskirts of the town centre. Large island bar. Food served at lunchtimes and evenings. Outside seating. Children welcome.

OPEN *11am–midnight Sun–Thurs; 11am–1am Fri–Sat.*

The Stag
1 Heath Road, Leighton Buzzard LU7 3AB
☎ *(01525) 372710*
Peter Gavin and Jacky Sharp

Tied to Fuller's with four real ales. Three from the brewery range (London Pride, ESB and Discovery) plus one guest, changed quarterly.

A traditional town pub with one wood-panelled bar and a local clientele. Regular live music, plus Tuesday night quiz. Traditional pub games available. Outside seating, car park.

OPEN *12–11pm.*

LUTON

The Bricklayers Arms
16–18 Hightown Road, Luton LU2 0DD
☎ *(01582) 611017* Alison Taylor

Five real ales from Everards, B&T, Tring, Nethergate and other local micro-breweries.

Bare boards and barrels set the tone in this traditional two-room pub, first known to be trading in 1834. Formerly owned by Banks and Taylor, now part of a small local chain. Lunchtime bar snacks served 12–2pm Mon–Fri. Sky TV, car park. Quiz night on Mondays. Close to the railway station and popular before and after Luton Town home games. No children.

OPEN *12–2.30pm and 5–11pm Mon–Thurs; 12–11pm Fri–Sat; 12–10.30pm Sun.*

The English Rose
46 Old Bedford Road, Luton LU2 7PA
☎ *(01582) 723889* Stan and Lisa Smith
www.englishroseluton.co.uk

Three rotating real ales, mostly from local breweries.

An award-winning street-corner freehouse close to the railway station. Food available 12–2pm Tues–Fri and 12–6pm Sat. Pool, quiz nights (Tues). Garden. Children welcome. Summer beer festival.

OPEN *12–11pm.*

The Globe
26 Union Street, Luton LU1 3AN
☎ *(01582) 728681* Ian Mackay

Greene King IPA and Caledonian Deuchars IPA plus a frequently changing guest. More brews are available at the regular beer festivals.

Enterprise Inns-owned, cosy, friendly one-bar street-corner pub, situated just outside the town centre. Strong local support, with bar games and teams a regular feature. Major sporting events shown. Small car park plus large patio with heated smoking area. Children allowed at meal times. Food served 11am–3pm Mon–Sat.

OPEN *11am–11pm.*

Mother Redcap
80 Latimer Road, Luton LU1 3XD
☎ *(01582) 730913* Jan Foster and Mike Shaw

Greene King tied house with IPA, Abbot and Old Speckled Hen plus a rotating guest.

Built in 1935 in the Tudor style, a typical drinkers' one-bar backstreet local. Beer garden and outside seating at the front. Car park. Pool, darts, juke box and fruit machines. Bar food available for lunches on Sunday. Children welcome until 7pm. Quiz nights on Thursdays. Monthly discos.

OPEN *11am–11pm Mon–Sat; 12–10.30pm Sun.*

MILLBROOK VILLAGE

The Chequers at Millbrook
Millbrook Village MK45 2JB
☎ *(01525) 403835* Thomas Polti

Something from Stonehenge (such as Pigswill, Heel Stone, Body Line, Great Bustard, Celebration, Danish Dynamite or Second to None) always available, on a rotating basis.

An Italian family-run pub specialising in pasta, chargrilled meat, fish and award-winning coffee. Food served 12–2pm and 7–9pm (Tues to Sat). Children allowed in the restaurant. Car park, beer garden. Off the A507 from Ridgmont.

OPEN *11.30am–2.30pm and 6.30–11pm Tues–Sat (closed Sun and Mon).*

ODELL

The Bell
Horsefair Lane, Odell MK47 7AU
☎ *(01234) 720254* Peter and Rachel Causton

Greene King tied house serving IPA and Abbot plus regularly changing seasonal and guest ales.

Thatched 300-year-old village pub with log fires, five rooms and a large beer garden backing onto the Great Ouse. Good food available 12–2pm daily and 7–9pm Mon–Sat. Children welcome, car park. Close to Harrold Country Park. North of Bedford, off the A6.

OPEN *11am–3pm and 6–11pm Mon–Sat; 12–4pm and 7–10.30pm Sun.*

POTTON

The Old Coach House
12 Market Square, Potton SG19 2NP
☎ *(01767) 260221* Thomas Kilroy
www.thomaskilroy.com

Potton Brewery's Shannon IPA, Village Bike and Shambles Bitter plus seasonal brews and three monthly-changing guests such as Timothy Taylor Landlord, Fuller's London Pride and Hook Norton Old Hooky.

A 17th-century coaching inn, with a cosy bar and lounge, dining room, two function rooms and 12 recently renovated rooms. Fine food served 12–2.30pm and 6–9.30pm Mon–Sat only. Off the A1 towards Cambridge (three miles from Sandy), the pub is in the market square.

OPEN *12–3pm and 5pm–late Sun–Thurs; 12–late Fri–Sat.*

The Rising Sun
11 Everton Road, Potton SG19 2PA
☎ *(01767) 260231* Kay Dunkley

 A Wells and Young's house serving Eagle IPA and St Austell Tribute, plus four guests changed twice a month from breweries such as Adnams, St Austell, Fuller's, Everards, Butcombe and Wadworth.

Spacious pub on several levels, with one large bar and small intimate areas leading off. Some parts date from around 1800 and there are low ceilings and beams. Recent refurbishment led to the discovery of a well. Upstairs restaurant and function room seats 50. Home-cooked pub food using locally sourced produce served 12–2.30pm and 6–9.30pm Mon–Fri and all day Sat–Sun and bank holidays. Outside patio, car park. Children welcome. Live traditional jazz on first Thursday of the month. Beer festival on May Day weekend. On the eastern edge of the historic market town of Potton, within easy driving distance of RSPB headquarters, Bedford, Cambridge and the Shuttleworth Aircraft collection.

OPEN *12–2.30pm and 6pm–12 Mon–Fri; 11am–midnight Sat–Sun.*

RAVENSDEN

The Blacksmith's Arms
Bedford Road, Ravensden MK44 2RA
☎ *(01234) 771496* Pat O'Hara

 Fuller's London Pride, Greene King IPA and Abbot and Marston's Pedigree plus occasional guests in summer.

A family-friendly, food-oriented village pub and restaurant in traditional style with oak beams and fireplaces. Food served throughout opening hours. Beer garden. Parking. Live music and quiz nights. North of Bedford.

OPEN *12–3pm and 6–11pm Mon–Sat; 12–10.30pm Sun.*

RIDGMONT

The Rose & Crown
89 High Street, Ridgmont MK43 0TY
☎ *(01525) 280245* Jane Brazier

A Charles Wells brew always available plus two guests that rotate, one weekly and one every quarter.

Traditional two-bar rural pub dating from 1827, with log fires. Food available 12–2pm and 7–9pm (except Sun evening). Separate dining area. Beer garden, function suite with bar, caravan park for 12 vans. Off junction 13 of the M1.

OPEN *12–11.30pm.*

SANDY

Sir William Peel
39 High Street, Sandy SG19 1AG
☎ *(01767) 680607* Lindsey Hehir

Everards Beacon plus three guest ales.

Opened in 1838 as the Lord Nelson, this welcoming and traditional pub was renamed after Captain Sir William Peel who, apart from his distinguished military service, built the railway line. No food. Outside seating and car park. Two minutes from the station.

OPEN *12–11pm Mon–Fri; 11am–11pm Sat; 12–10.30pm Sun.*

SHARNBROOK

The Swan with Two Nicks
High Street, Sharnbrook MK44 1PM
☎ *(01234) 871585* Craig and Fleur Baxter

Charles Wells Eagle IPA and Bombardier and Greene King Old Speckled Hen plus one guest beer.

Two-bar village pub with food available (snacks and full menu) 12–2.30pm and 6–9pm Mon–Thurs, 12–2.30pm and 6–10pm Fri–Sat, 12–2.30pm Sun (including roasts). Children welcome. Car park.

OPEN *11.30am–3pm and 5–11pm Mon–Fri; all day Sat–Sun.*

SHEFFORD

The Brewery Tap
14 North Bridge Street, Shefford SG17 5DH
☎ *(01462) 628448* Mr D Mortimer

B&T Shefford Bitter, Mild and Dragon Slayer plus seasonal B&T brews. Also at least one guest beer, perhaps from Wye Valley or Crouch Vale.

One-bar local beer house close to the brewery. Hot pies and rolls served at lunchtimes. Live music. Children allowed (family room and outside seating). Car park.

OPEN *11.30am–11pm Mon–Sat; 12–10.30pm Sun.*

SHILLINGTON

Musgrave Arms
16 Apsley End Road, Shillington, Hitchin SG5 3LX
☎ *(01462) 711286* Andy and Claire Dodd

Greene King IPA and Abbot Ale plus an occasional guest.

Traditional alehouse with two bars serving beers direct from the barrel. Full of character, with original beams and inglenook fireplaces. Dogs welcome in public bar. Home-cooked food served 12–2pm and 6–9pm Tues–Sat, and 12–4pm Sun. Patio, large garden, petanque pitches, ample parking. Children welcome inside and out. Between Barton-le-Clay and Hitchen.

OPEN *12–11pm Mon–Sat (closed Mon lunchtimes); 12–10.30pm Sun.*

SLAPTON

The Carpenters Arms
Horton Road, Slapton, Nr Leighton Buzzard
LU7 4DB
☎ *(01525) 220563*
Mike Byron and Alan Dugard

 Freehouse with four real ales, including Greene King IPA, Abbot Ale, Fuller's London Pride, plus a guest beer, changed when it runs out.

Character 14th-century public house with thatched roof. An excellent menu, from a resident chef who has worked at Clarence House and on the QEII, is served 12–3pm and 7–10pm Wed–Sat, with all food sourced locally where possible. Beer garden. Regular events, including themed nights, quiz nights and local folk music. Right on the Bedfordshire–Buckinghamshire border, two miles from Leighton Buzzard.

OPEN 12–12 (11pm Sun).

STUDHAM

The Red Lion
Church Road, Studham LU6 2QA
☎ *(01582) 872530* Garry and Ann Ellis

Five real ales, with Fuller's London Pride, Courage Best and something from Adnams among the regulars. One guest is changed weekly.

Traditional country pub overlooking Studham Common. Food served 12–2.30pm every day and 6–8.30pm Tues–Sat. Children welcome. Beer garden, car park. Close to Whipsnade Zoo and Dunstable Downs.

OPEN 12–3pm and 5–11pm Mon–Thurs; all day Fri–Sun.

SUTTON

John O'Gaunt Inn
30 High Street, Sutton, Sandy SG19 2NE
☎ *(01767) 260377* Les and Helena Ivall

Woodforde's Wherry, plus three or four guests, rotated fortnightly. These might include Black Sheep Bitter, Fuller's London Pride, Sharp's Doom Bar, Shepherd Neame Bishops Finger and Moorhouse's Pride of Pendle.

Traditional village inn, named after the fourth son of Edward III, the father of the Lancastrian dynasty. Open fires. Food available 12–2pm and 7–9pm. Skittles and boules. No music, except for occasional live folk music sessions. Morris dancing in the car park during the summer. Located between Biggleswade and Potton, off the B1042.

OPEN 12–2.30pm and 7–11pm.

TODDINGTON

Oddfellows Arms
2 Conger Lane, Toddington, Dunstable LU5 6BP
☎ *(01525) 872021*
David and Karen Morrissey

 Adnams Broadside plus Fuller's London Pride and two or three weekly-changing guest beers. Plus bottled Belgian beers.

A 15th-century pub and restaurant owned by Enterprise Inns. Food served 6.30–9pm Tues–Sat, 12.30–2.30pm Sat and 12.30–4pm Sun. Outside patio area. Spring and autumn beer festivals. M1 junction 12.

OPEN 5pm–close Mon–Fri; 12–close Sat–Sun.

Sow & Pigs
19 Church Square, Toddington, Dunstable
LU5 6AA
☎ *(01525) 873089*
www.sowandpigs.co.uk

Greene King IPA and Abbot Ale plus at least one guest.

A 19th-century, one-bar pub with real fires and a real reputation. Rolls and bar snacks. Hot food available (lunchtimes only). Upstairs room available for hire. Patio area, garden, car parking. Accommodation. This pub was run by Roger Martin for almost 30 years until his recent tragic death.

OPEN 11am–11pm; 12–10.30pm Sun.

TURVEY

Three Cranes
High Street, Turvey MK43 8EP
☎ *(01234) 881305* Tony Murphy
www.threecranes-turvey.com

Between three and five real ales, with something from Greene King plus two guests, changed monthly.

Ivy-covered, 17th-century coaching inn and restaurant set back from the Bedford to Northampton road. Food available 12–2.30pm Mon–Fri and 6–9pm Sat. Three bedrooms. Children welcome. Beer garden, car park. Ten miles west of Bedford, on the A428.

OPEN 11am–3pm and 5–11.30pm Mon–Fri (1am Fri); all day Sat–Sun.

WHIPSNADE

The Old Hunters Lodge
The Crossroads, Whipsnade LU6 2LN
☎ *(01582) 872228* Sharon Gentilecia

Freehouse serving Greene King Abbot and IPA plus one guest, changed weekly.

Thatched pub dating from the 15th century, with an open fire, one main bar and two restaurants. Bar and à la carte meals served 12–2pm and 7–9.30pm Mon–Fri, 12–2.30pm and 7–9.30pm Sat and 12–7pm Sun. Six bedrooms. Functions catered for. Large car park, large gardens. Theme nights. Handy for Whipsnade Zoo, Dunstable Downs and golf courses.

OPEN 11.30am–3pm and 6–11pm Mon–Sat; all day from 12 Sun.

WINGFIELD

The Plough Inn
Tebworth Road, Wingfield, Leighton Buzzard LU7 9QH
☎ *(01525) 873077* Roger and Theresa Burden

Fuller's house serving Discovery, London Pride and ESB, together with a seasonal brewery ale. Plus a guest beer, changed every couple of weeks.

A thatched olde-English pub, 350 years old, with low beams and conservatory. Food available at lunchtimes and evenings (not Sun evenings). Beer garden, car park. Children welcome. Between Toddington and Houghton Regis.

OPEN *12–12.*

YELDEN

The Chequers
High Street, Yelden MK44 1AW
☎ *(01933) 356383* Kathryn Filsell

Five real ales, including Fuller's London Pride, Shepherd Neame Spitfire and Greene King Abbot, plus two rotating guests.

Traditional village freehouse in the northernmost corner of Bedfordshire. Located close to game shooting venues with real beer, real cider and a real fire! Large beer garden. Homemade food available in separate restaurant area. Children allowed. Pool, darts, skittles (children welcome to play). Annual beer festival on the Whitsun bank holiday. Large car park.

OPEN *5–11pm Mon–Tues; 12–2.30pm and 5–11pm Weds–Thurs; 12–2.30pm and 4–11pm Fri; 12–11pm Sat; 12–10.30pm Sun.*

THE BREWERIES

BUTTS BREWERY LTD
Northfield Farm, Wantage Road, Great Shefford, Hungerford RG17 7BY
☎ *(01488) 648133*
www.buttsbrewery.com

JESTER 3.5% ABV
Light and refreshing.
BUTTS TRADITIONAL 4.0% ABV
Rich, golden and slightly fruity.
BIT O' POSH 4.2% ABV
Well rounded with a hint of spice.
BUTTS BLACKGUARD PORTER 4.5% ABV
Rich and chocolatey.
BUTTS BARBUS BARBUS 4.6% ABV
Hoppy and not oversweet.
GOLDEN BROWN 5.0% ABV
Potent and slightly spicy.
LE BUTTS BIERE 5.0% ABV
Crisp, European-style brewed with lager yeast and hops.
COPER 6.0% ABV
Classic, strong English ale.
Plus seasonal and occasional brews.

THE WEST BERKSHIRE BREWERY CO. LTD
The Old Bakery, Yattendon, Thatcham RG18 0UE
☎ *(01635) 202968*
www.wbbrew.co.uk

OLD FATHER THAMES 3.4% ABV
Fruit-flavoured pale ale.
MR CHUBB'S LUNCHTIME BITTER 3.7% ABV
Made with all English hops.
MAGG'S MAGNIFICENT MILD 3.8% ABV
Dark and not too sweet.
GOOD OLD BOY 4.0% ABV
Strongly hopped.
DR HEXTER'S WEDDING ALE 4.1% ABV
Dry, pale, almost lager-ish.
FULL CIRCLE 4.5% ABV
Distinctive hoppy flavour.
DR HEXTER'S HEALER 5.0% ABV
Fruity, light-coloured ale made from American hops.
Plus special, seasonal and occasional brews.

ZERODEGREES
9 Bridge Street, Reading RG1 2LR (Also a base in Bristol)
☎ *(0118) 9597959*
www.zdrestaurants.com/zerodegrees

PALE ALE 4.6% ABV
Floral and fruity.
WHEAT ALE 4.6% ABV
Vanilla and banana flavours.

THE PUBS

ALDWORTH
The Bell Inn
Aldworth, Nr Reading RG8 9SE
☎ *(01635) 578272*
HE Macaulay and IJ Macaulay

Five real ales including brews from Arkells and West Berkshire.

There has been a building on this site since 1340. Now a multi-award-winning village pub in the same family for generations. Hot crusty filled rolls and homemade soup available 11am–2.45pm and 6–10pm Tues–Sat; 12–2.45pm and 7–9pm Sun. Well-behaved children welcome. Car park, beer garden. Next door to the cricket ground. Two miles from Streatley on B4009 to Newbury.

OPEN *11am–3pm and 6–11pm Tues–Sat; 12–3pm and 7–10.30pm Sun (closed all day Mon except bank holiday lunchtimes).*

ASHMANSWORTH
The Plough
Ashmansworth, Nr Newbury RG20 9SL
☎ *(01635) 253047* Oliver Davies

Archers Village, Best and Golden always available.

Small, traditional pub serving beer direct from the cask. Light bar snacks available 12–1.45pm Wed–Sun. No children. Tiny car park accommodating three cars.

OPEN *12–2pm and 6–11pm Wed–Sat; 12–3pm and 7–10.30pm Sun. Closed all day Mon and Tues.*

BAGNOR
The Blackbird
Bagnor, Newbury RG20 8AQ
☎ *(01635) 40638* Howard and Liz English
www.theblackbird.co.uk

Freehouse with Jester and Barbus Barbus from the local Butts brewery, plus two guests such as Sharp's Doom Bar or Eden, Fuller's London Pride or Greene King Ruddles County.

Country pub dating from the 17th century, with open fires in winter and separate dining room. Traditional country pub food served 12–2pm and 6–9pm (not Sun evening). Large beer garden with children's play area. Families welcome. Plenty of country walks in the area. Next to the famous Watermill Theatre. Two miles from Newbury town centre – follow signs for the theatre.

OPEN *11.45am–2.30pm and 6–11pm Mon–Sat; 12–3pm Sun.*

BARKHAM

The Bull

Barkham Road, Barkham, Wokingham RG41 4TL
☎ *(0118) 976 0324*
Adrian and Susie Brunswick
www.thebullatbarkham.com

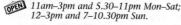 Adnams Bitter and Broadside plus one monthly-changing guest.

Grade II listed pub in building dating from 1728, retaining original features including a forge. Separate restaurant. Food served 12–2.15pm and 6–9.30pm (7–9pm Sun). Beer garden with alfresco dining area. Car park. On the B3349 between Wokingham and Arborfield.

OPEN *11am–3pm and 5.30–11pm Mon–Sat; 12–3pm and 7–10.30pm Sun.*

BEEDON

The Langley Hall Inn

Oxford Road, World's End, Beedon, Newbury RG20 9XW
☎ *(01635) 248332* Simon Liquorish

Two real ales, including West Berkshire Good Old Boy and a guest changed every two weeks.

Traditional country inn featuring wooden floors, scrubbed pine tables and simple decor. Small restaurant serves home-cooked food using fresh ingredients 12–2.30pm and 7–9.30pm Mon–Sat and 12.30–3pm Sun. Large garden, patio tables, petanque court, car park. Children under 10 welcome Sat and Sun lunchtimes, over-10s allowed at other times. Three en-suite double rooms. Take the Chieveley exit north of J13 roundabout, then Oxford Road for 1.5 miles.

OPEN *11.30am–3pm and 5.30–11pm Mon–Sat; 12.30–4.30pm Sun.*

BRIMPTON

Three Horseshoes

Brimpton Lane, Brimpton, Reading RG7 4TL
☎ *(0118) 971 2183*
Mike and Margaret Holmes

 Arkells 3B, Kingsdown and Moonlight.

Small, traditional country pub featuring a restaurant and public bars. Disabled access and toilets. Food served 12–2pm every day and 7–9.30pm Mon–Sat. Real fire, beer garden. Car park. Well-behaved children welcome. Off the A4 between Thatcham and Midgham.

OPEN *11am–3pm and 6–11pm Mon–Sat; 12–3pm and 7–10.30pm Sun.*

BURGHCLERE

The Carpenters Arms

Harts Lane, Burghclere, Newbury RG20 9JY
☎ *(01635) 278251* Simon Bell

An Arkells pub with 3B always available plus other brewery beers such as Kingsdown Ale and seasonals such as Noel, Summer Ale and Moonlight regularly featured.

A 180-year-old country pub with open log fire and beams. Full menu available lunchtimes and evenings (not Sun evening) in the conservatory restaurant. Terrace and garden, car park. Children allowed. Six miles from Newbury, off the A34 bypass, over the roundabout, head to Sandham Memorial Chapel, turn left at the T-Junction, and the pub is on the right.

OPEN *11am–3pm and 6–11pm Mon–Sat; 11am–11pm Sun.*

BURGHFIELD COMMON

The Bantam

Omers Rise, Burghfield Common, Reading RG7 3HJ
☎ *(0118) 983 2763* Karen McDermot

Arkells pub with 3B and Moonlight plus one seasonal ale.

Drinkers' pub in a 1960s building, featuring two bars (a sports bar and a cosy lounge), pool tables and darts. No food. Comedy nights, barbecues, weekend entertainment, fun days. Lounge bar available for private hire. Well-lit front parking. Children welcome. Situated behind local shops four miles from Reading.

OPEN *12–12.*

CAVERSHAM

The Baron Cadogan

22–4 Prospect Street, Caversham, Reading RG4 8JG
☎ *(0118) 947 0626* Rob Churly

Up to six hand pumps serving a constantly changing range of guests, with four or five different beers each week. Marston's Pedigree is a regular as are local brews from Loddon and Cottage.

A modern town Wetherspoon's pub with food available all day. Children allowed, if eating, until 9pm. Public car park behind the pub.

OPEN *9am–11pm (10.30pm Sun).*

CHIEVELEY

Ye Olde Red Lion

Green Lane, Chieveley, Newbury RG20 8XB
☎ *(01635) 248379* Robin Macdonald
www.yeolderedlion.com

Arkells 3B and Kingsdown Ale plus a seasonal Arkells brew.

Proper village pub dating back over 200 years, with open fires. Large restaurant with homemade food available 12–2.30pm and 6.30–9.30pm every day. Patio area at front. Two car parks. Functions and parties over 20 by prior arrangement. Walkers, cyclists, well-behaved children and dogs all welcome. Five letting rooms overlooking the 'secret garden' adjoining the pub. Leave the M4 at J13, heading briefly north towards Oxford (A34). Take the Chieveley slip road, left at the top, and the pub is 300 yards on the left.

OPEN *12–3.30pm and 6–11pm Mon–Fri; 12–12 Sat; 12–11pm Sun.*

COOKHAM DEAN
Jolly Farmer
Church Road, Cookham Dean, Maidenhead SL6 9PD
☎ *(01628) 482905* David and Laura Kelsey
www.jollyfarmercookhamdean.co.uk

Four hand pumps serve brews such as Young's Bitter and Brakspear Bitter, and guests from breweries such as Rebellion and Hop Back.

Traditional two-bar country pub near the church. Separate restaurant with food available every lunchtime, and 7–9pm in the evening (not Sun or Mon). Large garden. The pub is owned by the village.

OPEN *11.30am–11pm Mon–Sat; 12–10.30pm Sun.*

DONNINGTON
The Fox & Hounds
Oxford Road, Donnington, Newbury RG14 3AP
☎ *(01635) 40540* Julia Megarry
www.arkells.com

Arkells pub serving 3B and Moonlight plus one guest, changed quarterly.

Small country pub in a 300-year-old building, with gazebo, garden and friendly atmosphere. Food served 12–3pm and 7–9.30pm, with snacks available all day. Small private area for dining or meetings. Car park. Ramblers, cyclists and dogs welcome. Close to J13 of M4.

OPEN *11am–11pm.*

ETON
Waterman's Arms
Brocas Street, Eton, Windsor SL4 6BW
☎ *(01753) 861001* Gillian Chapman

Fuller's London Pride, Hog's Back TEA and Brakspear Bitter plus a guest such as Wychwood Hobgoblin.

Close to the river at Windsor Bridge and dating from 1542, the building was used as a morgue during the Great Plague. Good homemade food is served in a separate restaurant and the fireside bar 12–2pm and 6–9pm Mon–Fri, 12–9pm Sat and 12–5pm Sun. Beer garden. Children very welcome. Close to Windsor and Eton Riverside station.

OPEN *11.30am–11pm Mon–Sat; 12–10.30pm Sun.*

FRILSHAM
Pot Kiln
Frilsham, Yattendon RG18 0XX
☎ *(01635) 201366*
Michael and Katherine Robinson
www.potkiln.co.uk

Freehouse with West Berkshire Brick Kiln Bitter plus Mr Chubb's Lunchtime Bitter and Magg's Mild. There is also a West Berkshire guest, changed weekly.

Traditional pub, former home of the West Berkshire micro-brewery. Bar food available 12–2.30pm every day, and there is now a restaurant, open 12–2.30pm and 7–9pm. Large garden. Children welcome. Car park. From Newbury take B4009 into Hermitage. Turn right at The Fox, follow

Yattendon sign. Once in Yattendon, take first right to Frilsham, stay on road for one mile, and the pub is on the right.

OPEN *12–3pm and 6–11pm Mon–Fri; 12–11pm Sat; 12–10.30pm Sun.*

HERMITAGE
The Fox Inn
High Street, Hermitage RG18 9RB
☎ *(01635) 201545* Kay Binns
www.thefoxathermitage.co.uk

Fuller's London Pride, Shepherd Neame Spitfire and Masterbrew plus up to two guests, changed twice a week, such as Skinner's Cornish Knocker, Butcombe Blond, Young's Special and Sharp's Doom Bar or Eden Ale.

Traditional country village pub with good walks nearby. Timbered beams, woodburning stove, two bars and a dining room. Family friendly. Food served 12–2pm and 6.30–9pm Mon–Sat; 12–3pm Sun. Terraced garden, covered pergola and car park. On the B4009, close to J13 of the M4.

OPEN *12–2pm and 5–11pm Mon–Thurs; 12–12 Fri–Sat; 12–10.30pm Sun.*

HOLYPORT
The Belgian Arms
Holyport Street, Holyport, Maidenhead SL6 2JR
☎ *(01628) 634468* Jamie Sears

Brakspear Bitter and Special.

Typical English country pub next to the village pond, with a 250-year-old wisteria plant at its entrance. Cosy, with an open fire in winter. Conservatory leading to attractive beer garden where large willows screen a view of the village green. Food served 12–2.30pm on weekdays and 12–3pm Sun. Children and dogs welcome. Car park. From Junction 8/9 on M4 follow signs for Maidenhead, then take A330 Ascot/Bracknell road, turn left at Holyport Green and left again at the village pond.

OPEN *11am–3pm and 5.30–11pm Mon–Sat; 12–4pm and 7–10.30pm Sun.*

HURLEY
The Dew Drop Inn
Batts Green, Honey Lane, Hurley SL6 6RB
☎ *(01628) 824327* John and Helen Lake
www.thedewdropinn.co.uk

Brakspear Bitter, Special and a seasonal ale from Wychwood.

Classic brick-and-stone countryside pub dating back to the 17th century, with two bars and an extension added in 1999. Idyllic woodland setting with good walking nearby. Fresh, home-cooked food served 12–2.30pm and 7–9pm every day (except Sunday evening). Large car park and extensive garden. Children welcome. Look for a sharp turning halfway along Honey Lane with a smaller lane leading off. Follow this for 300 yards. Pub is on the right.

OPEN *11.30am–3pm and 5.30–11pm Mon–Fri; all day Sat–Sun.*

Green Man

Hinton Road, Hurst, Twyford RG10 0BP
☎ *(0118) 934 2599* Gordon and Simon Guile
www.thegreenman.uk.com

 Brakspear Bitter and Special plus seasonal beers, changed twice a month.

Licensed since 1602, this low-ceiling, oak-beamed classic country pub boasts real fires. No music or machines. Modern and varied British and Mediterranean food available 12–2.30pm and 6–9.30pm Mon–Sat, plus 12–9pm Sun (roasts 12–4pm only). Tables can be booked through the website. Large garden with children's play area. Large covered patio with heaters, plus additional covered and heated area for smokers. Turn off the A321 between Twyford and Wokingham. Hinton Road is next to the cricket club in Hurst.

OPEN *11am–3pm and 5.30–11pm Mon–Sat; 12–10.30pm Sun.*

Wheelwrights Arms

Davis Way, Hurst, Reading RG10 0TR
☎ *(0118) 934 4100* Kevin Morley

 A Wadworth-managed house with four Wadworth brews plus four guests (up to 20 different guests per month).

Traditional alehouse dating from the 1850s with low beams, real fire and an emphasis on conversation. Quiz night on Monday. Live bands last Sunday of the month. Food available 12–2pm and 6.30–9pm (not Sat or Sun evenings). Beer garden. Wi-Fi and dedicated smoking pavilion. Children allowed in restaurant only. Opposite Dinton Pastures on Twyford Road.

OPEN *11.30am–2.30pm and 5.30–11pm Mon–Fri; all day Sat–Sun.*

The Crown & Garter

Inkpen Common, Hungerford RG17 9QR
☎ *(01488) 668325* Gillian Hern

 Genuine freehouse with three or four real ales, including Timothy Taylor Landlord, West Berkshire Mr Chubbs and Good Old Boy plus Arkells Moonlight. Two are rotated every few days.

A pub full of history – James II is said to have stayed here. Dating from the 17th century and refurbished in December 2006 but retains its old fireplace and criss-crossed beams. Food prepared on the premises using local produce and served 12–2pm and 6.30–9.30pm Mon–Sat, and 12–2.30pm and 7–9.30pm Sun. AA 4 star dining award for 2008. Eight en-suite rooms and a large car park at the back. The area is ideal for walking, cycling, riding, fishing, or just relaxing! No babies or young children in the evenings. From J13 of the M4, follow A4 to Hungerford, then signs to Kintbury/ Inkpen Common; coming into Inkpen, the pub is on the left.

OPEN *5.30–11pm Mon–Tues; 12–3pm and 5.30–11pm Wed–Sat; 12–5pm and 7–10.30pm Sun.*

The Swan Inn

Craven Road, Lower Green, Inkpen, Hungerford RG17 9DX
☎ *(01488) 668326* Mary and Bernard Harris
www.theswaninn-organics.co.uk
enquiries@theswaninn-organics.co.uk

 Three Butts Real Ales always available, plus occasional guest beers.

Traditional 17th-century village hotel and freehouse. Ten en-suite bedrooms and a restaurant owned by organic beef farmers. AA and English Tourist Board recommended. Bar food available with organic food a speciality: 12–2pm and 7–9.30pm Mon–Sat, 12–3pm and 7–9pm Sun. Organic farm shop and butchery on the premises. Children allowed, walkers welcome. From M4 take J14 via Hungerford.

OPEN *11am–11pm Mon–Sat; 12–10.30pm Sun.*

The Dundas Arms

Station Road, Kintbury RG17 9UT
☎ *(01488) 658263* David Dalzell-Piper
www.dundasarms.co.uk

 Genuine freehouse with four ales, including Ramsbury Gold, Adnams Best and West Berkshire Good Old Boy, plus a guest, changed monthly.

A 250-year-old pub near the river and canal, with one bar and two rooms for dining. Food served 12–2pm Mon–Sat and 7–9pm Tues–Sat. Five en-suite rooms overlooking the river. Outside seating. Car parking for 50 cars. Well-behaved children welcome.

OPEN *11am–2.30pm and 6–11pm Mon–Sat; 12–2.30pm Sun (closed Sunday evenings).*

Bird in Hand

Bath Road, Knowl Hill RG10 9UP
☎ *(01628) 826622* Caroline Shone
www.birdinhand.co.uk

 Freehouse with five real ales, including Brakspear Original and four guests changed every few days from breweries such as Rebellion, Loddon, Vale, White Horse, Titanic and West Berkshire.

A 14th-century country inn and restaurant and Berkshire CAMRA Pub of the Year 2007. Traditional and European food served in the bar and restaurant 12–2.30pm and 6.30–10pm Mon–Sat; 12–9pm Sun. Private rooms available for meetings or dining. Accommodation in 15 en-suite rooms. Beer festivals May/June and October. From J8/9 of the M4 take the A4 towards Reading, and Knowl Hill is three miles along.

OPEN *7am–11pm Mon–Fri; 8am–11pm Sat; 8am–10.30pm Sun.*

LITTLEWICK GREEN

The Cricketers

Coronation Road, Littlewick Green SL6 3RA
☎ *(01628) 822888* Christine Broadbridge

Tied to Hall & Woodhouse serving Badger First Gold, Tanglefoot and King & Barnes Sussex plus a seasonal brew.

Traditional village green pub situated close to the old Bath Road (A4). Bar food, à la carte and specials menu available lunchtimes and evenings. Cricket regularly played on the green at weekends. Well-behaved children very welcome. En-suite accommodation available. Outside tables at front and enclosed garden at rear.

 12–3pm and 5–11pm Tues–Thurs; all day Fri–Mon.

NEWBURY

The Coopers Arms

Bartholomew Street, Newbury RG14 5LL
☎ *(01635) 47469* David and Tiff Reid

Tied to Arkells, serving 3B and a seasonal brew.

Friendly, town-centre locals' pub in an old-style building with a low ceiling. Lounge plus two smaller bars linked by a serving hatch. Pool and darts. Car park. No children. No food although baguettes available from next door. Call for directions.

 11am–11pm Mon–Sat; 12–10.30pm Sun.

The Gun

142 Andover Road, Wash Common, Newbury RG14 6NE
☎ *(01635) 47292* Roland Parker
www.thegunpubnewbury.moonfruit.co.uk

Tied to Courage, with Wadworth 6X and Adnams Broadside among the five real ales. Two guests change every few days and might include Cottage Champflower, Arkells 3B or beers from the Hampshire brewery such as Penny Black, Propose, Hare or King Alfred.

A pub with origins around the 15th century, featuring Victorian-style interior, two bars and a restaurant. Food served 12–4pm and 6–9pm. Garden, car park. Beer festival, live music and other events. On the junction of the A343 near the Rugby Club.

 12–11.30pm Sun–Thurs; noon–12.30am Fri–Sat.

The Monument

57 Northbrook Street, Newbury RG14 1AN
☎ *(01635) 41964* Simon Owens

Butts Traditional, Barbus Barbus and Blackguard, plus Theakston Old Peculier and an occasional guest.

This 400-year-old pub is the oldest in Newbury. Good food available all day and evening, including roasts on Sundays. Children and dogs very welcome. Live music Tues, Wed, Fri and Sat. Covered and heated garden open in summer – the roof is removable. Formerly the Tap and Spile.

 12–11pm Mon–Tues; 12–12 Wed–Thurs; 12–1am Fri–Sat; 12–11.30pm Sun.

The Rampant Cat

Broadlayings, Woolton Hill, Newbury RG20 9TP
☎ *(01635) 253474* Peter Hayward

Greene King IPA and Old Speckled Hen plus Wadworth 6X and Fuller's London Pride, with one of these rotating with a guest beer.

Serving the village community and surrounding areas for well over 250 years, this pub retains an olde-worlde atmosphere, with its open log fire, beams and shining brass. Homemade food served in the bar, conservatory and traditional restaurant overlooking the garden, 12–2pm Tues–Sun and 7–9pm Tues–Sat. Children and dogs welcome.

 12–2.30pm and 4–11pm Mon–Thurs; 12–11pm Fri–Sat; 12–10.30pm Sun.

The Red House

12 Hampton Road, Newbury RG14 6DB
☎ *(01635) 30584* Mr and Mrs Andrews

West Berkshire Mr Chubb's plus one guest, changed monthly, often from a local brewer.

A friendly local pub, with pool, darts, football team and golf society. Children allowed until 6pm. No garden. Limited parking.

 6–11pm Mon–Thurs; 6pm–1am Fri; 3pm–1am Sat; 12–10.30pm Sun.

PINKNEYS GREEN

The Stag & Hounds

Lee Lane, Pinkneys Green, Maidenhead SL6 6NU
☎ *(01628) 630268* Mark Hull

Freehouse with six hand pumps (four or five operating at any one time) serving a selection of rotating beers. Brews from Rebellion are a regular feature.

Friendly pub in a rural location, with a clientele mainly over the age of 30. Homemade food available 12–3pm and 6.30–9pm Tues–Sat and 12–3pm Sun. Function room and huge garden. Children allowed.

 12–3pm and 6–11pm Mon–Sat; 12–4pm and 7–10.30pm Sun. Open all day Sat–Sun in summer.

READING

Back of Beyond

104–8 Kings Road, Reading RG1 3BY
☎ *(0118) 959 5906* Rachel and Jason Lord

Ruddles ales served, plus four guests. Foreign beers and Weston's cider also served.

A traditional JD Wetherspoon's pub with beer garden, on the site of an old warehouse overlooking the river. Two minutes from the town centre and five minutes from the railway station. Food available 9am–11pm. Well-behaved children welcome. Beer festival twice a year.

 9am–midnight.

The Corn Stores

10 Forbury Road, Reading RG1 1SE
☎ *(0118) 951 2340* Fayez Ghaly
www.ilgusto.co.uk

Fuller's Chiswick Bitter, London Pride and ESB.

A wood-panelled town-centre pub on three floors converted from Walter Parsons seed merchants warehouse. The Il Gusto Italian restaurant is on the upper floors and food is available all day. The whole place is decorated with seed merchant memorabilia. Reading Science Fiction Group meets here on Monday evenings. Children welcome, meetings, parties and weddings catered for. Opposite the railway station.

OPEN *11.30am–11pm Mon–Sat; 12–10.30pm Sun.*

Hobgoblin

2 Broad Street, Reading RG1 2BH
☎ *(0118) 950 8119* Rob Wain

Owned by Community Taverns, with up to eight real ales, including three beers from the West Berkshire Brewery and five ever-changing guests from other micros. More than 5,000 real ales have been served here.

Small old-fashioned pub in the town centre with one bar and several small snugs at the rear. No food. Small outside seating area. Opposite the Oracle shopping centre.

OPEN *11am–11pm Mon–Sat; 12–10.30pm Sun.*

The Hop Leaf

163–5 Southampton Street, Reading RG1 2QZ
☎ *(0118) 931 4700*
Debbie and Malcolm Purvis and Laura Hayman

Eight hand pumps serve a range of Hop Back ales including Summer Lightning, GFB, Best, Crop Circle and Entire Stout. As well as five permanent beers, there are three guests, changed once or twice a week.

Refurbished pub in a late Victorian building on the edge of the town centre. Reading in Bloom gold winner 2005, and Pub of the Year award 2005. Pub games played, including darts and bar billiards. Children welcome until 6pm, dogs at all times. Meeting room available. Outside patio with heating. Beer festivals held twice yearly. Fifteen minutes from the station.

OPEN *4pm–12 Mon–Weds; 12–12 Thurs–Sun.*

The Retreat

8 St Johns Street, Reading RG1 4EH
☎ *(0118) 957 1593*
Bernie Whiten and Jane Marsden
www.retreatpub.co.uk

Seven hand pumps with Ringwood Best and Loddon Ferryman's Gold plus four ever-changing guest ales. Real cider also on offer.

Traditional, two-bar backstreet terraced pub, built as a house around 1850 and licensed in 1875. Two real ale and cider festivals per year (May and October). Music every Thursday and most Sundays (see website for details). Off Queens Road.

OPEN *4.30–11pm Mon–Thurs; 12–11.30pm Fri–Sat; 12–11pm Sun.*

ST NICHOLAS HURST

Wheelwrights Arms

Davis Way, St Nicholas Hurst, Reading RG10 0RT
☎ *(0118) 934 3100*
Kevin Morley and Helen Beighton

Wadworth house with eight real ales including JCB, 6X, Henry's IPA and Horizon. Four guests, changed regularly.

An 18th-century pub first licensed when the railways were introduced. One bar, quiet room, beer garden, smoking pavilion. Food served lunch and evenings Mon–Fri and lunch Sat–Sun. Car park. Opposite Dinton Pastures, halfway between Twyford and Winnersh.

OPEN *11.30am–3pm and 5.30–11pm Mon–Fri; all day Sat–Sun.*

SHEFFORD WOODLANDS

The Pheasant Inn

Ermin Street, Shefford Woodlands, Hungerford RG17 7AA
☎ *(01488) 648284* JG Ferrand
www.pheasant-inn.co.uk

Wadworth 6X, Loddon Hoppit and Butts Jester are the three real ales on offer at this freehouse.

Built in 1540 on the Roman road Ermin Street, this pub was originally called The Board House, and was renamed the Paraffin House in the 19th century. Food served 12–2.30pm and 7–9.30pm Mon–Sat; 12–4pm Sun. Meeting room, 11 en-suite letting rooms. Large car park. Garden (no children's facilities in garden). Handy for Newbury racecourse and Lambourn stables. From J14 of the M4, go 200 yards on the A338 to Wantage then turn left onto the B4000.

OPEN *11am–12.30am (may change by arrangement).*

SHINFIELD
Bell & Bottle
School Green, Shinfield, Reading RG2 9EE
☎ *(0118) 988 3563*
Antony Hodges and Jem Dance

 Four ales, including Wadworth 6X, Archers Best and Fuller's London Pride, plus a guest, changed weekly.

Three-bar, traditional pub with open fires, dating from 1800. Games room, patio, separate dining area. Large-screen TV. Food served 11.30am–3pm Tues–Sun. Beer garden, car park. Children welcome till 8.30pm. Live bands at weekends.

OPEN *11.30am–11.30pm Mon–Sat; 12–10.30pm Sun.*

SILCHESTER
The Calleva Arms
Silchester Common, Silchester, Reading RG7 2PH
☎ *(0118) 970 0305*
Simon and Sharon Bumpstead

A Fuller's pub with Chiswick, London Pride and Gale's HSB plus one guest ale, changed every four weeks.

A village pub with beams and open fires. Separate dining area and conservatory. Good food served 12–2pm and 6.30–9.30pm. Beer garden. Car park. Children allowed.

OPEN *11am–3pm and 5.30–11pm Mon–Thurs; 11am–3pm and 5.30–11.30pm Fri; 11am–11.30pm Sat; 12–11pm Sun.*

SINDLESHAM
The Walter Arms
Bearwood Road, Sindlesham, Wokingham RG41 5BP
☎ *(0118) 978 0260* Brian Howard

Adnams Broadside and Fuller's London Pride plus a guest ale such as Shepherd Neame Spitfire, Young's Special or Greene King Ruddles County.

Upmarket pub in Victorian building with three open fires. Popular with business lunchers for pre-ordering and rapid service – food is served 12–2.30pm and 6.15–9.30pm (booking essential). Only fresh produce used, with traditional dishes a speciality in the evenings. Fresh fish and seafood restaurant adjacent, open lunchtimes 12–3pm Wed–Fri and 7–10pm Tues–Sat (booking essential). Garden, parking for 80 cars. No children under 14. Situated on the main road.

OPEN *12–3pm and 5–11pm Mon–Sat; 12–4.30pm Sun.*

SLOUGH
The Rose & Crown
213 High Street, Slough SL1 1NB
☎ *(01753) 521114* Mr Jobling

Freehouse with four pumps serving a range of guest beers, which may include ales from Archers or Springhead breweries.

Traditional town pub with two small bars. Patio at front, garden at rear. No food. No children. Summer beer festival.

OPEN *11am–11pm Mon–Sat; 12–10.30pm Sun.*

SONNING
The Bull Hotel
High Street, Sonning, Reading RG4 6UP
☎ *(0118) 969 3901*
Dennis and Christine Mason
www.accommodating-inns.co.uk

 Fuller's tied house serving London Pride and Gale's HSB and Butser Bitter, plus a guest changed every six weeks.

A 16th-century olde-worlde village inn separated from the church next door by a patio and courtyard garden. One large lounge bar and a separate locals' bar. Log fires. Food available all day in summer; in winter food is served 12–2.30pm and 6.30–9pm, and all day Sat–Sun. Seven high-standard letting rooms (4 diamond silver award). Children allowed. Mentioned in BBC2's *Three Men in a Boat*. Off the A4 between Reading and Maidenhead.

OPEN *Summer: all day, every day. Winter: 11am–2.30pm and 5.30–11pm Mon–Fri; 11am–11pm Sat–Sun.*

STANFORD DINGLEY
The Bull Country Inn
Stanford Dingley, Reading RG7 6LS
☎ *(0118) 974 4409*
www.thebullatstanforddingley.co.uk

West Berkshire Skiff (exclusive to the pub) plus Good Old Boy, Brakspear Bitter and Arkells BBB. Weekly-changing guest ales also served.

Traditional family-owned 15th-century freehouse in centre of village, with two bars, a dining room and six bed and breakfast rooms. Menu offers excellent food at pub, not restaurant, prices. Food served 12–2.30pm and 6.30–9.30pm Mon–Sat, 12–2.30pm Sun. Children welcome, as long as the parents behave! Classic-car owners and motorsport enthusiasts particularly welcome. There is a large garden with lots of tables for summer. This pub closed in early 2008 and was due to reopen as we went to press.

OPEN *12–3pm and 6–11pm Mon–Sat; 12–3pm and 7–10.30pm Sun.*

The Old Boot Inn
Stanford Dingley, Reading RG7 6LT
☎ *(0118) 974 4292* John Haley

Three real ales, with beers from West Berkshire, Fuller's and Wells and Young's regularly featured, plus a guest changed every week or two.

A traditional, 18th-century, olde-worlde village freehouse with a conservatory and open fires, in a designated Area of Oustanding Natural Beauty. Bar and à la carte food available 12–2pm and 7–9.30pm. Beer garden, conservatory, car park. Children welcome.

OPEN *11am–3pm and 6–11pm.*

STOCKCROSS
The Rising Sun
Ermin St, Stockcross, Newbury RG20 8LG
☎ *(01488) 608131* Keith and Joan Holloway
www.therisingsun-stockcross.co.uk

 Up to five West Berkshire beers served, including their monthly specials.

Refurbished and opened in 2005 as the first West Berkshire Brewery tied pub. Three areas, quarry tiles, bare boards and carpeted dining area with an open log fire and woodburner when needed. Home-cooked English food available 12–2pm and 6.30–9pm. Beer garden. Darts, crib and other games. Live music – see website for details. The village is west of Newbury off the A34 bypass, on B4000.

OPEN *12–2.30pm and 6–11pm Mon–Fri; 11am–11pm Sat; 12–3pm and 7–10.30pm Sun.*

SUNNINGDALE
The Nags Head
28 High Street, Sunningdale SL5 0NG
☎ *(01344) 622725* Denise West

 Harveys XX Mild and Sussex Best Bitter plus a seasonal brew.

Traditional village pub and the only Harveys pub in Berkshire. Games-orientated public bar and spacious lounge bar. Cask Marque award. 'Pub grub' with daily special served 12–2pm Mon–Fri. Car park. Sky Sports on big screen. Large garden with smoking area. Between A30/A329 in Sunningdale village, nearly opposite the church.

OPEN *11.30am–11pm Mon–Sat; 12–10.30pm Sun.*

SUNNINGHILL
The Dukes Head
Upper Village Road, Sunninghill SL5 7AG
☎ *(01344) 626949* Philip Durrant

 Greene King owned house with IPA and Abbot usually available plus two hand pumps for guest ales or a Greene King seasonal ale when available.

A traditional village pub with three drinking areas. Specialising in Thai food (12–2.30pm and 6–10pm). Well-behaved children welcome. Upper Village Road runs parallel to the High Street. A beer festival is held once a year.

OPEN *11am–11pm Mon–Sat; 12–10.30pm Sun.*

THATCHAM
The White Hart
2 High Street, Thatcham RG19 3JD
☎ *(01635) 863251* Des Williams

 Three hand pumps with Greene King Abbot and Old Speckled Hen plus a guest.

Town-centre pub, catering for business people at lunchtimes and locals in the evenings. Lounge bar with dining area. Food served lunchtimes Mon–Fri and Sun. No darts, pool or TV. Outside patio, parking at rear. No children.

OPEN *11am–11pm Mon–Fri; 11am–3.30pm and 7–11pm Sat; 12–3.30pm and 7–10.30pm Sun.*

THEALE
The Red Lion
5 Church Street, Theale, Reading RG7 5BU
☎ *(0118) 930 2394* Karen Crabtree

 Owned by Punch Taverns, with Marston's Pedigree, Young's Bitter and Greene King Old Speckled Hen plus a guest rotated monthly.

Friendly Victorian village pub with beams, two fires and an old-fashioned cosy atmosphere. Food served 12–2pm and 6–9pm Mon–Sat and 1–3pm Sun. Small garden and summer patio (BBQs), skittle alley (converted for dining during busy periods). Children welcome until 8pm. Situated off the High Street.

OPEN *12–11pm (10.30pm Sun).*

TIDMARSH
The Greyhound
The Street, Tidmarsh RG8 8ER
☎ *(0118) 984 3557* Paul and Ann Woodford

 Fuller's London Pride, ESB and Chiswick Bitter plus a changing guest ale every two weeks.

A traditional thatched village inn dating from the 12th century with low beams and real fires. Food available 12–2.30pm Mon–Fri; 12–3pm Sat; 12–8pm Sun. Children allowed. On the main A340.

OPEN *11am–11pm Mon–Sat; 12–10.30pm Sun.*

TWYFORD
The Duke of Wellington
27 High Street, Twyford RG10 9AG
☎ *(0118) 9340456* Karen and Bill Suter

 A Brakspear tenancy selling Bitter, Oxford Gold and Wychwood Hobgoblin, plus a seasonal beer when available.

Village local in a 500-year-old building with beams, character and separate public and lounge bars. Large beer garden with children's play equipment and an outside patio. Traditional pub food available Mon–Sat 12–2pm. Children welcome. Car park at rear. Situated in the village centre, 100 metres from the traffic lights along High Street.

OPEN *11.30am–2.30pm and 5–11pm Mon–Thurs; 11.30am–2.30pm and 5pm–12 Fri; 11.30am–midnight Sat; 12–11pm Sun.*

The Golden Cross

38 Waltham Road, Twyford, Reading RG10 9EG
☎ *(0118) 934 0180* Mark Grey

Three hand pumps with Fuller's London Pride and a beer from West Berkshire plus a guest beer.

Locals' pub with restaurant area and beer garden. Food served every lunchtime and Tues–Sat evenings. Children allowed in the garden and restaurant only. Close to the station.

OPEN *11.30am–11pm Mon–Fri; 11am–11pm Sat; 12–10.30pm Sun.*

WALTHAM ST LAWRENCE
Bell

The Street, Waltham St Lawrence RG10 0JJ
☎ *(0118) 934 1788* Iain and Scott Ganson

Genuine freehouse with five frequently changing real ales from a range of independent and micro-breweries including Loddon and the West Berkshire Brewery, with West Berkshire No 1 the house brew.

A 14th-century half-timbered inn opposite the church in the middle of the village. Two drinking areas and a restaurant. Lots of oak panelling and beams. Room available for private hire. Huge beer garden. Food available 12–2pm and 7–9.30pm Mon–Fri, 12–11pm Sat and 12–10.30pm Sun. Between Maidenhead and Twyford.

OPEN *12–3pm and 5–11pm Mon–Fri; 12–11pm Sat; 12–10.30pm Sun.*

WARFIELD
The Cricketers

Cricketers Lane, Warfield RG42 6JT
☎ *(01344) 882910* Dawn and Paul Chance

Greene King IPA and Abbot plus one guest from breweries such as Wadworth or Bateman.

Small, rural pub situated in a quiet country lane. Three bars – public, saloon and middle – separate restaurant and garden. Food available 12–3pm and 6–9pm Mon–Sat; 12–8pm Sat–Sun plus Sunday carvery 12–3pm. Children welcome, play area in garden. Car park. Follow the B3022 from Bracknell towards Windsor; Cricketers Lane is found on the right-hand side of a sharp bend.

OPEN *11.30am–midnight Mon–Sat; 12–11pm Sun.*

WASH WATER
The Woodpecker

Wash Water, Newbury RG20 0LU
☎ *(01635) 43027* Andrew and Janet Cover

Arkells pub with 2B and 3B plus occasional beers such as Moonlight, Summer Ale or Noel Ale.

A 100-year-old beamed pub with no music, pool or games, just good food and drink! Food served 12–2pm (not Wed) and 7–9pm (not Sun). Outside seating at the front of the pub. Two car parks. No children. No credit cards. Off the A343.

OPEN *11.45am–2.45pm and 6–11pm Mon–Sat (closed Wed lunchtimes); 12–3pm and 7–10.30pm Sun.*

WHITE WALTHAM
The Beehive

Waltham Road, White Waltham SL6 3SH
☎ *(01628) 822877* Guy Martin
www.thebeehive-pub.com

Tied to Enterprise Inns with Brakspear Bitter, Fuller's London Pride and Greene King Abbot Ale plus a guest changed frequently, perhaps from Loddon or Rebellion breweries.

Rural pub with two large gardens, one south-facing overlooking the cricket pitch, and a separate restaurant. Food available 11.30am–2.30pm and 5.30–9.30pm Mon–Fri, 11.30am–9.30pm Sat and 12–8.30pm Sun. Children welcome. Monthly quiz nights, large car park, disabled facilities.

OPEN *11am–3pm and 5–11pm Mon–Thurs; 11am–midnight Fri–Sat; 12–10.30pm Sun.*

WINDSOR
Carpenters Arms

4 Market Street, Windsor SL4 1PB
☎ *(01753) 755961* Cilla Palmer

Constantly changing range of five ales, usually from craft brewers.

Traditional Victorian town pub situated in the cobbled streets between the Guildhall and the castle. There are three drinking areas on three levels. A pub since 1518, the cellars reputedly have passages leading into Windsor Castle. Food available all day.

OPEN *11am–11pm Mon–Sat; 12–10.30pm Sun.*

The Duke of Connaught

165 Arthur Road, Windsor SL4 1RZ
☎ *(01753) 840748* Mel Collinge

Greene King tied house with Greene King IPA and Abbot Ale plus two guests that change every one to two weeks.

Established in the 1870s as a beer retailer, this traditional Victorian building has open fireplaces and wooden floors inside. No pool tables, juke box or game machines. Homemade, traditional pub food and daily specials are served Mon–Sun lunchtimes (with a roast on Sunday) and Mon–Fri evenings. Enclosed courtyard garden. Children and dogs welcome. Half a mile from the River Thames and Windsor town centre, a ten-minute walk to Windsor Castle and local car parks. Take Junction 6 off the M4 towards Windsor, take the first turning towards the town centre and the pub is 500 yards down this road on the left.

OPEN *12–12 Mon–Thurs; noon–2am Fri–Sat; 12–11.30pm Sun.*

The Windsor Castle

Kings Road, Windsor SL4 2AP
☎ *(01753) 830677* Sarah Murfin

 Courage Best, Brakspear Bitter, Timothy Taylor Landlord plus a constantly changing guest beer which could be Wadworth 6X, Brains SA, Theakston XB, Adnams Explorer, Caledonian Deuchars IPA or XPA.

Traditional locals' pub situated directly opposite the panoramic Long Walk, within easy walking distance of Windsor Castle, the town centre and The Great Park. A range of food is available, including sandwiches, baguettes, homemade pies, pastas, salads and steaks, 12–2.30pm Mon–Sat, 6.30–9.30pm Tues–Sat and Sunday 12–5pm (booking strongly recommended). Dogs and children welcome.

OPEN *All day, every day (except Christmas Day, when open 12–2.30pm for festive drinks!).*

WINDSOR FOREST

The Duke of Edinburgh

Woodside Road, Windsor Forest SL4 2DP
☎ *(01344) 882736* Nicholas Tilt

 Tied to Arkells, serving 2B, 3B and Kingsdown Ale plus seasonal Arkells beers.

Traditional 100-year-old pub with restaurant. Public, saloon and back bar – lots of different nooks and crannies! Food available 12–2pm and 6.30–9pm Mon–Fri and 12–2pm Sun. Beer garden and car park. Five minutes from Ascot racecourse.

OPEN *11am–11pm Mon–Sat; 12–6pm Sun.*

WOKINGHAM

The Broad Street Tavern

29 Broad Street, Wokingham RG40 1AU
☎ *(0118) 977 3706* Clive Wallis
www.broadstreettavern.co.uk

 Wadworth house with 6X, Henry's IPA, Horizon and Bishop's Tipple plus one weekly guest such as Spectrum Old Stoatwobbler.

Catering mainly for the over 25s, with the largest beer garden in Wokingham. Food served 12–9.30pm Sun–Thurs and 12–10pm Fri–Sat. No children. South-East Berkshire CAMRA Pub of the Year in 2003, 2004 and 2005. Cask Marque accredited. Barbecues in summer, plus three or four beer festivals each year, including one for Belgian beers.

OPEN *12–11pm Mon–Wed; 12–12 Thurs–Sat (no entry after 11pm); 12–10.30pm Sun.*

THE BREWERIES

THE CHILTERN BREWERY

Nash Lee Road, Terrick, Aylesbury HP17 0TQ
☎ *(01296) 613647*
www.chilternbrewery.co.uk

 CHILTERN ALE 3.7% ABV
Creamy, smooth, light colour, clean finish.
BEECHWOOD BITTER 4.3% ABV
Pale ale, malty, nutty flavour.

OXFORDSHIRE ALES

Bicester Beers and Minerals, Unit 12 Pear Tree Farm Industrial Estate, Bicester Road, Marsh Gibbon, Bicester OX27 0GB
☎ *(01869) 278765*
www.oxfordshireales.co.uk

 TRIPLE B BEST 3.7% ABV
PRIDE OF OXFORD 4.2% ABV
MARSHMELLOW 4.7%

REBELLION BEER CO.

Bencombe Farm, Marlow Bottom, Marlow SL7 3LT
☎ *(01628) 476594*
www.rebellionbeer.co.uk

 IPA 3.7% ABV
Malt and fruit flavoured with crisp finish.
SMUGGLER 4.1% ABV
Smooth, with a dry aftertaste.
MUTINY 4.5% ABV
Hoppy and rich malty flavour.
Plus seasonal and occasional brews including:
BLONDE 4.3% ABV
OVERDRAFT ALE 4.3% ABV
ROASTED NUTS 4.6% ABV
RED 4.7% ABV
ZEBEDEE 4.7 % ABV

VALE BREWERY CO. LTD

Thame Road, Haddenham, Aylesbury HP17 8BY
☎ *(01844) 290008*
www.valebrewery.co.uk

 BLACK SWAN MILD 3.3% ABV
Smooth, dark ale.
NOTLEY ALE 3.3% ABV
Pale, malty ale.
WYCHERT ALE 3.9% ABV
Nutty and fruity flavoured.
BLACK BEAUTY 4.3% ABV
Malt flavours.
EDGAR'S GOLDEN ALE 4.3% ABV
Golden-coloured award winner.
HALCYON DAZE 4.3% ABV
Hoppy and golden.
GRUMPLING OLD ALE 4.6% ABV
Full bodied and moreish.
Plus seasonal and occasional brews.

THE PUBS

ASHENDON

Gatehangers

Lower End, Ashendon HP18 0HE
☎ *(01296) 651296* Laura Sangster
www.gatehangers.co.uk

 Two hand pumps offering Greene King IPA and Brakspear Bitter.

A 400-year-old country pub with a traditional atmosphere. Beamed in part with open fires and a large L-shaped bar. Bar food served at lunchtimes on Tues, Sat and Sun (roast) only, and every evening. Car park and garden. Children allowed. En-suite accommodation. Between the A41 and A418 west of Aylesbury, near the church. Twenty minutes to Oxford.

OPEN *6–11pm Mon, Wed and Thurs; 12–3pm and 6–11pm Tues and Fri; 12–11pm Sat; 12–3pm Sun.*

ASTON CLINTON

The Oak

119 Green End Street, Aston Clinton, Nr Aylesbury HP22 5EU
☎ *(01296) 630466*

A Fuller's house, serving the full range of brewery ales, plus guests.

Beamed pub with real fire and large beer garden. Food served at lunchtimes and evenings, and all day Sat–Sun. Quiz nights. Annual beer festival.

OPEN *All day, every day from 12.*

AYLESBURY

The Farmers' Bar

Kings Head Passage, Market Square, Aylesbury HP20 2RW
☎ *(01296) 718812* Claire Bignell

Award-winning pub run by the Chiltern Brewery, with Chiltern Ale, Beechwood Bitter, Three Hundreds Old Ale and others, plus a rotating guest.

In a 15th-century building owned by the National Trust with a cobbled yard for outside drinking. Food served 12–2pm Mon–Sat (3pm Sat) and 1–4pm Sun, plus 6–8pm (not Sun and Mon). Awards for quality of food and beer. Children welcome in large cobbled courtyard (though not inside the pub). Parking in nearby pay and display and multi-storey car parks.

OPEN *11am–11pm Mon–Sat; 12–10.30pm Sun.*

BEACONSFIELD

The Greyhound Bar

33 Windsor End, Beaconsfield HP9 2JN
☎ *(01494) 671315* Andrew Grant
www.greyhoundbar.co.uk

Fuller's London Pride plus a monthly-rotating guest beer from Rebellion.

A two-bar public house with separate dining area. Food served 12–3pm and 5–9pm. Function room available for hire, excellent beer garden. In Beaconsfield old town.

OPEN *All day, every day from 12.*

The Royal Standard of England

Forty Green, Beaconsfield HP9 1XT
☎ *(01494) 673382* Matthew O'Keeffe
www.rsoe.co.uk

Freehouse with Chiltern Ale, Rebellion IPA and Mild, Marston's Pedigree, Brakspear Bitter and Hop Back Entire Stout plus one guest, changed every three months. The guest might be Hop Back Summer Lightning or something from Westerham. Range of guest lagers also served, such as black lagers, wheat beers and micro-brewery lagers.

Claims to be one of the oldest pubs in England. It changed its name when Charles I had breakfast here while on the run from the Roundheads. Full of beams, log fires and lots of cosy corners. Food available 12–10pm. Best Sunday Lunch in Publican Food Awards 2007 and Chiltern Best Food Pub 2006. Huge car park (120 cars) and attractive beer garden. Children welcome. Between New Beaconsfield and Penn – follow brown tourist signs. Publican Awards: Freehouse of the Year and Pub of the Year 2009, speciality Beer Pub 2008.

OPEN *11am–11pm Mon–Sat; 12–10.30pm Sun.*

BELLINGDON

The Bull

Bellingdon HP5 2XU
☎ *(01494) 758163* Jude and Jerry Smeimon

Young's Bitter, Greene King IPA and Old Speckled Hen are among the brews usually available.

Country pub with one bar and beams, formerly a coaching inn. Food available at lunchtimes and evenings. Garden, car park, occasional live music. Children allowed.

OPEN *11am–11pm Mon–Sat; 12–10.30pm Sun.*

BLEDLOW

The Lions of Bledlow

Church End, Bledlow, Princes Risborough HP27 9PE
☎ *(01844) 343345* Mark McKeown

Freehouse serving Wadworth 6X and Marston's Pedigree plus perhaps something from Brakspear, Burton Bridge or Slaters. In addition, at least one local ale, such as Loddon Hoppit, Vale Wychert or Rebellion Mutiny.

A 16th-century, traditional, rambling pub with beams and stone floors. One long bar with two rooms. Food available at lunchtimes and evenings – there is a separate dining area. Garden, car park. Children allowed in dining area only. Look for the brown tourist sign at the bottom of B4009.

OPEN *12–3pm and 6–11pm (10.30pm Sun).*

BOURNE END

The Bounty

Riverside, Cockmarsh, Bourne End SL8 5RG
☎ *(01628) 520056* David Wright

Freehouse serving Rebellion IPA and Mutiny plus one monthly guest ale.

A former hotel dating from 1880, this family pub features one bar, a dining room, a large patio with benches, and lots of character. Food served 12–8pm. Children and dogs welcome. There is no road access – customers arrive on foot or by boat! Park at the railway station, cross the footbridge over the river and the pub is 100 metres upstream.

OPEN *12–11pm.*

BRADENHAM

The Red Lion

Bradenham Village, Nr High Wycombe HP14 4HF
☎ *(01494) 562212* Phil Butt

Freehouse with three real ales, perhaps including Red Lion Best, Butts Barbus Barbus and Archers IPA.

Pub and restaurant in a 19th-century building close to Bradenham Manor. Food served 11.30am–3pm and 5.30–9pm Tues–Sun. Beer garden, car park. On the A4010.

OPEN *11.30am–3pm and 5–10pm Tues–Sun.*

BRADWELL VILLAGE

Victoria Inn

Vicarage Road, Bradwell Village, Milton Keynes MK13 9AQ
☎ *(01908) 316355* Jon Davies

With Fuller's London Pride as a regular, this pub rotates around ten different ales each week, with three on at a time.

Originally a small farm house, the building dates back to 1610. One small ale-focused bar in this old-fashioned stone-built village pub. Highly reputable food served weekday lunchtimes. Beer garden, car park. Annual beer festival held August bank holiday. 'Beer 'n' Bun' race held on Good Friday. Function room available for hire in the summer. Located close to Central Milton Keynes train station.

OPEN *11am–midnight Mon–Sat; 12–10.30pm Sun.*

BUCKINGHAM

The Woolpack

Well Street, Buckingham MK18 1EP
☎ *(01280) 817972*
Dan Simpson and Rachael Turner
www.buckinghamwoolpack.co.uk

An Enterprise Inns tied house serving Black Sheep Best and Timothy Taylor Landlord plus two weekly-changing guests.

A 16th-century pub combining traditional and modern features. Food served 12–3pm and 6–9pm Mon–Sat, 12–3pm Sun. Riverside beer garden. Dogs and children welcome. Beer festivals held over end of May and August bank holidays. Small car park. Play area. From the A421, head for the town centre, go over the bridge and turn left.

OPEN *10am–11pm Mon–Thurs; 10am–midnight Fri–Sat; 12–10.30pm Sun.*

CADMORE END
Old Ship
Marlow Road, Cadmore End, High Wycombe HP14 3PF
☎ *(01494) 883496* Phil Butt

 Genuine freehouse offering beers from Wells and Young's, Archers and Sharps straight from the barrel plus two guests changed weekly.

Small, restored country pub dating from 1634, with one bar. Food served 12–2pm Tues–Sun and 6–9pm Mon–Sat. Beer garden. Children over 10 years welcome. Just off the M40 between Stokenchurch and Marlow.

OPEN *12–2.30pm and 5.30–11pm Mon–Sat (closed Mon lunch); 12–2.30pm and 7–10pm Sun.*

CHEARSLEY
The Bell Inn
The Green, Chearsley, Aylesbury HP18 0DJ
☎ *(01844) 208077* Oliver Babington

A Fuller's inn with Chiswick, London Pride and two other seasonal or guest ales, including something from Gale's.

Pretty, thatched, traditional village inn, 450 years old, set on the village green, with open fires and beams. One bar. Wholesome English menu served 12.30–2.30pm and 6.30–9pm. Large garden with children's play area, car park. Located off A418 between Long Crendon and Cuddington, and close to Thame, Aylesbury and Waddesdon Manor.

OPEN *11.30am–3pm and 5.30–11pm (10.30pm Sun); open all day on summer weekends.*

CHENIES
The Red Lion
Chenies Village, Rickmansworth WD3 6ED
☎ *(01923) 282722* Mike Norris

Freehouse with Lion Pride, brewed for the pub by Rebellion, plus Wadworth 6X and Vale Best Bitter. Other local beers also often served.

Owner-run, traditional pub that sells food, not a restaurant that sells beer! Front bar, back room and snug. Home-cooked meals served 12–2pm and 6.30–10pm (until 9.30pm Sun). No children. Car park. Outside seating on a small side terrace. From J18 on M25, pub is off the A404 between Little Chalfont and Chorleywood.

OPEN *11am–2.30pm and 5.30–11pm (6.30–10.30pm Sun).*

CHESHAM
The Black Horse
The Vale, Chesham HP5 3NS
☎ *(01494) 784656* Mick and Jan Goodchild

Greene King Old Speckled Hen, Adnams Bitter and a guest ale always available.

A 14th-century traditional coaching inn just outside Chesham, said to be the oldest pub in the Chilterns, and reputedly haunted! Now thriving again under former owners who moved away for 15 months. No music or machines. Log fire in winter. Food served 12–2.30pm. Large beer garden.

Children welcome. Two miles from the A41, off Nashleigh Hill.

OPEN *11am–3pm and 5.30–11pm Mon–Fri; all day Sat–Sun.*

The Queens Head
120 Church Street, Chesham HP5 1JD
☎ *(01494) 778690* Lisa Rafferty
www.fullers.co.uk

 Fuller's house with four real ales, including London Pride, ESB, Brakspear Bitter and a guest, changed monthly.

Homely, welcoming, traditional pub, over 350 years old, with open fires and loads of character. Thai menu in the bar available 12–9.30pm every day, with traditional English food and sandwiches 12–3pm. The Thai restaurant upstairs offers a full menu 6–10pm Mon–Sat, and is also available for functions. Car park, heated beer garden. Children welcome in all areas until 8.30pm. Quiz night every Thursday. Annual 'Tour de Pednor' charity bike ride.

OPEN *12–11pm Mon–Wed; 12–12 Thurs–Fri; 11am–midnight Sat; 11am–10.30pm Sun.*

COLESHILL
The Red Lion
Village Road, Coleshill, Nr Amersham HP7 0LH
☎ *(01494) 727020* John and Christine Ullman

Young's Bitter and Black Sheep Bitter plus a couple of guests, usually from a local brewery.

A village pub with beams and open fires. Regional Community Pub of the Year in 2005. A board lists every landlord since 1830. Home-cooked food available at lunchtimes and evenings (not Sun). Garden front and back, with children's area. Car park. Coleshill signposted at Water Tower on A355 Amersham–Beaconsfield road; pub is along the village road, opposite pond and church. Children welcome.

OPEN *10am–midnight Mon–Thurs; 10am–12.30am Fri–Sat; 11am–11.30pm Sun.*

CUBLINGTON
The Unicorn
High Street, Cublington LU7 0LQ
☎ *(01296) 681261* Shaun Walls
www.cublington.com

Genuine freehouse with four real ales. Shepherd Neame Spitfire, Brakspear Bitter, Greene King IPA and Bateman XXXB are regulars, and one of the beers is rotated every three weeks.

Traditional country pub dating from the 16th century, with open fires and low beams. One bar, separate restaurant and large beer garden with play area. Food, including specials, available 12–2.30pm and 6.30–9pm (except Sunday evenings). Large car park. Children and dogs welcome. Beer festivals every May Day bank holiday and at other times. Aylesbury Vale village pub winner. Between Leighton Buzzard and Aylesbury.

OPEN *12–3pm and 5–11.15pm Mon–Fri; all day Sat–Sun.*

DENHAM

The Falcon Inn

Village Road, Denham Village UB9 5BE
☎ *(01895) 832125*
David Brench and Marilyn Heath
www.falcondenham.com

 Four real ales available including Charles Wells Bombardier plus one guest rotated monthly. These might include Fuller's London Pride, Timothy Taylor Landlord and Hook Norton Old Hooky.

Award-winning 16th-century inn located in a preservation village. Pub and restaurant areas, attractive garden. Popular with walkers, the Colne Valley Regional Park is nearby. AA 4 star B&B accommodation. Food served 12–2.30pm and 5.30–9.30pm Mon–Sat; 12–4pm Sun. Also tapas 5–7pm. Close to Colne Valley Country Park, Bekonscot Model Village, Beaconsfield and Odds Farm. Three minutes from M40 junction 1.

OPEN *12–3pm and 5–11pm Mon–Thurs; all day Fri–Sun.*

EASINGTON

The Mole & Chicken

Easington, Nr Long Crendon HP18 9EY
☎ *(01844) 208387* Steve and Suzanne Bush
www.moleandchicken.co.uk

Freehouse serving Greene King Old Speckled Hen and IPA and a Hook Norton brew plus one guest. Fuller's London Pride and Wychwood The Dog's Bollocks are favourites.

Country pub and restaurant, with a slate floor, two fireplaces, and an oak bar, plus oak and antique pine furniture. Good food served 12–2.30pm and 7–9.30pm Mon–Sat, 12–9pm Sun. Beer garden with views over Oxford. Summer barbecues. Car park and accommodation. Children allowed. Call for directions.

OPEN *12–3pm and 6–11pm Mon–Sat; 12–10.30pm Sun.*

FARNHAM COMMON

The Foresters

The Broadway, Beaconsfield Road, Farnham Common SL2 3QQ
☎ *(01753) 643340* Tony and Maggie Jackson

Fuller's London Pride and Draught Bass plus one guest from a range of 30, changed several times a week.

A 1930s building set back from the road with pleasant shrubs and flowers all year round. One bar and 50-seater restaurant. No darts, no pool, no machines – just good beer and conversation. Food served 12–2.30pm and 6.30–10pm Mon–Sat and 12.30–9pm Sun. Large decked area seats 50 for drinking and dining. Near to the ancient woodlands of Burnham Beeches. Dogs on a lead and children welcome. On the A355 between Slough and Beaconsfield, or take the Beaconsfield turn-off on the M40.

OPEN *11am–11pm Mon–Sat; 12–10.30pm Sun.*

FRIETH

The Prince Albert

Moors End, Frieth, Henley-on-Thames RG9 6PY
☎ *(01494) 881683* Mike Robinson

 Brakspear Bitter plus Wychwood Hobgoblin or a seasonal beer.

Family-run 17th-century country pub, refurbished, with original features restored. There is an increasing emphasis on the food, which is served 12.15–2.30pm Mon–Sat, 12.30–3pm Sun and 7–9.30pm Fri–Sat. The food is served in the bar area and separate dining room, which can be booked. Pleasant beer garden. Children and dogs welcome. Travelling from Lane End to Frieth, turn right before the Frieth signs, towards Fingest.

OPEN *11am–11pm Mon–Sat; 12–10.30pm Sun.*

GREAT MISSENDEN

The Nag's Head

London Road, Great Missenden HP16 0DG
☎ *(01494) 862200* Alvin Michaels
www.nagsheadbucks.com

Genuine freehouse serving three/four real ales, such as Marlows Rebellion IPA, Fuller's London Pride, one of Tring brewery ales and Black Sheep Bitter. Two of the beers are changed weekly.

Attractive award-winning16th-century inn with ivy-clad exterior, low beams and ceilings and large open inglenook fireplace. Completely refurbished in 2008, now offering upgraded 4-star graded Inn accommodation and awarded a rosette for its culinary exellence, offering English traditional and French fusion menu. Food served 12–2.30pm and 6.30–9.30pm Mon–Sat; 12–3.30pm and 6.30–8.30pm Sun. Lovely garden looking onto the Chiltern Hills. Extended car park. Nearby walks and Roald Dahl Museum. Travel south from Great Missenden, one mile on London Road near Chiltern Hospital. Owned by the same people as the Bricklayer's Arms in Flaunden, Hertfordshire.

OPEN *12–11.30pm (6pm Sun, 11pm Sun, pre-bank holiday weekends).*

HADDENHAM

The Rising Sun

9 Thame Road, Haddenham HP17 8EN
☎ *(01844) 291744* John and Kris Mulqueen
www.johnmulqueen.co.uk

 Freehouse serving Vale Wychert Ale and Vale Best plus guest beers from a range of micro-breweries such as B&T, and others from Vale Brewery.

Village pub on the main road from Thame to Aylesbury. Very much a drinker's pub, with bar snacks only. Beer garden. Children allowed until 7.30pm.

OPEN *11am–3pm and 5–11pm Mon–Thurs; 11am–11pm Fri–Sat; 12–10.30pm Sun.*

HAMBLEDEN
Stag & Huntsman
Hambleden, Henley-on-Thames RG9 6RP
☎ *(01491) 571227* Andrew Stokes
www.stagandhuntsman.co.uk

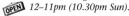 Freehouse with Rebellion IPA, Wadworth 6X and a weekly guest.

Popular, 400-year-old inn nestled in a typical Chiltern village, with three bars and a dining room. Bar and restaurant food available at lunchtimes and evenings. Accommodation. Large garden, car park. Children welcome. Annual beer festival. One mile from Mill End, off the A4155 between Henley-on-Thames and Marlow.

OPEN *11am–2.30pm and 6–11pm Mon–Fri; 11am–3pm and 6–11pm Sat; 12–3pm and 7–10.30pm Sun.*

HAWRIDGE
Full Moon
Hawridge Common, Nr Chesham HP5 2UH
☎ *(01494) 758959* Peter and Annie Alberto
www.thefullmoonpub.co.uk

Up to six real ales, including Adnams Bitter, Fuller's London Pride, Timothy Taylors Landlord and Draught Bass. The two guests are changed twice a week.

A 16th-century country pub with low beams, an inglenook fireplace and two restaurant areas. A wonderful setting, with the common in front and a windmill and fields behind. Outstanding food served at 12–2pm every day, 6.30–9pm Mon–Sat and 6–8pm Sun. Large garden, patio area with awning and heat lamps. Dogs on a lead welcome. Paddock hitching rail for horses. Cricket played on the common in summer. There is a walk to a nearby iron age fort. The pub is mid-way between Chesham, Berkhamstead, Tring and Wendover.

OPEN *12–11pm (10.30pm Sun).*

Rose & Crown
The Vale, Hawridge, Nr Chesham HP5 2UG
☎ *(01494) 758944* Sandra and Peter
www.theroseandcrownhawridge.co.uk

Four real ales, usually including Fuller's London Pride and something from the Tring brewery plus a couple of predominantly local guests.

One bar, two restaurants, a large garden and patio area. Food served 12–2pm and 6–9pm. Car parking. Beer festivals, live music Under new ownership since 2005 and voted regional CAMRA Pub of the Year 2007.

OPEN *12–3pm and 6–11pm Mon–Fri; 12–11pm Sat–Sun.*

HEDGERLEY
White Horse
Village Lane, Hedgerley SL2 3UY
☎ *(01753) 643225*
Dot Hobbs and Kevin Brooker

Genuine freehouse serving approx 1,000 different real ales annually. Seven at any one time, all drawn straight from the cask. Greene King IPA and Rebellion IPA are regulars, the others change daily. Real cider and Belgian draught beer also available.

A ward-winning, family-run, 15th-century village local. Two bars, log fires. Food served 12–2pm. Annual beer festival in late May. No machines, no music. Attractive garden behind plus outside seating in front. Good walking and bird sanctuary nearby.

OPEN *11am–2.30pm and 5.30–11pm Mon–Fri; 11am–11pm Sat; 12–10.30pm Sun.*

HIGH WYCOMBE
The Old Sun
Church Road, Lane End, High Wycombe HP14 3HE
☎ *(01494) 883959* Byron and Georgina Wolf
www.theoldsunpub.co.uk

 An Enterprise Inns pub serving Tring Jack O'Legs and Side Pocket for a Toad.

Recently refurbished and now bright, airy and welcoming. Various drinking and dining areas. Food served 12–2pm and 7–9pm Tues–Fri; 12–3pm and 7–9pm Sat; 12–3pm Sun. Car park. Quiz nights, Wii nights. Large beer garden with smoking shelter.

OPEN *12–12 Sun–Thurs; 1am Fri–Sat.*

IVER
The Swan
2 High Street, Iver SL0 9NG
☎ *(01753) 655776* Gary Nye and Sari Light
www.swaniver.co.uk

Freehouse serving a couple of brews from Fuller's, one of which is rotated every month.

Former coaching inn dating from the 16th century, with 50-seater restaurant and three bars, one of them external. The à la carte English and Italian menu is available 12–3pm and 6–10pm Tues–Sun. Ramblers' routes. Conference room for hire. Handy for Pinewood Studios, the M25 and Heathrow.

OPEN *12–12 Mon–Thurs; noon–2am Fri–Sat; 12–11pm Sun.*

LACEY GREEN
The Whip Inn
Pink Road, Lacey Green, Nr Princes Risborough HP27 0PG
☎ *(01844) 344060* Nick Smith

Freehouse serving over 700 different real ales a year on six hand pumps at any one time. Plus more than 20 wines available by the glass or bottle.

Country pub, over 150 years old. Attractive garden overlooking the oldest smock windmill in the country. Bar snacks and full menu 12–2.30pm and 6–8pm Mon; 12–2.30pm and 6.30–9pm Tues–Sat; 12–3pm Sun. Two beer festivals a year (May and October), with jazz during the day. Otherwise no music or machines.

OPEN *12–11pm (10.30pm Sun).*

LEY HILL
The Swan
Ley Hill, Near Chesham HP5 1UT
☎ *(01494) 783075* Nigel Byatt
www.swan-ley-hill.com

 Brakspear Bitter, Adnams Bitter, Fuller's London Pride and Timothy Taylor Landlord plus a couple of rotating guests such as Woodforde's Wherry, Hook Norton Hooky Bitter, King and Barnes Sussex, Black Sheep Bitter, Harvey's Best, Bateman's XB, Wychwood Hobgoblin, Caledonian Deuchars IPA and many more.

Characterful village inn dating from 1520, close to the Hertfordshire border. Low beams and log fires. Divided into two, with a bar on one side and restaurant on the other. Outside seating to the front, where the pub looks onto a cricket pitch, golf course and common plus large garden behind. Good food served 12–2.30pm and 7–9.30pm (not Sun or Mon evenings). Children welcome during the day.

OPEN *All day, every day in summer; in winter, 12–3pm and 5.15–11.30pm Mon–Sat; 12–10.30pm Sun.*

LITTLE MARLOW
The King's Head
Church Road, Little Marlow SL7 3RZ
☎ *(01628) 484407* Clive and Julie Harvison
www.kingsheadlittlemarlow.co.uk

 Owned by Enterprise Inns with four real ales: Fuller's London Pride, Timothy Taylor Landlord, Adnams Broadside and St Austell Tribute.

A 17th-century village pub situated on the A4155 between Marlow and Bourne End. Lounge bar, dining room, function room for 50–80 people. Large garden, petanque piste. Food served 12–2.15pm and 6.30–9.30pm Mon–Sat and 12–7pm Sun. Children welcome. Off the A404.

OPEN *11am–11pm Mon–Sat; 12–10.30pm Sun.*

LITTLE MISSENDEN
The Crown
Little Missenden HP7 0QD
☎ *(01494) 862571* Trevor How

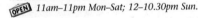 Freehouse with four or five real ales. Brews from Adnams, St Austell and Woodforde's are permanent fixtures, and the two weekly-rotating guests might include something from Hop Back, Vale, Hook Norton, Fuller's or Bateman breweries.

Country pub off the A413 coming from Amersham towards Aylesbury, with one bar and two real fires. Mixed clientele, no juke box or machines. Large sheltered garden, close to the river. Food served at lunchtimes only. Children allowed, but not in bar area. Run by the same family for nearly a century.

OPEN *11am–2.30pm and 6–11pm.*

LITTLEWORTH COMMON
The Jolly Woodman
Littleworth Road, Littleworth Common, Burnham SL1 8PF
☎ *(01753) 644350* Marianne Hancox
www.thejollywoodman.co.uk

 Five real ales which might include Fuller's London Pride, Tring Side Pocket for a Toad, Hop Back Summer Lightning, St Austell Tribute and Gribble Plucking Pheasant.

Traditional 17th-century family-run pub owned by Enterprise Inns in the middle of Littleworth Common. Lovely walks all around. Large bar and dining area, open fires, car park, large beer garden. Homemade traditional food available 12–2.30pm and 7–9.30pm Mon–Fri; 12–4pm and 7–9.30pm Sat; 12–4pm Sun. Children welcome at all times.

OPEN *11am–11pm Mon–Thurs; 11am–midnight Fri–Sat; 12–10.30pm Sun (8pm Jan–March).*

LOUDWATER
Derehams Inn
5 Derehams Lane, Loudwater, High Wycombe HP10 9RH
☎ *(01494) 530965* Graham Sturgess

Five beers including Fuller's London Pride, Brakspear Bitter and something from Loddon Brewery. Plus a couple of guests, changed weekly.

Small and cosy, family-run local freehouse dating from 1860 – an old-fashioned real ale pub. Bar food served 12–2pm Mon–Sat and 2–5pm Sun. Car park, beer garden. Annual beer festival. Off the A40, less than a mile from M40 J3.

OPEN *11.30am–3.30pm and 5.30–11pm Mon–Thurs; 11am–11pm Fri–Sun.*

MAIDS MORETON
The Wheatsheaf
Main Street, Maids Moreton, Buckingham MK18 1QR
☎ *(01280) 815433* Barry Teckoe

Freehouse serving Hook Norton Hooky Bitter and Tring Sidepocket For A Toad plus one guest rotated every other month. Plus a range of fine wines.

A traditional thatched English pub with inglenook fireplaces, a quaint snug bar and real atmosphere. Separate conservatory restaurant serving food 12–2.15pm Mon–Sun and 7–9.30pm Tues–Sat. Good quality bar food also available, much of it homemade. Children very welcome, highchairs provided. Beer garden with large range of play equipment. Off the A413.

OPEN *12–3pm and 6–11pm (10.30pm Sun, closed Mon evening).*

MARLOW

The Prince of Wales

1 Mill Road, Marlow SL7 1PX
☎ *(01628) 482970* Simon Peach

 Fuller's London Pride, Brakspear Bitter and Adnams Bitter plus a rotating guest changed monthly, perhaps something from Rebellion.

A traditional early-20th-century pub just off the high street, with a regular clientele of locals. Open plan with separate dining area. Traditional English food and Thai specials served lunchtimes, with comprehensive Thai menu in evening, plus take-away service. Two attractive patio areas. Large car park. Five en-suite bedrooms. Marlow town centre, with its famous bridge and weir, is two minutes' walk away. The pub is just off Marlow High Street on the way to the train station.

OPEN *11am–11pm Mon–Thurs; 11am–midnight Fri–Sat; 12–10.30pm Sun.*

The Two Brewers

St Peters Street, Marlow SL7 1NQ
☎ *(01628) 484140* Clive and Barry Mason
www.twobrewersmarlow.com

 Brakspear Bitter and Fuller's London Pride plus a beer from Rebellion such as IPA or Blonde.

Traditional pub in a 300-year-old building, with beams and fires. Patio, barn at the back and tables outside, near the river. Bar and restaurant food is available, and there is a 50-seater restaurant. Children are allowed, and well-behaved dogs are allowed in the bar.

OPEN *11am–11pm Mon–Thurs; 11am–midnight Fri–Sat; 12–10.30pm Sun.*

MARLOW BOTTOM

Three Horseshoes

Burroughs Grove, Marlow Bottom, Marlow SL7 3RA
☎ *(01628) 483109* Nigel Douglas

 Six beers from the local Rebellion Brewery. IPA, Mild, Smuggler and Mutiny plus one seasonal and one monthly guest.

Country pub with one large main bar incorporating a conservatory and two smaller drinking areas near the main entrance. A previous CAMRA Pub of the Year winner. Exposed brickwork and beams give the pub a rustic feel. Open fires, split-level seating. The pub is renowned for the quality and quantity of its food, served from an extensive menu 12–2.30pm and 5.45–9pm Mon–Thurs; 12–4.30pm and 5.45–9pm Fri–Sat; 12–3pm Sun. Beer garden, car park, annual beer festival. Children welcome. Two miles from M40 J4.

OPEN *11.30am–3pm and 5–11pm Mon–Thurs; 11.30am–11pm Fri–Sat; 12–5pm and 7–10.30pm Sun. Open all day bank holidays.*

MARSWORTH

The Anglers Retreat

Startops End, Marsworth, Nr Tring HP23 4LJ
☎ *(01442) 822250*
Pauline Payne and Jane Bishop
www.anglersretreatpub.co.uk

 Freehouse serving Tring's Side Pocket for a Toad and Fuller's London Pride plus two guests changed twice weekly.

Built around 1750 and still retaining original features, this pub has now been a freehouse for 15 years. Large bar and conservatory. Homemade food served 12–9pm Mon–Sat, 12–7pm Sun and bank holidays. Large beer garden with marquee shelter and aviary. Children and dogs welcome. Small car park, but larger one across the road. Located near the Grand Union Canal and Startops reservoir. Beer festivals held in April and October. Situated on the B489.

OPEN *11am–midnight Mon–Sat; 12–11.30pm Sun.*

The Red Lion

90 Vicarage Road, Marsworth, Tring HP23 4LU
☎ *(01296) 668366* Julie and Michael Brake

 Freehouse serving Fuller's London Pride and Vale Best plus two guests changed weekly.

A traditional 17th-century pub with lounge bar/dining room, snug and public bar with bar billiards, dartboard and open fires. Large beer garden. Food served 12–2.30pm Mon–Sun and 6–9pm Tues to Sat. Car park. Cask Marque accredited. Situated on Vicarage Road near the church and the canal.

OPEN *11am–3pm and 5–11pm Mon–Fri; 11am–3pm and 6–11pm Sat; 12–3pm and 7–10.30pm Sun.*

NEW BRADWELL

The New Inn

2 Bradwell Road, New Bradwell, Milton Keynes MK13 0EN
☎ *(01908) 312040* Michael Ward
www.bemerry.co.uk

 Wells and Young's tied house with four real ales. Charles Wells Eagle, Courage Directors and Best and Everards Tiger are regulars and the two guests are changed weekly.

Traditional canalside stone-built pub dating from 1804, refurbished in 2006, with a real fire in the public bar. Visitor mooring, lounge bar, front and rear beer garden, restaurant and function room. Food served 12–2pm and 5.30–8.30pm Mon–Sat, and Sunday carvery 12–3pm. Large car park. Dogs and walkers welcome.

OPEN *12–11pm (10.30pm Sun).*

NEWPORT PAGNELL

The Bull Inn

33 Tickford Street, Newport Pagnell MK16 9AE
☎ *(01908) 610325* Terry Fairfield

 Freehouse usually serving about five real ales, with a minimum of two changed each week. Favourites include Young's Special, Fuller's London Pride, Wadworth 6X and Adnams and Bateman brews. Others might be Shepherd Neame Spitfire, Hampshire Pride of Romsey, Jennings Sneck Lifter and Burton Bridge Top Dog Stout, to name but a few.

An old-fashioned coaching inn, just like pubs used to be! No music in lounge. Food at lunchtimes and evenings. Children allowed in restaurant only, if eating. Plenty of accommodation. Take M1, junction 14; pub next door to the Aston Martin Lagonda factory.

OPEN *11.30am–11pm Mon–Fri; 11am–11pm Sat; 12–10.30pm Sun.*

The Cannon

50 High Street, Newport Pagnell MK16 8AQ
☎ *(01908) 211495*
Adam Hepburn and Molly Hepburn

 A freehouse serving Banks's Bitter and Marston's Pedigree plus two guests, changing every week. These have recently included Jennings Dark Mild and Great Oakley Gobble.

Parts of this low-beamed building date back to circa 1480. Extended in 1780 with major additions in 1845, the Wilmers Cannon Brewery operated on the site from 1850–1910 when it was sold to ABC. Bought and turned back into a freehouse in 1994 by the present owners and decorated with military memorabilia. Regular live acoustic music plus folk jam sessions. No food.

OPEN *11am–11pm Mon–Thurs; 11am–midnight Fri–Sat; 12–11pm Sun.*

NORTH CRAWLEY

The Cock Inn

16 High Street, North Crawley, Newport Pagnell MK16 9LH
☎ *(01234) 391222* Lyn and John Russell

Wells and Young's pub with Charles Wells Eagle IPA and Greene King Old Speckled Hen plus a guest ale changed regularly.

Charming oak-beamed pub dating back to 1731 next to St Firmin's Church on the village square. Two bars, cosy function room. Food served every lunchtimes and Tues–Sat evenings. Children welcome until 9.30pm. Regular theme and music nights.

OPEN *12–3pm and 6–11pm (7–10.30pm Sun).*

PENN STREET

Hit or Miss

Penn Street, Amersham HP7 0PX
☎ *(01494) 713109* Mary Macken
www.hitormissinn.co.uk

Hall & Woodhouse tied house serving Badger Best, King & Barnes Sussex and seasonal beers such as Fursty Ferret or Tanglefoot.

Idyllic country pub dating from 1730 situated opposite the cricket ground. Plenty of nooks and crannies off one large bar and restaurant area with low beams and inglenook fireplace. Cricketing memorabilia decorate the walls. Meals are served 12–2.30pm and 6.45–9.30pm Mon–Sat; 12–8pm Sun. Lawn and patio. Private room available for hire. October beer festival. Children welcome. Off the A404 Amersham to Wycombe road.

OPEN *11am–11pm Mon–Sat; 12–10.30pm Sun.*

The Squirrel

Penn Street, Amersham HP7 0PX
☎ *(01494) 711291* Michael Macken
www.ourpubs.co.uk

Punch tied house serving beers from Brakspear and Adnams, plus Caledonian Deuchars IPA and a guest beer, changed weekly.

Single-bar 300-year-old village pub opposite the common, with plenty of character. Food served 12–2pm Mon–Sun and 7–9pm Mon–Sat. Front lawn overlooking common, woods and cricket ground. Large enclosed garden with play area at the back. Small private room (max. 20). Darts, car park. Off the A404 Amersham to Wycombe road.

OPEN *12–3pm and 5–11pm Mon–Fri; 12–11pm Sat; 12–10.30pm Sun.*

PRESTWOOD

The King's Head

188 Wycombe Road, Prestwood HP16 0HJ
☎ *(01494) 868101* Julie and Daniel Vallance

A Greene King pub serving a selection of the brewery's ales.

An old pub on the edge of the village. Tastefully refurbished. Food served at lunchtimes and evenings in the restaurant area, with two open fires and a relaxed atmosphere. Large car park. Large patio area with barbecue. Take the A4128 from High Wycombe.

OPEN *12–11pm (10.30pm Sun).*

QUAINTON
The George & Dragon
The Green, Quainton, Aylsebury HP22 4AR
☎ *(01296) 655436* Darren Curtis

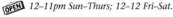 Five real ales including Fuller's London Pride, Black Sheep Bitter, Hook Norton Hooky Bitter and Tetley Mild, plus one weekly-changing guest.

Open fires, beams and wooden flooring feature in this pub, which has two bars, one dating back to the 1700s, a separate restaurant area and outside seating. Food is served 12–2pm Tues–Sun and 6–9pm Mon–Sat. There is a post office in the pub open 9.30am–11.30am on Mon and Wed. Children welcome. The village has a steam railway and a windmill.

OPEN *12–11pm Sun–Thurs; 12–12 Fri–Sat.*

SHERINGTON
The White Hart
1 Gun Lane, Sherington, Newport Pagnell MK16 9PE
☎ *(01908) 611953* Keith Shepherd
www.whitehartsherington.com

 Young's Bitter and Fuller's London Pride plus three ever-changing guest ales.

Three-hundred-year-old, award-winning, two-bar freehouse, hotel and restaurant. Wide variety of food served lunchtimes and evenings (not Sun). Large garden. Luxury accommodation in a converted barn. Annual May bank holiday three-day beer and sausage festival.

OPEN *12–3pm and 5–11pm Mon–Sat; 12–3pm and 7–10.30pm.*

STOKE POGES
Rose & Crown
Hollybush Hill, Stoke Poges SL2 4PW
☎ *(01753) 662829* Mr and Mrs Elliott

 Greene King tied house serving IPA and Abbot plus two guests, changing every four to six weeks.

Traditional village pub with two bars. Food served at lunchtimes (booking advisable on Sundays). Well-behaved children welcome. Beer garden with children's play area. Just off the B416 Slough to Gerrards Cross road, in the village of Stoke Poges.

OPEN *11am–11pm Mon–Thurs; 11am–midnight Fri–Sat; 12–11pm Sun.*

STONY STRATFORD
Vaults Bar
The Bull Hotel, 64 High Street, Stony Stratford MK11 1AQ
☎ *(01908) 567104* Stephen Gascoyne

 Six real ales, rotated on a regular basis.

An 18th-century coaching inn on the High Street. Food available 12–2pm (2.30pm Fri) and 6.30–9.30pm Mon–Fri; 12–9pm Sat–Sun. Outdoor patio area. Car park. Children welcome although there are no special facilities. Accommodation.

OPEN *12–11pm Mon–Thurs and Sat; 12–12 Fri; 12–10.30pm Sun.*

THE LEE
The Cock & Rabbit
The Lee, Great Missenden HP16 9LZ
☎ *(01494) 837540*
Gianfranco and Victoria Parola

 The permanent beer is Cock and Rabbit Bitter (brewed by Greene King). Other beers available may include Greene King IPA, Abbot Ale and Triumph.

A classic English pub with an Italian flavour. Facilities include a restaurant called Grazie Mille ('a thousand thank yous'), dining area and garden lounge. Food served lunchtimes and evenings, seven days a week. Large garden. Children allowed.

OPEN *12–2.30pm and 6–11pm Mon–Sat; 12–3pm and 7–10.30pm Sun.*

The Old Swan
Swan Lane, The Lee, Great Missenden HP16 9NU
☎ *(01494) 837239* JE and ME Joel
www.theoldswanpub.co.uk

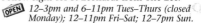 Freehouse with Brakspear Bitter and St Austell Tribute plus a weekly guest ale such as Fuller's London Pride.

A 16th-century freehouse retaining all the character of bygone days, with cosy bar featuring a real log fire. Refurbished restaurant serving delicious, locally sourced home-cooked food 12–2pm and 7–9pm. Large enclosed garden – perfect for families. Follow signs for St Leonards from The Lee.

OPEN *12–3pm and 6–11pm Tues–Thurs (closed Monday); 12–11pm Fri–Sat; 12–7pm Sun.*

THORNBOROUGH
The Lone Tree
Bletchley Road, Thornborough MK18 2DZ
☎ *(01280) 812334* Nichole McDonald
www.thelonetree.co.uk

 Five hand pumps deliver a constantly changing range of ales from independent brewers across the country.

Small roadside pub with a large choice of food available at lunchtimes and evenings. Car park and garden. Supervised children allowed.

OPEN *12–3pm and 5.30–11pm Mon–Sat; 12–10.30pm Sun.*

TYLERS GREEN

The Horse and Jockey

Church Road, Tylers Green HP10 8ES
☎ *(01494) 815963* Peter Darby
www.horseandjockeytylersgreen.com

 Leased from Punch, with six real ales, including Brakspear Bitter, Adnams Bitter and Broadside, Greene King Abbot and Fuller's London Pride plus a weekly guest such as Shepherd Neame Spitfire or Bishop's Finger.

Pub dating back to 1821, when it was converted from two cottages, and featuring horseshoe bar and traditional pub games such as darts and crib. Good home-cooked food served 12–2pm and 6–10pm. Steak night once a month. Quiz nights, golf days, football team, occasional beer festivals. From Beaconsfield go to Penn and turn left on School Road.

OPEN *11.30am–3pm and 5–11pm Mon–Thurs; 11.30am–midnight Fri–Sat; 12–11pm Sun.*

WENDOVER

The Red Lion Hotel

9 The High Street, Wendover HP22 6DU
☎ *(01296) 622266* Julia Cook

 Shepherd Neame Spitfire, Marston's Pedigree and a guest changed every month.

A 17th-century coaching inn with Oliver Cromwell connections, situated in beautiful Chilterns countryside, ideal for walkers. One bar, open fires, outside seating, patio. Breakfast served from 7am, lunch 12–3pm and dinner 6–10pm. Children welcome. Private room for hire. Accommodation. Car park.

OPEN *7am for breakfast; 10am–11pm.*

WESTON TURVILLE

The Chequers Inn

35 Church Lane, Weston Turville HP22 5SJ
☎ *(01296) 613298* Paul Boden
www.thechequers-westonturville.co.uk

 Adnams Bitter and Greene King IPA plus a weekly guest from breweries such as Black Sheep, Bateman and Hook Norton.

A 16th-century country inn with flagstone floors and open fireplace. Large patio at the front with tables and parasols. Dining area with a mixture of traditional English, Mediterranean-influenced and seafood meals and bar snacks. Food served 12–10pm. Opposite the church in the heart of the village.

OPEN *12–11pm.*

WHEELER END

The Chequers

Bullocks Farm Lane, Wheeler End, High Wycombe HP14 3NH
☎ *(01494) 883070*
Chris, Ray and Richard Dunse
www.thechequerswheelerend.co.uk

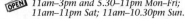 Fuller's inn serving London Pride, ESB and Discovery plus a guest, changed every two weeks.

A traditional 17th-century inn with attractive beer gardens, open fires, bar and restaurant. Home-cooked food, freshly prepared on the premises, served every lunchtimes and Tues–Sat evenings. Restaurant available for functions. Summer barbecues in the secluded rear garden. Children and dogs welcome. Car park at rear. On the Common, half a mile north of Lane End and four miles north of Marlow.

OPEN *11am–3pm and 5.30–11pm Mon–Fri; 11am–11pm Sat; 11am–10.30pm Sun.*

WING

The Cock Inn

26 High Street, Wing, Leighton Buzzard LU7 0NR
☎ *(01296) 688214*
Alberto Marcucci and Stuart Mosley

 Four weekly-changing guest beers from independent or micro-breweries which may include beers from Woodforde's, Thwaites, Brains or Cottage.

Privately owned, fine English country pub with log fires and good home-cooked food available every lunchtimes and evening in a separate restaurant and at the bar. Car park. Children welcome, high chairs available. Garden with play area.

OPEN *11.30am–3pm and 6–11pm Mon–Sat; 12–3pm and 7–10.30pm Sun.*

WOOBURN COMMON

The Royal Standard

Wooburn Common Road, Wooburn Common HP10 0JS
☎ *(01628) 521121* Mark Lloyd

Loosely tied to Enterprise Inns with up to ten real ales. Caledonian Deuchars IPA, St Austell Tribute and Hop Back Summer Lightning are regular fixtures, the others rotate. A porter or stout is always available.

Traditional, friendly, semi-rural locals' pub full of character and atmosphere, this proper real ale house has an open fire in winter, patio oven and separate restaurant. No garden. Food served 12–2.30pm (3pm Sun) and 6.30–9pm Tues–Sat. Located between Burnham, Taplow and Bourne End.

OPEN *12–11pm (10.30pm Sun).*

THE BREWERIES

CAMBRIDGE MOONSHINE BREWERY
28 Radegund Road, Cambridge CB1 3RS
☎ *07906 066794*

HARVEST MOON MILD 3.9% ABV
PIG ON THE MOON 3.9% ABV
CRYSTAL MOON 4.2% ABV
NIGHTWATCH PORTER 4.8% ABV
BLACK HOLE STOUT 5.0% ABV
MOONRAKERS GOLDEN ALE 5.0% ABV
PIG'S EAR PORTER 5.8% ABV
Plus seasonals and specials including:
RED WATCH 4.5% ABV

CITY OF CAMBRIDGE BREWERY LTD
Ely Road, Chittering, Cambridge CB5 9PH
☎ *(01223) 864864*
www.cambridge-brewery.co.uk

BOATHOUSE BITTER 3.7% ABV
A deep amber beer with a rich, chocolatey nose, supported by a little citrus hoppiness.
RUTHERFORD IPA 3.7% ABV
A copper-coloured IPA. A good clean bitterness with an aroma of floral and citrus notes.
HOBSON'S CHOICE 4.1% ABV
A light golden bitter with strong hops contributing to the refreshing bitter aftertaste.
SUNSET SQUARE 4.2% ABV
A smooth, crisp-tasting golden-coloured beer with a strong aroma. A blend of Atom Splitter and Hobson's Choice.
TRINITY 4.3% ABV
A full-flavoured blend of Boathouse and Atom Splitter, creating a lovely red beer with a subtle citrus nose and a hint of roast barley flavour.
ATOMIC ALE 4.5% ABV
Amber-coloured beer with plenty of character. Bursting with First Gold hoppiness.
DARWINS DOWNFALL 4.8% ABV
A blended fruity-flavoured bitter with a ruby-golden colour and tangy aftertaste.
PARKERS PORTER 5.0% ABV
A dark rich ruby-coloured fruity-flavoured bitter with a tangy aftertaste.
Seasonal:
JET BLACK 3.6% ABV
Uniquely styled black beer, mild but full in flavour and body. Available throughout the year.
MICH'AELMAS 4.4% ABV
Christmas ale. A deep reddish blend of Porter and Best Bitter creating a diverse mix of hops and malt not normally placed together. Ideal for the season. Available September–December.
PATRON SAINT 4.5% ABV
Brewed to celebrate St George's Day on the 23rd April. An amber beer with a rich malty nose backed by a hint of orange. Available in April.
HOLLY HEAVEN 5.4% ABV
A wonderfully full-bodied, full-flavoured Christmas beer. Deep rich copper in colour, with well-balanced malt and hops, both of which are present in abundance. Available October–December.
BRAMLING TRADITIONAL 5.5% ABV
Bramling hops are used to give attractive fruit flavour. Available October–March.

ELGOOD AND SONS LTD
North Brink Brewery, Wisbech PE13 1LN
☎ *(01945) 583160*
www.elgoods-brewery.co.uk

BLACK DOG MILD 3.6% ABV
Malty, dark mild with good balance.
CAMBRIDGE BITTER 3.8% ABV
Malt fruit flavours with dry finish.
GOLDEN NEWT 4.1% ABV
Prominent hop character and citrus aroma.
PAGEANT ALE 4.3% ABV
Rounded, balanced and bittersweet.
GREYHOUND STRONG BITTER 5.2% ABV
Bittersweet flavour.
Plus seasonal and occasional brews.

THE FENLAND BREWERY
Unit 2, Fieldview, Cowbridge Hall Road, Little Downham, Ely CB6 2UQ
☎ *(01353) 699966*
www.elybeer.co.uk

RABBIT POACHER 3.8% ABV
Light colour, fruity flavour.
ST AUDREY'S ALE (FENLAND IPA) 3.9% ABV
Fruity, amber-coloured ale.
BABYLON BANKS 4.1% ABV
Smooth, rich, malty and fruity.
OSIER CUTTER 4.2% ABV
Light-coloured with delicate, hoppy bouquet.
SMOKESTACK LIGHTNING 4.2% ABV
Dark chocolate hoppy mild.
SPARKLING WIT 4.5% ABV
SUFFOLK PUNCH 4.6% ABV
Amber bitter, slightly sweet, medium hopped.
DOCTOR'S ORDERS 5.0% ABV
Rounded flavour, subtle hoppy bite. Slightly sweet.
Plus seasonal and occasional brews including:
GOLDEN OXLIP 4.1% ABV
WINTER WARMER 5.5% ABV

HEREWARD BREWERY LTD
50 Fleetwood, Ely CB6 1BH
☎ *(01353) 666441*

BITTER 3.5% ABV
ST ETHELREDA'S GOLDEN 4.0% ABV
PORTA PORTER 4.3% ABV
OATMEAL STOUT 4.5% ABV
FLAT LAND BIG SKY 4.6% ABV
Plus seasonals.

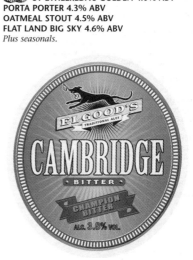

MILTON BREWERY, CAMBRIDGE LTD

Unit 111, Norman Industrial Estate, Cambridge Road, Milton CB4 6AT
☎ *(01223) 226198*
www.miltonbrewery.co.uk

MINOTAUR 3.3% ABV
Dark mild with rich chocolate malt flavour.
JUPITER 3.5% ABV
Golden with a hoppy flavour and bitter finish.
NEPTUNE 3.8% ABV
Crisp, nutty brew.
PEGASUS 4.1% ABV
Hoppy with balancing fruit, malt finish.
ELECTRA 4.5% ABV
Malty sweetness and powerful bitter finish.
CYCLOPS 5.3% ABV
Brewed with three malts and four hops for a full body, fruity and malt nose.
MAMMON 7.0% ABV
Dark winter warmer.
7 Wonders Range:
ARTEMIS 3.7% ABV
ZEUS 4.2% ABV
BABYLON 4.4% ABV
PYRAMID 4.4% ABV
PHAROS 4.7% ABV
MAUSOLEUM 4.9% ABV
COLOSSUS 5.6% ABV
The Imperator Range:
JUSTINIAN 3.9% ABV
CONSTANTINE 4.1% ABV
TIBERIUS 4.3% ABV
CLAUDIUS 4.9% ABV
NERO 5.0% ABV
AUGUSTUS 5.8% ABV
MARCUS AURELIUS 7.5% ABV
CALIGULA 8.5% ABV

OAKHAM ALES

2 Maxwell Road, Woodston, Peterborough PE2 7JB
☎ *(01733) 370500*
www.oakham-ales.co.uk

JHB (JEFFREY HUDSON BITTER) 3.8% ABV
Hoppy and fruity with dry finish.
WHITE DWARF 4.3% ABV
Piercing bitterness mellows to bone-dry finish.
BISHOPS FAREWELL 4.6% ABV
Elaborate fruity hops and grains with dry finish.
Plus seasonal and occasional brews including:
INFERNO 4.0% ABV
Dry fruity bitter.
JHB EXTRA 4.2% ABV
Peppery dry bitter.
ASYLUM 4.5% ABV
Amber bitter with grapefruit and berries tastes.
KALEIDOSCOPE 4.7% ABV
Deep red, mellow with rich hop finish.
HELTER SKELTER 5.0% ABV
Intense hops and fruit.
HARLEQUIN 4.9%ABV
Sharp and tangy with orange notes.
MOMPESSON'S GOLD 5.0% ABV
Bittersweet flavour, copper colour.
GRAVITY 5.1% ABV
Spicy hop character.
BLACK HOLE PORTER 5.5% ABV
Dark and malty.
OBLIVION 5.7% ABV
Strong fruity aroma.
ATTILA 7.5% ABV
Available from July.

UFFORD ALES

Ye Olde White Hart, Main Street, Ufford, Stamford PE9 3BH
☎ *(01780) 740250*
www.ufford-ales.co.uk

WHITE HART 3.8% ABV
IDLE HOUR 3.9% ABV
RED CLOVER 4.5% ABV
SETTING SUN 5.2% ABV
SNOW STORM 5.6% ABV

THE PUBS

ABBOTS RIPTON

The Three Horseshoes

Moat Lane, Abbots Ripton, Huntingdon PE28 2PA
☎ *(01487) 773440* Ronan McLister (licensee),
John Smith (manager)
www.thethreehorseshoes.com

Freehouse offering four real ales, including Adnams Bitter and Broadside, Oakham JHB and one or two weekly guests from breweries such as Nethergate and Newby Wyke.

Attractive thatched village pub with restaurant and accommodation. Food served 12–2pm and 6.30–9.30pm Tues–Sat; 12–2.30pm and 6.30–9pm Sun.

OPEN *Closed Mon; 11.30am–3pm and 6–11pm Tues–Sat; 12–3pm and 6–10pm Sun.*

ABINGTON PIGOTTS

The Pig & Abbot

High Street, Abington Pigotts, Nr Royston SG8 0SD
☎ *(01763) 853515*
Nicola Grundy and Pat Thomson
www.pigandabbot.co.uk

Adnams Best and Broadside and Fuller's London Pride always available, plus a constantly changing guest. Examples of ales served recently include Adnams Oyster, Woodforde's Wherry, Elgood's Cambridge Bitter, Nethergate Suffolk County and City of Cambridge Boathouse Bitter.

Cosy, Queen Anne period country pub with open fire, beams and a relaxed, friendly atmosphere. Home-cooked food to appeal to all tastes served 12–2pm and 7–9pm Mon–Fri, 12–3pm and 7–9.30pm Sat–Sun. Restaurant, beer gardens. Children welcome, and high chairs are available. Car park. Turn off the A1198 to Bassingbourn and look for signs. Accommodation planned. In Cambridgeshire, but with a Hertfordshire postal address.

OPEN *12–3pm and 6–11pm Mon–Fri; 12–11pm Sat; 12–10.30pm Sun.*

BOXWORTH
The Golden Ball
High Street, Boxworth CB3 8LY
☎ *(01954) 267397 Alan Maund*
www.goldenballhotel.co.uk

 Charles Wells pub.

Renovated bar in a 16th-century, part-thatched country hotel and restaurant in good walking country. Bar and restaurant food available 12–2.15pm and 6–9.30pm Mon–Sat, 12–9pm Sun. Meeting room, car park. Large, landscaped beer garden. Children allowed. Eleven bedrooms. Ten miles from Cambridge, six miles from St Ives close to the Cambridge Services on the A14.

OPEN *11.30am–11pm.*

BURWELL
The Fox
2 North Street, Burwell CB25 0BA
☎ *(01638) 741267 Bob and Lou Taylor*

Freehouse with an ever-changing range of real ales. Approx 300 served over the past two years.

Now with a Mexican restaurant in the pub's former pool room. Modern interior, large car park. English pub food also available, plus fresh fish and steaks. Food served Tues–Sat evenings.

OPEN *All day, every day.*

CAMBRIDGE
The Bird in Hand
73 Newmarket Road, Cambridge CB5 8EG
☎ *(01223) 351919 Trevor Critchlow*
www.bird-in-hand.fsnet.co.uk

Greene King IPA, XX Dark Mild, Old Speckled Hen and Ruddles County always on offer, plus one guest, changed every two months, such as Brakspear Bitter, Black Sheep Bitter or Jennings Cocker Hoop.

Traditional one-bar town pub with garden. No games or music. A French chef prepares the food on the French menu. Children not allowed.

OPEN *12–2pm and 5–11pm Mon–Thurs; 12–11pm Fri–Sun (10.30pm Sun).*

Cambridge Blue
85–7 Gwydir Street, Cambridge CB1 2LG
☎ *(01223) 471680*
Jethro and Terri Scotcher-Littlechild

An enormous range of real ales, with up to 12 at any one time. Woodforde's Wherry and Nethergate Dewdrop are regulars, the rest rotate from micro-breweries. Two real ciders and a perry also served.

Terraced side-street Victorian pub decorated with enamel signs and breweriana, with two bars and a large garden and a rowing theme. Food, including plenty of vegetarian options, available 12–2.30pm (until 4pm Sat–Sun) and 6–9pm. Children allowed in conservatory area until 9pm. Off Mill Road on the city side of railway bridge.

OPEN *12–11pm (10.30pm Sun) (in winter the pub closes 3–5.30pm Mon–Wed).*

Carlton Arms
Carlton Way, Cambridge CB4 2BY
☎ *(01223) 355717*
Jethro and Terri Scotcher-Littlechild
www.thecarltonarms.co.uk

At least six real ales, served straight from the cask. Timothy Taylor Landlord, Caledonian Deuchars IPA and a mild always available.

Under the same ownership as the Cambridge Blue. Food served 6–9pm daily plus 12–2pm Wed–Fri, 12–5pm Sat–Sun. Pool, darts, quizzes, TV. Car park, outside seating.

OPEN *Closed Mon; 5–11pm Tues; 12–2.30pm and 5–11pm Wed; 12–11pm Thurs–Sat; 12–10.30pm Sun*

The Eagle
8 Benet Street, Cambridge CB2 3QN
☎ *(01223) 505020 Peter and Daphne Peck*

Greene King tied house with IPA, Abbot and Old Speckled Hen, plus a monthly guest such as Hook Norton Old Hooky.

A 16th-century coaching inn with an impressive history and many original features. Tours on request. Traditional home-cooked food from the servery 12–10pm, plus à la carte evening menu. Large fireplace, beamed ceilings, panelled walls.

OPEN *11am–11pm Mon–Sat; 12–10.30pm Sun.*

The Free Press
7 Prospect Row, Cambridge CB1 1DU
☎ *(01223) 368337 Craig Bickley*
www.freepresspub.com

A Greene King tenancy with Abbot, IPA and XXX Mild ales always available, with two guest beers available. All ales served in oversized glasses to ensure you a full pint.

Famous East Anglian real ale house with a traditional atmosphere. Table games and newspapers available, real fires in winter and a sun-trap courtyard beer garden in summer. Genuine homemade bar food available at lunchtimes and evenings (not Sun evening). Mobile phone-free. Children welcome. Located near Grafton Shopping Centre.

OPEN *12–2.30pm and 6–11pm Mon–Fri; 12–11pm Sat; 12–3pm and 7–10.30pm Sun.*

The Kingston Arms
33 Kingston Street, Cambridge CB1 2NU
☎ *(01223) 319414*
Jane Fairhall and Paul Boggia
www.kingston-arms.co.uk

Hop Back Summer Lightning and Entire Stout, Timothy Taylor Landlord, Elgood's Black Dog Mild, Crouch Vale Brewer's Gold and Oakham JHB usually available plus up to four rotating guests.

Originally built for the railway workers, this pub is approximately 100 years old, and traditional with a modern twist. Food served 12–2pm and 6–9pm Mon–Thurs; 12–3pm and 6–9pm Fri–Sat. Free internet access and wireless access (two computers in the bar). Beer garden. Five minutes' walk from the station, off Mill Road.

OPEN *12–3pm and 5–11pm Mon–Thurs; 12–12 Fri–Sat; 12–11pm Sun.*

Live and Let Live

40 Mawson Road, Cambridge CB1 2EA
☎ *(01223) 460261* Peter Wiffin

Seven hand pumps serve Adnams Bitter, Everards Tiger and Nethergate Umbel Ale as regulars along with an ever-changing guest list, including brews from Oakham, Milton, Tring, B&T and Mighty Oak. An eighth pump serves a locally produced real cider. There is also a Belgian beer on draught. Several mini beer festivals held throughout the year.

Situated in central Cambridge, just off Mill Road, popular with students, business people and locals alike. The pub is 120 years old with a single bar, wooden furniture, floors and panelling plus real gas lighting. Beer and railway memorabilia. Extensive home-cooked menu with several vegetarian options available lunchtimes until 2pm and evenings until 9pm. Children allowed in eating area. Street parking.

OPEN *11.30am–2.30pm daily; 5.30–11pm Mon–Fri; 6–11pm Sat; 7–11pm Sun.*

The Mill

14 Mill Lane, Cambridge CB2 1RX
☎ *(01223) 357026* Tom Scanlon

Owned by the Passionate Pub Company, with Caledonian Deuchars IPA, Fuller's London Pride, Badger Tanglefoot and Wychwood Hobgoblin usually available. There is also a guest, which is changed weekly.

Traditional, homely one-room alehouse, over 200 years old, with oak floors and exposed brickwork, in a picturesque setting on the River Cam. Possibly the largest beer garden in England! Traditional home-cooked pub food served 12–3pm and 6–9pm Mon–Fri, 12–7pm Sat and 12–4pm Sun. Punting station nearby. Mill Lane is off Trumpington Road in an area known as 'Mill Pond', a five-minute walk from the market.

OPEN *12–11pm Sun–Wed; 12–12 Thurs–Sat.*

The Portland Arms

129 Chesterton Road, Cambridge CB4 3BA
☎ *(01223) 357268*
Haley Yoxall and Steve Pellegrini
www.theportland.co.uk

A Greene King tenancy with five real ales usually available. Greene King IPA, Abbot and XX Mild are the permanent beers, and guests, changed weekly, are also served.

A pub with three bars, one a traditional saloon, one a music venue (100 capacity), and one a games room with pool table, darts and TV. Full menu plus daily specials served 12–2.30pm and 5.30–8pm Mon–Sat. Beer garden. Beer festivals once a year. Situated on the outer Ring Road (A10).

OPEN *12–11.30pm Mon–Thurs; noon–12.30am Fri–Sat; 12–11pm Sun.*

St Radegund

129 King Street, Cambridge CB1 1LD
☎ *(01223) 311794* Terry Kavanagh

Genuine freehouse, with four real ales on offer, including Fuller's London Pride and beers from Milton such as Habit, Sackcloth (exclusive to the pub) and Nero stout.

The smallest pub in Cambridge, with one triangular bar and oodles of ambience and character. No mobile phones! No food. Children allowed on Sat afternoons only. The pub has its own cricket and rowing clubs. Opposite the Wesley church in King Street.

OPEN *5–11pm Mon–Fri; 12–11pm Sat; 6.30–11pm Sun.*

Wrestlers

337 Newmarket Road, Cambridge CB5 8JE
☎ *(01223) 566554* Mr PJ Phookha

A house tied to Wells and Young's, with seven real ales. Charles Wells Eagle IPA and Bombardier, Adnams Broadside, Badger Tanglefoot and Greene King Old Speckled Hen are the regulars; monthly guests are also featured.

The pub specialises in Thai food, served 12–3pm and 5–9pm Mon–Sat. Children welcome. Near to shops.

OPEN *12–3pm and 5–9pm Mon–Sat; closed Sun.*

CASTLE CAMPS

The Cock Inn

High Street, Castle Camps, Cambridge CB1 6SN
☎ *(01799) 584207* Lesley and Phil Clark

Freehouse serving Greene King IPA and Abbot plus a local guest, perhaps from Brandon, Nethergate or Cottage, changed weekly.

A two-bar village pub dating from 1725, originally used as accommodation and stables for the forge next door. Restaurant with food available 12–2pm and 6–9pm Mon–Sat, plus Sunday roasts 12–7pm. Beer garden, patio, smoking shelter. Car park. Three miles from Haverhill off the A1307.

OPEN *12–2pm and 6–11.30pm Mon–Fri; 12–11.30pm Sat–Sun.*

DOGSTHORPE

The Blue Bell Inn

Welland Road, Dogsthorpe, Peterborough PE1 3SA
☎ *(01733) 554890* Carole Worley

Tied to Elgood's, with five real ales. Black Dog Mild, Cambridge Bitter, Golden Newt and Greyhound plus a weekly changing guest beer from one of a variety of breweries.

One of the oldest pubs in Peterborough, a homely environment with traditional atmosphere and values. The landlady has been at the pub for 20 years (two years as landlady). Food served 11am–2pm Mon–Fri. Lounge bar with TV, plus bar with pool, darts and big screen for sports. Also small snug. Entertainment every Friday and Saturday (bands and discos), plus meat raffle every Sunday. Children welcome until 7pm. Beer garden with children's play area. Available for hire for events such as weddings and birthdays.

OPEN *11am–11pm Mon–Thurs; 11.30am–1am Fri; noon–1am Sat; 12–11pm Sun.*

DUXFORD
The Plough Inn
59 St Peters St, Duxford, Cambridge
☎ *(01223) 833170* Julie Nicholls

Everards Tiger, Original and Beacon, and Adnams Bitter plus one guest, perhaps another Adnams beer.

Thatched village pub with beer garden. Food available 12–2pm and 5–9pm Mon–Fri, and 12–6pm Sat–Sun. Live music Saturday. Children welcome (bouncy castle in garden!). Car park.

🍺 *11am–3pm and 5–11pm Mon–Thurs; 11am–11pm Fri–Sat; 12–10.30pm Sun.*

ELY
The Fountain
1 Silver Street, Ely CB7 4JF
☎ *(01353) 663122* John Borland

Freehouse with Adnams Bitter and Broadside plus Fuller's London Pride as permanent fixtures. A guest beer, changed weekly, could well be Charles Wells Bombardier.

A Victorian pub near the cathedral, renovated and modernised. No food. Children allowed until 9pm.

🍺 *5–11.30pm Mon–Fri; 12–2pm and 6–11.30pm Sat; 12–2pm and 7–11pm Sun.*

West End House
16 West End, Ely CB6 3AY
☎ *(01353) 662907* Stephen and Kim Baxter

Enterprise pub with four real ales, namely Shepherd Neame Spitfire, Adnams Best Bitter and two weekly guests such as Woodforde's Wherry, Badger Tanglefoot, Black Sheep Bitter and Elgood's Black Dog.

Four-bar pub dating from 1839, featuring beams, bare brickwork and lounge with log-burning stove. Large patio garden and covered, heated smoking area. Food served 12–3pm Mon–Sat. Well-behaved children allowed until 8.30pm. No dogs. Handy for Ely Cathedral, Oliver Cromwell's house and local museums. Follow the A10 to the city centre.

🍺 *12–3pm and 6–11pm Mon–Thurs; all day Fri–Sat; 12–4pm and 7–11pm Sun.*

ETTON
The Golden Pheasant
1 Main Road, Etton, Peterborough PE6 7DA
☎ *(01733) 252387* Jim Clark
www.goldenpheasant.net

Freehouse serving six real ales. Fuller's ESB and London Pride, Oakham JHB and Woodforde's Wherry are the regular beers, and the two guests are changed monthly.

This pub in an old Georgian farmhouse is set in an acre and a half of gardens, with a 100-seater marquee available for functions. Food available 12–2.30pm and 6–9pm Tues–Sun. Large beer garden, large car park. Children welcome. Situated on the 'Green Wheel' cycle route. Off the Helpston road, on the way to Stamford.

🍺 *12–2.30pm and 6–11pm Tues–Sun (closed all day Mon except bank holidays).*

FULBOURN
Six Bells
9 High Street, Fulbourn CB21 5DH
☎ *(01223) 880244* Hugo White

Punch pub with Adnams Bitter and Broadside, Greene King IPA and two pumps carrying different beers each week.

A 15th-century coaching inn full of cosy corners and cheerful characters. Good homemade food served every lunchtime and Tues–Sat evenings. Huge garden, funtion room with jazz twice a month. Children welcome. Near the nature reserve. Turn off the A11 and head for the centre of the village, or off the A14 at Fen Ditton through Feversham to Fulbourn.

🍺 *11.30am–2.30pm and 6–11pm Mon–Thurs; all day Fri–Sun.*

GLINTON
The Blue Bell
10 High Street, Glinton, Peterborough PE6 7LS
☎ *(01733) 252285* Mr Richard Taylor

Tied to Greene King and serving IPA and Abbot Ale plus two guests ales, changed every couple of months.

Traditional old village pub with separate restaurant and lots of character. Food served at lunchtime and evenings (not Mon evening). Beer garden, car park.

🍺 *12–2.30pm and 5–11pm Mon–Thurs; 12–12 Fri; 12–11pm Sat; 12–10.30pm Sun.*

GRANTCHESTER
The Blue Ball
57 Broadway, Grantchester CB3 9NQ
☎ *(01223) 840679* John Roos

Freehouse selling copious quantities of Adnams Bitter plus a rotating guest.

Popular village local established in 1767, with the emphasis very much on drinking. Bare boards, a real fire, pub games and plenty of character. Simple bar food available at lunchtimes. Live music nights, views across the meadows. Take J12 off the M11.

🍺 *12–3pm and 6–11pm Mon–Sat; 12–10.30pm Sun*

GRAVELEY
The Three Horseshoes
23 High Street, Graveley, Huntingdon PE18 9PL
☎ *(01480) 830992* Alfred Barrett

Freehouse with three pumps serving a variety of beers, which change weekly, mainly from independent breweries such as Marston's, Adnams and others.

A very old country inn, with no juke box or pool tables. Food at lunchtimes and evenings. Children allowed.

🍺 *11am–3pm and 6–11pm Mon–Sat; 12–2pm and 7–11pm Sun.*

GREAT ABINGTON

The Three Tuns

75 High Street, Great Abington, Cambridge CB21 6AB
☎ *(01223) 891467 Chris and Karen Adomeit*
www.thethreetuns-greatabington.co.uk

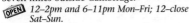 Freehouse with three real ales from a range of independent brewers.

Typical English country pub, nearly 500 years old. A Thai menu is available Mon–Sat lunchtimes and evenings. Large beer garden. Car park. Children welcome. Outside buffets catered for. Quiz nights. Live music. Seven miles outside Cambridge.

OPEN *12–2pm and 6–11pm Mon–Fri; 12–close Sat–Sun.*

HELPSTON

The Bluebell Inn

10 Woodgate, Helpston, Peterborough PE6 7ED
☎ *(01733) 252394 Aubrey S Ball*

 Freehouse with three Grainstore beers, Cooking Bitter, Ten Fifty and John Clare (exclusive to the pub). Up to three guests, changed weekly, from other local micro-breweries such as Elgood's and Tydd Steam, or from breweries further afield, such as Castle Rock, Fuller's and Adnams.

Inviting, traditional pub next door to the cottage of John Clare, the late peasant poet, with lots of character and local historical references. Food served 12–2pm Mon–Sat and 6.30–9pm Tues–Sat; 12–4pm Sun. Enclosed patio area and ample parking. Follow A15 out of Peterborough, leave A15 at the sign for Helpston and turn left at the staggered junction in the village.

OPEN *11.30am–2.30pm and 5–11pm Mon–Sat (until midnight Fri–Sat); 12–6pm Sun.*

HEMINGFORD GREY

The Cock

47 High Street, Hemingford Grey PE28 9BJ
☎ *(01480) 463609*
Oliver Thain and Richard Bradley
www.cambscuisine.com

 Freehouse with a policy of only serving beers brewed within an hour's drive of the pub. The four regular ales include Wolf's Golden Jackal and Buntingford IPA. Local cider sold: Oliver Cromwell.

Dating from the 16th century, situated in a pretty riverside village. One bar predominantly for locals and one separate bar/restaurant. Good food, including homemade sausages, always available. Winner of Cambridgeshire Dining Pub of the Year 2006–7 and 2007/8. Beer garden. Car park. Annual beer festival. Located between Huntingdon and Cambridge.

OPEN *12–3pm and 6–11pm.*

HINXTON

The Red Lion

32 High Street, Hinxton, Cambridge CB10 1QY
☎ *(01799) 530601 Alex Clarke*
www.redlionhinxton.co.uk

 Freehouse with Adnams Bitter, Woodforde's Wherry and Greene King IPA plus a mid-strength guest rotated weekly.

A 16th-century coaching inn at the heart of a conservation village half a mile north of junction 9 off the M11. Grade II listed building, with an original bar and a dining room in the impressive, sympathetic extension. Spacious walled garden plus paddock and stables overlooked by the village church. Food served 12–2pm and 6.45–9pm (9.30pm Fri–Sat). Well-behaved children and dogs welcome. Car park. Eight miles south of Cambridge with Audley End and Duxford air museum close by.

OPEN *11am–2.30pm and 6–11pm Mon–Sat; 12–4pm and 7–10.30pm Sun.*

HISTON

Red Lion

27 High Street, Histon CB24 9JD
☎ *(01223) 564437 Mark Donachy*

 At least seven real ales on offer at this freehouse, including Tring Blonde, Everards Tiger and Beacon, Oakham Bishop's Farewell and Elgood's Black Dog. The two guests (around five per week) could be Abbeydale Absolution, York Guzzler, Nethergate IPA, B&T Edwin Taylor Stout and Crouch Vale Brewers Gold.

Two-bar pub with huge display of breweriana and a coal fire in one of the bars. No machines or music. Food served 12–2pm. Darts, crib, petanque and cricket teams. Two annual beer festivals (Easter and first week in September). Monthly theme nights (booking necessary), such as curry night, Belgian night, Cockney night. Half a mile from the A14 – follow the signs for Histon.

OPEN *10.30am–2.30pm and 4–11pm Mon–Thurs; all day Fri–Sun.*

HOLYWELL

The Ferryboat Inn

Holywell PE27 4TG
☎ *(01480) 463227*
David and Niamh Baynham

Tied to Greene King, with IPA and Abbot plus additional beers, mainly available in the summer, including Greene King Old Speckled Hen and Ruddles County.

Remote pub in a rural setting down a country lane and overlooking the River Great Ouse. Ring for directions, if needed! Food-oriented, with meals available all day. Large bar and eating area with function room. Children welcome.

OPEN *11.30am–11pm Mon–Sat; 12–10.30pm Sun.*

HUNTINGDON

King of the Belgians

27 Main Street, Hartford, Huntingdon PE29 1XU
☎ *(01480) 52030*
James McAulay and Gwyneth Davies

Freehouse serving three guest beers from local breweries such as Cottage, Potton, Nethergate and Greene King.

A traditional pub in a Grade II listed building. Two bars. Pub food served 12–2pm (2.30pm Sun) and 6–9pm. Children welcome. Quiz nights. Sky Sports shown. Beer garden. Car park. Located in Hartford village, within Huntingdon.

OPEN *10am–3pm and 5–11pm Mon–Thurs; all day Fri–Sun.*

The Old Bridge Hotel

1 High Street, Huntingdon PE29 3TQ
☎ *(01480) 424300* Nina Beamond
www.huntsbridge.com

Adnams Best and City of Cambridge Hobson's Choice plus a guest beer.

Smart town-centre hotel that features a busy and welcoming bar. Restaurant meals and bar snacks served every day, with full afternoon teas. Well-behaved children allowed. Occasional live entertainment.

OPEN *11am–12pm every day*

KEYSTON

The Pheasant

Keyston, Huntingdon PE28 0RE
☎ *(01832) 710241* Taffeta Scrimshaw

Adnams Bitter plus two guests from a changing selection, with brews from Potton, City of Cambridge and other local micro-breweries appearing regularly.

A thatched inn in a quiet village, with oak beams and large open fires. Quality food served in the pub, and in the small restaurant. Food available lunchtimes and evenings. Car park. Children welcome.

OPEN *12–3pm and 6–11pm.*

LEIGHTON BROMSWOLD

The Green Man

37 The Avenue, Leighton Bromswold, Nr Huntingdon PE18 0SH
☎ *(01480) 890238* Toni Hanagan

Nethergate IPA plus three weekly guest beers (200 per year) perhaps from Adnams, Wells and Young's, Robinson's, Shepherd Neame, Brakspear, Fuller's, Wychwood, Shepherd Neame or Timothy Taylor.

Family-run, 17th-century, detached village pub decorated with water jugs and memorabilia. Bar food available 12–2pm Fri–Sun and 7–9pm Tues–Sat. Car park, beer garden. Children welcome. Skittles played. Barn for hire. Handy for fishing at Grafham Water and Rutland Water, with Wickstead Park only ten miles away. Off J17 of the A14 between Thrapston and Brampton Hut.

OPEN *12–3pm and 6.30–11pm Tues–Sun (closed all day Mon).*

LITTLE GRANSDEN

The Chequers

71 Main Road, Little Gransden, Sandy, Bedfordshire SG19 3DW
☎ *(01767) 677348* Bob and Wendy Mitchell

Freehouse with a minimum of three real ales (six at weekends). Nethergate IPA is always available, the others change daily. A micro-brewery was recently installed.

Friendly, award-winning pub with tap room, lounge, games room and large garden. Food on Friday evenings only (fish and chips!). Children welcome until 9pm. Car park. Close to the Bedfordshire border, halfway between Cambridge and Bedford.

OPEN *12–2pm and 7–11pm Mon–Thurs; 11am–11pm Fri–Sat; 12–10.30pm Sun.*

LONGSTOWE

The Red House

134 Old North Road, Longstowe PB3 7UT
☎ *(01954) 718480* Martin Willis
www.theredhouse-pub.co.uk

Freehouse with a selection of beers from small to medium-sized breweries around Britain. The house beer is Buntingford Highwayman IPA, the others change daily.

Traditional rural pub built in 1750 with one bar, beer garden and separate restaurant. Food available at lunchtimes and evenings on weekdays, all day at weekends (last food orders Sat 3pm). No games. Live music occasionally on Sundays. Grand piano in bar: with customers encouraged to play a tune if they can. Car parking. Children welcome. Between Royston and Huntingdon.

OPEN *12–3pm and 5.30–11pm Mon–Fri; 12–11pm Sat; 12–10.30pm Sun.*

MADINGLEY

The Three Horseshoes

Madingley CB3 8AB
☎ *(01954) 210221* Richard Stokes
www.huntsbridge.com

Adnams Best plus two guests, City of Cambridge being a regular.

A thatched inn with a bar and large garden. Imaginative food served in the bar, garden and conservatory-restaurant. Meals available 12–2pm and 6.30–9.30pm daily. Car park. Children welcome.

OPEN *11.30am–2.30pm and 6–11pm Mon–Sat; 12–3pm and 7–10.30pm Sun.*

MARCH

The Rose & Crown

41 St Peters Road, March PE15 9NA
☎ *(01354) 656705* Miss Jackie Millson

At least seven real ales served from a menu that changes on a daily basis.

A 150-year-old suburban pub. Winner of a CAMRA gold award. No juke box, no videos, no television, just a good old-fashioned friendly atmosphere and a games machine! Outside beer garden available in summer. Car parking for at least 15 cars.

OPEN *4–11.30pm Mon–Fri; 12–12 Sat; 12–3pm and 7–10.30pm Sun.*

MILTON
The Waggon & Horses
39 High Street, Milton CB24 6DF
☎ *(01223) 860313*
Nick and Mandy Winnington

 Elgood's Cambridge Bitter, Black Dog Mild, Golden Newt and a seasonal or guest ale from a varied range.

Imposing 1930s mock-Tudor building set back from the main road. Large child-friendly garden to rear. Note hat collection and eclectic pictures on walls. Bar billiards and darts. Food available 12–2pm and 6–9pm (7–9pm Thurs, Sat and Sun). Children allowed in pub under supervision (9pm curfew), as are animals on a lead. Child-friendly beer garden, small car park. Village at junction of A10 and A14.

OPEN *12–2.30pm and 5–11pm Mon–Fri (midnight Fri); 12–3pm and 6–11.30pm Sat; 7–10.30pm Sun.*

NEEDINGWORTH
The Queen's Head
30 High Street, Needingworth, Nr Huntingdon PE17 2SA
☎ *(01480) 463946* Fraser and Linda Macrae

 Up to three real ales, including beers such as Greene King Old Speckled Hen and Black Sheep Bitter.

Friendly pub, refurbished and extended. Fantastic restaurant with home-cooked food, served 12–2pm and 6–9pm Mon–Fri, all day Sat and 12–3pm Sun. Children allowed. Close to St Ives.

OPEN *12–2.30pm and 5–11pm Mon–Thurs; 12–2.30pm and 5pm–12.30am Fri; noon–12.30am Sat; 12–10.30pm Sun.*

NEWTON
Queen's Head
Fowlmere Road, Newton, Nr Cambridge CB22 7PG
☎ *(01223) 870436* David and Robert Short

 Genuine freehouse but has specialised in Adnams beers for over 30 years. Usually serves Bitter and Broadside plus one of the brewery's seasonal ales.

Dating from the 1680s (the landlords from 1729 are listed) with a later extension. Beside the village green (outside tables) with a public and saloon bar plus games room. Bar food served 12–2.30pm and 7–9.30pm. Car park, well-behaved children welcome, bar games. Three miles from M11 junction 10; less than two miles off the A10 at Harston.

OPEN *11.30am–2.30pm and 6–11pm Mon–Sat; 12–2.30pm and 7–10.30pm Sun.*

OLD WESTON
The Swan
Main Road, Old Weston, Huntingdon PE28 5LL
☎ *(01832) 293400* Jim Taylor

 Greene King Abbot, Adnams Best and Broadside at this freehouse, along with a guest beer changed weekly.

A 400-year-old beamed pub with a central bar, lounge, small restaurant and games room with bar skittles. Food served Sat–Sun lunchtimes and Wed, Fri and Sat evenings.

OPEN *6.30–11.30pm Mon–Fri; 12–3pm and 7–11pm Sat–Sun (10.30pm Sun).*

PETERBOROUGH
Bogart's Bar and Grill
17 North Street, Peterborough PE1 2RA
☎ *(01733) 890939* Thomas Melillo

 Six beers always available, from a varied selection, some changed weekly, some fortnightly. Everards Original, Tiger and Sunchaser are regulars, and beers from Full Mash and Oakham are often on offer.

Bogart's was built at the turn of the 20th century and has a horseshoe-shaped bar and an open-plan area, darts area and TV dining area. Outside there is a shelter for smokers and an ale bar. Plasma screen. Food served 12–9pm Tues–Sat, plus Sunday roast 12–6pm. Beer garden. Children welcome until 6pm. Disabled facilities. Beer festival every bank holiday, plus mini-festival every weekend during Jun–Aug. Live music at the start and end of every month, plus DJs on Thursday nights. Next to Westgate House car park.

OPEN *All day, every day (later openings Fri–Sat).*

The Brewery Tap
80 Westgate, Peterborough PE1 2AA
☎ *(01733) 358500*
Stuart Wright, Jessica Loock and Paul Hook
www.oakhamales.com

Freehouse linked to the Oakham Ales brewery, which brews on site and can be observed through a glass wall. Up to 12 pumps serving Oakham JHB, Bishop's Farewell and White Dwarf as plus a mild, and eight guests from all over the country, changed daily.

Open-plan 500-seater pub with relaxed sofa seating area and restaurant-style Thai food served at pub prices 12–2.30pm and 6–9.30pm Sun–Thurs, all day Fri–Sat. Extended opening hours on Fri and Sat, when there is entertainment, live music and DJs. Children welcome during food service times. Two in-house beer festivals each year. Public car parks nearby. Near Peterborough train, bus and coach stations.

OPEN *12–late (even later on Fri–Sat).*

Charters Real Ale Bar

Town Bridge, Peterborough PE1 1FP
☎ *(01733) 315700 Paul Hook*
www.bluesontheboat.co.uk/www.oakhamales.com

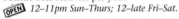 Twelve hand pumps offering four permanent and eight guest ales. Oakham JHB, White Dwarf, Inferno and Bishop's Farewell plus guest beers (500 a year) changing every other day, from breweries such as Dark Star, Whim, Milestone, Crouch Vale, Abbeydale, Newby Wyke and Leatherbritches.

A176-ft floating converted Dutch barge moored on the River Nene by the bridge in the centre of Peterborough, built in 1907 and now a real ale live music bar. Oriental restaurant on the upper deck, with food served 12–2.30pm and 6–10pm. Children welcome if accompanied by a responsible adult. Dogs allowed. Landscaped beer garden next to the river. Late-night entertainment Fri and Sat nights until 2am. Three or four outside beer festivals per year.

OPEN *12–11pm Sun–Thurs; 12–late Fri–Sat.*

Coalheavers Arms

5 Park Street, Fletton, Peterborough PE2 9BH
☎ *(01733) 565664*

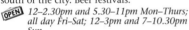 Milton Brewery ales including Minotaur, Jupiter and Pegasus plus guest beers from smaller breweries such as Bartrams, Rooster's and Black Sheep.

Backstreet boozer relaunched in 2002 by a local consortium including the Milton Brewery. No food. Outside seating. In the south of the city. Beer festivals.

OPEN *12–2.30pm and 5.30–11pm Mon–Thurs; all day Fri–Sat; 12–3pm and 7–10.30pm Sun.*

Hand & Heart

12 Highbury Street, Peterborough PE1 3BE
☎ *(01733) 564653 Eamon Bracken*

 Four well-kept real ales, changed weekly, from a range that might include Potton Village Bike, Wolf Granny Wouldn't Like It, Barnsley IPA, Elgood's Black Dog Stout and Kelham Island Pride of Sheffield.

A local community pub retaining many original 1930s features, with friendly, warm atmosphere. Open fire, wooden floors and large beer garden with lawn and flowers. Crib, darts and dominoes, but no juke box. Sandwiches and rolls are available on request. Children welcome in lounge bar until 6pm. Located 15 minutes' walk from town centre, off Lincoln Road.

OPEN *11am–11pm Mon–Sat; 12–10.30pm Sun.*

The Palmerston Arms

82 Oundle Road, Peterborough PE2 9PA
☎ *(01733) 565865 David McLennan*
www.palmerston-arms.co.uk

 Owned by Bateman since 2003, with up to 12 real ales, all dispensed by gravity direct from the cellar. The selection is ever-changing, but will usually include three or four Bateman brews, and five guests that rotate several times a week.

Two-bar alehouse, 400 years old, with traditional 1970s interior and 1950s furniture. No music, no games, no TV. Filled rolls served all day (subject to availability). Beer festivals, beer tasting, real ale home delivery service. Small courtyard area. No car park, no children, no private room. Dogs welcome. Half a mile from the town centre – see map on the website.

OPEN *4–11pm Mon; 12–11pm Tues–Thurs; 12–12 Fri–Sat; 12–11.30pm Sun.*

REACH

The Dyke's End

Fair Green, Reach, Cambridge CB25 0JD
☎ *(01638) 743816*
Simon Owers and Frank Feehan

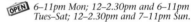 Genuine freehouse and home of the Devil's Dyke micro-brewery. Devil's Dyke Bitter and Woodforde's Wherry, plus two or three brews produced on site and changed on a weekly basis.

Saved from closure in 1998 by a village co-operative, this former farmhouse is now owned by a single villager who has added the micro-brewery and is now extending the bar area to cope with the increasing demand for a good, old-fashioned village pub. Food served 12–2pm and 7–9pm Tues–Sat; 12–2pm Sun. No food Mon. From Cambridge, follow signs to Newmarket, then Swaffham Priory, then Reach.

OPEN *6–11pm Mon; 12–2.30pm and 6–11pm Tues–Sat; 12–2.30pm and 7–11pm Sun.*

ST IVES

Oliver Cromwell

13 Wellington Street, St Ives PE27 5AZ
☎ *(01480) 465601 J P Schonfeldt*
www.theolivercromwell.co.uk

A genuine freehouse serving Adnams Broadside and Bitter, Oakham JHB and Woodforde's Wherry. Two guests changed weekly including Fuller's London Pride, Archers IPA and ales from Nethergate, Grainstore, Greene King, Caledonian and many more.

Very much the classic town local, this is an award-winning 300-year-old pub with a large panelled bar and heated covered area for smokers. Situated in the back streets, near the river. Food available Mon–Sat lunchtimes. From the bridge, walk down past the quay to find the pub.

OPEN *11am–11pm Mon–Thurs; 11am–12.30am Fri–Sat; 12–11pm Sun.*

The Royal Oak

13 Crown Street, St Ives PE27 4EB
☎ *(01480) 462586 Angie Davies*

Adnams Broadside, Wadworth 6X, Tetley Bitter and a Charles Wells beer.

Built in 1502 and now a Grade II listed building, this traditional-style pub in the town centre features a single bar. Food served 12–4pm. Children allowed until 7pm. Car park, beer garden.

OPEN *11am–11pm Mon–Sat; 12–10.30pm Sun.*

STILTON

The Bell Inn Hotel

Great North Road, Stilton, Peterborough PE7 3RA
☎ *(01733) 241066*
S A Robson and L McGivern
www.thebellstilton.co.uk

 A freehouse. Greene King IPA and Abbot, Oakham JHB and Fuller's London Pride, plus one or two guests each week. Daleside Blonde, Hop Back Crop Circle, Crouch Vale Brewers Gold and Castle Rock Harvest Pale have featured as guests.

Pub dating from at least 1500. The highwayman Dick Turpin is supposed to have hidden here, and Cromwell's troops visited during the English Civil War. The Bell is the birthplace of Stilton cheese, where it has been served since the 18th century. Today there is a village bar, residents' bar, bistro, restaurant and conference suite. Accommodation. Licensed as a wedding venue. Outdoor courtyard. Breakfast, lunch and dinner available daily.

OPEN *12–2.30pm and 6–11pm Mon–Thurs; 12–2.30pm and 6pm–12 Fri; 12–3pm and 6pm–12 Sat; 12–3pm and 7–11pm Sun.*

STOW CUM QUY

Prince Albert

Newmarket Road, Stow cum Quy CB5 9AQ
☎ *(01223) 813377* Mr and Mrs Henderson

 Five real ales including Greene King IPA. Guests might include Ash Vine Bitter and Shardlow Reverend Eaton's Ale.

Lively roadside pub built in 1830. Bar and à la carte restaurant, food served at lunchtimes and weekend evenings. Private functions catered for. Car park and garden. Children allowed. Just off A14 on the Newmarket road (A1303).

OPEN *11am–3.30pm and 5–11pm Mon–Fri; all day Sat–Sun.*

White Swan

Main Street, Stow cum Quy CB5 9AB
☎ *(01223) 811821*
Sandra and Colin Allsebrook

Woodforde's Wherry, Greene King IPA, Fuller's London Pride and Sharp's Doom Bar plus one guest beer changed weekly, perhaps from Adnams.

Village inn and restaurant serving a fine selection of real ales and quality wines, and offering a friendly atmosphere and a warm welcome for all, including families. Home-cooked food served 12–2.30pm every day (carvery on Sunday) and 6–8.30pm Mon–Sat. Beer garden and large car park. Close to Anglesey Abbey.

OPEN *12–3pm and 6–11pm Mon–Fri; 12–11pm Sat; 12–10.30pm Sun.*

SWAVESEY

The White Horse Inn

1 Market Street, Swavesey CB24 5QG
☎ *(01954) 232470* Will Wright
www.whitehorseswavesey.com

 An Enterprise Inns pub serving Caledonian Deuchars IPA plus two or three guests.

A village inn, dating from the early 17th century. Two bars with log fires, a pool room and bar billiards. Beer garden with patio and play area. Food served except Sun evenings. Children and dogs (on a lead) welcome. Annual beer festival every May bank holiday. Function room for private hire. Half a mile from the A14.

OPEN *12–3pm and 6–11pm Mon–Thurs; 12–3pm and 6pm–12.30am Fri; 11.30am–12.30am Sat; 12–11pm Sun.*

THRIPLOW

The Green Man

2 Lower Street, Thriplow SG8 7RJ
☎ *(01763) 208855* Ian Parr
www.greenmanthriplow.co.uk

 Genuine freehouse offering an ever-changing selection of up to four real ales. Beers from Milton, Adnams, Slaters and Woodforde's are favoured.

Open-plan, two-bar, 200-year-old pub by the village green, with small dining area. The pub is painted a striking blue! Bar and restaurant food available 12–2pm and 7–9pm Tues–Sat, 12–2pm Sun. Car park and garden. Annual pig race and daffodil festival. Two miles from M11 J10.

OPEN *12–3pm and 6–11pm Tues–Sat; 12–3pm Sun (closed Sun evening and all day Mon).*

WHITTLESEY

The Boat Inn

2 Ramsey Road, Whittlesey, Nr Peterborough PE7 1DR
☎ *(01733) 202488* Philip Quinn

Elgood's Brewery tied house serving Cambridge Bitter, Pageant Ale and GSB.

A 17th-century former coaching inn on a site mentioned in the Domesday Book. One large informal bar, plus separate lounge featuring the bow of a boat as the bar. Bed and breakfast accommodation. No food (except breakfasts for those staying). Large car park and garden featuring children's play area and covered patio. Seven miles from Peterborough. Ask for directions on reaching Whittlesey.

OPEN *Open from 7.30am Tues–Fri; from noon Sat–Mon.*

THE BREWERIES

RW RANDALL LTD
PO Box 154, Vauxlaurens Brewery, St Julian's Avenue, St Peter Port, Guernsey GY1 3JG
☎ *(01481) 720134*

ISLAND GOLD 3.4% ABV
CYNFUL 3.5% ABV
SIMPLE 3.5% ABV
PALE ALE 3.8% ABV
SLIPPING BULL 4.2% ABV
WICKED 4.2% ABV
ENVY 4.8% ABV
PATOIS ALE 4.8% ABV
GUILTY STOUT 5.2% ABV
Plus occasional brews.

THE PUBS

GUERNSEY

CASTEL
Hotel Fleur du Jardin
Kings Mills, Castel, Guernsey GY5 7JT
☎ *(01481) 257996* Keith Read
www.fleurdujardin.com

Freehouse serving Jersey Guernsey Sunbeam and Fuller's London Pride.

A 15th-century country inn in a converted farmhouse, with two bars, low beams, open fires and an olde-worlde atmosphere. Bar and restaurant meals served 12–2pm and 6–9.30pm (9pm Sun). Beer garden, car park. Just inland from Vazon Bay.

🍺 *11am–11.45pm Mon–Sat; 12–11pm Sun.*

FOREST
Venture Inn
New Road, (Rue de la Villiaze), Forest, Guernsey GY8 0HG
☎ *(01481) 263211* Tony and Kay Mollet

Randall's Patois plus seasonal or occasional brews.

Country pub in the heart of the farming community. Log fire in the lounge bar during winter months. Big-screen TV, pool and darts in the public bar. Food served May–Sept, 12–2pm and 6–9pm Mon–Sat; Oct–Apr, 12–2pm Mon–Thurs, 12–2pm and 6–9pm Fri–Sat. Car park. Children's menu.

🍺 *10.30am–11.45pm Mon–Sat.*

ST MARTINS
The Captain's Hotel
La Fosse, St Martins, Guernsey GY4 6EF
☎ *(01481) 238990* Alison Delamare
www.thecaptainshotel.co.uk

Two real ales, including Fuller's London Pride and a guest ale changed every couple of weeks, perhaps Shepherd Neame Spitfire, Greene King Old Speckled Hen, or something from Adnams, Black Sheep or Timothy Taylor.

A traditional family-run hotel, popular with locals and tourists. Lunch and dinner served daily in bar and bistro, with traditional bar meals, pizza, vegetarian dishes

and a wide selection of fresh fish. Parties catered for. Children and dogs welcome.

🍺 *11am–11pm Sun–Thurs; 11am–midnight Fri–Sat.*

ST PETER PORT
Albion House Tavern
Church Square, St Peter Port, Guernsey GY1 2LD
☎ *(01481) 723518* Amanda Roberts

Jersey Brewery house with Guernsey Sunbeam and occasional guests.

S pread over two floors with a large nautical-themed bar downstairs, sports bar and wine bar upstairs (great views) with pool tables. Food available 12–2.30pm daily, all day on Sundays and Mon–Thurs evenings. Children welcome. Situated right beside the Church.

🍺 *10.30am–11.45pm Mon–Thurs; 10.30am–12.45am Fri–Sat; 12–10pm Sun.*

The Banker's Draught
The Pollet, St Peter Port, Guernsey GY1 1WL
☎ *(01481) 723855* Suzanne and Glen Pontin

Jersey Brewery tied house serving Guernsey Sunbeam, with Fuller's London Pride and Shepherd Neame Spitfire among the guests.

A big pub with varied clientele – business people, tourists and families. Video games machines and video juke box, live bands occasionally. Food served at lunchtime only. Children allowed. Opposite the harbour exit.

🍺 *10am–11.45pm Mon–Thurs; 10am–12.45am Fri–Sat; 12–7pm Sun.*

Cock & Bull
2 Lower Hauteville, St Peter Port, Guernsey
☎ *(01481) 722660* Stephen Taylor

Freehouse serving Ringwood beers plus guests from breweries such as Stonehenge, Shepherd Neame, Hop Back, Greene King, Orkney, and many others. The range changes constantly.

L arge, friendly pub on three levels, with one bar and a traditional feel, voted Guernsey CAMRA Pub of the Year on many occasions. There is an outdoor smoking area. The varied clientele includes rugby supporters and plenty of university students. Quarterly beer festivals held. Live music three times a week including Irish music provided by the landlord and his wife on Thursday nights (with a little Irish dancing thrown in!). Visiting musicians are most welcome. Baroque ensemble third Monday of each month. Acoustic jam sessions every Tuesday night. Pool room, big-screen TV. Situated at the top of Cornet Street, on the way to Victor Hugo's house, and close to the Mignot Plateau, which offers one of the best views of Castle Cornet.

🍺 *11.30am–2.30pm and 4–11.45pm Mon–Thurs; 11.30am–12.45am Fri–Sat; closed Sun.*

The Cornerstone Café Bar

2 La Tour Beauregard, St Peter Port, Guernsey GY1 1LQ
☎ *(01481) 713832* William Cann
www.cornerstoneguernsey.co.uk

Freehouse with three hand pumps. Examples of beers served include Shepherd Neame Early Bird, Fuller's London Pride, Badger Best and Tanglefoot, Timothy Taylor Landlord, Young's Bitter and Greene King IPA. The local Randall's Patois is proving extremely popular with locals and visitors alike, and is now a regular feature.

Café/bar popular with locals and visitors. Comprehensive menu offering local fresh fish and bar food specials, daily roasts, homemade soups and chilli. Sandwiches and baguettes made while you wait. Food is served 10am–2.15pm and 6–8.15pm Mon–Weds and Sat, 8am–2.15pm and 6–8.15pm Thurs–Fri. Menu also available in French. Occasional live music, dart board and amusing jokes in the toilets.

(OPEN) *10am–12.45am Mon–Weds and Sat; 8am–12.45am Thurs–Fri; closed Sun.*

The Drunken Duck

La Charroterie, St Peter Port, Guernsey GY1 1EL
☎ *(01481) 726170* Cyril Dunne

The range on offer at this freehouse varies, with brews such as Wadworth 6X, Fuller's London Pride, Thwaites Lancaster Bomber, Badger Best and Tanglefoot, Adnams Broadside, Bateman XXXB, Young's Bitter and Greene King Old Speckled Hen and IPA, to name but a few.

A small, friendly pub, still painted yellow! Appeals to young and old alike, and is popular with a wide range of customers. Big-screen TV for major sporting events (GAA games shown live during the season), plus separate, quiet back bar. Food available Mon–Fri lunchtimes. Ample parking from 5pm and at weekends.

(OPEN) *11am–12.45am Mon–Sat; 12–11pm Sun.*

The Ship & Crown

Pier Steps, North Esplanade, St Peter Port, Guernsey GY1 2NB
☎ *(01481) 721368* Mark Pontin

Jersey Brewery pub with four real ales from a range including Marston's Pedigree, Fuller's London Pride, Timothy Taylor Landlord, and Greene King IPA, Abbot, Ruddles County and Old Speckled Hen. Changed on a daily basis.

Established in 1846, this traditional town pub has been in the Pontin family since 1979. It boasts excellent views over the harbour, and is popular with visitors and locals alike. It has a contemporary feel, though it has managed to retain its character. There are several wall displays of local shipwrecks and local history, including the German occupation during WW2. Traditional pub meals and daily specials are served 11am–9pm Mon–Thurs, 11am–6pm Fri–Sat and 12–9pm Sun. Car park. Children welcome while food is being served.

(OPEN) *10am–12.45am Mon–Sat; noon–12.45am Sun.*

ST SAMPSON

Pony Inn

Les Capelles, St Sampsons, Guernsey GY2 4GX
☎ *(01481) 244374* Isoken Ogbeide

Jersey Brewery tied house always serving either Guernsey Sunbeam or Pirates Ale.

A family-orientated two-bar pub with conservatory, patio, play area, Playstations and TV-screen games. Child-free zone for those who prefer a peaceful pint. Live music every Friday. Car park. Food available.

(OPEN) *10.30am–11.45pm.*

VALE

Houmet Tavern

Grande Havre, Vale, Guernsey GY6 8JR
☎ *(01481) 242214* Antony Green

Jersey Brewery tied house with one guest, changed every couple of weeks. Seasonal and special brews are sometimes featured, but the guest could be from anywhere.

Comfortable lounge bar overlooking the sea. Darts, pool, bar billiards. Beer garden. Car park. Food available Mon–Sat lunchtimes and Tues, Wed, Fri, Sat evenings. Children allowed, and there is a special children's menu available.

(OPEN) *10am–11.45pm.*

JERSEY

GROUVILLE

Seymour Inn

La Rocque, Grouville, Jersey JE3 9BU
☎ *(01534) 854558* Gary Boner

Jersey Guernsey Sunbeam and Jimmy's Bitter usually available.

Traditional country pub with two lounges, bar and beer garden. Food 12–2pm and 6–8pm Mon–Sat. Car park. Children welcome.

(OPEN) *10am–11pm Mon–Sat; 11am–11pm Sun.*

ST BRELADE

The Old Smugglers Inn

Ouaisne Bay, St Brelade, Jersey JE3 8AW
☎ *(01534) 741510* Andrew Walker

Genuine freehouse serving at least two real ales, perhaps including Greene King Abbot and something from Ringwood or Skinner's and changed on a daily basis. Traditional scrumpy also served.

Close to the beach and dating from the 18th century, this pub has no music or fruit machines. Good food, including a children's menu, is served every day. Children welcome. Large free car park. Beer festivals held Feb, March, Oct and Dec. Turn left towards Portelet at the top of St Aubins Hill, then right at the sign for Ouaisne, keep right, follow the hill, and the pub is at the bottom on the left.

(OPEN) *All day, every day.*

ST HELIER

The Lamplighter

9 Mulcaster Street, St Helier, Jersey JE2 3NJ
☎ *(01534) 723119* Sean Murphy

Eight real ales usually available. Beers from Wells and Young's, Jennings, Skinner's, Marston's, Stonehenge, Hop Back and Dark Star are often featured, plus guests.

Gas-lit pub with old wooden beams, rafters and soft, pewter bar top. The only Cask Marque accredited pub in the Channel Islands, and named Cask Pub of the Year in 2004, 2005 and 2006. Local CAMRA Pub of the Year 2006 and 2007, and holder of Beautiful Beer Gold award. Refurbished in July 2003 but with the character still intact. Live sport on satellite TV. Food served 12–3pm Tues–Fri and 12–4pm Sat –Sun (no food in the evening). Children welcome. Close to St Helier bus station.

OPEN *10am–11pm Mon–Sat; 11am–11pm Sun.*

The Prince of Wales Tavern

French Lane, St Helier, Jersey JE2 4SL
☎ *(01534) 737378* Graeme Channing

Tied to Randalls, with five real ales changing from time to time. A typical selection would be Ringwood Best, Skinner's Betty Stogs and Ginger Tosser, and Courage Cask and Directors.

A small, one-bar, 18th-century tavern in the middle of St Helier with character and ambience and a beautiful beer garden. No TV, no pool, no juke box, just background music. Food 11.45am–2.30pm April–Nov. No children. No car park. Next to the central market.

OPEN *10am–11.30pm Mon–Sat; 12–2pm Sun.*

ST OUEN

Le Moulin de Lecq

Greve de Lecq, St Ouen, Jersey JE3 2DT
☎ *(01534) 482818* Kenneth Jenkins

Freehouse offering local real ales such as Jersey Jimmy's Bitter and up to five guest ales such as Greene King Old Speckled Hen and Abbot or a Ringwood brew.

Built around a 12th-century flour mill with working parts still on view inside and outside the bar, this is one of the few remaining freehouses in Jersey. The water wheel was used during the German occupation to generate electricity for searchlights. Two bars and small upstairs lounge, large beer garden and adventure playground. Summer barbecues, beer festivals. Food served at lunchtimes and evenings. There is a new restaurant on the side of the pub. Children welcome. Very close to the beach.

OPEN *All day, every day.*

THE BREWERIES

BEARTOWN BREWERY
Bromley House, Spindle Street, Congleton
CW12 1QN
☎ *(01260) 299964*
www.beartownbrewery.co.uk

 GOLDIE HOPS 3.5% ABV
Pale, hoppy session bitter.
BEAR ASS 4.0% ABV
Aromatic, with smooth, dry malty flavour.
KODIAK GOLD 4.0% ABV
Sharp with citrus and hops with a bitter
aftertaste.
BEARSKINFUL 4.2% ABV
Golden, dry sharp flavour, with a hoppy, rich
malt aftertaste.
SPECIALITY HOPPY NEW BEAR 4.5% ABV
Malty bitter with good hop nose, available each
new year as a celebratory brew.
POLAR ECLIPSE 4.8% ABV
Rich dark oatmeal stout.
BLACK BEAR 5.0% ABV
Smooth, dark ruby mild.
BRUINS RUIN 5.0% ABV
Golden, smooth and full flavoured.
WHEAT BEAR 5.0% ABV
Crisp, refreshing award winner.
Plus seasonal and occasional brews.

BOROUGH ARMS BREWERY
The Borough Arms, 33 Earle Street, Crewe
CW1 2BG
☎ *(01270) 254999*

PALE ALE 3.9% ABV
NEVER BEHIND 4.5% ABV
EARLE THOMAS 5.7% ABV

COACH HOUSE BREWING CO. LTD
Wharf Street, Howley, Warrington WA1 2DQ
☎ *(01925) 232800*
www.coach-house-brewing.co.uk

COACHMAN'S BEST BITTER 3.7% ABV
Smooth, rich malt flavour, with some
fruit.
GUNPOWDER STRONG MILD 3.8% ABV
Full flavour, with slight bitter aftertaste.
HONEYPOT 3.8% ABV
Lightly hopped, medium bodied and golden.
FARRIERS BEST BITTER 3.9% ABV
Sweet at first but rich hoppy finish.
CROMWELL'S BEST BITTER 4.0% ABV
Smooth and well balanced.
DICK TURPIN PREMIUM BITTER 4.2% ABV
Strong session beer with toffee, malty palate.
DUCKWORTH'S DELIGHT 4.3% ABV
Mellow with a hoppy aftertaste.
FLINTLOCK PALE ALE 4.4% ABV
Light and golden with a touch of sweetness.
INNKEEPER'S SPECIAL RESERVE 4.5% ABV
Crisp and malty with balancing hops.
POSTLETHWAITE 4.6% ABV
Dry and fruity.
GINGER NUT PREMIUM BEER 5.0% ABV
Light colour, premium strength with a touch of
ginger.
POSTHORN PREMIUM 5.0% ABV
Rich, smooth and complex.
Plus seasonal and occasional brews.

FREDERIC ROBINSON LTD
Unicorn Brewery, Stockport SK1 1JJ
☎ *(0161) 480 6571*
www.frederic-robinson.com

 HATTERS 3.3% ABV
Fresh, with malt throughout.
OLD STOCKPORT BITTER 3.5% ABV
Golden, with a hoppy flavour.
UNICORN 4.2% ABV
Rich malt and hops with a long, dry finish.
DOUBLE HOP 5.0% ABV
Interesting hop flavour and bitterness.
OLD TOM 8.5% ABV
Superb, mellow winter warmer.
Plus specials and seasonal brews including:
DISSY BLONDE 3.8% ABV
FLASH HARRY 4.1% ABV
DARK HORSE 4.3% ABV
MR SCROOGE 4.4% ABV

NORTHERN BREWING LTD
Blakemere Brewery, Blakemere Craft Centre,
Chester Road, Sandiway, Northwich CW8 2EB
☎ *(01606) 301000*
www.norbrew.co.uk

ALL-NITER 3.8% ABV
ALL-DAYER 3.9% ABV
Pale and fruity.
SOUL RIDER 4.0% ABV
Straw-coloured bitter.
SPELLBINDER 4.1% ABV
Pronounced fruity aroma and flavour.
DANCER 4.2% ABV
Aromatic, intensely malty.
STAR 4.3% ABV
Made with European hops and traditional malt
varieties.
SOUL MASTER 4.4% ABV
Gold colour with citric and floral aromas.
45 4.5% ABV
Fruity and refreshing.
ONE-DER-FUL WHEAT 4.7% ABV
Subtle orange flavour.
SOUL TIME 5.0% ABV
Ruby colour with lemon undertones.
TWO TONE SPECIAL 5.0% ABV
Chocolatey-flavoured stout.

PARADISE BREWING COMPANY
Three Rivers Brewing Company Ltd, Vauxhall
Industrial Estate, Greg Street, Stockport SK5 7BR
☎ *(0161) 477 3333*
☎ *(01270) 780916*
www.paradisebrewery.co.uk

MARBURY MILD 3.6% ABV
FARMER'S FAVOURITE 4.0% ABV
DABBER'S WHEAT 5.0% ABV
NANTWICH ALE 5.4% ABV
RUM OLD ALE 6.3% ABV
Plus seasonal and occasional brews.

SPITTING FEATHERS BREWERY
Common Farm, Waverton, Chester CH3 7QT
☎ *(01244) 332052*
www.spittingfeathers.org

FAR HOUSE ALE 3.6% ABV
THIRST QUENCHER 3.9% ABV
OLD WAVERTONIAN 4.1% ABV
SPECIAL ALE 4.2% ABV
BASKETCASE 4.8% ABV
Plus seasonals.

STATION HOUSE BREWERY

Unit 1, Meadow Lane Industrial Park, Meadow Lane, Ellesmere Port CH65 4YT
☎ *(0151) 356 3000*
www.stationhousebrewery.co.uk

1ST LITE 3.8% ABV
Hints of grapefruit.
LADY O'THE STREAM 3.9% ABV
Three-hop mix.
ODE2JOY 4.1% ABV
Malty.
BUZZIN' 4.3% ABV
Tangy.
3 SCORE 4.5% ABV
Malty and raisin flavours.
LSC 5.0% ABV
Citrus tones.

THE STORM BREWING COMPANY

2 Waterside, Macclesfield SK11 7HJ
☎ *(01625) 431234*

BEAUFORTS 3.8% ABV
DESERT STORM 3.8% ABV
BITTER EXPERIENCE 4.0% ABV
TWISTER 4.0% ABV
BRAIN STORM 4.1% ABV
ALE FORCE 4.2% ABV
TORNADO 4.4% ABV
HURRICANE HUBERT 4.5% ABV
WINDGATHER 4.5% ABV
SILK OF AMNESIA 4.7% ABV
STORM DAMAGE 4.7% ABV
TYPHOON 5.0% ABV
Plus seasonal and occasional brews.

WC BREWERY LTD

Micklegate, Mickle Trafford, Chester CH2 4TF
thegents@wcbrewery.com

IP ALE 3.8% ABV
Hoppy, citrus notes.
GOLDEN CASCADE 4.0% ABV
Wheaty, malty, golden ale.
GYPSY'S KISS 4.1% ABV
Copper-coloured bitter.
SBD 5.0% ABV
Rich and fruity.
Plus seasonals and specials.

WEETWOOD ALES LTD

The Brewery, Weetwood Grange, Weetwood, Tarporley CW6 0NQ
☎ *(01829) 752377*
www.weetwoodales.co.uk

BEST BITTER 3.8% ABV
Rounded flavour, sharp bitter with hoppy aftertaste.
CHESHIRE CAT 4.0% ABV
Blonde ale with fruity, hoppy finish.
EASTGATE ALE 4.2% ABV
Golden, with fruity hoppiness.
OLD DOG PREMIUM BITTER 4.5% ABV
Deep colour, smooth and rich.
AMBUSH 4.8% ABV
Amber colour, fruity notes.
OAST-HOUSE GOLD 5.0% ABV
Pale and hoppy with a dry finish.

WOODLANDS BREWING COMPANY

Unit 5, Creamery Industrial Estate, Station Road, Wrenbury, Nantwich CW5 8EX
☎ *(01270) 620101*
www.woodlandsbrewery.co.uk

OLD WILLOW 4.1% ABV
Pale and fruity.
OAK BEAUTY 4.2% ABV
Mid-coloured bitter with hint of acorn.
WOODLANDS IPA 4.3% ABV
Lighter version of traditional IPA.
MIDNIGHT STOUT 4.4% ABV
Roasted barley flavour.
WOODLANDS BITTER 4.4% ABV
Dark tan colour, very little aftertaste.
GOLD BREW 5.0% ABV
Bitter with blended hop aftertaste.
Plus seasonal and occasional brews.

THE PUBS

ALDFORD

Grosvenor Arms

Chester Road, Aldford, Chester CH3 6HJ
☎ *(01244) 620228* Gary Kidd
www.grosvenorarms-aldford.co.uk

 Regular beers are Caledonian Deuchars IPA, Thwaites Original and Weetwood Eastgate, plus two rotating guest beers.

Charming Victorian pub on the Duke of Westminster's estate. It has well-spaced rooms and a great outside terrace leading into a large garden, which in turn leads onto the village green. Children welcome if supervised until 7pm. Food served daily 12–10pm (9pm Sun). Dogs allowed in tap room.

OPEN *11.30am–11.00pm Mon–Sat; 12–10.30pm Sun.*

ALTRINCHAM

The Old Market Tavern

Old Market Place, Altrincham WA14 4DN
☎ *(0161) 927 7062* Janet Casserley
www.oldmarkettavern.co.uk

A Punch Taverns pub. Bank Top Smokestack, Lightning and Volunteer, Phoenix Arizona and Caledonian Deuchars IPA plus up to seven guests. Oakham JHB, Hop Back Summer Lightning, Adnams Regatta, Dent Kamikaze, George Wright Drunken Duck and Coach House Gunpowder Strong Mild feature regularly.

A one-bar pub, built in 1600. Food served 12–2.30pm and 5–8pm Mon–Fri; 12–6pm Sat–Sun. Children welcome. Wed: quiz night; Sat and Sun: live music. Function room. Beer garden. Located on the A56, near the Cresta Court.

OPEN *12–11pm Sun–Mon; 12–12 Wed–Sat.*

APPLETON THORN

Appleton Thorn Village Hall

*Stretton Road, Appleton Thorn, Nr Warrington
WA4 4RT*
☎ *(01925) 268370* Mrs Karen Howard
 Five real ales, always different (over 1,500 served in last three years).

Charitable village club operated voluntarily by local residents. Membership not required for entry, though new members always welcome (£4 per year). Car park, garden, playing field, bowling green, pool and darts. Children welcome. From M6 Jct 20 or M56 Jct 10, follow signs for Appleton Thorn. Hall is 100m west of village church.

OPEN *8.30–11pm Thurs–Sat; 8.30–10.30pm Sun. Open lunchtimes (1–4pm) on first Sunday of each month.*

ASTON

Bhurtpore Inn

*Wrenbury Road, Aston, Nr Nantwich
CW5 8DQ*
☎ *(01270) 780917* Simon and Nicky George
www.bhurtpore.co.uk
 Eleven real ales usually on offer (1,100+ a year), all changed regularly, on average twice a week. Beers from Salopian, Weetwood, Moorhoue's, Slaters (Eccleshall), Abbeydale, Hornbeam and Allgates often feature. Also real cider and 150 bottled Belgian beers plus eight Belgian beers on draught.

The family has been connected with this comfortable, traditional, award-winning pub since 1849. Fresh bar and restaurant food 12–2pm and 6.45–9.30pm Mon–Fri and 12–9pm Sat-Sun. Car park, large beer garden. Well-behaved children allowed at lunchtime and in early evening up to 8pm. Annual beer festival in July, with 118 ales featured at the 2008 event. Located five miles south of Nantwich, west of the A530, between Nantwich and Whitchurch.

OPEN *12–2.30pm and 6.30–11pm Mon–Fri; 12–12 Fri, Sat; 12–11pm Sun.*

BOLLINGTON

The Poacher's Inn

95 Ingersley Road, Bollington SK10 5RE
☎ *(01625) 572086* Rob and Helen Ellwood
www.thepoachers.org
 Freehouse serving Timothy Taylor Landlord and Copper Dragon Best Bitter plus three changing guests.

A friendly, local community pub, 200 years old, stone-built, with a welcoming fire in winter. Food served 12–2pm and 6–9.30pm Tues–Sat; 12–9pm Sun. Beer garden. Car park. Private room for hire.

OPEN *5.30–11pm Mon (closed Mon lunch); 12–2pm and 5.30–11pm Tues–Fri; 12–2pm and 7–11pm Sat; 12–11pm Sun.*

Vale Inn

Adlington Road, Bollington SK10 5JT
☎ *(01625) 575147* Lee Wainwright
www.valeinn.co.uk
 Freehouse offering their own selection of cask ales and up to three from other local breweries.

A 150-year-old stone pub overlooking the cricket ground, with one room and an imposing stone bar. Food served 12–2.30pm and 6–9pm Mon–Wed; 12–2.30pm and 6–10pm Thur and Fri; 12–9pm Sat and Sun. Beer garden, car park. Regular beer festivals. Head north through Bollington and turn left at The Dog & Partridge.

OPEN *12–3pm and 5.30–11pm Mon–Fri; 12–11pm Sat–Sun.*

BROXTON

The Egerton Arms

Whitchurch Road, Broxton CH3 9JW
☎ *(01829) 782241*
Keith Wilson and Sian Stephens
A Marston's house, with two real ales from Jennings and Marston's. Beers are rotated monthly.

Large former hunting lodge, refurbished in 2006 and promising fantastic hospitality. Home-cooked food served 12–9.30pm every day. Families very welcome. Seven letting rooms. Large garden, large car park. Ten miles from Chester on the junction of the A41 and A534.

OPEN *12–11pm.*

BUNBURY

The Dysart Arms

*Bowes Gate Road, Bunbury, Nr Tarporley
CW6 9PH*
☎ *(01829) 260183*
www.dysartarms-bunbury.co.uk
Thwaites Best Bitter and something from Weetwood plus a couple of guest beers, changed frequently.

Dating from 1770, a classic English village pub with open fires and an abundance of oak furniture. Food served 12–9.30pm Mon–Sat and 12–9pm Sun. Beer garden, car park. Supervised children until 6pm. Disabled facilities. Beer festival on alternate years. Bunbury Mill, Beeston and Peckforton castles are nearby.

OPEN *11.30am–11pm Mon–Sat; 12–10.30pm Sun.*

BURLEYDAM
The Combermere Arms
Burleydam, Whitchurch SY13 4AT
☎ *(01948) 871223* Jon Astle-Rowe
www.combermerearms-burleydam.co.uk

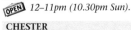 Thwaites Original and Mild, Sharp's Doom Bar and Weetwood Cheshire Cat. Two guests, changing every other day, such as Cotleigh Buzzard and Cottage Whippet Strikes Back.

Dating from the 18th century, with an eclectic layout of rooms off a central, three-sided bar. Real fires, beams, oak floors, old furniture. Food served 12–9.30pm. Children and dogs welcome. Beer gardens at front and back. Large car park. Located on the A525.

OPEN *12–11pm (10.30pm Sun).*

CHESTER
Albion Inn
Park Street, Chester CH1 1RN
☎ *(01244) 340345* Michael Mercer
www.albioninnchester.co.uk

A Punch Taverns pub. Timothy Taylor Landlord and Young's Bitter. One guest, changed quarterly, such as Coachman's Cheshire Gold or Titanic Steerage or Lifeboat.

The Albion is dedicated to the Great War and decorated with prints, pictures and articles of interest. No under-18s. Racegoers discouraged. Organic, free-range and locally sourced food available 12–2pm and 5–8pm (booking required). No food Sun evening. Two en-suite bedrooms available. Situated against the city walls between the Newgate and the river.

OPEN *12–3pm and 5–11pm Mon–Fri; 12–3pm and 6–11pm Sat; 12–2.30pm and 7–10.30pm Sun.*

Bear & Billet
94 Lower Bridge Street, Chester CH1 1RU
☎ *(01244) 311886* Alexandra Bruchez

Owned by Okells, with six real ales, including Okells Bitter and IPA plus three or four guests changed every couple of days, such as Weetwood Cheshire Cat, Oakham JHB, Bank Top Spitting Feathers and beers from Phoenix.

The birthplace of John Lennon's grandmother and once the home of the Earl of Shrewsbury, this timber-framed pub was built in 1664. Delicious home-cooked food served 12–9pm Mon–Sat and 12–7pm Sun. At the bottom of Lower Bridge Street, on the right.

OPEN *12–11pm Mon–Tues; 12–11.30pm Wed–Thurs; 12–12 Fri–Sat; 12–10.30pm Sun.*

Bromfield Arms
43 Faulkner Street, Hoole CH2 3BD
☎ *(01244) 345037* Chris Gilley

Part of the John Barras Co chain, with three real ales, including Caledonian Deuchars IPA, Charles Wells Bombardier, plus a guest beer, changed twice a week.

Warm, friendly local, a pub since 1871, with a real fire, one lounge and one traditional bar. Over the years, a music hall and a billiards room have operated here, and US officers were based here during World War 2. Food served 11am–9.30pm. Disabled facilities. Close to city centre and handy for Chester Zoo. In Hoole, just off Hoole Road, near the train station.

OPEN *11am–11.30pm.*

The Mill Hotel & Spa
Milton Street, Chester CH1 3NF
☎ *(01244) 350035* Gary and Gordon Vickers
www.millhotel.com

 CAMRA local Pub of the Year 2000 and 2004, offering five permanent real ales (including Weetwood Best, Coach House Mill Premium, Cains Traditional Bitter and brews from Phoenix). Guests change daily (approx. 2000 served every year) and always include a mild and either a stout or a porter. Requests welcome! Plus real cider.

Hotel bar and restaurant on the site of a once-working mill. Bar and restaurant food available at lunchtime and evenings. Canalside patio, restaurant boat lunch and dinner cruises. Accommodation available (130 bedrooms). Sky Sports on TV (with sound turned down). Families most welcome. Ample car parking.

OPEN *11am–11pm Mon–Sat; 12–10.30pm Sun.*

Old Harkers Arms
1 Russell Street, Chester CH3 5AL
☎ *(01244) 344525* Paul Jeffery
www.harkers.arms-chester.co.uk

Up to 12 real ales: Wadworth 6X, Thwaites Original and Weetwood Cheshire Cat plus a wide range of daily changing guests such as Titanic Stout, Crouch Vale Brewer's Gold, Weetwood Ambush, RCH Old Slug Porter and Marble Lagonda.

City of London-style two-bar boozer in a converted warehouse, built using reclaimed wood – the bar front is made from old mahogany doors, and the bar top from chemistry lab counters! Chester and South Clwyd CAMRA Pub of the Year in 2007. Food, from a changing seasonal menu with local produce, served 12–9.30pm every day. No children. Dogs allowed in the bar area. On the Shropshire Union Canal, just off City Road, two minutes from the train station.

OPEN *11.30am–11pm Mon–Sat; 12–10.30pm Sun.*

The Pheasant Inn
Higher Burwardsley, Tattenhall, Chester CH3 9PF
☎ *(01829) 770434* Andrew Nelson
www.thepheasantinn.co.uk

 Freehouse serving Weetwood Best, Eastgate and Old Dog plus one guest ale, changed by the firkin.

A 300-year-old inn nestling in the Peckforton Hills overlooking the Cheshire plains. Sandstone walls, log fires and a flower-filled courtyard. Food served 12–3pm and 6–9.30pm Mon, 12–9.30pm Tues–Thurs, 12–10pm Fri–Sat, 12–8.30pm Sun. Beer garden. Car park. Accommodation.

OPEN *11am–11pm.*

The Plough Inn

Plough Lane, Chester CH3 7PT
☎ *(01244) 336096* Philip Harland
www.theploughinnchester.co.uk

Tied to the Globe Pub Co, with between five and seven real ales on a typical night, with Theakston Best Bitter usually served. Guest ales including from local brewery Spitting Feathers changed weekly.

An 18th-century former cottage, this pub has been extended over the years. Central main bar with pub one side and restaurant on the other. Food served 12–3pm and 6–9pm Mon–Sat, 12–8pm Sun. Large beer garden and orchard. Landlord rears his own animals for the restaurant, including pigs, geese, turkeys and hens. Also grow their own vegetables according to the season. Three miles from Chester town centre, half a mile from children's theme park Crocky Trail. Situated between Waverton and Christleton with access from the A41 and A51.

OPEN *12–12 (11pm Sun).*

Telford's Warehouse

Tower Wharf, Chester CH1 4EZ
☎ *(01244) 390090* Jeremy Horrill
www.telfordswarehouse.com

Freehouse serving Timothy Taylor Landlord, a Weetwood ale and two weekly-changing guests.

Canal warehouse built in the 1790s by Thomas Telford. Remains in the original style, with beams, timbers and bare brick. Food served all day. Separate restaurant. Beer garden. Car park. Live music venue and art gallery. Situated over Shropshire Union Canal.

OPEN *12–12 (sometimes later).*

The Union Vaults

44 Egerton Street, Chester CH1 3ND
☎ *(01244) 400556* Trevor and Linda Craggs

Tied to Punch Taverns, with Everards Tiger always on offer, plus two guests rotated fortnightly. Examples include Punch Finest Cask Book, Fullers London Pride, Wadsworth 6X, Black Sheep.

A local pub with one bar, snug and lounge. Courtyard at rear with decking and seating, plus heated smoking area. One of only a few pubs with a bagatelle table. No food. Within five minutes' walk of the shops and railway station.

OPEN *10am–11pm Mon–Thurs; 10am–late Fri–Sat; 10am–10.30pm Sun.*

CONGLETON

The Beartown Tap

18 Willow Street, Congleton CW12 1RL
☎ *(01260) 270990* Steve King

The Beartown Brewery tap, with the full range of Beartown beers usually available. Six hand-pulled beers at any one time, with one a guest beer from another micro-brewery. Cider and Belgian beer on draught, plus over 30 bottled Belgian and Czech beers.

Traditional drinkers' town pub, quiet (no juke box), with no swearing! Dominoes, darts and crib. Function room upstairs, beer garden at rear. Brewery tours booked at the pub. Children allowed. Parking nearby.

OPEN *12–2pm and 4–11pm Mon–Thurs; 12–11pm Fri–Sat; 12–10.30pm Sun.*

The Castle Inn

Castle Inn Road, Dane-in-Shaw, Congleton CW12 3LP
☎ *(01260) 277505* Julie Parkinson

Timothy Taylor Landlord and Greene King Old Speckled Hen plus two guests, changed every three or four days.

Food-led country pub dating from the 18th century, set on the Biddulph Way and Gritstone Path on the Cheshire/Staffordshire border . Home-cooked food served all day, every day. Large beer garden with children's play area. Two large car parks. On the A527 between Congleton and Biddulph.

OPEN *12–11pm.*

The Queen's Head Hotel

Park Lane, Congleton CW12 3DE
☎ *(01260) 272546* Anna Gunner
www.queensheadhotel.org.uk

Eight real ales. Greene King Abbot and Charles Wells Bombardier are favourites, other beers might come from breweries such as Woodlands, Archers, Titanic, Cottage and Storm and are changed every couple of days.

A traditional community pub beside the Macclesfield Canal (with moorings). Food served all day. Garden with children's play area. Bed and breakfast accommodation.

OPEN *11am–midnight (late licence to 2am Fri–Sat).*

FRODSHAM

Helter Skelter

31 Church Street, Frodsham WA6 6PN
☎ *(01928) 733361* Nicholas Broome

Six real ales, including Weetwood Best Bitter (the house beer) plus five guests, changing every day or two.

Traditional real ale pub offering home-cooked food, with no juke box or games machine. Bar meals served 12–2.30pm and 5.30–8.30pm Mon–Sat, and 12–4pm Sun. The restaurant is open 6–9.30pm Thurs–Sat and 12–4pm Sun. Parking. Children allowed in restaurant. In the main shopping area, opposite Ennisbury Square car park.

OPEN *11am–11.30pm Mon–Sat; 12–10.30pm Sun.*

Netherton Hall

Chester Road, Frodsham WA6 6UL
☎ *(01928) 732342*

A Jennings brew is a permanent fixture, plus four other ales, perhaps Greene King Abbot and IPA, Timothy Taylor Landlord and something from Adnams.

A typical Cheshire country pub on the main road, with one large bar. Food served at lunchtimes and evenings, and all day Sunday. Well-behaved children allowed.

OPEN *11am–11pm Mon–Sat; 12–10.30pm Sun.*

GREAT SUTTON

The White Swan Inn

*Old Chester Road, Great Sutton, Ellesmere Port
CH66 3NZ*
☎ *(0151) 339 9284* David Morris

 Tied to Robinsons's and offering Old Stockport and Cumbria Way plus a quarterly guest.

A traditional community local with bar and lounge. Meals served at lunchtimes 12–2pm and 5–7pm Mon–Sat (except Tues) and 12–6pm Sun (three meats available for Sunday roast). Satellite TV, beer garden, car park, Wi-Fi. Quiz nights Mon and Thurs. Just off the A41.

OPEN *11.30am–midnight Mon–Sat; 12–12 Sun.*

HALEBANK

The Cock & Trumpet Inn

Halebank Road, Halebank, Widnes WA8 8NB
☎ *(0151) 425 3142* Tom Glover (manager)

 Two hand pumps serve Burtonwood Top Hat plus one guest, changed weekly, which could be Jennings Sneck Lifter or Shepherd Neame Bishop's Finger, though the aim is not to repeat beers too often.

Fairly modern community pub with two bars (games room and lounge). 'Pub grub' served. Beer garden with play area. Barbecues when weather permits. Car park. Children allowed up to 8pm. Five minutes from Runcorn Bridge, off Ditton Road.

OPEN *11.30am–11pm Mon–Sat; 12–10.30pm Sun.*

HANDFORTH

The Railway

Station Road, Handforth, Wilmslow SK9 3AB
☎ *(01625) 523472* Nick and Sue Quinn

Robinson's Unicorn Bitter and Hatter's Mild plus Robinson's seasonal beers, such as the award-winning Old Tom. Wide selection of Spanish wines.

Friendly, traditional pub with a main bar featuring railway memorabilia, a separate dining room dedicated to a Laurel and Hardy tribute, Traditional Vault. Relax in luxury leather room leading direcctly to spectacular smoking area and beer garden. Live sports shown, and live entertainment. Home-cooked food served 12–2pm and 12–4pm Sat–Sun. Authentic Spanish Tapas menu served Thurs 5.30–9pm. Opposite Handforth railway station.

OPEN *11am–11pm Sun–Thurs; 11am–midnight Fri–Sat.*

HANKELOW

The White Lion

Audlem Road, Hankelow, Nr Crewe CW3 0JA
☎ *(01270) 811288* Gareth and Carol Blythin
www.thewhitelionpub.com

Charles Wells Bombardier plus up to three guests, perhaps including local brews from Spitting Feathers or Weetwood Ales.

Traditional, 19th-century country pub opposite the village green and duck pond. Public bar, lounge bar and restaurant. Good food served 12–2pm Tues–Sun and 6.30–9pm Mon–Sat. Large beer garden, car park. August beer festival. On the A529 between Nantwich and Audlem.

OPEN *5.30–11pm Mon; all day Tues–Sun.*

HASSALL GREEN

The Romping Donkey

Hassall Green, Sandbach CW11 4YA
☎ *(01270) 765202* Steve Fennel

Greene King Abbot and Robinson's Best Bitter always featured.

A family-oriented pub with large beer garden. Food 12–9pm daily, with carvery, bar menu and à la carte. Children welcome. Large car park. Off the Alsager–Sandbach road, turn left at the New End pub.

OPEN *12–11pm (10.30pm Sun).*

HATCHMERE

Carriers Inn

Delamere Road, Hatchmere, Norley
☎ *(01928) 788258* Karen Ashton

Burtonwood house serving Bitter and Smooth plus two monthly guests. York Yorkshire Terrier is a regular.

Refurbished inn with restaurant and extensive beer garden overlooking the lake. Food available 12–3pm and 6–8pm daily. Pool table. Children allowed, with children's play area provided. On the B5152.

OPEN *11am–11pm Mon–Sat; 12–10.30pm Sun.*

HIGHER HURDSFIELD

George & Dragon

*61 Rainow Road, Higher Hurdsfield, Macclesfield
SK10 2PD*
☎ *(01625) 424300* D Molly Harrison

A beer from Storm Brewing Co. is among the brews usually available.

Traditional part-17th-century pub with food served 12–2pm Mon–Fri and Sun. Car park. Children welcome.

OPEN *12–3pm and 7–11pm Mon–Fri; 7–11pm Sat; 12–3pm and 7.30–10.30pm Sun.*

HYDE

The Sportsman

57 Mottram Road, Hyde SK12 2NN
☎ *(0161) 368 5000* Peter and Greg Banks

Genuine freehouse with up to eight real ales. Moorhouse's Black Cat Mild, Plassey Bitter, Hartington Bitter, Timothy Taylor Landlord, Phoenix Bantam and Pictish Brewers Gold are regulars, plus a couple of guests.

Traditional, early-Victorian community alehouse with two bars in the town centre. Open fires, function room, pool table, quiz nights etc. Car park. Beer festival in October. Close to Newton station.

OPEN *11am–2am Mon–Sat; noon–2am Sun.*

KINGSLEY

Horseshoe Inn

Hollow Lane, Kingsley WA6 8EF
☎ *(01928) 788466* Ron Varnett

 Burtonwood pub, with Burtonwood Bitter always on offer. The monthly guest could be Everards Tiger or a Ridleys brew.

Village community pub with an L-shaped bar and open fire. Food is available, and there is a dining area. Patio, car park. Children allowed.

OPEN *12–3pm and 5–11pm (10.30pm Sun).*

KNUTSFORD

The Cross Keys Hotel

King Street, Knutsford WA16 6DT
☎ *(01565) 750404* Andrew Burke
www.knutsfordcrosskeys.co.uk

 Enterprise Inns pub serving up to six real ales. Timothy Taylor Landlord, Caledonian Deuchars IPA plus guest ales from breweries such as Weetwood, Archers and Storm.

A 16th-century coaching inn with lounge, tap room and cellar restaurant. Housed in a 13-room hotel in the town centre. Food served 12–2pm every day. Outside seating area.

OPEN *11.30am–3pm and 5–11pm Mon–Thurs (until 11.30pm Thurs); 11.30am–midnight Fri–Sun.*

LANGLEY

Leather's Smithy

Clarke Lane, Langley, Nr Macclesfield SK11 0NE
☎ *(01260) 252313* Paul McMahon
www.leatherssmithy.co.uk

 Charles Wells Bombardier, Theakston Best and Greene King Old Speckled Hen plus one guest changed twice weekly. Wherever possible, guest beers are not repeated. Also 80 different whiskies.

Former smithy (originally run by William Leather), built in the 16th century in a beautiful area on the edge of Macclesfield Forest overlooking the Ridge Gate Reservoir (fishing possible). Food at lunchtime and evenings. Car park, garden, family/function room.

OPEN *12–3pm and 7–11pm Mon–Sat; 12–10.30pm Sun.*

LITTLE NESTON

The Harp Inn

19 Quayside, Little Neston CH64 0TB
☎ *(0151) 336 6980* A Jones

 An Admiral Taverns pub with up to six real ales. Timothy Taylor Landlord and Titanic Iceberg are the permanent beers, and the rest change every six weeks and might include Jennings Sneck Lifter or Cumberland, plus brews from Copper Dragon, Spitting Feathers, Coach House or Wadworth.

Over 400 years old, a pub with lots of history from the local mines, decorated with memorabilia and pictures. There are unspoilt views across to Wales, and the pub is popular with birdwatchers and walkers. Food served 12–2pm Tues–Fri. Grassed area

with tables and beer garden. Children and pets welcome. In Little Neston, turn down Marshlands Road, go to the very bottom and turn left – the pub is 200 yards along.

OPEN *12–12.*

MACCLESFIELD

The Railway View

Byrons Lane, Macclesfield SK11 7JW
☎ *(01625) 423657* Graham and Sue Calvert

 Freehouse with an ever-changing selection of real ales, with beers from Phoenix, Titanic, Copper Dragon, Weetwood, Moorhouse's and Archers regularly available, plus local breweries Storm and Beartown.

One-bar family pub with beams and log fires. Patio area, pool, darts. Football friendly – the pub is on the way to the ground, and away supporters are welcome.

OPEN *7–11pm Mon–Tues; 6–11pm Wed–Thurs; 4–11pm Fri; 12–11pm Sat; 12–10.30pm Sun.*

Waters Green Tavern

96 Waters Green, Macclesfield SK11 6LH
☎ *(01625) 422653* Brian McDermott

 Timothy Taylor Landlord and Greene King IPA plus guests from breweries such as Rooster's, Phoenix, Oakham and Whim, to name but a few.

A traditional pub with a real fire in winter. Home-cooked food served at lunchtime only. Children allowed if dining.

OPEN *11.30am–3pm and 5.30–11pm Mon–Fri; 11am–3pm and 7–11pm Sat; 12–3pm and 7–10.30pm Sun.*

MIDDLEWICH

The Big Lock

Webbs Lane, Middlewich CW10 9DN
☎ *(01606) 833489* Stuart Griffiths

 Phoenix Wobbly Bob and Black Sheep Bitter permanently available. The two guests, changed every fortnight and not repeated if possible, could be Marston's Pedigree, Charles Wells Bombardier, or anything from Beartown or Moorhouse's.

Traditional pub on the canal bank with outside balcony and benches overlooking the canal. Two public bars, restaurant and function room. Food served at lunchtimes and evenings, all day on Sun. Car park. Children allowed. Call for directions.

OPEN *11am–11pm Mon–Sat; 12–10.30pm Sun.*

MOBBERLEY
The Roebuck Inn
Mill Lane, Mobberley WA16 7XH
☎ *(01565) 873322* Jane Marsden
www.theroebuck.com

Freehouse with Timothy Taylor Landlord and Greene King Old Speckled Hen plus guests, changed weekly, that may include Greene King Abbot, Charles Wells Bombardier or something from Adnams.

A friendly country inn with a contemporary twist. Fresh locally sourced food served 12–2.30pm and 6–9.30pm Mon–Fri, 12–9.30pm Sat, and 12–4pm and 6–9pm Sun. Large three-tier beer garden. Private function room for hire. Car park available. Children welcome.

OPEN *12–3pm and 5–11pm Mon–Fri; 12–11pm Sat; 12–10.30pm Sun.*

NANTWICH
The Black Lion
29 Welsh Row, Nantwich CW5 5ED
☎ *(01270) 628711* Jill Llewellyn

Weetwood Best, Old Dog and Eastgate plus Titanic White Star always available on hand pump with Titanic Stout in bottles and real cider.

Former CAMRA Pub of the Year built in 1664, a traditional two-bar pub with exposed beams and wooden floors. No food. Children welcome during the day. Beer garden, conservatory. Live music several nights a week. On the A53 Old Chester Road, near the Shropshire Union canal.

OPEN *4–11pm Mon–Thurs; 12–11pm Fri–Sat; 12–10.30pm Sun.*

Oddfellows Arms
97 Welsh Row, Nantwich CW5 5ET
☎ *(01270) 624758* Roger Drinkwater

Tied to Burtonwood, with Burtonwood Bitter and Top Hat plus two monthly-changing guest beers (three each month).

Locals' pub, built circa 1640 with beams and open fires. Food served daily at lunch and early evening except Monday. Book for Sunday lunch. Garden. First pub into town from the canal. Children allowed until 9pm if eating. On the A534, the old Chester road from the town centre.

OPEN *12–3pm and 6–11pm Mon–Thurs (closed Mon lunch); 12–11pm Fri–Sat; 12–4pm and 7–10.30pm Sun.*

Wilbraham Arms
58 Welsh Row, Nantwich CW5 5EJ
☎ *(01270) 626419*

Marston's Pedigree and JW Lees Best Bitter always available.

Close to the town centre, near canal, with traditional Georgian frontage, bar and dining area. Bar food available at lunchtime and evenings. Accommodation. Children allowed in dining room. Small car park.

OPEN *12–11pm (10.30pm Sun).*

NESTON
The Harp Inn
19 Quayside, Neston CH64 0TB
☎ *(0151) 336 6980* Albert Jones

An Admiral Taverns tied house with Timothy Taylor Landlord, Greene King IPA and Abbot plus three guest ales. Changing up to every six weeks, these are often from breweries such as Holt.

Over 400 years old, with small bar and lounge. No juke box, TV, pool table, dartboard or games machines. Open fire in winter, beer garden in summer, with an unobstructed view of the Welsh mountains as far as the eye can see. A bird watcher's paradise! Food served 12–2pm Tues–Fri. Children and dogs welcome. Approximately one mile from Neston town centre.

OPEN *12–12.*

NORTHWICH
George and the Dragon
High Street, Great Budworth, Northwich CW9 6HF
☎ *(01606) 891317* Alan Todd

Punch Taverns pub serving Weetwood Cheshire Cat plus two guests, always from local independent breweries.

Built in 1700 and set in an idyllic village location. Food served 12–2pm and 6–9pm Mon–Sat; 12–6pm Sun. Children and dogs welcome. Private room for hire. Off the A559 at Great Budworth.

OPEN *12–3pm and 5–11.30pm Mon–Fri; 12–11.30pm Sat–Sun.*

NORTHWICH
Penny Black
110 Witton Street, Northwich CW5 1AB
☎ *(01606) 42029* Roger Cazaly

A Wetherspoon's pub. Marston's Pedigree and Greene King Abbot are regulars, plus up to eight guests, changed daily, from Storm, Phoenix, Moorhouse's, George Wright, Beartown and Wentworth.

Huge, black and white timber building, formerly a post office and sorting office, and dating from 1914. Sheltered outside area. Regular beer festivals featuring up to 60 beers. Food served 9am–10pm. Children welcome if eating. Located in the centre of Northwich, opposite Sainsburys.

OPEN *9am–midnight Sun–Thurs; 9am–1am Fri–Sat.*

OVER PEOVER

The Dog Inn

*Well Bank Lane, Over Peover, Nr Knutsford
WA16 8UP*
☎ *(01625) 861421* Steve Wrigley

A freehouse with five real ales. Hydes Bitter, Weetwood Best, Copper Dragon 1816 and Moorhouse's Black Cat are permanent fixtures, plus one guest, changed monthly.

A 200-year-old rural pub with front bar, tap room, dining room and accommodation. Food served 12–2.30pm and 6–9pm Mon–Sat; 12–8.30pm Sun. Front patio and rear beer garden. Children welcome. Large car park. Annual beer festival in July. Located in Peover Heath, signposted from Chelford roundabout.

OPEN *11.30am–3pm and 4.30–11pm Mon–Fri; 11.30am–11pm Sat; 12–10.30pm Sun.*

PENKETH

The Ferry Tavern

Station Road, Penketh, Warrington WA5 2UJ
☎ *(01925) 791117*
A Mulholland and J Maxwell
www.theferrytavern.com

Boddingtons Bitter (brewed by Hydes), Courage Directors and Greene King Old Speckled Hen plus two rotating guests, changed daily. Over 300 whiskies also served.

Built in the 11th century, this has been an alehouse for 300 years. Unique position on an island between the River Mersey and the St Helens canal. Open coal fires, riverside beer garden. CAMRA Pub of the Year for Cheshire 2002. Home-cooked fresh food served 12–2pm Mon–Fri. Car park. Children and well-behaved dogs welcome. On the Trans-Pennine Trail. Follow signs for 'Yacht Haven'.

OPEN *12–3pm and 5.30–11pm Mon–Fri; 12–11pm Sat; 12–10.30pm Sun.*

RODE HEATH

The Royal Oak

41 Sandbach Road, Rode Heath ST7 3RW
☎ *(01270) 875670* Stephen Fennell

Six real ales, with Tetley Bitter and Dark Mild, Boddingtons Bitter (brewed by Hydes) and Greene King Abbot the permanent beers. The two guests, rotated every six weeks, might be something like Charles Wells Bombardier and Camerons Strongarm.

Public house with bar, lounge and restaurant. Food served 12–9pm. Children are welcome, and there is a fully equipped play area. Car park. Located on the main Alsager to Sandbach road.

OPEN *12–11pm (10.30pm Sun).*

SANDBACH

Ring O'Bells

17 Wells Street, Sandbach CW11 1GT
☎ *(01270) 765731* Jane Robson

A Burtonwood house serving Bitter and Mild plus guests during the winter months.

A traditional one-bar locals' pub with darts, pool and a juke box. No food. Children allowed until 6pm.

OPEN *11am–11pm Mon–Sat; 12–10.30pm Sun.*

SAUGHALL

The Greyhound Inn

Seahill Road, Saughall, Chester CH1 6BJ
☎ *(01244) 880205* Carl Jones

Six rotating real ales, often including something from Timothy Taylor and the local Spitting Feathers brewery.

Village pub leased from Enterprise Inns and dating from the 15th century, with a bar, snug, lounge, restaurant and real log fires. Has an outdoor dining area, beer garden and play area. Home-cooked traditional British food with a few international favourites served 12–2pm and 6–9pm Mon–Sat, and 12–4pm Sun, with a curry night on Mondays. On the Welsh border, not far from the M56 and 15 minutes from Chester city centre.

OPEN *11am–11pm Mon–Thurs; 11am–11.30pm Fri–Sat; 12–10.30pm Sun.*

SMALLWOOD

The Bluebell Inn

*Spen Green, Smallwood, Sandbach, Crewe
CW11 2XA*
☎ *(01477) 500262* Sally Owen

Leased from Punch Taverns and serving Black Sheep Bitter plus three rotating guests.

Traditional local country pub, dating from the 16th century. Food served 12–2.30pm Tues–Sun; 5.30–7.30pm Tues–Thurs. Children and dogs welcome. Large beer garden. Situated between the A50 and A34.

OPEN *5.30–11pm Mon (closed Mon lunch); 12–3pm and 5.30–11pm Tues–Thurs; 12–11pm Fri–Sat; 12–10.30pm Sun.*

SWETTENHAM
The Swettenham Arms
Swettenham Village, Congleton CW12 2LF
☎ *(01477) 571284*
Jim and Frances Cunningham
www.swettenhamarms.co.uk

 Freehouse offering a Hydes Brewery ale and a Beartown ale plus three guests changed every two weeks.

A 13th-century inn located in an Area of Outstanding Natural Beauty. The inn is steeped in local history, being a former nunnery with its own resident ghost! Locally sourced and home-prepared food available 12–2.30pm and 7–9.15pm Mon–Sat; 12–9.15pm Sun. The Quinta arboretum and nature reserve is accessed through the picnic area at the side of the pub, offering 30 acres of open space, water and wooded areas. Spectacular lavender meadow in summer, plus cream teas. Popular live jazz evenings and themed cabaret nights throughout the year. From J18 M6.

OPEN *11.30am–3pm and 6–11pm Mon–Sat; 11.30am–11pm Sun.*

TUSHINGHAM
The Blue Bell Inn
Bell o'th Hill, Tushingham, Nr Whitchurch SY13 4QS
☎ *(01948) 662172*
Ginette Hanson and Jeremy Mark Ward

 Hanby Drawwell Bitter plus one or two others (now up to 80 per year), perhaps including beers from Ma Pardoes Old Swan and Cotleigh breweries.

D ating from 1667, this is said to be one of Cheshire's oldest pubs. Friendly and welcoming. No games machines or loud music. Food available 12–2pm and 6–9pm Tues–Sat and 12–2pm and 7–9pm Sun. Car park and garden. Children and dogs always very welcome. Four miles north of Whitchurch on the A41 Chester road.

OPEN *12–3pm and 6–11pm Tues–Sat; 7–11pm Sun. Closed all day Mon except bank holidays.*

WARRINGTON
The Tavern
25 Church Street, Warrington WA1 2SS
☎ *(01925) 577990*

 Town-centre freehouse with up to six real ales from a wide range of breweries.

F ormerly known as Wilkies, a one-room pub with floorboards and pine furniture. Popular for sport on TV. No food. Covered rear courtyard.

OPEN *2–11pm Mon–Thurs; 12–11pm Fri–Sat; 12–10.30pm Sun*

WILLEY MOOR
Willey Moor Lock Tavern
Tarporley Road, Nr Whitchurch SY13 4HF
☎ *(01948) 663274* Elsie Gilkes

 Five real ales served in summer, two in winter. Beers from Beartown, Hanby Ales, Cottage, Weetwood, Coach House, Wood, Springhead and Wychwood breweries are likely to feature.

S ituated next to a working lock on the Llangollen Canal, this pub was formerly a lock-keeper's cottage. Food served lunchtimes and evenings. Children welcome: there is a large garden with a play area. Car park. Situated two miles north of Whitchurch on A49. Pub found at end of driveway, pub sign on the road.

OPEN *12–2.30pm (2pm winter) and 6–11pm Mon–Sat; 12–2.30pm (2pm winter) and 7–10.30pm Sun.*

WINCLE
The Ship Inn
Barlow Hill, Wincle, Macclesfield SK11 0QE
☎ *(01260) 227217* Chris Knights

 JW Lees Bitter, Brewer's Dark and John Willie's among the four real ales on offer at this freehouse. Plus a seasonal brew from the same brewery, perhaps Dragon's Fire or Spring Cheer.

A ttractive 16th-century sandstone inn in a very popular walking area of the Peak District. Food served 12–2.30pm and 6.30–9pm Tues–Sat; 12–3pm Sun. Beer garden and car park. Beer festival at August bank holiday weekend. Children welcome.

OPEN *5–10pm Mon; 12–3pm and 6.30–11.30pm Tues–Thurs; 12–3pm and 5–11pm Fri; 12–11pm Sat; 12–10.30pm Sun.*

THE BREWERIES

ATLANTIC BREWERY

*The Atlantic Brewery, Treisaac Farm, Treisaac,
Newquay TR8 4DX*
☎ *(0870) 042 1714*
www.atlanticbrewery.com

GOLD ORGANIC SUMMER ALE 4.6% ABV
BLUE ORGANIC DARK ALE 4.8% ABV
RED ORGANIC CELTIC ALE 5.0% ABV

BLACKAWTON BREWERY

*Unit 7, Peninsula Park, Moorlands Trading
Estate, Saltash PL12 6LX*
☎ *(01752) 848777*
www.blackawtonbrewery.com

ORIGINAL BITTER 3.8% ABV
Well hopped. A popular session beer.
WEST COUNTRY GOLD 4.1% ABV
Summer beer, sweet malt, vanilla and fruit
flavours.
44 SPECIAL 4.5% ABV
Full bodied with rich nutty flavour.
EXHIBITION ALE 4.7% ABV
Pale colour, smooth, rich hop taste.
WINTER FUEL 5.0% ABV
Winter beer, malty and chocolatey.
HEADSTRONG 5.2% ABV
Rich, smooth and powerful with fruit flavour.
Plus seasonal and occasional brews.

BLUE ANCHOR

50 Coinage Hall Street, Helston TR13 8EL
☎ *(01326) 562821*
www.spingoales.com/brewery.html

SPINGO IPA 4.5% ABV
Clean tasting and hoppy.
SPINGO MIDDLE 5.0% ABV
Sweet Cornish bitter.
SPINGO BRAGGET 6.1% ABV
Apple and honey flavours.
SPINGO SPECIAL 6.6% ABV
Dark with sweetness to the taste.
At Christmas and Easter an extra special brew is
available at 7.6% ABV.
Plus seasonal brews.

DOGHOUSE BREWERY

Scorrier, Redruth TR16 5BN
☎ *(01209) 822022*

WET NOSE 3.5% ABV
BITER 4.0% ABV
SNOOZY SUZI 4.2% ABV
DOZY DOG 4.4% ABV
CORNISH CORGI 4.5% ABV
BOW WOW 5.0% ABV
Seasonals:
SEADOG 4.6% ABV
STAFFI 4.7% ABV
RETRIEVER 5.0% ABV
XMAS TAIL 5.0% ABV
WINTER TAIL 5.5% ABV
COLLIE WOBBLES 5.8% ABV

DRIFTWOOD BREWERY

*Driftwood Spars Hotel, Trevaunance Cove,
St Agnes TR5 0RT*
☎ *(01872) 552428*
www.driftwoodspars.com/Brewery.htm

CUCKOO ALE 4.5% ABV
Pale, malty brew.

KELTEK BREWERY

Candela House, Cardrew Way, Redruth TR15 1SS
☎ *(01209) 313620*
www.keltekbrewery.co.uk

MAGIK 4.0% ABV
Medium colour, underlying sweetness.
NATURAL MAGIK 4.6% ABV
Rich malt and hops with a hint of ginger biscuit.
KING 5.1% ABV
Pale bitter with fruity citrus nature.
KRIPPLE DICK 6.0% ABV
Dark, sharp taste, made using five different
grains.
BEHEADED 7.6% ABV
Dark, slightly sweet, strong malt flavour.
Plus seasonal and occasional brews.

LIZARD ALES LTD

*Unit 2a, Treskewes Industrial Estate, St Keverne,
Helston TR12 6PE*
☎ *(01326) 281135*

HELFORD RIVER 3.6% ABV
KERNOW GOLD 3.8% ABV
BITTER 4.2% ABV
FRENCHMAN'S CREEK 4.6% ABV
AN GOFF 5.2% ABV
Plus seasonals.

THE ORGANIC BREWHOUSE

*Unit 1, Rural Workshops, Higher Bochym,
Cury Cross Lanes, Helston TR12 7AZ*
☎ *(01326) 241555*
www.theorganicbrewhouse.com

HALZEPHRON GOLD 3.6% ABV
Golden with hints of passion fruit.
LIZARD POINT 4.0% ABV
Golden, dry, fruity.
SERPENTINE 4.5% ABV
Malty and hoppy. Ruby colour, balanced.
BLACK ROCK 4.7% ABV
Robust porter, tangy, hoppy.
WOLF ROCK 5.0% ABV
Sweet balance, dry malt finish.
CHARLIE'S PRIDE 5.3% ABV
Refreshing and hoppy.
Plus seasonal and occasional brews.

RING O'BELLS BREWERY

Pennygilliam Way, Launceston PL15 7ED
☎ *(01566) 777787*
www.ringobellsbrewery.co.uk

PORKER'S PRIDE 3.8% ABV
Malt and hops, clean in the finish.
BODMIN BOAR 4.3% ABV
Full flavoured and aromatic with a malty finish.
DRECKLY 4.8% ABV
Spicy aroma with heather and gorse notes.
SURF BOAR 5.0% ABV
Hoppy, with clean bitter finish.
TIPSY TROTTER 5.1% ABV
Dark, malty and wheaty with a bite.
SOZZLED SWINE 5.5% ABV
Ruby coloured and flowery.
Plus seasonal and occasional brews.

ST AUSTELL BREWERY CO. LTD

63 Trevarthian Road, St Austell PL25 4BY
☎ *(0845) 241 1122*
www.staustellbrewery.co.uk

IPA 3.4% ABV
Golden colour, delicate hop. Spicy notes.
TINNERS 3.7% ABV
Light and refreshing.
DARTMOOR BEST 3.9% ABV
Toffee apple flavours.
BLACK PRINCE 4.0% ABV
Full-bodied fruity and molasses flavour.
TRIBUTE 4.2% ABV
Hoppy flavour and citrus nose.
PROPER JOB 4.5% ABV
Pine aroma. Hoppy, grassy taste.
HSD 5.0% ABV
Full bodied and complex. Raisin/toffee aroma
and dried fruit taste.

SHARP'S BREWERY

Sharp's Brewery, Rock, Cornwall PL27 6NU
☎ *(01208) 862121*
www.sharpsbrewery.co.uk

CORNISH COASTER 3.6% ABV
Honeyed and malty with a dry, hoppy
finish.
DOOM BAR BITTER 4.0% ABV
Spicy, resinous with hoppy notes.
EDEN ALE 4.4% ABV
Hoppy with a hint of malty sweetness.
SHARP'S OWN 4.4% ABV
Rich roasted and malty sweet.
ATLANTIC IPA 4.8% ABV
Crisp light sweetness, giving way to hoppy
dryness.
SPECIAL 5.2% ABV
Jellied fruit aroma and subtle roasted notes.
Plus seasonal and occasional brews.

SKINNER'S BREWING CO.

Riverside, Newham Road, Truro TR1 2DP
☎ *(01872) 271885*
www.skinnersbrewery.com

SPRIGGAN ALE 3.8% ABV
Light golden and hoppy.
BETTY STOGS BITTER 4.0% ABV
Distinctly hoppy.
HELIGAN HONEY 4.0% ABV
Light and hoppy with honey overtones.
GREEN HOP 4.2% ABV
Zingy, clean, green-tinged ale.
KEEL OVER 4.2% ABV
Classic mid-strength bitter. Smooth finish.
POPPY ALE 4.2% ABV
Classic Cornish bitter. Charity fund-raiser.
CORNISH KNOCKER 4.5% ABV
Clean and golden with a fresh aroma.
FIGGY'S BREW 4.5% ABV
Dark, full flavoured and smooth.
PENNY COME QUICK 4.5% ABV
Dark, creamy full oatmeal stout.
CORNISH BLONDE 5.0% ABV
Deceptively light with a citrus finish.
Plus speciality and occasional brews.

WHEAL ALE BREWERY

Paradise Park, Trelissick Road, Hayle TR27 4HY
☎ *(01736) 753974*

MILLER'S ALE 4.3% ABV
OLD SPECKLED PARROT 5.5% ABV
PICKLED PARROT 6.6% ABV

WOODEN HAND BREWERY

Unit 2b, Grampound Road Industrial Estate,
Grampound Road, Truro TR2 4TB
☎ *(01726) 884596*
www.woodenhand.co.uk

BLACK PEARL 4.0% ABV
Dry, tangy finish.
CORNISH BUCCANEER 4.3% ABV
Fruity, hoppy, dry finish.
CORNISH MUTINY 4.8% ABV
Slight biscuity flavour.
Plus speciality and occasional brews.

THE PUBS

ALTARNUN

The Rising Sun

Altarnun, Nr Launceston PL15 7SN
☎ *(01566) 86636* Andy Mason

Three to five real ales, changed
constantly. Brews from Sharp's, Cotleigh,
Greene King and Skinner's are often featured.

A 16th-century, single-bar moorland inn
with olde-worlde charm, open fires and
slate/hardwood floor. Bar and à la carte meals
available 12–2.30pm and 7–9.30pm daily.
The emphasis is on fresh food and local
produce, with everything made on the
premises, from bread to desserts. Darts and
pool teams. Camping facilities and
accommodation in three en-suite rooms.
Patio to rear, beer garden at front. Ample
parking. Children welcome (family/dining
room). Close to hiking trails. One mile off
the A30, seven miles west of Launceston.

OPEN *11am–3pm and 5.30–11pm Mon–Fri;
11am–11pm Sat; 12–10.30pm Sun. Open
all day, every day during summer season.*

ASHTON

The Lion & Lamb

Fore Street, Ashton, Nr Helston TE13 9RE
☎ *(01736) 763227* Barrie Martin

Up to four real ales from a range of local
independent brewers such as Sharp's and
Skinner's. Beers changed weekly.

A bout 200 years old, with one large bar
and separate restaurant area. Food served
12–2pm and 5.30–9pm daily. Beer garden at
rear, patio at front. Children welcome. Car
park. Close to St Michael's Mount, Lands End
and Flambards theme park. On the A394
between Helston and Penzance.

OPEN *12–12.*

BLISLAND

Blisland Inn

The Green, Blisland, Nr Bodmin
PL30 4JF
☎ *(01208) 850739*
Gary and Margaret Marshall

Freehouse with eight pumps, with guests changing every couple of days. Cornish ales are regulars.

Old-fashioned traditional pub on one of the last village greens left in Cornwall. The picturesque village has a lovely church that was one of Betjamin's favourites. Built using local stone, the pub has granite mullioned windows and real fires. Lounge, bar, family room and games. Food served 12–2pm and 6.30–9.30pm. Children allowed in family room. May is the month of mild – there is a Mild Festival all through the month! Very close to the Camel Trail and Bodmin Moor.

OPEN *11.30am–11pm Mon–Sat;*
12–10.30pm Sun.

BODMIN

The Masons Arms

5–9 Higher Bore Street, Bodmin PL31 2JS
☎ *(01208) 72607* David and Dionne Morgan

Sharp's Cornish Coaster and Doom Bar plus two weekly guests such as Greene King Abbot, Otter Ale, Adnams IPA, Marston's Pedigree, Theakston XB or Skinner's Cornish Knocker.

A 300-year-old, friendly, traditional Cornish drinkers' pub at the heart of the community. Three bars, old beams, slate floors and a warm welcome. Darts room, pool room, family room. Dogs welcome. Located on the main road, so easy to find.

OPEN *12–11.30pm (11pm Sun).*

BOSCASTLE

The Cobweb Inn

Boscastle PL35 0HE
☎ *(01840) 250278* Adrian and Ivor Bright

St Austell Tribute, Sharp's Doom Bar and Greene King Abbot plus a range of guest ales.

Atmospheric 17th-century freehouse, close to the harbour and run by the same family since 1969. Food served lunchtimes and evenings. Car park. Family room and restaurant. Outside seating. The pub is across the road from the car park at the bottom of the village, near the harbour.

OPEN *11am–11pm Mon–Fri; 11am–midnight*
Sat; 12–10.30pm Sun.

BUDE

The Bush Inn

Crosstown, Morwenstow, Bude EX23 9SR
☎ *(01288) 331242* Edwina Tape
www.bushinn-morwenstow.co.uk

A freehouse. St Austell HSD, plus a range of guest ales from Cornish breweries, such as Skinner's Betty Stogs, Sharp's Doom Bar and St Austell Tribute.

Cosy 13th-century country pub, just off the south-west coast path between Bude and Hartland. Food, from fresh local produce, served all day: full menu, light snacks and cream teas. Children and dogs welcome, children's menu available. Car park. Large garden with scenic views. Children's play area. Accommodation.

OPEN *11am–midnight.*

CHARLESTOWN

Rashleigh Arms

Quay Road, Charlestown, St Austell PL25 3NJ
☎ *(01726) 73635* Neville and Enid Andrews

St Austell house with HSD, Tribute and Tinners plus Skinner's Betty Stogs and Wadworth 6X on offer, plus a guest.

Grade II listed inn with locals' public bar, quiet lounge bar, restaurant, and a warm, friendly welcome. Bar and restaurant food served 12–3pm (carvery 12–2pm). Large outside seating area and beer garden. Live music Sat evenings. Eight en-suite letting rooms. Large car park. Children welcome. Close to the Eden Project and beautiful Charlestown harbour (home of square riggers). Follow signs for Charlestown from the St Austell bypass.

OPEN *11am–11pm (midnight Fri–Sat).*

CRACKINGTON HAVEN

Coombe Barton Inn

Crackington Haven, Bude EX23 0JG
☎ *(01840) 230345* Dawn and Stephen Oliver
www.coombebarton.co.uk

Freehouse offering up to four real ales. Sharp's Safe Haven (brewed especially for the pub following the 2004 flood), Doom Bar and St Austell Tribute are regulars, plus various guests, particularly in high season, with beers from Skinner's often on offer.

A family-run pub overlooking the beach in a beautiful cove. Once the house of the captain of the local slate quarry. Food served 12–2.30pm and 6.30–9.30pm, with a children's menu and Sunday carvery. Large family room. Six rooms available for bed and breakfast plus two self-catering cottages and a large function room for hire (ideal for weddings). Car park. Off the A39.

OPEN *Summer: 11am–11pm Sun–Thurs;*
11am–midnight Fri–Sat. Winter:
11am–3pm and 6–11pm Mon–Fri;
11am–11pm Sat; 12–11pm Sun.

CRANTOCK

Old Albion

Langurroc Road, Crantock, Newquay TR8 5RB
☎ *(01637) 830243*
James Hardy and A Cockcroft

Skinner's and St Austell beers plus three guests, changed frequently, perhaps including Fuller's London Pride, Smiles Best and something from Ring O'Bells, plus extra guests in summer.

A country pub, which used to be used for smuggling beer, situated next to the church in Crantock. Homemade food served at lunchtime and evenings in bar area. Children allowed in family room.

OPEN *12–11pm.*

CROWLAS
The Star Inn
Crowlas, Penzance TR20 8DX
☎ *(01736) 740375* Peter Elvin

Freehouse with five real ales, changed daily, so that at least 15 beers are on offer each week.

Locals' village pub in a late Victorian purpose-built hotel. Large bar with raised seating area. Dining room (no food served in the bar). Pool, darts, occasional live music. Beer garden, car park. Children allowed. Accommodation. On the A30, four miles from Penzance.

OPEN *11.30am–11pm Mon–Sat; 12–10.30pm Sun.*

CUBERT
The Smugglers' Den Inn
Trebellan, Cubert, Newquay TR8 5PY
☎ *(01637) 830209* Paul Partridge
www.thesmugglersden.co.uk

Freehouse with Skinner's Smugglers Ale, St Austell Tribute and Sharp's Doom Bar plus a guest changed on a weekly basis.

A 16th-century thatched country pub with a reputation locally for good ale, wine and food. Large bar, two courtyards, real fires, function room for private hire, family room. Food available lunchtime from 12 and evenings from 6pm. Beer garden with children's play area. Children allowed. Large car park. Ale & Pie festival annually in May. Situated on the A3075 Newquay–Redruth road. Turn towards Cubert village and take first left.

OPEN *Summer: 11.30am–11pm. Winter: 11.30am–2.30pm Thurs–Sun; 6–11pm Mon–Sat.*

EDMONTON
The Quarryman
Edmonton, Wadebridge PL27 7JA
☎ *(01208) 816444*
Terence and Wendy de-Villiers Kuun

A four-pump freehouse, with guest beers changed every two or three days. Favourites include Skinner's and Sharp's brews plus Timothy Taylor Landlord and Hop Back Summer Lightning.

Old Cornish inn that originally housed workers for the slate quarries. Food served at 12–2.30pm and 6–9pm, with sizzling steaks a speciality. Large courtyard for summer eating. Well-behaved children allowed. Opposite the Royal Cornwall Showground.

OPEN *12–11pm.*

FALMOUTH
Oddfellows Arms
2 Quay Hill, Falmouth TR11 3HA
☎ *(01326) 318530* Victoria Sear
www.oddfellowsarms.uk.com

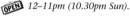Freehouse serving the local Sharp's Special and Eden Ale plus one constantly changing guest beer.

Cosy backstreet local, full of great local characters. One main bar, rear pool room. No food. Close to the railway station, just off Falmouth main street at the 'maritime' end of town.

OPEN *12–11pm (10.30pm Sun).*

The Quayside Inn
41 Arwenack Street, Falmouth TR11 3JQ
☎ *(01326) 312113*
Paul and Katherine Coombes

Up to eight beers always available. Sharp's Special and Doom Bar, Skinner's Cornish Knocker and Heligan Honey plus a range of four rotating guests.

Twice-yearly beer festivals at this quayside pub overlooking the harbour. Two bars – comfy upstairs lounge and downstairs real ale bar. Food available all day, every day in summer, and at lunchtimes and evenings in winter (skillet house with food cooked in skillets). Outside seating on quayside. Parking. Children very welcome – children's menu. On Custom House Quay.

OPEN *Both bars open all day in summer. Top bar open all day in winter.*

FOWEY
King of Prussia
3 Town Quay, Fowey, PL23 1AT
☎ *(01726) 833694* Colin Phillips
www.kingofprussiafowey.com

A St Austell house with two of the brewery's ales available.

Seventeenth-century one-bar pub and restaurant on the quayside with six en-suite bedrooms. Food served 12–9pm. Children welcome.

OPEN *11am–11pm*

GOLANT
The Fisherman's Arms
Fore Street, Golant, Fowey PL23 1LN
☎ *(01726) 832453* Anne-Marie Phillis
www.golant.net

Three real ales, including Sharp's Doom Bar Bitter.

A village pub on the banks of the River Fowey. Food at lunchtime and evening. Garden. Beer festival every August bank holiday weekend. Children and dogs welcome. Near St Austell and the Eden Project.

OPEN *12–3pm and 6–11pm Mon–Fri; 12–11pm Sat; 12–10.30am Sun; all day, every day July–August.*

GORRAN HAVEN

Llawnroc Inn

33 Chute Lane, Gorran Haven, St Austell
PL26 6NU
☎ *(01726) 843461* Alan Freeman and Reg Luff
Four real ales (three in winter), including Llawnroc Ale (exclusively brewed by Sharp's) and Sharp's Doom Bar, plus two guest ales such as Fuller's London Pride, Greene King Abbot or Shepherd Neame Spitfire.

Relaxing, family-run hotel with beautiful sea views and a terraced garden, situated in an old fishing village. Food served 12–1.45pm and 6.30–9.45pm in summer and 12–2pm and 6.30–9pm in winter. Car park. Children welcome. From St Austell continue past Heligan Gardens and after Gorran Haven, turn right.

OPEN *12–11pm (10.30pm Sun).*

GUNNISLAKE

Rising Sun Inn

Calstock Road, Gunnislake PL18 9BX
☎ *(01822) 832201* David and Caroline Heery
www.risingsuninn.co.uk
Freehouse with three or four real ales, including brews from Sharp's and Skinner's, Draught Bass and guests.

Warm and friendly 17th-century traditional stone freehouse with two bars and a dining area. Log fires and live music. No TV or games machines. Award-winning beer garden with views over the Tamar valley. Good walking and fishing.

OPEN *12–2pm and 5–11pm Mon–Sat; 12–3pm and 7–10.30pm Sun.*

HAYLE

Bird in Hand

Trelissick Road, Hayle TR27 4HY
☎ *(01736) 753974* Mr Miller
Home of the Wheal Ale Brewery. A range of own brews always available, plus two guest beers, perhaps including Greene King Abbot or Shepherd Neame Spitfire.

An old coach house with one bar. Live music. Food at lunchtimes and evenings (summer only). Children allowed.

OPEN *11am–11pm Mon–Sat; 12–10.30pm Sun.*

HELSTON

The Blue Anchor

50 Coinagehall Street, Helston TR13 8EX
☎ *(01326) 562821*
One of only four pubs in Britain which has brewed continuously for centuries and still produces its famous Spingo ales, from a Victorian word for strong beer.

This thatched town pub was originally a monks' rest home in the 15th century. Brewing continued on the premises after the Reformation and the Blue Anchor is now believed to be the oldest brewpub in Britain. Garden, children's room, skittle alley, function room. Accommodation available.

OPEN *10.30am–11pm Mon–Sat; 12–10.30pm Sun.*

KILKHAMPTON

The London Inn

Kilkhampton EX23 9QR
☎ *(01288) 321665* Stewart and Lorraine Davey
Sharp's Doom Bar always available, plus one guest.

A 16th-century pub with unusual hard-wood bar front. The pub has a reputation for good-quality food, served in the restaurant or the snug, 12–2pm and 6.30–9pm. Beer gardens to front and rear. Children and dogs welcome if kept under control. Ample parking space nearby. Located at the centre of the village on the main A39.

OPEN *All day, every day.*

LAUNCESTON

The Eliot Arms

Tregadillet, Launceston
☎ *(01566) 772051* Chris Hume
Sharp's Doom Bar and Courage Best plus a guest such as Fuller's London Pride, changed monthly.

Ivy-clad pub with open fires, slate floors and high-backed settles, packed with collections of pub memorabilia, snuff, clocks, prints and photos, bank notes and horse brasses! Food served 12–2pm and 6–9pm, including children's menu. Outside tables. Car park. Just off the A30 after the Devon and Cornwall border.

OPEN *11.30am–11pm Mon–Thurs (11.30am–3pm in winter); 11am–midnight Fri–Sat; 12–10.30pm Sun.*

LELANT DOWNS

The Watermill

Lelant Downs, Nr St Ives TR27 6LQ
☎ *(01736) 757912* Frank Symes
www.eatoutcornwall.com
Freehouse with Sharp's Doom Bar plus two guests, changed after every cask, such as Fuller's London Pride and beers from Princetown, Skinner's and Black Sheep.

A 17th-century watermill that still has a working waterwheel. Bar, restaurant, and large garden with mill stream. Food served lunchtimes and evenings. Family-friendly. Car parking. Beer festival last weekend in June. Close to St Ives and Hayle beaches. From the the A30 at St Ives, turn off and head for St Ives, after 500 yards turn left, and the pub is 100 yards on the right.

OPEN *12–11pm.*

LERRYN

The Ship

Lerryn, Nr Lostwithiel PL22 0PT
☎ *(01208) 872374* Jonathan Pusey
www.theshipinnlerryn.co.uk

 Five beers, usually two from Sharp's, two from Skinner's plus Bass, with the selection from these breweries changing.

A 16th-century inn in an idyllic riverside location in the upper reaches of the Fowey Estuary, with restaurant and beer garden. Food available 12–9.30pm Easter–Oct; 12–3pm and 6–9pm Nov–March. Five B&B rooms and two cottages. Children welcome. Fantastic walks by the river, plus golf, riding and beaches nearby. Convenient for Eden Project. Three miles off the A390 from Lostwithiel.

OPEN *10am–midnight Easter–Oct; 10am–3pm and 5.30pm–12 Nov–March.*

LOSTWITHIEL

The Royal Oak Inn

Duke Street, Lostwithiel PL22 0AG
☎ *(01208) 872552* Joe Lado and Steve Pitt
www.royaloakrestaurant.co.uk

 Up to six real ales, including beers such as Sharp's Doom Bar, Fuller's London Pride, Greene King Old Speckled Hen and Abbot. Two or three of the beers are rotated a couple of times a month.

P opular 13th-century inn catering for all tastes. Two bars and a restaurant serving freshly cooked food 12–2pm and 6–9pm. Beer garden with heaters. Car park. Children and dogs welcome. Refurbished en-suite rooms available. Private functions catered for. Only seven miles from the Eden Project, just off the A390 going into Lostwithiel.

OPEN *11am–11pm.*

NANCENOY

Trengilly Wartha Inn

Nancenoy, Constantine, Nr Falmouth TR11 5RP
☎ *(01326) 340332* Will and Lisa Lea
www.trengilly.co.uk

Freehouse offering three or four real ales, with brews from Skinner's, St Austell, Lizard and Sharp's among the favourites. All rotate weekly.

A country freehouse and bistro in six acres of valley gardens and meadows. Bar food served 12–2.15pm and 6.30–9.30pm. Car park, garden and children's room. Eight bedrooms, function room for up to 30 people. Dogs welcome. Just south of Constantine – follow the signs.

OPEN *11am–3pm and 6.30–11pm.*

NEWBRIDGE

The Fountain Inn

Newbridge, Penzance TR20 8QH
☎ *(01736) 364075* Shelton Pendar

St Austell brewery tied house, offering five real ales in summer, three in winter. Hicks and Proper Job plus seasonals and specials changed at least monthly.

V ery quaint pub in a Cornish hamlet. One bar, two restaurants. Food served every lunchtime and evening. Children welcome. Car park. Beer garden. Off the A3071 between Penzance and St Just.

OPEN *Winter: 11.20am–2pm and 5pm–close. Summer: 11am–close.*

PAR

The Rashleigh Inn

Polkerris, Par PL24 2TL
☎ *(01726) 813991* Jon and Samantha Spode
www.therashleighinnpolkerris.co.uk

 Genuine freehouse with six real ales in summer, four in winter. Local brews such as Sharp's Doom Bar and Skinner's Cornish Blonde are regulars, but any beer from any independent brewer in the country could be featured.

A beachfront stone pub, formerly a coastguard station. Approximately 300 years old, with a sun terrace overlooking St Austell bay. Situated directly above the sandy beach, with safe bathing in the bay. Bar, lounge and restaurant. Bar meals available 12–2pm and 6–9pm; bar snacks and cream teas 3–5pm. Children welcome. Car park. 15 minutes from the Eden Project, two miles to Fowey. From Par, follow signs to Menabilly, Polkerris and the beach. Located at the bottom of a steep hill down to the beach.

OPEN *11am–11pm Mon–Sat; 12–10.30pm Sun.*

PENRYN

Seven Stars

73 The Terrace, Penryn TR10 8EL
☎ *(01326) 373573* Rob Brinkhof

Skinner's Heligan Honey, Cornish Knocker and Spriggan Ale plus Blue Anchor Jubilee IPA on offer at this freehouse.

B elieved to have been built in 1454, a pub known for its quality beer and nice atmosphere. Named Best Community Pub 2007 for Cornwall under the Best Bar None scheme. Beer garden used for smokers. No food, but takeaway meals can be eaten in the pub. In the centre of Penryn, near the clock.

OPEN *11am–1am Mon–Sat; noon–1am Sun.*

PENZANCE

The Crown

1 Victoria Square, Penzance TR18 2EP
☎ *(01736) 351070* Joshua Dunkley
www.thecrownpenzance.co.uk

A freehouse. Skinner's Heligan Honey and Otter Ale plus a guest such as Timothy Taylor Landlord or Keltec Majik. Also a good wine list and extensive spirits.

A small backstreet pub with ample outdoor seating. Home-cooked food served 12–2.30pm and 6.30–9pm Thurs–Sun (not Sun evening) in winter; daily in summer. No TV. Open fire. Quiet Snug with no music. Fresh ground coffee.

OPEN *12–12 Sun–Thurs; noon–12.30am Fri–Sat.*

Globe & Ale House

Queen Street, Penzance TR18 4BJ
☎ *(01736) 364098* Mr and Mrs Cripps

Freehouse with up to eight real ales. Something from local Skinner's and Sharp's usually features, plus a constantly changing range of real ales from any independent or micro-brewery from Cornwall to Orkney!

An alehouse with live music once a week and quiz nights. Food served lunchtimes and evenings, but no separate dining area. No children.

OPEN *11am–11pm Mon–Sat; 12–10.30pm Sun.*

Mexico Inn

Long Rock, Penzance TR20 8JD
☎ *(01736) 710625* Martin and Ceri Britten

Freehouse with Skinner's Betty Stogs and Sharp's Doom Bar or Eden Ale usually available.

One-bar local village inn, over 200 years old. Traditional pub food served 12–2.30pm and 6–9pm Mon–Sat; 12–8.30pm Sun in the bar or the separate restaurant. Children welcome in the conservatory. Beer garden. Small car park. Situated near St Michael's Mount and Flambards theme park. Two miles outside Penzance; follow brown sign from the A30.

OPEN *11.30am–2.30pm and 5pm–12 Mon–Sat; 12–11pm Sun.*

Mounts Bay Inn

Promenade, Wherry Town, Penzance TR18 4NP
☎ *(01736) 360863*
Denis Mayor and Shirley O'Neill

Skinner's Cornish Knocker plus two guests in the summer, changed weekly, which could be from any independent or micro-brewery.

A warm welcome awaits in this characterful olde-worlde pub. Food served lunchtimes and evenings. Local authority car park situated opposite the pub. Quiz nights. No children allowed inside the pub, although welcome on small side terrace, which has seating.

OPEN *11am–11pm Mon–Sat; 12–10.30pm Sun.*

PIECE

The Countryman

Piece, Carnkie, Redruth TR16 6SG
☎ *(01209) 215960* N Lake

Courage Best and Directors, Greene King Old Speckled Hen, Theakston Old Peculiar and Sharp's 'No Name' as the house brew. Plus three guests changed depending on popularity, such as Sharp's Doom Bar and Special, Heligan Honey and Skinner's Cornish Knocker.

Traditional country freehouse, built from solid granite in the mid 19th century to service the local mines. Two bars, games and pool room, veranda, beer garden and smoking area. Families welcome. Large car park. Situated on the Pool to Four Lanes Road, off the Camborne turning.

OPEN *11am–midnight Sun–Thurs; 11am–1am Fri–Sat.*

POLPERRO

The Blue Peter Inn

The Quay, Polperro, Nr Looe PL13 2QZ
☎ *(01503) 272743*
Caroline and Steve Steadman

A selection of Sharp's and St Austell ales plus daily guest beers, with the emphasis on smaller independent breweries from all over the country. Local draught scrumpy also served.

Small, atmospheric, traditional pub with beamed ceilings, log fires and a family room. Children and pets welcome. Excellent lunch menu available every day, with local crab and scallops a speciality. Live music Fri and Sat nights plus Sun afternoons. Situated at the end of the fish quay.

OPEN *11am–11pm Mon–Sat; 12–10.30pm Sun.*

The Old Mill House Inn

Mill Hill, Polperro PL13 2RP
☎ *(01503) 272362* Jan Perry
www.oldmillhouseinn.com

Freehouse offering Skinner's Old Mill Ale, Sharp's Doom Bar and other guest ales.

Originally a 16th-century mill, now a white-painted, homely, cottage-style pub. Licensed for civil weddings (www.polperro weddings.co.uk). One bar plus lounge area and restaurant. Food available 9am–2pm and 7–9pm in season and evenings only in winter. Tapas also available. Pool table. Log fire in winter. Well-behaved children and dogs welcome. Car parking for residents only. Accommodation. Beer garden. Cash point. In the centre of the village.

OPEN *9am–12.30am (alcohol served 10am–midnight).*

PORT GAVERNE

Port Gaverne Hotel

Port Gaverne, Port Isaac PL29 3SQ
☎ *(01208) 880244* Graham Sylvester

Four real ales. Sharp's Doom Bar Bitter, Cornish Coaster and Eden and St Austell Tribute are among the beers regularly on offer.

A 16th-century hotel with two bars, 100 yards from the sea on the coast between Tintagel and Padstow. Interesting photographs showing the history of the slate and pilchard industries. Food served 12–2.30pm and 6.30–9pm. Beer garden, car park. Accommodation available (15 bedrooms). Children welcome.

OPEN *11am–11pm Mon–Sat; 12–10.30pm Sun.*

PORTHALLOW
The Five Pilchards Inn
Porthallow, St Keverne, Helston TR12 6PP
☎ *(01326) 280256* Brandon Flynn
www.fivepilchards.com

A four-pump freehouse with brews from Skinner's and Sharp's usually available.

A 300-year-old Cornish seafaring pub, with a conservatory featuring a waterfall. Interesting display of ship's accessories, including figure heads, binnacles and telegraphs, plus ship models. Food served 12–2pm and 7–9.30pm. A juicing machine juices whole oranges. Courtyard with tables and umbrellas. Children welcome.

OPEN *12–2.30pm and 6–11pm.*

PORTHLEVEN
Atlantic Inn
Peverell Terrace, Porthleven, Helston TR13 9DZ
☎ *(01326) 562439* Leigh and Adrian Santi
www.theatlanticinn.co.uk

Freehouse with Skinner's ales such as Figgy's Brew and Betty Stogs plus St Austell Tribute and Proper Job IPA.

Newly refurbished, traditional seaside pub in a village location (signposted), with live entertainment every Saturday. Food served lunchtimes and evenings from an extensive menu, reasonably priced. Children allowed.

OPEN *11am–11pm (10.30pm Sun).*

PORTREATH
Basset Arms
Tregea Terrace, Portreath TR16 4NS
☎ *(01209) 842077* Eric Wilkes and Sue Laity

Sharp's Doom Bar, Wadworth 6X and Skinner's Heligan Honey, plus one guest in summer, such as Skinner's Betty Stogs.

Friendly local pub with a good atmosphere, situated opposite Portreath Bay with its sandy beach. Separate restaurant. Food served 12–2pm and 6–9pm. Outdoor tables on patio, large car park. Children's play area. Three miles from the A30 – follow the signs to Portreath.

OPEN *11am–11pm Mon–Thurs; 11am–midnight Fri–Sat; 11am–10.30pm Sun.*

QUINTRELL DOWNS
The Two Clomes
East Road, Quintrell Downs, Nr Newquay TR8 4PD
☎ *(01637) 871163* CT Schofield

Genuine freehouse with Sharp's Doom Bar and Skinner's Figgy's Brew plus two weekly guests in summer.

Converted and extended old farm cottage built from Cornish stone, with real open fire and a cosy, warm atmosphere. Famous for fresh fish and shellfish served by Newquay's premier chef. Beer garden. Car park. Bingo and quiz on Saturdays. Charity events. Available for group bookings. Take the A392 from Newquay to Quintrell Downs (three miles), straight on at the roundabout, then second right.

OPEN *Winter: 12–3pm and 6–11pm. Summer: all day, every day.*

ST AGNES
Driftwood Spars
Trevaunance Cove, Quay Road, St Agnes TR5 0RT
☎ *(01872) 552428* Louise Treseder
www.driftwoodspars.com

A freehouse. Two Driftwood Brewery Beers (7 different beers brewed on site), Sharp's Doom Bar, St Austell Tinners and Tribute. Plus two monthly-changing guests such as Sharp's Eden, St Austell HSD, Skinner's Heligan Honey, Hop Back Summer Lightning and other mainly Cornish beers.

Built in the 1650s and adjacent to the south west coastal path, 200 yards from the beach. Bars and seaview dining room serving local produce 12–2.30pm and 6.30–9.30pm. Accommodation. Large car park. Children and dogs welcome. Live music Sat and some Fridays. Small on-site brewery. From the A30, take the B3277 through St Agnes to the seafront.

OPEN *11am–11pm (1am Fri–Sat).*

ST CLEER
The Stag Inn
Fore Street, St Cleer, Liskeard PL14 5DA
☎ *(01579) 342305* Pam Dawson

Freehouse, with Sharp's Own, Greene King Abbot and something from Skinner's always available, plus a guest ale changed weekly.

A 17th-century moorland inn with TV and dining area. Food served 12–2pm and 6.30–9pm. An annual beer festival takes place in June. Well-behaved children welcome. En-suite accommodation. Two miles from Liskeard, close to the Eden Project.

OPEN *12–11pm (10.30pm Sun).*

ST IVES
The Castle Inn
16 Fore Street, St Ives TR26 1AB
☎ *(01736) 796833* Hilary Aspinall

Up to six real ales, including any Skinner's ale. Up to five of the pumps change daily, offering a range of real ales.

Food served lunchtimes and evenings May–Sept.

OPEN *11am–midnight Mon–Thurs; 11am–1am Fri–Sat; 12–12 Sun.*

ST JUST

The King's Arms

Market Square, St Just, Penzance TR19 7HF
☎ *(01736) 788545* R and K Robinson

St Austell Brewery tied house offering Tinners and Tribute plus HSD when available, and seasonal St Austell ales. Cask Marque awarded.

A 14th-century cosy pub with family atmosphere. One bar with lots of nooks and crannies, low ceilings, open fires. Outside seating at the front, parking on the square. Occasional live music, weekly in summer, free weekly quiz night. Food available 12–2pm in winter, 12–2.30pm and 6–9.30pm in summer. Children and dogs welcome. Bed and breakfast.

OPEN *11am–12.30am.*

The Star Inn

1 Fore Street, St Just, Penzance TR19 7LL
☎ *(01736) 788767* Colin McClary

St Austell house with HSD, Tinners, Tribute and Dartmoor generally available.

Old mining pub with a horseshoe bar and artefacts on the walls. Bar food available 12–8pm during the summer. Accommodation. Children welcome, children's room provided. Beer garden with outside seating. Live music.

OPEN *11am–11pm Mon–Sat; 12–10.30pm Sun.*

ST MAWES

Victory Inn

Victory Steps, St Mawes, TR2 5DQ
☎ *(01326) 270324* Philip Heslip
www.victory-inn.co.uk

Sharp's Doom Bar and two guests, changed fortnightly in summer and monthly the rest of the year.

A 16th-century fisherman's pub near the harbour. One main bar, a downstairs dining room, an upstairs restaurant with roof terrace, and two en-suite guest rooms. Food served 11.30am–2.30pm and 6.30–9.30pm, with seafood a speciality. The restaurant can be booked for functions. Barbecues in summer, outside seating areas. Child- and dog-friendly. In the centre of St Mawes, up a side street next to the harbour.

OPEN *All day, every day.*

STITHIANS

Seven Stars

Church Road, Stithians
☎ *(01209) 860003* Phil Preen

Up to four almost exclusively Cornish real ales such as Sharp's Doom Bar or Special and Skinner's Betty Stogs Bitter.

Beamed, stone-floored one-room village local built as a farmhouse extension in the 19th century. Outside drinking area. Food lunchtimes (not Tues) and Weds–Sat evenings. Saturday night is music night.

OPEN *12–2.30pm and 7–11pm Mon–Fri; all day Sat; 12–3pm and 7–10.30pm Sun.*

STRATTON

King's Arms

Howell's Road, Stratton, Bude EX23 9BX
☎ *(01288) 352396* Steven Peake

A 17th-century freehouse serving Sharp's Doom Bar Bitter, Exmoor Ale and Otter Ale. Two guests are changed weekly. Traditional cider served during the summer season. Cask Marque awarded.

Traditional pub with quality, value-for-money bar meals served 12–2pm and 6.30–9pm, including a very popular Sunday lunch. Takeaway fish and chips also available. Quiz nights on Tuesdays. Well-behaved children and nice dogs are welcome. Ten minutes' drive from beautiful beaches and rugged coastal walks. Accommodation.

OPEN *12–11pm.*

TINTAGEL

The Trewarmett Inn

Trewarmett, Tintagel PL34 0ET
☎ *(01840) 770460* John and Liz Heard
www.thetrewarmettinn.co.uk

Freehouse with beers from local breweries Skinner's and Sharp's plus one guest.

A 200-year-old coaching inn with a small cosy bar featuring woodburner, beamed ceilings and slate floors. Separate restaurant serving food 6.30–9pm Mon–Fri; 12–2pm and 6.30–9pm Sat–Sun. Children allowed in the restaurant and beer garden. Car park. Annual beer festival in September. Off the B3263 between Tintagel and Delabole.

OPEN *Lunchtimes in summer; evenings all year.*

TREBARWITH

The Mill House Inn

Trebarwith, Tintagel PL34 0HD
☎ *(01840) 770200*
www.themillhouseinn.co.uk

The three permanent beers include Sharp's Own and Doom Bar Bitter plus a guest ale rotated every month.

A 16th-century mill over a trout stream, set in seven acres of woodland half a mile from the sea. Bar and restaurant food lunchtimes and evenings, featuring excellent cuisine in an informal atmosphere. Car park, garden and terrace. Barbecues on the terrace in summer. Accommodation (all en-suite). Children welcome.

OPEN *12–11pm (10.30pm Sun).*

TREGREHAN

The Britannia Inn

Tregrehan Par, Tregrehan PL24 2SL
☎ *(01726) 812889*
Richard Rogers and Philip Lafferty
www.britanniainn.net

This freehouse has four permanent real ales and two guests.

Very popular, busy pub with two bars, a restaurant and function room. Food served at lunchtime and evenings (all day in season). Children allowed in the dining area. Large beer garden with children's play area. Close to the Eden Project.

OPEN *11am–11pm Mon–Sat; 12–10.30pm Sun.*

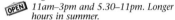

TRESPARRETT
The Horseshoe Inn
Tresparrett, Camelford PL32 9ST
☎ *(01840) 261240* Pat Codack
www.thehorseshoeinn.co.uk

 Freehouse serving three or four real ales from breweries including Sharp's and Skinner's.

A 19th-century village pub situated in Thomas Hardy country. Slate floors, beamed ceilings and open fire. Single bar with ample seating and dining area, plus separate games room. Outside seating and beer garden. Food served lunchtime and evening. Located off the A39 at Otterham Station.

OPEN *12–3pm and 6.30–11pm.*

TRURO
The City Inn Hotel
Pydar Street, Truro TR1 3SP
☎ *(01872) 272623* Keren Wilson

Up to seven real ales, usually including local beers from Skinner's and Sharp's.

Community-oriented, 200-year-old character pub with a friendly atmosphere. Food served 12–2pm and 6–9pm. Games room. Children welcome. Beer garden. Accommodation. Function room. Close to the north coast (9 miles) and Falmouth (11 miles). Located next to Carrick District council offices.

OPEN *10am–11pm Mon–Thurs; 10am–midnight Fri–Sat; 12–11pm Sun.*

The Old Ale House
7 Quay Street, Truro TR1 2HD
☎ *(01872) 271122* Mark and Bev Jones

Six to eight real ales served straight from the cask. Regulars include beers from Fuller's, St Austell, Exmoor, Skinner's and Wooden Hand, and most are rotated daily.

Traditional alehouse in the city centre with old furniture. Food available 12–2.45pm and 6.30–8.45pm Mon–Fri, 12–3pm Sat and 12–2.30pm Sun. Private room for hire. Three beer festivals a year. Only five minutes' walk from Skinner's Brewery (tours available), opposite Truro bus station.

OPEN *11am–11pm Mon–Sat; 12–10.30pm Sun.*

WIDEMOUTH BAY
The Bay View Inn
Marine Drive, Widemouth Bay, Bude EX23 0AW
☎ *(01288) 361273* David and Cherylyn Keene
www.bayviewinn.co.uk

Freehouse offering three real ales drawn straight from the cask, Skinner's Bay View Sunset (exclusive to this pub) and Betty Stogs plus Sharp's Doom Bar.

Traditional old-style seaside pub decorated with local views. Two bars, garden, children's play area, large car park. Decking from which to witness the sunsets. Food available all day from April to September, 12–2.30pm and 6.30–9.30pm at other times. Dining and family room. Accommodation with stunning views of the sea. Children allowed in designated rooms.

OPEN *All day, every day (although for two hours only on Christmas Day).*

ZELAH
Hawkins Arms
High Road, Zelah, Truro TR4 9HU
☎ *(01872) 540339*
Richard and Amanda Baylin

Freehouse with four real ales, Skinner's Zelah Mist and Otter Bitter being permanent fixtures. Another Skinner's beer plus two other guests are also served, and these are rotated weekly.

A 17th-century country-style pub with exposed stone walls, real fire and atmospheric bar. Food served at lunchtime and evenings. Beer garden and courtyard. Large car park. Children welcome. Good walks in the area, plus local gardens, award-winning campsites and beaches. Follow the brown signs from the A30.

OPEN *11am–3pm and 5.30–11pm. Longer hours in summer.*

ZENNOR
The Gurnard's Head
Nr Zennor, St Ives TR26 3DE
☎ *(01736) 796928*
Charles and Edmund Inkin
www.gurnardshead.co.uk

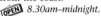 Rotating brews from local breweries including St Austell, Skinners and Sharp's.

Owned by the same people as the Felin Fach Griffin near Brecon. With a fine reputation for its food but still committed to its real ale. Food served 12–3pm and 6–10pm. Accommodation. Off the B3306, 500 yards from the coast.

OPEN *8.30am–midnight.*

The Tinners Arms
Zennor, St Ives TR27 3BY
☎ *(01736) 796927*
Richard Motley and Grahame Edwards
www.tinnersarms.com

Sharp's Doom Bar and Special and St Austell Tinners are always available.

Freehouse in a lovely 14th-century building, with stone floor, beams and open fires. Function room is used as a family room in bad weather in summer. Lunch and supper served. Large garden with tables overlooking coastline. Occasional live music. Children allowed, but not in the main bar. Luxury accommodation available (two double en-suite rooms and two singles). Only half a mile from the South West coastal path. Off the B3306 St Ives road.

OPEN *11am–11pm Mon–Sat; 12–10.30pm Sun.*

THE BREWERIES

BARNGATES BREWERY LTD
*The Drunken Duck Inn, Barngates, Ambleside
LA22 0NG*
☎ *(01539) 436575*
www.drunkenduckinn.co.uk

CAT NAP ALE 3.6% ABV
Fruity and zesty with strong hop aroma.
CRACKER ALE 3.9% ABV
Clean, smooth, long bitter finish.
PRIDE OF WESTMORLAND 4.1% ABV
Berry aromas, malty hop flavour.
WESTMORLAND GOLD 4.2% ABV
Refreshing and bittersweet.
TAG LAG 4.4% ABV
Golden colour, spicy hop aroma, dry finish.
RED BULL TERRIER 4.8% ABV
Malt flavour, spicy aftertaste.
CHESTERS STRONG & UGLY 5.2% ABV
Slightly fruity, roasted malt flavours.

BECKSTONES BREWERY
*Upper Beckstones Mill, The Green, Millom
LA18 5HL*
☎ *(01229) 775294*

LEAT 3.6% ABV
Thirst-quenching, fruity, flowery,
modern-style quaffing ale.
IRON TOWN 3.8% ABV
Standard bitter, darker in colour with malty
bitter aftertaste.
HEMATITE 4.2% ABV
Dark strong ale, very malty.
Plus seasonals and specials including:
BLACK DOG FREDDY 3.6% ABV
BEER O'CLOCK 3.9% ABV
BORDER STEANS 4.1% ABV
Scottish-style beer.

BITTER END BREWPUB
15 Kirkgate, Cockermouth CA13 9PJ
☎ *(01900) 828993*
www.bitterend.co.uk

COCKERMOUTH PRIDE 3.8% ABV
CALL OUT 4.2% ABV
CUDDY LUGS 4.3% ABV
SKINNER'S OLD STRONG 5.5% ABV
Plus seasonals and specials including:
WHEAT BEER 4.1% ABV
CZECHUMBERLAND 4.5% ABV

THE CONISTON BREWING CO. LTD
The Coppermines Road, Coniston LA21 8HL
☎ *(01539) 441133*
www.conistonbrewery.com

BLUEBIRD BITTER 3.6% ABV
Light, clean, hoppy aroma, dry finish.
BLUEBIRD PREMIUM XB 4.2% ABV
Pale ale with citrus notes.
OLD MAN ALE 4.2% ABV
Fruit aroma, full bodied, balanced.
Plus specials.

CUMBRIAN LEGENDARY ALES
*Old Hall Brewery, Hawkshead, Ambleside
LA22 0QF*
☎ *(01539) 436436*

WICKED JIMMY 3.6% ABV
KING DUNMAIL 4.2% ABV
BUTTERMERE BEAUTY 4.8% ABV
CLAIFE CRIER 5.0% ABV
Plus specials.

DENT BREWERY
Hollins, Cowgill, Dent LA10 5TQ
☎ *(01539) 625326*
www.dentbrewery.co.uk

DENT BITTER 3.7% ABV
Mild hop flavour and slightly sweet.
AVIATOR 4.0% ABV
Full, rounded hop flavour.
RAMBRAU 4.5% ABV
Very pale, sweet and hoppy.
RAMSBOTTOM STRONG ALE 4.5% ABV
Medium-dark, caramel flavour.
KAMIKAZE 5.0% ABV
Very pale, good hop flavour and creamy
maltiness.
T'OWD TUP 6.0% ABV
Powerful stout. Roast barley, bite and softness.
Plus monthly brews.

DERWENT BREWERY
*Units 2a–2b, Station Road Industrial Estate,
Silloth, Wigton CA7 4AG*
☎ *(01697) 331522*

CARLISLE STATE BITTER 3.7% ABV
PARSON'S PLEDGE 4.0% ABV
WINTER GOLD 4.1% ABV
HANSI'S OKTOBERFEST 4.2% ABV
HOFBRAU 4.2% ABV
WHITWELL & MARKS PALE ALE 4.4% ABV
Plus seasonal and occasional brews including:
LATE SUMMER 4.0% ABV
BILL MONKS ALE 4.5% ABV

FOXFIELD BREWERY
*Prince of Wales, Foxfield, Broughton in Furness
LA20 6BX*
☎ *(01229) 716238*
www.princeofwalesfoxfield.co.uk
A constantly changing range of ales. The only
permanent ale is:

DARK MILD 3.4% ABV
FLEUR DE LYS 3.6% ABV
SANDS 3.6% ABV
BRIEF ENCOUNTER 4.1% ABV
Plus seasonals and specials.

GREAT GABLE BREWING CO.
Wasdale, Nr Gosforth CA20 1EX
☎ *(01946) 726229*
www.greatgablebrewing.com

LIAR 3.4% ABV
GREAT GABLE 3.7% ABV
Hoppy aroma.
WRY'NOSE 4.0% ABV
Zesty, summery beer.
WASD'ALE 4.4% ABV
Ruby colour, strong aftertaste.
SCAWFELL 4.8% ABV
Roasted wheat, malty flavours.
Plus occasional brews.

HARDKNOTT BREWERY
The Woolpack Inn, Boot, Holmrook, Eskdale
CA19 1TH
☎ *(01946) 723230*
www.woolpack.co.uk/ales.htm

WOOLPACKER 3.7% ABV

HAWKSHEAD BREWERY COMPANY
Hawkshead Brewery, Staveley Mill Yard, Staveley
LA8 9LR
☎ *(01539) 822644*
www.hawksheadbrewery.co.uk

HAWKSHEAD BITTER 3.7% ABV
Light coloured, with hops.
ULVERSTON PALE ALE 4.1% ABV
Fruity and dry.
HAWKSHEAD RED BITTER 4.2% ABV
Red and dry, with malt.
LAKELAND GOLD 4.4% ABV
Taste of fruit and hops.
BRODIE'S PRIME 5.0% ABV
Dry and spicy.
Plus seasonal and occasional brews.

HESKET NEWMARKET BREWERY
Old Crown Barn, Hesket Newmarket, Wigton
CA7 8JG
☎ *(01697) 478066*
www.hesketbrewery.co.uk

GREAT COCKUP PORTER 3.0% ABV
Nearly black, smooth and malty.
BLENCATHRA BITTER 3.2% ABV
Ruby coloured and hoppy.
HAYSTACKS 3.7% ABV
Pale and zesty.
SKIDDAW SPECIAL BITTER 3.7% ABV
Gold coloured and full flavoured.
HELVELLYN GOLD 4.0% ABV
Straw coloured with a hoppy aroma.
DORIS'S 90TH BIRTHDAY ALE 4.3% ABV
Full flavoured, hints of butterscotch, with fruit
throughout.
SCAFELL BLONDE 4.4% ABV
Hoppy with almost citrus finish.
CATBELLS PALE ALE 5.0% ABV
Dangerously easy to drink.
OLD CARROCK STRONG ALE 6.0% ABV
Rich, smooth and strong.

JENNINGS BROS PLC
The Castle Brewery, Cockermouth CA13 9NE
☎ *(0845) 1297185*
www.jenningsbrewery.co.uk

JENNINGS DARK MILD 3.1% ABV
Malty and sweet.
BITTER SMOOTH 3.5% ABV
Distinctively dark and nutty.
JENNINGS BITTER 3.5% ABV
Nutty and mellow, with malt.
CUMBERLAND ALE 4.0% ABV
Gold coloured, rich and smooth.
CUMBERLAND CREAM 4.0% ABV
Golden with barley flavours.
COCKER HOOP 4.6% ABV
A well-hopped premium bitter.
SNECK LIFTER 5.1% ABV
Robust and slightly sweet.
Plus seasonals including:
TOM FOOL 4.0% ABV
Amber coloured, in the style of a light mild.
CRAG RAT 4.3% ABV
Golden-coloured bitter.

FISH KING 4.3% ABV
Refreshing, brewed with a new variety of hops.
GOLDEN HOST 4.3% ABV
Pronounced hop character.
MOUNTAIN MAN 4.3% ABV
Red, toffee-flavoured bitter.
WORLD'S BIGGEST LIAR 4.3% ABV
Biscuit flavour, dry finish.
HONEY BOLE 4.5% ABV
Straw colour, honey finish.
RED BREAST 4.5% ABV
Chestnut colour, balanced hop flavour.

KESWICK BREWING COMPANY
The Old Brewery, Brewery Lane, Keswick
CA12 5BY
☎ *(01768) 780700*
www.keswickbrewery.co.uk

THIRST PITCH 3.8% ABV
THIRST ASCENT 4.0% ABV
THIRST RUN 4.2% ABV
Plus seasonals including:
THIRST QUENCHER 4.0% ABV
THIRST BLOSSOM 4.1% ABV
THIRST FALL 4.3% ABV
THIRST LOVE 4.3% ABV
THIRST WINTER 4.4% ABV
THIRST BLOOD 6.0% ABV
THIRST NOEL 6.0% ABV

LOWESWATER BREWERY
Kirkstile Inn, Loweswater, Cockermouth
CA13 0RU
☎ *(01900) 85219*
www.kirkstile.com

MELBREAK BITTER 3.7% ABV
Hoppy bitter.
RANNERDALE 4.0% ABV
Golden with citrus tones.
GRASMOOR ALE 4.3% ABV
Roasted malt flavour.
KIRKSTILE GOLD 4.3% ABV
Flavours of banana and mango.

ABRAHAM THOMPSON'S BREWING COMPANY
Flass Lane, Barrow in Furness LA13 0AD
☎ *07708 191437*

DARK MILD 3.5% ABV
LICKERISH STOUT 4.0% ABV
BEST MILD 4.1% ABV
PORTER 4.2% ABV
BARLEY STOUT 5.2% ABV
LETARGION 9.0% ABV

THE TIRRIL BREWERY
Unit 11, Brougham Hall, Brougham, Penrith
CA10 2DE
☎ *(01768) 863219*

BEWSHERS BITTER 3.8% ABV
Golden, with hop flavours.
BROUGHAM ALE 3.9% ABV
Amber coloured, delicate hops.
OLD FAITHFUL 4.0% ABV
Fruity and pale golden.
1823 4.1% ABV
Dark, but not heavy bitter.
ACADEMY 4.2% ABV
Full flavoured, malt taste.

ULVERSTON BREWERY

c/o 59 Urswick Road, Ulverston LA12 9LJ
☎ *(01229) 584280*

HARVEST MOON 3.9% ABV
WHAT THE DICKENS 4.0% ABV
LAUGHING GRAVY 4.1% ABV
LONESOME PINE 4.3% ABV
BAD MEDICINE 6.0% ABV
Plus seasonals and specials.

WATERMILL BREWING COMPANY

The Watermill Inn, Ings, Nr Staveley, Kendal LA8 9PY
☎ *(01539) 821309*

COLLIE WOBBLES 3.7% ABV
W'RUFF NIGHT 5.0% ABV
Plus seasonals and specials.

YATES BREWERY LTD

Ghyll Farm, Westnewton, Wigton CA7 3NX
☎ *(01697) 321081*
www.yatesbrewery.co.uk

BITTER 3.7% ABV
Hoppy and fruity.
FEVER PITCH 3.9% ABV
Fruity lager style.
SUN GODDESS 4.2% ABV
Lager style with hoppy aroma.
Seasonals:
SUMMER FEVER 3.9% ABV
SPRING FEVER 4.7% ABV
BEST CELLAR 5.8% ABV
Christmas brew, strength varies from year to year.

THE PUBS

ALLONBY

Ship Hotel

Main Street, Allonby, Maryport CA15 6QF
☎ *(01900) 881017* Steve and Valerie Ward
www.theshipallonby.co.uk

Yates Bitter plus another Yates beer, changed monthly.

Overlooking the Solway Firth, a 300-year-old hotel with considerable history. Home-cooked bar meals served 12–3pm Sat–Sun and 6–11pm Tues–Sun in winter, and every lunchtime and evening in summer. Car park, dogs welcome, accommodation.

OPEN *12–3pm and 7–11pm (10.30pm Sun). Closed Mon, Tues and Weds lunchtimes in winter.*

ALSTON

The Cumberland Inn

Townfoot, Alston CA9 3HX
☎ *(01434) 381875* Guy Harmer
www.alstoncumberlandhotel.co.uk

Freehouse with Yates Bitter plus three rotating guests and three real ciders.

A Victorian brick building, converted from a private house in the 1940s. One bar, plus separate restaurant. Bar meals, specials and sandwiches available 12–9pm. External patio area. Children and pets welcome. Car park. Cycle storage. Accommodation. On the A686 between Penrith and Hexham, next to Henderson's garage.

OPEN *12–11pm (closed Christmas day only).*

The Golden Rule

Smithy Brow, Ambleside LA22 9AS
☎ *(01539) 432257* John Lockley

Frederic Robinson tied house with six Robinson's ales. Hatters Dark, Oldham Bitter, Hartleys XB and Cumbria Way are permanents, plus two seasonal brews.

A self-proclaimed 'no frills' pub. No pool or juke box. Machines and darts in separate room. Selection of pork pies, scotch eggs and filled rolls usually available. Beer garden and patio. Private room available. Well-behaved children allowed. Off the A591 towards Kirkstone.

OPEN *11am–midnight.*

Queens Hotel

Market Place, Ambleside LA22 9BU
☎ *(015394) 32206* Terry Davie
www.queenshotelambleside.com

Freehouse with up to six real ales, with local brews favoured. Yates Bitter should be one of them while others are likely to come from Jennings, Moorhouse's, Coniston, Hawkshead and Black Sheep.

Victorian town-centre hotel, with one traditional bar and a refurbished cellar bar. Food available 12–9.30pm. Children welcome. Accommodation in 26 en-suite bedrooms.

OPEN *10am–midnight.*

The Royal Oak Appleby

Bongate, Appleby CA16 6UB
☎ *(017683) 51463* Kyle Macrae
www.royaloakappleby.co.uk

Black Sheep Bitter, Hawkshead Bitter and Hesket Newmarket Doris's 90th Birthday are among the beers regularly served. One changed weekly.

Totally refurbished genuine tap room, over 400 years old, with panelled oak and lots of character. Darts and dominoes. Refurbished lounge bar with real fire. Informal dining, 55-cover restaurant and private dining room, with food served all day, every day. Children welcome. Off-road parking. Nine en-suite rooms and a two-bedroom holiday cottage. One mile from the A66 between Scotch Corner and Penrith.

OPEN *11am–midnight.*

ARMATHWAITE

Fox & Pheasant

Armathwaite, Carlisle CA4 9PY
☎ *(01697) 472400 Paul Jordan*
www.thefoxandpheasant.co.uk

 Owned by Robinson's Brewery since 2003 and now exclusively selling their ales. Unicorn, Double Hop and Dark Hatter's Mild permanently available.

A 17th-century traditional coaching inn and fishing lodge with log fires and beamed ceilings, overlooking the River Eden, in a small village. Two bars, three eating areas. Outside seating. Food served 12–2pm and 6–9pm Mon–Fri and 12–9pm Sat–Sun. Children allowed. En-suite accommodation, parties catered for. On the Carlisle to Settle railway line, two miles east of the A6 between Carlisle and Penrith.

OPEN *11am–11pm.*

ASPATRIA

The Swan Inn

West Newton, Nr Aspatria CH7 3PQ
☎ *(01697) 320627 Roger Thorne*

 Freehouse with two Hesket Newmarket beers such as Doris's 90th Birthday Ale and High Pike.

C ountry village pub dating back about 400 years. Food served in the bar and lounge 6.30–9pm Wed–Sat; 12–3pm and 6.30–9pm Sun. Children welcome. Beer garden. Car park. Two miles from both Aspatria and the Solway coast.

OPEN *6.30–11pm Wed–Sat; 12–3pm and 6.30–11pm Sun.*

BARNGATES

The Drunken Duck Inn

Barngates, Ambleside LA22 0NG
☎ *(015394) 36347 Stephanie Barton*
www.drunkenduckinn.co.uk

 The home of the Barngates brewery, with four ales on offer from a range including Cracker Ale, Tag Lag, Cat Nap, Pride of Westmorland, Westmorland Gold, Red Bull Terrier and K9. Two are rotated weekly.

D elightful 400-year-old inn, set in beautiful countryside and oozing olde-worlde charm. Tempting restaurant and modern, stylish accommodation. Amusing story behind the pub name – ask the landlady! Food available 12–2.30pm and 6–9pm. Car park. Children are welcome, but there are no special facilities.

OPEN *11.30am–11pm Mon–Sat; 12–10.30pm Sun.*

BOOT

Brook House Inn

Boot, Eskdale CA19 1TG
☎ *(01946) 723288 Gareth and Sarah Thornley*
www.brookhouseinn.co.uk

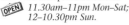 Freehouse with Timothy Taylor Landlord and Hawkshead Bitter plus up to four rotating guests from breweries such as Yates, Moorhouse's and Barngates, to name but a few.

T he main building dates from 1888. The bar area was added in 1994 but is tastefully decorated to be in keeping with the original character. Bar, snug, restaurant and private room for hire. Food served 12–8.30pm. Children welcome. Beer garden. Car park. Accommodation. Annual beer festival held in June.

OPEN *All day, every day except Christmas day.*

The Woolpack Inn

Boot, Eskdale, Holmrook CA19 1TH
☎ *(01946) 723230*
Dave Bailey and Ann Wedgwood
www.woolpack.co.uk

 Home of the Hardknott Brewery, with a range including Woolpacker, Lauters Lamm and Light Cascade plus many others. The pub serves Cumbrian real ales from its own and other micro-breweries.

T his traditional Lakeland inn dates from the 16th century but has a Victorian façade. One public bar and one residents' bar for those staying in the hotel. Individual innovative food produced with locally sourced ingredients served 12.30–2.30pm and 7–9pm, booking advised. Cold snacks available all day. Children and pets welcome. Beer garden in picturesque setting. Two car parks. Regular live music. Annual beer festival held in June. Located at the top of the Eskdale valley, at the foot of Hardknott Pass.

OPEN *11am–11pm March–October. Variable opening November–February.*

BRAMPTON

White Lion Hotel

Highcross Street, Brampton CA8 1RP
☎ *(01697) 72338 Gemma Connelly*

 Black Sheep Bitter, Coniston Bluebird and a guest ale, perhaps from Hawkshead.

A 17th-century former coaching inn in the centre of a busy market town. Two bars, log fires, restaurant, award-winning flower displays. Good food served 12–2.30pm and 5–9pm (12–9pm Sun). Ten bedrooms available plus a function room. Children welcome; no pets. Ten miles from Carlisle, three from Hadrian's Wall.

OPEN *9am–11.30pm (10.30pm Sun).*

BROUGHTON IN FURNESS

The Manor Arms

The Square, Broughton in Furness LA20 6HY
☎ *(01229) 716286* David Varty

 Up to eight well-kept real ales. Brews from Yates, Rooster's and Copper Dragon plus rotating guests changed frequently. New brews, winter warmers – you name it, they have probably served it!

A 17th-century freehouse in a picturesque square, with a welcoming atmosphere. Two real fires. Regular CAMRA Pub of the Year award-winner (West Pennines Pub of the Year 2007). Bar snacks available all day until 10pm, including toasties, rolls, homemade soup, Cumberland sausage and bacon buns. The pub has outside seating overlooking the square. Two real fires, including one Adams fireplace. Beer festivals held twice a year. Three en-suite rooms (two doubles, one twin). Pool table. Free street parking. Between Ulverston and Coniston – from J36 of the M6, take A590 to Greenod and A5092 to Broughton.

OPEN *12–12 (11pm Sun).*

BROUGHTON MILLS

The Blacksmiths Arms

Broughton Mills, Broughton in Furness LA20 6AX
☎ *(01229) 716824* Michael and Sophie Lane
www.theblacksmithsarms.com

 Genuine freehouse offering three real ales. Clarke's Classic Blonde is permanent, Jennings, Hawkshead, Barngates, Moorhouse's and Dent are favoured brewers, with Jennings Cumberland Ale occasionally.

A pub since 1748 and still totally unspoilt, in walking country off the A593. Four small rooms, wooden tables and beams, real fires, flagstone floors. Terraced outside area to front. Food served 12–2pm (not Mon) and 6–9pm. Great walking country. Car park to rear. Children and dogs welcome. Beer festival in November. On the A593 between Coniston and Broughton in Furness, turn left two miles from Broughton.

OPEN *5–11pm Mon; 12–2.30pm and 5–11pm Tues–Fri; 12–11pm Sat; 12–10.30pm Sun.*

BUTTERMERE

Fish Hotel

Buttermere, Cockermouth CA13 9XA
☎ *(01768) 770253* John Richardson
www.fish-hotel.co.uk

 Hotel and freehouse with up to six real ales. Jennings Bitter and Sneck Lifter, Hesket Newmarket Haystacks and Keswick Brewing Co. Thirst Run are regular fixtures. Two guest ales from Jennings and Hesket Newmarket, changed weekly.

One of the oldest inns in the Lake District. Situated between the two lakes of Buttermere and Crummock Water. Food served 12–2pm and 6–9pm. Children welcome. No dogs allowed in the bar. Large car park. Beer garden. B&B accommodation. Off the A591 towards Borrowdale Valley.

OPEN *10.30am–3pm and 6–11pm Mon–Fri; 10.30am–11pm Sat; 10.30am–10.30pm Sun.*

CARLISLE

Woodrow Wilsons

48 Botchergate, Carlisle CA1 1QS
☎ *(01228) 819942* Craig Walker (manager)

Wetherspoon's pub with at least nine real ales. Greene King Abbot, Marston's Pedigree and Jennings Bitter are regulars plus six rotating guests, often from local breweries.

Typical Wetherspoon's town-centre pub in a stone-fronted building. Food available all day. Children welcome to dine until 8pm. Car park. Two beer festivals a year plus a monthly featured brewery festival.

OPEN *9am–midnight (12.30am Fri–Sat).*

CARTMEL

Cavendish Arms

Cavendish Street, Cartmel LA11 6QA
☎ *(01539) 536240* Richard English
www.thecavendisharms.co.uk

Jennings Cumberland and Charles Wells Bombardier plus a guest which changes every month.

A 450-year-old coaching inn, with bar area with low ceilings and beams, plus separate restaurant and riverside drinking area. Food available 12–2pm and 6–9pm. Car park, seven en-suite bedrooms. From the village square, go through the ancient archway and the pub is on the right.

OPEN *11am–11pm Mon–Sat; 12–10pm Sun.*

The King's Arms

The Square, Cartmel LA11 6QB
☎ *(01539) 536220*
Richard and Angela Grimmer

Part-tied to Enterprise Inns, with up to four real ales. Hawkshead Bitter and Moorhouse's Blond Witch are permanent fixtures, with one or two guests, usually either Barngates Tag Lag, Hawkshead Red or Marston's Pedigree.

Archives show that there has been a pub on this site for 900 years. The current building has a relaxed and traditional atmosphere with exposed beams and brasses, and a cobbled area in the outside front area, looking onto the village square. Riverside restaurant serving food 12–2.30pm and 5.30–8.45pm Mon–Fri; 12–8.45pm Sat–Sun. Times vary in winter. Children and dogs welcome. Function room. Close to Cartmel racecourse, off the A590.

OPEN *11am–11pm (10.30pm Sun).*

CHAPEL STILE
Wainwrights Inn
Chapel Stile, Langdale, Chapel Stile, Ambleside LA22 9JD
☎ *(01539) 438088*
Tina Darbyshire and Ben Clarke

Freehouse: Jennings, Cumberland and Sneck Lifter are main offerings, with four other pumps serving beers from Yates, Dent, Derwent, Tyrill, Stringers, Barngates and Hawkshead, to name but a few.

Traditional Lakeland pub with stone-flagged floors and open fire, originally part of a 200-year-old farmhouse. Food served 12–2pm and 6–9pm. One main bar, beer garden and patio overlooking the hills. Children and dogs welcome. Car park at front and rear. Head towards Ambleside and follow signs for Langdale.

OPEN *11.30am–11pm.*

CLEATOR
The Brook Inn
93 Trumpet Terrace, Cleator CA23 3DX
☎ *(01946) 811635* Kirsty J Bennett

Freehouse offering four real ales. Timothy Taylor Landlord and Hawkshead Lakeland Gold permanent; two guests, one from Yates Brewery and one from any independent brewer. Winner of CAMRA Pub of the Season 2005.

Built in 1808, this is a traditional street-corner pub. Open fires, candlelit atmosphere. Homemade food, from locally sourced ingredients whenever possible, served 12–2pm daily and 7–9pm Mon–Thurs and Sat. Children, dogs, bikes, boots and backpacks welcome! Traditional pub games. Thurs: quiz night. Fri: live music. On the A5086 Egremont to Cockermouth road, opposite St Mary's church. Half a mile from the coast-to-coast route.

OPEN *11am–midnight Sun–Thurs; 11am–1am Fri–Sat.*

COCKERMOUTH
The Bitter End
15 Kirkgate, Cockermouth CA13 9PJ
☎ *(01900) 828993* Susan Askey
www.bitterend.co.uk

Home to the Bitter End Brewery with own brews always available. Cuddly Lugs and Cockermouth Pride are usually on the menu. Also Jennings Bitter, Cumberland and Sneck Lifter and one or two guests, changed weekly.

A very traditional brewpub with open fires and background music. No machines or juke box. Food served at lunchtime and evenings. Children allowed. Tuesday is quiz night.

OPEN *11.30am–2.30pm and 6–11pm Mon–Thurs; 11.30am–3pm and 6–11pm Fri–Sat; 11.30am–3pm and 7–10.30pm Sun.*

The Bush
Main Street, Cockermouth CA13 9JS
☎ *(01900) 822064* Maureen Williamson

Jennings house with six hand pumps. The full Jennings range is usually on offer, plus one guest which could be any local ale.

A very warm, friendly town-centre pub with open fires. In operation since 1817. Food served at lunchtime only. Children and dogs welcome in the afternoons.

OPEN *11am–11pm Mon–Sat; 12–10.30pm Sun.*

CONISTON
The Black Bull Hotel
1 Yewdale Road, Coniston LA21 8DU
☎ *(01539) 441335/441668* Ronald Bradley
www.conistonbrewery.com

Genuine freehouse but with the Coniston Brewery located behind it. Offers Coniston Bluebird, Bluebird XB, Old Man and Blacksmith's Ale plus seasonals and specials and up to two rotating guests from other micro-breweries.

A 16th-century coaching inn in the centre of Coniston, with one bar, oak beams and log fire. No juke box, piped music or fruit machines. Outside seating area. Separate restaurant. Good food served all day until 9pm. Children and dogs welcome. Car park. Accommodation (15 en-suite rooms).

OPEN *11am–11pm Mon–Sat; 12–10.30pm Sun. Closed Christmas Day.*

The Sun Hotel and 16th Century Inn
Coniston LA21 8HQ
☎ *(01539) 441248* Alan Piper
www.thesunconiston.com

Freehouse with five pumps and a cool cellar! Local beers are regularly featured, with Coniston Bluebird and Hawkshead brews particularly popular. Other guests might include Black Sheep Special, Moorhouse's Black Cat or something from Yates or Barngates. Breweries from further afield (Wychwood, Shepherd Neame, Greene King, Exmoor, Fuller's and Wells and Young's) also feature.

This 16th-century pub has a 19th-century hotel attached, accommodating 25 people in good-value refurbished bedrooms. Situated on rising ground to overlook the village and enjoying excellent mountain views. One bar, a new conservatory and terrace overlooking the beer garden, outside seating at front, side, rear and in garden. Good-value food from à la carte menu and specials board served lunchtimes and evenings in the conservatory restaurant and bar; the wine list has 40 wines. Children and dogs welcome. Situated on the hill leading up to the Old Man of Coniston,100 yards above Coniston village, turn left at the bridge.

OPEN *11am–11pm (10.30pm Sun).*

CROSTHWAITE

The Punch Bowl Inn

Crosthwaite, Lyth Valley, Crosthwaite
LA8 8HR
☎ *(01539) 568237*
www.the-punchbowl.co.uk

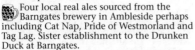

 Four local real ales sourced from the Barngates brewery in Ambleside perhaps including Cat Nap, Pride of Westmorland and Tag Lag. Sister establishment to the Drunken Duck at Barngates.

Luxurious Lake District hotel and restaurant next to the church in Crosthwaite in the heart of the Lyth Valley. The building dates from the 17th century with lots of low beams, log fires and slate floors. Lunch served 12–6pm and dinner 6–9.30pm. Nine bedrooms.

OPEN *12–11pm, breakfast from 8.30am for non-residents.*

CURTHWAITE

The Royal Oak

Curthwaite, Nr Wigton CA7 8BG
☎ *(01228) 710219* Marcus and Laura Denby

 Three real ales: Jennings Cumberland plus two guests.

A 17th-century Grade II listed country pub and restaurant. Food served 12–2pm and 6–9pm. Darts. Children welcome. Six miles from Carlisle.

OPEN *12–2.30pm and 5–11pm Mon–Sat;12–10.30pm Sun.*

DALTON IN FURNESS

Black Dog Inn

Black Dog Road, Holmes Green, Dalton in Furness LA15 8JP
☎ *(01229) 462561*
James Howarth and Andrew Turner

 Genuine freehouse with six constantly changing real ales, rotated weekly, with at least three local beers where possible.

Old coaching inn and local institution situated at the site of the tollgates on the ancient Furness Abbey to Scotland road. Extensively refurbished in keeping with a traditional country pub atmosphere, with open fires and exposed beams. No games machines or music. Food served 12–8.30pm Tues–Sat and 12–5pm Sun. Accommodation. Large car park, beer garden. Families and children welcome. Beer festivals. Situated just 1km from South Lakes Wildlife Park, and 20 minutes from the Lake District. Follow the elephant signs for the Wildlife Park, and the pub is half a mile further along the same road.

OPEN *11am–late Mon–Sat; 12–late Sun.*

The Brown Cow Inn

10 Goose Green, Dalton in Furness LA15 8LQ
☎ *(01229) 462553* CL Bell
www.browncowinndalton.co.uk

Five real ales all rotate every few days at this freehouse, with breweries such as Hawkshead, Coniston, Barngates, Ulverston, Moorhouse's and Dent featuring regularly.

A 900-year-old family-oriented pub with low ceilings, beams, coal fire and 100-seater restaurant. Food served 12–9pm. Large beer garden, car park. Two letting properties. Close to the Lakes, Furness Abbey and South Lakes Animal Park. Off the A590 to Dalton, on Abbey Road next to the Chequers Hotel.

OPEN *12–12.*

DENT

The George & Dragon Hotel

Main Street, Dent LA10 5QL
☎ *(01539) 625256* Paul and Judith Beeley
www.thegeorgeanddragondent.co.uk

Owned by the Dent Brewery, offering Aviator, Kamikaze, Ramsbottom and T'owd Tup Golden Fleece plus 5 more hand pulls including cask cider. Cask Marque Feb 2009. The only place in Dent selling Dent beers all year round. Brewery Trip can be arranged, booking needed, max. groups of 10 persons.

Two-bar traditional Dales pub in a picturesque rural village. Food served 12–2.30pm and 6–9pm. Two twin rooms, five doubles, two family and one single. Car park to the right of the pub. Children and dogs welcome. Good walking, fishing and golf nearby. Ten miles from junction 37 of the M6.

OPEN *10.30am–11pm Mon–Thur; 10.30-1pm Fri-Sat; 10.30am–11pm Sun.*

The Sun Inn

Main Street, Dent LA10 5QL
☎ *(01539) 625208* Martin Stafford

Three to five beers from all over the country, from breweries such as Inveralmond, Jarrow, Hambleton and Blackadder.

A traditional country pub in the cobbled main street close to the George & Dragon. Friendly atmosphere, large beer garden, dining area. Food served 12–2pm and 6.30–8.30pm all year round. Children welcome until 9pm.

OPEN *11am–11pm Mon–Sat; 12–10.30pm Sun.*

ELTERWATER

The Britannia Inn

Elterwater, Ambleside LA22 9HP
☎ *(01539) 437210* Clare Woodhead
www.britinn.co.uk

Freehouse serving Coniston Britannia Inn Special and Bluebird, Jennings Bitter, plus three guests changed every barrel from a variety of local and national breweries.

Quintessential English Lakeland inn in the middle of a picturesque village four miles from Ambleside within the Langdale Valley. Around 500 years old. Small oak-beamed rooms with log fires in winter. Full menu served 12–2pm and 6.30–9.30pm, plus snacks 2–5.30pm. Separate dining area. Large outside seating area plus car park. Nine en-suite rooms, with special mid-week rates. Children and dogs welcome. Autumn beer festival, quiz night most Sundays.

OPEN *11am–11pm.*

FOXFIELD
The Prince of Wales
Foxfield, Broughton-in-Furness LA20 6BX
☎ *(01229) 716238* Stuart Johnson
www.princeofwalesfoxfield.co.uk

The home of the Foxfield Brewery, which operates from an adjoining converted stables. Up to six hand pumps dispense a constantly changing range of interesting beers. There is always a mild and something from Tigertops (in Wakefield) and Foxfield breweries, both of which are owned and run by the Johnsons. Belgian beers, plus over 80 malts and blended whiskies.

Award-winning 'no-frills' real ale house, for real ale lovers, in the hamlet of Foxfield. CAMRA Cumbria Pub of the Year 2005 and 2007, and ACORP Community Rail Pub of the Year 2005. Homemade snacks served 12–7pm Fri–Sun. Car park. B&B. Traditional pub games. Themed (stouts, porters, strong ales etc) beer weekends. Disabled access and toilet. Opposite Foxfield station.

OPEN *2.45pm–11pm Wed–Thurs; 12–11pm Fri–Sat; 12–10.30pm Sun; closed Mon–Tues.*

GARRIGILL
George & Dragon Inn
Garrigill, Alston CA9 3DS
☎ *(01434) 381293*
www.garrigill-pub.co.uk

Genuine freehouse with Black Sheep Bitter and three guest ales in summer, fewer in winter.

Very rural but popular 17th-century inn with good atmosphere and good food. Handily placed for the Pennine Way. Flagstone floor, open fires, by the village green. Food served 12–1.30pm in summer, 7–8.30pm all week. Children and dogs welcome. Four miles south of Alston.

OPEN *Easter–Nov: 12–2pm and 7–11pm Mon–Fri; 12–11pm Sat; 12–4pm and 7–10.30pm Sun. Winter: 7–11pm Mon–Thurs; 12–2pm and 7–11pm Fri; 12–11pm Sat; 12–4pm and 7–10.30pm Sun.*

GRASMERE
The Traveller's Rest
Grasmere LA22 9RR
☎ *(01539) 435604* R Collins
www.lakedistrictinns.co.uk

Jennings tied house, offering four real ales. Jennings Bitter, Cumberland and Sneck Lifter are on the menu along with a guest which might be Black Sheep Bitter, Coniston Bluebird or another beer from an independent brewery, according to availability and demand.

A 16th-century inn with one bar, beer garden, games room and bed and breakfast (en-suite accommodation). Food served 12–3pm and 6–9.30pm (winter); 12–9.30pm (summer). Families and dogs always welcome. Half a mile north of Grasmere village, on A591.

OPEN *11am–11pm (10.30pm Sun).*

Tweedies Bar
Red Bank Road, Grasmere LA22 9SW
☎ *(01539) 435300*
Brian Roberts and James Heaton Goodall
www.dalelodgehotel.co.uk

Freehouse with Caledonian Deuchars IPA, the full Timothy Taylor range and the full Yates range, plus three guests, one English, one Scottish and one local.

A pub since 1976, but previously a retirement home, and named after a man who made and sold tweed in the area. One bar, traditional in style but with a modern twist, and one of the largest beer gardens in Cumbria. Food served 12–3pm and 6–9pm (pizzas till 9.45pm); 12–4pm and 6.30–9pm Sun. Children and dogs welcome. Attached to the Dale Lodge Hotel with 11 en-suite rooms.

OPEN *12–11pm Mon–Wed; 12–12 Thurs–Sun.*

GREAT CORBY
The Corby Bridge Inn
Great Corby, Carlisle CA4 8LL
☎ *(01228) 560221* Dave Maxwell

Thwaites Original and Lancaster Bomber plus a rotating guest, changed twice a week, which could be from anywhere in the country. Extensive list of malt whiskies also on offer.

Grade II listed freehouse built in 1838, originally a railway hotel and fully refurbished in 2006. One bar, pool room, darts and dining area. Bar menu and evening meal menu available, with lunch and dinner served Mon–Thurs and all day Fri–Sun. Four en-suite rooms. Large car park, patio, beer garden. Approximately four miles from junction 43 of M6, off the A69, or 300 yards from Wetheral railway station.

OPEN *12–11pm (10.30pm Sun).*

GREAT LANGDALE
Old Dungeon Ghyll Hotel
Great Langdale, Ambleside LA22 9JY
☎ *(01539) 437272* Neil Walmsley
www.odg.co.uk

Up to seven real ales at this freehouse. Yates Bitter, Jennings Cumberland Ale, Black Sheep Special, Theakston XB and Old Peculier plus two guests changed weekly. Scrumpy also served.

Interesting National Trust property at the head of the Langdale Valley, a listed building with large open fire and spectacular mountain views. Food served 12–2pm and 6–9pm. Accommodation. Beer garden, car park. Seven miles from Ambleside, at the head of the B5343.

OPEN *11am–11pm.*

GREAT SALKELD
The Highland Drove Inn
Great Salkeld, Nr Penrith CA11 9NA
☎ *(01768) 898349* Donald and Paul Newton
www.highland-drove.co.uk

 Theakston Black Bull and John Smiths Cask plus a guest beer changed every barrel.

Friendly, family-run freehouse. Bar, lounge and separate games room plus an upstairs restaurant. Bar and restaurant food served 12–1.45 pm (not Mon) and 6.30–8.45pm (8.30pm Sun). Beer garden, private room for up to 24. Accommodation available in five en-suite bedrooms. Situated behind the church.

OPEN *12–2.30pm and 6pm–12 (closed Mon lunch).*

GREAT STRICKLAND
The Strickland Arms
Great Strickland, Penrith CA10 3DF
☎ *(01931) 712238* Anton and Penny Flaherty
www.thestricklandarms.co.uk

A Marston's Brewery tied house serving Marston's ales, plus Jennings Cumberland. Also two guest ales, such as Brakspears Oxford Gold, Wychwood Hobgoblin, Ringwoods Bold Forester. The choice changes monthly.

An 18th-century pub, formerly a farmhouse and barn. Food served in a separate dining area 12–2.30pm and 5.30–9.30pm, and in Bar, Terrace and Garden. Children most welcome. Pet-friendly. Secluded beer garden and walled terrace. Accommodation. Car park. Located six miles south of Penrith, just off the A6.

OPEN *12–2.30pm and 5pm–12; all day Sat–Sun.*

HAYTON
Stone Inn
Hayton, Brampton, Nr Carlisle CA8 9HR
☎ *(01228) 670896* Johnnie and Susan Tranter

Thwaites Bitter and Mild plus two local guest brews, often from the Allendale brewery.

A traditional village pub rebuilt in 1815. Toasted sandwiches available at all times at the bar and private dinner parties are arranged in the dining room but the focus is on beer. Coach parties can be catered for if booked in advance. The pub has a car park, and is situated four miles east of M6 junction 43, just off the A69.

OPEN *10am–3pm and 5.30–11pm Mon–Fri; 10am–11pm Sat; 12–3pm and 7–10.30pm Sun.*

HESKET NEWMARKET
The Old Crown
Hesket Newmarket, Caldbeck, Wigton CA7 8JG
☎ *(01697) 478288* Lewis and Linda Hogg
www.theoldcrownpub.co.uk

Freehouse specialising in Hesket Newmarket brews. Up to eight available with Old Carrock Strong Ale, Skiddaw Special, Catbells Pale Ale, Doris's 90th Birthday Ale, Blencathra Bitter and Great Cockup Porter always on the menu.

Small, old-fashioned pub, with two bars, bought by a co-operative of more than 125 locals in 2003. Voted the UK's eighth best pub in a *Morning Advertiser* poll. The Hesket Newmarket Brewery is in a barn behind the pub and tours can be arranged for six or more people. Food served at lunchtime (Tues–Sun) and evenings (Tues–Sat) in the new garden restaurant. Children allowed. On the edge of the Lake District National Park, the only pub in the village. The Prince of Wales dropped in in February 2004!

OPEN *5.30–11pm Mon; 12–3pm and 5.30–11pm Tues–Sat; 12–3pm and 7–10.30pm Sun.*

INGS
The Watermill Inn
Ings, Nr Staveley, Kendal LA8 9PY
☎ *(01539) 821309* Brian Coulthwaite
www.watermillinn.co.uk

 Sixteen beers are usually available (500 per year), including Black Sheep Bitter, Coniston Bluebird and Theakston Old Peculier. Guest ales may come from the Hop Back, Cotleigh, Ridleys, Shepherd Neame, Exmoor, Summerskills, Coach House, Yates and Wadworth breweries. There is now a micro-brewery with a viewing window on site, and the regular beers brewed include Collie Wobbles (3.7%), W'Ruff Night (5%) and Bit'er Ruff (4.1%).

Formerly a wood mill, now a traditional, family-run pub full of character with two bars, log fires, brasses and beams and a relaxing atmosphere. A new extension has added a beer cellar and brewery viewing window from the main bar. No juke box or games machines. Many times winner of Westmorland Pub of the Year and other prizes. Food served 12–4.30pm and 5–9pm every day. Car park, garden, seats and tables by the river. Disabled toilets. Children allowed in one bar, dogs in the other. Accommodation. From the M6, junction 36, follow the A591 towards Windermere. One mile past the second turning for Staveley. Turn left after the garage, before the church.

OPEN *12–11pm (10.30pm Sun).*

IREBY
The Lion
The Square, Ireby, Wigton, Carlisle CA7 1EA
☎ *(01697) 371460* Brad and Amanda Leader
www.irebythelion.co.uk

A three-pump freehouse offering Derwent Carlisle State Bitter, Jennings Bitter and a guest, which might come from Yates, Coniston, Hawkshead or Hesket Newmarket.

This traditional village freehouse features oak panels, an open fire and wooden floor. Back bar/games room for darts. Food served 6–9pm Tues–Sat and 7–9pm Sun. Children welcome.

OPEN *6–11pm Mon–Thurs; 6pm–12 Fri–Sat; 12–3pm and 7–11pm Sun.*

KENDAL
Burgundy's Wine Bar
19 Lowther Street, Kendal LA9 4DH
☎ *(01539) 733803* M Pennington

Freehouse with four real ales. Beers from Yates and Hawkshead are always on offer, plus two guests, changed every couple of days.

Traditional town pub, formerly the Kendal Labour Exchange, built in the early 19th century. One split-level bar with a continental feel and a relaxed atmosphere. No food. Live music on Thursdays. Beer terrace. Children allowed. Next to the Town Hall. Hosts the Cumbria Micro Beer Challenge in April.

OPEN *6.30–11pm Tues–Weds; 11am–3.30pm and 6.30pm–12 Thurs–Sat (11pm Thurs); 7pm–12 Sun.*

Ring o' Bells
39 Kirkland, Kendal LA9 5AF
☎ *(01539) 720326* Clive Graham

Four real ales, with two regular features and a couple of rotating guests, changed every few days.

Unspoilt 17th-century pub in the grounds of the parish church. Bar food available at lunchtimes and evenings. Dining room seating 14. Parking. Children allowed. Accommodation. Take M6 junction 36, then follow the A590 and A591 to the A6 in Kendal.

OPEN *12–11pm (10.30pm Sun).*

KINGS MEABURN
The White Horse Inn
Kings Meaburn, Penrith CA10 3BU
☎ *(01931) 714256* Jon and Dawn Hamilton

A freehouse. No permanent beers, just two constantly changing guests. All beers come from local micro-breweries, such as Yates, Barngates, Keswick, Dent, Hesket Newmarket, Tirill and Derwent.

An early-19th-century coaching inn with real fire and lots of character. One bar area plus private room. Home-cooked food – including real chips! – served every evening (except Wed) and lunchtimes Sat–Sun. Children welcome, with a healthy children's menu. No juke box, pool table or fruit machines. Car park and beer garden. Annual beer festival featuring 50 Cumbrian beers and ciders – a great community event.

OPEN *7pm–12 Mon–Wed; 6pm–12 Thurs–Fri; (closed weekday lunch); 12–2pm and 6pm–12 Sat; 12–12 Sun.*

KIRKBY LONSDALE
The Snooty Fox
Main Street, Kirkby Lonsdale LA6 2AH
☎ *(01524) 271308* Paul Riley

Three or four real ales with Black Sheep Bitter, Timothy Taylor Landlord and Hawkshead Lakeland Gold among the beers regularly featured.

Jacobean inn with original stonework and beams, two bars and nine en-suite bedrooms. Award-winning food served lunchtime and evenings. Beer garden, private car park, semi-private dining room. Children and dogs welcome. Just off the market square.

OPEN *11am–11pm Sun–Thurs; 11am–midnight Fri–Sat.*

The Sun Inn
6 Market Street, Kirkby Lonsdale LA6 2AO
☎ *(01524) 271965* Lucy and Mark Fuller
www.sun-inn.info

A freehouse. Hawkshead Bitter, Timothy Taylor Landlord, Jennings Cumberland and Marston's Pedigree.

Built in the 17th-century and set in a busy market town, close to the Lake District and the Yorkshire Dales. A blend of old and new in the décor, with real log fires and a contemporary restaurant. Locally sourced food available 12–2.30pm and 7–9pm. Dog friendly. Accommodation.

OPEN *10am–11pm.*

KIRKSANTON
King William IV
Kirksanton, Nr Millom LA18 4NN
☎ *(01229) 772009* Pete and Karen Rodger

Freehouse with Jennings Cumberland Ale always available, with regular guest ales during the summer.

A 200-year-old country pub with oak beams and real fires. Four letting rooms available for bed and breakfast. Dining area. Food at lunchtimes and evenings. Children allowed. On the main road from Millom to Whitehaven.

OPEN *12–3pm and 7–11pm.*

LOWESWATER
Kirkstile Inn
Loweswater, Cockermouth CA13 0RU
☎ *(01900) 85219* Roger and Helen Humphreys
www.kirkstile.com

Freehouse and home of the Loweswater Brewery, offering Melbreak Bitter, Kirkstile Gold and Grasmoor Dark Ale plus guests such as Coniston Bluebird and Yates Bitter.

Award-winning, family-owned 16th-century inn with its own micro-brewery. Bar and separate dining room. Food served 12–3pm and 6–9pm. Children welcome. Dogs allowed until 6pm. Car park. Comfortable accommodation. Situated seven miles from Cockermouth.

OPEN *11am–11pm (except Christmas Day).*

NETHER WASDALE

The Screes Inn

Nether Wasdale, Seascale CA20 1ET
☎ *(01946) 726262* Nick and Rachel Putnam
www.thescreesinnwasdale.com

Freehouse, with Jennings Cumberland, Yates and Black Sheep brews plus a guest, changed weekly, from independents such as Derwent.

An 18th-century family-run pub with split-level bar, log fire, separate dining area and small function room. Beer garden, car park. Magnificent views of the fells. Food served 12–2.30pm and 6–9pm. Accommodation (five en-suite rooms). Children welcome. Folk music sessions. Four miles from Gosforth on the A595.

OPEN *All day, every day (except Christmas and New Year's Day).*

RAVENSTONEDALE

The King's Head Hotel

Ravenstonedale CA17 4NH
☎ *(015396) 23284*

Black Sheep Bitter and at least four guest ales. An annual beer festival is held in August.

A 16th-century inn created out of four cottages. Beams, real fires, games and family room. Food served at lunchtimes and evenings. Off the A685.

OPEN *11am–11pm Mon–Sat; 12–10.30pm Sun.*

SATTERTHWAITE

The Eagle's Head

Satterthwaite, Nr Ulverston LA12 8LN
☎ *(01229) 860237* Rob and Rebecca Bruce

Freehouse serving Moorhouse's Eagles Head and Grizedale and Theakston Best. Also one monthly-changing guest.

Dating from the 16th century, the building was originally a farmhouse with attached barn. Now an open-plan L-shaped single bar. Food served 12.30–2.30pm and 7–8.30pm Tues–Sun. Children welcome. Dogs welcome (under control). Limited parking, but parking also permitted in village lane. Beer garden. Popular with cyclists and walkers. Located in the heart of Grizedale National Forest, four and a half miles from Hawkshead.

OPEN *7–11pm Mon (closed Mon lunch); 12–2.30pm and 7–11pm Tues–Thurs; 12–2.30pm and 6.30–11pm Fri–Sat; 12–2.30pm and 7–11pm Sun. Longer opening hours during peak holiday season.*

SAWREY

Tower Bank Arms

Nr Sawrey, Ambleside LA22 0LF
☎ *(01539) 436334* Anthony Hutton
www.towerbankarms.com

A freehouse. Five Cumbrian Ales offered on hand pump, often with more available directly from the cellar. Always with Hawkshead Bitter and a range of classic and seasonal beers. Brodies Prime and Lakeland Gold, Barngate's Mothbag, Tag Lag, Cracker and Pride of Westmorland, Keswick Thirst Ascent and Thirst Run, and Ulverston Lonesome Pine are popular.

A 17th-century Lakeland inn, situated next to Beatrix Potter's farm, Hilltop. Cosy atmosphere with log fire, flagstone floor and friendly service. Bar, restaurant and beer garden. Food, from locally sourced produce, served 12–2pm and 6–9pm (8pm Sun and Bank Holidays, and Sun-Thurs in winter). Children and dogs welcome.

OPEN *Summer:11.30am–11pm Mon–Sat; 12–10.30pm Sun. Winter: 11.30am-2pm daily (Sundays 12-2.30pm); 5.30-10.30pm Sun-Thurs; 5.30-11pm Fri-Sat.*

SEATHWAITE

Newfield Inn

Seathwaite, Broughton in Furness LA20 6ED
☎ *(01229) 716208* Paul Batten

Freehouse with four real ales, including Jennings Cumberland Ale and Sneck Lifter. Two weekly changing guests from a selection of Cumbrian beers.

Dating from around the early 17th century, with traditional slate floors and real fire. A family-friendly, real Lakeland pub, popular with outdoor enthusiasts for its stunning views. No juke box or games machines. Food served 12–9pm. Children welcome. Large beer garden with children's play area. Six miles off the A595 at Duddon Bridge.

OPEN *11am–11pm.*

STAVELEY

Eagle & Child Inn

Kendal Road, Staveley LA8 9LP
☎ *(01539) 821320*
Richard and Denise Coleman
www.eaglechildinn.co.uk

Freehouse serving Hawkshead Bitter and Gold permanently. Plus three guests, on constant rotation.

Georgian double-fronted inn with bar, restaurant, function room, riverside beer garden and decking area. Food served 12–2.30pm and 6–9pm. Accommodation in five hotel-style en-suite rooms with colour TV. Rates available for B&B or dinner, B&B.

OPEN *11am–midnight.*

Hawkshead Brewery Beer Hall

Staveley Mill Yard, Staveley LA8 9LR
☎ *(01539) 822644* Alex Brodie
www.hawksheadbrewery.co.uk

The brewery tap for Hawkshead Brewery. Available beers are: Red, Lakeland Gold, Bitter, Brodies Prime, Lakeland Lager, Organic Stout an whatever else the brewery is brewing at the time. Guest beers occasionally. Twice yearly Beer Festival of SIBA champion beers. Traditional and modern bottled beers, plus cider and a good range of wines.

Established three years ago as the bar, function room and visitors' centre of the brewery, into which it looks. Evening functions available. Food available all day. Dogs welcome.

OPEN *12–5pm Mon-Tues; 12-6pm Weds-Sun. (Evenings are available private hire.)*

STONETHWAITE

Langstrath Country Inn

Stonethwaite, Keswick CA12 5XG
☎ *(017687) 77239* Sara and Mike Hodgson
www.thelangstrath.com

Freehouse with Black Sheep Bitter and Jennings Bitter plus two weekly guests. Examples include Hawkshead Bitter, Jennings Cocker Hoop, Tirrels beers. Wines by the glass and 20+ malt whiskies.

A 17th-century country inn with real fires and eight en-suite bedrooms. Food served in bar and restaurant 12–2.15pm and 6–9pm (full-time chef). Beer garden, car park. From Keswick, take the B5289 to Borrowdale and turn left to Stonethwaite just after Rosthwaite.

OPEN *Closed Mon; 12–10.30pm Tues–Sun.*

STRAWBERRY BANK

The Mason's Arms

Strawberry Bank, Cartmel Fell LA11 6NW
☎ *(01539) 568486* Helen Parker
www.strawberrybank.com

Five real ales, including Timothy Taylor Landlord and brews from Black Sheep and Hawkshead. Other guests are from all over the country, e.g. Greene King Old Speckled Hen, Caledonian Deuchars IPA and beer from Barngates brewery. Good selection of fruit beers and bottle-conditioned beers. Hoegaarden and Budvar also available.

R ural freehouse set in the middle of nowhere! Slate floor and open fires. Terrace with 12 tables overlooking the valley. Self-catering studio apartments available. Homemade food served at lunchtime and evenings, with a good vegetarian and vegan selection. Children allowed.

OPEN *11.30am–3pm and 6–11pm Mon–Thurs; all day Fri–Sun.*

TALKIN

Blacksmith's Arms

Talkin, Nr Brampton CA8 1LE
☎ *(016977) 3452* Donald Jackson
www.blacksmithstalkin.co.uk

Beers from the Geltsdale brewery, Copper Dragon and Yates plus a guest ale.

A 17th-century blacksmith's, now a freehouse with real open fires, accommodation and restaurant. Good food served at lunchtime and evenings. Close to Hadrian's Wall and Brampton Golf Course, and ten miles from Carlisle. Off junction 43 of the M6, on the A69 to Brampton.

OPEN *12–3pm and 6–11pm.*

TIRRIL

The Queen's Head

Tirril, Penrith CA10 2JF
☎ *(01768) 863219*
Daniel Gault and Emma Papa

Offers four beers from the Tirril Brewery plus one other ale on a guest pump.

A 300-year-old freehouse, once owned by the Wordsworth family, situated on the B5320, with stone walls and beams. Two bars, Grade II listed. The small village of Tirril once boasted two breweries, one being at this inn. It was closed in 1899, and reopened 100 years later in October 1999 by the present landlord, in an outhouse at the rear of the pub. The brewery moved to nearby Brougham Hall in 2002. The pub itself is a Cask Marque winner. Food served 12–2pm and 6–9.15pm, with a separate dining area available. Cumbrian Beer and Sausage Festival held annually on second weekend of August. Another festival in February. Children allowed. Seven en-suite rooms. On the B5320.

OPEN *12–3pm and 6–11pm Mon–Thurs; 12–12 Fri–Sat; 12–10.30pm Sun.*

TROUTBECK

The Queen's Head Hotel

Troutbeck, Windermere LA23 1PW
☎ *(01539) 432174* Mark Stewardson
www.queensheadhotel.com

Freehouse with six real ales. Coniston Bluebird and something from Hawkshead, Jennings and Tirril are probably among them plus a couple of guests.

A food-oriented pub and hotel in a 17th-century coaching inn with log fires, oak beams and stone floors. Accommodation in 16 bedrooms. Seating area outside. Food served 12–2pm and 6.30–8.45pm. Children welcome. On the A592, two miles from Lake Windermere.

OPEN *11am–11pm Mon–Sat; 12–10.30pm Sun.*

ULDALE

The Snooty Fox Country Inn

Uldale, Wigton CA7 1HA
☎ *(01697) 371479* JJ and P Barker
www.snootyfox-uldale.com

Freehouse usually serving Jennings Cumberland Ale, Yates Bitter and Black Bull and Robinson's Hatter Mild.

T ypical rural country inn dating from the 17th century. Open fires and beamed ceilings give a historic atmosphere. Food served every evening (except Wednesday) 6.30–8.30pm and Sun lunch 12–1.45pm. Beer garden and patio. Accommodation. Off the A591 Keswick to Carlisle.

OPEN *6.30–11pm Mon–Sat (closed lunchtimes); 12–2pm and 6.30–11pm Sun.*

WALTON

The Centurion Inn

Walton, Nr Brampton CA8 2DH
☎ *(016977) 2438* MJ Davies
www.centurioninn.com

Jennings Cumberland and Timothy Taylor Landlord plus a guest or seasonal special.

Two hundred years old and known as the Black Bull until 1974. On the actual route of Hadrian's Wall, a family-run community freehouse with restaurant and bed and breakfast accommodation. Food suitable for a variety of diets served 6–8pm every day plus 12–2pm Sat–Sun, then all day, every day from Easter onwards. Children welcome. Beer garden, car park.

OPEN *Winter: 5.30–11pm Mon–Fri; 12–11pm Sat; 12–10.30pm Sun. From Easter onwards: 11am–11pm (10.30pm Sun).*

WASDALE HEAD

Wasdale Head Inn

Wasdale Head, Nr Gosforth CA20 1EX
☎ *(01946) 726229* Howard Christie
www.wasdale.com

Home of the Great Gable Brewery, with up to nine of the brewery's own beers plus others from other Cumbrian breweries such as Jennings, Dent, Derwent, Coniston and Foxfield.

Traditional pub with a beer garden, set in the Lake District National Park. CAMRA Cumbria Pub of the Year 2006. Food served 12–9pm (8.30pm in winter). Children allowed (if on a lead!). Bar, sitting room, dining room and 11 bedrooms plus self-catering apartments. Barbecue nights in summer. Excellent base for walking and climbing. Situated beneath England's highest mountain, beside her deepest lake.

OPEN *11am–11pm Mon–Sat; 12–10.30pm Sun.*

WINTON

The Bay Horse Inn

Winton, Kirkby Stephen CA17 4HS
☎ *(01768) 371451* Mr Gott

 Freehouse offering six real ales, all rotated, and all hand-pulled from the cask. Regulars include Fuller's London Pride, Hawkshead Best Bitter, Stones Bitter (brewed by Everards) and Black Sheep Bitter.

A pub dating from the late 1600s, off the A685, two miles north of Kirkby Stephen. Lounge bar, panelled walls, beams, two open fires, flag floors. Public and lounge bars with central servery. Modern 50-seater dining area. Food served at lunchtimes and evenings. Children allowed.

OPEN *6pm–12 Mon; 12–3pm and 6pm–12 Tues–Sun.*

THE BREWERIES

BOTTLE BROOK BREWERY
10 Church Street, Kilburn, Belper DE56 0LU
☎ *07971 189915*

 MEANDERING MILD 4.1% ABV
CELTIC PORTER 4.5% ABV
FULL MOON 4.6% ABV
TOLL BAR BITTER 4.7% ABV
MIDNIGHT MASH 5.1% ABV
DEEP WELL 5.2% ABV
BLACK BESS 7.4% ABV

BRUNSWICK BREWERY
*The Brunswick Inn, 1 Railway Terrace, Derby
DE1 2RU*
☎ *(01332) 290677*

MILD 3.6% ABV
BITTER 3.7% ABV
TRIPLE HOP 4.0% ABV
SECOND BREW 4.2% ABV
RAILWAY PORTER 4.3% ABV
TRIPLE GOLD 4.5% ABV
OLD ACCIDENTAL 5.0% ABV
PILSENER 5.0% ABV
FATHER MIKE'S DARK RICH RUBY 5.8% ABV
BLACK SABBATH 6.0% ABV
Plus monthly specials.

CALLOW TOP BAD RAM BREWERY
*Callow Top Holiday Park, Buxton Road,
Sandybrook, Ashbourne DE6 2AQ*
☎ *(01335) 344020*
www.callowtop.co.uk/brewery

DR SAMUEL JOHNSON 4.5% ABV
Full bodied with a balance of malt and
hop flavours.
WOGGLE DANCE 4.5% ABV
Full bodied with a hint of honey.
BAD RAM 5.0% ABV
Full-bodied ale with a hoppy aftertaste.
FIERY FRED 5.2% ABV
Dark and full bodied with a malty aftertaste.
CALLOW TOP IPA 5.25% ABV
Full-strength Indian pale ale

DERBY BREWING CO. LTD
*Unit 11, Masons Place, Nottingham Road, Derby
DE21 6AQ*
☎ *(01332) 242888*
www.derbybrewing.co.uk

TRIPLE HOP 4.1% ABV
Well balanced, smooth.
BUSINESS AS USUAL (HARRIS HAWK) 4.4% ABV
Malty bitter.
OLD INTENTIONAL 5.0% ABV
Full-bodied bitter.
Plus seasonals and specials including:
GOLD'N'PERLE 4.5% ABV
MUTZ NUTZ 4.5% ABV
OUTRAGEOUSLY DARK 4.5% ABV
NO HALF MEASURES 4.8% ABV

DERVENTIO BREWERY LTD
Trusley Brook Farm, Trusley, Ashbourne DE6 5JP
☎ *07816 878129*
www.derventiobrewery.co.uk

CENTURIAN 4.3% ABV
VENUS 5.0% ABV
Plus seasonals and specials.

EDALE BREWERY CO. LTD
*Ruskin Villa, Hope Road, Edale, Hope Valley
S33 7ZE*
☎ *(01433) 670289*
www.edalebrewery.co.uk

KINDER RIGHT TO ROAM 3.9% ABV
KINDER TRESPASS 4.0% ABV
BACK FOR BITTER 4.2% ABV
BLACK TOR BITTER 4.2% ABV
KINDER DOWNFALL 5.0% ABV
KINDER STOUTER 5.0% ABV
KINDER WASAILE 6.0% ABV
RINGING ROGER 6.0% ABV
Plus seasonals and specials.

FALSTAFF BREWING COMPANY
*The Falstaff Freehouse, 74 Silverhill Road,
Normanton, Derby DE23 6UJ*
☎ *(01332) 342902*
www.falstaffbrewery.co.uk

LENNY HENRY 4.0% ABV
Grapefruit and tangerine citrus flavours.
NORMAN WISDOM 4.0% ABV
Dried apricot, hoppy undertones.
BILLY CONNOLLY 4.2% ABV
Malt nose, dry citrus hop.
CHARLIE CHAPLIN 4.2% ABV
Citrus notes.
SPIKE MILLIGAN 4.4% ABV
Subtle toffee flavour.
A FIST FULL OF HOPS 4.5% ABV
Amber colour, dry and hoppy.
FRENCH & SAUNDERS 4.5% ABV
PHOENIX 4.7% ABV
Copper colours, lots of body with a sweeter taste.
BEBBINGTON ARMS 4.8% ABV
THE OLD SILK MILL 4.8% ABV
THE SMILING ASSASSIN 5.2% ABV
Syrupy quality, copper colour, deceptively
strong.
THE GOOD THE BAD AND THE DRUNK 6.2% ABV
Rich vine fruits, malty nose.
ERM 10.5% ABV
Full-bodied with fruity bitter flavour and hints of
caramel.
Plus numerous wide-ranging specials and seasonals.

FUNFAIR BREWING COMPANY
Canal Street, Ilkeston DE7 8DR
☎ *07970 540186*

GALLOPERS 3.8% ABV
SHOWMAN'S GOLD 4.4% ABV
SHOWMAN'S BITTER 4.6% ABV
BRANDY SNAP 4.7% ABV
DODGEM 4.7% ABV
CAKE WALK 6.0%

HOWARD TOWN BREWERY
Hawkshead Mill, Hope Street, Glossop SK13 7SS
☎ *(01457) 869800*
www.howardtownbrewery.co.uk

BLEAKLOW 3.8% ABV
MONK'S GOLD 4.0% ABV
WREN'S NEST 4.2% ABV
DINTING ARCHES 4.5% ABV
GLOTT'S HOP 5.0% ABV

LEADMILL BREWERY

Unit 1, Park Hall Farm, Parkhall Road, Denby, Ripley DE5 8PX
☎ *(01332) 883577*

MASH TUN BITTER 3.6% ABV
OLD OAK BITTER 3.8% ABV
OLD MOTTLED COCK 4.3% ABV
STRAWBERRY BLONDE 4.4% ABV
ROLLING THUNDER 4.5% ABV
CURLY BLONDE 4.6% ABV
MAPLE PORTER 4.7% ABV
SNAKE EYES 4.7% ABV
AGENT ORANGE 4.9% ABV
ALIVE AND KICKING 5.0% ABV
BORN IN THE USA 5.0% ABV
B52 5.2% ABV
GHOST RIDER 5.4% ABV
BEAST 5.7% ABV
NEMESIS 6.4% ABV
WEAPON OF MASS DESTRUCTION 6.7% ABV
Plus seasonals.

LEATHERBRITCHES BREWERY

The Bentley Brook Inn, Fenny Bentley, Ashbourne DE6 1LF
☎ *(01335) 350278*
www.leatherbritches.co.uk

GOLDINGS 3.6% ABV
GINGER SPICE 3.8% ABV
ASHBOURNE 4.0% ABV
BELTER 4.4% ABV
BELT N BRACES 4.4% ABV
DOVEDALE 4.4% ABV
GINGER HELMET 4.7% ABV
HAIRY HELMET 4.7% ABV
BESPOKE 5.0% ABV
BENTLEY BROOK BITTER 5.2% ABV
Plus monthly specials.

PEAK ALES

The Barn Brewery, Cunnery Barn, Chatsworth, Bakewell DE45 1EX
☎ *(01246) 583737*
www.peakales.co.uk

SWIFT NICK 3.8% ABV
DALESMAN 4.0% ABV
BAKEWELL BEST BITTER 4.2% ABV
WILL'S GLORY 5.0% ABV
Plus seasonals.

SPIRE BREWERY

Unit 2–3, Gisborne Close, Ireland Business Park, Staveley, Chesterfield S43 3JT
☎ *(01246) 476005*
www.spirebrewery.co.uk

ENCORE 3.9% ABV
Amber coloured, hoppy.
LAND OF HOP AND GLORY 4.5% ABV
Biscuity.
CHESTERFIELD BEST BITTER 4.8% ABV
Resinous hoppy ending.
Plus seasonals.

JOHN THOMPSON BREWERY

John Thompson Inn, Ingleby Lane, Ingleby DE73 1HW
☎ *(01332) 862469*

JTS BITTER 4.1% ABV
JTS GOLD 4.5% ABV
JT 80 4.7% ABV
ST NICK 5.0% ABV

THORNBRIDGE HALL COUNTRY HOUSE BREWING COMPANY

Thornbridge Hall, Ashford in the Water DE45 1NZ
☎ *(01629) 641000*
www.thornbridgebrewery.co.uk

WILD SWAN 3.5% ABV
White gold colour, bitter lemon and spicy flavour.
BROTHER RABBIT 3.7% ABV
Sweet with bitter finish.
LORD MARPLES 4.0% ABV
Honey and caramel notes.
BLACKTHORN ALE 4.4% ABV
Golden and fruity.
KIPLING 5.2% ABV
Grassy nose with kiwi fruits, bitter finish.
JAIPUR 5.9% ABV
Honey flavoured with bitter finish.
ST PETERSBURG 7.7% ABV
Chocolatey, malt flavour and coffee finish.
Plus specials.

TOLLGATE BREWERY

Unit 8 Viking Business Centre, High Street, Woodville, Swadlincote DE11 7EH
☎ *(01283) 229194*

WOODENBOX BITTER 4.3% ABV
RED STAR IPA 4.5% ABV
TGL TOLLGATE LIGHT 4.5% ABV
BILLY'S BEST BITTER 4.6% ABV
Plus seasonal and one-off brews.

TOWNES BREWERY

Speedwell Inn, Lowgates, Staveley, Chesterfield S43 3TT
☎ *(01246) 472252*

GOLDEN BUD 3.8% ABV
SPEEDWELL BITTER 3.9% ABV
LOCKFORD 4.0% ABV
LOWGATE LIGHT 4.1% ABV
STAVELEY CROSS 4.3% ABV
BLUE WIND BREW 4.4% ABV
IPA 4.5% ABV
MUFFIN ALE 4.5% ABV
PYNOT PORTER 4.5% ABV
Very dark and wholesome.
STAVELEYAN 4.9% ABV
Plus monthly and seasonal brews.

WHIM ALES

Whim Farm, Hartington, Buxton SK17 0AX
☎ *(01298) 84991*

ARBOR LIGHT 3.6% ABV
HARTINGTON BITTER 4.0% ABV
KASCADE 4.4% ABV
HARTINGTON IPA 4.5% ABV
STOUT JENNY 4.8% ABV
ARMADILLO 4.9% ABV
Plus occasional brews.

THE PUBS

APPERKNOWLE
The Barrack Hotel
Barrack Road, Apperknowle S18 4AU
☎ *(01246) 416555* John and Rachel Eggleston
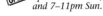 Freehouse with five real ales, changed regularly according to customer choice. Kelham Island Pale Rider and Abbeydale Moonshine feature regularly, as do beers from Bradfield, Acorn, Spire and Cottage.

Stone-built traditional country pub dating from 1852. Situated in a walking area, it claims to have the best views in the county across the valley. Food served 6–8pm Tues–Fri and 12–4pm Sun. Beer garden, patio, car park. Off the old Sheffield–Chesterfield road in Unstone, up the hill to Eckington and the pub is on the left.

OPEN *6pm–12 Mon–Fri; 7pm–12 Sat; 12–4pm and 7–11pm Sun.*

ASHBOURNE
The Green Man and Blacks Head Royal Hotel
St John Street, Ashbourne DE6 1GH
☎ *(01335) 345783*
Philippa Golonko and Paul Gregory
www.gmrh.com
 Freehouse with up to five real ales. Greene King Abbot Ale and Leatherbritches Dr Johnson are permanents, plus three other pumps serving a range of ales from local micro-breweries. Also one real cider.

Two bars: the Johnson bar, which has a modern feel and three plasma-screen TVs showing sports; and the Boswell bar, which is oak-panelled with a traditional atmosphere and no music. Food served 12–3pm and 6–8.30pm Mon–Fri; 12–9pm Sat–Sun (all day in summer or when busy). Children welcome. Car park. Accommodation in 18 hotel rooms. Annual beer festival over August bank holiday. Two function rooms for hire. Off the A515 in Ashbourne town centre.

OPEN *11am–11pm Mon–Wed; 11am–midnight Thurs; 11am–1am Fri; 11am–2am Sat; 12–11pm Sun.*

ASHOVER
Old Poets Corner
Butts Road, Ashover S45 0EW
☎ *(01246) 590888* Kim Beresford
www.oldpoets.co.uk
Freehouse with its own micro-brewery, Ashover, in a garage in the grounds. Up to four Ashover ales plus up to five guests changed every couple of days.

Mock-Tudor building with one large bar, coal fire, beamed ceilings and hops creating a traditional atmosphere. Food served 12–2pm and 6.30–9pm Mon–Fri; 12–3pm and 6.30–9pm; 12–3pm Sun, plus curry night Sunday. Function room for hire. Accommodation. Two beer festivals each year. Tues: acoustic night. Wed: quiz night. Live music. Three miles from Matlock, six miles from Chesterfield.

OPEN *12–11pm.*

BAKEWELL
Monsal Head Hotel (The Stables)
Monsal Head, Nr Bakewell DE45 1NL
☎ *(01629) 640250* Sarah Belfield
www.monsalhead.com
Five to eight real ales, including Theakston Best and Lloyds Monsal. The guests are changed weekly, and come from breweries such as Whim, Thornbridge and Peakstones.

Part of a hotel, the pub was originally the stables for horses working for the local railway. Situated in the middle of the Peak District National Park, overlooking beautiful views and surrounded by popular walking countryside. Food served 12–9.30pm (9pm Sun). Accommodation. Residents' lounge.

OPEN *8.30–9.30am for breakfast; 12–11pm.*

BELPER
The Cross Keys
Market Place, Belper DE56 1FZ
☎ *(01773) 599191* Colin and Matt Sinclair
Bateman tied house with up to six real ales. Bateman XB and XXB, Draught Bass and a house beer, Golden Keys, plus a varied guest beer programme, many from micro-brewers. Also real cider and perry, and a range of bottled and draught Belgian beers.

Dating from the 18th century, this is a traditional community pub retaining its original bar and separate lounge. Traditional pub games including pool, bar billiards and ring the bull. Bar snacks served 1–11pm. Well-behaved children and dogs welcome. Beer garden. Annual beer festival in October.

OPEN *From 1pm every day.*

BOLSOVER
The Blue Bell
57 High Street, Bolsover S44 6HF
☎ *(01246) 823508* Kevin Maidens
www.bolsover.uk.com
 Marston's tied house serving one Marston's ale, one Jennings and four monthly changing guests.

A 300-year-old coaching inn with a traditional atmosphere. No juke box or loud music, and pride is taken over the 'no bad language' policy. Food served 12–3pm and 5–7pm Mon–Fri; 12–2pm Sat–Sun. Beer garden with spectacular views. Annual beer festival.

OPEN *12–3.30pm and 5pm–12 Mon–Thurs; 12–3.30pm and 6.30pm–12 Sat; 12–3.30pm and 7pm–12 Sun.*

BRAMPTON

The Royal Oak

41–3 Chatsworth Road, Brampton, Chesterfield S40 2AH
☎ *(01246) 277854 Mr and Mrs M Mount*

Freehouse with a large selection of real ales. The five regulars include beers from Theakston, Whim, Marston's and Everards, and five guests are rotated weekly.

A traditional local pub with friendly staff and regulars of all ages. Two bars, timber ceilings and an open fire. Live music, quizzes, pub games and big-screen TV. Annual music and beer festivals. Beer garden, car park, play area. Marquee for hire. No food. Five minutes from the town centre, Queen's Park cricket ground and football ground.

OPEN *11.30am–midnight Sun–Thurs; 11.30am–1am Fri–Sat.*

BUXTON

George Bar and Brasserie

The Square, Buxton SK17 6AZ
☎ *07523 209881 James Hopkinson*

Four real ales including beers from Timothy Taylor and Black Sheep, George Ale from Leatherbritches and a rotating guest.

The original George Hotel was built in 1772. One bar, restaurant and function room, plus large outdoor seating area overlooking the Opera House. Brasserie due to open in September 2008. Food served 12–2.30pm and 5.30–10.30pm. Handy for Buxton's two summer festivals. In the centre of town, next to the Opera House and the Pavilion Gardens.

OPEN *10am–1am (midnight Sun).*

BUXWORTH

Navigation Inn

Bugsworth Canal Basin, Buxworth, High Peak, Nr Whaley Bridge SK23 7NE
☎ *(01663) 732072 Lynda and Alan Hall*
www.navigationinn.co.uk

Freehouse with at least four real ales. Timothy Taylor Landlord and Marston's Pedigree are regulars plus a range of constantly changing guest beers.

A 200-year-old stone inn on the site of a restored canal basin in Derbyshire's High Peak. Full of interesting memorabilia and canalwares. Lounge bar with log fire, separate restaurant, play area, games room and stone-floored snug. Food served 12–3pm and 5.30–9.30pm Mon–Fri, 12–9.30pm Sat–Sun. Beer festival held at the end of June. En-suite accommodation. Two miles from Whaley Bridge.

OPEN *11am–11pm Mon–Sat; 12–10.30pm Sun.*

CHESTERFIELD

The Arkwright Arms

Chesterfield Road, Duckmanton, Chesterfield S44 5JG
☎ *(01246) 232053*
John Chadwick and Kathy Shorrock
www.arkwrightarms.co.uk

Timothy Taylor Landlord and Greene King Abbot always on offer at this freehouse, plus five guests, changed every couple of days, all from local breweries such as Spire, Ashover, Ossett, Brampton, The Brew Company, and Thornbridge Hall. Ten ciders, two perries, and a selection of Belgian beers.

Mock-Tudor-fronted pub with two bars, dining room and beer garden. Food available 12–2.30pm every day; 5–7.30pm Mon–Thurs and 5–8pm Fri. Pool table. Large car park. Beer festivals Easter and August bank holiday. From J29 of the M1 head for Bolsover Castle. CAMRA awards: East Midlands Pub of the Year 2008, and Cider and Perry East Midlands Pub of the Year 2008.

OPEN *11am–11pm Mon–Thurs; 11am–midnight Fri–Sat; 11am–10.30pm Sun.*

The Derby Tup

387 Sheffield Road, Whittington Moor, Chesterfield S41 8LS
☎ *(01246) 454316 Mr Hughes*

Black Sheep Bitter, Whim Hartington, Timothy Taylor Landlord, Marston's Pedigree and Greene King Abbot plus four pumps serving a constantly changing range of guest ales (500 per year).

Old and original, beamed with three rooms and open fires. Home-cooked food available 11am–2pm daily and 6–8pm Thurs–Sat; Thai, Indian and vegetarian food are specialities. Parking nearby, children allowed. Sunday quiz, occasional live music.

OPEN *11.30am–3pm and 5–11pm Mon–Tues; 11.30am–11pm Wed–Sat; 12–4pm and 7–10.30pm Sun.*

Industry Inn

49 Queen Street, Chesterfield S40 4SF
☎ *(01246) 554123 Stewart Lawson*

Admiral Taverns pub with Jennings Sneck Lifter and three rotating guests such as Springhead Roaring Meg, Spire Sgt Pepper Stout and Acorn Northdown Blonde.

Pre-war pub with three rooms, small beer garden and car park. Food served 12–2pm and 5.30–8pm Mon–Sat; all day Sun. Children welcome. Ten minutes' walk from centre of Chesterfield, five minutes from the football ground.

OPEN *12–3pm and 5pm–late Mon–Fri; 12–late Sat–Sun.*

The Market

95 New Square, Chesterfield S40 1AH
☎ *(01246) 273641 Keith Toone*

Greene King Abbot, Timothy Taylor Landlord and Tetley Bitter are regularly featured. Two rotating guest ales also served (300 per year).

A one-bar market pub, with dining area in bar. Food served 11am–2.30pm Mon–Sat. In the small market square.

OPEN *11am–11pm Mon–Sat; 7.30–10.30pm Sun.*

The Peacock Inn

412 Chatsworth Road, Chesterfield S40 3BQ
☎ *(01246) 275115* John Bradbury

Enterprise Inns pub. Caledonian Deuchars IPA, Black Sheep Best Bitter and Adnams Broadside plus one guest beer from a local brewery.

Mock-Tudor pub, dating from the mid 19th-century on the main road to the Peak District. Two bars, one with open fire and one a games room with darts and dominoes. No food. Large beer garden and outside seating area at the front. On the main A619 west of town.

OPEN *12–11pm.*

The Portland Hotel

West Bars, Chesterfield S40 1AY
☎ *(01246) 245410*
Kevin and Debbie Lancaster
www.jdwetherspoon.co.uk

JD Wetherspoon's pub. Greene King Abbot and Marston's Pedigree plus a selection of guest ales from local breweries.

One bar attached to a hotel. Friendly atmosphere. Food served 7am–11pm Mon–Fri; 8am–11pm Fri–Sun. Children welcome until 9pm. Beer and wine festivals held throughout the year. Large beer garden. Private room available.

OPEN *7am–midnight Mon–Fri; 8am–1am Sat–Sun. Serving alcohol from 9am daily.*

The Rutland Arms

23 Stephensons Place, Chesterfield S40 1XL
☎ *(01246) 205857* Ken and Jane Randall

Eight real ales at any one time (16+ per week). Caledonian Deuchars IPA, Greene King Abbot, Timothy Taylor Landlord and Boddingtons Bitter (brewed by Hydes) are the permanent beers, but guests might be from breweries such as Brampton, Abbeydale, Naylors, Kelham Island, Thornbridge, Copper Dragon and Whim.

A pub since 1906, with a warm, friendly environment and a mainly wooden interior. Close to Chesterfield's famous crooked spire. One central bar and seating in two rooms. Parties and functions catered for. Regular mini beer festivals. Small outside seating area overlooking church grounds. Accompanied children welcome if dining. Food served 11am–9pm early in the week, 11am–7pm weekends.

OPEN *11am–11pm Mon–Wed; 11am–midnight Thurs–Sat; 12–11pm Sun.*

COAL ASTON

The Cross Daggers

Brown Lane, Coal Aston, Nr Dronfield S18 3AJ
☎ *(01246) 412728* Anthony Hutchinson

Black Sheep Bitter, Theakston Best and Tetley Bitter usually available. The first two of these are changed occasionally.

Traditional, friendly two-room pub, originally two cottages but knocked into one to create a beerhouse in 1851. Large,

well-looked-after beer garden. No food. Plenty of walks in the area. Occasional entertainment on Sundays, but no loud music! In the village square.

OPEN *4–11pm Mon–Fri; 5–11pm (or midnight) Sat; 12–3pm and 7–11pm Sun.*

CROMFORD

The Boat Inn

Scarthin, Cromford, Matlock DE4 3QF
☎ *(01629) 823282*
Kevin White and Debbie White

Freehouse with a Hartington or Springhead ale and Marston's Pedigree plus all sorts of guests, from local micro-breweries whenever possible.

Village pub built about 1772, near the market square. A 24-seater restaurant, Frets, has been added. Two bars, log fires, beer garden. Regular music nights and pub quizzes, plus beer festivals three times a year. Bar snacks at lunchtimes and evenings plus Sunday lunches. Children allowed. Dogs welcome.

OPEN *11.30am–3pm and 6–11pm Mon–Fri; all day Sat–Sun.*

DALE ABBEY

The Carpenters Arms

Dale Abbey, Ilkeston DE7 4PP
☎ *(0115) 932 5277* John Heraty
www.thecarpentersarms.biz

Tied to Punch Retail, serving Marston's Pedigree and Adnams Bitter plus two other beers from local and national breweries such as Wells and Young's and Greene King.

A traditional village pub in picturesque walking country, family-run since the 1930s. Children's play area and beer garden, family room and large car park. Cask Marque accredited. Food served at lunchtimes and evenings. Children not allowed in bar. Three miles from junction 25 off the M1.

OPEN *12–3pm and 6–11pm (7–10.30pm Sun).*

DENBY

The Old Stables Bar

Unit 5, Park Hall, Park Hall Road, Denby, Nr Ripley DE5 8PX
☎ *(01332) 883577* Richard Creighton

Owned and run by the nearby Leadmill Brewery, with a selection of beers from the huge Leadmill range plus a couple of guests. Up to ten real ales at any one time.

Opened in January 2003 in a 200-year-old stable building. One small bar, sawdust on the floor. Fresh cobs and snacks available. Brewery tours by arrangement. Outside seating. Children welcome until 9pm. One mile south of Denby Pottery.

OPEN *4–11pm Fri; 12–11pm Sat; 12–10.30pm Sun.*

DERBY

The Alexandra Hotel

203 Siddals Road, Derby DE1 2QE
☎ *(01332) 293993* Mark Robins

Up to ten real ales. Castle Rock Nottingham Gold, York Yorkshire Terrier and Belvoir Star Bitter plus seven ever-changing guests, including a mild.

Built as a coffee and chop house in 1865. Now trading as a comfortable award-winning pub decorated with wooden floors and a railway and brewery theme. Bar food (cold snacks) at lunchtimes. Darts, background music. Four en-suite bedrooms. Car park and garden. Five minutes' walk from Derby Midland Railway Station.

OPEN *11am–11pm Mon–Sat; 12–3pm and 7–10.30pm Sun.*

Babington Arms

11–13 Babington Lane, Derby DE1 1TA
☎ *(01332) 383647* Tom Taylor
www.jdwetherspoon.co.uk

Wetherspoon's pub with 15 pumps featuring as many new beers as possible, including local brews and guests from far and wide. Regulars include Marston's Pedigree and Burton Bitter, Greene King Abbot, Wyre Piddle Marcos King of the Watusi and Derby Penny's Porter.

A former furniture shop converted into a pub in 1997, with single bar, wood panelling and doors that open out onto a terrace in summer. Food served 9am–11pm. Brewery feature weekends and regular beer festivals. Children welcome to eat until 6pm. Derby CAMRA City Pub of the Year 2006. Up the hill from Waterstones bookshop.

OPEN *9am–midnight Sun–Thurs; 9am–1am Fri–Sat.*

The Brunswick Inn

1 Railway Terrace, Derby DE1 2RU
☎ *(01332) 290677* Graham Yates
www.brunswickinn.co.uk

Tied to Everards, with 16 real ales available, including seven brewed on the premises Marston's Pedigree, Timothy Taylor Landlord and Everards Beacon. Guests, changed weekly, might include local Derby brews and beers from Burton Bridge, RCH, Oakhams, Tring, Bath, York and Kelham Island.

Built in 1841–2 as the first purpose-built railwaymen's pub in the world. The birthplace of the Railway Institute, an educational establishment for railway workers. It fell into dereliction in the early 1970s and trading ceased in April 1974. The Derbyshire Historic Buildings Trust started restoration work in 1981. The pub reopened in October 1987 and the installation of the brewing plant followed in 1991. The first beer was produced on 11 June that year. Brewery tours are available. Food served 11.30am–2.30pm Mon–Weds; Thurs and Sat 11.30am–5pm; 11.30am–7pm Fri. Beer festival early October. Parking, garden, children's room, function and meeting rooms. Jazz on Thursdays. Turn right from the railway station and the pub is just 100 yards away.

OPEN *11am–11pm Mon–Sat; 12–10.30pm Sun.*

The Crompton Tavern

46 Crompton Street, Derby DE1 1NX
☎ *(01332) 733629* Mr and Mrs Bailey

Marston's Pedigree and Timothy Taylor Landlord plus four guest beers (200 per year) perhaps from Fuller's, Coach House, Kelham Island, Banks & Taylor or Burton Bridge breweries. A porter or stout is normally available.

Small pub just outside the city centre. Popular with locals and students. Cobs and sandwiches available daily. Car park and garden. Children allowed in garden.

OPEN *11am–11pm Mon–Sat; 12–10.30pm Sun.*

The Falstaff

74 Silver Hill Road, Normanton, Derby DE23 6UJ
☎ *(01332) 342902* Jim Hallows
www.falstaffbrewery.co.uk

The Falstaff Brewery, attached to the pub, reopened in December 2003. The pub now serves four real ales, three from the brewery and a guest from another micro-brewery.

Friendly former hotel built in 1886 and tucked away in the back streets of Derby. One main bar serves three rooms, and the lounge has a real fire. Outside seating area. Wheelchair access. Brewery tours by arrangement. From the city, take the Normanton Road to the painted mini-island, turn right, take the first available right, then the next right.

OPEN *12–11pm (10.30pm Sun).*

The Flowerpot

25 King Street, Derby DE1 3DZ
☎ *(01332) 204955* Sylvia Manners

Marston's Pedigree and Whim IPA plus at least seven (and sometimes 20) guest beers (500+ per year) from all over the UK. Whim, Oakham, Archers, Samuel Smiths, Leatherbritches, Burton Bridge, Salamander, Shardlow, Newby Wyke and Titanic brews have all featured. The pub's own brewery, the Headless Brewing Co, opened in 2007 and has three regular beers, First Bloom, King Street Ale and Owd Reg, plus one-off specials.

Traditional friendly town pub with parts of the building dating from the late 17th century. Age range of regulars is 18 to 95. Ground-level cellar bar has a unique 'beer wall', through which customers can see ale being cared for and dispensed straight from the barrel. Homemade food served 12–2.30pm Mon, Tues, Wed; 12–5.30pm Sun. Garden area. Function room with capacity for up to 250 people. Wheelchair access to all areas. Children welcome till 7.30pm. Car park 30 yards away. Situated on the A6 just off the inner ring road, 300 yards north of the Cathedral.

OPEN *11am–11pm Mon–Thurs; 11am–midnight Fri–Sat; 12–11pm Sun.*

The Rowditch Inn

246 Uttoxeter New Road, Derby DE22 3LL
☎ *(01332) 343123* Jan and Steve Birkin

Freehouse with three or four real ales, including Marston's Pedigree and a wide range of rotating guests from all over the country.

A traditional beer house with one servery covering a lounge bar, traditional snug and beer garden. Real fires. No food, no children. Regular beer festivals. On the main road, a mile from the city centre.

OPEN *12–2pm Sat–Sun; 7–11pm daily.*

The Smithfield

Meadow Road, Derby DE1 2BH
☎ *(01332) 370429* Roger and Penny Myring
www.thesmithfield.co.uk

Freehouse with Whim Hartington IPA and either Whim Arbor Light or Oakham JHB plus up to five guests changing two or three times a week. Fuller's London Pride and beers from Rooster's and Oakham regularly featured.

Traditional, friendly atmosphere. Lounge with open fire and pub games plus a family room. Food served 12–2pm only. Children allowed until 8pm. Ring for directions.

OPEN *11am–11pm Mon–Sat; 12–10.30pm Sun.*

ELMTON

The Elm Tree Inn

Elmton, Nr Creswell, Worksop S80 4LS
☎ *(01909) 721261*

Up to six real ales. Three Black Sheep beers plus Tetley Bitter and a couple of guests.

Olde-worlde pub with separate rooms and a restaurant that serves good food at lunchtimes and evenings. Children welcome. Extensive garden.

OPEN *11am–11pm Mon–Sat; 12–10.30pm Sun*

FENNY BENTLEY

The Bentley Brook Inn

Fenny Bentley, Ashbourne DE6 1LF
☎ *(01335) 350278* Hazel and Richard Foulkes
www.bentleybrookinn.co.uk

Home to the Leatherbritches Craft Brewery, Fenny's Restaurant and Leatherbritches Fine Food Shop. Leatherbritches cask and bottle-conditioned beers, brewed on site, are always available, plus Marston's Pedigree and guest beers. Up to three real ales at any one time with the menu changing daily.

A traditional, 16th-century country inn (AA 3 star, 11 en-suite rooms including a family suite) with large garden, children's play area and a friendly atmosphere. Facilities for weddings and conferences. Food served all day, every day April–Sept; from Oct to March the kitchen is closed 3–5.30pm every day. Large car park. Children welcome. Dog-friendly bar and accommodation. Various events all year round. Close to Alton Towers, two miles north of Ashbourne on the A515 to Buxton.

OPEN *All day, every day.*

The Coach & Horses

Fenny Bentley, Ashbourne DE6 1LB
☎ *(01335) 350246* John and Matthew Dawson

Family-run freehouse offering a continually changing range of award-winning cask ales. Marston's Pedigree always available, plus two guests, rotated daily.

A traditional 17th-century coaching inn with background music and beer garden. Food served every day 12–9pm. Winner of Derbyshire Food and Drink Award 2003/4 and highly commended 2005/6 (both awards in Pub/Bistro section). Children welcome. On the A515, two miles from Ashbourne towards Buxton.

OPEN *11am–11pm.*

FOOLOW

The Bull's Head Inn

Foolow, Nr Eyam, Hope Valley S32 5QR
☎ *(01433) 630873* Les and Marilyn Bond

Four real ales, including beers from Adnams, Black Sheep and Peak Ales, rotated regularly.

This 200-year-old family-run pub has lots of original features, including inglenook fireplace, log fires and flagged floors. Good food available 12–2pm and 6.30–9pm Tues–Sat; 12–2pm and 5–8pm Sun. Children and dogs welcome. Three beautifully appointed en-suite bedrooms. Car park. Off the A623 near Stoney Middleton.

OPEN *12–3pm and 6–11pm Tues–Sat (closed Mon).*

GLOSSOP

The Globe

144 High Street West, Glossop SK13 8HJ
☎ *(01457) 852417* Ron Brookes
www.globemusic.org

Freehouse with up to six real ales. Brewing takes place on the premises and home brews are always on offer, plus a selection of guest ales.

A two-bar Georgian pub and micro-brewery since 2006. Vegetarian food served from 5pm. Award-winning beer garden. Car park. Live music venue. On Glossop high street, next to Tesco.

OPEN *5pm–close Mon, Wed–Sat; 1pm–close Sun (closed Tues).*

The Star Inn

2 Howard Street, Glossop SK13 7DD
☎ *(01457) 853072*
Paul Hurditch and Vivien Hurditch

Punch Taverns pub serving Black Sheep Bitter plus a range of guest ales which regularly includes Oakham JHB and White Dwarf and beers from breweries such as Phoenix, Howard Town, Abbeydale, Kelham Island and Newby Wyke. Also Old Rosie cider.

Built in 1837 with one main bar and a vault room. No food. Children welcome until 7pm. Car park. Accommodation. Covered and heated smoking area, dog-friendly. Situated in the High Peak on the edge of the Peak District National Park.

OPEN *4–11pm Mon–Tues; 2–11pm Wed–Thurs; 2pm–12 Fri; 12–12 Sat; 12–10.30pm Sun.*

HADFIELD

The New Lamp

Bankbottom, Hadfield, Glossop SK13 1BY
☎ *(01457) 860490 Derrick Wellings*

Three ever-changing beers such as Daleside Old Legover, Everards Tiger, Black Sheep Bitter, and Shepherd Neame Spitfire or Bishop's Finger.

Built in the 1800s during the construction of the reservoirs and railways, this was used as a meeting place by ladies of the night and workmen! Families, walkers and well-behaved dogs welcome. Food served 12–2.30pm Wed–Fri and all day Sat–Sun. Sunday quiz night, regular bands. Pool and darts teams. Off Woodhead Pass at Tintwistle, or take the A57 and follow signs for Hadfield.

OPEN *12–11pm Mon–Wed; 12–12 Thurs–Sat; 12–10.30pm Sun.*

HALLFIELDGATE

Shoulder of Mutton

Hallfieldgate Lane, Hallfieldgate, Shirland, Nr Alfreton, DE55 6AA
☎ *(01773) 834992 Wendy Morris*

John Smiths Bitter plus two further pumps providing up to ten different real ales each week, usually sourced from micro-breweries.

Freehouse established in 1601 in a stone building that was previously two cottages. Large well-kept beer garden with beautiful views overlooking a valley. One small room with a juke box with over 50,000 songs, and a larger room with comfortable seating areas. Walkers welcome. Children welcome in the garden only. No food served, but customers are welcome to bring sandwiches. Won CAMRA 2006 Chesterfield Campaigning Excellence Award.

OPEN *12–11pm Mon, Wed–Sat; 7pm–11pm Tues; 12–10.30pm Sun.*

HATHERSAGE

The Little John Hotel

Station Road, Hope Valley S32 1DD
☎ *(01433) 650225 Stephanie Bushell*
www.littlejohnhotel.co.uk

Genuine freehouse with four or five real ales, including Little John Ale, brewed for the pub by Wentworth. Other beers change daily, and might include beers from Sharp's, Kelham Island, Storm and Wentworth, to name but a few.

A late-18th-century inn owned by the same licensee since 1991. Food prepared by the pub's long-serving chef Richard Mosely is served 12–2pm and 5–10pm Mon–Fri; 12–10pm Sat; 12–8.30pm Sun. Beer garden. Car park. Children welcome. Private room for function hire. Occasional beer festivals.

OPEN *12–12.*

HAYFIELD

The Royal Hotel

Market Street, Hayfield SK22 2EP
☎ *(01663) 742721 DA Ash*
www.theroyalhayfield.co.uk

One Hydes ale always available, plus five constantly changing guest ales from breweries all over the UK, such as Enville, Rooster's, York, Howard Town, Salopian, Mauldons and Triple FFF.

A 15th-century pub with one main bar, dining area, function room and accommodation. Food served every day. Patio area. Annual beer festival in October. Next to the cricket ground.

OPEN *All day, every day.*

HEMINGTON

The Jolly Sailor

Main Street, Hemington, Derby DE74 2RB
☎ *(01332) 810448 Margaret and Peter Frame*

Eight real ales, with Greene King Abbot, Marston's Pedigree and Sharp's Doom Bar among the permanent fixtures. The three rotating guests could be Abbeydale Absolution, Fuller's ESB, Whim Hartington IPA, Timothy Taylor Landlord or something from Burton Bridge, Tower, Leatherbritches, Newby Wyke or Oldershaws. Old Rosie, Westons Perry and Aspells also on pump.

A 17th-century village pub, full of character and with a hospitable atmosphere. Run by the same couple since 1990. Food served 12–2pm Mon–Sat. The two patios are heated. No children's facilities. Car park. Next to Castle Donington (junction 24 on M1).

OPEN *11.30am–2.30pm and 4.30–11pm Mon–Fri; 11.30am–11pm Sat; 12–10.30pm Sun.*

HOLYMOORSIDE

Lamb Inn

16 Loads Road, Holymoorside, Chesterfield S42 7EU
☎ *(01246) 566167 Alan Goucher*

Freehouse with six real ales: Timothy Taylor Landlord, Black Sheep Bitter and Daleside Blonde, plus three guests such as Fuller's London Pride, Bateman XB, Shepherd Neame Spitfire, Everards Tiger and beers from Adnams, Black Sheep, Peak, Thornbridge and Abbeydale.

Two-room village country pub built in 1760, with real fire, beer garden and car park. No food. Hikers welcome (on removal of boots!). On the edge of the Peak District, and handy for Chesterfield's crooked spire. From Chesterfield follow signs for Manchester, Holymoorside is three miles away.

OPEN *5–11pm Mon–Thurs; 4–11pm Fri; 12–3pm and 7–11pm Sat–Sun.*

HOPE

Cheshire Cheese Inn

Edale Road, Hope, Hope Valley S33 6ZF
☎ *(01433) 620381* David Helliwell
www.cheshirecheesehope.co.uk

Freehouse with five real ales. Regular brewers include Black Sheep, Hartington and Archers.

Historic pub dating from 1573, first licensed in 1578. Three areas. Food served 12–2pm and 6.30–9pm. Beer garden. Close to the Pennine Way, Chatsworth, Castleton and Haddon Hall, with good walks nearby. On the Edale Road, off the A6187 at Hope.

OPEN *12–3pm and 6.30–11pm Mon–Fri; 12–12 Sat; 12–10.30pm Sun.*

HORSLEY WOODHOUSE

Old Oak Inn

176 Main Street, Horsley Woodhouse, Ilkeston DE7 6AW
☎ *(01332) 881299* Roger and Frances Warren

Brewery tap for the Leadmill Brewery, with a selection from the brewery's range of 40-plus beers, plus a couple of constantly changing guests. Nine real ales at any time.

A 150-year-old former village freehouse bought by the brewery in October 2003 and saved from potential demolition. Three rooms, covered courtyard with garden and field behind. Beer festivals held in May and December. Fresh cobs and bar snacks available. Children welcome in the back rooms.

OPEN *4–11pm Mon–Wed; 3–11pm Thurs–Fri; 12–11pm Sat; 12–10.30pm Sun.*

ILKESTON

Spring Cottage

1 Fulwood Street, Ilkeston DE7 8AZ
☎ *(0115) 932 3153* Mr Wootton

 Tied to Punch Taverns, with two guests changed daily, which may include Wadworth 6X, Marston's Pedigree, Greene King Abbot Ale and Old Speckled Hen or Shepherd Neame Spitfire.

Traditional town pub with two bars and background music. Children's room. The lounge doubles as a dining area. Food at lunchtimes and evenings. Children allowed. Near the main shopping area on one-way system.

OPEN *11am–3pm and 6–11pm Mon–Thur; 11am–4pm and 6–11pm Fri; 11am–5pm and 7–11pm Sat; 12–3pm and 7–10.30pm Sun.*

ILKESTON JUNCTION

Dewdrop Inn

24 Station Street, Ilkeston Junction DE7 5TE
☎ *(0115) 932 9684* John Cooke

Five real ales, with Timothy Taylor Best Bitter and Oakham Bishop's Farewell permanently served, with Castle Rock Harvest Pale and beers from Oakham, Funfair and local micro-breweries among the beers regularly on offer. Erewash Valley CAMRA Pub of the Year 2008 and 2009.

Old-style Victorian three-room pub dating from 1881, with real fire, real ale and real friendly atmosphere! Winner of numerous awards. Outside drinking area with covered, heated smoking area. Barnes Wallis stayed here during World War II. There is a 1960s juke box, a pool table and a family room. Cobs only served, with black pudding a speciality. East of the town centre on the A6096, by the railway bridge.

OPEN *12–11pm (10.30pm Sun).*

INGLEBY

John Thompson Inn

Ingleby, Melbourne DE73 1HW
☎ *(01332) 862469* Nick Thompson

Home of the John Thompson Brewery, which re-introduced brewing to Derbyshire in 1977. Three ales in winter, four in summer, with the beers including JTS XXX, JT Gold, Rich Porter and JT 80.

Converted 15th-century oak-beamed farmhouse, with a collection of paintings and antiques. Food served 12–2pm Tues–Sat. Close to the River Trent. Car park. Children's room and large garden.

OPEN *6–11pm Mon; 11am–2.30pm and 6–11pm Tues–Sat; 12–10.30pm Sun.*

KEGWORTH

The Red Lion

24 High Street, Kegworth DE74 2DA
☎ *(01509) 672466* John Briggs
www.redlionkegworth.com

Freehouse with up to eight real ales from any independent brewery. Beers changed every few days.

A Georgian building with three bars. Food served 12–2.30pm and 6–8pm Mon–Fri; 12–2.30pm Sat; 12–3pm Sun. Beer garden. Car park. Accommodation. Two minutes from J24 of the M1.

OPEN *All day, every day.*

KIRK IRETON

The Barley Mow Inn

Main Street, Kirk Ireton, Ashbourne DE6 3JP
☎ *(01335) 370306* Mary Short

 Six real ales. Whim Hartington IPA and beers from Hook Norton, Leatherbritches, Storm and Archers might be a typical selection, with several of the brews rotating every week.

Imposing stone village inn dating from 1683, with new stone front wing. Three rooms with small central bar, exposed beams and quarry tiles. Fresh cobs only served 12–2pm. Children are permitted inside the pub at lunchtime. Garden area at front. Car park. Accommodation in five en-suite rooms, with evening meals available for residents. No music. Close to Carsington Water, Alton Towers and Chatsworth. From junction 25 of the M1 take the A6 north, then the B5023.

OPEN *12–2pm and 7–11pm (10.30pm Sun).*

LITTON

The Red Lion

The Green, Church Lane, Litton SK17 8QU
☎ *(01298) 871458* Suzy Turner

 Oakwell Barnsley Bitter plus two guests from local breweries such as Peak Ales, Abbeydale, Whim or Thornbridge. Guests changed weekly on a rotating basis.

A traditional village pub, dating from 1797, with roaring fires and plenty of character, situated on a village green. Cask Marque accredited. Home-cooked pub food served 12–2pm and 6–8pm Mon–Wed; 12–8.30pm Thurs–Sun. The village green is used as a beer garden in summer! From the A623 Chesterfield road, take the turning marked Cressbrook and Litton.

OPEN *12–11pm Mon–Thurs; 12–12 Fri–Sat; 12–10.30pm Sun.*

MAKENEY

The Holly Bush Inn

Holly Bush Lane, Makeney, Milford DE56 0RX
☎ *(01332) 841729* JJK Bilbie

 Marston's Pedigree and Greene King Ruddles County plus four guests (200+ per year) that may include Brains Dark, Exmoor Gold, Fuller's ESB, Marston's Owd Roger, Greene King Abbot and Old Speckled Hen, Timothy Taylor Landlord and brews from Bateman. Also scrumpy cider.

G rade II listed former farmhouse with flagstone floors and open fires. Bar food at lunchtime, barbecues in summer. Regular beer festivals. Car park and children's room. Private parties welcome. Just off the main A6 at Milford, opposite the Makeney Hotel.

OPEN *12–3pm and 5–11pm Mon–Thurs; 12–11pm Fri–Sun.*

MATLOCK

The Thorntree Inn

48 Jackson Road, Matlock DE4 3JQ
☎ *(01629) 580295*
Pat Stevenson and Emma Wright

 Seven real ales, with Adnams Bitter, Black Sheep Bitter, Draught Bass and Timothy Taylor Landlord always available, plus a weekly guest.

O lde-worlde community pub with a large covered patio, heated on chilly evenings, offering unrivalled views over Matlock and the valley. Food available 12–2pm Tues–Fri. Children allowed, but no special facilities. From Crown Square in Matlock, go up the hill on Bank Road, turn into Smedley Street, then second right into Smith Road, and the pub is at the top on the left.

OPEN *6–11pm Mon–Tues; 12–2pm and 6–11pm Wed–Thurs; 12–2pm and 5pm–12 Fri; 12–11pm Sun.*

MELBOURNE

The Blue Bell Inn

53 Church Street, Melbourne DE73 1EJ
☎ *(01332) 865764* Kevin Morgan
www.themelbournebluebell.co.uk

 Owned by the Shardlow Brewing Company, with Reverend Eaton's Ale, Golden Hop, Narrowboat and Melbourne Mild always on offer together with seasonal and guest ales.

T raditional family pub frequented by friendly drinkers! Bar, lounge and restaurant refurbished in 2006. Good-quality pub food available 12–2pm (roasts on Sun) with a pizza menu 6–9pm Mon–Sat. Sky Sports TV in the bar. Covered and heated patio. Summer barbecues. Two en-suite letting rooms (one double, one family). Accompanied children welcome. Situated near Melbourne Hall and parish church. Close to the Cloud Trail.

OPEN *11am–11pm Mon–Sat; 12–10.30pm Sun.*

The Paddock Hotel

222 Station Road, Melbourne DE73 8BQ
☎ *(01332) 862566*
Linda and Harvey Goodchild
www.paddockhotel.co.uk

 Freehouse with Shardlow's Reverend Eaton's Ale and Marston's Pedigree usually available.

A small pub within a family-run hotel with nine en-suite bedrooms and a restaurant. Two warm and friendly bars. Food served 6.30–9pm Mon–Sat and 12–4pm Sun. Children allowed. On the outskirts of the village. Secure parking.

OPEN *5.30–11pm Mon–Sat; 12–5pm Sun.*

OAKERTHORPE

Anchor Inn

Chesterfield Road, Oakerthorpe, Alfreton DE55 7LP
☎ *(01773) 833575* John Lymbery
www.anchor.greycomp.co.uk

 Freehouse with three real ales from the Cropton Brewery. Two Pints, Honey Gold and Monkmans Slaughter are regulars plus seasonal ales.

A n 18th-century pub with two bars and two separate restaurants. Food served 12–3pm and 7–9pm. Large car park, outdoor seating area, disabled access and facilities. Close to Wingfield Manor, Crich Tramway Museum, Matlock Bath, Bakewell, Chatsworth, Gulliver's Kingdom and Heights of Abraham. Take J28 off the M1 onto the A38 and follow the Alfreton and Matlock signs.

OPEN *Closed Mon except bank holidays; 12–3pm and 6–11pm Tues–Fri; 12–11pm Sat; 12–10.30pm Sun.*

OCKBROOK
The Royal Oak
55 Green Lane, Ockbrook DE72 3SE
☎ *(01332) 662378* Olive Wilson

At least three constantly rotating real ales usually on offer from a wide selection of breweries, plus Draught Bass.

Traditional village pub built in 1762. The landlady has run the pub for over 50 years! One bar, no juke box or pool table. Lunch is available every day, plus evening meals 6–8pm Mon, Wed, Thurs, Fri, and there is a separate dining area. Function room with bar, two beer gardens (one for adults, one for children), darts, car park. Annual beer festival in October. Children welcome. M1 junction 25, take the A52 to Derby and follow to Ockbrook.

OPEN *11.30am–2.30pm (3pm Sat) and 6.30–11pm Mon–Sat; 12–3pm and 7–10.30pm Sun.*

OLD TUPTON
The Royal Oak Inn
Derby Road, Old Tupton, Chesterfield S42 6LA
☎ *(01246) 862180* John Pridmore

Charles Wells Bombardier, Caledonian Deuchars IPA, John Smiths Cask, Adnams Bitter and Marston's Pedigree usually available plus one guest, changed weekly.

A 100-year-old pub with restaurant serving food lunchtimes and evenings. Children allowed. Three miles south of Chesterfield.

OPEN *Noon–1am.*

OVER HADDON
The Lathkil Hotel
School Lane, Over Haddon, Nr Bakewell DE45 1JE
☎ *(01629) 812501* Robert Grigor-Taylor
www.lathkil.co.uk

Freehouse featuring up to five real ales. Whim Hartington Bitter and Everards Tiger are permanent features but the three guests change several times a week, with brews from Peak, Spire, Sharps, Phoenix, Lloyds and Storm among those regularly on offer.

A pub since 1820, with stunning views over the Lathkil Dale and beyond. Traditional bar plus dining/family room. Occasional TV for sporting events. Food served in the bar and dining room 12–2pm (until 2.30pm Sat–Sun), and 6–8pm Bar meals Sun–Thurs and in the restarant only 7–9.45pm Fri and Sat. Children welcome at lunchtimes, over-14s only in the bar. Four en-suite bedrooms, beer garden, car park. Two miles south-west of Bakewell.

OPEN *11.30am–3pm and 6.30–11pm Mon–Fri (11.30am–11pm in summer); 11.30am–11pm Sat; 12–10.30pm Sun.*

RIPLEY
The Nags Head
Butterley Hill, Ripley DE5 3LT
☎ *(01773) 746722* Steve Marshall

 A freehouse serving Adnams Bitter and Marston's Pedigree plus two or three guests each week including Belvoir Star, Timothy Taylor Landlord and ales from Cottage and Falstaff.

Built around 1900, this friendly two-roomed local hosts live music every Sunday afternoon and is close to Butterley Railway Centre. No food. Located on the Alfreton Road, out of Ripley.

OPEN *3pm–12 Mon–Thurs; noon–1am Fri–Sat.*

ROWARTH
Little Mill Inn
Rowarth, High Peak SK22 1EB
☎ *(01663) 743178* K Mackenzie

Freehouse always offering Banks's Bitter and Marston's Pedigree, plus four guest ales, changed weekly.

Old-style pub in the middle of nowhere with a waterwheel at the side. Two bars, live music once a week, quiz and bingo nights. Upstairs restaurant area. Food served all day. Children allowed. Isolated, but fully signposted.

OPEN *11am–midnight Mon–Sat; 12–10.30pm Sun.*

SHARDLOW
The Old Crown Inn
Cavendish Bridge, Nr Shardlow DE72 2HL
☎ *(01332) 792392* Monique Johns

Tied to Marston's, with Pedigree always available plus up to seven guests, changed frequently.

A 17th-century coaching inn with olde-worlde bar with log fire in winter, water jugs hanging from the beams, and a display of old coaching and railway memorabilia on the walls. Homemade food and children's menu available 12–2pm and 5–8pm Mon–Thurs, 12–2pm Fri, 12–7pm Sat and 12–3pm Sun. En-suite accommodation. Beer garden with play area. Children and dogs welcome. Two beer festivals per year. Five minutes from junction 2 of the A50.

OPEN *11am–midnight.*

SHIRLAND
The Hay
135 Main Road, Shirland DE55 6BA
☎ *(01773) 835383* Malcolm C Mackenzie

Freehouse with five real ales plus one traditional cider. Fuller's London Pride and Kimberley Mild are permanent, plus weekly-changing guests from breweries such as Skinner's, Beowulf, Berrow, Burton Bridge, Thornbridge and Salamander. Also one traditional cider.

Traditional village pub dating from the 19th century, comprising one cosy U-shaped bar. Brewery posters form an appropriate decoration. No food. Outside patio. Car park. Regular beer festivals. Located seven miles from Matlock and the Peak District, off the A61.

OPEN *6–11.30pm Mon; 4.30–11.30pm Tues–Thurs; 4.30pm–12 Fri; 12–12 Sat; 12–11.30pm Sun (closed weekday lunchtimes).*

SMALLEY

The Bell Inn

Main Road, Smalley, Ilkeston DE7 6EF
☎ *(01332) 880635* Angela Bonsall

 Freehouse with seven or eight real ales at any one time. Adnams Broadside, Mallard Duckling, Whim Hartington Bitter and Hartington IPA plus Oakham JHB usually available and either XXX or XB from Bateman. Fuller's London Pride and Sharp's Doom Bar occasionally on offer.

A two-roomed, Victorian-style pub. Food available 11.30am–2pm and 6–8.30pm. Accommodation. Children welcome in the garden.

OPEN *11.30am–2.30pm and 5–11pm Mon–Thurs; all day Fri–Sun.*

STANLEY COMMON

The White Post

237 Belper Road, Stanley Common, Ilkeston DE7 6FT
☎ *(0115) 930 0194* Paul Hancock
www.myspace.com/thewhitepost

 Part of Woodman Taverns, a privately owned chain of three pubs. A freehouse with four real ales, including Marston's Pedigree and Jennings Cockerhoop, plus two guests, changing constantly. One pump always has something from Funfair, while another has beers from other micro-breweries.

Traditional village pub with open-plan layout. Quality home-cooked food from the award-winning chef served 6–9.30pm Mon; 12–3pm and 6-9.30pm Tues-Fri; 12-9.30pm Sat; 12–6pm Sun. Function room and large beer garden. Children welcome. Car park. Four beer festivals each year, on the last weekends in May, June, July and August. On the A609 between Smalley and Ilkeston.

OPEN *6–11pm Mon, 12–3pm and 6pm–11pm Tues–Thurs; 12–3pm and 6pm–1am Fri; noon–1am Sat; 12–11pm Sun.*

STAVELEY

Speedwell Inn

Lowgates, Staveley, Chesterfield S43 3TT
☎ *(01246) 472252* Alan Wood

 Freehouse whose owners run the Townes Brewery on the premises. At least four Townes brews such as Sunshine and Golden Bud always available, plus guests.

A traditional pub with occasional live music. No food. No children.

OPEN *6–11pm Mon–Thurs; 5–11pm Fri; 12–11pm Sat; 12–10.30pm Sun.*

SWANWICK

The Steampacket

15 Derby Road, Swanwick, Alfreton DE55 1AB
☎ *(01773) 602172* Garry Dawe

Punch Taverns pub with Wychwood Hobgoblin, Adnams Bitter, Black Sheep Bitter, Bateman XB, Everards Tiger and Jennings Cumberland Ale usually available.

Quiet village local with two bars and a real fire. No food. Beer garden. Car park. Two beer festivals held each year, in April and October. Close to the Midland Railway

Centre and Crich Tramway Museum.
OPEN *12–11.30pm Sun–Thurs; 12–12 Fri–Sat.*

SWINSCOE

The Dog & Partridge Country Inn

Swinscoe, Nr Ashbourne DE6 2HS
☎ *(01335) 343183* M Stelfox
www.dogandpartridge.co.uk

Greene King Old Speckled Hen and Marston's Pedigree plus one guest beer changed on a weekly basis.

A country inn with olde-worlde beamed bar and log fire in winter. Restaurant and garden. Cosy lounges and sunny conservatory. Bar and restaurant food available all day, including breakfasts. Car park. Indoor and outdoor children's play areas, highchairs and special children's menu. Six miles from Alton Towers on the A52 between Ashbourne and Leek.
OPEN *7.30am–11pm.*

TICKNALL

The Staff of Life

7 High Street, Ticknall DE73 7JH
☎ *(01332) 862479* Christopher and Kaye Nix
www.thestaffoflife.co.uk

 Between four and six real ales. Marston's Pedigree and Timothy Taylor Landlord are the permanent features, and the other guests are rotated every week. Additional real ales available during summer months, and they can be served from the hand pull and straight from the cask located in the temperature controlled cellar.

An 18th-century oak-beamed freehouse refurbished to a high standard. Traditional country pub in a beautiful area, with an extensive range of cask ales and roaring fires to welcome visitors. Extensive lunchtime and evening menus offer good-quality homemade food. Private guest accommodation at competitive rates. Wonderful beer garden open all year round. Ten minutes' walk to the grounds of Calke Abbey. On the main road from Ticknall to Ashby.
OPEN *11.30am–3pm and 6–11pm Mon–Sat; 12–3pm and 6.30–10.30pm Sun. Open all day Sat–Sun during summer months.*

TIDESWELL

The George Hotel

Commercial Road, Tideswell, Buxton SK17 8NU
☎ *(01298) 871382* Phil Fairey
www.george-hotel-tideswell.co.uk

Tied to Hardys & Hansons' Kimberley Brewery, so with Kimberley Bitter and Olde Trip always available plus a guest, changed monthly.

Olde-worlde coaching house dating back to 1730, with three bars and a separate dining area. Food served 12–2pm and 6–9pm. Beer garden. Function room. Accommodation (five bedrooms). Children and pets welcome. Off the A623 Chesterfield to Manchester road.
OPEN *11am–3pm and 6–11pm Mon–Fri; all day Sat–Sun.*

TROWAY
Gate Inn
Main Road, Troway, Nr Dronfield S21 5RU
☎ *(01246) 413280*
A Browes and KM Grines

Theakston Best Bitter and two guests rotating monthly.

Friendly North Derbyshire country pub with the same owner since 1994. Popular with walkers. Real fires and wooden beams and an award-winning garden. Car park. Off the B6056.

(OPEN) *12–3pm and 7–11pm (10.30pm Sun).*

WARDLOW MIRES
Three Stags' Heads
Wardlow Mires, Tideswell SK17 8RW
☎ *(01298) 872268* Geoff and Pat Fuller

Abbeydale Black Lurcher (brewed exclusively for the Three Stags' Heads), Absolution and Matins permanently available, plus occasional guests.

Small 17th-century Peak District farmhouse pub with stone-flagged bar and its own pottery workshop. Unspoilt, with no frills, no piped muzak, no games machines. Live folk/Irish music at weekends. Bar food at lunchtime and evenings. Car park. Older children allowed (no babes-in-arms or toddlers). On the A623 at the junction with the B6465.

(OPEN) *7–11pm Fri; 11am–11pm Sat; 12–10.30pm Sun (closed during the week).*

WHALEY BRIDGE
Shepherd's Arms
7 Old Road, Whaley Bridge, High Peak SK23 7HR
☎ *(01663) 732384* Susan Greenwood

Marston's tenancy, where Marston's Bitter and Pedigree are always available, plus two guest beers, changed monthly.

Traditional pub, 400 years old, with scrubbed tables in the old-fashioned tap room, a comfortable lounge, and two real fires in winter. No food. Large beer garden – the only one in the village! Car park. The lounge is available for private functions mid-week. Walkers welcome – ring in advance if sandwiches required. Child- and dog-friendly. Ten minutes' walk from High Peak Canal and from the beautiful Goyt Valley. Just off the A6.

(OPEN) *3pm–12 Mon–Fri; noon–1am Sat–Sun.*

WHITEHOUGH
The Oddfellows Arms
Whitehead Lane, Whitehough, Chinley, High Peak SK23 6EJ
☎ *(01663) 750306*
JA Newton and A Holland

Tied to Marston's, so always offers Marston's Bitter and Pedigree, plus one guest, changed monthly.

A one-bar country pub. Food served 12–7pm Mon–Sat and 12–5pm Sun. Children allowed.

(OPEN) *11am–11pm Mon–Sat; 12–10.30pm Sun.*

WIRKSWORTH
The Royal Oak
North End, Wirksworth DE4 4FG
☎ *(01629) 823000* John and Avis Drury

Freehouse serving Whim IPA and Hartington Bitter, Timothy Taylor Landlord and Draught Bass, plus two rotating guests, changed two or three times a week.

Mid-town locals' local, in a three-storey, mid-terrace building. One main lounge, bar area and tap/games room. Bar snacks available (no cooked food). Beer garden. Close to Wirksworth historic railway and Black Rock local beauty spot.

(OPEN) *8–11.30pm Mon–Sat; 12–3pm and 7.30–11pm Sun.*

WOOLLEY MOOR
The White Horse Inn
Badger Lane, Woolley Moor, Alfreton DE55 6FG
☎ *(01246) 590319*
Forest Kimble and Keith Hurst

Freehouse with three or four real ales, which often include Jennings Lakeland or Cumberland, Ruddles Best Bitter, Adnams Broadside, Black Sheep Bitter and Fuller's London Pride.

A two-bar pub with lounge and conservatory for dining. Adventure playground, football goalposts, outside seating on three patios with 25 tables, disabled facilities. Food usually served 12–2pm and 6–9pm Mon–Sat and 12–8pm Sun. Hours more limited in January and February.

(OPEN) *12–3pm and 6–11pm Mon–Sat; 12–10.30pm Sun.*

THE BREWERIES

BARUM BREWERY LTD
*c/o Reform Inn, Pilton High Street, Pilton,
Barnstaple EX31 1PD*
☎ *(01271) 329994*
www.barumbrewery.co.uk

BSE 3.7% ABV
XTC 3.9% ABV
GOLD 4.0% ABV
ORIGINAL 4.4% ABV
BARUMBURG 4.6% ABV
LIQUID LUNCH 4.6% ABV
DARK STAR 4.8% ABV
BREAKFAST 5.0% ABV
TECHNICAL HITCH 5.3% ABV
CHALLENGER 5.6% ABV
BARNSTABLASTA 6.6% ABV

THE BEER ENGINE
Newton St Cyres, Nr Exeter EX5 5AX
☎ *(01392) 851282*
www.thebeerengine.co.uk

RAIL ALE 3.8% ABV
Amber coloured, malty nose and flavour
of fruit.
PISTON BITTER 4.3% ABV
Sweetness throughout, with some bitterness in
the finish.
SLEEPER HEAVY 5.4% ABV
Red, with fruit, sweetness and some bitterness.

BLACKDOWN BREWERY
*Unit C6 Dunkeswell Park, Honiton, Exeter
EX14 4LE*
☎ *(01404) 890096*
www.blackdownbrewery.co.uk

DEVON'S PRIDE 3.8% ABV
BLACKDOWN GOLD 4.3% ABV
BLACKDOWN SMOOTH 4.3% ABV
BLACKDOWN PREMIUM 4.7% ABV
BLACKDOWN DARK SIDE 5.0% ABV
Plus seasonal brews.

THE BRANSCOMBE VALE BREWERY
*Great Seaside Farm, Branscombe, Seaton
EX12 3DP*
☎ *(01297) 680511*

BRANOC 3.8% ABV
Golden and malty with a light hop
finish.
DRAYMAN'S BEST BITTER 4.3% ABV
BRANSCOMBE VALE BEST 4.6% ABV
House beer, may be sold under different names.
Seasonals:
ANNIVERSARY ALE 4.6% ABV
Light coloured with clean, crisp hoppy flavour.
Feb only.
HELL'S BELLS 4.8% ABV
October to March. Smooth, mellow and hoppy.
SUMMA THAT 5.0% ABV
Golden, light and hoppy throughout. Mar–Oct.
OLD MAN OF THE SEA 5.4% ABV
YO HO HO 6.0% ABV
From November onwards. Fruity, and flavour
packed.
Plus occasional brews.

BURRINGTON BREWERY
*Homelands Business Centre, Burrington,
Umberleigh EX37 9JJ*
☎ *(01805) 622813*
www.burringtonbrewery.co.uk

RUBY NEWT 3.6% ABV
Ruby red mild.
BARLEY MOW 3.8% ABV
Dry and fruity.
TIPPLED NEWT 3.8% ABV
Copper colour with bitter bite.
AZZA NEWT 4.0% ABV
Light and dry, brewed with barley malt.
OPUS 4.0% ABV
Wheaty and golden.
ALCHEMY 4.2% ABV
Reddish, fruity and dry.
DNA (DARK NEWT ALE) 4.4% ABV
Rich copper colour with malt, wheat and barley
flavours.
NEWT N WRIGGLY 4.6% ABV
Dry and hoppy with chocolatey notes.
NEWT-RITION 5.2% ABV
Brewed with a mix of English and American
hops.

CLEARWATER BREWERY
*2 Devon Units, Hatchmoor Industrial Estate,
Torrington EX38 7HP*
☎ *(01805) 625242*

COLLEY VILLAGE PRIDE 3.7% ABV
CAVALIER 4.0% ABV
EBONY AND IVORY 4.2% ABV
TORRIDGE BEST 4.4% ABV
1646 4.8% ABV
OLIVER'S NECTAR 5.2% ABV
Plus occasional brews.

COMBE MARTIN BREWERY
*4 Springfield Terrace, Combe Martin, Ilfracombe
EX34 DEE*
☎ *(01271) 883507*

HANGMANS 3.9% ABV
PAST TIMES 3.9% ABV
SHAMMICK ALE 6.2% ABV

COUNTRY LIFE BREWERY
The Big Sheep, Abbotsham, Bideford EX39 5AP
☎ *(01237) 420808*
www.countrylifebrewery.co.uk

OLD APPLEDORE 3.7% ABV
Dark red colour, roasted malt flavour.
GOLDEN PIG 4.7% ABV
Gold coloured and well rounded.
COUNTRY BUMPKIN 6.0% ABV
Dark with malty sweetness.
Plus occasional brews including:
POT WALLOP 4.4% ABV

EXE VALLEY BREWERY

Land Farm, Silverton, Exeter EX5 4HF
☎ *(01392) 860406*
*www.siba-southwest.co.uk/breweries/exevalley/
index.htm*

EXE VALLEY BITTER 3.7% ABV
A full-bodied bitter based on an old West
Country recipe.
BARRON'S HOPSIT 4.1% ABV
A well-hopped bitter using Challenger hops.
DOB'S BEST BITTER 4.1% ABV
A finely balanced bitter with that extra touch of
hops.
DEVON GLORY 4.7% ABV
A distinctive beer made from the finest Devon
malt.
MR SHEPPARD'S CROOK 4.7% ABV
Premium bitter, full flavour of Devon malt and
Challenger hops.
EXETER OLD BITTER 4.8% ABV
A smooth, well-hopped, strong beer.
Seasonals:
DEVON SUMMER 3.9% ABV
SPRING BEER 4.3% ABV
AUTUMN GLORY 4.5% ABV
DEVON DAWN 4.5% ABV
WINTER GLOW 6.0% ABV

GARGOYLES BREWERY

Court Farm, Holcombe Village, Dawlish EX7 0JT
☎ *07773 444501*

SUMMER ALE 3.8% ABV
BEST BITTER 4.2% ABV

THE JOLLYBOAT BREWERY (BIDEFORD) LTD

*The Coach House, Buttgarden Street, Bideford
EX39 2AU*
☎ *(01237) 424343*

GRENVILLE'S RENOWN 3.8% ABV
FREEBOOTER 4.0% ABV
MAINBRACE 4.2% ABV
Light chestnut colour, late hopped for aroma.
PRIVATEER 4.8% ABV
Full flavoured and hoppy. Mixed hop.
Seasonals:
BUCCANEERS 3.8% ABV
Nut-brown colour and hoppy. Summer.
CONTRABAND 5.8% ABV
Christmas feasting ale/porter. Cascade hop.
Plus occasional brews.

O'HANLON'S BREWING CO. LTD

Great Barton Farm, Whimple, Exeter EX5 2NY
☎ *(01404) 822412*
www.ohanlons.co.uk

FIREFLY 3.7% ABV
Crisp and tangy session beer.
WHEAT BEER 4.0% ABV
Citrus tinted with a hint of spice.
DRY STOUT 4.2% ABV
Smoky with plenty of bite.
YELLOWHAMMER 4.2% ABV
Sweet, malty and with a touch of citrus.
GOODWILL 4.8% ABV
ORIGINAL PORT STOUT 4.8% ABV
Dry and lingering on the palate.
ROYAL OAK 5.0% ABV
Amber with a malty hop fragrance.
Plus special brews.

OTTER BREWERY

Mathayes Farm, Luppit, Honiton EX14 4SA
☎ *(01404) 891285*
www.otterbrewery.com

BITTER 3.6% ABV
Pale brown. Hoppy, fruity aroma.
BRIGHT 4.3% ABV
Light and delicate with long malty finish.
ALE 4.5% ABV
HEAD 5.8% ABV
Smooth, strong and malty.
Plus seasonal and occasional brews.

PRINCETOWN BREWERIES LTD

Station Road, Princetown, Yelverton PL20 6QX
☎ *(01822) 890789*
www.princetownbreweries.co.uk

DARTMOOR IPA/BEST 4.0% ABV
Pale, refreshing and hoppy.
HOP JACK 4.0% ABV
Amber colour, hop aroma.
JAIL ALE 4.8% ABV
Full bodied, mid-brown, sweet in the aftertaste.

RED ROCK BREWERY

Higher Humber Farm, Bishopsteignton TQ14 9TD
☎ *07894 035094*
www.redrockbrewery.com

BACK BEACH 3.8% ABV
RED ROCK 4.2% ABV
DRIFTWOOD 4.3% ABV
BREAKWATER 4.6% ABV

SCATTOR ROCK BREWERY

*Unit 5, Gidley's Meadow, Christow, Exeter
EX6 7QB*
☎ *(01647) 252120*
www.scattorrockbrewery.com

TEIGN VALLEY TIPPLE 4.0% ABV
Tawny with plenty of hops.
DEVONIAN 4.5% ABV
Fruity and moreish.
GOLDEN VALLEY 4.6% ABV
VALLEY STOMPER 5.0% ABV
*Plus the Tor Collection (monthly brews named after
local tors), and seasonal brews including:*
SCATTOR CLAUS 4.7% ABV
SCATTOR BRAIN 4.8% ABV
TOTALLY BRAIN DEAD 8.0% ABV

SOUTH HAMS BREWERY LTD

Stokely Barton, Stokenham, Kingsbridge TQ7 2SE
☎ *(01548) 581151*
www.southhamsbrewery.co.uk

DEVON PRIDE 3.8% ABV
XSB 4.2% ABV
WILD BLONDE 4.4% ABV
EDDYSTONE 4.8% ABV
SUTTON COMFORT 4.5% ABV

SUMMERSKILLS BREWERY
Unit 15, Pomphlett Farm Industrial Estate,
Broxton Drive, Billacombe, Plymouth PL9 7BG
☎ *(01752) 481283*
www.summerskills.co.uk

CELLAR VEE 3.7% ABV
Crystal malt and hop flavours.
HOPSCOTCH 4.1% ABV
Light, malt flavour.
BEST BITTER 4.3% ABV
Pale, with malty flavour and honey hints.
TAMAR 4.3% ABV
Malt and roasted barley flavours.
Seasonals:
NORM'S FIRST BREW 4.2% ABV
O'SUMMERSKILLS SHAMROCK STOUT 4.4% ABV
DEVON PILLS LOUTENBERG 4.5% ABV
DUNE PALE ALE 4.5% ABV
MENACING DENNIS 4.5% ABV
WINTER WARMER 4.6% ABV
FAT FREE BEER 4.7% ABV
WHISTLE BELLY VENGEANCE 4.7% ABV
NINJA BEER 5.0% ABV
INDIANA'S BONES 5.6% ABV

TARKA ALES
Yelland Manor Farm, Fremington EX31 3DT
☎ *07870 670804 or (01837) 811030*

GOLDEN POOL 4.3% ABV
TOM NODDY 4.3% ABV
Plus seasonals and occasionals.

TEIGNWORTHY BREWERY,
The Maltings, Teign Road, Newton Abbot
TQ12 4AA
☎ *(01626) 332066*

REEL ALE 4.0% ABV
Hoppy, dry session beer.
SPRING TIDE 4.3% ABV
Sweet, copper-coloured brew, with hops
throughout.
OLD MOGGIE 4.4% ABV
Gold coloured, with hops and citrus, ideal for
hot summer weather.
Seasonals:
BEACHCOMBER 4.5% ABV
AMY'S ALE 4.8% ABV
HARVESTER 5.0% ABV
MARTHA'S MILD 5.3% ABV

TOPSHAM AND EXMINSTER BREWERY
Unit 5, Lions Rest Estate, Station Road,
Exminster, Exeter EX6 8DZ
☎ *(01392) 823013*
www.topexe.co.uk

FERRYMAN ALE 4.5% ABV

WARRIOR BREWING COMPANY
Matford House, Old Matford Lane, Matford,
Exeter EX2 8XS
☎ *(01392) 221451*

BEST BITTER 4.0% ABV
TOMAHAWK 4.0% ABV
GERONIMO 4.9% ABV

THE PUBS

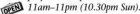
ABBOTSKERSWELL

Court Farm Inn
Wilton Way, Abbotskerswell, Newton Abbot
TQ12 5NY
☎ *(01626) 361866* Mr Parker

Flowers IPA (brewed by Badger) and Otter
Ale regularly available.

Large, busy and foody. Typical Devonshire
longhouse with two bars. Food-led.
Children welcome. Garden. Car park.
OPEN *12–2pm and 6–9pm Mon–Sat; 12–8pm
Sun.*

APPLEDORE

Beaver Inn
Irsha Street, Appledore, Nr Bideford EX39 1RY
☎ *(01237) 474822* Graham Stone

Freehouse with two or three frequently
changing real ales, usually from West
Country micro-breweries.

Popular, centuries-old waterside town pub,
formerly a smugglers' den. Wonderful
location overlooking the estuary with views
from the restaurant and patio. One bar. Food
lunchtime and evening seven days a week.
Children welcome. Pool table in the games
room. Handy for local beaches. Close to the
main quayside car park.
OPEN *11am–11pm (10.30pm Sun).*

Coach & Horses
5 Market Street, Appledore, Nr Bideford EX39 1PW
☎ *(01237) 420821* Mr and Mrs Rose

Freehouse serving Country Life's Old
Appledore plus four other real ales,
perhaps Shepherd Neame Spitfire or Charles
Wells Lock, Stock and Barrel.

Cosy backstreet pub – a traditional 17th-
century alehouse with real fire, real food
and a warm welcome. Children welcome.
Beer garden. Park on the quay.
OPEN *10am–midnight Mon–Sat; 12–10.30pm
Sun.*

AVONWICK

The Turtley Corn Mill
Avonwick, South Brent TQ10 9ES
☎ *(01364) 646100* Lesley and Bruce Brunning
www.avonwick.net

Summerskills Tamar plus other local
brews such as Butcombe Blonde, St
Austell Tribute, Otter Ale, Princetown Jail and
IPA. Plus a good range of wines.

Renovated and refurbished former mill set
in six acres of grounds beside the River
Glazebrook. Good food served 12–9.30pm
daily. No music, fruit machines or pool
tables. Children welcome until 7pm. Large
car park. Half a mile off the A38.
OPEN *11.30am–11pm Mon–Sat; 12–10.30pm
Sun.*

AXMINSTER

The Red Lion

Lyme Street, Axminster EX13 5AU
☎ *(01297) 32016*

 Enterprise Inns pub with four brews from local independent breweries. The range changes weekly.

A 16th-century traditional one-bar inn, a typical local boozer. Pub grub served daily. No children. Darts, pool, skittles and Sky Sports.

OPEN *12–12.*

AXMOUTH

Harbour Inn

Axmouth, Seaton EX12 4AF
☎ *(01297) 20371 David Squire*

 Freehouse offering Otter Ale, Flowers Original and Flowers IPA (both brewed by Badger).

A 12th-century traditional-style pub with a large games room attractive to families. Food every session except Sunday night in the winter – home-produced lamb is the speciality. Children welcome. Car park. Garden. Pool table and skittle alley.

OPEN *11am–3pm and 6–11pm.*

The Ship Inn

Axmouth, Nr Seaton EX14 4AF
☎ *(01297) 21838 RJ Chapman*

 Wadworth 6X and the local Otter Bitter are permanent fixtures, and seasonal brews are also served.

C reeper-clad village inn, trading in a traditional way. Two friendly bars, à la carte restaurant area, and beer garden with magnificent rural and estuary views. Food served 12–2pm and 6–9pm. Family room and skittle alley. Off the A3052 Lyme Regis to Exeter road.

OPEN *11am–2.30pm and 6–11.30pm (times vary according to the season).*

BAMPTON

The Exeter Inn

Tiverton Road, Bampton EX16 9DY
☎ *(01398) 331345 James Pattison*
www.exeter-inn.com

Two real ales, often including Exmoor Ale, plus guests such as Cotleigh Seahawk or Tawny and Otter Bitter.

A 15th-century traditional Devonshire longhouse, with open fire, two bars, private dining room and 11 en-suite bedrooms. Food served 12–2.30pm and 6–9pm. Outside seating, large car parks. Local food and ale festivals. Fishing, shooting, walking, cycling and other outdoor activities are available. Take junction 27 off the M5 toward Tiverton and then go along the A296 to Bampton.

OPEN *11am–11pm.*

BARNSTAPLE

Monkey Island

14 Castle Street, Barnstaple EX31 1DR
☎ *(01271) 375964 Phil Kelland*

At least three brews from a constantly changing range of beers, direct from independent breweries around the UK.

A true freehouse with one bar, a friendly, local atmosphere and the usual pub games. There has been a pub on this site since 1650. Juke box, live music (mainly blues/rock) and discos. Car park. No children. Bikers welcome. On the ring road opposite the old railway station and adjacent to the castle mound and Tarka Trail cycle route.

OPEN *11am–midnight.*

BEER

Barrel O'Beer

Fore Street, Beer EX12 3EQ
☎ *(01297) 20099 Roberta Hunt*
www.barrelobeer.com

 Genuine freehouse offering four real ales, frequently Fuller's London Pride and St Austell Dartmoor, two or three brews from Exe Valley, and seasonal ales. Guests are rotated every few months.

A traditional, family-run pub with a friendly welcome, serving real ale and local seafood. Clean and unfussy in historic fishing village. Food is locally sourced when possible and served 12–2pm and 6–9pm (not Wed and Sun evenings in winter). Children over 5 welcome. Close to beach.

OPEN *11.30am–2.30pm and 5.30–11pm Mon–Fri; 11.30am–11pm Sat; 12–2.30pm Sun. Opening hours extended (all day) during peak season and reduced in winter.*

BELSTONE

The Tors

Belstone, Okehampton EX20 1QZ
☎ *(01837) 840689 Ann and Tony Cooper*

 Freehouse serving Sharp's Doom Bar and St Austell Tribute, with Palmers IPA sometimes available.

O ld granite pub in a building dating from around 1892, in a pleasant Dartmoor village. One bar, dining room, darts, patio and outside seating overlooking the moor. Food served 12–3pm every day (longer in summer). Three en-suite letting rooms (family, twin and single). Dining room seats 40 for functions.

OPEN *11am–3pm and 6–11pm Mon–Sat; 12–4pm and 7–11pm Sun; all day, every day in the summer.*

BIDEFORD

The Kings Arms

The Quay, Bideford EX39 2HW
☎ *(01237) 475196 Paul Phipps*

Jollyboat Grenville Renowned, Butcombe Bitter and Greene King Abbot Ale.

P leasant market-town pub in a building dating from 1560, with beams and log fires. One big bar, patio. Food served lunchtimes. Children allowed.

OPEN *11am–11pm.*

BLACKAWTON

The George Inn

Main Street, Blackawton, Totnes TQ9 7BG
☎ *(01803) 712342* Bob and Tracey Clark

Freehouse serving Teignworthy Springtide, Princetown Jail Ale and Palmers Copper Ale plus a guest beer, changed fortnightly. The emphasis is on local micro-breweries.

Traditional, relaxed village pub with dining room. The wooden-floored bar has a large woodburning stove and a lovely view. Traditional pub food with a weekly specials board served 12–2pm (except Mon) and 6–9pm every day. Two en-suite B&B rooms. Beer garden, patio, car park. Private room for hire (up to 15 people). Children and dogs welcome. Annual beer festival end of April/early May. Just down the road from Woodlands Leisure Park, off the B3122 Dartmouth to Totnes/ Kingsbridge Road.

OPEN *6–11pm Mon; 12–3pm and 6–11pm Tues–Fri; 12–11pm Sat–Sun.*

BRANSCOMBE

The Fountain Head Inn

Branscombe, Nr Seaton EX12 3AG
☎ *(01297) 680359*
Jon Woodley and Teresa Hoare (landlords) and Graham Williams (licensee)

Branscombe Vale Branoc and Jolly Jeff plus one rotating guest.

A 500-year-old character inn with open log fires, one main bar and a restaurant. Food served 12–2pm and 6.30–9pm. Beer terrace at the front. Car park. Children welcome in specified areas. Spitroast and barbecue on Sunday evenings in summer. Beer festival held in mid-June.

OPEN *11am–3pm and 6–11pm Mon–Sat; 12–3pm and 6–10.30pm Sun.*

The Masons Arms

Branscombe Village EX12 3DJ
☎ *(01297) 680300* Carol and Colin Slaney
www.masonsarms.co.uk

Five real ales, including Otter Bitter and Masons Ale and Branscombe Vale Branoc, plus a guest, changed twice a week. An annual beer festival takes place each July.

Originally a one-bar Devon cider house in the middle of a row of cottages, now a thatched freehouse comprising the lot. Beams, slate floors, stone walls and open fires. Front terrace and side garden. Good food served 12–2pm and 7–9pm (Devon dining pub of the year 2004). A 17–mile drive from Exeter and a 12–minute walk from the sea. Accommodation (24 bedrooms), conference room, car park. At the bottom of the village off the A3052.

OPEN *9am–11pm Mon–Sat; 12–10.30pm Sun.*

BRENDON

The Rockford Inn

Brendon, Nr Lynton EX35 6PT
☎ *(01598) 741214* C Carter
www.therockfordinn.com

 Three real ales, including beers from St Austell, Cotleigh and others, plus beers brewed at the pub itself. All beers are rotated weekly.

A 17th-century inn next to the East Lyn river, with a small brewery inside the pub. Four comfortable bars, open fire and murals painted by a famous local artist. Food served 12–3pm and 7–9.30pm every day. Small beer garden and riverside seating. Children and dogs welcome. Accommodation. Handy for walks along the river to see stunning scenery and wildlife, including red deer and otters. Just outside the village of Brendon, at Rockford.

OPEN *12–3pm and 7–11pm (10.30pm Sun).*

BROADHEMPSTON

The Coppa Dolla Inn

Broadhempston, Nr Totnes TQ9 6BD
☎ *(01803) 812455* James Boase

Freehouse serving Wadworth 6X and Fuller's London Pride.

Dating from 1745, a country pub with restaurant area and delightful beer garden. Log fires in winter. Homemade food (including two-in-one pies) served 12–2.30pm and 6–9.30pm (7–9.30pm Sun). Children welcome. Room for hire, car park. Easy to find, once you're in Broadhempston.

OPEN *11.30am–3pm and 6–11pm Mon–Sat; 12–3pm and 7–10.30pm Sun.*

BUCKFASTLEIGH

The White Hart

2 Plymouth Road, Buckfastleigh TQ11 0DA
☎ *(01364) 642337* Geoff Hutchings

Freehouse with Teignworthy Beachcomber, Gale's HSB and a house ale always on the menu, plus one guest, changed every two days.

An olde-worlde pub, Grade II listed, with flagstone floors and log fires. One bar, background music. Partitioned dining area and family room. Food served at lunchtimes and evenings (not Sun evening). Three bed and breakfast rooms (two en-suite). Children allowed.

OPEN *12–11pm Mon–Sat (10.30pm Sun).*

CHAGFORD

The Bullers Arms

7 Mill Street, Chagford TQ13 8AW
☎ *(01647) 432348* Maurice and Wendy Cox
www.thebullersarms.co.uk

Enterprise Inns tenancy usually offering three real ales. Otter Bitter is regularly featured, and the two guests, rotated every few months, might be something like St Austell Tribute and Bays Gold.

Pleasant old Dartmoor coaching inn offering a warm, friendly welcome. Courtyard garden, accommodation. Food served 12–2pm (12–6pm Sunday carvery) and 6.30–9pm every day; there are two mid-week carveries every month. Take away pizzas available from 9pm each evening. Children and dogs welcome. Regular entertainment, live music, quizzes. Close to the village square.

OPEN *10am–3pm and 5–11pm Mon–Thurs; all day Fri–Sun.*

CHERITON BISHOP
The Old Thatch Inn

Cheriton Bishop, Dartmoor EX6 6JH
☎ *(01647) 24204*
David London and Serena London
www.theoldthatchinn.com

Freehouse, privately own and managed, with Otter Ale, O'Hanlon's Royal Oak and Sharp's Doom Bar and a weekly guest such as O'Hanlon's Yellowhammer or Original Port Stout, Exmoor Ale or Fox, Skinner's Betty Stogs or Princetown Jail Ale.

This traditional 16th-century thatched inn is now a Grade II listed building. Fresh food is served 12–2pm and 6.30–9pm. South-facing garden, car park. Children and dogs very welcome. Close to Dartmoor, Fingle Bridge and Castle Drogo. Half a mile from the A30, ten miles south of Exeter.

OPEN *11.30am–3pm and 6–11pm.*

CHIPSHOP
The Chipshop Inn

Chipshop, Gulworthy, Nr Tavistock PL19 8NT
☎ *(01822) 832322* Steve and Lynn Callender

Freehouse offering Sharp's Doom Bar and Shepherd Neame Spitfire plus a guest, changed monthly.

Once a 19th-century shop owned by the local mine owners and used to exchange penny tokens (chips) for goods. Now a friendly rural pub in Dartmoor. Food served 12–2pm and 6.30–9pm (and, yes, they do serve chips). Restaurant offers food 7–9pm Tues–Sat. Garden, courtyard and car park. Children welcome. Skittle alley and darts. Function room for hire. On the Gullworthy to Lamerton road between the A390 and the B3362.

OPEN *12–2.30pm and 5–11pm Mon–Fri; 12–11pm Sat; 12–10.30pm Sun.*

CHITTLEHAMPTON
The Bell

The Square, Chittlehampton EX37 9QL
☎ *(01769) 540368* Mark and Lynn Jones
www.thebellatchittlehampton.co.uk

Up to ten real ales, with three on pump, the rest on stillage. Beers will be from breweries such as Cotleigh, Timothy Taylor, Exmoor, Badger, Sharp's, Otter, Black Sheep and Skinner's, and are rotated cask by cask, day by day!

Purpose-built village community pub in an unusual 1888 building. CAMRA North Devon Pub of the Year 2007. Home-made food available 12–2pm and 6–9pm. Conservatory, dining area, beer garden, smoking shelter, orchard, alpacas. Children, and dogs on leads, welcome. En-suite accommodation. Massive car park. Disabled toilets.

OPEN *11am–3pm and 6pm–12 Mon–Fri; all day Sat–Sun and bank holidays.*

CHUDLEIGH
Bishop Lacy

Fore Street, Chudleigh TQ13 0HY
☎ *(01626) 854585* Robin Bishop

Genuine freehouse offering Princetown Jail Ale and Fuller's London Pride plus one or two guests changed monthly.

An inn dating back to the middle ages with two bars, open fires, beams and lots of character. Food served 12–2.30pm Tues–Sun. Beer festivals held. Private room for hire.

OPEN *12–12 (1am Fri–Sat).*

CLEARBROOK
The Skylark Inn

Clearbrook, Yelverton PL20 6JD
☎ *(01822) 853258*

Three locally-sourced real ales usually including Otter Tribute.

Friendly staff and the best black cherry cheesecake ever tasted!

OPEN *11.30am–11.30pm Mon–Sat; 12–10.30pm Sun.*

COCKWOOD
The Anchor Inn

Cockwood, Nr Starcross EX6 8RA
☎ *(01626) 890203*
Terry Morgan and Alison Sanders
www.anchorinncockwood.com

Six regular real ales on offer. Otter Ale, Fuller's London Pride, Greene King Abbot, Bass, Adnams Broadside and Timothy Taylor Landlord usually available.

Charming low-beamed smugglers' inn furnished in dark wood. Food served 12–10pm (9.30pm Sun), seafood a speciality. Children welcome. Car park. Powderham Castle is just up the road, and there are several holiday parks nearby. From Exeter M5 J29 follow the A389 towards Dawlish.

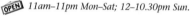

OPEN *11am–11pm Mon–Sat; 12–10.30pm Sun.*

COLEFORD
The New Inn

Coleford, Crediton EX17 5BZ
☎ *(01363) 84242* Simon and Melissa Renshaw
www.thenewinncoleford.co.uk

Freehouse with Otter Ale and Sharp's Doom Bar plus two rotating guests.

A 13th-century thatched pub, with lots of oak beams, in a sleepy conservation village. Restaurant and bar meals available 12–2pm and 7–10pm (9.30pm Sun). Large, terraced riverside garden. Seven luxury en-suite bedrooms. Children welcome. Car park. Off the A377 outside Crediton.

OPEN *12–2.30pm and 6–11pm Mon–Sat; 7–10.30pm Sun.*

COLYTON
Gerrard Arms

Rosemary Lane, Colyton EX24 6JN
☎ *(01297) 552588* Roy Turner

Freehouse offering Branscombe Vale Branoc and Bass plus a regular guest beer throughout the year.

Cosy one-bar local in pleasant village. Food every lunchtime, also every evening in summer but only Fri and Sat nights in winter. Children welcome. Garden. Skittle alley. Small beer festivals at Easter and August bank holiday, with six guest beers.

OPEN *11am–3pm and 5.30pm–12 Mon–Fri (1am Fri); 11am–3pm and 6pm–1am Sat; 12–3pm and 7pm–12 Sun.*

COMBEINTEIGNHEAD

The Wild Goose Inn

Combeinteignhead, Nr Newton Abbot TQ12 4RA
☎ *(01626) 872241* Jeremy English

 Freehouse offering seven real ales, all from West Country breweries such as Teignworthy, Skinner's, Otter, O'Hanlon, Princetown and Sharp's, rotated weekly.

A 17th-century, traditional, family-owned and -run country village pub, originally a Devon longhouse. Extensive menu with an emphasis on homemade fare, with fresh fish and vegetarian dishes always available 12–2pm and 7–9.30pm, plus Sunday roast. Secluded beer garden overlooking farmland and the 14th-century church. Families, dogs and muddy boots welcome. Live music on Friday night, quiz Sunday night, regular theme nights. Easter beer festival. Take the Shaldon road from the main Penn Inn roundabout on the A38.

OPEN *11am–2.30pm and 5.30–11pm Mon–Sat; 12–3pm and 7–11pm Sun.*

COMBE MARTIN

The Castle Inn

High Street, Combe Martin EX34 0HS
☎ *(01271) 883706* Allan Stephenson
www.castleinn.info

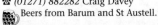 Four real ales at this freehouse. Brews from Cotleigh, Barum, Clearwater and guests from other local brewers are often on offer, and are regularly rotated.

A village pub with two bars, function room (150 capacity) and log fire. Live sports shown on two big screens. Bar food served 12–12 seven days a week. Darts, skittles, pool. Children and dogs welcome. Beer garden, large car park. Halfway up the village.

OPEN *Noon–2.30am.*

Ye Olde George & Dragon

Castle Street, Combe Martin EX34 0HX
☎ *(01271) 882282* Craig Davey

 Beers from Barum and St Austell.

V illage pub, club and restaurant in a 400-year-old building, with three bars. Meals served throughout. Pool, darts, patio. Children allowed. Ring for directions, as it is easy to miss.

OPEN *4–11pm Mon–Wed; 4pm–1am Thurs–Sat; 12–10.30pm Sun.*

CREDITON

The Crediton Inn

28A Mill Street, Crediton EX17 1EZ
☎ *(01363) 772882* Diane Heggadon

Freehouse with Sharp's Doom Bar and Fuller's London Pride plus two to six guests changed every few days. Branscombe Vale and Cotleigh beers are often featured.

F riendly local, with refurbished bar, wood-burning fire, skittle alley and function room. Local CAMRA Pub of the Year 2005.

Home-cooked food served 12.30–2.30pm and 7.30–9pm Fri–Sat. Buffets available for pre-booked functions in bar or function room. No children, dogs on leads. Car park. Beer festival in November. Occasional quiz/theme nights. Part of the Tarka Trail. On the Tiverton road, five minutes from the railway station.

OPEN *11am–11pm Mon–Sat; 12–2pm and 7–10.30pm Sun.*

The Lamb Inn

The Square, Sandford, Crediton EX17 4LW
☎ *(01363) 773676* Mark Hildyard
www.lambinnsandford.co.uk

 Freehouse serving Beer Engine Rail Ale, Bath Ales Barnstormer and Rooster's Yankee plus a daily-changing guest.

A real-ale-focused pub dating from the 16th century. Three open fires, two bars, one cinema/conference room and a large cobbled and lawned beer garden. Plans for en-suite accommodation. Live music monthly. Children and dogs welcome. Parking available 200 yards away at local village hall. On the A377 to Crediton.

OPEN *9am–11.30pm Mon–Fri; 11am–midnight Sat–Sun.*

DARTMOUTH

The Cherub Inn

13 Higher Street, Dartmouth TQ6 9RB
☎ *(01803) 832571* Laurie Scott
www.the-cherub.co.uk

 Freehouse with Cherub Best Bitter (Summerskills) and three other real ales that change every month but may well include something from Sharp's.

O ne-bar pub dating from 1380, very small with beams, character and open fire. Air-conditioned cellar. Gastro-food lunchtimes and evenings. Over-7s only in the restaurant at certain times, no under-14s in the bar.

OPEN *11am–11pm.*

DODDISCOMBSLEIGH

The Nobody Inn

Doddiscombsleigh, Nr Exeter EX6 7PS
☎ *(01647) 252394* Susan Burdge
www.nobodyinn.co.uk

 Nobody's House Ale (brewed by Branscombe) plus two guest beers changed every day, which may include beers from Otter, Blackawton, Exmoor, Exe Valley and Cotleigh.

A 16th-century inn with a charming, traditional bar, a refurbished restaurant, beams, inglenooks and fireplaces. Food available: bar food lunch 12–2pm; evenings bar and restaurant meals 6.30–9.30pm Fri–Sat, 7–9pm Sun. Five impeccably refurbished bedrooms. Car park and garden. Well-behaved children and dogs welcome. Three miles southwest of Exeter racecourse, 100 yards from the village church.

OPEN *11am–11pm Mon–Sat; 12–10.30pm Sun.*

DOLTON

The Royal Oak

The Square, Dolton, Winkleigh EX19 8QF
☎ *(01805) 804288* Peter Sandbach

Two or three real ales rotate weekly, and might include Sharp's Will's Resolve, Timothy Taylor Landlord, Clearwater Cavalier and beers from the Tarka brewery.

Large village pub in a 14th/16th-century building, with restaurant, two main bars and snug. Food served 12–3pm (not Mon–Wed during winter) and 6–9.30pm during the week, 12–9.30pm at weekends. Pool table, darts, skittles and table football. Function room, beer garden. Accommodation. Car parking available. Families welcome, dogs on leads. Five miles from Winkleigh off the Crediton to Torrington Road, at the top end of the village.

OPEN *12–12 (in winter the opening hours Mon–Wed are 5.30–11.30pm).*

DUNSFORD

The Royal Oak Inn

Dunsford EX6 7DA
☎ *(01647) 252256* Mark Harrison
www.troid.co.uk

Greene King Abbot Ale, Princetown Jail Ale and Sharp's Cornish Coaster plus up to three rotating guest beers.

Light, open Victorian village pub. Food 12–2pm and 7–9pm (except Mon). Children welcome. Car park, courtyard, garden, pool. Live music. Quiz night (Thurs). Accommodation in a converted barn. Within the Dartmoor National Park in an Area of Outstanding Natural Beauty.

OPEN *12–2.30pm and 7–11pm.*

EAST PRAWLE

Pigs Nose Inn

East Prawle, Kingsbridge TQ7 2BY
☎ *(01548) 511204* Peter Webber
www.pigsnoseinn.co.uk

Three real ales on offer at this freehouse, namely Eddystone and Devon Pride, both from South Hams, and Bays Gold.

A 500-year-old smugglers' pub, the most southerly in Devon, with snug, pool room, showers and outside tables. Food served 12–2pm and 6–9pm. Dogs and children very welcome, plus adults on their best behaviour! South Devon CAMRA Pub of the Year 2005. Country Pub of the Year 2008–9 *Devon Life* magazine.

OPEN *12–3pm and 6–11pm-ish.*

EXETER

The Brook Green Tavern

31 Well Street, Exeter EX4 6QL
☎ *(01392) 495699* Josephine Johnson

Tied to Punch Taverns, with six real ales, including London Pride and Spitfire, plus various guest ales are rotated weekly.

A Tudor building with small beer garden and small car park. One bar, one small room upstairs, accommodation. No food. Near Exeter City football club and St James railway station.

OPEN *4pm–12.30am Mon–Thurs; 4pm–1.30am Fri; noon–1.30am Sat; noon–12.30am Sun.*

Double Locks Hotel

Canal Bank, Exeter EX2 6LT
☎ *(01392) 256947* Phil and Rach Uffendell
www.doublelocks.co.uk

Nine real ales in summer, six in winter, with Wells and Young's brews always on offer, plus rotating guest beers from local breweries. Local cider also served all year round.

Victorian lock-keeper's cottage situated on the lock gates of the canal. Outside stable bar and barbecue. Full menu, snacks and specials served all day in summer, and at lunch and dinner in winter. Large beer garden, children's play area, car park. Live music at weekends. Beer festival at May Day. Dogs welcome. By car, take Clapperbrook Lane East, off Marsh Barton.

OPEN *Summer: 11am–midnight Mon–Sat; 11am–10.30pm Sun. Winter hours may vary.*

Great Western Hotel

St David's Station Approach, Exeter EX4 4NU
☎ *(01392) 274039* R Kaushall

Fuller's London Pride, Adnams Broadside and Bitter and a beer from Exe Valley plus guests to make ten different beers during the week and 14 at weekends. These may include Branscombe Vale Branoc, Timothy Taylor Landlord, O'Hanlon's Yellowhammer, Orkney Dark Island and Greene King Old Speckled Hen.

Traditional freehouse within a hotel. Exeter and East Devon CAMRA Pub of the Year 2001, South West CAMRA Pub of the Year 2002. Staff pride themselves on looking after their customers. Thirty-five bedrooms with en-suite facilities. Background music. Live music on bank holidays. Food served all day. Children allowed.

OPEN *11am–11pm Mon–Sat; 12–10.30pm Sun.*

The Imperial

New North Road, Exeter EX4 4AH
☎ *(01392) 434050* Paul Dixey
www.jdwetherspoon.co.uk

A Wetherspoon's pub. Greene King Abbot and IPA and Marston's Pedigree. Plus 11 daily-changing guest ales from the south-west, such as O'Hanlon's Yellowhammer, Exmoor Stag, Otter Bright and Skinner's Betty Stogs.

A Victorian former hotel with three bars and four acres of gardens. Regular beer festivals featuring local breweries. Food served 9am–11pm. Children welcome until 9.30pm. Meeting room. Situated outside the city centre, near Exeter University and the railway station.

OPEN *9am–midnight Sun–Thurs; 9am–1am Fri–Sat.*

The Wellhouse Tavern

Cathedral Yard, Exeter EX1 1HD
☎ *(01392) 223611* David Colegate
www.michaelcaines.com

One of Devon's biggest freehouses, with Otter Ale and Sharp's Doom Bar, plus (most of the time) O'Hanlon's Yellowhammer, and a minimum of three guests, changing daily. Examples include beers from Archers, Teignworthy, Red Rock, Scattor Rock, Cottage, Cotleigh and Blackawton.

Connected to the self-proclaimed oldest hotel in Britain, with a Roman cellar complete with skeleton and ghost! Beautiful views of Exeter Cathedral. First-class food from the Michelin-starred kitchen of chef Michael Caines MBE (widely known for his appearance on the TV show *Great British Menu*), served 12–5.30pm Mon–Sat and 12–2.30pm Sun. Sponsors the ale tent at the Exeter Food and Drink Festival. The pub's management includes a CAMRA regional judge and a Taste of the West ale and cider judge. At least two ale and two cider festivals a year. Monthly local brewery tours April to August on weekday evenings.

OPEN *11am–11pm Mon–Thurs; 11am–midnight Fri–Sat; 12–10.30pm Sun.*

EXMOUTH

The Grove

The Esplanade, Exmouth EX8 1BJ
☎ *(01395) 272101* Darren and Jen Paterson

Wells and Young's pub always offering Charles Wells Bombardier plus one or two of the seasonal ales. Eight bottled ales from Wells and Young's also served.

Friendly pub with a bar and dining area upstairs and a large downstairs bar, plus a huge garden area and large balcony with ocean views. Food served 12–10pm, with seafood a speciality. Families and dogs welcome. Quiz on Thursday nights. Disabled access and toilets. Baby-changing facilities. Very close to the beach.

OPEN *11am–11pm.*

GEORGEHAM

Rock Inn

Rock Hill, Georgeham EX33 1JW
☎ *(01271) 890322* Andy and Debbie
www.therockinngeorgeham.co.uk

Five real ales from a rotating range that may well include something from Exmoor, Dartmoor and Cotleigh breweries.

Classic Devon village pub about a mile north of Croyde and three south of Woolacombe. One main stone-flagged bar, plus pool room and conservatory. Outside seating in garden at rear. Car parking opposite. Food served 12–2.30pm and 6.30–9.30pm. Handy for north Devon's surfing beaches.

OPEN *11am–4pm and 6pm–12 Mon–Sat; 12–11pm Sun.*

HALWELL

Old Inn

Halwell, Nr Totnes TQ9 7JA
☎ *(01803) 712329* B Crowther

Freehouse serving RCH East Street Cream plus one guest, changed sporadically, from a range of micro-breweries.

A food and beer village inn dating from the 18th century, with dining area and beer garden. Food at lunchtimes and evenings. Accommodation. Children allowed. Car park. Norman church next door. On the main A381 between Totnes and Kingsbridge.

OPEN *11am–3pm and 6–11pm Mon–Sat; 12–3pm and 6–10.30pm Sun.*

HATHERLEIGH

Tally Ho Country Inn

14 Market Street, Hatherleigh EX20 3JN
☎ *(01837) 810306* Ady Taylor

Offers Cavalier, Torridge Best and Oliver's Nectar from the Clearwater brewery.

An inn that used to be the town bakery. Bar and restaurant food available at lunchtimes and evenings. Garden, accommodation. Children allowed.

OPEN *11am–2.30pm and 6–11pm.*

HOLBETON

Mildmay Colours

Fore Street, Holbeton, Plymouth PL8 1NA
☎ *(01752) 830248* Chris Hopkins

Mildmay Colours Bitter (brewed by Skinner's), Skinner's Cornish Knocker and O'Hanlon's Royal Oak plus one guest each month, such as O'Hanlon's Yellowhammer.

Traditional old inn with terrace, beer garden and tables, games room and function room. Pub food, plus specials and steaks, served 12–2.15pm every day and 6–9pm Mon–Sat. Accommodation in six en-suite rooms. Large car park and children's play area. Children and pets under supervision welcome. Handy for beach and coastal walks.

OPEN *11.30am–3pm and 6–11pm Mon–Sat; 12–3pm and 6.30–10.30pm Sun.*

HONITON

The Holt

178 High Street, Honiton EX14 1LA
☎ *(01404) 47707* Joe and Angus McCaig
www.theholt-honiton.com

Partly tied to Otter Brewery, with four Otter ales: Bitter, Bright, Ale and Head.

Opened in May 2005 as Otter Brewery's first pub. Open-plan kitchen, lively bar and upstairs restaurant. Modern Mediterranean food served 12–2pm and 7–9pm (10pm Thurs–Sat), with rare roast beef Sunday lunches a speciality. Live Jazz nights. Film club.

OPEN *11am–3pm and 5.30–11pm Mon–Sat; 12–4pm Sun (closed Sun evening).*

HORNDON
The Elephant's Nest
Horndon, Nr Mary Tavy PL19 9NQ
☎ *(01822) 810273* Peter Wolfes

Palmers IPA and Copper, St Austell HSD plus one changing guest, perhaps Exmoor Gold or Otter Bright. Also draught cider.

This 16th-century Dartmoor inn with a large garden and log fires has a collection of 'Elephant's Nests' written in different languages on the beams in chalk. Bar food and à la carte menu at lunchtimes and evenings. Car park and children's room. Follow A386 into Mary Tavy. Take the road signposted Horndon for just under two miles.

OPEN *12–3pm and 6–11pm Tues–Sat; 12–3pm Sun; closed Sun evening and Mon.*

HORSEBRIDGE
The Royal Inn
Horsebridge TL19 8PJ
☎ *(01822) 870214* Catherine Eaton

Freehouse with a Cotleigh and a Sharp's brew plus two guests also offered in the summer.

An old pub with open fires, patio and beer garden. Food lunchtimes and evenings. Children allowed at lunchtime only.

OPEN *12–3pm and 6.30–11pm (10.30pm Sun).*

IDDESLEIGH
Duke of York
Iddesleigh, Winkleigh EX19 8BG
☎ *(01837) 810253*
Jamie Stuart and Pippa Hutchinson

Freehouse with real ales served straight from the barrel; no pumps used. Adnams Broadside, Cotleigh Tawny, Sharp's Doom Bar, O'Hanlon's Yellowhammer and Exe Valley Dob's Best Bitter will often feature, with three of these changing every week.

A 15th-century pub in a rural setting, with inglenook, beams and a friendly atmosphere. No juke box, no fruit machines, no karaoke. Separate dining area. Food served all day, every day. Children allowed. Accommodation available in seven en-suite rooms. In mid-Devon, five miles from Winkleigh on the B3220.

OPEN *11am–11pm Mon–Sat; 12–10.30pm Sun.*

INSTOW
The Bar
Marine Parade, Instow EX39 4HY
☎ *(01271) 860624* Yasmin Braund

Sharp's Doom Bar, Cotleigh Tawny, Fuller's London Pride and St Austell Tribute are regularly featured, with two rotating every few weeks.

Harbourside pub overlooking River Torridge, with cosy bar and outside seating. Extensive menu and daily specials, including seafood, served 12–11pm every day in main season, plus morning coffee and tea from 9.30am. Children and pets welcome. Near historic quay, sandy beach and Tarka Trail. A mile and a half from A39, two and a half miles from Bideford.

OPEN *9.30am–11.30pm (12am at weekends).*

Wayfarer Inn
Lane End, Instow EX39 4LB
☎ *(01271) 860342* Royston Dennis
www.thewayfarerinstow.co.uk

Enterprise Inns pub serving one Sharp's and one Skinner's ale plus one guest.

A traditional family-run pub situated in a pretty coastal village, one minute from the beach. Restaurant offering an extensive menu including locally caught fish, serving food 12–3pm and 6–9pm. Sun-trap beer garden. Accommodation with B&B. Children welcome. Three gold AA stars. Off the B3233 from Barnstaple.

OPEN *11am–11pm.*

KILMINGTON
The New Inn
Kilmington, Axminster EX13 7SF
☎ *(01297) 33376*

Beers from JC and RH Palmer including Copper Ale, IPA and seasonal brews such as Dorset Gold.

The building dates back to the 14th century and was rebuilt after a fire in 2004. A thatched village pub with large beer garden and skittle alley. Food served lunchtimes and evenings.

OPEN *11am–2.30pm and 7–11pm Mon–Fri; 11am–3pm and 6–11pm Sat; 12–4pm and 7–10.30pm Sun.*

KINGSBRIDGE
The Pilchard Inn
Burgh Island, Bigbury-on-Sea, Nr Kingsbridge TQ7 4BG
☎ *(01548) 810514* Anthony Orchard
www.burghisland.com

Freehouse serving alternating local brews from St Austell and Teignworthy breweries, and cider from Heron Valley.

Small pub dating from the 14th century on a tidal island. Owned and run by the owners of the island, with its famous Art Deco hotel. Food served every lunchtime. Early booking suggested for curry night on Fridays, and 'fishy' night on Saturdays. Children welcome. Top bar reserved for hotel residents and regulars. Beer garden. Accessed by sea tractor, when the tide is in!

OPEN *11am–11.30pm.*

KINGSWEAR
The Ship Inn
Higher Street, Kingswear, Dartmouth TQ6 0AG
☎ *(01803) 752348* Colin and Heather Lang
www.theshipinnkingswear.co.uk

Four or five real ales, perhaps including Fuller's London Pride, Greene King IPA, Adnams Bitter and Otter Ale.

Traditional 15th-century pub next to the church. Two bars, log fires plus dining room. Food served 12.30–2.30pm and 7–9.30pm Mon–Sat. Views of the River Dart. Quiz night Tues, games night Thurs. Outside seating. Local CAMRA Pub of the Year 2006.

OPEN *11am–11.30pm Mon–Sat; 12–11pm Sun.*

LAPFORD
The Old Malt Scoop Inn
Lapford, Nr Crediton EX17 6PZ
☎ *(01363) 83330* Colin Comasso

Marston's Pedigree, Otter Best, Sharp's Doom Bar and Special Ale plus a couple of guests. Also traditional cider.

This 16th-century freehouse is open for morning coffee, bar snacks, meals and cream teas. There are inglenook fireplaces, beamed ceilings, panelled walls, skittle alley, beer garden, patio areas and car park. Children are allowed in the sun lounge and one of the bars. Lapford is on the A377 between Crediton and Barnstaple. Follow brown tourist signs near village. The inn is at the centre of the village, opposite the church.

OPEN *12–4pm and 6–11pm Mon–Fri; 12–11pm Sat; 12–4pm and 7–11pm Sun.*

LOWER ASHTON
The Manor Inn
Lower Ashton, Teign Valley EX6 7QL
☎ *(01647) 252304* Joseph and Diane O'Toole

Freehouse serving Teignworthy Reel Ale and Exmoor Ale plus two weekly guests such as Cotleigh Snowy, Fuller's London Pride, Courage Directors or Teignworthy Neap Tide and Ebb Tide.

Informal rural pub in the heart of the scenic Teign Valley. All meals are home-cooked, and are served 12–2.30pm and 6–9pm Mon–Sat, 1–5pm Sun. Children are welcome until 7pm, and the pub is dog-friendly. Car park. Located just off the B3193, about five miles from Chudleigh.

OPEN *12–2.30pm and 6–11pm Mon–Thurs; all day Fri–Sun except bank holidays.*

LUNDY ISLAND
Marisco Tavern
Lundy Island, Bristol Channel EX39 2LY
☎ *(01237) 431831* Derek Green
www.lundyisland.co.uk

A freehouse. St Austell Old Light and Lundy Experience (both house ales).

The self-proclaimed hub of island life, with a warm and welcoming atmosphere. Log fire in winter, picnic garden in summer. Island produce, when available, served in a separate restaurant 8–10.30am, 12–2.30pm and 6–9pm.

OPEN *11am–11pm for drinks, but the door is open 24/7.*

LUTTON
The Mountain Inn
Old Chapel Road, Lutton, Nr Ivybridge PL21 9SA
☎ *(01752) 837247* Jane Owen

A freehouse. Princetown Jail Ale and three guests such as Royal Oak ESB, Brains Rev James, Otter Tawny and Shepherd Neame Bishops Finger.

A 17th-century country village pub. One bar, lounge area, open fire. Children and dogs welcome. Annual beer festival. Cask Marque awarded. Food served 12–2pm and 6–9pm every day except Tues.

OPEN *12–close (4.30pm Tues).*

LYMPSTONE
Redwing
Church Road, Lympstone EX8 5JT
☎ *(01395) 222156* Dave and Jackie Moir

Greene King Abbot, Palmers IPA and Otter Bitter are permanents, plus one guest.

Atmospheric local in attractive village on the River Exe estuary. Home-cooked food every session except Sunday evening. Children over 5 welcome in the restaurant area. Garden and car park.

OPEN *11am–3pm and 6–11pm Mon–Fri; all day Sat–Sun.*

MARY TAVY
The Mary Tavy Inn
Lane Head, Mary Tavy PL19 9PN
☎ *(01822) 810326* Mr Brown

Freehouse serving Princetown Jail Ale and two guests that often include something from Sharp's.

Unpretentious and welcoming 400-year-old roadside community pub which has undergone complete refurbishment. Public bar and restaurant. Children welcome. Food every session. Accommodation. Garden and car park. Pool and darts. On the A386.

OPEN *All day, every day.*

MILTON COMBE
Who'd Have Thought It
Milton Combe, Yelverton PL20 6HP
☎ *(01822) 853313* Chris Lisney
www.whodhavethoughtitdevon.co.uk

Skinners beers plus Dartmoor Jail Ale always available.

Lovely pub, friendly staff, excellent ale. Seasonal menu with daily specials.

OPEN *12–3pm and 6–11pm; 10.30pm Sun.*

MONKLEIGH
The Bell Inn
Monkleigh, Bideford EX39 5JS
☎ *(01805) 622338*
www.bellinnmonkleigh.mysite.wanadoo-members.co.uk

Genuine freehouse offering Barum Original plus two guests changed every two weeks from a wide range including Clearwater, Sharp's and Burrington.

A 16th-century thatched village pub with one bar and three drinking areas including a lounge and dining area. Food served 12–9pm. Pool and darts, live music, entertainment, beer garden (the local village shop operates from here). Car park. Children allowed.

OPEN *11am–11pm Mon–Sat; 12–10.30pm Sun.*

MORTEHOE

The Chichester Arms

Chapel Hill, Mortehoe, Woolacombe EX34 7DU
☎ *(01271) 870411* John and Marsha Huxtable

 Barum Original and a Cottage brew plus two guests, changed every week or two.

Mortehoe's original village inn, built as cottages for the church wardens in 1620. Converted in 1820, it is basically unchanged since and is still partly gas lit, although it does also have its own electricity generator. Homemade traditional meals and fresh seafood served 12–2pm and 6.30–9pm every day in the award-winning restaurant. Beer garden, children's room. Families welcome. Car park. One mile from Woolacombe's famous beach.

OPEN *Winter: 12–2.30pm and 6–11pm. Summer: 12–12.*

NEWTON ABBOT

Dartmouth Inn

63 East Street, Newton Abbot TQ12 2JP
☎ *(01626) 353451* Francis McBride

Princetown Dartmoor IPA plus four regularly changing guest beers (up to 500 per year) which may include RCH East Street Cream, Sarah Hughes Dark Ruby Mild, Teignworthy Springtide and Sutton Knickerdroppa Glory. Plus their own brews, Mischief and Rascal.

This 450-year-old pub is reputed to be the oldest inn in Newton Abbot. Beautiful beer garden, a previous Bloom of Britain winner. Regional CAMRA Pub of the Year winner on several occasions. Five minutes' walk from the station. Bed and breakfast.

OPEN *11am–11pm Mon–Sat; 12–10.30pm Sun.*

NEWTON POPPLEFORD

Cannon Inn

High Street, Newton Poppleford EX10 0DW
☎ *(01395) 568266* Karen Worts

Sharp's Doom Bar, plus two or three weekly guests such as Ringwood Best Bitter, Otter Bitter and Theakston Old Peculier.

Welcoming village pub with real log fires in the winter. Separate dining area serves 'proper' pub food, locally sourced and cooked fresh to order, and available 12–2.30pm and 6–9.30pm. Accommodation. Beer garden, skittle alley and car park.

OPEN *11am–2.30pm and 5.30–11pm Mon–Sat; 12–2.30pm and 6–10.30pm Sun.*

NEWTON ST CYRES

The Beer Engine

Sweetham, Newton St Cyres, Nr Exeter EX5 5AX
☎ *(01392) 851282* Mike and Jan Tutty
www.thebeerengine.co.uk

Rail Ale, Piston Bitter and Sleeper Heavy brewed on the premises and always available. Seasonals brewed occasionally.

The brewery was established along with a cellar bar in the basement of a former station hotel in 1983. It has now expanded

to produce three brews and supplies local pubs and wholesalers. Homemade food available at lunchtimes and evenings. Car park, garden. Children allowed.

OPEN *11am–11pm Mon–Sat; 12–10.30pm Sun.*

NORTH TAWTON

Fountain Inn

Exeter Street, North Tawton EX20 2HB
☎ *(01837) 82551*

Freehouse with St Austell Daylight Robbery, Charles Wells Bombardier, and Greene King Old Speckled Hen always available.

A large, lively and friendly pub. Separate dining area. Food at lunchtimes and evenings. Well-behaved children allowed.

OPEN *11.30am–2.30pm and 5.30–11pm Mon–Fri; all day Sat–Sun.*

Railway Inn

Whiddon Down Road, North Tawton EX20 2BE
☎ *(01837) 82789* Claire and Bert Bolt

Freehouse always serving Teignworthy Reel Ale. The two guests, changed every few days, might include beers such as Skinner's Cornish Knocker and something from Blackawton.

Unique, hidden, rural Victorian pub offering a warm, friendly welcome. It was built to house the railway engineers when the line was being constructed, and features one bar, a dining room and a garden. Food available in the evenings (except Thurs). Children welcome. Car park. In the middle of Devon, four miles from Dartmoor and one mile south of North Tawton.

OPEN *6–11pm Mon–Thurs; 12–3pm and 6–11pm Fri–Sat; 12–3pm and 7–10.30pm Sun.*

NOSS MAYO

The Ship Inn

Noss Mayo PL8 1EW
☎ *(01752) 872387* Charlie and Lisa Bullock
www.nossmayo.com

 Freehouse serving Summerskills Tamar and Princetown Jail Ale plus a guest changed every few months, such as Butcombe Blonde or something from Bath Ales.

A waterside village pub with great character and a warm welcome, featuring a library full of books and an open fire. A room called 'The Bridge' overlooks the water, while downstairs is a traditional bar with stone and wood floors. Food 12–9.30pm. The car park is tidal! Beer garden. In the centre of Noss Mayo.

OPEN *11am–11pm Mon–Sat; 12–10.30pm Sun.*

OKEHAMPTON

Plymouth Inn

26 West Street, Okehampton EX20 1HH
☎ *(01837) 53633* Jeff and Dee Smith

Freehouse, with beers served straight from the barrel. Accent on brews from the West Country, though others are often featured.

A country-style town pub with restaurant, beer garden and function room. Local CAMRA Pub of the Year 2002. Mini beer festivals and occasional folk bands. Food at lunchtime and evenings. Children allowed; function room doubles as children's room.

OPEN *11am–midnight.*

OTTERY ST MARY

The Kings Arms

Gold Street, Ottery St Mary EX10 1GT
☎ *(01404) 812486* Graham Hudson

Branscombe Vale Summa That and Branoc are generally available, plus Hell's Bells in the winter.

U npretentious town-centre local with large-screen TV. Car park. Pool and darts. Two beer festivals held each year. Karaoke Sun evening.

OPEN *6–11pm Mon–Fri; 11am–11pm Sat; 12–10.30pm Sun.*

PAIGNTON

The Isaac Merritt

54–8 Torquay Road, Paignton TQ3 3AA
☎ *(01803) 566066* Colin Bianco
www.jdwetherspoon.co.uk

JD Wetherspoon's pub serving Marston's Pedigree and Burton and Greene King Abbot Ale plus a house ale: Isaac's Own, brewed for the pub by Sharp's. Up to seven guests from a range of independent breweries across the south-west.

O pened in 1997, in a building converted from an indoor market and named after the inventor of Singer sewing machines. A locals' pub with a focus on real ale. Food 9am–11pm daily. Plans for a beer garden. Mini-beer festival every week, where the focus is on one brewery at a time with at least four of their beers at a reduced price. Also takes part in the national JD Wetherspoon's beer festivals. Children welcome.

OPEN *9am–midnight.*

PARKHAM

The Bell Inn

Rectory Lane, Parkham, Bideford EX39 5PL
☎ *(01273) 451201* Michael and Rachel Sanders
www.thebellinnparkham.co.uk

Four real ales at this freehouse, including Fuller's London Pride, Greene King IPA and Sharp's Doom Bar, plus a guest, changed every cask, such as Skinner's Betty Stogs, Country Life Old Appledore, RCH Steam Sale or Exmoor Fox.

S teeped in history, this 13th-century thatched village inn has traditional oak beams, cob walls and open fires. Renowned by locals for its homemade, traditionally cooked food, which is served 12–1.30pm and 5 or 6pm–8.30 or 9pm. Beer festival first weekend in June. From the A39 turn inland and go through Horns Cross.

OPEN *12–2pm and 5pm–12.*

PETER TAVY

Peter Tavy Inn

Peter Tavy, Tavistock PL19 9NN
☎ *(01822) 810348* Chris and Jo Wordingham

Freehouse serving Princetown Jail Ale, Sharp's Doom Bar and Blackawton Original on a permanent basis plus one or two guests that might include beers such as St Austell HSD and Cotleigh Golden Seahawk.

C harming 15th-century inn serving good food and real ale in an attractive Dartmoor village. Two large rooms, flagstone floors, low beams and real fires. Children and dogs welcome. Beer garden, patio and car park. Located within Dartmoor National Park. Walkers and cyclists welcome. One mile off the A386 two miles north of Tavistock.

OPEN *12–3.30pm and 6–11pm (10.30pm Sun).*

PILTON

The Reform Inn

Reform Street, Pilton, Barnstaple EX31 1PD
☎ *(01271) 323164* Esther and Gavin Davies

A wide variety of Barum ales always available.

F riendly village pub, a former ale/cider house, with a music focus. Sandwiches available. Pool table and shove ha'penny, plus a skittle alley that is available for hire. Live music at weekends. The Barum Brewery is situated behind the pub, but is separately owned.

OPEN *11.30am–11pm Mon–Thurs; 11.30am–midnight Fri–Sat; 12–11pm Sun.*

PLYMOUTH

The Boringdon Arms

Turnchapel, Plymouth PL9 9TQ
☎ *(01752) 402053* Barry and Elizabeth Elliott
www.boringdonarms.co.uk

A Punch Taverns pub with brews from Butcombe, Otter, Plymouth Pride, Summerskills and RCH.

A n old terraced pub with lounge and public bar. Food served 12–2pm and 6–9pm Mon–Sat; 12–2pm and 6–8pm Sun. Courtyard, conservatory and beer garden. Accommodation. Six beer festivals per year. Close to Mountbatten Water Sports Centre and on a coastal path.

OPEN *11am–midnight Mon–Sat; 12–11.30pm Sun.*

The Clifton
35 Clifton Street, Greenbank, Plymouth PL4 8JB
☎ *(01752) 266563* Mr Clark

Clifton Classic (house beer brewed by Summerskills) always on offer. Two guests, changed weekly, may include beers from anywhere in the UK, with Orkney Dark Island a particular favourite.

A locals' pub, with one bar and Sky TV for football. No food. No children. Not far from the railway station.

OPEN *3.30–11pm Mon–Thurs; 11am–11pm Fri–Sat; 12–10.30pm Sun.*

Porters
20 Looe Street, Plymouth PL4 0EA
☎ *(01752) 662485* Denise Vessey

Six real ales, changed every two or three days. Sharp's Doom Bar, Greene King Old Speckled Hen and Fuller's London Pride regularly featured.

Town-centre pub with exposed brickwork and lots of bric-à-brac. Background music. Raised area at top of pub for eating. Beer garden. Food served at lunchtimes and evenings. Children allowed.

OPEN *12–11pm (9pm Sun).*

The Prince Maurice
3 Church Hill, Eggbuckland, Plymouth PL6 5RJ
☎ *(01752) 771515* RG Dodds

Eight real ales, including Summerskills Best, RCH East Street Cream, Sharp's Doom Bar and Adnams Broadside, plus many and various guest beers.

Small, 17th-century detached freehouse with two bars and log fires. Regular CAMRA Pub of the Year winner. Weekday lunchtime bar snacks. Car park, patio. In the city suburbs, to the north.

OPEN *11am–3pm and 7–11pm Mon–Thurs; 11am–11pm Fri–Sat; 12–10.30pm Sun.*

Sippers
18 Millbay Road, Plymouth PL1 3LH
☎ *(01752) 670668* Pierre and Hazel Renon
www.sipperspub.co.uk

An Enterprise Inns pub with Greene King Old Speckled Hen, Marston's Pedigree, Otter Ale and a Butcombe brew.

A character food-led pub just off the city centre and situated by Millbay ferry port. Food served 11.30am–2.30pm and 5.30–9.30pm. Children welcome. Beer garden.

OPEN *11am–midnight Mon–Sat; 11am–11pm Sun.*

Thistle Park Brewhouse
32 Commercial Road, Plymouth PL4 0LE
☎ *(01752) 204890* Quintin Style

Five brews from South Hams always available, namely XSB, Devon Pride, Eddystone Light, Wild Blonde and Old Pedantic.

Polished wooden floors feature in this maritime pub with roof terrace and Thai restaurant. Food served lunchtimes and evenings every day. Live music Sat and Sun 4–6pm. Great loos! Beer garden, private

room. Beer festivals. Well-behaved children allowed. Handy for Warner Village.

OPEN *10am–2am.*

The Boringdon Arms
13 Boringdon Terrace, Turnchapel, Nr Plymstock PL9 9TQ
☎ *(01752) 402053* Barry Elliott
www.bori.co.uk.

Butcombe Bitter and RCH Pitchfork plus four guests beers (250 per year) from Orkney (north), Butts (south), Skinner's (west), Scott's (east) and all points in between.

Ex-quarrymaster's house with a good atmosphere. No juke box. Live music on Saturday nights. Bar food available at lunchtimes and evenings. Conservatory, plus beer garden and courtyard in the old quarry to the rear of the pub. Accommodation. Bi-monthly beer festivals. Located at the centre of the village, four miles south-east of Plymouth, on south coast footpath. Signposted from the A379.

OPEN *11am–midnight Mon–Sat; 12–10.30pm Sun.*

The Blacksmith's Arms
Plymtree, Cullompton EX15 2JU
☎ *(01884) 277474*
Bruce Blackmore and Rachel Stephens

Freehouse serving O'Hanlon's Yellowhammer plus one guest which might be O'Hanlon's Firefly or St Austell Tinner's Ale. Guest changed weekly.

A 19th-century community pub with one bar and beamed ceilings. Food served every evening and Sat–Sun lunchtimes. Children welcome. Skittles. Separate pool room. Boules piste. Beer garden. Small car park. Signposted from A373.

OPEN *6–11pm Mon–Sun; 11am–3pm Sat; 12–4pm Sun.*

The Prince of Wales
Tavistock Road, Princetown PL20 6QF
☎ *(01822) 890219* Mr and Mrs Baker

Princetown Jail Ale and Dartmoor IPA plus one guest, with beers from St Austell a regular feature.

Family-run bar in a 150-year-old building, full of character. The pub has a dining area and a separate restaurant seating 60, which can be booked for functions. Food is available all day. Children allowed. En-suite bed and breakfast. Car park.

OPEN *11am–11pm Mon–Sat; 12–10.30pm Sun.*

RINGMORE
The Journey's End
Ringmore, Nr Kingsbridge TQ7 4HL
☎ *(01548) 810205* Juliet Kane
www.thejourneysendinn.co.uk

 Sharp's Doom Bar is the house bitter, with two other guests, changed weekly. These include Princetown Jail Ale and Teignworthy Neap Tide.

A 13th-century inn offering good food and a sun-drenched beer garden! Food served 12.30–2.45pm and 6–9.30pm. Function room for private dinners available. Families and dogs welcome. Large car park. Lovely coastal walks nearby. Turn off A38 at Modbury, continue through Modbury, turn right at St Anne's Chapel, drive into Ringmore and park opposite the church. The inn is 150 metres down the hill.

OPEN *12–3pm and 6pm–close Tues–Sun (closed Monday). Open all day at the weekends.*

ST GILES IN THE WOOD
The Cranford Inn
St Giles In The Wood, Torrington EX38 7LA
☎ *(01805) 623309* Steve Lock
www.cranfordinn.com

 Genuine freehouse with its own brewery - The Fremington Brewery. Fremington Beer (IPA and Nugget), plus 1 guest ale.

Old character country pub with low ceilings and beer garden. Top-quality food served every lunchtime and evening. All produce is sourced locally, and home-smoked food and homemade sausages are available. Well-behaved children are allowed – the staff are the judges of 'well-behaved'! Between Torrington and Umberleigh on the B3227.

OPEN *12–2.30pm and 6–11pm Mon–Fri; all day Sat–Sun.*

SIDBURY
The Hare & Hounds
Putts Corner, Sidbury, Sidmouth EX10 0QQ
☎ *(01404) 41760*
Lindsey and Tracy Chun and Graham Cole
www.hareandhounds-devon.co.uk

 Part of the small Heartstone Inns chain with three local real ales in winter, four in summer, namely Otter Bitter and Ale and Branscombe Best. Guests come from Otter, Branscombe and other local breweries.

A large, characterful, rural pub specialising in quality food and real ale. Renowned locally for its carvery. Food served 12–9.15pm. Comfy sofas, family room. Extensive gardens with stunning views down the Sid Valley to the sea. Two large car parks. Outdoor children's play area. Halfway between Honiton and Sidbury on the A375.

OPEN *10am–11pm Mon–Sat; 11am–10.30pm Sun.*

Red Lion
Fore Street, Sidbury EX10 0SD
☎ *(01395) 597313* Margaret Bolt

 Freehouse serving Wadworth 6X and Otter Bitter plus one guest, changed weekly.

Friendly traditional local, a former coaching inn, with wooden beams and brasses. This 400-year-old pub has parts that were rebuilt following a fire in 1836, and is situated in a quaint 'chocolate-box' Saxon village with a Norman church. Food served 12–2pm and 6.30–9pm (not Sun evening) – the chef has worked in a Michelin-star restaurant in London. Children welcome. Garden. Darts and skittles. B&B accommodation. Occasional beer festival. Crealy Park donkey sanctuary is nearby, and the seaside is only a mile and a half away.

OPEN *12–3pm and 6–11pm (midnight Fri–Sat).*

SIDMOUTH
The Swan Inn
37 York Street, Sidmouth EX10 8BY
☎ *(01395) 512849* Adrian Ricketts

 A Wells and Young's pub offering the full range, including seasonal brews.

A traditional pub. Local fish is a speciality. Food served 12–2pm and 6–9pm. Beer garden, close to the river. Beer festivals in the summer. A hundred yards on the left past the lifeboat station.

OPEN *11am–2.30pm (3pm Sat) and 5.30–11pm (10.30pm Sun).*

SILVERTON
The Lamb Inn
Fore Street, Silverton EX5 4HZ
☎ *(01392) 860272* Alan Isaac

 Freehouse offering three real ales. The selection might include Cotleigh Tawny, Exe Valley Dobs or Hop Back Back Row. Guests changed every four to six weeks. All gravity fed.

Village pub with stone floors, stripped timber and old pine tables. Home-cooked food served 12–2pm and 7–9.15pm. Children welcome. Disabled facilities. Function room for hire with its own bar and skittle alley. Close to Killerton House (NT). One mile from A396.

OPEN *11.30am–2.30pm and 6–11pm Mon–Fri; 11am–11pm Sat–Sun.*

Silverton Inn
Fore Street, Silverton, Nr Exeter EX5 4HP
☎ *(01392) 860196* Shane Radmore
www.silvertoninn.com

 Theakston Best and O'Hanlon's Royal Oak plus a weekly guest such as Exmoor Fox, Wadworth 6X or Cotleigh Tawny. Many local beers featured.

Traditional Victorian pub offering homemade cooking, great beer and accommodation. Food served 6–8pm Mon–Fri, 11am–1.30pm Sat and 12–2pm Sun. Comfortable single, twin and double rooms available all year. Handy for Westpoint, M5 and Exeter, with Killerton House, a National Trust property, only a mile away.

OPEN *12–2.30pm and 6–11pm Mon–Fri; 11am–midnight Sat; 12–10.30pm Sun.*

SLAPTON
The Tower Inn
Church Road, Slapton, Nr Kingsbridge TQ7 2PN
☎ *(01548) 580216*
Andrew and Annette Hammett
www.thetowerinn.com

 Butcombe Bitter, St Austell Tribute and Badger Tanglefoot plus two guests, changed monthly.

A 14th-century inn with a superb garden, low ceilings and log fires. Bar and restaurant food available 12–2pm and 7–9pm. Car park. Accommodation (three en-suite double rooms). Hidden in the centre of the village at the foot of the old ruined tower. Between Dartmouth and Kingsbridge on the A379.

OPEN *12–3pm and 6–11pm (7–10.30pm Sun); closed Sun night and all day Mon in winter.*

SOUTH BRENT
Royal Oak
Station Road, South Brent, TQ10 9BE
☎ *(01364) 72133* Andrew and Carol Doree
www.royaloaksouthbrent.co.uk

 Teignworthy Reel Ale, Beachcomber and one guest, constantly changing between local and national brews. Dark Island, Princetown, Adnams, Skinners and Red Rock breweries have all featured.

A Victorian village community freehouse. Bar area and upstairs restaurant and function room. Five B&B rooms and a new bistro overlooking the courtyard. Fresh homemade food at good prices served 12–2pm and 6–9pm Mon–Sat and 12–2.30pm and 6–8.30pm Sun. South Devon CAMRA Pub of the Year 2007. Wi-Fi available in the bar area. Situated on the edge of Dartmoor. Leave the A38 towards South Brent, and the pub is in the centre of the village.

OPEN *12–11pm Sun–Thurs; 12–11.45pm Fri–Sat.*

SOUTH MOLTON
The Sportsman's Inn
Sandyway, South Molton EX36 3LU
☎ *(01643) 831109* Martin Macro
www.sportsmansinn.co.uk

 Freehouse offering two real ales, with beers from Exmoor and St Austell the regular favourites, plus weekly changing guests.

Former tellers' cottages for the Royal Forest of Exmoor, with beams, fireplaces and a well in the bar! Bar snacks, à la carte menu and specials served 12–2pm (seasonal) and 7–9pm (all year), plus Sunday carvery. Pool and skittles. Beer garden, function room. Three double en-suite B&B rooms. Car park. Between the villages of North Molton and Withypool.

OPEN *7–11pm Mon–Sat; 12–3pm and 7–11pm Sun. Also open 12–2.30pm Wed–Fri from April to Sept.*

SOUTH ZEAL
Oxenham Arms
South Zeal, Okehampton EX20 2JT
☎ *(01837) 840244* Mark Payne
www.theoxenhamarms.co.uk

Freehouse offering two or three real ales including Sharp's Doom Bar plus guests changed at least weekly.

A truly magnificent 12th-century coaching inn nestling right on the edge of Dartmoor. Exciting restaurant, with food available at all times. Wonderful garden. Children and dog friendly. Just off the old A30 to Okehampton.

OPEN *11am–11pm.*

SPREYTON
The Tom Cobley Tavern
Spreyton, Nr Crediton EX17 5AL
☎ *(01647) 231314* Roger and Carol Cudlip

Freehouse with up to 20 real ales from a huge range. Popular beers include Woodham Cornish Mutiny, Cotleigh Barn Owl and Peregrine, Clearwater Cavalier and Oliver's Nectar, O'Hanlon's Royal Oak and Cottage Evening Star.

This is the pub from which, in 1802, Uncle Tom Cobley left to go to Widecombe Fair. The inn dates from 1589 and is situated in the heart of a quiet, unspoilt village. CAMRA National Pub of the Year 2006. Homemade food served at all opening times. Children welcome. Indoor BBQ. Accommodation in six rooms (three en-suite). Beer garden. In easy reach of Dartmoor, Exmoor and beaches.

OPEN *All day, every day, except Mon lunchtime.*

STAVERTON
Sea Trout Inn
Staverton, Nr Totnes TQ9 6PA
☎ *(01803) 762274* Nick and Nicky Brookland

A Palmers pub offering IPA, Gold and 200.

Many people's idea of the idyllic Devon inn. Nice local feel to public bar and a large lounge bar. Food served every session, on very big plates! Children welcome. Car park and garden. Accommodation.

OPEN *11am–3pm and 6–11pm Mon–Sat; 12–3pm and 7–10.30pm Sun.*

STICKLEPATH
Devonshire Inn
Sticklepath, Okehampton EX20 2NW
☎ *(01837) 840626*
John and Ann Verner-Jeffreys

Freehouse serving St Austell Tinners and Hicks Special Draught straight from the barrel and cooled from passing stream.

Thatched pub with loads of character. Keys hang from low beams, and there is a big fireplace and strange photographs. Food if ordered in advance, also bar snacks. Children allowed but not in bar area. Car park. Garden. Dogs welcome. Accommodation only with dogs. Bar billiards and other games.

OPEN *11am–3pm and 5–11pm Mon–Thur; all day Fri–Sat; 12–3pm and 7–10.30pm Sun.*

STOKENHAM

The Tradesman's Arms

Stokenham, Kingsbridge TQ7 2SZ
☎ *(01548) 580313* Nick Abington Abbott
www.thetradesmansarms.com

 The permanent beers here are Brakspear Bitter, Bass, South Hams Devon Pride and either Porter or Eddystone, also from South Hams. The Porter or Eddystone is served direct from the cask, and a guest beer is changed regularly.

Welcoming, picturesque country pub with lots of character, half 14th-century thatched and half Georgian with slates. Three separate areas with a fire in each. Restaurant-quality food served every session except Mon night. Beer garden, car park. Just off the A379 (follow brown tourist signs), overlooking the village green. One mile from Slapton Sands, famous for D-Day practice landings, and half a mile from South Hams Brewery.

OPEN *11.30am–3pm and 6pm–12. Open all day Sat–Sun in good summer weather.*

TALATON

Talaton Inn

Talaton, Ottery St Mary EX5 2RQ
☎ *(01404) 822214* Jan Walasckowski

 Freehouse with beers from Otter and O'Hanlon's plus two guests, changed monthly, such as Theakston Old Peculiar, Fuller's London Pride and Greene King Abbot.

A 16th-century inn with two bars, a restaurant and skittle alley. Outside seating to front of pub. Covered smoking area. Dogs and children welcome. Food served 12–2.15pm and 7–9.15pm. Take the old A30 to Fairmile from Ottery St Mary, and follow signs to Talaton village.

OPEN *12–3pm and 6–11pm.*

TAVISTOCK

The Halfway House

Grenofen, Tavistock PL19 9ER
☎ *(01822) 612960* Peter Jones

 Freehouse serving Sharp's Doom Bar Ale, Sharp's Special, Fuller's London Pride and Shepherd Neame Spitfire plus one guest.

Country inn on the A386. Public bar. Background music. Separate dining and lounge bar. Food, with emphasis on the homemade, served every lunchtime and evening. Children allowed. Pets welcome. En-suite accommodation available.

OPEN *11.30am–2.30pm and 5.30–11pm Mon–Sat; 12–3pm and 6.30–10.30pm Sun.*

The Trout & Tipple

Parkwood Road, Tavistock PL19 0JS
☎ *(01822) 618886*
www.troutandtipple.co.uk

 Princetown Brewery Jail Ale plus three guests.

A traditional country pub with bar, dining room, games room and outdoor patio. Food served 12–2pm and 6.30–9pm Mon–Sat (except Tues lunch); 12–2pm and 7–9pm Sun. Children and dogs welcome. Car park.

Regular beer festivals. On the A386 towards Okehampton.

OPEN *12–2.30pm and 6–11pm Mon; 6–11pm Tues; 12–2.30pm and 6–11pm Wed–Sat; 12–2.30pm and 7–10.30pm Sun (6.30pm in summer).*

TEIGNMOUTH

The Blue Anchor

Teign Street, Teignmouth TQ14 8EG
☎ *(01626) 772741* Paul Fellows

 Freehouse serving Adnams Broadside, Marston's Pedigree and Teignworthy Reel Ale. Three guests, changed two or three times a week, include favourites such as Greene King Abbot, Fuller's ESB or something from Bateman or Branscombe Vale.

Small, very boozy, locals' pub. Old, with log fire. Rolls only. No children. Beer garden.

OPEN *11am–11pm Mon–Sat; 12–10.30pm Sun.*

TOPSHAM

Bridge Inn

Bridge Hill, Topsham, Nr Exeter EX3 0QQ
☎ *(01392) 873862*
Caroline Cheffers-Heard
www.cheffers.co.uk.

 Nine or ten real ales from breweries such as Branscombe Vale, Exe Valley, Otter, Blackawton, Teignworthy, Adnams and O'Hanlon's.

This 16th-century pub overlooking the River Clyst has been in the same family since 1897 through four generations. Good, simple bar food at lunchtime. Car park with outside seating. Two miles from M5 junction 30. Topsham is signposted from the exit. In Topsham, follow the yellow signpost (A376) to Exmouth.

OPEN *12–2pm daily; 6–10.30pm Mon–Thurs; 6–11pm Fri–Sat; 7–10.30pm Sun.*

The Globe Hotel

Fore Street, Topsham EX3 0HR
☎ *(01392) 873471* Liz Hodges
www.globehotel.com

 Freehouse offering St Austell Dartmoor, Sharp's Doom Bar, Fuller's London Pride and Otter Ale plus one guest.

A 16th-century coaching inn with oak-panelled bar, at the heart of an AA 2 star hotel with café and restaurant. Modern British food served 12–2pm and 7–9.30pm Mon–Sat; breakfasts and lunches on Sun until 2pm. Car park. Folk club every Sun. Annual Town Criers festival on August bank holiday.

OPEN *11am–11pm Sun–Thurs; 11am–midnight Fri–Sat.*

Children allowed. On the A377 between
Barnstaple and Exeter.

TORQUAY

Chelston Manor

Old Mill Road, Torquay TQ2 6HW
☎ *(01803) 605142* Matt and Ferne
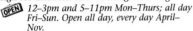Three guests, including beers such as
Sharp's Doom Bar, Shepherd Neame
Spitfire, Otter Ale and St Austell Tribute.

Unique olde-worlde pub in the heart of
Torquay. Home-cooked meals served 12–
2.30pm and 6–9.30pm. Large walled beer
garden. Car park. Children welcome. Follow
sign for Chelston and Cockington Village.

OPEN *12–3pm and 5–11pm Mon–Thurs; all day
Fri–Sun. Open all day, every day April–
Nov.*

Crown & Sceptre

2 Petitor Road, St Marychurch, Torquay TQ1 4QA
☎ *(01803) 328290* RD Wheeler
Eight real ales, including Young's Special,
Courage Best, Ottter Ale, Tribute,
Tanglefoot and Greene King Old Speckled
Hen, and two other guest ales.

A two-bar traditional local pub, around 200
years old. No TV or juke box. Food at
lunchtimes only. Music Tuesday and
Saturday. Children welcome. Beer garden, car
park. Handy for Babbacombe Model Village,
Cliff Railway and Bygones museum.

OPEN *12–11pm Sun–Thur; 12–12 Fri–Sat.*

TUCKENHAY

Maltsters Arms

Bow Creek, Tuckenhay, Nr Totnes TQ9 7EQ
☎ *(01803) 732350*
Quentin and Denise Thwaites
www.tuckenhay.com
Freehouse serving Princetown Dartmoor
IPA plus two or three guests, with
regulars from Teignworthy, South Hams,
Scattor Rock, Blackawton, Cottage and
Exmoor. Over 150 different guests served last
year. Young's Special London Ale (bottle
conditioned) is also stocked.

Country pub with separate eating area
overlooking the river. B&B in themed
rooms. Barbecues on the river bank.
Occasional live music, annual beer festival.
Food served 12–3pm and 7–9.30pm (except
Christmas Day), with cream teas in summer.
Darts, chess, backgammon and shut the box.
No piped music or gaming machines.
Children allowed in certain areas. Free
moorings for boats. In the middle of
nowhere – if you find Tuckenhay, you'll find
the pub.

OPEN *11am–11pm (12–2pm Christmas Day).*

UMBERLEIGH

The Rising Sun

Umberleigh EX37 9DU
☎ *(01769) 560447* Malcolm Andrew Hogg
Cotleigh Tawny Bitter and Barn Owl.

Inn in a traditional building, with
restaurant, patio and nine bedrooms. Local
folk musicians have jamming sessions every
Monday (not bank holidays). Car park.

Children allowed. On the A377 between
Barnstaple and Exeter.

OPEN *11.30am–3pm and 6–11pm (10.30pm
Sun).*

WEST DOWN

The Crown Inn

The Square, West Down EX34 8NF
☎ *(01271) 862790* Ray and Margaret Pearce
Freehouse with Barum Original and
Greene King Abbot plus one guest beer,
changed regularly.

A small 17th-century village pub with open
fire and delightful garden. Food served in
separate restaurant 12–2pm and 6.30–9pm,
with seafood and homemade local dishes a
speciality. Children welcome. B&B
accommodation. Car park. Handy for
Exmoor and the beaches at Croyd and
Woolacombe. Follow tourist signs between
Braunton and Ilfracombe and Lynton Cross
and Mullacott Cross.

OPEN *12–2.30pm and 6.30–11pm.*

WESTCOTT

Merry Harriers Inn

*Merry Harriers, Westcott, Nr Cullompton
EX15 1SA*
☎ *(01392) 881254*
Simon and Annabel McCabe
O'Hanlon's Yellowhammer and Firefly,
Cotleigh Tawny, Exmoor Ale and up to
two seasonal ales are always available at this
freehouse.

A traditional country pub dating back 400
years, on the site of an old forge. Food
made from locally sourced produce served
every day 12–2pm and 6.30–9pm. Children
welcome. Beer garden. Skittle alley. Function
room for hire. Car park. Accommodation. On
the B3181 near Cullompton.

OPEN *12–3pm and 6pm–12 (subject to seasonal
variation).*

WESTWARD HO!

Pig on the Hill

West Pusehill, Westward Ho!, Bideford EX39 5AH
☎ *(01237) 425889* Simon Curtis
www.pigonthehill.co.uk
The original home to the Country Life
Brewery, with the four beers rotated on
the pumps.

Friendly country inn in rural setting with
food available each session. Games room,
garden, terrace and children's play area.
Petanque club. Car park.

OPEN *12–3pm and 6.30–11pm Mon–Sat; 12–
3pm and 7–10.30pm Sun.*

WHIDDON DOWN
Post Inn
Exeter Road, Whiddon Down, Okehampton EX20 2QT
☎ *(01647) 231242* Miriam Short

 Freehouse always offering three or four local brews but always changing, perhaps something from Exe Valley or Scattor Rock.

Popular roadside pub. Serves a nice pint but also food-orientated. One bar for three areas. Children welcome. Car park. Patio.

OPEN *11am–11pm Mon–Sat (closed all day Tues); 12–10.30pm Sun.*

WHIMPLE
New Fountain Inn
Church Road, Whimple, Exeter EX5 2TA
☎ *(01404) 822350* Paul Mallett

Freehouse with Teignworthy Reel Ale and Beachcomber served straight from the barrel.

Family-run village pub, around 200 years old, with two bars on two tiers. Food served 12–2pm every day, plus 6.30–9pm Mon–Sat and 7–9pm Sun. Children and dogs welcome. The heritage centre situated in the pub car park is open Easter to the end of September (2–4pm Wed and 10am–3.30pm Sat and bank holidays). Three miles from the Daisymount junction of the A30, halfway between Exeter and Honiton.

OPEN *12–2.30pm and 6.30–11pm Mon–Sat; 12–2.30pm and 7–10.30pm Sun.*

WINKLEIGH
The Kings Arms
Fore Street, Winkleigh EX19 8HQ
☎ *(01837) 83384*
Julia Franklin and Chris Guy

Sharp's Doom Bar and Cornish Coaster plus Butcombe Bitter are usually available. Also two Winkleigh ciders – Sam's Dry and Poundhouse.

Traditional, thatched country pub with oak beams and log fire, in the centre of a pretty village. Bars and separate dining rooms. Freshly prepared food available 11am–9.30pm Mon–Sat and 12–9pm Sun. Small beer garden. Dogs and children welcome. Follow signs 'To the village', and the pub is in the centre of the square.

OPEN *11am–11pm Mon–Sat; 12–10.30pm Sun.*

WOOLACOMBE
The Old Mill
Ossaborough Road, Woolacombe EX34 7HJ
☎ *(01271) 870237* D Huxtable

A beer from the Barum brewery is usually available, plus a couple of guests, changed weekly.

A 17th-century former mill overlooking Cleavewood House, with characteristic bar and original features. Food is served 12–9pm. Children are welcome, and there is an adventure playground. Outdoor dining, patio heaters, barbecues in the summer. Live entertainment. Take the first right-hand turning out of Woolacombe.

OPEN *Summer: 12–11pm. Closed Nov–Feb.*

YARDE DOWN
Poltimore Arms
Yarde Down, South Molton EX36 3HA
☎ *(01598) 710381* Richard Austen

Freehouse with real ales served straight from the barrel. Cotleigh Tawny Ale is always available, and during the summer there may well be a guest.

Dates back to 1600. Has its own generator for electricity. Food served; a very large menu. Children allowed. In the middle of nowhere; best to ring for directions.

OPEN *12–2.30pm and 6.30–11pm Mon–Sat; 12–2.30pm and 7–10.30pm Sun.*

YEOFORD
The Mare & Foal
The Village, Yeoford, Crediton EX17 5JD
☎ *(01363) 84348*
Alex and Karen Duxbury-Watkinson

Freehouse serving a range of real ales from independent breweries, including Sharp's, Badger, Peninsula, Teignworthy, Black Sheep, Otter and more.

Built in 1867 as a railway hotel with many owners and now consisting of two bars, three open fires, dining room, skittle alley and pool room. Homemade food from local produce cooked to order 12–2pm Tues–Sun and 6–9pm Mon–Sun. Children, dogs and walkers welcome. Large garden with pond. Car park. Two beer festivals per year. Three miles outside Crediton on Tarka train line. Seven miles from the A30 at Cheriton Bishop.

OPEN *12–3pm-ish Tues–Sun; 6pm–close Mon–Sun.*

THE BREWERIES

DORSET BREWING COMPANY (THE QUAY BREWERY)
Brewers Quay, Hope Square, Weymouth DT4 8TR
☎ *(01305) 777515*
www.fineale.com

WEYMOUTH HARBOUR MASTER 3.6% ABV
Rounded and easy-drinking.
SUMMER KNIGHT 3.8% ABV
Award-winning wheat beer. Available May–Oct.
WEYMOUTH BEST BITTER 4.0% ABV
Gold and well balanced.
WEYMOUTH JD 1742 4.2% ABV
Quenching bittersweet flavour.
STEAM BEER 4.5% ABV
Chocolate undertones, crisp bitterness.
JURASSIC 4.7% ABV
Medium body with honey hints.
DURDLE DOOR 5.0% ABV
Clean taste, with marmalade notes.
SILENT KNIGHT 5.8% ABV
Dark wheat beer. Seasonal

GOLDFINCH BREWERY
47 High East Street, Dorchester DT1 1HU
☎ *(01305) 264020*

TOM BROWN'S BEST BITTER 4.0% ABV
Hoppy throughout.
FLASHMAN'S CLOUT STRONG ALE 4.5% ABV
Occasional.
MIDNIGHT BLINDER 5.0% ABV
Sweet malt with balancing hoppiness.

HALL AND WOODHOUSE LTD
The Brewery, Blandford St Mary DT11 9LS
☎ *(01258) 452141*
www.badgerbrewery.com
www.hall-woodhouse.co.uk

KING AND BARNES SUSSEX 3.5% ABV
Clean, hoppy taste.
EXTRA SMOOTH 3.8% ABV
Smooth and creamy toffee aromas with citrus hop notes.
BADGER FIRST GOLD 4.0% ABV
Spicy, orange notes.
BADGER ORIGINAL 4.6% ABV
Smooth and fruity.
TANGLEFOOT 4.9% ABV
Pale, full fruit, with bittersweet finish.
Plus seasonal beers including:
FURSTY FERRET 4.4% ABV
FESTIVE FERRET 4.5% ABV
HOPPING HARE 4.5% ABV
RIVER COTTAGE STINGER 4.5% ABV

ISLE OF PURBECK BREWERY
Bankes Arms Hotel, Manor Road, Studland, Swanage BH19 3AU
☎ *(01929) 450225*

FOSSIL FUEL 4.1% ABV
SOLAR POWER 4.3% ABV
IPA 4.5% ABV
STUDLAND BAY WRECKED 4.5% ABV

JC AND RH PALMER LTD
The Old Brewery, West Bay Road, Bridport DT6 4JA
☎ *(01308) 422396*
www.palmersbrewery.com

COPPER ALE 3.7% ABV
Fruit throughout.
BEST BITTER 4.2% ABV
Well balanced and good hop character.
DORSET GOLD 4.5% ABV
Golden with delicate fruity hoppiness. Seasonal.
200 PREMIUM ALE 5.0% ABV
Smooth, full flavoured and complex.
TALLY HO! 5.5% ABV
Nutty and full flavoured. Seasonal.

SHERBORNE BREWERY
257 Westbury, Sherborne DT9 3EH
☎ *(01935) 817307*
www.sherbornebrewery.co.uk

257 3.9% ABV
CHEAP STREET 4.4% ABV
Plus seasonals.

THE PUBS

ASKERSWELL

The Spyway Inn
Askerswell, Dorchester DT2 9EP
☎ *(01308) 485250*
Kevin, Vivien and Tim Wilkes
www.spyway-inn.co.uk

Local ales from Otter, Exmoor and Butcombe. The selection changes every couple of months.

A friendly, 16th-century cottage inn with log fires, cosy bar and two dining areas. Home-cooked food from local produce served every day, with daily specials and Sunday roasts. Children welcome. Car park. Lovely, large, award-winning beer garden overlooking the rolling Dorset hills. Three en-suite letting rooms. Three miles from Bridport, off the A35 in the direction of Dorchester.

OPEN *12–3pm and 6pm–12 (all day in summer).*

BEAMINSTER

The Greyhound Inn
11 The Square, Beaminster DT8 3AW
☎ *(01308) 862496* Steven and Sally Stanners

Palmers house offering Best or IPA, Copper Ale and 200 plus Dorset Gold in summer, Tally Ho! in winter.

Small, warm and friendly one-bar local set right on the town square. Food served 12–2pm and 6.30–9pm (7–9pm Sun). Children welcome. Table skittles and darts. Parking on the square.

OPEN *11.30am–3pm and 6.30–11pm Mon–Fri; 11.30am–11pm Sat; 12–3pm and 7–11pm Sun.*

BENVILLE

The Talbot Arms

Benville, Dorchester DT2 0NN
☎ *(01935) 83381* Brian Dash

Freehouse serving Branscombe Vale Drayman's Best Bitter plus one guest, another beer from Branscombe Vale, or one from a wide range of other breweries.

A country pub/restaurant with beer garden. Food served lunchtimes and evenings. Campsite. Children allowed.

OPEN *11am–11pm.*

BLANDFORD FORUM

The Railway Hotel

Oakfield Street, Blandford Forum DT11 7EX
☎ *(01258) 456374* Nigel Jones

Genuine freehouse with Badger First Gold and Ringwood Best always available, plus two guests from regional and micro-brewers based in Dorset, Hampshire, Wiltshire, Somerset, Devon, Cornwall, IOW and the Channel Islands.

Victorian-built in 1864 as a hotel for the local railway line which closed in 1966. Now a sports-oriented community local with multiple TV stations, interactive quizzes and traditional pub games such as shove ha'penny, skittles, pool, darts and cribbage. Full menu available at all times. Heated smoking area with TVs. Children welcome. Annual beer festival on May Day bank holiday weekend, featuring the breweries from the south and south-west listed above. Function room. Just off the one-way system near the town centre. On the X8 bus route from Poole

OPEN *11am until the last person leaves (usually 3 or 4am Mon–Thurs and between 6 and 9am Fri–Sun). No admission after 1am at weekends.*

BOURNEMOUTH

The Goat & Tricycle

27–9 West Hill Road, Bournemouth BH2 5PF
☎ *(01202) 314220* James and Trish Blake

Wadworth 6X, Henry's Original IPA and JCB always available plus eight regularly changing guests.

A ward-winning traditional pub with family area and courtyard. No juke box, background music only. No children in the bar. Food served 12–2pm and 6–9pm.

OPEN *12–3pm and 6–11pm Mon–Sat; 12–3pm and 7–10.30pm Sun.*

Moon in the Square

4–8 Exeter Road, Bournemouth BH2 5AQ
☎ *(01202) 652090* Dave and Terri Lea

Eight or nine real ales, including Ringwood Best, Marston's Pedigree, Burton Ale, Greene King Abbot and Shepherd Neame Spitfire, plus a couple of guests.

A traditional Wetherspoon's pub a few minutes from the sea. Two floors, two bars. Food served all day (steak and curry nights). Beer garden. Disabled facilities. Children welcome.

OPEN *10am–11pm (10.30pm Sun).*

The Porterhouse

113 Poole Road, Westbourne, Bournemouth BH4 9BG
☎ *(01202) 768586*
Jonathan and Andrea Blackie

Ringwood Brewery tied house serving Best, Fortyniner, Old Thumper and one seasonal brew plus one guest from another independent brewery. Also Farmer's Tipple real cider.

Former wine bar, now a traditional one-bar pub located on the main road. Food served 12–3pm. A quiet pub with no music. No children. Dogs welcome. Voted CAMRA's East Dorset Pub of the Year six times.

OPEN *11am–11pm Mon–Thurs; 11am– midnight Fri–Sat; 12–11pm Sun.*

BRADPOLE

The King's Head Inn

Bradpole, Bridport DT6 3DS
☎ *01308 422520* Barry Lurkins

Palmers house, with Palmers IPA and Copper Ale permanently available. Other beers from Palmers, such as 200, Tally Ho! and Dorset Gold, appear as guests.

Traditional 400-year-old village pub with two bars and a dining area. Food served. Entertainment and quiz nights once a month. Garden and patio. Two letting rooms. Parking. Well-behaved children and dogs allowed. On the main Bridport to Yeovil road.

OPEN *11am–2.30pm and 6–11pm Mon–Sat; 12–2.30pm and 6–10.30pm Sun.*

BRANKSOME

Branksome Railway Hotel

429 Poole Road, Branksome, Poole BH12 1DQ
☎ *(01202) 769555*
Christopher and Hannah Allner

Enterprise pub with two real ales usually on offer.

Victorian pub built in 1894 with two bars and a relaxed atmosphere. Friday night disco, requested music played. Food served 7am–3pm. En-suite accommodation, including one room with disabled facilities including stairlift. Well-behaved children welcome. Large car park at rear. Located on the A35, opposite Branksome Railway Station.

OPEN *All day, every day.*

BRANSGORE
The Three Tuns Country Inn
*Ringwood Road, Bransgore, Christchurch
BH23 8JH*
☎ *(01425) 672232* Nigel Glenister
www.threetunsinn.com

Enterprise Inns pub with Ringwood Best
and Fortyniner, Caledonian Deuchars
IPA, Timothy Taylor Landlord, Porter
(Winter), Bold Forester, Doombar, St Austell,
Exmoor Gold and Teahouse (all subject to
availability).

A 17th-century traditional thatched pub
and restaurant with lounge, snug and 60-
cover restaurant. No music, TV or games.
Food served 12.15–2.15pm and 6.15–9.15pm;
12–9.15pm Sun. Egon Ronay recommended
and two AA rosettes. Family garden with
barbecue and garden benches. Old Barn
event area, petanque court, terraced area
seating 60. Dogs and well-behaved children
welcome. Turn off the A31 Lyndhurst to
Christchurch road at Hinton, follow the signs
for Bransgore.

OPEN *11.30am–11pm Mon–Sat; 12–10.30pm
Sun.*

BRIDPORT
The Crown Inn
59 West Bay Road, Bridport DT6 4AX
☎ *(01308) 422037* Simon and Shelly Warry

Traditional Palmers house with the full
range of the brewery's beers available.

F amily-run pub in a very old building on
the edge of town. One bar, dining area,
garden and rear patio. Food available all day.
Live music most Saturdays. Children allowed.
On the main A35, look out for the entrance
50 yards on right-hand side of the B3157.

OPEN *12–11pm (10.30pm Sun).*

BUCKHORN WESTON
The Stapleton Arms
*Church Hill, Buckhorn Weston, Gillingham
SP8 5HS*
☎ *(01963) 370396* Kaveh Javvi
www.thestapletonarms.com

Freehouse with four or five real ales,
including Butcombe Bitter and Cheddar
Ales Potholer. The guests, changed every
couple of days, might be Moor Brewery JJJ
I.P.A., Roosters Yankee, Matthews Brown Ale,
Moor Peat Porter, or Keystone Large One, to
name but a few. Draught ciders and 32
bottled beers.

R ecently refurbished English pub ten
minutes' drive from Longleat. Food served
12–3pm and 6–10pm (9.30pm Sun). Dining
room, beer garden, large car park. Children
welcome. Four en-suite bedrooms. Between
the A303 and A30, south of Wincanton.

OPEN *11am–3pm and 6–11pm Mon–Fri;
11am–11pm Sat–Sun.*

BUCKLAND NEWTON
Gaggle of Geese
Buckland Newton, Nr Dorchester DT2 7BS
☎ *(01300) 345249*
Tim Scarisbrick and Angela Grinsted
www.gaggleofgeese.co.uk

Award-winning freehouse serving
Ringwood Fortyniner and Best plus
Butcombe Best and a weekly guest ale.

C ommunity village pub built in the 1800s,
set in extensive five-acre gardens with a
children's play area. Food served 12–2pm and
6.30–9pm Mon–Sat and 12–2pm Sun in the
bar and dining room. Well-behaved children
and dogs welcome. Skittle alley. Local
attractions include Sticky Wicket wild flower
garden and Henly Hillbillies quad bikes and
minis plus the Cerne Abbas giant. Nine miles
from Sherborne, ten miles north of
Dorchester off the B3143.

OPEN *12–3pm and 6.30–11pm Mon–Sat;
12–2.30pm and 7–10.30pm Sun.*

BURTON BRADSTOCK
Anchor Inn
*High Street, Burton Bradstock, Nr Bridport
DT6 4QF*
☎ *(01308) 897228*
Andrew Overhill and Neil Cadle
www.dorset-seafood-restaurant.co.uk

Two real ales, namely Otter Ale and
St Austell Tribute.

P leasant pub with two bars, one a
restaurant specialising in a wide variety of
seafood. Food served lunchtimes and
evenings every day. Children welcome. Car
park. Accommodation. On the main Bridport
to Weymouth road (B3157).

OPEN *Lunchtimes and evenings every day.*

CATTISTOCK
The Fox & Hounds
Duck Street, Cattistock DT2 0JH
☎ *(01300) 320444* Scott and Liz Flight
www.foxandhoundsinn.com

Palmers IPA, Copper and 200 or Gold
plus occasional guests.

A 17th-century village inn with large fires,
flagstones and a separate restaurant.
Relaxing atmosphere. Homemade, local,
seasonal food available. Parking, garden and
play area opposite. Dogs more than welcome.
Campsite nearby. Accommodation. On the
A37, look out for the sign for Cattistock, just
past the Clay Pigeon Shooting Club from
Yeovil or the sign on the road from
Dorchester.

OPEN *7–11pm Mon (closed Mon lunch); 12–
2.30pm and 7–11pm Tues–Sun.*

CERNE ABBAS

Royal Oak

23 Long Street, Cerne Abbas DT2 7JG
☎ *(01300) 341797* Tony and Chris Green

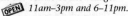 Tied to Hall and Woodhouse, with Badger Best, Tanglefoot and Fursty Ferret available.

A low-ceilinged 16th-century pub decorated with brasses and cups. A friendly comfortable tourist gastropub that hasn't lost its character. Food served 12–2pm and 6.30–9pm. Children welcome. Courtyard. Located in the centre of the village.

OPEN *11am–3pm and 6–11pm.*

CHARMOUTH

The Royal Oak

The Street, Charmouth DT6 6PE
☎ *(01297) 560277* Karen and Brian Prevett

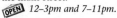 Tied to Palmers, with Copper Ale, IPA and 200 available.

A friendly village pub built in the 1870s, with beams and one through bar. Bar snacks available at lunchtime, with evening meals also served during the summer. Darts, table skittles and pool. Children allowed. On the main street.

OPEN *12–3pm and 7–11pm.*

CHETNOLE

The Chetnole Inn

Chetnole, Sherborne DT9 6NU
☎ *(01935) 872337* Mike and Jude
www.thechetnoleinn.co.uk

 Freehouse with Branscombe Vale Branoc Ale and Sharp's Doom Bar plus many other rotating local real ales.

Inn with a restaurant, bar area, snug, skittle alley and three en-suite letting bedrooms. Food served lunchtimes and evenings. Flagstones, log burners, antique pine furniture, plus a beer garden complete with ducks! Great base for walking. Dogs welcome in the snug bar, well-behaved children allowed.

OPEN *11.30am–2.30pm and 6.30–11pm Mon–Sat; 12–3pm and 7–11pm Sun.*

CHIDEOCK

The Anchor Inn

Seatown, Chideock, Bridport DT6 6JU
☎ *(01297) 489215* Paul Wiscombe

 Palmers house with IPA and Palmers 200 plus Tally Ho! and Copper occasionally.

Situated in the centre of a little cove, nestled under the Golden Cap Cliff which is the highest point on the south coast. A World Heritage site, Area of Outstanding Natural Beauty, with National Trust land all around. Food available all day in summer, lunchtimes and evenings in winter. Well-behaved children and dogs allowed. Beer garden with terraces overlooking the sea and the south west coastal path. From A35 travel south to Chideock.

OPEN *Summer (end May–September): all day, every day. Winter: 11am–2.30pm and 6–11pm (10.30pm Sun).*

CHILD OKEFORD

Saxon Inn

Gold Hill, Child Okeford DT11 8HD
☎ *(01258) 860310* Peter and Helen
www.saxoninn.co.uk

Four real ales, including Ringwood Best, something from Butcombe, plus a variety of popular brews from around the country.

Friendly, traditional, old village pub with two cosy log fires. Good, tasty, home-cooked food from a varied menu served every day except Sunday evenings. Beautiful oak outdoor dining area. At the rear of the pub is a country garden with ample seating. Four sumptuous en-suite B&B rooms.

OPEN *12–2.30pm and 7–11pm Mon–Fri; 12–3pm and 7–11pm Sat; 12–11pm Sun.*

CHRISTCHURCH

The Ship

48 High Street, Christchurch
☎ *(01202) 484308* Nicole Thomas

Ringwood Fortyniner and Best and Greene King Abbot Ale plus occasional guests.

Steeped in history, with a welcoming atmosphere and excellent staff, this claims to be the oldest (and busiest!) pub in Christchurch. A wide range of traditional and special food, including breakfasts served daily in the summer (lunchtimes only in winter). Children welcome. Beer garden. Car park. Situated on main street opposite Woolworths.

OPEN *11am–11pm Mon–Sat; 12–10.30pm Sun.*

CHURCH KNOWLE

The New Inn

Church Knowle, Wareham BH20 5NQ
☎ *(01929) 480357*
M Estop, R Estop, A Estop and MD Estop
www.newinnchurchknowle.co.uk

Wadworth 6X, Flowers Original (brewed by Badger) and Greene King Old Speckled Hen are regulars. Large wine cellar.

A 16th-century stone and thatched country inn that has been run by the same family since 1985, and has featured in several food guidebooks. Food served 12–2.35pm and 6–9.15pm, with fish dishes a speciality. Large new function room (Purbeck Lounge), large smoking area, large garden that seats over 100 and large car park at rear. Campsite. A mile and a half from Corfe Castle.

OPEN *11am–3pm and 6–11pm.*

CORFE CASTLE

The Fox Inn

8 West Street, Corfe Castle BH20 5HD
☎ *(01929) 480449* AL Brown

Freehouse generally serving about four real ales straight from the barrel at any one time. Fuller's London Pride, Greene King Old Speckled Hen and Wadworth 6X are regulars.

A traditional, old-fashioned, olde-worlde pub dating back to 1568. A long and narrow building with a garden overlooking the castle. Food every session.

OPEN *11am–3pm (2.30pm in the winter) and 6.30–11pm.*

The Greyhound

The Square, Corfe Castle BH20 5EZ
☎ *(01929) 480205* Jacci Pestana
www.greyhoundcorfe.co.uk

Three real ales changing weekly. Examples include Ringwood Best, Sharp Doombar, Lady of the Lake, Glastonbury Ales, Altons Pride, fff Brewery etc. We aim to provide beer enthusiasts with a good variety and changing selection.

A 15th-century coaching inn, said to be the most photographed pub in Britain, with lots of small rooms. There is a lovely terrace and beer garden, where the best views of the castle and steam train are to be had. Children, cyclists, walkers and dogs are all welcome. Freshly prepared seasonal food made daily, including locally sourced fish, beef, pork and venison. We are renowned for our beer festivals in May and August with over 40-60 real ales and cider. Sausage and cider festival in October. Seafood festival in September. Live music including jazz, rockabilly, blues and acoustic musicians weekly.

OPEN *All day, every day.*

CORFE MULLEN

Coventry Arms

Mill Street, Corfe Mullen BH21 3RH
☎ *(01258) 857284* John Hugo

Owned by Enterprise Inns, serving beers straight from the cask, including Timothy Taylor Landlord, Gale's Best and a rotating guest.

A 500-year-old, one-bar country pub with food served at lunchtimes and evenings in a separate dining area. Children allowed. Large beer garden. Beer festival every May Day bank holiday. Located on the main A31, two miles from Wimborne.

OPEN *11am–3pm and 5.30–11pm Mon–Fri; all day Sat–Sun.*

CORSCOMBE

The Fox Inn

Corscombe, Nr Beaminster DT2 0NS
☎ *(01935) 891330* Clive Webb

Exmoor Ale and Butcombe Bitter are the permanent beers, with one guest ale in the summer.

A 16th-century thatched country pub, with log fire, flagstone floors and beams. No music. A wide variety of food is served in the pub's four dining areas. Garden, car park. Four letting rooms. Well-behaved children allowed. On the Halstock road, on the outskirts of Corscombe.

OPEN *12–3pm and 7–11pm (10.30pm Sun) (afternoon closing times may vary).*

CRANBORNE

The Sheaf of Arrows

The Square, Cranborne BH21 5PR
☎ *(01725) 517456* Rex Neville

Ringwood Best and Wadworth 6X, plus a guest, changed every two weeks, usually a local ale.

Small, friendly village local in the peaceful village of Cranborne, handy for lovely walks in the surrounding countryside. One large bar, function room, skittle alley and beer garden. Restaurant open 12–2.30pm and 7–9.30pm daily. En-suite accommodation. Next door to Cranborne Manor Gardens and Garden Centre, between Wimbourne and Fordingbridge.

OPEN *11am–11pm.*

DORCHESTER

Blue Raddle

Church Street, Dorchester DT1 1JN
☎ *(01305) 267762*
Christine and Richard Townsend

Sharp's Doom Bar and Otter Bitter plus two guest ales, changed as they run out.

Small, quiet, market-town pub with local atmosphere, a pub since 1850. Food served 12–2pm every day and 7–9pm Thurs–Sat. No children. In central Dorchester (old town), within walking distance of attractions.

OPEN *6.30pm–close Mon; 11.30am–3.30pm and 6.30pm–late Tues–Sat; 12–3.30pm Sun.*

The Giant Inn

24 Long Street, Cerne Abbas, Dorchester DT2 7JF
☎ *(01300) 341441* Anneliese Coats
www.thegiantinncerneabbas.co.uk

A varying selection of two real ales, such as St Austell Tribute, Wadworth Henry's IPA or something from Greene King.

Rebuilt in 1896 from a 15th-century original building, this is a friendly, traditional pub. No food. Pool table. Skittle alley. Beer garden. Named after, and close to, the famous Cerne Abbas giant hill carving.

OPEN *6–11pm Mon–Fri; 12–11pm Sat–Sun.*

Tom Brown's

47 High East Street, Dorchester DT1 1HU
☎ *(01305) 264020* Alan Finch

Home to the Goldfinch brewery, with three of their beers available.

A pub for locals and drinkers, with no food. Darts. Juke box.

OPEN *11am–3pm and 5.30–11pm Mon–Thur; all day Fri–Sat; 12–4pm and 7–10.30pm Sun.*

EAST CHALDON

Sailor's Return

East Chaldon, Dorchester DT2 8DN
☎ *(01305) 853847* Michael Pollard
www.sailorsreturn.com

Freehouse with six real ales, including Strongs from Hampshire Brewery and Ringwood Best, plus four other beers changed as they run out. Regional brewers are favoured.

Historic country pub dating from the late 1860s, with one main bar, one smaller bar, and a 50-seater restaurant. Food served 12–9.30pm in summer, 12–2pm and 6–9pm in winter. Children welcome in restaurant, dogs allowed in bar. Beer garden, plus tables at front of pub. Beer festival at spring bank holiday. Main car park with very large grassed extension. One mile from the A352 – follow the signs on the main road.

OPEN *Summer: all day, every day. Winter: 11am–3pm and 6–11pm.*

EVERSHOT

Acorn Inn

28 Fore Street, Evershot DT2 0JW
☎ *(01935) 83228* John Metcalf
www.acorn-inn.co.uk

 Real ales including beers such as Doombar, Golden Arrow and Dorset and Somerset ale. One or two guest ales athat change every week.

Quality 16th century coaching inn, that Thomas Hardy called 'The Sow & Acorn' in 'Tess of the d'Urbervilles'. Set in picturesqe West Dorset village of Evershot, this lovely old stone-built Inn boasts worthy history. Originally known as The Kings Arms, it once brewed its own ales with water drawn from the source of the River From. 400 years of charm and character. Beamed bars, log fires. Nestlling among rolling hills in Area of Outstanding Natural Beauty, and close to British Hertiage Coast – perfect base for exploring or walking. Food served in bars or restaurant, using best fresh local ingredients. Two oak panelled bars. Between Yeovil and Dorchester.

OPEN *11am–11.30pm.*

EYPE

The New Inn

Eype DT6 6AP
☎ *(01308) 423254* Steve Tuck

 Palmers tied house, with four pumps serving the range of Palmers brews.

Traditional village pub on the Jurassic Coast, half a mile from the sea, with a tranquil atmosphere and superb countryside views. Cosy bar, separate dining area, terraced decking and garden. Home-cooked food served 12–2pm and 6–9pm. Children and dogs welcome. Ideal 'pit-stop' for walkers. Just off the A35, one mile west of Bridport. Signposted.

OPEN *11am–3pm and 6–11pm Mon–Sat; 12–3pm and 7–10.30pm Sun. All day during holiday season.*

FARNHAM

The Museum Inn

Farnham, Nr Blandford Forum DT11 8DE
☎ *(01725) 516261* David Sax
www.museuminn.co.uk

Freehouse with Ringwood Best and Timothy Taylor Landlord plus a weekly guest such as Gale's HSB, Fuller's London Pride, Palmers Tally Ho! or Hop Back Summer Lightning.

Part-thatched 17th-century inn. Food is served in all areas of the pub, including the Shed Restaurant, which is open Fri–Sun and available for private hire. Food available 12–2.30pm and 7–9.30pm. Eight letting rooms.

OPEN *12–3pm and 6–11pm.*

GILLINGHAM

Phoenix Inn

The Square, Gillingham SP8 4AY
☎ *(01747) 823277* Adrian Clarke

 Tied to Hall and Woodhouse, with Badger Sussex Bitter and First Gold plus seasonal ales (Festive Feasant, Hopping Hare, Stinger or Fursty Ferret). No keg or smooth!

Friendly one-bar pub with separate restaurant, dating from the 15th century but rebuilt in the 17th century. At one time it was a hotel, and had its own brewery. Food served every session except Sunday and Monday nights. Well-behaved children and dogs welcome. Patio and courtyard. Car park 50 yards away. Handy for local country houses and the coast. At the bottom of the High Street, turn into the Square.

OPEN *10am–2.30pm Mon; 10am–2.30pm (3pm Sat) and 7–11pm Tues–Sat; 12–3pm and 7–10.30pm Sun.*

The Smouldering Boulder

Queen Street, Gillingham SP8 4DZ
☎ *(01747) 823988* John Beresford
www.thesmoulderingboulder.co.uk

Fuller's London Pride and Wadworth 6X plus guest beers.

A 400-year-old freehouse re-opened in July 2008 following extensive refurbishment. Comfortable bar and restaurant with mood lighting and a contemporary feel. Food served 12–3pm and 6.30–9pm including children's menu. Tea and coffee served all day. Large garden with decking for smokers. Families welcome. Quiz every Sunday at 8pm.

OPEN *10am–late.*

HINTON ST MARY

The White Horse

Hinton St Mary, Sturminster Newton DT10 1NA
☎ *(01258) 472723* Joy Moss

Freehouse serving three well-kept real ales, including beers from Hidden, Sharp's, Ringwood and Archers, rotated every couple of weeks.

A traditional 17th-century character pub in a pretty location, with real fires and a warm welcome. Lounge bar and dining room serving real English home-cooked food 12–2pm Tues–Sun and 6–9pm Tues–Sat. Cosy public bar, with no juke box. Families and pets welcome. Heated smoking shelter, beer garden and large car park. There are fabulous walks from historic Cut Mill to Sturminster Newton. Charlie Dimmock's Millennium Garden and William Fox Pitt Equestrian centre are nearby.

OPEN *12–3pm and 6–11pm (not Mondays).*

HURN

Avon Causeway Hotel

Hurn, Christchurch BH23 6AS
☎ *(01202) 482714* Keith Perks

Up to seven real ales, including Wadworth 6X, Ringwood Best and Old Thumper, plus guests.

Quaint country hotel, ten minutes from Bournemouth. Formerly Hurn railway station, the pub is decorated with lots of railway bric-à-brac. CAMRA and Cask Marque approved. Food served at lunchtimes and evenings in a separate large lounge, plus all day at weekends (carvery on Sundays). Murder mystery nights are a feature, and make use of an old Victorian carriage. Beer garden with large children's play area. Inside, children are allowed in dining area only. The main pub and restaurant are disabled friendly. There are 12 en-suite rooms.

(OPEN) *All day, every day.*

LODERS

The Loders Arms

Loders, Nr Bridport DT6 3SA
☎ *(01308) 422431* Graham and Louise Rowe
www.thelodersarms.com

Palmers 200, IPA and Copper Ale always available.

Country village pub, a traditional Dorset longhouse, over 200 years old. Home-cooked food using local produce usually served 12–2.30pm and 6.30–9pm (times vary). Fires, dining area, garden, patio and car park. Occasional live music in garden. Families and dogs welcome.

(OPEN) *11.30am–3pm and 6–11pm Mon–Sat; 12–10.30pm Sun.*

LOWER BURTON

The Sun Inn

Lower Burton, Nr Dorchester DT2 7RX
☎ *(01305) 250445* Lucy Fenwick
www.sun-inn-dorchester.co.uk

Three real ales, perhaps including Butcombe Bitter and Otter Ale.

A traditional coaching inn with the motto 'Good Food, Good Beer and Good Cheer'. Carvery and bar menu served 12–2.30pm and 6.30–9.30pm Mon–Sat and 12–9.30pm Sun. Beer garden, courtyard, large car park and outdoor play area. Disabled facilities. Children's menu and high chairs available. Situated half a mile from Dorchester town centre on the Sherborne road.

(OPEN) *11am–11pm Mon–Sat; 12–10.30pm Sun.*

LYME REGIS

The Nag's Head

Silver Street, Lyme Regis DT7 3HS
☎ *(01297) 442312* Robin Hamon

Freehouse with up to four ales, perhaps including Ringwood Best, Fortyniner and Otter Ale.

Former coaching inn with one main bar divided into two areas plus a pool room. Background music. Large walled beer garden and covered smoking area with outstanding panoramic views across Lyme Bay. Outdoor

log fire on busy nights and weekends during winter. Sky Sports in bar and sometimes on the deck outside. Live music every Saturday and some Wednesdays. Three en-suite bedrooms. Sea views across the bay to Portland.

(OPEN) *All day, every day until late.*

The Volunteer Inn

31 Broad Street, Lyme Regis DT7 3QE
☎ *(01297) 442214* JP O'Donnell

Fuller's London Pride and house ale Donegal, which is brewed by Branscombe Vale, are always available. Two constantly changing guest ales served. Regulars include Otter Bitter and Ale, Exmoor Ale and Sharp's Doom Bar. Three ciders also on offer, including cask-conditioned traditional still cloudy cider.

A small, friendly pub with separate dining area and extensive bar menu; the emphasis is on food, drink and conversation. Food available 12–2pm and 6–9pm Tues–Sat, 12–2pm Sun. Children allowed in the dining area only. Located on the main high street, at the top of the hill.

(OPEN) *11am–11pm Mon–Sat; 12–10.30pm Sun.*

MANSTON

The Plough

Shaftesbury Road, Manston, Sturminster Newton DT10 1HB
☎ *(01258) 472484*
www.theploughatmanston.co.uk

Palmers IPA and Copper and Wadworth 6X plus one guest ale, changed weekly.

Traditional beamed pub, approximately 400 years old. Food served 12–2pm and 6–9pm Mon-Sat; 12–4pm and 6–9pm Sun. Children welcome. Large beer garden. Car park. Annual three-day beer festival in July. On the B3091 between Shaftesbury and Sturminster Newton.

(OPEN) *Mon-Sat 11.30am-2.30pm and 6-11pm; Sun noon-10.30pm.*

MARSHWOOD

The Bottle Inn

Marshwood, Bridport DT6 5QJ
☎ *(01297) 678254* Shane Pym
www.thebottleinn.co.uk

Freehouse with Otter Bitter available on a permanent basis. Greene King Old Speckled Hen is a regular and there are often guest beers from the Quay and Branscombe Vale breweries.

A quirky, unspoilt thatched pub built in 1585. Sells organic coke and has a good range of vegetarian meals on its menu. Garden with strange horse in playground. Car park. Skittle alley. Children welcome (family room). Annual beer festival, world stinging-nettle-eating championship and a wickerman burnt at Hallowe'en. On the B3165 between Crewkerne and Lyme Regis.

(OPEN) *12–3pm and 6.30–11pm; closed Mon (except bank holidays).*

MIDDLEMARSH

The Hunters Moon

Middlemarsh, Sherbourne DT9 5QN
☎ *(01963) 210966* Brendan Malone

 Four frequently changing real ales from breweries such as St Austell, Sharp's and Otter.

Characterful country inn, carefully renovated to enhance the rustic nature of the original pub. Fresh home-cooked food served 12–2pm and 7–9.30pm (9pm Sun). Sunday carveries. Booking for food recommended. Car park. Beer garden facing due west, enjoying all of the evening summer sun. Accommodation. No dogs. Set deep in Thomas Hardy country, in the village in which he set his novel *The Woodlanders*. Convenient for the Cerne and Piddle river valleys.

OPEN *11am–11.30pm Mon–Sat; 12–10.30pm Sun.*

NETTLECOMBE

Marquis of Lorne Inn

Nettlecombe, Nr Bridport DT6 3SY
☎ *(01308) 485236* Julie and David Woodroffe
www.marquisoflorne.com

 Palmers pub with Palmers 200, IPA and Copper permanently served, plus Tally Ho! and Gold featured seasonally.

Dating back to 1870 as a pub, with two bars, two restaurants and beautifully laid-out gardens with all-round views of the countryside. Bar snacks and full à la carte menu served 12–2pm and 6.30–9.30pm. Large car park. Seven en-suite rooms with full facilities. Many varied walks in the area. Six miles from the coast, with Lyme Regis and Weymouth within easy reach. See website for directions.

OPEN *11.30am–2.30pm and 6.30pm–late Mon–Sat; 12–2.30pm and 7–11pm Sun.*

NORTH WOOTTON

The Three Elms

North Wootton, Nr Sherborne DT9 5JW
☎ *(01935) 812881* Howard Manning

 Fuller's London Pride, Otter Bitter and Butcombe brews always available.

This busy rural roadside pub contains the landlord's collection of 1,600 model cars and lorries in display cabinets around the walls. Bar and restaurant food, including a large vegetarian selection, available 12–2pm and 6.30–10pm daily. Children allowed. Accommodation. Great views. Situated on the A3030 Sherborne to Sturminster Newton road, two miles from Sherborne.

OPEN *11am–2.30pm Mon–Sat, 12–3pm Sun; 6.30–11pm Mon–Sat, 7–10.30pm Sun.*

PIDDLEHINTON

The Thimble

14 High Street, Piddlehinton DT2 7TD
☎ *(01300) 348270*

 Local brews such as Palmers Copper and IPA, Ringwood Best and Old Thumper and Hop Back Summer Lightning.

Thatched village inn beside the River Piddle with beams, fireplaces and a glass-covered well. Food lunchtimes and evenings. Floodlit garden. Children and dogs welcome.

OPEN *12–2.30pm and 7–11pm (10.30pm Sun).*

PIDDLETRENTHIDE

The Poacher's Inn

Piddletrenthide, Dorchester DT2 7QX
☎ *(01300) 348358* Sarah Harris
www.thepoachersinn.co.uk

 Fuller's London Pride and Shepherd Neame Spitfire plus one guest such as Palmers Copper.

A 17th-century country inn with riverside garden. Food served until 9pm every day. Decking and swimming pool in the garden. Children welcome. Parking at the rear. Well-behaved dogs welcome. Accommodation. Six miles north of Dorchester.

OPEN *All day, every day.*

PLUSH

The Brace of Pheasants

Plush DT2 7RQ
☎ *(01300) 348357* Phil and Carol Bennett
www.braceofpheasants.co.uk

Freehouse offering Ringwood Best plus two rotating guests, changed every three days, such as Timothy Taylor Landlord, Otter Ale, Palmers Copper Ale, Sharp's Doom Bar and beers from Cottage.

A 16th-century thatched village inn, formerly two cottages and a smithy. Private dining/conference room, restaurant area, plus lovely English country garden. Bar meals and snacks and à la carte restaurant food served 12.30–2.30pm and 7.30–9.30pm Tues–Sun. Featured in the Michelin guide for eating out in pubs. Children welcome. Superb walks to Dorset Gap. Fifteen minutes north-east of Dorchester.

OPEN *12–3pm and 7–11pm Tues–Sun; closed Mon except bank holidays.*

POOLE

Angel Inn

28 Market Street, Poole BH15 1NF
☎ *(01202) 666431* Colin Barter

Tied to Ringwood Brewery, with Best, Fortyniner, Old Thumper and seasonal ales plus a weekly guest from a wide range.

Grade II listed and in the old town. One horseshoe-shaped bar with log-burning stove. Food served 12–2.30pm. Beer terrace at rear and outside seating at front. Close to the harbour, opposite the Guild Hall Museum.

OPEN *11am–11pm Mon–Sat; 12–10.30pm Sun.*

Bermuda Triangle Freehouse

10 Parr Street, Nr Ashley Cross, Lower Parkstone,
Poole BH14 0JY
☎ *(01202) 748087* Gisela Crane,
John Hewitson and Steve Wilson

Four real ales constantly changing.
A freehouse that likes to support as many
micros as possible.

An interesting theme pub and regular local
CAMRA Pub of the Year. Three German
lagers on draught. Good music, great
atmosphere. Bar food served weekday
lunchtimes. Car park. Near Ashley Cross.

OPEN *12–3pm and 5–11pm Mon–Thurs;*
12–12 Fri–Sat; 12–11pm Sun.

The Blue Boar

29 Market Close, Poole BH15 1NE
☎ *(01202) 682247* Gary Parker

Tied to Fuller's, with six real ales,
including London Pride, Chiswick, ESB
and Discovery, plus a guest changed every
two weeks.

Unusual three-bar pub in a restored 18th-
century listed mansion, with a large
collection of military and nautical artefacts.
Cellar bar with live entertainment Wed, Fri
and Sat. Food served 11.30am–2.30pm.
Function room available. Off the High Street,
opposite the multi-storey car park.

OPEN *Summer: all day, every day.*
Winter 11am–3pm and 5–11pm Mon–
Fri; all day Sat–Sun.

The Brewhouse

68 High Street, Poole BH15 1DA
☎ *(01202) 685288* Paul Slocombe

Tied to Milk Street Brewery and
showcasing the brewery's range, plus
guest ales.

Welcoming pub with a varied clientele.
Pool table and darts team. Pub has
narrow frontage on High Street, so could
easily be missed.

OPEN *All day, every day.*

Sandacres Free House

3 Banks Road, Sandbanks, Poole BH13 7PW
☎ *(01202) 707244* Peter Fay
www.thesandacres.co.uk

Ringwood Best and Old Thumper, plus
one guest pump, frequently Greene King
Abbot and other local and national beers.

A large, modern-style waterside pub in
Poole Harbour with lovely views. One
large bar, children's area, pool room, outside
seating overlooking the harbour. Disabled
facilities with no steps. Food served 12–2pm
and 7–9.15pm Mon–Sat; 12–8pm Sun.
Children allowed until 9pm. Close to
Sandbanks beach, and en route to Studland
Ferry. Located on the approach to Sandbanks.

OPEN *11.30am–3pm and 6–11pm Mon–Sat;*
12–11pm Sun.

PORTLAND

The Clifton

50 Grove Road, Portland DT5 1DA
☎ *(01305) 820473* Mark Pollard

Freehouse with three ever-changing real
ales from Dorset brewers. Also a real cider.

Popular with Prince Charles and Prince
Andrew in their Navy days, this pub has
two bars and a separate restaurant. Food
11am–9pm. Beer garden with children's play
area and lots of animals. Accommodation.
Beer festival every May bank holiday.
Situated 300 yards past the football ground.

OPEN *11am–11pm.*

PULHAM

Halsey Arms

Pulham, Dorchester DT2 7DZ
☎ *(01258) 817344* Holly and Gef Royal
www.halseyarms.co.uk

Enterprise pub serving three real ales.
There is always a Ringwood beer and one
from a local brewery such as Yeovil, plus
another, perhaps Greene King Abbot or
Timothy Taylor Landlord.

Traditional pub with public bar, restaurant
and a friendly atmosphere, set in the
Dorset countryside. Food served all day, with
carvery on Sunday. Children and dogs
welcome. Car park. On the road between
Sturminster Newton and Dorchester.

OPEN *All day, every day.*

PYMORE

The Pymore Inn

Pymore Road, Bridport DT6 5PN
☎ *(01308) 422625* Barry and Irene Clapham

Freehouse with three real ales. St Austell
Tribute, Dartmoor and Tinners are
regulars, and there is a quarterly guest.

Formerly a country residence, 180 years old
and converted into a pub in the 1920s.
One bar, dining area, log-burning fireplace.
Food served 12–2pm and 6.30–9pm. Beer
garden, large car park. Close to the market
town of Bridport and the Jurassic Coast
(Charmouth, Lyme Regis and West Bay).

OPEN *12–3pm and 6–11pm.*

SANDFORD ORCAS

The Mitre Inn

Sandford Orcas DT9 4RU
☎ *(01963) 220271*
Cheryl Holloway and Allen Page

Greene King Abbot, Old Speckled
Hen and Wychwood Hobgoblin are
typical of the three real ales, changed weekly.

Friendly, traditional stone-clad pub with
flagstone floors and open fires. No piped
music. Fresh food using local produce served
12–2pm and 7–9.30pm Tues–Sat; 12–2pm and
7–9pm Sun. Dogs, well-behaved children and
muddy boots are no problem. Car park. Beer
garden. Off the B3145, off the Sherborne-
Marston road, or direct from Sherborne, three
miles north-east along Crombe Lane.

OPEN *7–11pm Mon (closed Mon lunch);*
11.30am–2.30pm and 7–11pm Tues–Fri;
11.30am–3pm and 7–11pm Sat; 12–3pm
and 7–10.30 Sun.

SHAFTESBURY

Ship Inn

Bleke Street, Shaftesbury SP7 8JZ
☎ *(01747) 853219* Mark Tilbrook

 Badger Tanglefoot and Best plus one constantly changing guest.

An old-style pub in attractive building with lots of small rooms. Decorated with plenty of pictures of ships. Food every session except Sunday night. Children welcome. Garden. Games including crib, pool, darts and boules.

OPEN *11am–11pm Mon–Sat; 12–10.30pm Sun.*

SHERBORNE

The Digby Tap

Cooks Lane, Sherborne DT9 3NS
☎ *(01935) 813148* Oliver Wilson
www.digbytap.co.uk

 Twenty different beers served each week from a range of 100 per year. Four at any one time. Brews from the Wells and Young's, Bath Ales, Sharp's, Teignworthy, Ringwood, Exmoor, Otter, Scatter Rock, St Austell, Butcombe, Church End, Archers, Cotleigh, Hop Back, Mole's and Cottage breweries, plus other regional producers.

A traditional, local, one-bar pub with three rooms and flagstone floors. Bar snacks available 12–1.45pm (not on Sundays). Children are welcome at lunchtime only. Outside seating in summer. Just 100 yards from the abbey, towards the railway station.

OPEN *11am–11pm Mon–Sat; 12–3pm and 7–11pm Sun.*

Skippers

1 Terrace View, Horsecastles, Sherborne DT9 3HE
☎ *(01935) 812753* Sandra and Chris Frowde

Former cider house, and a Wadworth pub since 1991 serving Henry's IPA, 6X and Old Timer plus Butcombe Bitter as a permanent guest.

Pleasant town local. Decorated with toy farm animals, school photos, a ten-shilling note and a letter from Margaret Thatcher – like a free museum! Food every session, large menu but retaining significant drinking area. Children welcome. Beer garden and car park. Just off the A30.

OPEN *11am–2.30pm and 6–11pm Mon–Sat; 12–2.30pm and 7–10.30pm Sun.*

SHROTON

The Cricketers

Shroton, Nr Blandford Forum DT11 8QD
☎ *(01258) 860421*
Andrew and Natasha Edwards
www.thecricketersshroton.co.uk

Ringwood Best and two other ales always available; guests may include Otter Best, Otter Ale, Butcombe Tradiational Ale, St Austell Tribute, Piddle Ale.

Friendly freehouse with pretty garden and children's play area, situated between the village green and Hambledon Hill. Good for walking. Good food from a blackboard menu available lunchtimes and evenings (not Sun evenings). One luxury en-suite bed and breakfast garden room. Children allowed. Large beer garden. Located just off the A350 between Blandford and Shaftesbury.

OPEN *11.30am–3pm and 6.30–11pm Mon–Sat; 12–3pm and 7–10.30pm Sun. Open all day Sat–Sun from May–Sept.*

STOURTON CAUNDLE

Trooper Inn

Stourton Caundle, Sturminster Newton DT10 2JW
☎ *(01963) 362405* Kevin and Zena Staunton

Award-winning freehouse with three real ales including Otter bitter permanently.

A small 16th-century pub, a former meeting place for the 11th Hussars. Food served Tues–Sun 12–2pm, Weds–Sat 6.30–8.30pm. Skittle alley and function room for 80 people. Beer garden with children's play area. Session music 4th Sunday of month, and pub quiz 3rd Sunday of month, everyone welcome. Maypole dancing on May Day bank holiday. Beer festival featuring 20 real ales and 10 ciders, Whitsun bank holiday. One mile off the A3030, a mile and a half off the A354.

OPEN *12–2.30pm and 6.30–11pm daily (closed Mon lunchtime).*

STRATTON

Saxon Arms

The Square, Stratton, Nr Dorchester DT2 9WG
☎ *(01305) 260020* Rod and Janette Lamont

Freehouse offering Ringwood Best and Timothy Taylor Landlord plus two guests, changed weekly, from breweries such as Butcombe, Dorset, Cottage, Hop Back and Fuller's. Large selection of malt whiskies and fine wines.

Flintstone, thatched village pub next to the church and overlooking the green. Award-winning chef, with food served 11.30am–2.15pm and 6–9pm Mon–Thurs; 11.30am–2.30pm and 6–9.30pm Fri–Sat; all day Sun. Dorset Food and Drink Awards finalist. Patio, car park. The pub is dog-friendly. There are good walks nearby. Located just off the A37, three miles from Dorchester.

OPEN *11am–3pm and 5.30pm–late Mon–Fri; all day Sat–Sun.*

STUDLAND

The Bankes Arms

Manor Road, Studland BH19 3AU
☎ *(01929) 450225*
Tim and Jenny Lightbown

Freehouse with nine hand pumps. The one permanent beer is chosen at the annual beer festival, held every August and featuring beers from 30 breweries. The winner remains a permanent fixture for the whole year. The eight guests, changed daily, might be from breweries such as Cottage, Smiles, Wychwood, Badger or Isle of Purbeck.

Country village inn overlooking the sea, with two fires, beams and dining area. The only pub in the village! Award-winning food available. Fruit machine, live music, cliff-top beer garden. Car park. Eight en-suite letting rooms. Children allowed.

OPEN *11am–11pm Mon–Sat; 12–10.30pm Sun.*

SWANAGE
The Red Lion
63 High Street, Swanage BH19 2LY
☎ *(01929) 423533*
Karen Cattle and Jodi Haines

Timothy Taylor Landlord, Caledonian Deuchars IPA, Ringwood Best plus a selection of guests, perhaps from Palmers.

A traditional and cosy family-run, two-bar local, approximately 300 years old. Food served 12–3pm and 6–9pm. Car park and large garden. Children welcome. Pool and darts. Live music. Accommodation available in the annexe. Three minutes' walk from the square and beach.

OPEN *All day, every day.*

TARRANT MONKTON
The Langton Arms
Tarrant Monkton, Nr Blandford Forum DT11 8RX
☎ *(01258) 830225* Barbara Cossins
www.thelangtonarms.co.uk

Freehouse serving four real ales, including Ringwood Best Bitter and two guests, changed when they run out.

An attractive 17th-century thatched inn with two bars, function room and à la carte restaurant in a converted stable and conservatory. Open 7 days a week, bar and restaurant serve food 12–2.30pm and 6–9.30pm Mon–Fri; all day Sat–Sun. Large car park, beer garden. Children are welcome, and there is a children's play area. Functions catered for, including wedding receptions, civil ceremonies, family celebrations and business meetings. Accommodation. Less than two miles off the A354 Blandford to Salisbury road, five miles north of Blandford.

OPEN *11.30am–midnight.*

TRENT
The Rose & Crown
Trent, Nr Sherborne DT9 4SL
☎ *(01935) 850776* Heather and Stuart
www.roseandcrowntrent.co.uk

Wadworth pub with four ales always on offer, plus a guest ale.

A 15th-century thatched rural pub with a large beer garden. Good-quality locally sourced food served 12–3pm and 6–9.30pm Tues–Fri; 12–10pm Sat; 12–4pm Sun. Restaurant available for large functions. Live music, including jazz. Themed evenings for food. Just off the A30 between Sherborne and Yeovil.

OPEN *12–3pm and 6–11pm Tues–Fri; 12–11pm Sat; 12–10pm Sun..*

VERWOOD
Albion Inn
Station Road, Verwood BH31 7LB
☎ *(01202) 825267* Rex Neville

An Enterprise Inns pub, with Ringwood Best Bitter always available.

Former railway-owned hotel, with a traditional two-bar layout. Food served at lunchtimes and evenings. Patio and garden plus children's garden.

OPEN *All day, every day.*

WAREHAM
The Duke of Wellington
7 East Street, Wareham BH20 4NN
☎ *(01929) 553015* Kevin Mitchell
www.dukeofwellington.biz

Freehouse serving up to six real ales. Brews from Ringwood, Studland and Hop Back plus three guests changed at least weekly. Also good range of wines.

A traditional 16th-century pub with one bar, restaurant and beer garden. CAMRA Regional Pub of the Year 2008. No juke box or machines. Food served 12–2pm and 6–9pm Mon–Sat; 12–9pm Sun. Large car park. Theme evenings. Accommodation. At the entrance to the Jurassic coastline.

OPEN *11am–11pm (later Fri–Sat).*

WAYTOWN
Hare & Hounds
Waytown, Bridport DT6 5LQ
☎ *(01308) 488203* Marian and Peter Smith

Palmers tenancy offering Best Bitter, 200 and Copper Ale plus Dorset Gold in the summer and Tally Ho! in winter.

Classic unspoilt and friendly 300-year-old cottage, converted to a pub around 1850, with bar, snug, a dining room for 20–25, and wonderful views from the beer garden. Food available 12–2pm and 6.30–9pm Mon–Sat; 12–2pm and 7–9pm Sun in summer, 12–2pm Sun in winter. Dogs and walkers welcome. Car park. Darts, Sunday quiz nights in winter. From the B30668 Bridport to Beaminster, go to Netherbury and follow signs to the pub. Difficult to find, but worth it!

OPEN *11.30am–3pm and 6.30–11pm Mon–Sat; 12–3pm and 7–11pm Sun.*

WEYMOUTH
The Boot
High Street West, Weymouth DT4 8JH
☎ *(01305) 770327* Giles Emley

Ringwood tied house featuring the full range including Best Bitter, Fortyniner, Old Thumper and seasonal brews such as XXXX Porter, plus a wide range of guests on an additional pump. Real cider also served. CAMRA Wessex Regional Pub of the Year 2005.

With foundations dating from 1346, and in business since the 17th century, this is the oldest pub in Weymouth. One bar area with comfortable rooms for sitting at either end. Also seating on the pavement outside. Behind the fire station.

OPEN *All day, every day.*

King's Arms

15 Trinity Road, Weymouth DT4 8TJ
☎ *(01305) 770055* Mr and Mrs Glynn

Ringwood Best and Fortyniner always available plus Bass.

Dating from the 16th century, subsequently altered but remains an olde-worlde quayside pub with separate dining area. Lounge bar with original beams, public bar with tiles. Pool table. Food served every lunchtime and Wed–Sat evenings. Children and dogs allowed.

OPEN *All day, every day.*

The Weatherbury Hotel

7 Carlton Road North, Weymouth DT4 7PX
☎ *(01305) 786040*
Brenda Smith and Roy Williams

Fuller's London Pride is a permanent fixture plus three rotating guests that may include something from Cottage, Hop Back or Otter.

A busy, family-run town local with a large bar in a residential area. Snacks served 12–2pm and 5–8pm. Car park, patio garden and dining area (where children are allowed). En-suite accommodation. Dart board and pool table. Sky Sports on TV. Coming in to Weymouth, turn right off the Dorchester road. Five minutes from the beach and train station.

OPEN *12–12 (1am Fri–Sat).*

Wellington Arms

13 St Alban Street, Weymouth OT4 8PY
☎ *(01305) 786963*
Martin and Chris Whitehorn

Now owned by Marston's, with Ringwood Best and something from Jennings usually available, plus a rotating guests such as Wadworth 6X .

A pub since 1850, this family-run local was originally leased from and then owned by Eldridge Pope before being sold to Marston's in 2007. Popular with holidaymakers and locals. Food served 12–7pm Mon–Thurs; 12–9pm Fri–Sat; 12–5pm Sun.

OPEN *10am–1am.*

The Lamb Inn

Burley Road, Winkton BH23 7AN
☎ *(01425) 672427* Ben Mullings
www.lambwinkton.co.uk

Four real ale pumps, serving Timothy Taylor Landlord, Ringwood Best and Fortyniner, plus one guest, changed every two months, such as St Austell Tribute, Wadworth 6X, Charles Wells Bombardier or Greene King Old Speckled Hen.

Situated on the edge of the New Forest, this traditional country inn has two bars, an open fire and a large restaurant. Food available 12–3pm and 6–9pm Mon–Sat and 12–3.30pm Sun. Beer garden and heated patio areas. Car parks front and rear. Live music, quiz night. Near New Forest walks. Between Sopley and Burton, signposted from Stoney Lane rounabout.

OPEN *11am–11pm.*

The Square & Compass

Worth Matravers, Nr Swanage BH19 3LF
☎ *(01929) 439229* Charles Newman

Classic freehouse with Ringwood Best on permanently and up to four guests depending on the time of year – perhaps Tanglefoot or something from Hop Back. Beers served straight from the cask.

An unspoilt, unchanged and extremely popular place, this has been a pub for more than 300 years. Originally built for the local stonemasons. Excellent views of the sea. Basic food such as homemade pasties. Real fires, beer garden. Games in the winter. Children welcome.

OPEN *12–3pm and 6–11pm (closed Sun evenings) in the winter; all day in the summer.*

The Wyke Smugglers

76 Portland Road, Wyke Regis, Weymouth DT4 9AB
☎ *(01305) 760010* Kelly Moore

Two real ales changed every week or two. Beers regularly featured include Greene King Old Speckled Hen and Abbot, Adnams Broadside, Wadworth 6X, Charles Wells Bombardier and brews from Wells and Young's and Black Sheep.

Traditional pub on the outskirts of Weymouth, with lounge bar, pool bar, car park and beer garden. No food. Function room and skittle alley for hire. Children welcome. Music festivals held in summer. On the main Weymouth to Portland road.

OPEN *12–12.*

The White Hart

High Street, Yetminster DT9 6LF
☎ *(01935) 872338* James Bayfield

Two or three real ales, perhaps from Otter, Butcombe, St Austell or Ringwood, rotated every couple of days.

A 16th-century thatched inn, with open fire and one large bar with separate areas. Food served 12–2pm and 7–9pm (until 9.30pm Fri and Sat, and until 8pm Sun). New full disabled facilities. Outside smoking shelter. Pool room, separate skittle alley that is suitable for functions. Large beer garden, car park at rear. Occasional folk nights, karaoke and other musical evenings. Village is just a few miles off the A37.

OPEN *12–3pm and 7pm–12.*

THE BREWERIES

CAMERONS BREWERY LTD
Lion Brewery, Hartlepool TS24 7QS
☎ *(01429) 266666*
www.cameronsbrewery.com

CAMERONS CREAMY 3.6% ABV
BANNER BITTER 4.0% ABV
SPRING KNIGHTS (MAR–JUN) 4.0% ABV
STRONGARM 4.0% ABV
SUMMER KNIGHTS (JUL–AUG) 4.0% ABV
TROPHY SPECIAL 4.0% ABV
AUTUMN KNIGHTS (SEPT–OCT) 4.2% ABV
CASTLE EDEN ALE 4.2% ABV
NIMMO'S XXXX 4.4% ABV
LONG LEG 4.8% ABV
WINTER KNIGHTS (NOV–FEB) 5.0% ABV

CONSETT ALE WORKS
The Grey Horse, Sherburn Terrace, Consett DH8 6NE
☎ *(01207) 502585*
www.thegreyhorse.co.uk

3 GIANTS 3.2% ABV
Dark mild.
MUTTON CLOG 3.8% ABV
Bittersweet with hints of citrus.
PADDY'S DELIGHT 3.8% ABV
Single hop beer.
STEEL TOWN 3.8% ABV
Hoppy with bitter finish.
TARGET ALE 4.0% ABV
Smooth bitter.
CONROY'S STOUT 4.1% ABV
Seasonal for St Patrick's Day.
POTT CLOCK 4.2% ABV
Lager-type beer.
RED DUST 4.2% ABV
Tawny, slightly sweet and malty.
SWORDMAKER 4.5% ABV
Full bodied and fruity.
ANGEL ALE 5.0% ABV
Gold-coloured bitter.
C2C 5.0% ABV
Hoppy bitter.
DERWENT DEEP 5.0% ABV
Roasted barley flavour.
DEVIL'S DIP 9.0% ABV
Dark ruby.

THE DURHAM BREWERY
Unit 5a, Bowburn North Industrial Est., Bowburn DH6 5PF
☎ *(0191) 377 1991*
www.durham-brewery.co.uk

The White Range:
SUNSTROKE 3.6% ABV
MAGUS 3.8% ABV
WHITE GEM 3.9% ABV
WHITE HERALD 3.9% ABV
WHITE GOLD 4.0% ABV
WHITE AMARILLO 4.1% ABV
WHITE VELVET 4.2% ABV
WHITE CRYSTAL 4.3% ABV
WHITE BULLET 4.4% ABV
WHITE CENTENNIAL 4.4% ABV
INVINCIBLE 4.5% ABV
WHITE FRIAR 4.5% ABV
WHITE SAPPHIRE 4.5% ABV
CUTHBERT'S CROSS 4.7%
WHITE BISHOP 4.8% ABV

The Gold Range:
DURHAM GOLD 3.7% ABV
BEDE'S GOLD 4.2% ABV
DURHAM COUNTY 4.4% ABV
BISHOP'S GOLD 4.5% ABV
PRIORS GOLD 4.5% ABV
MAGNIFICAT 6.5% ABV
BENEDICTUS 8.4% ABV
The Dark Range:
DURHAM RUBY 3.7% ABV
BLACK VELVET 4.0% ABV
CANNY LAD 4.3% ABV
DARK SECRET 4.3% ABV
EVENSONG 5.0% ABV
NINE ALTARS 5.2% ABV
SANCTUARY 6.0% ABV
TEMPTATION 10% ABV

THE FOUR ALLS BREWERY
Ales of Kent Brewery Ltd, Four Alls Hotel, Ovington, Richmond DL11 7BP
☎ *(01833) 627302*

IGGY POP 3.6% ABV
BITTER 3.8% ABV
30/- 3.8% ABV
RED ADMIRAL 3.9% ABV
SMUGGLER'S GLORY 4.8% ABV

HILL ISLAND BREWERY
Unit 7, Fowlers Yard, Back Silver Street, Durham DH1 3RA
☎ *07740 932584*

BITTER 4.0% ABV
DUN COW BITTER 4.0% ABV
CATHEDRAL ALE 4.3% ABV
GRIFFIN'S IRISH STOUT 4.5% ABV
Plus seasonals.

WEAR VALLEY BREWERY
The Grand Hotel, South Church, Bishop Auckland DL14 6DU
☎ *(01388) 601956*
www.the-grand-hotel.co.uk

EXCALIBUR 3.8% ABV
GRAND CANNY 'UN 3.8% ABV
AMOS ALE 4.1% ABV
AUCKLAND ALE 4.3% ABV
MORNING AFTER 4.8% ABV

THE PUBS

BARNARD CASTLE

The Black Horse Hotel
10 Newgate, Barnard Castle DL12 8NG
☎ *(01833) 637234* Mr Landon

A Castle Eden pub with Castle Eden Bitter and Nimmo's XXXX always on offer.

Rural pub in a stone building dating from the 17th century, formerly a coaching inn. Food available – the pub is famous for its steaks. Function room, pool room, snug area and private dining area for small parties. Occasional live music. Car park at rear. Five letting rooms. Children allowed.

OPEN *7–11pm Mon–Tues; varies on Wed–Thurs; 11am–11pm Fri–Sat; 12–10.30pm Sun.*

The Red Lion

Cotherstone, Barnard Castle DL12 9QE
☎ *(01833) 650236* ER Robinson

Freehouse with Charles Wells Bombadier and Jennings Cumberland Ale plus one guest, changed frequently.

Dating from 1738, a stone-built coaching house with exposed beam ceilings and an open fire. Food served in a separate restaurant 7–9.30pm Fri; 12–2pm and 7–9.30pm Sat; 12–2pm and 7–9pm Sun. Children and dogs welcome. Dominoes popular with the locals. Beer garden. Car park. Small functions catered for.

OPEN *7–11pm Mon–Fri; 12–3pm and 7–11pm Sat; 12–4pm and 7–10.30pm Sun.*

BILLY ROW

Dun Cow Inn (Cow Tail)

Old White Lea, Billy Row, Crook
Steve Parkin

One or two Darwin beers regularly available from a changing selection, which may include Richmond Ale.

Established in 1740, this pub is only open four nights a week and has a unique atmosphere.'A bit of a good crack.' The current licensee has been here since 1960. Car park. Well-behaved children welcome.

OPEN *8–11pm Wed, Fri, Sat; 8–10.30pm Sun.*

BIRTLEY

The Barley Mow Inn

Durham Road, Birtley, Chester le Street DH3 2AG
☎ *(0191) 410 4504* Trevor Hudspith

An Enterprise Inns pub. Black Sheep Bitter. At least six guest ales, changed at least once a week. The range of mainly local breweries featured includes Wylam, Mordue, Jarrow, Rudgate, Northumberland, Darwin and Daleside.

A large, brick-built, 1930s suburban pub. Public bar with pool and darts. Split-level lounge with dining area. Food available 11am–8pm Mon–Fri; 11am–6pm Sat; 11.30am–4pm Sun. Annual beer festival, first weekend in February. Sat: live music; Sun: quiz. Parking.

OPEN *11am–midnight Mon–Sat; 10am–11.30pm Sun.*

BISHOP AUCKLAND

Newton Cap

Newton Cap Bank, Bishop Auckland DA14 7PX
☎ *(01388) 605445* Christine Peart

Tied to Castle Eden. One guest ale, changed monthly, and the policy is not to repeat beers if possible.

This has been a pub since the 19th century. Pool room, lounge, patio. No food. Car parking space available. Accompanied children allowed, but not in evenings. Situated on the outskirts of town, two miles from the bus station.

OPEN *12–4pm and 7–11pm (10.30pm Sun); closed Tues lunch.*

BOLAM

The Countryman

Dunwell Lane, Bolam, Nr Darlington DL2 2UP
☎ *(01388) 832418* Paul and Alison Stabler
www.thecountrymanbolam.co.uk

Black Sheep Bitter, Theakston Best and a guest ale (perhaps from Camerons). Guests will increasingly be sourced from local breweries.

A 200-year-old one-bar country pub, with beams and coal fires, that reopened at Easter 2004 after almost two years standing vacant and unoccupied. Food available (Monday is steak night), with two meals for £6.95 every day except Monday, plus special deals for pensioners. Garden, car park for 50 cars. Children are welcome, and there is a children's area available. Off the A68 between Darlington and West Buckland.

OPEN *12–3pm (not Mon) and 6–11pm.*

CHESTER LE STREET

The Butcher's Arms

Middle Chare, Chester Le Street DH3 3QD
☎ *(0191) 387 3973* Leon and Liz Rawson

Marston's tied house serving Pedigree and Jennings Cumberland plus three guests, changed monthly, such as Wadworth 6X, Caledonian Deuchars IPA, Hook Norton Old Hooky, Bateman XB, Brains St Davids, Everards Tiger and Young's Waggle Dance.

Located in the town centre, this traditional one-bar pub is the oldest in Chester Le Street. Full menu and lunchtime specials served 11am–2.30pm Mon–Sat and 12–2pm Sun. Accommodation in four letting rooms. Four miles from Durham, seven miles from Metro centre, and very close to Durham County Cricket ground. Off the front street opposite Lambton Arms Hotel.

OPEN *11am–3pm and 6.30–11pm Mon–Sat; 11.30am–3pm and 7–11.30pm Sun. (Plans to open all day in future – phone for details.)*

CONSETT

The Grey Horse

115 Sherburn Terrace, Consett DH8 6NE
☎ *(01207) 502585* Kath Croft

Home of the Consett Ale Works Brewery, with three permanent beers: White Hot, Steeltown and Red Dust, and also permanent, Westons Old Rosie Scrumpy 7.3%. Four guests every week from breweries Hadrian, Jarrow, Daleside, Northumberland and many others.

Brewpub with traditional interior including two log fires in winter. The building dates from 1848, and the pub features one lounge and one bar, but no juke box, loud music or TV. Beer festivals held twice a year. Derwent reservoir is nearby. Two minutes' walk from Consett town.

OPEN *12–12.*

CORNSAY

The Black Horse Inn

Cornsay, Durham DH7 9EL
☎ *(0191) 373 4211* Gary and Jane Nattrass

 Freehouse offering Black Sheep plus four weekly-changing guests.

A former coaching inn with original features and a cosy, friendly atmosphere. Beer garden. No food. Traditional pub games, including darts. Annual beer festival every Easter. Car park. Function room available. Located just off the A68 between Tow and Lanchester.

OPEN *7–11pm Mon–Sat; 8–10.30pm Sun.*

CROOK

The White Swan

66 Hope Street, Crook DL15 9HT
☎ *(01388) 764478* John Varley

 Admiral Taverns tied house serving two constantly changing guest ales.

S mall, friendly pub with music from the '60s to the present day at weekends. No food. Outdoor patio.

OPEN *12–close.*

CROXDALE

The Daleside Arms

Front Street, Croxdale, Durham DH6 5HY
☎ *(01388) 814165*
Michael and Sandra Patterson

 Freehouse with three real ales, changed weekly.

A traditional pub in a rural setting dating from 1817, with public bar, lounge and restaurant area. Two outside seating areas, function room for hire. Food served 4–9pm Wed–Fri and 12–2pm Sat–Sun. Three en-suite letting rooms. Weekly folk club Tues evenings. Beer and folk festival June and October every year. Very large car park. Three miles from Durham northbound on A167, 500 metres off the B6288.

OPEN *4pm–12 Mon–Thurs; noon–1am Fri–Sat; 11am–midnight Sun.*

DARLINGTON

Number Twenty 2

Coniscliffe Road, Darlington DL3 7RG
☎ *(01325) 354590* Ralph Wilkinson
www.villagebrewer.co.uk

Ten or eleven real ales, including the main house beer, Village Brewer White Boar. Five or six beers arc constantly changing guests from micros and small regional breweries. Ten wines by the glass and nine continental beers on tap are also served.

A ward-winning bar on the edge of the town centre mainly serving the over-30s. Food available 12–2pm. Parking nearby.

OPEN *12–11pm Mon–Sat.*

The Quakerhouse

1–3 Mechanics Yard, Darlington DL3 7QF
☎ *07845 666643* Stephen Metcalfe
www.quakerhouse.net

Nine real ales, with Jarrow Rivet Catcher always available. The eight constantly changing guests might include Valhalla Sjolmet Stout, College Green Belfast Blonde, Country Life Golden Pig and Wharf Robin from the Brew Wharf brewery. Old Rosie Cider also served.

B uilt as three houses in the late 1700s, this pub has one main bar and a friendly atmosphere. Function room for hire. Filled rolls usually available. Disabled facilities. Well-behaved children welcome. All-year beer festival with 60 real ales each month. Live music Wed nights. Close to market and shops, through the alley between Binns and the card shop, off High Row.

OPEN *11am–11pm Mon–Thurs; 11am–midnight Fri–Sat; 12–11pm Sun.*

The Railway Tavern

8 High Northgate, Darlington DL1 1UN
☎ *(01325) 464963* C Greenhow

Tied to Enterprise, this pub offers Wadworth 6X and Bateman XXXB on a fairly regular basis. Guests include beers from Durham, Mordue, Timothy Taylor, Northumberland, Rudgate, Marston Moor and others.

T his small local pub was probably the first 'Railway Inn' in the world, as it is situated 150 metres from the first passenger station in the world. The land on which it stands was owned by the Pease family, founders of the Darlington–Stockton Railway. On the main road through Darlington, the pub has two bars, one of which has pool and darts, and features live music on Friday nights. Children allowed if supervised.

OPEN *12–11pm.*

Tap & Spile

99 Bondgate, Darlington DL3 7JY
☎ *(01325) 381679* Patrick Freeman

Four guest ales, constantly changing, from small breweries in the north-east or regional micro-breweries. Examples include beers from Wylam, Hambleton, Goose Eye, Old Bear, Daleside, Jarrow, Wensleydale and Hill Island.

T raditional town-centre local with function room available. Live music Sundays and occasionally Thurs and Sat. Quiz on Mondays. Pool table. Well-behaved children welcome until 2pm. Outside café pavement licence. Disabled facilities. Late licence at weekends.

OPEN *11.30am–11pm Mon–Wed; 11.30am–midnight Thurs; 11.30am–2am Fri–Sat; 12–12 Sun.*

DURHAM

The Dun Cow

37 Old Elvet, Durham DH1 3HN
☎ *(0191) 386 9219* Mike Leonard

Enterprise Inns house serving Camerons Castle Eden Ale, Caledonian Deuchars IPA and Black Sheep Bitter.

Grade II building, part of which dates back to the 16th century. Bar snacks, sandwiches and toasties available. Children welcome. Close to the riverbank and the university cricket ground in the centre of the beautiful city of Durham.

OPEN *11am–11pm.*

Ye Old Elm Tree

12 Crossgate, Durham DH1 4PS
☎ *(0191) 386 4621* Dave Cruddace

Regular guests, two rotating every two weeks, may include Fuller's London Pride, Greene King Old Speckled Hen or Bateman XXXB.

An alehouse dating from 1601, in the centre of Durham city, off Framwellgate Bridge. Two guest rooms, beer garden and patio. The bar is built round an elm tree. Quiz and folk nights held. Light snacks at lunchtime and evenings. Children allowed.

OPEN *12–3pm and 6–11pm Mon–Fri; 11am–11pm Sat; 12–4pm and 7–10.30pm Sun.*

The Victoria Inn

86 Hallgarth Street, Durham DH1 3AS
☎ *(0191) 386 5269* Michael Webster
www.victoriainn-durhamcity.co.uk

Freehouse serving only local beers, including Big Lamp Bitter, Wylam Gold Tankard and three daily guests, such as Durham Magus and Jarrow Swinging Gibbet.

Totally unspoilt late-Victorian layout, owned by the same family for more than 30 years. Six first-class en-suite bedrooms – voted one of the best 50 B&Bs in the country by the *Independent* newspaper in 2007. Local CAMRA Pub of the Year on five occasions. No food. Five minutes' walk to the cathedral and castle.

OPEN *11.45am–3pm and 6–11pm Mon–Sat; 12–3pm and 7–10.30pm Sun.*

The Waterhouse

65 North Road, Durham DH1 4SQ
☎ *(0191) 370 6540* Alistair Lane
www.jdwetherspoon.co.uk

JD Wetherspoon's pub with up to five real ales from local and national independent breweries. Greene King Abbot Ale and Marston's Pedigree are usually permanent, the rest change every few days.

A modern pub with one bar and a warm, friendly atmosphere. Food served 9am–11pm. Takes part in the JD Wetherspoon's national beer festival, plus quarterly beer festivals featuring local breweries. Opposite the bus station.

OPEN *9am–midnight.*

The Woodman Inn

23 Gilesgate, Durham DH1 1QW
☎ *(0191) 386 7500* Peter Seed
www.peterspub.co.uk

Always a good selection of real ales, six on tap at any time, including local brewers Durham Brewery. Also source real ale from all over the British Isles. Plus a good selection of whiskies and spirits.

Traditional friendly local pub. One of the oldest pubs in Durham City, unspoiled by modern times, a real pub. Bar snacks (toasted sandwiches, etc) available. Beer garden. Accommodation. Situated at the top of Claypath bank, within easy walking distance of local attractions.

OPEN *12–12.*

FERRYHILL STATION

The Surtees Arms & Yard of Ale Brew Co Ltd

Chilton Lane, Ferryhill Station DL17 0DH
☎ *(01740) 655724* Alan Hogg

Freehouse serving Yard of Ale beers brewed on site plus two guest ales and a cask cider. Cask Marque accredited. Brewery established 2008. Two CAMRA awards.

A traditional pit village pub built in 1872. Bar, lounge, dining room and function room. Bar snacks available, Sunday lunch 12–2.30pm. Children welcome in lounge. Beer festivals May and Oct. Two miles from J60 off the A1M.

OPEN *4–11pm Mon–Thurs; 4–12pm Fri; 12pm–12am Sat; 12–11.30pm Sun.*

FOREST IN TEESDALE

The High Force Hotel

Forest in Teesdale, Nr Barnard Castle DL12 0XH
☎ *(01833) 622222* Mike Clegg
www.highforcehotel.com

Former home of the High Force Brewery, the beers are now brewed in Sunderland by Darwin. But Forest XB and Cauldron Snout still available plus Theakston Best.

A 19th-century hunting lodge still with original character intact. Two bars, log fires. Food served 12–2.30pm daily and 7–8.45pm Tues–Sat. Children welcome. Accommodation, car park. Easy to find, opposite the High Force waterfall on the B6277.

OPEN *11am–11pm Mon–Sat; 12–10.30pm Sun.*

FRAMWELLGATE MOOR

Tap & Spile

*27 Front Street, Framwellgate Moor, Durham
DH1 5EE*
☎ *(0191) 386 5451* Lesley Fyfe
www.tapandspile.co.uk

 Up to eight beers. Caledonian Deuchars IPA is a regular, the rest of the range changes constantly. A recent guest menu featured Hook Norton Hooky Dark, Shepherd Neame Spitfire, Inveralmond Ossian, Exmoor Silver Stallion, Hampshire Thunderbolt, Bateman XXXB and Theakston Old Peculier. Cask Marque accredited.

A traditional pub with a main bar, family room and games room for darts and billiards. Pet-friendly. Bar snacks only. Children welcome until 9pm. Two miles north of Durham city centre, on the old A1.

 12–3pm and 6–11pm Mon–Sat; 12–3pm and 7–10.30pm Sun.

GREAT LUMLEY

The Old England

*Front Street, Great Lumley, Nr Chester le Street
DH3 4JB*
☎ *(0191) 388 5257* Fred Barkess

Three real ales from breweries such as Jennings and Black Sheep. All are rotated at least weekly.

A pub/restaurant set off the road, with a 200-seat lounge, 150-seat bar, separate dining area, darts, dominoes, pool. Big screen showing live sport. Food served 6.15–9pm Mon–Sat and 12–2pm Fri–Sun. Quiz nights Tues and Thurs. Large car park at rear. Close to Durham County Cricket ground.

11am–11pm Mon–Thurs; 11am–midnight Fri–Sat; 12–10.30pm Sun.

HARTLEPOOL

The Causeway

Stranton, Hartlepool TS24 7QT
☎ *(01429) 273954* Geoff Eccleshall

Marston's tied house serving Marston's Bank's Bitter and Old Empire, Camerons Strongarm and Jennings Dark Mild plus one monthly-changing guest. CAMRA Pub of the Year 2006.

Victorian pub built circa 1900 by JW Camerons as the brewery tap. Bar, servery, two snugs and a music room. Pub grub served 12–3pm Tues–Sat; BBQs in garden at weekends in summer. Children and dogs welcome. Beer garden. Live music nights. Behind Camerons brewery, next to Stranton church.

11am–11pm Mon–Wed; 11am–11.30pm Thurs; 11am–midnight Fri–Sat; 12–10.30pm Sun.

Tavern

56 Church Street, Hartlepool TS24 7DX
☎ *(01429) 222400* Chris Sewell

Camerons Strongarm and three guest beers, such as Orkney Dark Island or something from the Jennings range.

Traditional town-centre one-bar pub with upstairs, open-plan dining area. Home-cooked food served 11am–2pm and 5–8pm Mon–Sat, 12–4pm Sun. Children welcome until 8pm and they eat half price. Situated close to the railway station.

11am–3pm and 5–11pm Mon–Fri; 11am–11pm Sat; 12–3pm and 7–10.30pm Sun.

HEIGHINGTON

The Bay Horse

28 West Green, Heighington, Darlington DL5 6PE
☎ *(01325) 312312* John Blythe

 Enterprise Inns pub serving Black Sheep Bitter plus up to three guests, which are currently Timothy Taylor Landlord, Caledonian Deuchars IPA and Adnams Broadside but this changes constantly.

A 300-year-old pub in the BBC's Perfect Village competition winning location for 2006. Two bars, lounge and separate restaurant. Food served 12–3pm and 5.30–9.30pm. Children welcome. Car park. Beer garden. Eight miles from Darlington.

11am–midnight.

HETT HILLS

The Moorings Hotel

Hett Hills, Chester le Street DH2 3JU
☎ *(0191) 370 1597* John S Archer
www.themooringsdurham.co.uk

 Freehouse with two real ales rotating twice weekly, from local brewries such as Consett, Mordue, Rudgate and Jarrow.

Family-run hotel and bar/bistro. Traditional food all day from 11.45am. Beer garden and secure car parking. Nine en-suite rooms. On the B6313 from Chester le Street, two miles from the viaduct.

11.45am–late.

HIGH HESLEDEN

The Ship Inn

High Hesleden, Hartlepool TS27 4QD
☎ *(01429) 836453* Peter and Sheila Crosby
www.theshipinn.net

 A freehouse. Seven real ales, changing all the time. All the beers served come from indepenent microbreweries.

Cosy country pub close to historic Durham city. Food available. Accommodation in six deluxe en-suite chalets, awarded 4 stars by Visit Britain. Function room available.

6–11pm Tues–Fri; 12–3pm and 6–11pm Sat; 12–9pm Sun; closed Mon.

KIRK MERRINGTON

The Half Moon Inn

*Crowther Place, Kirk Merrington, Nr Spennymoor
DL16 7JL*
☎ *(01388) 811598* Mrs Crooks

 Something from Durham Brewery always available in this freehouse. Favourite guest beers might come from the Kitchen Brewery, or include Elgood's Black Dog and Hart Squirrels Hoards.

Traditional pub on the village green, with one room, games area and car park. Bar meals at lunchtime and evening. Children allowed until 8pm.

All day, every day.

LEAMSIDE

The Three Horseshoes

Pit House Lane, Leamside DA4 6QQ
☎ *(0191) 584 2394* Martin Thompson

 Six real ales including Timothy Taylor Landlord and five others from local, micro and independent breweries.

Traditional two-bar English pub. Food served at lunchtimes and evenings. Beer garden and outside areas. Private dining room. Large car park. Children welcome. Five minutes from Durham.

OPEN *11am–midnight Mon–Sat; 12–11pm Sun.*

MIDDLESTONE VILLAGE

The Ship Inn

Low Row, Middlestone Village, Bishop Auckland DL14 8AB
☎ *(01388) 810904* Graham Snaith

 Freehouse with up to six real ales. Timothy Taylor Landlord is a regular fixture and ales from local breweries such as Durham, Daleside and Big Lamp are popular. The range changes constantly.

Well-appointed traditional pub with a small bar and lounge. Built into the hillside in walking country, it offers panoramic views. CAMRA North East Pub of the Year 2001, 2002 and 2004. Restaurant on first-floor balcony doubles as a function room. Food served every day except Tues. Children allowed if parents are eating. Spring and winter beer festivals. Directions on website.

OPEN *4–11pm Mon–Thurs; 12–11pm Fri–Sat; 12–10.30pm Sun.*

NEASHAM

The Fox & Hounds

24 Teesway, Neasham, Darlington DL2 1QP
☎ *(01325) 720350* Claire Blenkin

 Two real ales usually on offer. Black Sheep Special, Jennings Cumberland Ale and Timothy Taylor Landlord are regularly featured, and are changed once a week.

Typical country pub, 100 years old, with two bars, a restaurant and conservatory. Food served 12–2pm and 6.30–9pm daily except Mondays, and Sunday evenings. Large beer garden by the River Tees. Conservatory available for hire. Children welcome. Five minutes from Darlington football stadium.

OPEN *7–11pm Mon; 12–3pm and 6–11.30pm Tues–Sat (midnight Fri–Sat); all day Sun.*

NEWTON AYCLIFFE

The Blacksmith's Arms

Preston-le-Skerne, Newton Aycliffe DL5 6JH
☎ *(01325) 314873*
Brenda Whear and Bev Hayman

 Three real ales, rotated every nine gallons, from a range including Durham Ghost, Timothy Taylor Landlord and beers from York, Hambleton, Jarrow and many other breweries.

Charming 18th-century old blacksmiths' shop with restaurant, lounge and snug. Food served 11.30am–2pm and 6–9.30pm Tues–Sun. Large beer garden. Children welcome. Disabled toilets and full access. Large car park. Turn off the A167 at the Gretna pub; The Blacksmith's Arms is half a mile down Ricknall Lane.

OPEN *11.30am–2.30pm and 6.30–11pm Tues–Sat; all day Sun.*

NO PLACE

Beamish Mary Inn

No Place, Beamish, Nr Stanley DH9 0QH
☎ *(0191) 370 0237* Graham Ford
www.beamishmary.co.uk

 Up to ten real ales. Black Sheep Special and Bitter and Jennings Cumberland Ale, plus No Place (a beer brewed specially by Big Lamp Brewery) and Theakston Old Peculier. Other guests come from small local breweries.

Built in 1897, a family-run traditional freehouse in a former mining village. Two bars, open fires and a large collection of memorabilia from the 1920s and 1930s. Live music at least three nights a week in the converted stables. Food served 12–2pm and 6–9pm (not Sun evening) in a separate restaurant area. B&B, function room. Children welcome until 8pm. Beer festival on the last weekend in January. Half a mile from the Beamish museum.

OPEN *All day, every day.*

NORTH BITCHBURN

Famous Red Lion

North Bitchburn Terrace, Nr Crook DL15 8AL
☎ *(01388) 763561* Keith Young

 Freehouse with three real ales always available. A house brew (Jenny Ale) is a regular fixture plus brews from Camerons, Northumberland, Black Sheep, Timothy Taylor, Rudgate, Hart and Derwent breweries which change every week.

An easy-to-find, typical, olde-worlde inn, stone-built with open fires, one bar, a beamed ceiling, small patio and a separate restaurant. Food served 12–2pm (not Mon) and 7–9.30pm. Families welcome, car park at rear.

OPEN *12–3pm (not Mon) and 6.30–11pm (10.30pm Sun).*

ROOKHOPE

The Rookhope Inn

Rookhope, Nr Stanhope, Bishop Auckland DL13 2BG
☎ *(01388) 517215* Alan Jackson
www.rookhope.com

 Freehouse offering a choice of three constantly changing guest ales, over 100 a year, with beers from Greene King, Black Sheep, Marston's, Timothy Taylor and Allendale making regular appearances.

A 17th-century listed pub with log fires, real beams and a resident ghost. Live music most Saturdays. Three rooms: lounge bar, games bar and dining room. Hot food and sandwiches available. Five en-suite bedrooms. On the coast-to-coast cycle route. Children and dogs welcome.

OPEN *12–3pm and 6pm–12 Sun–Fri (1am Fri); noon–1am Sat.*

SEDGEFIELD

The Dun Cow Inn

43 Front Street, Sedgefield TS21 3AT
☎ *(01740) 620894* Geoff Rayner

Four real ales, with two rotated every couple of weeks. Breweries such as Black Sheep, Hambleton, Theakston, Mordue and Rudgate are among the favourites.

S mall hotel in a pretty building with two large bars and a separate restaurant. Six en-suite bedrooms. Food available 12–2pm and 6.30–9.30pm Mon–Sat and 12–8.30pm Sun. Car park at the rear. Situated in the centre of the village, identifiable by its impressive flowers and shrubs all year round. Racecourse nearby.

OPEN *11am–3pm and 6–11pm Mon–Sat; 12–11pm Sun.*

SHADFORTH

The Shadforth Plough

South Side, Shadforth, Durham DH6 1LL
☎ *(0191) 372 0375* Claire Robinson

 Marston's Pedigree plus guests changed weekly, with brews from Hill Island regularly featured.

A traditional country pub, with bar, lounge and restaurant extension. Food served 12–2.30pm and 6–9.20pm Mon–Sat; 12–3pm and 6–9pm Sun. Beer garden. Children welcome. Close to Durham city centre.

OPEN *12–3pm and 6–11pm Mon–Fri; 12–11pm Sat; 12–10.30pm Sun.*

TANTOBIE

The Highlander

White-le-Head, Tantobie, Nr Stanley DH9 9SN
☎ *(01207) 232416* CD Wright

 Up to 100 beers per year changed weekly, including something from Thwaites, Timothy Taylor, Black Sheep and Marston's, plus beers from many other smaller breweries as available.

O ne bar has games and music (pool, darts, etc). Also a small lounge and dining area. Hot food available on weekday evenings and weekend afternoons. Car park, beer garden and function room. Children welcome. Occasional accommodation (ring to check). One mile off the A692 between Tantobie and Flint Hill.

OPEN *7.30–11pm Mon–Fri; 12.30–3pm and 7.30–11pm Sat–Sun.*

WOLVISTON

The Ship Inn

Wolviston, Billingham TS22 5JX
☎ *(01740) 644420* Edna Sanderson

 Three guest ales available at all times, changed up to twelve times a week.

O ld village pub, with food served 12–1.45pm and 5–8.45pm (no food Sun evening). Two weekly music quizzes, one weekly general knowledge quiz. Beer garden. Function room. Just off the A19 to Hartlepool.

OPEN *12–3pm and 5–11pm.*

THE BREWERIES

BLANCHFIELD'S BREWERY
3 Fleet Hall Road, Rochford SS4 1NF
☎ *(01702) 530053*

BLACK BULL MILD 3.6% ABV
IPA TWIST 3.6% ABV
PORTER BULL 4.3% ABV
WHITE BULL WHEAT BEER 4.4% ABV
GOLDEN BULL 4.6% ABV
RAGING BULL BITTER 4.9% ABV
Plus seasonal brews.

BRENTWOOD BREWING COMPANY
c/o 372 Ongar Road, Brentwood CM15 9JH
☎ *(01277) 375760*
www.brentwoodbrewing.co.uk

CANARY BEAVER 3.8% ABV
Golden, hoppy.
SPOOKY MOON 3.8% ABV
Chocolate and fruity flavours.
CHESTNUT STOUT 3.9% ABV
Roast chestnut flavour.
BRENTWOOD BEST 4.2% ABV
Reddish, hoppy bitter.
HOPE AND GLORY 4.5% ABV
Hoppy.
SUMMER VIRGIN 4.5% ABV
Citrus aroma and flavour.
BIG BROWN BEAR 4.8% ABV
Malt and hop flavours.
Plus seasonals including:
BLIND DATE 4.1% ABV
HEAVENLY BODY 4.3% ABV
VOLCANO 4.6% ABV
CLOCKWORK ORANGE 6.5% ABV

CROUCH VALE BREWERY LTD
23 Haltwhistle Road, South Woodham Ferrers,
Chelmsford CM3 57A
☎ *(01245) 322744*
www.crouch-vale.co.uk

ESSEX BOYS BITTER 3.5% ABV
Plenty of malt and hop flavour.
BLACKWATER MILD 3.7% ABV
Smooth, dark and malty.
BREWERS GOLD 4.0% ABV
Hoppy with tropical fruit aromas.
CROUCH BEST 4.0% ABV
Malt and fruit, some hops.
Plus seasonals including:
ESSEX BLONDE 4.7% ABV
ANCHOR STREET PORTER 4.9% ABV
AMARILLO 5.0% ABV
BREWERS GOLD EXTRA 5.2% ABV

FAMOUS RAILWAY TAVERN BREWING CO.
The Famous Railway Tavern Co., 58 Station
Road, Brightlingsea, Colchester CO7 0DT
☎ *(01206) 302581*

CRAB & WINKLE 3.7% ABV
FOG ALE 3.7% ABV
BLADDERWRACK STOUT 4.7% ABV
FIRESIDE PORTER 4.7% ABV
HISTORIC NETTLE ALE 5.0% ABV
Plus seasonals and specials.

THE FELSTAR BREWERY
Felsted Vineyard, Crix Green, Felsted, Dunmow
CM6 3JT
☎ *(01245) 361504*
www.felstarbrewery.co.uk

FELSTAR 3.4% ABV
Golden brown bitter, balanced malt and hops.
CRIX FOREST 4.0% ABV
Dark mild, undertones of raspberry.
SHALFORD 4.0% ABV
Bitter brewed with three different hops.
GOOD KNIGHT 5.0% ABV
Smoky spicy tones.
HOPPY HEN 5.0% ABV
Spicy yet malty.
PECKIN' ORDER 5.0% ABV
Lager style.
DANCIN' HEN 6.0% ABV
Malty and powerful.
Plus seasonal brews.

THE GEORGE & DRAGON,
Churchend, Foulness Island, Southend-on-Sea
SS3 9XQ
☎ *(01702) 219460*
www.georgeanddragonpub.co.uk

BEATER'S BEST BITTER 5.0% ABV

MALDON BREWING CO. LTD
The Stable Brewery, Silver Street, Maldon
CM9 4QE
☎ *(01621) 840925*
www.maldonbrewing.co.uk

A DROP OF NELSON'S BLOOD 3.8% ABV
BLUE BOAR BITTER 4.0% ABV
Malty, uses 1st Gold hops.
HOTEL PORTER 4.1% ABV
A dark beer of 'stout' character.
PUCK'S FOLLY 4.2% ABV
A light beer with lots of Goldings hops and a hint of grapefruit.
EDWARD BRIGHTS STOUT 4.5% ABV

MERSEA ISLAND BREWERY
Mersea Island Vineyard, Rewsalls Lane,
East Mersea, Colchester CO5 8SX
☎ *(01206) 381830*
www.merseawine.com

MERSEA MUD 3.8% ABV
Smooth and malty.
YO BOY 3.8% ABV
Gold colour with a hint of fruit.
SKIPPERS 4.8% ABV
Dark, hoppy bitter.
MERSEA MONKEYS 5.0% ABV
Lingering hops and malt.
OYSTER 5.0% ABV
Brewed with local Mersea Island oysters added to it.

MIGHTY OAK BREWING CO.
14b West Station Yard, Spital Road, Maldon CM9 6TW
☎ *(01621) 843713*
www.mightyoakbrewery.co.uk

IPA 3.6% ABV
Pale golden. Good hoppy bitterness.
OSCAR WILDE MILD 3.7% ABV
Mellow and nutty dark mild.
MALDON GOLD 3.8% ABV
Light golden ale with biscuity malt flavours.
BURNTWOOD BITTER 4.0% ABV
Deep copper coloured, clean bitterness and complex malt flavours.
SIMPLY THE BEST 4.4% ABV
A tawny-coloured ale with crisp, light bitterness.
ENGLISH OAK 4.8% ABV
Full malt amber ale with strong hop finish.
Plus seasonal brews including:
SEA LEGS 3.7% ABV
JACK FROST 3.8% ABV
PROP UP THE BAR 3.8% ABV
TO THE LIGHTHOUSE 3.8% ABV
EAST COAST ALE 4.0% ABV
SPINNAKERED 4.0% ABV
TILLER GIRL 4.2% ABV
OH BUOY 4.4% ABV
TELL T'ALE 4.4% ABV

PITFIELD ORGANIC BREWERY
London Road, Great Horkesley, Colchester
☎ *0845 8331492*
www.pitfieldbeershop.co.uk

BITTER 3.7% ABV
EAST KENT GOLDINGS 4.2% ABV
ECO WARRIOR 4.5% ABV

STAR BEERMAKING COMPANY
Mystique Too, Steeple, Southminster CM0 7RT
☎ *07980 530707*

GOLD STAR 3.6% ABV
IPA 4.5% ABV
Plus seasonals.

THE PUBS

ALTHORNE
The Black Lion
Burnham Road, Althorne CM3 6BT
☎ *(01621) 740241* John Windle
www.theblacklionpub.co.uk

Adnams Bitter plus up to three local ales brewed by Farmer's including Puck's Folly, A Drop of Nelson's Blood and Sweet Farmer's Ale.

Grade II listed building dating from the 1750s and under the same management for more than two decades. Food served 12–2pm and 7–9.30pm. Car park, garden with large children's play area. Restaurant available for private hire. Guide dogs only.

OPEN *Closed Mon; 12–3pm and 7–11.30pm Tues–Sat; 12–3pm and 7–10.30pm Sun.*

BARKING
The Britannia
1 Church Road, Barking IG11 8PR
☎ *(020) 8594 1305* John and Rita Pells

Wells and Young's pub serving Young's Special and Bitter plus a winter warmer from October and various specials in summer.

An old-fashioned community alehouse with public bar, saloon/lounge bar and snug. Patio. Food available at lunchtimes and evenings. No children. Can be extremely difficult to find – ring if need be.

OPEN *11am–11pm*

BASILDON
The Moon on the Square
1–15 Market Square, Basildon SS14 1DF
☎ *(01268) 520360* Nick Merenda

Wetherspoon's pub serving nine beers, with Marston's Pedigree and Greene King IPA always available. Guests changed weekly, from a list that includes Adnams Clipper, Badger Tanglefoot, Charles Wells Bombardier, Ringwood Fortyniner, amongst many other independents.

Busy market pub (note early opening) with one large bar. A mixed clientele of business customers and lunchtime shoppers. Food served all day. Children allowed only at tables.

OPEN *9am–midnight Sun–Thurs; 9am–1am Fri–Sat.*

BILLERICAY
The Coach & Horses
36 Chapel Street, Billericay CM12 9LU
☎ *(01277) 622873* Terry Roberts

Greene King IPA and Abbot and Adnams Bitter plus weekly-changing guest beers. Tries to stock independent breweries' beers whenever possible.

Small town pub with one bar. Friendly locals and good regular clientele. Food available 12–2.20pm and 6–9pm Mon–Sat, 12–7pm Sun. Beer garden, car park. No children. Next to Waitrose.

OPEN *10am–11pm Mon–Sat; 12–10.30pm Sun.*

BIRDBROOK
The Plough
The Street, Birdbrook CO9 4BJ
☎ *(01440) 785336* Richard Holman

Greene King IPA plus rotating guest beers.

A 16th-century thatched genuine freehouse in picturesque village, with low-beamed ceilings, cosy, interlinking lounge, dining area and public bar. Beer garden and patio. Follow signs to Birdbrook from A1017.

OPEN *12–2pm and 6.30–11pm Tues–Thurs; 12–12 Fri–Sun.*

BLACK NOTLEY

The Vine Inn

105 The Street, Black Notley, Nr Braintree CM77 8LL
☎ *(01376) 324269* Tony Keogh

 Independent freehouse with Adnams Bitter plus two guest ales, often from local counties. Beers from Mighty Oak are regularly available.

Country pub dating from 1640 with an old barn end, a minstrel's gallery and lots of beams. Main area is split 50/50, bar and restaurant. Food served at lunchtimes and evenings. Children allowed in restaurant (for meals) and on patio. A couple of miles outside Braintree on the Notley Road.

OPEN *12–2.30pm and 6.30–11pm Mon–Sat; 12–4pm and 7–10.30pm Sun.*

BRENTWOOD

The Rising Sun

144 Ongar Road, Brentwood CM15 9DJ
☎ *(01277) 213749* Colin and Dawn Smith

Admiral Taverns pub offering Timothy Taylor Landlord and Brakspear Bitter plus one guest.

Small, locals' pub, rebuilt about 70 years ago from an older original building. No food. Well-behaved children welcome. Beer garden, covered smoking area. Small car park. Small function room. On the A128.

OPEN *3–11.30pm Mon–Thurs; 3pm–12 Fri; 12–12 Sat; 12–11pm Sun.*

The Swan

123 High Street, Brentwood CM14 4RX
☎ *(01277) 211848* Chrisandra Bester

Greene King IPA, Abbot and Old Speckled Hen on hand pump plus up to four weekly-changing guests such as Timothy Taylor Landlord, Ringwood Best and Fortyniner plus seasonal ales from all over the UK served on gravity.

A 13th-century pub with a friendly atmosphere. Mainly a locals' pub with quiet background music. Food served at lunchtimes but parties catered for outside these hours. Small patio garden to be extended. No children or under-21s.

OPEN *11am–11pm Mon–Wed; 11am–11.30pm Thurs; 11am–midnight Fri–Sat; 12–11pm Sun.*

BRIGHTLINGSEA

The Famous Railway Tavern

58 Station Road, Brightlingsea CO7 0DT
☎ *(01206) 302581* David English

 Brewpub with home brews plus Crouch Vale Best, a dark mild, a stout and a real cider always available, plus up to five guests from local breweries. Gravity-fed in winter.

Friendly, traditional pub with real fire and floorboards. No fruit machines or juke box in the public bar. Garden, children's room. Table football, shove ha'penny, darts, cribbage, dominoes. Campsite opposite, 11 pubs within walking distance. Buskers'

afternoon held once a month between October and April. Annual cider festival held during first week of May.

OPEN *5–11pm Mon–Thurs; 3–11pm Fri; 12–11pm Sat; 12–3pm and 7–10.30pm Sun.*

BURNHAM–ON–CROUCH

The Anchor Hotel

The Quay, Burnham-on-Crouch CM0 8AT
☎ *(01621) 782117* Kevin Veal

Greene King IPA and Adnams and Crouch Vale brews plus three guests from breweries such as Titanic or Wells and Young's. Seasonal ales also stocked.

A locals' pub with a broad clientele in a small seaside town with seating on the sea wall. Two bars, two dining areas. Food available at lunchtimes and evenings. Children allowed in the restaurant. Live music on Thursdays. Accommodation available in four en-suite rooms.

OPEN *All day, every day.*

Ye Olde White Harte Hotel

The Quay, Burnham-on-Crouch CM0 8AS
☎ *(01621) 782106* John Lewis

Adnams Bitter and Crouch Vale Best available.

Red-brick, riverside inn built in the 1600s with many original beams and fireplaces, both in the public rooms and in the bedrooms. No machines, no music. Waterside restaurant open 12–2pm and 7–9pm every day with local fish a speciality. Nineteen rooms in the hotel, where there is a separate residents' lounge. Well-behaved children welcome.

OPEN *All day, every day.*

The Queen's Head

26 Providence, Burnham-on-Crouch CM0 8JU
☎ *(01621) 784825* Jim and Lin Morton
www.queensheadburnham.com

Gray's house with Mighty Oak Maldon Gold plus up to three guests from small, often local independent breweries, changed regularly (over 200 served in 2007), plus Weston's Traditional Scrumpy Cider.

Recently, sympathetically refurbished hidden gem in a quiet side street run by the local CAMRA membership secretary. Dating from 1850, this is a traditional locals' pub offering quality real ale and genuine homemade food, including Essex Huffers baked on the premises using local flour, and the Landlord's own Curries and Chillis. Food served 12–2.30pm Tues–Sun. Small, secluded courtyard garden. Beer festival August bank holiday. Providence is a narrow turning off the High Street, opposite the Clock Tower and there is a public car park over the road from the pub. Walkers, cyclists, dogs etc. welcome.

OPEN *12–11pm every day.*

The Ship Inn

High Street, Burnham-on-Crouch CM0 8AA
☎ *(01621) 785057* Tony and Brenda Tofari

Adnams house with Bitter and Broadside plus the same brewery's Regatta through the summer, and various other guests through the rest of the year.

Refurbished country town pub with open-plan bar, but clever separation of eating and drinking areas. Outside seating on the quiet High Street. En-suite accommodation. Food served lunchtimes (12–2.30pm) and evenings (7–9.30pm). Well-behaved children allowed at restaurant tables.

OPEN *11am–11pm Mon–Sat; 12–10.30pm Sun.*

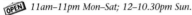

CASTLE HEDINGHAM

The Bell Inn

10 St James Street, Castle Hedingham CO9 3EJ
☎ *(01787) 460350*
Penny Doe and Kylie Turkoz-Ferguson
www.hedinghambell.co.uk

Up to five real ales, including Mighty Oak IPA and Maldon Gold, plus Adnams Best and rotating guests served straight from the barrel. Plus real cider.

Former coaching inn with a friendly atmosphere, a pub for 500 years. Four rooms, two with bars, real fires, function room. Food available 12–2pm and 7–9pm. Vine-covered patio, large walled orchard garden. Children, dogs and horses welcome. Live music, Sunday quiz night. Beer festival on the third weekend in July. Handy for the castle and for the nearby steam trains.

OPEN *12–3pm and 6–11pm Mon–Thurs; 12–12 Fri–Sat; 12–11pm Sun.*

CHELMSFORD

The Cricketers

143 Moulsham Street, Chelmsford CM2 0JT
☎ *(01245) 261157* Mr Harley

Gray's house with Greene King IPA and Abbot plus two guests from Mighty Oak and others.

City-centre local with pool table and Sky Sports. Bar food served at lunchtimes.

OPEN *11am–11pm Mon–Sat; 12–10.30pm Sun.*

The Endeavour

Duke Street, Chelmsford CM2 6AW
☎ *(01245) 257717* Mike Mitchell

Gray's house with Greene King IPA and Abbot, and Mighty Oak Maldon Gold plus two guests, with Woodforde's Wherry a regular visitor.

A cosy 17th-century pub with original features, large open fire and two bars. Originally named to commemorate Cook's ship, it also celebrates the Space Shuttle of the same name. The pub also boasts a rare 'Russian Black' terrier bitch. Theme nights every so often. Food served Mon–Sat lunchtimes with specials. Fresh fish from Lowestoft on Fridays and steak night on Saturdays. Sunday lunch. Booking essential for Sat evening and Sun lunch.

OPEN *11am–11pm Mon–Sat; 12–10.30pm Sun.*

The Queen's Head

30 Lower Anchor Street, Chelmsford CM2 0AS
☎ *(01245) 265181* Mike Collins

Crouch Vale-owned house. Crouch Vale Best and Brewer's Gold always available, plus guests, always including a mild, stout or porter. Guests come from a range of independent breweries such as St Peter's, Otter, RCH, Skinner's, Sharp's and Orkney.

A traditional alehouse a mile from the cricket ground. Built in 1895 but totally refurbished – one bar with real fires, courtyard and beer garden. Pub games, no music. Food available 12–2.30pm Mon–Sat, with homemade pies and locally produced beer sausages a speciality. No children. Large car park. Annual beer festival in September. Close to Essex CCC.

OPEN *12–11pm Sun–Thurs; 12–11.30pm Fri–Sat.*

The Railway Tavern

63 Duke Street, Chelmsford CM1 1HT
☎ *(01245) 356995* Chris and Rick Day

Gray and Sons house with Greene King IPA and Abbot plus two guests from around the country changed weekly, plus a draught cider.

Long, narrow one-bar pub converted from 19th-century railway cottages. Situated immediately opposite the main station entrance. Secluded beer garden. Food served 11.30am–3pm, with specials changed daily. Children welcome in beer garden only.

OPEN *11am–midnight.*

The White Horse

25 Townfield Street, Chelmsford CM1 1QJ
☎ *(01245) 269556* Rianna Read

Seven real ales usually served. Greene King IPA, Adnams Broadside, Theakston Mild, Fuller's London Pride and Young's Bitter are the permanent beers, plus two guests, rotated every couple of weeks.

Traditional one-bar pub full of pub games, including bar billiards, skittles, and darts. Food available 12–3pm Mon–Fri. Smoking area provided. An ideal stop after a cattle-truck commute! Turn right from the rear of the railway station.

OPEN *12–11.30pm Mon–Thurs; 12–12 Fri; 11am–midnight Sat; 12–11pm Sun.*

The Woolpack

23 Mildmay Road, Chelmsford CM2 0DN
☎ *(01245) 259295* D Gentry and M Jones

Greene King tied house with IPA, Ruddles Best and two seasonal Greene King ales. Also two guests changed monthly.

A late-Victorian backstreet local with two bars and traditional pub games. Quiz night Tues. Acoustic music on the last Sunday of the month. Food, specialising in eight types of sausage, served 12–2.30pm and 5–8pm Mon–Fri; 12–4pm Sun. Patio. Outside covered smoking area. Small car park. In the centre of Chelmsford, just off Parkway.

OPEN *12–11pm Sun–Thurs; 12–12 Fri–Sat.*

COLCHESTER

The Bricklayers

27 Bergholt Road, Colchester CO4 5AA
☎ *(01206) 852008* Fred Veasey

An award-winning Adnams pub featuring the full range of the brewery's beers plus up to five wide-ranging guest ales. Crone's cider also served.

Two-bar town pub not far from the station. Food served Sun–Fri lunchtimes. Good Sunday lunch 12–2pm. Conservatory and outside seating.

OPEN *11am–3pm and 5.30–11pm Mon–Thurs; all day Fri–Sat; 12–3pm and 7–11pm Sun.*

The Hospital Arms

123–5 Crouch Street, Colchester CO3 3HA
☎ *(01206) 542398* Ros and Lindsey
www.colchester-hospitalarms.co.uk

Adnams house with Bitter, Broadside, Explorer and Old, plus three guests, such as Woodfordes Wherry, Timothy Taylors Landlord, St Austell Tribute, Black Sheep Bitter, Everards Sunchaser, Crouch Vale Brewers Gold, Bateman Valiant, Castle Rock Elsie Mo and Wadworth Summersault. Award winning Adnams 'Best Pub'.

Traditional English alehouse, winner of several awards. Home-cooked food served 12–2pm, including very popular traditional Sunday lunches. Outside patio area – an oasis in the summer – plus courtyard smoking facilities. Just outside the town centre, opposite the Essex County Hospital, on Lexden Road.

OPEN *All day, every day from noon.*

Odd One Out

28 Mersea Road, Colchester CO2 7ET
☎ *(01206) 513958* John Parrick

Genuine freehouse with Archers Best and a dark ale always available plus up to five guests, often from East Anglian breweries, changed every few days. Four traditional ciders including one organic brew.

Friendly pub with 50s-style décor about 100 yards up the Mersea Road from St Botolph's roundabout. Open fires, beer garden, no music, room for hire. Cheese rolls available most of the time. Also has a good range of whiskies (10 Irish, 50 single malt).

OPEN *4.30–11pm Mon–Thurs; 12–11pm Fri; 11am–11pm Sat; 12–10.30pm Sun.*

COXTIE GREEN

The White Horse

173 Coxtie Green Road, Coxtie Green, Brentwood CM14 5PX
☎ *(01277) 372410* Colin Gibbs
www.whitehorsecoxtiegreen.co.uk

Freehouse offering six real ales: Fuller's London Pride and something from Brentwood plus four guests changed every few days, from all over the country.

A friendly pub with public bar and lounge. Large garden with secure children's play area. Food served 12–2.30pm Mon–Sat. Car park. Two miles from J28 of the M25.

OPEN *All day, every day.*

DEDHAM

The Sun Inn

High Street, Dedham CO7 6DF
☎ *(01206) 323351* Piers Baker
www.thesuninndedham.com

Four real ales on tap from small breweries, including the award-winning Brewer's Gold from Crouch Vale. Also botanically brewed ginger beer and Victorian lemonade. Extensive wine list of over 40 bottles, 15 available by the glass.

Independent freehouse with oak floorboards, a rare oak bar top, exposed beams, original artwork, character furniture and four open fires. Modern British food from locally sourced produce served 12–2.30pm and 6.30–9.30pm. Children welcome. Beer garden and terrace. Car park. Shop.

OPEN *12–11pm Mon–Sat; 12–6pm Sun (11pm bank holidays).*

EPPING

The Forest Gate Inn

Bell Common, Epping CM16 4DZ
☎ *(01992) 572312* Robin Stokes

A freehouse. Adnams Bitter and Broadside and Nethergate IPA. Guests such as Woodforde's Wherry and Palmers Tally Ho! served on a seasonal basis.

A 16th-century character pub. Bar snacks served 12–2pm and 6–9.30pm. Well-behaved children and dogs welcome. Beer garden. Car park. Private room.

OPEN *10am–2.30pm and 5–11pm Mon–Fri; 10am–3pm and 5–11pm Sat; 12–3.30pm and 6.30–10.30pm Sun.*

The Moletrap

Tawney Common, Epping CM16 7PU
☎ *(01992) 522394* Mr and Mrs Kirtley

Freehouse with Fuller's London Pride plus ever-changing guests from all over the country with the emphasis on independent and micro-breweries.

A 250-year-old listed building which has been extended. Outside seating. Food served at lunchtime and evenings. Well-behaved children allowed. Down a rural country lane, but only five minutes' drive from Epping.

OPEN *Winter: 11.30am–2.30pm and 6.30–11pm. Summer: 11.30am–3pm and 6–11pm.*

FEERING

The Sun Inn

3 Feering Hill, Feering, Nr Kelvedon CO5 9NH
☎ *(01376) 570442* Andy Howard

Now tied to Shepherd Neame, with five or six real ales on offer, Bishop's Finger, Spitfire, Master Brew, Kents Best and a seasonal ale. Guests from Shepherd Neame are changed monthly.

Heavily timbered former mansion, richly decorated with carved beams and open fires in winter, full of charm and character. Traditional, with no TVs, games machines or music. Bar and restaurant food 12–2.30pm and 6–9.30pm. Car park, beer garden and beer tent. Small functions (up to 28 persons) catered for. Children welcome. Turn off the Kelvedon bypass from the north or south.

 12–3pm and 5.30–11pm Mon–Sat; all day Sun.

FINGRINGHOE

The Whalebone

Chapel Road, Fingringhoe, Colchester CO5 7BG
☎ *(01206) 729307* Mr and Mrs Burroughes

 Freehouse with four guest ales.

A traditional village pub with exposed beams, refurbished to high standards. Beer garden with views across the Roman River Valley. Car park, children welcome. Food served daily. Three miles from Colchester. From the A12, follow signs to Colchester. At the roundabout at the end of Southway, follow Fingringhoe.

 12–3pm and 5.30–11pm Mon–Fri; all day Sat–Sun.

FYFIELD

The Queen's Head

Queen Street, Fyfield, Nr Ongar CM5 0RY
☎ *(01277) 899231*
Daniel Lamprecht and Penelope Miers

Adnams Best and Broadside plus four constantly changing guests from a range of independent and micro-breweries. Extensive wine list, plus scrumpy cider, cognacs, whiskies and brandies.

A friendly 15th-century freehouse, heavily beamed with two fireplaces and a riverside garden. Character tables, some in private booths. Food served 12–2.30pm and 7–9.30pm (not Sun evening). Beer garden by the River Roding. No under-14s. In the centre of Fyfield, three miles from Ongar.

 11am–3.30pm and 6–11pm Mon–Sat; 12–3.30pm and 7–10.30pm Sun.

GESTINGTHORPE

The Pheasant

Audley End, Gestingthorpe CO9 3AU
☎ *(01787) 461196*
James and Diana Donoghue

Maldon's Pleasant Pheasant and Nethergates IPA plus a guest ale from Greene King which is changed fortnightly.

Multi-roomed, 400-year-old freehouse, refurbished throughout with oak floors and wood-burning stoves. There is one bar and two dining areas. Bar billiards. There is a comprehensive menu of freshly prepared home-cooked food, sourced locally where possible. Bar snacks, à la carte meals, specials, vegetarian dishes and children's menu available 12–2.30pm and 6.30–9.30pm Tues–Sat; Sunday 12–3pm, including roasts. Garden with extensive views over the Essex countryside. Large car park. Children are welcome: the pub has a children's play area. Private function room. Well signposted, just north of Halstead, the only pub in the village.

 6–11pm Mon; 12–2.30pm and 6–11pm Tues–Fri; 12–3pm and 6–11pm Sat; 12–3pm and 7–10.30pm Sun.

GOLDHANGER

The Chequers Inn

The Square, Goldhanger, Nr Maldon CM9 8AS
☎ *(01621) 788203*
Philip Glover and Dominic Davies
www.thechequersgoldhanger.co.uk

Punch Taverns house serving Caledonian Deuchars IPA, Flowers IPA (brewed by Badger) and Everards Tiger plus three guests such as Goff's Jouster or Hydes Jekyll's Gold.

Traditional English pub on a village square, built in 1410. Food served 12–3pm and 6.30–9pm every day except Sun evening. Traditional pub games such as shove ha'penny and bar billiards. Beer garden. Car park. 400 yards from the B1026.

 11am–11pm Mon–Sat; 12–10.30pm.

GRAYS

The White Hart

Argent Street, Grays RM17 6HR
☎ *(01375) 373319* Chris and Benice Ryley
www.whitehartgrays.co.uk

Crouch Vale Brewers Gold is one of the four beers on offer, plus three guests, changed several times a week. Examples include Sharp's Special, York Centurion's Ghost, Dark Star Original, Phoenix Wobbly Bob and Acorn Old Moor Porter.

Built in 1938 to replace the old building that stood in front of it, the pub has two large bars with a private room at the rear for parties and meetings. Large beer garden with exterior TV screen, two large car parks, ten letting rooms. Barbecues on summer weekends. Annual winter beer festival in Jan/Feb. Short walk from Grays Beach Playground, and three minutes from Grays station and town.

 12–11.30pm Sun–Thurs; 12–12 Fri–Sat.

GREAT BROMLEY

The Snooty Fox

Frating Road, Great Bromley, Colchester CO7 7JW
☎ *(01206) 251065* Wayne Munn

Up to four real ales, often sourced from local or other micro-brewers and changing constantly.

A 17th-century village freehouse with a log burner creating a cosy atmosphere. Good-quality food in the bar and in a flagstone-floor restaurant. Large car park and over an acre of meadow. Close to Beth Chatto's gardens.

 12–2.30pm and 5.30–11pm.

GREAT DUNMOW

The Swan Inn

The Endway, Great Easton, Great Dunmow CM6 2HG
☎ *(01371) 870359* David and Karen Scott
www.swangreateaston.co.uk

 Freehouse serving Adnams Bitter. Guest ales mainly from local and smaller regional brewers, such as The Saffron Brewery, Crouch Vale, Nethergates, Mighty Oak, and the Nottingham brewery Magpie.

A 15th-century village freehouse with lounge bar, public bar with pool table and darts and separate restaurant. Fresh, homemade food (even the marmalade and chocolates!) served 12–2pm Mon–Sun and 7–9pm Mon–Sat. Pretty beer garden. Children welcome. Car park. Superior B&B accommodation. Rated as a 4-star inn by the English Tourist Board and recommended by Condé Nast Johansens. Signposted off the B184, three miles north of Dunmow.

OPEN *12–3pm and 6–11pm Mon–Sat; 12–3pm and 7–10.30pm Sun (closed winter Sundays – when the clocks change).*

GREAT YELDHAM

The Waggon & Horses

High Street, Great Yeldham CO9 4EX
☎ *07000 924466 (WAGGON)* Mike Shiffner
www.waggonandhorses.net

 A Greene King ale plus two weekly-changing guests.

A traditional freehouse. Food served 12–2pm and 7–9pm Mon–Sat; all day Sun. Accommodation. Beer garden. Convenient for Stansted airport, Constable country and the Colne Valley railway. On the A1017 between Braintree and Haverhill.

OPEN *11am–11pm.*

HARLOW

The Queens Head

26 Churchgate Street, Harlow CM17 0JT
☎ *(01279) 427266* Robert Webster

 Freehouse with Adnams Bitter and Broadside, Nethergate IPA and a frequently changing guest, often from Nethergate, Crouch Vale or Mighty Oak.

B uilt in 1530 and converted into a pub around 1700, this traditional, old-fashioned, beamed pub has two bars and a patio garden. Good pub food served 12–2.30pm and 6–9.30pm. Car park. Follow signs from the A414 in Harlow to Churchgate Street.

OPEN *11.30am–3pm and 5–11pm Mon–Sat; 12–4pm and 7–10.30pm Sun.*

HATFIELD BROAD OAK

The Cock Inn

High Street, Hatfield Broad Oak CM22 7HF
☎ *(01279) 718306*
Pam Holcroft and Dave Sulway

 Adnams Best and Fuller's London Pride plus guests.

T raditional country freehouse with open fires, private function room, car park, disabled access and outside seating. Food served at lunchtimes and evenings. Well-behaved children allowed.

OPEN *12–2.30pm and 6–11pm Mon–Sat; all day most Sundays.*

HERONGATE TYE

The Olde Dog Inn

Billericay Road, Herongate Tye, Brentwood CM13 3SD
☎ *(01277) 810337* Sheila Murphy
www.theoldedoginn.co.uk

 Genuine freehouse with seven real ales, including Fuller's London Pride, Greene King Abbot and Crouch Vale Olde Dog IPA, plus two rotating beers changed weekly and a further two guest beers changed twice a week. Real cider also served.

A friendly, traditional family-owned and -run Essex weatherboard inn, over 500 years old, with low beams, open fires and several distinct areas. In the same family since 1978. Main bar, separate large dining area, background music, garden. Homemade food using locally sourced ingredients served 12–2.30pm and 6.15–9pm Mon–Fri (until 9.30pm Fri), 12–9.30pm Sat and 12–7pm Sun. Secluded beer garden, large car park. Good base for some excellent country walks. Well-behaved children allowed. Located on a sharp bend on the Billericay Road, off the A128.

OPEN *11am–3pm and 6–11pm Mon–Fri; 12–11pm Sat; 12–10.30pm Sun.*

HIGH RODING

The Black Lion

3 The Street, High Roding, Great Dunmow CM6 1NT
☎ *(01371) 872847* Andy Coleman

 A Greene King tied house, serving IPA plus one guest from the brewery's seasonal range.

B uilt in 1397, this olde-worlde country village pub features beams and open fires. Food served 12–3pm and 7–9pm Mon–Fri, all day Sat, 12–3.30pm Sun. Children welcome – the pub has an enclosed garden. Lawned area, car park. Regular live music and quiz nights. On the main B4187.

OPEN *12–3pm and 6–11pm Mon–Fri; 12–11pm Sat; 12–10.30pm Sun.*

HORNDON ON THE HILL

The Bell Inn

High Road, Horndon on the Hill SS17 8LD
☎ *(01375) 642463* John and Christine Vereker
www.bell-inn.co.uk

 Seven real ales, with Greene King IPA, Crouch Vale Brewers Gold and Draught Bass permanently featured, plus four beers rotated weekly.

Attractive 600-year-old village coaching inn with two bars and a restaurant. The courtyard has seating, and is filled with hanging baskets in summer. Award-winning restaurant and bar food available 12–1.45pm and 6.30–9.45pm Mon–Fri (no food bank holiday Mon); 12–2.30pm and 7–9.45pm Sun. Accommodation (16 bedrooms). Car park for 50 cars. Private room for hire. On the B1007 off the A13 or A128, junction 30/31 of M25.

OPEN *11am–2.30pm and 5.30–11pm Mon–Fri; 11am–3pm and 6–11pm Sat; 12–4pm and 7–10.30pm Sun.*

HUTTON

The Chequers

213 Rayleigh Road, Hutton, Brentwood CM13 1PJ
☎ *(01277) 224980* Dianne Thomas

Greene King IPA and Adnams Broadside plus a fortnightly guest such as Everards Tiger, Brains SA, Greene King Abbot, Hook Norton Old Hooky, Shepherd Neame Spitfire or Marston's Pedigree.

A 16th-century traditional local with public bar and saloon bar. Regular live music, karaoke, large-screen TV, pool, darts. No food. Large family beer garden – families welcome. Occasional BBQs in summer. On the A129 halfway between Brentwood and Billericay, and ten minutes' walk from Shenfield station.

OPEN *12–11.30pm Sun–Wed; noon–12.30am Thurs–Fri; 11am–12.30am Sat.*

KIRBY-LE-SOKEN

Red Lion

32 The Street, Kirby-le-Soken, Frinton-on-Sea CO13 0EF
☎ *(01255) 674832*

Up to six real ales, with Greene King IPA a permament fixture. The others rotate constantly.

Allegedly haunted, this 14th-century village alehouse is leased from Enterprise Inns. Food available at lunchtime and evenings. Large beer garden with decking area and children's play area. Annual beer festival in August.

OPEN *12–11pm.*

LAYER DE LA HAYE

The Donkey & Buskins

High Road, Layer de la Haye, Colchester CO2 0HU
☎ *(01206) 734774* Alan Sharman

Freehouse serving three or four real ales from local breweries such as Mighty Oak, Crouch Vale, Adnams or Greene King, or from further afield such as Black Sheep or St Austell. Winner of CAMRA's Most Improved Pub 2005–06.

English rural pub dating from 1840. No juke box, machines, pool or darts. Two bars, three restaurant areas. Traditional pub food, mostly homemade, served 12–2.30pm and 6–9pm Mon–Fri; 12–9.30pm Sat; 12–7.30pm Sun. Children welcome, with healthy children's menu available. Fun pub quiz every Sunday night. Large, enclosed beer garden. Annual mini beer festival. B&B accommodation. Close to Colchester Zoo. From the A12, follow signs to Colchester Zoo, then signs to Layer.

OPEN *11.30am–3pm and 5.30–11.30pm Mon–Fri; 11.30am–11.30pm Sat; 12–11pm Sun.*

LEIGH-ON-SEA

The Broker Free House

213–17 Leigh Road, Leigh-on-Sea SS9 1JA
☎ *(01702) 471932*
Alan and Elaine Gloyne and family
www.brokerfreehouse.co.uk

 Shepherd Neame Spitfire, Ridleys Tolly Original and Young's Tiger plus two guests, which regularly include Fuller's London Pride, Young's Bitter and beers from Mighty Oak, Woodforde's, Harveys, Mansfield, Bateman and Cottage breweries. Often serves 14 different beers over 10 days.

Family-run, family-friendly freehouse, catering for 18–102 year olds! One big bar, beer garden, children's licence and dedicated children's area. Sunday night is live music or quiz night. Food served at lunchtimes and evenings (except Sunday evenings). Children allowed.

OPEN *11am–3pm and 6–11pm Mon–Wed; 11am–11pm Thurs–Sat; 12–10.30pm Sun.*

The Elms

1060 London Road, Leigh-on-Sea SS9 3ND
☎ *(01702) 474687* Adrian and Rachel

Shepherd Neame Spitfire plus more than 100 guests every year from smaller breweries such as Ridleys. Beer festival.

A Wetherspoon's pub. Modern bar with an old-looking exterior. Outside seating. Food served 10am–10pm. Curry nights Mon–Thurs 6–10pm. Well-behaved children allowed until 6pm. Coffee available in the morning.

OPEN *All day, every day.*

LITTLE CLACTON
The Apple Tree
The Street, Little Clacton CO16 9LF
☎ *(01255) 861026* Paul Lead and Alan Short

Fuller's London Pride, Adnams Southwold Bitter and Mighty Oak Oscar Wilde plus seasonal guest beers. A total of three real ales available at any time. All beers are served straight from the barrel.

A traditional freehouse. Food served in a separate restaurant at lunchtimes and Friday and Saturday evenings. Car park and garden. Follow the 'old' road into Clacton (i.e. not the bypass).

OPEN *12–11pm (10.30pm Sun). Closed Sun evenings in winter.*

LITTLE OAKLEY
Ye Olde Cherry Tree Inn
Clacton Road, Little Oakley, Harwich CO12 5JH
☎ *(01255) 886290* Steve and Ruth Munn
www.harwich.net/savethecherrytree

Adnams Best plus three rotating guests and real cider.

Traditional country pub overlooking the sea, around 600 years old, with one bar and beer garden, plus traditional pub games. Home-cooked food served 12–2pm and 7–9pm, with Sunday roasts. Walkers welcome, dogs allowed. Quiz night first Sunday of the month. Annual beer festival. Near to historic Harwich and the port, Hamford View golf range, and Harwich golf, rugby and football clubs. On the Harwich to Clacton road.

OPEN *12–2.30pm and 5–11pm.*

LITTLE TOTHAM
The Swan
School Road, Little Totham CM9 8LB
☎ *(01621) 892689* John Pascoe
www.theswanpublichouse.co.uk

Genuine freehouse with a well-deserved reputation for its real ale. Brews available include Mighty Oak Oscar Wilde Mild, Totham Parva and Maldon Gold, Crouch Vale Brewer's Gold, Woodforde's Wherry, Adnams Bitter and Broadside, Nethergate IPA, Red Fox, Fox and Hind, Farmers Ales Pucks Folly, and regularly changing guests from Mauldons, Nethergate, Skinner's, Wibblers and Clark's. All beers are gravity fed straight from the cask (up to 25 casks in the cellar at any one time). Weston's cider is also on offer, including Old Rosie, Traditional and Perry.

CAMRA's National Pub of the Year 2002 and 2005 and NFU Countryside Rural Pub of the Year 2003, this is a traditional English country pub in a Grade II listed building with heavy beams, low ceilings and a large open fire for chilly winter evenings. Good food available Tues–Sat lunchtimes, and evenings with roasts on Sundays. Separate dining area. No swearing. No vests/singlets/backwards hats. Children welcome – with well-behaved parents! Annual beer festival in June, with live entertainment and barbecue. Muddy boots and dogs welcome. Situated off the B1022 Colchester–Maldon road, near Tiptree.

OPEN *11am–11pm Mon–Sat; 12–10.30pm Sun.*

LITTLE WAKERING
The Castle Inn
81 Little Wakering Road, Little Wakering, Southend-on-Sea SS3 0JW
☎ *(01702) 219295* Victoria Yeates

Up to four real ales changed several times a week, perhaps including Young's Special, Thwaites Double Century, Palmers IPA and Everards Pitch Black.

A 200-year-old alehouse, with two bars, a large garden and covered smoking area. Large car park, children welcome. Food served at lunchtimes and early evenings. Well placed for walkers and cyclists.

OPEN *12–12.*

LITTLE WALDEN
The Crown
Little Walden, Saffron Walden CB10 1XA
☎ *(01799) 427266* Robert Webster

Privately owned freehouse with four or five real ales, including Greene King IPA and Adnams Best Bitter. The guest, changed every few weeks, might be beers from Cambridge or Woodforde's.

Dating from 1757, this pub includes a bar and a separate restaurant area. Continental, classic English and fish specialities served 11.30am–2.30pm and 6–10pm. Plans to add seven rooms for B&B. Take the B184 from the M11 and follow signs for Saffron Walden.

OPEN *11.30am–3pm and 6–11pm.*

LITTLEBURY
The Queen's Head
High Street, Littlebury, Nr Saffron Walden CB11 4TD
☎ *(01799) 522251* Paul and Alison Lloyd

Greene King tied house with IPA, Morland Original and two guests.

A 16th-century coaching inn with exposed beams, a snug and two open fires. Good food available 12–2pm Tues–Sun and 6–9pm Tues–Sat, all home-cooked using freshly prepared ingredients to create interesting restaurant-style meals rather than traditional pub grub. Designated smoking area, large car park and beer garden. Children welcome. En-suite accommodation. On the B1383, between Newport and junction 9 of the M11.

OPEN *12–3pm Tue–Sat; 5.30–11pm Mon–Sat; 12–3pm and 7–10.30pm Sun.*

LOUGHTON
The Victoria Tavern
165 Smarts Lane, Loughton IG10 4BP
☎ *(020) 8508 1779* James Stuchfield

A Punch Taverns pub. Timothy Taylor Landlord, Adnams Bitter and Greene King IPA plus two guests, changed every two or three days. Guest beers have included Harveys Sussex, Brakspear Organic, Saltaire Blonde and Hook Norton Old Hooky.

Victorian-style pub situated in the heart of Epping Forest. Food served 12–2.30pm and 6–9pm Mon–Sat; 12–4pm Sun. Family beer garden. Under-21s only allowed inside if dining. Parking.

OPEN *11am–3pm and 5–11pm Mon–Sat; 12–10.30pm Sun.*

MALDON
The Blue Boar Hotel
Silver Street, Maldon CM9 4QE
☎ *(01621) 855885* John Wilsdon
www.blueboarmaldon.co.uk

Freehouse operating its own micro-brewery. Four Farmer's Ales brews plus Adnams Bitter always available, with one monthly-changing guest. Beers served under gravity in the back bar.

A 15th-century coaching inn with two bars, an open fire, antiques and pictures to complement the traditional atmosphere. Food served lunchtimes and evenings. Children welcome in the back bar. Attached to a hotel with 27 rooms and a large function room. Car park. Opposite All Saints Church in Maldon High Street.

OPEN *11am–11pm Mon–Sat; 12–10.30pm Sun.*

The White Horse
26 High Street, Maldon CM9 5PJ
☎ *(01621) 851708* Gary and Wendy Cooper

Shepherd Neame tied house. Bishop's Finger, Spitfire and Master Brew and ales from Real Kentish always available, plus one rotating guest.

Typical high-street pub offering homemade food at lunchtimes and evenings, with specials changed daily. Patio. Pool table. Children allowed. B&B accommodation.

OPEN *All day, every day.*

MANNINGTREE
Manningtree Station Buffet
Station Road, Lawford, Manningtree CO11 2LH
☎ *(01206) 391114* Paul Sankey

Greene King Abbot, IPA and Old Speckled Hen are permanent fixtures, and the two guest ales are changed monthly.

Station buffet built in 1846. Very popular breakfast menu served every day until 1pm. Sky Sports. Fun atmosphere in the evenings. Small beer garden. Live music monthly. Children welcome.

OPEN *5.30am–11pm Mon–Fri; 8am–11pm Sat; 8am–2pm Sun (longer if football on Sky).*

MARGARETTING
The White Hart Inn
Swan Lake, Margaretting CM4 9JX
☎ *(01277) 840478* Liz Haines
www.thewhitehart.uk.com

Freehouse with a minimum of six real ales, usually eight. The four resident ales are Mighty Oak IPA and Oscar Wilde Mild and Adnams Best and Broadside. Also three guests, changed every few days and never repeated within 12 months.

The original part of the building is over 400 years old, and converted from cottages. New conservatory at the rear, set in one acre of well-cared-for gardens. Food served 12–2pm Mon; 12–2pm and 6–9.30pm Tues–Fri; 12–2.30pm and 6–9pm Sat; 12–5pm and 6–9pm Sun. Children welcome in garden, where there is a play area, duck pond, rabbits, goats and an aviary. Large car park. Summer beer festival in June. Winter beer festival in October. Located just outside Margaretting, between the A12 and the B1007.

OPEN *11.30am–midnight Mon–Fri; 12–12 Sat; 12–11pm Sun.*

MILL GREEN
The Viper
Mill Green Road, Mill Green, Nr Ingatestone CM4 0PT
☎ *(01277) 352010*
Donna Torris and Peter White

Five regularly changing real ales, including a mild. These may include up to three Viper Ales brewed exlusively for the pub by Mighty Oak and Nethergate, plus something from Wolf, Crouch Vale, Oakham or other breweries around the country. A traditional cider is always available. Two beer festivals held each year (Easter and September).

Small, traditional, unspoilt country pub with award-winning garden. Bar food available at lunchtimes (12–2pm Mon–Fri, 12–3pm Sat–Sun). Car park. Children allowed in garden only. Take the Ivy Barn road off the A12. Turn off at Margaretting. Two miles north-west of Ingatestone.

OPEN *12–3pm and 6–11pm Mon–Fri; 12–11pm Sat; 12 –10.30pm Sun.*

MORETON
The Nag's Head
Church Road, Moreton, Nr Ongar CM5 0LF
☎ *(01277) 890239* Stephen Little

Greene King tied house serving IPA, Old Speckled Hen and Ruddles County.

A country pub with food served at lunchtimes and evenings in a separate dining area. Named Ridleys Best Real Ale Pub (supported by Chelmsford CAMRA) in 2005.

OPEN *11.30am–3.30pm and 6–11pm Mon–Fri; all day Sat–Sun (all day Fri–Sun in summer).*

NORTH FAMBRIDGE

The Ferry Boat Inn

North Fambridge CM3 6LR
☎ *(01621) 740208* Sylvia Maltwood
www.ferryboatinn.net

Three hand pumps serving Greene King Morland Original, Ruddles County, Abbot or IPA.

Five-hundred-year-old freehouse beside the River Crouch. Food served 12–2pm and 7–9.30pm Mon–Sat, 12–2.30pm and 7–9pm Sun. Accommodation available in six en-suite rooms in a separate building.

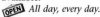 *11.30am–3pm and 6.30–11pm (10.30pm Sun).*

ONGAR

The Cock Tavern

218 High Street, Ongar CM5 9GB
☎ *(01277) 362615* Ian and Mary Goodman

Greene King IPA and three guests, changed regularly.

A 500-year-old locals' pub. Pub games. Food served all day. Live music every Sat. Small outside area. Car park. Function room available.

 All day, every day.

ORSETT

The Foxhound

High Road, Orsett RM16 3ER
☎ *(01375) 891295* Jackie Firman

Tied house with one pump offering a regularly changing guest beer, perhaps from Elgood's, Fuller's, O'Hanlon's, Everards, Wells and Young's, York, Millennium, Hampshire, Phoenix or Shepherd Neame, among others.

Traditional, two-bar country pub with local pictures and memorabilia covering the walls. Saloon lounge bar with open fire and 'tree'. Bar and restaurant food available every lunchtime and Wed–Sat evenings. Traditional roasts on Sundays. Darts and pub games in public bar. Dogs welcome. Patio. Large car park. Well-behaved children welcome in the restaurant.

 11am–3.30pm and 6–11pm Mon–Fri; 11am–11.30pm Sat; 12–4pm and 7–11pm Sun.

PEBMARSH

The King's Head

The Street, Pebmarsh, Nr Halstead CO9 2NH
☎ *(01787) 269306* KR and SA Smith

Woodforde's Wherry and Greene King IPA plus two guest ales.

A richly timbered freehouse dating from around 1450, with restaurant, large bar area and pool room. A range of traditional homemade meals available 12–2pm and 6–9pm Tues–Thurs; 12–2.30pm and 6–9.30pm Fri–Sat. Barbecues in season. Large car park, outside seating for over 100 on the forecourt, patio and beer garden. Children's play area. One mile off the A131 Halstead to Sudbury road.

12–3pm and 6pm–12 Tues–Thurs (closed Mon); 12–12 Fri–Sat; 12–8pm Sun.

PLESHEY

The White Horse

The Street, Pleshey, Chelmsford CM3 1HA
☎ *(01245) 237281* Mike and Jan Smail
www.thewhitehorsepleshey.co.uk

Freehouse serving Young's PA or Winter Warmer plus a guest.

One-bar village pub in a 15th-century building in an historic, picturesque village setting. One bar and three eating areas, large garden, car park. Food served 11.30am–3pm and 7–11pm Tues–Sat, 12–4.30pm Sun. Large beer garden, plenty of parking, gift shop, function room. Children welcome. Live jazz nights (see website).

Closed Mon. 11.30am–3pm and 7–11.30pm Tues–Sat; 12–5pm Sun.

RADWINTER

The Plough Inn

Radwinter, Nr Saffron Walden CB10 2TL
☎ *(01799) 599222* Emma Welch

Freehouse with Greene King IPA plus two or three rotating guests perhaps including something from Adnams, Archers, Saffron, Brandon or Green Tye.

A 17th-century traditional English pub, with one bar, two open fires and good views of the countryside. Food available 12–2pm and 6.30–9pm Mon–Sat, 12–3pm Sun. Children and dogs welcome. Large beer garden and patio. Restaurant available for hire or special parties. Themed nights every few months. Good country walks. At the junction of B1053 and B1054, four miles east of Saffron Walden.

12–3pm and 6–11pm Mon–Sat; 12–3pm and 7–9pm Sun.

RICKLING GREEN

The Cricketer's Arms

Rickling Green, Quendon, Saffron Walden CB11 3YG
☎ *(01799) 543210* Barry Hilton
www.thecricketersarms.com

Three real ales, from a list including Greene King IPA and Jennings Cumberland, plus one guest beer.

Heavily timbered building dating from 1590, with two restaurants. Food (mostly restaurant meals) served 12–2.30pm and 6–9.30pm. Private function room and conference room. Nine en-suite bedrooms. Cricket Days. Handy for Audley End House and Stansted Airport. Facing the cricket green, just off the B1383 at Quendon.

8am–midnight.

RIDGEWELL
The White Horse
Mill Road, Ridgewell CO9 4SG
☎ *(01440) 785532* Robin Briggs

Freehouse serving a constantly changing range of real ales on gravity, which may include beers from Mighty Oak, Nethergate and Maldon, plus many others from small breweries.

Rural village pub with games room, pool table and darts. Single bar covered in old pennies (4,200 in all). Large restaurant, beer patio, car park and lodge. Food served at lunchtimes and evenings. Children allowed. Located on the A1017 between Halstead and Haverhill.

OPEN *12–3pm Wed–Sat (closed Mon and Tues lunch); 6–11pm Mon–Sat; 12–10.30pm Sun.*

ROCHFORD
The Golden Lion
35 North Street, Rochford SS4 1AB
☎ *(01702) 545487* Sue Williams

Greene King Abbot, Crouch Vale Brewer's Gold and Adnams Bitter plus three guests, changed every few days.

A 16th-century traditional-style freehouse with one bar, beams and brasses, a log-burning fire and a small beer garden. No food. South East Essex CAMRA Pub of the Year 2007 and 2008. Outside courtyard garden with covered smoking area. Well-behaved dogs welcome.

OPEN *11am–11pm Sun–Thurs; 11am–midnight Fri–Sat.*

ROMFORD
The Moon & Stars
103 South Street, Romford RM1 1NX
☎ *(01708) 730117* Sarah Saye

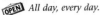Wetherspoon's pub with Greene King Abbot and Shepherd Neame Spitfire among the beers always available. Four guest ales change on a weekly basis.

Large bar, dining area, outside seating, disabled facilities. Food available all day. Children allowed outside only.

OPEN *All day, every day.*

SAFFRON WALDEN
The Old English Gentleman
11 Gold Street, Saffron Walden CB10 1EJ
☎ *(01799) 523595* Jeffrey and Cindy Leach

Enterprise Inns tied house serving Greene King Abbot, Timothy Taylor Landlord, Woodforde's Wherry and one guest.

A traditional one-bar pub dating from the 18th century. Food served at lunchtimes only. Patio garden area. Just off Saffron Walden High Street.

OPEN *11am–11pm Sun–Mon; 11am–midnight Tues–Thurs; 11am–1am Fri–Sat.*

SHALFORD
The George Inn
The Street, Shalford CM7 5HH
☎ *(01371) 850207* Steve Alderson
www.thegeorgeshalford.co.uk

Greene King IPA, Adnams Bitter, Woodforde's Wherry and Nelson's Revenge, plus beer from the local Shalford Brewery and guests changed weekly.

A 15th-century inn with one bar, the last remaining pub in Shalford (there were five at one time). Food available 12–2.30pm and 6.30–9pm Mon–Sat and 12–3pm Sun. Children welcome. Patio garden, car park. Annual beer festival. Close to picturesque Finchinfield. Situated on the main road between Braintree and Finchinfield.

OPEN *12–3pm and 5pm–12 Mon–Fri; all day Sat–Sun and bank holidays.*

SOUTHEND-ON-SEA
Last Post
Weston Road, Southend-on-Sea SS1 1AS
☎ *(01702) 431682* Robin Duberley

Greene King Abbot plus up to six daily-changing guests such as Greene King Old Speckled Hen or Hop Back Summer Lightning. Anything and everything from brewers of real ale considered.

Busy two-bar operation with disabled access and toilets. No music, a real drinkers' pub. Food served all day, every day. No children. Opposite the railway station.

OPEN *10am–11pm.*

SOUTHMINSTER
The Station Arms
39 Station Road, Southminster CM0 7EW
☎ *(01621) 772225* Martin Park

Freehouse with four or five real ales, with the selection changing daily. Local brewers feature regularly, including Crouch Vale, Mighty Oak and Farmer's Ales, and others from Adnams and Dark Star.

Welcoming, one-bar, Essex weatherboard pub with open fire and traditional pub furniture. Pub games played. Courtyard to the rear. No food. Street parking. Children welcome in yard and barn to the rear of the pub. Two beer festivals held each year, with 30 real ales at each (last weekend of January and late May bank holiday). Just 200 yards from Southminster railway station.

OPEN *12–2.30pm and 6–11pm Mon–Fri; 12–11pm Sat; 12–4pm and 7–10.30pm Sun.*

STANFORD RIVERS
The Woodman
155 London Road, Stanford Rivers, Ongar
☎ *(01277) 362019*
David and Gina MacDonald

Shepherd Neame Master Brew, Spitfire and Bishop's Finger regularly available.

Wooden-clad, 14th-century inn set in three acres. Food served all day. Car park. Children's play area.

OPEN *11am–11pm Mon–Sat; 12–10.30pm Sun.*

STEEPLE

The Star Inn

The Street, Steeple, Southminster CM0 7LF
☎ *(01621) 772646* Simon and Carole Plumb
www.starinnsteeple.co.uk

Genuine freehouse with Adnams Best and Mighty Oak Burntwood plus a guest or two from small independent breweries.

Friendly country pub dating back to the 17th century, with a large main bar and two restaurants. Good food available 6–9pm Mon, 12–2.30pm and 7–9pm Tues–Wed, 12–2.30pm and 6–9pm Thurs–Sat, 12–4pm Sun. Plenty of space outside for drinking, eating and keeping an eye on well-behaved children. Pool, darts, occasional live music. Accommodation and caravan site. Steeple is a small village a mile or so north of the River Blackwater on the Latchingdon–Bradwell road.

(OPEN) *12–11pm.*

STISTED

The Dolphin

Stisted, Braintree CM77 8EU
☎ *(01376) 321143*
Ashley and Aimee Winsbury-Cutts

Tied to Greene King with IPA always on offer, plus another beer such as Old Speckled Hen.

Traditional locals' pub – three cottages knocked into one. Food available 12–9.30pm every day. Beer garden, car park. Children not allowed. On the main A120 from Stansted and Colchester.

(OPEN) *12–11pm.*

STOCK

The Hoop

21 High Street, Stock CM4 9BD
☎ *(01277) 841137* Michelle Corrigan
www.thehoop.co.uk

Six real ales. Brews from Brentwood and Adnams are always on offer, plus guests, changed daily.

Friendly local pub with restaurant. Home-cooked food served 12–2.30pm and 6–9pm. Beer garden, barbecues in summer. Beer festival end of May/start of June. Take the B1007 from the A12 Chelmsford bypass, then take the Galleywood–Billericay turn-off.

(OPEN) *11am–11pm Mon–Sat; 12–10.30pm Sun.*

STOW MARIES

The Prince of Wales

Woodham Road, Stow Maries CM3 6SA
☎ *(01621) 828971* Robert Walster

Fuller's Chiswick plus any four guests (too many to count) including a mild and a stout/porter from small independent and the better regional brewers.

A traditional Essex weatherboard pub with real fires and Victorian bakehouse. Bar food available at lunchtimes and evenings. Car park, garden and family room. Under two miles from South Woodham Ferrers on the road to Cold Norton.

(OPEN) *11am–11pm Mon–Sat; 12–10.30pm Sun.*

TILLINGHAM

Cap & Feathers

8–10 South Street, Tillingham, CM0 7TH
☎ *(01621) 779212*
Jane Norris and Alan Mulholland

Adnams Bitter and Broadside plus two guests such as Mighty Oak Burntwood or Maldon Gold plus other brews from smaller independents.

A 15th-century weatherboard pub in a pretty village setting. Food served 12–4pm and 6–9pm daily plus 12–9pm in the restaurant Wed–Sat. Family-friendly, with a children's room and dedicated play area in the garden. Four rooms to let. Occasional live music and theme nights.

(OPEN) *11am–midnight Mon–Fri; 11am–1am Sat; 12–11.30pm Sun.*

TOOT HILL

The Green Man and Courtyard Restaurant

Toot Hill, Nr Ongar CM5 9SD
☎ *(01992) 522255* Diane Whitworth

Crouch Vale Best plus two guests changing twice weekly such as an Adnams brew or Fuller's London Pride. No strong bitters over 4.3% ABV.

Country freehouse with two restaurants, one bar, courtyard and beer garden. Food served at lunchtimes and evenings. Children aged 11+ allowed. Five letting rooms available.

(OPEN) *11am–3pm and 6–11pm (10.30pm Sun).*

WENDENS AMBO

The Bell

Royston Road, Wendens Ambo CB11 4JY
☎ *(01799) 540382* Elizabeth Fetzer

Adnams Bitter and Broadside plus three or four guests from small independents and micro-breweries.

Built in 1576, beamed with open fires in winter. Home-cooked food available 12–2pm and 6–9pm Mon–Fri, 12–3pm and 6–9pm Sat, 12–3pm Sun (no food Sun evenings except through summer). Extensive wine list. Car park, dining terrace overlooking pond, three and a half acres of landscaped gardens with wilderness walk to river. Children's golf. Family-friendly garden with areas of water inaccessible to toddlers.

(OPEN) *11.30am–2.30pm and 5–11pm Mon–Thurs; all day Fri–Sun.*

WHITE RODING
The Black Horse
Chelmsford Road, White Roding CM6 1RF
☎ *(01279) 876322* Jim Thorp

 Greene King house with IPA, Abbot and Ruddles Extra Smooth on offer, plus one changing guest.

Atraditional, family-oriented 16th-century country pub with two bars and a restaurant. Public bar offers darts, cribbage and pool. Monthly events such as quizzes and live music. There is even a resident ghost! Food served all day Wed–Sun, including regularly changing specials and fish boards, roasts on Sunday 12–9pm. Lots of homemade goodies available. Well-behaved children welcome in dining area. Barbecues in summer. Parties catered for. Late licence for events. Dogs allowed outside. Next to Brett's Farmshop, on the A1060 between Chelmsford and Bishops Stortford.

OPEN *11.30am–2.30pm and 5–11pm Mon–Wed; all day Thurs–Sun.*

WITHAM
The Woolpack
7 Church Street, Witham CM8 2JP
☎ *(01376) 511195* Jan Mooney

 Bateman XB, Maldon Gold and Archers Best plus one weekly changing guest.

Traditional freehouse, around 200 years old, with traditional décor. Very much a locals' pub. Team-oriented (darts, pool, cribbage etc). No food. No children. Dogs welcome. Live music monthly.

OPEN *11.30am–11pm Mon–Thurs; 11.30am–midnight Fri–Sat; 12–10.30pm Sun.*

WOODFORD GREEN
The Cricketers
299–301 High Road, Woodford Green IG8 9HQ
☎ *(020) 8504 2734* Mr and Mrs Woolridge

 Owned by McMullen, so AK Original, and Country Best Bitter always served, with specials and seasonals when available.

Semi-rural pub with lounge and public bars and beer garden. Food available 12–2pm Mon–Sat, with OAP specials Mon–Thurs. Children allowed till 6.30pm in the lounge bar only. Situated near the statue of Winston Churchill. Local CAMRA Pub of the Year 2005.

OPEN *11am–11pm Mon–Fri; 11.30am–11pm Sat; 12–10.30pm Sun.*

WOODHAM FERRERS
The Bell Inn
Main Road, Woodham Ferrers, Chelmsford CM3 8RF
☎ *(01245) 320443* DL Giles and S Rowe

 Ridleys IPA and Adnams Bitter plus five guest beers often from Farmers, Adnams, Crouch Vale or Cottage.

Friendly village pub with cosy bars and open fire in winter. Freshly cooked food served 12–2.30pm and 7–10pm Mon–Fri, 12–10pm Sat–Sun. Car park. No children.

OPEN *11am–3pm and 6–11pm Mon–Fri; 11am–11pm Sat; 12–10.30pm Sun.*

WOODHAM MORTIMER
The Hurdlemaker's Arms
Post Office Road, Woodham Mortimer, Maldon CM9 6ST
☎ *(01245) 225169*
Paul and Katherine Johnson

 Gray's tied house serving Greene King IPA and Abbot and three guests, changed every few days.

A400-year-old building with exposed beams, log fire and two bars, one reserved for food. Food served 12–2.30pm and 6.30–9pm. Children welcome. Large beer garden. Large car park. Annual beer festival.

OPEN *12–3pm and 5–11pm Mon–Fri; 12–3pm and 6.30–11pm Sat; 12–11pm Sun.*

WOODHAM WALTER
The Bell
The Street, Woodham Walter, Maldon CM9 6RF
☎ *(01245) 223437* Brian and Jenn Barnard

Freehouse with Greene King IPA plus two guest pumps serving real ales from a wide range with around six different ales per month from the smaller independent and micro-breweries.

Atraditional 16th-century village inn with beams, one large bar and a dining room. No machines. Background music from the 1930s and 1940s. Beer garden. Food available lunchtimes and evenings in a separate dining room. Children allowed.

OPEN *12–3pm and 6–11pm Mon–Sat; 12–6pm Sun.*

THE BREWERIES

BATH ALES LTD
Unit 3–7, Plot A2, Caxton Industrial Estate, Tower Road North, Warmley, Bristol BS30 8XN
☎ *(0117) 947 4797*
www.bathales.com

SPA 3.7% ABV
Pale and citrusy.
GEM 4.1% ABV
Hoppy and malty.
BARNSTORMER 4.5% ABV
Rich in fruit and malt.
WILD HARE 5.0% ABV
Plus seasonals and occasionals including:
FESTIVITY 5.0% ABV
RARE HARE 5.2% ABV

BATTLEDOWN BREWERY
The Keynsham Works, Keynsham Street, Cheltenham GL5 6EJ
☎ *07734 834104*
www.battledownbrewery.com

SAXON 3.8% ABV
Dry and golden.
TURNCOAT 4.5% ABV
Malty and dark.
BRIGAND 4.7% ABV
Fruity and amber.

BRISTOL BEER FACTORY
c/o Tobacco Factory, Raleigh Road, Southville, Bristol BSE 1TF
☎ *(0117) 902 6317*
www.bristolbeerfactory.co.uk

RED 3.8% ABV
NO 7 4.2% ABV
SUNRISE 4.4% ABV
GOLD 5.0% ABV

COTSWOLD SPRING BREWERY
Dodington Spring, Dodington, Chipping Sodbury BS37 6RX
☎ *(01454) 323088*
www.cotswoldbrewery.co.uk

OLDE ENGLISH ROSE 4.0% ABV
CODRINGTON CODGER 4.2% ABV
CODRINGTON ROYAL 4.5% ABV

DONNINGTON BREWERY
Upper Swell, Stow-on-the Wold, Cheltenham GL54 1EP
☎ *(01451) 830603*

BB 3.5% ABV
XXX 3.5% ABV
SBA 4.6% ABV
Smooth and malty.

EAGLES BUSH BREWERY
The Salutation, Ham, Berkeley GL13 9QH
☎ *(01453) 810284*

MERLIN 3.6% ABV
KESTREL 3.7% ABV
OSPREY DARK 3.9% ABV

FREEMINER BREWERY LTD
Whimsey Road, Steam Mills, Cinderford, Royal Forest of Dean GL14 3JA
☎ *(01594) 827989*
www.freeminer.com

BITTER 4.0% ABV
Biscuit brown, hoppy.
MORSES LEVEL 4.0% ABV
Chocolatey with floral notes.
STRIP AND AT IT 4.0% ABV
Summer bitter, hoppy.
SPECULATION ALE 4.8% ABV
Ruby red, chocolatey.
CELESTIAL STEAM GALE 5.0% ABV
(also sold under the name STAIRWAY TO HEAVEN)
Bitter with floral hop.
GOLD STANDARD 5.0% ABV
Hoppy and golden.
SLAUGHTER PORTER 5.0% ABV
Dark mild.
TRAFALGAR IPA 6.0% ABV
Sunset brown, hoppy bitter.
DEEP SHAFT 6.2% ABV
Malty smokiness.

GOFF'S BREWERY LTD
9 Isbourne Way, Winchcombe, Cheltenham GL54 5NS
☎ *(01242) 603383*
www.goffs.biz

JOUSTER 4.0% ABV
Tawny colour, hoppy, with fruity hints.
WHITE KNIGHT 4.7% ABV
Hoppy and golden.
Seasonals:
EXCALIBUR 3.8% ABV
Golden, well balanced.
TOURNAMENT 4.0% ABV
Amber colour, floral aroma.
GUINEVERE 4.1% ABV
Slight spiciness.
MORDRED 4.2% ABV
Malty with fruity nose.
GALAHAD 4.3% ABV
Full-bodied brown ale.
MERLIN 4.3% ABV
Straw-coloured, hoppy bitter.
CAMELOT 4.4% ABV
Dark amber and malty.
LAUNCELOT 4.5% ABV
Floral nose, clean and hoppy.
LAMORAK 5.0% ABV
Malty bitter, dry finish.
BLACK KNIGHT 5.3% ABV
Chocolate malt aromas. Winter porter.
Plus 12 special beers and beers commissioned to mark private occasions.

NAILSWORTH BREWERY
The Cross, Bath Road, Nailsworth GL6 0HH
☎ *07878 448377*
www.nailsworth-brewery.co.uk

THE DUDBRIDGE DONKEY 3.6% ABV
Sweet.
THE ARTIST'S ALE 3.9% ABV
Citrus.
THE MAYOR'S BITTER 4.2% ABV
Blackcurrant flavours.
THE VICAR'S STOUT 4.5% ABV
Chocolatey.
THE TOWNCRIER 4.7% ABV
Grassy.

NORTH COTSWOLD BREWERY
Ditchford Farm, Moreton-in-Marsh
GL56 9RD
☎ *(01608) 663947*
www.northcotswoldbrewery.co.uk

PIGBROOK BITTER 3.8% ABV
GENESIS 4.0% ABV
Seasonals:
MAYFAIR MILD 4.1% ABV
SUMMER SOLSTICE 4.5% ABV
WINTER SOLSTICE 4.5% ABV
HUNG, DRAWN 'N' PORTERED 5.0% ABV
STOUR STOUT 5.0% ABV
Plus occasional brews.

SEVERN VALE BREWING COMPANY
Woodend Lane, Cam, Dursley GL11 5HS
☎ *(01453) 547550*
www.severnvalebrewing.co.uk

VALE ALE 4.0% ABV
DURSLEY STEAM BITTER 4.2% ABV
DANCE BITTER 4.5% ABV
MONUMENTALE 4.5% ABV
SEVERN SINS 5.2% ABV

STANWAY BREWERY
Stanway, Cheltenham GL54 5PQ
☎ *(01386) 584320*
www.stanwaybrewery.co.uk

COTTESWOLD GOLD 3.9% ABV
Light and refreshing ale with a delicate
hop aroma.
STANNEY BITTER 4.5% ABV
Quenching amber beer. Summer only.
LORDS-A-LEAPING 4.5% ABV
Dark and full bodied. Winter only.

STROUD BREWERY
c/o 141 Thrupp Lane, Thrupp, Stroud GL5 2DG
☎ *07891 995878*
www.stroudbrewery.co.uk

TOM LONG 3.8% ABV
RED COAT 3.9% ABV
BUDDING 4.5% ABV
FIVE VALLEYS 5.0% ABV
WOOLSACK 5.0% ABV
Plus seasonals including:
DING DONG 5.0% ABV

ULEY BREWERY LTD
The Old Brewery, The Street, Uley, Dursley
GL11 5TB
☎ *(01453) 860120*
www.uleybrewery.com

HOGSHEAD PA 3.5% ABV
BITTER 4.0% ABV
LAURIE LEE'S BITTER 4.5% ABV
OLD RIC 4.5% ABV
OLD SPOT PRIZE ALE 5.0% ABV
PIG'S EAR STRONG ALE 5.0% ABV
Plus occasional brews.

WHITTINGTONS BREWERY
Three Choirs Vineyard, Newent GL18 1LS
☎ *(01531) 890223*
www.whittingtonbrewery.co.uk

NINE LIVES 3.6% ABV
SUMMER PALE ALE 4.0% ABV
CATS WHISKERS 4.2% ABV

WICKWAR BREWERY CO. LTD
The Old Brewery, Station Road, Wickwar
GL12 8NB
☎ *0870 7775671*
www.wickwarbrewing.co.uk

COOPERS 3.5% ABV
Full-flavoured pale ale.
BRAND OAK BITTER 4.0% ABV
Characterful and well balanced.
COTSWOLD WAY 4.2% ABV
Rich amber, smooth, well balanced beer.
ISOMBARD KINGDOM BRUNEL 4.5% ABV
Malty and fruity.
MR PERRETT'S TRADITIONAL STOUT 5.9% ABV
A powerful stout with a liquorice and chocolate
taste.
STATION PORTER 6.1%ABV
Intricate, well-rounded blend of flavours.
Plus seasonal and occasional brews.

ZERODEGREES
53 Colston Street, Bristol SS1 5BA (Also a base
in Reading)
☎ *(0117) 925 2706*
www.zdrestaurants.com/zerodegrees

PALE ALE 4.6% ABV
Floral and fruity.
WHEAT ALE 4.6% ABV
Vanilla and banana flavours.

THE PUBS

ALDERTON

The Gardeners Arms
Beckford Road, Alderton, Nr Tewkesbury
GL20 8NL
☎ *(01242) 620257*
Michael and Wendy Wakeman
www.gardenersarms.biz

Freehouse serving five changing real ales
on a guest basis, no permanents,
although Greene King IPA is a regular. Cask
Marque accredited, 7 years running.

A late-15th-century thatched pub and
restaurant in a quiet rural village. Family-
run with a friendly atmosphere. Home-
cooked food, including seasonal local
produce such as strawberries and asparagus,
available every day. Children welcome and
dogs allowed in some areas. Large beer
garden with boules area. Smaller functions
catered for. Live music on Friday evenings.
Large car park. Two real ale festivals each
year: Boxing Day and May spring bank
holiday. Accommodation available during
the week of the Cheltenham Gold Cup only.

OPEN 5-11pm Mon-Sat; all day Sun. (Close at
10pm in winter months.)

AMBERLEY
Black Horse

Littleworth, Amberley, Stroud GL5 5AL
☎ *(01453) 872556* Sharon O'Flynn

Up to five real ales including Archers Best, Stroud Tim Long, Butcombe Bitter and Timothy Taylor Landlord. The guest beers might include Bath Spa. Also real cider.

Two-bar village inn with spectacular views across the Nailsworth valley from the conservatory and rear garden. Outside seating. Food available at lunchtimes and evenings. Recently changed hands again.

OPEN *11am–11pm.*

AMPNEY ST PETER
Red Lion

Ampney St Peter, Cirencester GL7 1SL
☎ *(01285) 851596* John Barnard

Freehouse serving Hook Norton Hooky Bitter and Timothy Taylor Landlord.

A unique little gem of a pub, 400 years old. Only three different landlords since 1887, present one (very friendly) has been here since 1975. Two small rooms, one in which the beer is served. No food. Car park. Children allowed in the games room.

OPEN *6–10pm Mon–Sat; 12–2pm and 7–10.30pm Sun.*

APPERLEY
Coal House Inn

Gabb Lane, Apperley GL19 4DN
☎ *(01452) 780211* Mrs McDonald

Severn Vale Ale plus two changing guests.

Country freehouse on the east bank of the River Severn. Home-cooked food served lunchtimes and evenings, 'Portuguese Steak on a Stone' a speciality. Large car parks and riverside garden. Children allowed. Moorings for boats (24 hours). Apperley is signposted on B4213 south of Tewkesbury. Follow signs for Coalhouse Wharf from village centre.

OPEN *April–Sept: 12–2.30pm and 6–11pm; Oct–Mar: 12–2.30pm and 7–11pm; 12–3pm and 7–10.30pm Sun (all year).*

ASHLEWORTH
The Boat Inn

The Quay, Ashleworth GL19 4HZ
☎ *(01452) 700272*
Ron, Elisabeth and Louise Nicholls
www.boat-inn.co.uk

Always something from the Wye Valley and RCH breweries plus four changing guests, from breweries such as Church End and Hook Norton.

Small friendly 15th-century cottage pub on the River Severn, with outside covered area for smokers. Filled rolls and snacks served 12–2pm. Beer garden on the banks of the river. Annual beer festival in June. Car park. Children welcome. Ashleworth is signposted off the A417 north of Gloucester; The Quay is signed from the village.

OPEN *11.30am–2.30pm and 6.30–11pm Tues–Fri (closed all day Mon, and Wed lunchtime); 11.30am–3pm and 6.30–11pm Sat–Sun. Opens at 7pm in winter.*

AVENING
The Bell

29 High Street, Avening, Tetbury GL8 8NF
☎ *(01453) 836422*
Tony Seward and Simon Taylor

Freehouse with Uley Bitter, Greene King IPA and St Austell Tribute the permanent beers.

Traditional Cotswold pub dating from before 1866 with bar and restaurant. Pub grub and à la carte food available 12–2.30pm and 6–9.30pm Tues–Sat; 12–3.30pm Sun (closed Sun night and all day Mon). Bench tables at the front. Parking on the front road. Well-behaved children welcome. No accommodation. Handy for Gatcombe Park Horse Trials and craft fayre, local golf courses and Westonbirt Arboretum. Three and a half miles from Tetbury, three miles from Nailsworth.

OPEN *12–3pm and 5.30–11pm Tues–Sat; 12–4pm Sun (closed Sun night and all day Mon).*

AWRE
The Red Hart Inn at Awre

Awre, Newnham GL14 1EW
☎ *(01594) 510220*
Maria Griffiths and Martin Cape

Freehouse with Fuller's London Pride, Bass and Freeminer Bitter plus up to four guests changing weekly, including something from Wickwar, Wye Valley, Archer's, Whittington's or Goff's. The landlord's policy is to support smaller breweries as much as possible.

A beamed hostelry dating from 1483 with one bar area. Outside seating in front garden. Homemade bar snacks and à la carte menu available using local ingredients at lunchtime and evenings. Food available 12–2pm and 7–9pm Mon–Sun. Children welcome. Set in a tranquil hamlet environment. Accommodation available. Turn off A48 between Newnham and Blakeney.

OPEN *12–3pm and 6–11pm Mon–Sat (check in winter); 12–3pm and 7–10.30pm Sun.*

BIRDLIP
The Golden Heart

Nettleton Bottom, Nr Birdlip GL4 8LA
☎ *(01242) 870261*
Catherine Stevens and David Morgan
www.thegoldenheart.co.uk

Four real ales, including beers from the Festival Brewery plus guest such as Goff's Jouster, Otter Bitter, Young's Winter Warmer and Archers Golden.

A centuries-old traditionally constructed freehouse with five rooms and an open fireplace. Full menu, including prize-winning meat from national shows, snacks and vegetarian choices, served 12–3pm and 6–10pm Mon–Thurs; 12–10pm Fri–Sat (cold food only 3–6pm); 12–10pm Sun. Children and dogs welcome. Large beer garden. En-suite accommodation. Two private rooms and a marquee for hire. A good base for exploring the Cotswolds; advice offered regarding other good village pubs and hidden gems! On the A417 between Cheltenham and Cirencester.

 11am–3pm and 5.30–11pm Mon–Thurs; 11am–11pm Fri–Sat; 12–10.30pm Sun.

BLAISDON
The Red Hart Inn
Blaisdon, Nr Longhope GL17 0AH
☎ *(01452) 830477* Guy and Louise Wilkins

Hook Norton Hooky Bitter is one of two brews regularly available plus three guest beers from Uley, Slaters, Wickwar, Exe Valley, Otter, Sharp's, Wells and Young's, Fuller's and many more.

Traditional 16th-century English village pub with stone floor, low-beamed ceiling and open fire. Large bar area and separate restaurant with food available 12–2pm and 6.30–9pm. Barbecue area and large garden with children's play area. Car park. Off the A48, north of Westbury-on-Severn.

 12–2.30pm and 6–11pm Mon–Sat; 12–3pm and 7–10.30pm Sun.

BLEDINGTON
The Kings Head Inn
The Green, Bledington OX7 6XQ
☎ *(01608) 658365*
Archie and Nicola Orr-Ewing
www.kingsheadinn.net

Four real ales, from breweries such as Hook Norton, Vale, Wye Valley and North Cotswold. Three of the beers are rotated after each firkin.

Quintessential, 15th-century Cotswold stone freehouse located on the village green with brook and attendant ducks. Retains olde-worlde charm of pews, settles, flagstone floors, beams, antique furnishings and inglenook fireplace. Courtyard seating area. Tasteful accommodation in 12 en-suite rooms. Food served 12–2pm and 7–9pm (9.30pm Fri–Sat). Children welcome. Large car park. On the B4450.

 11am–2.30pm and 6–11pm Mon–Sat; 12–3pm and 7–10.30pm Sun.

BLOCKLEY
Great Western Arms
Station Road, Blockley GL56 9DT
☎ *(01386) 700362* Andy and Sharon Pearce

Hook Norton pub, with Hooky and Old Hooky the favourite brews.

Friendly local in classic Cotswold pretty village, serving real ale and real homemade food every day. Children welcome. Large car park and beer terrace garden. A great place for walkers – cars can be left and orders for lunch placed before you set off on your walk!

 12–2.30pm and 6–11pm Mon–Fri; 11am–11pm Sat; 12–10.30pm Sun.

BOURTON-ON-THE-HILL
Horse & Groom
Bourton-on-the-Hill, Moreton-in-Marsh GL56 9AQ
☎ *(01386) 700413* Tom and Will Greenstock
www.horseandgroom.info

Three real ales, with Purity Pure Gold on permanently and two regularly changing guests. Locally brewed Cotswold Premium Lager and Wheat Lager also served.

Refurbished Cotswold dining pub, light and airy with a nice combination of character and contemporary decor. Freshly prepared homemade food from a regularly changing menu served 7–9pm Mon, 12–2pm and 7–9pm Tues–Sat and 12–2.30pm Sun. Large garden to rear, ample parking. Children welcome. Five double en-suite rooms. Near Sezincote House, Batsford Arboretum, Bourton House and Broadbury Tower. On the A44 at the top of the village.

 6–11pm Mon; 11am–2.30pm and 6–11pm Tues–Sat; 12–3pm Sun.

BOX
The Halfway House
Box, Minchinhampton, Stroud GL6 9AE
☎ *(01453) 832631*
www.halfwayhousebox.com

At least four real ales, with local breweries such as Wickwar, Stroud and Nailsworth prominently featured.

Freehouse on the edge of Minchinhampton Common with two dining areas. Food served 12–2pm and 7–9.30pm Mon–Sat and 12–3pm Sun. Landscaped garden with giant chessboard and Jenga. Large car park. Disabled parking, lift and toilets.

 8.30am–11pm.

BREAM
The Rising Sun
High Street, Bream, Forest of Dean GL15 6JF
☎ *(01594) 564555* Jo Gash and John Lillie
www.therisingsunbream.co.uk

Genuine freehouse serving three real ales, four at weekends, constantly rotating.

A friendly traditional pub. Food served 12–2pm and 6.30–9pm (from 7pm Sat–Sun). Children and dogs welcome. Car park and beer garden. Darts. B&B accommodation.

 12–2.30pm and 6.30–11pm Mon–Sat; 12–3pm and 7–11pm Sun.

BRISTOL
The Bridge Inn
16 Passage Street, Bristol BS2 0JF
☎ *(0117) 949 9967* Robert Clarke

Freehouse that has Bath SPA and Gem as permanents, plus a guest, perhaps another Bath Ales beer such as Wild Hare, changed every few weeks.

Probably the smallest pub in Bristol, it has office-based clientele during the day and a mixed bunch in the evening. Food served 11.30am–2.45pm Mon–Fri and 12–2pm Sat. Plenty of on-street parking. Five minutes from Temple Meads station.

 11.30am–11pm (or later) Mon–Fri; 12–11pm Sat; 7–10.30pm Sun.

The Cornubia

142 Temple Street, Bristol BS1 6EN
☎ *(0117) 925 4415*
Ben Jobbins and Lorraine McNair

 Hidden Brewery pub with Pint, Quest, Old Sarum, Pleasure and one seasonal, plus two guests, changed daily or weekly, such as Millstone and Burton Bridge brews. Range of tap and bottled ciders.

Built in 1775, a real pub offering a lovely warm atmosphere. Home-cooked food served 11.30am–9pm. Two seating areas, smoking tent, car park. Good selection of jazz and blues music. Behind Temple Mead fire station.

(OPEN) *11.30am–11pm Mon–Fri; 12–11pm Sat; 12–6pm Sun.*

Hort's

49 Broad Street, Bristol BS1 2EP
☎ *(0117) 925 2520* Jamie Reed
www.hortsbristol.co.uk

Now owned by Wells and Young's so with Bombardier and Young's Bitter, plus Bath Gem, St Austell Tribute, Courage Directors and rotating guests.

A deceptively large city-centre pub that was completely refurbished in 2006. Good food served 12–8.30pm Mon–Sat, 12–4pm Sun. Pool tables. Outside patio area.

(OPEN) *All day, every day.*

The King's Head

60 Victoria Street, Bristol BS1 6DE
☎ *(0117) 927 7860* Jane Wakeham

Four real ales: Sharp's Doom Bar and Atlantic IPA, Bath Gem and Wadworth 6X.

Small, friendly pub, full of atmosphere and character, dating from around 1660. Part of the bar has a wooden tramcar design complete with bells and mirrors. Featured in CAMRA Heritage Pub Guide. Food available 12–2pm Mon–Fri. Pavement tables in summer. Between Bristol Bridge and Temple Meads station.

(OPEN) *11am–11pm Mon–Fri; 7–11pm Sat; 12–3pm and 7–11pm Sun.*

The Old Fish Market

59–63 Baldwin Street, Bristol BS1 1QZ
☎ *(0117) 921 1515* Jaume Escoriza
www.fullers.co.uk

Fuller's tied house serving London Pride, ESB and Discovery plus Butcombe Original. Also one guest, changed monthly.

A 130-year-old building, trading as a pub since 1998. A Thai and English menu is available 12–3pm and 5–10pm Mon–Fri; 12–10pm Sat; 12–5pm Sun. Children welcome in the daytime. Big-screen TV for sports. Separate covered courtyard. Located next to Bristol Bridge.

(OPEN) *12–11pm Sun–Thurs; 12–12 Fri–Sat.*

The Orchard Inn

12 Hanover Place, Bristol BS1 6XT
☎ *(0117) 926 2678* Hugh Black

Freehouse with Bath Ales Gem and Sharp's Doom Bar plus two guests from breweries such as Mole's and Butcombe. Guests change monthly. Also draught cider.

One-bar street-corner local. Food served daily. Located off Cumerland Road, right next to the SS Great Britain, the ferry service to Arnolfini and the Bristol floating harbour. Enjoy walks along the quayside.

(OPEN) *12–3pm and 5–11pm Mon–Sat; 12–3pm and 7.30–10.30pm Sun. Longer hours in summer.*

Shakespeare Tavern

68 Prince Street, Bristol BS1 4QZ
☎ *(0117) 929 7695* Malcolm Mant

Five real ales on offer at this Greene King pub: Abbot, IPA, Old Speckled Hen, and two guest ales.

A two-bar pub in a Georgian mansion dating from 1726 – an old merchant house on the docks. Open fire, bare floor boards, wood panelling. Food available 12–9pm every day, including Sunday roasts. Quiz night Tuesday 8pm. Children allowed until 6pm.

(OPEN) *11am–11pm Sun–Thurs; 11am–midnight Fri–Sat.*

BRISTOL–BEDMINSTER

Robert Fitzharding

24 Cannon Street, Bedminster, Bristol BS3 1BN
☎ *(0117) 966 2757* Simon Fitton

 Wetherspoon's pub with a range of up to ten real ales. Regulars include Butcombe Bitter and Gold, Bath Gem, Marston's Pedigree, Greene King Abbot and Brains SA, and guests might be something like Exmoor Best, Badger Tanglefoot or Bath Barnstormer.

City suburb pub with one bar, decorated in a traditional style. Food served 9am–11pm every day. Seating at the front and beer garden at the rear. Two major beer festivals held each year. Children welcome until 9pm. Ten minutes' walk from the centre of Bristol, between East Street and North Street.

(OPEN) *9am–midnight Sun–Thurs; 9am–1am Fri–Sat.*

The Windmill

14 Windmill Hill, Bedminster, Bristol BS3 4LU
☎ *(0117) 963 5440* Joby Andrews
www.thewindmillbristol.com

Freehouse with three cask ales from the Bristol Beer Factory, namely Red, Sunrise and No. 7, brewed less than two miles from the pub.

Restored in 2006, the pub is now a thriving focal point of the community. Food served all day until 10pm. Turn left from Bedminster train station, and the pub is 20 yards on the right.

(OPEN) *11am–11pm Mon–Thurs; 11am–midnight Fri–Sat; 12–10.30pm Sun.*

The Annexe

Seymour Road, Bishopston, Bristol BS7 9EQ
☎ *(0117) 949 3931* Teresa Rogers

Smiles Best, Marston's Pedigree and Greene King IPA plus one guest changing daily.

A town pub with disabled access, children's room, garden, darts etc. Bar food available at lunchtime and restaurant food in the evenings. Children allowed until 8.30pm in the conservatory only.

11.30am–2.30pm and 6–11pm Mon–Fri; 11.30am–11pm Sat; 12–10.30pm Sun.

The Eldon House

6 Lower Clifton Hill, Bristol, BS8 1BT
☎ *(0117) 922 1271* Emma Harper

Bath Ales Spa, Gem and one weekly changing guest such as St Austell Proper Job, Butcombe Gold or Triple FFF Moondance.

End-of-terrace, 150-year-old freehouse with many original features. Live music every weekend. Food served 12–2pm and 6–9pm Mon–Sat and excellent Sunday lunches served 12–4pm. Opposite QEH School, off Clifton Triangle.

12–11pm Mon–Thurs; 12–12 Fri; 12–11pm Sat; 12–10.30pm Sun.

The Hope & Anchor

38 Jacobs Wells Road, Clifton, Bristol BS8 1DR
☎ *(0117) 929 2987*
Nikki Hughes and Hugh Simpson-Wells

Freehouse offering up to six different real ales, changing all the time but quite likely something from Butcombe or a micro-brewery such as Blindmans Brewery.

A laid-back, almost intellectual atmosphere with wooden floors, wooden tables and sophisticated haircuts. Food all day, every day. Beer garden at back. Chess and backgammon.

12–11pm.

The Penny Farthing

115 Whiteladies Road, Clifton, Bristol BS8 2PB
☎ *(0117) 973 3539* Charles Corston

Henry's IPA and 6X from Wadworth, Adnams Broadside, Badger Tanglefoot, Bath Gem and Butcombe Bitter are regulars plus three rotating guests. Charles Wells Bombardier is a favourite.

Popular character pub with strange decorations including a penny farthing. One bar. Food served 12–8.30pm Mon–Thurs and 12–6pm Fri–Sun. Small patio.

11am–11pm Mon–Thurs; 11am–midnight Fri–Sat; 12–10.30pm Sun.

The Port of Call

3 York Street, Clifton, Bristol BS8 2YE
☎ *(0117) 973 3600* Roger Skuse

Usually six permanent real ales plus another six guests, which are rotated every couple of days. Popular brews include Caledonian Deuchars IPA, Sharp's Doom Bar and Cornish Coaster and Butcombe Blonde.

A traditional one-bar pub dating from 1788. No music or machines. No children. Food served 12–2.15pm and 5.30–9pm Mon–Fri; 12–9pm Sat; 12–5pm Sun. Booking for food advisable. Beer garden.

12–2.30pm and 5.30–11pm Mon–Fri; 12–11pm Sat; 12–5pm Sun.

The Quinton House

2 Park Place, Clifton, Bristol BS8 1JW
☎ *(0117) 907 7858* Shirley Haskins

Four real ales, including Greene King Abbot, Butcombe Bitter, Wadworth 6X and Courage Best.

Cosy, traditional city local off the Clifton Triangle. Wood-clad walls and a warm atmosphere. Food served 12–2pm and 4.30–11.30pm.

11.30am–2.30pm and 4.30–11pm Mon–Fri; 12–11.30pm Sat; 12–10.30pm Sun.

The Royal Oak

50 The Mall, Clifton Village, Bristol BS8 4JG
☎ *(0117) 973 8846* Simon Dauncey

Enterprise Inns house with five real ales, including Greene King IPA, Sharp's Doom Bar and Cornish Coaster. Also Courage Best and Bass.

A friendly local decorated with sports (especially rugby) memorabilia and 1970s Smirnoff posters. Dogs and children welcome. Food served 12–2.30pm. Darts, dominoes and chess to play.

12–11pm Mon–Sat; 12–4pm Sun.

The Victoria

2 Southleigh Road, Clifton, Bristol BS8 2BH
☎ *(0117) 974 5675* Francesca Arnold
www.dawkins-taverns.co.uk

Six real ales on the pumps at this freehouse, with Matthews Brassknocker and Goff's Jouster always on offer. The four guests are changed when the barrel finishes, so usually every couple of days, and examples include Cheddar Best Bitter, Jollyboat Hart of Oak.

Small pub (30 seats) in a Grade II listed Victorian building with candles and a real fire. Tucked away off Whiteladies Road, next to the newly re-opened Clifton Lido, so quite a hidden gem. Over 30 different types of snack! Quiz 8pm Tues. St George's Beer festival in April, with over 25 real ales and ciders, plus cider festival at August bank holiday. Turn left in Whiteladies Road opposite the BBC building, the pub is behind St Paul's Road and the reservoir.

4–11pm Mon–Fri; 12–11pm Sat; 12–10.30pm Sun.

BRISTOL–COTHAM
The Cat & Wheel
207 Cheltenham Road, Cotham, Bristol BS6 5QX
☎ *(0117) 942 7862*
Scott Waldron and Jan Friend

Mole's pub with Mole's Rucking Mole and Courage Best plus a Mole's seasonal guest.

A two-bar pub, one with a traditional, relaxed atmosphere, the other more lively, with pool, table football, darts and juke box. No food. Quiz on Thursdays, live music on Fridays. By the arches on Cheltenham Road.

OPEN *3pm–12.30am Mon–Thurs; 2pm–12.30am Fri; noon–12.30am Sat–Sun.*

The Highbury Vaults
164 St Michael's Hill, Cotham, Bristol BS2 8DE
☎ *(0117) 973 3203* Bradd Francis

Wells and Young's tied house serving Young's Bitter, Special and seasonal ales, plus Brains SA, Charles Wells Bombardier, Bath Gem and St Austell Tribute. Two of these are rotating guests.

Traditional two-bar alehouse in the heart of university land and hospitals, reputed to be where condemned men had their last meal. Original front bar, snug including jug and bottle. Lots of atmosphere for young and old, students and locals. Food served Mon-Fri 12–2pm and 5.30–8.30pm; 12–2.30pm Sat; 12–3pm Sun. Heated rear patio garden. Children welcome. No dogs. Annual charity (street) music festival on August bank holiday Sunday. At the top of St Michael's Hill.

OPEN *12–12 (11pm Sun).*

BRISTOL–HOTWELLS
Adam & Eve
7 Hope Chapel Hill, Hotwells, Bristol BS8 4ND
☎ *(0117) 929 1508*
James and Karen Thompson

Enterprise Inns tied house serving ales such as Bath Ales Gem, RCH Pitchfork and Wye Valley HPA. Guests changed at least fortnightly.

Traditional, old, wood-panelled bar. Food served 12–3pm and 6–9pm Tues–Fri; 12–9pm Sat; 12–5pm Sun. Children welcome. Board games and book exchange.

OPEN *All day, every day.*

The Bag O'Nails
141 St Georges Road, Hotwells, Bristol BS1 5UW
☎ *(0117) 940 6776* James Dean
www.bagonails.org.uk

Six or seven different beers available on a rotating basis from smaller, independent and micro-breweries. The pub's own web page gives details of the beers stocked.

A small, quiet, traditional gas-lit city-centre pub with one bar, situated on the Hotwells roundabout just 25 yards from the dock. Two beer festivals held each year in April and November. No children.

OPEN *12–2.15pm and 5.30–11pm Tue–Thurs; all day Fri–Sun; closed Mon.*

Merchant's Arms
5 Merchant's Road, Hotwells, Bristol BS8 4PZ
☎ *(0117) 904 0037* John Lansdall

Bath Ales pub offering SPA, Gem and Barnstormer, plus one seasonal ale, usually from Bath, and occasional guests.

Small, friendly one-bar pub that is popular with locals, an old-fashioned place where good conversation takes place. Pork pies, pasties and toasties available all sessions. Quiz on Thursdays. Well-behaved children welcome until 7pm. Popular with Bristol City fans on match days – away fans welcome. Close to Bristol Docks, next to the flyover (ferry available from city centre).

OPEN *12–2.30pm and 5–11pm Mon–Thur; 12–11pm Fri–Sat; 12–10.30pm Sun.*

BRISTOL–KINGSDOWN
The Bell Inn
21 Alfred Place, Kingsdown, Bristol BS2 8HD
☎ *(0117) 907 7563* Anna Luke

Freehouse regularly offering Abbey Bellringer, RCH Pitchfork, Archers Golden plus occasional guests.

A proper, traditional English one-bar pub with a warm and friendly atmosphere. Customers an eclectic mix of all ages, mainly local. Candlelight in the evenings. No food. No children. Situated off St Michael's Hill, at the back of the BRI hospital.

OPEN *4.30–11pm Mon–Sat; 12–2pm and 7–10.30pm Sun.*

Hare On The Hill
41 Thomas Street North, Kingsdown, Bristol
☎ *(0117) 908 1982* James Blackwell

Bath Ales SPA, Gem, Barnstormer, SPA Extra (summer) and Festivity (winter) plus one or two guest beers, all above 4.8% ABV. Their own Rare Hare is also offered and they specialise in beer swaps.

Popular, Bath Ales award-winning pub. Bar food served lunchtimes and evenings. Sunday roasts 12.30–3.30pm. Well-behaved children welcome, but no special facilities.

OPEN *12–2.30pm and 5–11pm Mon–Thurs; 12–11pm Fri–Sat; 12–10.30pm Sun.*

The Hillgrove
53 Hillgrove Street North, Kingsdown, Bristol BS2 8LT
☎ *(0117) 944 4780* Glen Dawkins

Goff's Tournament, Matthews Brassknocker and Cheddar Best Bitter, plus five guests, always including one dark beer. Also up to 15 wines served by the glass. Genuine imported lagers.

Victorian street-corner local, established in 1854. Great character features such as 1920s art deco stained glass windows. Open-plan layout but with two distinct lounges containing comfortable Chesterfields. CAMRA Pub of the Year for Bristol and District 2007. Beer garden with heated sheltered area. Two annual beer festivals. Located up the hill from 'Stokes Croft', near the Bristol Royal Infirmary.

OPEN *4pm–12 Sun–Thurs; 4pm–1am Fri–Sat.*

BRISTOL–KNOWLE
Knowle Hotel
Leighton Road, Knowle, Bristol BS4 2LL
☎ *(0117) 977 7019* Paul and Debra Cheesley

 Courage Best, Fuller's London Pride and Wadworth 6X are permanent, and one guest ale is also served.

Alarge typical locals' bar, in the middle of a residential area, with separate lounge and wonderful views over the city. Sports channels in bar. Reasonably priced food served 12–8pm Sat, and 12–5pm Sun. (No food served during week.) Beer garden. Two miles from city centre.

OPEN *4–11pm Mon–Wed; 3–11pm Thurs–Fri; 12–11pm Sat; 12–10.30pm Sun.*

BRISTOL–MONTPELIER
Cadbury House
68 Richmond Road, Montpelier, Bristol BS6 5EW
☎ *(0117) 924 7874* Clair Trick

Sharp's Doom Bar and Bath Ales Gem plus one rotating guest, perhaps Young's Special or Shepherd Neame Spitfire.

Locals' pub in a residential area. Clientele a mix of regulars and students. Large beer garden. Bar meals lunchtime and evening. Children allowed until 9pm.

OPEN *All day, every day.*

BRISTOL–SOUTHVILLE
Coronation
18 Dean Lane, Southville, Bristol BS3 1DD
☎ *(0117) 940 9044* Lorna Joseph

Five beers from the Hop Back brewery plus one guest (changed monthly).

Arelaxed and busy traditional one-bar local. Pizzas served 6–9pm. Supervised children welcome during the day. Chess and draughts to play.

OPEN *3–11pm Mon–Fri; 12–11pm Sat; 12–10.30pm Sun.*

BRISTOL–TOTTERDOWN
The Shakespeare
1 Henry Street, Totterdown, Bristol BS3 4UD
☎ *(0117) 907 8818*
Emma and Warwick Newton
www.theshakey.co.uk

Enterprise Inns tied house with Bath Gem, Sharp's Cornish Coaster and Falstaff (brewed exclusively for them) as permanent fixtures, plus two guest ales, changed twice a week.

Built in 1871, this pub features an open-plan U-shaped bar with outdoor drinking areas at the front and back of the building. DJs every night, frequent music quizzes and Sunday BBQs in summer, Sunday lunch in winter. Children allowed until 6pm. Three annual real ale festivals held on each bank holiday, featuring 12 guest beers and cider. From Temple Meads station, turn left up Wells Road, turn right at The Three Lamps and it is 100 yards up on the left.

OPEN *4.30–11pm Mon–Thurs; 4.30pm–12 Fri; 12–12 Sat; 12–10.30pm Sun.*

BRISTOL–WESTBURY ON TRYM
The Post Office Tavern
17 Westbury Hill, Westbury on Trym, Bristol BS9 3AH
☎ *(0117) 940 1233* Russell Fitz-Hugh

Up to six beers: Otter Bitter, Bath Gem, Butcombe Bitter, Bass and Courage Best, plus a guest changed each month.

Early-20th-century freehouse full of post office memorabilia specialising in real ale and pizzas. Food served 12–2pm (12.30–3pm Sun) and 7–9pm (not Sun). On-street parking, small patio, happy hours. No children under 14. On main road in Westbury village.

OPEN *11am–11pm Mon–Sat; 12–3pm and 7–10.30pm Sun.*

The Prince of Wales
84 Stoke Lane, Westbury on Trym, Bristol BS9 3SP
☎ *(0117) 962 3715* Richard Ellis

Freehouse generally serving Fuller's London Pride, Butcombe Bitter, Bath SPA and Brakspear Bitter, plus one guest, perhaps Timothy Taylor Landlord.

Afriendly and busy real ale local, decorated with cricket memorabilia. Food lunchtime only Mon–Sat. Garden with children's play area.

OPEN *11am–3pm and 5.30–11pm Mon–Fri; all day Sat; 12–4pm and 7–10.30pm Sun.*

The Victoria Inn
20 Chock Lane, Westbury on Trym, Bristol BS9 3EX
☎ *(0117) 950 0441* Alastair and Fiona Deas
www.thevictoriapub.co.uk

Wadworth tied house serving 6X and Henry's IPA plus Butcombe Bitter and two guests changed fortnightly.

Village pub with a real community feel – it has its own cricket team, and hosts regular meetings of the local hockey teams, Scout leaders, allotment keepers and bellringers. A welcoming place to enjoy the company of old friends and make some new ones! Cask Marque accredited. Food served 12–2pm every day and 6–9pm Mon–Sat, with fresh fish served Tues–Sat. Beer garden. Fortnightly quiz on Mondays, occasional live music, themed menu evenings.

OPEN *12–2.30pm and 6–11pm Mon–Sat; 12–3pm and 7–10.30pm Sun.*

The White Horse
High Street, Westbury on Trym, Bristol BS9 3DZ
☎ *(0117) 950 7622* Derek Roberts

Sharp's Doom Bar, and a brew from Wychwood, Brakspear or Butcombe.

An olde-worlde pub, part of which dates from 1400. Three small bars and one large area. Outside patios. No food. No children. Opposite the post office.

OPEN *11am–11pm Mon–Sat; 12–10.30pm.*

BROAD CAMPDEN
The Bakers Arms
Broad Campden, Chipping Campden GL55 6UR
☎ *(01386) 840515* Sally and Ray Mayo

Freehouse with Charles Wells Bombardier, Donnington BB and brews from Stanway always available, plus two rotating guest ales.

Small, friendly Cotswold country pub with open fire. Bar food available every lunchtime and evening; all day in the summer. Car park, garden, patio and children's play area. In a village between Chipping Campden and Blockley. Local CAMRA Pub of the Year 2005.

OPEN *Summer: 11.30am–11pm Mon–Sat; 12–10.30pm Sun. Winter: 11.30am–2.30pm and 4.45–11pm Mon–Fri; 11.30am–11pm Sat; 12–10.30pm Sun.*

CHARLTON KINGS
Merryfellow
2 School Lane, Charlton Kings, Cheltenham GL53 8AU
☎ *(01242) 525883* Jim Dockree

Sharp's IPA and Doom Bar, Shepherd Neame Spitfire and a Hook Norton brew.

Classic village pub offering value-for-money food and a selection of ales. No food Mon–Tues. Car park, garden, skittle alley and function room. Children welcome.

OPEN *All day, every day.*

CHELTENHAM
Adam & Eve
10 Townsend Street, Cheltenham GL51 9HD
☎ *(01242) 690030* Mrs Gasson

Arkells 2B, 3B and seasonals always on offer.

Simple side-street pub that could be somebody's front room. Skittle alley and darts. Children allowed in patio area.

OPEN *10.30am–2.30pm and 4–11pm Sun–Fri; all day Sat.*

The Jolly Brewmaster
39 Painswick Road, Cheltenham GL50 2EZ
☎ *(01242) 772261* Danielle Wheatley

Enterprise Inns house with six constantly changing cask ales. Examples include Sharp's Doom Bar, Northumberland Bucking Fastard, Purity Pure Ubu, Wye Valley Dorothy Goodbody and Badger Tanglefoot. Eight ciders also served.

One-bar backstreet pub, dating from the 1850s, located in an affluent area. Sociable horseshoe-shaped bar and a hidden gem of a garden. Sunday roasts available, no other food. Annual cider festival in June or July. Cheltenham CAMRA pub of the year for 2008 and 2009.

OPEN *12–11pm (10.30pm Sun).*

The Kemble Brewery Inn
27 Fairview Street, Cheltenham GL52 2JF
☎ *(01242) 243446* Chris Baylis

Six real ales, including many independent locals and favourite nationals.

This small, friendly, backstreet local dating from 1850 is one of the few remaining real ale pubs in Cheltenham, and features a Mediterranean-style courtyard garden. Food served lunchtimes with a sumptuous weekly Sunday roast. Within walking distance of football ground and racecourse.

OPEN *12–11pm Sun–Thurs; 12–12 Fri–Sat.*

Sudeley Arms
Prestbury Road, Cheltenham GL52 2PN
☎ *(01242) 510697* Gary Hyett

Part tied to Enterprise Inns. Goff's Jouster and St Austell Tribute, plus two weekly-changing guests such as Brains SA, Wickwar Bob, Gale's HSB, Ringwood Fortyniner or Wychwood Hobgoblin.

Located on the edge of the town centre, the last pub before the racecourse and football ground. No food. Close to Pittville park and pump rooms. Five minutes' walk from the town.

OPEN *11am–11pm.*

The Swan
35–7 High Street, Cheltenham GL50 1DX
☎ *(01242) 584929* Stephen Hall

A Marston's tied house serving three daily-changing real ales. In additional to Marston's, beers from Jennings, Otter and Thwaites are regularly featured. CAMRA Pub of the Year 2005–07.

A 17th-century coaching inn with a contemporary and smart interior. Food served 12–9pm every day. Children allowed until 7pm. Beer garden. Car park.

OPEN *12–12.*

Tailors
4 Cambray Place, Cheltenham GL50 1JS
☎ *(01242) 255453* Cherri Dandridge

A Wadworth-managed house serving 6X, IPA and JCB.

Comfortable, traditional pub in the town centre, full of character. Cellar bar is a function room. Two lovely beer gardens. Four big-screen TVs. Landlady was a recent finalist in the licensee of the year. Good-value pub meals served Mon–Sat lunchtimes only. Children welcome.

OPEN *All day, every day.*

The Lygon Arms

High Street, Chipping Camden GL55 6HB
☎ *(01386) 840318*
IG Potter, HM Potter and S Davenport
www.lygonarms.co.uk

 Freehouse with Hook Norton Hooky Bitter plus two guests, changing weekly, from any independent brewery.

A 16th-century, family-owned and -run coaching inn, with traditional bar area, dining room and picturesque courtyard for outside dining in summer. One bar, courtyard and beer garden, car parking at rear. En-suite accommodation in 12 bedrooms. Traditional English food prepared with local produce served 12–2.30pm and 6–10pm every day. Children welcome.

OPEN *Winter: 11am–3pm and 6–11pm. Summer: 11am–11pm.*

The Volunteer Inn

Lower High Street, Chipping Campden GL55 6DY
☎ *(01386) 840688*
Mark Gibson and Peter Miskerik
www.thevolunteerinn.com

 Wychwood Hobgoblin, Wickwar Cotswold Way, Hook Norton Hooky Bitter and a guest, perhaps something from Donnington or Battledown, rotated every couple of months.

A 17th-century country inn at the start of the Cotswold Way with two bars, log fires and lots of war memorabilia. Beer garden leading to the River Cam. Food served 12–2.30pm, plus Indian cuisine in the restaurant 5–10.30pm. Children welcome: there is a children's play area in the garden. Nine letting rooms (six en-suite). Garden available for private hire. At the lower end of the High Street.

OPEN *11am–3pm and 5–11pm Mon–Sat; 12–3pm and 5–10.30pm Sun.*

Beaufort Hunt

Broad Street, Chipping Sodbury, Bristol BS37 6AG
☎ *(01454) 312871* Mr Arnall

 Greene King IPA plus one guest, perhaps Fuller's London Pride.

Old-style village pub with courtyard. Food available at lunchtime. Children aged 14–18 allowed in lounge bar only if eating. Under-14s not allowed.

OPEN *11am–2.30pm and 5–11pm (10.30pm Sun).*

The Bear Inn

12 Dyer Street, Cirencester GL7 2PF
☎ *(01285) 653472* Lianne

 Mole's Brewery tied house serving Mole's Best plus one guest.

Town-centre pub, refurbished in the style of an old coaching inn. Home-cooked food served at lunchtimes and evenings. Children allowed until 6.30pm.

OPEN *All day, every day.*

Corinium Hotel & Restaurant

12 Gloucester Street, Cirencester GL7 2DG
☎ *(01285) 659711* Tim Waller
www.coriniumhotel.co.uk

 Cotleigh Tawny and Uley brews plus a guest beer, changing regularly, from an independent brewery.

A 16th-century wool merchant's house, now a hotel, bar and restaurant popular with locals. Wide selection of food served 12–2pm and 6.30–9pm. Accommodation in 15 rooms. Walled beer garden. Children welcome in restaurant and garden. Car parking. Five minutes' walk from the town centre. Close to Cirencester Park and Corinium Museum.

OPEN *11am–11pm (midnight Fri–Sat; 10.30pm Sun).*

The Drillman's Arms

84 Gloucester Road, Cirencester GL7 2JY
☎ *(01285) 653892* Richard Selby

 Freehouse serving Archers Best, Wickwar Cotswold Way and Young's Bitter plus one guest.

Village pub with log fire and function room. Food served at lunchtime and evenings. Children allowed.

OPEN *11am–3pm and 5.30–11pm Mon–Fri; all day Sat; 11am–4pm and 7–10.30pm Sun.*

Twelve Bells

Lewes Lane, Cirencester GL7 1EA
☎ *(01285) 644549* RJ Ashley

 Freehouse serving five different real ales but always changing – more than 350 last year.

A traditional pub offering good beer, good grub in pleasant atmosphere. Don't be fooled by the ordinariness of the outside, this is a real find. One bar with three quieter side rooms. Children welcome. Car park and garden.

OPEN *11am–11pm (closed for an hour in the afternoon).*

The Lamb Inn

The Cross, Clearwell, Nr Coleford GL16 8JU
☎ *(01594) 835441* FJ Yates and SY Lewis

 Wye Valley Bitter plus three guests which may include Bath Gem, Blindman's Mine Beer or beers from Stonehenge and other micro-breweries.

A 19th-century stone-built freehouse with later additions. No food, machines or music and the beer is served straight from the barrel. Well-behaved children welcome till 8.30pm. Small snug with old settle. Open fires, beer garden, car park. Handy for Clearwell Caves, Cinderbury Iron Age Village, Wye Valley and local campsites. Situated 200 yards from Clearwell Cross on the Newland and Redbrook road.

OPEN *6–11pm Wed–Thurs; 12–3pm and 6–11pm Fri–Sat and bank holidays; 12–3pm and 7–10.30pm Sun.*

COATES

The Tunnel House Inn

Tarlton Road, Coates, Cirencester GL7 6PU
☎ *(01285) 770280* Rupert Longsdon
www.tunnelhouse.com

 A freehouse. Beers from Uley, Hook Norton and Wickwar. Plus one or two guests, from breweries such as Bath Ales, Wickwar, Stroud, Nailsworth and Cheltenham.

Built in the 18th century to house the workers of the Severn and Thames canal, this is a rural pub on the edge of a wood deep in the Cotswolds. Everyone welcome: real ale enthusiasts, families, dogs. Food served 12–2.15pm and 6.45–9.15pm. Follow the brown signs from the A438 from Circencester to Tetbury.

OPEN *11.30am–3.30pm and 6–11.30pm Mon–Thurs; all day Fri–Sun.*

COLEFORD

The Angel Hotel

Market Place, Coleford GL16 8AE
☎ *(01594) 833113* Barry Stoakes

Two constantly changing real ales from a wide range of breweries.

Dating from the 17th century and situated in the Forest of Dean, this was once used as a town hall but is now a tastefully refurbished nine-room hotel with real ale bar. Courtyard and beer garden. Separate nightclub attached (Fri and Sat only). Food served 12–2.30pm and 7–9pm daily with a tea shop open from 7am–noon and 2.30–5pm. Children welcome.

OPEN *From 7am (for breakfast) and 10.30am–11pm (1am in nightclub).*

COWLEY

Green Dragon Inn

Cockleford, Cowley, Cheltenham GL53 9NW
☎ *(01242) 870271*
Jonathan Mather and Sally Wigg
www.green-dragon-inn.co.uk

Butcombe Bitter, Hook Norton Hooky Bitter and Courage Directors are regularly available at this freehouse.

Traditional Cotswold inn with stone-clad floors and roaring log fires in winter. Function room and patio overlooking lake. Nine en-suite accommodation. Food served 12–2.30pm and 6–10pm Mon–Fri, 12–10pm Sat, 12–3.30pm and 6–9pm Sun. Car park. Off the A435 between Cheltenham and Cirencester.

OPEN *11am–11pm Mon–Sat; 12–11pm Sun.*

CRANHAM

The Black Horse Inn

Cranham, Gloucester GL4 8HP
☎ *(01452) 812217* David Job

Four real ales generally available including Wickwar BOB, plus probably something from Archers.

An unspoilt traditional village inn perched on the side of a hill. Cosy lounge, classic country public bar complete with strange stag head, and dining room upstairs. No food

on Sunday evening. Car park and garden. Children allowed.

OPEN *12–2.30pm and 6.30–11pm (8–10.30pm Sun). Closed some Mondays in the winter.*

DIDMARTON

The King's Arms

The Street, Didmarton, Nr Badminton GL9 1DT
☎ *(01454) 238245* Mr and Mrs Sadler
www.kingsarmsdidmarton.co.uk

 Uley Bitter plus two guests changed every few weeks, with examples including Stroud Budding and beers from Otter and Bath breweries.

A coaching inn dating from 1652, with two bars and a restaurant, refurbished in 2007. Accommodation – four rooms in the pub and three luxury self-catering cottages. Good food available 12–2.30pm and 6–9.30pm Mon–Sat; 12–7.45pm Sun. AA 4 diamond rating, and mentioned in various guide books. See website for directions, sample menu and room information.

OPEN *11am–11pm Mon–Sat; 12–11pm Sun.*

DOYNTON

The Cross House Inn

High Street, Doynton BS30 5TF
☎ *(0117) 937 2261* André Large

Enterprise Inns pub with five real ales. Bath Ales Gem, Greene King Old Speckled Hen, Wickwar BOB and Timothy Taylor Landlord are regular features.

One bar locals' pub, about 300 years old, with a small restaurant. Food served 11.30am–2pm and 6–9.15pm Mon–Sat (10pm Sat); 12–2pm and 7–9pm Sun. Children welcome. Beer garden. Car park. Off the A420.

OPEN *11.30am–3pm and 6–11pm Mon–Sat; 12–4pm and 7–10.30pm Sun.*

DUNTISBOURNE ABBOTS

Five Mile House

Gloucester Road, Duntisbourne Abbots, Cirencester GL7 7JR
☎ *(01285) 821432* Jon and Jo Carrier
www.fivemilehouse.furryfeet.tv,
www.fivemilehouse.co.uk

 Freehouse serving three different distinctive beers of varying strength. Young's PA, Donnington BB, Wye Valley Butty Bach and Stroud Budding are among the beers often featured.

A warm welcome is guaranteed at this traditional 17th-century country pub, winner of the Good Pub Guide's Best Pub 2007, with old bar, family room and garden. Award-winning food served 12–2.30pm and 6–9.30pm Mon–Sat and 12–2.30pm and 7–9pm Sun (no food Sunday evenings Oct–April). Children welcome with well-behaved adults! Marquee for hire in summer. Plenty of parking. Just off the A417 on what was the Roman Ermine Street, 200 yards downhill from services.

OPEN *12–2.30pm and 6–11pm (7–10.30pm Sun).*

DURSLEY
Old Spot Inn
Hill Road, Dursley GL11 4JQ
☎ *(01453) 542870* Stephen Herbert
www.oldspotinn.co.uk

At least eight ales, with Butcombe Bitter and Uley Old Ric the permanent features. Guests are changed weekly or monthly, and might include Otter Bitter, Severn Vale Dance, Bath Gem, Goff's White Knight, Nailsworth Artist's Ale and Stroud Tom Long.

Cosy freehouse in an old school house. Food served 12–3pm Mon–Sun. One main bar with additional rooms at either end. Parking. Four beer festivals every year, plus monthly beer promotions, brewery visits and guest speakers. Gloucestershire CAMRA Pub of the Year for 4 consecutive years, national winner 2007. On the Cotswold Way.

OPEN *11am–11pm.*

EBRINGTON
The Ebrington Arms
Ebrington, Nr Chipping Campden GL55 6NH
☎ *(01386) 593223* Claire and Jim Alexander
www.theebringtonarms.co.uk

Local beers such as Goff's Jouster, Uley Bitter, Bass and Tom Long.

CAMRA's North Cotswolds Pub of the Year 2009. Traditional 17th-century Cotswold inn. Bar and separate dining room in the 'Old Bakehouse'. Homemade food served 12–2.30pm and 6–9pm Tues–Sat and 12–3.30pm Sun. AA Rosette rated and in Michelin Pub Guide (for food). Three 4-star en-suite rooms. Large beer garden. Music nights. Car park. Saturday breakfasts open to the public (9.30–11am). Close to Hidcote Manor Gardens and Chipping Campden.

OPEN *12–3pm and 6–11pm Tues-Sat (closed Mon except bank holidays); 12–close Sun. From Easter, open all day Fri-Sun for summer.*

ELDERSFIELD
The Butchers Arms
Lime Street, Eldersfield, Gloucester GL19 4NX
☎ *(01452) 840381* James and Elizabeth Winter
www.thebutchersarms.net

Freehouse with two or three real ales (one in winter) with the selection changing regularly. Examples include Wye Valley Butty Bach, Bitter and Dorothy Goodbody's, RCH Pitchfork, Bath Gem, Malvern Hills Black Pear, Swedish Nightingale and Dr Gully's IPA.

A 16th-century rural inn with a daily changing menu. Food served 12–1pm Wed–Sun and 7–8.30pm Tues–Sat. On the A417 towards Ledbury, follow sign for Corse Lawn and take the Lime Street turning.

OPEN *12–2.30pm and 7pm–12am Tues–Sun; closed Mon.*

FORD
The Plough Inn
Ford, Temple Guiting GL54 5RU
☎ *(01386) 584215* Craig Brown
www.theploughinnatford.co.uk

Donnington Brewery house always serving BB and SBA.

A 13th-century Cotswold stone inn. Food served at lunchtimes and evenings. Children allowed. Located on the main road between Stow-on-the-Wold and Tewkesbury, opposite the Jackdaws Castle racing stables.

OPEN *All day, every day.*

FORTHAMPTON
Lower Lode Inn
Forthampton, Nr Tewkesbury GL19 4RE
☎ *(01684) 293224* Samantha Snape

Freehouse with Hook Norton Old Hooky and Donnington on permanent plus up to four guests depending on the season.

Riverside inn dating from the 15th century. Popular with locals but also a destination pub in the summer. Accommodation. Food every session. Car park and garden. Children welcome. Pool, darts.

OPEN *12–3pm and 6–11pm Mon–Thur; all day Fri–Sun; closed Mon and Tues lunchtime in the winter.*

FRAMPTON COTTERELL
The Rising Sun
43 Ryecroft Road, Frampton Cotterell, Nr Bristol BS17 2HN
☎ *(01454) 772330* Kevin Stone

A popular freehouse with Butcombe Bitter, Wadworth 6X, Cotleigh Tawny, Sharp's Doom Bar and Draught Bass plus one guest, changed weekly.

Friendly, single-bar local that likes to support the smaller brewers. Food served 12–2pm and 6.30–9.30pm Mon–Sat (until 10pm Sat) and 12–9pm Sun. Skittle alley. Off Church Road.

OPEN *11.30am–3pm and 5.30–11pm Mon–Thurs; 11.30am–midnight Fri–Sat; 12–11.30pm Sun.*

FRANCE LYNCH
The King's Head
France Lynch, Stroud GL6 8LT
☎ *(01453) 882225* Mike Duff
www.kingsheadfrancelynch.co.uk

Freehouse serving Young's Bitter, Sharp's Doom Bar and Otter plus a guest beer that changes frequently.

Small, traditional, country pub with large garden. No juke box. Live music every Monday evening. Food served at lunchtimes and evenings. Children's play area.

OPEN *12–2.30pm and 6–11pm Mon–Sat; 12–2.30pm and 7–10.30pm Sun.*

GLOUCESTER
Dick Whittington's
100 Westgate Street, Gloucester GL1 2PE
☎ *(01452) 502039*

Up to eight real ales, too many to mention as they change on a daily basis.

A traditional real ale pub in a 15th-century Grade II listed building. Homemade food available 12–9pm Mon–Sat and 12–3pm Sun. Beer garden, private room for hire. Children welcome. Near the cathedral, in the city centre.

OPEN *11am–11pm Mon–Sat; 12–10.30pm Sun.*

England's Glory

66–8 London Road, Gloucester GL1 3PB
☏ *(01452) 302948* Andy and Marie Smith
www.englandsgloryglos.co.uk

 Wadworth-managed house with Henry's IPA, 6X, JCB and Horizon, plus occasional seasonal Wadworth guests.

Two-bar pub on the outskirts of town. Food available 11.30am–2pm and 6–9pm Mon–Fri; all day from 11.30pm Sat; 12–3pm Sun. Disabled access and toilet, skittle alley, two beer gardens, large car park. Children welcome. Big screens, quiz night on Sundays.

OPEN *Open all day, every day April–Nov. Winter: 11.30am–2.30pm and 5–11pm Mon–Thurs; 11.30am–midnight Fri; 11.30am–11pm Sat; 12–10.30pm Sun.*

The Linden Tree

73–5 Bristol Road, Gloucester GL1 5SN
☏ *(01452) 527869* Gordon Kinnear

 Wadworth 6X, Henry's IPA, and JCB plus up to four guest beers, which may include Badger Tanglefoot.

A true country pub in the heart of Gloucester, south of the city centre. Large refurbished Georgian Grade II listed building. Bar food available lunchtimes and evenings (except Sat and Sun night). Parking, skittle alley, function room. Children allowed if eating. Accommodation. Cask Marque approved. Follow the Bristol road from the M5.

OPEN *11.30am–2.30pm and 6–11pm Mon–Fri; 11am–11pm Sat; 12–10.30pm Sun.*

New Inn Hotel

16 Northgate Street, Gloucester GL1 1SF
☏ *(01452) 522177* Yunis Akhtar
www.newinngloucester.co.uk

 Eight to ten real ales, including Butcombe Gold and Blond or Brunel, Wychwood Hobgoblin and regularly changing guests from Hook Norton, Festival, Bath, RCH, Church End and Wye Valley.

Friendly, relaxed pub with courtyard, built in 1455 and considered one of the country's finest medieval galleried inns. Four bars and a coffee shop. Restaurant and bar meals served 12–2.30pm and 6–9pm Mon–Sat and 12–3pm Sun (carvery). Coffee shop open 9am–4pm Mon–Sat, 10am–4pm Sun. Regency Suite for hire for meetings and events, including weddings (civil licence). Accommodation in 34 bedrooms. In the town centre.

OPEN *11am–11pm Mon–Thurs; 11am–midnight Fri–Sat; 12–10.30pm Sun.*

The Queen's Head

Tewkesbury Road, Longford, Gloucester GL2 9EJ
☏ *(01452) 301882* Martin Hand

 Freehouse featuring Butcombe Gold, Butty Bach, Hooky Bitter, Otter and Timothy Taylor Landlord. Winner of CAMRA Gloucestershire Pub of the Year 2006.

A 250-year-old two-bar pub. Food served 12–2pm and 6–9.30pm every day. No children. On the A38 Tewkesbury–Gloucester road.

OPEN *11am–3pm and 5.30–11pm.*

The Regal

32 St Aldate Street, King's Square, Gloucester GL1 1RP
☏ *(01452) 332344* Michael Ayers

 Wetherspoon's pub. Greene King Abbot and Shepherd Neame Spitfire usually available plus Brains SA, Rooster's Leghorn or other guests changed on a weekly basis. Real cider.

Large town pub in a converted cinema with disabled access and toilets. Beer garden. Food served all day. Children allowed up to 6pm (5pm Saturday). Regular beer festivals.

OPEN *All day, every day.*

GRETTON

The Royal Oak

Gretton Road, Gretton GL54 5EP
☏ *(01242) 604999* Andy Robertson

 Owned by Goff's Brewery and serving Jouster, Tournament and White Knight, as well as Greene King Old Speckled Hen, John Smith's Bitter and Wickwar BOB. Plus one guest ale changing weekly.

Much bigger than it seems, the pub has a tasteful and light extension. Panoramic views. Huge car park and play area – even has its own tennis court. Food available. Children welcome.

OPEN *12–3pm and 6–11pm Mon–Sat; 12–4pm and 7–10.30pm Sun.*

HAM

The Salutation Inn

Ham, Berkeley GL13 9QH
☏ *(01453) 810284* Mr SA Fisher

 Four real ales, changed weekly.

Friendly country pub with three bars, the home of the Eagles Bush Brewery. Food served 12–2pm and 5–8pm Tues–Sat and 12–2pm Sun. Beer garden, skittle alley, car park. Situated half a mile south of Berkeley Castle.

OPEN *5–11pm Mon; 12–2.30pm and 5–11pm Tues–Fri; 12–11pm Sat; 12–10.30pm Sun.*

HANHAM MILLS

The Old Lock & Weir

Ferry Road, Hanham Mills, Bristol BS15 3NU
☏ *(0117) 967 3793* Karen State

 Freehouse serving a range of real ales, usually four in winter and six in summer. Wadworth 6X, Charles Wells Bombardier, Bath Gem and Greene King Old Speckled Hen usually available, plus two guests, changed monthly, perhaps Fuller's London Pride or Wickwar IKB.

A 300-year-old riverside pub, very quaint with bags of character, with one bar, four drinking areas and real log-burning fire. Dart board. Food available 12–2.30pm and 6.30–8.30pm Mon–Sat, 12–3pm Sun. Three riverside patio gardens, car park. Children and dogs welcome. Beer festival at August bank holiday. On the River Avon at Hanham.

OPEN *11am–11pm Mon–Sat; 12–10.30pm Sun.*

HAWKESBURY UPTON
The Beaufort Arms
High Street, Hawkesbury Upton GL9 1AU
☎ *(01454) 238217*
www.beaufortarms.com

Three real ales, four at weekends, always including Wickwar BOB, and constantly rotating guests from Butcombe, Bath, Severn Vale, RCH, Bristol Beer Factory and Wickwar. Screech Cider from Wickwar also served.

Characterful Cotswold inn built in 1602, with two traditional bars, dining room in converted stables, function room and skittle alley. Food served 12–2.30pm and 7–9.30pm every day. Picturesque beer garden. Disabled facilites. Car park. Close to Westonbirt Arboretum and the Badminton Estate, and 400 yards from the Cotswold Way. Located five miles north of J18 (Todmarton) of the M4, just off the A46 Bath–Stroud road.

OPEN *12–11pm (10.30pm Sun).*

KINGSWOOD
Dinneywicks Inn
The Chippings, Kingswood, Wotton under Edge GL12 8RT
☎ *(01453) 843328* Mr and Mrs Thomas

Wadworth house serving 6X and IPA, with other seasonal guests such as Adnams Broadside.

A refurbished village pub with garden and petanque court. Children allowed.

OPEN *11.30am–3pm and 6–11pm (all day Sat in winter); 12–3pm and 7–10.30pm Sun.*

LITTLETON UPON SEVERN
The White Hart Inn
Littleton upon Severn, Nr Bristol BS35 1NR
☎ *(01454) 412275* Jamie and Diane Reed

Wells and Young's pub always offering Young's Bitter and Special, plus Waggle Dance in the summer and Winter Warmer for the colder months. Two guest brews change monthly.

Near the Severn Bridges and Thornbury Castle, a 400-year-old former farmhouse with log fires. Bar food served 12–2pm (2.30pm at weekends) and 6.30–9.30pm (6–9pm Sun). Children are welcome in the garden room. Car park. Fifteen miles from the centre of Bristol. Signposted from Elberton village. Good local walks.

OPEN *12–2.30pm and 6–11.30pm Mon–Fri; 12–11.30pm Sat; 12–10.30pm Sun.*

LONGBOROUGH
The Coach & Horses Inn
Longborough Village, Moreton-in-Marsh GL56 0QJ
☎ *(01451) 830325* Connie Emm

Donnington tied house with XXX and Best Bitter served.

Old, original Cotswold locals' inn in lovely village setting with good views from patio. Children welcome at lunchtime and early evening. Walkers are very welcome, and can eat their own sandwiches on the premises.

OPEN *11am–3pm and 7–11pm (10.30pm Sun).*

LONGHOPE
The Glasshouse Inn
May Hill, Longhope GL17 0NN
☎ *(01452) 830529* Steve and Gill Pugh

Freehouse regularly serving Butcombe Bitter and Fuller's London Pride, plus two guests, changed weekly. All are served straight from the barrel.

Old-fashioned country pub with garden. Food served 12–2pm and 7–9pm Mon–Sat, 12–2pm Sun (for roasts only). There are three chefs – English, Thai and Lithuanian – so the menu is always interesting! No children under 14 allowed. Beer garden. Off the A40, by May Hill.

OPEN *11.30am–3pm and 6.30–11pm Mon–Sat; 12–3pm Sun.*

LOWER APPERLEY
The Farmer's Arms
Ledbury Road, Lower Apperley GL19 4DR
☎ *(01452) 780307* Maurice Estop
www.farmersarmslowerapperley.co.uk

Wadworth 6X and Henry's IPA are permanent ales, and the guest beer is changed monthly.

An 18th-century food-oriented inn with one bar, oak beams and open fires. Run by the same family as The New Inn, Church Knowle (Dorset). Bar and restaurant food available at lunchtimes and evenings. Dining area seats 100. Car park and garden. Accommodation. Weddings and other functions catered for. B4213 Ledbury Road, four miles south of Tewkesbury.

OPEN *11am–2.30pm and 6–11pm Tues–Sun; closed Mon except in late July and August.*

LYDNEY
The Swan
Pillowell, Lydney GL15 4QU
☎ *(01594) 562477* Matthew Tye

Freehouse usually serving Marston's Pedigree and an Archers beer, changed weekly.

Small local set in the centre of the Forest of Dean, over 100 years old, and a pub for most of that time. Two bars, lots of local characters, plus darts and quoits teams. Food served 12–2pm and 7–9pm every day. Beer garden, private room, car park. Children welcome. Small car park. Local attractions include Wye Valley, Forest of Dean, caves, rope walks, Dean Heritage Museum. From Lydney, head towards Whitecroft, then Pillowell.

OPEN *All day, every day.*

MARSH GIBBON
The Plough Inn
Church Street, Marsh Gibbon, Bicester OX27 0HQ
☎ *(01869) 278759 Bob Cockbill*

Genuine freehouse with Greene King IPA and Oxfordshire Ales Triple B and Marshmellow always available. Marshmellow is occasionally replaced with a one-off brew from Oxfordshire Ales.

A 17th-century coaching inn, stone-built with original beams and open fires. Public bar with pool, darts and dominoes. Lounge bar and restaurant. Food served 12–9.30pm daily (Easter–Oct); 3–9.30pm Mon–Thurs; 3–9.30pm Fri; 12–9.30pm Sat–Sun (winter). Large beer garden with enclosed children's adventure playground. Live music nights and steak nights. Large car park. Just off the A41 east of Bicester.

OPEN *Easter–Oct: 12–11pm. Winter: 3–11pm Mon–Thurs; 12–close Fri–Sun.*

MARSHFIELD
The Catherine Wheel
39 High Street, Marshfield, Chippenham SN14 8LS
☎ *(01225) 892220 Amanda Allison*
www.thecatherinewheel.co.uk

Freehouse offering Abbey Ales Bellringer and Courage Best as permanent fixtures, and a guest changed every four to six weeks, typically Bristol Beer Factory's Red.

This 17th-century old coaching inn features a main bar area and two restaurants with open fires. Food served lunchtimes and evenings Mon–Sat, 12–4pm Sun. B&B accommodation available, beer courtyard, private conference room, car park, children and dogs welcome, free Wi-Fi. Located on the A420 between Bristol and Chippenham, 10 mins from Junction 18 of the M4, 15 mins from Bath.

OPEN *12–3pm and 6–11pm Mon–Thurs; 12–3pm and 6pm–12 Fri; 12–12 Sat–Sun.*

MAYSHILL
The New Inn
Badminton Road, Mayshill, Nr Frampton Cotterell
☎ *(01454) 773161 Dave McKillop*

One brew from Cotswold Spring Brewery and three guests from far and wide, changed two or three times a week.

A listed building dating from 1650, retaining many original features. Lounge bar, fireside lounge and restaurant. Food served every lunchtime and evening. Well-behaved and supervised children welcome. Beer garden. Car park. On the A432.

OPEN *11.45am–3pm and 6–10.30pm Mon–Tues; 11.45am–3pm and 6–11pm Wed–Sat; 12–10pm Sun.*

MEYSEY HAMPTON
The Masons Arms
28 High Street, Meysey Hampton, Nr Cirencester GL7 5JT
☎ *(01285) 850164*

Former freehouse rescued from closure in 2009 by Arkells, so now with a selection of the brewery's real ales plus guests.

Village local serving the rural community that has changed hands twice in recent years. Closed for six months in early 2009 but now back in business. No garden but next to the village green. Food served lunchtime and evenings (not Sunday). Accommodation. Small car park.

OPEN *11.30am–3pm and 6–11pm Mon–Thurs; 11.30am–11pm Fri–Sat; 12–12pm Sun.*

MORETON-IN-MARSH
Inn on the Marsh
Stow Road, Moreton-in-Marsh GL56 0DW
☎ *(01608) 650709 Wayne Branagh*

Banks's Original, Marston's Pedigree and Best are permanents, plus one guest changed weekly.

A one-bar pub in a building dating from around 1850 that started life as a bakery. Typical pub food served 12–2pm and Oriental, Dutch and English meals served 7–9pm. Children welcome at lunchtime and until 9pm in the evening. Outside smoking garden, car park. Dutch game 'sjoelen' played. Handy for Cotswolds attractions, including arboretum, wildlife parks, fishing lakes and stately homes. On the main Fosse Way (A429).

OPEN *12–3pm Mon–Sun (from 11am Tues); 7–11pm Sun–Wed; 6–11pm Thurs–Sat.*

NAILSWORTH
Village Inn
The Cross, Fountain Street, Nailsworth GL6 0HH
☎ *(01453) 835715*

Home of the flourishing Nailsworth Brewery, with four home brews and a couple of guests from other independents such as Mole's and Spinning Dog.

Reopened in 2006 in the heart of the town with the brewery located in the basement. Several multi-level rooms with wooden floors and panels. Real fires. Food served at lunchtime and evenings (pies a speciality).

OPEN *11am–11pm Sun–Wed; 11am–midnight Thurs–Sat.*

The Weighbridge Inn
Longfords, Minchinhampton, Nr Nailsworth GL6 9AL
☎ *(01453) 832520 Howard Parker*
www.2in1pub.co.uk

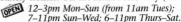Uley Laurie Lee and Old Spot plus Wadworth 6X usually available.

This 17th-century inn was built as a weighbridge for local mills, and now acts as a community pub with many original features. Hundreds of old keys from the mill hang from the ceiling providing a curious decoration. Famous for its 2-in-1 pie – customers choose a second filling to go with cauliflower cheese – a 25-year-old recipe.

Food served 12–9.30pm daily (it is advisable to book). Large beer garden with lovely views. Car park for 50 vehicles. Well-behaved children welcome. On the B4014 between Nailsworth and Avening.

OPEN *12–11pm (10.30pm Sun).*

NAUNTON
The Black Horse Inn
Naunton, Cheltenham GL54 3AB
☎ *(01451) 850565* Peter and Joanne Bate
A Donnington tied pub serving BB and SBA.

Built in 1870, a small and pleasant country local in a pretty Cotswold village – popular with walkers. Flagstone floors, exposed beams, oak pews and iron-framed tables. A main bar plus dining room. Food served 12–2.30pm and 6.30–9pm. Patios at front and back (no garden). Car park. Children welcome. Darts. Accommodation.

OPEN *11am–3pm and 6–11pm Mon–Fri; all day Sat–Sun.*

NEWENT
The George Hotel
Church Street, Newent GL18 1PU
☎ *(01531) 820203* Rhodri Yeandle
www.georgehotel.uk.com
Four real ales, changed every six weeks. Regulars include Hancock's HB (brewed by Brains) and brews from Whittingtons, Goff's and Battledown.

A 17th-century coaching inn with lounge, bar and restaurant. Food served 6–9.30pm Mon–Sat. Live music Fri nights. Car park. Annual beer festival in September. Garden, function room for hire. Accommodation: en-suite rooms and holiday flats. Located in the village centre, opposite St Mary's Church.

OPEN *11am–close.*

NEWLAND
The Ostrich Inn
Newland, Nr Coleford GL16 8NP
☎ *(01594) 833260* Kathryn Horton
Character country pub boasting eight real ales that are changed continuously. Some of the most frequent and popular include Hook Norton Old Hooky, Sharp's Doom Bar, Timothy Taylor Landlord and Uley Pig's Ear.

This 13th-century inn opposite the Cathedral of the Forest has beams, log fire, settles and candles. Well-known for its meals using local produce – bar and restaurant food available at lunchtime and evenings. Garden.

OPEN *12–2.20pm and 6.30–11pm Mon–Fri; 12–3pm and 6–11pm Sat; 12–3pm and 6.30–10.30pm Sun.*

NORTH WOODCHESTER
Royal Oak
Church Road, Woodchester GL5 5PQ
☎ *(01453) 872735* Bunny and John Firth
Sharp's Doom Bar, Greene King Old Speckled Hen and Abbot plus something from Stroud are the permanent offerings, and there is also a monthly guest.

Delightful 16th-century village inn with log fires, stone floors and a warm and friendly ambience. Small, private sunny patio, private room for hire (holds up to 20 people). Bar menu served Wed–Sat evenings, and the 25-cover restaurant offers fresh, locally produced food 12–2pm and 7–9.30pm Wed–Sat plus Sunday carvery 12–3.30pm (booking necessary).

OPEN *7–11.30pm Mon–Tues; 12–2.30pm and 6.30–11.30pm Wed–Sat; 12–4.30pm and 7.30–11pm Sun.*

OAKRIDGE LYNCH
Butchers Arms
Oakridge Lynch, Nr Stroud GL6 7NZ
☎ *(01285) 760371* PJ Coupe and BE Coupe
Archers Best Bitter, Young's Bitter, Greene King Abbot Ale and Wickwar BOB plus an occasional guest beer.

Friendly, 200-year-old village pub with log fires, exposed beams and attractive garden. Separate restaurant. Food served in the bar each lunchtime and evening (except Sun evening and all day Monday). Restaurant open 7.30–9.30pm Wed–Sat and Sun lunchtimes. Car park. Children welcome in the restaurant and small dedicated room off bar area. Signposted from the Eastcombe to Bisley road.

OPEN *12–3pm and 6–11pm Mon–Sat; 12–4pm and 7–10.30pm Sun.*

OLD DOWN
The Fox Inn
The Inner Down, Old Down, Bristol BS32 4PR
☎ *(01454) 412507*
Philip Biddle and Lynn Fleming
Freehouse serving six real ales, with Sharp's Doom Bar, Mole's Best, Flowers IPA (brewed by Badger) and Bass, plus two constantly changing guests.

A very traditional pub, with wooden floors, low ceilings and wood burner. Food served 12–2pm and 6–9pm. Large beer garden and parking at rear with children's adventure play area. One bar and children's room.

OPEN *12–3pm and 6–11pm Mon–Sat; all day Sun.*

OLD SODBURY
Dog Inn
Old Sodbury, Nr Bristol BS37 6LZ
☎ *(01454) 312006* JB, JL and NS Harris
Wadworth 6X, Wickwar BOB and Fuller's London Pride are permanent features.

Very popular cosy rural pub with plenty of oak beams. Food available lunchtime and evening each day. Juke box. Accommodation. Children welcome in the large garden which includes a play area. Parking.

OPEN *11am–11pm Mon–Sat; 12–10.30pm Sun.*

OLDBURY ON SEVERN
The Anchor Inn
Church Road, Oldbury on Severn BS35 1QE
☎ *(01454) 413331*
MJ Dowdeswell and M Sorrell

Freehouse offering Otter Bitter, Butcombe Bitter, Theakston Old Peculier and Draught Bass plus a guest every Thursday.

A 16th-century country pub in a Grade II listed building. Two bars and a dining area. Boasts one of the largest boules pistes in the country. Home-cooked food served at lunchtimes and dinner every day. Large car park. Children welcome in the dining room. Private room for hire. Handy for the Severn Way walk.

OPEN *11.30am–3pm and 6.30–11pm Mon–Fri; open all day Sat–Sun.*

PILL
The Star Inn
13 Bank Place, Pill, Nr Bristol BS20 0AQ
☎ *(01275) 374926* Miss Hurst

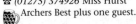Archers Best plus one guest.

L ocal village pub with a wide range of customers. Parking. Owners put strong emphasis on food (not available Monday). Junction 19 off the M5.

OPEN *12–3pm and 6–11pm.*

POPE'S HILL
The Greyhound Inn
The Slad, Pope's Hill, Newnham, Gloucester GL14 1JX
☎ *(01452) 760344*
Dave Bathers and Grace Loving

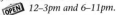Genuine freehouse serving Fuller's London Pride plus Wyre Piddle and Timothy Taylor brews.

A country pub with one large L-shaped bar, log fires, dining area and large garden. Food served 12–3pm and 6–9pm. Children welcome. Car park. Good walking country on the edge of the Forest of Dean. On the A4151.

OPEN *11am–11pm.*

PRESTBURY
The Royal Oak
43 The Burgage, Prestbury, Cheltenham GL52 3DL
☎ *(01242) 522344* Simon Daws
www.royal-oak-prestbury.co.uk

Timothy Taylor Landlord and two guests, plus traditional ciders.

C lassic 16th-century country pub formerly owned by cricketer Tom Graveney. Food served 12–2pm and 6.00–9pm Mon–Sat, all day Sun. Beer garden, patio, function room and car park. Children welcome in dining room and garden. Beer festivals in May and August.

OPEN *10.30am (for coffee)–11pm.*

PUCKLECHURCH
Rose & Crown
Parkfield Road, Pucklechurch BS16 9PS
☎ *(0117) 937 2351* Paula and James Meredith
www.wadworth.co.uk

Wadworth house with 6X and Henry's IPA plus Bath Gem permanently available. There is always at least one guest, rotated every couple of months.

T raditional village pub that retains its olde-worlde charm. Food served 12–2pm and 6–9.30pm Mon–Thurs, 12–9.30pm Fri–Sun (light bites only 2.30–6.30pm) – best to book in advance. Car park, beer garden and play area. Children welcome in the dining room.

OPEN *11.30am–3pm and 6–11pm Mon–Thurs; 11.30am–11pm Fri–Sat; 12–10.30pm Sun.*

The Star Inn
37 Castle Road, Pucklechurch BS16 9RF
☎ *(0117) 937 2391* Tanya Brice

Wadworth 6X and Bass served straight from the barrel plus guest ales and a range of traditional ciders.

A popular and friendly village local that has a real sense of community. Beer festival held third week in June with 25 guest ales. Opposite the playing fields that double as a beer garden. Children welcome. Food every session except Sun evening. Car park.

OPEN *11am–11pm.*

QUEDGELEY
Little Thatch Hotel
Bristol Road, Quedgeley, Gloucester GL2 4PQ
☎ *(01452) 720687* J McDougall

Three constantly changing beers, perhaps Woodforde's Norfolk Nog or something from Goff's or Oakhill.

B lack and white timber-frame hotel built in 1350 with recent addition. Food served 12–2pm and 7–9.30pm Mon–Fri and 7–10pm Sat. Car park. Children welcome.

OPEN *12–2.30pm and 6.30–10.30pm Mon–Fri; 7–10.30pm Sat; 12–3.30pm and 7–10.30pm Sun.*

SAPPERTON
The Bell
Sapperton GL7 6LE
☎ *(01285) 760298*
Pat Le Jeune and Paul Davidson
www.foodatthebell.co.uk

Four real ales, probably including Wickwar Cotswold Way, Uley Old Spot and Bath Gem Ale.

R estored and renovated village inn arranged with three separate but connecting rooms. Beams, wooden floors, real fires. Award-winning food served 12–2pm and 7–9.30pm (9pm Sun). Outside seating in an elegant front garden. Car park and provision for tying up your horse.

OPEN *11am–2.30pm and 6.30–11pm Mon–Sat; 12–3pm and 7–10.30pm Sun*

The Daneway

Sapperton, Nr Cirencester GL7 6LN
☎ *(01285) 760297*
Elizabeth and Richard Goodfellow

Wadworth house offering 6X, Henry's IPA and Horizon plus regular guests.

Built in 1784, this beamed pub is set in some wonderful Gloucestershire countryside. It features a lounge and public bar, plus small family room. No piped music, machines or pool but traditional pub games. Bar food is available at lunchtime and meals in the evening. Car park, garden, children allowed. Less than two miles off the A419 Stroud–Cirencester road.

OPEN *11am–2.30pm and 6.30–11pm (closed Mon evening).*

SHEEPSCOMBE

The Butcher's Arms

Sheepscombe, Painswick GL6 7RH
☎ *(01452) 812113*
Johnny and Hilary Johnston

Brews from Wye Valley, Mole's and Otter.

A country pub built in the 1600s, with log fires, panoramic views and sheltered gardens. Bar and restaurant food served 12–2.30pm and 7–9.30pm Mon–Sat, and all day from 12 on Sun. Car park. Children welcome. Close to Prinknash Abbey and Painswick Rococo Gardens. Situated off A46 north of Painswick (signposted from main road).

OPEN *11.30am–3pm and 6.30–11pm Mon–Sat; 12–11pm Sun.*

SLAD

Woolpack Inn

Slad Road, Slad, Stroud GL5 7QA
☎ *(01452) 813429*
Dan Chadwick and Jon Byford
www.woolpackslad.com

Uley Bitter, Old Spot and Pig's Ear plus guests such as Timothy Taylor Landlord and Stroud Budding.

Haunt of the late Laurie Lee (*Cider with Rosie*) and situated in the beautiful Slad Valley. Food served 12–2.30pm Mon–Sat; 6.30–9pm Tues–Sat; 12–4pm Sun. Car park. Small garden and beer terrace. Children welcome.

OPEN *All day, every day.*

SLIMBRIDGE

Tudor Arms

Shepherds Patch, Slimbridge GL2 7BP
☎ *(01453) 890306* Richard and Samantha Sims
www.thetudorarms.co.uk

Six real ales on offer at this freehouse: Wadworth 6X, Uley Pig's Ear, seasonal ales from Palmers and Wickwar, plus two guests changed weekly. Breweries such as Mole's, Wye Valley, Sharp's, Severn Vale, Bath, Cottage and Goff's often feature.

The original part of the pub dates back to the 17th century. Skittle alley, pool tables, function room, heated patio. Gloucester CAMRA Country Pub of the Year 2007 and 2008. Food served 12–9pm. Two car parks, 12-bedroomed lodge refurbished to high standard Mar 2009. Families welcome. From J13 or J14 of M5 follow the signs to Slimbridge WWT.

OPEN *11am–11pm Mon–Sat; 12–10.30pm Sun.*

SLING

The Miners Arms

Sling, Coleford GL16 8LH
☎ *(01594) 836632* Brian and Yvonne

Freeminer Bitter and Speculation Ale always available.

Traditional country inn with one bar, in tourist area. Nice walking and views. Large garden, juke box and live music twice a week. Food served all day. A la carte restaurant. Children's play area. Situated on the main road from Chepstow to Coleford and the Forest of Dean.

OPEN *All day, every day.*

SNOWSHILL

The Snowshill Arms

Snowshill, Broadway WR12 7JU
☎ *(01386) 852653* David J Schad

A Donnington-owned house with SBA and BB usually available.

Rural family pub in the heart of the Cotswolds. The open-plan bar has a log fire in winter. Food lunchtimes and evenings. Children welcome, with play area in garden for use under parental supervision. Car park.

OPEN *11am–2.30pm and 6–11pm Mon–Sat; 12–3pm and 7–10.30pm Sun.*

SOMERFORD KEYNES

Bakers Arms

Somerford Keynes, Cirencester, GL7 6DN
☎ *(01285) 861298* Paul Fallows

Three real ales including Butcombe Bitter and something from Archers plus a weekly-rotating guest such as Wickwar Cotswold Way, Bath Gem, Box Steam Tunnel Vision or something from the Stroud brewery.

Former bakery in the heart of the Cotswold Water Park. Open fires in winter. Large garden with children's play area. Famous for its summer barbecues. Food served 12–2.30pm and 6–9pm Mon–Sat, all day Sun. Off the A419.

OPEN *11am–11pm Mon–Thurs; 11am–midnight Fri–Sat; 12–11pm Sun.*

SOUTH WOODCHESTER

The Ram Inn

Station Road, South Woodchester, Nr Stroud
GL5 5EL
☎ *(01453) 873329* Tim Mullen

 Six ales usually available. Uley Old Spot, Stroud Budding and Tom Long, Goff's Jouster and Butcombe Bitter plus guests such as Cotswold Spring New English Rose and Otter Ale are regularly featured. A couple of the beers are changed every month.

This bustling old Cotswold pub was built around 1601. Beautiful village setting, with wonderful views. Food served 12–2.30pm and 6.30–9pm every day. Children welcome. Plenty of outside seating, and real fires in the winter. Car park. Excellent walking nearby. Follow brown tourist signs from the A46 Stroud to Nailsworth road.

OPEN *11am–11pm.*

STOW-ON-THE-WOLD

The Golden Ball Inn

Lower Swell, Stow-on-the-Wold GL54 1LF
☎ *(01451) 830247* Steve and Maureen Heath

Tied to the nearby Donnington Brewery, so BB and SBA are always available.

A 17th-century, Cotswold stone, village local with two bars, a dining room and log fires in winter. Accommodation available in three en-suite rooms. Homemade food using local produce served 12–2.30pm and 6.30–9pm Mon–Sat and 12–4pm Sun. Large car park, beer garden. Children welcome. On the B4068, one mile from Stow-on-the-Wold, handy for Bourton-on-the-Water and Moreton-in-Marsh.

OPEN *12–3pm and 6–11pm Mon–Fri; noon–1am Sat; 12–11.30pm Sun.*

The Queen's Head

The Square, Stow-on-the-Wold GL54 1AB
☎ *(01451) 830563* John Bate

Donnington house offering both BB and SBA.

A 16th-century traditional English pub, one of many inns in this historic market town. Stone floor, hops on the ceiling, and friendly. Food available 12–2.30pm and 6.30–8.30pm (except Sun evening). Attractive beer garden. Dogs welcome. Situated in the main town square.

OPEN *11am–11pm.*

STROUD

Golden Fleece

Nelson Street, Stroud GL5 2HN
☎ *(01453) 764850*
Wendy Lewis and Anne O'Neill-Thomas

 Enterprise Inns tied house with Caledonian Deuchars IPA and Fuller's London Pride plus two rotating guests changed every 4–6 weeks.

This old-style drinking-led pub has three small rooms, one bar and many cosy corners. Food served Sat–Sun and occasional weekdays. Beer garden. Children welcome. Small function room available.

OPEN *12–3pm and 5–11pm Mon–Thurs; 12–12 Thurs–Sun.*

SWINEFORD

The Swan Inn

Bath Road, Swineford, Bitton, Bristol
☎ *(0117) 932 3101* Peter Abram

Bath Ales house with Gem, SPA, Barnstormer and Festive plus seasonal guests.

Unpretentious friendly local halfway between Bath and Bristol. One bar, two rooms. Food every session except Sunday evening. Children allowed if eating. Small car park. Small garden. Refurbished in 2006.

OPEN *11am–3pm and 5–11pm.*

TETBURY

Snooty Fox

Market Place, Tetbury GL8 8DD
☎ *(01666) 502436* Marc Gibbons
www.snooty-fox.co.uk

Otter Bitter, Wickwar IKB and Nailsworth Mayor's Bitter.

A 16th-century coaching inn on a prime site in the heart of this market town. The airy bar has a wooden floor and large log fire. Good food served at lunchtime and evenings. Outside seating. Accommodation.

OPEN *All day, every day.*

TEWKESBURY

The Berkeley Arms

8 Church Street, Tewkesbury GL20 5PA
☎ *(01684) 293034* Mr Ian Phillips

Wadworth Henry's IPA, 6X and JCB always available, plus a seasonal ale and one guest which may include Badger Tanglefoot, Wadworth Old Timer, Greene King Old Speckled Hen and Charles Wells Bombardier.

Small, homely 15th-century pub. Cask Marque accredited. Bar and restaurant food available. Street parking. The restaurant can be hired for functions. Children allowed in the restaurant.

OPEN *11am–3pm and 5–11pm Mon–Thur; all day Fri–Sat; 12–4pm and 7–10.30pm Sun.*

The White Bear

Bredon Road, Tewkesbury GL20 5BU
☎ *(01684) 296614* Gerry and Jane Boazman

 Freehouse serving Bass plus three guest beers from breweries such as Goff's, St George's and Freeminer, changed regularly. Three real ciders also available.

A family-run pub with one bar and a friendly atmosphere. No food. Darts, pool, skittles. Large garden, car park. Children and dogs welcome.

OPEN *10am–midnight.*

TODENHAM
The Farriers Arms

Todenham, Moreton-in-the-Marsh GL56 9PF
☎ *(01608) 650901* Nigel and Louise Kirkwood
www.farriersarms.com

Hook Norton Hooky Bitter plus two rotating guest ales changed weekly, perhaps Purity Pure UBU or something from Black Sheep.

Dating from 1650, this Cotswold stone pub is situated near the church in a beautiful village. Home made food served 12–2pm Mon–Sat and 12–2.30pm Sun plus 6–9pm Mon–Sat and 6.30–9pm Sun. Beer garden. Library. Beer festivals. Children welcome. Dogs on leads allowed in bar area. Signposted from Moreton-in-Marsh and the A3400.

OPEN *12–3pm and 6–11pm Mon–Sat; 12–3pm and 6.30–11pm Sun.*

ULEY
Old Crown Inn

The Green, Uley, Dursley GL11 8SN
☎ *(01453) 860502*

Freehouse but handily placed for the nearby brewery and with Uley Bitter and Pig's Ear regularly available, plus three weekly changing guests from breweries such as Cotleigh, Wye Valley, Hook Norton, Hampshire and Hop Back.

A village pub with games room, garden and accommodation. Pub food served at lunchtimes and evenings, plus all day Sat–Sun. Cream teas available 2.30–6pm Mon–Fri. Children allowed.

OPEN *11.30am–3pm and 7–11pm (10.30pm Sun). Open all day, every day in summer.*

WATERLEY BOTTOM
The New Inn

Waterley Bottom, North Nibley, Nr Dursley GL11 6EF
☎ *(01453) 543659* Les Smitherman

Cotleigh Tawny, Wye Valley Hereford Pale Ale and Butty Bach plus rotating guests (up to 200 per year).

Remote freehouse with two bars, set in a beautiful valley. Fresh homemade food available 12–2pm and 6.30–9pm Tues–Sun (8.30pm Sun) – booking is recommended. Car park and garden. Two or three beer festivals per year. Dogs and children welcome. En-suite accommodation. From North Nibley, follow signs for Waterley Bottom.

OPEN *6–11pm Mon; 12–2.30pm and 6–11pm Tues–Fri; all day Sat–Sun.*

WHITECROFT
The Miners Arms

Whitecroft, Forest of Dean GL15 4PE
☎ *(01594) 562483* Mario Constantinides
www.minersarmswhitecroft.co.uk

A freehouse with a constantly changing selection of five real ales, all served on a guest basis. Regular breweries featured include Wye Valley, Butcombe, Banks', Whittington, Sharp's, Cottage, Severn Vale, Wickwar, Bateman, Marston's, Goff's and Freeminer.

Sporting pub with skittle alley and three league teams, and regulars' bar with quoits table and two league teams. Boules pitch. Also a main bar and conservatory. Home-cooked food served all day every day including Sunday lunches. Large garden. Accommodation. Children and dogs welcome. Follow signs to Whitecroft from Lydney on the A48 Chepstow–Gloucester road.

OPEN *Noon–12.30am.*

WHITMINSTER
The Old Forge

Bristol Road, Whitminster GL2 7NY
☎ *(01452) 741306*
Carolyn Cake and Graham Jones

Butcombe Bitter, Shepherd Neame Spitfire and Greene King IPA plus a guest changed weekly. Examples include Greene King Old Speckled Hen, Flowers Original (brewed by Badger) and Saltaire Amarillo Gold.

A 16th-century village pub with low-beamed ceiling, a friendly atmosphere and plenty of character. Food served 12–3pm and 6–9pm Mon–Fri (no food Mon evenings Oct–March); 12–9pm Sat–Sun and bank holidays. Patio garden with traditional games such as chess and noughts and crosses. Heated smoking shelter. Families welcome. Car park. Off J12 of the M5, on the A38.

OPEN *12–11pm (10.30pm Sun).*

WINTERBOURNE
The Cross Hands

85 Down Road, Winterbourne BS36 1BZ
☎ *(01454) 850077* Peter Hughes

Five real ales, one permanent, four weekly-changing guests, from a variety of breweries.

An old country pub with one bar and beer garden. Large covered smoking area. No food. Children welcome. Dog friendly. BBQs to rent and pig roasts! One mile from the M32.

OPEN *All day, every day.*

WINTERBOURNE DOWN

The Golden Heart

*Down Road, Winterbourne Down, Bristol
BS36 1AU*
☎ *(01454) 773152*
Nick Gilmartin and Claire Johnson

Theakston Old Peculier and Wadworth 6X permanently available.

A 16th-century Somerset inn, set in Kendalshire. A traditional country pub, with one bar and a table-service restaurant. Food, including specials board, served 12–3pm and 5–9.30pm Mon–Fri (all day in summer), and all day Sat–Sun. Beer garden to the front and rear. Quiz on Weds. Themed food nights. Can cater for small functions (but no function room). Well-behaved children welcome.

OPEN *12–11pm Sun–Thurs; 12–12 Fri–Sat.*

WOOLASTON COMMON

The Rising Sun Inn

Woolaston Common, Lydney GL15 6NU
☎ *(01594) 529282* Phil and Yvonne Brockwell

Freehouse with Wye Valley Bitter and Butcombe Bitter plus a guest changed weekly.

T wo-bar, low-ceiling country pub decorated with currencies from around the world and with great views of the Forest of Dean. Food served 12–2pm and 6.30–9.30pm Mon–Sat (closed Wed lunch) and 12–2pm and 7–9pm Sun. Car park, patio, beer garden. One mile from camping facilities.

OPEN *12–2.30pm (not Wed) and 6.30–11.30pm Mon–Sat; 12–3pm and 7–11.30pm Sun.*

WOTTON UNDER EDGE

The Swan Hotel

16 Market Street, Wotton under Edge GL12 7AS
☎ *(01453) 843004* Rob Cinnamond
www.swanhotelwotton.co.uk

Genuine freehouse, sourcing most of its four real ales from local micro breweries, Butcombe, Youngs, and two guests. Large selection of unusual malt whiskies.

E ighteenth century coaching inn, full of character with exposed walls, beamed ceilings, three open fires. Two bars - Sky TV and gaming machines in public bar. Food served in bars or separate restaurant, extensive choice of traditional dishes,10am–2pm and 6–9pm. Six en-suite bedrooms. Popular with walkers on the Cotswold Way, in Wotton under Edge town centre, next to the town hall, close to free public car park.

OPEN *7.30am–midnight.*

THE BREWERIES

BALLARDS BREWERY LTD
The Old Sawmill, Nyewood GU31 5HA
☎ *(01730) 821301*
www.ballardsbrewery.org.uk

MIDHURST MILD 3.4% ABV
Lightly hopped, well malted.
BEST BITTER 4.2% ABV
Copper colour, dry aftertaste.
WILD 4.7% ABV
Rich malt flavour.
NYEWOOD GOLD 5.0% ABV
Award winner.
WASSAIL 6.0% ABV
Tawny red and fruity.
Seasonals:
GOLDEN BINE 3.8% ABV
Light floral flavour. Available March–April.
ON THE HOP 4.5% ABV
Spicy, zingy taste. Available September–October.
WHEATSHEAF 5.0% ABV
Banana and clove flavours.Available May–June.
DUADEKADEMON 5.5% ABV
Well balanced. Available July–August.
OLD BOUNDER SERIES 9.4% ABV
Malty and fruity. Available December–January.

THE CRONDALL BREWING COMPANY LTD
Lower Old Park Farm, Dora's Green Lane, Crondall, Farnham GU10 5DX
☎ *(01252) 319000*

CRONDALL'S BEST 4.0% ABV
SOBER AS A JUDGE 4.0% ABV
MITCHELL'S DREAM 4.5% ABV
Plus seasonals and specials including:
MR T'S WEDDING ALE 3.8% ABV
GHOULIES 4.3% ABV
ROCKET FUEL 4.5% ABV
STOCKING FILLER 6.0% ABV

THE FLOWERPOT BREWERY
Formerly The Cheriton Brewhouse
Flowerpots Inn, Cheriton, Alresford SO24 0QQ
☎ *(01962) 771534*

FLOWERPOTS BITTER 3.8% ABV
POTS ALE 3.8% ABV
GOODEN'S GOLD 4.7% ABV
Plus seasonal and occasional brews.

HAMPSHIRE BREWERY LTD
6–8 Romsey Industrial Estate, Greatbridge Road, Romsey SO51 0HR
☎ *(01794) 830529*
www.hampshirebrewery.com

KING ALFRED'S BITTER 3.8% ABV
Amber, light, refreshing and complex.
STRONGS 3.8% ABV
A deep copper best bitter, with rich malt complexity.
IRONSIDE 4.2% ABV
Amber, with crisp hop flavour and bitter finish.
LIONHEART 4.5% ABV
Refreshing with subtle hop finish.
PRIDE OF ROMSEY 5.0% ABV
Aromatic with good bitter flavour.
Plus occasional and seasonal beers.

ITCHEN VALLEY BREWERY LTD
Prospect Commercial Park, Prospect Road, Arlesford SO24 9QF
☎ *(01962) 735111*

GODFATHERS 3.8% ABV
FAGIN'S 4.1% ABV
HAMPSHIRE ROSE 4.2 ABV
WINCHESTER ALE 4.2% ABV
PURE GOLD 4.8% ABV
Plus corporate and seasonal brews.

OAKLEAF BREWING COMPANY
Unit 7, Clarence Wharf Industrial Estate, Mumby Road, Gosport PO12 1AJ
☎ *(023) 9251 3222*
www.oakleafbrewing.co.uk

MAYPOLE MILD 3.8% ABV
Rich, dark, sweet mild.
OAKLEAF BITTER 3.8% ABV
Clean and aromatic.
NUPTU' ALE 4.2% ABV
Crisp, pale ale.
HEART OF OAK 4.5% ABV
Bittersweet aroma, chocolatey finish.
HOLE HEARTED 4.7% ABV
Floral and fruity flavours.
BLAKE'S GOSPORT BITTER 5.2% ABV
Strong, dark, intensely malty.
Plus seasonal, special and bottled beers.

THE RED SHOOT BREWERY
Toms Lane, Linwood, Ringwood BH24 3QT
☎ *(01425) 475792*
http://website.lineone.net/~red_shoot/Index.htm

FOREST GOLD 3.8% ABV
TOMS TIPPLE 4.8% ABV

RINGWOOD BREWERY LTD
138 Christchurch Road, Ringwood BH24 3AP
☎ *(01425) 471177*
www.ringwoodbrewery.co.uk

BEST BITTER 3.8% ABV
Dry, tangy, fruity finish.
FORTYNINER 4.9% ABV
Strong hop balance, bittersweet finish.
OLD THUMPER 5.6% ABV
Spicy aroma with a hint of apples.
Seasonals:
BOONDOGGLE 4.0% ABV
Available May–September.
BOLD FORESTER 4.2% ABV
Available February–May.
HUFFKIN 4.4% ABV
Available September–November.
XXXX PORTER 4.7% ABV
Available November–February.

STUMPY'S BREWERY
Unit 5, Lyecroft Farm Industrial Park, Upper Swanmore, Swanmore, Southampton SO32 2QQ
☎ *(01329) 664902*
www.stumpysbrewery.com

DOG DAZE 3.8% ABV
HOP A DOODLE DOO 4.0% ABV
HOT DOG 4.5% ABV
OLD GINGER 4.5% ABV
OLD STUMPY 4.5% ABV
BOSUNS CALL 5.0% ABV
HAVEN 5.0% ABV
SILENT NIGHT 5.0% ABV
TUMBLEDOWN 5.0% ABV
IKB 7.2% ABV

SUTHWYK ALES
Offwell Farm, Southwick, Fareham PO17 6DX
☎ *(023) 9232 5252*
www.suthwykales.com

BLOOMFIELDS BITTER 3.8% ABV
LIBERATION 4.2% ABV
SKEW SUNSHINE ALE 4.6% ABV

TRIPLE FFF BREWING CO.
Unit 3, Magpie Works, Station Approach,
Four Marks, Alton GU34 5HN
☎ *(01420) 561422*
www.triplefff.com

ALTON'S PRIDE 3.8% ABV
Golden brown and full of flavour.
PRESSED RAT AND WARTHOG 3.8% ABV
Ruby with blackcurrant notes.
MOONDANCE 4.2% ABV
Amber coloured, balanced bitter.
STAIRWAY 4.6% ABV
Summer fruits flavour.
COMFORTABLY NUMB 5.0% ABV
Fruity flavour, mellow aroma.
LITTLE RED ROOSTER 5.0% ABV
Dark with chocolate aftertaste.
Plus seasonal brews.

WHITE STAR BREWERY LTD
The Brewery, Clewers Lane, Waltham Chase
SO32 2LP
☎ *(01489) 893926*
www.whitestarbrewery.com

BEST BITTER 3.5% ABV
U-X-B 3.8% ABV
MAJESTIC 4.2% ABV
DARK DESTROYER 4.7% ABV
STARLIGHT 5.0% ABV
CAPSTAN 6.0% ABV
Plus seasonal brews.

THE WINCHESTER BREWERY LTD
Unit 19, Longbridge Industrial Park, Floating
Bridge Road, Southampton SO14 3FL
☎ *07764 949157*
www.winchesterbrewery.com

WINCHESTER BEST BITTER 3.7% ABV
Balance of malt and hops.
SUMMER '76 4.2% ABV
Lightly golden, hopped.
WEST WINDOW 4.5% ABV
Hoppy bitter.
TRUSTY SERVANT 4.7% ABV
Caramel hints.
SWITHUN GOLD 5.0% ABV
Hoppy and gold coloured.
Plus seasonals and occasionals including:
CHORISTER 4.4% ABV
CURSED EMPIRE DARK BREW 4.7% ABV
SOLOIST 6.3% ABV

THE PUBS

ALDERSHOT
The White Lion
20 Lower Farnham Road, Aldershot GU12 4EA
☎ *(01252) 323832* Ian Andrews

Six real ales, including Alton Pride, Moondance and Pressed Rat & Warthog, all from Triple FFF. The three guests, changed every week or so, might be beers from Surrey Hills, Crouch Vale, Hidden, Dark Star or King.

Traditional-style pub dating from the early 1900s, featuring wooden floors and an open fire. Saloon and public bars, beer garden. Food served 12–9pm. Live music, quiz nights, open mic nights. From the A331 towards Aldershot turn left into Lower Farnham Road.

OPEN *12–11pm Mon–Thurs; 12–12 Fri–Sat; 12–10.30pm Sun.*

ANDOVER
The George
Vernham Dean, Andover SP11 0JY
☎ *(01264) 737279* Matt and Adele Tyson

Fuller's London Pride, Gale's GB and Bass plus one monthly-changing guest.

A traditional country village pub with exposed beams. Food available lunchtime and evenings either at the bar or in a separate dining area. Beer garden and front patio. Children's play area. Pool table.

OPEN *6–11pm Mon; 12–3pm and 6–11pm Tues–Sat; 12–4pm Sun.*

AXFORD
The Crown Inn
Axford, Nr Preston Candover, Basingstoke
RG25 2DZ
☎ *(01256) 389492* Paul Francois

Freehouse with three real ales, generally something from the Triple FFF brewery in Alton (such as Alton's Pride and Moondance) plus Flowerpots Bitter.

Busy, two-bar country pub with a warm atmosphere. Homemade food available at lunch and evenings (all day at weekends during summer). Large garden with patio to the rear. Car park. Well-behaved children and dogs welcome. Situated on the Candover Valley road (B3046) between Basingstoke and Arlesford. Five miles from the M3.

OPEN *12–3pm and 6–11pm Mon–Fri; 12–11pm Sat–Sun.*

BANK

The Oak Inn

Pinkney Lane, Bank, Lyndhurst SO43 7FE
☎ *(023) 8028 2350*
Martin Sliva and Zuzana Frankova

Fuller's managed house with four ales in winter, five in summer, which could include Timothy Taylor Landlord, Ringwood Fortyniner, Fuller's London Pride, Gale's HSB and Ringwood Best Bitter. Also two rotating guest ales, changed weekly.

Established in 1750 as a cider house, this country pub situated in the New Forest has become a must-visit for people in the area. Low ceilings, one main bar. Traditional English dishes and four or five fish dishes available daily 12–2.30pm and 6–9.30pm. Very sunny beer garden, large car park. Children under 14 not permitted after 6pm. From Lyndhurst, follow the A35 to Christchurch, after a mile follow the signs for Bank and take the turning on the left.

OPEN *11.30am–3.30pm and 6–11pm Mon–Fri; 11.30am–11.30pm Sat; 12–10.30pm Sun.*

BEAUWORTH

The Milbury's

Beauworth, Alresford SO24 0PB
☎ *(01962) 771248* Ken Rice

Freehouse serving Milbury's Best (house beer), Theakston Old Peculier and Caledonian Deuchars IPA plus two guests, changing every couple of months, and may be something like Timothy Taylor Landlord.

A 17th-century country pub with dining area and beer garden. Food available 12–2pm and 6.30–9.30pm Mon–Fri, 12–3pm and 7–9.30pm Sat–Sun. Children allowed.

OPEN *12–11pm.*

BENTWORTH

The Star Inn

Bentworth, Alton GU34 5RB
☎ *(01420) 561224* Matt Williams

Freehouse serving Ringwood Best, Fuller's London Pride and Butcombe Best plus one guest changed weekly.

Built in 1843, this pub has one bar, a dining room and beer garden. Food is served lunchtimes and evenings Mon–Sat and all day Sun.

OPEN *12–3.30pm and 5pm–12 Mon–Thurs; 12–12 Fri–Sun.*

The Sun Inn

Bentworth, Nr Alton GU34 5JT
☎ *(01420) 562338* Mary Holmes

Ringwood Best, Flowerpots Bitter, Stonehenge Pigswill and Timothy Taylor Landlord plus four guest ales changed frequently. Regulars include Fuller's London Pride, Gale's HSB, Hogs Back TEA and brews from Adnams.

Delightful, flower-decked 17th-century freehouse on the edge of the village. Three interconnecting rooms, each with low-beamed ceiling, real log fire and authentic brick or wood floor. No music or fruit machines. Home-cooked food available 12–2pm and 7–9.30pm. Beer garden, car park. Children and dogs welcome. Good walks nearby. Off the A339 Alton to Basingstoke road.

OPEN *12–3pm and 6–11pm Mon–Sat; 12–10.30pm Sun.*

BRAISHFIELD

Wheatsheaf

Braishfield Road, Romsey SO51 0QE
☎ *(01794) 368372* Peter and Jenny Jones

Enterprise Inns tied house offering Ringwood Best and Timothy Taylor Landlord plus three guests that change on a weekly basis.

Around 300 years old, this pub boasts an eclectic mix of furnishings and bric-à-brac. One main bar with various rooms leading off. Award-winning food available 12–2.30pm and 6–9.30pm daily. Large beer garden and patio, large car park. The owners have their own herd of rare-breed pigs and chickens, as well as a vegetable garden – all for use in their kitchen! Wonderful views.

OPEN *11am–midnight.*

CHALTON

The Red Lion

Chalton, Waterlooville PO8 0BG
☎ *(023) 9259 2246* David Browning
www.fullers.co.uk

Fuller's managed house, serving Gale's HSB, Fuller's London Pride, Discovery and ESB plus one guest changed monthly, from a range of Fuller's and Gale's seasonal beers.

This is reputed to be the oldest pub in Hampshire (1147), and features a period bar with inglenook fireplace, two other bars, dining room and large beer garden with views of the South Downs. Food available 12–9pm Mon–Thurs, 12–9.30pm Fri–Sat and 12–8pm Sun. Children welcome at any time. Dogs allowed in the public bar. Come off the A3 at the exit between Horndean and Petersfield and follow the signs.

OPEN *11am–11pm Mon–Sat; 11.45am–10.30pm Sun.*

CHARTER ALLEY

The White Hart

White Hart Lane, Charter Alley, Tadley RG26 5QA
☎ *(01256) 850048* Howard Bradley
www.whitehartcharteralley.com

Freehouse with West Berkshire Magg's Magnificent Mild, Palmers IPA and Triple FFF Alton's Pride plus guests.

A village pub built in 1818 next to the village forge, overlooking open countryside, and with oak beams and open fires. Home-cooked food available 12–2pm daily and 7–9pm Tues–Sat. Terraced beer garden/patio, restaurant. En-suite accommodation in nine letting rooms. Five miles northwest of Basingstoke.

OPEN *12–2.30pm and 7–11pm Mon–Sat; 12–10.30pm Sun.*

CHAWTON
The Greyfriar
Winchester Road, Chawton, Nr Alton GY34 1SB
☎ *(01420) 83841* Peter and Fran Whitehead

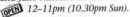 Tied to Fuller's, serving London Pride and ESB plus a guest ale, changing weekly or monthly.

This 17th-century coaching inn is situated in Jane Austen's home village of Chawton. One main bar, and a smaller separate one serving bar snacks. Food served lunchtimes 12–2pm and 7–9.30pm Mon–Fri, 12–2.30pm and 7–9.30pm Sat, 12–3pm Sun and 6–8pm. Beer garden at rear with sheltered smoking area. Private room available from 12–11pm for up to 18 people. Car park. Cask Marque accredited. Well-behaved children and dogs welcome. Located on four-mile circular pub walk composing the Watercress Line, Chawton House Library and Jane Austen's house.

OPEN *12–11pm (10.30pm Sun).*

CHERITON
The Flower Pots Inn
Cheriton, Alresford SO24 0QQ
☎ *(01962) 771318* Paul Tickner and Jo Bartlett

 A traditional inn and home of the Flowerpots Brewery. Three beers from the micro-brewery, namely Flowerpots Bitter, Wheatsheaf Best and Goodens Gold, plus occasional and seasonal brews throughout the year.

Former farmhouse now an unspoilt two-bar inn on the edge of the village. Bar food is available every lunchtime and Mon–Sat evenings. Car park, garden, en-suite accommodation. Children not allowed in the pub. Six miles east of Winchester, off the A272.

OPEN *12–2.30pm and 6–11pm Mon–Sat; 12–3pm and 7–10.30pm Sun.*

CHURCH CROOKHAM
The Foresters
Aldershot Road, Church Crookham, Fleet GU52 9EP
☎ *(01252) 616503*
Steve and Glenice Nicolopulo

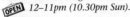 Timothy Taylor Landlord and Fuller's London Pride are among the real ales available.

A jovial landlord presides over this roadside inn with a tile-roofed verandah. There is a stone hearth, half-panelled walls and a friendly atmosphere within. Good food served 12–9pm. Large beer garden and car park. On the southern outskirts of Fleet just south of the Basingstoke Canal.

OPEN *12–11pm (10.30pm Sun).*

CLANFIELD
The Bat & Ball
Hyden Farm Lane, Clanfield, Waterlooville PO8 0UB
☎ *(023) 9263 2692* Tony and Jane Drinkwater

Fuller's pub serving Gale's HSB and London Pride plus one guest changed weekly.

A pub widely known as the 'cradle of cricket' – where the modern rules of cricket were first made. Food served 12–2pm and 6.30–9pm Mon–Fri, 12–9pm Sat–Sun. Beer garden, car park. Children welcome. Located between Hambledon and Clanfield.

OPEN *12–3pm and 6pm–close Mon–Fri; 12–close Sat–Sun.*

DUNDRIDGE
The Hampshire Bowman
Dundridge, Bishops Waltham, Southampton SO32 1GD
☎ *(01489) 892940* Heather Seymour
www.hampshirebowman.com

A freehouse with Bowman Ales Swift One and Ringwood Fortyniner. Two guests changed monthly, including Hop Back Crop Circle, Stonehenge Spire, Hogs Back TEA, Harviestoun Bitter and Twisted, Nethergate Umbel Magna, Oakleaf Hole Hearted and Suthwyk Ales Skew.

Old-fashioned brick-floored country pub, circa 1860. No music, machines or mobile phones. Newly converted stable bar. Food served 12–2pm and 6.30–9pm Mon–Thurs; 12–9pm Fri–Sun. Large beer garden with children's play equipment. Car park. Very dog friendly. Children under 14 allowed until 9pm. Annual summer beer festival. From the main Bishops Waltham roundabout take the B3035 to Dundridge.

OPEN *12–11pm (10.30pm Sun).*

EASTON
The Cricketers Inn
Easton, Near Winchester SO21 1EJ
☎ *(01962) 779353* Alan and Barbara Gover

Marston's pub serving Ringwood Best plus three guests changed after every barrel, from brewers across the country.

A local village pub with a cricketing theme. Two bars and a drinking terrace. Homemade food served 12–2pm and 7–9pm in winter and 12–2.30pm and 7–9.30pm in summer. En-suite accommodation, large car park, conference room. Children welcome. Good fishing and walking locally. Between Winchester and Alresford.

OPEN *12–3pm and 6–11pm (7–10.30pm Sun). Open longer in summer.*

ECCHINSWELL
The Royal Oak
Ecchinswell, Nr Newbury RG20 4UH
☎ *(01635) 298280* Mrs A Noonan and Mr Lay

Two guest ales, changed weekly, are served straight from the cask. Wadworth 6X and Fuller's London Pride are regulars, with other beers featured if requested!

Small village pub with two bars, a dining area, fireplaces and beams. Food served. Pool, darts, TV, beer garden, car park. Children allowed. Situated just over seven miles south of Newbury.

OPEN *12–11pm (10.30pm Sun).*

FAREHAM

The Lord Arthur Lee

100–108 West Street, Fareham PO16 0EP
☎ *(01329) 280447* Joanne Weller

 Wetherspoon's pub with ten real ales rotating daily, could include Greene King Abbot, Marston's Pedigree or Burton Bitter.

This pub hosts two beer festivals each year. Beer garden. Food served 9am–11pm daily. Children welcome.

OPEN *9am–midnight Sun–Thurs; 9am–1am Fri–Sat.*

Osborne View Hotel

67 Hill Head Road, Fareham PO14 3JP
☎ *(01329) 664623* Paul Reynolds

 Hall and Woodhouse (Badger) tied pub with up to eight real ales. Badger Best, IPA and Tanglefoot always featured, plus a range of ales from Gribble Brewery.

A seafront pub on three levels. Sea views, parking. Food available at lunchtimes and evenings, and all day on Sundays. Children and dogs welcome.

OPEN *11am–11pm (10.30pm Sun).*

FARNBOROUGH

The Prince of Wales

184 Rectory Road, Farnborough GU14 8AL
☎ *(01252) 545578* Julie and Peter Moore

 Ten-pump freehouse with Hogs Back TEA, Fuller's London Pride, Hop Back Summer Lightning, Ringwood Fortyniner and Young's Bitter the permanent beers, plus four guests, continually changing. Session beers below 4.0% ABV appear on a monthly basis. Ales from micro-breweries across the country are featured. An annual beer festival is held in mid-October.

Traditional country drinking pub in an old building on the edge of town. Local CAMRA Pub of the Year 2003 and 2005. No music, games or darts. Food available Mon–Sat lunchtimes. Marquee outside during summer, car park. Children allowed only in marquee. Round the corner from Farnborough North Station.

OPEN *11.30am–2.30pm and 5.30–11pm Mon–Fri (open from 11am Fri); 11.30am–11pm Sat; 12–10.30pm Sun.*

FREEFOLK

The Watership Down Inn

Freefolk, Nr Whitchurch RG28 7NJ
☎ *(01256) 892254* Anthony Lamden

Real ale available on five pumps, serving Young's Bitter and a constantly changing range of guest ales, usually from smaller breweries and including a mild.

Built in 1840, renamed after the Richard Adams novel that was set locally, a one-bar community pub with an open fire and pretty garden with many outside tables. Bar and restaurant food served 11.30am–2.30pm and 6–9.30pm Mon–Sat, 12–2.30pm and 7–8.30pm (or thereabouts) Sun, plus conservatory that seats 30 diners. Car park, new children's play area. Children allowed in

the restaurant. Local CAMRA Pub of the Year 2002 and 2005. On the B3400 between Whitchurch and Overton.

OPEN *11.30am–3pm and 6–11pm Mon–Sat; 12–3pm and 7–10.30pm Sun.*

FRITHAM

The Royal Oak

Fritham SO43 7HJ
☎ *(023) 8081 2606*
Pauline and Neil McCulloch

Freehouse with seven real ales, namely Ringwood Best and Fortyniner, Hop Back Summer Lightning and something from Bowman, plus three constantly changing guests, often from Keystone, Oakleaf, Hidden or Stonehenge.

A 15th-century thatched pub with three small bars, looking out over both the New Forest and the pub's own farm. Food served 12–3pm. No debit or credit cards accepted. Large beer garden. Children, dogs and well-behaved parents welcome! Beer festival in September. From J1 of the M27 follow the B3078 towards Fordingbridge, then the signs to Fritham.

OPEN *11am–3pm and 6–11pm Mon–Fri; 11am–11pm Sat; 12–10.30pm Sun.*

FROGHAM

The Forester's Arms

Abbots Well Road, Frogham, Fordingbridge SP6 2JA
☎ *(01425) 652294* M Harding

Wadworth tied house serving 6X, JCB, Bishop's Tipple and Henry's IPA plus two seasonal or special brews such as Mayhem Odda's Light.

Country inn in the New Forest area. Dartboard, garden with children's play area. Food available at lunchtimes and evenings in a separate restaurant. Children and dogs welcome.

OPEN *11am–3pm and 6–11pm Mon–Sat; 12–3pm and 7–10.30pm Sun.*

FROXFIELD

The Trooper Inn

Alton Road, Froxfield, Petersfield GU32 1BD
☎ *(01730) 827293* Mr Matini
www.trooperinn.com

Freehouse serving Ringwood Fortyniner and Best plus a couple of weekly changing guests from breweries such as Ballard's.

A country pub with dining area, function room and garden. Food available 12–2pm and 6.30–9pm Tues–Sat (until 9.30pm Fri–Sat); 12–2.30pm Sun. There is an eight-bedroom hotel attached to the pub – phone for reservations. Children allowed.

OPEN *12–3pm and 5–11pm (closed Sun evenings and Mon lunchtime, except bank holiday weekends).*

GOSPORT

The Clarence Tavern

1 Clarence Road, Gosport PO12 1AJ
☎ *(023) 9252 9726* Patrick and Teresa Noonan

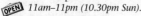 Beers from the Oakleaf Brewery range are always available. Beer festivals at Easter and August bank holiday.

A Victorian pub with food available all day in separate dining area. Outside terrace seating. Darts. Golf society. Three en-suite bedrooms. Car park. Function room.

 11am–11pm (10.30pm Sun).

Queens Hotel

143 Queens Road, Gosport
☎ *(023) 9258 2645* Sue Lampon

 Freehouse serving brews from Wells and Young's, Rooster's, Ringwood and Hook Norton plus two rotating guests.

P opular backstreet local, a genuine freehouse, with a good selection of ales. Snacks and rolls served at lunchtimes only. No children.

 5–11pm Mon–Thurs; 11.30am–2.30pm and 5–11.30pm Sat; 12–3pm and 7–11pm Sun.

HAMBLE

The King & Queen

High Street, Hamble, Southampton SO31 4HA
☎ *(023) 8045 4247* Kelly Smith

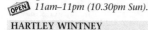 Enterprise Inn with Fuller's London Pride, Wadworth 6X, Adnams Best and Ringwood Fortyniner always available.

A sailing pub with log fires and bar billiards. Serving food at lunchtimes and evenings. Children allowed in the lounge.

11am–11pm (10.30pm Sun).

HARTLEY WINTNEY

The Waggon & Horses

High Street, Hartley Wintney, Nr Hook RG27 8NY
☎ *(01252) 842119* Niall Scott

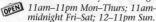 Freehouse with Gale's HSB and Courage Best plus one guest, rotated every day or two.

T ypical village pub with public bar, saloon bar, log fires and secluded courtyard-style beer garden. Food available Mon–Sat lunchtimes only. Children welcome. On the A30 between Camberley and Basingstoke.

11am–11pm Mon–Thurs; 11am–midnight Fri–Sat; 12–11pm Sun.

HAWKLEY

The Hawkley Inn

Pococks Lane, Hawkley, Nr Liss GU33 6NE
☎ *(01730) 827205* Jeannie Jamieson
www.hawkleyinn.co.uk

Freehouse with up to ten constantly changing real ales from breweries such as Triple FFF, King, Ballard's, Itchen Valley, Hop Back, Hogs Back, Sharp's, Dark Star, Suthwyck and Goddards, to name but a few.

Q uirky village pub in a lovely rural location, with two bars. Recently refurbished but retaining its unique decor. The main building dates from the 1800s, and was extended in 2006. Homemade food served 12–2pm and 7–9.30pm Mon–Fri, 12–3pm and 7–9.30pm Sat, and 12–3pm and 7–9pm Sun. Popular garden. Beer festival on first full weekend in June. Children welcome until 8pm. Dogs welcome. Five luxury en-suite bedrooms, including one disabled room. Stunning countryside with many interesting footpaths and bridleways. Two miles from Liss and the A3.

12–3pm and 5.30–11pm Mon–Fri; 12–11pm Sat; 12–10.30pm Sun.

HILLHEAD

The Crofton

48 Crofton Lane, Hillhead PO14 3QF
☎ *(01329) 314222* Ian and Jenny Readman

Tied to Punch Taverns, with Oakleaf Bitter and Hole Hearted, Caledonian Deuchars IPA and Adnams Broadside plus three rotating guests.

T his 1960s-built community pub has two bars with a separate function room. Beer garden. Large car park. Beer festivals held in October. Skittle alley. Very near the sea. Dogs and children welcome.

 11am–11pm Mon–Sat; 12–10.30pm Sun.

HINTON AMPNER

The Hinton Arms

Petersfield Road, Hinton Ampner, Alresford SO24 0NH
☎ *(01962) 771252* Roger and Angela Mattia

Hinton's Own and Hinton's Sportsman, brewed specially by the Hampshire Brewery, and Ringwood Best are permanent, plus one guest from Bowman Ales, changed every six weeks.

F riendly, unspoiled 17th-century coaching inn with one large bar and log fire. Homemade food available 12–2.45pm and 6–9.45pm. Large beer garden and patio. Children welcome. Located next door to the popular Hinton Ampner House and Gardens (National Trust). On the A272 Winchester to Petersfield road.

11am–3pm and 5.30–11.30pm. Open 11am–11pm at weekends in summer.

HORNDEAN

The Brewer's Arms

1 Five Heads Road, Horndean, Waterlooville PO8 9NW
☎ *(023) 9259 1325* Mick Jenkins

Enterprise Inns tied house serving Courage Director's, Ringwood Best and Fuller's London Pride plus three guest ales at the weekends.

A 1920s-style building with two bars. No food. Car park and beer garden. Dogs welcome.

5–11pm Mon; 12–2pm and 5–11pm Tues–Wed; 5–11pm Thurs; 12–2pm and 5pm–12 Fri; 12–4pm and 6pm–12 Sat; 12–3pm and 7–11pm Sun.

Ship & Bell Hotel

6 London Road, Horndean, Waterlooville PO8 0BZ
☎ *(023) 9259 2107* Rebecca Hoy

 Fuller's managed house, with ESB, London Pride and Gale's HSB plus a guest changed every two weeks from a wide range.

The former Gale's brewery tap, a two-bar village pub with separate dining area and accommodation. First mentioned as a pub in 1686. Food served 12–3pm and 5–9pm Mon–Thurs; 12–9pm Fri–Sat; 12–6pm Sun. Fourteen en-suite rooms, recently refurbished. Eight miles north of Portsmouth.

OPEN *11am–11pm Mon–Sat; 12–10.30pm Sun.*

LASHAM

The Royal Oak

Lasham Village, Nr Alton GU34 5SJ
☎ *(01256) 381213* Aaron and Dionne Calder
www.royaloak.uk.com

 Freehouse serving up to six real ales. Triple FFF Moondance, Ringwood Best and Gale's HSB are the permanent beers, and there are two or three guests, changed monthly.

Charming pub in a building dating from 1780, with beams and real fires. Food available 12–2.30pm and 6–9pm Tues–Sat, and all day on Sun. Two bars (lounge and public), large attractive beer garden with covered seating area. Children welcome in the lounge. Located next to Lasham Airfield, which is signposted. A picture-postcard village. Signposted from the A339 Alton to Basingstoke road.

OPEN *12–11pm.*

LINWOOD

The Red Shoot Inn & Brewery

Toms Lane, Linwood, Ringwood BH24 3QT
☎ *(01425) 475792* Simon and Judith Karelus

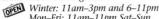 Wadworth 6X and Henry's IPA plus Red Shoot's own beers (Forest Gold, Tom's Tipple and Muddy Boot) always available.

This Wadworth-owned New Forest pub is home to the Red Shoot Brewery. Traditional home-cooked food served 12–2.30pm and 6–9pm Mon–Fri and all day Sat–Sun in winter; all day, every day in summer. Attractive beer garden. Campsite adjacent. Children and dogs welcome. Beer festivals in April and October. Live bands every Sunday throughout the year. Car park. Signposted from A338 at Ellingham.

OPEN *Winter: 11am–3pm and 6–11pm Mon–Fri; 11am–11pm Sat–Sun. Summer: all day, every day.*

LISS

The Jolly Drover

London Road, Hillbrow, Liss, Nr Petersfield GU33 7QL
☎ *(01730) 893137* Barry Coe

 Enterprise Inns pub serving Sharp's Doom Bar and Timothy Taylor Landlord plus Triple FFF Alton's Pride as a guest.

One bar drover-built pub dating from 1820, with 40-seater dining room and covered patio and garden. Accomodation in six en-suite rooms. Food served 12–2pm and 7–9.30pm Mon–Sat; 12–2.30pm Sun. Children welcome. Situated near Goodwood racecourse and Queen Elizabeth country park. On the old A3 between Petersfield and Liphook, at the junction between Liss and Rogate.

OPEN *11am–2.30pm and 6–11pm Mon–Thurs; 11am–2.30pm and 6pm–12 Fri–Sat; 12–5pm Sun (closed Sun evenings).*

LITTLE LONDON

The Plough Inn

Silchester Road, Little London, Tadley RG26 5EP
☎ *(01256) 850628*

 Freehouse with Ringwood Best and Ringwood seasonals available plus a wide selection of guest ales.

Situated on the edge of Pamber Forest, this 330-year-old pub has exposed beams and a secluded garden for summer, log fires in winter. Hot, filled baguettes served at lunchtime and evening. Children allowed. Regional CAMRA Pub of the Year 2007.

OPEN *12–2.30pm and 5.30–11pm Mon–Fri; 12–2.30pm and 6–11pm Sat; 12–3pm and 7–10.30pm Sun.*

LYMINGTON

The Kings Head Inn

Quay Hill, Lymington SO41 3AR
☎ *(01590) 672709* Paul R Stratton

 An Enterprise Inns leased pub. Fuller's London Pride and Gale's HSB. Three weekly changing guests, from breweries such as Adnams, Ringwood, Timothy Taylor and Shepherd Neame.

A 300-year-old pub with oak beams and one bar divided into three sections. A clean modern style with wooden floors, scrubbed wooden tables each set with different chairs and candles. Children and dogs welcome. Food served all day, every day. Extensive wine list including vintage Champagne. Small patio garden. Situated at the bottom of the High Street, 200 metres from the quay.

OPEN *11am–3pm and 6pm–12 Mon–Thurs; all day Fri–Sun.*

LYNDHURST

New Forest Inn

Emery Down, Lyndhurst SO43 7DY
☎ *(023) 8028 4690* Christopher Leverton
www.thenewforestinn.co.uk

 Leased from Enterprise Inns, with Ringwood Best Bitter and three guests (19 different ones each week), such as Palmers 200, Triple FFF Stairway, Hogs Back Hop Garden Gold, Archers Golden, Hidden Quest and Wychwood Hobgoblin.

An 18th-century pub set in the New Forest, with one bar, separate function room for 25 people and large beer garden. Food served 12–2pm and 6–9pm Mon–Fri; 12–3pm and 6–9.30pm Sat; 12–4pm Sun. Children welcome at lunchtimes. Car park. Annual beer festival. Handy for visits to the New Forest, and located centrally for Salisbury, Bournemouth, Southampton and Lymington. Turn off the A35 from Lyndhurst towards Bournemouth, signposted Emery Down.

OPEN *11.30am–2.30pm and 6–11pm; 11.30am–11pm Sat; 12–10.30pm Sun. Open all day, every day in summer.*

MEONSTOKE

The Bucks Head

Bucks Head Hill, Meonstoke, Southampton SO32 3NA
☎ *(01489) 877313*
Martin and Maggie Davenport

 Greene King house serving IPA and Old Speckled Hen plus one guest.

Rural country pub, part 16th century and part 19th century on the banks of the River Meon. Both the separate restaurant and the public bar have log fires. Food available 12–2pm (until 4pm Sat) and 6.30–9pm Mon–Sat, and 12–3pm Sun. Large riverside garden plus smaller beer garden, large car park. Accompanied children welcome. Five en-suite B&B rooms. On the South Down Trail, near Winchester Hill and the disused Watercress Line. Just off the A32 Fareham to Alton road.

OPEN *12–3pm and 6–11pm Mon–Fri; 12–11pm Sat; 12–10.30pm Sun.*

MICHELDEVER

The Half Moon & Spread Eagle

Winchester Road, Micheldever SO21 3DG
☎ *(01962) 774339*
Sam Dean and Debbie Thickett
www.thehalfmoonspreadeagle.webeden.co.uk

 Greene King tenancy with two of the brewery's beers plus a monthly guest.

Popular traditional one-bar country pub built in the early 1700s. Superb à la carte menu plus bar meals served 12–2pm and 6–9pm Mon–Sat plus lunchtimes Sundays. Large car park and beer garden. Children and dogs welcome – there is a children's play area. Purpose-built outside heated smoking area with seating. Good walks nearby in Micheldever Woods. Less than a mile off the A33, six miles north of Winchester, 12 miles south of Basingstoke.

OPEN *12–3pm and 6–11pm (10.30pm Sun); open all day at weekends in summer.*

OVINGTON

The Bush Inn

Ovington, Nr Alresford SO24 0RE
☎ *(01962) 732764* Nick and Cath Young

 Wadworth tied house serving 6X and Henry's IPA plus Bishop's Tipple, Malt 'n' Hops, Summersault, Old Timer and other regular guest ales.

Built in the 17th-century on the Pilgrims' Way, this is an old-fashioned pub with central wooden bar, high-backed seats and pews, a real fire and stuffed animals on the walls. No music, no fruit machines, no darts, no pool table, just a warm, welcoming atmosphere. Lovely beer garden with streams/rivers nearby. Award-winning pub, Cask Marque accredited. The food on offer makes use of carefully sourced produce, and the dishes range from traditional to cosmopolitan and modern. Food served 12–2.30pm and 7–9.30pm Mon–Sat and 12–4pm and 7–8.30pm Sun. Limited space for children indoors. Disabled facilites. Large car park. Situated off the A31 between Winchester and Alresford.

OPEN *11am–3pm and 6–11pm Mon–Sat; 12–3pm and 7–10.30pm Sun. Open all day bank holiday weekends in summer, and school summer holidays.*

PORTCHESTER

The Cormorant

181 Castle Street, Portchester PO16 9QX
☎ *(023) 9237 9374* Carol and Mike Frewing
www.thecormorant.co.uk

 Ringwood Best, Gale's HSB and Hop Back Summer Lightning are permanent features, and there is also a seasonal guest.

Originally called The Swan, this is the last pub in Old Portchester and dates back over 300 years. Large restaurant, with food served 12–2.30pm and 6–9.30pm Mon–Sat and 12–5pm Sun. Large car park, outside patio area. Well-behaved children welcome. Nearby attractions include Portchester Castle, Port Solent Marina, and walks round Portsmouth Harbour. On the A27 Portsmouth to Fareham road, follow signs for Portchester Castle. The pub is next to the castle car park.

OPEN *11.30am–11pm Mon–Sat; 12–10.30pm Sun.*

PORTSMOUTH

The Connaught Arms

119 Guildford Road, Fratton, Portsmouth PO1 5EA
☎ *(023) 9264 6455* Sue Law

 Up to six beers usually available. Hop Back Summer Lightning is a permanent feature, plus three regularly changing guests. Old Rosie cider also on offer.

Comfortable pub hidden in the back streets of Fratton, famous for its interesting range of pasties. Bar menu available 11.45am–2.30pm Mon–Sat; pasties available every session. Roasts on Sundays. Well-behaved children welcome until 7pm. Beer garden. Situated at the junction of Penhale and Guildford roads.

OPEN *All day, every day.*

The Dolphin

41 High Street, Old Portsmouth PO1 2LV
☎ *(023) 9282 3595*
Pete Croft and Jackie Rumary

 Fuller's London Pride, Wadworth 6X, Timothy Taylor Landlord, Gale's HSB, Ringwood Fortyniner, Greene King Abbot and IPA and Adnams Broadside always available.

A 16th-century coaching inn with wood and flagstone floors. Historic area with good walks nearby. The pub boasts Nelson's signature on a piece of glass in the bar! À la carte menu and bar food available 12–2.30pm and 6.30–9pm. Small function room and outside patio area. Children allowed. Directly opposite the cathedral in Old Portsmouth.

11am–3pm and 6–11pm Mon–Fri; all day Fri–Sun.

The Isambard Kingdom Brunel

2 Guildhall Walk, Portsmouth PO1 2DD
☎ *(023) 9229 5112* Vicky Head

 Six to seven real ales served, including Ringwood Old Thumper, Greene King Abbot and a selection of guest ales, changed every few days.

Friendly town pub in a Grade II listed building. Food served all day with meal deals available. Cask Marque approved. Children's licence. Conference rooms for hire. Outside drinking in the summer. Near the Guildhall.

9am–midnight Sun–Thurs; 9am–1am Fri–Sat.

The Tap

17 London Road, North End, Portsmouth PO2 0BQ
☎ *(023) 9261 4861*

 Up to 11 beers available including Greene King Ruddles Best and Ringwood Old Thumper. Guests (100 per year) could include Ringwood Best, Badger Tanglefoot and Gale's HSB. Micro-breweries particularly favoured.

A one-bar drinking pub in the town centre with no juke box or fruit machines. Formerly the brewery tap for the now defunct Southsea Brewery. Bar meals available at lunchtime. Street parking opposite, small yard, disabled toilet. Children not allowed.

10.30am–11pm Mon–Sat; 12–10.30pm Sun.

The Wellington

62 High Street, Portsmouth PO1 2LY
☎ *(023) 9234 3110* K Preston and A Whitelaw

Greene King IPA plus one guest from a brewery such as Fuller's, Wells and Young's, Shepherd Neame or Adnams rotated each month.

A traditional community pub with a friendly atmosphere and a reputation for good food, served 11.30am–3pm daily and 6.30–9pm Tues–Sat, plus 12–7pm on Sunday.

Patio beer garden. Children and dogs welcome. At the end of the high street, close to the beach and opposite Portsmouth Cathedral. Parking permits available at the bar.

11.30am–midnight Mon–Thurs; 11am–1am Fri–Sat; 12–11.30pm Sun.

The Winchester Arms

99 Winchester Road, Portsmouth PO2 7PS
☎ *(023) 9266 2443* Paul Fewings

 Beers from Oakleaf Brewery always served, with Nuptu'Ale, Blake's Gosport Bitter and Hole Hearted permanently available. Plus two rotating guests.

Small, backstreet, community village pub, where everybody is treated as a friend. Food served at weekends 2–7pm only. Live music from local musicians every Sunday, with occasional karaoke and discos. Light-hearted pub quiz every Monday evening, darts, football and cricket teams. Wed night, open mic. Children allowed in snug, tap and patio garden.

4–11pm Mon; 2–11pm Tues–Fri; 12–11pm Sat; 12–10.30pm Sun.

The White Horse Inn

Priors Dean, Nr Petersfield GU32 1DA
☎ *(01420) 588387* Paula and Georgina Stuart
www.stuartinns.com

 A former Gale's tied house, now owned by Fuller's and serving HSB, Butser and various Gale's seasonals plus Ringwood Fortyniner. Four or five permanents and two or three rotating guests.

Olde-world pub untouched for years, with log fires and ticking clocks. Two bars and a restaurant. Food available at lunchtime and evening. Children welcome in restaurant. Car park and garden. June beer festival with up to 40 ales, live music and camping. Tricky to find. Between Petersfield and Alton, five miles from Petersfield, seven miles from Alton.

12–3pm and 6–11pm Mon–Sat; 12–3pm and 7–10.30pm Sun.

Inn on the Furlong

12 Meeting House Lane, Ringwood BH24 1EY
☎ *(01425) 475139* Dale and Nicky Wheller
www.ringwoodbrewery.co.uk

Ringwood Brewery pub, serving Best, Fortyniner, Bold Forester and Old Thumper plus a seasonal beer.

An old building with one bar, conservatory and patio. Food available 12–9pm. Main car park opposite. Live music every Tuesday, market Wednesdays, quiz nights. Opposite the Tourist Information Centre.

11am–11pm Mon–Thurs; 11am–midnight Fri–Sat; 12–11pm Sun.

ROTHERWICK

The Falcon

The Street, Rotherwick, Hook RG27 9BL
☎ *(01256) 762586* Andy Francis
www.thefalconrotherwick.co.uk

Enterprise pub with Fuller's London Pride and a fortnightly guest.

Traditional family-run village pub/restaurant with one large bar and roaring fires in winter. Beer garden and patio. Large car park. Bar and full restaurant menu available 12–2pm and 7–9.30pm Mon–Sat; in winter 12–3.30pm Sun, in summer 12–2pm and 7–9pm Sun, including Sunday roasts. Booking advisable for meals. No high chairs. Leave Hook on the B3349 towards Reading.

OPEN *11am–2.30pm and 6–11pm Mon–Sat; 12–3pm and 7–10.30pm Sun.*

SELBORNE

The Selborne Arms

High Street, Selborne GU34 3JR
☎ *(01420) 511247* Nick and Hayley Carter
www.selbornearms.co.uk

Genuine freehouse serving Ringwood Fortyniner, Suthwyk Bloomfields and Courage Best plus two guests from a wide range of local breweries, changed every firkin.

A 17th-century building housing a traditional country pub in the historic village of Selborne, with original beams, log fires and a friendly atmosphere. Two separate bars and an intimate dining room. A wide range of freshly prepared local food is served 12–2pm and 7–9pm daily. Large beer garden with separate children's play area. Covered, heated outdoor area. Host of the village beer festival. Lots of fantastic walks nearby, plus Gilbert White's house and Oates Museum. Between Alton and Liss on B3006.

OPEN *11am–3pm and 6–11pm Mon–Sat; 12–11pm Sun.*

SHEDFIELD

The Wheatsheaf Inn

Botley Road, Shedfield, Southampton SO32 2JG
☎ *(01329) 833024*
Tim Shepherd and Jo Bartlett

Freehouse serving Flowerpots Bitter plus beers from Oakleaf, Ringwood and many other local micro-breweries. All ales gravity-fed.

Country pub with open log fire and garden. Food available at lunchtime plus Tues and Wed evenings. There is a beer festival held on the late Spring Bank Holiday weekend. Jazz and blues every Saturday night.

OPEN *All day, every day.*

SOUTHAMPTON

The Alexandra Beer Emporium

6 Bellevue Road, Southampton SO15 2AY
☎ *(023) 8033 5071* Joseph Khalil
www.myspace.com/thealexsouthampton/

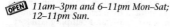

Enterprise Inns leased house serving Fuller's London Pride, Timothy Taylor Landlord, Ringwood Best and Hop Back Summer Lightning.

One of the last remaining traditional pubs in the town centre, with wooden floors throughout and a real working fireplace. Also boasts one of the largest beer gardens in the centre, with heaters. A large, dedicated football following. Table football, darts, pool. Sky TV projector, big-screen TV and four others inside the pub. Food available 12–4pm every day. No children. North of the city centre, just off London Road.

OPEN *11am–11pm Mon–Fri; 12–11pm Sat–Sun.*

Bevois Castle

63 Onslow Road, Bevois Valley, Southampton SO14 0JL
☎ *(023) 8033 0350* Dave and Sandy Bulpitt

Three beers from the Hampshire Brewery plus a rotating guest.

Small, traditional pub with real fire. Darts and pool. Strong football following. Full menu available 11am–2pm. Courtyard garden. No children's facilities. Car park.

OPEN *11am–11pm (10.30pm Sun).*

The Crown Inn

9 Highcrown Street, Southampton SO17 1QE
☎ *(023) 8031 5033* Steve Grimble

An Enterprise house with Timothy Taylor Landlord, Fuller's London Pride, Ringwood Best, Flowers IPA (brewed by Badger) and Draught Bass.

A country pub in the town. Food available 12–2.30pm every day; 6–9.30pm Mon–Thurs, 6–10pm Fri–Sat, 7–9pm Sun. Children welcome, but there are no special facilities or children's menu. Off The Avenue, down Highfield Lane then the second left.

OPEN *11am–11pm.*

The Duke of Wellington

36 Bugle Street, Southampton SO14 2AH
☎ *(023) 8033 9222*
Norman and Carole Trainor
www.southampton-pubs.co.uk/dukeofwellington

Wadworth house offering Henry's IPA, 6X and something from Ringwood plus three constantly changing guests.

Built in 1220, this is the oldest pub in Southampton. Cask Marque approved. Food available in a separate dining area 12–2.30pm daily and 6–8.30pm Mon–Sat. Function room. Children welcome in the dining area.

OPEN *11am–11pm Mon–Sat; 12–10.30pm Sun.*

The Eagle

1 Palmerston Road, Southampton SO14 1LL
☎ *(023) 8033 3825* Bob Warren

Enterprise Inns tenancy with four real ales. Wadworth 6X and beers from Timothy Taylor, Ringwood and Fuller's/Gale's are regularly featured, and one beer is rotated every week.

Traditional pub in the towncentre, in a Tudor building with wooden beams and a friendly atmosphere. Football-focused during the season, cricket-focused in summer. Food available all day. In the centre of Hoglands Park, opposite Debenhams.

OPEN *10am–midnight.*

The Guide Dog

38 Earls Road, Southampton SO14 6SF
☎ *(023) 8022 5642 Paul B Barden*

This freehouse has seven ales available at all times from various local and national breweries. Bowman Swift One is permanent, plus six rotating guests which change daily.

Previously The Valley Inn, this pub reopened in 1984 under its current name. A quiet pub with a single bar. No fruit machines, pool tables or juke box – just old-fashioned conversation! Food available when Southampton FC are playing at home. Annual beer festival in October. Large selection of foreign bottled beers and fruit beers available. Dogs welcome. Dartboard. Ideal pre- or post-match venue for games held at St Mary's Stadium for both home and away supporters. Nearest rail station is St Denys, approximately ten minutes away.

3–11pm Mon–Thurs; 12–11pm Fri–Sun.

The Humble Plumb

Commercial Street, Bitterne, Southampton SO18 6LY
☎ *(023) 8043 7577 KR and D Jukes*

Wadworth tied house with ten ales; four permanent fixtures from Wadworth and six guests, rotating daily.

This typical olde-worlde family-run pub was built in 1812 and is Cask Marque accredited. It has two bars, a beer garden, patio and background music. Quiz nights on Monday, meat draw on Sunday afternoon. Bar meals available 12–2pm Mon–Sun and 6–8pm Thurs–Sat. Children under 14 welcome until 7pm, children over 14 welcome until 9pm. Dogs on leads welcome. Large car park. 15 minutes from Southampton city centre. Five minutes off the M27, taking junction 7 towards Bitterne/West End.

11.30am–2.30pm and 5–11pm Mon–Thurs; 11.30am–11pm Fri–Sat; 12–10.30pm Sun.

The Platform Tavern

Town Quay, Southampton SO14 2NY
☎ *(023) 8033 7232 Stewart Cross*
www.platformtavern.com

Freehouse with Fuller's London Pride and Itchen Valley Godfathers plus two rotating guests which can be changed in a matter of hours!

A pub since 1873, this building consists of part of the old city walls. Very individual décor and atmosphere, separate fish restaurant, one bar. Food served in the café 9am–noon daily, in the pub 12–9pm daily. Fresh fish available 7–10pm Thurs–Sat. Licensed pavement area in front of pub. Children welcome in restaurant. Frequent live jazz and blues music. Located opposite the town quay.

9am–midnight.

South Western Arms

38–40 Adelaide Road, St Denys, Southampton SO17 2HW
☎ *(023) 8032 4542 Ryan and Shona Pickering*

Leased from Enterprise Inns, with Caledonian Deuchars IPA plus eight guests changed every firkin. Mainly features local breweries such as Bowman, Hampshire, Triple FFF, Oakleaf, Itchen Valley and Gribble.

Close to the football ground, this pub has a beer garden, heated smoking shelter and car park. Two beer festivals a year. No food. On the south side of St Denys railway station.

12–11pm Sun–Thurs; 12–12 Fri–Sat.

The Standing Order

30 High Street, Southampton SO14 3HT
☎ *(023) 8022 2121 Adrian Crocco*

Wetherspoon's pub serving Ringwood Fortyniner and Old Thumper, Greene King Abbot, Courage Best and Directors, Marston's Pedigree plus two guests changed every couple of days.

Traditional high-street pub. Food available all day.

9am–midnight Sun–Thurs; 9am–1am Fri–Sat.

The Stile

163 University Road, Southampton SO17 1TS
☎ *(023) 8058 1124 Andy Ebdy*

Five constantly changing real ales.

A city-based student pub with food served all day. Beer garden. Children welcome for dining.

11am–11pm.

Waterloo Arms

101 Waterloo Road, Southampton SO15 3BS
☎ *(023) 8022 0022 Robert and Linda Roach*

Hop Back pub serving Summer Lightning, GFB, Entire Stout, Crop Circle and Best plus guests, rotated weekly on one pump, perhaps King and Barnes Festive, Woodforde's Wherry or something from the Hampshire Brewery.

Local, traditional village pub with conservatory and garden. Food available 12–3pm and 7–9pm. Children allowed.

All day, every day.

SOUTHSEA

The Artillery Arms

Hester Road, Milton, Southsea, Portsmouth PO4 8HB
☎ *(023) 9273 3610*
Mike and Annette Bradshaw

Freehouse with up to eight real ales including Gale's GB and HSB, Ringwood Old Thumper and Fortyniner plus a couple of guests changed every two weeks.

A traditional, two-bar local community pub with garden. Snacks available all day at weekends. Beer festival held at the end of May. Small parking area. Children welcome.

12–3pm and 5–11pm Mon–Thurs; 12–11pm Fri–Sat; 12–10.30pm Sun.

The Old Oyster House

291 Lockway Road, Milton, Southsea,
Portsmouth PO4 8LH
☎ *(023) 9282 7456* Paul and Cath Russell

Four real ales, including beers such as Greene King Abbot, Ringwood Best, Shepherd Neame Spitfire and Wychwood Hobgoblin, with two of these changed every three weeks.

Built in 1919, a busy local pub with friendly staff and a friendly atmosphere, alongside the Langstone canal, in a small fishing community. Two bars, beer garden, log fire in winter. Function room for hire. Large public car park opposite. Barbecues in summer. At the bottom of Lockswary Road, opposite Milton Locks.

OPEN *Winter: 4–11pm Mon–Thurs;*
12–12 Fri–Sat; 12–10.30pm Sun.
Summer: 12–12 (10.30pm Sun).

The Sir Loin of Beef

152 Highland Road, Southsea PO4 9NH
☎ *(023) 9282 0115* Paul Jevons

Eight beers on tap, including Hop Back Summer Lightning and seven weekly guests from breweries such as Downton, King, Lloyds, Cottage, Fuller's, Hogs Back, Arundel, Irving, Flowerpots and Hidden.

Freehouse dating from the early 1900s with horseshoe-shaped bar. Food served 11am– 3pm and evenings during the monthly beer festival. Head towards Easney, and the pub is on the main road.

OPEN *11am–11.30pm Mon–Thurs; 11am–*
midnight Fri–Sat; 12–11.30pm Sun.

The Wine Vaults

43–7 Albert Road, Southsea PO5 2SF
☎ *(023) 9286 4712* Rod Bailey

Former freehouse bought by Fuller's in 2005 and now serving beers from the brewery's range.

Friendly, traditional pub with varied clientele and good atmosphere. Food is served 12–9pm daily, and there is also a brasserie menu. Well-behaved over-5s welcome, but there are no special facilities. Located directly opposite Kings Theatre.

OPEN *12–11pm (10.30pm Sun).*

STEEP

The Harrow Inn

Steep, Nr Petersfield GU32 2DA
☎ *(01730) 262685*
Denise and Claire McCutcheon

A freehouse. Ringwood Best, Oakleaf Bitter, Bowman Swift One, Palmer IPA, Suthwyk Bloomfields and Hop Back GFB.

A 16th-century, family-run inn with two bars: one with inglenook fireplace, the other Victorian. Little has changed in this pub over the years. Homemade food prepared from traditional family recipes 12– 2pm and 7–9pm (not Sun evenings). Children only allowed in the beer garden. Dogs welcome. Car park.

OPEN *12–2.30pm and 6–11pm Mon–Fri;*
11am–3pm and 6–11pm Sat; 12–3pm
and 7–10.30pm Sun (closed Sun nights
Oct–Apr).

TICHBORNE

Tichborne Arms

Tichborne, Alresford SO44 0NA
☎ *(01962) 733760* Mr and Mrs Roper

Four real ales from back bar stillage, including Palmers Copper and Dorset Gold, Ringwood Best and guests such as Hop Back Summer Lightning, Bowman Swift One or Triple FFF Moondance.

Thatched freehouse surrounded by countryside, ideal as a base for walking. Home-cooked food available lunchtimes and evenings. Large garden and car park. Dogs welcome. Close to Watercress Line.

OPEN *11.30am–3pm and 6–11pm.*

TITCHFIELD

The Wheatsheaf Inn

1 East Street, Titchfield, Fareham PO14 4AD
☎ *(01329) 842965* Adrienne De Noia

Freehouse serving Fuller's London Pride and Woodforde's Wherry plus two guests changed weekly. Examples may include Hook Norton Hooky Bitter and Exmoor Gold.

A village pub with dining area, open fire, patio and garden. Food available at lunchtimes and evenings. Children allowed in the dining area only.

OPEN *12–3pm and 6–11pm Mon–Thurs; all day*
Fri; 12–3pm and 6–11pm Sat; 12–3pm
and 7–10.30pm Sun.

WEYHILL

Weyhill Fair

Weyhill Road, Weyhill, Nr Andover SP11 0PP
☎ *(01264) 773631* Robert and Catherine Eyre
www.weyhillfair.co.uk

Fuller's London Pride, Chiswick and seasonal beers plus three guests (approx. 200 per year) including brews from Butcombe and Ramsbury.

Friendly local offering traditional English bar food 12–9pm. Cask Marque award winner. Small function room. Beer festival in July. Car park, garden and family room. Close to Hawk Conservancy and Thruxton circuit. On the A342 west of Andover.

OPEN *11am–3pm and 6–11pm Mon–Thurs;*
11am–3pm and 5–11pm Fri; 12–11pm
Sat; 12–10.30pm Sun.

WHITSBURY

The Cartwheel

Whitsbury Road, Whitsbury, Nr Fordingbridge
SP6 3PZ
☎ *(01725) 518362* Ed and Liz Freeman

Ringwood pub serving up to five real ales from the brewery range plus one guest, changed regularly.

A relaxed, friendly locals' pub with exposed beams and open fire, in good walking country. Bar and restaurant food available 12–2pm and 6–9pm. Car park and garden. Families welcome. Annual beer festival (20 brews) in August. Signposted from the A338. Turn south out of Salisbury onto the Fordingbridge road at Breamore.

OPEN *11am–3pm and 5.30–11pm Mon–Fri;*
11.30am–midnight Sat; 12–11pm Sun.

WINCHESTER

The Black Boy

1 Wharf Hill, Winchester SO23 9NQ
☎ *(01962) 861754* David Nicholson
www.theblackboypub.com

Freehouse offering five real ales, with Flowerpots Bitter, Ringwood Best and Hop Back Summer Lightning always available plus two guests, changed several times a week. Examples include beers from Triple FFF, Itchen Valley, Hampshire and Archers.

The pub features eclectic old furnishings, rugs and real fires, but no juke box or fruit machines. Homemade pub grub served Tues evening to Sun lunch. Just off Chesil Street, handy for visits to the Black Rat restaurant next door.

OPEN *12–11pm Mon–Thurs; 12–12 Fri–Sat; 12–10.30pm Sun.*

The Old Gaol House

11 Jewry Street, Winchester SO23 8RZ
☎ *(01962) 850095* Gareth Hughes

Wetherspoon's pub with Shepherd Neame Spitfire, Greene King Abbot and Hop Back Summer Lightning among the beers permanently served, plus four guests from a wide range of independent breweries.

Large pub offering food 10am–10pm Mon–Sat and 12–9.30pm Sun. Accompanied children welcome 12–5pm if eating, with children's menu, high chairs and baby-changing facilities available.

OPEN *10am–11pm Mon–Sat (10.30pm Sun).*

WINSOR

The Compass Inn

Winsor Road, Southampton SO40 2HE
☎ *(023) 8081 2237* Mop Draper

Enterprise Inns tied house, serving Ringwood Best, Fuller's London Pride, Gale's HSB and Greene King Abbot Ale plus a feature ale.

Traditional pub with a large local following. Logburner and cosy atmosphere. Pool table. Traditional, good value for money pub food served 12–2pm and 6.30–9pm daily. Beer garden. Beer festivals held over May and August bank holidays. Children and dogs welcome. Music nights held frequently. Near Paulton's Park and the New Forest. Take Junction 2 off the M27, following signs to Ower/Green Pastures. Go past Green Pastures caravan site and take the next right at the crossroads.

OPEN *11am–11pm.*

WOLVERTON

George & Dragon

Wolverton, Tadley RG26 5ST
☎ *(01635) 298292*

Genuine freehouse serving Greene King Abbot, Wadworth Henry's IPA, Fuller's London Pride and Ringwood Best, plus one rotating guest.

Approximately 300 years old with beams, flagstone floors and log fires, this welcoming pub features one large bar. Home-cooked food available 12–2pm and 6.30–9.30pm, with roasts on Sundays. Beer garden, large car park, courtyard. En-suite bedrooms available for letting. Function room. Located one mile off the A339.

OPEN *12–3pm and 5.30–11pm.*

THE BREWERIES

ARROW BREWERY
The Wine Vaults, 37 High Street, Kington HR5 3BJ
☎ (01544) 230685

BITTER 4.0% ABV
QUIVER 5.0% ABV

DUNN PLOWMAN BREWERY
Arrow Court Industrial Estate, Lower Hergest, Kington HR5 3ER
☎ 07907 169449

BREWHOUSE BITTER 3.8% ABV
EMERALD ALE 3.9% ABV
EARLY RISER 4.0% ABV
STING HONEY BEER 4.2% ABV
KINGDOM BITTER 4.5% ABV
OLD JAKE STOUT 4.8% ABV
SHIRE HORSE ALE 5.5% ABV
CROOKED FURROW 6.5% ABV
Plus occasionals.

MARCHES ALES
The Old Hop Kilns, Claston Farm, Dormington HR1 4EA
☎ (01584) 878999

FOREVER AUTMN 4.2% ABV
LUDLOW GOLD 4.3% ABV
DORMINGTON GOLD 4.5% ABV
ST LAWRENCE ALE 4.5% ABV

MAYFIELDS BREWERY
Mayfields Farm, Bishops Frome WR6 5AS
☎ (01531) 640015

NEMESIS 3.8% ABV
OBLIVION 5.5% ABV
Plus seasonals and specials.

SHOES BREWERY
Three Horseshoes Inn, Norton Canon, Hereford HR4 7BH
☎ (01544) 318375

NORTON ALE 3.5% ABV
CANON BITTER 4.2% ABV
PEPPLOE'S TIPPLE 6.0%
FARRIER'S ALE 14.0%

SPINNING DOG BREWERY
The Victory, 88 St Owen Street, Hereford HR1 2QD
☎ (01432) 342125
www.spinningdogbrewery.co.uk

HEREFORDSHIRE ORGANIC BITTER 3.7% ABV
HEREFORDSHIRE OWD BULL 3.9% ABV
HEREFORD LIGHT ALE 4.0% ABV
MUTLEY'S DARK 4.0% ABV
MUTLEY'S PITSTOP 4.0% ABV
TOP DOG 4.2% ABV
CELTIC GOLD 4.5% ABV
HARVEST MOON 4.5% ABV
MUTLEY'S REVENGE 4.8% ABV
MUTTS NUTTS 5.0% ABV
Plus seasonals and occasionals including:
SPRINGER 4.0% ABV
SANTA PAWS 5.2% ABV

WILD'S BREWERY LIMITED
Unit 6, Whitehill Park, Industrial Estate, Weobly, Hereford HR4 8QE
☎ (01544) 319333
www.wildsbrewery.com

NIGHT 4.5% ABV
Malty, hoppy taste.
WILD BLONDE 4.5% ABV
Clear, blonde and hoppy, hint of vanilla.
Plus seasonals and specials.

WYE VALLEY BREWERY
Stoke Lacey, Bromyard, Hereford HR74HG
☎ (01885) 490505
www.wyevalleybrewery.co.uk

WYE VALLEY BITTER 3.7% ABV
Delicate hoppy flavour, bitter finish.
HEREFORD PALE ALE 4.0% ABV
Smooth and citrusy.
BUTTY BACH 4.5% ABV
Smooth, gold, full bodied.
Plus seasonals and specials including Dorothy Goodbody's selection:
GOLDEN ALE 4.2% ABV
WHOLESOME STOUT 4.6% ABV
COUNTRY ALE 6.0% ABV

THE PUBS

ASTON CREWS

The Penny Farthing
Aston Crews, Nr Ross-on-Wye HR9 7LW
☎ (01989) 750366

Marston's Pedigree and Bitter and Wadworth 6X plus a guest beer (ten per year) such as Shepherd Neame Spitfire, Greene King Old Speckled Hen or something from Robinson's or Hook Norton breweries.

A country inn and restaurant. Bar and restaurant food available at lunchtimes and evenings. Car park and garden. Children allowed in the restaurant. Turn off the A40 Ross-on-Wye to Gloucester road at Lea, on to the B4222 (signposted to Newent). The Penny Farthing is one mile down this road.

OPEN *12–3pm and 7–11pm.*

AYMESTREY

The Riverside Inn
Aymestrey, Leominster HL6 9ST
☎ (01568) 708440 Richard Gresko
www.theriversideinn.org

Two real ales: expect Butty Bach and a seasonal brew from Wye Valley, and Dorothy Goodbody's Golden Ale or something else from the Wye Valley range.

A 16th-century rural coaching inn with original beams, one main bar, dining area and a riverside garden which is floodlit at night. Award-winning bar and restaurant food available at lunchtimes and evenings. Children of all ages permitted in the dining area. Function room and car park. Accommodation. Dogs welcome. On the A4110 northwest of Leominster.

OPEN *11am–3pm and 6–11pm (10.30pm Sun). Closed Mon lunchtimes.*

BISHOP'S FROME
The Chase Inn
4 Bridge Street, Bishop's Frome, Nr Worcester WR6 5BP
☎ *(01885) 490234* Richard and Helen Baker

 A Marston's pub with Pedigree and Burton Bitter plus one guest, changed fortnightly. This could be another Marston's brew or something from Jennings, Wadworth or further afield.

A country inn built in 1860 and refurbished in 2007, with a 40-seat restaurant, public bar, separate pool/darts area and outside heated smoking area. Food served 12–9pm daily, from an extensive menu plus specials. Corporate entertaining provided. There is also a takeaway service. Five en-suite B&B bedrooms, plus two with shared bathroom. Children welcome. Large car park with disabled space. Between Bromyard and Ledbury, follow the brown information signs.

OPEN *12–11pm (10.30pm Sun).*

Green Dragon
Bishop's Frome, Nr Worcester WR6 5BP
☎ *(01885) 490607* Simon and Alison Durrant
www.thegreendragoninn.com

Six real ales from Theakstons, Timothy Taylor, Wye Valley and elsewhere. Snowdonia Ale from Purple Moose brewery in Portmadoc is now a permanent feature.

Seventeenth-century village inn with low beams, flagstone floors, fireplaces in every room and a multi-level beer garden. Function room. Food available 5.30–8.30pm. Regular beer festivals.

OPEN *5–11pm Mon–Thurs; 4–11.30pm Fri; 12–11.30pm Sat; 12–4pm and 7–11pm Sun.*

BROMYARD
The Rose & Lion Inn
5 New Road, Bromyard HR7 4AJ
☎ *(01885) 482381* Mrs Herdman

Wye Valley tied house always serving Bitter, Hereford Pale Ale, Dorothy Goodbody's, Butty Bach and Wholesome Stout. Plus one weekly-changing guest, sometimes a seasonal Wye Valley ale such as Springtime, or brews such as Coach House Gunpowder Strong Mild.

An award-winning, two-bar drinking house. Old, traditional building carefully renovated, with garden. No food. Children allowed in the garden only.

OPEN *11am–3pm and 6–11pm Mon–Fri; all day most Sat–Sun.*

DORMINGTON
The Yew Tree
Priors Frome, Dormington HR1 4EH
☎ *(01432) 850467* Len Gee
www.lengees.info

Wye Valley Butty Bach and usually another Wye Valley Bitter, plus a guest such as Bishops Castle Three Tons or 1642, Wickwar Bob or Golden Valley Gloucester or 410. One beer at 4.5% and another weaker for most of the year; a stronger ale at around 5.0% at Christmas.

This 200-year-old country freehouse and restaurant with log fire and wood-burner has beams that are 500 years old. Home-cooked food available 12–2pm and 7–9pm. Three bars, 50-seater restaurant, large garden with great views towards the Black Mountains. Car park plus room for coaches. No accommodation. Children allowed. Close to Newbridge Farm Park and two rivers for fishing.

OPEN *12–2pm and 7–11pm (closed Tues).*

EWYAS HAROLD
The Dog Inn
Village Centre, Ewyas Harold HR2 0EX
☎ *(01981) 240598* T Blows
www.thedoginn.net

Freehouse serving ten to twelve real ales every week.

A 14th-century olde-worlde village inn with bar, restaurant, games room. Two letting rooms available for B&B. Bar snacks and evening meals served 12–3pm and 7–9pm. Annual beer festival. Close to the Black Mountains and Brecon Beacons. Ideal location for walking, in the heart of the Golden Valley. On the A465, 12 miles south of Hereford.

OPEN *10am–midnight.*

HAMPTON BISHOP
Bunch of Carrots
Hampton Bishop, Hereford HR1 4JR
☎ *(01432) 870237* Paul and Katharine Turner

Spinning Dog Organic Bitter, Butcombe Bitter and Courage Directors regularly available.

Traditional country inn with open fires and stone-clad floors, beer garden and function room. Food served lunchtimes and evenings Mon–Thurs and all day Fri–Sun. Large car park. Beer garden, children's play area. Situated two miles from Hereford city centre on the B4224, close to the River Wye.

OPEN *10am–3pm and 6–11pm Mon–Thurs; 10am–11pm Fri–Sat; 12–10.30pm Sun.*

HAY-ON-WYE

Bull's Head

Craswall, Nr Hay-on-Wye HR2 0PN
☎ *(01981) 510616* Gaynor and Mark

 Freehouse with three real ales on a typical night, including Wye Valley Butty Bach and various guest beers, often from Spinning Dog, changed weekly. Eight real ciders also served.

On the Welsh border but just in Herefordshire, nestling at the foot of the Black Hill, in the Black Mountains. Flagstone floors, open fires and a rustic atmosphere. Excellent food made from local produce served 12–9.30pm in bar and beamed restaurant. Large beer garden, three large fields for rough camping, plus corral for horse riders. Popular with walkers. Three pet-friendly letting rooms for B&B. Isolated, but not to be missed.

OPEN *11am–11pm Mon–Sat; 12–10.30pm Sun. Open for coffee from 10am.*

HEREFORD

The Barrels

69 St Owen Street, Hereford HR1 2JQ
☎ *(01432) 274968* Peter Amor

Once the home of the Wye Valley Brewery, this pub still stocks Wye Valley brews. Bitter, Hereford Pale Ale, Butty Bach and Golden Ale are regulars, and two beers rotate.

A town boozer. One of the last multi-roomed public houses in Hereford. Clientele a mix of old regulars and students. Cask Marque accredited, and Hereford CAMRA Pub of the Year 2006. Occasional live music. Improved decking area in garden. Old brewery converted to function room. No food.

OPEN *All day, every day.*

The Bridge Inn

Kentchurch, Hereford HR2 0BY
☎ *(01981) 240408*

Freehouse offering three guest ales, which could include Greene King IPA, Black Sheep or Wessex Ale. Changed constantly, with up to six per week.

A 16th-century listed building on the River Monnow on the England/Wales border. One bar, separate restaurant. Food served Wed–Sun. One en-suite letting room available. Beer festivals held on May and August bank holidays. Large car park. Beer garden with children's play area. Halfway between Hereford and Abergavenny on the A465.

OPEN *5–11pm Mon–Tues; 11am–3pm and 5–11pm Wed–Sat; 12–4pm and 7–11pm Sun.*

Lichfield Vaults

11 Church Street, Hereford HR1 2LR
☎ *(01432) 267994* John Cray

 Greene King Abbot is a regular plus two rotating guests.

Traditional, historic town-centre pub with one bar and a mixed clientele. Food served 12–8pm Mon–Sat and 12–6pm Sun.

Beer garden, children welcome until 3pm.
OPEN *11am–11pm Mon–Sat; 12–10.30pm Sun.*

The Victory

88 St Owen Street, Hereford HR1 2QD
☎ *(01432) 274998* James Kenyon
www.spinningdogbrewery.co.uk

Home of the Spinning Dog Brewery, with up to eight real ales, four from Spinning Dog and four from elsewhere. Three real ciders also served. Two annual beer festivals held (May Day and October).

A two-bar boozer with a nautical theme. Live music on Saturday and Sunday evenings. Beer garden. Food served lunchtimes and evenings Mon–Sat, vegetarian meals available and roasts on Sundays 12–5pm. Homemade real ale sausages available all week. Children allowed. Cask Marque accredited. Beer garden. The publican runs a visitors' book which is an absolute must for 'tickers'! Brewery tours available. Function room available. In Hereford town centre.

OPEN *Summer: 12–12. Winter: 3pm–12.*

KINGTON

Ye Olde Tavern

22 Victoria Road, Kington HR5 3BX
☎ *(01544) 231933* Steve and Gaye Dunn

Home of the Dunn Plowman brewery, so offering a good selection from the range.

Long-time local boozer, refurbished and reopened in 2002, the county's CAMRA Pub of the Year in 2004.

OPEN *5.30–11pm Mon–Fri; 12–3pm and 6–11pm Sat; 12–3pm and 6–10.30pm Sun.*

The Queen's Head

Bridge Street, Kington HR5 3DW
☎ *(01544) 231106*

Owned by the nearby Dunn Plowman Brewery and run as the brewery tap, with the full range of brews always available.

A 400-year-old refurbished pub in the old market town. Food available all day Tues–Sun. Beer garden. Petanque court. Accommodation. Children allowed.

OPEN *11.30am–11pm (10.30pm Sun).*

LEA

The Crown Inn

Gloucester Road, Lea, Nr Ross-on-Wye HR9 7JZ
☎ *(01989) 750407* Gary Hogsden

Four real ales available. Wye Valley Butty Bach, Brains Rev James and Charles Wells Bombardier are regular features, plus a rotating guest perhaps from Hook Norton or Spinning Dog.

Fifteenth-century rural coaching inn with a warm welcome always assured. One large bar, beer garden, car park, restaurant. Bar and à la carte meals served 12–2.30pm and 6–9pm every day. Children and pets welcome. New games room can cater for large parties. Close to Royal Forest of Dean, Symonds Yat, Gloucester and Hereford. Walkers welcome. Situated on the A40 Ross-on-Wye to Gloucester road.

OPEN *11am–11pm Mon–Sat; 12–10.30pm Sun.*

LEDBURY
The Horseshoe Inn
The Homend, Ledbury HR8 1BP
☎ *(01531) 632770* Hylton Haylett

Timothy Taylor Landlord and Fuller's London Pride plus one local guest ale. Cask Marque accredited.

Friendly, traditional black and white pub centrally located in Ledbury, a pretty market town close to the Malvern Hills and Eastnor Castle. Dating from the 1700s, the pub has one olde-worlde bar, low beams and a log fire. Good, mostly locally sourced, food available at lunchtimes. Pretty beer garden and heated patio area. Occasional live music (call for details). Dog-friendly any time!

OPEN *All day, every day, from 11am Mon–Sat and from 12 Sun.*

The Prince of Wales
Church Lane, Ledbury HR8 1DL
☎ *(01531) 632250* Les Smith
www.powledbury.com

Freehouse with Banks's Bitter, Sharp's Doom Bar and Brains Reverend James permanently on offer plus one guest. A range of continental bottled and draught beers also available, plus draught perry in summer.

Timber-framed building dating from circa 1570. Front and back bar, lots of character, swearing prohibited! Cask Marque accredited. Food available 12–2pm. Small patio area. Live music with 'folk jam sessions' Wednesday evenings. In the town centre, behind the Market House, towards the church.

OPEN *11am–11pm (10.30pm Sun).*

LEOMINSTER
The Grape Vaults
Broad Street, Leominster HR6 8BS
☎ *(01568) 611404* Julie Saxon

Owned by Punch Taverns, serving five real ales from local breweries: Hobsons, Ludlow, Spinning Dog, Mayfields, Wye Valley, Woods.

A small, unspoilt Victorian Grade II listed pub in the town centre, beamed and with two real fires. No games machines. Locally sourced food served 12–2pm and 5.30–9pm. Close to Leominster Priory, within walking distance of the train station.

OPEN *11am–11pm Mon–Thurs; 11am–midnight Fri–Sat; 12–11pm Sun.*

LETTON
The Swan Inn
Letton, Hereford HR3 6DH
☎ *(01544) 327304* Jenny Howells

Two pumps, with beers from Wye Valley usually available, often including Butty Bach.

A traditional roadside one-bar freehouse with pool table, darts and a beer garden with petanque. Food available until 9.30pm. Children welcome. Accommodation available. Car park. Located on the A438 Hereford–Brecon road, 12 miles out of Hereford.

OPEN *12–3pm and 5.30–11pm.*

LINTON
The Alma Inn
Linton, Ross-on-Wye HR9 7RY
☎ *(01989) 720355* Graham and Linda Webb
www.lintonfestival.org/almainnlinton

Freehouse serving three ales during the week and up to five at the weekends. Butcombe Bitter and Oakham JHB prevail and guests beers are drawn from local brewers Malvern Hills, Goff's, Freeminer, Ludlow, Teme Valley, Wye Valley, Woods, Three Tuns and RCH.

Victorian village pub dating back to 1876 with three public rooms. The main bar and pool room accommodate 80–90 people. A separate bar seats up to 30 people. No food, though they will arrange for occasions such as weddings and funerals. Very large beer garden, car park. Host to the sellout annual outdoor Linton Festival. Winner of various Herefordshire Pub of the Year awards. Nearby attractions include the Wye Valley and the Forest of Dean. Take junction 3 off the M50 and turn left on leaving the motorway.

OPEN *6–11pm Mon–Fri; 12.30–3.30pm and 6–11pm Sat; 12.30–3.30pm and 7–11pm Sun.*

MUCH DEWCHURCH
The Black Swan Inn
Much Dewchurch, Hereford HR2 8DJ
☎ *(01981) 540295*
Arwell Davies and Gillian Constance

Brews from Timothy Taylor, Hook Norton, Bateman and Rhymney often feature, with two changed monthly.

A 14th-century inn with open fires and a warm friendly atmosphere. Restaurant in lounge. Homemade food available 12–2pm and 7–10pm. Car park front and rear, patio. Children welcome. Dogs on a lead allowed. Near Golden Valley, seven miles north of Ross-on-Wye, off the A49.

OPEN *12–3pm and 5.30–11pm Mon–Sat; 12–3pm and 7–10.30pm Sun.*

NORTON CANON
Three Horse Shoes Inn
Norton Canon, Hereford HR4 7BH
☎ *(01544) 318375* Frank Goodwin

Home of the Shoes Brewery, with a selection of brews always available.

Two bars and a games room, with grassed area for summer use. Situated on the A480. No food. Car park. Children welcome.

OPEN *6–11pm Mon–Tues and Thurs–Fri; 12–3pm and 6–11pm Wed; 11am–11pm Sat; 12–10.30pm Sun.*

PETERSTOW
The Red Lion
Winters Cross, Peterstow, Ross-on-Wye HR9 6LH
☎ *(01989) 730202 David Anthony Rapson*

 Enterprise Inns tied house serving Bath Ales SPA and Gem, Wye Valley Golden Ale, Timothy Taylor Landlord and Otter Bitter plus one guest changed weekly.

A traditional single-bar pub and restaurant with beams and log fires. Food served 12–2.30pm and 6–9pm Tues–Sun. Beer garden, car park and children's play equipment. Situated on the A49 Ross–Hereford road.

OPEN *12–3pm and 5.30–11pm Tues–Fri; 12–11pm Sat–Sun.*

ROSS-ON-WYE
The Crown & Sceptre
Market Place, Ross-on-Wye HR9 5NX
☎ *(01989) 562765 Les Trute and Sarah Dean*

 An Enterprise Inn serving Wye Valley Bitter, Fuller's London Pride and Greene King Abbot Ale. A couple of rotating guests such as Greene King Old Speckled Hen, Shepherd Neame Spitfire or Gale's HSB are also available at busy times.

A town pub with a friendly atmosphere and mixed clientele. One bar, patio and garden. Homemade food including up to ten specials served all day. Well-behaved children allowed.

OPEN *All day, every day.*

STAPLOW
The Oak Inn
Staplow, Nr Ledbury HR8 1NP
☎ *(01531) 640954 Hylton Haylett*

A freehouse with Wye Valley Bitter, Brains Rev James and Timothy Taylor Landlord plus one guest changed twice weekly.

Country pub and restaurant, dating from the 17th century, located two miles north of Ledbury on the Bromyard road. Recently reopened after refurbishment, there are three cosy bar areas with log-burning stoves, flagstone floors and wooden beams. Rustic restaurant area with open plan kitchen serving locally sourced food 12–2.30pm and 6.30–9.30pm daily (booking advisable). Interesting selection of exclusive wines. Car park. Garden. Dogs welcome.

OPEN *12–3pm and 5.30–11pm.*

WELLINGTON
The Wellington
Wellington, Nr Hereford HR4 8AT
☎ *(01432) 830367 Ross Williams*
www.wellingtonpub.co.uk

 Genuine freehouse with Hobsons Best Bitter, Wye Valley HPA and Butty Bach.

Traditional single-bar country pub in a Victorian building, with a restaurant in the converted stables. Food served 12–2pm (not Mon) and 7–9pm (not Sun). No games, no TV. Annual beer festival in July. Beer garden, car park. Children welcome. Just off the A49 between Hereford and Leominster.

OPEN *6–11pm Mon; 12–3pm and 6–11pm Tues–Sat; 12–4pm Sun (closed Sun evenings and Monday lunchtimes).*

YARPOLE
The Bell Inn
Green Lane, Yarpole, Nr Leominster HR6 0BD
☎ *(01568) 780359 Claude and Cedric Bosi*
www.thebellinnyarpole.co.uk

 Enterprise Inns pub with Hook Norton Hooky Bitter, Timothy Taylor Landlord and Wye Valley Hereford Pale Ale permanently available.

Black and white fronted typical village pub, complete with original cider press and beautiful extensive gardens. Food served 12–2.30pm Tues–Sat and 6.30–9.30pm Tues–Sun. Large car park. Children welcome, dogs welcome in the bar. Nearby attractions include historic Ludlow, Croft Castle and some amazing walks. On the B4361 between Ludlow and Leominster

OPEN *12–3pm and 6.30–11pm Tues–Sat; 12–3pm Sun.*

THE BREWERIES

ALEHOUSE PUB AND BREWERY

The Farmer's Boy, 134 London Road, St Albans AL1 1PQ
☎ *07872 985918*
www.alehousebrewery.co.uk

SIMPLICITY 3.6% ABV
VERULAM CLIPPER IPA 4.0% ABV
NEW AGE STOUT 4.3% ABV
ROBUST PORTER 4.3% ABV
TECHNICIAN'S PALE 4.3% ABV
VERULAM FARMER'S JOY 4.3% ABV
BUTT'S PARK BITTER 4.4% ABV
Plus specials, many on a one-hop theme.

BUNTINGFORD BREWERY CO. LTD

Greys Brewhouse, Therfield Road, Royston SG8 9NW
☎ *(01763) 250749*
www.buntingford-brewery.co.uk

HIGHWAYMAN IPA 3.6% ABV
Moderately hoppy, toffee aftertaste.
PARGETTERS MILD 3.7% ABV
Dark with honey notes.
CHALLENGER 3.8% ABV
Golden, packs a surprising punch.
BRITANNIA 4.4% ABV
Bitter made from five malts.
Seasonals:
ISAAC'S FLYING COACH 3.9% ABV
NIGHT OWL 4.2% ABV
PALE ALE 4.3% ABV
OATMEAL STOUT 4.4% ABV
92 SQUADRON 4.5% ABV
ROYSTON RED 4.8% ABV
SILENCE 5.2% ABV

GREEN TYE BREWERY

Green Tye, Much Hadham SG10 6JP
☎ *(01279) 841041*
www.gtbrewery.co.uk

UNION JACK 3.6% ABV
MUSTANG MILD 3.7% ABV
SNOWDROP 3.9% ABV
Quenching, balanced hop flavour, with some sweetness.
XBF 4.0% ABV
AUTUMN ROSE 4.2% ABV
Red-brown best bitter.
EAST ANGLIAN GOLD 4.2% ABV
GREEN TIGER 4.2% ABV
Light copper-coloured bitter.
MAD MORRIS 4.2% ABV
Golden and quenching with citrus fruit tanginess.
WHEELBARROW 4.3% ABV
Balanced hop, malt and fruit flavours. Easy drinker.
COAL PORTER 4.5% ABV
Flavour-packed porter. Winter brew.
CONKERER 4.7% ABV
Mid-brown best bitter.

MCMULLEN & SONS LTD

The Hertford Brewery, 26 Old Cross, Hertford SG14 1RD
☎ *(01992) 584911*
www.mcmullens.co.uk

ORIGINAL AK 3.8% ABV
COUNTRY BEST BITTER 4.3% ABV
Plus seasonals.

RED SQUIRREL BREWERY

146 Mimram Road, Hertford SG14 1NN
☎ *(01992) 501100*
www.redsquirrelbrewery.co.uk

CONSERVATION BITTER 4.1% ABV
Malty with chocolate notes.
RED SQUIRREL GOLD 4.2% ABV
Malty golden ale.
Seasonals:
DARK RUBY MILD 3.7% ABV
RED SQUIRREL BITTER 3.9% ABV
IPA 4.1% ABV
SCOTTISH ALE 4.3% ABV
PREMIUM ALE 4.5% ABV
ROSE GOLD SUMMER ALE 4.5% ABV
WHEAT BEER 4.5% ABV
STOUT 4.9% ABV
HONEY PORTER 5.0% ABV
ORIGINAL ENGLISH IPA 5.0% ABV

SAFFRON BREWERY

Unit 2, Pledgdon Hall Farm, Henham, Bishop's Stortford CM22 6BJ
☎ *(01279) 850923*
www.saffronbrewery.co.uk

MUNTJAC 3.7% ABV
Floral notes, slightly sweet bitter.
EPA 3.9% ABV
Blackcurrant spice, hop aroma.
PLEDGDON ALE 4.3% ABV
Copper colour, hints of citrus and biscuit.
Plus seasonals.

SAWBRIDGEWORTH BREWERY

The Gate, 81 London Road, Sawbridgeworth CM21 9JJ
☎ *(01279) 722313*
www.the-gate-pub.co.uk

IPA 3.6% ABV
SELHURST PARK FLYER 3.7% ABV
'ERBERT 3.8% ABV
VIKING 3.8% ABV
IS IT YOURSELF? 4.2% ABV
STOUT 4.3% ABV
BROOKLANDS EXPRESS 4.6% ABV
PILEDRIVER 5.3% ABV
Plus specials.

THE TRING BREWERY COMPANY LTD

Units 12–13 Akeman Business Park, 81–2 Honours Yard, Akeman Street, Tring HP23 6AF
☎ *(01442) 890721*
www.tringbrewery.com

SIDE POCKET FOR A TOAD 3.6% ABV
Crisp, dry, citrus finish.
JACK O'LEGS 4.2% ABV
Full fruit and hoppy flavour.
COLLEY'S BLACK DOG 5.2% ABV
Malty, with walnut hints.
Plus occasional and seasonal beers including:
FANNY EBBS SUMMER ALE 3.9% ABV
TAPSTER 4.0% ABV
HUCK ME BUCK 4.4% ABV
SANTA'S HELPER 4.8% ABV

THE PUBS

ALDBURY

The Greyhound

19 Stocks Road, Aldbury, Tring HP23 5RT
☎ *(01442) 851228* Tim O'Gorman
www.greyhoundaldbury.co.uk

 Badger (Hall and Woodhouse) Brewery tied pub serving Badger Best, Tanglefoot and Sussex.

Historic inn in a pretty village with an inglenook fireplace, two bars, two dining areas including a conservatory, and courtyard garden. Food available 12–2.30pm and 6.30–9.30pm Mon–Sat. Children and dogs welcome. Conservatory and accommodation. Close to Ashridge Forest, Tring Museum, Whipsnade Zoo and local canals and reservoirs. Off junction 8 of the M1 and junction 10 of the M25 – take the Tring exit and follow signs for Aldbury (three miles).

OPEN *11am–11pm Mon–Sat; 12–10.30pm Sun.*

Valiant Trooper

Trooper Road, Aldbury, Tring HP23 5RW
☎ *(01442) 851203* Tim O'Gorman

Five real ales, including Fuller's London Pride, Oakham JHB and Tring Jack O'Legs, plus two regularly rotating guest ales.

The deeds for this freehouse date back to 1752, when it was called The Royal Oak. The name was changed to The Valiant Trooper in 1803, allegedly because the Duke of Wellington once met his troops here. Three bars and a separate restaurant. Exposed beams and open fires. Food served 12–2pm and 6.30–9.15pm Mon–Sat (not Mon evening); 12–2.30pm Sun. Large beer garden, car park. Children and dogs welcome. Beer festivals in May and August. Beautiful village setting surrounded by National Trust woodland and monument.

OPEN *11.30am–11pm Mon–Sat; 12–10.30pm Sun.*

AMWELL

Elephant & Castle

Amwell Lane, Amwell, Wheathampstead AL4 8EA
☎ *(01582) 832175*

Greene King IPA, Abbot and Morland plus a guest ale.

Located in buildings almost 500 years old, with three bars on different levels. There is a 200ft well in the middle of the bar. No music or machines. Bar meals available at lunchtimes and evenings (not Sunday or Monday evenings). Car park, two gardens (one for adults only). Children not allowed in back bar. Not easy to find – ask in Wheathampstead or ring for directions.

OPEN *12–2.30pm and 5.30–11pm Mon–Fri; all day Sat–Sun.*

ASHWELL

The Bushel & Strike

Mill Street, Ashwell SG7 5LY
☎ *(01462) 742394* Mark Stier
www.bushelandstrike.co.uk

 Wells and Young's pub with four real ales, including Charles Wells Bombardier, plus one guest beer changed monthly.

Located in a pretty village, a two-bar pub with large restaurant, patio, barbecue and small garden. Food served lunchtimes and evenings. Large car park, large restaurant suitable for functions and parties. Live music licence. Families are welcome, and there is a large garden and play area. From junction 10 of the A1 turn right and follow the signs – the pub is next to the tallest church in Hertfordshire.

OPEN *12–3pm and 6–11pm Mon–Thurs; 12–3pm and 5–11pm Fri; 12–11pm Sat; 12–10.30pm Sun.*

AYOT ST LAWRENCE

The Brocket Arms

Ayot St Lawrence AL6 9RT
☎ *(01438) 820250* Howard and Suzy Sharp
www.brocketarms.com

Greene King IPA, Abbot and Brocket Bitter plus guest ales.

A 14th-century oak-beamed village pub with attractive walled garden and accommodation. Under new management and extensively refurbished. Bar and restaurant food served at lunchtimes and evenings (except Sunday nights). Parking. Dogs welcome. Close to Shaw's Corner, home of George Bernard Shaw.

OPEN *12–11pm.*

BALDOCK

The Old White Horse

1 Station Road, Baldock SG7 5BS
☎ *(01462) 893168* Margaret Patterson
www.oldwhitehorse.com

Enterprise Inn serving B&T Shefford Bitter plus two guests, rotated every three months, with beers such as Shepherd Neame Spitfire and Wychwood Hobgoblin examples of those on offer.

A former coaching inn with a restaurant offering a cosmopolitan menu. Food served 12–2.30pm and 6.45–9.30pm Mon–Fri (until 10pm Fri), 12–10pm Sat and 12–6pm Sun. All-day tapas menu also available. Beer garden, car park. On the first Sunday of the month there is live jazz at 3pm and quiz at 8pm. Beer festival August bank holiday weekend. Wine festival also held.

OPEN *11am–11pm Sun–Thurs; 11am–midnight Fri–Sat.*

BARKWAY

The Tally Ho

London Road, Barkway, Royston SG8 8EX
☎ *(01763) 848389* Paul Danter
www.tallyho-barkway.co.uk

 Nine different ales on offer every week, through three barrels at a time. The focus is on a varied spectrum of strengths from breweries nearby and across the country, the local Buntingford Brewery ales among them. Also over 60 different malt whiskys, 13 gins, 9 rums and over 170 different spirits in all. All real ale prices are the same regardless of ABV.

A traditional pub with traditional values – no fruit machines, no pool tables, no music, no TV. Oak-panelled bar with armchairs, a restaurant, two gardens and terraces, car park. Homemade food available 12–2pm and 6.30–9pm. Children allowed, with well-behaved parents! On the B1368.

OPEN *11am–11pm Mon–Sat; 12–4pm Sun (closed Sun evening).*

BARLEY

The Fox & Hounds

High Street, Barley, Nr Royston SG8 8HU
☎ *(01763) 848459* Aaron Clayton (landlord), Gabby Sale (manager)

Owned by Punch Taverns, offering Greene King IPA and Adnams Bitter.

Dating from the mid 1600s, this pub was formerly known as The Waggon and Horses, and is one of the only pubs in the country with the gantry still standing across the road. Warm and welcoming with an inglenook fireplace and original beams. Newly refurbished restaurant serves homemade food from an extensive and changing menu. Food served 12–3pm and 6–10pm Tues–Fri; 12–10m Sat; 12–6pm Sun. New delicatessen offers continental and locally sourced produce, from Spanish and Italian hams to French cheeses and chocolates. Car park, beer garden. Well-behaved children welcome.

OPEN *12–3pm and 6–11pm Tues–Thurs; 12–3pm and 6pm–12 Fri; 12–12 Sat; 12–7pm Sun.*

BARNET

Moon Under Water

148 High Street, Barnet EN5 5XP
☎ *(020) 8441 9476* Gareth Fleming

Wetherspoon's pub serving Greene King IPA and Abbot plus Shepherd Neame Spitfire plus three guests such as Hop Back Summer Lightning which are changed on a weekly basis.

Olde-worlde town pub with one large bar, a dining area and big beer garden. Food available from 11am–10pm. No children.

OPEN *All day, every day.*

BENINGTON

The Lordship Arms

42 Whempstead Road, Benington, Nr Stevenage SG2 7BX
☎ *(01438) 869665* Alan Marshall

Genuine freehouse with eight real ales. Black Sheep Best Bitter, Fuller's London Pride and Crouch Vale Brewers Gold are permanent fixtures, plus five guest beers. Specialises in ales from small independent and micro-breweries. Also draught cider.

Cosy village freehouse with real fires and a display of telephone memorabilia. Hot and cold bar snacks available 12–2pm Mon–Sat. Home-cooked roast lunches served on Sundays (booking advisable). Curry night on Wednesdays (7–9pm). Car park and large garden. Take the A602 exit off the A1(M), turn left. Signposted Aston, Benington.

OPEN *12–3pm and 6–11pm Mon–Sat; 12–3pm and 7–10.30pm Sun.*

BERKHAMSTED

The Lamb

277 High Street, Berkhamsted HP4 1AJ
☎ *(01442) 862615* Philip Lampey

Tring Ridgeway, Fuller's London Pride, Adnams Bitter and Greene King IPA available.

Traditional two-bar local. Good homemade food served 12–2pm plus regular quiz and curry nights. Patio beer garden.

OPEN *11am–11pm Mon–Sat; 12–10.30pm Sun.*

BISHOP'S STORTFORD

The Half Moon

31 North Street, Bishop's Stortford CM23 2LD
☎ *(01279) 834500* Fiona Davies

Six real ales. Caledonian Deuchars IPA, Fuller's London Pride and Wychwood Hobgoblin are regular fixtures, with three rotating guests changed every week.

A two-bar town pub with snug, function room, courtyard and secluded garden. Sandwiches available at lunchtimes, plus barbecues in summer. On the corner of North Street and the A1250.

OPEN *11am–midnight.*

BUNTINGFORD

The Crown

17 High Street, Buntingford SG9 9AB
☎ *(01763) 271422* Colin Harrington

Genuine freehouse serving three real ales. Everards Tiger and Young's Bitter are always on offer, plus one guest pump.

Two-bar pub in the town centre, a pub since 1630 and with the same landlord since 1989. Patio, garden. No juke box, fruit machines or TV. The real ale comes first, but food is served most of the time, with fish and chips available Thursday and Friday. Function room. Theme nights. In the town centre, just off the bypass.

OPEN *12–3pm and 6–11pm (closed Sun night).*

BUSHEY

Swan

25 Park Road, Bushey WD23 3EE
☎ *(020) 8950 2256*
Peter, Gavin and Marian White

Young's Bitter and Special plus Jennings Cumberland and Wadworth 6X always on offer.

A friendly one-bar local in a residential street, built in 1866 and retaining its traditional character. No fruit machine or juke box, just real fires, a dart board and a piano. Bar snacks served.

OPEN *All day, every day.*

COLNEY HEATH

Crooked Billet

88 High Street, Colney Heath, St Albans AL4 0NP
☎ *(01727) 822128* W Kasprak

Freehouse with Tring Side Pocket for a Toad and three guests, changed daily. Examples include Pot Belly Pigs Do Fly, Church End Vicar's Ruin and York Yorkshire Terrier.

A 200-year-old traditional village pub with quarry-tiled floors and an open fire. Well-established among locals as a popular venue for lunch, and always very busy on Sundays. Homemade food served 12–2pm every day and 6.30–8.30pm Fri. Large garden overlooking open fields, children's play equipment, large car park. From the A1M at Hatfield take the A414 to St Albans. Colney Hatch is signposted at the elongated roundabout, and the pub is 400 yards on the left.

OPEN *11am–2.30pm Mon–Sat; all day Sun.*

FLAMSTEAD

The Spotted Dog

8 High Street, Flamstead, St Albans, AL3 8BS
☎ *(01582) 840984* Des Scarboro

Tring Brock Bitter plus two guests, which might include Adnams Broadside.

C hanged hands in 2006 and revitalised since, already with a reputation for good food. Regular curry (Tuesday) and quiz nights (Mondays).

OPEN *12–3pm and 5pm–12 Mon–Thurs; noon–12.30am Fri–Sun.*

FLAUNDEN

Bricklayers Arms

Hogpits Bottom, Flaunden HP3 0PH
☎ *(01442) 833322* Alvin Michaels
www.bricklayersarms.com

Freehouse serving Fuller's London Pride and Greene King IPA and Old Speckled Hen plus two guests which could include Timothy Taylor Landlord or something from Tring.

O rginally built from local flint and brick in 1722 as two cottages, with another dwelling attached in the early 18th century, this award-winning pub retains its original character with low ceilings, exposed original beams and log fires. A Grade II listed building with a traditional, homely feel. Food, both traditional English and French

fusion, is served 12–2.30pm and 6.30–9.30pm Mon–Sat, 12–4pm and 6.30–8.30pm Sun. Featured in *Michelin Eating Out in Pubs* and in the *Michelin Guide 2009*; awarded *Hertfordshire's Good Pub Guide* 'Dining Pub of the Year 2009' for the second year in a row. Produce sourced and farmed locally. Beer garden and large car park. Hard to find, so take a map!

OPEN *12–11.30pm (11pm Sun).*

GREEN TYE

The Prince of Wales

Green Tye, Much Hadham SG10 6JP
☎ *(01279) 842517* Gary Whelan
www.thepow.co.uk

Home of the Green Tye Brewery, so with beers from the range available plus a guest from an independent brewery.

F ormer McMullen's tied house turned back into a village freehouse in 1991 and run in conjunction with the Green Tye Brewery since 1999. Food served at lunchtimes. Car park and beer garden. Children allowed. Monthly folk club. Beer festivals in May and September.

OPEN *12–3pm and 5.30–11pm Mon–Fri; all day Sat–Sun.*

HARPENDEN

The Carpenter's Arms

14 Cravells Road, Southdown, Harpenden AL5 2JP
☎ *(01582) 460311* John Tibble

Adnams Bitter, Greene King Abbot and another pump featuring a wide range of guests, usually from a local brewery or micro.

B uilt in the early 1800s and leased from Enterprise Inns, the smallest pub in town, but very friendly and named the local CAMRA Pub of the Year for 2005. Full of motoring memorabilia plus a real fire. Run by the same landlord for around 20 years. Food served at lunchtime. Car park. Beer garden. Cricket and golf teams. Just off the A1081.

OPEN *11am–3pm and 5.30–11pm Mon–Sat; 12–3pm and 7–10.30pm Sun.*

Cross Keys

39 High Street, Harpenden AL5 2SD
☎ *(01582) 763989* Mike Artz

Real ale on four pumps, often including Timothy Taylor Landlord, Fuller's London Pride and Rebellion IPA. One of these is regularly rotated.

P ub in a 16th-century listed building, said to be the oldest pub in town, with a pewter bar counter and pump station. Low oak beams, open fires, beer garden. Food served at lunchtime (not Sunday). In Harpenden town centre.

OPEN *All day, every day.*

The Oak Tree

15 Leyton Green, Harpenden AL5 2TG
☎ *(01582) 763850* Margaret Lehmann

Formerly a freehouse, now tied to Wells and Young's so with Charles Wells Bombardier and Eagle IPA available. But still serving four guests, perhaps including Adnams Bitter, Everards Tiger, Marston's Pedigree and St Austell HSD.

Traditional family-run, one-bar town house with real fires, plus seats to the front and beer garden behind. Barbecues. Home-cooked food available 12–3pm. Children allowed at lunchtimes if eating.

OPEN *11am–11pm.*

HERONSGATE

The Land of Liberty, Peace & Plenty

Long Lane, Heronsgate WD3 5BS
☎ *(01923) 282226*
Gill Gibson and Martin Few
www.landoflibertypub.com

Six real ales, with Tring Liberty Ale and Red Squirrel Conservation the regulars, plus four changing whenever the barrel runs out. Breweries featured include Dark Star, York, Buntingford, Mighty Oak, Downton, Hop Back and other micros. Real cider and perry available all year.

Single-bar pub built in the 1820s, traditional in style and decorated with breweriana. Traditional pub food, including regularly changing specials, served 12–2.30pm Mon–Sat Bar snacks available all day. Large garden includes The Pavilion, a large, covered decking area. Large car park. Boules pitch and garden games, including Aunt Sally. Children welcome in the garden, but not in the bar (which is also mobile-free!). Regular beer festivals held, including winter ales, Easter and August bank holiday. CAMRA National Pub of the Year runner-up 2008 and local branch winner four consecutive years. Regular events – see website. From J17 of the M25 take the Heronsgate exit, and the pub is less than a mile away, on the right.

OPEN *11am–11pm (midnight Fri–Sat); 12–11pm Sun.*

HERTFORD

The Black Horse

29–31 West Street, Hertford SG13 8EZ
☎ *(01992) 583630*
Tony Dawes and Linda Howe
www.blackhorseherts.co.uk

Greene King IPA and Abbot plus at least one guest.

Community local with the biggest beer garden in town. Food served at lunchtimes and evenings. Quiz night Sun.

OPEN *12–2pm and 5.30–7.30pm Mon; 5–11pm Tues; 12–2.30pm and 5–11pm Weds–Fri; 12–11pm Sat–Sun.*

Old Cross Tavern

8 St Andrew Street, Hertford SG14 1JA
☎ *(01992) 583133* Nigel Beviss

Freehouse regularly serving Dark Star Hophead, Red Squirrel Gold, Timothy Taylor Landlord plus four changing guests.

This centrally located pub holds beer festivals twice a year. Food served lunchtimes Tues–Sat. Log fire, patio garden.

OPEN *4–11pm Mon; 12–11pm Tues–Sat; 12–10.30pm Sun.*

The White Horse

33 Castle Street, Hertford SG14 1HH
☎ *(01992) 501950* Nigel Crofts
www.castlestreetparty.org.uk

Fuller's Chiswick, London Pride, ESB and Discovery plus Adnams Southwold usually available, plus up to five guest beers from micro-brewers the length and breadth of the country, changing continuously. Spring and autumn beer festivals held, each featuring up to 60 micro-brewery beers.

Classic 15th-century alehouse, renowned for its selection of cask ales, despite being a Fuller's tied pub. Two bars, and a traditional bar billiards room used for functions upstairs. Home-cooked food served 12–2pm Mon–Sat, with roasts on Sunday. Supervised children welcome in the upstairs area. Well-behaved dogs always welcome. Near the castle. Outside seating.

OPEN *12–2.30pm and 5.30–11pm Mon–Thurs; all day Fri–Sun.*

HERTINGFORDBURY

The Prince of Wales

244 Hertingfordbury Road, Hertingfordbury, Hertford SG14 2LG
☎ *(01992) 581149* Louise Evans

Freehouse with three real ales always available.

A one-bar country pub with extension and garden. Food available 12–2pm and 6–9pm Tues–Sat (no food Mondays) and 12–4pm Sun. Accommodation. Children allowed.

OPEN *12–11pm Mon–Thurs; 12–12 Fri–Sat; 12–10.30pm Sun.*

HITCHIN

The Red Lion

Kings Walden Road, Great Offley, Hitchin SG5 3DZ
☎ *(01462) 768281* Jason and Louise Archer

Freehouse serving Young's Bitter and Fuller's London Pride plus two or three guest ales – never the same one twice!

A 17th-century traditional English village pub. Top bar used during sports events and a main bar with a large open fire. Live entertainment every other week. Food served in the conservatory 12–2.15pm and 6.30–9.15pm Mon–Sat and 12–5pm Sun. Five en-suite accommodation rooms. Beer garden with decking areas. Annual beer festival. Situated off the A505 between Hitchin and Luton.

OPEN *12–12 (10.30pm Sun).*

The Sunrunner

24 Bancroft, Hitchin SG4 0NS
☎ *(01462) 440717* Kevin MacNamara

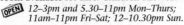 Freehouse with up to nine real ales. Potton Shannon IPA and Fuller's London Pride are regular fixtures. Up to seven guests, changed daily, from a huge range. Also two real ciders.

Town pub in an old building, with lots of character, beams and one large bar. Original wood floors and fireplaces. Food served 12–2.30pm Mon–Thurs and 12–3pm Fri–Sun. Also 7–9pm Tues and Thurs. Private room available for hire. Children allowed.

OPEN *12–3pm and 5.30–11pm Mon–Thurs; 11am–11pm Fri–Sat; 12–10.30pm Sun.*

ICKLEFORD

The Cricketers

107 Arlesey Road, Ickleford, Hitchin SG5 3TH
☎ *(01462) 422766* Mathew Walker

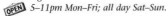 Wells and Young's tied house with four beers usually available. These are likely to be Charles Wells Bombardier and Eagle IPA plus Adnams Best and a guest rotated every two weeks.

A one-bar traditional country pub with wood-burning stove and various nooks and crannies. No food. No children. Accommodation, beer garden, car park, quiz nights (Wednesday) and midsummer music festival. On the high street, at the far end of the village.

OPEN *5–11pm Mon–Fri; all day Sat–Sun.*

The Plume of Feathers

Upper Green, Ickleford, Hitchin SG5 3YD
☎ *(01462) 432729*
TA Thompson and CL Napper

Leased from Enterprise Inns, with six real ales on offer. Adnams Best, Wadworth 6X and Flowers IPA (brewed by Badger) plus three other brews from a constantly changing range.

A 300-year-old open-plan traditional village pub with country pub garden. Traditional homemade food served lunchtimes and evenings. Car park. Beer festival at Whitsun bank holiday. Near the church, good local walks. On the A600 Hitchin to Bedford road.

OPEN *11.30am–3pm and 6–11.30pm Mon–Thurs; 11.30am–midnight Fri–Sat; 12–11pm Sun.*

KIMPTON

The White Horse

22 High Street, Kimpton, Nr Hitchen SG4 8RJ
☎ *(01438) 832307* Peter and Janet Johnson

McMullen AK and Country plus a guest changed every six weeks.

Grade II listed conversion of three cottages dating from the 16th century in the heart of an ancient village. The first was licensed in the 1820s, with an extension to include the rest in 1989. Log fires and a priest hole included. Bar and restaurant food served lunchtimes and evenings (not Monday). Theme nights, private functions. Outside decked area and garden. Car park.

Shaw's Corner and Knebworth House nearby. Between Knebworth and Harpenden.

OPEN *12–3pm and 6–11pm Mon–Sat; 12–4pm and 7–10.30pm Sun.*

OLD KNEBWORTH

The Lytton Arms

Park Lane, Old Knebworth SG3 6QB
☎ *(01438) 812312* Anthony Smith

Up to ten real ales with something from Fuller's, Adnams and Mighty Oak probably among them. The wide-ranging guests change every day. Note also the Belgian beers and malt whiskies.

Traditional English freehouse on the edge of Knebworth Park, built in 1837 and completely refurbished in late 2004. Beamed with open fires. Home-cooked food available 12–2.30pm and 6.30–9.30pm on weekdays, all day Sat and 12–5pm Sun. Large car park, front terrace, rear garden and children's room. Four beer festivals a year. Located halfway between Knebworth and Codicote.

OPEN *11am–11pm Mon–Sat; 12–10.30pm Sun.*

PERRY GREEN

The Hoops

Perry Green, Much Hadham SG10 6EF
☎ *(01279) 843568* Michael O'Connor
www.thehoopsinn.co.uk

Greene King IPA and Young's Special plus a local guest ale, perhaps McMullens AK.

A 17th-century, family-run, one-bar pub in a small hamlet situated close to the Henry Moore Foundation and Sculpture Park and directly opposite Henry Moore's house. Tastefully extended in keeping with the period. Separate dining room. Large garden with outside seating, two patios, barbecue and large car park. Bar and restaurant food available 12–2pm and 6.30–9.30pm Tues–Fri, all day Sat–Sun. Children allowed.

OPEN *12–3pm and 6.30–11pm Mon–Fri; 12–11pm Sat; 12–10.30pm Sun.*

POTTER'S CROUCH

The Holly Bush

Ragged Hall Lane, Potter's Crouch, St Albans AL2 3NN
☎ *(01727) 851792* Ray Taylor
www.thehollybushpub.co.uk

Fuller's Chiswick, London Pride and ESB plus seasonal brews. The licensee is an award-winning Fuller's cellarman and the quality of his beers reflects it.

Spotless pub with a country cottage feel tucked down a back lane between Bedmond and St Albans. One low-beamed bar on two levels with various alcoves and seating areas. Award-winning garden. Simple good value bar food served Mon–Sat 12–2pm; traditional pub favourites served 6–9pm Wed–Sat and 12–2.30pm Sunday (roasts often available). Children welcome in the garden only.

OPEN *12–2.30pm and 6–11pm Mon–Sat; 12–2.30pm and 7–10.30pm Sun.*

PRESTON
The Red Lion
The Green, Preston, Nr Hitchin SG4 7UD
☎ *(01462) 459585* Tim Hunter

Wells and Young's beers served, plus an ever-changing range of four guests, from local independents and micros.

CAMRA-award-winning, 300-year-old village green pub with log fires, named the *Morning Advertiser* Best Village Pub for East Anglia in 2007. The first pub in Britain to be owned by the local community. Food served 12–2pm and 7–9pm (except Tues and Sun). Car park. Large beer garden. Plans to extend the restaurant area.

OPEN *12–3pm and 5.30–11pm Mon–Fri; Sat varies; 12–3pm and 7–10.30pm Sun.*

PUCKERIDGE
Crown & Falcon
33 High Street, Puckeridge, Ware SG11 1RN
☎ *(01920) 821561* Ian and Rachel Norman
www.crown-falcon.demon.co.uk

Freehouse serving Adnams Bitter and McMullens AK plus two guests, changed weekly.

Tudor timber building dating back to 1530. Bar and dining area. Food served 12–2pm and 7–9pm Mon–Wed, 12–2pm and 3.30–9pm Thurs, 12–2pm and 6–9.30pm Fri, 12–2pm and 7–9pm Sat, 12–3pm Sun.

OPEN *11.30am–2.30pm and 5.30–11pm Mon–Fri; 12–3pm and 6.30–11pm Sat; 12–4.30pm and 4–11pm Sun.*

REDBOURN
The Hollybush
Church End, Redbourn, St Albans AL3 7DU
☎ *(01582) 792423* Bernadette Laventure

Adnams Bitter, Brakspear Bitter and Special plus a rotating guest, perhaps from a local (Tring or Vale) brewery.

Operating since 1696 in a pretty street, this former freehouse is now owned by Brakspear. Open fires and exposed beams. Food available at lunchtime. Hall available for private functions and folk club on Thursdays. Garden. Car park.

OPEN *11am–2.30pm and 5.30–11pm Mon–Fri; 12–3pm and 7–11pm Sat–Sun.*

REED
The Cabinet
High Street, Reed, Nr Royston SG8 8AH
☎ *(01463) 848366*
www.thecabinetatreed.co.uk

Cabinet Bitter plus up to three guests, always changing but often including something from Nethergate.

A 16th-century weatherboarded pub with two rooms. Bar and restaurant food served lunchtimes and evenings. Children's room. Large garden. A watering hole for 500 years. On A10 south of Royston.

OPEN *12–3pm and 6–11pm (10pm Sun).*

ROYSTON
The White Bear
49 Kneesworth Street, Royston SG8 5AQ
☎ *(01763) 242458* Shirley Smeeton

Freehouse serving City of Cambridge Hobson's Choice, Greene King IPA and Charles Wells Bombadier plus three weekly-changing guests.

Town-centre pub dating back to the 1800s, with a wide range of customers of all ages. Food served 11am–3pm and 6–9pm. Front and rear beer gardens. Car park. Accommodation available. All welcome.

OPEN *11am–midnight.*

ST ALBANS
The Blacksmith's Arms
56 St Peter's Street, St Albans AL1 3HG
☎ *(01727) 855761* Sue and Noel Keane

Six real ales (over 250 a year), with Wadworth 6X and Timothy Taylor Landlord regularly served, plus a wide variety of guests from around the country. The only supplier of City of Cambridge beer in St Albans. Regular Beer of the Month feature, and free tasters on all products. Six Belgian beers also stocked.

A Hogshead pub with one bar. Food served 12–9pm Mon–Thurs, 12–7pm Fri–Sun. Background music. Large garden – children welcome in garden until 5.30pm. Located on the main road.

OPEN *11am–11pm Mon–Sat; 12–10.30pm Sun.*

The Boot Inn
4 Market Place, St Albans AL3 5DG
☎ *(01727) 857533* Will Hughes

Leased from Punch Taverns, serving Black Sheep Bitter and a Wells and Young's brew plus five constantly changing guest ales.

Built around 1450, this one-bar market pub is situated beside the standalone clock tower in the town centre. Food served at lunchtimes. Car parks nearby in shopping centre. Near St Albans Abbey.

OPEN *11am–midnight Mon–Thurs; 11am–1am Fri–Sat; 12–11.30pm Sun.*

The Duke of Marlborough
110 Holywell Hill, St Albans AL1 1DH
☎ *(01727) 858982* Mr Tossoun

Greene King Old Speckled Hen and Fuller's London Pride plus a guest.

Two-bar pub dating from 1875, decorated in a sports and theatre theme. Food served 12–6pm Mon–Fri plus Sun roasts. Beer garden, covered patio, car park. Children welcome. Next to Verulamium Park and Town. The first pub at the bottom of Holywell Hill.

OPEN *12–11pm (10.30pm Sun).*

The Farmer's Boy

134 London Road, St Albans AL1 1PQ
☎ *(01727) 800029* Heidi Bancroft

Home of the Verulam Brewery since 1996, so with Farmer's Joy and Clipper always on offer, plus Timothy Taylor Landlord, Fuller's London Pride and guests from local and national brewers. Bottled Belgian beers also stocked.

A friendly one-bar town brewpub, around 200 years old with low ceilings. Refurbished, but retaining its character. Home-cooked, traditional food served 12–3pm every day and 6–8pm Mon–Fri. Lovely garden, featuring morris dancers in summer, and regular live music. Five minutes from centre of town, ten minutes from station.

OPEN *11am–11pm Mon–Sat; 12–10.30pm Sun.*

The Garibaldi

61 Albert Street, St Albans AL1 1RT
☎ *(01727) 855046* P Day

Fuller's pub with four real ales plus one rotating guest, changed every two weeks.

B ackstreet Victorian local with homemade pub food available at lunchtime and Thai food in the evenings. Beer garden. Down Holywell Hill from the town centre, close to the cathedral.

OPEN *12–11pm (10.30pm Sun).*

The Lower Red Lion

34–6 Fishpool Street, St Albans AL3 4RX
☎ *(01727) 855669*
Chris Adkins and Kevin Yelland
www.lowerredlion.com

Genuine freehouse with up to eight real ales. Fuller's London Pride and Oakham JHB are consistent fixtures, plus six guests (at least 750 per year) from all over the country. Beer festivals held on average every six weeks (check website for dates). One of the landlords brews the beers at the Verulam Brewery, under the name 'Alehouse'.

T wo-bar traditional coaching house dating from the 17th century in the conservation area of St Albans close to the abbey and Roman Verulamium. A wide-ranging clientele. No music or games machines. Home-cooked food is available 12–2pm Mon–Fri and 12–3pm Sunday. Car park, function room and garden. Accommodation. No children.

OPEN *12–2.30pm and 5.30–11pm Mon–Fri; 12–11pm Sat; 12–10.30pm Sun.*

The Mermaid

98 Hatfield Road, St Albans AL1 3RL
☎ *(01727) 837758* Graham Varney

Former Everards pub, with up to five real ales. Everards Tiger and Adnams Bitter are regularly served, plus three guests, changed weekly.

L ively one-bar locals' pub in a Victorian building, with darts, crib and domino teams, two football teams and a backgammon club. Food served 12–2pm Mon–Fri. Sky Sports. Patio garden. On the main road, close to St Albans town centre.

OPEN *All day Mon–Sat; 12–7pm Sun.*

The Plough

Tyttenhanger Green, Nr St Albans AL4 0RW
☎ *(01727) 857777* Mike Barrowman

Up to seven real ales on offer from various breweries, with up to five rotating frequently.

P opular country freehouse in a rural setting on the outskirts of St Albans housed in a building 100 years old that was once the village bakery. Bar food available at lunchtime only (12–2pm). Real fires. Car park, front terrace and beer garden. Family room.

OPEN *11.30am–2.30pm and 6–11pm Mon–Sat; 12–3pm and 7–10.30pm Sun and bank holidays.*

The Rose & Crown

St Michael's Street, St Albans AL3 4SG
☎ *(01727) 851903* Ruth Courtney

Adnams Bitter, Fuller's London Pride, Shepherd Neame Spitfire and Greene King IPA plus a guest, perhaps from Black Sheep or Timothy Taylor.

A 16th-century pub in the same part of town as The Lower Red Lion. Beams and open fires. Food (especially speciality sandwiches) served at lunchtime, plus Mon–Sat evenings; roasts served Sunday lunchtime. Live music every Monday evening and folk music every Thursday evening. Family room. Garden.

OPEN *11.30am–3pm and 5.30–11pm Mon–Fri (all day in summer); all day Sat–Sun.*

White Hart Tap

4 Keyfield Terrace, St Albans AL1 1QJ
☎ *(01727) 860974* Stephen McConnell
www.whitetharttap.co.uk

Caledonian Deuchars IPA, Fuller's London Pride and two guest beers, which change on a weekly basis.

O ne-bar local with large garden. Food served at lunchtimes and evenings. Live music first Saturday of the month.

OPEN *12–11pm.*

The White Lion

91 Sopwell Lane, St Albans AL1 1RN
☎ *(01727) 850540* David Worcester
www.thewhitelionph.co.uk

Owned by Punch Taverns with Fuller's London Pride, Black Sheep Bitter and four rotating guests changed at the end of every barrel.

A nother fine 16th-century St Albans pub, this one located just off Holywell Hill. Two bars. Large, attractive garden with children's play area. Summer barbecues. Food served 12–2pm (3pm at weekends) and 6–8.30pm. Live music on Tuesdays and Fridays. A beer festival is held over the August bank holiday.

OPEN *12–2.30pm and 5.30–11pm Mon–Fri; 12–11pm Sat; 12–10.30pm Sun.*

ST LEONARDS
The White Lion
Jenkins Lane, St Leonards, Nr Tring HP23 6NW
☎ *(01494) 758387* Michelle Stratton

Punch pub serving Greene King IPA and three guests changed weekly.

Approximately 500 years old, this pub has one bar with separate smaller rooms and a restaurant. Food served 12–2.30pm and 6–9pm Sat, 12–2.30pm Sun. Small function room for hire. Children welcome. Beer festival held every May. Large scenic gardens with children's play equipment. Car park, lifeboat and resident ghost, 'Mrs Bishop'! Located near Chesham and Tring.

OPEN *11.30am–midnight Mon–Sat; 12–10.30pm Sun.*

ST PAUL'S WALDEN
The Strathmore Arms
London Road, St Paul's Walden, Nr Hitchin SG4 8BT
☎ *(01438) 871654* Danny Blackwell

Five real ales are usually available, with Fuller's London Pride and Buntingford Golden Plover the permanent fixtures, plus three guests, changed after each barrel. More than 2,100 different beers served in five years. Cider and perry also served.

Built in 1858, on the Bowes-Lyon family estate, CAMRA's Hertfordshire Pub of the Year 2004. One bar, a beer garden and good food served 12–2pm Tues–Thurs; 12–2pm and 6–9pm Fri–Sat. Children welcome. Three beer festivals a year. Car park. On the B651.

OPEN *6–11pm Mon; 12–2.30pm and 5–11pm Tues–Thurs; all day Fri–Sun.*

SANDRIDGE
The Green Man
High Street, Sandridge AL4 0NS
☎ *(01727) 854845* Michael and Lesley Eames

A range including Adnams Bitter, something from Greene King and Bateman XXXB. Plus two guests changed every three weeks and served straight from the cask.

Solid red-brick pub built in the 1880s and formerly owned by Benskins. Food served at lunchtimes and Friday and Saturday evenings. Family room. Garden. Car park. Good walking and cycling. In the centre of the village.

OPEN *11am–3pm and 5.30–11pm Mon–Thurs; 11am–11pm Fri–Sat; 12–10.30pm Sun.*

SAWBRIDGEWORTH
The Gate
81 London Road, Sawbridgeworth CM21 9JJ
☎ *(01279) 722313* Tommy Barnett, Gary Barnett and Tracy Barnett
www.the-gate-pub.co.uk

Enterprise Inns pub with eight real ales, offering Timothy Taylor Landlord, Harveys Sussex Bitter, Rebellion IPA and Woodforde's Wherry, plus guests changed daily. Examples include Fuller's ESB, Young's Special, Caledonian Deuchars IPA and beers from the Northumberland brewery. The Sawbridgeworth brewery is on site, and the whole range is available. Well over 6,000 beers served in ten years.

A traditional pub with two bars, with a focus on darts and all sports. Over 2,000 pump clips decorate the beams. Food available 12–2pm. Regular beer festivals, including a big one at the August bank holiday weekend (over 100 beers). Small car park for 20/25 cars. Outside seating. Between Harrow and Bishop Stortford.

OPEN *11.30am–2.30pm and 5.30–10.45pm Mon–Thur; all day Fri–Sun.*

STAPLEFORD
Papillon at the Woodhall Arms
17 High Road, Stapleford SG14 3NW
☎ *(01992) 535123* Phil Gonzalez
www.papillon-woodhallarms.co.uk

Four real ales from Adnams, Wells and Young's, Greene King, Everards, Eccleshall, Cottage and Nethergate. Guests are changed regularly.

Food-oriented English/continental pub/restaurant. The restaurant and conservatory each seat 50 people, and there is an extra restaurant seating 25, plus a party room for 10. Food available 12–2pm and 6.30–10.30pm Mon–Sat, 12–2.30pm and 6.30–9.30pm Sun. Beer garden. Children allowed. Accommodation available in 10 letting rooms. Car park for 50 cars. On the A119 between Hertford and Stevenage.

OPEN *11am–3pm and 5–11pm Mon–Sat; 12–4pm and 7–10.30pm Sun.*

STEVENAGE
Our Mutual Friend
Broadwater Crescent, Stevenage SG2 8EH
☎ *(01438) 312282* Keith Neville

Seven real ales usually available from independent and micro-brewers. Caledonian Deuchars IPA is a permanent feature, and the guests, changed when they run out, usually include a mild or a stout. Cider and perry also served.

Comfortable, friendly, 44-year-old two-bar pub, named after the Dickens novel. Pool, darts and various pub games. North Herts CAMRA Pub of the Year 2006 and 2007. Food served 12–1.30pm. Live bands, beer festival in January. Patio, car park. Close to Stevenage football ground. No under-18s. Off the A602 next to the Esso Station.

OPEN *12–11pm Mon–Thurs; 12–11.30pm Fri–Sat; 12–3pm and 8–11pm Sun.*

TONWELL

The Robin Hood & Little John

14 Ware Road, Tonwell SG12 0HN
☎ *(01920) 463352* Mr J Harding

 Freehouse with up to four beers, Greene King IPA as a permanent offering, plus three changing every fortnight or so.

A 300-year-old, traditional village pub with beams and open fire, two miles from Hertford. One bar on split levels and restaurant. B&B in eight twin rooms (five of them en-suite). Food available 12–2pm and 6.30–9pm.

OPEN *12–3pm and 5.30–11pm Mon–Sat; 12–3pm and 7–10.30pm Sun.*

TRING

The King's Arms

King Street, Tring HP23 6BE
☎ *(01442) 823318*
John Francis, Thomas and Victoria North

 Freehouse with five real ales. Wadworth 6X is a permanent fixture plus guests from a wide-ranging list of smaller breweries including local Tring ales.

T raditional town pub built in the 1830s with distinctive Regency architecture and a covered and heated beer garden. Real fires. Home-cooked food available at lunchtimes and evenings. No machines, music or television but darts and traditional pub games and free Wi-Fi access. Children allowed. Local CAMRA Pub of the Year 2003–2006.

OPEN *12–2.30pm and 7–11pm Mon–Thurs; 12–3pm and 7–11pm Fri; 11.30am–3pm and 7–11pm Sat; 12–4pm and 7–10.30pm Sun.*

Robin Hood

1 Brook Street, Tring HP23 5ED
☎ *(01442) 824912*
Terry Johnson and Stewart Canham
www.therobinhoodtring.co.uk

 Fuller's Chiswick, London Pride, ESB and Discovery plus a guest ale.

A nother Hertfordshire pub run by a Fuller's master cellarman (see also The Holly Bush, Potter's Crouch). Once a street-corner cottage, with low beams and real fires. Local CAMRA Pub of the Year 2008. Food (especially fish) served at lunchtime and evenings (not Sunday evening). Conservatory and flower-filled courtyard with heating.

OPEN *11.30am–3pm and 5.30–11pm Mon–Fri; 12–4pm and 6.30–11pm Sat; 12–4pm and 7–11pm Sun.*

WARESIDE

Chequers Inn

Wareside, Nr Ware SG12 7QY
☎ *(01920) 467010* Douglas Cook

 Freehouse with Adnams Best and Broadside plus up to four regularly changing guests such as Archers Dark Mild, Young's Special or Greene King IPA. All beers are served straight from the cask racked behind the bar.

A tiny village pub with parts of the building dating from the 13th century and parts from the 17th century. Three bars, wooden beams and two open fires. Food available at lunchtimes and evenings (not Sunday) in a 40-seater restaurant. Bench seating outside, hog roast on bank holidays. Live band on Sundays. Children allowed. Just outside Ware. Accommodation.

OPEN *12–3pm and 6–11pm Mon–Sat; all day Sun.*

WATFORD

The Southern Cross

41–3 Langley Road, Watford WD17 4PP
☎ *(01923) 256033* John Ross and Joan Bayliss

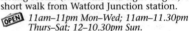 Caledonian Deuchars IPA, Charles Wells Bombardier, Theakston Mild and up to three guest ales.

O nce a hotel, now a large, suburban inn on the main road with large drinking area and central bar. Food served daily until 9pm. Quiz nights three times a week. Ten letting rooms (two twins and eight singles). A short walk from Watford Junction station.

OPEN *11am–11pm Mon–Wed; 11am–11.30pm Thurs–Sat; 12–10.30pm Sun.*

WESTON

The Cricketers

Damask Green Road, Weston SG4 7DA
☎ *(01462) 790273* Tony Szpak
www.rhubarb-inns.co.uk

 Three real ales usually available. Fuller's London Pride, Greene King IPA and a weekly guest ale comprise a typical trio.

P reviously called The Thatched House, now owned by Rhubarb Inns, a two-bar Victorian-style freehouse in a village near Baldock. Large garden including petanque pitch and children's play area. Home-cooked food, including fresh fish daily, served at lunchtimes and evenings Tues–Sat plus Sunday lunchtime. Car park. Near junction 9 on the A1(M).

OPEN *12–2.30pm and 5.30–11pm Mon–Fri; all day Sat–Sun.*

WHITWELL
The Maiden's Head
67 High Street, Whitwell, Nr Hitchin SG4 8AH
☎ *(01438) 871392* Mike Jones

McMullen tied house with AK Original and Country Best available plus two guests, changed monthly.

An unspoilt, two-bar village pub in a 17th-century timbered building with an open fire. Large rear garden. Licensees in place since the early 1980s. Darts, dominoes and good banter. Food available 12–2pm Mon–Sat and 6.30–9pm Wed–Sat. No children. Near a rare breeds farm with tea shop, local watercress beds and a maze of footpaths! Close to the Bowes-Lyon estate, the late Queen Mother's ancestral home, and handy for Luton Airport and the market town of Hitchin. Between Stevenage and Luton. On the B656 Hitchen to Codicote road.

OPEN 12–3pm and 5–11pm Mon–Fri; 12–4pm and 6–11pm Sat; 12–4pm and 7–10.30pm Sun.

WIDFORD
The Green Man
High Street, Widford, Ware SG12 8SR
☎ *(01279) 842846* Linda and Melvyn James

Adnams Bitter and McMullen AK are the regular beers at this freehouse plus a guest, changed every week, perhaps from Green Tye, Moor or Mighty Oak.

Traditional pub with one large bar and a lounge/dining area. Darts, pool, beer garden. Food served until 8pm Mon–Sat, 12–6pm Sun. Children welcome. Large car park. Accommodation available. Easy to find on the main road from Bishop's Stortford to Ware (B1004).

OPEN 12–3pm and 5.30–11pm Mon–Thurs; 12–11pm Fri–Sat; 12–10.30pm Sun.

WILD HILL
The Woodman
45 Wildhill Lane, Wild Hill, Hatfield AL9 6EA
☎ *(01707) 642618* Graham Craig

McMullen ales, Greene King Abbot and IPA plus three guests from independent and micro-breweries such as Rooster's, Hampshire, Mighty Oak or York.

A popular country village pub with garden. Sandwiches available at lunchtime (no food on Sundays or bank holidays). No children. Car park.

OPEN 11.30am–2.30pm and 5.30–11pm Mon–Sat; 12–2.30pm and 7–10.30pm Sun.

WILLIAN
The Fox Inn
Baldock Lane, Willian, Letchworth SG6 2AE
☎ *(01462) 480233* Cliff Nye
www.foxatwillian.co.uk

Freehouse serving Fuller's London Pride, Adnams Best Bitter, Woodforde's Wherry plus one guest ale changed every barrel. Winner of Best Cask Beer Pub 2009 (South East) award.

One bar with adjacent restaurant, this old pub was refurbished in 2005 and is now under new ownership. AA Rosette-awarded restaurant. Food served daily 12–2pm in the bar and restaurant, 6.45–9.15pm in the restaurant only. Car parking available. Plasma screen TV for live sports. Beer garden. Popular walking trails nearby.

OPEN 12–12 (11pm Sun).

THE BREWERIES

THE MOUNT MURRAY BREWING CO. LTD

Bushys Brewery, Braddan IM4 1JE
☎ *(01624) 661244*
www.bushys.com

CASTLETOWN BITTER 3.5% ABV
Golden and floral.
RUBY MILD 3.5% ABV
Red and well balanced.
BUSHY'S BITTER 3.8% ABV
Fresh, clean, hoppy.
SUMMER ALE 3.8% ABV
Lager style.
CELTIBRATION 4.0% ABV
Refreshing hoppy bitter.
MANANNAN'S CLOAK 4.0% ABV
Smooth and creamy.
SHUTTLEWORTH SNAP 4.0% ABV
Refreshing.
OYSTER STOUT 4.2% ABV
Made with oysters.
CLASSIC 4.3% ABV
Full fruit, rich ruby ale.
OLD BUSHY TAIL 4.5% ABV
Reddish brown with treacle tones.
PISTON BREW 4.5% ABV
Ruby with hints of toffee.
LOVELY JUBBLY 5.2% ABV
Sweet and malty.
The Manx Collection and specials also available.

OKELL & SONS LTD

Falcon Brewery, Kewaigue, Douglas IM2 1QG
☎ *(01624) 661120*
www.okells.co.uk

MILD 3.4% ABV
Hint of oranges.
BITTER 3.7% ABV
Gold, hoppy, dry finish.
SMOOTH 3.7% ABV
Hoppy, full malt flavour.
CASTLETOWN ALE 4.0% ABV
Dry, citrus bitter.
MACLIR 4.4% ABV
Light wheat beer.
DR OKELL'S IPA 4.5% ABV
Spicy, lemon notes.
OKELL'S AILE 4.8% ABV
Liquorice- and coffee-flavoured porter.
Plus seasonal brews including:
SUMMER STORM 4.2% ABV
Hints of vanilla.
ST NICK 4.5% ABV
Dark and fruity.

OLD LAXEY BREWING CO. LTD

Shore Hotel, Old Laxey Hill, Laxey IM4 7DA
☎ *(01624) 861509*

BOSUN BITTER 3.8% ABV

THE PUBS

BALLAUGH

The Raven Inn

Main Road, Ballaugh IM7 5EG
☎ *(01624) 896128* Alan Carr

Three real ales, generally from Okells, plus a guest ale changed weekly.

Small, friendly former coaching inn built in 1780 next to Ballaugh Bridge on the TT course. English and Thai food served 12–2.30pm every day and 6–8.30pm Mon–Sat. One main bar, outside drinking area. Children welcome. Car park.

OPEN *12–11pm Sun–Thurs; 12–12 Fri–Sat.*

CASTLETOWN

The Sidings

Station Road, Castletown IM9 1EF
☎ *(01624) 823282* David Quayle

 Up to ten real ales. Regular fixtures should include Bushy's Castletown Bitter, Bitter and Ruby Mild plus Robinson's Old Stockport and Unicorn. Guests might be from Moorehouses, Hook Norton, Hydes, Thwaites, Robinsons, York, Black Sheep, Bradfield or other breweries.

Welcoming, traditional, beer-orientated pub which was once the railway station and is now situated alongside it. Church pews and coal fires. Chip-fat-free atmosphere! Food served 12–2pm Mon–Sat. Car park. Beer garden. Children welcome at lunchtime only. Annual beer festival in Tynwald Week, with over 50 real ales.

OPEN *11.30am–11pm Sun–Thurs; 11.30am–midnight Fri–Sat.*

DOUGLAS

The Albert Hotel

3 Chapel Row, Douglas IM1 2BJ
☎ *(01624) 673632* Harry Creevy

Freehouse serving Okells Mild, Bitter and Jough Manx Ale (the house bitter) plus a rotating guest.

Town-centre, popular working man's local next to the bus terminal and close to the quay. No food. No children. Cask Marque approved.

OPEN *10am–11pm Mon–Thurs; 10am–midnight Fri–Sat; 12–11pm Sun.*

Old Market Inn

Chapel Row, Douglas IM1 2BJ
☎ *(01624) 675202* Breda Watters

 Okells Bitter regularly served, with something from Theakston often available as well.

A friendly atmosphere is to be found in this small, 17th-century backstreet tavern with open fire, popular with all ages. No food. Children welcome. On North Quay at the end of Strand Street.

OPEN *9am–midnight.*

Saddle Inn

Queen Street, Douglas IM1 1LH
☎ *(01624) 673161* Bob Fenner
Okells Bitter and Mild.

Friendly one-bar 17th-century coaching tavern, a proper old pub, where they don't stand on ceremony! Limited bar snacks and baps. Pool table, darts, Sky TV. Lots of TT memorabilia on display. Popular with bitter drinkers. Situated on the quayside.

OPEN *11.30am–11pm Sun–Wed;*
11.30am–midnight Thurs–Sat.
Open later during TT Races.

LAXEY

Queens Hotel

New Road, Laxey
☎ *(01624) 861195* James Robert Hamer
Freehouse offering Bushy's Ruby Mild and Export plus three guest beers.

Friendly village pub with single, open-plan bar and pool area. Large beer garden and adjacent to the electric railway. Live music some Saturday nights. The Laxey wheel is nearby. Toasted sandwiches available. Car park. B&B accommodation available all year.

OPEN *12–11pm Sun–Thurs; 12–12 Fri–Sat.*

The Shore Hotel

Old Laxey, Laxey IM4 7DA
☎ *(01624) 861509* Trevor Latus
www.shorehotel.im
A brewpub, home of the Old Laxey Brewing Company, so with Bosun Bitter always on offer. Largest selection of single malt whisky on the island, with over 130 Scotch and Irish whiskies on sale.

Friendly 18th-century village pub with river frontage close to the harbour and beach, featuring nautical charts and oil paintings of steam drifters. Food served in the bar or the large riverside beer garden 12–2pm and 6–8pm Mon–Sat and 12–4pm Sun. Annual blues festival, with live acoustic music most Sat evenings. Free wi-fi access. Large car park. Midway between Douglas and Ramsey, follow signs to Laxey Harbour.

OPEN *12–12.*

PEEL

The White House

2 Tynwald Road, Peel IM5 1LA
☎ *(01624) 842252* Jamie Keig
Freehouse with up to nine real ales. Okells Mild and Bitter, Bushy's Bitter, Flowers Original (brewed by Badger) and Timothy Taylor Landlord plus up to four guests from all over the country.

A traditional family-run pub unaltered since the 1930s with one central servery and four small adjoining rooms. CAMRA listed and Cask Marque approved. Live Manx music most Saturday nights. TV. Light bar snacks served in the bar area. Children allowed until 9pm. Beer garden, pool and function room, car park, TV and pub games. At the other end of Atholl Street from the bus station.

OPEN *11am–midnight.*

PORT ST MARY

Albert Hotel

Athol Street, Port St Mary IM9 5DS
☎ *(01624) 832118* Pat O'Meara
Serves Bushy's Bitter, Bushy's Old Bushy Tail, Okells Bitter and one rotating guest, changed every couple of weeks.

A traditional pub, approximately 100 years old, with one lounge bar and one public bar. Two open fires, friendly atmosphere. Lovely sea views from both bars. Food served 12–2pm Mon–Sat (also 6–9pm Sat), toasties available all day. Three en-suite rooms available for letting. Beer garden, private room available (30–40 people). Near Port St Mary harbour.

OPEN *11am–midnight Sun–Thurs; 11am–2am Fri–Sat.*

RAMSEY

Ellan Vannin

Market Square, West Ramsey IM8 1JU
☎ *(01624) 812131* Mark Antony Williams
Freehouse serving Bushy's Bitter and Castletown plus two guest ales, changed weekly.

A true locals' pub renowned for its real ales. No food.

OPEN *12–12 Mon–Thurs; noon–1am Fri–Sun.*

The Stanley Hotel

West Quay, Ramsey IM8 1DW
☎ *(01624) 812258* Colin Clarke
Okells Bitter and a guest, changed on a weekly basis.

A small pub close to the harbour, by the swing bridge. No food, no children.

OPEN *12–11pm Sun–Thurs; 12–12 Fri–Sat.*

The Trafalgar Hotel

West Quay, Ramsey IM8 1DW
☎ *(01624) 814601* James Kneen
Freehouse serving Black Sheep Bitter, Okells Bitter and Moorhouse's Black Cat Mild plus one guest beer, constantly changing. Examples of guests include Shepherd Neame Spitfire, a Flowers brew (from Badger) or something from Wychwood.

Small, friendly, traditional quayside pub dating from 1870, known for its character, well-kept ales and realistic prices! No machines or other gimmicks. Cask Marque approved. No food. Private room available. Darts, TV. Not far from the swing bridge.

OPEN *11am–11pm Mon–Thurs;*
11am–12.30am Fri–Sat;
11.30am–3.30pm and 8–11pm Sun.

SULBY

The Sulby Glen Hotel

Sulby Crossroads, Sulby, Nr Ramsey IM7 2HR
☎ *(01624) 897240*
Rosemary and Eddie Christian
www.sulbyglenhotel.net

 Genuine freehouse serving Bushy's Traditional, Okells Bitter, Bushy's Ruby Mild plus one guest ale, rotated every second barrel.

This traditional country inn has three bars and a separate dining room. Open fire. Occasional evening entertainment. Eleven en-suite rooms available for letting. Beer patio, private room available for hire, car park. Beer festival. Children welcome. Near the wildlife park, shopping centre, race circuit and golf course. Follow the signs from Douglas to Ramsey along the A18, then take the A3 to Peel; the pub is four miles down there on the main road. Or take the A1 towards Peel followed by the A3 to Ramsey – it is halfway on the way to Ramsey.

OPEN *12–12.*

THE BREWERIES

GODDARDS BREWERY

Barnsley Farm, Bullen Road, Ryde PO33 1QF
☎ *(01983) 611011*
www.goddards-brewery.co.uk

SPECIAL BITTER 4.0% ABV
Well balanced with good hoppiness.
FUGGLE DEE DUM 4.8% ABV
Golden, full bodied and spicily aromatic.
Seasonals:
ALE OF WIGHT 4.0% ABV
Pale, refreshing and fruity. May–June.
DUCK'S FOLLY 5.2% ABV
Light colour, strong and hoppy. September.
INSPIRATION 5.2% ABV
Floral and exotic. March–April.
WINTER WARMER 5.2% ABV
Dark and smooth. November–February.

YATES' BREWERY

The Inn at St Lawrence, St Lawrence, Ventnor PO38 1XG
☎ *(01983) 731731*
www.yates-brewery.co.uk

UNDERCLIFFE EXPERIENCE 4.1% ABV
Amber with clean citrus notes.
YATES BLONDE 4.5% ABV
Dry and fruity.
HOLY JOE 4.9% ABV
Malty bitter with a distinct tang.
WIGHT WINTER/ST LAWRENCE ALE 5.0% ABV
Ruby, malty and chocolatey.
YATES SPECIAL BITTER 5.5% ABV
Gold with tart, fruit notes.

THE PUBS

ARRETON

The Dairyman's Daughter

Main Road, Arreton PO30 3AA
☎ *(01983) 539361* Lee Hext
www.arretonbarns.co.uk

Up to eight real ales, including brews from Ventnor, Goddards, Yates of St Lawrence, Ringwood and further afield.

Traditional, beamed pub located in a craft village, with a host of agricultural memorabilia. Large sheltered terrace, live traditional music most nights, beer and brewery shop. Top-quality hot and cold food served all day. Car park. The village features glass-blowing, woodworking, ceramic crafts, a Saxon church, an ancient carp pond and the Maritime and Lifeboat Experience. On the main Newport to Sandown road.

OPEN *10.30am–11pm.*

The White Lion

Main Road, Arreton, Newport PO30 3AA
☎ *(01983) 528479* Katie Cole
www.white-lion-arreton.com

Leased from Enterprise Inns serving Fuller's London Pride, Badger First Gold and Timothy Taylor Landlord.

A 300-year-old coaching inn in a picturesque country village. One bar, two restaurants, family room. Patio has views of the village. Delicious home-cooked food served 12–9pm every day. Function room available, small car park (with more parking opposite the pub), children under 14 welcome in family room. On the main Newport to Sandown road (A3056).

OPEN *11am–11pm Mon–Sat; 12–10.30pm Sun.*

BEMBRIDGE

The Crab & Lobster

32 Forelands Field Road, Bembridge PO35 5TR
☎ *(01983) 872244* Richard and Adrian Allan
www.crabandlobsterinn.co.uk

Greene King IPA and Goddards Fuggle Dee Dum plus Flowers Original (brewed by Badger).

Family pub and restaurant overlooking the Bembridge Ledge, with outstanding sea views. Large lounge area, bar and à la carte restaurant featuring locally caught seafood, available all year round (12–2.30pm and 6–11pm). Children and dogs welcome. Car park. Five en-suite rooms available.

OPEN *11am–11pm Mon–Sat; 12–10.30pm Sun.*

The Windmill Inn

1 Steyne Road, Bembridge PO35 5UH
☎ *(01983) 872875* Martin Bullock

 Genuine freehouse with ales from Goddards and Ventnor Breweries, plus a rotating guest changed monthly.

A large detached freehouse offering delightful dining as well as cosy corners for those just wanting a quiet drink. Food served 12–9pm daily. Accommodation is available in the form of 14 rooms and 7 self-catering cottages, all of a high standard. Large car park. Near to beach and harbour. Located in the middle of Bembridge village, East Wight.

OPEN *All day, every day.*

BRADING

The Yarbridge Inn

Yarbridge, Brading PO36 0AA
☎ *(01983) 406212* Paul Jenner

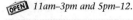 Freehouse serving Ringwood Best plus seven rotating guests, changed very regularly. In four years they have had over 1300 different guest ales. Tend to use very small micro-breweries so always have a unique range.

B uilt in the early 1800s, the main feature of this traditional pub is its railway theme. One main bar. Food served 12–2.15pm and 5–8.15pm daily (but not on Mondays during winter). Beer patio. Children welcome. Annual beer festival. Car park. Situated on the main road between Brading and Sandown, a five minute walk from Brading station.

OPEN *11am–3pm and 5pm–12.*

BRIGHSTONE

The Countryman

Limerstone Road, Brighstone PO30 4AE
☎ *(01983) 740616* Karen and Russ O'Keefe

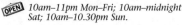 Ringwood Best and Fortyniner plus Marston's Pedigree are among the beers usually available. A guest ale is regularly rotated, and Old Rosie cider is also served.

S ituated in a countryside setting in the south-west of the island, this pub with character bar, restaurant and snug was built in the 1930s and has panoramic views of the coast and sea from the beer garden. Well-known locally for food which is available 12–3pm in winter, 12–9pm in summer. Car park. Children welcome. Large function room with its own bar and magnificent views. Festivals are encouraged. Handy for beaches and dinosaur park, two miles from Brightstone village, about 400 yards along Shorewell Road.

OPEN *10am–11pm Mon–Fri; 10am–midnight Sat; 10am–10.30pm Sun.*

CALBOURNE

The Blacksmith's Arms

Calbourne Road, Calbourne, Newport PO30 5SS
☎ *(01983) 529263* Simon Willis

Four real ales, including Badger Best, Tanglefoot and Gribble Fursty Ferret, plus a rotating guest ale.

C ountryside pub with restaurant and panoramic views of the island and the Solent. Nearly 400 years old and reportedly haunted. Log fires and flagstones. Large garden. Food available (locally caught seafood) all day, every day. Children welcome (there is a play area). On the main Newport to Calbourne road beside a footpath that forms part of the Tennyson Trail.

OPEN *All day, every day.*

The Sun Inn

Sun Hill, Calbourne PO30 4JA
☎ *(01983) 531231* S Mobley

An Enterprise Inns pub. One or two real ales in winter, two or three in summer. The range changes constantly and often contains local ales such as Goddards Fuggle de Dum and Ventnor Pistol Night.

A pproximately 105 years old and a traditional village pub. Two bars, restaurant, large car park and beer garden. Food served 12–9pm (8pm winter). Well-behaved children and dogs welcome. Situated at a crossroads in the centre of Calbourne, near Winkle Street.

OPEN *Summer: 11am–11pm. Winter: 11am–10.30pm.*

CHALE

The Wight Mouse Inn

Church Place, Newport Road, Chale PO38 2HA
☎ *(01983) 730431*
Tony Russell and Shirley Amner
www.innforanight.co.uk

Wide range of cask ales, including Badger First Gold and Tanglefoot plus limited edition seasonal ales.

A 17th-century coaching house of immense charm and character. It was a favourite haunt of European royalty, society and literary figures in the heyday of the island as a holiday venue for the smart set. Food served all day. The restaurant has a children's play area, outdoor eating and excellent disabled facilities. Car park for more than 150. Accommodation in ten rooms with views of either the coastline or St Catherine's Down.

OPEN *11am–11pm.*

COWES

The Anchor Inn

High Street, Cowes PO31 7SA
☎ *(01983) 292823* Andy Taylor

Wadworth 6X and Fuller's London Pride plus four guests, usually from local or independent breweries. Goddards Fuggle Dee Dum and Inspiration Ale and Badger Tanglefoot are popular.

H igh-street pub built in 1704. Three bars, garden. Stable bar with music Fri–Sat.

Food available 12–9.30pm. Children allowed in the garden and middle eating area.

OPEN *All day, every day.*

The Duke of York

Mill Hill Road, Cowes PO31 7BT
☎ *(01983) 295171*
Barry and Sally Cass, and Traci Read

Three real ales, with Goddards Fuggle Dee Dum permanently featured, plus guests such as Goddards Special or something from Ringwood.

Traditional town pub and restaurant, over 200 years old, with a maritime theme. The present landlord has been here since 1969. Homemade food served 12–2.30pm and 6.30–10.30pm, with fresh fish a speciality. Children and dogs welcome. Car park. Accommodation. Cold, wet yachtsmen welcome!

OPEN *11am–midnight.*

The Griffin Inn

Godshill PO38 3JD
☎ *(01983) 840039* Andrew Still

Greene King Old Speckled Hen and Marston's Pedigree are regular brews, and local beers such as Goddards Special Bitter and Ventnor Golden are also featured.

Open-plan family pub in a Gothic-style stone building. The superb garden includes a pond, wendy house, play area, basketball hoop, and hedge maze in the shape of a griffin, made up of 2,500 privet trees. Food is served from the Adults' and Children's Menus plus Specials board.

OPEN *10.30am–11pm Mon–Sat; 12–10.30pm Sun.*

The Sun Inn

Hulverstone, Newport PO30 4EH
☎ *(01983) 741124* Chris Cole

Leased from Enterprise Inns with four real ales, changed every barrel.

A 600-year-old thatched stone pub, with stone floors in the bar, separate restaurant and views of the Channel. Log burner and fireplace in winter, plus a very large beer garden for use in summer. Food is available 12–9pm every day, from an extensive menu and daily specials board. Large car park, private room for hire. Curry nights on Thursdays in winter, plus fortnightly quizzes. Beer festival second weekend in July. Children welcome, and dogs welcome in main bar. The pub is half a mile north-east of Brook, just off the Military road, five minutes' drive from Chessel Pottery.

OPEN *11am–11pm Mon–Sat; 12–10.30pm Sun.*

The Bargeman's Rest

Little London Quay, Newport PO30 5BS
☎ *(01983) 525828* Dan McCarty

Freehouse with six real ales, often including Ringwood Best and Fortyniner, Ventnor Golden, Yates' Undercliff Experience and something from Goddards.

Huge, traditional seafaring family pub. The two bars are decorated with artefacts of marine interest, and the pub has an outside terrace and a function room. Food is available 12–9pm every day. Children, dogs and muddy boots are all welcome.

OPEN *10.30am–11pm Mon–Sat.*

Prince of Wales

36 South Street, Newport PO30 1JE
☎ *(01983) 525026*
R Watson and B Murgatroyd

Punch Taverns pub with three ales, varying weekly.

Built in 1929, this mock-Tudor corner pub has two bars. Snacks such as toasties and pies are available 11.30am–3.30pm. Located in the town centre opposite Morrisons. Children not allowed, dogs welcome. Smoking area at back.

OPEN *10.30am–11.30pm.*

The Waverley

2 Clatterford Road, Newport PO30 1PA
☎ *(01983) 522338*
Rachel and Stephen Kennedy

Four ales, all rotating guests – never the same one twice!

A large Victorian pub dating back to the 1890s with high ceilings and three bars. Food served 12–2pm and 6–9.30pm daily. Six letting rooms available. Two beer gardens. Function room available. TV, pool tables. Located at the top of the hill in Carisbrooke.

OPEN *12–12.*

The Horse & Groom

Main Road, Ningwood PO30 4NW
☎ *(01983) 760672* Martin Bullock

Three ales from breweries such as Goddards, Ventnor, Wells and Young's and Wadworth.

This renovated coaching inn has oodles of character! Food served 12–2.30pm and 5.30–9pm daily (a limited menu is available between these times). Large car park. Children's play area with bouncy castle, mini football pitch and recent addition of crazy golf. Located on the main Newport–Yarmouth road (A3054).

OPEN *All day, every day.*

NITON

The Buddle Inn

St Catherine's Road, Niton PO38 2NE
☎ *(01983) 730243* Ray Benwell

Six real ales always on tap, including Adnams Best (the landlord's favourite, so they never run out!), and their own Buddle Bitter brewed exclusively for them by Yates of St Lawrence. Local wine and cider served when available, together with a wide and interesting selection of soft drinks for the non-drinker.

A 16th-century, stone-built former farmhouse with oak beams, flagstone floors and open fires. Good food available at lunchtimes and evenings. Car park, dining room and garden with fine views. Children allowed. Near St Catherine's Lighthouse.

OPEN *All day, every day.*

White Lion Inn

High Street, Niton PO38 2AT
☎ *(01983) 730293*
James Dickson and Shelley Quigley

 An Enterprise Inns pub with Greene King Abbot Ale and Old Speckled Hen plus Draught Bass permanently available, and one local guest ale rotated daily.

F amily pub composed of a dining room, function room, small corner bar and main bar on the lower level. Homemade food available, from both a main menu and specials board, 12–2.15pm and 6–9pm daily (plus roasts available on Sun). Attractive beer garden with children's play area. Dogs welcome. Annual beer festival at Christmas. Located in the centre of Niton village.

OPEN *11am–11pm Mon–Thurs;
11am–midnight Fri–Sat.*

NORTHWOOD

Traveller's Joy

85 Pallance Road, Northwood, Cowes PO31 8LS
☎ *(01983) 298024* Derek Smith
www.tjoy.co.uk

Locally brewed Goddards Special Bitter is the regular ale, plus a range of seven guests from all around the country changed every week.

D ates back to 1799, a former private house in rural surroundings. A multiple winner of the local CAMRA Pub of the Year award. A single bar serves all areas. Food is available at lunchtime and evenings and a traditional roast lunch is served on Sundays. Large car park. Garden with patio. Two pool/children's rooms. Conservatory available for hire. On the main Cowes to Yarmouth road.

OPEN *11am–2.30pm and 5pm–12 Mon–Thurs;
11am–midnight Fri–Sat; 12–3 and
7pm–12 Sun.*

ROOKLEY

The Chequers Inn

Niton Road, Rookley PO38 3NZ
☎ *(01983) 840314* Debbie Lazelle
www.chequersinn-iow.co.uk

Greene King Old Speckled Hen and Gale's HSB are among the permanent features, plus two guests, changed every couple of months.

T raditional pub with beams, log fires and a flagstone floor. Food served all day. Gaming machines, garden with great views, car park. Children allowed – there is a play area and a family room.

OPEN *11am–11pm Mon–Sat; 12–10.30pm Sun.*

Rookley Inn

Main Road, Rookley PO38 3LU
☎ *(01983) 721800* Jacqui Morton

Two real ales on offer at this freehouse, changed every three days, with beers such as Greene King Old Speckled Hen and Goddards Special Bitter often featured.

A family-oriented pub on a holiday park, with stage, restaurant and patio area. Food served all day from 10am until late. Entertainment. The patio overlooks two lakes, where fishing is available. Children welcome. Accommodation consists of static caravans, bungalows and tenting and touring sites. Car park. From Rookley, take the main road from Newport Head to Shanklin, and the pub is just before Godshill.

OPEN *All day, every day from 11am.*

RYDE

S Fowler & Co

41–3 Union Street, Ryde PO33 2LF
☎ *(01983) 812112* Sharon Longley

A Wetherspoon's house, serving Greene King Abbot, Marston's Pedigree and Courage Directors plus up to six guest ales, changing every few days, with favourites including Hop Back Summer Lightning, Badger Tanglefoot and Charles Wells Bombardier.

T raditional town pub, recently refurbished, with food available all day. Children allowed until 9pm. Beer festivals held twice a year (May and October).

OPEN *9am–midnight Sun–Thurs; 9am–1am Fri–Sat.*

The Railway

68 St Johns Road, Ryde PO33 2RT
☎ *(01983) 615405*
Janet Brown and Garret True

 Greene King IPA, Oakleaf Farmhouse and Adnams Broadside plus a rotating guest ale, which changes weekly.

A n olde-worlde pub with flagstone floor, stone walls, beamed ceiling and open fire. Food available at weekends only (12–4pm and 6–9pm). Well-behaved children allowed. No car park. Situated opposite St John's railway station.

OPEN *11am–11pm Mon–Sat; 12–10.30pm Sun.*

The Simeon Arms

Simeon Street, Ryde PO33 1JG
☎ *(01983) 614954* Jamie Clarke

Goddards Special Bitter and Courage Directors plus a weekly changing guest, which is often a beer from Archers.

Locals' backstreet drinking pub dating from 1865 with one large bar, function room, family room, beer garden and large outdoor smoking area (front and back). Food available 12–3pm every day and Fri–Sun evenings. Ask for directions.

OPEN *11am–11.30pm Mon; 11am–11pm Tues–Wed; 11am–midnight Thurs–Sat; 12–11.30pm Sun.*

Solent Inn

7 Monkton Street, Ryde PO33 1JW
☎ *(01983) 563546*
Helen and Graham Fastnedge

Leased through Punch Taverns with five or six ales. Banks's Bitter is permanent, with the others on constant rotation.

Built in the late 18th century, this Grade II listed building is known as the longest-serving pub in the area. Two newly redecorated bars. Food served 12–6pm Mon–Fri. Third in CAMRA Best Island Pub 2008. Beer garden with smoking area. Outdoor dining area. Located just off the Ryde esplanade.

OPEN *11am–11.30pm Mon–Wed; 11am–12.30am Thurs–Sat; 12–10.30pm Sun.*

The Wishing Well

Pondwell Hill, Ryde PO33 1PX
☎ *(01983) 613222* Adrian Allen

Freehouse serving Greene King Abbot. Two guests might be Badger Fursty Ferret, or something from Goddards or Ventnor.

Family pub with one main bar, fireplace, patio and wishing well. Elevated decking gives superb views down the valley to the sea. Games room with pool table and TV. Food served 12–2.30pm and 6–9.30pm. New disabled facilities. Children and dogs allowed. Car park.

OPEN *11am–3pm and 5.30–11pm Mon–Sat; 12–3pm and 5.30–10.30pm Sun.*

SANDOWN

The Castle Inn

12–14 Fitzroy Street, Sandown PO36 8HY
☎ *(01983) 403169* David Radcliffe

Freehouse offering Young's Bitter and Special plus two guests.

Locals' pub run by locals, where visitors are welcomed with a smile. One bar, courtyard garden. Darts, pool, shove-ha'penny, bar billiards, skittle alley and cribbage. Family room. Five minutes' walk from beach, shops, pier and other attractions.

OPEN *12–11pm Sun–Wed; 12–12 Thurs–Fri; 11am–midnight Sat.*

SHALFLEET

The New Inn

Main Road, Shalfleet PO30 4NS
☎ *(01983) 531314* Martin Bullock

Tied house serving four real ales from breweries such as Goddards, Ventnor, Greene King and Marston's.

Built in 1743, this inn has flagstone floors, inglenook fireplaces and scrubbed pine tables. Food served 12–2.30pm and 6–9.30pm daily. Awarded the Isle of Wight Dining Pub of the Year several times. Located at the foot of the New Town estuary, on the main Newport–Yarmouth road (A3054).

OPEN *All day, every day.*

SHANKLIN

The Crab Inn

High Street, Shanklin PO37 6NS
☎ *(01983) 862363* Derry Derbyshire

Something from Goddards plus one monthly-changing guest beer.

Traditional family dining pub with patio, built in the 17th century. No music, games or TV. Children allowed.

OPEN *11am–11pm Mon–Sat; 12–10.30pm Sun.*

The King Harry's Bar

6 Church Road, Shanklin PO37 6NU
☎ *(01983) 863119* Clive and Nicola Ottley

Freehouse with four or five ales in the summer, three in the winter. Fuller's ESB is a permanent fixture with the others rotating every three or four days.

A 19th-century thatched property with two bars and large gardens. Floodlit at night, overlooking the chines (remains of ancient river valleys). Food served in the bar at lunchtime, and in their steak restaurant in the evenings. Four rooms available for B&B. Entertainment Fri evenings. Function room available. Located in centre of village of Shanklin. Ten minutes' walk from the beach, close to shops. Not suitable for young children. Fifteen minutes from train station, on main bus route from Ryde to Ventnor.

OPEN *Summer: 11am–midnight.*
Winter: 4–10pm Mon–Fri; 12–11pm Sat; Sun 12–6pm.

The Steamer Inn

Shanklin Esplanade, Shanklin PO37 6BS
☎ *(01983) 862641* Duncan Scott (manager)

Ventnor Golden, Badger Best and Tanglefoot and Goddards Fuggle Dee Dum plus two guests, which might include Greene King Abbot, Adnams Regatta (in summer) or a Yates of St Lawrence ale.

A nautical theme which includes memorabilia and a seafront terrace. Get 'wrecked' here!! Food, including local seafood, available all day in summer, lunchtimes and evenings in winter. Children welcome, children's menu available.

OPEN *11am–11pm Mon–Sat; 12–10.30pm Sun.*

The Village Inn

Old Village Church Road, Shanklin PO37 6NU
☎ *(01983) 862764* Paul Ottley

 Ventnor Golden plus a guest ale.

Two-bar pub with beams and fireplaces. Children welcome, separate family bar upstairs. Food available 12–2.30pm and 6–10pm daily. Beer garden.

OPEN *11am–11pm Mon–Sat; 12–10.30pm Sun.*

TOTLAND BAY

The Broadway Inn

The Broadway, Totland Bay PO39 0BL
☎ *(01983) 755333* Kim and Dave Filby

 Four real ales in summer, two in winter. Timothy Taylor Landlord and Shepherd Neame Spitfire are regulars, and brews from the local Yate's, Goddards and Ventnor breweries are usually represented, rotated at least weekly.

A two-bar public house in a 100-year-old building with a historical connection to Marconi. It became a pub in 1951. Food available 12–2.30pm and 6–9pm Mon–Sat. Real coffee also served. Beer terraces, private room for hire. Live music every weekend. Nearby attractions include Alum Bay and the Needles. On the B3322 between Yarmouth and Alum Bay.

OPEN *Summer: 11am–late. Winter: 11am–3pm and 6–11.30pm.*

Highdown Inn

Highdown Lane, Totland Bay PO39 0HY
☎ *(01983) 752450* Susan White
www.highdowninn.com

 Three real ales: Wadworth 6X and beers from Ringwood and Adnams.

Ideal ramblers' pub, nestling at the foot of Tennyson Down, only half a mile from Alum Bay and the Needles. Muddy boots and dogs welcome! Known locally as a pub for good food and real ales. Newly refurbished restaurant and letting rooms. Runner-up in the Ushers Food Competition. Food available in the restaurant, two small bars or garden patio area 12–3pm and 6–9pm daily. Children are catered for with their own menu and play area within a large garden. En-suite accommodation also available throughout the year, offering comfortable rooms with countryside views. Half a mile from the Needles – follow Alum Bay Old Road to Freshwater Bay.

OPEN *Winter: 11am–3pm and 6–11pm; potentially all day in summer.*

VENTNOR

The Spyglass Inn

The Esplanade, Ventnor PO38 1JX
☎ *(01983) 855338* Neil and Stephanie Gibbs

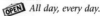 Badger Best and Tanglefoot and Ventnor Golden plus three guests. Goddards Fuggle Dee Dum and beers from Yates of St Lawrence, Badger (Hall & Woodhouse), Ventnor Ales and Scarecrow are often available. Two real ale festivals every year, in spring and October.

A seafaring pub situated on the sea wall. Food available 12–9.30pm every day. Large outside terraces. Children, dogs and muddy boots welcome. Live music every evening.

OPEN *11am–11pm.*

The Volunteer Inn

30 Victoria Street, Ventnor PO38 1ES
☎ *(01983) 852537* Mike and Heather Janvrin

 Leased from Victoria Inns with up to eight regularly changing ales. The locally produced Ventnor Golden Bitter is always available, plus other local brews and Greene King Old Speckled Hen and Abbot Ale.

This award-winning freehouse is the smallest pub on the island, and a haven for adult drinkers. Traditional wooden floors, lively conversation and gourmet pickled eggs, but no chips, children, fruit machines or juke box. Annual October beerfest with over 24 real ales. Muddy boots and (cat-proof) dogs welcome.

OPEN *All day, every day.*

WHIPPINGHAM

Folly Inn

Folly Lane, Whippingham PO32 6NB
☎ *(01983) 297171*
Andy and Cheryl Greenwood

 Greene King tied house with Old Speckled Hen and IPA plus something local from Goddards.

Perched on the banks of the River Medina, an open-plan country pub seating 200, with large patio, garden area and breathtaking views. Full menu and specials board, with breakfasts 9–11am, lunches 12–5pm and evening meals 5–11pm. Live music Fri and Sat in summer. Based on a river mooring for 230 boats and pontoon with mooring – a water taxi runs from the pontoon to the mooring during summer. Showers available 24 hours. A mile up-river from Cowes. Children welcome, car park. Well signposted. Close to Butterfly World, Robin Hill Adventure Park and Amazon World.

OPEN *9am (for breakfasts)–11pm (10.30pm Sun).*

WROXALL

The Four Seasons Inn

2 Clarence Road, Wroxhall PO38 3BY
☎ *(01983) 854701* Richard and Sonia Lowe

Ringwood Best, Gale's HSB and Shepherd Neame Spitfire usually available.

A pub with a warm welcome for children and dogs. Food available in the bar or in a separate restaurant 12–2pm and 6–9.15pm. Honorary member of CAMRA. Beer garden with outside seating, car park. Located off the main road but visible from it, on the junction with Manor Road.

OPEN *All day, every day.*

YARMOUTH

The Bugle Coaching Inn

The Square, Yarmouth PO41 0NS
☎ *(01983) 760272* Ray Benwell
www.buglecoachinginn.co.uk

Six real ales, with beers from Greene King, Yates of St Lawrence and Wadworth the regular features, plus three guests, changed every week or two.

A 17th-century coaching inn fronting the town square, with two bars and a beer garden. Food is available lunchtimes and evenings, including a specials menu featuring locally caught fresh fish. Nine letting bedrooms. Children always welcome. Courtyard beer garden, car park.

OPEN *All day, every day.*

The Wheatsheaf

Bridge Road, Yarmouth PO41 0PH
☎ *(01983) 760456* Mrs Keen

Goddards Fuggle Dee Dum, Wadworth 6X, Greene King Old Speckled Hen and a Brakspear bitter.

Traditional, food-oriented former coaching house with two bar areas, separate eating area, two family areas, conservatory and garden. An extensive menu is available at lunchtimes and evenings. Children allowed. Near the ferry.

OPEN *All day, every day.*

THE BREWERIES

ALES OF SCILLY BREWERY LTD
Porth Mellon, St Mary's TR21 0JY
☎ *(01720) 423233*

 NATURAL BEAUTY 4.2% ABV
SCUPPERED 4.6% ABV
Plus seasonals and Christmas specials.

THE PUBS

ST AGNES

Turk's Head
St Agnes TR22 0PL
☎ *(01720) 422434* Nicki and Rob Anderson

 Always two real ales at this popular freehouse. St Austell Turk's Ale and Ales of Scilly Scuppered are regulars, plus frequent guests.

Welcoming pub on the sparsely populated island of St Agnes, a 20-minute boat ride from the main island of St Mary's and well worth the sometimes choppy journey. Situated bang on the quayside, the Turk's Head used to be home to a lifeboat station. It has been a pub since 1974 but the stone building dates from much earlier times. It has a main bar, a garden bar overlooking the sea and a restaurant room, as well as a raised beer garden and benches outside the pub, which can be overflowing with customers on sunny afternoons. Food is served 12–2.30pm and 6–9pm March–Oct – its pasties are legendary. Children are welcome. Twin-bedded en-suite room for B&B.

OPEN *10.30am–4pm and 6pm–11.30pm; open all day in July and August.*

ST MARY'S

The Atlantic Inn
Hugh Street, St Mary's TR21 0HY
☎ *(01720) 422323*
Stephanie Todd and Grahame Rickard

At least four pumps dedicated to real ale at this St Austell Brewery-owned pub in the heart of Hugh Town. IPA, Tribute, HSD and Proper Job are the regulars but the selection varies according to the brewery's output.

An outdoor terrace, a real sun-trap that was extended in April 2008, overlooks the harbour – at high tide the water literally laps at the walls. The one large bar with low, beamed ceilings and a smattering of nautical memorabilia attracts a mix of tourists and locals. Connected to the bar is a spacious restaurant serving tourist favourites including fresh crab sandwiches; food is served all day, seven days a week. Children are welcome.

OPEN *11am–11pm Mon–Sat; 12–10.30pm Sun.*

Bishop & Wolf
Hugh Street, St Mary's TR21 0LL
☎ *(01720) 422790* Richard and Rachel

Three real ale pumps at this St Austell tied pub serving a selection of well-kept Cornish-brewed St Austell beers such as Tinners Ale, Tribute and HSD, with the selection varying according to the brewery's output. There is also a brew from the local Ales of Scilly brewery during the summer.

In the centre of bustling Hugh Town, there is one main bar, with pool room and an enclosed patio area. Upstairs dining area. Homemade food and fish specials served lunchtimes and evenings every day, and children are welcome.

OPEN *11am–11pm (10.30pm Sun). Open 9am in summer for breakfast.*

Mermaid Inn
The Bank, St Mary's TR21 0HY
☎ *(01720) 422701*
Irene Connolly and Ray Brown

As well as Greene King IPA you'll always find one pump dedicated to local beer from the Ales of Scilly brewery at this Unique Pub Company hostelry.

This quayside pub is always busy with locals, sailors and tourists – many of whom arrive on the Scilly Isles' main island, St Mary's, on the ferry which docks just around the corner. The décor is strictly nautical with bits of boats on the walls and flags signed by visiting sailors adorning the ceiling. There is one main bar, a restaurant upstairs and a cellar bar, open in the summer only. Children are welcome and food is served every day, lunchtimes and evenings.

OPEN *11am–11pm (10.30pm Sun).*

Old Town Inn
Old Town Lane, St Mary's TR21 0NN
☎ *(01720) 422442* Nicholas and Bridie Smith

Freehouse serving three real ales, two of them regulars – Scuppered and Natural Beauty – which come from nearby island brewery, the Ales of Scilly. The other is likely to be a guest ale with a Cornish flavour, perhaps something from Sharp's.

The Old Town Inn opened as a pub in 1996 but the building, which was once a wood workshop belonging to the local Ennor Castle estate, dates back to 1744. Inside are original old beams and a wood-burning stove. There are two beer gardens and a games room. Children are welcome. There is also a function suite attached to the pub and three en-suite B&B rooms available. The pub attracts a mixture of locals and tourists, and serves food at lunchtimes and evenings, seven days a week.

OPEN *12–3pm and 6–11pm (10.30pm Sun).*

Porthcressa Inn

Littleporth, St Mary's TR21 0JG
☎ *(01720) 423488*
Richard Smith and Rachel Gaulton

Genuine freehouse with four real ales in summer (fewer in winter). Ales of Scilly Scuppered plus one other from the island brewery and ales from Skinner's and elsewhere.

Former café, converted to a pub in the 1990s and run by the same people as The Bishop & Wolf. Claims to be the cheapest pub on the island. One large L-shaped bar with large patio overlooking Porthcressa Bay. Pool, darts. Food served 12–2pm and 5.30–8.30pm (all day in high season). Children welcome. Nightclub in the basement.

OPEN *11am–11pm (1am in basement).*

Scillonian Club

The Parade, St Mary's TR21 0LP
☎ *(01720) 422720* Sarah and Mark Twynham

Freehouse with three real ales, always including St Austell Tribute, plus two guests, changed weekly.

This 85-year-old former private club is now a freehouse, and is on the first floor of a terraced house in Hugh Town, St Mary's. Newly refurbished open-plan bar with sofas and a games area for pool and darts. Large snooker room with two full-size tables. The 60-seater Lyonnesse restaurant has fabulous harbour views. Home-cooked food is served 12–2pm and 6–8.30pm every day, plus breakfasts and tea/coffee from 9am in high season. Local produce is used where possible, and all tastes and needs are catered for (including coeliac, gluten-free and vegetarian diets). Outside balcony area also has views of the town, beach and harbour. Regular live music by local bands. Children welcome. The only venue in Isles of Scilly with Sky TV, with sporting events shown on giant screen. Regular quizzes in aid of local charities. Weekly bridge and whist sessions. Annual real ale festival. Card room and restaurant available for private hire. Disabled lift. Easily accessible from the town, the pub is almost opposite the park, next to the Stone Shop.

OPEN *11.30am–11pm Mon–Sat; 12–10.30pm Sun. Open 9am in high season for breakfasts and tea/coffee.*

New Inn

New Grimsby, Tresco TR24 0QE
☎ *(01720) 422844* Robin Lawson

Up to five pumps dedicated to real ale at this island freehouse. Beers from Skinner's and the local Ales of Scilly brewery on St Mary's. Occasional guest ales are served and beer festivals of four days each are held twice a year, in May and September.

Part of a row of workers' cottages in the village of New Grimsby. Leased from the Duchy of Cornwall by the Dorrien Smith family, who also own the island's hotel. The main bar area includes comfy battered leather sofas, pool table and dartboard; the beer garden has views of nearby island Bryher. In recent years the New Inn hotel has been extended to include a café and an outdoor swimming pool which is open to pub guests. Food is served 12–2pm (plus reduced menu during the afternoon) and 7–9pm (from 6pm in high season). Breakfast is also available in high season. Live music every two–three weeks. Children are welcome in the pub until 9pm.

OPEN *All day, every day.*

THE BREWERIES

P & DJ GOACHER

Unit 8, Tovil Green, Business Park, Burial Ground Lane, Tovil, Maidstone ME15 6TA
☎ *(01622) 682112*
www.goachers.com

REAL MILD ALE 3.4% ABV
Chocolatey dark mild.
MAIDSTONE FINE LIGHT ALE 3.7% ABV
Floral character.
BEST DARK ALE 4.1% ABV
Full bodied and rich.
CROWN IMPERIAL STOUT 4.5% ABV
Roasted barley flavour.
Occasionals including:
GOLD STAR STRONG ALE 5.1% ABV
OLD 1066 6.7% ABV

HOPDAEMON BREWERY COMPANY LTD

Unit 1, Parsonage Farm, Seed Road, Newnham, Sittingbourne ME9 0NA
☎ *(01795) 892078*
www.hopdaemon.com

GOLDEN BRAID 3.7% ABV
INCUBUS 4.0% ABV
SKRIMSHANDER IPA 4.5% ABV
DOMINATOR 5.1% ABV
Occasionals including:
BEWITCHED 3.7% ABV
GOLDEN DOVE 5.0% ABV
GREEN DAEMON 5.0% ABV
LEVIATHAN 6.0% ABV

LARKINS BREWERY LTD

Larkins Farm, Hampkin Hill Road, Chiddingstone, Edenbridge TN8 7BB
☎ *(01892) 870328*

TRADITIONAL ALE 3.4% ABV
CHIDDINGSTONE BITTER 4.0% ABV
BEST 4.4% ABV
PORTER 5.2% ABV

THE MILLIS BREWING COMPANY LTD

Formerly The Gravesend Brewing Co
St Margrets Farm, St Margrets Road, South Darenth, Dartford DA4 9LB
☎ *(01474) 566903*

OAST SHOVELLERS BITTER 3.9% ABV
Copper colour, tart and tangy.
DARTFORD WOBBLER 4.3% ABV
Tawny, full flavoured, with roast in the finish.
KENTISH RED ALE 4.3% ABV
Malty with fruit notes.
THIEVES 'N' FAKIRS 4.3% ABV
Complex fruit, hops and malt flavours.
Plus seasonals and occasionals.

THE NELSON BREWING COMPANY

Unit 2, Building 64, The Historic Dockyard, Chatham ME4 4TE
☎ *(01634) 832828*
www.nelsonbrewingcompany.co.uk

VICTORY DARK MILD 3.5% ABV
Roast hop aftertaste.
ROCHESTER BITTER 3.7% ABV
Pale ale, lingering bitter aftertaste.
PIECES OF EIGHT 3.8% ABV
Malty bitter.
TRAFALGAR BITTER 4.1% ABV
Honey and nut flavours.
LOOSE CANNON 4.4% ABV
Roasted hop flavour.
DOGWATCH STOUT 4.5% ABV
Chocolatey stout.
FRIGGIN' IN THE RIGGIN' 4.7% ABV
Bittersweet and malty.
NELSON'S BLOOD 6.0% ABV
Warming and nutty.
Plus occasionals and specials.

RAMSGATE BREWERY LTD

Unit 1, Hornet Close, Isle of Thanet, East Kent Coast CT10 2YD
☎ *(01843) 868453*
www.ramsgatebrewery.co.uk

GADDS' NO.7 3.8% ABV
Dry bitter.
GADDS' SANDBOY KENT PALE ALE 3.8% ABV
Fruity pale ale.
GADDS' DARK MILD ALE 4.0% ABV
Full of chocolate and roast taste.
GADDS' SEASIDER 4.3% ABV
Pale amber, clean crisp aftertaste.
GADDS' NO.5 4.4% ABV
Easy drinker.
GADDS' OLD PIG BROWN ALE 4.8% ABV
Available Sept–early Nov. Rich and malty.
GADDS' NO.3 5.0% ABV
Pale and quenching, brewed with local hops.
GADDS' STORM WARNING 5.0% ABV
Caramel flavour, sweet hoppy finish.
GADDS' DOGBOLTER WINTER PORTER 5.6% ABV
Nov–Mar.
Plus specials.

SHEPHERD NEAME LTD

17 Court Street, Faversham ME13 7AX
☎ *(01795) 532206*
www.shepherd-neame.co.uk

MASTER BREW BITTER 3.7% ABV
Clean, dry with touch of sweetness.
MASTER BREW SMOOTH 3.7% ABV
Creamy and hoppy.
BEST BITTER 4.1% ABV
Biscuity sweetness.
EARLY BIRD 4.3% ABV
Feb–May. Light and malty, floral aroma.
SPITFIRE PREMIUM KENTISH STRONG ALE 4.5% AVB
Golden with a subtle hint of toffee.
SPITFIRE SMOOTH 4.5% ABV
Creamy award winner.
BISHOPS FINGER KENTISH STRONG ALE 5.0% ABV
Nut brown with fruity flavour.

THE SWAN MICROBREWERY

Swan On The Green, The Green, West Peckham, Maidstone ME18 5JW
☎ *(01622) 812271*
www.swan-on-the-green.co.uk

GINGER 3.6% ABV
Pale with spicy oriental notes.
O.F. MILD 3.6% ABV
Easy drinker.
WHOOPER 3.6% ABV
Straw coloured and fruity.
BLONDE 4.0% ABV
Clean, refreshing, with organic malt.
TRUMPETER 4.0% ABV
English bitter.
PORTSIDE 4.2% ABV
Dark, hoppy with a bottle of port added to each cask.
WEISSE 4.5% ABV
Slightly spicy, continental style.
BEWICK 5.3% ABV
Hoppy bitter.

THE WESTERHAM BREWERY COMPANY

Grange Farm, Pootings Road, Edenbridge TN8 6SA
☎ *(01732) 864427*
www.westerhambrewery.co.uk

FINCHCOCK'S ORIGINAL 3.5% ABV
Hoppy bitter.
BLACK EAGLE SPECIAL PALE ALE 'SPA' 3.8% ABV
Dry and biscuity.
GRASSHOPPER KENTISH BITTER 3.8% ABV
Dark and malty.
BRITISH BULLDOG 'BB' 4.3% ABV
Rich and full bodied.
GENERAL WOLFE '1759' MAPLE ALE 4.3% ABV
Autumn only.
GOD'S WALLOP CHRISTMAS ALE 4.3% ABV
Christmas only.
PUDDLEDOCK PORTER 4.3% ABV
Winter only.
IPA 4.8% ABV
Occasional.
SEVENOAKS BITTER '7X' 4.8% ABV
Dry and malty with biscuit tones. Occasional.
WESTERHAM SPECIAL BITTER ALE '1965' 5.0% ABV
Occasional.

WHITSTABLE BREWERY

c/o 29 Beach Walk, Whitstable CT5 2BP
☎ *(01622) 851007*
www.whitstablebrewery.info

EAST INDIA PALE ALE 4.2% ABV
Highly hopped.
OYSTER STOUT 4.5% ABV
Dry, chocolate flavour.
RASPBERRY WHEAT BEER 5.2% ABV
Sharp finish.
WHEAT 5.2% ABV
Banana flavour.

ASHFORD

Hooden on the Hill

Silver Hill Road, Willesborough Lees, Ashford TN24 0NY
☎ *(01233) 662226*
Howard Lapish and Kelly Loft

Young's Bitter and Greene King IPA plus a usually stronger guest beer.

Oldest and busiest pub in suburban Ashford, beamed and candlelit with hops in the ceiling and worth escaping the town centre to enjoy, or simply to witness regular customers forming an orderly queue to be served! One bar, friendly staff and menu specialising in Mexican food. Full range of Gales country wines generally in stock. Food available 12–2pm and 6–10pm Mon–Sat; 12–10pm Sun. Children and dogs allowed. Large garden. Leave town-centre one-way system heading east on A292 (Hythe Road), and shortly before reaching M20 turn left into Lees Road at Esso service station. Lees Road becomes Silver Hill Road and pub is on left about 300 yards after underpassing M20.

OPEN *12–11pm (10.30pm Sun).*

BADLESMERE

The Red Lion

Ashford Road, Badlesmere Lees, Faversham ME13 0NX
☎ *(01233) 740320* Kim Sharrock
www.redlion-badlesmere.co.uk

Shepherd Neame Master Brew, Fuller's London Pride and Greene King Abbot Ale plus Shepherd Neame Mild popular among guest beers.

An English rural pub dating from the mid 1500s with a large beer garden and heaps of character. Well known locally for real ale and live music. Food available 12–2.15pm and 7–9pm Tues–Thurs and Sat; 12–2.15pm Fri; 12–2.30pm Sun. Children are welcome, and the pub is dog-friendly. Beer festivals at Easter and August bank holiday. Free camping. On the A251 (Ashford Road) between Faversham and Ashford.

OPEN *12–3pm and 6–11pm Mon–Thurs (closed Mon lunch); 12–3pm and 5pm–12 Fri; 12–12 Sat; 12–10.30pm Sun.*

BARFRESTONE

The Yew Tree Inn

Barfrestone, Dover CT15 7JH
☎ *(01304) 831619* Margaret and Chris Cruse

Genuine freehouse with five beers: two permanents and three guests. Strong emphasis on local breweries, Ramsgate (Gadds) and Hopdaemon in particular, although a vast range from throughout the country is stocked duringthe year.

Unspoilt traditional village pub with wooden floors and pine-scrubbed tables; built only in 1927 because of a fire to the previous building, but giving the impression of being much older. One bar and two other rooms. Food available 12–3pm and 6.30–8.30pm Mon–Thurs, 12–3pm and 6–9.30pm Fri, 12–9.30pm Sat and 12.30–5pm Sun, with traditional roast. Children allowed; dog-friendly; tethering bar for horses outside. Patio garden. Long two miles north-east of A2; look for the yew tree! OS:264501.

OPEN *12–11pm.*

BETHERSDEN

The George

The Street, Bethersden, Ashford TN26 3AG
☎ *(01233) 820235* Tony Le Beau

A freehouse. Charles Wells Bombardier, Young's Bitter, Harveys Sussex Best, Greene King Old Speckled Hen plus a beer from Brakspear or Wychwood.

A village local with public bar and saloon bar. Traditional pub food served 12–2pm and 6.30–9pm Tues–Sat; 12–3pm Sun (no food Mon). Children welcome. Beer garden. Car park. Two beer festivals each year: St George's Day and summer. Located midway between Ashford and Tenterden on the A28.

OPEN *12–11pm.*

BEXLEYHEATH

Robin Hood & Little John

78 Lion Road, Bexleyheath DA6 8PF
☎ *(020) 8303 1128* Ray Johnson

Freehouse serving eight cask-conditioned beers. Brains Reverend James, Harveys Best, Fuller's London Pride, Adnams Best and Brakspear Bitter are regular features, the other two brews change monthly.

One-bar, village-type pub with wood-panelled walls and old Singer sewing machine tables. Beer garden. Food available at lunchtime only, Mon–Sat. Off Bexleyheath Broadway. CAMRA Greater London Pub of the Year in 2005, and local CAMRA Pub of the Year 2005 and 2006.

OPEN *11am–3.30pm and 5.30–11pm (7–11pm Sat; 7–10.30pm Sun).*

Wrong 'Un

234–6 The Broadway, Bexleyheath,
☎ *(020) 8298 0439* Terry Fitzgerald

A Wetherspoon's pub with Greene King Abbot, Shepherd Neame Spitfire and Marston's Pedigree among the permanent beers, plus two guests, changed every few days.

Light, spacious pub with traditional décor and a relaxed atmosphere. Extensive menu available 9am–11pm every day. Disabled facilities. Car park. Families welcome. At the centre of The Broadway, a short drive from the shops.

OPEN *9am–midnight.*

BLUE BELL HILL

The Lower Bell

201 Old Chatham Road, Blue Bell Hill, Aylesford ME20 7EF
☎ *(01634) 861127* Laurence Walker

Greene King tied house offering IPA and Abbot Ale permanently, with up to two other beers from the brewery's portfolio, but note the landlord accepts it would be folly, strengthwise, to pit Greene King Old Speckled Hen against Abbot Ale – so he doesn't!

Built about 100 years ago, the pub gets its name from a bell signalling system used by stagecoaches on the single-track road to the top of the hill. One bar, separate dining area and restaurant/function suite on two levels. Food available 12–2.30pm and 6–9.30pm, with traditional roast Sun lunchtime. Homemade pies and fresh fish are specialities. Children allowed but not dogs. Patio garden. At foot of sliproad west of A229 (Blue Bell Hill).

OPEN *11am–11pm Mon–Sat; 12–10.30pm Sun.*

BOUGH BEECH

The Wheatsheaf at Bough Beech

Hever Road, Bough Beech TN8 7NU
☎ *(01732) 700254* Elizabeth Currie
www.wheatsheafatboughbeech.com

Harveys Sussex Best plus two or three guests, such as the local Westerham Brewery British Bulldog and Grasshopper, plus other Westerham seasonal brews.

A historic pub, steeped in history. Local tradition claims that part of the pub was once a hunting lodge owned by Henry V and dates from the late 14th century. Prominent gables, large Tudor chimneys and fireplaces dominate the structure. A varied collection of artefacts decorate the interior. Food served 12–10pm. Situated between Edenbridge and Tonbridge on the B2027, close to Hever Castle, the childhood home of Anne Boleyn.

OPEN *11am–11.30pm Mon–Fri; 11am–midnight Sat; 11am–11pm Sun.*

BOUGHTON ALUPH

The Flying Horse

The Lees, Boughton Aluph, Ashford TN25 4HH
☎ *(01233) 620914* Simon Chicken

 Fuller's London Pride and Greene King IPA, plus two other beers, with Shepherd Neame Spitfire proving a good seller.

A 15th-century beamed pub on edge of cricket green with two natural wells rediscovered under small back bar. Two bars and restaurant; accommodation. Food available 12–3pm and 6–9pm Mon–Fri; all day Sat–Sun. Dogs welcome, children allowed in restaurant only. Garden. Just off A251 at Boughton Lees (despite Boughton Aluph address).

OPEN *12–11pm Mon–Wed; noon–1am Thurs–Sat; 12–11pm Sun.*

BOUGHTON MONCHELSEA

The Cock Inn

Heath Road, Boughton Monchelsea, Maidstone ME17 4JD
☎ *(01622) 743166* Dave and Jo Whitehurst

 Wells and Young's tied house offering Young's PA, Special and a seasonal ale.

A 15th-century beamed inn with inglenook fireplace and restaurant. The pub was featured in the film *Kind Hearts and Coronets*. Food served 12–2.30pm and 6–9pm Mon–Sat and 12–4pm Sun. Large beer garden. Dog-friendly. Off junction 8 of the M20, on the B2163, four miles from Leeds Castle and handy for the Greensand Way walk.

OPEN *11am–11pm Mon–Sat; 12–10.30pm Sun.*

BOXLEY

The King's Arms

The Street, Boxley, Maidstone ME14 3DR
☎ *(01622) 755177* Daren and Clare Parker

 Fuller's London Pride, Greene King IPA and Gale's HSB, plus one guest, such as Harvey's Sussex, changed every few weeks.

Village pub mindful of good causes, with some parts of the building dating from the 12th century. One power bar in two distinct sections, with hops prevalent. Food available 12–2.30pm and 6–9pm (9.30pm Sat) and all day Sun, with traditional Sunday roast 'until it runs out'. Children allowed; dog-friendly. Weddings catered for with room for a marquee in the large garden. Excellent walks nearby. In the heart of the village of Boxley.

OPEN *11am–11pm Mon–Sat; 12–10.30pm Sun.*

BOYDEN GATE

The Gate Inn Marshside

Marshside, Chislet, Canterbury CT3 4EB
☎ *(01227) 860498* Chris Smith

Shepherd Neame tied house offering Master Brew Bitter and Spitfire, with whatever seasonal beer is appropriate, all served directly from the cask.

Parts of the pub are 200 years old, but not the 'beams' in the single hopped bar. Couple of side rooms, too, all with tiled floors and illustrating that this has long been the centre of village life, from rugby and

distance running to mummers' plays each Christmas. Food available 11am–2pm and 6–9pm Mon–Sat; 12–2pm and 7–9pm Sun. No food Mon and Tues evenings in winter. Well-behaved children and dogs allowed. Large garden complete with stream and ducks, though 'canard' was not seen on the menu! Long mile south of A299 (Thanet Way). OS:220656.

OPEN *11am–2.30pm and 6–11pm Mon–Sat; 12–4pm and 7–10.30pm Sun.*

BRENCHLEY

Halfway House

Horsmonden Road, Brenchley TN12 7AX
☎ *(01892) 722526* Richard Allen

 Freehouse with Harveys Sussex, Westerham 1965, Goacher's Fine Light, Rother Valley Mild, plus two to four constantly rotating guests. Real ales and cider served straight from the barrel.

Built in the early 18th century, this former coaching inn has beams and open fires, and is set in two acres of land. No music, TV, fruit machines or pool tables. One main bar and four other drinking/dining areas. CAMRA West Kent Pub of the Year 2006 and 2007, and Kent Pub of the Year 2006. Food served lunchtimes and evenings Mon–Sat, lunchtimes only Sun. Three en-suite letting rooms available. Large beer garden, children's play area. Car park. Beer festivals held over Whitsun and August bank holidays, featuring 45 real ales. Located between the villages of Brenchley and Horsmonden.

OPEN *12–11pm.*

BROADSTAIRS

The White Swan

17 Reading Street, Broadstairs CT10 3AZ
☎ *(01843) 863051* Kathryn J Barnes

Freehouse serving Adnams Best plus five rotating guests, changed every seven to ten days. Examples include Surrey Hills Albury Ruby, Whitstable Kentish Reserve, Ramsgate East Kent Pale Ale, Oakleaf Hole Hearted and Timothy Taylor Landlord.

Village pub in a 100-year-old building, though there was a pub on this site for many years previously. Traditional, with two bars – saloon and public (with price difference!). Saloon is cosy with comfortable furniture, while the public bar is more simply furnished, with pool table, fruit machine and piped music. No loud music, no TV, no children. Food served 12–2pm and 7–9.30pm Mon–Sat; 7.30–9pm Sun. Car park at rear. Close to North Foreland Lighthouse, beautiful sandy bays and coastal walks. Take A25 into Thanet and follow signs for Broadstairs, then Kingsgate. The pub is between St Peter's and Kingsgate, near North Foreland Golf Club.

OPEN *11.30am–2.30pm and 6–10pm Mon, 6–11pm Tues; 11.30am–2.30pm and 5–11pm Weds–Fri; 11.30am–11pm Sat; 11.30am–5pm in winter months. Summer to be confirmed.*

BROMLEY

The Red Lion

10 North Road, Bromley BR1 3LG
☎ *(020) 8460 2691*
Chris and Siobhan Humphrey

Greene King Abbot and IPA along with Harvey's Sussex are always available. Supported by two continually changing guest ales from various famous and infamous breweries.

Friendly local offering food every day.

OPEN *11am–11pm.*

BROMPTON

King George V

1 Prospect Row, Brompton ME7 5AL
☎ *(01643) 842418* John Brice

Adnams Bitter, plus a rotating dark mild, strong beer and weak beer changed very frequently. More than 30 bottled Belgian real ales. Cask Marque accredited.

Built in 1690, an oak-beamed pub with lots of memorabilia from nearby Chatham dockyard and local army barracks. Small beer garden. Steam traction engines outside on some Suns, and many special events for St George's Day, etc. Food served 12–2pm Mon–Sat, 6.30–8.30pm Tues–Sat, and roast lunch 1–4pm Sun. Live acoustic music last Sun every month. Quiz or poser set every Sunday – no quizmaster but a set of questions. Four letting rooms including a four-poster and family room.

OPEN *11.45am–11pm (plus late licence).*

CANTERBURY

The Canterbury Tales

12 The Friars, Canterbury CT1 2AS
☎ *(01227) 768594* Chris Smith

Shepherd Neame Spitfire, Fuller's London Pride, Young's PA and Greene King IPA usually available with one rotating every month.

Lively country-style 18th-century pub in town-centre setting, used by locals as well as actors from the Marlowe Theatre opposite. Bar food available 12–9pm. The Aztec, a separate restaurant upstairs, opens 6–9.30pm and specialises in both North and South American dishes. Dogs allowed; children also, but not in main bar. Two private function rooms available. Nearest railway station is Canterbury West.

OPEN *Noon–1am (11pm Sun).*

King's Head

204 Wincheap, Canterbury CT1 3RY
☎ *(01227) 462885* M Longley

Freehouse serving Harveys Sussex Best and Greene King IPA, plus one ever-changing guest.

This friendly 15th-century oak-beamed inn features a cosy bar decorated with hops. Pub games such as darts and billiards. Food served 12–2pm and 5–9pm Mon–Fri (but not Tues evenings), 12–3pm and 5–9pm Sat, 12–3pm and 7–9pm Sun. B&B available with parking. Beer garden. Bat & trap played during summer months. Children welcome. Close to Canterbury Cathedral. Located 500 yards from Canterbury East railway station, on A28 from city centre towards Ashford.

OPEN *12–2.30pm and 4.45pm–12 Mon–Thurs; 12–12 Fri–Sat; 12–11.30pm Sun.*

The Phoenix

67 Old Dover Road, Canterbury CT1 3DB
☎ *(01227) 464220* Linda Barker
www.thephoenix-canterbury.co.uk

Young's Bitter, Charles Wells Bombardier and Greene King Abbot Ale, plus three guests, changed every couple of days.

Pub with a friendly atmosphere built in 1962 after the Bridge House Tavern, formerly on the site, burnt down. One large bar, no music or machines. Food available 11am–9pm Mon–Wed, Fri and Sat; 12–2pm Thurs; 12–3pm and 7–8.30pm Sun, with traditional roast. Beer garden. B&B. Beer festival in December. South-east of town centre, close to county cricket ground.

OPEN *11am–11pm Mon–Sat; 12–4pm and 7–11pm Sun. Late licence available.*

Simple Simon's

Radigunds Hall, 3–9 Church Lane, Canterbury CT1 2AG
☎ *(01227) 762355*

Up to six real ales available from an ever-rotating range. Plus real cider.

Set in a 14th-century building with plenty of low beams, flagstones, real fires and lots of atmosphere. Good food at lunchtime and evenings. Large courtyard beer garden and car park. Live bands at weekends. Popular with students.

OPEN *All day, every day.*

The Unicorn

61 St Dunstan's Street, Canterbury CT2 8BS
☎ *(01227) 463187* Lorenzo Carnevale-Maffé
www.unicorninn.com

Shepherd Neame Master Brew Bitter and Caledonian Deuchars IPA, plus two other beers, one changed every few days, the other every month.

Welcoming pub in listed building dating from 1604, with one large bar housing bar billiards table. Food available 12–2.30pm and 5–8pm Mon–Fri and 12–7pm Sat. Children welcome until 7.30pm. Large beer garden. Close to Westgate Gardens and Towers, and only a short walk from the cathedral. On A290 near Canterbury West railway station.

OPEN *11.30am–midnight Sun–Thurs; 11.30am–1am Fri–Sat.*

CAPEL

The Dovecote Inn

Alders Road, Capel, Tonbridge TN12 6SU
☎ *(01892) 835966* Nick and Shelley Page

Harveys Sussex Best Bitter, Westerham Bulldog, Adnams Broadside and Badger Sussex Bitter permanently served. There are usually two guests at weekends, changed by popular demand.

Situated among picturesque terraced cottages, this friendly village pub is about 200 years old. One beamed, seriously hopped bar and dining area, large patio and children's play area. Food available 12–2.15pm and 7–9pm Tues–Sat; 12–3pm Sun, with traditional roast. Children allowed but not dogs. Large car park. Short mile west of, and signed from, A228 between Tonbridge Wells and Paddock Wood.

OPEN *5.30–11pm Mon; 12–3pm and 5.30–11pm Tues–Fri; 12–3pm and 6–11.30pm Sat; 12–close Sun.*

CHARING
The Bowl Inn
Egg Hill Road, Charing, Ashford TN27 0HG
☎ *(01233) 712256* Alan and Sue Paine
www.bowl-inn.co.uk

Fuller's London Pride plus three other beers, regularly featuring brews such as Adnams Southwold, Whitstable IPA and Westerham Sevenoaks 7X, changed when the barrel ends.

Traditional 16th-century country pub on top of the North Downs above Charing, in an Area of Outstanding Natural Beauty. Inglenook open log fire, heated patio area, large beer garden with open country views. Bar snacks served until 9.30pm every day, with Kent-sourced products used whenever possible. Huge car park. Camping area and accommodation. Beer festival in mid-July. Nearby attractions include Bishop's Palace in Charing, and Leeds Castle. A mile and a half from Charing, signposted from A20 and A252.

OPEN *Winter: 4–11pm Mon–Thurs; 12–12 Fri–Sat; 12–11pm Sun. Summer: open at 12 every day.*

CHATHAM
The Alexandra
43 Railway Street, Chatham ME4 4RJ
☎ *(01634) 830545*
Lesley Lewis and David Hughes-Jones
www.alexandrachatham.co.uk

Shepherd Neame tied house offering Master Brew Bitter and Spitfire permanently, plus a seasonal beer.

Victorian pub renovated to include quiet room off the one airy bar, conservatory leading to beer garden and upstairs function room. Shepherd Neame Most Improved Cellar 2006 and Most Improved Pub 2007. Food available 12–3pm Mon–Sat; 12–3pm Sun, with traditional roast. Live music 5–7pm every Sun and at other times. Tuesday is quiz night. Children allowed in conservatory and garden until 7pm. Effectively situated on traffic island just down from Chatham station.

OPEN *11am–11pm Mon–Sat; 12–10.30pm Sun.*

The Tap 'n' Tin
24 Railway Street, Chatham ME4 4JT
☎ *847926* Dave Gould

Greene King IPA, Abbot Ale and Old Speckled Hen, plus up to three other beers, one of which is often Goacher's Gold Star.

Lively pub just down hill from Chatham railway station and with largely young clientele. Four bars: one on ground floor, one in pool room and two upstairs. Snacks only. Dogs allowed; children in patio area only. On edge of one-way system, under arches; A2 passes overhead.

OPEN *4–11pm Sun–Wed; 4pm–2am Thurs; noon–3am Fri–Sat.*

CHIDDINGSTONE HOATH
The Rock Inn
Ryewell Hill, Hoath Corner, Chiddingstone, Edenbridge TN8 7BS
☎ *(01892) 870296* Bob Dockerty

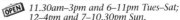The only Larkins tied house, less than two miles from the brewery and offering Traditional Ale, Chiddingstone and Best, plus a seasonal beer.

A 450-year-old rural drinkers' pub that should not be missed. Two bars, one with a distinctive brick floor, large wood-burning stove and octagonal, wooden pump handles. 'Ring the bull' played in the public bar, with a real bull's head. Food available 12–2.30pm and 7–9.30pm Tues–Sat, plus 12–3pm Sun. Dogs allowed but not children. Garden. Long two miles south of B2027. OS:497431.

OPEN *11.30am–3pm and 6–11pm Tues–Sat; 12–4pm and 7–10.30pm Sun.*

CLAYGATE
The White Hart
Benover Road, Claygate, Marden TN12 9PL
☎ *(01892) 730313* Russell and Sue Roberts
www.thewhitehart.biz

Genuine freehouse with Adnams Bitter, Fuller's London Pride and Goacher's Fine Light Ale permanent fixtures on hand pump, and a varying guest beer served directly from the cask.

Victorian pub with two bars and separate restaurant area, run by a man fiercely loyal to the contacts (e.g. Phil Goacher) he has made in his years in the trade, and for whom nothing seems too much trouble. Succulent food available 12–2.30pm and 7–9.30pm, with traditional Sunday roast. Children and dogs allowed. Massive garden. On B2162, three miles east of Paddock Wood.

OPEN *11am–11pm Mon–Sat; 12–10.30pm Sun.*

COWDEN

The Fountain

30 High Street, Cowden, Edenbridge TN8 7JG
☎ *(01342) 850528* Maria and John E'Vanson

 Harveys tied house offering Sussex Pale Ale and Sussex Best Bitter permanently, with any of the brewery's other products flowing from the third hand pump.

A 17th-century village pub with two small oak-beamed bars and separate dining area. Restaurant-style food at pub prices available 12–2.30pm and 7–9.30pm Tues–Sat; 12–2.30pm Sun, with traditional roast. Children not encouraged; dogs allowed. Large rear garden; small front patio. Barely a quarter of a mile from East Sussex boundary, short mile north of A264. OS:465404.

OPEN *6–11pm Mon; 11.30am–3pm and 6–11pm Tues–Sat; 12–10.30pm Sun.*

DARTFORD

The Malt Shovel

3 Darenth Road, Dartford DA1 1LP
☎ *(01322) 224381*
James and Shirley McGourlay

 Young's tied house since 1983 permanently offering Wells and Young's brews, plus one seasonal guest.

Beer has been sold on the site since 1873, while parts of the tap room date back 200 years before that. Two low-ceilinged bars and conservatory strongly favoured by diners. Food, prepared by the resident chef, available 12–3pm Mon–Sat, 6.30–9pm Wed–Sat, and 12–4pm Sun. Children welcome. Patio garden. Morris dancers. Only just outside town centre, but safe from the weekend 'strolling masses'. Close to A226, east side of town.

OPEN *11am–11pm Mon–Sat; 12–10.30pm Sun.*

The Wat Tyler

80 High Street, Dartford DA1 1DE
☎ *(01322) 272546*
Michael Aynge and Tracey Barrow
www.wattylerinn.co.uk

 Courage Best and John Smith's Cask plus three guests changed frequently such as Black Sheep Riggwelter, Theakston Old Peculier, Millis Thieves 'n' Fakirs and Everards Pitch Black.

Olde-worlde pub, over 600 years old, with one through bar. B&B available. No food. Children welcome until 6pm, but dogs not allowed.

OPEN *9am–11pm Mon–Thurs; 9am–midnight Fri–Sat; 10.30am–10.30pm Sun.*

DEAL

The Prince Albert

187–9 Middle Street, Deal CT14 6LW
☎ *(01304) 375425* M Harlick

 Freehouse serving three guest ales on constant rotation from local micro-breweries.

This 18th-century pub is set in a rural conservation area. Open-plan main bar and separate dining room. Food served Wed–Sat evenings and Sun lunch. B&B accommodation available. Beer garden. Located in the town centre, a short distance from the sea front.

OPEN *6–11pm Mon–Sat; 12–11pm Sun.*

The Ship Inn

141 Middle Street, Deal CT14 6JZ
☎ *(01304) 372222* Penny and Ray Dennis

A freehouse. Five real ales on offer, from independent breweries, stocked according to availability. Caledonian Deuchars IPA and Hop Back ales have featured.

Dating from 1712 and set in a historic town. No food. Beer garden.

OPEN *11am–11pm Mon–Sat; 12–11pm Sun.*

DENTON

The Jackdaw

The Street, Denton, Canterbury CT4 6QZ
☎ *(01303) 844663* Caroline and Bob Hopkins

An Enterprise Inns pub serving Shepherd Neame Spitfire and Ringwood Best, plus three weekly-changing guest ales from breweries such as 1648, Broughton, Nelson, Ramsgate, Wychwood, Wooden Hand and Hart.

This 17th-century inn features one bar with two open fires, and an 80-cover restaurant. Food served 10am–9.30pm daily. Beer gardens at front and back. Car park. Located nine miles south of Canterbury on the A260 towards Folkestone.

OPEN *10am–11pm.*

EAST FARLEIGH

The Farleigh Bull

Lower Road, East Farleigh, Maidstone ME15 0HD
☎ *(01622) 726282* Jon West and Jan Tolley

Fuller's London Pride, Shepherd Neame Master Brew and Harvey's Bitter.

Victorian pub with self-contained function room and large L-shaped dining room/bar. Food available 12–3pm and 6–9pm Mon–Sat; 12–5pm Sun, with traditional roast dinners served with a choice of meats and fresh market vegetables, all home-cooked. Families welcome. Two large gardens, one with a play area for children and dogs, the other with ponds for the adults. Paved patio area, pets' corner. On B2010, two miles south-west of Maidstone.

OPEN *12–11pm (10.30pm Sun).*

EAST MALLING
King & Queen
1 New Road, East Malling ME19 6DD
☎ *(01732) 842752* David C Drury

Rotating guest ales from breweries such as Westerham, Wells and Young's and Harveys.

A500-year-old traditional country pub in the same ownership since 2000, with one bar and separate dining areas. Food available, both bar food and an à la carte menu in the restaurant 12–9pm Mon–Sat, 12–4pm Sun. Large secluded beer garden. Function room. Near The Hop Farm in Beltring. Situated in the old part of East Malling, opposite the church.

OPEN *10am–11pm Mon–Fri; 11am–11pm Sat; 11am–9pm Sun.*

The Rising Sun
125 Mill Street, East Malling ME19 6BX
☎ *(01732) 843284*
Peter Kemp and Paul Fincham

Freehouse where products from Goacher's and Shepherd Neame are usually available, plus a third beer from virtually anywhere, though generally a stronger one.

Locals' pub in a terrace of mill cottages with one U-shaped bar. Vast selection of standard-priced single-malt whiskies. Food available 12–2.15pm Mon–Fri; then only snacks until late afternoon. Dogs allowed but not children. Large paved garden. League darts played every weekday evening. Short mile south of A20. OS:697572.

OPEN *12–11pm (10.30pm Sun).*

EDENBRIDGE
The King & Queen
81 High Street, Edenbridge TN8 5AU
☎ *(01732) 862139* Jenny Edney

Shepherd Neame tied house offering Best Bitter and Spitfire permanently, with whatever seasonal beer is appropriate.

Dating back to 1650, this welcoming pub has one beamed and hopped bar, separate dining area, several nooks and crannies and real fires. Food 12–2.30pm daily, with traditional Sunday roast, and 7–9pm Sat (phone to ask on other evenings). Familes welcome, though a sign above the bar warns 'Children left unattended will be sold to the circus' – riled, Jenny could be awesome; dogs discouraged. Garden. On B2026, southern end of town.

OPEN *11am–3pm and 6–11pm Mon–Fri; 11am–11pm Sat; 12–5pm and 7–10.30pm Sun.*

ELHAM
The Rose & Crown
High Street, Elham, Canterbury CT4 6TD
☎ *(01303) 840226*
Patrick Clarke and Alison Kirby
www.roseandcrownelham.co.uk

A Shepherd Neame pub with Master Brew, Best, Spitfire and Bishops Finger, plus a seasonal ale.

A16th-century country inn, full of traditional features including five open fires. Extensive homemade à la carte menu using only fresh produce served 12–2.30pm and 6.30–9pm. Restaurant seating 70, beer terrace, large family gardens with a selection of outdoor games. Children and dogs allowed. Car park. Six deluxe en-suite rooms. Five minutes from Channel Tunnel, ten minutes from the port of Dover and ten minutes from historic Canterbury. From junction 12 of the M20, head for Lymings, or take the Barham turning off the A2.

OPEN *All day, every day.*

FAIRSEAT
The Vigo Inn
Gravesend Road, Fairseat, Sevenoaks TN15 7JL
☎ *(01732) 822547* Peter and Peta Ashwell

Wells and Young's and Harveys products permanently occupy four of the five hand pumps, the other being reserved for a variable guest beer.

Old drovers' inn with two bars: one built in the 15th century, the other in the 16th. Simple food and bar snacks available. A must for anybody who values the traditions of a no-nonsense English pub. Located on the North Downs Way, on the A227, a country mile north-east of A20.

OPEN *6–11pm Mon–Fri; 12–4pm and 6–11pm Sat; 12–4pm and 7–10.30pm Sun.*

FARNBOROUGH
The Woodman
50 High Street, Farnborough BR6 7BA
☎ *(01689) 852663* Terry Pritchard

Shepherd Neame Master Brew, Spitfire and a seasonal brew.

Avillage pub in a quiet location, with a large garden, grapevine canopy and many hanging baskets, window boxes and tubs. Food served 12–2pm Mon–Sat and lunchtime roasts every Sunday. Children welcome. Car park. Located just off the A21, three miles from Bromley, signposted 'Farnborough Village'.

OPEN *All day, every day.*

FARNINGHAM
The Chequers
High Street, Farningham, Dartford DA4 0DT
☎ *(01322) 865222*
Alan Vowls and Karen Jefferies

Fuller's London Pride and ESB and Timothy Taylor Landlord, with something from Oakham virtually certain to feature among up to six other beers from smaller breweries.

Three-hundred-year-old beamed village pub with one bar, close to River Darenth in Brands Hatch area. Food available 12–2.30pm Mon–Sat. Children and dogs allowed. Street-corner site about 250 yards from A20.

OPEN *11am–11pm Mon–Sat; 12–10.30pm Sun.*

FAVERSHAM

The Anchor Inn

52 Abbey Street, Faversham ME13 7BP
☎ *(01795) 536471 David and Fran Little*
www.theanchorinnfaversham.com

Shepherd Neame tied house offering Master Brew Bitter, Best Bitter and Spitfire plus whatever seasonal beer is appropriate.

A 17th-century pub, long associated with the brewery. Two bar areas, one of which is a 26-seat restaurant with à la carte menu. Food available 12–3pm (not Mon) and 6–9pm Mon–Sat and 12–4pm Sun, with traditional roast. Popular with families, and dog-friendly. Comfortable smoking area. Large beer garden. Occasional live music. North of town centre, within walking distance, close to Standard Quay.

OPEN *12–11pm Sun–Thurs; 12–12 Fri–Sat.*

The Crown & Anchor

41 The Mall, Faversham ME13 8JN
☎ *(01795) 532812 Marion M Koncsik*

Shepherd Neame tied house offering Master Brew Bitter, Best Bitter and Spitfire are added to coincide with brewery's hop festival.

The pub was already serving beer when Shepherd Neame acquired it in 1859. One L-shaped bar and separate games room. Food available 12–2.30pm Mon–Fri. Goulash is a speciality. Just off A2, south of town centre.

OPEN *10.30am–3pm and 5.30–11pm Mon–Fri; 10.30am–4pm and 6–11pm Sat; 12–2.30pm and 7–10.30pm Sun.*

The Elephant Inn

31 The Mall, Faversham ME13 8JN
☎ *(01795) 590157 James and Kim Pearson*

A genuine freehouse that usually has five hand pumps dispensing a constantly changing range of beers, mainly from local micro-breweries.

Traditional locals' pub with friendly atmosphere dating back to the 17th century. Single bar and enclosed garden, function room and barbecue available for private use. Swale CAMRA Pub of the Year 2007. Supervised children welcome away from the bar. Between A2 and the town centre, south of the railway line and within walking distance of the station.

OPEN *3–11pm Tues–Fri; 12–11pm Sat; 12–10pm Sun (closed 7pm Sun in winter).*

The Shipwright's Arms

Hollowshore, off Ham Road, Oare, Faversham ME13 7TU
☎ *(01795) 590088 Derek and Ruth Cole*

Genuine freehouse serving beers only from Kent breweries directly from the cask. Goacher's Dark Mild, Original and Shipwrecked (the house ale) plus Hopdaemon Golden Braid and Whitstable IPA are regular features.

Unspoilt 17th-century former smugglers' inn with one service bar and lots of nooks and crannies. Food available 12–2.30pm every day and 7–9pm (not Sun);

traditional Sunday roast. Large garden. Children allowed in designated areas. On Ham Marshes, long mile north of Faversham; follow signs for Oare, then for the pub itself. OS:017636.

OPEN *Summer: 11am–3pm and 6–11pm Mon–Fri; 11am–4pm and 6–11pm Sat; 12–10.30pm Sun. Winter: As summer, but closed Mon and 4–6pm Sun. May close early on winter evenings if no customers (wise to phone first).*

FINGLESHAM

The Crown

The Street, Finglesham, Deal CT14 0NA
☎ *(01304) 612555 David and Jackie Cooper*
www.thecrownatfinglesham.co.uk

Genuine freehouse with five real ales typically available, and changed weekly, favouring micro-breweries. Guest beers could be Gadds-20 Beer, Hopdeaman, beers from Whitstable Brewery, and many others.

A twelfth-century building, set in 2 acres of land, with a beautiful beer garden, and complete with brick BBQ. A 52-cover restaurant offers above-average cuisine, catering for theme nights, weddings, functions. Food served 12–3pm and 6–9pm (Sun from 12). Little hamlet set beween Deal and Sandwich.

OPEN *12am–3pm and 6pm–midnight Mon–Thurs; open all day Fri, Sat, Sun.*

FOLKESTONE

The Chambers

Cheriton Place, Folkestone CT20 2BB
☎ *(01303) 223333 CP and E Smith*

This freehouse serves Ringwood Old Thumper, Hopdaemon Skrimshander, Ramsgate Gadds' No. 5, an Adnams ale plus one guest changed every two to four weeks.

This two-bar pub is located in a basement with an eclectic mix of styles, old and new. Mixed customer base with good ale following. Fresh homemade food available, with weekly specials and Mexican specialities, 12–2pm Mon, 12–2pm and 7–9pm Tues–Thurs, 12–2pm Fri, 12–2pm and 7–9pm Sat. Weekly live music and DJs twice a week. Steak night every Tues. Licensed coffee shop with pavement seating. Monthly quiz nights. Annual ale festival held at Easter. Private parties catered for, outside catering and bar available.

OPEN *12–11pm Mon–Thurs; noon–1am Fri–Sat; 7–10.30pm Sun.*

The Lifeboat

42 North Street, Folkestone CT19 6AF
☎ *(01303) 252877* Mike and Laura Edson

A true freehouse with four to seven real ales, including Harveys Sussex and Timothy Taylor Landlord plus weekly-changing guests.

Classic backstreet locals' pub in listed building on the fringes of what tourist area Folkestone has left. Beer has been sold on site since 16th century. One beamed bar with background music. Light food available. Dogs welcome, plus children until 7.30pm. Beer garden with BBQ and stage for bands. About 100 yards from seafront; follow signs to Folkestone Harbour.

OPEN *12–12 (11pm Sun).*

GILLINGHAM

The Dog & Bone

21 Jeffrey Street, Gillingham ME7 1DE
☎ *(01634) 576829* David Skinner

Four constantly changing beers, with styles and strengths to suit everyone. Priced identically.

Traditional pub with one L-shaped bar, large conservatory/dining area and games room. Bar food available 12–2.30pm Tues–Sat; restaurant meals Tues–Sat from 6pm; traditional Sunday roast 12–2.30pm. Garden. On corner of James Street, a few minutes from Gillingham railway station.

OPEN *11am–11pm Mon–Sat; 12–10.30pm Sun.*

The Frog & Toad

Burnt Oak Terrace, Gillingham ME7 1DR
☎ *(01634) 852231* David Gould
www.thefrogandtoad.com

Fuller's London Pride plus three other regularly changing beers, priced identically. Belgian beers also available.

Lively one-bar street-corner freehouse with no fruit machines or juke boxes. Good-value, freshly made sandwiches. Children and dogs allowed in the large garden only. Two annual beer festivals. Virtually due north of Gillingham railway station.

OPEN *12–11pm (10.30pm Sun).*

The Will Adams

73 Saxton Street, Gillingham ME7 5EG
☎ *(01634) 575902* Peter and Julie Lodge

Hop Back Summer Lightning plus up to four more beers on bank holiday weekends, two at other times.

One-bar local that was originally the Anglo Saxon; renamed by present licencees. Will Adams was a famous local explorer. Burgers, homemade chillis and pies available 12–2pm Sat only. Dogs allowed. Situated on corner of Lock Street at High Street end of Canterbury Street.

OPEN *7–11pm Mon–Fri; 12–3pm and 7–11pm Sat; 12–4pm and 8–10.30pm Sun.*

GOUDHURST

The Green Cross

Station Road, Goudhurst TN17 1HA
☎ *(01580) 211200* Lou and Caroline Lizzi

Genuine freehouse with Harveys Sussex Best Bitter plus weekly-changing guests in summer.

Built as station hotel on western edge of village and as such provides welcome space away from endless traffic congestion. One basic bar and separate restaurant area, where seafood is the speciality. Food available 12–3pm and 7–9.30pm; traditional Sunday roast. Children allowed but not dogs. Small garden. From the A21 Lamberhurst roundabout take the turn for Goudhurst (A26/A262). The pub is two miles along on the right, next to the Bentley garage.

OPEN *11.30am–3pm and 6.30–11pm Mon–Sat; 12–3pm and 7–10.30pm Sun, but closed Sunday evenings in winter (phone first).*

GRAVESEND

The Crown & Thistle

44 The Terrace, Gravesend DA12 2BJ
☎ *(01474) 326049*
Phil Bennett and Jackie Hall
www.crownandthistle.org.uk

Freehouse with Daleside Shrimpers and four other beers, one of which will be above 5% ABV. The fact that in the first 20 months of his tenure, the landlord turned round some 800 different beers speaks for itself about the range.

Pub since 1849 and probably the best-kept secret in town, at least until it was named CAMRA National Pub of the Year in 2004. One beamed bar, separate hopped dining area. Run by a Gravesend local with a terrific feel for beer, who is eager to put something back into his locale and already does a vast amount of fund-raising for the RNLI. Bar snacks, Chinese and Thai food available 12–3pm with Indian, Chinese and Thai food – to eat in or to take away – an evening feature from 6–10pm. Children welcome, but are asked to leave by 9pm if not eating; dog-friendly. Large, paved, south-facing garden. Situated in narrow corridor between A226 and River Thames. OS:651743.

OPEN *11am–11pm Mon–Sat; 12–10.30pm Sun.*

The Jolly Drayman

1 Love Lane, Wellington Street, Gravesend DA12 1JA
☎ *(01474) 352355* Tim and Andrea Fordred
www.jollydrayman.com

Everards Tiger plus up to three other beers, ranging from 3.5% to 5.5% ABV in strength.

Country-style pub in town-centre location and a pub since 1843. Housed in part of Wellington Brewery building. One beamed bar, airy conservatory and separate dining area; accommodation. Food available 12–2.30pm Mon–Sat; 12–4pm Sun, including traditional roast; 7–9.30pm Tues–Sun. Children not allowed in bar but well-behaved dogs are. Garden. Just south of A226.

OPEN *11.30am–11pm Mon–Sat; 12–10.30pm Sun.*

The Somerset Arms

10 Darnley Road, Gravesend DA11 0RU
☎ *(01474) 533837 Edward and Pat Kerr*

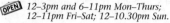 Six beers from a range of hundreds per year, the landlord making the best of being allowed 'guest' brews.

Former Fremlins street-corner pub, now tied to Enterprise Inns and catering for all tastes. One large U-shaped bar, but with quiet nooks and crannies in which to ease away the pains caused by town-centre shopping. Homemade fresh food available 11am–3pm Mon–Sat. No children in evening nor dogs at any time. Discos Friday and Saturday nights, but an over-21 restriction deters the marauding masses; you can still enjoy the beer. Close to Gravesend railway station on B262, on south-west fringes of one-way system.

OPEN *11am–midnight.*

GREAT CHART

The Hoodeners Horse

The Street, Great Chart, Ashford TN23 3AN
☎ *(01233) 625583 Ralph Johnson*

Young's Special plus one rotating guest.

Old English pub with one bar decorated with hops. Varied menu specialising in Mexican food. Full range of Gale's country wines generally in stock. Food available 12–2pm and 6–10pm Mon–Sat; 12–3pm and 5–9pm Sun. Children allowed. Garden. Situated in middle of village on former route of A28.

OPEN *11am–3pm and 5–11pm Mon–Thurs; 11am–11pm Fri–Sat; 11am–10.30pm Sun.*

HALSTEAD

The Rose & Crown

Otford Lane, Halstead, Sevenoaks TN14 7EA
☎ *(01959) 533120*
Joy Brushneen and Robert Baker

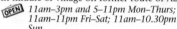 Genuine freehouse serving Larkins Traditional Ale and Whitstable EIPA plus three or four guests, from breweries such as Cotleigh, Oakham and RCH, changed every few days.

Victorian Grade II listed flint building with two bars; primarily a drinkers' pub. Food available 12–7pm Mon–Sat, and 12–3pm Sun (booking advisable for Bob's Sunday Roast!). There is also an all-day menu available on Sunday 3–7pm. Beautiful enclosed garden with covered seating area. Dogs allowed on leads. Pool and darts available. One mile west of A224, opposite primary school.

OPEN *12–12.*

HARVEL

Amazon & Tiger

Harvel Street, Harvel, Meopham DA13 0DE
☎ *(01474) 814705 Mick Whitehouse*

Genuine freehouse with three beers varying on a weekly basis.

Typical village pub that caters for all age groups. Two bars. Food available 12–2.30pm Mon–Sat; 7–9pm Fri and Sat; 12–4pm Sun, with traditional roast. Children and

dogs allowed. Garden overlooking cricket ground. Headquarters and spiritual home of Harvel Hash House Harriers, 'the drinking club with a running problem'. Short mile east of A227.

OPEN *12–3pm and 6–11pm Mon–Thurs; 12–11pm Fri–Sat; 12–10.30pm Sun.*

HASTINGLEIGH

The Bowl Inn

The Street, Hastingleigh, Ashford TN25 5HU
☎ *(01233) 750354 Ron and Annie Blown*

Freehouse serving Adnams Bitter, Fuller's London Pride, Harveys and Ramsgate brews and a weekly-changing guest.

A traditional pub dating back to the 1740s. Two bars. Games room including pool table and dartboard. No juke box or games machines. Sandwiches available at weekends. Large beer garden. Annual beer festival over the August bank holiday ties in with the village carnival.

OPEN *5–11pm Tues–Fri; 12–12 Sat–Sun (closed Mon).*

HERNE

The Butcher's Arms

29a Herne Street, Herne CT6 7HL
☎ *(01227) 371000 Martyn Paul Hillier*
www.micropub.co.uk

Freehouse with four or five real ales. Dark Star Hophead, Harveys Best, Fuller's ESB and JW Lees Harvest Ales are permanent, and one or two guests rotate, based on customers' choices. One soft drink, two wines, but no lager or spirits!

Opened in 2005 in a converted butchers shop, this has no bar, no food and one toilet. All beers are on gravity, and there is a 10% discount for takeaways. Opposite the church in Herne on the A291, six miles from Canterbury.

OPEN *12–1.30pm and 6–10.30pm Tues–Sun.*

HOOK GREEN

The Elephant's Head

Furnace Lane, Hook Green, Lamberhurst TN3 8LJ
☎ *(01892) 890279 George and Sue May*

Harveys tied house offering Sussex Pale Ale, Sussex Best Bitter and Armada Ale, with any of the brewery's seasonal products, except for Knots of May Light Mild.

Built as a farm dwelling in 1489, this splendidly isolated stone building gained its present name and full licence in 1808. Two beamed and hopped bars, one with a cosy off-shoot, separate dining area and airy conservatory. Food available 12–2.30pm daily, with traditional roast on Sunday; 7–9.30pm Tues–Thu; 6.30–9.30pm Fri and Sat. A barbecue may be hired for private functions. Children and dogs on leads allowed. Large garden with paved patio. On B2169, long mile west of Lamberhurst; half a mile from East Sussex boundary.

OPEN *Summer: 11am–3pm and 5–11pm Mon–Fri; 11am–11pm Sat; 12–10.30pm Sun; no afternoon closing in school summer holidays (except perhaps if it's raining). Winter: As summer, but lunchtime opening 12 all week.*

HORTON KIRBY
The Bull
Lombard Street, Horton Kirby, Dartford DA4 9DF
☎ *(01322) 862274*
Lynne Prentice and Garrett Phipps

Freehouse with four ales, a constantly changing range from brewers all over the country.

A warm and welcoming Victorian village pub, built in the early 1900s. One main central horseshoe-shaped bar. Home-cooked food using fresh ingredients from local suppliers available 12–2pm Tues–Wed, 12–2pm and 7–9.30pm Thurs–Fri, 1–3pm and 7–9.30pm Sat, 1–4pm Sun. Large, landscaped beer garden with stunning views over the Darent Valley. Regular barbecues held in summer. Regular live music events. Dogs welcome on a lead in the garden. Located five miles from Dartford, three miles from junction 3A of the M25.

OPEN *4–11pm Mon; 12–11pm Tues–Thurs; 12–12 Fri; 1pm–12 Sat; 12–10.30pm Sun.*

IGHTHAM COMMON
The Old House
Redwell, Ightham TN15 9EE
☎ *(01732) 882383* Richard Boulter

Genuine freehouse serving Daleside Shrimpers, Otter Bitter and Oakham Jeffrey Hudson Bitter plus one or two others, all served lovingly directly from the cask.

W ords cannot describe this Grade II listed building that, despite its limited opening hours, deserves to be in every beer/pub guide, whatever the parameters. Two bars: one beamed and dating from the 17th century with a vast open fire, the other – more of a 'snug' – a couple of hundred years younger. More than 100 single-malt whiskies. No food. Dogs allowed; children also if kept tethered. No sign outside; look for a row (lit at night) of cottages on the north side of the lane. Less than half a mile from both the A25 and A227. OS:590559.

OPEN *7–9pm Tues; 7pm–close Wed–Mon; 12–3pm Sat–Sun.*

LADDINGFORD
The Chequers Inn
Lees Road, Laddingford, Nr Yalding ME18 6BP
☎ *(01622) 871266* Charles and Tracey Leaver

Adnams Bitter, Fuller's London Pride and Young's Bitter plus two guest ales.

B uilt in the 15th century, this weatherboarded building has been a farmhouse in its time. One oak-beamed bar leading to patio and at times a large marquee; accommodation. Food available 12–2.30pm and 7–9.30pm, with traditional Sunday roast. Children and dogs allowed. Large garden with livestock and an extensive play area. Award-winning flower displays in summer. Annual real ale festival held every April. A mile east of A228, south/south-west of Yalding.

OPEN *12–3pm and 5–11pm Mon–Fri; 12–11pm Sat; 12–10.30pm Sun.*

LEEDS
The George Inn
4 Lower Street, Leeds ME17 1RN
☎ *(01622) 861314* Jenny and Geoff Griffiths

Shepherd Neame tied house with Master Brew and a seasonal ale from the brewery. Spitfire also available from time to time. Recent guests have included East Anglian and St Austell beers.

B uilt in 1692 and the nearest pub to Leeds Castle, with many little areas to hide away in. The dining room seats 27, and there is a new patio for smokers. Food available 12–9pm Mon–Sat, and 12–8pm Sunday. Car park, beer garden. Well-behaved children and dogs welcome. Quiz every 1st Tues of month. Good centre for walkers, and handy for the castle and church. From junction 8 of the M20, follow signs for Leeds Castle. Continue past the gates, and this is the first pub you come to.

OPEN *11am–11pm Mon–Sat; 12–10.30pm Sun.*

LUDDESDOWN
The Cock Inn
Henley Street, Luddesdown, Gravesend DA13 0XB
☎ *(01474) 814208* Andrew Turner
www.cockluddesdowne.com

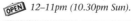Freehouse offering seven real ales, with brews from Adnams, Harveys and Goacher's usually featured. Guest ales might be from Burton Bridge, Westerham, Cottage and Woodforde's.

A 16th-century traditional beamed and hopped two-bar pub set in idyllic countryside on North Downs escarpment, complete with open fires. Food served 12–9pm (until 8pm Sun). Cask Marque accredited. No children inside pub or rear garden, please; dogs more than welcome. Fully heated outside covered smoking area. Conservatory and small garden. A long half mile east of B2009 and Sole Street station, from which there is a direct footpath. OS:664672.

OPEN *12–11pm (10.30pm Sun).*

LYNSTED
The Black Lion
Lynsted Lane, Lynsted ME9 0RJ
☎ *(01795) 521229* CM Morgan

Freehouse serving Goacher's Fine Light, Real Mild, Best Dark and Crown Imperial Stout.

A purpose-built Jacobean alehouse with two bars. Food served 12–2pm and 6–9pm daily. Accommodation available. Private function room. Beer garden, car park. Close to Canterbury, Faversham, Belmont House, Leeds Castle and Doddington Place. Located just off the A2 at Teynham.

OPEN *11am–3pm and 6–11pm Mon–Sat; 12–3pm and 7–10.30pm Sun.*

MAIDSTONE

The Pilot

24 Upper Stone Street, Maidstone ME15 6EU
☎ *(01622) 691162* Joe Houlihan

 Harveys tied house with six hand pumps, offering Sussex XX Mild Ale, Sussex Best Bitter and Armada Ale plus whatever seasonal beers are appropriate.

The county town's little marvel. Grade II listed building that houses all things good about country pubs in an urban location. Two bars, with a third room tucked away for peace and quiet should you need it. Food available 12–3pm Tues–Fri, 7–9pm Mon–Sat and Sunday lunches 1–4pm. Live music Saturday night and Sunday lunch. Children and dogs allowed. Garden with some 'interesting' brickwork – see landlord for details. In one-way system on A229 leaving town southwards, but sufficiently far from drinking halls not to attract the weekend blundering chunderers.

OPEN *12–3pm and 6–11pm Mon–Fri; 12–4pm and 7–11pm Sat; all day Sun.*

The Rifle Volunteers

28 Wyatt Street, Maidstone ME14 1EU
☎ *(01622) 758891* Alan and Wendy Marlow

 One of only two Goacher's tied houses, offering realistically priced Real Mild Ale, Fine Light Ale and Crown Imperial Stout permanently.

Street-corner local in Grade II listed building. One basic bar. Food available 12–2pm. No children; dogs tolerated. Patio garden. On junction of Union Street close to town centre, but offers nothing to attract weekend 'strollers'.

OPEN *11am–3pm and 6–11pm Mon–Sat; 12–3pm and 7–10.30pm Sun.*

MARGATE

The Orb

243 Ramsgate Road, Margate CT9 4EU
☎ *(01843) 220663* Dennis McGrellis

Shepherd Neame tied house offering Master Brew Bitter permanently, with Best Bitter, Spitfire or whatever seasonal beer is appropriate.

Built at the end of the 15th century, this pub is situated on the town's outskirts close to a large hospital. One bar, separate dining area and games room. Food available 12–2.30pm Mon–Fri; 12–5pm Sun, with traditional roast. Children welcome; dog-friendly. Outside drinking area. On A254.

OPEN *11am–11pm Mon–Sat; 12–10.30pm Sun.*

The Spread Eagle

25 Victoria Road, Margate CT9 1LW
☎ *(01843) 293396*
Michelle Galvin and Mark Hodges

Fuller's London Pride and Young's Bitter plus two guest beers changed weekly.

Traditional Victorian backstreet local with one bar, dining area and garden with gazebo. Six-foot projection screen showing Sky Sports. Traditional home cooking using fresh ingredients served 11am–7pm Mon–Sat

and 12–4pm Sun (including Sunday roasts). Children and dogs welcome. Room for small parties (anniversaries, Christenings etc), with catering if required. Fifteen minutes' walk from Margate seafront and Dreamland amusement park. Just off B2055, behind St John's church.

OPEN *11am–11pm Mon–Thus; 11am–midnight Fri–Sat; 12–10.30pm Sun.*

MARSH GREEN

The Wheatsheaf Inn

Marsh Green Road, Marsh Green, Edenbridge TN8 5QL
☎ *(01732) 864091* Neil Foster
www.thewheatsheaf.net

 Genuine freehouse with Harveys Sussex Best Bitter plus up to six constantly changing other beers. Among the favourites are Fuller's London Pride, Everards Tiger Best Bitter and other brews from Harveys.

Built around the middle of the 19th century, this traditional village pub has one large, circular bar with numerous serving areas and several small off-shoots. Food available 12–2pm and 7–9.30pm Mon–Fri; 12–2.30pm and 7–9.30pm Sat; 12–2.30pm, with traditional roast, and 7–9pm Sun. Children and dogs allowed, all kept on leads, please. Conservatory and garden. Only just in Kent, on B2028.

OPEN *11am–11pm Mon–Sat; 12–10.30pm Sun.*

NORTHBOURNE

Hare & Hounds

The Street, Northbourne CT14 0LG
☎ *(01304) 365429* Bruce Doodney

Punch Taverns tied house serving Harveys Sussex, Flowers IPA, Adnams Best and a weekly-changing guest ale.

A 16th-century rural pub with one main bar. Extensive food menu (including vegetarian) available daily for lunch and dinner. Beer garden. Car park. Children welcome. Annual beer festival held in June. Located off the A256.

OPEN *12–3pm and 6–11pm.*

NORTHFLEET

The Campbell Arms

1 Campbell Road, Gravesend DA11 0JZ
☎ *07708 280727* Christine Jeffries

 Courage Best, Young's Bitter and Daleside Shrimpers, plus two weekly changing guests including Otter Bright, RCH Pitchfork or something from Wooden Hand brewery.

Backstreet freehouse in a listed building over 100 years old. Children welcome. Garden and barbecue area, with barbecue food often available in the summer. Leaving Gravesend town centre, follow Pelham Road, take the second turning on the right on to Lennox Road and then the first left.

OPEN *12–11pm (10.30pm Sun).*

OAD STREET
The Plough & Harrow
Oad Street, Borden, Sittingbourne ME9 8LB
☎ *(01795) 843351* Mark Lockyer

Freehouse with Goacher's Mild and Original, Hardys and Hansons Olde Trip and Shepherd Neame Master Brew plus one guest beer, changed every three months.

Small two-bar country pub dating from the 1600s, with low beamed ceilings and lots of breweriana. Restaurant seating 40, beer garden. Bar snacks and à la carte meals available 12–2pm Mon, 12–2.30pm and 6–9.30pm Tues–Sat and 12–4pm Sun (roasts). Families welcome. Car park. Weddings and other events catered for. Craft centre opposite. Close to M2 J5 and M20 J7.

OPEN *11am–11pm Mon–Thurs; 11am–midnight Fri–Sat; 12–10.30pm Sun.*

OLD ROMNEY
The Rose & Crown
Swamp Road, Old Romney, Romney Marsh TN29 9SQ
☎ *(01797) 367500* Michael Hoverd
www.roseandcrown-oldromney.co.uk

Freehouse with Greene King IPA and Courage Directors plus local beer Rother Valley Level Best. Guest beers are served during the summer months. Biddenden and Bushels cider also featured.

Built towards the end of the 17th century and a pub since 1806. Two bars, conservatory and separate games room; accommodation. Food available 12–2.30pm and 6–8.30pm Mon–Fri; 12–9pm Sat; 12–8.30pm Sun (12–4pm Sun in winter); traditional Sunday roast. Children and dogs allowed. Large garden. Signed from A259.

OPEN *11.30am–11pm Mon–Sat; 12–10.30pm Sun.*

OTFORD HILLS
The Fox & Hounds
Romney Street, Otford Hills, Sevenoaks TN15 6XR
☎ *(01959) 525428* Phil Tatler

Freehouse serving four constantly rotating guest ales from breweries such as Archers and Cottage. Also feature a weekly guest ale at £1.80 a pint.

This 400-year-old former woodman's cottage became a public house in 1700. Beams and open fire. One main bar and restaurant. Food, including local game and farm produce, available Tues–Sun. Large child-friendly garden. Marquee available for functions. Large car park at rear, smaller one at front. Restaurant available for hire for up to 60 people, garden holds around 200 people. Many walks nearby on the North Downs. Beer and folk festivals held May and August. Situated three miles up Bower Lane from Eynsford war memorial. A two-mile walk from Otford, Shoreham or Eynsford railway stations, along country footpaths.

OPEN *11am–midnight.*

PECKHAM BUSH
Bush, Blackbird & Thrush
194 Bush Road, Peckham Bush, East Peckham TN12 5LN
☎ *(01622) 871349* Natalie and Jon Surtees

Shepherd Neame tied house offering Master Brew Bitter and Spitfire permanently, with whatever seasonal beer is appropriate, all served directly from the cask.

A 14th-century building that stands alone amid spacious farmland. One beamed bar and separate restaurant area. Food available 12–2pm and 6.30–9pm Tues–Sat; 12–2.30pm Sun, with traditional roast. Children and dogs allowed, the pub having its own hound, Bremner, who, despite the landlord supporting Leeds United, will 'bite yer leg' only if seriously provoked. Massive garden with plenty of activities for children. Long half-mile west of East Peckham village. OS:663499.

OPEN *12–3pm and 6pm–close.*

PENSHURST
The Bottle House Inn
Smarts Hill, Penshurst TN11 8ET
☎ *(01892) 870306* Gordon and Val Meer
www.thebottlehouseinnpenshurst.co.uk

Harveys Best and Larkins Traditional.

Family-run freehouse built in 1492 as a farm building and finally granted a full licence in 1938. Beams, real fires, wooden tables and a series of interconnecting rooms. Good food served all day, every day (12–9.30pm). Terrace and garden. Rural location takes some finding. Check website or ring for directions.

OPEN *11am–11pm (10.30pm Sun).*

PETTS WOOD
Sovereign of the Seas
109 Queensway, Petts Wood, Orpington BR5 1DG
☎ *(01689) 891606* Robert Barfoot

Wetherspoon's pub serving Shepherd Neame Spitfire. Two guests might include Hop Back Summer Lightning or Timothy Taylor Landlord. Guests changed weekly.

A community pub with one big bar, a dining area and disabled facilities. Outside patios in summer. Food available all day. No children.

OPEN *All day, every day.*

PLAXTOL

The Papermakers Arms

The Street, Plaxtol, Sevenoaks TN15 0QJ
☎ *(01732) 810407* June and Doug Edmondson

Harveys Sussex Bitter and an Adnams ale, with a third beer that changes barrel by barrel.

Traditional village pub, the Edwardian building providing a spacious bar and resultant relaxed atmosphere. Pool, darts, cribbage, and bat and trap. Reasonably priced homemade meals available 12–2pm and 7–9pm Mon–Sat; 12.30–3.30pm Sun. Car park. Live music once a fortnight. Off the A227 Tonbridge to Igtham Road.

OPEN *12–3pm and 6–11pm Mon–Thurs; all day Fri–Sun.*

RAINHAM

The Angel

Station Road, Rainham, Gillilngham ME8 7UH
☎ *(01634) 360219* Matthew Greig

An Admiral Tavern pub with an Adnams beer plus two rotating guests, which change daily.

Dating back to the late 17th century, this pub has won CAMRA Pub of the Year several times. One large bar. Large beer garden. Children welcome. Pool table, large TV. Snacks available on Sundays.

OPEN *12–11pm Sun–Thurs; 12–12 Fri–Sat.*

The Mackland Arms

213 Station Road, Rainham ME8 7PS
☎ *(01634) 232178*
Godfrey Page and Trinna White

Shepherd Neame tied house offering Master Brew Bitter permanently, plus seasonal ales.

Very popular small pub with one L-shaped bar and friendly licensees. No food or children; dogs allowed. Beer garden and patio. On B2004, close to Rainham railway station.

OPEN *10am–11pm Mon–Sat; 12–10.30pm Sun.*

RAMSGATE

The Artillery Arms

36 West Cliff Road, Ramsgate CT11 9JS
☎ *(01843) 853282* Chris and Michele Parry

Genuine freehouse with Charles Wells Bombardier plus four other beers on a constantly rotating basis.

Small street-corner hostelry with welcoming atmosphere and justifiably CAMRA Thanet Pub of the Year for 2002 and 2003. Grade II listed building constructed at start of the 19th century, featuring leaded stained-glass windows depicting Royal Artillery horseback scenes, hand-painted by soldiers after the Napoleonic Wars. No hot food but doorstep sandwiches made fresh to order nearly all day Mon–Sat. No children. Close to marina, perhaps 200 yards from seafront.

OPEN *12–11pm (10.30pm Sun).*

Churchill Tavern

19–22 The Paragon, Ramsgate CT11 9JX
☎ *(01843) 587862* Peter Matthews

Charles Wells Bombadier, Fuller's London Pride, Ringwood Old Thumper, plus three frequently changing guests, including Gale's HSB, Everards Sunchaser or local specials from the Ramsgate or Whitstable breweries.

A freehouse overlooking the marina with views across the sea to France on a clear day. Located in an historic building dating from 1816 which was once the Isabella Baths, converted to the Paragon Hotel in 1868 and is now part of a language school. Children welcome. Beer festivals. Smoking terrace. Food served 12–3pm and 6.30–10pm.

OPEN *11.30am–2am.*

Montefiore Arms

1 Trinity Place, Ramsgate CT11 7HJ
☎ *(01843) 593265* Andy Breeze

Ramsgate Gadds' No.7 plus two guests changed every three days. Beers from Dark Star, Burton Bridge and Wye Valley often feature. Biddenden cider also served.

Named after Sir Moses Montefiore, this friendly town local dates from 1850 and has one bar and a family room. It is run by the owner at all times. No food. No juke box or fruit machines. Various theme nights. Off Hereson Road, near Dumpton Park.

OPEN *12–2.30pm and 7–11pm Mon–Sat (closed Wed); 12–3pm and 7–10.30pm Sun.*

RECULVER

The King Ethelbert Inn

Reculver Lane, Reculver CT6 6SU
☎ *(01227) 374368* Marc and Mandy Wing

Shepherd Neame Master Brew plus up to two other beers, one of which is usually from a Kent micro-brewery.

Built in 1843, this is a reliable pub for seasiders and walkers alike, being on Saxon Shore Way and overlooking the Thames estuary. One circular beamed bar with large dining area. Food available 12–3pm and 6–9pm Mon–Fri; 12–5pm and 6.30–9pm Sat–Sun, with traditional roasts on Sun. Children allowed until 9pm; dogs, on a lead, any time. Children's play area. Long mile north of A299 (Thanet Way).

OPEN *11am–11pm Mon–Thurs; 11am–midnight Fri–Sat; 12–11pm Sun.*

ROCHESTER
The Britannia Bar Café
376 High Street, Rochester ME1 1DJ
☎ *(01634) 815204*
John Baker and Colin Boyes

 Goacher's Fine Light plus two guest beers that change maybe twice a week.

This pub has one bar and a sunny patio. Breakfast available 10–11.45am Mon–Sat, then snacks, sandwiches and meals until 3pm; roast only on Sundays, 12–3pm. Evening menu available 6–9pm Mon–Thurs. Close to seamless join between Chatham and Rochester High Streets, just east of Rochester railway station on corner of Hospital Lane.

OPEN *10am–11pm Mon–Thurs; 10am–2am Fri–Sat; 12–10.30pm Sun.*

The Cooper's Arms
10 St Margarets Street, Rochester ME1 1TL
☎ *(01634) 404298* Mark and Zoe Stephenson

 Freehouse with three beers, Courage Best and Directors plus one rotating guest changed two or three times a week. Examples include Fuller's London Pride, Charles Wells Bombardier, Nelson Trafalgar Bitter and Rochester Bitter, and Theakston Cooper's Butt.

Mentioned in the Domesday Book, this two-bar weatherboard pub is thought to be the oldest inn in Kent. Food available 12–2pm Mon–Sat and 12.30–2.30pm Sun. Children allowed in garden and paved terrace area; dogs in pub but not when food is being served. Barbeques on Friday nights in summer. Behind High Street, near castle and cathedral.

OPEN *11am–11pm Mon–Thurs; 11am–midnight Fri–Sat; 12–10.30pm Sun.*

The Man of Kent Alehouse
6–8 John Street, Rochester ME1 1YN
☎ *(01634) 818771*
Robert Jaegar and Heather Mason
www.manofkent.org.uk

 Six varying beers on eight hand pumps available at any one time, with Kent micro-breweries strongly favoured. Kent wines, ciders and soft drinks also served.

Street-corner local with one L-shaped bar. No fruit machines or juke box, but there are board games and cards. Dogs allowed; children allowed in garden only. Music on Sun, Wed and Thurs nights. The pub has its own cycling club. Behind the old police station, close to Star Hill junction at end of Rochester High Street 'proper'.

OPEN *2–11pm Mon; 1–11pm Tues–Thurs; 1pm–12 Fri; 12–12 Sat; 12–11pm Sun.*

ST MARGARET'S BAY
The Coastguard
The Bay, St Margaret's Bay CT15 6DY
☎ *(01304) 853176* Nigel and Sam Wydymus
www.thecoastguard.co.uk

 At least three real ales available, probably including Adnams Bitter and a Kentish brew. Extensive wine and whisky menus.

Situated beneath the white cliffs and with justifiable claims to be Britain's closest pub to mainland Europe. Family-run freehouse and restaurant with the focus on using fresh local produce. Food served 12.30–2.45pm and 6.30–8.45pm.

OPEN *11am–11pm Mon–Sat; 12–10.30pm Sun.*

SANDWICH
The Fleur de Lis Hotel
6–8 Delf Street, Sandwich CT13 9BZ
☎ *(01304) 611131* Bryan Williams

 Verini Taverns tied house serving Wadworth 6X and Greene King IPA plus one guest from a local brewery changed every day or two.

Built in 1785, this former corn exchange has a large bar, restaurant and 11-room hotel. Food served all day, with the bar menu available until 9.30pm and the à la carte menu in the evenings Mon–Sat. Located in the town centre.

OPEN *7am–11pm Mon–Fri; 8am–11pm Sat; 8am–10.30pm Sun (alcohol served from 10am).*

SEAL
The Crown
16 High Street, Seal, Sevenoaks TN15 0AJ
☎ *(01732) 761023* J Avis

 Enterprise Inns tied house serving Westerham Finchcock's Original, Harveys Sussex Best Bitter and ales from Wells and Young's.

This 16th-century former coaching inn has one large open bar and garden. Food served lunchtimes daily (including Sunday roast) and Thurs evenings. Function room, car park. Children welcome. Large beer garden. Indoor pub games such as darts and pool. Bat & trap and petanque in the summer. Located in Seal, on the A25 from Sevenoaks to Maidstone.

OPEN *12–close.*

SELLING
The Rose & Crown
Perry Wood, Selling ME13 9RY
☎ *(01227) 752214*
Tim Robinson and Vanessa Grove
www.roseandcrownperrywood.co.uk

 A freehouse. Harveys Best and Adnams Southwold. One or two guests, changed regularly, often from local breweries such as Gadds, Goacher's or Nelson, but could be from any independent nationwide.

A 16th-century English country pub, said to be haunted! Set in 150 acres of woodland. Decorated in a traditional style, with hops, horse brasses, corn dollies and old photographs of the pub and the surrounding area. One large bar, snug and restaurant, serving food 12–2pm Mon–Sun and 7–9.00pm Tues–Sun. Large beer garden with children's play area..

OPEN *11.30am–3pm Mon (closed Mon evening); 11.30am–3pm and 6–11pm Tues–Sat; 12–3.30pm and 7–10.30pm Sun.*

SEVENOAKS

Anchor

32 London Road, Sevenoaks TN13 1AS
☎ *(01732) 454898 Barry Dennis*

Tied house serving Harveys plus a rotating guest, changed weekly.

This one-bar locals' pub is approximately 100 years old and located in the town centre. Food served 11am–2.30pm Mon–Fri, 11am–2pm Sat and 12–3pm Sun. Knole House is a five minute drive from here.

OPEN *11am–3pm and 6–11pm Mon–Fri; 10.30am–5pm and 7–11pm Sat; 12–5pm and 7–11pm Sun.*

The Oak Tree

135 High Street, Sevenoaks TN13 1UP
☎ *(01732) 472615 Philip Hannon*

A pub serving Courage Best, Westerham Special Bitter Ale and British Bulldog plus a rotating guest changed monthly.

A 16th-century alehouse with a modern twist! Food served 10am–9pm daily. Private room. Children welcome. Sports shown on plasma screen. A ten-minute walk from Knole Park.

OPEN *11am–midnight (10.30pm Sun).*

SITTINGBOURNE

The Red Lion

58 High Street, Sittingbourne ME10 4BP
☎ *(01795) 472706*
Richard Mason

Fuller's London Pride and Shepherd Neame Spitfire plus a seasonal guest such as Shepherd Neame Master Brew or Early Bird, or something from Black Sheep.

A 14th-century former coaching inn with a wealth of history and a myriad of famous visitors over the years. Now a busy town-centre pub with one long bar and separate dining area, which gel together in the evening, when pizza and pasta help to create a relaxed atmosphere. Fabulous summer evenings spent in the courtyard listening to live music and drinking good beer. Range of Gale's country wines. Food available 12–2.30pm and 6–10pm Mon–Sat; 12–3pm Sun, with traditional roast. No children or dogs inside, but they can be accommodated in garden courtyard. Follow the A2 into Sittingbourne.

OPEN *11am–11pm Mon–Thurs; 11am–1am Fri–Sat; 12–11pm Sun.*

SMARDEN

The Chequers Inn

The Street, Smarden, Ashford TN27 8QA
☎ *(01233) 770217 Mick and Jan Denny*
www.thechequerssmarden.com

Three real ales usually available, with Greene King Abbot, Old Speckled Hen and IPA, plus Fuller's London Pride and beers from Harveys regularly featured, and changed every couple of days.

Timber-framed pub built in 1385, with beamed bars and three dining areas. Accommodation. Food available 12–2.30pm and 6–9.30pm. Children and dogs allowed.

Large garden with delightful pond, offering best of rural tranquility. Four letting rooms. Function room. On B2077.

OPEN *11am–11pm Mon–Sat; 12–10.30pm Sun.*

SNARGATE

The Red Lion

Snargate, Romney Marsh TN29 9UQ
☎ *(01797) 344648 Doris and Kate Jemison*

Up to five beers available directly from the cask, Kent breweries (Goacher's Light in particular) virtually guaranteed to be featured. Also local real cider.

Unspoilt 16th-century pub bursting with character. In the Jemison family since 1911. One bar and a couple of side rooms, all adorned with local items of interest. No food. Gale's country wines an innovative feature. Children welcome but not in main bar. Large garden. On B2080 about a mile south-east of Appledore station.

OPEN *12–3pm and 7–11pm Mon–Sat; 12–3pm and 7.30–10.30pm Sun.*

SOUTHFLEET

The Wheatsheaf

8 Highcross Road, Southfleet, Westwood DA13 9PH
☎ *(01474) 833210 Gerry and Nick Cox*

Owned by Punch Taverns, with five real ales. Fuller's London Pride, Charles Wells Bombardier, Greene King IPA and Old Speckled Hen are likely to be among them.

Beamed village pub that dates from 1408 and run by the same family for many years. One extended bar dominated by hops and separate restaurant area that doubles as function room. Food available 12–2.30pm and 7–9.30pm (7–9pm Sun), with traditional roast Sunday lunchtime. Children and dogs allowed, the latter encouraged to stay away from diners, please. Large garden; equally impressive pond. Still at the bottom of the crib league after many years of trying. Long mile south of A2.

OPEN *11am–11pm Mon–Sat; 12–10.30pm Sun.*

SPELDHURST

The George & Dragon

Speldhurst Hill, Speldhurst, Tunbridge Wells TN3 0NN
☎ *(01892) 863125 Julian Leefe-Griffiths*
www.speldhurst.com

Freehouse with Harveys Sussex Best Bitter and Hadlow and Larkins Traditional Ale plus one seasonal guest from Westerham, namely Summer Perle or Puddledock Porter.

Originally a Wealden hall house, built at the beginning of the 13th century but understandably modified since. Two restaurants, two real fires, gardens front and back, and friendly staff. Food served 12–2.30pm and 7–9pm Mon–Sat, and 12–3.30pm Sun. Named Restaurant of the Year in Alistair Sawday's Guide. Children welcome. Disabled access and toilets. Two miles west of Tunbridge Wells.

OPEN *11am–11pm Mon–Sat; 12–10.30pm Sun.*

SUTTON VALENCE
The Swan
Broad Street, Sutton Valence, Maidstone ME17 3AJ
☎ *(01622) 843212* Martin and Toby

Harveys Sussex Best, Young's Bitter, Woodforde's Wherry and Sharp's Doom Bar are the regular beers, and there is also a weekly guest.

Grade II listed building constructed in 1367 with Grade I stable block at rear, it became an inn 100 years later and is the oldest continuously operating pub in Kent. Food available 12–3pm and 6–9pm Mon–Sat and 12–5.30pm Sun. Children and dogs welcome. Spacious beer garden with wonderful views over Kent Weald.

OPEN *11am–midnight.*

TEMPLE EWELL
The Fox
14 High Street, Temple Ewell, Dover CT16 3DU
☎ *(01304) 823598* Steve Grayson

Tied to Enterprise Inns, with Greene King Abbot and Caledonian Deuchars IPA more or less permanently available, plus two monthly-changing guests.

A typical village pub with open log fire and beer garden. Food served 12–2pm and 7–9pm Mon–Sat; 12–2pm Sun. Children's play area. Skittle alley. Car park.

OPEN *11.30am–3pm and 6–11pm Mon–Sat; 12–4pm and 7–11pm Sun.*

TENTERDEN
The William Caxton
West Cross, Tenterden TN30 6JR
☎ *(01580) 763142* Giles Davies

Shepherd Neame tied house offering Master Brew Bitter and Spitfire permanently plus whatever seasonal beer is appropriate.

Food-oriented pub built in 1580. Two oak-beamed bars with hops prevalent and inglenook. Separate dining area, accommodation. Fresh food available 12–2.30pm (12–3pm Sat and Sun) and 7–10pm (7–9pm Sun); traditional Sunday roast. Children and dogs allowed. Garden. On junction of A28 and B2082.

OPEN *11am–11pm Mon–Sat; 12–10.30pm Sun.*

TONBRIDGE
The New Drum
54 Lavender Hill, Tonbridge TN9 2AU
☎ *(01732) 365044* Jason Bevis

Genuine freehouse with Harveys Sussex Best Bitter, plus two other beers.

Traditional backstreet local that began life as two terraced cottages, with one L-shaped bar and mixed clientele. No food. Children and dogs allowed. For its location, the pub has an unexpectedly large garden, and patio. South of the railway and town centre, therefore relatively safe from weekend 'revelry', but it can be crowded when live football is being televised. North off A2014.

OPEN *11am–11pm Mon–Sat; 12–10.30pm Sun.*

TROTTISCLIFFE
The Plough
Taylors Lane, Trottiscliffe, West Malling ME19 5DR
☎ *(01732) 822233* David Dyer

Adnams Best Bitter and Broadside and Harveys Sussex Best.

A traditional one-bar 14th-century public house, licensed since 1817, with open fires, beamed ceiling and a warm, friendly welcome. Food available every lunchtime and Tues–Sat evenings. Children and dogs allowed. Small patio. Off the A227 near junction of M20 and M26.

OPEN *11.30am–3pm and 6 (6.30 Sat)–11pm Mon–Sat; 12–3pm Sun.*

TUNBRIDGE WELLS
The Beacon
Tea Garden Lane, Rusthall, Nr Tunbridge Wells TN3 9JH
☎ *(01892) 524252* John and Di Cullen

Freehouse with Harveys Best, Timothy Taylor Landlord and Larkins Traditional.

Originally built in 1895 as a private house for Sir Walter Harris, this building was also used as a hostel for Jewish refugees during the Second World War. Food served 12–2.30pm and 6.30–9.30pm Mon–Sat, 12–5pm and 6.30–9.30pm Sun. Three en-suite bedrooms available for letting. Set in 17 acres of land including three lakes. Car park. Outdoor dining area. Private room available for hire. Near Hever Castle, Penshurst Place and The Pantiles. On the A264 to East Grinstead, one mile from Tunbridge Wells.

OPEN *11am–11pm.*

The Rose & Crown
47 Grosvenor Road, Tunbridge Wells TN1 2AY
☎ *(01892) 522427* Graham Rumsey

Greene King IPA and Timothy Taylor Landlord plus two guests, changed every two weeks.

Traditional Victorian pub in the town centre, with two connecting bars and function room. Darts, cribbage and all traditional pub games regularly played. Traditional pub grub served 11.30am–2.30pm and 5–7pm Mon–Fri, 12–5pm Sat and roasts 12–4pm Sun. Customers must be over 21. Beer festivals held. Just north of main shopping precinct on A26.

OPEN *10am–11pm Mon–Sat; 12–10.30pm Sun.*

Sankey's
39 Mount Ephraim, Tunbridge Wells TN4 8AA
☎ *(01892) 511422*
Guy, Matthew and Adam Sankey

Freehouse serving Larkins Traditional and Harveys Best always available, plus a selection of brews from around the world.

A traditional town-style bar with huge collection of enamel signs and other breweriana. Two bars and a brasserie. Food served 12–3pm Mon, 12–3pm and 6–10pm Tues–Fri and all day Sat. Garden. Regular spit roasts. Available to hire.

OPEN *11am–11pm.*

UNDERRIVER
The White Rock Inn
Carter's Hill, Underriver, Sevenoaks TN15 0SB
☎ *(01732) 833112* Frank and Maria Scott
www.thewhiterockinn.co.uk

 Genuine freehouse serving Harveys Sussex Best Bitter and Westerham ales.

Oldest part of the pub dates back to 1820, but there were buildings on the site for hundreds of years before that. Two beamed bars, restaurant and separate games area. Food available 12–3pm. Fresh fish and Aberdeen Angus steaks are specialities. Children allowed only if eating; no dogs. Extensive garden and patio. Two miles (by road) east of A21, midway between Sevenoaks and Tonbridge. OS:556521.

OPEN *12–3pm and 6–11pm Mon–Sat; 12–3pm and 7–10.30pm Sun.*

UPPER UPNOR
The Tudor Rose
29 High Street, Upper Upnor, Rochester ME2 4XG
☎ *(01634) 715305* Roger Rennie

 Freehouse with Young's Bitter and Special plus four other beers that constantly change.

A 16th-century pub with one main bar, several off-shoots and 20-seat restaurant. Food available 12–2.30pm Mon–Sat; 7–9.30pm Tues–Sat. Children allowed. Large walled garden with play area. Half a mile river side of A228; follow signs for Upnor Castle.

OPEN *11am–11pm Mon–Sat; 12–4pm and 7–10.30pm Sun.*

WALMER
The Berry
23 Canada Road, Walmer, Deal CT14 7EQ
☎ *(01304) 362411* Chris Barnes

 Freehouse with Harveys Best plus at least two changing guest ales.

Formerly The Green Berry, this 1860s-built popular family-run community pub specialises in a changing variety of ales from local and regional brewers. Beer terrace. Small car park, unrestricted free parking on road. Function room available for hire with private bar. Located directly off the Deal–Dover coastal road, a five-minute walk from the beach and easy walking distance from Deal and Walmer castles.

OPEN *11am–2.30pm and 5.30–11.30pm Mon and Wed; 5.30–11.30pm Tues and Thurs; 11.30am–2.30pm and 5.30pm–12 Fri; 11am–midnight Sat; 11.30am–11.30pm Sun.*

WEST MALLING
The Lobster Pot
47 Swan Street, West Malling ME19 6JU
☎ *(01732) 843265* Polly Fetherstonhaugh

 Up to six cask ales, rotating every few days, from breweries such as Harveys, Adnams, Caledonian, Hook Norton, Hop Back, Wells and Young's and Ringwood.

Traditional, friendly, 300-year-old pub with two bars, a restaurant and a function room for events and meetings. Home-cooked pub food available 12–2.30pm Tues–Sat and 12–3pm Sun–Mon (roasts on Sunday). Skittle alley. Quiz on Mondays, arts class on Tuesdays. Beer festival in August. Just off the A228 at the bottom of Swan Street.

OPEN *12–11pm (10.30pm Sun).*

WEST PECKHAM
The Swan on the Green
The Green, West Peckham, Maidstone ME18 5JW
☎ *(01622) 812271* Gordon Milligan
www.swan-on-the-green.co.uk

 Brewpub, with the extensive range of beers produced on the premises. Seasonals and specials also brewed, any celebration being excuse enough.

Country pub at heart of small village community with emphasis on good food and beer brewed by a man (Gordon) who seems at total peace with his lot. First licensed in 1685 but, for a pub with beams, hops and a wooden floor, it has a deceptively modern feel in its one extended light bar. Food available 12–2.15pm and 7.15–9.15pm Mon–Sat (not Mon evenings); 12–2.15pm Sun, with traditional roast. Children and dogs allowed. Seated drinking area outside the pub, as well as across the road on the Green itself. Short mile west of A228. OS:644524.

OPEN *11am–3pm and 6–11pm Mon–Fri (closed Mon evenings); 11am–4pm and 6–11pm Sat; 12–4pm and 7–10.30pm Sun. Times may differ seasonally and if there are cricket matches or other events on the Green.*

WHITSTABLE
The Old Neptune
Marine Terrace, Whitstable CT5 1EJ
☎ *(01227) 272262* Keith Flynn

 Fuller's London Pride plus one other beer.

Weatherboarded pub dating from the middle of the 19th century, complemented by authentic Thomson and Wootton Brewery windows and floor and bar that slope towards Whitstable Bay. Mixture of 'fast' foods, char-grilled steaks and fish fresh from harbour available 12–6pm throughout summer, but at weekends only in winter. No children after 7pm. Outside drinking area. Adjacent to beach.

OPEN *11am–11pm Mon–Thurs; 11am–12.30am Fri–Sun.*

Ship Centurion Arminius
111 High Street, Whitstable CT5 1AY
☎ *(01227) 264740*
Janet, Roland and Armin Birks

Freehouse serving Adnams Bitter and Elgood's Black Dog Mild plus up to three frequently changing guest beers, one of which is usually a stronger bitter. The only place in Whitstable where cask mild is available. Genuine continental lagers also served.

One-bar town pub, first licensed in 1750, with sun lounge/24-seat dining area, where children with well-behaved parents are allowed at all times. Genuine home-cooked snacks available 12–3pm and 6–9pm Mon–Fri; special menu served 12–3pm Sat; no food Sun except selection of seafood, sausages or chicken drumsticks on bar at lunchtime. Live music every Thurs. Four TVs. CAMRA Regional Pub of the Year 2007. On B2205, west end of town.

OPEN *11am–11pm Mon–Sat; 12–7pm Sun.*

WITTERSHAM
The Swan Inn
1 Swan Street, Wittersham TN30 7PH
☎ *(01797) 270913* Ray and Angela Pratt
www.swan-wittersham.co.uk

Harveys Sussex Best Bitter, Goacher's Fine Light Ale and Rother Valley Smild are permanent fixtures on hand pump, with up to four other beers – either brewed locally or 'unusual offerings' from elsewhere – available directly from the cask.

An old drovers' pub on Isle of Oxney and only just in Kent, this focal point for the village has a landlord passionate about draught beer. Two bars. Food available 12–3pm and 6–9pm Sun–Fri; all day Saturday. Children and dogs allowed. Beer garden. Beer festivals in February and August, cider festival in May. On B2082, about five miles north of Rye.

OPEN *11am–midnight Mon–Thurs; 11am–2am Fri–Sat; 12–12 Sun.*

WOODLANDS
The Rising Sun
Cotmans Ash Lane, Woodlands, Nr Kemsing, Sevenoaks TN15 6XD
☎ *(01959) 522683* Peter and Michelle Hunter

Genuine freehouse that offers an amazing range of real beers. Five are usually available, which may reduce to four in the worst of the winter; the pump clips offer a treasure trove.

Once in the door of this heavily beamed 400-year-old pub, you won't want to leave; it is a reviving experience. One long bar and separate dining area, with additional nooks and crannies and open fire. Food available 12–2pm and 7–9.30pm, with traditional 'home-reared' Sunday roast that is served in the evening if there is any left from lunchtime. Dogs, children, muddy boots and probably pet goats allowed, the future of the countryside being of obvious importance to anybody involved in any way with the pub. Large garden with ample facilities for children. Off the beaten track very close to

North Downs Way, but, like a handful of other watering holes in the county (see Chiddingstone Hoath, Fairseat, Ightham Common and Snargate), it is seriously worth the effort digging out if you believe that nostalgia is not what it used to be! Best approached by turning off A20 at West Kingsdown opposite Portobello Inn (road signed to Knatts Valley) into School Lane, then three miles of rural roads. OS:563599.

OPEN *11am–3pm and 6–11pm Mon–Sat; 12–3pm and 7–10.30pm Sun.*

WORTH
The St Crispin Inn
The Street, Worth, Deal CT14 0DF
☎ *(01304) 612081* Tyrone Mayes
www.stcrispininn.com

Greene King IPA, Black Sheep Bitter, Shepherd Neame Spitfire and Harveys Sussex plus a guest such as Timothy Taylor Landlord, Shepherd Neame Master Brew or Bishops Finger or something from Adnams.

Busy oak-beamed pub built in 1420 and licensed since 1690. Lovely warm old-fashioned pub with large conservatory, lounge bar and restaurant. Food available 12–2pm and 6–9pm Mon–Fri; 12–2.15pm and 6–9pm Sun. Large garden, parking. Large patio area with sheltered glass area, outside changing baby area and toilet facilities. BBQs. Play area and rat and trap, plus large bouncy castle in summer. Private parties welcome and catered for. Coaches welcome. Short half-mile east of A258.

OPEN *12–2.30pm and 6–11pm Mon–Sat; 12–9pm Sun (closed 5pm on Sunday in winter).*

YALDING
The Walnut Tree
Yalding Hill, Yalding ME18 6JB
☎ *(01622) 814266* BM Jenner

Enterprise Inns pub serving Timothy Taylor Landlord, Harveys Sussex, Westerham Finchcock's and Fuller's London Pride.

A traditional 15th-century-built pub with beams and inglenooks. Two bars. Food served lunchtimes and evenings Mon–Thurs, all day Fri–Sun. Specialises in high-quality home-cooked food prepared entirely from fresh produce, most sourced locally. Located in the medieval village of Yalding between Paddock Wood and Maidstone.

OPEN *12–3pm and 6–11pm Mon–Thurs; all day Fri–Sun.*

THE BREWERIES

THE BOWLAND BEER CO. LTD

The Bowland Brewery, Bashall Barn, Twitter Lane, Bashall Town, Clitheroe BB7 3LQ
☎ *(01200) 428825 or 07952 639465*
www.bowlandbrewery.com

HUNTERS MOON 3.7% ABV
Chocolate and coffee hints.
SAWLEY TEMPTED 3.7% ABV
Rounded fruit flavours.
BOWLAND GOLD 3.8% ABV
Gold-coloured bitter, with plenty of hops.
CHIPPING STEAMER 3.9% ABV
Citrus and green apple flavours.
HEN HARRIER 4.0% ABV
Citrus and peach flavours.
BOWLAND DRAGON 4.2% ABV
Golden and fruity.
Plus seasonals.

BRYSONS OF LANCASTER BREWERS

Newgate Brewery, White Lund Industrial Estate, Morecambe LA3 3PT
☎ *(01524) 39481*

WESTMORLAND BITTER 3.6% ABV
LANCASHIRE BITTER 3.8% ABV
UNION FLAG 3.9% ABV
HURRICANE BITTER 4.1% ABV

DANIEL THWAITES BREWERY PLC

Penny Street, Blackburn BB1 5BU
☎ *(01254) 686868*
www.thwaites.co.uk

THWAITES DARK SMOOTH 3.0% ABV
THWAITES DARK MILD 3.3% ABV
THWAITES BITTER 3.4% ABV
THWAITES SMOOTH BEER 3.4% ABV
THWAITES ORIGINAL 3.6% ABV
THOROUGHBRED 4.0% ABV
DANIEL'S 4.2% ABV
LANCASTER BOMBER 4.4% ABV
DOUBLE CENTURY 4.8% ABV
Seasonals including:
WAINWRIGHT 4.1% ABV
FLYING SHUTTLE 4.6% ABV

HART BREWERY

The Cartford Hotel, Cartford Lane, Little Eccleston, Preston PR3 0YP
☎ *(01995) 671686*

DISHY DEBBIE 4.0% ABV
GOLDEN BEST 4.0% ABV
ICE MAIDEN 4.0% ABV
LORD OF THE GLEN 4.0% ABV
SQUIRREL'S HOARD 4.0% ABV
BAT OUT OF HELL 4.5% ABV
NEMESIS 4.5% ABV
Occasionals and specials.

HOPSTAR BREWERY

The Black Horse, 72 Redearth Street, Darwen BB3 2AF

BUMBLE BEA 3.5% ABV
CHILLI BEER 3.8% ABV
DIZZY DANNYALE 3.8% ABV
JAX ALE 4.0% ABV
SMOKY JOE'S BLACK BEER 4.0% ABV
SPINNING JENNY 4.0% ABV
DEGREE 4.1% ABV
Plus seasonals and specials.

THE MILLSTONE BREWERY LIMITED

Unit 4, Vale Mill, Micklehurst Road, Mossley OL5 9JL
☎ *(01457) 835835*
www.millstonebrewery.co.uk

THREE SHIRES BITTER 4.0% ABV
WINDY MILLER 4.1% ABV
GRAIN STORM 4.2% ABV
TRUE GRIT 5.0% ABV
Occasionals and specials:
A MILLER'S ALE 3.8% ABV
SUMMER DAZE 4.1% ABV
AUTUMN LEAVES 4.3% ABV
SQUARE PEG 4.3% ABV
MILLSTONE EDGE 4.4% ABV
CHRISTMAS RUBY 4.7% ABV

MOONSTONE BREWERY

The Ministry of Ale, 9 Trafalgar Street, Burnley BB11 1TQ
☎ *(01282) 830909*
www.ministryofale.co.uk

BLACK STAR 3.4% ABV
BLUE JOHN 3.6% ABV
ONYX 3.8% ABV
TIGER'S EYE 3.8% ABV
MOONSTONE DARKISH 4.2% ABV

MOORHOUSE'S BREWERY LTD

4 Moorhouse Street, Burnley BB11 5EN
☎ *(01282) 422864*
www.moorhouses.co.uk

BLACK CAT 3.4% ABV
Refreshing.
PREMIER BITTER 3.7% ABV
Full flavoured with good hoppiness.
PRIDE OF PENDLE 4.1% ABV
Smooth and well rounded.
BLOND WITCH 4.5% ABV
Blond ale.
PENDLE WITCHES BREW 5.1% ABV
Complex, sweet malt and fruit flavour.
Plus special monthly brews.

PICTISH BREWERY

Unit 9, Canalside Industrial Estate, Woodbine Street East, Rochdale OL16 5LB
☎ *(01706) 522227*
www.pictish-brewing.co.uk

BREWER'S GOLD 3.8% ABV
Spicy hop aroma. Core beer.

Either one or the other of the two beers below will be available at any one time:
CELTIC WARRIOR 4.2% ABV
Malty with hop aromas.
ALCHEMIST'S ALE 4.3% ABV
Mid-brown, hoppy finish.
Plus occasionals.

PORTER BREWING COMPANY LTD

Rossendale Brewery, The Griffin Inn, Hud Rake, Haslingden, Rossendale BB4 5AF
☎ *(01706) 214021*
www.pbcbreweryinstallations.com

 FLORAL DANCE 3.6% ABV
BITTER 4.2% ABV
RAILWAY SLEEPER 4.2% ABV
ROSSENDALE ALE 4.2% ABV
PORTER 5.0% ABV
SUNSHINE 5.3% ABV
Plus occasionals and specials.

RED ROSE BREWERY

Unit 4 Stanley Court, Heys Lane Industrial Estate, Great Harwood BB6 7UR
☎ *(01254) 877373*
www.redrosebrewery.co.uk

ACCRINGTON STANLEY ALE 3.6% ABV
Malty with citrus finish.
TREACLE MINERS 3.9% ABV
Sweetish and liquoricy.
FELIX 4.2% ABV
Dry, hoppy.
OLD BEN 4.3% ABV
Light coloured and refreshing.
PADDY O'HACKERS GENUINE IRISH STOUT 4.6% ABV
Coffee notes.
OLDER EMPIRE IPA 5.5% ABV
Hop aroma, floral bitter.
CARE TAKER OF HISTORY 6.0% ABV
Sweetish, malty.
Plus seasonals and specials.

THE THREE B'S BREWERY

Unit 5, Laneside Works, Stockclough Lane, Feniscowles, Blackburn BB2 5JR
☎ *(01254) 207686*
www.threebsbrewery.co.uk

STOKERS SLAKE 3.6% ABV
Dark mild with creamy chocolate notes.
BOBBIN'S BITTER 3.8% ABV
Golden bitter, nutty grain.
TACKLER'S TIPPLE 4.3% ABV
Full hop flavour and biscuit tones.
DOFF COCKER 4.5% ABV
Straw coloured, flowery taste.
Plus seasonals and specials including:
PINCH NOGGIN 4.6% ABV
Bitter.
KNOCKER UP 4.8% ABV
Porter.
SHUTTLE ALE 5.2% ABV
Strong pale ale.

THE PUBS

ACCRINGTON

The George Hotel

185 Blackburn Road, Accrington BB5 0AF
☎ *(01254) 383441*

Four beers from an ever-changing list that might include Titanic Stout, Cains FA and Goose Eye Bitter.

A friendly freehouse with an open-plan bar area and separate restaurant in converted stables. Bar and restaurant food available at lunchtimes and evenings. Street parking, garden/patio area. Children allowed. Accommodation. Close to the railway and bus stations.

OPEN *12–11pm (10.30pm Sun).*

ADLINGTON

The Spinner's Arms

23 Church Street, Adlington, Chorley PR7 4EX
☎ *(01257) 483331* Steven Gilmartin

Freehouse with five real ales. Timothy Taylor Landlord, Coniston Bluebird and Moorhouse's Black Cat Mild on the bar permanently, plus daily guests such as Caledonian Deuchars IPA, Moorhouse's Premier or Blond Witch, George Wright's Drunken Duck, Crouch Vale Brewer's Gold or something from Durham. Saxon Ruby Tuesday traditional cider.

Built in the late 1880s with small beer garden at the front. Quiz night Tuesday 9.15pm. Bingo night is Wednesday. Lunchtime meals now served 12-2pm Tues-Sat and 12-6pm Sun. Parties catered for. On the A6, as it passes through Adlington.

OPEN *12–11pm Sun–Thurs; 12–12 Fri–Sat.*

ARKHOLME

The Bay Horse Hotel

Arkholme, Carnforth
☎ *(01524) 221425* Peter Dawson Jackson

Two real ales changed every two weeks.

Typical, unspoilt country pub. Food served Tues–Sun 11.30am–2pm and 6–9pm Tues–Sun. Car park, bowling green (crown). Children and dogs welcome. From junction 35 of the M6, follow the Kirkby Lonsdale signs for five miles.

OPEN *11.30am–2.30pm and 6pm–close Tues–Sun.*

AUGHTON

The Derby Arms

Prescot Road, Aughton L39 6TA
☎ *(01695) 422237* Janice Brogden

 Freehouse with three rotating guest ales. Selection changes up to four times per week. CAMRA Pub of the Year 2007.

A traditional country pub which has undergone a sympathetic refurbishment. Real fires, real people, real friendly! Home-cooked traditional and 'unusual' pub food served 11.30am–2pm and 5.30–8pm Mon–Thurs; 11.30am–8pm Fri; 9.30am–5pm Sat; 12–4.30pm Sun (bank hols 11.30am–8pm). Beer garden. Car park. Quiz nights Tues and Thurs. Close to Aintree racecourse, en route from M58 to Southport.

OPEN *11.30am–midnight Mon–Fri; 9am–midnight Sat; 12–12 Sun.*

BACUP

The Crown Inn

Greave Road, Bacup OL13 9HQ
☎ *(01706) 873982* Tracey Clough

Freehouse serving Pictish Brewery's Gold and Crown IPA plus one guest, changed up to three times a week.

Local, traditional alehouse with flagged floors, open fires and a friendly atmosphere. Sandwiches (locally renowned) always available; hot food served evenings and weekends. No children. No dogs. Beer garden. Car park. Annual folk festival and Lancashire black pudding festival. Function room available. Off Todmorden Road.

OPEN *5pm–close Mon–Fri; 12–close Sat–Sun.*

BARROWFORD

George & Dragon

217 Gisburn Road, Barrowford BB9 6JD
☎ *(01282) 612929* Margaret Wood

Enterprise Inns pub with three real ales, including Moorhouse's Premier and two guests, changed every few days. There will always be one beer from Bowland and one from another local micro-brewery.

An inn since at least 1778, it had its own brewhouse in 1780 and was known as the Bridge End. Now a community village pub, a meeting place for several local sports teams. No food. Close to the Pendle Heritage Centre and just a short walk from Barrowford Locks on the Leeds–Liverpool Canal. On the A682.

OPEN *3pm–12 Mon–Wed; 12–12 Thurs; noon–1am Fri–Sat; 12–12 Sun.*

BISPHAM GREEN

The Eagle & Child

Malt Kiln Lane, Bispham Green, Nr Ormskirk L40 3SG
☎ *(01257) 462297* David Anderson

Freehouse with up to five real ales. Thwaites Bitter is a regular fixture plus rotating guests, perhaps from Phoenix, Moorhouse's, Timothy Taylor, Southport, Cains and elsewhere.

Old-fashioned country pub with flagstone floors, antique furniture and an open fire. Bowling green, croquet lawn, beer garden. Food served 12–2pm and 5.30–8.30pm (9pm on Fri–Sat), 12–8.30pm Sun. Large function room available to hire. Children and dogs welcome.

OPEN *12–3pm and 5.30–11pm Mon–Sat; all day Sun.*

BLACKBURN

The Cellar Bar

39–41 King Street, Blackburn
☎ *(01254) 698111* Dan Hook

Two regularly changing beers, often from Moorhouse's, Three B's, Castle Eden, Dent, Jennings or RCH.

Buried underground in the first mayor of Blackburn's family home and the oldest Georgian house in the town, this pub has a cosy atmosphere, real fire, live music and the biggest beer garden in Blackburn. No food. Car park. Children welcome.

OPEN *11am–11pm Mon–Tues; 11am–1am Wed–Fri; 7pm–1am Sat; 7–10.30pm Sun.*

The Postal Order

15 Darwen Street, Blackburn BB2 2BY
☎ *(01254) 676400* Neil and Sharon Longley

Wetherspoon's pub serving several guest ales. Thwaites Mild is a regular, and other guests might include Exmoor Fox, Gale's GB and Cotleigh Barn Owl.

Large, traditional town pub near the Cathedral. One long bar with two separate areas. Food served all day. Children welcome.

OPEN *All day, every day.*

BLACKPOOL

The New Road Inn

244 Talbot Road, Blackpool FY1 3HL
☎ *(01253) 628872* Zoe Pomies

Jennings tied house, with Sneck Lifter, Dark Mild and Cumberland plus up to three guests, which could be from any independent brewery.

A 1930s pub with an Art Deco interior. Central bar, games room and back room. Food served 11am–2pm and 4–7pm Mon–Sat; cold food available all day. Front parking spaces. Outside heated smoking area. Sun and Mon: karaoke nights; Wed: quiz night; Fri: boozy bingo. Situated close to Blackpool North railway station, opposite Mecca Bingo.

OPEN *10.30am–close Mon–Sat; 11am–close Sun.*

The Saddle Inn

286 Whitegate Drive, Blackpool FY3 9PH
☎ *(01253) 767827* Alan Bedford

Thwaites Original. Six guest ales, changed every three days, from breweries including Hawkshead, Copper Dragon, Timothy Taylor, Fuller's, Elgood's and many more.

Dating from 1764, this is Blackpool's oldest pub. A single-bar with eight cask pumps and the largest outside terrace in town. Food served 12–3pm and 5–8pm Mon–Wed; 12–3pm and 5–9pm (steak night); 12–4pm Fri–Sun. Winner of CAMRA's Blackpool, Fylde and Wyre Pub of the Year 2007 and 2008.

OPEN *12–11pm Sun–Thurs; 12–12 Fri–Sat.*

The Shovels

260 Common Edge Road, Blackpool FY4 5DH
☎ *(01253) 762702* Steve and Helen Norris

Theakston Best Bitter plus five guest beers from breweries such as Hart. Micro-breweries favoured whenever possible. Annual beer festival held in the last week of October/first week of November, with up to 80 cask ales.

Freehouse in a suburban location. CAMRA Blackpool Fylde, & Wyre Pub of the Year 2001 and 2003. One bar, real fire, front patio, disabled access/toilet. Dining area, conservatory. Good food served 12–9.30pm. Children welcome. Just off the M55 on main road from Blackpool to Lytham St Annes.

OPEN *11.30am–11pm Mon–Wed; 11.30am–midnight Thurs–Sat; 12–11pm Sun.*

BRETHERTON

The Blue Anchor Inn

21 South Road, Bretherton, Nr Leyland PR26 9AB
☎ *(01772) 600270* Michele Fielden

Timothy Taylor Landlord, Marston's Pedigree and Moorhouse's Black Cat plus three guests, which might be something from Hart, Phoenix, Marston's, Moorhouse's, Boggart Hole Clough, Cottage or Blackpool.

Busy traditional village pub with large beer garden and play area. Food served 12–2pm and 5–9pm Mon–Fri and all day at weekends and bank holidays, with carvery alongside usual menu and specials 5–9pm Sat and all day Sun from 12. Children welcome. Car park.

OPEN *12–2pm and 5pm–close (11pm Mon–Thurs, 1am Fri); noon–1am Sat–Sun and bank holidays.*

BURNLEY

Bridge Bier Huis

2 Bank Parade, Burnley BB11 1UH
☎ *(01282) 411304* Simon Scott
www.thebridgebierhuis.co.uk

Freehouse with Hydes Original plus four or five guests, usually from micro-breweries.

A 100-year-old building with one bar, serving an open-plan pub and separate snug. Modern, with mixed clientele. Food served 12–3pm. No juke box, fruit machines or pool table. Fringe venue for Burnley Blues Festival. Occasional open mic and jam sessions. Behind Charter Walk shopping centre. CAMRA's Regional Pub of the Year 2008.

OPEN *Closed Mon–Tues; 12–12 Wed–Thurs; noon–2am Fri–Sat; 12–12 Sun. Doors close one hour before last orders.*

The Ministry of Ale

9 Trafalgar Street, Burnley BB11 1TQ
☎ *(01282) 830909* Michael Jacques

Home of the Moonstone Brewery, with two home ales plus at least two guests, which could be a Moonstone special or a beer from any independent brewery, but especially local ones such as Phoenix, Bank Top and Moorhouse's.

Modern café-style brewpub situated on the edge of town. No food. No children.

OPEN *5–11pm Mon–Thurs (closed lunchtimes); 12–11pm Fri–Sat; 12–10.30pm Sun.*

The Sparrow Hawk Hotel

Church Street, Burnley BB11 2DN
☎ *(01282) 421551* Jeffrey Mallinson
www.sparrowhawkhotel.co.uk

Freehouse offering seven or eight cask ales, including guest bitters, stouts, porters and ciders from breweries throughout the country as well as northern favourites. Moorhouse's brews generally feature.

A country-style inn in the town centre, with one bar, restaurant and accommodation. Food served 12–2pm and 5–9.30pm, all day at weekends. Entertainment Thurs–Sun. Blues and beer festivals held.

OPEN *12–2pm Mon–Fri; 5–11pm Mon–Weds; 5pm–12 Thurs; 5pm–2am Fri; all day Sat–Sun.*

CHORLEY

Malt 'n' Hops

50–2 Friday Street, Chorley PR6 0AH
☎ *(01257) 260967* David Wright

Beartown Kodiak plus seven rotating guest beers, changing constantly.

Bought in 2004 by the Beartown Brewery in Congleton, a Victorian-style, one-bar character pub with a friendly atmosphere. No food, no pool table. Small beer garden ('Ale Yard'). Dogs welcome. Close to the station, so ideal for trainspotters and commuters.

OPEN *12–11pm (10.30pm Sun).*

CLAYTON-LE-MOORS
The Albion
243 Whalley Road, Clayton-le-Moors,
Accrington BB5 5HD
☎ *(01254) 238585* Lucille McGlauchlin

Two or three real ales usually on offer from various local micro-breweries, including such beers as Moorhouse's Pride of Pendle, Bank Top Flat Cap, Three B's Doff Cocker and Bowland Oak.

A traditional real ale pub offering a friendly welcome, extensively refurbished, with one main bar and separate comfy room and games room. Canalside location with large beer garden. No food. Sky Sports on large screen, pool table. Karaoke every Sunday 2–7.30pm, live entertainment once a month. Disabled access and toilet. Families welcome. Car park. On the A680 Accrington to Clitheroe road, by the bridge over the Leeds–Liverpool Canal.

OPEN *4pm–12 Mon–Fri; noon–1am Sat; 2–11pm Sun.*

CLITHEROE
The New Inn
Parson Lane, Clitheroe BB7 2JN
☎ *(01200) 423312* Mr and Mrs Lees

Whitbread house with a guest beer policy serving Fuller's London Pride, Marston's Pedigree and a Moorhouse's brew plus a guest, changed weekly, from smaller breweries if possible. Beers featured have included Greene King Abbot, Gale's HSB and Wadworth 6X.

An old English pub with one bar and an open fire, plus adjoining rooms. No music or games, but folk club on Friday nights. Children allowed in designated area. No food.

OPEN *All day, every day.*

CLIVIGER
Queens
412 Burnley Road, Cliviger, Nr Burnley
☎ *(01282) 436712* Alec Heap

Freehouse with four real ales from a wide range of micro-breweries.

Simple one-bar alehouse. No pool table, juke box or bandits. No food. Children welcome, but there are no special facilities. On the A646 between Burnley and Todmorden.

OPEN *1–11pm.*

COLNE
Black Lane Ends
Skipton Old Road, Colne BB8 7EP
☎ *(01282) 863070*
www.copperdragon.uk.com

Part-tied to Copper Dragon, with Golden Pippin, Best Bitter and 1816, plus two weekly guests from breweries such as Phoenix, Ossett, Daleside and Bowland.

Old drovers' inn with one bar and real fires all year round. Traditional home-cooked food served 12–3pm and 6–9pm Mon–Fri; all day Sat–Sun. Beer garden with children's play area and BBQ. Car park. On the Skipton–Colne road.

OPEN *All day, every day.*

CRAWSHAWBOOTH
The White Bull
612 Burnley Road, Crawshawbooth BB4 8AJ
☎ *(01706) 260394* Chhanu Miah

Formerly tied to Beartown, now a freehouse with three permanent real ales and one guest.

Quiet traditional village pub. Old building, with beams, Indian restaurant upstairs (no food in the pub) and beer garden. Children allowed. Car park.

OPEN *5–11pm Mon–Fri; 12–11pm Sat; 12–10.30pm Sun.*

CROSTON
The Black Horse
Westhead Road, Croston, Nr Chorley PR5 7RQ
☎ *(01772) 600338* Mr A Edmundson

Six traditional cask bitters and one mild, from breweries such as Black Sheep, Caledonian, Jennings, Moorhouse's, Greene King, Phoenix and Timothy Taylor, plus smaller micro-breweries. Two beer festivals held each year around April and October.

This traditional village freehouse serves bar and restaurant food at lunchtimes and evenings, at very competitive prices. Car park, beer garden, bowling green and French boules pitch are all available, and specially organised parties and meals can be catered for. In the village of Croston, close to Chorley, between Preston and Southport.

OPEN *All day, every day.*

DALTON
The Beacon Inn
Beacon Lane, Dalton WN8 7RR
☎ *(01695) 632323* Brian Doyle

Owned by Marston's, with Jennings Mild, Bitter and Cumberland plus two guests, perhaps Fuller's London Pride or a Castle Eden brew.

This country pub is much used by ramblers as it is situated by Ashurst Beacon Point. Also handy for Beacon Golf Club. Food served 12–9pm Tues–Sat, 12–8pm Sun. Car park. Large beer garden. Function room available for hire. Children welcome.

OPEN *12–11pm (10.30pm Sun).*

DARWEN

Black Horse

72 Redearth Road, Darwen BB3 2AF
☎ *(01254) 873040* Andy Harding
www.theblackun.co.uk

Freehouse with up to five real ales, including Bank Top Flat Cap and Three B's Stokers Slake plus something from the Hopstar range and guests from micro-brewers. Four beer festivals a year.

Family-run community pub set back from the town centre off the A666. Contact point for the Hopstar Brewery. One small bar with lounge and diner separated by a corridor to games room and beer garden. Food served at lunchtimes. Outside seating.

OPEN *12–11pm (10.30pm Sun).*

Greenfield Inn

Lower Barn Street, Darwen BB3 2HQ
☎ *(01254) 703945* Carol Wood

Timothy Taylor Landlord, Greene King Abbot and Charles Wells Bombardier plus two guests.

A traditional one-room pub with beer garden. Food served at lunchtime and evenings. Children allowed. Situated on the outskirts of Darwen.

OPEN *12–11pm (10.30pm Sun).*

DIGGLE

The Diggle Hotel

Station Houses, Diggle, Oldham OL3 5JZ
☎ *(01457) 872741* Geoff Hibbert
www.saddleworthlife.com/digglehotel

Tied to Enterprise Inns, with Black Sheep Bitter, Timothy Taylor Landlord and Copper Dragon Black Gold plus two monthly-changing guests.

Built for the navvies digging Standedge Canal Tunnel, which is the longest, highest, deepest canal tunnel in Britain, this pub is over 200 years old. Sandwiches, homemade pies and steaks served 12–2.30pm and 5.30–9pm Mon–Fri; 12–9pm Sat–Sun. Small snug room to seat 20 for private hire. Beer garden. Newly refurbished en-suite accommodation from 2009. Two car parks. Fortnightly brass band concerts in summer. One mile from the Pennine Way.

OPEN *12–3pm and 5pm–12 Mon–Fri; noon–1am Sat; 12–12 Sun.*

EARBY

The Red Lion

70 Red Lion Street, Earby BB18 6RD
☎ *(01282) 843395* Janet Taylor

Freehouse with Thwaites Dark Mild, Timothy Taylor Landlord and a Copper Dragon Brewery ale plus three weekly-changing guests.

A lounge with character and a tap room. Children welcome. Food served daily. Waterfalls two minutes away.

OPEN *12–3pm and 5–11.30pm Mon–Thurs; all day Fri–Sun.*

ECCLESTON

Original Farmers Arms

Towngate, Eccleston, Chorley PR7 5QS
☎ *(01257) 451594* Barry Newton

Tied to Enterprise Inns with Timothy Taylor Landlord and ales from Phoenix and Moorhouse's always on offer. Up to four weekly-changing guests.

A one-bar pub in a traditional setting, 200 years old. Homemade food served 12–10pm in a busy separate restaurant. Children welcome. Beer garden. B&B accommodation. Quiz nights. Live music. Situated five miles from the M6 J27 on the B5250; close to Camelot Theme Park and Bygone Times.

OPEN *All day, every day.*

ENTWHISTLE

The Strawbury Duck

Overshores Road, Entwhistle, Bolton BL7 0LU
☎ *(01204) 852013* Danny Byrne

Five real ales available. Moorhouse's Pendle Witches, Black Sheep Special and Strawbury Duck Ale (brewed by Bank Top) are permanent fixtures, and a wide variety of guests is also served, including Young's Waggle Dance, Charles Wells Bombardier and beers from Phoenix, Three B's and Greene King.

Over 300 years old, this one-bar pub with several dining areas is nestled in between two reservoirs, next to Entwhistle Railway Station. Extensive menu, reasonably priced and catering for everyone, available 12–9pm Mon–Sat and 12–8pm Sun. Rooms available for hire, with small private functions catered for. Accommodation, beer garden, car park. Beer festival every August. Children welcome.

OPEN *12–11pm.*

FLEETWOOD

Wyre Lounge Bar

Marine Hall, The Esplanade, Fleetwood FY7 6HF
☎ *(01253) 771141*

Eight beers always available, including Moorhouse's brews. Also 200+ guest beers per year which may come from Wells and Young's, Banks's and Timothy Taylor.

Part of the Marine Hall Sports Complex. Food available at lunchtime. Car park, garden, function room. No children.

OPEN *11am–4.30pm and 7–11pm Mon–Sat; 12–4pm and 7–10.30pm Sun.*

GREAT HARWOOD

The Dog & Otter

Cliffe Lane, Great Harwood, Blackburn BB6 7PG
☎ *(01254) 885760* Catherine Darnley

Jennings Bitter and Cumberland Ale plus two rotating guest ales, perhaps Fuller's London Pride or a Marston's brew.

Traditional pub dating back to 1750 with two bar areas. Separate restaurant. Patio area with tables and outdoor heaters, lights and plants. Traditional pub food including specials served 12–2pm and 5–9pm. Children allowed.

OPEN *12–11pm.*

The Royal Hotel

Station Road, Great Harwood, Blackburn BB6 7BA
☎ *(01254) 883541* Janice and Peter Booth

Former home to the Red Rose micro-brewery, a freehouse with up to eight constantly changing beers (over 350 per year; more than 1,000 under the present landlords) including two from Red Rose, which now operates from a nearby industrial estate. Regular guests include brews from Hart, Anglo-Dutch, Barngates, Picks and Cropton.

Victorian pub/hotel with public bar, separate dining area, separate live music area and beer garden. English Tourist Council 3-diamond accommodation. Food available. No football, no discos, no karaoke! Live music Fri (mainly blues and folk). Children allowed, disabled facilities. Great Harwood is between Blackburn, Accrington and Clitheroe.

OPEN *12–11pm (10.30pm Sun).*

The Victoria Hotel

St John's Street, Great Harwood BB6 7EP
☎ *(01254) 885210* Jean Baxter

Freehouse with Bowland Gold plus up to seven constantly changing beers from any independent brewery.

Grade II listed building with one bar area and six separate rooms. No food. Children welcome. Large south-facing beer garden, formerly a bowling green. Annual beer festival. Situated approximately five miles from Accrington and Blackburn.

OPEN *4pm–12 Mon–Thurs; 3pm–1am Fri; 12–12 Sat–Sun.*

GRIMSARGH

The Plough

187 Preston Road, Grimsargh, Preston PR2 5JR
☎ *(01772) 652235* Karen and Francis McGrath
www.theploughgrimsargh.co.uk

Timothy Taylor Landlord, Hawkshead Bitter, Moorhouse's Pride of Pendle and Copper Dragon Black Gold plus one weekly-changing regional guest.

A 250-year-old traditional village pub. Single bar, three dining areas and lounge area. Regional food served 12–2.30pm and 6–9pm Tues–Sat; 12–6pm Sun (no food Mon). Children welcome. Beer garden. Car park. Bowling green. Weekly quiz. Annual beer festival in autumn. Private parties accommodated. On the B6243 between Preston and Longridge.

OPEN *All day, every day.*

HASLINGDEN

The Griffin Inn

84–6 Hud Rake, Haslingden, Rossendale BB4 5AF
☎ *(01706) 214021* Geoff and Cangui Oliver

Home of the Rossendale Brewery, which is in the basement. A brewpub with Floral Dance, Bitter, Porter, Sunshine, Railway Sleeper and Rossendale Ale brewed and served on the premises, plus an occasional guest beer and a regular, ever-changing traditional cider.

Traditional no-frills alehouse and community local 'quiet pub' on the northern edge of town, offering traditional pub games and a real fire. No pool, loud music or entertainment. No food. No children.

OPEN *All day, every day.*

HEAPEY

Top Lock

Copthurst Lance, Heapey, Chorley PR6 8LS
☎ *(01257) 263376* Philip Entwistle

Nine hand pumps, always serving one mild and one stout or porter. All the beers are constantly rotating, and might include brews from Timothy Taylor, Coniston, Durham, Wentworth, Hop Back, Hawkshead, Black Sheep, York, Ulverston, Bank Top, Stonehenge and Exmoor, to name but a few. European beers on tap and bottles.

Stone-built canalside pub in a rural location, ideal for pre- and post-walk drinks and meals. Home-cooked menu available 12–8pm every day. Two Indian chefs on site produce authentic Indian Cuisine every evening. Children allowed until 9pm. Private car park for pub users only.

OPEN *12–12.*

HESKIN

The Farmer's Arms

85 Wood Lane, Heskin PR7 5NP
☎ *(01257) 451276* Andrew Rothwell
www.farmersarms.co.uk

Six or seven real ales, with Jennings Cumberland, Caledonian Deuchars IPA, Marston's Pedigree, Greene King Old Speckled Hen and beers from Copper Dragon and Timothy Taylor often available. Guests are rotated weekly.

Award-winning olde-worlde two-bar inn in a 17th-century building, named Village Pub of the County in 2005. Food served all day, every day. Accommodation, children's play area, beer garden, large car park. Nearest attractions are Camelot Theme Park and Bygone Times. Situated off Junction 27 of M56 on B5250.

OPEN *12–11pm (10.30pm Sun).*

HEST BANK

The Hest Bank

2 Hest Bank Lane, Hest Bank, Lancaster LA2 6DN
☎ *(01524) 824339* Garrat Lymer

Timothy Taylor Landlord, Black Sheep Bitter, Caledonian Deuchars IPA plus three guests, changed weekly.

A 16th-century, canalside coaching inn, first licensed in 1554. Two bars. No pool table. Food served 12–9pm every day (including Christmas Day). Children welcome. Beer garden. Car park. Beer festivals. Function room and meeting room available. Off the A6 north of Lancaster, follow signs for Hest Bank.

OPEN *11.30am–11pm (10.30pm Sun).*

HOGHTON

The Sirloin Inn

Station Road, Hoghton PR5 0DD
☎ *(01254) 852293* Wayne Keough
www.thyme-out.net

Serving weekly-changing bitters and milds from various brewers, such as Archers, Bank Top, Three B's, Hydes and Moorhouse's.

This 16th-century former coaching inn is a hidden gem with beamed ceilings and open fires. Five-star food served from the Thyme kitchen Fri–Sun in the pub. Large car park. Outdoor decking area. Private function room for hire. Thyme restaurant on the first floor open Tues–Sun for lunch and dinner – Hi-Life Diners' award for Best Lancashire Restaurant 2007. Close to Hoghton Tower.

OPEN *4pm–close Mon–Thurs; 12–close Fri–Sun.*

LANCASTER

The Borough

3 Dalton Square, Lancaster LA1 1PP
☎ *(01524) 64170* Hannah and Martin Horner
www.theboroughlancaster.co.uk

Freehouse offering seven real ales: Thwaites Original and Wainwright, Hawkshead Bitter and Bowland Hen Harrier, plus three guests changed every week from breweries such as Bank Top, Brysons, Barngates and Ulverston.

Georgian townhouse with front pub, dining room, private dining room and garden to rear. Michelin-recommended menu full of local produce, with food served 12–2.30pm every day. Well-behaved children and dogs welcome. In the town centre, near the statue of Queen Victoria.

OPEN *Noon–12.30am.*

The Sun Hotel and Bar

63–5 Church Street, Lancaster LA1 1ET
☎ *(01524) 66006* Dominic Kiziuk
www.thesunhotelandbar.co.uk

Freehouse with four beers from the pub's own Lancaster brewery, such as Blonde or Red, plus Thwaites Lancaster Bomber and Wainwright, something from Jennings and one or two guests from around the country. CAMRA Lunesdale Pub of the Year 2006–07; *The Publican* Freehouse Pub of the Year 2008–09; *Daily Telegraph* Perfect Pub of the Year 2006–07.

Built on the site of Stoop Hall, dating from the medieval era, and first licensed in 1680. Situated in the heart of Lancaster with luxury, modern, 4-star (English Tourist Board) accommodation attached. Breakfast served 7.30–10.30am Mon–Fri; 8–11am Sat; 8.30–11am Sun. Lunch served 12–3pm (3.30pm Sun). Cheeseboards available all day, every day, plus new supper menu. Children welcome (away from the bar area). Beer garden. Monthly beer festivals. Meeting room available. Located in the centre of town, just off the A6.

OPEN *7.30am–midnight Mon–Thurs; 7.30am–1am Fri; 8am–1am Sat; 8.30am–11.30pm Sun.*

The Waterwitch

The Towpath, Aldcliffe Road, Lancaster LA1 1SU
☎ *(01524) 63828*

Up to eight real ales, almost exclusively from local independent breweries. Bryson's, Hart, Thwaites and Abbey often feature. Plus bottled beers and wheat and fruit beers on draught.

A genuine canalside inn converted from a stable block in 1978, with real fires and a garden. Upstairs restaurant. Good food available 12–3pm and 6–9.30pm Mon–Sat, 12–6pm Sun. Live music on Sunday nights.

OPEN *11am–11pm Mon–Sat; 12–10.30pm Sun.*

The White Cross

Quarry Road, Lancaster LA1 4XT
☎ *(01524) 33999* Tim Tomlinson

A wide range of real ales including Caledonian Deuchars IPA and Tirril Old Faithful. Six guests, changed fortnightly, from breweries such as Copper Dragon, Moorhouse's, Hawkshead, Tirril, Theakston and Coniston.

Built in the former warehouse of a Victorian mill and sitting on the canalside, only a few minutes' walk from the city centre. Food available 12–9pm Mon–Sat; 12–6pm Sun. Tues: quiz night; Sun: roasts. Large outdoor seating area. Parking. Annual Beer and Pie Festival in April. Located just off the ring road, behind the town hall.

OPEN *11.30am–midnight Mon–Thurs; 11.30am–1am Fri–Sat; 12–12 Sun.*

LEA TOWN

The Saddle Inn

Sidgreaves Lane, Lea Town, Preston PR4 0RS
☎ *(01772) 726616* Lauren Emmett

Thwaites tied house, serving Bitter and Lancaster Bomber plus a guest, changed every week or two.

Traditional one-bar country pub. Food served 12–8.30pm Mon–Sat and 12–7.30pm Sun. Front and rear beer garden, play area, large car park. Children welcome. Regular special events, including beer festivals. Two miles off Blackpool Road.

OPEN *11am–11pm.*

LITTLE ECCLESTON

The Cartford Hotel

Cartford Lane, Little Eccleston, Preston PR3 0YP
☎ *(01995) 670166* Andrew Mellodew

The Hart Brewery operates from the premises producing a range of 16 beers for sale in the hotel and some local freehouses. Up to eight beers available at any one time: two Hart ales and Fuller's London Pride plus five or six guests from a range of over 3,000 other beers so far.

A 400-year-old family pub. One large bar, large garden with children's play area. Quiet eating area with food available at lunchtime and evenings. Brewery tours by appointment. Occasional beer festivals. Car park. Games room. Accommodation. CAMRA's Lancashire Pub of the Year.

OPEN *12–3pm and 6.30–11pm Mon–Sat; all day Sun.*

LITTLEBOROUGH

The Moorcock Inn

Halifax Road, Blackstone Edge, Littleborough OL15 0LD
☎ *(01706) 378156*
Pauline and Allan Ashworth

Freehouse with Timothy Taylor Landlord plus three constantly changing guests.

Originally a farmhouse built in 1641, now a privately owned country inn with traditional beamed bar and outside terrace. Bar food and à la carte food served in separate restaurant served 11.30am–2.30pm and 5.30–9.30pm Mon–Fri; 11.30am–9.30pm Sat; 11.30am–9pm Sun. Beer garden. Accommodation. Large car park. Functions catered for. Four miles from M62 J21 on the A58 one mile from Littleborough.

OPEN *11.30am–close.*

LONGRIDGE

The Corporation Arms

Lower Road, Longridge, Preston PR3 2YJ
☎ *(01772) 782644* Kevin Proctor

Freehouse with three weekly-changing real ales from a wide variety of breweries.

Typical country inn dating from the 17th century. One bar, beer garden, accommodation. Food, including bar snacks, served all day. Superb view of the Ribble Valley.

OPEN *11am–close Mon–Sat; 12–10.30pm Sun.*

LONGTON

The Dolphin Inn

Marsh Lane, Longton, Preston PR4 5JY
☎ *(01772) 612032* Zena Slinger

Freehouse serving four cask ales, including Timothy Taylor Landlord, Greene King IPA and guest ales changing every few days.

A traditional country pub with two bars including one suited to families that leads to a conservatory. Children's play area. Real fire. Food served all day until 8pm, including daily specials and a children's menu. Situated on the Ribble Way and thus an ideal base for walkers.

OPEN *All day, every day.*

LYTHAM

The Taps

12–15 Henry Street, Lytham FY8 5LE
☎ *(01253) 736226* Ian Rigg

Up to eight real ales, two permanent fixtures (including a house brew from Titanic) and six frequently rotating guests from a vast selection of breweries located all over the British Isles. A mild is usually available.

Olde-English town pub with one bar and coal fires. The yard behind is heated. Viewing cellar. Disabled facilities and toilets. Food served at lunchtime only Mon–Sat. Children allowed only if dining.

OPEN *11am–11pm Sun–Thurs; 11am–midnight Fri–Sat.*

MAWDESLEY

The Black Bull

Hall Lane, Mawdesley L40 2QY
☎ *(01704) 822202* Tony McAughey

Punch Taverns pub serving five real ales. Timothy Taylor Landlord, Black Sheep Bitter, JW Lees Bitter and Jennings Cumberland permanently available, plus one guest.

Listed building dating from 1580, with a traditional feel and open fire. Two bars. Food served 12–2pm and 6.30–9pm Mon–Fri; 12–2.30pm and 6–9pm Sat; 12–8pm Sun. Beer garden. Car park.

OPEN *12–12 (11pm Sun).*

Robin Hood Inn

Bluestone Lane, Mawdesley, Nr Ormskirk L40 2RG
☎ *(01704) 822275* David Cropper
www.robinhoodinn.co.uk

Enterprise Inns house serving Timothy Taylor Landlord, Caledonian Deuchars IPA, Jennings Cumberland and three guests.

Originally dating from the 15th century, but altered in the 19th century, this is a friendly country pub, owned by the same family for the last 30 years. One public bar; upstairs restaurant. Bar food served 12–2.30pm and 5.30–9.30pm Mon–Fri; 12–9.30pm Sat–Sun. Restaurant open 6–9.30pm Tues–Sun. Families welcome. Beer garden with children's play area. Car park with disabled spaces and ramp access. Functions fully catered for. Located on the three-way crossroads between Croston, Eccleston and Mawdesley.

OPEN *12–11pm Mon–Thurs; 12–close Fri–Sat; 12–10.30pm Sun.*

MITTON

The Three Fishes

Mitton Road, Mitton, Nr Whalley BB7 9PQ
☎ *(01254) 826888* Ian Walton
www.thethreefishes.com

A Ribble Valley inn. Thwaites Bomber, Wainwrights and Original, plus one monthly-changing guest, such as Bowland Hen Harrier.

A 400-year-old inn which, after years of neglect, was renovated by Ribble Valley Inns in 2004. Now an award-winning pub offering a relaxed atmosphere, sun terrace in summer and crackling fires in winter. Traditional British food, locally sourced where possible, served 12–2pm and 6–9pm Mon–Sat (5.30pm Sat); 12–8.30pm Sun (all day bank holidays). Children welcome, they are provided with fun sheets and stickers, and offered a healthy children's menu also sourced from fresh produce. Car park.

OPEN *12–11pm (10.30pm Sun).*

MOSSLEY

The Rising Sun

235 Stockport Road, Mossley, Ashton-under-Lyne OL5 0RQ
☎ *(01457) 834436* Rais Devine

Freehouse serving Archer's Village, Shaws Golden Globe, Black Sheep Best and one local guest.

Traditional real-ale pub, over 200 years old. Four drinking areas around a central bar, with wood-burning stove and quaint and friendly atmosphere. No food. Small car park. Live music Tues night. Views of Saddleworth, good for rambling and walks. On the A670.

 5pm–12.

ORMSKIRK

The Hayfield

County Road, Ormskirk L39 1NN
☎ *(01695) 571157* Godfrey Hedges

Cains Mild is among the beers always on offer, plus eight guests from a variety of breweries, including Jennings, Phoenix, Slaters (Eccleshall), Rooster's, Black Sheep, Weetwood, Moorhouse's and Robinson's.

Busy freehouse with a warm, friendly atmosphere. Food served 12–3pm and 5.30–8.30pm Mon–Sat plus 12–7.30pm Sun. No children's facilities. Car park. On the main A59 road in Ormskirk.

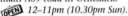 *12–11pm (10.30pm Sun).*

The Queen's Head

30 Moor Street, Ormskirk L39 2AQ
☎ *(01695) 574380* Elaine Wright

Up to three real ales, Tetley Bitter and Mild on cask permanently, and four guest ales changed daily, including Classic Blonde, Hooky Gold, Bombardier and Early Bird. Scored 100/100 by cask mark, 2009.

Classic one-bar pub with beer garden, plasma screen for live sports, and smoking pagoda. Food served 12–7pm.

All day, every day.

The Yew Tree

Grimshaw Lane, Ormskirk L39 1PD
☎ *(01695) 572261* Leslie Baker

Cain's Bitter, Robinson's Bitter and Caledonian Deuchars IPA plus two weekly-changing guests.

A traditional tap room bar, with separate lounge, food served 12–2.30pm and 5.30–7.30pm Mon–Sat (8pm Sat); 12–2.30pm Sun. Children welcome. Beer garden. Car park. Just outside Ormskirk town centre.

12–3pm and 5–11.30pm Mon–Fri; 11.30am–midnight Sat; 12–4pm and 7.30–11pm Sun.

PENDLETON

The Swan with Two Necks

Pendleton, Clitheroe BB7 1PT
☎ *(01200) 423112* Stephen John Dilworth

Freehouse with Copper Dragon Golden Pippin, Bargates Cat Nap, Phoenix Navvy and Bank Top Flat Cap permanently available.

A typical English village pub, dating from 1772, with real fires in winter and beer garden in summer. A pretty setting, nestling under Pendle Hill, with the village stream running through. Darts and dominoes. No music or juke box. Food served 12–1.45pm Wed–Sat; 7–9pm Wed–Thurs; 6–9pm Fri–Sat; 12–6.30pm Sun (no food Mon–Tues). Children welcome. Near Clitheroe Castle, signed Pendleton off the A59.

7–11pm Mon; closed Tues; 12–2pm and 7–11pm Wed–Thurs; 12–2.30pm and 6–11pm Fri–Sat; 12–10.30pm Sun.

POULTON LE FYLDE

Thatched House

12 Ball Street, Poulton le Fylde FY6 7BG
☎ *(01253) 891063* Valerie Ballentine

Five real ales usually available. Regular beers include Charles Wells Bombardier, Boddingtons and Theakston Best Bitter plus two rotating guest beers one of which is usually from the Hart Brewery.

Its unusal location in the graveyard of the parish church in the centre of town means that you are always guaranteed a warm welcome in this award-winning and unspoilt traditional pub. No food, children or music.

11am–11pm Mon–Sat; 12–10.30pm Sun.

PRESTON

The Black Horse

166 Friargate, Preston PR1 2EJ
☎ *(01772) 204855*

Robinson's house with Hatters Dark Mild, Cumbria Way, Best Bitter, Unicorn, Double Hop and Old Tom available plus seasonal and occasional brews.

Built in 1898 and once a hotel, now a classic multi-roomed town-centre pub in a listed building. Amazing interior décor with tiled walls and panelled bars plus a mosaic floor.

 11am–11pm Mon–Sat; 12–4pm Sun.

The Fox & Grapes

15 Fox Street, Preston PR1 2AB
☎ *(01772) 561149* Sharon Fishwick

A Scottish and Newcastle tied house. Three guest ales available, changed every barrel. Breweries featured have included Hydes, Harviestoun and Theakston.

Old-fashioned boozer's boozer with a large collection of beer mats on the walls and a collection of motorbike memorabilia. Football table. Darts. No food. Situated five minutes from the railway station, off Fishergate.

12–11pm Mon–Thurs; 12–12 Fri–Sun.

The Guild

99 Fylde Road, Preston PR1 2XQ
☎ *(01772) 252870* Karen McCart

Greene King pub with IPA, Abbot and Old Speckled Hen plus a weekly guest.

Drinkers' pub in a listed building on the outskirts of town with large bar and zoned areas. Food 12–9pm, including roasts on Sundays. Excellent beer garden, including heated smoking area. Pool table. Quiz night Monday. Car park. Buffets available.

OPEN *11am–11pm Mon–Wed; 11am–midnight Thurs–Sat; 12–11pm Sun.*

New Britannia Inn

6 Heatley Street, Preston PR1 2XB
☎ *(01772) 253424* Nick Robinson

An Enterprise Inns pub serving six real ales. Marston's Pedigree and Timothy Taylor Landlord. Two regularly changing guests, from breweries such as Salamander, York, Bowland, Bradfield, Northern and Ossett.

An open-plan, city-centre pub, traditionally furnished. Food served 11am–2pm Mon–Sat; 12–4pm Sun. Pool table. Open mic nights Wed. Charity nights. Three beer festivals each year. Smoking area. Turn off Ringway at Friargate towards the university, Heatley Street is second on the left.

OPEN *11am–11pm Mon, Tues, Thurs; 11am–midnight Wed, Fri, Sat; 12–11pm Sun.*

The Old Black Bull

35 Friargate, Preston PR1 2AT
☎ *(01772) 823397* Stan Eaton

A beer from Cains is among those permanently served. The eight guest beers are changed every couple of days, and might include Timothy Taylor Landlord and Fuller's London Pride.

Old traditional pub in the town centre. Food served until 4pm. Pool and darts, patio. Live music on Saturday nights. Children allowed during the daytime.

OPEN *10.30am–11pm Mon–Sat; 12–10.30pm Sun.*

The Old Vic

78 Fishergate, Preston PR1 2UH
☎ *(01772) 254690* Mike Wood

At least four, but sometimes as many as seven, real ales on offer. All served on a guest basis, but popular favourites include Caledonian Deuchars IPA, Shepherd Neame Spitfire, Marston's Pedigree and Charles Wells Bombardier.

Formerly known as the Victoria and Railway Hotel, this is over 200 years old and has a traditional atmosphere with beams and a horseshoe-shaped bar. Food served 12–5pm. Children welcome. Beer garden. Car park. Opposite the mainline railway station.

OPEN *11.30am–midnight.*

The Stanley Arms

Lancaster Road, Preston PR1 1DA
☎ *(01772) 254004* Niall Johnson

Six ales are usually on offer, including beers such as Greene King Old Speckled Hen and Ruddles County.

A traditional pub in a Grade II listed building, newly refurbished with chill-out 'Crystal Lounge' upstairs and outside drinking patio. Very busy at weekends. Food available 10am–7pm. Children welcome. Next to the Guild Hall, near Avenham Park, and just 30 seconds from Preston bus station.

OPEN *11am–11.30pm Sun–Thurs; 11am–1.30am Fri–Sat.*

SADDLEWORTH

The White Hart at Lydgate

Stockport Road, Lydgate, Saddleworth DL4 4JJ
☎ *(01457) 872566* Charles Brierley
www.thewhitehart.co.uk

Freehouse with JW Lees Bitter, Black Sheep Bitter and Timothy Taylor Landlord and Golden Best plus one weekly-changing guest.

Stone-built pub, 220 years old, a former prison, police station, weaver's cottage and Second World War lookout station. Food served in a separate brasserie, a restaurant, and private dining and function rooms. Full menu of traditional home-cooked food served every day for breakfast, lunch and dinner. Large car park. Limited accommodation. Civil wedding licence. Two miles east of Oldham on the A668.

OPEN *All day, every day.*

STANDISH

The Crown at Worthington

19–21 Platt Lane, Standish WN1 2XF
☎ *(01257) 421354* Daniel and Tracy Prance
www.thecrownatworthington.co.uk

Freehouse serving five constantly rotating guests from small micro-breweries – local, regional and national.

A 100-year-old country inn with lounge bar, restaurant and ten letting rooms. Food served lunchtimes and evenings Mon–Fri, all day Sat–Sun. Beer festivals held twice a year. Function room and private dining room. Decked sun terrace. Car park. Near junction 27 of the M6 and junction 6 of the M61. Located just off the A5106 between Wigan and Chorley.

OPEN *12–11pm.*

TRAWDEN

The Sun Inn

Back Colne Road, Trawden BB8 8PG
☎ *(01282) 867985*
Wayne Forster and Faye Medcalf

Freehouse currently serving a range of four Copper Dragon ales.

A rural pub dating from 1780 with two bars and a function room in a converted barn. Food served Tues–Sun. Children welcome. Two car parks. Beer garden. Tues: jazz night. Thurs: quiz night. Two private rooms for hire, including civil wedding ceremony licence. Located in popular walking country.

OPEN *5pm–close Mon–Fri; all day Sat–Sun. Summer: all day Thurs–Sun.*

UPHOLLAND

The White Lion

10 Church Street, Upholland, Skelmersdale WN8 0ND
☎ *(01695) 622727* Alan and Tracy Branagan

Tied to Thwaites, with Original and one or two other Thwaites cask ales.

Village pub built in the 16th century, with many of the original features still present. One bar, open fires. No food. Traditional pub games such as darts and dominoes, big-screen TV. Beer garden and car park.

OPEN *6–11pm Mon–Thurs; 5pm–12 Fri; 1pm–12 Sat; 1–10.30pm Sun.*

WADDINGTON

The Lower Buck

Church Lane, Waddington, Nr Clitheroe BB7 3HU
☎ *(01200) 423342* Andrew Warburton

Moorhouse's Premier, Black Cat and Pride of Pendle plus Timothy Taylor Landlord and Bowland Hen Harrier together with a monthly-changing guest.

The quintessential country pub with four open fires and a separate dining room. Traditional homemade pies and bar snacks served 12–2.30pm and 6–9pm Mon–Fri; 12–9pm Sat–Sun. Children welcome. Disabled facilities and access. Beer gardens front and rear. Private room. Located two miles from historic Clitheroe in the Ribble Valley, an Area of Outstanding Natural Beauty.

OPEN *All day, every day.*

WHALLEY

The Dog Inn

55 King Street, Whalley BB7 9SP
☎ *(01254) 823009* Norman H Atty

Five or six real ales, with one or two Moorhouse's beers usually available, plus weekly and monthly guests. Local breweries are often given preference.

A 17th-century building that has been knocked about a bit! It has a traditional interior with lots to see. Home-prepared and -cooked food served 12–2.30pm every day. Beer garden. Children and dogs welcome. The village has excellent shops for clothes, antiques etc.

OPEN *11am–12.30am Mon–Sat; 12–11.30pm Sun.*

The Swan Hotel

62 King Street, Whalley BB7 9SN
☎ *(01254) 822195* Louise and Gary Clough

Two cask ales, generally Timothy Taylor Landlord and a guest which could be something from Bowland Brewery.

Thriving 17th-century coaching inn in the heart of the beautiful Ribble Valley village of Whalley, offering a vibrant, well-stocked bar and modern, comfortable surroundings. Winners of a Beautiful Beer Gold Award. Food served all day. Lovely refurbished en-suite rooms.

OPEN *All day, every day.*

WHARLES

The Eagle & Child Inn

Church Road, Wharles, Nr Kirkham
☎ *(01772) 690312* Brian Tatham

Two real ales, perhaps from Clark's, Wadworth or Eccleshall.

Relaxed atmosphere and lovely antiques in this Grade II listed thatched country inn (circa 1650) on the Fylde coast. No food. Large car park. Well-behaved children welcome, subject to licensing regulations.

OPEN *7–11pm Mon–Sat; 12–4pm and 7–10.30pm Sun.*

WHEELTON

The Dresser's Arms

9 Briers Brow, Wheelton, Chorley PR6 8HD
☎ *(01254) 830041* Stuart Swanton

A true freehouse with eight hand pumps. Timothy Taylor Landlord, Moorhouse's Pendle Witches, Wheelton Big Frank's Bitter, Theakston Old Peculier, Caledonian Deuchars IPA and Phoenix Arizona could be among the beers on offer. Six are changed weekly, or sooner if they run out.

A village pub with oak beams, real fires and a cosy atmosphere. Food available 12–2.30pm Mon–Fri and all day Sat–Sun, with separate Cantonese restaurant upstairs. Beer garden and outside smoking area. Car park. Quiz night Tuesday, curry night Thursday. Children allowed.

OPEN *11am–12.30am Sun–Thurs; 11am–1am Fri–Sat.*

THE BREWERIES

BARROWDEN BREWERY
The Exeter Arms, 28 Main Street, Barrowden, Rutland LE15 8EQ
☎ *(01572) 747247*

 FARMER BOYS 3.6% ABV
BEACH BOYS 3.8% ABV
YOUNG BOYS BITTER 4.1% ABV
FUN BOY FOUR 4.4% ABV
BEVIN BOYS 4.5% ABV
NAUGHTY BOY'S BITTER 4.8% ABV
Plus seasonal and occasional brews.

BELLS BREWERY AND MERCHANTS LTD
The Workshop, Lutterworth Road, Ullesthorpe, Lutterworth LE17 5DR
☎ *(01455) 209940*
www.bellsbrewery.co.uk

COSBY'S 3.7% ABV
MAN IN THE MOON 3.9% ABV
RAINMAKER 4.0% ABV
MAD COW 4.3% ABV
DREAMCATCHER 4.7% ABV
SIR FRANK WHITTLE'S JET ALE 5.8% ABV
MUCKY DOG 6.0% ABV
Plus seasonals and specials.

BELVOIR BREWERY LTD
Crown Business Park, Station Road, Old Dalby, Melton Mowbray LE14 3NQ
☎ *(01664) 823455*
www.belvoirbrewery.co.uk

WHIPPLING GOLDEN BITTER 3.6% ABV
BEAVER BITTER 4.3% ABV
Hoppy, smooth malt beer.
Memory Lane Beers:
STAR MILD 3.4% ABV
Dark and malty.
STAR BITTER 3.9% ABV
Crisp and dry.
Occasionals:
GORDON BENNETT 4.1% ABV
Chestnut colour, hoppy aroma.
PEACOCK'S GLORY 4.7% ABV
Light and hoppy.
OLD DALBY 5.1% ABV
Roasted flavour.

BREWSTERS BREWING CO. LTD
Penn Lane, Stathern, Melton Mowbray LE14 4JA
☎ *(01949) 861868*
www.brewsters.co.uk

HOPHEAD 3.6% ABV
Brewed from a blend of English and American hops.
MARQUIS 3.8% ABV
Tawny and malty.
DAFFYS ELIXIR 4.2% ABV
Pale, golden and hoppy.
HOP A DOODLE DOO 4.3% ABV
Copper colour and fruity.
RUTTERKIN 4.6% ABV
Slightly sweet, rich and flavoursome.
BELLYDANCER 5.2% ABV
Dark ruby and fruity.
Plus the Wicked Woman Range of changing beers, each brewed to a new recipe but always at 4.3% and changed every four to six weeks.

DOW BRIDGE BREWERY
3 Rugby Road, Catthorpe, Lutterworth LE17 6DA
☎ *(01788) 869121*

BONUM MILD 3.4% ABV
Traditional dark mild. Roast malt flavour with chocolate hints.
ACORIS 3.8% ABV
BITTER 3.8% ABV
RATAE'D 4.3% ABV
Straw coloured. Strong hop aroma, with bitter hop finish.
FOSSE ALE 4.8% ABV
Plus seasonals.

EVERARDS BREWERY LTD
Castle Acres, Norborough LE19 1BY
☎ *(0116) 2014100*
www.everards.co.uk

 BEACON BITTER 3.8% ABV
Award winning, fresh, clean taste.
SUNCHASER 4.0% ABV
Delicate spicy overtones and hints of peach.
TIGER BEST BITTER 4.2% ABV
Good body, dry hopped.
EVERARDS ORIGINAL 5.2% ABV
Copper-brown and sweetish.
Plus seasonal beers including:
SLY FOX 4.0% ABV
PITCH BLACK 4.3% ABV
SLEIGH BELL 4.5% ABV

THE GRAINSTORE BREWERY
Davises Brewing Co. Ltd, Station Approach, Oakham, Rutland LE15 6RE
☎ *(01572) 770065 (Brewery tours)*
www.grainstorebrewery.co.uk

RUTLAND PANTHER 3.4% ABV
COOKING BITTER 3.6% ABV
Golden and well balanced.
TRIPLE B 4.2% ABV
Malty sweetness with balancing hop flavours.
STEAMIN' BILLY BITTER 4.3% ABV
FORTH KING 4.5% ABV
GOLD 4.5% ABV
THREE KINGS 4.5% ABV
TIPPING ALE 4.5% ABV
TEN FIFTY 5.0% ABV
Easy-drinking sweet maltiness, with bitter finish.
RUTLAND BEAST 5.3%ABV
NIP 7.3% ABV
Plus seasonals and occasionals including:
BILLY'S LAST BARK 3.9% ABV
NO2 4.0% ABV
RUTLAND ROUSER 4.2% ABV

LANGTON BREWERY
Grange Farm, Nelham Road, Thorpe, Langton, Market Harborough LE16 7TU
☎ *07840 532826*

CAUDLE BITTER 3.9% ABV
BUZZ LIGHTBEER 4.2% ABV
BOWLER STRONG ALE 4.4% ABV
BOXER HEAVYWEIGHT 5.2% ABV
Plus seasonals and occasionals including:
BANKER'S DRAUGHT 4.2% ABV
HOP ON 4.4% ABV
BELLE 4.5% ABV

PARISH BREWERY

6 Main Street, Burrough-on-the-Hill, Melton Mowbray LE14 2JQ
☎ *(01664) 454801*

MILD 3.8% ABV
PARISH SPECIAL BITTER 3.9% ABV
FARM GOLD 4.0% ABV
SOMERBY PREMIUM BITTER 4.0% ABV
BURROUGH BITTER 4.8% ABV
POACHER'S ALE 6.0% ABV
BAZ'S BONCE BLOWER 11.0% ABV
Plus occasionals.

SHARDLOW BREWING COMPANY LTD

Old Brewery Stables, British Waterways Yard, Cavendish Bridge, Shardlow, Derby DE72 2HL
☎ *(01332) 799188*

CHANCELLOR'S REVENGE 3.6% ABV
CAVENDISH DARK 3.7% ABV
SPECIAL BITTER 3.9% ABV
GOLDEN HOP 4.1% ABV
NARROWBOAT 4.3% ABV
CAVENDISH GOLD 4.5% ABV
REVEREND EATON'S ALE 4.5% ABV
WHISTLE STOP 5.0% ABV
5 BELLS 5.2% ABV
6 BELLS 6.0% ABV
Plus seasonals and occasionals.

WICKED HATHERN BREWERY

The Willows, 46 Derby Road, Hathern, Loughborough LE12 5LD
☎ *(01509) 842585 or 07946 361069*

WHB (WICKED HATHERN BITTER) 3.8% ABV
ALBION SPECIAL 4.0% ABV
COCKFIGHTER 4.2% ABV
HAWTHORN GOLD 4.5% ABV
SOAR HEAD 4.8% ABV
Occasionals:
DERBY PORTER 4.8% ABV
GLADSTONE TIDINGS 5.1% ABV
Available Christmas only.

THE PUBS

ASHBY DE LA ZOUCH

The Ashby Court Hotel

34 Wood Street, Ashby de la Zouch LE65 1EL
☎ *(01530) 415176* Philip Lathbury

Freehouse with three real ales. Marston's Pedigree plus two rotating guests.

Mock-Tudor town pub with spacious restaurant behind and a good-sized beer garden. Food served 12–2pm and 7–9pm Mon–Sat, 12–4pm Sun. Accompanied children allowed. Car park.

OPEN *12–2.30pm Weds–Fri; 5–11pm Mon–Fri; 11.30am–11pm Sat; 12–5 and 7–10.30pm Sun.*

AYLESTONE

The Black Horse

65 Narrow Lane, Aylestone
☎ *(0116) 283 2811* Stuart and Pauline Fraser

Everards Beacon, Tiger, Original and seasonal ales plus guest beers from Old English Ale Club.

Village community pub in a 19th-century building. Lounge, bar, snug, function room, long alley skittles, garden. Food available.

OPEN *12–2.30pm and 5–11pm Mon–Thurs; 12–11pm Fri–Sat; 12–4pm and 7–10.30pm Sun.*

BARROW ON SOAR

The Navigation

Mill Lane, Barrow on Soar LE12 8LQ
☎ *(01509) 412842* Neil Stevens

Belvoir Star Bitter, Greene King Abbot, Timothy Taylor Landlord and Adnams Bitter plus two monthly guests.

Traditional English countryside canal pub with large beer garden and function room, benefiting from a bridge crossing the River Soar. Children welcome. Boating available. Regular BBQs in summer. Can be difficult to find, so ask locally or phone. Follow signs for Barrow Boating from A6.

OPEN *Noon–12.30am.*

BARROWDEN

The Exeter Arms

Main Street, Barrowden, Rutland LE15 8EQ
☎ *(01572) 747247* Martin Allsopp

Home of the Barrowden Brewing Company. A full range of brews is always available (and only sold here). Also various guests such as Fuller's London Pride, Greene King IPA and seasonal ales from various brewers. The aim is only to repeat the guest beers a maximum of three times a year.

A very traditional country pub, situated off the beaten track. One bar, huge garden. Brewery tours by appointment only. Food available Tues–Sun lunchtimes and Tues–Sat evenings. Accommodation consists of two twin rooms and one double. Children allowed. Ring for directions.

OPEN *11am–2.30pm and 6–11pm (10.30pm Sun, closed Mon lunchtime).*

CATTHORPE

Cherry Tree

Main Street, Catthorpe LE17 6DB
☎ *(01788) 860430* Phil and Sue Cartwright

Freehouse with Adnams Bitter plus three constantly rotating guests from various breweries nationwide.

Small village pub dating back to the 1860s with real fires, one main bar, two rooms and a south-facing patio. Food served Mon and Fri lunchtimes and 5–9pm Mon–Sun. Beer garden. Car park. Beer festivals held. Children welcome. A mile and a half from Stanford Hall.

OPEN *12–2.30pm and 5–11pm Mon–Fri; 12–11pm Sat–Sun.*

CLIPSHAM

The Olive Branch

Main Street, Clipsham, Rutland LE15 7SH
☎ *(01780) 410355* Sean Hope and Ben Jones
www.theolivebranchpub.com

 Grainstore Olive Oil (the house brew) and two other real ales often from other local breweries.

Originally three farm workers' cottages and a pub since 1890, this multi-award-winning gastropub with rooms deserves its formidable reputation. Revitalised, refurbished and reopened by the present team after closing in 1997, it features several adjoining rooms plus outside seating areas. Good food served 12–2pm and 7–9.30pm. Accommodation is in the Beech House opposite. Two miles from the A1.

OPEN *12–3pm and 6–11pm Mon–Fri; all day Sat–Sun.*

EAST LANGTON

The Bell Inn

Main Street, East Langton, Market Harborough LE16 7TW
☎ *(01858) 545278* Peter Faye

 Freehouse with locally brewed Langton Caudle Bitter and Bowler Ale plus Greene King Abbot and IPA. Also an excellent range of wines.

A traditional Grade II listed county pub in the heart of the Leicestershire countryside. Friendly village pub atmosphere. Freshly prepared food available at lunchtimes (not Mon in winter) and evenings, from light bites to full meals. Traditional roasts on Sundays. Two en-suite letting rooms. Located three miles north of Market Harborough on the B6047.

OPEN *Winter: closed Sun evening and Mon; 12–2.30pm and 7–11pm Tues–Sat; 12–4.30pm Sun. Summer: 12–2.30pm and 7–11pm.*

FOXTON

Foxton Locks Inn

Bottom Lock, Gumley Road, Foxton LE16 7RA
☎ *(0116) 279 1515* Stephanie Hamblin

 Caledonian Deuchars IPA, Theakston Old Peculier and two fortnightly-changing guests.

Modern development housed in buildings which pre-date 1814. Food served 12–3pm and 6–8.45pm daily. Large beer garden overlooking the canal with two heated terraces. Children and dogs very welcome. Disabled access. Private function room with terrace to hire opening autumn 2008. Situated near picturesque country park, follow signs to the Bottom Lock.

OPEN *11am–11pm (closed Christmas Day).*

FRISBY ON THE WREAKE

The Bell Inn & Brasserie

2 Main Street, Frisby on the Wreake LE7 2NJ
☎ *(01664) 434237* Barry and Lynn Turner

 Freehouse with Black Sheep Bitter, plus two guests changed weekly, perhaps Cottage Brunel or Swordfish, or Grainstore Triple B.

A 250-year-old olde-worlde village pub with one bar and decked outside area. Food served at lunchtime (not Mon) and evenings (not Sun). Car park, restaurant. Children welcome. On the A607 Melton to Leicester road.

OPEN *6–11pm Mon; 12–3pm and 6–11pm Tues–Sat; 12–3pm Sun.*

GLENFIELD

The Dominion

Tournament Road, Glenfield
☎ *(0116) 231 3789* Peter Flaherty

 Everards pub with Beacon and Tiger plus one guest, perhaps Everards Original, or a seasonal beer.

Estate community pub offering pool, snooker, darts and games machines. Food served. Garden and patio, car park. Children allowed.

OPEN *11am–3pm and 5–11pm Mon–Thurs; 11am–11pm Fri–Sat; 12–10.30pm Sun.*

GLOOSTON

The Old Barn Inn

Andrews Lane, Glooston, Nr Market Harborough LE16 7ST
☎ *(01858) 545215* Adam Townsley

Four beers (30 per year) from brewers such as Adnams, Hook Norton, Fuller's, Wadworth, Oakhill, Nene Valley, Ridley, Bateman, Thwaites, Leatherbritches, Mauldons, Cotleigh and Greene King.

A 16th-century village pub in rural location with a log fire, no juke box or games machines. Bar and restaurant food available in evenings and Sunday lunchtime. Car park. Catering for parties, receptions and meetings. Well-behaved children and dogs welcome. Accommodation. On an old Roman road between Hallaton and Tur Langton.

OPEN *6–11pm Mon; 12–2.30pm and 6–11pm Tues–Sat; all day Sun.*

HOSE

The Rose & Crown

43 Bolton Lane, Hose, Melton Mowbray LE14 4JE
☎ *(01949) 860424* Robin Stroud

Up to eight real ales available from a wide range, changing constantly.

Not easy to find at the back of the village, this modernised open-plan bar has an olde-worlde lounge with open fire, attractive bar with darts and pool plus background music. Beamed restaurant open Weds and Thurs evenings, Fri and Sat lunchtimes and evenings and Sun lunch. Large car park and gardens. Room for camping and caravans.

OPEN *5.30–11pm Mon–Thurs; 12–11pm Fri–Sun.*

KEGWORTH

Red Lion

24 High Street, Kegworth DE74 2DA
☎ *(01509) 672466* John Briggs
www.redlionkegworth.com

Eight real ales, including Adnams Bitter, Greene King Abbot, Banks's Original and Castle Rock Preservation, plus four rotating guests, all from micro-breweries and independents.

Freehouse in a Georgian building, with three bars and a large garden. Food served every lunchtime and Mon–Fri evenings every day. Accommodation. From J24 of the M1 take the A6 to the centre of the village and turn right into High Street.

OPEN *All day, every day.*

KIRBY MUXLOE

The Royal Oak

Main Street, Kirby Muxloe, Leicester LE9 2AN
☎ *(0116) 239 3166* Mr Jackson

Everards house serving Tiger, Beacon and Old Original. Also two guest pumps serving beers such as Greene King Abbot Ale, Nethergate Old Growler or an Adnams brew.

Food-oriented village pub. Modern building with traditional decor. Function facilities. Disabled access. Garden. Food available at lunchtimes and evenings. Children allowed.

OPEN *11am–3pm and 5.30–11pm (10.30pm Sun).*

LEICESTER

The Ale Wagon

27 Rutland Street, Leicester LE1 1RE
☎ *(0116) 262 3330* Stephen Hoskins

Hoskins Brewery house with four Hoskins ales always available, plus two or three guests from other micro-breweries.

A 1930s red-brick corner pub, originally built as a hotel. Food available lunchtimes and evenings. Located on the corner of Rutland Street and Charles Street.

OPEN *11am–11pm Mon–Sat; 12–10.30pm Sun.*

The Barley Mow

149 Granby Street, Leicester LE1 6SB
☎ *(0116) 254 4663* Kimberley Stones

Everards Tiger, Beacon, Sunchaser and Original plus one or two guests, changed every two weeks.

A 200-year-old regulars' pub on the edge of the city centre, with one large bar area and friendly staff and customers. Traditional pub fayre is served in the upstairs area, which is also a coffee shop, 7.30am–3.30pm Mon–Fri and 9am–4.30pm Sat. Smokers' courtyard. Real Ale Club Mon, karaoke Wed. Regular quiz nights. Large pay & display car park nearby. Children welcome until 7pm. Meeting place for Sci-Fi Club and Dungeons & Dragons. One minute from the train station, just off the A6 towards the city centre.

OPEN *11am–11pm Mon–Sat (open 10.30am Sat on match days); 12–6pm Sun.*

The Black Horse

1 Foxon Street, Leicester LE3 5LT
☎ *(0116) 254 0030* Phil Gomersall

Everards pub with up to six real ales including Beacon, Tiger and Elgood's Black Dog plus three guests.

Characterful, cosy locals' pub on Braunstone Gate. Two rooms. Live music (Tues, Thurs, Sat) and regular quizzes (Weds and Sun).

OPEN *3pm–12.*

Criterion Free House

44 Millstone Lane, Leicester LE1 5JN
☎ *(0116) 262 5418* RD Hunt

Up to 12 real ales available on hand pump, including Oakham brews and beers from a wide range of micro-breweries, changed daily. A further 12 ales from gravity in the cellar are served for beer festivals. Over 100 international bottled beers also on offer.

City-centre pub with two rooms, a lounge and a games room that is available for private parties. Food served 12–2.15pm and 5.30–9pm, with pub grub Sun–Mon and homemade pizzas Tues–Sat. Beer patio. Darts and dominoes teams. Pop music quiz Tues night, general knowledge quiz Weds night, live music Thurs and Sat. Caters for football and rugby supporters. Four real ale festivals and one cider festival a year. No children after 8pm. Inside the ring road, 15 minutes from the train station near De Montfort University.

OPEN *12–11pm (10.30pm Sun). Late bar extensions for special events and private parties.*

The Globe

43 Silver Street, Leicester LE1 5EU
☎ *(0116) 262 9819* Janet Kerr

Tied to Everards, with the full range of the brewery's beers plus up to four guest ales, changed frequently.

Built in 1723, this regular local drinkers' pub has two bar areas and an upstairs pool room. Food served every day 12–7pm. Close to The Shires shopping centre.

OPEN *11am–11pm Mon–Thurs; 11am–1am Fri–Sat; 12–10.30pm Sun.*

The Hat & Beaver

60 Highcross Street, Leicester LE1 4NN
☎ *(0116) 262 2157* Tony Cartwright

Hardys & Hansons tied house serving Mild, Best Bitter and Olde Trip plus seasonal and occasional ales.

Traditional 19th-century town-centre pub with two rooms. Pub games. Filled cob rolls available at lunchtimes and on request. Children allowed until 6pm. On the edge of the city.

OPEN *12–3pm and 6–11pm Mon–Thur; 12–11pm Fri–Sat; 12–10.30pm Sun.*

Marquis Wellington

139 London Road, Leicester LE2 1EF
☎ *(0116) 254 0542*
www.marquiswellington.com

An Everards pub with three or four of the brewery's ales including Beacon and Tiger plus up to four guests.

Recently refurbished and under new management, an Edwardian alehouse with ornate frontage serving home-cooked food 12–7pm daily. Beer garden. Large-screen TVs showing Sky Sports, quiz night (Mon) and open mic night (Thurs). On the edge of the city, close to the railway station and university.

OPEN *All day, every day.*

Molly O'Gradys

14 Hotel Street, Leicester LE1 5AW
☎ *(0116) 251 8992* Lorraine Anderson

Everards Beacon and Tiger are always available at this Everards pub.

The only true Irish pub in Leicester, in an old building, with fireplaces and bright, clean wooden interior. Irish TV, regular live music, with big bands at weekends. Food served at lunchtimes, including Irish Sunday dinners on Sunday. Children welcome during the day only, in the back bar. Situated just off the market place.

OPEN *11am–11.30pm Mon–Thurs; 11am–2am Fri–Sat; 12–12 Sun.*

Shakespeare's Head

Southgates, Leicester LE1 5SH
☎ *(0116) 262 4378* Ruth Rodger
www.shakespeareshead.co.uk

Barnsley Bitter and Old Tom (mild) from the Oakwell Brewery.

Oakwell Brewery managed house built in the 1960s and keeping the character of the period. Two rooms leading from a large glass- fronted foyer. Pub games. No car park. Rolls on Fri; Sat and Sun lunch served 12–2pm. Located in the city's historical quarter near the cathedral, off St Nicholas Circle.

OPEN *12–12 Mon–Thurs; noon–1am Fri–Sat; 12–11pm Sun.*

The Swan & Rushes

19 Infirmary Square, Leicester LE1 5WR
☎ *(0116) 233 9167* Grant Cook

Bateman XB, Oakham JHB and Bishop's Farewell plus six guests, constantly rotating. There is usually a dark on at least one pump. No nationals. Also a range of imported beers, mainly from Germany, and over 100 top-quality bottled beers.

A triangular pub, built around 1930, with a comfortable interior and a small garden with outside seating. Food available Wed–Sun lunchtimes and Wed and Fri evenings. Weekly quiz nights on Thursdays and live entertainment on Saturdays. Located at the southern end of Oxford Street.

OPEN *12–3pm and 5–11pm Mon–Thurs (midnight Thurs); 12–12 Fri–Sat; 12–11.30pm Sun.*

Vin IV

24 King Street, Leicester LE1 6RL
☎ *07976 222378 or 07974 932186*
Paul Summers and Daksha Patel
www.outofthevaults.com

Up to 12 real ales available, all from micro-breweries and all competitively priced.

Opened in 2004 by the team that ran The Vaults down the road. One long bar, wooden floor, church pew seating. Special events including regular beer festivals (check website). No food, but customers are welcome to order in food, and plates and cutlery are provided.

OPEN *12–11pm (10.30pm Sun).*

The Albion Inn

Canal Bank, Loughborough LE11 1QA
☎ *(01509) 213952* Mr Hartley

Robinson's Best, Brains Dark and something from the Wicked Hathern Brewery plus guests such as Shepherd Neame Spitfire and Early Bird, Black Sheep Special or brews from Greene King.

Traditional two-bar pub with garden, situated on the canal bank. Disabled access. Food available at lunchtimes and early evenings. Well-behaved children allowed. Car park.

OPEN *11am–3pm and 6–11pm (10.30pm Sun).*

The Swan in the Rushes

21 The Rushes, Loughborough LE11 5BE
☎ *(01509) 217014* Ian Bogie
www.swanintherushes.co.uk

Castle Rock Harvest Pale, Sheriff's Tipple, and Elsie Mo, and Adnams Bitter, plus five guest beers and a mild. About 15 guest beers are sold each week.

A cosmopolitan town-centre alehouse, smart yet down to earth, with two bars and a friendly atmosphere. Extended in 2007 to include new kitchen, new family room, drinking terrace and large function room with bar and skittle alley. Home-cooked food served 12–3pm daily; 6–9pm Mon–Sat; 12-5pm Sun. Car park with bicycle rack. B&B accommodation. Two beer festivals held annually, in spring and November. Wireless internet access available. On the A6, behind Sainsbury's.

OPEN *11am–11pm Mon–Thurs; 11am–midnight Fri–Sat; 12–11pm Sun.*

Tap & Mallet

36 Nottingham Road, Loughborough LE11 1EU
☎ *(01509) 210028* Steve Booth

Jennings Dark Mild, Abbeydale Matins, Marston's Burton Bitter and Oakham JHB plus five guests perhaps from Abbeydale, Archers, Church End, Rooster's, Oakham, Oldershaws, Skinners or Thornbridge, to name but a few. Traditional cider also served, usually from Thatchers.

This one-bar Victorian pub features a large beer garden with grass, trees, parrots, rabbits and various other animals! Private room for hire. Well-behaved children are allowed, and there is a children's play area. Close to the Great Central Steam Railway and Taylor's Bell Foundry Museum. Halfway between the railway station and the town centre on the A60.

 5pm–2am Mon–Fri; 11.30am–2am Sat–Sun. May close earlier, depending on trade.

The Three Nuns

30 Churchgate, Loughborough LE11 1UD
☎ *(01509) 611989* Steve Wesson

 Everards pub serving Tiger, Beacon and Original, plus one guest, changed every two weeks, often including Everards Lazy Daze and Perfick.

The second oldest pub in town, with wood-panelled interior. Food available. Live rock bands on Saturdays. Garden seating area, car park. Children allowed until 8pm.

 11am–11pm Mon–Thurs; 11am–midnight Fri–Sat; 12–11pm Sun.

MARKET BOSWORTH
Ye Olde Red Lion

1 Park Street, Market Bosworth CV13 0LL
☎ *(01455) 291713* Eddie Davies

 Tied to Banks's, serving Bitter and Original plus Marston's Pedigree. The two guests are changed every few days, and include something from Frankton Bagby once a month, with beers from Church End, Lloyds and Cottage making regular appearances. Seasonal and celebration ales are also featured.

Small market-town pub, over 400 years old, very close to the countryside. Beams and fires in winter. Food is served every day at lunchtime, plus Tues–Sat evening. Live jazz once a month, quiz night on first Sunday of month, Irish music four times a year (call for details). Patio, car park, four letting rooms. Children allowed.

 11am–2.30pm and 5.30–11pm Mon–Fri; 11am–11pm Sat; 11am–3pm and 7–10.30pm Sun.

MEDBOURNE
The Nevill Arms

12 Waterfall Way, Medbourne, Market Harborough LE16 8EE
☎ *(01858) 565288* Mark Kemp

Freehouse with four real ales. Samuel Smith's OBB and Fuller's London Pride are always available, plus two guests, perhaps St Austell Tribute, Wychwood Hobgoblin or Greene King IPA.

Built in 1868 as a coach house, this traditional country pub has one main bar, new 70-seater restaurant and large new courtyard. There is additional seating on benches near the brook. Function room available for weddings and other events. Food served 12–2pm (until 3.30pm Sun) and 6.30–9.30pm. Ten en-suite rooms, including

bridal suite and one with a four-poster bed. On the B664 between Market Harborough and Uppingham.

 12–close.

NEWTON BURGOLAND
The Belper Arms

Main Street, Newton Burgoland LE67 2SE
☎ *(01530) 270530* Nick Plews
www.belperarms.co.uk

Punch Taverns tied pub serving Black Sheep Bitter, Bass and Marston's Pedigree plus two weekly-changing guests.

Reputed to be the oldest pub in Leicestershire, circa 1290, this traditional English country inn consists of one main bar with a separate dining and function area. Food served 12–3pm and 6–9pm Mon–Fri, 12–5pm Sat and 12–6pm Sun. Large beer garden with children's play area and floodlit petanque court, cricket nets and putting green. Caravan and camping club facilities. Annual beer festival over August bank holiday. Regular live entertainment.

 12–close.

OADBY
The Cow & Plough

Stoughton Farm, Gartree Road, Oadby LE2 2FB
☎ *(0116) 272 0852* Barry and Elisabeth Lount
www.steamin-billy.co.uk

Freehouse with an ever-changing range of beers, many from micro-breweries. Home of Steamin' Billy beers (brewed in Burton), with Steamin' Billy Bitter always available. Steamin' Billy seasonals include BSB, Country Bitter, Lazy Summer and Skydiver.

Converted barn on a working farm, with ornate Victorian bar and large conservatory. Twice CAMRA East Midlands Pub of the Year. A restaurant has been added in a converted dairy with sandwiches and fresh, modern English food available at lunchtimes and evenings. Bar snacks in the pub. Large car park. Live jazz/blues. Off the A6 out of Leicester.

 11am–3pm and 5–11pm Mon–Fri; 12–11pm Sat–Sun.

OAKHAM
The Grainstore Brewery Tap

Station Approach, Oakham, Rutland LE15 6RE
☎ *(01572) 770065* Tony Davis

The home of The Grainstore Brewery, so Cooking Bitter, Triple B, Ten Fifty and Rutland Panther are always available plus Silly Billy, Rutland Beast and Phipps IPA.

A traditional three-storey old grainstore, situated next to the railway station. One bar; outside seating. Live jazz on first Sunday afternoon of the month, and live blues on third Sunday evening of the month. Brewery tours by appointment. Pub grub at lunchtimes only. The Rutland Beer Festival is held over the August bank holiday.

 11.30am–11pm Mon–Thur; 11am–midnight Fri-Sat; 11am-11pm Sun.

OLD DALBY

The Crown Inn

Debdale Hill, Old Dalby, Nr Melton Mowbray LE14 3LF
☎ *(01664) 823134* Alan and Lorraine Hale

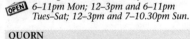 Four real ales, some served straight from the cask behind the bar. These are likely to include Marston's Pedigree, Charles Wells Bombadier and Theakston Old Peculier. Regular guests are featured, often from the local Belvoir brewery.

Built in 1590, a pub with six small rooms, oak beams, open fires, antique furniture and prints. Large patio and terrace with orchard at bottom of the garden. Beer served from cellar near back door. Bar and restaurant food served at lunchtime (not Mon) and evenings (not Sun or Mon). Car park, petanque pitch. Children welcome. Many special events throughout the year. From Nottingham on the A606, turn right at Nether Broughton for Old Dalby.

OPEN *6–11pm Mon; 12–3pm and 6–11pm Tues–Sat; 12–3pm and 7–10.30pm Sun.*

QUORN

The Manor House

Woodhouse Road, Quorn, Loughborough LE12 8AL
☎ *(01509) 413416* Phil Triggs
www.themanorhouseatquorn.co.uk

 Punch pub with Timothy Taylor Landlord and Black Sheep Bitter among the five real ales on offer. Two guests, changed every two weeks, might be Greene King Old Speckled Hen, Hook Norton Old Hooky, Fuller's London Pride, Shepherd Neame Spitfire or a Bateman brew.

Former hotel that was reopened in 2005, with restaurant seating 80, separate bar, private function room and huge beer garden. Food, including daily specials, served 12–2.30pm and 5–10pm Mon–Fri; all day Sat–Sun. Winner and runner-up in Leicestershire and Rutland restaurant awards. Ample parking.

OPEN *12–11pm Mon–Thurs; 12–12 Fri–Sat; 12–10pm Sun.*

RATBY

The Bull's Head

23 Main Street, Ratby LE6 0LN
☎ *(0116) 239 3256* Phil and Marny Jones

 Up to six real ales including Everards Beacon, Tiger and Original plus a seasonal brew. Guests from a huge range of independent brewers, small and large.

Three-bar pub on the main road in the heart of Ratby. Good food served 12–2pm Mon–Fri and 12–3pm Sun, 6–9pm on Tues and Thurs–Sat. Special events and live entertainment including karaoke nights. Large garden with childen's play area. Beer festivals held twice a year.

OPEN *11am–3pm and 5–11pm Mon–Thurs; 11am–11pm Fri–Sat; 12–5pm and 7–10.30pm Sun.*

SADDINGTON

The Queens Head

Main Street, Saddington
☎ *(0116) 240 2536*
Christine and Steve Bebbington

 Everards Beacon and Tiger plus alternating guests.

A nicely situated, award-winning country inn and restaurant. The garden has lovely views over Saddington Reservoir. Previous Leicestershire Tourist Board Pub Meal of the Year winner. Food served 12–2pm and 6.30–9pm, but not on Sunday evenings. Large car park. Situated near to Fleckney.

OPEN *11am–3pm and 5.30–11pm (10.30pm Sun).*

SHAWELL

White Swan Inn

Main Street, Shawell, Nr Lutterworth LE17 6AG
☎ *(01788) 860357* Mike and Susan Walker

 Greene King Abbot and IPA plus a regularly changing guest ale.

Built in the main street of a small hamlet in around 1700, it retains many original features. Local skittles in the bar. Restaurant and dining area. Seating to the front of the pub. Food served all opening times. Accommodation available, including log cabins. Car park. Children welcome. Located five minutes from M1, M6, A14 and A5.

OPEN *7–11pm Tues–Sat; 12–3pm Sun (closed all day Mon, Tues–Sat lunchtimes and Sun evenings).*

SHEARSBY

Chandler's Arms

Fenny Lane, Shearsby, Nr Lutterworth LE17 6PL
☎ *(0116) 247 8384* Steve Compton

 Usually four, but up to seven, real ales, including Black Sheep Bitter, Dow Bridge Acris and guests from national, regional and micro-breweries.

A 17th-century red-brick farmhouse and chandlers converted to a pub in the 19th century. Overlooking the village green, it has a three-tier garden and two lounges. Food served lunchtimes and evenings except Mondays. Children welcome. Follow signs for Shearsby from A5199.

OPEN *12–3pm and 7–11pm Mon–Fri; all day from 12 Sat–Sun (closed Mon lunchtimes in winter).*

SMISBY
The Tap House
Anwell Lane, Smisby, Ashby de la Zouch LE65 2TA
☎ *(01530) 413604* Thompson

Freehouse with three real ales. Marston's Pedigree, Greene King Old Speckled Hen and Bass would be a typical selection, and one of the beers is rotated weekly.

Family bar and restaurant, with open fires in winter. A traditional pub with traditional pub food and carvery available lunchtimes and evenings Tues–Sun. Separate accommodation. Function facilities. Children welcome. Beer garden with barbecue area and outdoor pool table. Large outdoor TV screen showing live Sky Sports. On the A511 Ashby to Burton road, at the end of Smisby village.

OPEN *5.30–11pm Mon; 12–2.30pm and 5.30–11pm Tues–Fri; all day Sat–Sun.*

SOMERBY
The Stilton Cheese Inn
High Street, Somerby LE14 2QB
☎ *(01664) 454394* Jeff and Carol Evans
www.stiltoncheeseinn.co.uk

Five real ales always on offer. Marston's Pedigree, Grainstore Ten Fifty and Tetley Cask are among the regulars, plus two constantly changing guest beers (around six different ones each week).

A 16th-century stone freehouse, with beams, two rooms and an upstairs restaurant seating 40. Decorated throughout with dried hops and hunting prints. The beams are covered in pump clips from previous guest beers. Food served daily 12–2pm and 6–9pm (7–9pm Sun). Children welcome. Patio with seating for 20. Three B&B rooms available.

OPEN *12–3pm and 6–11pm Mon–Sat; 12–3pm and 7–11pm Sun.*

STATHERN
The Red Lion Inn
2 Red Lion Street, Stathern, Melton Mowbray LE14 4HS
☎ *(01949) 860868* Ben Jones
www.theredlioninn.co.uk

Freehouse with three constantly rotating beers, such as Brewsters Marquis Bitter, Belvoir Peacock's Glory, Oldershaw Newton's Drop and Grainstore Ten Fifty.

Dating back to 1653, a pub with a traditional rustic feel featuring open fires, flagstone floors and exposed beams. The dining room used to be a skittle alley! Lovely food using local produce served 12–2pm and 7–9.30pm Tues–Sat; 12–3pm Sun. Enclosed rear patio garden with access to children's play area. Close to Belvoir Castle, and ideal as a base for country walks. From the A52 follow signs to Belvoir Castle, then the signs for Stathern.

OPEN *Closed Mon; 12–3pm and 6–11pm Tues–Thurs; 12–11pm Fri–Sat; 12–6.30pm Sun.*

SUTTON BASSETT
The Queen's Head
Main Street, Sutton Bassett, Market Harborough LE16 8HP
☎ *(01858) 463530* Melvyn Foot

Freehouse with up to eight real ales, including Timothy Taylor Landlord, Adnams Bitter and Greene King IPA plus a selection of guests running into hundreds of different brews each year.

Friendly country pub with traditional décor, real fires, front and back bars. Disabled facilities on ground floor. Patio, beer garden and petanque court. Food served at lunchtimes and evenings. Large parties and functions catered for. Children allowed. Prettily situated with views of the Welland valley. Annual beer festival.

OPEN *12–2.30pm and 5–11.30pm Mon–Fri; all day Sat–Sun.*

SWINFORD
The Chequers
High Street, Swinford LE17 6BL
☎ *(01788) 860318* Brian Priest
www.chequersswinford.co.uk

Punch Taverns house with up to three real ales, changed on a monthly basis.

Traditional, family-friendly village pub. Food (with children's menu) served 12–2pm and 6–9pm Tues–Sat; 12–2pm Sun. Children welcome. Beer garden with children's play area, including separate toddler area. Traditional pub games. Car park. Beer festivals. Situated half a mile from M1 J19.

OPEN *6–11pm Mon (closed Mon lunch); 12–2.30pm and 6–11pm Tues–Thurs; 12–3pm and 6–11pm Fri–Sat; 12–3pm and 7–10.30pm Sun.*

SWITHLAND
The Griffin Inn
174 Main Street, Swithland LE12 8TJ
☎ *(01509) 890535* John and Sue Colledge
www.griffininnswithland.com

Three Everards ales always on offer, plus three regularly changing guests.

A cosy, unspoilt, traditional coaching inn with log fires. Bar snacks, seafood specials and restaurant food 12–9pm Mon–Fri, 12–9.30pm Sat, 12–8pm Sun. Large car park, patio and garden. Skittle alley. Function room and private dining areas. In Charnwood Forest, between Loughborough and Leicester.

OPEN *All day, every day.*

THORPE SATCHVILLE

The Fox Inn

*Main Street, Thorpe Satchville, Melton Mowbray
LE14 2DQ*
☎ *(01664) 840257*
Yves and Elisabeth Ogrodzki

Freehouse with beers from John Smith's and Theakston among the three real ales.

Country pub built in 1938, refurbished in November 2005 as a French bistro and restaurant. Food is available Tues lunch to Sat evening, plus 12–3pm Sun. Beer garden, patio, petanque. Large car park. Between Melton Mowbray and the A47, on the B6047.

OPEN *12–3pm, 6.30–11pm Tues–Sat; 12–3pm Sun.*

THURNBY

The Swallow

Station Road, Thurnby LE7 9PU
☎ *(0116) 241 9087* Ross Allibone

Everards Tiger, Beacon and Old Original always served at this Everards tied house. The two guests might include Greene King Old Speckled Hen, something from Adnams, or seasonals like Everards Lazy Daze.

Community pub built in the sixties, with two bars, conservatory, garden and play area. Food is served. Live music Sat and Sun evenings. Disabled facilities, car park. Children allowed until 8pm.

OPEN *11.30am–11pm Mon–Fri; 11am–11pm Sat; 12–10.30pm Sun.*

WALTHAM-ON-THE-WOLDS

The Marquis of Granby

High Street, Waltham-on-the-Wolds LE14 4HA
☎ *(01664) 464212* Melanie Dawson

Everards pub with Tiger and Original plus something from Adnams permanently available, together with one guest, changed every couple of weeks, often a beer from Everards such as Perfick.

A 400-year-old village pub with beams and fires. Food served. Occasional live music. Garden and patio. Children allowed.

OPEN *12–2.30pm and 5.30–11.30pm Mon–Fri; 11am–11pm Sat; 12–10.30pm Sun.*

WIGSTON MAGNA

The Horse & Trumpet

Bull Head Street, Wigston Magna LE18 1PB
☎ *(0116) 288 6290* Andy Moone

Tied to Everards, and always featuring Original, Tiger and Beacon.

Characterful community local in a very old building, with one open-plan bar. Food served at lunchtimes. Live music on Thurs evenings. Patio, skittle alley, function room, car park. No children.

OPEN *11am–2.30pm and 5–11pm Mon–Thurs; 11am–11pm Fri; 11am–2.30pm and 6–11pm Sat; 12–10.30pm Sun.*

WYMESWOLD

The Three Crowns

*45 Far Street, Wymeswold, Loughborough
LE12 6TZ*
☎ *(01509) 880153* Marcia Constable
www.thethreecrownsatwymeswold.co.uk

Marston's Pedigree and Adnams Bitter are permanent features, and the two guests are changed every week.

Typical village pub, over 300 years old, with original beams, open fires and a traditional atmosphere. Food available 12–9pm Tues–Sat and 12–4pm Sun–Mon. Sky TV, pool and table football. Outside decking, children's play area, private room for hire (capacity 60). Car park. Beer festivals. In the middle of the village, opposite the church.

OPEN *12–11pm.*

THE BREWERIES

GEORGE BATEMAN & SONS LTD
*Salem Bridge Brewery, Mill Lane, Wainfleet,
Skegness PE24 4JE*
☎ *(01754) 880317*
www.bateman.co.uk

DARK MILD 3.0% ABV
Dark and fruity, some roast malt, hoppy
finish.
XB 3.7% ABV
Distinctive, refreshing dry bitterness.
BATEMAN'S VALIANT 4.2% ABV
Gold coloured and refreshing.
SALEM PORTER 4.7% ABV
Dry, nutty, rich malt and superb hop flavours.
XXXB 4.8% ABV
Multi-faceted malt and fruit character.
Plus a seasonal and special selection.

BLUE BELL BREWERY
*Sycamore House, Lapwater Lane,
Holbeach St Marks PE12 8EX*
☎ *(01406) 701000*
www.bluebellbrewery.co.uk

SESSION ALE 3.7% ABV
OLDE HONESTY 4.1% ABV
OLD FASHIONED 4.8% ABV

THE BLUE COW INN AND BREWERY
*29 High Street, South Witham, Nr Grantham
NG33 5QB*
☎ *(01572) 768432*

THIRLWELL'S BEST BITTER 3.8% ABV
THIRLWELL'S CUDDY 3.8% ABV
WITHAM WOBBLER 4.2% ABV

DARKTRIBE BREWERY
*25 Doncaster Road, Gunness, Scunthorpe
DN15 8TG*
☎ *(01724) 782324*
www.darktribe.co.uk

DIXIE'S MILD 3.6% ABV
Dark, tasty award-winner.
HONEY MILD 3.6% ABV
Dark with a hint of honey.
FULL AHEAD 3.8% ABV
Dry-hopped bitter.
ALBACORE 4.0% ABV
Beautifully pale and hoppy.
RED DUSTER 4.0% ABV
RED ROCK 4.2% ABV
STERN WHEELER 4.2% ABV
BUCKET HITCH 4.4% ABV
DIXIE'S BOLLARDS 4.5% ABV
Ginger beer.
DR GRIFFIN'S MERMAID 4.5% ABV
OLD GAFFER 4.5% ABV
GALLEON 4.7% ABV
TWIN SCREW 5.1% ABV
DARK DESTROYER 9.7% ABV

FUGELESTOU ALES
*Fulstow Brewery, 6 North Way, Fulstow, Louth
LN11 0XH*
☎ *(01507) 363642*
www.fulstowbrewery.co.uk

FULSTOW COMMON 3.8% ABV
Copper colour and malty taste.
MARSH MILD 3.8% ABV
Toffee overtones to chocolatey dark mild.
NORTHWAY IPA 4.2% ABV
Crisp with citrus aroma, dry finish.
PRIDE OF FULSTOW 4.5% ABV
Blackcurrant fruit notes.
SLEDGEHAMMER STOUT 8.0% ABV
Plus specials.

HIGHWOOD BREWERY LTD
Home Farm, Scawby, Brigg DN20 9AF
☎ *(01652) 654514*
www.tom-wood.com

FATHER'S PRIDE 4.5% ABV
Malty nose, sweet with caramel hints.
JOLLY PLOUGHMAN'S 5.0% ABV
Malty and smoky, copper colour.
Plus wide range of seasonals and specials.

NEWBY WYKE BREWERY
*Willoughby Arms Cottages, Station Road,
Little Bytham, Grantham NG33 4RA*
☎ *(01780) 411119*
www.newbywyke.co.uk

SIDEWINDER 3.8% ABV
GRANTHAM GOLD 4.2% ABV
HMS REVENGE 4.2% ABV
STAMFORD GOLD 4.4% ABV
BEAR ISLAND 4.6% ABV
WHITE SQUALL 4.8% ABV
CHESAPEAKE 5.5% ABV
Plus seasonals and occasionals.

OLDERSHAW BREWERY
12 Harrowby Hall Estate, Grantham NG31 9HB
☎ *(01476) 572135*
www.oldershawbrewery.com

MOWBRAY'S MASH 3.7% ABV
Pale and hoppy.
HIGH DYKE 3.9% ABV
Gold coloured with good hoppiness.
OSB 4.0% ABV
Easy drinking and hoppy.
ALMA'S BREW 4.1% ABV
Malty and flowery.
NEWTON'S DROP 4.1% ABV
Golden and hoppy.
CASKADE 4.2% ABV
Light, clean-tasting.
ERMINE ALE 4.2% ABV
Pale and refreshing hoppiness.
AHTANUM GOLD 4.3% ABV
New Zealand hops.
GRANTHAM STOUT 4.3% ABV
ISAAC'S GOLD 4.5% ABV
Golden bitter with hoppy aroma.
OLD BOY 4.8% ABV
Golden chestnut colour with good balance.
ALCHEMY 5.3% ABV
Golden with good hop flavour.
*Plus a large range of occasional and special brews
including:*
GRANTHAM DARK 3.6% ABV
SUNNYDAZE 4.0% ABV
YULETIDE 5.2% ABV

POACHERS BREWERY
439 Newark Road, North Hykeham LN6 9SP
☎ *(01522) 807404*
www.poachersbrewery.co.uk

- TREMBLING RABBIT 3.4% ABV
- SHY TALK 3.7% ABV
- POACHERS PRIDE 4.0% ABV
- POACHERS DEN 4.2% ABV
- POACHERS TRAIL 4.2% ABV
- BLACK CROW 4.5% ABV
- POACHERS DICK 4.5% ABV
- JOCK'S TRAP 5.0% ABV
- TROUT TICKLER 5.5% ABV
- SANTA'S COME 6.5% ABV

RIVERSIDE BREWERY
Unit 1 Church Lane, Wainfleet, Skegness PE24 4BY
☎ *(01754) 881288*
www.wainfleet.info/shops/brewery-riverside.htm

- LIGHT BRIGADE 3.9% ABV
- MAJOR 3.9% ABV
- DESERT RAT 4.8% ABV

WILLY'S BREWERY
17 High Cliff Road, Cleethorpes DN35 8RQ
☎ *(01472) 602145*

- WILLY'S ORIGINAL 3.9% ABV
- BURCOM BITTER 4.2% ABV
- WILLY'S LAST RESORT 4.3% ABV
- WILLY'S WEISS BOUY 4.5% ABV
- COXSWAIN'S SPECIAL BITTER 4.9% ABV
- WILLY'S OLD GROYNE 6.2% ABV

THE PUBS

ALLINGTON
The Welby Arms
The Green, Allington, Grantham NG32 2EA
☎ *(01400) 281361* Matt Rose and Anna Cragg

Six real ales. Timothy Taylor Landlord, Ringwood Old Thumper, Badger Tanglefoot and Phoenix Wobbly Bob often feature.

Traditional freehouse on the village green with beams, log fires and terrace. Two bars, snug and 70-seater restaurant. Disabled access. Baguettes or soup available at lunchtime in the bar, plus restaurant food 12–2pm and 6.30–9pm. En-suite accommodation. Well-behaved children welcome at lunchtimes. Car park. Close to the Vale of Belvoir and Belvoir Castle.

OPEN *12–2.30pm (3pm Sat, 4pm Sun) and 6–11pm (10.30pm Sun).*

AUBOURN
The Royal Oak
Royal Oak Lane, Aubourn, Lincoln LN5 9DT
☎ *(01522) 788291*
Robert Varley and Rachael Blakebrough
www.royaloakaubourn.co.uk

Bateman XB, Greene King Abbot, Adnams Broadside and Black Sheep Bitter plus a guest beer changed twice a week.

A traditional village pub with character, open fires and beams. One bar, two rooms and separate restaurant. Bar food available 12–2pm and 6.30 or 7–9pm Mon–Fri, plus 12–9.30pm Sat–Sun. Car park and heated patio plus private orchard and beer garden. Weekly quiz nights. Functions catered for. Children welcome until 8.30pm. South of Lincoln, off the A46.

OPEN *12–2.30pm and 7–11pm (6.30–11pm Fri–Sat; 7–10.30pm Sun).*

BARNACK
The Snooty Millstone
Millstone Lane, Barnack, Nr Stamford PE9 3ET
☎ *(01780) 740296* Joanna Osinska
www.snootyinns.com

Everards Old Original and Tiger plus Adnams Bitter plus a guest beer changed once a week.

The inn was built in 1672 of Barnack stone which was quarried nearby. The interior has been refurbished, but retains its olde-worlde feel. Large courtyard, function room. Food served 12–2.30pm and 6.30–9.30pm. Live music night first Tuesday of the month. Barbecues on Sundays throughout the summer. Jazz nights and 'meet the artists' nights. Children welcome. On the B1443, the only pub in the village.

OPEN *All day, every day from 12.*

BARTON UPON HUMBER
The Sloop Inn
81 Waterside Road, Barton upon Humber DN18 5BA
☎ *(01652) 637287* The 'Strange' Family
www.sloopinn.net

Freehouse serving Tom Woods Shepherd's Delight and Bomber Country plus two guest ales, changed at least weekly.

A family-run pub dating from 1848 with original features and a nautical theme. One bar, four seating areas. Food available every lunchtime and evening. Children allowed. Pool table and darts board. Located close to the Humber Bridge.

OPEN *11am–11pm Mon–Sat; 12–10.30pm Sun.*

BELCHFORD
The Bluebell Inn
Main Road, Belchford LN9 6LQ
☎ *(01507) 533602* Darren and Shona Jackson

Black Sheep Best and Greene King IPA. Local breweries at Fulstow and Wainfleet supply guest beers every week.

Village pub full of character on the Louth road north of Horncastle. Restaurant serves imaginative food 12–2pm Tues–Sun and 6.30–9pm Tues–Sat. Listed in *Michelin Pub Food Guide*. Garden, car park, children welcome.

OPEN *11.30am–2.30pm and 6.30–11pm Tues–Sat; 12–4pm Sun (closed Sun night and Mon).*

BLYTON

The Black Horse Inn

93 High Street, Blyton, Nr Gainsborough DN21 3JX
☎ *(01427) 628277* Mark Harrison

 Greene King IPA and three rotating guests from breweries such as Bateman, Highwood, Black Sheep and other local micro-breweries.

An 18th-century village freehouse with wood burners and open fires. Homemade food served 12–2pm and 6–9pm Tues–Sat; 12–7pm Sun. Traditional pub games. Big-screen TV. Beer garden. Car park. On the A159 Gainsborough to Scunthorpe.

OPEN *Closed Mon; 12–2.30pm 5pm–12 Tues–Fri; 12–12 Sat–Sun.*

BOSTON

The Carpenter's Arms

Witham Street, Boston PE21 6PU
☎ *(01205) 362840* Peter Reid

Bateman house serving XB plus two changing guests which are often other Bateman brews but also sometimes Marston's Pedigree, Greene King IPA or Old Speckled Hen, Tanners Jack and others.

Traditional one-bar town pub with games room, a real fire and outside seating during summer months. Food available 7–10pm Mon (spice night), 12–2pm and 4–7pm Wed–Fri, 12–5pm Sat–Sun. Well-behaved children allowed.

OPEN *11am–11pm Mon–Sat; 12–10.30pm Sun.*

The Eagle

144 West Street, Boston PE21 8RE
☎ *(01205) 361116* Andrew Rudolf

Five real ales, perhaps including Banks's Bitter, Castle Rock Harvest Pale, Everards Tiger, Bateman XXXB, Adnams Broadside and Hop Back Summer Lightning. May operate up to eight real ales during beer festivals.

A traditional local on the outskirts of Boston town centre. Two bars (one public, one lounge), real fires, pool room and function room (the venue for monthly meetings of the folk club). Regular beer festivals held throughout the year and brewery trips.

OPEN *11am–11pm Mon–Sat; 12–10.30pm Sun.*

BRANT BROUGHTON

The Generous Briton

72 High Street, Brant Broughton LN5 0RZ
☎ *(01400) 272119* Ian Philip

Adnams Bitter, Bateman XB and Greene King IPA usually available.

A rural Pub of the Year with exposed brick and beamed ceilings. Food available at lunchtime and evening. Piped music.

OPEN *12–2.30pm and 6–11pm Mon–Sat; 12–2.30pm and 7–10.30pm Sun.*

BRIGG

The Yarborough Hunt

49 Bridge Street, Brigg DN20 8NS
☎ *(01652) 658333* Pete Smith

Tom Wood Best and Greene King IPA plus four guests, including Tom Wood seasonal ales, which change every couple of days. Also Belgian beers and malt whiskies.

The building dates from the 1700s and was once the Sergeants Brewery tap. Closed for 30 years but restored, refurbished and reopened in 2003. Four rooms plus a walled patio garden. No food, but customers are welcome to bring their own. Just off the A18, three miles from junction 4 of the M180.

OPEN *11am–11pm Sun–Wed; 10am–midnight Thurs; 11am–midnight Fri; 10am–midnight Sat.*

BURTON-ON-STATHER

The Ferry House Inn

Burton-on-Stather, Nr Scunthorpe DN15 9DJ
☎ *(01724) 721504* Steve Smith

Freehouse with one or two casks from craft brewers available during the week, always two at weekends. Cask Marque awarded.

Riverside pub with nautical theme, steeped in history. Food served in the riverside restaurant during the summer, Sunday carvery all year. Beer garden with bouncy castle and summer barbecues – a summer-time family pub. Bikers and walkers welcome. Live bands. Annual beer festival and hog roast during August bank holiday. Located almost two miles from Normanby Hall Country Park.

OPEN *5–11.30pm Mon–Fri; 12–12 Sat–Sun.*

CAYTHORPE

The Red Lion Inn

62 High Street, Caythorpe, Grantham NG32 3DN
☎ *(01400) 272632* John Cork

Freehouse serving Adnams Bitter and Everards Tiger.

A 17th-century country inn with roaring open fires in the bar, separate restaurant seating 60, and a relaxed atmosphere. Food available 12–2pm and 6–9.30pm Mon–Sat (until 10pm Sat) and 12–4pm Sun. Restaurant available for private hire. Car park, patio. Just off the A607 between Grantham and Lincoln.

OPEN *12–2.30pm and 6–11pm Mon–Sat; 12–6pm Sun.*

CLAYPOLE

Five Bells Inn

95 Main Street, Claypole, Newark NG23 5BJ
☎ *(01636) 626561* Martin Finney

Freehouse with Greene King IPA and Tetleys Cask plus two guests, changed often, from breweries such as Oldershaws, Milestone, Springhead, Rudgate, Acorn, Bradfield and Wold Top.

Village pub built around 1850, with separate restaurant. Food served 6–9pm Mon, 12–2pm Tues–Wed, 6–9pm Sat and 12–4pm Sun. Four en-suite rooms, large garden with play area, large car park. Local attractions include Belvoir Castle, Newark showground, Peak District (one hour), Newark town, Sherwood Forest, Lincoln, Nottingham and Sheffield. Two miles from the A1 Newark/Balderton junction.

OPEN *4–11pm Mon; 11am–11pm Tues–Sat; 12–10.30pm Sun.*

CLEETHORPES

No 2 Refreshment Rooms

Station Approach, Cleethorpes DN35 8AX
☎ *07905 375587* P Rowntree and D Sparkes

Freehouse with three permanent real ales, from breweries such as Cottage, Hardys & Hansons and Wickwar, plus three rotating guests.

Situated at Cleethorpes station. No food. 'Beer garden' provided at the station. Fifty yards from seafront.

OPEN *9am–1am Mon–Sat; 10am–midnight Sun.*

DYKE

The Wishing Well Inn

Main Street, Dyke, Nr Bourne PE10 0AF
☎ *(01778) 422970* Jackie Maplethorpe

Everards Tiger, Greene King Abbot, Oakham JHB and Fuller's London Pride are among the regular beers served at this freehouse. Four of the five beers are changed every week.

Attractive country inn in a 200-year-old building, a pub for over a century. Food served 12–3pm and 6–9pm Mon–Sat and all day Sun. Beer garden, children's play garden, car park. B&B in 12 rooms. Weddings catered for. Just outside Bourne on the A15.

OPEN *11am–3pm and 5–11pm Mon–Sat; 12–10.30pm Sun.*

EAST BUTTERWICK

The Dog & Gun

High Street, East Butterwick, Nr Scunthorpe DN17 3AJ
☎ *(01724) 782324* Dixie Dean

Freehouse and home of the Darktribe Brewery. Two Darktribe brews always on offer, plus occasional guests.

Unspoilt village pub overlooking the banks of the River Trent. One traditional bar with log fire, one with dart board. No food. Car park. Situated four miles from the A18 at Gunness.

OPEN *5–11pm Mon–Fri; 12–11pm Sat–Sun.*

FRAMPTON

The Moores Arms

Church End, Frampton, Nr Boston PE20 1AD
☎ *(01205) 722408* Steve Upsall

Three real ales from a wide range that changes every month.

A 16th-century one-bar freehouse and restaurant off the A16 Boston to Spalding road. Food served all day until 10pm. Beer garden, car park.

OPEN *11am–11pm Mon–Sat; 12–10.30pm Sun.*

FROGNALL

The Goat

155 Spalding Road, Frognal, Market Deeping, Nr Peterborough PE6 8SA
☎ *(01778) 347629* Graham Stokes

Five real ales from a wide variety of micro-breweries and brewpubs nationwide, always including a strong ale (over 6%), the rest rotated weekly. One real cider and a range of Belgian bottled beers also served, plus over 50 single Scottish malts.

Traditional English country freehouse dating from 1647. Full bar menu served 12–2pm and 6.30–9pm Mon–Sat and all day Sun. Functions catered for. Beer festival each July. Car park, large beer garden with play equipment, family dining area. Situated on the B1525 between Market Deeping and Spalding. Summer beer festival in late July.

OPEN *11.30am–3pm and 6–11pm Mon–Sat; all day Sun.*

GAINSBOROUGH

The Eight Jolly Brewers

Ship Court, Silver Street, Gainsborough DN21 2DW
☎ *(01427) 677128* Ben Langdale

Eight real ales, including Glentworth Lightyear and regularly changing guests from breweries such as Bateman, Oakham, Abbeydale, Salamander, Copper Dragon, Cottage, Acorn, Oldershaw, Maypole and Rudgate.

A 300-year-old freehouse, this Grade II listed building is a country pub in the town centre. Based in a former carpenter's yard and overlooking the River Trent and Riverside gardens, it has one bar and a large seating area upstairs. Traditional pub games on request. Local CAMRA Pub of the Year 2006 and 2007. Patio area and car park. No food. No children. Live music every Thursday, plus charity events all year round. Located near the Guildhall. Easy parking.

OPEN *11am–midnight Mon–Sat; 12–12 Sun.*

GRAINTHORPE

The Black Horse Inn

Mill Lane, Grainthorpe, Louth LN11 78U
☎ *(01472) 388229* Neill Jarvis and Jane Impey

Freehouse with four real ales. Tom Wood Best and Fuller's London Pride are the permanent beers, and the two guests are rotated weekly.

English country pub built in the 1850s, with an open fire in the comfortable lounge, plus second bar with pool table, darts and juke box. Food served 12–2pm and 5–9pm Wed–Sat, plus Sunday lunches 12–2pm. Spacious beer garden, car park. Children welcome till 9pm. Located in the village, off the A1031.

 7–11pm Mon–Tues; 12–11.30pm Wed–Sun.

GRANTHAM
The Blue Bull

64 Westgate, Grantham NG31 6LA
☎ *(01476) 570929* Tracy Madsen

 Four cask ales, with beers from Newby Wyke, Thornbridge, Oakham and Abbeydale rotated on a daily basis.

Pub dating from the 1850s, with public bar, lounge and games room. Bar food available 11am–4pm on weekdays, plus 12–4pm for Sunday lunch. Lounge available for private functions. Outside decking, car park. Children welcome. Three minutes from the mainline BR railway station, on the corner of Westgate and Dysart Rd.

 11am–11pm Mon–Sat; 12–11pm Sun.

The Blue Pig Inn

9 Vine Street, Grantham NG31 6RQ
☎ *(01476) 563704* D R Foster
www.thebluepiginnatbravehost.com

 An Enterprise Inns pub. Timothy Taylor Landlord and Caledonian Deuchars IPA plus three guests, changed weekly. Guests have included ales from Archers, Oldershaw and Brewsters. Also Thatchers cider.

Reputed to be one of only four Tudor dwellings to survive the disastrous fire that swept Grantham in 1660. Situated on the corner of Vine Street and Swinegate, today it is a friendly and historic three-bar pub. Food served 11am–2.30pm and 4.30–9pm.

 11am–midnight.

The Houblon Inn

Oasby, Nr Grantham NG32 3NB
☎ *(01529) 455215* Hazel Purvis

 Everards Tiger plus three or four guests such as Oldershaw Old Boy, Jennings Sneck Lifter, Black Sheep Bitter, Newby Wyke Grantham Gold or Brains Reverend James.

Stone building dating from circa 1650 retaining many original features. Stone and tiled floors, open wood-burning fire. Two rooms, one central bar, traditional with a modern twist. Food served 12–2pm and 6.30–9.30pm Tues–Sat; 12–2.30pm Sun. Gravel garden with comfortable seating, boules and chess. Accommodation. Close to Belton House and Grimsthorpe Castle. Off the A52 at Boston.

 12–2.30pm and 6.30–11pm Tues–Fri; 12–2.30pm and 6–11pm Sat; 12–3pm and 7–10.30pm Sun.

GRIMSBY
Swigs

21 Osborne Street, Grimsby DN31 1EY
☎ *(01472) 354773* Jeanette Broughton

 Willy's Original plus three guests.

A real drinker's pub, one of the first real ale pubs in Grimsby with authentic character and opened by the owner of the first micro-brewery in the area. Food served 9.30am–2pm Mon–Sat; 12–5pm Sun. No children. Situated in the town centre, near the bus station.

 9am–midnight.

HARMSTON
The Thorold Arms

High Street, Harmston, Lincoln LN5 9SN
☎ *(01522) 720358*
Julie Haycraft and Alison Welch
www.thoroldarms.co.uk

 Four real ales, all from micro-breweries across the UK, and all changing constantly.

A rural inn in a 17th-century building, a pub for over 200 years. One comfortable bar and separate dining room. Food served lunchtimes (Wed–Sun) and evenings (à la carte) Wed–Sat. Traditional Sunday lunches, fish and chips Wednesday evenings. No children's menu. Featured in the *Good Pub Food Guide 2008*, and East Midlands CAMRA Pub of the Year 2006 and 2007. National finalist 2008. Small car park/drinks area. Disabled access and toilets. Annual beer and music festival August bank holiday. Black tie dinners, New Year's Eve, Burns Night, St George's and Trafalgar nights. Seven miles south of Lincoln – see website for map and directions.

 6–11pm Mon–Tues; 12–3pm and 6–11pm Wed–Sat; 12–3pm and 7–11pm Sun.

HEMINGBY
Coach and Horses

Hemingby, Horncastle LN9 5QF
☎ *(01507) 578280* Keith and Debbie Stride
http://coachandhorses.website.orange.co.uk

 Three real ales, with Riverside Dixon's Major and Bateman Dark Mild always available plus a guest changed every few days from an independent brewery such as Tom Wood, Cottage, Oldershaw, Black Hole or Fulstow.

Traditional village pub on the edge of the Lincolnshire Wolds. One main room with open fire, low beams and brasses plus games room for pool and darts with a digital TV and Internet access. Food served 12–2pm Wed–Sun and 6–8pm Wed–Fri, 7–10pm Sat. Two outside smoking areas plus beer garden with children's play area. Camping and caravanning in field to the rear. Large car park. Halfway between Lincoln and Skegness.

 7–11pm Mon–Tues; 12–2.30pm and 6–11pm Wed–Fri; 12–2.30pm and 7–11pm Sat; 7–10.30pm Sun.

KIRKBY ON BAIN

The Ebrington Arms

*Main Street, Kirkby on Bain, Woodhall Spa
LN10 6YT*
☎ *(01526) 354560*
Ronnie and Cathy Moncrieff

Genuine freehouse with Woodforde's Wherry and beers from Greene King, Bateman and Tom Wood permanently available, plus two guest ales from breweries such as Timothy Taylor, Hook Norton, Fuller's and Wychwood.

A typical English country pub with a good reputation for beer and food. Part of the building dates from 1610. Food available 12–2.30pm and 6–9pm, booking recommended. Children allowed until 9pm. Pets also welcome. Large beer garden. Car park.

OPEN *12–2.30pm and 6–11pm.*

LAUGHTERTON

The Friendship Inn

Main Road, Laugherton, Lincoln LN21 2JZ
☎ *(01427) 718681* Diane Humphreys

Freehouse with Marston's Pedigree plus guests, which may well be something from Brewster's, Slaters (Eccleshall) or another micro-brewery.

A traditional, friendly one-bar village pub. Log fires, garden, disabled access. Food lunchtimes and evenings (except Sun evening) in a designated dining area. Children allowed.

OPEN *11.30am–2.30pm and 6–11pm Mon–Sat;
12–3pm and 7–10.30pm Sun.*

LINCOLN

Dog & Bone

10 John Street, Lincoln LN2 5BH
☎ *(01522) 522403* Alex Doak and Eve Quinn

Tied to Bateman, so with XB, XXXB and Valiant plus one or two seasonal Bateman beers, changed monthly. There is an occasional guest from another brewery.

T raditional community pub dating from 1856 with two small bars (one being the lounge) and two open fires. Food served 12–2.30pm Tues–Sat. Summer and winter beer festivals. Monthly folk music session, book exchange service. Half a mile along Monks Road from the city centre.

OPEN *7–11pm Mon; 12–3pm and 7–11pm
Tues–Sun.*

The Golden Eagle

21 High Street, Lincoln LN5 8BD
☎ *(01522) 521058* Tracy Harris
www.goldeneagle.org.uk

Tynemill Ltd freehouse with seven real ales, with Everards Beacon, Castle Rock Harvest Pale and Bateman XXXB the permanent beers, plus guests each week.

O ld coaching house with lounge, bar and petanque court. Big-screen TV for sports. Function room available, beautiful beer garden. Car park. Children allowed until 9pm. At the south end of the High Street.

OPEN *11am–11pm Sun–Thurs; 11am–midnight
Fri–Sat.*

The Green Dragon Inn

Magpie Square, Broadgate, Lincoln LN2 5BH
☎ *(01522) 567155*
www.greendragonpub.co.uk

Lincoln's first microbrewery with 12 real ales on tap at any time.

O lde worlde pub in a lovely setting by the river. Good food and very friendly staff.

OPEN *12–11pm Sun–Tues; 12–12 Wed; 12–
11pm Thurs; noon–1am Fri–Sat.*

The Jolly Brewer

27 Broadgate, Lincoln LN2 5AQ
☎ *(01522) 528583* Emma Chapman
www.thejollybrewer.co.uk

Five real ales at this freehouse, including Young's Bitter, Timothy Taylor Landlord and The Jolly Brew (from a local brewery that allows the pub to use it as a house brew – drinkers are encouraged to guess which brewery!).

O ld coaching inn with unique art deco interior and beer garden. Food served 12–2pm Mon–Sat and 5–7pm Mon–Fri. Five minutes' walk from bus and train station.

OPEN *12–11pm Sun–Tues; 12–12 Wed; 12–
11pm Thurs; noon–1am Fri–Sat.*

The Portland

50 Portland Street, Lincoln LN5 7JX
☎ *(01522) 560564*
Annette Bannon and Phil Seed

Greene King IPA, Bateman XB, Shepherd Neame Spitfire and John Smith Cask are among the six to eight beers usually on offer, with up to four guests changed a couple of times a week.

R elaxed pub, with beer garden and outside smoking area. Music, TV, pool, darts, dominoes. Bar food available every day, plus traditional Sunday lunch 12–3pm. Karaoke nights, quiz nights, occasional live music. Children welcome. Car park. Off the high street, close to the train and bus stations.

OPEN *11am–11pm Mon–Thurs; 11am–
12.30am Fri–Sat; 12–10.30pm Sun.*

The Queen in the West

12–14 Moor Street, Lincoln LN1 1PR
☎ *(01522) 880123* SD Holmes

Timothy Taylor Landlord, Charles Wells Bombardier, Greene King Old Speckled Hen and two weekly-changing guests.

A two-bar pub dating from 1865. No food. No children. Off the A57 at Lincoln.

OPEN *12–3pm and 5.30–11pm Mon–Thurs; all
day Fri–Sun.*

Sippers Freehouse
26 Melville Street, Lincoln LN5 7HW
☎ *(01522) 527612* Joan Keightley

Hop Back GFB and Summer Lightning plus Marston's Pedigree always available plus three regularly changing guest beers (mostly from micro-breweries).

Traditional city-centre pub. Food served lunchtimes and evenings Mon–Sat, lunchtime only Sun. Private functions catered for. Families welcome with children until 8.30pm.

OPEN *11am–3pm and 5–11pm Mon–Thurs; 11am–11pm Fri–Sat; 7–10.30pm Sun.*

The Strugglers
83 Westgate, Lincoln LN1 3BG
☎ *(01522) 535023* Alan Watts

Punch Taverns pub with eight rotating beers. No permanent fixtures, but regulars include Timothy Taylor Landlord, Fuller's London Pride, Greene King Abbot, Bateman Mild, Black Sheep Bitter and Everards Old Original.

A character pub standing below the walls of Lincoln Castle in the city centre. One busy bar, plus a cosy snug with real fire. Food served lunchtimes Tues–Sat, and bank holidays. Well-maintained beer garden, covered in winter. Annual beer festival in October.

OPEN *All day, every day.*

The Tap & Spile
21 Hungate, Lincoln LN1 1ES
☎ *(01522) 534015* Peter Hladun
www.tapandspilelincoln.co.uk

Up to eight real ales available from a rotating list of about 20, with the selection changing daily. Charles Wells Bombardier, Caledonian Deuchars IPA and Black Sheep Best are regular features, and around half are from local SIBA breweries.

Traditional town tavern with a rich diversity of customers from all walks of life. Cask Marque accredited. Heated beer garden. Regular live blues music on Fridays, jam sessions Sunday teatimes. At the top of the high street turn left, the pub is 200 yards on the left opposite the Cheese Society.

OPEN *12–12 (1am Fri–Sat).*

The Victoria
6 Union Road, Lincoln LN1 3BJ
☎ *(01522) 536048* Neil Renshaw

Bateman pub with up to nine beers, including Castle Rock Harvest Pale and Bateman XB, Valiant and Salem Porter. Four guests, including a mild, are changed every few days.

A traditional, two-bar Victorian terraced pub with a large patio, in the city by the west gate of the castle. Same licensee for ten years (and has worked there for 20 years). Bar food available 12–2.30pm Mon–Fri, 11am–2.30pm Sat and 12–2pm Sun. Enlarged beer garden next to the castle wall. Hallowe'en beer festival every year. Next to the castle, at the west gate.

OPEN *11am–midnight Mon–Thurs; 11am–1am Fri–Sat; 12–12 Sun.*

LITTLE BYTHAM
The Willoughby Arms
Station Road, Little Bytham, Grantham NG33 4RA
☎ *(01780) 410276* Kip and Lynda Hulme

Freehouse with six real ales on offer, half from local micro-breweries and half from around the country. Bateman XB is the house ale and other regulars include Abbeydale Absolution plus beers from Hopshackle, Ufford and Great Oakley.

Beamed, traditional stone country pub around 150 years old. It was originally the railway booking office and waiting room. Situated in a pretty village that is recorded in the Domesday Book, the pub enjoys stunning countryside views from the large beer garden. Tasty, home-cooked food lunchtime and evening. Live music several times a month. Beer festivals on bank holidays. High-quality en-suite B&B available. Six miles north of Stamford.

OPEN *All day, every day.*

LOUTH
The Wheatsheaf Inn
62 Westgate, Louth LN11 9YD
☎ *(01507) 606262* Barry Allen

Timothy Taylor Landlord plus beers from Black Sheep and Daleside, changed twice weekly.

Dating from 1648, a two-bar pub with flag floors and coal fires. Food served 12–2.30pm. Outside smoking extension. Car park. Situated behind St James's Church.

OPEN *All day, every day.*

The Woodman Inn
134 Eastgate, Louth LN11 9AA
☎ *(01507) 602100* Dave Kilgour

Greene King Abbot plus two guests, such as Wadworth 6X, Charles Wells Bombardier and brews from Cotleigh and Abbeydale. Other specials from micro-breweries when possible.

Situated on the edge of town, this pub has a film theme. Two bars, one a live rock and blues music venue. Food available at lunchtime only. Children allowed.

OPEN *11am–4pm and 7–11pm Mon–Fri; all day Sat; 12–3.30pm and 7–10.30pm Sun.*

MARKET RASEN
The White Hart
Magna Mile, Ludford, Market Rasen LN8 6AD
☎ *(01507) 313489* Michael Sharpe

Genuine freehouse with up to five constantly rotating real ales. Fulstow Marsh Mild is a regular, others could come from any micro-brewery.

Thought to have first been used as a pub in 1742, this two-roomed village pub is close to Viking Way. Louth CAMRA Country Pub of the Year 2007. Homemade food, locally sourced, Wed–Sun evenings and Fri–Sun lunch. Three real fires. Guest accomodation separate to pub. On the A631 between Louth and Market Rasen.

OPEN *5.30–11pm Mon–Thurs; 12–2pm and 5.30–11pm Fri; 12–2.30pm and 6–11pm Sat; 12–4pm and 7–11pm Sun.*

NORTH KELSEY

The Butchers Arms

*Middle Street, North Kelsey, Market Rasen
LN7 6EH*
☎ *(01652) 678002* Steve Cooper

 Freehouse predominantly serving Tom Wood Highwood beers, plus one constantly changing guest.

Small, old-style village pub. One bar. No music or games. Outside seating. Children allowed.

OPEN *4–11pm Mon–Fri; 12–11pm Sat–Sun.*

OLD BOLINGBROKE

The Black Horse Inn

Moat Lane, Old Bolingbroke, Nr Spilsby PE23 4HH
☎ *(01790) 763388* Eugenie Phillips

 Young's Bitter plus three guest ales, changed every cask. Old Rosie Cider also served.

A traditional freehouse with open fire in a picturesque royal village ideal for countryside walks. Restaurant-quality food and bar snacks available at pub prices using local produce and organic veg. Food served 12–2.30pm and 7–9.30pm Wed–Sun; Grimsby haddock and chips on Fri; speciality menu Sat night; Sunday lunches. Disabled access. Dog friendly, with outside areas. Seasonal beer festivals. Car park. Located between the A158 and A16.

OPEN *7–11.30pm Tues; 12–3pm and 7–11.30pm Wed–Sun. No entry after 11pm.*

PINCHBECK

The Bull Inn

1 Knight Street, Pinchbeck, Spalding PE11 3LA
☎ *(01775) 723022* Heather and John Allen

 A genuine freehouse serving three or four real ales at all times. Range changes weekly.

Friendly and intimate pub with public bar, lounge bar, large restaurant, outside patio and beer garden. Food (restaurant à la carte, bar snacks or specials) served every lunchtime and evening. Air-conditioned. Car park. In the centre of Pinchbeck village.

OPEN *12–2.30pm and 5.30pm–12 Mon–Fri; 12–12 Sat; 12–11pm Sun.*

ROTHWELL

The Blacksmith's Arms

Hillrise, Rothwell LN7 6AZ
☎ *(01472) 371300* Rachel Flello

Freehouse with five real ales, namely Black Sheep Bitter and Tom Wood Shepherd's Delight plus three guests, changed after every barrel.

A 400-year-old haunted pub, with oak beams, real fires and candles in the dining area. CAMRA Country Pub of the Year 2007. Bar and restaurant food 12–2pm and 5.30–9pm Mon–Thurs; 12–2pm and 5.30–9.30pm Fri; 12–2pm and 6–9.30pm Sat; 12–3pm and 6–9pm Sun. Curry night 7.30–11pm Thurs. Car park, garden and function room/restaurant/entertainment room. Pool table and dart board. Quiz on Monday nights. Children welcome. Park area to the side. In a picturesque village, surrounded by rolling hills. Two minutes from the Viking Way, and on National Cycle Route 1. Two miles off the A46 between Caistor and Swallow.

OPEN *11.30am–3pm and 5–11pm Mon–Fri; all day Sat–Sun.*

SCAMBLESBY

The Green Man

Old Main Road, Scamblesby, Louth LN11 9XG
☎ *(01507) 343282* Tim and Anne Eyre

 An ever-changing selection of real ales. Regular features include Black Sheep Bitter plus brews from Wells and Young's.

A country pub with lounge and public bar. Pub meals served 12–8.30pm Mon–Sat, 12–7.30pm Sun. Children allowed.

OPEN *12–12.*

SCOTTER

The White Swan

7 The Green, Scotter, Nr Scunthorpe DN21 3UD
☎ *(01724) 762342* Dean Garner

 Tom Woods beer plus three or four rotating guests, changed at least fortnightly.

Set in the village of Scotter, in quiet and relaxing surroundings. General bar, cocktail bar and full à la carte restaurant. Food served 11.30am–2.30pm and 6.30–10pm Mon–Thurs, 11.30am–10pm Fri–Sat, 11.30am–9pm Sun. A pretty, riverside setting with roaming ducks! Car park.

OPEN *11.30am–3.30pm and 6.30pm–12.30am Mon–Thurs; 11.30am–12.30am Fri–Sat; 11.30am–11.30pm Sun.*

SCUNTHORPE

Bird in the Barley

Northfield Road, Messingham, Scunthorpe DN17 3SQ
☎ *(01724) 764744* William and Debby Jackson

 Tied to Marston's with Pedigree and Jennings Sneck Lifter on offer, plus two monthly guests.

Delightful olde-worlde pub. Good homemade pub food served 12–2pm and 6–9pm. Beer garden, ample parking. Children welcome.

OPEN *Closed Mon; 11am–3pm and 5.30–11pm Tues–Sun.*

The Honest Lawyer

70 Oswald Road, Scunthorpe DN15 7PG
☎ *(01724) 849906* Allan Edgar

Freehouse with Timothy Taylor Landlord and a Daleside brew plus six rotating guests.

Opened in 1990 with a judicial theme. Food every lunchtime and evening. Children welcome. Outside patio. Just outside the town centre, near the museum.

OPEN *11am–11pm Mon–Thurs; 11am–midnight Fri–Sat; 12–11pm Sun.*

The Malt Shovel

219 Ashby High Street, Scunthorpe DN16 2JP
☎ *(01724) 843318*
Simon Hall and Belinda Fisher

Seven real ales, including Exmoor Gold and Tom Wood Dark Mild, plus guests changed every few days. Guests are two pale beers, one traditional (brown) beer and one stout or porter.

Housed in an old cinema, but trading as a pub since the 1990s. Two bars, one pool table and 14 full-size snooker tables. Food served 12–2pm and 4–8pm Mon–Sat; 12–7pm Sun. Beer garden.

OPEN *10am–11pm Sun–Thurs; 10am–midnight Fri–Sat.*

SKEGNESS

The Vine Hotel

Vine Road, Seacroft, Skegness PE25 3DB
☎ *(01754) 610611* Nigel Dorman

Bateman ales are a permanent feature, including XB, XXXB and Mild, plus two monthly-changing guest beers.

Claiming to be the oldest and most famous hotel in Skegness, it dates from the 1770s. RAC/AA 3-star Best Western Hotel set in tranquil gardens, boasting two cosy bars with wooden beams and open fires, a fine dining restaurant alongside and 24 en-suite rooms. Food served 12–2.15pm and 6–9.15pm Mon–Fri, 12–9.15pm Sat–Sun. Extensive parking. Children welcome. At the southern end of Skegness.

OPEN *11am–11pm Mon–Sat; 12–10.30pm Sun.*

SOUTH WITHAM

The Blue Cow Inn

29 High Street, South Witham, Nr Grantham NG33 5QB
☎ *(01572) 768432* Simon Crathorn

Home of The Blue Cow brewery since 1997, with two home-brewed ales, Best Bitter and Witham Wobbler, on offer.

A heavily beamed, 13th-century coaching inn with stone floors and open fires. Food available 10.30am–9.30pm, including children's menu. No juke boxes or pool tables. Accommodation commended by the English Tourist Board – six en-suite rooms. Beer garden, car park. One mile from the A1, between Stamford and Grantham.

OPEN *10.30am–11pm Mon–Sat; 12–10.30pm Sun.*

SPALDING

The Lincolnshire Poacher

11 Double Street, Spalding PE11 2AA
☎ *(01775) 766490* Gary Bettles

Greene King IPA and Fuller's London Pride are the permanent beers here.

Old country inn located in the town, overlooking the River Welland. Food every lunchtime, and Tues–Sat evenings. Children welcome until 9pm. Large patio with tables and seating. Accommodation. Private parties. Adjacent to Spalding Water Taxi.

OPEN *11am–midnight.*

STAMFORD

The Green Man

29 Scotgate, Stamford PE9 2YQ
☎ *(01780) 753598* Tony Shilling

Seven real ales, with Hop Back Summer Lightning and Caledonian Deuchars IPA always on offer, plus five guests.

Olde-worlde pub dating from 1796 with a single L-shaped bar, oak beams, low ceilings and wooden floors. Decorated with beer/ale artefacts. Food available 12–2.30pm. Children allowed until 7pm. Large beer garden (off road). Three letting rooms. Located on the old A1 through Stamford, five minutes' walk from the town centre.

OPEN *11am–midnight.*

The Periwig

7 All Saints Place, Red Lion Square, Stamford PE9 2AG
☎ *(01780) 762169* Eddy Renner

A genuine freehouse offering Oakham JHB, Fuller's London Pride, Ufford Idle Hour and two guests changed every week.

A town pub in a 17th-century building with modernised interior. Food, including cheeseboards, available 12–7pm. Live band once a month. Children allowed.

OPEN *11am–11pm Mon–Tues; 11am–midnight Wed–Thurs; 11am–1am Fri–Sat; 12–10.30pm Sun.*

The Tobie Norris

2 St Paul's Street, Stamford PE9 2BE
☎ *(01780) 753800* Mick Thurlby
www.tobienorris.com

Five real ales including locally brewed Ufford Ales, plus Adnams Bitter and guests from near and far including Milestone of Newark, Lancaster, Abbeydale, Burton Bridge, Slaters, Oldershaws and many more.

An ancient pub full of history and with a terrific interior. Owned by the RAF Association for the second half of the 20th century, reopened as a pub in 2006. Seven rooms over three floors plus an outside drinking area. Food served 12–2.30pm (3pm Sat–Sun) and 6–9pm Mon–Thurs. Dogs and children over 10 welcome.

OPEN *11.30am–11pm Mon–Thurs; 11.30am–12am Fri–Sat; 11.30am–10.30pm Sun.*

TETFORD
White Hart Inn
East Road, Tetford LN9 6QQ
☎ *(01507) 533255* V Garnett

 Freehouse serving Adnams Bitter, Fuller's London Pride, Greene King Abbot and a guest beer.

Opposite the church in the heart of the village, a beamed pub with several bars. The main bar is at the back with a huge settee in front of an open fire. Award-winning food served 12–2pm and 7–9pm Tues–Sat. Fish fresh from Grimsby on Fri and Sat. Roast lunches 12–2.30pm on Sun. Accommodation, outside seating, function room, large car park. Children welcome in the lounge bar. Dogs welcome. Walking country, seven miles from Horncastle, nine miles from Louth.

OPEN *Closed Mon; 12–3.30pm and 7–11pm Tues–Sun.*

THORNTON CURTIS
Thornton Hunt Inn
Thornton Curtis, Nr Ulceby DN39 6XW
☎ *(01469) 531252*
Peter and Stephanie Williams
www.thornton-inn.co.uk

 Freehouse with Timothy Taylor Landlord and a Highwood beer such as Hop Bunny Hop, changed every two or three months.

Family-run inn in a Grade II listed building. Traditional homemade meals available, including pies, Lincolnshire sausage & mash, healthy salads, fresh sandwiches, steaks and a selection of homemade desserts, plus children's and vegetarian menus. Food served 12–2pm and 6.30–9pm. Past winner of Lincolnshire Taste of Excellence award and winner of Taste of Lincolnshire Best Pub Meal 2008. Beer garden with extensive children's fun trail. Six comfortable en-suite rooms, including one on the ground floor with disabled access. Rooms have a separate entrance, and are decorated to 4-star Visit Britain standards.

OPEN *12–3pm and 6.30–11pm.*

WAINFLEET
Mill Bar
Bateman's Visitor Centre, Salem Bridge Brewery, Mill Lane, Wainfleet PE24 4JE
☎ *(01754) 882017/882009* Lesley Young
www.bateman.co.uk

 A Bateman Brewery tied house. Only Bateman ales on offer, XB and XXXB permanently, plus three rotating seasonals and specials.

The brewery tap at Bateman Brewery, housed in the old windmill part of the site, which dates from 1874. Food served 12–2pm; evenings by appointment only. Children welcome. Outdoor games area including traditional old pub games. Beer garden. Car park. Two beer festivals held each year. Located five miles south of Skegness on the A52.

OPEN *11.30am–3.30pm; evenings by appointment only.*

WHAPLODE ST CATHERINE
The Bluebell Inn
Cranesgate South, Whaplode St Catherine, Spalding PE12 6SN
☎ *(01406) 540300* John Lusher

 Three Bluebell Brewery brews produced on the premises plus a guest from further afield.

A pub and restaurant with one main bar and a snug with a woodburner. Pool and darts. Beer garden with occasional barbecues in summer. Restaurant open Tues–Fri evenings, Sat lunchtime and evening and all day Sun. Children allowed. Brewery visits arranged. Car park. Situated in the middle of nowhere, seven miles from Spalding, so do ring for directions.

OPEN *7–11pm Tues–Fri; 12–3pm and 7–11pm Sat; 12–10.30pm Sun.*

WILLOUGHBY
The Willoughby Arms
Church Lane, Willoughby, Nr Alford LN13 9SU
☎ *(01507) 462387* Tom Myles

 A Bateman Brewery tied house. XB plus up to four guest ales from any independent brewery. Also a good range of wines.

Self-proclaimed Mecca for lovers of fine ales, wines and fresh food. Victorian beamed bar with real fire and separate restaurant. Food served 12–2pm and 7–9pm (bookings only) Tues–Sat; 12–2.30pm Sun. Award-winning flower display and garden. Car park. Annual beer festival. Small private functions catered for. Turn off the A1028 at Skendleby towards Willoughby.

OPEN *7pm–close Mon (closed Mon lunch); 12–2pm and 7pm–close Tues–Sun.*

WOOLSTHORPE-BY-BELVOIR
The Chequers
Main Street, Woolsthorpe-by-Belvoir, Grantham NG32 1LV
☎ *(01476) 870701* Justin Chad
www.chequers-inn.net

Freehouse with Hardys and Hansons Olde Trip, Belvoir Bitter and Brewsters Marquis usually available, plus three guest ales rotated regularly to include other local breweries.

A 17th-century country pub with olde-worlde decor. Open fires, beams, snug and separate restaurant. Five-acre garden and private cricket field. Four en-suite bedrooms. Restaurant food available 12–2.30pm and 5.30–9.30pm Mon–Sat and 12–4pm and 6.30–8.30pm Sun. Children allowed. Next to Belvoir Castle.

OPEN *12–3pm and 5.30–11pm Mon–Sat; 12–10.30pm Sun (closes at 7pm on Sun in winter).*

THE BREWERIES

BATTERSEA BREWERY COMPANY

43 Glycena Road, Battersea SW11 5TP
☎ *(020) 7978 7978*
www.batterseabrewery.com

PAGODA 3.7% ABV
BATTERSEA BITTER 4.0% ABV
Copper coloured with hints of malt.
POWER STATION PORTER 4.9% ABV
Dark, dry, traditional London beer.

FULLER, SMITH & TURNER PLC

Griffin Brewery, Chiswick Lane South W4 2QB
☎ *(020) 8996 2000*
www.fullers.co.uk

CHISWICK 3.5% ABV
Flowery and fresh.
DISCOVERY 3.9% ABV
Zesty and fruity blonde beer.
LONDON PRIDE 4.1% ABV
Malty base, distinctive hop flavours.
INDIA PALE ALE 4.8% ABV
Distinctive bitterness and aroma.
HONEY DEW 5.0% ABV
Golden, organic beer.
LONDON PORTER 5.4% ABV
Smooth, rich, chocolatey.
ESB 5.5% ABV
Brewed from pale ale and crystal malts.
Seasonals:
SUMMER ALE 3.9% ABV
May–August only.
JACK FROST 4.5% ABV
November–January only.
OLD WINTER ALE 4.5% ABV
Winter months only.

THE GRAND UNION BREWERY LTD

Brewhouse Lock, 10 Abenglen, Betam Road,
Hayes UB3 1SS
☎ *(020) 8573 9888*
www.gubrewery.co.uk

BITTER 3.7% ABV
Well hopped and refreshing.
GOLD 4.2% ABV
Golden-coloured ale. Aromatic and clean-tasting.
HONEY ALE 4.3% ABV
Sweet, but hoppy.
LIBERTY BLONDE 4.2% ABV
Light and refreshing.
GRAND UNION ONE HOP 4.5% ABV
Brewed with a different hop each time.
SPECIAL 4.5% ABV
Full flavoured and nicely hopped.
STOUT 4.8% ABV
Dark and satisfying. Full bodied with bittersweet chocolate and roasted flavours.
HONEY PORTER 4.9% ABV
Rich and smooth. Dark and very satisfying.
Plus seasonals and specials.

MEANTIME BREWING CO. LTD

The Greenwich Brewery, 2 Penhall Road SE7 8RX
☎ *(020) 8293 1111*
www.meantimebrewing.com

HELLES BEER 4.4% ABV
PALE ALE 4.7% ABV
ORGANIC PILSNER 5.4% ABV
COFFEE BEER 6.0% ABV
GRAND CRU WHEAT 6.3% ABV
CHOCOLATE 6.5% ABV
GRAND CRU RASPBERRY 6.5% ABV
LONDON PORTER 6.5% ABV
OLD SMOKED BOCK 6.5% ABV
IPA 7.5% ABV

PITFIELD BREWERY

The Beer Shop, 14 Pitfield Street N1 6EY
☎ *0845 8331492*
www.pitfieldbeershop.co.uk

ORIGINAL BITTER 3.8% ABV
EAST KENT GOLDINGS 4.2% ABV
ECO WARRIOR 4.5% ABV
Plus occasionals. Certified organic brewery.

TWICKENHAM FINE ALES LTD

The Crane Brewery, Unit A, Ryecroft Works,
Edwin Road, Twickenham TW2 6SP
☎ *(020) 8241 1825*
www.twickenham-fine-ales.co.uk

CRANE SUNDANCER 3.7% ABV
Crisp and hoppy session bitter.
ADVANTAGE ALE 4.0% ABV
Amber colour, roasty aroma.
TWICKENHAM ORIGINAL 4.2% ABV
Ruby coloured, malty best bitter.
Plus seasonals and specials including:
TWICKENHAM IPA 4.5% ABV
Lively, traditional India Pale Ale.
STRONG & DARK 5.2% ABV
Dark winter ale.

THE PUBS

LONDON CENTRAL

EC1

The Artillery Arms

102 Bunhill Row EC1V 8ND
☎ *(020) 7253 4683 Peter Brogan*

Fuller's pub with Chiswick, London Pride and ESB plus seasonal brews and a guest ale from a wide range of independent breweries.

An attractive Victorian building tucked away behind Old Street. Named after the Honourable Artillery Company, which is based over the road. Food available 12–3pm Mon–Fri. Upstairs function room.

⊖ Nearest Tube: Old Street.

🍺 *12–11pm Mon–Sat (10.30pm Sun).*

The Bishops Finger

9–10 West Smithfield EC1A 9JR
☎ *(020) 7248 2341* Paul Potts

Shepherd Neame house with four real ales supplied by the brewery, including seasonal brews.

Located next to Smithfield Market, a two-bar pub with first-floor bar available for private hire. Food served at lunchtime and dinner Mon–Fri.

⊖ Nearest Tube: Farringdon/Barbican.

OPEN 11am–11pm Mon–Fri.

Butcher's Hook & Cleaver

61–3 West Smithfield EC1A 9DY
☎ *(020) 7600 9181* Paul Bancroft

Fuller's pub with Chiswick, London Pride, Discovery and ESB plus seasonal brews.

Traditional award-winning alehouse, formerly a bank and butcher's wholesale shop right next to Smithfield Market. Attractive wooden facade and large bar and mezzanine areas. Ale and pie menu available 12–9pm Mon–Fri. Claims to serve the best bangers and mash in Smithfield, plus Smithfield steaks. Function room available for hire at the weekends.

⊖ Nearest Tube: Farringdon.

OPEN 11am–11.30pm Mon–Fri.

The Eagle

139 Farringdon Road EC1
☎ *(020) 7837 1353* Michael Belben

Four hand pumps, with Charles Wells Eagle IPA and Bombardier always available.

A gastropub with a reputation for good food, which is available 12.30–2.30pm Mon–Fri (3.30pm Sat and Sun) and 6.30–10.30pm Mon–Sat. On a busy main road close to *The Guardian* and *The Observer* newspaper offices. Outside seating.

⊖ Nearest Tube: Farringdon.

OPEN 12–11pm Mon–Sat; 12–5pm Sun. Closed bank holidays.

The Harlequin

27 Arlington Way EC1R 1UY
☎ *(020) 7837 9035*

Timothy Taylor Landlord and Black Sheep Bitter always available.

Tucked behind Sadlers Wells theatre and often heaving with an interval; and after-show crowd as a result. A small, friendly one-bar pub with wooden floors. Bar snacks and home-cooked food available. Free Wi-Fi, occasional live music. Limited outside seating

⊖ Nearest Tube: Angel

OPEN 12–11pm (plus late licence).

Jerusalem Tavern

55 Britton Street, Clerkenwell EC1M 5UQ
☎ *(020) 7490 4281* Cheryl Jacob
www.stpetersbrewery.co.uk

St Peter's Brewery tied house serving six of the cask range, usually including Best Bitter, Organic Best Bitter, Golden Ale, a fruit beer and a dark beer. Many more in bottles.

A small, restored 18th-century listed coffee house near Smithfield with plenty of atmosphere, no music or machines. Limited outside seating. Food available 12–3pm Mon–Fri and 5–9.30pm Tues–Thurs. Dogs welcome.

⊖ Nearest Tube: Farringdon.

OPEN 11am–11pm Mon–Fri. Available for private hire at weekends.

The Masque Haunt

168–72 Old Street EC1V 9PB
☎ *(020) 7251 4195* Anthony Booker

JD Wetherspoon's pub with up to eight real ales. Many of the usual suspects (Fuller's London Pride, Marston's Pedigree, Greene King Abbot etc) plus guests perhaps from Grand Union and other smaller independents.

On the ground floor of a modern office building on the corner of Old Street and Bunhill Row. Food served 9am–11pm daily.

⊖ Nearest Tube: Old Street.

OPEN 9am–11.30pm (11pm Sun).

Melton Mowbray

18 Holborn EC1 2LE
☎ *(020) 7405 7077* Christie Graham

Fuller's house with Chiswick, London Pride, ESB and Discovery plus one or two guest ales, changed every couple of weeks.

Traditional English pub with food and ales to suit, popular with City workers. Traditional home-cooked food served 11am–8pm Mon–Thurs and 11am–5pm Fri, including daily specials. Private function room available free of charge. Easy walking distance from both St Paul's Cathedral and the West End.

⊖ Nearest Tube: Chancery Lane.

OPEN 11am–11pm Mon–Fri.

Old China Hand

8 Tysoe Street, Islington EC1 4RQ
☎ *(020) 7278 7678* Rowena Smith
www.clerkenwellbar.com

Freehouse serving two to three real ales from micro-breweries only, all rotating weekly, with almost always one from O'Hanlon's. Around 20 bottled beers from all over the world also available.

Close to Sadlers Wells Theatre, a wine bar serving real ales from small breweries. Winner of a Responsible Drinks Retailing Award 2006 and the *Morning Advertiser* London Newcomer Pub of the Year 2006, and finalist in *The Publican* Nationwide Newcomer Pub of the Year Award 2006. Food (dim sum) served 12–3pm and 6–10pm Mon–Fri and 6–10pm Sat, made by the former head chef from the Dorchester Hotel's Oriental Restaurant. Two screens showing rugby and football on request. Function room upstairs available for small parties and meetings, with the entire pub available for hire for larger events. Between Angel and Farringdon tube stations.

⊖ Nearest Tube: Angel/Farringdon.

OPEN 12–12 Mon–Thurs; noon–1am Fri–Sat.

The Old Fountain

3 Baldwin Street, EC1V 9NU
☎ *(020) 7253 2970*
www.oldfountain.co.uk

Up to eight constantly rotating real ales. Fuller's London Pride plus a huge range of microbrews. A recent visit featured beers from Dark Star, City of Cambridge, Saltaire, Ascot, Cairngorm, Red Squirrel and Whitstable, but many others also feature.

Traditional, unassuming back-street freehouse with three drinking areas and a central bar plus a beer garden to one side. Run by the Durrant family since 1964. Freshly-cooked food including specials served 12-2.30pm plus pizzas in the evening. TV, fish tank and darts. Just off City Road, local CAMRA pub of the year 2009.

⊖ Nearest Tube: Old Street

OPEN *11am–11pm Mon–Fri; closed Sat–Sun.*

Ye Olde Mitre

1 Ely Court, Ely Place, Off Hatton Garden EC1 6SJ
☎ *(020) 7405 4751* Eamon and Kathy Scott

Leased from Punch and offering Adnams Bitter and Broadside, Caledonian Deuchars IPA and a guest (up to four per week). Recent guests came from Rooster's, Dark Star, Phoenix and Orkney. Additional real ales featured during the Great British Beer Festival, and the Milds for May Festival. Real cider.

Unspoilt, historic two-bar tavern built in 1546 within the grounds of what was the Bishop of Ely's London palace. No music, no TV, no machines. Outside drinking area. Small upstairs function room for hire. Hot and cold snacks (including toasties) served 11.30am–9pm. Sorry, no children. In an alley between numbers 8 and 9 Hatton Garden.

⊖ Nearest Tube: Chancery Lane/Farringdon.

OPEN *11am–11pm Mon–Sun; closed Sat–Sun and bank holidays but opens for the weekend of the Great British Beer Festival in early August.*

Sekforde Arms

34 Sekforde Street EC1 0HA
☎ *(020) 7253 3251* Kevin McElroy

Wells and Young's house with Young's PA and Special and Charles Wells Bombardier plus a seasonal brew.

Very much a traditional locals' pub on the edge of the City with one main bar and a private function room available for hire. Food served 12–3pm Mon–Fri; 5–9pm Wed–Fri (last orders 8.30pm). Traditional roast, Sun 12–4pm, last orders 3.30pm. Young children only allowed Sun 12–3pm. Outside drinking area. In central Clerkenwell, a short walk from Farringdon station.

⊖ Nearest Tube: Farringdon.

OPEN *Noon–11pm Mon–Wed; 11am–11pm Thur–Fri; 12–8pm or (more likely in summer) 9pm Sat.*

The Sutton Arms

16 Great Sutton Street EC1V 0DH
☎ *(020) 7253 2462* Michael Duignan

Freehouse with Fuller's London Pride, Timothy Taylor Landlord and Greene King IPA available.

Historic one-bar pub in Clerkenwell frequented by a range of City types – builders, artists and designers as well as office workers. Food served 12–3pm Mon–Fri (booking recommended), plus evening buffets. Upstairs bar available for private hire all day. The whole pub is available for functions at weekends. There are extensions to drinking hours for functions and other special events.

⊖ Nearest Tube: Farringdon.

OPEN *11am–11pm Mon–Fri.*

The Three Kings

7 Clerkenwell Close EC1R 0DY
☎ *(020) 7253 0483* Deke Eicher

Owned by Enterprise Inns with three real ales that might include Timothy Taylor Landlord, Caledonian Deuchars IPA, Fuller's London Pride and Hopback Summer Lightning.

Popular and eclectic Clerkenwell pub opposite St James' Church in a building dating from 1791. Food served 12–3pm and 6–11pm Mon–Fri. Can get busy at the end of the week as the crowds spill on to the pavement when the front windows are open. Proper jukebox.

⊖ Nearest Tube: Farringdon.

OPEN *12–11pm Mon–Sat.*

OTHER REAL ALE PUBS IN EC1

The Betsey Trotwood
(SHEPHERD NEAME)
Farringdon Road EC1R 3BL ☎ *(020) 7253 4285*

City Pride (FULLER'S)
28 Farringdon Lane, Clerkenwell EC1R 3AU
☎ *(020) 7608 0615*

Fence
67–9 Cowcross Street, Farringdon EC1M 6BP
☎ *(020) 7250 3414*

Legion
348 Old Street EC1 ☎ *(020) 7729 4411*

The Printworks (WETHERSPOON)
113–17 Farringdon Road EC1R 3AP
☎ *(020) 7713 2000*

Sir John Oldcastle (WETHERSPOON)
29–35 Farringdon Road EC1M 3JF
☎ *(020) 7242 1013*

Viaduct (FULLER'S)
126 Newgate Street EC1A 7AA
☎ *(020) 7600 1863*

EC2

Dirty Dicks

202 Bishopsgate EC2M 4NR
☎ *(020) 7283 5888* Ian Martin

 Wells and Young's house with up to four real ales, including Young's PA, SPA and Winter Warmer and Charles Wells Bombardier.

Dating from approximately 1745, an old-style friendly local in the city, with three fully air-conditioned bars, function area and lunchtime restaurant. Food served 12–9.30pm Mon–Sat, 11.30am–8pm Sunday (roasts served). All bars available for free hire. Free car park after 6.30pm. Near Liverpool Street Station, and handy for Petticoat Lane and Spitalfields Market.

⊖ Nearest Tube: Liverpool Street.

OPEN *11am–midnight Mon–Thurs; 11am–1am Fri–Sat; 11.30am–10.30pm Sun.*

Old Doctor Butler's Head

2 Mason's Avenue, Moorgate EC2V 5BY
☎ *(020) 7606 3504* Christopher Gouldson
www.shepherd-neame.co.uk

Shepherd Neame house with the full range of Spitfire, Master Brew, Bishop's Finger, Best and a guest ale.

Traditional-style pub dating from 1610, just off Moorgate, with gas lamps in the bar area. Food is served 12–3pm Mon–Fri, and for private bookings in the evening. Famous for steak and kidney pudding! First-floor restaurant, second-floor function room for hire, whole pub can be hired at weekends. Close to the Guildhall.

⊖ Nearest Tube: Moorgate/Bank.

OPEN *11am–11pm Mon–Fri.*

The Phoenix

26 Throgmorton Street EC2N 2AN
☎ *(020) 7588 7289* Mike Wren
www.traditionalpubslondon.co.uk

Greene King pub serving four or five real ales, including IPA, Abbot, Old Speckled Hen plus a one or two guests changed monthly, such as Black Sheep Best, Ringwood Best, Greene King Fireside or Ridleys Old Bob.

A traditional, one-bar city pub, this was the first non-smoking pub in London (December 2003). Formerly a bank, it occupies a listed building close to the Bank of England and is Cask Marque accredited. Food available 12–9pm Mon–Fri. Disabled access, complimentary Wi-Fi.

⊖ Nearest Tube: Bank.

OPEN *11am–11pm Mon–Fri.*

OTHER REAL ALE PUBS IN EC2

City House

86 Bishopsgate EC2N 4AU ☎ *(020) 7256 8325*

Finch's (WELLS AND YOUNG'S)

12a Finsbury Square EC2A 1AS
☎ *(020) 7588 3311*

Fleetwood (FULLER'S)

36 Wilson Street EC2M 2TE
☎ *(020) 7247 2241*

The Greene Man (WETHERSPOON)

1 Poultry, Bank Station EC2R 8EJ
☎ *(020) 7248 3529*

Hamilton Hall (WETHERSPOON)

Unit 32, Liverpool Street Station EC2M 7PY
☎ *(020) 7247 3579*

Magpie

12 New Street EC2M 4TP ☎ *(020) 7929 3889*

Red Herring (FULLER'S)

49 Gresham Street EC2V 7ET
☎ *(020) 7606 0399*

Telegraph (FULLER'S)

11 Telegraph Street EC2R 7AR
☎ *(020) 7920 9090*

EC3

The Chamberlain Hotel

132 The Minories EC3N 1NT
☎ *(020) 7680 1500* Liz McLelland
www.thechamberlainhotel.com

Owned by Fuller's with up to five real ales, including London Pride and ESB plus seasonal brews.

A pub-style bar in a four-star hotel two minutes from the Tower of London. Food served 11am–9.30pm Mon–Sat, 12–9.30pm Sun. There are 64 en-suite bedrooms.

⊖ Nearest Tube: Aldgate.

OPEN *11am–11pm Mon–Sat; 12–10.30pm Sun.*

The Counting House

50 Cornhill EC3V 3PD
☎ *(020) 7283 7123* Colin George

Fuller's house with five real ales: Chiswick, London Pride, Discovery, ESB and Gale's HSB.

Built in 1893, this was a bank until 1997, with a domed ceiling, gallery and dark wood panelled and marble walls. One island bar, three function rooms. Traditional pies and more available 12–10pm Mon–Fri. Open Sat and Sun for private hire only.

⊖ Nearest Tube: Bank/Monument.

OPEN *11am–11pm Mon–Fri.*

The Crosse Keys

9 Gracechurch Street EC3V 0DR
☎ *(020) 7623 4824* Jason Blower
www.jdwetherspoon.co.uk

Wetherspoon's pub usually offering around ten real ales, with Fuller's London Pride, Greene King Abbot, Shepherd Neame Spitfire and Marston's Pedigree always available. Guests, changed daily, might be from Burton Bridge, Titanic, Brains, Grainstore, Oakham, to name but a few. Draught cider also served.

Imposing former bank headquarters in the heart of the City of London, carefully converted and retaining many original features. Huge main room with central island bar and three smaller rooms. Cinema-sized screen for sporting events. Food available all day until 11pm (6pm Sat). Private rooms available for hire. Children welcome. Beer festivals held twice a year.

⊖ Nearest Tube: Monument.

 *9am (for breakfast)–midnight Mon–Thurs;
9am–1am Fri; 9am–7pm Sat.*

The Elephant

119 Fenchurch Street EC3M 5BA
☎ *(020) 7623 8970 R Paffey*

 Wells and Young's house with three real ales, including Young's Bitter, Special and a seasonal (Waggle Dance or Winter Warmer) brew.

Two-bar old-style pub serving food at lunchtimes.

⊖ Nearest Tube: Monument.

 *11am–9pm Mon–Wed; 11am–11pm
Thurs–Fri.*

The Hoop & Grapes

47 Aldgate High Street EC3
☎ *(020) 7265 5171 Hugh Ede*

Fuller's London Pride plus three guests, which could well include Timothy Taylor Landlord, Brakspear Special and Best, Badger Best, Adnams Bitter and Extra, Charles Wells Bombardier, Eagle or IPA, Shepherd Neame Spitfire, Hook Norton Old Hooky or Wychwood Hobgoblin or Special. An average of 50 different beers served every year.

A 400-year-old pub just inside the Square Mile. Bar food served every lunchtime 12–3pm, with table service available. No children.

⊖ Nearest Tube: Aldgate.

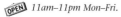 *11am–10pm Mon–Wed; 11am–11pm
Thurs–Fri; closed Sat–Sun.*

The Walrus & Carpenter

45 Monument Street EC3R 8BU
☎ *(020) 7626 3362 JE Mannion*

Fuller's London Pride and Timothy Taylor Landlord are permanent fixtures, plus three or four guest ales, changed at least weekly. Examples include Timothy Taylor Golden Best, Wadworth Henry's IPA, Arundel Sussex Gold and Highgate Pride & Joy. Beers are not often repeated.

Nicholson's house over three floors with a dining room (specialising in sausages served 12–10pm), wine/champagne bar and main bar. Outside drinking area. Children welcome in the dining room. Functions catered for.

⊖ Nearest Tube: Tower Hill.

 *11am–11pm Mon–Fri.*

OTHER REAL ALE PUBS IN EC3

Cock and Woolpack
(SHEPHERD NEAME)
6 Finch Lane EC3V 3NA ☎ *(020) 7626 4799*

East India Arms (SHEPHERD NEAME)
67 Fenchurch Street EC3M 4BR
☎ *(020) 7265 5121*

Hog's Head
29 St Mary Axe EC3A 8AA ☎ *(020) 7929 0245*

Hog's Head
America Square EC3N 2LS ☎ *(020) 7702 2381*

Hung Drawn and Quartered
(FULLER'S)
26–7 Great Tower Street EC3R 5AQ
☎ *(020) 7626 6123*

Lamb Tavern (WELLS AND YOUNG'S)
10–12 Leadenhall Market EC3V 1LR
☎ *(020) 7626 2454*

The Liberty Bounds
(WETHERSPOON)
15 Trinity Square EC3N 4AA
☎ *(020) 7481 0513*

Peacock
41 Minories EC3N 1DT ☎ *(020) 7488 3630*

Swan (FULLER'S)
Ship Tavern Passage, 77–80 Gracechurch Street EC3V 0AS ☎ *(020) 7283 7712*

The Three Lords (WELLS AND YOUNG'S)
27 The Minories EC3N 1DD ☎ *(020) 7481 4249*

Willy's Wine Bar
(WELLS AND YOUNG'S)
107 Fenchurch Street EC3 5JB
☎ *(020) 7480 7289*

Wine Lodge (WELLS AND YOUNG'S)
Sackville House, 145 Fenchurch Street EC3M 6BL ☎ *(020) 7626 0918*

EC4

The Old Bank of England
194 Fleet Street EC4 2LT
☎ *(020) 7430 2255 Jo Farquahar*

Fuller's flagship alehouse with London Pride, Chiswick, Discovery and ESB plus a seasonal brew.

An impressive conversion of a Victorian building that was once part of the Bank of England annexed to the law courts. Styled in brass and wood. Walled courtyard. Two separate rooms for dining, in which food is available 12–9pm Mon–Thurs and 12–8pm Fri. Full bar menu, including popular pies. Traditional afternoon tea served 2.30–5.30pm Mon–Fri. Two function rooms, buffets, weddings, weekend hire. No children.

⊖ Nearest Tube: Temple.

 *11am–11pm Mon–Fri; closed Sat–Sun,
although available for private party hire.*

The Black Friar

174 Queen Victoria Street EC4
☎ *(020) 7236 5650* David Tate

Adnams Bitter, Fuller's London Pride, Greene King Old Speckled Hen and Timothy Taylor Landlord plus two rotating guests changed every week or two.

Popular and original pub on the edge of the City now owned by Mitchells and Butler. Built in 1860 on the site of an old monastery with a remarkable interior. Bar food available 11.30am–9pm Mon–Sun. Children allowed. Outside standing area.

✪ Nearest Tube: Blackfriars.

11am–11pm Mon–Sat; 12–9.30pm Sun.

City Retreat

74 Shoe Lane EC4A 3BQ
☎ *(020) 7353 7904* Carol Joyce

Tied to Wells and Young's with Young's Bitter, Special and a seasonal brew such as Winter Warmer.

Very traditional house with one bar and a local feel. The landlady and her son are always behind the bar and many of the customers are regulars. Food available at lunchtime. Functions catered for (at weekends as well).

✪ Nearest Tube: Chancery Lane.

11am–11pm Mon–Fri.

Hoop & Grapes

80 Farringdon Street EC4A 4BL
☎ *(020) 7353 8808* Alex Fletcher
www.shepherd-neame.co.uk

Shepherd Neame pub serving Spitfire, Master Brew, Bishops Finger and Whitstable Bay plus a seasonal guest.

Built in 1721, this Grade II listed pub once offered refreshment during the night for the carriers and porters from Farringdon and Smithfield markets. Also used in the 18th century for 'Fleet Weddings', at which prisoners from the nearby Fleet Prison could be married and enjoy a wedding breakfast before returning to prison. Now has two bars, two beer gardens and a function room for hire. Food served 12–5pm Mon–Fri. Just around the corner from St Paul's Cathedral and Fleet Street.

✪ Nearest Tube: Farringdon.

11am–11pm Mon–Fri; available for private hire at weekends.

Shaws Booksellers

31–4 St Andrew's Hill EC4V 5DE
☎ *(020) 7489 7999* Adam Sykes (manager)

Fuller's house with London Pride and a guest ale from either the brewery range or further afield.

A gastropub on the ground floor of a converted paper merchants that used to serve the Fleet Street newspaper business. Still with original features but a refurbishment has added a more contemporary flavour. Lunch served 12–3pm and 5–9pm Mon–Fri, from a daily changing menu.

✪ Nearest Tube: Blackfriars.

12–11pm Mon–Fri.

The Williamsons Tavern

1 Groveland Court EC4
☎ *(020) 7248 5740* Andrew Murduck

Part of the Nicholson's group, with Timothy Taylor Landlord and Fuller's London Pride plus three guests, changed weekly.

Perhaps London's oldest hostelry and a former home of the Lord Mayor of London, a three-bar pub situated off Bow Lane. Food available 10am–10pm. Well-behaved children allowed.

✪ Nearest Tube: Mansion House.

11am–midnight Mon–Fri; closed Sat–Sun.

OTHER REAL ALE PUBS IN EC4

Banker (FULLER'S)

Cousin Lane EC4R 3TE ☎ *(020) 7283 5206*

The Bell

29 Bush Lane EC4R 0AN ☎ *(020) 7626 7560*

Fine Line (FULLER'S)

1 Bow Churchyard EC4M 9PQ
☎ *(020) 7248 3262*

Harrow (FULLER'S)

Whitefriars Street EC4Y 8JJ ☎ *(020) 7427 0911*

Vintry (FULLER'S)

Abchurch Yard, Off Abchurch Lane EC4N 5AX
☎ *(020) 7280 9610*

WC1

The Bountiful Cow

51 Eagle Street WC1R 4AP
☎ *(020) 7404 0200* Roxy Beaujolais

Adnams Best and Broadside, Harvey's Bitter and usually one other real ale.

From the same stable as the Seven Stars (WC2), a refurbished steak and ale house serving food all day.

✪ Nearest Tube: Holborn.

All day, every day.

Calthorpe Arms

252 Gray's Inn Road WC1X 8JR
☎ *(020) 7278 4732* Adrian and Tessa Larner

Popular Wells and Young's tenancy serving Young's Bitter, Special and seasonal or occasional brews.

Former CAMRA North London Pub of the Year. A one-bar street-corner local. Upstairs function/dining room. Food served every lunchtime 12–2.30pm and 6–9.30pm Mon–Fri. Outside seating. Available for private hire.

✪ Nearest Tube: Russell Square.

11am–11pm Mon–Sat; 12–10.30pm Sun.

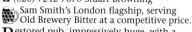

Cittie of Yorke

22 High Holborn WC1V 6BN
☎ *(020) 7242 7670* Stuart Browning

Sam Smith's London flagship, serving Old Brewery Bitter at a competitive price.

Restored pub, impressively huge, with a history dating back to 1430 although it was completely rebuilt in 1923. Enormous back bar with vaulted ceiling, side booths and adjoining wood-panelled room. Cellar bar open in evenings. Bar food available 12–9pm Mon–Sat. Well-behaved children allowed.

⊖ Nearest Tube: Chancery Lane.

OPEN *11.30am–11pm Mon–Sat; closed Sun and bank holidays.*

The College Arms

18 Store Street WC1E 7DH
☎ *(020) 7436 4697* Paul Davies
www.collegearmswc1.co.uk

Freehouse serving Adnams Broadside, Shepherd Neame Spitfire and Greene King IPA plus one guest, rotating monthly, such as Fuller's London Pride.

Formerly The University Tavern, now a one-bar pub with large open-plan basement seating area situated next door to England & Wales College of Law, so very student-oriented. Pool, darts, plus Wi-Fi throughout. Food available 12–9pm Mon–Fri. Pavement benches with awning for smoking in comfort. No children or dogs. Situated off Tottenham Court Road.

⊖ Nearest Tube: Goodge Street.

OPEN *11am–11pm Mon–Fri. Available for private hire Sat–Sun.*

Dolphin Tavern

44 Red Lion Street WC1R 4PF
☎ *(020) 7831 6298* Kim Charley

Enterprise Inn serving Adnams Bitter and Broadside and Greene King Old Speckled Hen plus one guest changed every three months.

A one-bar local close to Conway Hall in Holborn. Food 12–3pm Mon–Sat. Off Theobalds Road.

⊖ Nearest Tube: Holborn.

OPEN *11am–11pm Mon–Fri; 12–5pm Sat; closed Sun.*

The Ivy House

8–10 Southampton Row WC1B 4AE
☎ *(020) 7831 6999* Nick Goodhall

Freehouse serving Charles Wells Bombardier and two guest brews such as Everards Tiger and Wadworth 6X.

Former bank in a Gothic-style, Grade II listed building. Over two floors. Food served 12–3.30pm and 5.30–8.30pm Mon–Sat. Function room available for hire.

⊖ Nearest Tube: Holborn.

OPEN *11am–11pm Mon–Sat; closed Sun.*

The King's Arms

11a Northington Street, Bloomsbury WC1N 2JF
☎ *(020) 7405 9107* Kelly Spicer

Greene King IPA, Timothy Taylor Landlord and Adnams Broadside plus one rotating guest.

A one-bar, office workers' pub in a legal and media professional area. Thai cuisine and English food served 12–9.45pm Mon–Fri. Outdoor seating, two large-screen TVs for sports coverage, games room with darts, pool and table football.

⊖ Nearest Tube: Chancery Lane.

OPEN *11am–11pm Mon–Fri; closed Sat–Sun.*

The Lamb

94 Lamb's Conduit Street WC1N 3LZ
☎ *(020) 7405 0713* Suzanne Simpson

Young's PA and Special plus a Wells and Young's seasonal brew and a guest such as Charles Wells Bombardier.

Popular Wells and Young's pub in a Grade II listed building with original features and a snug. Upstairs function room available for hire. Food available 12–9pm. No children. Outside seating to front and rear.

⊖ Nearest Tube: Russell Square/Holborn.

OPEN *11am–midnight Mon–Sat; 12–10.30pm Sun.*

Mabel's Tavern

9 Mabledon Place WC1H 9AZ
☎ *(020) 7387 7739* Tom Milne

Shepherd Neame house with five real ales: Best, Spitfire, Master Brew, Bishop's Finger and a seasonal brew.

Traditional English pub with single bar and two raised areas with fire place. Food served 12–9.30pm Mon–Thurs, 12–8.30pm Fri–Sun. North London CAMRA Pub of the Year 2006.

⊖ Nearest Tube: Euston/King's Cross.

OPEN *11am–11pm Mon–Wed; 11am–midnight Thurs–Sat; 12–10.30pm Sun. 1am licence for pre-booked parties.*

The Museum Tavern

49 Great Russell Street WC1B 3BA
☎ *(020) 7242 8987* Tony Williamson

Up to six beers, including Fuller's London Pride. The others might include Timothy Taylor Landlord, Bateman XXB, Shepherd Neame Bishops Finger and Greene King Old Speckled Hen.

Dating back to 1885 and originally called the Dog and Duck, it changed its name to reflect its location opposite the British Museum. The front and back bars are listed buildings. Food available all day. Outside seating area. No children. Board games.

⊖ Nearest Tube: Holborn/Tottenham Court Road.

OPEN *11am–11pm Mon–Sat; 12–10.30pm Sun and bank holidays.*

The Old Nick

20–2 Sandland Street WC1R 4PZ
☎ *(020) 7430 9503* Megan Robinson

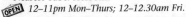 Owned by Hall & Woodhouse, with three real ales available.

Formerly The Three Cups and owned by Young's, changed hands in late 2003 and then expanded into the café next door and underwent refurbishment. One long bar. Food served 12–3pm Mon–Fri. Off Red Lion Street.

⊖ Nearest Tube: Holborn.

OPEN *12–11pm Mon–Thurs; 12–12.30am Fri.*

Pakenham Arms

1 Pakenham Street WC1X 0LA
☎ *(020) 7837 6933* Michael Furey
www.capitalpubcompany.com

 Up to six real ales, which might include Fuller's London Pride, Timothy Taylor Landlord and something from Adnams and Greene King plus two guests from other smaller breweries, changed every few weeks. Two brews from Sharp's on a recent visit.

Large, popular local near Mount Pleasant sorting office with extended opening hours as a result. Breakfast (9.30–11.30am), lunch (11.30am–2pm) and dinner (6–9pm) available on weekdays with food 9am–6pm at weekends. Some brews are sold at reduced prices. Outside seating. All major sports shown.

⊖ Nearest Tube: King's Cross/Russell Square.

OPEN *9am–1am (10.30pm Sun).*

Penderel's Oak

283–8 High Holborn, Holborn WC1V 7PF
☎ *(020) 7242 5669* Robert Douglas

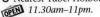 JD Wetherspoon's pub serving up to nine real ales. All the regulars plus several rotating guests.

Two-bar pub on two floors with contrasting atmospheres. Food served all day. Beer festivals held twice a year.

⊖ Nearest Tube: Holborn.

OPEN *9am–1am*

Princess Louise

208–9 High Holborn WC1V 7BW
☎ *(020) 7405 8816*

 A Sam Smith's pub with Old Brewery Bitter (at less than £2 a pint) plus the brewery's range of bottled beers available.

Lacks the real ale range of its freehouse days, but still a central London landmark and most impressively refurbished after closing during 2007. Downstairs and upstairs bars, with real coal fires. Food served, with pies a speciality.

⊖ Nearest Tube: Holborn.

OPEN *11.30am–11pm.*

Rugby Tavern

19 Great James Street WC1N 3ES
☎ *(020) 7405 1384*

 Shepherd Neame tied house serving Master Brew, Spitfire and a seasonal brew.

Popular Victorian street-corner locals' pub with two bars. Outside seating in summer. Upstairs dining/function room available for hire. Food available 12–2.30pm and 5.30–8.30pm Mon–Fri.

⊖ Nearest Tube: Holborn.

OPEN *11am–11pm Mon–Fri; closed weekends.*

Skinners Arms

114 Judd Street WC1H 9NT
☎ *(020) 7837 6521* Anthony Monks

 Greene King IPA and Abbot plus Timothy Taylor Landlord are usually among the three to six beers on offer. Guests are changed every few weeks.

A Victorian one-bar pub tastefully refurbished in traditional style. Outside drinking area. Food served 12–3pm and 5.30–9pm. Close to Camden Town Hall, the whole pub is available for private hire at weekends.

⊖ Nearest Tube: King's Cross.

OPEN *11am–11pm Mon–Sat; 12–10.30pm Sun.*

Swan

7 Cosmo Place WC1N 3AP
☎ *(020) 7837 6223*

 Up to six real ales available, including Greene King IPA and Abbot plus guests.

One-bar pub down a pedestrian alley between Southampton Row and Queen's Square. Outside seating. Food available all day.

⊖ Nearest Tube: Russell Square.

OPEN *11am–11pm Mon–Sat; 12–10.30pm Sun.*

OTHER REAL ALE PUBS IN WC1

Dolphin

47 Tonbridge Street WC1H 9DW
☎ *(020) 7692 7116*

The Plough

27 Museum Street WC1A 1LH
☎ *(020) 7636 7964*

Queen's Larder (GREENE KING)

1 Queen Square WC1N 3AR
☎ *(020) 7837 5627*

WC2

The Crown

43 Monmouth Street WC2H 9DD
☎ *(020) 7836 5861* Mr Brocklebank

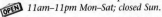 Adnams ale is usually available plus up to four guest ales. Greene King Old Speckled Hen and Marston's Pedigree are regular features.

A traditional, two-bar pub near Seven Dials. Generally quiet, with background music and a mixed clientele. Food available all day. No children.

⊖ Nearest Tube: Leicester Square.

OPEN *11am–11pm Mon–Sat; closed Sun.*

The Edgar Wallace

40 Essex Street WC2R 3JE
☎ *(020) 7353 3120 Shane Feeney*
www.edgarwallacepub.com

Eight real ales, including Edgar's Pale Ale (brewed for the pub by Nethergate) and Adnams Bitter plus around 20 different rotating guests every week. A typical weekly selection might include B&T Shefford, Crouch Vale Brewer's Gold, Elland Beyond the Pale, Prestonpans Gothenberg Porter, Kelburn Goldihops, Mordue Geordie Pride, Downton Forest King, Brakspear Bitter, Oakham JHB, St Austell Tribute and Twickenham Naked Ladies. Regular seasonal beer festivals held – see website for details.

Dating from 1777 in legal territory down a small side street between the river and the Strand. Popular with barristers and solicitors. Upstairs bar available for hire.
✛ Nearest Tube: Temple.
OPEN *11am–11pm Mon–Fri.*

Knights Templar

95 Chancery Lane WC2A 1DT
☎ *(020) 7831 2660*
Gerard Swards, Jan Swards and Graeme Hind

Ten real ales, including Greene King's Abbot, Shepherd Neame Spitfire and eight guest ales, changing on a regular basis.

A large Grand Wetherspoon conversion from bank to pub right in the legal heart of the city. Extensive food menu available all day. Balcony upstairs. Pub available for hire, especially at weekends, just right for a Celebration, Private Function or Wedding celebration. Marriage license granted.
✛ Nearest Tube: Chancery Lane.
OPEN *9am–11.30pm Mon–Fri; 11am–7pm Sat; closed Sun.*

Lamb & Flag

33 Rose Street WC2
☎ *(020) 7497 9504*
Gerard Swords, Jan Swords and Graeme Hind

Charles Wells Eagle IPA and Young's Special, Courage Best and Directors, plus four guests a week, such as Adnams Best, Charles Wells Bombardier, Greene King IPA and Abbot and Wells and Young's seasonal brews.

Oldest pub in Covent Garden, built in the 1630s and once known as the 'Bucket of Blood' for its bare-knuckle fistfights! Food served 11.30am–3pm Mon–Fri and 12–5pm Sat–Sun. No juke box or piped music, no games machines. Free live jazz on Sundays 7.30–10.30pm. Accompanied children welcome at lunchtimes.
✛ Nearest Tube: Leicester Square.
OPEN *10am–11pm Mon–Thurs; 10am–11.30pm Fri–Sat; 12–10.30pm Sun.*

Marquess of Anglesey

39 Bow Street WC2E 7AU
☎ *(020) 7240 3216 Steve Williamson*

Wells and Young's house with Young's Bitter, Special and a seasonal ale such as Waggle Dance or Winter Warmer.

In the heart of Covent Garden, opposite the Royal Opera House. Food available from 12.
✛ Nearest Tube: Covent Garden.
OPEN *11am–11pm.*

The Round House

1 Garrick Street, Covent Garden WC2E 9AR
☎ *(020) 7836 9838 Matt James*
www.thespiritgroup.com

Five real ales, including Theakston Old Peculier, Fuller's London Pride, and three guests rotated every month.

A small, one-bar real ale house in a prominent location with no juke box or machines. Old brass tap on bar and strike plates for matches. Food available 12–9pm. Over 18s only. Background music. Outside smoking area, plus seating with heaters and awnings.
✛ Nearest Tube: Leicester Square.
OPEN *11am–11pm Mon–Thurs; 11am–midnight Fri–Sat; 12–10.30pm Sun.*

The Round Table

26 St Martin's Court WC2N 4AL
☎ *(020) 7836 6436 Gregory Baird*

Charles Wells Bombardier and Fuller's London Pride always on offer plus a guest ale changing every week.

A lively pub with a friendly atmosphere just off Charing Cross Road. Full menu available all day. Children allowed until 7pm. Separate function room available. Comedy on Sunday and Tuesday nights.
✛ Nearest Tube: Leicester Square.
OPEN *11am–11pm Mon–Sat; 12–10.30pm Sun.*

The Seven Stars

53 Carey Street WC2A 2JB
☎ *(020) 7242 8521 Roxy Beaujolais*

Freehouse with real ales such as Adnams Best, Crouch Vale Brewer's Gold, and brews from Harvey's.

Built in 1602 and originally known as The League of Seven Stars after the seven provinces of the Dutch Republic – the Thames was nearer in those days, and Dutch merchant ships moored locally. An unspoilt, one-bar freehouse behind the Royal Courts of Justice. Grade II listed, it was tactfully restored and enhanced when the present licensees took over, and is now winning awards for its cooking, conviviality and style. More recently it was extended into the former secondhand legal wig shop next door, a room still known as The Wig Box. Barristers, reporters and pit musicians from West End theatres are regular customers. A remaining Elizabethan feature is the steep staircase to the lavatories. Food available all day until 9pm. The pub cat, Tom Paine, is no longer tolerant of dogs.
✛ Nearest Tube: Holborn/Temple.
OPEN *11am–11pm Mon–Fri; 12–11pm Sat–Sun.*

Shakespeare's Head

64–8 Kingsway, WC2B 6BG
☎ *(020) 7404 8846* Chris Cole

 Another Wetherspoon's pub in Holborn with up to eight real ales.

A one-bar pub with the usual company policies. Food served all day. Handy location near the top of The Strand.

⊖ Nearest Tube: Holborn/Temple.

OPEN *9am–midnight Sun–Thurs; 9am–1am Fri–Sat.*

Ship & Shovell

1–3 Craven Pasage WC2N 5PH
☎ *(020) 7839 1311* Mac and Louise

 Owned by Hall & Woodhouse, so Badger Gold, Sussex and Tanglefoot always available plus a seasonal brew such as Hopping Hare, Pickled Partridge, River Cottage Stinger and Festive Pheasant.

Two-bar pub, over 300 years old, named after the famous English admiral Sir Cloudesley Shovell. Unique in being on either side of a foot passage. Food served 12–3.30pm Mon–Fri and 12–4pm Sat. Available for private parties. Situated near the famous 'arches' (as in the song!).

⊖ Nearest Tube: Embankment/Charing Cross.

OPEN *11am–11pm Mon–Sat (closed Sun).*

OTHER REAL ALE PUBS IN WC2

The Bloomsbury (SHEPHERD NEAME)
236 Shaftesbury Avenue WC2H 8EG
☎ *(020) 7379 9811*

Cross Keys
31 Endell Street WC2H 9EB
☎ *(020) 7836 5185*

Fine Line (FULLER'S)
77 Kingsway WC2B 6SR ☎ *(020) 7405 5004*

Freemason's Arms (SHEPHERD NEAME)
81–2 Long Acre WC2E 9NG
☎ *(020) 7836 3115*

Harp
47 Chandos Place WC2N 4HS ☎ *(020) 7836 0291*

Hogshead
5 Lisle Street, Leicester Square WC2H 7BF
☎ *(020) 7437 3335*

Hogshead
23 Wellington Street WC2E 7DA
☎ *(020) 7836 6930*

Marquis of Granby
51–2 Chandos Place WC2 ☎ *(020) 7836 7657*

Montagu Pyke (WETHERSPOON)
105–7 Charing Cross WC2H 0BP
☎ *(020) 7287 6039*

The Moon under Water
(WETHERSPOON)
28 Leicester Square WC2H 7LE
☎ *(020) 7839 2837*

Nag's Head (McMULLEN'S)
10 James Street WC2E 8BT
☎ *(020) 7836 4678*

The Salisbury
90 St Martin's Lane WC2N 4AP
☎ *(020) 7836 5863*

LONDON EAST

E1

Black Bull

199 Whitechapel Road E1 1DE
☎ *(020) 7247 6707* Anthony McCann

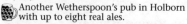 Freehouse but serving Nethergate beers including Suffolk County, Old Growler and seasonal brews. Beers are rotated as soon as they run out.

Busy, popular one-bar East End local dating from 1740, when it was a coaching inn, with a Tudor-style exterior and a mixed clientele. Sandwiches served 12–3pm. Local CAMRA Pub of the Year 2005. Large-screen TV showing sports. Opposite the Royal London Hospital Green, on the corner of Whitechapel Road and Vallence Road.

⊖ Nearest Tube: Whitechapel.

OPEN *11am–11pm.*

Brown Bear

139 Leman Street E1 8EY
☎ *(020) 7481 3792* Rob Porter

Fuller's London Pride, Adnams Bitter and a guest beer, changed every week, from an interesting selection of independent breweries.

Well-run, friendly, traditional one-bar alehouse on the edge of the City. Wooden floors and panelling. English and Thai food served 11am–9pm. Limited outside seating in summer. Private functions can be catered for.

⊖ Nearest Tube: Tower Hill/Aldgate East.

OPEN *11am–11pm Mon–Fri.*

Goodman's Field

87–91 Mansell Street, E1 8AN
☎ *(020) 7680 2850* Ian Taylorson

A relatively recent addition to the JD Wetherspoon stable, serving five well-kept brews from the usual range. Fuller's London Pride, Shepherd Neame Spitfire and Greene King Abbot are usually available, the other two pumps rotate.

Modern, big and bright ground-floor street-corner location on the edge of the City close to the Tower of London. Named after the owner of the land, which was once a field on which cloth was dried. Food served all day until 9pm (breakfasts from 7.30am, steak club 5–10pm Tuesday; curry club all day Thursday).

⊖ Nearest Tube: Tower Hill.

OPEN *7.30am–11pm Mon–Fri; 10am–11pm Sat; 10am–10.30pm Sun.*

Pride of Spitalfields

3 Heneage Street, Spitalfields E1 5LJ
☎ *(020) 7247 8933* Ann Butler

One or two brews from Fuller's, plus seasonals and weekly-changing guests, perhaps including Crouch Vale Best and Hadrian & Border Gladiator.

Friendly, small and comfortable side-street pub just off Brick Lane, attracting a good mixed clientele. Survived serious fire damage in June 2000. Homemade food served at lunchtime. Children welcome. Standing room outside in summer. Turn left out of Aldgate East tube station (Whitechapel Art Gallery end), left again then take the third side street on the left.

⊖ Nearest Tube: Aldgate East.
OPEN *11am–11pm Mon–Sat; 12–10.30pm Sun.*

The Shooting Star

125–9 Middlesex Street E1 7JF
☎ *(020) 7929 6818* Kathryn Rolfe

A Fuller's pub with Chiswick, Discovery, London Pride, ESB and a seasonal brew usually available.

Large street-corner pub close to Petticoat Lane. Cellar bar available for hire. Food available 12–9pm Mon–Fri.

⊖ Nearest Tube: Liverpool Street.
OPEN *11am–11pm Mon–Fri.*

Dispensary
19A Leman Street E1 8EN ☎ *(020) 7702 1406*

The Half Moon (WETHERSPOON)
213–23 Mile End Road, Stepney Green E1 4AA
☎ *(020) 7790 6810*

Mint (FULLER'S)
12 East Smithfield E1 9AP ☎ *(020) 7702 0370*

Cape
Thomas More Square, Nesham Street E1W 1YY
☎ *(020) 7702 9222*

The White Swan (SHEPHERD NEAME)
21–3 Alie Street E1 8DA ☎ *(020) 7702 0448*

E2

The Approach Tavern

47 Approach Road, Bethnal Green E2 9LY
☎ *(020) 8980 2321* Jo Nylander

Freehouse serving Fuller's ESB, Discovery, Chiswick and London Pride plus Adnams Bitter.

A friendly pub with good atmosphere, decorated with photographs. Art gallery upstairs, heated beer garden in front. Food available 12–2.30pm and 6–9.30pm Mon–Fri; 12–9.30pm Sat; 12–4pm Sun. Children and dogs welcome. Seasonal beer festivals held. Close to Museum of Childhood and Victoria Park.

⊖ Nearest Tube: Bethnal Green.
OPEN *12–11pm Sun–Thurs; noon–1am Fri–Sat.*

OTHER REAL ALE PUBS IN E2

The Camden's Head
(WETHERSPOON)
456 Bethnal Green Road, Bethnal Green E2 0EA
☎ *(020) 7613 4263*

The Camel
277 Globe Road, Bethnal Green E2 0JD
☎ *(020) 7739 6654*

E3

The Coborn Arms

8 Coborn Road, Bow E3 2DA
☎ *(020) 8980 3793* Peter and Norma Footman

Bought by Young's in 1984 and later extended, with Young's Bitter and Special always available plus a seasonal or occasional brew.

A large, busy but comfortable and friendly one-bar locals' pub. Two side rooms for games and TV viewing. Homemade food available 12–2pm and 6–9pm Mon–Fri and 1–9pm Sat–Sun. Outside seating. No children. Named after Priscilla Coborn, a local benefactor.

⊖ Nearest Tube: Bow Road/Mile End.
OPEN *11am–11pm Mon–Sat; 12–10.30pm Sun.*

OTHER REAL ALE PUBS IN E3

The Crown
223 Grove Road, Victoria Park E3 5SN
☎ *(020) 8880 7261*

The Eleanor Arms
(SHEPHERD NEAME)
460 Old Ford Road, Bow E3 5JP
☎ *(020) 8981 2263*

The Matchmaker (WETHERSPOON)
580–6 Roman Road, Bow E3 5ES
☎ *(020) 8709 9760*

The Morgan Arms
43 Morgan Street, Bow E3 5AA
☎ *(020) 8980 6389*

Palm Tree
127 Grove Road, Bow E3 5RP
☎ *(020) 8980 2918*

E4

Kings Ford
250–2 Chingford Mount Road, Chingford E4 8JL
☎ *(020) 8523 9365*

Popular Wetherspoon's pub with the chain staples such as Greene King Abbot, Wadworth 6X, Shepherd Neame Spitfire etc, plus three or four guests.

A busy pub not far from Walthamstow Greyhound Stadium beyond the North Circular Road. Food served all day.
OPEN *11am–11pm Mon–Sat; 12–10.30pm Sun.*

OTHER REAL ALE PUBS IN E4

Royal Oak
219 Kings Head Hill, Chingford E4 7PP
☎ *(020) 8529 1492*

E5

The Anchor & Hope

15 High Hill Ferry, Clapton E5 9HG
☎ *(020) 8806 1730* Matthew Withey

Fuller's pub, serving ESB and London Pride plus one guest, changed weekly.

One of Fuller's smallest pubs, a traditional real ale house with one bar, popular with locals, although everyone is welcome. Right on the River Lea footpath, with outside seating looking across to Walthamstow Marshes. Food served 12–5pm. Children and dogs on leads welcome. Ten minutes' walk along the river from Lea Bridge Road.

OPEN *12–11pm (10.30pm Sun).*

OTHER REAL ALE PUBS IN E5

Eclipse

57 Elderfield Road, Clapton E5 0LF
☎ *(020) 8986 1591*

Princess of Wales

(WELLS AND YOUNG'S)

146 Lea Bridge Road, Clapton E5 9QB
☎ *(020) 8533 3463*

E6

Millers Well

419–23 Barking Road, East Ham E6 2JX
☎ *(020) 8471 8404*

Wetherspoon's pub with six regular brews including Greene King Abbot, Wadworth 6X and Shepherd Neame Spitfire plus a couple of guests.

A former wine bar, converted and extended. Food available all day, every day.

⊖ Nearest Tube: Plaistow.

OPEN *11am–11pm Mon–Sat; 12–10.30pm Sun.*

E7

The Hudson Bay

1–5 Upton Lane, Forest Gate E7 9PA
☎ *(020) 8471 7702* Anthony Baptiste

Wetherspoon's outlet with seven real ales. Marston's Pedigree, Courage Best and Directors plus Greene King Abbot are the regulars. The other three rotate.

Modern pub named after the Hudson Bay Company formed by Sir John Henry Pelly, who came from the area. Food served all day from breakfast onwards. Large beer garden, car park, regular beer festivals.

OPEN *9am–midnight (1am Fri–Sat).*

E8

The Dove

24 Broadway Market E8 4QJ
☎ *(020) 7275 7617*

Freehouse with at least six real ales. Young's Special, Timothy Taylor Landlord, Greene King Old Speckled Hen, Archers Golden, Fuller's London Pride and Crouch Vale Brewers Gold could well be among them. Also specialises in Belgian beers.

Popular, good-natured street-corner institution right on the market that has expanded into several adjoining rooms. They take their food almost as seriously as their beers here, available at lunchtime and evenings daily. The unisex toilets are a feature.

OPEN *All day, every day*

Pembury Tavern

90 Amhurst Road, Hackney E8 1JH
☎ *(020) 8986 8597* Stephen Early
www.individualpubs.co.uk/pembury

Semi-tied to Milton Brewery. Ten real ales, four or five guests and the rest from Milton. Milton Sparta and Nero are permanent features.

Almost destroyed by fire in the late 1990s, bought by the Milton Brewery and reopened after a major refurbishment in 2006. A 19th-century building in a prominent East London location and, like the Oakdale Arms in Harringay (owned by the same company), with a reputation for its real ale. One large bar area with high ceiling and wooden floor. Food served 12–3pm and 6–9pm Mon–Sat and 12–9pm Sun (see website for menu, which changes daily). Bar billiards, pool, and lots of board games. Beer festivals held three times a year. Convenient for Hackney Downs and Hackney Central railway stations.

OPEN *12-11.30pm Mon-Thurs; 12-12.30am Fri-Sat; 12-11pm Sun.*

Pub on the Park

19 Martello Street, Hackney E8 3PE
☎ *(020) 7275 9586*

Fuller's Discovery and London Pride, Greene King IPA and Gale's HSB plus rotating guests.

On the edge and overlooking London Fields with an extensive, decked outside terrace area. One open-plan bar. Food served at lunchtimes and evenings.

OPEN *All day, every day.*

OTHER PUBS IN E8

Baxter's Court (WETHERSPOON)

282–4 Mare Street, Hackney E8 1HE
☎ *020 8525 9010*

The Spurstowe Arms

68 Greenwood Road, Hackney E8 1AB
☎ *(020) 7254 4316*

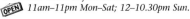

E10
The Drum
557–9 Lea Bridge Road, Leyton E10 7EQ
☎ *(020) 8539 9845* Rebecca Brown
www.jdwetherspoons.com

JD Wetherspoon's pub since 1986, serving four regional ales and six interesting guests from around the country at any one time. Greene King Abbot, Marston's Pedigree, Burton Bitter, and Courage Directors are among the staples.

One of the smaller, older members of the chain, refurbished after a fire. A busy local serving food all day (until 10pm Mon–Sat, 9.30pm Sun). Local CAMRA Pub of the Year 2003 and 2004. One bar. Children welcome until 6pm. Beer garden and regular beer festivals.

⊖ Nearest Tube: Walthamstow Central.
OPEN *10am–11pm (10.30pm Sun).*

King William IV
816 High Road, Leyton E10 6AE
☎ *(020) 8556 2460* Michael Debono

A popular pub with at least five real ales. Fuller's London Pride and ESB always available together with an ever-changing menu of interesting guests sourced from all over the country. Brewing has restarted in the restored Sweet William brewery behind the pub.

A traditional and genuine East London freehouse with two large bars and a beer garden. Authentic Thai menu available 12–10pm Tues–Sat, 12–9.30pm Sun. Children welcome until 7pm. Quiz on Sunday evenings.

⊖ Nearest Tube: Leyton/Walthamstow Central.
OPEN *11am–11pm Mon–Sat; 12–10.30pm Sun.*

E11
The Birkbeck Tavern
45 Langthorne Road, Leytonstone E11 4HL
☎ *(020) 8539 2584* Kathleen Wilson

Freehouse with four real ales, changed every few days, and from various breweries.

A friendly, backstreet community pub in a late Victorian building. Two bars, function room, pool, darts and garden. Rolls only on football days, other snacks available weekdays. Children allowed in the large garden. Local CAMRA award-winner. Music on Saturday nights. Fortnightly quiz.

⊖ Nearest Tube: Leyton.
OPEN *11am–11pm Sun–Thurs; 11am–midnight Fri–Sat.*

The Sir Alfred Hitchcock
147 Whipps Cross Road, Leytonstone E11 1NP
☎ *(020) 8532 9662* Michelle and Jason Flack

Freehouse with three or four real ales, perhaps including Black Sheep Bitter and Fuller's London Pride.

Large, rambling pub opposite Hollow Ponds. Log fires. Refurbished restaurant specialising in steaks, burgers and seafood and serving at lunchtimes (12–3pm Mon–Sat, 1–5pm Sun) and evenings (7–10.30pm Mon–Sat). Quiz nights. Children welcome. Accommodation.

⊖ Nearest Tube: Leytonstone.
OPEN *11am–11pm Mon–Sat; 12–10.30pm Sun.*

OTHER REAL ALE PUBS IN E11
George (WETHERSPOON)
High Street, Wanstead E11 2RL
☎ *(020) 8989 2921*

Nightingale
51 Nightingale Lane, Wanstead E11 2EY
☎ *(020) 8530 4540*

Walnut Tree (WETHERSPOON)
857–61 High Street, Leytonstone E11 1HH
☎ *(020) 8539 2526*

E14
The Grapes
76 Narrow Street, Limehouse E14 8BB
☎ *(020) 7987 4396* Barbara Haigh

Formerly a managed house, now independently owned. Adnams Bitter always available, plus Marston's Pedigree and Timothy Taylor Landlord. The selection may change occasionally.

Established in 1583, rebuilt in 1720, a popular, long, narrow riverside pub with a considerable history and splendid views of the Thames. Bar and restaurant food (especially seafood) available at lunchtime and evenings (not Sun evening). Dogs welcome, children and mobile phones not welcome. No TV or juke box. Small outside decked area.

⊖ Nearest Tube: Limehouse/Westferry DLR.
OPEN *12–3pm and 5.30–11pm Mon–Wed; 12–11pm Thurs–Sat; 12–10.30pm Sun.*

The Oporto Tavern
43 West India Dock Road E14 8EZ
☎ *(020) 8987 1530* Alan Rogers

Wadworth 6X, Greene King IPA and Bass plus one guest rotated monthly.

Set in a Victorian building. One bar, TV, darts, pool and racing club. Hot food, including specials, and baguettes available 12–3pm with roasts on Sun. Children allowed in outside areas.

⊖ Nearest Tube: Westferry DLR.
OPEN *11am–11pm Mon–Sat; 12–10.30pm Sun.*

OTHER REAL ALE PUBS IN E14
Cat & Canary (FULLER'S)
Building FC2, 1–24 Fisherman's Walk, Canary Wharf E14 4DJ ☎ *(020) 7512 9187*

Fine Line (FULLER'S)
10 Cabot Square, Canary Wharf E14 4QB
☎ *(020) 7513 0255*

The George
114 Glengall Grove, Millwall E14 3ND
☎ *(020) 7987 2954*

The Ledger Building
(WETHERSPOON)

4 Hertsmere Road, West India Quay E14 4AL
☎ *(020) 7536 7770*

Queens Head (WELLS AND YOUNG'S)

8 Flamborough Street E14 7LS
☎ *(020) 7791 2504*

E15

The Golden Grove
146–8 The Grove, Stratford E15 1NS
☎ *(020) 8519 0750* Karen Catchpole

Greene King Old Speckled Hen and Shepherd Neame Spitfire among the five brews always available plus three guests such as Hop Back Summer Lightning but changed almost daily.

Large, popular Wetherspoon's pub with one bar, dining area, no music, disabled access and beer garden. Food available all day, 10am–10pm. Children allowed for meals until 6pm. Car park.

⊖ Nearest Tube: Stratford.

OPEN *10am–11pm (10.30pm Sun).*

King Edward VII
47 Broadway, Stratford E15 4BQ
☎ *(020) 8534 2313* Kendall Cordes
www.kingeddie.co.uk

Tied to Enterprise Inns, with four real ales, all rotated every couple of weeks. Regulars include Charles Wells Bombardier, Woodforde's Wherry, Archers IPA and Nethergate Suffolk County.

Original, two-bar traditional London tavern dating from 1812 with lots of wood, gas lamps, beams and mirrors. Courtyard garden and seating at the front. Food served 12–3pm and 5–10pm Mon–Fri; 12–10pm Sat; 12–9pm Sun. Children welcome. Sunday quiz night, live music Thurs. Private function room.

⊖ Nearest Tube: Stratford.

OPEN *12–11pm Mon–Wed; 12–12 Thurs–Sat; 12–11.30pm Sun.*

E17

The Village
31 Orford Road, Walthamstow E17 9NL
☎ *(020) 8521 4398* Richard Donkin

Five real ales, with Fuller's London Pride, Greene King Abbot and Adnams Broadside usually on offer, plus two guests which could come from any independent brewery. Greene King IPA is a favourite.

A residential pub with one bar and a snug area. Large garden. Food available every lunchtime. Children allowed in snug area or the garden until 6pm.

⊖ Nearest Tube: Walthamstow Central.

OPEN *12–11pm (10.30pm Sun).*

OTHER REAL ALE PUBS IN E17

Nag's Head
9 Orford Road, Walthamstow E17 9LP
☎ *(020) 8520 9709*

E18

Hogshead
184 George Lane, South Woodford E18 1AY
☎ *(020) 8989 8542*

LONDON NORTH

N1

The Barnsbury
209–11 Liverpool Road, Islington N1 1LX
☎ *(020) 7607 5519* Jeremy Gough
www.thebarnsbury.co.uk

Freehouse serving three real ales. Timothy Taylor Landlord and Fuller's London Pride plus a monthly-rotating guest.

One-bar gastropub with scrubbed wooden floor and small walled garden. Good food served 12–3pm and 6.30–11pm.

⊖ Nearest Tube: Angel.

OPEN *12–11pm (10.30pm Sun).*

Compton Arms
4 Compton Avenue, Islington N1 2XD
☎ *(020) 7359 6883*
Scott Plomer and Eileen Sheslock

Greene King pub, with three Greene King beers plus a guest rotated every week.

A small, unspoilt local tucked away near Highbury Corner. Courtyard garden for smokers. Food available 12–2.30pm and 6–8.30pm Mon–Fri, 12–4pm Sat–Sun. Beer garden. Sky on big-screen TV for major sports. Quiz night on Sunday.

⊖ Nearest Tube: Highbury and Islington.

OPEN *12–11pm (10.30pm Sun).*

The Crown
116 Cloudesley Road, Islington N1 0EB
☎ *(020) 7837 7107* Katie Lewin

Up to four real ales. Tied to Fuller's, so London Pride, ESB and/or Discovery plus seasonals but also a guest from Hook Norton, Adnams etc.

Street-corner pub off Liverpool Road in a Grade II listed building. Wood panels, comfy sofas, screens around the island bar. Beer garden in front. Good food served 12–3pm and 6–10.30pm Mon–Sat, 12–9.30pm Sun.

⊖ Nearest Tube: Angel.

OPEN *12–11pm (10.30pm Sun).*

Duke of Cambridge
30 St Peter's Street N1 8JT
☎ *(020) 7359 3066* Geetie Singh
www.dukeorganic.co.uk

Freehouse with four real ales, including beers from the Pitfield and St Peter's breweries and a guest, rotating every fortnight.

The first organic pub in the UK, opened in 1998 but built in 1851. Food served 12.30–3pm and 6.30–10.30pm Mon–Fri; 12.30–3.30pm and 6.30–10.30pm Sat; 12.30–3.30pm and 6.30–10pm Sun. Children welcome. No music, no TV, no juke box, no games machines.

⊖ Nearest Tube: Angel.

OPEN *12–11pm (10.30pm Sun).*

Marquess Tavern

32 Canonbury Street, Islington N1 2TB
☎ *(020) 7354 2975*
Will Beckett and Huw Gott
www.themarquesstavern.co.uk

Wells and Young's house with Young's Waggle Dance, Special and Bitter, plus Charles Wells Bombardier and Summer Solstice.

A traditional Victorian pub with horseshoe-shaped bar. Voted Gastropub of the Year 2006 by *Time Out*. Food served 6–10pm Mon–Fri and 12–10pm Sat–Sun. Outdoor tables at front of pub, beautiful dining room at rear. Bar billiards.

⊖ Nearest Tube: Highbury & Islington.
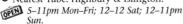 *5–11pm Mon–Fri; 12–12 Sat; 12–11pm Sun.*

The Nobody Inn

92 Mildmay Park, Newington Green N1 4PR
☎ *(020) 7249 6430* Margaret Smyth

Two or three real ales available, with Fuller's London Pride and Black Sheep Bitter among the regulars.

Street-corner pub on the N1/N16 border with one large bar and three distinct sections including a large pool/TV room. Food served 12.30–2.30pm and 6–10pm Mon–Fri; 12–6pm Sat and 12–4pm Sun.

⊖ Nearest Tube: Highbury & Islington.
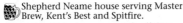 *12–12 Mon–Thurs; noon–1am Fri–Sat; 12–11pm Sun.*

The Prince Arthur

49 Brunswick Place, Charles Square N1 6EB
☎ *(020) 7253 3187* C Dean

Shepherd Neame house serving Master Brew, Kent's Best and Spitfire.

One-bar Victorian corner pub off City Road serving the business community. Sandwiches and pies available 12–4pm. Children welcome. Near Hoxton Square.

⊖ Nearest Tube: Old Street.
 11am–midnight Mon–Fri; 12–6pm Sat–Sun.

The Wenlock Arms

26 Wenlock Road, Hoxton N1 7TA
☎ *(020) 7608 3406*
Steven Barnes and Will Williams
www.wenlock-arms.co.uk

A genuine freehouse with up to eight real ales. Adnams Best and a mild always on offer. The rest of the menu is an ever-changing selection from brewers up and down the country (see the website for details).

A popular street-corner, one-bar pub with a big real ale reputation. Established in 1835 next door to the Wenlock Brewery, which closed in 1962. Sandwiches only available all day until 9pm. Children welcome until 9pm. Live music on Fri and Sat evening and Sun lunchtime. Quiz on Thurs. Function room available. Occasional mini beer festivals. Close to the Regents Canal, off City Road.

⊖ Nearest Tube: Old Street/Angel.
 12–12 (plus optional late licence).

William IV

7 Shepherdess Walk N1 7QE
☎ *(020) 7490 1542* Henry Davis
www.williamthefourth.co.uk

Three real ales. Fuller's London Pride, Black Sheep Bitter and Flowers IPA (brewed by Badger) are likely candidates.

Refurbished pub with an award-winning interior and reputation for good food (12–3pm and 6–10pm Mon–Sat; 12–4pm Sun). Two bars and available for private hire.

⊖ Nearest Tube: Old Street.
 All day, every day.

OTHER REAL ALE PUBS IN N1

The Angel (WETHERSPOON)

3–5 High Street, Islington N1 9LQ
☎ *(020) 7837 2218*

The Baring

55 Baring Street N1 3DS ☎ *(020) 7359 5785*

The Castle

54 Pentonville Road, Islington N1 9HF
☎ *(020) 7713 1858*

Charles Lamb

16 Elia Street, Islington N1 8DE
☎ *(020) 7837 5040*

Drapers Arms

44 Barnsbury Street, Islington N1 1ER
☎ *(020) 7619 0348*

Earl of Radnor (FULLER'S)

106 Mildmay Grove N1 ☎ *(020) 7241 0318*

George & Vulture (FULLER'S)

63 Pitfield Street, Hoxton N1 6BU
☎ *(020) 7253 3988*

Grand Union (GRAND UNION)

153 Upper Street N1 1RA ☎ *(020) 7226 0808*

Hemingford Arms

158 Hemingford Road N1 1DF
☎ *(020) 7607 3303*

Hope & Anchor (GREENE KING)

207 Upper Street N1 ☎ *(020) 7354 1312*

Island Queen

87 Noel Road, Islington N1 8HD
☎ *(020) 7704 7631*

Lord Clyde

340–2 Essex Road N1 3PB ☎ *(020) 7288 9850*

Narrow Boat

119 St Peters Street N1 8PZ ☎ *(020) 7288 0572*

Scolt Head

107a Culford Road N1 4HJ ☎ *(020) 7254 3965*

The Wellington

119 Balls Pond Road N1 4BL
☎ *(020) 7275 7640*

The White Swan (WETHERSPOON)

255–6 Upper Street, Islington N1 1RY
☎ *(020) 7288 9050*

N2

Madden's Ale House

130 High Road, East Finchley N2 7ED
☎ *(020) 8444 7444*

Greene King Abbot, Wadworth 6X, Fuller's London Pride and Adnams Broadside plus up to eight guests (300 per year) including Ridleys Witchfinder Porter, Ringwood Old Thumper and Fortyniner. Also country wines.

A converted shop on the High Road. Bar food available at lunchtime. Children allowed.

✪ Nearest Tube: East Finchley.
OPEN *11am–11pm Mon–Fri; 12–10.30pm Sun.*

OTHER REAL ALE PUBS IN N2

Old White Lion

121 Great North Road, East Finchley N2 0NW
☎ *(020) 8365 4861*

N4

The Oakdale Arms

283 Hermitage Road, Harringay N4 1NP
☎ *(020) 8800 2013* Stephen Early
www.individualpubs.co.uk/oakdale

Six real ales, usually four from Milton and two guests. Milton Sparta and Dionysus are fixtures, and the others are changed when the cask runs out. Milton Nero is an occasional stout.

Built as an off-licence around 1930, this two-bar pub was named CAMRA North London Pub of the Year 2005. The public bar has a pool table and dart board. Beer garden. No food.

✪ Nearest Tube: Seven Sisters/Manor House.
OPEN *12–11pm (10.30pm Sun).*

The Salisbury

1 Grand Parade, Green Lanes N4 1JX
☎ *(020) 8800 9617* David Lewis

Fuller's London Pride, ESB and Discovery plus one guest rotated every month.

Built in 1898, a magnificent and imposing listed, late-Victorian gin palace restored by the Remarkable Restaurants company. Spectacular wrought-iron entrance leads into three large and impressive bars. Food served 6–10pm Mon–Fri, 12–10pm Sat and 12–6pm Sun. Private room for hire. Children welcome. Live bands and DJ at weekends, quiz on Monday.

✪ Nearest Tube: Turnpike Lane/Manor House.
OPEN *5pm–12 Mon–Wed; 5pm–1am Thurs; 5pm–2am Fri; noon–2am Sat; 12–11.30pm Sun.*

OTHER REAL ALE PUBS IN N4

The White Lion of Mortimer

(WETHERSPOON)

125–7 Stroud Green Road, Stroud Green N4 3PX
☎ *(020) 7561 8880*

N6

The Flask

77 Highgate West Hill N6 6BU
☎ *(020) 8348 7346* Andrew Cooper

Adnams Broadside, Timothy Taylor Landlord, Hop Back Summer Lightning and Fuller's Chiswick plus a couple of guests. Owned by Mitchells & Butlers.

Popular, former coaching inn in the heart of Highgate village. Built in 1663, still with many original features. Large paved outside seating area and a new garden bar with barbecue. Food available 12–3pm and 6–10pm (all day on summer weekends). Children and dogs welcome. Beer festival in May.

✪ Nearest Tube: Highgate.
OPEN *12–11pm (10.30pm Sun).*

OTHER REAL ALE PUBS IN N6

The Gatehouse (WETHERSPOON)

1 North Road, Highgate N6 4BD
☎ *(020) 8340 8054*

Wrestlers

98 North Road, Highgate N6 4AA
☎ *(020) 8340 4297*

N7

The Coronet

338–46 Holloway Road, Holloway N7 6NJ
☎ *(020) 7609 5014* David Leach

JD Wetherspoon's house with up to ten real ales. Regulars include Greene King Abbot, Courage Directors, Marston's Pedigree and Theakston Best plus guests rotated every few days.

Converted cinema with lots of cinema memorabilia. Food served all day from 10am. Disabled access, patio area, no music. Children allowed if eating in family area until 9pm. Close to Arsenal's new stadium.

✪ Nearest Tube: Holloway Road.
OPEN *9am–11.30pm.*

OTHER REAL ALE PUBS IN N7

The Duchess of Kent

441 Liverpool Road N7 8PR
☎ *(020) 7609 7104*

N8

The Three Compasses

62 High Street, Hornsey N8 7NX
☎ *(020) 8340 2729*
Alison and Nigel Oxford and Mike Smith

Leased pub offering six real ales, perhaps including Timothy Taylor Landlord, Caledonian Deuchars IPA and Fuller's London Pride, plus three guests often from smaller independent breweries rotated every few days.

Refurbished and revitalised in 2004 and already winning awards. A Victorian pub with original features. Food served all day until an hour before closing. Children over 14 allowed. Quiz nights (Mon), games nights, live music, special events. Private room available for hire.

OPEN *11am–11pm Mon–Thurs; 11am–midnight Fri–Sat; 12–11pm Sun.*

The Toll Gate
26–30 Turnpike Lane N8 0PS
☎ *(020) 8889 9085* John Wootton

Wetherspoon's pub with 11 real ales, including Greene King Abbot, Shepherd Neame Spitfire, Courage Directors, Marston's Pedigree and Ridleys Old Bob plus guests rotated every few days.

In business since 1988, so an early member of the chain. Traditional décor, diverse clientele. One horseshoe bar. Food available 10am–10pm. Beer garden, two annual beer festivals, children welcome.

⊖ Nearest Tube: Turnpike Lane.

OPEN *10am–11pm Mon–Sat (10.30pm Sun).*

OTHER REAL ALE PUBS IN N8
Harringay Arms
153 Crouch Hill, Crouch End N8 9HX
☎ *(020) 8340 4243*

Queen's Hotel (WELLS AND YOUNG'S)
26 Broadway Parade, Crouch End N8 9DE
☎ *(020) 8340 2031*

Three Compasses
62 High Street, Hornsey N8 7NX
☎ *(020) 8340 2729*

N9
The Lamb Inn
52–4 Church Street, Lower Edmonton N9 9PA
☎ *(020) 8887 0128*
Michael Knight and Jay Zinzan (managers)
www.myspace.com/thelambpub

Freehouse with five ales. Charles Wells Bombardier, Adnams Broadside and Courage Best are permanent, and the others rotate every six to twelve weeks.

A modern, community pub with one large bar, dining area and disabled access. All live sport shown. Weekly quiz night. Hot food available 12–9pm, including roast on Sunday. No children.

OPEN *11am–11pm Mon–Thurs; 11am–midnight Fri–Sat; 12–11pm Sun.*

OTHER REAL ALE PUBS IN N9
Beehive
24 Little Bury Street, Edmonton N9 9JZ
☎ *(020) 8360 4358*

N10
Maid of Muswell
121 Alexandra Park Road, N10 2DP
☎ *(020) 8365 4851*

N12
Elephant Inn
283 Ballards Lane, Finchley N12 8NR
☎ *(020) 8343 6110* Lucy Burch

Fuller's house with London Pride, ESB, Discovery and a guest ale available.

Charming three-bar pub with lounge, sports room with big-screen TV and public bar. Courtyard garden. Private parties catered for, children welcome until 7pm. Food available (Thai menu available) 12–10pm daily. Just before Tally Ho Corner.

OPEN *11am–11pm Mon–Thurs; 11am–midnight Fri–Sat; 12–10.30pm Sun.*

OTHER REAL ALE PUBS IN N12
The Tally Ho (WETHERSPOON)
749 High Road, North Finchley N12 0BP
☎ *(020) 8445 4390*

N13
The Whole Hog
430–4 Green Lanes, Palmers Green N13 5XG
☎ *(020) 8882 3597* Rebecca Smith

Formerly a Wetherspoon's pub, now privately owned. Regular ales include Greene King IPA and Courage Directors, plus guests from Red Squirrel, Dark Star and Crouch Vale.

A traditional pub with two bars on split levels. Landlady won local CAMRA Pub of the Year awards while at The Drum in Leyton. Beer festivals, 'meet the brewer' nights, quiz night Thursday. Food served from 12–10pm Mon–Sat (9.30pm Sun). No children.

OPEN *10am–11pm Mon–Sat; 12–10.30pm Sun.*

OTHER REAL ALE PUBS IN N13
Alfred Herring (WETHERSPOON)
316–22 Green Lanes N13 5TT
☎ *(020) 8447 8261*

N14
The New Crown (WETHERSPOON)
80–4 Chase Side, Southgate N14 5PH
☎ *(020) 8882 8758*

N16
The Rochester Castle
145 Stoke Newington High Street, Stoke Newington N16 0YN
☎ *(020) 7249 6016* Jenny Kittermark

Greene King Abbot, Shepherd Neame Spitfire and Fuller's London Pride among the beers plus seven guests selected from the extended Wetherspoon's range. Something changes every day.

A huge Wetherspoon's pub (among the oldest in the chain) with one big bar, patio, disabled access and facilities. No music. Dining area in rear conservatory. Food available all day (breakfasts from 10am). Children welcome for meals. Beer garden. Two beer festivals each year.

OPEN *All day, every day.*

The Rose & Crown

199 Stoke Newington Church Street N16 9ES
☎ *(020) 7254 7497* M Hill

Independently run but tied to Scottish Courage, with three real ales available. Adnams Bitter and Marston's Pedigree are permanent fixtures plus a guest changed every few days.

Traditional street-corner pub built in 1806. Real fires. Food served 12–2.30pm Mon–Fri and 12–3.30pm Sat–Sun. Children allowed until 7pm. Tuesday is quiz night. Four guest rooms. Opposite Clissold Park, on the 73, 476 and 393 bus routes.

OPEN *11.30am–midnight.*

OTHER REAL ALE PUBS IN N16

The Birdcage
58 Stamford Hill, N16 6XS ☎ *(020) 8806 6740*

The Daniel Defoe
(WELLS AND YOUNG'S)
102 Stoke Newington Church Street N16
☎ *(020) 7254 2906*

The Londesborough
36 Barbauld Road N16 0SS ☎ *(020) 7254 5865*

The Prince
59 Kynaston Rd N16 0EB ☎ *(020) 7923 4766*

The Shakespeare
57 Allen Rd N16 8RY ☎ *(020) 7254 4190*

The Three Crowns
175 Stoke Newington High Street N16 0LH
☎ *(020) 7275 8659*

N17

The New Moon
413 Lordship Lane, Tottenham N17 6AG
☎ *(020) 8801 3496* Tom Connelly

Freehouse with Wyre Piddle Piddle in the Wind plus three guests stocked to customer order. Tick list with monthly winners. Badger Tanglefoot is popular.

A large town pub with three bars, dining area, patio, disabled access and facilities. Food available at lunchtimes and evenings. Children allowed.

OPEN *All day, every day.*

N18

The Gilpin's Bell (WETHERSPOON)
50–4 Fore Street, Upper Edmonton N18 2SS
☎ *(020) 8884 2744*

N19

North Nineteen
194–6 Sussex Way, Archway N19 4HZ
☎ *(020) 7281 2786*

N21

The Orange Tree

18 Highfield Road, Winchmore Hill N21 3HD
☎ *(020) 8360 4853* John Maher

Greene King IPA and Abbot, Ruddles Best and County plus a guest.

Comfortable, traditional one-bar house with pub games and beer garden. Regular CAMRA award winner. Food served 12–2.30pm (3.30pm on Sun). Children welcome in beer garden. Plenty of parking nearby. Located off Green Lanes, enter through Carpenter Gardens.

OPEN *12–11pm (10.30pm Sun).*

OTHER REAL ALE PUBS IN N21

Dog and Duck
74 Hoppers Road, Winchmore Hill N21 3LH
☎ *(020) 8886 1987*

The King's Head
1 The Green, Winchmore Hill N21 1BB
☎ *(020) 8886 1988*

N22

The Phoenix Bar

Alexandra Palace, Wood Green N22 7AY
☎ *(020) 8365 4356* Prasanna Jayawardena
www.alexandrapalace.com

Freehouse with Fuller's London Pride and two rotating guests.

Well worth the trip for the view alone. At the main entrance of Alexandra Palace, built in 1873 on top of a hill and looking down over Central London. Indoor and outdoor beer gardens. Food available. Children welcome.

OPEN *10.30am–11pm.*

OTHER REAL ALE PUBS IN N22

Wetherspoon's
5 Spouters Corner, High Road, Wood Green
N22 6EJ ☎ *(020) 8881 3891*

LONDON NORTH WEST

NW1

The Albert

11 Princess Road, Primrose Hill NW1 8JR
☎ *(020) 7722 1886* Christie Graham

Greene King IPA and Charles Wells Bombardier and a guest ale.

Victorian pub with modern appeal. One bar, garden, conservatory, outside seating at front. Close to the canal. Food served 12–2.30pm and 6–10pm Mon–Fri, all day Sat–Sun. Dogs and children welcome. Near London Zoo.

⊖ Nearest Tube: Camden Town/Chalk Farm.
OPEN *11am–11pm Mon–Sat; 12–10.30pm Sun.*

The Betjeman Arms

St Pancras International Station NW1 2QP
☎ *(020) 7923 5440*

Adnams Bitter, Fuller's London Pride and Sharp's Betjeman Bitter available.

Impressive gastropub run by Geronimo Inns within the station complex. Watch the Eurostar trains from the outside terrace. One bar and two dining rooms. Food served all day, including breakfast and daily specials.
 Nearest Tube: King's Cross.
OPEN *10am–11pm.*

Bree Louise
69 Coburg Street, NW1 2HH
☎ *(020) 7267 8240* Craig Douglas

 Freehouse serving up to ten real ales, five of them on hand pump and five straight from the cask. The selection changes daily, but Timothy Taylor Landlord and something from Sharp's and Adnams are usually available. Plus more than 100 bottled beers.

Formerly known as The Jolly Gardners, a one-room, street-corner, refurbished alehouse close to Euston station. Big-screen TV and outside seating. Food served 11.30am–3pm and 5.30–10.30pm. The pies are a speciality. Discounts for card-carrying CAMRA members.
 Nearest tube: Euston/Euston Square
OPEN *11am–11pm.*

The Doric Arch
1 Eversholt Street, Euston NW1 1DN
☎ *(020) 7383 3359* James Lunt

Up to nine real ales, including at least two Fuller's brews. The rest come from a wide range of independents and micros. Westons Vintage and Old Rosie also served.

Congenial upstairs bar with polished wood floors, featuring regular exhibitions of railway paintings. Large screens, Sky TV. Food served 12–3pm and 4–8.30pm Mon–Fri, 12–5pm Sat–Sun. Children's certificate until 9pm. In front of the bus station outside the mainline railway station.
 Nearest Tube: Euston.
OPEN *11am–11pm Mon–Sat; 12–10.30pm Sun.*

The Engineer
65 Gloucester Avenue, Primrose Hill NW1 8JH
☎ *(020) 7722 0950* Karen Northcote
www.the-engineer.com

Charles Wells Bombardier and Hook Norton Best plus one guest, changed every six months.

One of London's original gastropubs, situated in trendy Primrose Hill. Intimate bar area and separate dining facilities on ground floor, plus two large dining rooms upstairs (available for private hire). Courtyard garden at rear. Food served 9am–11.30am, 12–3pm and 7–10.30pm Mon–Sat; 9am–noon, 12.30–4pm and 7–10.30pm Sun. Children welcome. Situated between Camden Town, Regents Park and Primrose Hill.
 Nearest Tube: Chalk Farm/Camden Town.
OPEN *9am–11pm (10.30pm Sun).*

The Euston Flyer
83–7 Euston Road NW1 2RA
☎ *(020) 7383 0856* Stephen Finch

Tied to Fuller's, so with the full brewery range plus up to five guests from brewers such as Dark Star and Cottage.

Large, traditional pub opposite the British Library. Food served all day (12–9pm). Large TV screens, occasional beer festivals, areas available for private hire.
 Nearest Tube: King's Cross.
OPEN *11am–midnight.*

The Lansdowne
90 Gloucester Avenue, Primrose Hill NW1
☎ *(020) 7483 0409* Amanda Pritchett

Owned by Mitchells & Butlers with up to four real ales, perhaps including Caledonian Deuchars IPA and Everards Tiger.

Another original gastropub. Good restaurant serving food 12.30–3pm and 7–10pm plus bar food and pizzas in the afternoon (12.30–7pm). Outside seating in summer. Children welcome.
 Nearest Tube: Chalk Farm.
OPEN *5–11.30pm Mon; 12–11.30pm Tues–Sat; 12–11pm Sun.*

The Metropolitan Bar
7 Station Approach, Marylebone Road NW1 5LA
☎ *(020) 7486 3489* Colin Pawson

Wetherspoon's pub with Charles Wells Bombardier, Ringwood Fortyniner, Greene King Abbot and Marston's Pedigree among the brews usually available. Plus four guests from a wide range of independents.

Large open design. A one-bar pub above Baker Street tube station. Food served all day. Beer festivals held twice a year.
 Nearest Tube: Baker Street.
OPEN *9am–11pm Mon–Sat; 10am–10.30pm Sun.*

Spread Eagle
141 Albert Street, Camden NW1 7NB
☎ *(020) 7267 1410* Amanda Lowis

Wells and Young's house serving Young's Bitter and Special and Charles Wells Bombardier plus a seasonal guest.

Traditional, Victorian pub that claims to be Camden's best local. Varied menu served 12–9pm every day. Outside seating. Families welcome. Handy for Regents Park, London Zoo and Camden Market. Two minutes' walk up Parkway from tube station – the pub is on the left.
 Nearest Tube: Camden Town.
OPEN *11am–11pm Mon–Thurs; 11am–midnight Fri–Sat; 12–10.30pm Sun.*

Square Tavern
26 Tolmers Square NW1 2PE
☎ *(020) 7388 6010* Davis Simmonds
www.youngs.com

Wells and Young's house with Young's Bitter and Special plus a guest such as Charles Wells Bombardier, changed every couple of months.

One main bar, with large outside seating area. Adjoining wine bar is available for private functions. Homemade traditional food served 12–8.30pm Mon–Fri. Away from the traffic just off Hampstead Road.
 Nearest Tube: Euston Square/Warren Street.
OPEN *11am–11pm Mon–Fri.*

Devonshire Arms (WYCHWOOD)
33 Kentish Town Road NW1 8NL
☎ *(020) 7284 0562*

The Man in the Moon
(WETHERSPOON)
40–2 Chalk Farm Road, Camden NW1 8BG
☎ *(020) 7482 2054*

Princess of Wales
22 Chalcot Road, Primrose Hill NW1 8LL
☎ *(020) 7722 0354*

Queens (WELLS AND YOUNG'S)
9 Regents Park Road, Primrose Hill NW1 8XD
☎ *(020) 7586 9498*

Quinns
65 Kentish Town Road NW1 8NY
☎ *(020) 7267 8240*

NW2

The Beaten Docket
55–6 Cricklewood Broadway, Cricklewood NW2 3DT
☎ *(020) 8450 2972* John Hand

Shepherd Neame Spitfire and Greene King Abbot plus at least two constantly changing guests from the Wetherspoon's range.

A two-bar Wetherspoon's pub on the A5 (Edgware Road) as it passes through Cricklewood with dining area and patio. Music, but no games. Food available all day. No children.

⊖ Nearest Tube: Kilburn Park.

OPEN *All day, every day.*

NW3

The Duke of Hamilton
23 New End, Hampstead NW3
☎ *(020) 7794 0258* Mary Wooderson

Freehouse serving Fuller's brews plus guests and real cider.

Close to the New End Theatre, a 200-year-old pub that has won several local CAMRA awards thanks to the quality of its beer. Snacks only. Outside seating. Children allowed.

⊖ Nearest Tube: Hampstead.

OPEN *12–11pm (10.30pm Sun).*

The Hollybush
22 Holly Mount, Hampstead NW3 6SG
☎ *(020) 7435 2892* Robert Tudgey
www.hollybushpub.com

Tied to Punch Taverns, with Harvey's Best, Adnams Bitter and Broadside and Fuller's London Pride available plus a guest rotated once or twice a week.

Charming, wood-panelled local, close to Hampstead Heath. Private room, dining room. Food available 12–11pm Mon–Sat and 12–10.30pm Sun.

⊖ Nearest Tube: Hampstead.

OPEN *12–11pm (10.30pm Sun and bank holidays).*

The Horseshoe
28 Heath Street, Hampstead NW3 6TE
☎ *(020) 7431 7206* Jasper Cuppaidge

One or two McLaughlin's home brews plus guests from breweries such as Sharp's, Hogs Back and Adnams.

Former Wetherspoon's taken over in 2006 and now with its own micro-brewery. Already winning awards and with an emphasis on good food in the split-level dining area which is served 12.30–3.30pm (12–4.30pm Sun) and 6.30–10pm (6.30–9.30pm Sun).

⊖ Nearest Tube: Hampstead.

OPEN *10am–11pm (10.30pm Sun).*

The Magdala
2A South Hill Park, Hampstead NW3 2SB
☎ *(020) 7435 2503* Christiane Baehr

Greene King IPA and Fuller's London Pride always available. Rotating seasonal guest ale always on offer.

Victorian café, bar and restaurant famed for being the place where Ruth Ellis shot her lover. Two bars, one a traditional oak-panelled pub lounge, the other a lighter café-style bar. Food served 12–2.30pm and 6–10pm Mon–Fri, 12–10pm Sat, 12–9.30pm Sun. Small beer garden. Private restaurant/function room. Family- and dog-friendly. Right on Hampstead Heath.

⊖ Nearest Tube: Hampstead/Belsize Park.

OPEN *11am–11pm Mon–Thurs; 11am–midnight Fri–Sat; 12–10.30pm Sun.*

Ye Olde White Bear
Well Road, Hampstead NW3 1LJ
☎ *(020) 7435 3758* Chris Ely

Up to six real ales, all rotating, from all over the UK. Examples include Sharp's Doom Bar, Titanic White Star and beers from Otter, Exmoor, Brains, Jekylls, Highgate, Wood and St Austell.

Comfortable, friendly, traditional pub built in 1704 and well maintained. Cosy and dark in winter, outside drinking area in summer. Food served 12–9pm.

⊖ Nearest Tube: Hampstead.

OPEN *11am–11pm Mon–Sat; 12–10.30pm Sun.*

The Spaniards Inn
Spaniards Road, Hampstead NW3 7JJ
☎ *(020) 8731 6571* David Nichol

Five real ales, often including Adnams Bitter, Marston's Old Empire, Fuller's London Pride and Harveys Best plus two seasonal guests changed monthly.

Built in 1585, this inn is mentioned in Dickens' *Pickwick Papers*, and claims to be the highest in London. Large beer garden with outside bar. Food served 11am–10pm Mon–Fri and 10am–10pm Sat–Sun. Real fires, private rooms. Quarterly beer festivals, including Spaniards Festival over Easter. Children and dogs are welcome, and there is an automatic dog wash! Car park. Directly opposite Hampstead Heath, on the 210 bus from Golders Green.

OPEN *11am–11pm Mon–Fri; 10am–11pm Sat–Sun.*

OTHER REAL ALE PUBS IN NW3

Flask (WELLS AND YOUNG'S)
14 Flask Walk, Hampstead NW3 1HE
☎ (020) 7435 4580

Wetherspoon's (WETHERSPOON)
O2 Centre, 255 Finchley Road NW3 6LU
☎ (020) 7433 0920

NW4

Greyhound (WELLS AND YOUNG'S)
Church End NW4 4JT ☎ (020) 8457 9730

NW5

The Bull & Last
168 Highgate, Kentish Town NW5 1QS
☎ (020) 7267 3641 Amanda Rimmer

Greene King IPA and Fuller's London Pride always available.

One-bar former coaching inn built in 1863, now a gastropub. Good food served 12–3pm and 6.30–10pm Mon–Fri, 12–10pm Sat–Sun. Upstairs dining room available for functions. Close to Hampstead Heath.

⊖ Nearest Tube: Kentish Town.

11am–11pm Mon–Sat; 12–10.30pm Sun.

The Junction Tavern
101 Fortess Road, Kentish Town NW5 1AG
☎ (020) 7485 9400
Jacky Kitching and Chris Leech
www.junctiontavern.co.uk

Caledonian Deuchars IPA plus guest ales, with more than a dozen rotated every week and sourced from independent brewers.

Longstanding institution on a busy street corner. Food served 12–3pm (4pm Sat and Sun) and 6.30–10.30pm (9.30pm Sun). Dining room, conservatory and garden. Regular beer festivals. There is a discount for card-carrying CAMRA members on the first Monday of every month.

⊖ Nearest Tube: Kentish Town.

12–11pm (10.30pm Sun).

The Pineapple
51 Leverton Street, Kentish Town NW5 2NX
☎ (020) 7284 4631 Francis and Chloe Powell

Freehouse serving Fuller's London Pride, Marston's Pedigree plus a rotating guest, which might be Adnams Bitter or Explorer.

Victorian freehouse in a listed building saved from a property developer by its regulars. Food served 12–2.30pm in the bar downstairs and in the dining room 7–10pm (Tues–Sat). Beer garden, conservatory.

⊖ Nearest Tube: Kentish Town.

12–11pm (10.30pm Sun).

OTHER REAL ALE PUBS IN NW5

Dartmouth Arms
35 York Rise, Dartmouth Park NW5 1SP
☎ (020) 7485 3267

The Lord Palmerston
33 Dartmouth Park Hill NW5 1HU
☎ (020) 7485 1578

Oxford
256 Kentish Town Road NW5 2AA
☎ (020) 7485 3521

NW6

Queens Arms (WELLS AND YOUNG'S)
1 Kilburn High Road, Kilburn NW6 4SE
☎ (020) 7624 5735

NW8

The Clifton Hotel
96 Clifton Hill, St John's Wood NW8 0JT
☎ (020) 7372 3427
www.capitalpubcompany2.com

Freehouse (part of a small independent chain) with four beers, all rotating seasonally. Examples include Sharp's Doom Bar and Cornish Coaster, Adnams Broadside and Explorer, and Hogs Back TEA.

Traditional pub in a converted house in St John's Wood. Fresh-cooked menu 12–3pm and 6–9.30pm Mon–Sat; 12–4pm and 6.30–9pm Sun (roasts). Dogs welcome. Children allowed until 7pm, later if they are eating. Situated off Abbey Road, close to Lord's cricket ground.

⊖ Nearest Tube: St John's Wood.

12–11pm (10.30pm Sun).

NW9

JJ Moons (WETHERSPOON)
553 Kingsbury Road, Kingsbury NW9 9EL
☎ (020) 8204 9675

The Moon Under Water (WETHERSPOON)
10 Varley Parade, Colindale NW9 6RR
☎ (020) 8200 7611

NW10

Grand Junction Arms (WELLS AND YOUNG'S)
Canal Bridge, Acton Lane, Willesden NW10 7AD ☎ (020) 8965 5670

The Misty Moon (WETHERSPOON)
25–6 Manor Park Road, Harlesden NW10 4JE
☎ (020) 8961 6570

The Outside Inn (WETHERSPOON)
312–14 Neasden Lane, Neasden NW10 0AD
☎ (020) 8452 3140

William IV
786 Harrow Road, Kensal Green NW10
☎ (020) 8969 5944

FURTHER NORTH AND NORTH WEST

HARROW

The Castle
30 West Street, Harrow HA1 3EF
☎ *(020) 8422 3155* Helena Ackroyd

 Fuller's house with London Pride and ESB permanently on offer, plus the seasonal Fuller's ale.

Quiet pub with no music or pool. Central bar and beer garden. Food served 12–9pm Mon–Sat and lunchtime roasts on Sundays. Children and dogs welcome. Follow signs to Harrow School and Harrow on the Hill, West Street is located next to Harrow School Outfitters shop.

OPEN *11am–11pm Mon–Sat; 12–10.30pm Sun.*

The Moon on the Hill
373–5 Station Road, Harrow HA1 2AW
☎ *(020) 8863 3670* Trevor Briggs

 JD Wetherspoon's pub with up to six ales, Greene King Abbot, Courage Best and Marston's Pedigree plus three guests, changed daily.

A friendly town-centre pub, with a trendy yet traditional atmosphere, forming part of the weekend pub circuit. Food available every day 9am–10pm, with grill night on Tuesday, curry club on Thursday, and Sunday lunches. Ale and wine club on Wednesday. Children allowed, if eating, until 9pm. Situated in the town's shopping district, two minutes from the bus and train stations.

OPEN *9am–midnight Sun–Thurs; 9am–12.30am Fri–Sat.*

PINNER

The Village Inn
402–8 Rayners Lane, Pinner HA5 5DY
☎ *(020) 8868 8551* Avi Collins

 Greene King Abbot, Courage Best and Marston's Pedigree, plus four guests changed every day or two.

Small community pub with a traditional atmosphere, where customers choose the beers, and where charity events are often held. Food served 9am–11pm every day. Children welcome. Heated beer garden at the back and outside seating at the front. Car park. To find, turn left at the station.

OPEN *9am–midnight Mon–Thurs; 9am–12.30am Fri–Sat; 9am–11pm Sun.*

STANMORE

The Malthouse
7 Stanmore Hill, Stanmore HA7 3DP
☎ *(020) 8420 7265* Benny Lazar

Freehouse serving a range of up to four constantly changing real ales. Favourites include Timothy Taylor Landlord, Fuller's London Pride and Wadworth 6X.

A modern pub decorated in an old style with character and atmosphere. Late licence. Live music Thurs–Sun. Garden, disabled access. Food available at lunchtimes

plus pizzas in the evenings. Children allowed. Theme nights.

OPEN *11am–11pm Mon–Tues; 11am–midnight Wed–Thurs; 11am–1am Fri–Sat; 12–12 Sun.*

LONDON SOUTH EAST

SE1

The Bridge House
218 Tower Bridge Road SE1 2UP
☎ *(020) 7407 5818*
Steve McGinn and Wayne Seddon

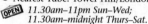 Adnams tied house, with Best, Broadside and Explorer on offer, plus a guest rotated weekly.

The closest bar to Tower Bridge, 100 years old and spread over three floors. Dining room, function rooms for hire. Freshly prepared food served 11.30am–10.30pm daily. As well as Tower Bridge, the pub is handy for the Tower of London, London Dungeons, HMS Belfast, the GLA building and the Design Museum.

↔ Nearest Tube: Tower Hill/London Bridge.

OPEN *11.30am–11pm Sun–Wed; 11.30am–midnight Thurs–Sat.*

Bunch of Grapes
2 St Thomas Street, Borough SE1 9RS
☎ *(020) 7403 2070* Rod Lindley

Wells and Young's house serving Young's Bitter and Special and Charles Wells Bombardier plus a seasonal ale.

A very busy traditional pub close to Guy's Hospital and Borough Market, dating from the 1850s. Popular with tourists, city commuters and market traders. Beer garden, heated outside courtyard. Open log fire. Food served 9am–9pm Mon–Fri, 9am–8pm Sat and 12–8pm Sun (roasts on Sundays).

↔ Nearest Tube: London Bridge.

OPEN *9am–midnight Mon–Sat; 12–11pm Sun.*

The Charles Dickens
160 Union Street SE1 0LH
☎ *(020) 7401 3744* Andrew Keeshan
www.thecharlesdickens.co.uk

Freehouse serving up to six real ales, including Adnams Best and guests, changed daily, such as Nethergate Umbel Ale and beers from Harveys and Hogs Back, Nethergate, Mighty Oak and a host of micro-brewers.

Comfortable, traditional pub in a Victorian building, with bar and open-plan kitchen. Food served at 12–3pm and 6–9pm, plus Sunday lunch 12–6pm. Beer garden and patio.

↔ Nearest Tube: Southwark.

OPEN *12–11pm Mon–Fri; 12–6pm Sat–Sun.*

The Fire Station Bar & Restaurant

150 Waterloo Road SE1 8SB
☎ *(020) 7620 2226* Tom Alabaster

 Marston's pub with a mixture of permanent and guest beers, changed regularly, with beers from Marston's and Fuller's regularly served.

Popular conversion of a huge fire station beside Waterloo station, with busy bar and semi-formal dining room. Fresh food and daily specials served 11am–11pm Mon–Sat and 12–9.30pm Sun. Children allowed until 9pm. Close to the Old Vic Theatre. Next to the Jubilee line exit of Waterloo Station.

Θ Nearest Tube: Waterloo.

 *11am–midnight (10.30pm Sun).*

Founders Arms

52 Hopton Street, Blackfriars SE1 9JH
☎ *(020) 7928 1899* Paul Raynor
www.foundersarms.co.uk

 Young's managed house, with Young's Bitter, Special and either Waggle Dance or Winter Warmer available, plus Charles Wells Bombardier.

Contemporary riverside pub featuring large outside dining and drinking area with amazing views of the city and river. Food served 10am–10pm Mon–Fri; 9am–10pm Sat–Sun. Children welcome. Next to Tate Modern and the Globe Theatre at the southern end of the Millennium Bridge.

Θ Nearest Tube: Southwark/Blackfriars.

 *10am–11pm Mon–Thurs; 10am–midnight Fri; 9am–midnight Sat; 9am–11pm Sun.*

The George Inn

77 Borough High Street, Borough SE1 1NH
☎ *(020) 7407 2056* Scott Masterson

 Greene King Abbot, IPA and Old Speckled Hen plus a house brew (brewed by Greene King) among the beers always available, plus at least one guest (often seasonal).

Famous galleried 17th-century pub, now owned by the National Trust, on a site where a pub has stood for considerably longer. Some say it is older then The Tabard, another famous Southwark pub built in 1307 and demolished in 1875. Four interconnecting bars open onto a large courtyard. Upstairs restaurant and function rooms available for hire. Food available 12–5pm every day and 6–9pm Mon–Sat, and in the restaurant 5–10pm Mon–Sat. Children allowed.

Θ Nearest Tube: London Bridge.

 *11am–11pm Mon–Sat; 12–10.30pm Sun.*

The Globe Tavern

8 Bedale Street SE1 9AL
☎ *(020) 7407 0043*

 Adnams and Wells and Young's brew always available, plus a guest such as Greene King Abbot, Old Speckled Hen or Marston's Pedigree.

A traditional pub close to Borough Market made famous by its appearance in the film *Bridget Jones's Diary*. Background music, bar billiards, game machines. Disabled access. Bar snacks available 12–3pm. No children.

Θ Nearest Tube: London Bridge.

 *11am–11pm Mon–Fri; closed Sat–Sun but available for private hire.*

Leather Exchange

15 Leathermarket Street SE1 3HN
☎ *(020) 7407 0295* Alasdair Rawlinson
www.theleatherexchange.co.uk

 Tied to Fuller's, with London Pride and Discovery available.

A contemporary pub in Bermondsey, attracting a local office crowd and young urbanites from in and around the area. It was built in 1879 as the London Leather Exchange. The original auctioneers' dining room is now the pub's upstairs dining room, complete with grand piano and real fire in winter. Lively downstairs bar. Good food served 12–3pm and 6–10pm Mon–Sat, and 12–4.30pm Sun, with gourmet burgers a speciality. The upstairs lounge is available for party bookings for up to 50 people.

Θ Nearest Tube: London Bridge.

 *12–11pm Mon–Thurs; 12–12 Fri–Sat; 12–10.30pm Sun.*

Lord Clyde

27 Clennam Street, Borough SE1 1ER
☎ *(020) 7407 3397* Martin Fitzpatrick

 Young's Bitter, Fuller's London Pride, Adnams Bitter, Shepheard Neame Spitfire and Greene King IPA usually available, although the line-up is altered every couple of months.

There has been an inn on this site for 300 years, though the present building was constructed in 1913. In the Fitzpatrick family for three generations, since 1956, and leased from Enterprise Inns. A traditional London 'boozer' close to the main South Bank attractions. The back bar can be reserved for darts matches or parties. Food served all day Mon–Fri.

Θ Nearest Tube: Borough.

 *11am–11pm Mon–Fri; 12–11pm Sat; 12–6pm Sun.*

The Market Porter

9 Stoney Street, Borough Market SE1 9AA
☎ *(020) 7407 2495* Tony Hedigan

 Harveys Sussex Best plus up to eight often-changing guests (20 per week) from a huge range of independent breweries small and large.

Traditional pub within a rejuvenated Borough Market. The threat of demolition because of the Crossrail project has now receded. Food available at lunchtime. Function room available seven days per week for private functions, meetings, etc. NB early-morning opening.

Θ Nearest Tube: London Bridge.

 *6.30–8.30am and 11am–11pm Mon–Sat; 12–10.30pm Sun.*

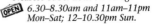

The Rake

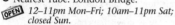

14 Winchester Walk,
Borough Market SE1 9AG
☎ *(020) 7407 0557* Andrew Carwood

At least six draught ales on offer from a remarkable and ever-changing global range, two are likely to be British and might include the infamous Thomas Hardy Ale (11.7% ABV), uniquely available here on draught. Plus an enormous range of bottled beers, lagers, ciders and perrys.

Opened in 2006 and surely the smallest pub in London, with room for only 44 people (allegedly) inside. The decked beer garden outside means you stand a chance of getting a seat. Run by the people behind Utobeer, the Borough Market beer specialists. Food available.

☉ Nearest Tube: London Bridge.

OPEN *12–11pm Mon–Fri; 10am–11pm Sat; closed Sun.*

Rose & Crown

47 Colombo Street, Blackfriars SE1 8DP
☎ *(020) 7928 4285* Anna and Matt Quick

Shepherd Neame tied house serving Master Brew, Best Bitter, Spitfire and a seasonal brew, rotated every season.

Classic, traditional, 350-year-old pub. Ground-floor bar plus upstairs bar and restaurant area. Large beer garden seating 200+ people adjoining church gardens. Food available 12–2.30pm Mon–Fri, including bar menu and five daily fresh specials. Function room available for hire. No children. Close to River Thames, London Eye and Tate Modern.

☉ Nearest Tube: Southwark.

OPEN *11.30am–11pm Mon–Fri.*

Royal Oak

44 Tabard Street SE1 4JU
☎ *(020) 7357 7173*
John Porteous and Frank Taylor

Well-kept Harveys XX Mild, Pale, Best Bitter and Armada plus seasonal brews and Thatcher's Heritage cider.

The capital's only Harveys tied house, tucked away off Borough High Street. An unspoilt oasis and well worth uncovering. Two bars plus upstairs function room. Food available Mon–Fri lunch and dinner; Sat dinner; Sun lunch. No children.

☉ Nearest Tube: Borough.

OPEN *11am–11pm Mon–Fri; 12–11pm Sat; 12–6pm Sun.*

OTHER REAL ALE PUBS IN SE1

Barrowboy & Banker (FULLER'S)

6–8 Borough High Street SE1 9QQ
☎ *(020) 7403 5415*

Horniman at Hays

Hay's Galleria, Tooley Street SE1 2HD
☎ *(020) 7407 1991*

Mad Hatter (FULLER'S)

3–7 Stamford Street SE1 9NT
☎ *(020) 7401 9222*

Mulberry Bush (WELLS AND YOUNG'S)

89 Upper Ground SE1 9PP ☎ *(020) 7928 7940*

The Pommeler's Rest

(WETHERSPOON)

196–8 Tower Bridge Road SE1 2UN
☎ *(020) 7378 1399*

Prince William Henry

(WELLS AND YOUNG'S)

216–19 Blackfriars Road SE1 8NL
☎ *(020) 7928 2474*

Rockingham Arms (WETHERSPOON)

119 Newington Causeway SE1 6BN
☎ *(020) 7940 0890*

Ship (FULLER'S)

68 Borough Road SE1 1DX ☎ *(020) 7403 7059*

Simon the Tanner

(SHEPHERD NEAME)

231 Long Lane, Bermondsey SE1 4PR
☎ *(020) 7403 2911*

Wetherspoon's

Metro Central Heights, Newington Causeway,
Elephant and Castle SE1 6PB
☎ *(020) 7940 0890*

Wheatsheaf (WELLS AND YOUNG'S)

6 Stoney Street, Borough Market SE1 9AA
☎ *(020) 7407 7242*

SE3

The British Oak

109 Old Dover Road, Blackheath SE3
☎ *(020) 8858 1082*

Princess of Wales

1A Montpelier Row, Blackheath SE3
☎ *(020) 8297 5911*

SE4

The Brockley Barge

(WETHERSPOON)

184 Brockley Road, Brockley SE4 2RR
☎ *(020) 8694 7690*

SE5

Fox on the Hill

149 Denmark Hill, Camberwell SE5 8EH
☎ *(020) 7738 4756* Peter Martin

Shepherd Neame Spitfire and Hop Back Summer Lightning among the brews always available plus a wide range of guests.

A large, modern Wetherspoon's pub with one bar, dining area, garden and disabled facilities. Food available all day. Children allowed in dining area only.

OPEN *All day, every day.*

The Hermit's Cave

28 Camberwell Church Street, Camberwell SE5 8QU
☎ *(020) 7703 3188* Brendan Gannon

Up to six beers, including Daleside Shrimpers, Fuller's London Pride, Shepherd Neame Spitfire and Greene King Old Speckled Hen. The guests rotate regularly and usually come from micro-brewers.

Built in 1902 and run by the same landlord for many years, this traditional, beamed pub with original etched windows serves bar food 11am–5pm daily. Street parking. No children.

⊖ Nearest Tube: Oval.

OPEN *11am–11pm Mon–Sat; 12–10.30pm Sun.*

OTHER REAL ALE PUBS IN SE5

Hoopers Bar and Cafe

28 Ivanhoe Road, Camberwell SE5 8DH
☎ *(020) 7733 4797*

SE6

Catford Ram

9 Winslade Way, Catford SE6 4JU
☎ *(020) 8690 6206*
P Pawson and G Dickenson

Wells and Young's house with Young's Bitter, Special and Waggle Dance available.

Just off Catford Broadway, by the theatre, a massive 1970s one-bar operation. Raised seating area. Food served 11am–3pm and 5–9pm Mon–Fri, 11am–3pm Sat and 12–4pm Sun. Children welcome for Sunday lunch.

OPEN *All day, every day.*

OTHER REAL ALE PUBS IN SE6

The London & Rye (WETHERSPOON)

109 Rushey Green, Catford SE6 4AF
☎ *(020) 8697 5028*

SE8

The Dog & Bell

116 Prince Street, Deptford SE8 3JD
☎ *(020) 8692 5664*
Adam Perfitt and Anmolia Singh Perfitt
www.thedogandbell.com

Five beers. Fuller's London Pride and ESB are regulars, while the three guests, sometimes changed daily or even hourly, might be beers from Nethergate, Dark Star or Pitfield. Plus 20 Belgian bottled beers.

Built in 1849 among the docks, this three-roomed pub has a mixed clientele, including regulars who travel distances to drink there. Food available 12–3pm and 6–10pm, including traditional Sunday lunch. Beer garden, party hire, free car parking. Children and babies welcome. Popular Sunday night quiz, regular theme nights, including curry nights and Belgian beer tasting. Two minutes from Deptford Station, close to Greenwich and DLR.

OPEN *12–11pm (10.30pm Sun); late licence for special functions.*

SE9

The Banker's Draft (WETHERSPOON)

80 High Street, Eltham SE9 1FT
☎ *(020) 8294 2578*

SE10

Ashburnham Arms

(SHEPHERD NEAME)
25 Ashburnham Grove, Greenwich SE10
☎ *(020) 8692 2007*

Cutty Sark

4–7 Ballast Quay, Greenwich SE10 9PD
☎ *(020) 8858 3146*

The Gateclock (WETHERSPOON)

210 Creek Road, Greenwich SE10 9RB
☎ *(020) 8269 2000*

Plume of Feathers

19 Park Vista, Greenwich SE10 9LZ
☎ *(020) 8858 1661*

Richard I (WELLS AND YOUNG'S)

52–4 Royal Hill, Greenwich SE10 8RT
☎ *(020) 8692 2996*

The Royal George

(SHEPHERD NEAME)
2 Blissett Street, Greenwich SE10 8UP
☎ *(020) 8692 9666*

Spanish Galleon (SHEPHERD NEAME)

48 Greenwich Church Street, Greenwich SE10 9BL ☎ *(020) 8293 0949*

Trafalgar Tavern

Park Row, Greenwich SE10 9NW
☎ *(020) 8858 2437*

SE11

Prince of Wales

48 Cleaver Square, Kennington SE11 4EA
☎ *(020) 7735 9916* Ewa Korzeniowska

Shepherd Neame house with Kent's Best, Spitfire and a brewery seasonal ale (Early Bird in spring, Goldings in summer, Late Red in autumn and Porter in winter).

Built in 1901, a cosy pub in the corner of an attractive Georgian square with one bar, open fire in winter, outside seating in summer. Background music. Food served 12–2.30pm and 6–9pm Mon–Thurs; 12–2.30pm Fri–Sat; traditional roasts 12–3pm Sun. Car parking is free at weekends only.

⊖ Nearest Tube: Kennington.

OPEN *12–11pm (10.30pm Sun).*

OTHER REAL ALE PUBS IN SE11

Court Tavern (SHEPHERD NEAME)

42 Renfrew Road, Lambeth SE11 4NA
☎ *(020) 7840 0878*

SE12

Crown (WELLS AND YOUNG'S)
117 Burnt Ash Hill, Lee SE12 0AJ
☎ *(020) 8857 6607*

The Edmund Halley (WETHERSPOON)
25–7 Lee Gate Centre, Lee Green SE12 8RG
☎ *(020) 8318 7475*

SE13

The Jolly Farmers
354 Lewisham High Street, Lewisham SE13 5JH
☎ *(020) 8690 8402*
Julien and Chantel Crawford

Enterprise Inns pub, with between two and six real ales, all changed weekly. Beers from Sharp's, Skinner's, Adnams, Wells and Young's, Black Sheep, Shepherd Neame, Ringwood and Greene King are regularly served.

One-bar pub with a country feel. Good mix of clientele. Background music. Home-cooked food served 12–3.30pm Tues–Fri and 12.30–2.30pm Sun. Themed evenings. Beer garden. Children welcome before 6.30pm and if dining. Close to High Street, Lewisham Hospital and Register Office.

OPEN *11am–11pm Mon–Sat; 12–10.30pm Sun.*

The Watch House
198–204 Lewisham High Street, Lewisham SE13 6JP
☎ *(020) 8318 3136* Mark Stevenson

Hop Back Summer Lightning among the brews always available plus up to five guests from breweries such as Bateman, JW Lees, Nethergate and Cotleigh.

A town-centre Wetherspoon's pub with a mature clientele. No music. Patio, disabled facilities. Food available all day. Children allowed until 7pm.

OPEN *All day, every day.*

SE15

The Gowlett
62 Gowlett Road, Peckham SE15 4HY
☎ *(020) 7635 7048* Jonny and Claire Henfrey
www.thegowlett.com

Four real ales from a large, rotating list, with Adnams Bitter usually available. Three guests (12 a week) such as Moorhouse's Pride of Pendle, Sharp's Eden, Timothy Taylor Landlord, Otter Ale or Caledonian Deuchars IPA.

Named local CAMRA Pub of the Year 2005. Food (stone-baked pizzas) served 12.30–4.30pm and 6.30–10.30pm Mon–Fri; 12.30–10.30pm Sat; 12.30–9pm Sun. Children and dogs welcome until 9pm. Covered and heated beer terrace. DJs on Sun.

OPEN *12–12 Mon–Thurs; noon–1am Fri–Sat; 12–11.30pm Sun.*

OTHER REAL ALE PUBS IN SE15

The Kentish Drovers
(WETHERSPOON)
77–9 Peckham High Street, Peckham SE15 5RS
☎ *(020) 7277 4283*

SE16

Blacksmith's Arms
257 Rotherhithe Street SE16 1EJ
☎ *(020) 7237 1349* Gordon D'Arcy

Fuller's House with London Pride and ESB plus Adnam's Bitter and a guest ale, changed every two weeks.

Next to the Hilton Hotel, a traditional, 100-year-old pub with one horseshoe-shaped bar and a games room. Food served 12–2.30pm Mon–Fri, all day Sat–Sun. Thai menu available each evening from 6pm. Enclosed rear patio garden.

OPEN *12–11pm (10.30pm Sun).*

The Clipper
562 Rotherhithe Street SE16 5EX
☎ *(020) 7237 2022*
JR Springate/J Reed (manager)

Fuller's London Pride plus one guest.

Opposite the Hilton Hotel, a one-bar pub with restaurant that seats 40. Garden with BBQ facilities. Close to the river. Food served 12–10pm. Available for private hire.

OPEN *11am–11pm Mon–Sat; 12–10.30pm Sun*

Moby Dick
6 Russell Place, Greenland Dock, Surrey Quays SE16 1PL
☎ *(020) 7231 6719 or (020) 7394 8597*
Joe Springate

Fuller's pub with London Pride and ESB plus two guests, changed fortnightly.

Fifteen years old, in a dockside setting, with glass walls. Food served 12–10pm daily. Outside benches, entertainment nearby, function room for up to 100. Children welcome.

⊖ Nearest Tube: Canada Water/Surrey Quays.

OPEN *11am–midnight Mon–Sat; 12–10.30pm Sun.*

OTHER REAL ALE PUBS IN SE16

Ship (WELLS AND YOUNG'S)
39–47 St Marychurch Street, Rotherhithe SE16 4JE ☎ *(020) 7237 4103*

The Surrey Docks (WETHERSPOON)
185 Lower Road, Rotherhithe SE16 2LW
☎ *(020) 7394 2832*

SE18

Rose's Free House (aka Prince Albert)
49 Hare Street, Woolwich SE18 6NE
☎ *(020) 8854 1538* Sharon Bouchere

Between three and six brews from a huge and varied range. Always changing, with 20–25 different beers a week.

Popular, one-bar, old-style wood-panelled pub. Bar snacks available all day (not Sun), but the clientele is here for the beer! Four twin bedrooms available. One minute from Woolwich Ferry.

OPEN *11am–11pm Mon–Sat; 12–3pm Sun.*

OTHER REAL ALE PUBS IN SE18

The Anglesea Arms

(SHEPHERD NEAME)

91 Woolwich New Road, Woolwich SE18 6EF
☎ *(020) 8317 0834*

The Great Harry (WETHERSPOON)

7–9 Wellington Street, Woolwich SE18 6NY
☎ *(020) 8317 4813*

Old Mill

1 Old Mill Road, Woolwich SE18 1QG
☎ *(020) 8244 8592*

SE19

The Postal Order (WETHERSPOON)

33 Westow Street, Crystal Palace SE19 3RW
☎ *(020) 8771 3003*

Railway Bell (WELLS AND YOUNG'S)

14 Cawnpore Street SE19 1PF
☎ *(020) 8670 2844*

SE20

Moon & Stars

164–6 High Street, Penge SE20 7QS
☎ *(020) 8776 5680* Rebecca Jordan

 Shepherd Neame Spitfire, Greene King IPA and Abbot and Hop Back Summer Lightning among the beers always available, plus up to five guests from a huge list.

A large Wetherspoon's pub in a former cinema. Disabled facilities. Dining area, beer garden. Food available all day from 10am. No children. Beer festivals twice yearly.

[OPEN] *10am–11pm (10.30pm Sun).*

SE21

Crown & Greyhound (aka The Dog)

73 Dulwich Village SE21
☎ *(020) 8299 4976* Ann Taylor

 Young's Bitter, Fuller's London Pride and an Adnams brew usually available.

Formerly two pubs, this huge refurbished Victorian alehouse sits in the heart of Dulwich, with split-level garden and conservatory. Food available at lunchtime and evenings. Children welcome in parts.

[OPEN] *11am–11pm Mon–Sat; 12–10.30pm Sun.*

SE22

The Clock House

(WELLS AND YOUNG'S)

196a Peckham Rye SE22 9QA
☎ *(020) 8693 2901*

Herne Tavern

2 Forest Hill Road SE22 0RR ☎ *(020) 8299 9521*

SE23

Blythe Hill Tavern

319 Stansted Road, Forest Hill SE23 1JB
☎ *(020) 8690 5176* Con Riordan

 At least four real ales including one from the local Westerham Brewery. Fuller's

London Pride, Adnams Broadside, Timothy Taylor Landlord and Harveys Best could feature.

Traditional late-Victorian street-corner pub on the South Circular Road with three rooms and an Irish influence. No food. Large outside drinking area. Former local CAMRA pub of the year.

[OPEN] *11am–12am*

The Capitol

11–21 London Road, Forest Hill SE23 3TW
☎ *(020) 8291 8920* Ripon Kazi

 Between five and eight real ales from the Wetherspoon's range, including Greene King Abbot and Old Speckled Hen, Marston's Pedigree and Shepherd Neame Spitfire, plus three guests, changed every two days.

Former cinema converted in 2001, with many original features retained. One bar, beer garden, large screen for sports coverage. Children welcome until 9pm. Food served 9am–11pm (including breakfast), with curry night on Tues, steak night on Thurs and roast on Sunday. Beer festivals held twice a year. On the South Circular Road, close to Forest Hill station.

[OPEN] *9am–midnight.*

OTHER REAL ALE PUBS IN SE23

The Railway Telegraph

(SHEPHERD NEAME)

112 Stanstead Road, Forest Hill SE23 1BS
☎ *(020) 8699 6644*

SE24

The Florence

131–133 Dulwich Road, Herne Hill SE24 0NG
☎ *(020) 7326 4987*
www.florencehernehill.com

 Home to a new microbrewery producing Weasel bitter and Dam Tasty Beaver plus guests such as Adnams Broadside.

Former sports bar reopened in spring 2007, opposite Brockwell Park. Open fires, conservatory, outside beer terrace, wifi. Food served until 10pm (9.30pm Sun). Dogs and children welcome.

⊖ Nearest Tube: Brixton

[OPEN] *12pm–12am (1am Fri–Sat)*

OTHER REAL ALE PUBS IN SE24

Tulse Hill Tavern

150 Norwood Road, Tulse Hill SE24 9AY
☎ *(020) 8674 9754*

SE25

The Alliance

91 High Street, South Norwood SE25 6EA
☎ *(020) 8653 3604* Mr Murphy

 Greene King Abbot and Courage Best plus two guest ales, rotating every four days.

A traditional, popular one-bar pub built in 1860 with leaded windows and wooden beams. No food. No children's room. Close to Norwood Junction railway station and Crystal Palace FC.

[OPEN] *11am–11pm Mon–Sat; 12–10.30pm Sun.*

Clifton Arms

21 Clifton Road, South Norwood SE25 6NJ
☎ *(020) 8771 2219* Mark Farrington

Three or four real ales, with some rotated every two weeks. Adnams Broadside and Best Bitter, Fuller's London Pride and Hogs Back TEA are regularly featured.

Local community pub built in 1863, close to Selhurst Park, so particularly busy on football days/evenings. Sky Sports. Darts and pool. Small menu available. Children welcome. Outdoor smoking facilities and beer garden. Quiz night last Thursday of month, karaoke, discos and occasional live music. The pub supports children's charities.

OPEN *12–11pm Mon–Wed; 12–12 Thurs–Sat; 12–10.30pm Sun.*

Portmanor

Portland Road, South Norwood SE25 4UF
☎ *(020) 8655 1308* Joan Brendan Kelly

Fuller's London Pride, Greene King Abbot Ale and up to five guest beers regularly available, perhaps from Hogs Back, Flagship or other small independents.

Popular freehouse with a good atmosphere and upstairs restaurant. Food served 11am–3pm and 5–9.30pm Mon–Fri, 12–9pm Sat (7pm Sun). No children. Quiz night (Thurs). Disco at weekends.

OPEN *11am–11pm Mon–Sat; 12–10.30pm Sun.*

OTHER REAL ALE PUBS IN SE25

The William Stanley

(WETHERSPOON)

7–8 High Street, South Norwood SE25 6EP
☎ *(020) 8653 0678*

SE26

Dulwich Wood House

39 Sydenham Hill SE26 6RS
☎ *(020) 8693 5666* Stephen Harkin

Wells and Young's house with Young's Bitter, Special and the brewery's seasonal ales available.

Built in 1857, designed by Sir Joseph Paxton for a local farmer and leased by Young's since 1889. Traditional, friendly pub with wood-panelled rooms, restaurant and large garden plus outside seating at the front. Food served 12–3pm and 6–9pm (12–4pm Sun). Private functions catered for. Car park. Close to Crystal Palace, Sydenham Hill is the nearest station.

OPEN *11am–11pm Mon–Sat; 12–10.30pm Sun.*

The Windmill

125–31 Kirkdale, Sydenham SE26 4QJ
☎ *(020) 8291 8670* Steve Jarvis

Wetherspoon's pub with Fuller's London Pride and Shepherd Neame Spitfire plus at least three guests.

A former furniture shop occupying spacious premises with garden. Food available all day.

OPEN *11am–11pm Mon–Sat; 12–10.30pm Sun.*

OTHER REAL ALE PUBS IN SE26

Bricklayers' Arms

(WELLS AND YOUNG'S)

189 Dartmouth Road, Sydenham SE26 4QY
☎ *(020) 8699 1260*

SE27

Hope (WELLS AND YOUNG'S)

49 High Street, West Norwood SE27 9JS
☎ *(020) 8670 2035*

LONDON SOUTH WEST

SW1

Buckingham Arms

62 Petty France, Westminster SW1H 9EU
☎ *(020) 7222 3386* Kristin Foord
www.buckinghamarms.com

Tied to Wells and Young's, with Young's PA and SPA and Charles Wells Bombardier served, plus a seasonal brew.

Built in 1780 with one bar and serving a business clientele. No music or pool tables. Food served 11am–9pm Mon–Fri; 12–4pm Sat–Sun. Pub for hire on Sat and Sun evenings – phone for details. Close to Buckingham Palace and Scotland Yard.

⊖ Nearest Tube: St James's Park.

OPEN *11am–11pm Mon–Fri; 12am–6pm Sat–Sun.*

The Captain's Cabin

4–7 Norris Street SW1Y 4RJ
☎ *(020) 7930 4767* Mervyn and Julie Wood

Greene King IPA and Fuller's London Pride plus two constantly changing guests.

Traditional two-bar pub dating from the early 1900s, with a central staircase and open balcony. Food served 12–9pm. Top bar available for private hire. No children. Close to the building where BBC radio stations were housed during and after World War II.

⊖ Nearest Tube: Piccadilly Circus.

OPEN *11am–11pm Mon–Sat; 12–10.30pm Sun.*

Cask & Glass

39–41 Palace Street, Victoria SW1
☎ *(020) 7834 7630*
Michael and Brigitte McAree

Shepherd Neame house with Spitfire, Best and Master Brew always available.

The smallest pub in Westminster, mid-Victorian with an olde-worlde ambience. Sandwiches and toasties available at lunchtimes. Outside tables and chairs in summer. Award-winning floral displays. Between Buckingham Palace Road and Victoria Street.

⊖ Nearest Tube: Victoria.

OPEN *11am–11pm Mon–Fri; 12–8pm Sat; closed Sun.*

Duke of Wellington

63 Eaton Terrace, Belgravia SW1W 8TR
☎ *(020) 7730 1782/3103* John and Helen Bond

Another Shepherd Neame House, with Master Brew, Spitfire and Bishop's Finger always available.

Set in a former library, a late-19th-century, friendly and traditional English local. Food served 11am–3pm and 6–9pm Mon–Sat (not Sun). Children welcome. Outside street tables. Three minutes from Sloane Square.

⊖ Nearest Tube: Sloane Square.
All day, every day.

Jugged Hare

172 Vauxhall Bridge Road, Victoria SW1V 1DX
☎ *(020) 7828 1543* Magda Wojtun
www.juggedhare.co.uk

Fuller's pub serving Chiswick, London Pride, Discovery, ESB and the brewery's seasonal ales. The licensee was the 2006 Fuller's Cellarman of the Year.

A former branch of NatWest and now a pub with a great atmosphere. Fresh, homemade traditional English food served 12–9.30pm every day. Gallery available for private hire. On the corner of Rochester Row and Vauxhall Bridge Road.

⊖ Nearest Tube: Victoria.
11am–11pm Mon–Sat; 12–10.30pm Sun.

Lord Moon of the Mall

16–18 Whitehall SW1A 2DY
☎ *(020) 7839 7701* Jason Blower
www.jdwetherspoons.co.uk

Wetherspoon's pub serving Marston's Pedigree, Shepherd Neame Spitfire and Greene King Abbot plus up to seven guests, changed every day or two, such as Ringwood Fortyniner, Exmoor Gold and beers from Wychwood.

Impressive former bank with high ceilings, arches and oak fittings. Disabled facilities. Breakfast served 9am–noon, plus full menu 9am–11pm. Next to Trafalgar Studios.

⊖ Nearest Tube: Charing Cross.
9am–11.30pm Mon–Thurs; 9am–midnight Fri–Sat; 9am–11pm Sun.

Marquis of Granby

41 Romney Street, Westminster SW1P 3RF
☎ *(020) 7227 0941* Gwylym Arthur

Part of the Nicholsons chain with four real ales available. Fuller's London Pride, Caledonian Deuchars IPA and two guests rotated weekly.

A two-bar operation off Smith Square and a couple of minutes from the Houses of Parliament, with a traditional downstairs bar and an upstairs bar and restaurant providing table service at lunch and a function room in the evening. Food served 12–10pm. Beer festivals held twice a year (usually February and October). Children welcome in the upstairs bar.

⊖ Nearest Tube: Westminster.
11am–11pm Mon–Fri.

Morpeth Arms

58 Millbank SW1P 4RW
☎ *(020) 7834 6442* Peter Henderson

Wells and Young's pub with Young's Bitter, Special and two seasonal Wells and Young's beers available.

Traditional one-bar pub built in 1847. The cellars were once prison cells where convicts awaiting transport to Australia were held. Food served 12–10pm. Private room for hire. Children allowed in upstairs room only. Near Tate Britain.

⊖ Nearest Tube: Pimlico.
11am–11pm Mon–Sat; 12–10.30pm Sun.

Nags Head

53 Kinnerton Street SW1X 8ED
☎ *(020) 7235 1135* Kevin Moran

Genuine freehouse serving Adnams Best, Broadside and Regatta.

Tucked down an attractive mews street off Wilton Place, an unspoilt, traditional drinking house in the heart of Belgravia. Conversation abounds, but mobile phones must not be used on the premises! Two wood-panelled bars on different levels (the bar area is between the two). Some outside seating. Good homemade food available 11am–9.30pm. Near Hyde Park Corner.

⊖ Nearest Tube: Knightsbridge.
11am–11pm.

Rising Sun

46 Ebury Bridge Road, Pimlico SW1W 8PZ
☎ *(020) 7730 9519* Mary Tabone

Tied to Wells and Young's, with Young's Bitter plus Winter Warmer or Charles Wells Bombardier. Two guests are changed fortnightly.

A two-bar pub frequented by locals, office workers and tourists. Food served 12–2.30pm and 6–9pm Mon–Sat, and 12–3pm Sun (roasts). Outside seating at front, smoking garden and heated patio at back. Private room for hire. At the bottom of Buckingham Palace Road.

⊖ Nearest Tube: Victoria/Sloan Square.
11am–midnight Mon–Fri; 12–12 Sat; 12–11pm Sun.

Sanctuary House Hotel

33 Tothill Street SW1 9LA
☎ *(020) 7799 4044* Sol Yepes
www.sanctuaryhousehotel.com

Another Fuller's pub, so with Chiswick, London Pride, ESB and Discovery always available.

Bar attached to small hotel in the heart of Westminster serving traditional English pub food until 9pm every day. Children welcome. Accommodation. Handy for Big Ben, Westminster Abbey, London Eye, Buckingham Palace and Scotland Yard.

⊖ Nearest Tube: St James's Park.
11am–11pm Mon–Sat; 12–10.30pm Sun.

The Speaker

46 Great Peter Street, Victoria SW1P 2NA
☎ *(020) 7222 1749* Dennis Reed
www.pleisure.com/speaker

Young's Bitter and Shepherd Neame Spitfire always available, plus daily rotating guest beers on our two guest ale pumps from a portfolio of over 200 micro brewers.

One-bar pub dating back to 1840 – a 'real' pub with no music, no fruit machines and no screens. Regular beer festivals featuring lots of different beers. Snacks available all day until 10pm. Bus routes: 11, 211, 24, 148, 507.

⊖ Nearest Tube: St James's Park.

OPEN *12–11pm Mon–Fri. Closed weekends and bank holidays.*

Star Tavern

6 Belgrave Mews West SW1X 8HT
☎ *(020) 7235 3019*
Jason Tinklin and Karen Tinklin
www.fullers.co.uk

A Fuller's tied pub with Discovery, London Pride, Chiswick and ESB plus a seasonal guest.

Tucked away down a small, cobbled mews street off Belgrave Square. Bars on two floors (upstairs available for functions and private dining). Food available 12–4pm and 6–9pm Mon–Fri, 12–5pm Sun. (Kitchen closed Sat.) Local CAMRA Pub of the Year 2005.

⊖ Nearest Tube: Hyde Park Corner/ Knightsbridge.

OPEN *11am–11pm Mon–Sat; 12–10.30pm Sun.*

Westminster Arms

9 Storey's Gate SW1
☎ *(020) 7222 8520* Gerry and Marie Dolan

Freehouse with a range of real ales that might include Adnams Bitter, Greene King Abbot, Wadworth 6X and a special house brew.

A large, busy, politician's pub handy for Westminster, serving restaurant food on weekday lunchtimes (not Wednesdays) and bar snacks at other times. Children in the restaurant only.

⊖ Nearest Tube: St James's Park/ Westminster.

OPEN *All day Mon–Fri; 11am–8pm Sat; 12–6pm Sun.*

Wilton Arms

71 Kinnerton Street, Belgravia SW1X 8ED
☎ *(020) 7235 4854* Val Knight

Shepherd Neame tied house with Spitfire, Master Brew and Bishop's Finger available.

Opened in 1826, one of two decent pubs on the street (known locally as the Village Pub). Several separate eating and drinking areas, plus a conservatory in the old garden which is available for private hire. Food served 12–9.30pm Mon–Fri and 12–3pm Sat. Children welcome. Handy for Harrods, Harvey Nichols and Hyde Park.

⊖ Nearest Tube: Knightsbridge.

OPEN *All day, every day (closed bank holidays).*

OTHER REAL ALE PUBS IN SW1

Adam and Eve

81 Petty France SW1H 9EX ☎ *(020) 7222 4575*

Antelope (FULLER'S)

22 Eaton Terrace SW1W 8EZ
☎ *(020) 7824 8512*

Fox & Hounds (WELLS AND YOUNG'S)

29 Passmore Street SW1W 8HR
☎ *(020) 7730 6367*

Horse & Groom (SHEPHERD NEAME)

7 Groom Place, Belgravia SW1X 7BA
☎ *(020) 7235 7949*

The Phoenix in Victoria

14 Palace Street, Victoria SW1E 5JA
☎ *(020) 7828 8136*

Red Lion

23 Crown Passage SW1Y 6PP
☎ *(020) 7930 4141*

Royal Oak (WELLS AND YOUNG'S)

2 Regency Street SW1 4EZ ☎ *(020) 7834 7046*

Wetherspoon's (WETHERSPOON)

Unit 5 Victoria Island, Victoria Station SW1V 1JT
☎ *(020) 7931 0445*

The Willow Walk (WETHERSPOON)

25 Wilton Road, Victoria SW1V 1LW
☎ *(020) 7828 2953*

SW2

The Crown & Sceptre

2a Streatham Hill, Brixton SW2 4AH
☎ *(020) 8671 0843* Sean Pulford

Shepherd Neame Spitfire among the brews always available plus two guests such as Hop Back Summer Lightning and ales from Adnams or Cotleigh.

A Wetherspoon's conversion with a big bar, dining area, front and rear patios. Food available all day. Children in garden only.

⊖ Nearest Tube: Balham.

OPEN *All day, every day.*

OTHER REAL ALE PUBS IN SW2

Hope & Anchor

(WELLS AND YOUNG'S)
123 Acre Lane, Brixton SW2 5UA
☎ *(020) 7274 1787*

SW3

Cooper's Arms

87 Flood Street, Chelsea SW3 5TB
☎ *(020) 7376 3120*

Wells and Young's pub serving Young's Bitter and Special, and Charles Wells Bombardier.

Traditional London local with village atmosphere. Food served from the main menu 12–3pm and 6–10pm, with light bites available 3–6pm. Garden. Just off King's Road.

⊖ Nearest Tube: Sloane Square.

OPEN *11am–11pm Mon–Sat; 12–10.30pm Sun.*

The Crown

153 Dovehouse Street, Chelsea SW3 6LB
☎ *(020) 7352 9505*
Alan Carroll and Karen Moore
Adnams Best Bitter, Fuller's London Pride plus a guest beer.

Traditional central London pub. Food served 12–3pm Mon–Fri. Well-behaved over-14s welcome. All major sports events shown on plasma screen. Situated 100 yards off Fulham Road, between the Brompton and Royal Marsden hospitals.

⊖ Nearest Tube: South Kensington.
⟨OPEN⟩ *11am–11pm Mon–Sat; 12–10.30pm Sun.*

OTHER REAL ALE PUBS IN SW3

The Builders Arms

13 Britten Street, Chelsea SW3 3TY
☎ *(020) 7349 9040*

Phene Arms

9 Phene Street, Chelsea SW3 ☎ *(020)7352 3294*

The Phoenix

23 Smith Street, Chelsea SW3 4BB
☎ *(020) 7730 9182*

SW4

Bread & Roses

68 Clapham Manor Street, Clapham SW4 6DZ
☎ *(020) 8498 1779* Ben Van Stellingwerff
www.breadandrosespub.com
Freehouse owned by the Worker's Beer Company with Worker's Ale (a house ale brewed by Smiles), Timothy Taylor Landlord, Adnams Explorer and Battersea Bitter the permanent beers, plus one guest.

Bright, modern pub with bar, function room and rear and front heated gardens. Disabled access and toilets. Food available 12–3pm and 7–9pm Mon–Fri; 12–3pm and 6–9.30pm Thurs–Fri; 11am–12.30pm (breakfast), 1–4pm and 6–9.30pm Sat; 11am–12.30pm (breakfast) and 1–6pm Sun. Children welcome until 9pm. Weekly quiz nights, theme nights. Annual beer festival. Convenient for underground, and Clapham High Street overland station.

⊖ Nearest Tube: Clapham Common/ Clapham North.
⟨OPEN⟩ *12–11.30pm Mon–Fri; 11am–11.30pm Sat; 11am–11pm Sun.*

The Windmill on the Common

South Side, Clapham Common SW4 9DE
☎ *(020) 8673 4578* David Martin
Wells and Young's house with Young's Bitter, Special and seasonal brews available.

A substantial and popular Victorian pub, built on the site of the home of the founder of Young's brewery. Good accommodation. Bar and restaurant food available 12–10pm every day. Children welcome in the dining room, which doubles as a function room available for private hire. Outside seating.

⊖ Nearest Tube: Clapham Common/ Clapham South.
⟨OPEN⟩ *11am–midnight Mon–Sat; 12–11pm Sun.*

OTHER REAL ALE PUBS IN SW4

Fine Line (FULLER'S)

182–4 Clapham High Street SW4 7UG
☎ *(020) 7622 4436*

Manor Arms

128 Clapham Manor Street SW4 6ED
☎ *(020) 7622 2894*

SW5

Blackbird (FULLER'S)

209 Earls Court Road SW5 9AR
☎ *(020) 7835 1855*

SW6

The Fulham Mitre

81 Dawes Road, Fulham SW6 7DU
☎ *(020) 7386 8877* Louis Amato
www.fulhammitre.com
Leased from Enterprise Inns with three real ales rotated every few months, perhaps including Fuller's London Pride, Caledonian Deuchars IPA and Brakspear Bitter.

Award-winning 'upmarket local' in the heart of residential Fulham. Refurbished in a modern and attractive style with wooden floors and a decked beer garden. Food served 12.30–2.30pm and 6.30–9.30pm daily.

⊖ Nearest Tube: Fulham Broadway.
⟨OPEN⟩ *12–11pm (10.30pm Sun).*

The Imperial

577 King's Road SW6 2EH
☎ *(020) 7736 8549* Andrew and Tim Haggard
Haggards Horny Ale and Charles Wells Bombardier always available plus Haggards Imp Ale at select times during the year. The pub lease belongs to the owners of Haggards Brewery and this is the principal outlet for their beers, which are brewed in Battersea.

A bright, airy, modern town pub with covered rear garden. Lively atmosphere. Food served every lunchtime and weekday evenings. Traditional roasts on Sundays. No children. Situated on the junction with Cambria Street.

⊖ Nearest Tube: Fulham Broadway.
⟨OPEN⟩ *11am–11pm Mon–Sat; 12–10.30pm Sun.*

The White Horse

1–3 Parsons Green, Fulham SW6 4UL
☎ *(020) 7736 2115*
www.whitehorsesw6.com

Harveys Sussex Best, Adnams Broadside and Highgate Mild plus a house brew and a wide range of guests including Rooster's Yankee, Oakham JHB and all sorts of seasonal brews. Bottled beers from around the world.

A large, comfortable Victorian pub overlooking Parsons Green, known as the 'Sloany Pony' and featuring the 'Coach House' restaurant. Brunch is served on Saturdays, 11am–4pm, and on Sundays. Regular beer festivals, including an Old Ale Festival (last Saturday of November), a Wheat Beer Festival (May) and the 'Beauty of the Hops' competition (June). Function room for private dinner parties, tastings and presentations. Parking, terrace/garden. Children allowed.

⊖ Nearest Tube: Parsons Green.
OPEN *11am–11pm Mon–Sat; 12–10.30pm Sun.*

OTHER REAL ALE PUBS IN SW6

The Duke on the Green

(WELLS & YOUNGS)

235 New King's Road, Fulham SW6 4XG
☎ *(020) 7736 2777*

SW7

The Anglesea Arms

15 Selwood Terrace, Chelsea SW7 3QG
☎ *(020) 7373 7960* Jenny Podmore
www.capitalpubcompany.co.uk

Five real ales, including Adnams Bitter and Broadside, Fuller's London Pride, Hogs Back TEA and Brakspear Oxford Gold plus one rotating guest such as Sharp's Doom Bar, Archers Golden, Hogs Back Hopgarden Gold or Timothy Taylor Landlord.

Lively, easy-to-find, 200-year-old pub with a traditional atmosphere. No background music or juke box. Modern English and world cuisine available 12–3pm and 6.30–10pm Mon–Fri, 12–10pm Sat, 12–9.30pm Sun. It is advisable to book. Wood-panelled dining room open in evenings and at weekends and available for private hire. Heated terraced garden area at front. Cask Marque winner. Children and dogs welcome. Between Fulham Road and Old Brompton Road.

⊖ Nearest Tube: South Kensington.
OPEN *11am–11pm Mon–Sat; 12–10.30pm Sun.*

OTHER REAL ALE PUBS IN SW7

The Tea Clipper

19 Montpelier Street, Knightsbridge SW7 1HF
☎ *(020) 7589 5251*

SW8

The Mawbey Arms

7 Mawbey Street, Lambeth SW8
☎ *(020) 7622 1936* Kellie and Tony Tooley

Freehouse serving Young's Bitter, Shepherd Neame Master Brew and a guest ale rotated at least weekly, such as Sharp's Eden or Doom Bar, or something from Bateman.

Local pub dating from the early 1800s, with one horseshoe-shaped bar. Large beer garden, recently revamped, with outside TV for sports. Food served 11am–3pm Mon–Fri. Darts. Children welcome. Off Wandsworth Road.

⊖ Nearest Tube: Vauxhall/Stockwell.
OPEN *11am–11pm Mon–Sat; 12–10.30pm Sun.*

The Priory Arms

83 Lansdowne Way, Stockwell SW8 2PB
☎ *(020) 7622 1884* Gary Morris

Adnams Bitter, Hop Back Summer Lightning and Harveys Best Bitter always available, with up to three guests, mainly from smaller regional breweries and especially micro-breweries.

Popular, genuine freehouse. Regular CAMRA regional Pub of the Year. Bar food available at lunchtimes, with traditional roasts on Sundays. Quiz night (Sun). Outside seating.

⊖ Nearest Tube: Stockwell.
OPEN *11am–11pm Mon–Sat; 12–10.30pm Sun.*

Surprise

16 Southville, South Lambeth SW8 2PP
☎ *(020) 7622 4623* Marie Leo

Owned by Wells and Young's, with Young's Bitter, Special and either Waggle Dance or Winter Warmer available.

Traditional one-bar local tucked away down a quiet cul-de-sac off Wandsworth Road. Food served 12–3pm Mon–Sat, 12–4pm Sun. Large patio area, boules pitch. BBQs in summer.

OPEN *11am–11pm Mon–Sat; 12–10.30pm Sun.*

OTHER REAL ALE PUBS IN SW8

The Fentiman Arms

64 Fentiman Road, Oval SW8 1LA
☎ *(020) 7793 9796*

The Hope (SHEPHERD NEAME)

7 Heather Close, South Lambeth SW8 3BS
☎ *(020) 7622 2987*

Mason's Arms (FULLER'S)

169 Battersea Park Road, Battersea SW8 4BT
☎ *(020) 7622 2007*

Plough Inn (WELLS AND YOUNG'S)

518 Wandsworth Road, Lambeth SW8 3JX
☎ *(020) 7622 2777*

Riverside (WELLS AND YOUNG'S)

5 St George Wharf, Vauxhall SW8 2LE
☎ *(020) 7735 8129*

SW9

The Beehive

407–9 Brixton Road, Brixton SW9 7DG
☎ *(020) 7738 3643* Francis M Wairegi

 Four or five real ales, including Shepherd Neame Spitfire, Greene King Abbot and Marston's Pedigree, plus guests such as Hook Norton Old Hooky.

A one-bar Wetherspoon's pub designed in a traditional English style, with many of the building's original features incorporated. Food served all day, every day, and there is a dining area at the rear of the pub. No external drinking or dining facilities. Located at the heart of Brixton town centre.

⊖ Nearest Tube: Brixton.

OPEN *9am–11pm.*

Trinity Arms

45 Trinity Gardens, Brixton SW9 8DR
☎ *(020) 7274 4544* Fergal O'Hanlon

An award-winning Wells and Young's pub with Young's Bitter, Special and seasonal brews.

In a quiet Victorian square in the middle of Brixton, a one-bar local that also attracts drinkers from further afield to its comfortable interior and beer garden plus front patio. Food served at lunchtimes. Close to the town hall. Local CAMRA Pub of the Year 2005.

⊖ Nearest Tube: Brixton.

OPEN *11am–11pm Mon–Sat; 12–10.30pm Sun.*

OTHER REAL ALE PUBS IN SW9

Hogshead

409 Clapham Road SW9 ☎ *(020) 7274 2472*

SW10

Chelsea Ram

32 Burnaby Street, Chelsea SW10 0PL
☎ *(020) 7351 4008* Liam Carlisle

Wells and Young's tied house selling Young's Bitter and Special plus Charles Wells Bombardier.

Popular, colourful, cheerful gastropub off King's Road. Children welcome. Outside seating. Good food served 12–3pm and 6.30–10pm (12–9.30pm Sun). Private room. Children and dogs welcome.

⊖ Nearest Tube: Fulham Broadway.

OPEN *11am–11pm Mon–Sat; 12–10.30pm Sun.*

Finch's

190 Fulham Road SW10 9PN
☎ *(020) 7351 5043* Amanda J Lowis
www.youngs.co.uk

Wells and Young's managed house, with Young's Bitter and Special available.

Traditional one-bar pub with large screens showing all major sporting events. Very popular in the evening with young affluent Chelsea people. Food served 12–10pm Mon–Sat, 12–5pm Sun. Close to Chelsea and Westminster Hospital, and only seven minutes from Stamford Bridge.

⊖ Nearest Tube: Fulham Broadway.

OPEN *11am–midnight Mon–Sat; 12–12 Sun.*

OTHER REAL ALE PUBS IN SW10

The World's End

459 King's Road, Chelsea SW10 0LR
☎ *(020) 7376 8946*

SW11

The Castle

115 High Street, Battersea SW11 3JR
☎ *(020) 7228 8181* Gill Markwell

Tied to Wells and Young's with Young's Bitter, Special and either Waggle Dance or Winter Warmer available.

French country farmhouse feel, open fire in the main bar, snug bar with leather sofas. Food served 12–3pm (4.30pm Sun) and 7–10pm daily. Patio beer garden, car park. Snug bar used for private parties.

OPEN *12–11pm.*

The Woodman

60 Battersea High Street SW11 3HX
☎ *(020) 7228 2968* Michael Foster
www.thewoodmanbattersea.co.uk

Tied to Hall and Woodhouse, so with Badger Best, Tanglefoot and Fursty Ferret plus an occasional guest. Cask Marque accredited.

Popular, colourful gastropub off Battersea Square, traditional, but with a modern twist and comfortable, contemporary design. Welcoming island bar, leather sofas, big beer garden and function area – a great space for big parties and functions. Food served 12–3pm and 6.30–10pm daily. Children and families welcome. Close to Battersea Park.

OPEN *11am–11pm Mon–Sat; 12–10.30pm Sun.*

OTHER REAL ALE PUBS IN SW11

The Asparagus (WETHERSPOON)

1–13 Falcon Road, Battersea SW11 2PT
☎ *(020) 7801 0046*

Bank (FULLER'S)

31–7 Northcote Road, Battersea SW11 1NJ
☎ *(020) 7924 7387*

Beehive (FULLER'S)

197 St John's Hill, Wandsworth SW11 1TH
☎ *(020) 7207 1267*

Duke of Cambridge

(WELLS AND YOUNG'S)
228 Battersea Bridge Road SW11 3AA
☎ *(020) 7223 5662*

Eagle Ale House

104 Chatham Road, Battersea SW11 6HG
☎ *(020) 7228 2328*

Fine Line (FULLER'S)

31–7 Northcote Road, Battersea SW11 1NJ
☎ *(020) 7924 7387*

The Latchmere

503 Battersea Park Road, Battersea SW11
☎ *(020) 7223 3549*

Plough (WELLS AND YOUNG'S)
89 St John's Hill, Clapham Junction SW11 1SY
☎ *(020) 7228 9136*

Grove
39 Oldridge Road, Balham SW12 8PN
☎ *(020) 8673 6531*

Young's Bitter, Special and a guest brew always available.

A former Victorian hotel with an oak-floored public bar area, a saloon bar for families and a restaurant. Real log fire. Food served at lunchtime and evenings daily. Popular Sunday roasts. Summer patio and big-screen TVs.

⊖ Nearest Tube: Balham/Clapham South.

OPEN *11am–11pm.*

Moon Under Water
194 Balham High Road, Balham SW12 9BP
☎ *(020) 8673 0535 James Glover*

A Wetherspoon's house with Hop Back Summer Lightning and Shepherd Neame Spitfire permanently available, plus two guest beers.

A friendly local. No music. Food served all day, every day. No children.

⊖ Nearest Tube: Balham.

OPEN *11am–11pm Mon–Sat; 12–10.30pm Sun.*

The Nightingale
97 Nightingale Lane, Balham SW12 8NX
☎ *(020) 8673 1637 Lee and Keris de Villiers*
www.nightingalewalk.org.uk

Wells and Young's house with Young's Bitter and Special plus Charles Wells Bombardier, together with a Wells and Young's seasonal ale.

B uilt in 1853 and bought by Young's in 1920, this is a traditional, local community pub with one horseshoe-shaped bar. Food served 12–10pm every day. Disabled toilets and access. Beer garden. Darts. Children welcome till 9pm. Quiz evening. Annual Nightingale charity walk, usually in May. Publicans' Community Pub 2009 award.

⊖ Nearest Tube: Balham.

OPEN *11am–midnight Mon–Sat; 12–12 Sun.*

OTHER REAL ALE PUBS IN SW12
Duke of Devonshire
(WELLS AND YOUNG'S)
39 Balham High Road SW12 9AN
☎ *(020) 7673 1363*

Jackdaw & Rook (FULLER'S)
96–100 Balham High Road SW12 9AA
☎ *(020) 8772 9021*

Bulls Head
373 Lonsdale Road, Barnes SW13 9PY
☎ *(020) 8876 5241 Dan and Liz Fleming*

Wells and Young's pub serving Young's Bitter, Special and Charles Wells Bombardier and seasonal brews such as Winter Warmer as appropriate. Also many lagers, 200 wines, 32 champagnes and 60 whiskies.

B eside the Thames on the south side of Barnes Bridge, known for its live jazz music every evening and on Sundays. Good reputation for fresh, home-cooked food in the bar 12–10.30pm every day, plus Thai food in The Stable restaurant in the evenings. Children welcome in eating area. Popular on Boat Race day. Outside seating. New soundproofing has ensured this pub's future.

OPEN *12–12.*

Coach & Horses
27 High Street, Barnes SW13 9LW
☎ *(020) 8876 2695 Lesley Greenstreet*

Wells and Young's house serving Young's Bitter, Special and seasonal brews.

P opular former coaching inn with single bar and friendly atmosphere. Large garden. Food available 12–10.30pm, with barbecues in summer. Function room available for hire. Children welcome in the garden.

OPEN *11am–midnight Mon–Sat; 12–12 Sun.*

Red Lion
2 Castlenau, Barnes SW13 9RU
☎ *(020) 8748 2984*
Claire Morgan and Angus McKean

Tied to Fuller's with London Pride, Discovery and ESB plus a seasonal guest.

L arge Victorian community pub with food served 11am–3pm and 6–10pm on weekdays, all day until 10pm at weekends. Handy for the London Wetlands Centre.

OPEN *11am–11pm Mon–Sat; 12–10.30pm Sun*

OTHER REAL ALE PUBS IN SW13
White Hart (WELLS AND YOUNG'S)
The Terrace, Riverside, Barnes SW13 9NR
☎ *(020) 8876 5177*

Charlie Butler (WELLS AND YOUNG'S)
40 High Street, Mortlake SW14 8SN
☎ *(020) 8878 2310*

Hare & Hounds (WELLS AND YOUNG'S)
216 Upper Richmond Road, Sheen SW14 8AH
☎ *(020) 8876 4304*

Jolly Gardeners
(WELLS AND YOUNG'S)
36 Lower Richmond Road, Mortlake SW14 7EX
☎ *(020) 8876 1721*

Railway Tavern
(HALL & WOODHOUSE)
11 Sheen Lane, Mortlake SW14 8HY
☎ *(020) 8878 7361*

SW15

The Bricklayer's Arms
32 Waterman Street, Putney SW15 1DD
☎ *(020) 8780 1155*
www.bricklayers-arms.co.uk

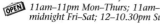 The only pub in London to serve the full range of Timothy Taylor beers. Many special events and beer festivals offering a much wider range.

Family-run award-winning freehouse close to Putney Bridge. Built in 1826, it is the oldest pub in Putney and has been rejuvenated by the present owners. Food served at lunchtimes and evenings. Curry nights, barbecues and Sunday roasts. Parking outside from 6.30pm. CAMRA's regional Pub of the Year.

⊖ Nearest Tube: Putney Bridge.
OPEN *12–11pm (10.30pm Sun).*

Green Man
Wildcroft Road, Putney Heath, Putney SW15 3NG
☎ *(020) 8788 8096*
Agnieszka Bulejak and Joel Pyke

Tied to Wells and Young's with Young's Bitter and Special, Charles Wells Bombardier and a Wells and Young's seasonal brew.

Traditional pub dating from around 1700, often a refuge after battles in years gone by. Putney Heath is notorious for its history of highwayman, and rumour has it that Dick Turpin once stashed his guns in an upstairs room of the pub. There is no danger of highwaymen now – just a cosy, welcoming pub with a fantastic garden, great beers and scrumptious menu. Food served 12–3pm and 6–9pm Mon–Thurs; 12–10pm Fri–Sat; 12–9pm Sun. Children welcome. Near Putney Heath, on the No.14 bus.

⊖ Nearest Tube: East Putney.
OPEN *11am–11pm Mon–Thurs; 11am–midnight Fri–Sat; 12–10.30pm Sun.*

The Railway
202 Upper Richmond Road, Putney SW15 6TD
☎ *(020) 8871 4497* Julie Allen

Wetherspoon's house serving the usual suspects such as Greene King Abbot and Shepherd Neame Spitfire plus guests.

Another in the chain, but with a railway theme. Serving standard Wetherspoon's food all day. Upstairs bar. Children welcome.
⊖ Nearest Tube: East Putney.
OPEN *11am–11pm Mon–Sat; 12–10.30pm Sun.*

OTHER REAL ALE PUBS IN SW15

Angel (WELLS AND YOUNG'S)
11 High Street, Roehampton SW15 4HL
☎ *(020) 8788 1997*

Boathouse (WELLS AND YOUNG'S)
32 Brewhouse Lane, Putney SW15
☎ *(020) 8789 0476*

The Coat and Badge
8 Lacy Road, Putney SW15 1NL
☎ *(020) 8788 4900*

Duke's Head (WELLS AND YOUNG'S)
8 Lower Richmond Road, Putney SW15 1JN
☎ *(020) 8788 2552*

Half Moon (WELLS AND YOUNG'S)
93 Lower Richmond Road, Putney SW15 1EU
☎ *(020) 8780 9383*

P Shannon and Sons (FULLER'S)
46–8 High Street, Putney SW15
☎ *(020) 8780 5437*

Spotted Horse (WELLS AND YOUNG'S)
122 Putney High Street SW15 1RG
☎ *(020) 8788 0246*

The Telegraph
Telegraph Road, Putney Heath SW15 3TU
☎ *(020) 8788 2011*

Whistle & Flute (FULLER'S)
46–8 High Street, Putney SW15 1SQ
☎ *(020) 8780 5437*

SW16

Bedford Park (WELLS AND YOUNG'S)
233 Streatham High Road, Streatham SW16 6EN
☎ *(020) 8769 2836*

Five Bells (GREENE KING)
68–70 Streatham High Road, Streatham SW16 1DA
☎ *(020) 8696 7587*

The Holland Tringham
(WETHERSPOON)
107–9 Streatham High Road, Streatham SW16 1HJ ☎ *(020) 8769 3062*

The Moon Under Water
(WETHERSPOON)
1327 London Road, Norbury SW16 4AU
☎ *(020) 8765 1235*

Pied Bull (WELLS AND YOUNG'S)
498 Streatham High Road SW16 3BQ
☎ *(020) 8764 4033*

SW17

JJ Moons
56a High Street, Tooting SW17 0RN
☎ *(020) 8672 4726* Angela Murphy
www.jdwetherspoons.com

 Owned by Wetherspoon's, with eight real ales available. Greene King Abbot, Shepherd Neame Spitfire, Marston's Pedigree and Courage Best plus two guests rotated twice a week.

Opened in 1991, a warm, friendly open-plan one-bar pub. Food served all day. Family area (children welcome).
⊖ Nearest Tube: Tooting Broadway.
OPEN *10am–midnight.*

Castle (WELLS AND YOUNG'S)

38 High Street, Tooting SW17 0RG
☎ *(020) 8672 7018*

The Gorringe Park Hotel
(WELLS AND YOUNG'S)

29 London Road, Tooting SW17 9JR
☎ *(020) 8648 4478*

Leather Bottle (WELLS AND YOUNG'S)

538 Garratt Lane, Tooting SW17 0NY
☎ *(020) 8946 2309*

Prince of Wales (WELLS AND YOUNG'S)

646 Garratt Lane, Tooting SW17 0PB
☎ *(020) 8946 2628*

SW18

Alma

499 Old York Road, Wandsworth SW18 1TF
☎ *(020) 8870 2537*
Daniel and Anna Bragger (managers)
www.thealma.co.uk

Wells and Young's managed house, with Young's Bitter, Special, a seasonal ale and Charles Wells Bombardier.

Victorian pub with green tiles, domed roof and rare, original painted mirrors and woodwork. Open, central bar and separate restaurant. Function room on first floor. Good food served 11am–4pm and 6–10.30pm for the main menu, and 12-10.30pm for the bar menu. Wedding licence held. Car park at rear. Directly opposite Wandsworth Town Railway Station.
⊖ Nearest Tube: Southfields.
OPEN *11am–midnight Mon–Sat; 12–11pm Sun.*

The Cat's Back

86–8 Point Pleasant, Wandsworth SW18 1NN
☎ *(020) 8877 0818* Roger Martin
www.thecatsback.com

Four bitters on offer, rotated constantly.

Unique, friendly ground-floor pub with one bar and a first-floor restaurant. Food served in bar and restaurant 11am–10.30pm. Children welcome. Dogs allowed in downstairs bar only. One minute from Wandsworth Park.
⊖ Nearest Tube: East Putney/Putney Bridge.
OPEN *All day, every day (from 11am).*

Queen Adelaide

35 Putney Bridge Road, Wandsworth SW18 1NP
☎ *(020) 8874 1695* Tim Lees

Wells and Young's house with Young's Bitter, Special and a seasonal ale available.

Refurbished in 2005, this pub now has a fantastic garden area with covered patio and dining area. Food from an extensive menu served 12–10pm, with waitress service.
⊖ Nearest Tube: East Putney.
OPEN *12–11pm Sun–Wed; 12–12 Thurs–Sat.*

The Rose & Crown

134 Putney Bridge Road, Wandsworth SW18 1NP
☎ *(020) 8871 4497* Daniel Williamson

Former Wetherspoon's pub now in different hands but still with eight real ales. Courage Best and Directors and Fuller's London Pride generally available, the rest rotate every barrel.

Pub with an outside drinking area, and with food served all day. Children welcome. Darts played.
⊖ Nearest Tube: East Putney/Putney Bridge.
OPEN *10am–close Mon–Sat.*

The Ship Inn

41 Jew's Row, Wandsworth SW18 1TB
☎ *(020) 8870 9667*
www.theship.co.uk

Young's Bitter, Special and seasonal brews such as Waggle Dance, Winter Warmer or St George's Ale.

Popular Victorian riverside pub with large conservatory, indoor and outdoor restaurant. The large garden has an outside bar and BBQ facilities. Good food (meat from the Gotto farm) available 12–10.30pm (10pm Sun).
OPEN *10am–11pm Mon–Sat; 12–10.30pm Sun.*

Spread Eagle

71 High Street, Wandsworth SW18 4LB
☎ *(020) 8877 9809* Steve and Sandra Turner

Young's Bitter, Special and Winter Warmer or Waggle Dance always available.

Opposite the former brewery in the centre of Wandsworth, a three-bar Victorian alehouse with classic interior. Two function rooms. Food served every day.
OPEN *All day, every day.*

Brewer's Inn (WELLS AND YOUNG'S)

147 East Hill, Wandsworth SW18 2QB
☎ *(020) 8874 4128*

Brewery Tap (WELLS AND YOUNG'S)

68 High Street, Wandsworth SW18 2LB
☎ *(020) 8875 7005*

County Arms (WELLS AND YOUNG'S)

345 Trinity Road, Wandsworth SW18 3SH
☎ *(020) 8874 8532*

Crane (WELLS AND YOUNG'S)

14 Armoury Way, Wandsworth SW18 3EZ
☎ *(020) 8874 2450*

The East Hill

21 Alma Road, Wandsworth SW18 1AA
☎ *(020) 8874 1833*

Fox & Hounds (WELLS AND YOUNG'S)

29 Passmore Street SW18 8HR
☎ *(020) 7730 6367*

Freemasons

2 North Side, Wandsworth Common SW18 2SS
☎ *(020) 7326 8580*

Gardeners Arms (WELLS AND YOUNG'S)

268 Merton Road, Southfields SW18 5JL
☎ *(020) 8874 7624*

Grapes (WELLS AND YOUNG'S)

39 Fairfield Street, Wandsworth SW18 1DX
☎ *(020) 8874 3414*

The Grid Inn (WETHERSPOON)

22 Replingham Road, Southfields SW18 5LS
☎ *(020) 8874 8460*

Halfway House (WELLS AND YOUNG'S)

521 Garratt Lane, Earlsfield SW18 4SR
☎ *(020) 8946 2788*

The Hop Pole (SHEPHERD NEAME)

64 Putney Bridge Road, Wandsworth SW18 1HR
☎ *(020) 8870 8188*

Kings Arms (WELLS AND YOUNG'S)

96 High Street, Wandsworth SW18 4LB
☎ *(020) 8874 1428*

Old Sergeant (WELLS AND YOUNG'S)

104 Garratt Lane, Wandsworth SW18 4DJ
☎ *(020) 8874 4099*

Pig & Whistle (WELLS AND YOUNG'S)

481 Merton Road SW18 5LB
☎ *(020) 8874 1061*

Waterfront (WELLS AND YOUNG'S)

*Baltimore House, Juniper Drive, Battersea
SW18 1TZ* ☎ *(020) 7228 4297*

SW19

The Brewery Tap

68–9 High Street, Wimbledon Village SW19 5EE
☎ *(020) 8947 9331* John Grover

 Five real ales, including Adnams Bitter and Fuller's London Pride, plus three guests changed after each firkin.

Small and cosy one-bar Victorian freehouse in the heart of Wimbledon village, with customers of all ages. Food available 12–2.30pm every day and 6–9pm Tues–Thurs. Satellite sports, digital juke box, quiz night (Mon).

✪ Nearest Tube: Wimbledon.

OPEN *11am–11pm Mon–Thurs; 11am–
midnight Fri–Sat; 12–10.30pm Sun.*

Crooked Billet

*15 Crooked Billet, Wimbledon Common
SW19 4RQ*
☎ *(020) 8946 4942* Mr and Mrs J Griffin

 Wells and Young's house with Young's Bitter, Special and either Winter Warmer or Waggle Dance.

Late-17th-century pub with a mock-Tudor interior. One bar plus restaurant. Food served 12.30–3pm and 6.30–10pm. Large outside area and the Common is one minute away.

OPEN *11am–11pm Mon–Sat; 12–10.30pm Sun.*

Rose & Crown

55 High Street, Wimbledon SW19 5BA
☎ *(020) 8947 4713* Nichola Green
www.roseandcrownwimbledon.co.uk

 Another Wells and Young's house with Young's Bitter, Special and Charles Wells Bombardier plus one seasonal ale (Winter Warmer, Golden Zest, Ram Rod or St George's Ale).

Traditional 16th-century pub with 13 modern en-suite bedrooms. Charming, olde-worlde, with Grade I listed bar. Delightful courtyard with patio heaters. Heated patio area. Food served 12–10pm Mon–Sat and 12–9.30pm Sun. Children welcome in conservatory and courtyard until 8pm. In the heart of Wimbledon Village, ten minutes from the A3.

OPEN *11am–11pm Mon–Sat; 12–10.30pm Sun.*

The Sultan

78 Norman Road, South Wimbledon SW19 1BT
☎ *(020) 8544 9323* Angela Shaw

The only pub in London owned by the Salisbury-based Hop Back Brewery, so serving GFB, Thunderstorm, Summer Lightning, Crop Circle and other seasonal ales.

Two-bar, street-corner local. All beers sold at reduced price (£1.70) on Wednesdays. Garden. Quiz night (Tues). No food. Local CAMRA Pub of the Year 2003 and *Time Out's* London Pub of the Year 2004.

✪ Nearest Tube: Colliers Wood/South Wimbledon.

OPEN *12–11pm (10.30pm Sun).*

The Trafalgar

23 High Path, Merton SW19 2JY
☎ *(020) 8542 5342* David and Karen
www.thetraf.com

Freehouse with up to six real ales, including Dark Star Hophead, Gale's HSB and guests from all over Britain.

Traditional street-corner 'local' five minutes from South Wimbledon Tube. South-west London CAMRA Pub of the Year 2008. Food served 12–2pm Mon–Fri and a themed dinner on the second Thurs of each month (7.30–9pm). Sky TV.

✪ Nearest Tube: South Wimbledon.

OPEN *Lunchtimes and evenings.*

OTHER REAL ALE PUBS IN SW19

Alexandra (WELLS AND YOUNG'S)

*33 Wimbledon Hill Road, Wimbledon
SW19 7NE* ☎ *(020) 8947 7691*

Dog & Fox (WELLS AND YOUNG'S)

24 Wimbledon High Street SW19 5EA
☎ *(020) 8946 6565*

Hand in Hand (WELLS AND YOUNG'S)

*6 Crooked Billet, Wimbledon Common
SW19 4RQ* ☎ *(020) 8946 5720*

Princess of Wales
(WELLS AND YOUNG'S)
98 Morden Road, Merton SW19 3BP
☎ *(020) 8542 0573*

Wibbas Down Inn (WETHERSPOON)
6–12 Gladstone Road, Wimbledon SW19 1QT
☎ *(020) 8540 6788*

SW20
The Edward Rayne
(WETHERSPOON)
8–12 Coombe Lane, Raynes Park SW20 8ND
☎ *(020) 8971 0420*

LONDON WEST

W1
Ain't Nothin' But ... Blues Bar
20 Kingly Street W1R 5PZ
☎ *(020) 7287 0514* Kevin Hillier
www.aintnothinbut.co.uk

 Adnams Best and Broadside plus a guest which changes every few days. Examples include Fuller's London Pride and Honey Dew, Young's Waggle Dance, Charles Wells Bombardier, Greene King Old Speckled Hen, Everards Beacon and Tiger, Bateman Salem Porter and brews from Badger and Wychwood.

Opened in 1993, this is a typical New Orleans-style blues bar with live music seven days a week (including all day Sat and Sun). Good old-fashioned drinkers' bar with mixed clientele. One main bar, small dance floor and seating area. Food served during opening hours. Over-18s only. No outside area. Bar available for hire outside opening hours. Situated between Regent Street and Carnaby Street behind Hamley's Toy Shop.

↔ Nearest Tube: Oxford Circus.

OPEN *6pm–1am Mon–Wed; 6pm–2am Thurs; 5pm–2.30am Fri; 3pm–2.30am Sat; 3pm–12 Sun.*

The Argyll Arms
18 Argyll Street W1 1AA
☎ *(020) 7734 6117* Mike Tayara

Seven beers, including Wadworth 6X and an ever-changing selection that might feature Fuller's London Pride, Hop Back Summer Lightning, Felinfoel Double Dragon, Timothy Taylor Landlord, Charles Wells Bombardier and brews from Jennings, Ringwood, Black Sheep or Tomintoul.

A 300-year-old pub with a remarkable interior located just off Oxford Circus and owned by the Duke of Argyll. Refurbished and air-conditioned. Bar and restaurant food available all day until 10pm. Function room. Children allowed in play area.

↔ Nearest Tube: Oxford Circus.

OPEN *11am–11pm Mon–Wed; 11am–midnight Thurs–Sat; 12–10.30pm Sun.*

The Carpenters Arms
12 Seymour Place W1H 7NE
☎ *(020) 7723 1050* Philip Riddle

 Beers from Harvey's and Adnams usually available, plus a great range of other ales such as Hop Back Summer Lightning, Everards Tiger, Wadworth 6X or something from Black Sheep, Hardys & Hansons or Oakhill.

A charming traditional freehouse with a warm welcome. Small and intimate one-bar house which is a great favourite with locals, business people and tourists alike. Food served on weekday lunchtimes. Cask Marque awarded.

↔ Nearest Tube: Edgware Road/Marble Arch.

OPEN *11am–11.30pm Mon–Thurs; 11am–midnight Fri–Sat; 12–10.30pm Sun.*

The Clachan
34 Kingly Street W1R 5LB
☎ *(020) 7734 2659*

Nicholson's house serving up to five ales that may well include Fuller's London Pride, Greene King IPA, Timothy Taylor Landlord and guests.

Behind Liberty's, just off Carnaby Street, a two-bar central London alehouse with upstairs restaurant which can also be used as a function room. Food served 12–10pm every day.

↔ Nearest Tube: Oxford Circus.

OPEN *11am–11pm Mon–Sat; 12–10.30pm Sun.*

Golden Eagle
59 Marylebone Lane W1U 2NY
☎ *(020) 7935 3228* Gary Grimes

St Austell Tribute and Fuller's London Pride plus two guest beers rotated monthly.

Genuine Victorian freehouse five minutes from Oxford Street. Licensed since 1852. One bar. Sing-a-long piano nights (Tue, Thurs, Fri 8.30–11pm). Handy for the Wallace Collection and the Wigmore Hall.

↔ Nearest Tube: Bond Street.

OPEN *11am–11pm Mon–Sat; 12–7pm Sun.*

The Guinea
30 Bruton Place, Mayfair W1J 6NL
☎ *(020) 7409 1728* Carl Smith
www.theguinea.co.uk

Wells and Young's pub serving Young's Bitter, Special and seasonal brews (Winter Warmer, Waggle Dance, St George's Ale).

Established in 1673 and tucked away in a mews street just off Berkeley Square with a fine restaurant at the rear. Food served 12.30–2.30pm Mon–Fri and 6.30–10.30pm Mon–Sat. Private room for hire.

↔ Nearest Tube: Bond Street/Green Park.

OPEN *11am.30–11pm Mon–Fri; 6.30–11pm Sat; closed Sun and bank holidays.*

Shaston Arms
4–6 Ganton Street W1S 7QN
☎ *(020) 7287 2631* Sally Graham

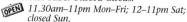 Owned by Hall & Woodhouse, so serving Badger Best and Tanglefoot, plus King & Barnes Sussex. A guest ale changes twice a year.

Opened in December 2000 in a former wine bar off Carnaby Street at the top end of Soho. The curious layout sees the bar in one room with much of the seating next door. Wooden floors, cosy in winter, cosmopolitan in summer. Food available 12–4.40pm (5pm Sat).

⊖ Nearest Tube: Oxford Circus.
🍺 *11.30am–11pm Mon–Fri; 12–11pm Sat; closed Sun.*

The Spice of Life
6 Moor Street, Cambridge Circus, Soho W1D 5NA
☎ *(020) 7437 7013* Andrew Ranum
www.spiceoflifesoho.com

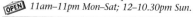 McMullen's house, with two brewery beers and a guest ale available.

Built in 1898, with two bars. Food available 12–9pm daily. Next to the Palace Theatre (*Les Miserables*). Live music every night in the basement bar.

⊖ Nearest Tube: Leicester Square.
🍺 *11am–11pm Mon–Sat; 12–10.30pm Sun.*

The Windmill
6–8 Mill Street, Mayfair W1R 9TE
☎ *(020) 7491 8050* Pauline Smith
www.windmillmayfair.co.uk

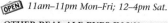 Wells and Young's house serving Young's Special, Charles Wells Bombardier and a seasonal brew.

Cosy, traditional and comfortable alehouse with two bars and a private room available for hire. Award-winning food served 12–9.30pm Mon–Fri, 12–4pm Sat. Close to Oxford Street and the London Palladium, off Regent Street.

⊖ Nearest Tube: Oxford Circus.
🍺 *11am–11pm Mon–Fri; 12–4pm Sat.*

OTHER REAL ALE PUBS IN W1
Carlisle Arms
2 Bateman Street, Soho W1D 4AE
☎ *(020) 7479 7951*

Coach & Horses
5 Bruton Street, Mayfair W1J 6PT
☎ *(020) 7629 4123*

Coach & Horses (SHEPHERD NEAME)
5 Hill Street, Mayfair W1J 5LD
☎ *(020) 7355 0300*

Dog & Duck
18 Bateman Street, Soho W1D 3AJ
☎ *(020) 7494 0697*

Duke of Wellington
94a Crawford Street, W1H 2HQ
☎ *(020) 722 49435*

Golden Lion
25 King Street SW1Y 6QY
☎ *(020) 7925 0007*

Grafton Arms (GREENE KING)
72 Grafton Way W1 ☎ *(020) 7387 7923*

The Hope
5 Tottenham Street W1T 2AJ
☎ *(020) 7637 0896*

Horse & Groom (SAM SMITHS)
128 Great Portland Street W1W 6PS
☎ *(020) 7580 4726*

Iron Duke (FULLER'S)
11 Avery Row, Mayfair W1X 9HA
☎ *(020) 7629 1643*

Jack Horner (FULLER'S)
236 Tottenham Court Road W1P 9AE
☎ *(020) 7636 2868*

King & Queen
1 Foley Street W1W 6DL ☎ *(020) 7636 5619*

Masons Arms (HALL & WOODHOUSE)
51 Upper Berkeley Street W1H 7QW
☎ *(020) 7723 2131*

The Moon & Sixpence
(WETHERSPOON)
183–5 Wardour Street W1V 3FB
☎ *(020) 7734 0037*

Newman Arms
23 Rathbone Street W1T 1NG
☎ *(020) 7636 1127*

Old Monk
24-6 Maddox Street W1R 9PG
☎ *(020) 7499 3775*

One Tun (WELLS AND YOUNG'S)
58–60 Goodge Street W1T 4ND
☎ *(020) 7209 4105*

Pillars of Hercules
7 Greek Street, Soho W1 ☎ *(020) 7437 1179*

Ship (FULLER'S)
116 Wardour Street W1F 0TT
☎ *(020) 7437 8446*

Sun & 13 Cantons (FULLER'S)
21 Great Pultney Street W1R 3DB
☎ *(020) 7734 0934*

Wargrave Arms (WELLS AND YOUNG'S)
42 Brendon Street W1H 5HS ☎ *(020) 7723 0559*

W2
Fountain's Abbey
109 Praed Street W2 1RL
☎ *(020) 7723 2364* David Harrison

Five real ales, including beers such as Fuller's London Pride, Young's Bitter and Charles Wells Bombardier, plus guests rotated weekly.

A large, Victorian-style alehouse, opened in 1824, just across the street from where Fleming discovered penicillin! Original fireplace. Sports bar upstairs with large screen, two pool tables, darts – the room is also available for hire. Food available 12–9.30pm. Two-minute walk from tube station.

⊖ Nearest Tube: Paddington.

OPEN *11am–11pm Mon–Sat; 12–10.30pm Sun.*

Mad Bishop & Bear
1st Floor, The Lawn, Paddington Station W2 1HB
☎ *(020) 7402 2441* David Lewis

Tied to Fuller's with up to five beers from the brewery range plus a guests such as St Austell Tribute.

V ery handy place to wait for a train. Large, open-plan bar dominated by a huge chandelier. Large-screen TV. Food, including breakfast, served all day from 8am–9pm. Plenty of outside seating.

⊖ Nearest Tube: Paddington.

OPEN *8am–11pm Mon–Weds and Sat; 8am–11.30pm Thurs–Fri; 10am–10.30pm Sun.*

The Mitre
24 Craven Terrace W2 3QH
☎ *(020) 7262 5240* Sarah Grundy
www.mitrebayswater.com

Real ales including Greene King IPA, Adnams Bitter, Hogs Back TEA, Charles Wells Bombardier and Fuller's London Pride plus occasional guests.

S treet-corner freehouse restored and refurbished in a Grade II listed building. Food available at lunchtime and evenings. Outside seating, basement bar and upstairs function room for hire.

⊖ Nearest Tube: Lancaster Gate.

OPEN *All day, every day*

Prince Edward
73 Princes Street, Bayswater W2 4NY
☎ *(020) 7727 2221* David Durling

Hall & Woodhouse pub with four real ales. Badger First Gold, Tanglefoot and King & Barnes Sussex are permanently featured, and there is also a seasonal guest.

T raditional-style pub in an Edwardian building. Large, circular bar in the middle, open fire and many original features. Food served 12–3pm and 5.30–10pm Mon–Fri and 12–10pm Sat–Sun, including daily specials and Sunday roasts. Outside pavement licence with tables and chairs. Private bar below available for private hire. Children welcome till 8pm.

⊖ Nearest Tube: Bayswater.

OPEN *12–11.30pm (11pm Sun).*

The Victoria
10A Strathearn Place, Paddington W2 2NH
☎ *(020) 7724 1191*
Chris Cochran and Helen Wilson

Tied to Fuller's, so with Discovery, London Pride and ESB always available plus a guest from Fuller's or Gale's, changed regularly.

V ictorian alehouse with many original features and elegant dining and function rooms. Outside patio can cope with 35 people. Quiz night on Tues. Food served 12–9.30pm Mon–Sat, 12–9pm Sun (Sunday roast available). Five minutes from Hyde Park.

⊖ Nearest Tube: Paddington.

OPEN *11am–11pm (10.30pm Sun).*

OTHER REAL ALE PUBS IN W2
Kings Head
33 Moscow Road W2 4AH ☎ *(020) 7229 4233*

Monkey Puzzle
(HALL & WOODHOUSE)
30 Southwick Street W2 1JQ
☎ *(020) 7723 0143*

The Tyburn (WETHERSPOON)
18–20 Edgware Road W2 2EN
☎ *(020) 7723 4731*

W3
Kings Head
214 High Street, Acton W3 9NX
☎ *(020) 8992 0282* Carl and Shabina Flynn

Tied to Fuller's so with Chiswick, London Pride and ESB always available plus a seasonal brew.

V ictorian community pub on the high street. One bar, one function room (available for hire). Comedy and live music nights. Sporting events shown. Food served 12–3pm and 5–9pm Mon–Fri, 12pm–8pm Sat–Sun.

OPEN *11am–11pm Mon–Sat; 12–11pm Sun.*

OTHER REAL ALE PUBS IN W3
Castle (FULLER'S)
Victoria Road, North Acton W3 6UL
☎ *(020) 8992 2027*

Kings Arms (FULLER'S)
Acton Vale, Acton W3 7JT ☎ *(020) 8743 2689*

The Red Lion & Pineapple
(WETHERSPOON)
281 High Street, Acton W3 9PJ
☎ *(020) 8896 2248*

W4

The Bell & Crown

11–13 Thames Road, Strand on the Green, Chiswick W4 3PL
☎ *(020) 8994 4164* Frank McBrearty

Fuller's tied house with London Pride, Chiswick and ESB permanently on offer. Fuller's seasonal ales served as available.

Backing on to the Thames, with excellent views, this substantial pub has a 40-seater dining area/conservatory and outside seating. Food available 12–10pm daily (8pm Sun). Children allowed, under supervision.

⊖ Nearest Tube: Gunnersbury.

OPEN *11am–11pm (10.30pm Sun).*

The George & Devonshire

8 Burlington Lane, Chiswick W4 2QE
☎ *(020) 8994 1859* Anthony Shields

Another Fuller's tied house with London Pride, Chiswick and ESB permanently on offer. Fuller's seasonal ales also served.

The building dates from 1790, and still has the public/saloon bar split. Food served 12–3pm and 5–8pm Mon–Thurs; 12–3pm and 6–9pm Fri–Sat; 12–4pm Sun. Car park, beer garden with heated area for smokers, children welcome. Function room for hire. Live music most Saturdays. Close to Fuller's Brewery and the river.

⊖ Nearest Tube: Turnham Green.

OPEN *12–11pm.*

OTHER REAL ALE PUBS IN W4

Crown & Anchor

374 Chiswick High Road, Chiswick W4 5TA
☎ *(020) 8995 2607*

Duke of York (FULLER'S)

107 Devonshire Road, Chiswick W4 2HU
☎ *(020) 8994 4624*

George IV (FULLER'S)

185 Chiswick High Road, Chiswick W4 1DR
☎ *(020) 8994 4624*

Mawson Arms (FULLER'S)

Mawson Lane, Chiswick W4 2QD
☎ *(020) 8994 2936*

Old Pack Horse (FULLER'S)

434 Chiswick High Road, Chiswick W4 5TF
☎ *(020) 8994 2872*

Pilot (FULLER'S)

56 Wellesley Road, Chiswick W4 4BZ
☎ *(020) 8994 0828*

W5

The Plough Inn

297 Northfield Avenue, Ealing W5 4XB
☎ *(020) 8567 1416* Andrew Durn

Tied to Fuller's with Chiswick, Discovery, London Pride and ESB plus Gale's HSB and one rotating guest.

One of the oldest pubs in the area. Food served 12–10pm. Large beer garden with children's play area. Jazz and quiz nights.

⊖ Nearest Tube: Northfields.

OPEN *All day, every day with extended hours most nights.*

The Red Lion

13 St Mary's Road, Ealing W5 5RA
☎ *(020) 8567 2541* Jonathan and Victoria Lee

Fuller's Chiswick, London Pride, ESB and Discovery plus a seasonal brew.

Small, traditional, Grade II listed, one-bar Fuller's pub, approximately 100 years old, although a Red Lion has stood here for over 350 years! No music or machines. Large patio garden. Food served 12–3pm and 7–9.30pm Mon–Sat, 12–5pm Sun. Children allowed in garden only. Situated opposite Ealing Studios. Local CAMRA Pub of the Year 2005 and 2006. Opposite Ealing Studios.

⊖ Nearest Tube: Ealing Broadway.

OPEN *11am–11pm Sun–Wed; 11am–midnight Thurs–Sat.*

TJ Duffy's

282 Northfield Avenue, Ealing W5 4UB
☎ *(020) 8932 1711* Margaret Deesy
www.tjduffy.com

Fuller's London Pride and Greene King Abbot plus a regularly changing guest.

Freehouse with one main bar and beer garden. Food served 12–2.30pm and 6–9pm. Small parties catered for.

⊖ Nearest Tube: Northfields.

OPEN *11am–11pm Mon–Sat; 12–10.30pm Sun.*

OTHER REAL ALE PUBS IN W5

Castle (FULLER'S)

36 St Mary's Road, Ealing W5 5RG
☎ *(020) 8567 3285*

Fox & Goose Hotel (FULLER'S)

Hanger Lane, Ealing W5 1DP
☎ *(020) 8998 5864*

Grapevine

Questors Theatre, 12 Mattock Lane, Ealing W5 5BQ ☎ *(020) 8567 0071*

Hogshead

46–7 The Mall, Ealing W5 3TJ
☎ *(020) 8579 3006*

Rose & Crown (FULLER'S)

Church Place, St Mary's Road, Ealing W5 4HN
☎ *(020) 8567 2811*

Townhouse (FULLER'S)

The Broadway, Ealing W5 2PH
☎ *(020) 8810 0304*

Wheatsheaf (FULLER'S)
41 Haven Lane, Ealing W5 2HZ
☎ *(020) 8997 5240*

The Blue Anchor
13 Lower Mall, Hammersmith Bridge W6 9DJ
☎ *(020) 8748 5774* Louis Amato
www.blueanchorpub1772.com

Tied to Enterprise Inns, with three real ales changed every three months, perhaps Brains SA, Caledonian Deuchars IPA, Sharp's Doom Bar or something from Adnams.

Small, cosy, historic pub on the river towpath near Hammersmith Bridge. First licenced in 1772. The ground floor is a traditional panelled river pub, upstairs there is a separate bar with great views of the river. Upstairs 'River Room' available for hire. Food available 12–9pm Mon–Fri, 12-8.30pm Sat–Sun. An obvious venue for watching the Boat Race and other river events. Handy for riverside walks. On the north side of the Thames, the first pub past Hammersmith Bridge.

⊖ Nearest Tube: Hammersmith.
OPEN *11am–11pm.*

The Cross Keys
57 Black Lion Lane, Hammersmith W6 9BG
☎ *(020) 8748 3541* Michael Franklin

Fuller's London Pride and a seasonal ale usually available.

A traditional pub with back garden open in summer. Food served 12–3pm and 6–9pm Mon–Sat, 12–5pm Sun. Quiz night on Thurs, live music once a month. Darts and board games. Big-screen TV for sports events. Children welcome before 9pm.

⊖ Nearest Tube: Stamford Brook.
OPEN *12–11pm Mon–Thurs; 12–12 Fri–Sat; 12–10.30pm Sun.*

Dove
19 Upper Mall, Hammersmith W6 9TA
☎ *(020) 8748 9474* Nick Kiley
www.fullers.co.uk

A Fuller's house, with London Pride, Discovery and ESB always available plus the seasonal brews.

Classic English inn steeped in history, full of character and old English charm. Charles II and Nell Gwynne met here, and two plaques on the wall list famous regulars through the years. Backing on to the Thames near Hammersmith Bridge. Owned by Fuller's since 1845. Features the smallest bar in Britain, but with plenty of space (inside and out) elsewhere. Food available 12–3pm and 5–10pm Mon–Fri; 12–10pm Sat and 12–7pm Sun. No machines or music. Beer garden on the Thames. Dogs welcome, children not allowed.

⊖ Nearest Tube: Hammersmith/Ravenscourt Park.
OPEN *11am–11pm Mon–Sat; 12–10.30pm Sun.*

Thatched House
115 Dalling Road, Hammersmith W6 0ET
☎ *(020) 8748 6174* Tom Gavaghan
www.thatchedhouse.com

Up to four real ales available including Young's Bitter and Special, Charles Wells Bombardier and seasonal ales.

Traditional alehouse also catering to the wine bar crowd. One large bar plus conservatory and beer garden. Food served 12–10pm daily.

⊖ Nearest Tube: Ravenscourt Park.
OPEN *12–11.30pm Sun–Thurs; noon–12.30am Fri–Sat.*

OTHER REAL ALE PUBS IN W6

Andover Arms (FULLER'S)
57 Aldensley Road W6 0DL
☎ *(020) 8741 9794*

Brook Green Hotel
(WELLS AND YOUNG'S)
170 Shepherds Bush Road W6 7PB
☎ *(020) 7603 2516*

Hammersmith Ram
(WELLS AND YOUNG'S)
81 King Street, Hammersmith W6 9HW
☎ *(020) 8748 4511*

Latymers (FULLER'S)
157 Hammersmith Road, Hammersmith W6 8BS
☎ *(020) 8748 3446*

Plough & Harrow (WETHERSPOON)
124 King Street, Hammersmith W6 0QU
☎ *(020) 8735 6020*

Salutation (FULLER'S)
154 King Street, Hammersmith W6 0QU
☎ *(020) 8748 3668*

Stonemasons Arms (FULLER'S)
54 Cambridge Grove, Hammersmith W6 0LA
☎ *(020) 8748 1397*

The William Morris
(WETHERSPOON)
2–4 King Street, Hammersmith W6 0QA
☎ *(020) 8741 7175*

The Dolphin
13 Lower Boston Road, Hanwell W7 3TX
☎ *(020) 8810 1617* John Connolly

Marston's Pedigree, Brakspear Bitter, Greene King Old Speckled Hen, Fuller's London Pride, Wadworth 6X or Gale's HSB usually available. A guest beer such as Badger Tanglefoot often on offer, too.

Olde-worlde character pub with wooden floors, lovely beer garden and restaurant. Food served 12–2.30pm and 6–9pm Tues–Sun. Kitchen closed Sun evening and Monday. Children welcome, with separate children's menu available. Small car park. Located off one-way system to Uxbridge Road or follow Boston Road to end.

OPEN *12–11pm (10.30pm Sun).*

The Fox

Greene Lane, Olde Hanwell W7 2PJ
☎ *(020) 8567 3912*
www.thefoxpub.co.uk

 Fuller's London Pride, Timothy Taylor Landlord and Black Sheep Bitter plus two guests, always changing, from breweries such as Twickenham, Archers, Cottage, Highwood, Wychwood, Kelham Island and Daleside. There is also a hand-selected wine list.

Unique family-run inn dating from around 1845, in a peaceful spot within yards of the Grand Union Canal at the junction of the Brent River and Hanwell flight of locks. Well-appointed Victorian bar and enclosed beer garden, a welcome pit-stop for ramblers, canal enthusiasts, real ale connoisseurs, cyclists and dog walkers, where children are also welcome. Freshly cooked, locally sourced food served: weekday lunches 12–3pm, brunch on Sat 12–4pm, traditional Sunday roasts 12.30–3pm; evening meals 6–9.30pm; children's menu available. Renowned Thursday quiz night and annual Easter and October beer festivals. Regular summer BBQs and live music nights. Local CAMRA Pub of the Year 2005 and 2007. Off Boston Road, a ten minute walk from Hanwell railway station, or E8 bus from Boston Manor tube station.

11am–11pm Mon–Sat; 12–10.30pm Sun.

OTHER REAL ALE PUBS IN W7

Viaduct (FULLER'S)

221 Uxbridge Road, Hanwell W7 3TD
☎ *(020) 8567 1362*

White Hart (FULLER'S)

324 Greenford Avenue, Hanwell W7 3DA
☎ *(020) 8578 1708*

W8

Churchill Arms

119 Kensington Church Street W8 7LN
☎ *(020) 7727 4242* Gerry O'Brien
www.fullers.co.uk

Another Fuller's house, so with Chiswick, London Pride, ESB and seasonal brews.

A popular, atmospheric, 1930s, award-winning locals' pub with plenty of Churchill family memorabilia (they celebrate his birthday in style). Thai food available 12–9.30pm Mon–Sat, 12–8pm Sun. Conservatory.

⊖ Nearest Tube: Notting Hill Gate.

11am–11pm Mon–Sat; 12–10.30pm Sun.

Windsor Castle

114 Campden Hill Road W8 7AR
☎ *(020) 7243 9551* Sally Hemmingway

Fuller's London Pride, Timothy Taylor Landlord and Adnams Broadside usually available plus guests.

Dating from 1835 on the brow of the hill. Three drinking areas with wooden floors and panelled walls. Large garden. Food served 12–10pm.

11am–11pm Mon–Sat; 12–10.30pm Sun.

OTHER REAL ALE PUBS IN W8

Britannia (WELLS AND YOUNG'S)

1 Allen Street, Kensington W8 6UX
☎ *(020) 7937 6905*

Uxbridge Arms

13 Uxbridge Street, Notting Hill Gate W8 7TQ
☎ *(020) 7727 7326*

W9

The Truscott Arms

55 Shirland Road, Maida Vale W9 2JD
☎ *(020) 7286 0310* Barbara Slack

Fuller's London Pride, Greene King IPA and Abbot plus other Fuller's beers.

Local community pub with one large centre bar. Secluded rear beer garden. Food served 12–3pm and 6–9pm Mon–Sat, plus 12–3pm Sun for traditional roasts and summer barbecues (weather permitting). Children are welcome until 7pm.

⊖ Nearest Tube: Warwick Avenue.

11am–11pm Mon–Sat; 12–10.30pm Sun.

Warrington Hotel

93 Warrington Crescent, Maida Vale W9 1EH
☎ *(020) 7286 2929* J Brandon

Brakspear Special, Young's Special, Fuller's London Pride and ESB plus one or two guest beers perhaps from Rebellion.

A splendid example of a Victorian public house with art nouveau stained glass, marble bar and fireplace. A family-owned freehouse which has been a popular meeting place for many years. Thai food served in the bar 12–2.30pm and in the upstairs restaurant 6–11pm. No children. Outside seating.

⊖ Nearest Tube: Warwick Avenue.

11am–midnight Mon–Sat; 12–10.30pm Sun.

OTHER REAL ALE PUBS IN W9

Grand Union (FULLER'S)

45 Woodfield Road W9 2BA
☎ *(020) 7286 1886*

W11

Duke of Wellington

179 Portobello Road W11 2ED
☎ *(020) 7727 6727* Stuart Down

Tied to Wells and Young's with Young's Bitter, Special and a seasonal ale available.

Traditional 200-year-old pub with lots of character, at the heart of Portobello Market. One island bar. Food served 9.30am–11pm Mon–Sat and 11.30am–10pm Sun. Functions catered for. Children welcome. Special events, such as St George's Day, celebrated.

⊖ Nearest Tube: Ladbroke Grove.

9am–midnight Mon–Fri; 8am–midnight Sat; 11.30am–10.30pm Sun.

The Elgin

96 Ladbroke Grove W11 1PY
☎ *(020) 7229 5663* Delwynne Fife

Charles Wells Bombardier and Greene King IPA available plus a guest rotated every two weeks.

Built in the 1850s, the original wooden interior with stained-glass windows and mirrors remain. Soft seating and dining areas plus private room for hire. Food served 12–9.30pm Mon–Sat, 12–8.30pm Sun. Three plasma screens and big screen for sports. Under-18s welcome until 6pm. Close to Portobello Road.

✪ Nearest Tube: Ladbroke Grove.

OPEN *12–11pm Mon–Thurs; 12–11.30pm Fri–Sat; 12–10.30pm Sun.*

OTHER REAL ALE PUBS IN W11

Cock & Bottle

17 Needham Road, Notting Hill W11 2RP
☎ *(020) 7229 1550*

W12

Crown & Sceptre

57 Melina Road, Shepherds Bush W12 9HY
☎ *(020) 8743 6414* Rachel Watson

Owned by Fuller's, with London Pride, a seasonal brew and one guest available.

Cosy gastropub in the heart of the local community. Good-sized beer garden, on-street parking. Food served 12–3pm and 6–10pm Mon–Fri, 12–10pm Sat and 12–9pm Sun. Quiz every Monday at 9pm.

✪ Nearest Tube: Goldhawk Road/Shepherds Bush/Stamford Brook.

OPEN *12–11pm (10.30pm Sun).*

OTHER REAL ALE PUBS IN W12

Central Bar (WETHERSPOON)

W12 Shopping Centre, Shepherds Bush Green W12 8PH ☎ *(020) 8746 4290*

The Eagle

215 Askew Road W12 9AZ ☎ *(020) 8746 0046*

Vesbar (FULLER'S)

15–19 Goldhawk Road, Shepherds Bush W12 8QQ
☎ *(020) 8762 0215*

W13

Duke of Kent

2 Scotch Common, Ealing W13 8DL
☎ *(020) 8911 7820* Kieron O'Donnell

Three real ales from Fuller's, plus one guest.

Grade II listed Georgian pub. Traditional features and modern twists. Beer garden with heated patio. Limited parking, disabled facilities. Food served 12–3pm and 5–9pm Mon–Thurs, 12–9.30pm Fri–Sun. Off the A40 at Perivale, just beyond Scotch Common.

OPEN *11.30am–11pm Mon–Sat; 12–10.30pm Sun.*

OTHER REAL ALE PUBS IN W13

Drayton Court Hotel (FULLER'S)

2 The Avenue, Ealing W13 8PH
☎ *(020) 8997 1019*

W14

Britannia Tap

150 Warwick Road, West Kensington W14 8PS
☎ *(020) 7602 1649* Dale Neil

Tied to Wells and Young's with Young's Bitter, Special and either Waggle Dance or Winter Warmer plus a guest such as Smiles Bristol Bitter.

Tiny pub with award-winning walled garden. Good-priced Thai food available 12–12 daily. Five minutes from Olympia.

✪ Nearest Tube: Kensington.

OPEN *11am–midnight Mon–Sat; 12–11pm Sun.*

OTHER REAL ALE PUBS IN W14

Crown & Sceptre

34 Holland Road, Kensington W14 8BA
☎ *(020) 780 1866*

Seven Stars (FULLER'S)

253 North End Road, Kensington W14 9NS
☎ *(020) 7385 3571*

Warwick Arms (FULLER'S)

160 Warwick Road, Kensington W14 9OS
☎ *(020) 7603 356*

FURTHER WEST

ASHFORD

Kings Fairway

91 Fordbridge Road, Ashford TW15 2SS
☎ *(01784) 423575* Linda Bowman

An Ember Inns pub. Fuller's London Pride. Five guests, changed every two or three days. Regulars include Adnams Broadside, Brains SA, Otter Gold and Ale, Okells IPA and Highgate Whisky Ale.

A one-bar pub with home-style décor. Over-14s allowed, if eating. Food served 12–9pm. Car park.

OPEN *12–11pm Sun–Thurs; 12–12 Fri–Sat.*

BRENTFORD

The Magpie & Crown

128 High Street, Brentford TW8 8EW
☎ *(020) 8560 5658* Charlie and Steve Bolton

Freehouse with four pumps serving a range of good-priced ales such as Brakspear Bitter, Greene King IPA, something from Cottage and many, many more including local brews from Grand Union and Twickenham.

A mock-Tudor pub. One bar that claims to have served 1,600 real ales. English and Thai food served at lunchtime and evenings. No children. Quiz nights on Thursday. Also serves draught European beers, plus ciders and perry.

OPEN *11am–11pm (10.30pm Sun).*

EGHAM
The Crown
38 High Street, Egham TW20 9DP
☎ *(01784) 432608* Lin Bowman

The permanent beers are Adnams Broadside in winter and Adnams Regatta in summer, and the two or three guests, changed weekly, are from a wide range of breweries.

Very busy town pub with one bar, dining area and garden. Plenty of food available! Twice-yearly beer festivals held, with around ten beers at each. Occasional live music.

11.30am–11pm Mon–Sat; 12–10.30pm Sun.

FELTHAM
Moon on the Square
30 The Centre, Feltham TW13 4AU
☎ *(020) 8893 1293* Bagrat Shahbazian

Greene King Abbot plus four guests, changing all the time, from breweries such as Brakspear, Cotleigh, Hook Norton and Exmoor.

One big bar plus dining area in which food is available all day. Children allowed until 3pm.

All day, every day.

HOUNSLOW
Moon Under Water
84–6 Staines Road, Hounslow TW3 3LF
☎ *(020) 8572 7506* Peter Johnson

Greene King Abbot and Old Speckled Hen plus Courage Best and up to five guests from an extended list which is constantly changing. Examples include Nethergate Old Growler, Twickenham Strong & Dark, Bateman XXXB and beers from Weltons, and the pub sells 2,600 pints every week.

Well-known, no-frills Wetherspoon's pub that has had stable management for eight years, and has been winning awards for the past six years. Food available 10am–11pm (9.30pm Sun). Patio, disabled facilities. Children allowed until 8pm.

10am–11pm (10.30pm Sun).

ISLEWORTH
The Red Lion
94 Linkfield Road, Isleworth TW7 6QJ
☎ *(020) 8560 1457* Paul Andrews
www.red-lion.info

Beers offered: nine real ales on pump at any one time. Young's Bitter is the house brew. Beer of the Month promotions have featured Harviestoun Bitter and Twisted, Timothy Taylor Landlord, Branscombe Vale Branoc, Otter Ale, Woodforde's Wherry, Marston's Pedigree and Crouch Vale Brewers Gold. Other regular guests include beers from Daleside, Oakham, Hogs Back, Hop Back and Blue Anchor. Monday nights from 6pm all real ales £2 per pint. Tasting notes and knowledgable staff available.

A large, friendly, locals' pub in a back street near Isleworth (BR) station, situated in an early-Victorian residential area close to Twickenham Rugby Ground and Richmond.

Regular live music and a generally relaxed atmosphere. Two bars and a large landscaped garden with regular BBQs in the summer. Corporate hospitality facilities available. Listed in *Time Out* Top 50 Pubs in London 2003 and local CAMRA Pub of the Year 2003 and 2004. Children allowed in the garden. Jam Night on Weds. Quiz night is Thurs. Beer festivals (May and August bank holidays) feature 50 real ales and ciders. Check website for 'Mini Beer Festivals' and special events.

All day, every day.

LALEHAM
The Feathers
The Broadway, Laleham, Nr Staines TW18 1RZ
☎ *(01784) 453561* Terry de Young

Genuine freehouse serving five real ales, all of which rotate on a daily basis. The emphasis is on beer from micro-breweries.

Approximately 150 years old, a pub with one bar supplying two separate areas. Wood beams, fitted furniture, plasma-screen TV, pub games. Food served 12–3pm and 6–9pm Mon–Fri, 12–8pm Sat and 12–5pm Sun. Beer garden at front and back. Car park, children welcome. Beer festival (30 real ales) held on the first weekend of July.

11am–11pm Mon–Sat; 12–10.30pm Sun.

STAINES
The Angel Hotel
Angel Mews, High Street, Staines TW18 4EE
☎ *(01784) 452509* John Othick

Freehouse with up to four real ales including two from Hogs Back, varying according to the season.

A town pub and restaurant with patio and 12 bedrooms. Food available all day.

All day, every day.

The Bells
124 Church Street, Staines TW18 4ZB
☎ *(01784) 454240* Mr and Mrs Winstanley

Tied to Wells and Young's, with Young's Special and Triple A always served, plus one guest from Smiles.

Village pub with village atmosphere, with two bars, function room and beer garden. Food available. Children allowed in designated areas.

11am–11pm Mon–Sat; 12–10.30pm Sun.

The George
2–8 High Street, Staines TW18 4EE
☎ *(01784) 462181* Barbara Westwood

Fuller's London Pride and Greene King Abbot plus four guests such as Marston's Pedigree, Shepherd Neame Spitfire and Greene King Old Speckled Hen. Always a good selection of brews from all over the UK. Guests changed frequently.

Large, two-level Wetherspoon's pub. No music, dining areas upstairs and down, disabled access and toilets. Food available 10am–10pm Mon–Sat, 10am–9.30pm Sun; alcohol served from 10am except on Sundays. Children allowed, if eating, until 9pm Sun–Thurs and until 6pm Fri–Sat.

All day, every day.

The Hobgoblin

14–16 Church Street, Staines TW18 4EP
☎ *(01784) 452012* Simon Barker

Freehouse serving Wychwood Hobgoblin and three local guests, changed weekly, from breweries such as Twickenham, Hogs Back and Church End, and micro-breweries such as Waylands. Bottles ales from Wychwood also available.

A town-centre pub with plenty of character, frequented by the 21–35 age group in evenings, with an older clientele at lunchtimes. An old building with wooden floors and beams. Small walled beer garden with heating. Live music Thursdays and Sundays. Mexican food available 12–8pm.

OPEN *12–11pm Sun–Thurs; noon–1am Fri–Sat.*

The Wheatsheaf & Pigeon

Penton Road, Staines TW18 2LL
☎ *(01784) 452922* John and Elaine Cornish
www.thewheatsheafandpigeon.co.uk

Freehouse serving Fuller's London Pride and Courage Best Bitter plus two rotating guests.

Situated 150 yards from the River Thames, and dating from the late 19th century, this is a truly family-run pub with one bar and a cottage restaurant. Food served 12–2.30pm and 6–9pm Tues–Fri (no food Mondays); 12–9pm Sat; 12–5pm Sun. Large outside seating area, including garden. August bank holiday event with tug-o-war, barbecue and band. Located between Staines and Laleham, off Laleham Road.

OPEN *11am–11pm Mon–Sat; 12–10.30pm Sun.*

TEDDINGTON

The Lion

27 Wick Road, Teddington TW11 9DN
☎ *(020) 8977 3199* John Brandon
www.thelionpub.co.uk

Freehouse serving five real ales, including Fuller's London Pride and guests such as Caledonian Deuchars IPA, Sharp's Cornish Coaster and many more.

Traditional Victorian pub and former local CAMRA Pub of the Year. Food served 12–2.30pm and 6–9pm Mon–Sat, 12.30–3pm Sun. Live music and quiz nights. Function room available. Occasional barbecues in the beer garden plus an annual beer festival. Children's play area. Five minutes' walk from Hampton Wick station.

OPEN *11am–11pm Mon–Sat; 12–10.30pm Sun.*

TWICKENHAM

The Eel Pie

9–11 Church Street, Twickenham TW1 3NJ
☎ *(020) 8891 1717* Tom and Kate McAuley

Badger Best, Tanglefoot and IPA and King & Barnes Sussex always available, plus two guests which may include Gribble Brewery's Fursty Ferret or Pig's Ear, or possibly from time to time, Timothy Taylor Landlord, Oakham JHB or Slaters Top Totty.

Cosy, traditional pub with laid-back atmosphere situated just off the main street in Twickenham. A newcomer is welcome either to keep themselves to themselves, or to be the life and soul of the party! Food available 12–4pm daily. Children allowed, children's menu available.

OPEN *11am–11pm Mon–Sat; 12–10.30pm Sun.*

Up 'N' Under

33–5 York Street, Twickenham TW1 3JZ
☎ *(020) 8891 3940* Aimy Lovell

Up to four real ales stocked, and changed on a monthly basis. Caledonian Deuchars IPA and Fuller's London Pride are favourites.

A stylish, dimly lit bar and gastropub serving traditional food, which is available 12–4pm and 6–10pm daily. Greek/Mediterranean restaurant upstairs. All sports shown on big-screen TV. Function room, disabled facilities. Children welcome. Two minutes from the station.

OPEN *Noon–12.30am Sun–Thurs; noon–1am Fri–Sat.*

UXBRIDGE

The Load of Hay

33 Villier Street, Uxbridge UB8 2PU
☎ *(01895) 234676* Gary Carpenter

Genuine freehouse with Fuller's London Pride plus three real ales from breweries such as Archers, Cottage, Vale and Rebellion, rotated every few days.

Once the site of the stables of the Elthorne Light Militia (hence the name), a pub since the 1870s on the outskirts of town, near the university. University clientele during the daytime and locals in the evenings. Two bars and beer garden. Food available 12–2.45pm and 7–9.45pm Mon–Sat, 12–4pm and 7–9.30pm Sun. Children welcome until 9pm in the smaller bar area and the garden. Live music on Fri–Sat nights. In a secluded location – ring for directions if necessary.

OPEN *11am–11pm Mon–Sat; 12–10.30pm Sun.*

The Swan & Bottle

Oxford Road, Uxbridge UB8 1LZ
☎ *(01895) 234047* Claire Chapman

Greene King Old Speckled Hen and Fuller's London Pride plus a guest from Brakspear.

A traditional 18th-century tavern next to the Grand Union canal, the ideal setting for any occasion. Children welcome, disabled access and toilets. Food available 11am–10pm. Huge car park. Off J16 of the M25.

OPEN *11am–11pm.*

The Three Tuns

24 High Street, Uxbridge UB8 1JN
☎ *(01895) 233960* Brian Gallagher

Marston's Pedigree, Fuller's London Pride and Adnams Bitter always on offer.

Traditional town-centre pub with beams, fires, conservatory, beer garden and patio for 80 people. Food available (not Sundays), and there is a separate dining area. Children allowed if eating. Opposite the Tube Station.

OPEN *11am–11pm Mon–Sat; 12–10.30pm Sun.*

THE BREWERIES

ALL GATES BREWERY
Brewery Yard, Off Wallgate, Wigan WN1 1JU
☎ 07971 013982
www.allgatesbrewery.com

 YOUNG PRETENDER 3.8% ABV
Citrus flavours, pale.
NAPOLEON'S RETREAT 3.9% ABV
Malty, rounded, copper colour.
50 MARKS 4.0% ABV
Golden ale.
BRIGHTBLADE 4.0% ABV
Lemon and spice notes.
UNUSUAL SUSPECT 4.0% ABV
Straw colour, sweet finish.
BOTTOMS UP 4.2% ABV
Dry aftertaste.
HASTY KNOLL 4.2% ABV
Slightly sweet.
REVEREND RAY 4.6% ABV
Red, hoppy.
Plus seasonals and occasionals.

BANK TOP BREWERY LTD
The Pavillion, Ashworth Lane, Bolton BL1 8RA
☎ (01204) 595800
www.banktopbrewery.com

BIKES, TRIKES AND BEER 3.6% ABV
Pale, floral aroma.
BRYDGE BITTER 3.8% ABV
Pale, citrus aftertaste.
GAME, SET & MATCH 3.8% ABV
Blackcurrant flavour, hoppy aftertaste.
DARK MILD 4.0% ABV
Liquorice tones.
FLAT CAP 4.0% ABV
Citrus aroma, hoppy citrus finish.
GOLD DIGGER 4.0% ABV
Spicy hints.
OLD SLAPPER 4.2% ABV
Blonde and fruity.
SAMUEL CROMPTON'S ALE 4.2% ABV
Grapefruit notes.
VOLUNTEER BITTER 4.2% ABV
Floral aftertaste.
PAVILION 4.5% ABV
Pale and hoppy.
PORT O' CALL 5.0% ABV
Barley flavour, port overtones.
SANTA'S CLAWS 5.0% ABV
Copper colour, hoppy and fruity.
SMOKESTACK LIGHTNIN' 5.0% ABV
Straw coloured and hoppy.
Plus special brews.

BAZENS' BREWERY
Bazen Brewing Co Ltd, Unit 6 Knoll Street Industrial Park, Knoll Street, Salford M7 2BL
☎ (0161) 708 0247
www.bazensbrewery.co.uk

 BLACK PIG MILD 3.6% ABV
Chocolatey.
PACIFIC BITTER 3.8% ABV
Amber and malty.
FLATBAC 4.2% ABV
Blonde with citrus notes.
BLUE BULLET 4.5% ABV
Single hop.
KNOLL STREET PORTER 5.2% ABV
Plus seasonal and special brews including:
ZEBRA BEST BITTER 4.3% ABV
Crisp and malty.
EXSB 5.5% ABV
Orange peel flavours.

BOGGART HOLE CLOUGH BREWING COMPANY LTD
Unit 13 Brookside Works, Clough Road, Moston, Manchester M9 4SP
☎ (0161) 277 9666
www.boggart-brewery.co.uk

BOGGART BITTER 3.8% ABV
BOG STANDARD 4.0% ABV
LOG END 4.0% ABV
ANGEL HILL 4.2% ABV
BOGGART'S BREW 4.3% ABV
THE DARK SIDE 4.4% ABV
SUNDIAL 4.7% ABV
STEAMING BOGGART 9.0% ABV

GREENFIELD REAL ALE BREWERY LTD
Unit 8 Waterside Mills, Chew Valley Road, Greenfield, Saddleworth OL3 7PF
☎ (01457) 879789
www.greenfieldrealale.co.uk

AMMON'S BITTER 4.0% ABV
BLACK FIVE 4.0% ABV
CELEBRATION 4.0% ABV
DOVESTONES BITTER 4.0% ABV
GREENFIELD ALE 4.0% ABV
GUY'S CRACKER 4.0% ABV
BILL'S O' JACK'S 4.1% ABV
DELPH DONKEY 4.1% ABV
CASTLESHAW 4.2% ABV
DENSHAW 4.2% ABV
DOBCROSS BITTER 4.2% ABV
EVENING GLORY 4.2% ABV
HOW DARE EWE 4.2% ABV
ICE BREAKER 4.2% ABV
PRIDE OF ENGLAND 4.2% ABV
UPPERMILL ALE 4.2% ABV
BRASSED OFF 4.4% ABV
FLYING SHUTTLE 4.4% ABV
FRIEZLAND ALE 4.4% ABV
ICICLE 4.4% ABV
INDIAN'S HEAD 4.4% ABV
LONGWOOD THUMP 4.5% ABV
HOPPED AND STONED 4.6% ABV
Plus seasonal beers and for special events to order.

J W LEES & CO.
Greengate Brewery, Middleton Junction, Manchester M24 2AX
☎ (0161) 643 2487
www.jwlees.co.uk

DARK SMOOTH 3.4% ABV
GB MILD 3.5% ABV
Smooth and sweet, with a malt flavour and a dry finish.
EXTRA SMOOTH BITTER 3.9% ABV
GREENGATE SMOOTH 3.9% ABV
BITTER 4.0% ABV
Refreshing maltiness, with a citrus aftertaste.
SCORCHER 4.2% ABV
Summer fruits and hops flavour.
MOONRAKER 7.5% ABV
Rounded sweetness, with balancing bitterness.

JOSEPH HOLT PLC

Derby Brewery, Empire Street, Cheetham, Manchester M3 1JD
☎ *(0161) 834 3285*
www.joseph-holt.com

MILD 3.2% ABV
Malty with good hoppiness.
BITTER 4.0% ABV
Powerful, hoppy and bitter throughout.

HYDES' ANVIL BREWERY LTD

46 Moss Lane West, Manchester M15 5PH
☎ *(0161) 226 1317*
www.hydesbrewery.co.uk

1863 3.5% ABV
Amber colour, slightly sweet.
HYDES MILD 3.5% ABV
Caramel taste.
OWD OAK 3.5% ABV
Dark colour with roast caramel flavour.
HYDES BITTER 3.8% ABV
Spicey hops and malt.
JEKYLL'S GOLD 4.3% ABV
Citrus aroma, fruity taste.
XXXX 6.8% ABV
Toffee taste and aroma.

THE LAB BREWERY

Lowes Arms, 301 Hyde Road, Denton M34 3FF
☎ *(0161) 336 3064*
www.lowesarms.co.uk

JET AMBER 3.5% ABV
IPA 3.8% ABV
FROG BOG BITTER 3.9% ABV
SWEET CLOG 4.0% ABV
WILD WOOD 4.1% ABV
BROOMSTAIRS BITTER 4.3% ABV
Plus seasonals.

LEYDEN BREWING COMPANY LIMITED

The Lord Raglan Hotel, Mount Pleasant, Nangreaves, Bury BL9 6SP
☎ *(0161) 764 6680*
www.leydenbrewery.com

NANNY FLYER 3.8% ABV
LIGHT BRIGADE 4.2% ABV
CROWNING GLORY 6.8% ABV
Very wide range of seasonals produced including:
BALACLAVA 3.8% ABV
BLACK PUDDING 3.9% ABV
FOREVER BURY 4.5% ABV
RAGLAN SLEEVE 4.6% ABV

MARBLE BREWERY

73 Rochdale Road, Manchester M4 4HY
☎ *(0161) 819 2694*
www.marblebeers.co.uk

N/4 3.8% ABV
Fruity hop, sweetness.
MANCHESTER BITTER 4.2% ABV
Light and full flavoured.
GINGER MARBLE 4.5% ABV
Light ginger beer with underlying spiciness.
UNCUT AMBER 4.7% ABV
Malty, sweet, yeasty.
LAGONDA IPA 5.0% ABV
Citrus flavour with dry, bitter finish.
CHOCOLATE HEAVY 5.5% ABV
Clean bitter with chocolatey flavour and slight fruitiness.
Plus seasonals and occasionals.

MAYFLOWER BREWERY

Mayflower House, 15 Longendale Road, Standish, Wigan WN6 0UE
☎ *(01257) 400605 or 07748 744781*
www.mayflowerbrewery.co.uk

DARK OAK 3.5% ABV
MYLES BEST BITTER 3.7% ABV
LIGHT OAK 4.0% ABV
SPECIAL BRANCH 4.2% ABV
Plus seasonals and occasionals.

OWL BREWING COMPANY LTD

The Hope Inn, 32 Greenacres Road, Oldham OL4 1HB
☎ *07889 631366*
www.owlbrew.co.uk

HORNY OWL 3.8% ABV
Dark red bitter with fruit tones.
YON OWL 3.8% ABV
Light, hoppy bitter.
GREENACRES GOLD 4.2% ABV
Honey-coloured, fruity bitter.
NIGHT OWL 4.2% ABV
Dark chocolatey porter.
RUSSETT OWL 4.2% ABV
Medium bitter.
Plus specials and seasonals.

PHOENIX BREWERY

Oak Brewing Co., Green Lane, Heywood OL10 2EP
☎ *(01706) 627009*

BANTAM BITTER 3.5% ABV
NAVVY 3.8% ABV
BEST BITTER 3.9% ABV
MONKEY TOWN MILD 3.9% ABV
ARIZONA 4.1% ABV
PALE MOONLIGHT 4.2% ABV
BLACK BEE 4.5% ABV
OLD OAK ALE 4.5% ABV
WHITE MONK 4.5% ABV
THIRSTY MOON 4.6% ABV
WEST COAST IPA 4.6% ABV
DOUBLE GOLD 5.0% ABV
DOUBLE DAGGER 5.1% ABV
WOBBLY BOB 6.1% ABV
Plus seasonal brews.

SADDLEWORTH BREWERY

Church Inn, Running Hill Gate, Uppermill, Oldham OL3 6LW
☎ *(01457) 820902*

CLOG DANCER 3.6% ABV
SADDLEWORTH MORE 3.8% ABV
BERT CORNET BITTER 4.0% ABV
ST GEORGE'S 4.0% ABV
HARVEST MOON 4.1% ABV
Some sweetness, but bitter in the finish.
HONEY SMACKER 4.1% ABV
HOPSMACKER 4.2% ABV
ROBYN'S BITTER 4.8% ABV
SHAFT BENDER 5.4% ABV
Occasionals:
XMAS CAROL 7.4% ABV

SHAWS BREWERY
Park Works, Park Road, Dukinfield SK16 5LX
☎ *(0161) 330 5471*

 BEST BITTER 4.0% ABV
A session beer typical of the north of England with a lingering aftertaste.
PURE GOLD 4.0% ABV
A pale ale with a dry, hoppy finish. Made using American hops.
GOLDEN GLOBE 4.3% ABV
Full-bodied and pale. Dry.
IPA 4.8% ABV
Premium pale ale designed to wean the Stella boys!
Occasionals:
TAME VALLEY ALE 4.3% ABV
Similar to Best Bitter but with more body and less bite in the aftertaste.
Plus monthly specials.

THREE RIVERS BREWING COMPANY
Delta House, Greg Street, Reddish, Stockport SK5 7BS
☎ *(0161) 477 3333*
www.3riversbrewing.com

 G.M.T. 3.8% ABV
Easy drinking, gold coloured with malty undertones.
AQUARIAN ALE 4.0% ABV
A russet amber ale brewed to reflect the most inventive of the zodiac signs.
HARRY JACKS 4.1% ABV
Rich, with fruit and malt.
MANCHESTER IPA 4.2% ABV
Classic Indian pale ale, made with genuine Manchester-grown hops.
PILGRIMS PROGRESS 4.2% ABV
Full bodied, with caramel tones.
OXBOW 4.5% ABV
Robust bitter with spice and citrus.
BLACK MOON 4.8% ABV
A rich, dark and unique stout brewed under licence from the Storm Brewing Company based in Bali, Indonesia. A full-bodied beer, smooth yet bitter with genuine Balinese chocolate included in the recipe.
CRYSTAL WHEAT 5.0% ABV
Brewed under licence from Beechams Bar in St Helens, this is a spicy, classic beer produced with Slovenian hops.
JULIE'S PRIDE 5.0% ABV
Fruit flavour, full-bodied bitter.
OLD DISREPUTABLE 5.2% ABV
Award-winning brew with hints of coffee and chocolate and a smooth finish.
SUITABLY IRISH 5.6% ABV
Irish bitter stout, very moreish.
Seasonals:
MURPHY'S LAW 4.5% ABV
YUMMY FIGGY PUDDING 7.5% ABV

THE PUBS

ASHTON-UNDER-LYNE

The Station Hotel
2 Warrington Street, Ashton-under-Lyne OL6 6XB
☎ *(0161) 330 6776*
Pauline Town

 The permanent beers are Holt Bitter, John Smith's and two that are specially brewed, Millstone Off the Rails and Holt Morrigan. The five guest beers are changed every couple of days and are usually from brewers in the North West.

Beautiful Victorian pub in the heart of Ashton's historic Old Town district, with railway memorabilia, period features and lots of old-fashioned charm. Soup, sandwiches and snacks served from noon onwards, with plans for a more extensive hot menu. Large beer garden with patio, lawn and fruit trees, and large conservatory furnished with Chesterfields and coffee tables. Lounge and snug both have open wood fires and table service. Separate pool room. Accompanied children welcome until 7pm. Tues night acoustic Celtic folk, Wed night quiz, Sun open mic. Occasional live bands. Four beer festivals a year. Snug available free of charge for private functions.

OPEN *12–12 (1am Fri–Sat).*

The Witchwood
152 Old Street, Ashton-under-Lyne OL6 7SF
☎ *(0161) 344 0321*
Graham Rees (licensee),
Davina Fitzpatrick (manager)
www.thewitchwood.co.uk

Nine real ales. Beers from Joseph Holt and John Smith's are the regular features, and the seven guest ales from independent brewers nationwide are changed every couple of days.

Award-winning real ale bar and separate live music venue (200 capacity, four to seven gigs a week, all types of music) in a Victorian building, a music venue since 1991. Sandwiches, soup and ploughmans available at lunchtimes from noon – new menu due summer 2008. Beer garden. Over-18s only. Beer festivals three times a year, plus regular themed mini-festivals. Free mailing list service. On the edge of the town centre, near the magistrates court and library.

OPEN *Bar: 12–12. Music venue: 8pm–12 Mon–Wed; 8pm–1am Thurs–Sun (times may vary depending on gigs).*

ASPULL

The Victoria Inn

50 Haigh Road, Aspull, Wigan WN2 1YA
☎ *(01942) 830869*
Kelly Thorpe and Lee Burrows
www.allgates-brewery.com

 Tied to All Gates, with Napoleon's Retreat, Young Pretender, and Hasty Knoll plus rotating guests on two pumps, including other All Gates brews such as Hop Gun and Shining Lite, and beers from breweries such as Shardlow, Slaters and Castle Rock.

Proper local pub with a warm, friendly atmosphere situated close to Haigh Country Park. Vault with pub games and Sky Sports, plus relaxed loung area with Sky TV (not on all the time!). Cold bar snacks and sandwiches. No children. Beer festivals and theme nights. Car park.

OPEN *1pm–close.*

ATHERTON

The Pendle Witch

2–4 Warburton Place, Atherton, Manchester M46 0EQ
☎ *(01942) 884537* Joan Houghton
www.moorhouses.co.uk

 Tied to Moorhouse's with Black Cat, Premier, Pendle Witches Brew, Pride of Pendle and Blond Witch plus one or two guests and a Moorhouse's seasonal ale.

A town-centre gem, sensitively refurbished and now featuring a dining conservatory and sun-trap garden/patio with giant parasols and heating. Quality meals served 12–4pm Mon–Fri, 12–6pm Sat and 12–4pm Sun. Spacious games rooms offering pool and big-screen TV. Beer festivals every bank holiday and alongside the annual Bent 'n' Bongs event. Situated off Market Street, close to the railway station.

OPEN *11am–midnight.*

BOLTON

Ainsworth Arms

606 Halliwell Road, Bolton BL1 8BY
☎ *(01204) 840671* Tony Bretherton

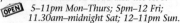 Timothy Taylor Landlord and Black Sheep Best Bitter plus a couple of Tetley beers and one guest, changed weekly.

One-bar rural pub, first licensed in 1836. Cards, darts and dominoes room, bar area and lounge. Food served 12–2pm Sat–Sun. Half a mile from Smithhills Hall, at the junction of Halliwell Road and the A58.

OPEN *5–11pm Mon–Thurs; 5pm–12 Fri; 11.30am–midnight Sat; 12–11pm Sun.*

The Flag Inn

Arnold Road, Egerton, Bolton BL7 9HL
☎ *(01204) 598267* Sharon Jones

 A Greene King tied house offering two local Bank Top ales, up to ten cask ales which rotate, and a vintage draught cider. Cask Marque accredited.

An original local with flag floor, real fire and three TVs showing Sky Sports. Views of the working cellar. Food served 12–2.30pm, 7 days a week. Covered outside smoking area. Beer garden with small patio. Children welcome until 7pm.

OPEN *12–11pm Sun–Thurs; 12–12 Fri–Sat.*

The Hen & Chickens

143 Deansgate, Bolton BL1 1EX
☎ *(01204) 389836* Anthony Coyne

Three guest ales, such as Charles Wells Bombardier, Jennings Cumberland, Greene King IPA and Marston's Pedigree. These are changed whenever they run out.

Traditional but smart real ale pub dating back to the 17th century with historical links to the Crimean War. Located on the fringe of the town centre close to the bus station. One central bar. Homemade food served at lunchtime only Mon to Sat (11.30am–2pm). Children welcome at lunchtime. Entry policy at night.

OPEN *11.30am–11pm Mon–Sat; 6.30pm–10.30pm Sun.*

Howcroft Inn

36 Pool Street, Bolton BL1 2JU
☎ *(01204) 526814*

Timothy Taylor Landlord, Tetley Bitter and a Bank Top brew plus guests, often from micro-breweries.

A traditional one-bar pub five minutes' walk from the town centre on the north side of town. Has appeared on the CAMRA/English Heritage pub interiors list. Beer garden and bowling green. Food served every lunchtime 12–2pm, and on Sundays 12–4pm. Children allowed.

OPEN *12–11pm Sun–Thurs; 12–12 Fri–Sat.*

Sweet Green Tavern

127 Crook Street, Bolton BL3 6DD
☎ *(01204) 392258* Kevin Banks
www.sweetgreentavern.com

Freehouse with a wide range of real ales. The 11 beers are all rotated weekly and include brews from Sharp's plus local breweries Bazens', Bank Top, Phoenix, Hopstar, and others.

Dating from 1831, and formerly tied to a number of different pub chains and breweries, this is now a traditional local freehouse with a focus on real ale. Featured as pub of the week on *Al Murray's Happy Hour* (ITV) in January 2008. One bar, one snug, coal fire, no swearing allowed. No food, though customers may bring their own. Beer garden. Small car park. Licensed for civil wedding ceremonies. Away supporters welcomed on Bolton Wanderers FC match days. Located right next to Bolton railway station.

OPEN *11am–11pm.*

BURY

The Lord Raglan

Walmersley Old Road, Nangreaves, Bury BL9 6SP
☎ *(0161) 764 6680* Brendan Leyden

 The home of the Leyden Brewing Company with the full range of ales brewed on the premises and always available. Plus up to three rotating guests exchanged with another local micro-brewery. Two annual beer festivals held late June/early July and in September.

Victorian two-bar pub and restaurant. Food available 12–2pm and 7–9.30pm Mon–Thurs, 12–2pm and 5–9.30pm Fri and all day Sat–Sun. Beer garden. Car park. Children allowed. Brewery visits by arrangement. Take the M66 to J1 Ramsbottom, turn left onto the A56 and then first left at traffic lights. The pub is just over a mile on the left.

OPEN *12–2.30pm and 7–11pm Mon–Thurs; 12–2.30pm and 5–11pm Fri; 12–11pm Sat; 12–10.30pm Sun.*

Dusty Miller

87 Crostons Road, Bury BL8 1AL
☎ *(0161) 764 1124* Barrie Powers

 Moorhouse's pub with Premier, Pendle Witches Brew, Black Cat and Blond Witch plus one guest ale, changed every week.

Traditional local pub with lounge bar and vault/pool room bar. Parking opposite. Children welcome until 7.30pm. Beer garden and smoking area. Pub games, Sky Sports and quiz night on Thursday with supper. On the outskirts of Bury, towards Ramsbottom, at the junction of Crostons Road and Tottington Road.

OPEN *1pm–12 Mon–Thurs; 1pm–1am Fri; noon–1am Sat; 12–12 Sun.*

CHEETHAM

The Queen's Arms

4–6 Honey Street, Redbank, Cheetham M8 8RG
☎ *(0161) 834 4239* Dave Price

 Eight beers, usually including Timothy Taylor Landlord and Phoenix Bantam plus six guests from a constantly changing list. Also a wide range of Belgian beers.

A traditional town pub built in the 1800s and subsequently extended. Bar food available at lunchtime and until 8pm every day. Street parking, children's play area and garden. Five minutes' walk from Manchester Victoria Station.

OPEN *12–11pm (10.30pm Sun).*

CHORLTON

The Marble Beer House

57 Manchester Road, Chorlton M21 9PW
☎ *(0161) 881 9206* Helen and Vicky Creer

 Marble Arch brewery pub with four totally organic Marble beers always on offer. Two guests, changed every couple of days, will be from micro-breweries, and there is also a hand pump for seasonal Marble ales.

Café bar with wooden floors and tasteful furniture, reminiscent of an Amsterdam brown café. Conservatory, outside seating area. Organic snacks are available all day. Children allowed until 5pm. Situated in the heart of Chorlton. The number 86 bus from the city centre stops just outside.

OPEN *12–11pm Mon–Wed; 12–12 Thurs–Sat; 12–11.30pm Sun.*

The Sedge Lynn

21a Manchester Road, Chorlton M21 9PN
☎ *(0161) 860 0141* Dan Stoddard

 Wetherspoon's pub with six beers, including Marston's Pedigree, Theakston Old Peculier and four guests, changed every couple of days.

A pub in a Temperance Hall built in 1907, named CAMRA's Best Building Conversion in 2000. Food served 12–9pm. Beer garden. Two beers festivals a year.

OPEN *9am–11pm Sun–Thurs; 9am–midnight Fri–Sat.*

DENTON

Lowes Arms

301 Hyde Road, Denton M34 3FF
☎ *(0161) 336 3064* Peter and Jillian Wood

 Home of the Dane Town Brewery, offering four own brews: Valkyrie, Warriors Might, Thors Thunderbolt and Elixir of Life. Phoenix and Hornbeam beers are also served.

Large pub with traditional décor and a friendly atmosphere. Separate lounge, dining area and vault bar, plus large beer terrace with fountain. Snacks and full à la carte menu served lunchtime and evening. Children allowed if eating. Beer festival every summer. By bus from Manchester (201) or by train to Hyde Central.

OPEN *12–3pm and 5–11pm Mon–Thurs; 12–12 Sat–Sun.*

DIDSBURY

Fletcher Moss

1 William Street, Didsbury M20 6RQ
☎ *(0161) 438 0073* Ken Mallion
www.hydesbrewery.com

Hydes tied house serving Bitter, Mild, Jekyll's Gold and a seasonal brew.

This pub is one of the best in Hydes' estate. It was extended in 2002 to include a spacious conservatory area. It retains a strong local identity and is popular at weekends as it is one of the few pubs in the area that does not serve food.

OPEN *12–11pm (10.30pm Sun).*

EDGELEY
Olde Vic
1 Chatham Street, Edgeley, Stockport SK3 9ED
☎ *(0161) 480 2410*
Steve Brannan and Johanne Quinn

 Five pumps serve a wide range of constantly changing beers, often switched daily. Chilled Weston's cider is also on offer.

A small, cosy pub with coal fire in the winter and a large, secure beer garden (complete with marquee-style covering for inclement weather!). No food. Two minutes' walk from Stockport railway station.

> 5–11pm Mon–Fri; 7–11pm Sat; 7–10.30pm Sun (closed every lunchtime).

HAWKSHAW
The Red Lion Hotel
81 Ramsbottom Road, Hawkshaw, Bury BL8 4JS
☎ *(01204) 856600* Carl Owen

Freehouse offering Jennings Bitter and Cumberland Ale and Bank Top Flat Cap plus a weekly-changing guest.

Former coaching inn on the A676 Burnley road, now a traditional pub and restaurant with quality fixtures and fittings. Award-winning home-cooked food served lunchtimes and evenings, plus all day Sat–Sun. Five en-suite bedrooms. Large car park. Children welcome. Handy for Bury Market and the Trafford Centre. On the A676 Bolton to Burnley road.

> 12–3pm and 6–11pm Mon–Fri; all day Sat–Sun.

HEATON CHAPEL
The Hinds Head
Manchester Road, Heaton Chapel, Stockport SK4 2RB
☎ *(0161) 431 9301* Terence Murphy

Greene King Old Speckled Hen, Timothy Taylor Landlord, Marston's Pedigree and Black Sheep Bitter plus one monthly-changing guest.

Award-winning pub with extensive lawned beer garden and lovely hanging baskets. CAMRA listed for its beer and food. Meals are served 12–2pm and 7–9pm Mon–Sat and 12–4.30pm Sun. Children welcome at all times in the beer garden and inside the pub if dining. Large car park.

> 11.30am–11pm Mon–Sat; 12–10.30pm Sun.

HEYWOOD
The Wishing Well
89 York Street, Heywood OL10 4NS
☎ *(01706) 620923* TM Huck and Alan Berry

Genuine freehouse with eight real ales. Moorhouse's Pride of Pendle, Phoenix Wigwam and White Monk, Black Sheep Bitter, Timothy Taylor Landlord and Boddingtons Bitter (brewed by Hydes) are usually on offer, plus two rotating guests from a vast range of independent and micro-breweries.

Traditional two-bar pub, with dining area. Clientele is a rare mix of old and young, creating a very welcoming atmosphere. Food available in a separate restaurant next door open 6–9.30pm Tues–Sat. Children allowed until 6pm. Football, TV. On the Rochdale road.

> 12–close.

HINDLEY
The Edington Arms
186 Ladies Lane, Hindley, Wigan WN2 2QJ
☎ *(01942) 259229* Mr Terry Gaskell

Joseph Holt tied house serving Holt Mild and Bitter plus a seasonal ale.

An old coaching house built in 1896, with two bars, two large comfortable rooms, and two open fires. Three televisions, pool, darts. No food. Popular quiz on Wednesdays, karaoke and live music. Car park, beer garden, function room with bar. New facilities for smokers. Well-behaved children welcome. Next to Hindley railway station.

> 12–11.30pm Sun–Thurs; noon–12.30am Fri–Sat.

HYDE
The Cheshire Ring
72 Manchester Road, Hyde SK14 2BJ
☎ *(0161) 368 1826* Wayne Taylor

At least four brews from the Beartown range (perhaps Ambeardextrous, Kodiak Gold, Bearskinful and Polar Eclipse stout), plus three regularly changing guests. Also Thatcher's cider in bottle and on hand pump, and occasionally cider from Peel Walls in Scotland. Czech beers on draught, Budwar Dark and a good selection of bottled European beers (no Stella or alcopops!).

Owned by the Beartown Brewery. Friendly and welcoming, with cold homemade sandwiches available at lunchtime. Function room for 70 with its own bar. Children welcome until 7pm. Close to Hyde Central metro.

> 2–11pm Mon–Wed; 1–11pm Thurs–Sun.

The Sportsman
57 Mottram Road, Hyde SK14 2NN
☎ *(0161) 368 5000* Peter and Greg Banks

Genuine freehouse with up to eight real ales. Moorhouse's Black Cat Mild, Plassey Bitter, Hartington Bitter, Timothy Taylor Landlord, Phoenix Bantam and Pictish Brewers Gold are regulars, plus a couple of guests.

Traditional, early Victorian community alehouse with two bars in the town centre. Plans to serve food in the near future. Open fires, function room, pool table, quiz nights etc. Car park. Beer festival in October. Close to Newton station.

> 11am–2am Mon–Sat; noon–2am Sun.

MANCHESTER
Bar Fringe
8 Swan Street, Manchester M4 5JN
☎ *(0161) 835 3815* Carmen Contreras

Freehouse with five real ales, changed when they run out. Beers from Bank Top and Boggart Hole Clough are permanently featured and the two guests, changed regularly, could be from Spinning Dog, Salamander, Cottage or Derwent breweries. Traditional cider plus draught Belgian and fruit beers are also stocked and there are regular promotional offers. Wide selection of foreign bottled beers, and guest crisps!

Pub on the outskirts of the town centre, in a building over 100 years old, with traditional long, narrow, Belgian brown bar. On a beer circuit in the northern quarter of Manchester. Food available 10.30am–8pm Sun–Thurs and 12–4pm Sat–Sat. One bar, pinball table, beer garden. Five beer festivals held every year. No children.

🅾 *10.30am–11pm Sun–Wed; 10.30am–midnight Thurs; 10.30am–12.30am Fri–Sat.*

The Britons Protection
50 Great Bridgewater Street, Manchester M1 5LE
☎ *(0161) 236 5895* Gwen Partridge

Punch Taverns house with up to five real ales. Jennings Cumberland and Robinsons Unicorn are permanents, plus two guest ales from breweries such as Coach House, Howard Town, Storm, Hydes and Robinsons, to name a few. Also over 210 whiskies.

An award-winning 195-year-old pub steeped in tradition. Multiple rooms lead off in every direction; the clientele range from young professionals to classical musicians and everything in between. Food served 11am–2pm Mon–Fri; 12–3.30pm Sat–Sun. Beer garden. Function room for hire. Located in the city centre, opposite the Bridgewater Hall and next to the G-mex.

🅾 *11am–11pm Mon–Thurs; 11am–midnight Fri–Sat; 12–10.30pm Sun.*

The Knott
374 Deansgate, Manchester M3 4LY
☎ *(0161) 839 9229* Frank Mullen

Freehouse with two Marble Brewery beers plus three rotating guests.

Built into a railway arch in the historic Castlefield area of Manchester. One bar with open-style kitchen and outside balcony. Food served 12–8pm.

🅾 *12–11.30pm Sun–Wed; 12–12 Thurs; noon–12.30am Fri–Sat.*

The Lass o'Gowrie
36 Charles Street, Manchester M1 7DB
☎ *(0161) 273 6932* Gareth Kavanagh
www.thelass.co.uk

Up to nine real ales served. Regulars include 'Betty's Best' - our house ale brewed by Outstanding Brewing Co, Conwy Ales, Allgates, Bank Top, Coach House, Howard Town, Titanic, Black Sheep, IPA, Hardy and Hanson's Kimberley and Olde Trip.

A gem of a Victorian pub, tastefully clad in authentic Threllfall tiling and offering a friendly atmosphere. All the food is made on the premises, including the celebrated range of home-baked pies, and is available every day from opening time until 8pm (except Sundays, when we finish at 6pm). Customers are welcome to play our free vintage video games, use the traditional snug, which is eclectically decorated with comic art and an unrivalled library of *Viz* annuals to leaf through. Also an outside balcony opened by Johnny Vegas in 2009, which is a dream for riverside dining, quaffing and outside smoking. Located in the city centre, close to the BBC and therefore ideal for 'star spotting'! Parking behind the pub courtesy of EuroParcs. Within five minutes' walk of Oxford Road and Piccadilly Stations.

🅾 *12–11pm Mon–Wed; 12–12 Thurs–Sat; 12–10.30pm Sun.*

Marble Arch Inn
73 Rochdale Road, Manchester M4 4HY
☎ *(0161) 832 5914* J Rogers

Ten real ales, six from the on-site Marble Brewery (including one seasonal) and four from guest micro-breweries. The guests change weekly, and a real cider is also served.

Listed building with striking original interior, a fine example of Manchester's Victorian heritage. The only organic brewpub in England, it is the home of the multi-award-winning Marble Brewery. A changing menu of snacks and hearty meals is served 12–8pm Mon–Sat and 12–8pm Sun. Homemade pies featuring the brewery's own organic real ale are especially popular. Winner of Manchester's Food and Drink Festival Pub of the Year 2006. Brewery tours by appointment. Occasional beer festivals, with one major one in the summer. Between Victoria and Piccadilly train stations, ten minutes' walk from the centre of Manchester.

🅾 *11.30am–11pm Mon–Thurs; 11.30am–midnight Fri; 12–12 Sat; 12–10.30pm Sun.*

Paradise Brewery Bar

Market Hall, Arndale Centre, Manchester M4 3AQ
☎ *(01745) 832966* Ron Hamner
www.paradisebrewery.net

Three real ales from the Paradise Brewery range. Plus bottled beers.

Unique licensed bar showcasing the Paradise brews in the food court of the Manchester market centre.

OPEN *11am–6pm Mon–Sat (until 8pm Thurs); 11am–4pm Sun.*

Peveril of the Peak

127 Great Bridgewater Street, Manchester M1 5JQ
☎ *(0161) 236 6364*

Copper Dragon Golden Pippin, Charles Wells Bombardier, Boddingtons Bitter (brewed by Hydes), Caledonian Deuchars IPA and Timothy Taylor Landlord could be among the brews on offer, plus other guests.

Named after the Sir Walter Scott novel, a street-corner pub with glazed external brickwork and a beautifully preserved original interior. Public bar, lobby plus two further roooms. No food.

OPEN *11.30am–3pm and 5–11pm Mon–Fri; 7–11pm Sat; 7–10.30pm Sun.*

Sandbar

120 Grosvenor Street, All Saints, Manchester M1 7HL
☎ *(0161) 273 1552* Stephen Gingell
www.sandbaronline.net

Freehouse with six pumps, one always a dark ale and one a cider. Beers from Moorhouse's and Timothy Taylor plus three guests changed frequently, including something from Phoenix and All Saints (one an exclusive brew).

A city-centre café bar carved out of an old Georgian townhouse. One main bar and benches outside, plus new landscaped courtyard to rear. Food served 12–3pm Mon–Fri, including traditional pub meals and Polish specialities, all prepared on the premises. Free Wi-Fi internet access, juke box, exhibitions. Off the A34 by the University.

OPEN *12–11pm Mon–Wed; 12–12 Thurs; noon–2am Fri; 4pm–12 Sat; closed Sun.*

The Smithfield Hotel

37 Swan Street, Manchester M4 5JZ
☎ *(0161) 839 4424* Mr Poole

Freehouse with Robinson's Hatters Dark Mild and a home brew, Smithfield Hotel Bitter, always available. Up to five guests from other independents, changed two or three times a week.

Dating from the 18th century, with one long bar, lounge area and hotel accommodation attached. No food.

OPEN *12–11pm (10.30pm Sun).*

The White Lion

43 Liverpool Road, Manchester M3 4NQ
☎ *(0161) 832 7373* Rose Wong

Enterprise Inns house with four real ales. Regulars include Marston's Pedigree, Timothy Taylor Landlord, Fuller's London Pride and brews from Black Sheep or Cumberland.

One-bar, one-room, traditional city-centre pub. Home-cooked English pub food served 12–6pm; Chinese food available 12–11pm. Large beer garden. Located in the historical area of Manchester near the Science and Industry Museum.

OPEN *11am–11pm Sun–Thurs; 11am–midnight Fri–Sat.*

Tandle Hill Tavern

14 Thornham Lane, Slattocks, Middleton, Manchester M24 2SS
☎ *(01706) 345297* Mike

JW Lees tied house with Mild and Bitter available.

A must on a visit to North Manchester. The pub is set in a rural setting and can be accessed via a rough track/unmetalled road from either Rochdale Road, Royton (A671) or Rochdale Road, Middleton (A664). It is a true surviving example of a country pub situated next to a farm. One of a dying breed. Visitors are made to feel welcome by the landlord and the roaring fires in winter, and the JW Lees beers are the best-kept for miles around. Soup and sandwiches available at lunchtime at weekends only. Good walks locally in Tandle Hill Country Park. Children welcome.

OPEN *7–11pm Mon–Fri; 12–11pm Sat; 12–10.30pm Sun.*

Ashton Arms

28–30 Clegg Street, Oldham OL1 1PL
☎ *07963 505393* Jo Potter

Freehouse serving Cains Bitter plus five constantly changing guests from local breweries such as Greenfield, Millstone and Phoenix. Beer festivals Easter and October.

The centrepiece of this open-plan pub is a large real fire that complements the real ale and real food served by Jo and her staff. Food 12–6pm Mon–Sat. Children welcome.

OPEN *All day, every day.*

The Albion Freehouse and Bistro

600 Whitworth Road, Rochdale OL12 0SW
☎ *(01706) 648540* Damian Grundy

Seven real ales available. The selection might include Timothy Taylor Best Bitter, Landlord and Golden Best, JW Lees Bitter, plus Moorhouse's Black Cat Mild, Pendle Witches Brew and Blond Witch, with two of the beers rotated at least weekly.

Traditional three-roomed freehouse with open fires and a welcoming atmosphere. One TV room. No machines. Excellent pub food is available 12–2.30pm and 5–9pm

Mon–Fri (10pm Thurs–Fri); all day until 9pm Sat–Sun. *Morning Advertiser* Northwest Freehouse of the Year 2006. Terrace garden at rear. Nearby moorland walks and Healy Dell Nature Reserve. On the A671 in the foothills of the Pennines a mile and a half from Rochdale town centre.

 12–2.30pm and 5–11pm Mon–Fri (1am Fri); noon–1am Sat; 12–10.30pm Sun.

Cask & Feather

1 Oldham Road, Rochdale OL16 1UA
☎ *(01706) 711476*
Anthony Hutchinson and Jackie Grimes
 Up to four real ales on offer, with beers from Phoenix and Moorhouse's regularly featured, plus two guests, changed every couple of weeks.

An old-style castle-fronted pub dating from 1814 and close to the town centre. Large bar, beer garden at the rear, function room. Food available 11am–2.30pm Sat–Sat and 12–3pm Sun. Located on the main road near the station.

 11am–1am Mon–Wed; 11am–2am Thurs–Sat; noon–2.30am Sun.

Cemetery Inn

470 Bury Road, Rochdale OL11 5EU
☎ *(01706) 645635* Mark Porter
 Freehouse offering a range of up to seven beers, including Timothy Taylor Landlord, Jennings Cumberland and Black Sheep Bitter, plus up to four rotating guests, changed every week.

Victorian pub with log fires, dating from 1865 and sympathetically refurbished. Bar area is split into three rooms. Food served daily 12–2.30pm and 5–7.30pm Mon–Fr; 12–6pm Sun. The menu includes locally sourced sausages and Lancashire cheeses. Children welcome until 7pm. Small car park. Upstairs room available for meetings.

 All day, every day.

The Flying Horse Hotel

37 Packer Street, Rochdale OL16 1NJ
☎ *(01706) 646412*
Samantha Bonde and Ben Boothman
www.theflyinghorsehotel.co.uk
 Freehouse serving Lees Bitter, Timothy Taylor Landlord and Phoenix Pale Moonlight plus two weekly-changing guests.

A 200-year-old hotel in the centre of Rochdale. Also features a club called Mystique, strictly for over-21s. Food served 12–9pm Mon–Thurs, 12–5pm Sat–Sun. Accommodation. Beer garden. Private room available. Car park. Located by the town hall.

 11am–midnight.

The Crescent

20 The Crescent, Salford M5 4PF
☎ *(0161) 736 5600* Mrs J Davies
 Crescent Bitter (house beer) plus up to ten others (150 per year) primarily from local breweries, including Oak, Moorhouse's, Titanic and Marston's. Other guests from all around the country. Occasional beer festivals.

Sprawling pub with a comfortable atmosphere, frequented by students and locals alike. Bar food available at lunchtime. Car park. Traditional pub games. Opposite Salford University. The nearest station is Salford Crescent, on the main A6.

 12–11pm Mon–Fri; 7.30–11pm Sat; 12–3pm and 7.30–10.30pm Sun.

Eagle Inn (The Lamp Oil)

18 Collier Street, Greengate, Salford M3 7DW
☎ *(0161) 832 4919* Paul and Sharon Wilson
 Joseph Holt tied house serving Mild and Bitter.

A classic example of a backstreet boozer with a unique friendly atmosphere. Three small rooms including a tap room, a games room and a snug. Live entertainment with karaoke at weekends. Ask about why it is affectionately known as the Lamp Oil.

 11am–11pm Mon–Sat; 12–10.30pm Sun.

The Kings Arms

11 Bloom Street, Salford M3 6AN
☎ *(0161) 832 3605* Jon Cooper
 Freehouse serving six real ales. Moorhouse's Blonde Witch, Bazens' Pacific, Caledonian Deuchars IPA and Timothy Taylor Landlord are permanent, plus three guests from a range of 30 regulars.

Established in 1883, one bar, downstairs snug, upstairs in-house theatre/music venue/artists' studio. Food served 12–6.30pm Mon–Fri; from noon Sat–Sun. Beer garden. Small car park. Located close to Salford Central railway station.

 12–11pm Mon–Thurs; 12–12 Fri–Sat; 12–6pm Sun.

New Oxford

Bexley Square, Salford M3 6DB
☎ *(0161) 832 7082* Tim Flynn
 Rotating range of ten real ales including a house brew from Northern Brewing. Plus three Belgian brews on draft and real cider.

CAMRA's regional Pub of the Year for 2007, a continental-style real ale bar reopened in 2005. Home-cooked food served 11am–6pm. Outside seating with heated area for smokers. Quiz night on Tues, live music on Sun. Regular beer festivals. Off Chapel Street, a ten-minute walk from Deansgate.

 11am–11pm Mon–Fri; 12–12 Sat; 3–11pm Sun.

STALYBRIDGE

The Buffet Bar

Stalybridge Railway Station, Stalybridge SK15 1RF
☎ *(0161) 303 0007*
John Hesketh and Sylvia Wood
www.buffetbar.freewebspace.com

 Seven or eight real ales, including a constantly changing range of guest beers from independent breweries. Around 6,600 guest beers served in 11 years. Draught cider and a large selection of continental beers are also on offer.

Unique and authentic buffet bar built in 1865, like a small museum, with a real fire, real ale and real people! Bar food available at most times. Private room, quiz nights. Parking. Children allowed. On platform one at Stalybridge railway station.

OPEN *11am–11pm Mon–Sat; 12–10.30pm Sun.*

Q Inn

3–5 Market Street, Stalybridge SK15 2AL
☎ *(0161) 303 9157* Lynda Wilson

 Hydes Brewery tied house serving the two Hydes beers plus one weekly changing guest.

The pub with the shortest name in Britain forms part of the Stalybridge Eight – eight pubs in the town offering 37 different beers. Brick walls, coal fire and a flagstone floor. Upstairs games room for pool, darts and cards. Children welcome until 6pm. Large beer garden. Annual beer festival over the August bank holiday. A short walk from the railway station.

OPEN *3–11pm Mon–Thurs; 12–11pm Fri–Sat; 12–10.30pm Sun.*

The White House

1 Water Street, Stalybridge SK15 2AG
☎ *(0161) 303 2288* Steve and Jeanette Foy

Hydes Brewery tied house serving Bitter and 1863 plus a beer from the Craft range, changed every two months.

A traditional pub with low ceilings, refurbished and very comfortable. Full menu available 12–3pm. Live entertainment twice monthly on a Sunday evening. No children. In a central location, opposite the bus station.

OPEN *11am–11pm Mon–Thurs; 11am–late Fri–Sat; 12–late Sun.*

STOCKPORT

Arden Arms

23 Millgate, Stockport SK1 2LX
☎ *(0161) 480 2185* Joe Quinn and Steve King
www.ardenarms.com

Robinson's tied house serving Unicorn and Hatters Mild plus a Robinson's seasonal brew such as Double Hop and in winter Old Tom.

Late-Georgian coaching inn in the centre of Stockport retaining the classical multi-roomed layout. Cobbled stabled courtyard at rear. One central bar, three rooms and hallway. Food available lunchtimes Mon–Fri; until 4pm Sat–Sun. Children welcome. Large beer garden. Darts team. Private parties catered for. Finalist in the CAMRA national Pub of the Year competition 2004.

OPEN *12–12.*

The Crown Inn

154 Heaton Lane, Heaton Norris,
Stockport SK4 1AR
☎ *07836 682 031* Steve Alexander
www.thecrowninn.uk.com

 Sixteen hand pumps serve an ever-expanding range of beers from breweries far and wide. There are dedicated pumps for Bank Top, Pictish and Copper Dragon, and there is always one mild and a stout or porter. Real cider also available.

A quaint, pre-Victorian multi-roomed pub under Stockport's stunning railway viaduct, with log fires in winter and large beer garden. Home-cooked food served 12–3pm Mon–Fri. Stockport and South Manchester CAMRA Pub of the Year 2008, national pub of the year runner-up 2008. Live music every week, plus weekly quiz night. Children welcome. A two-minute walk from Mersey Square, and very handy for the bus and railway stations.

OPEN *12–11pm (10.30pm Sun).*

Nursery Inn

Green Lane, Heaton Norris, Stockport SK4 2NA
☎ *(0161) 432 2044* Simon Wetton

Hydes Brewery tied house with Bitter, Mild, Owd Oak and Jekyll's Gold permanently available. Up to two guest ales, such as Jumping Jack, and a guest bitter.

Heritage pub in a conservation area. Built in 1939 with many original features such as a wood-panelled lounge. Food served every lunchtime. Children welcome. Beer garden. Bowling green, with bowling parties catered for. Car park. Private room for hire. Located five minutes from Stockport, 15 minutes from Manchester.

OPEN *11.30am–11pm Mon–Thurs; 11.30am–11.30pm Fri; 11.30am–midnight Sat; 12–11.30pm Sun.*

STRINES
The Sportsman
105 Strines Road, Strines, Stockport SK6 7GE
☎ *(0161) 427 2888* Sue and Joe Stockton
www.the-sportsman-pub.co.uk

Boddingtons Bitter (brewed by Hydes) and something from Cains always available, plus three guest beers changing regularly.

A 200-year-old, two-roomed pub with a lounge/dining room and a snug. Wonderful views over the Goyt Valley and an ideal base for walking in the Peak District and Peak Forest canal. Home-cooked food available 12–2pm and 6–9pm Mon–Sat and 12–8pm Sun. Car park, garden. Take the A626 from Stockport and then the B6101.

OPEN *12–3pm and 5–11pm Mon–Fri; all day Sat–Sun.*

UPPERMILL
The Church Inn and Belfry Function Suite
Church Lane, Off Church Road, Uppermill, Saddleworth
☎ *(01457) 820902 or 872415*
Julian Paul Taylor

Home of the Saddleworth Brewery with all brews usually available, plus occasional guest beers. Brewery visits by arrangement.

C ountry freehouse set in a beautiful, historic location with panoramic views and a lovely patio area. Peacocks, horses, ducks, geese, cats, dogs and hens too. Caters for all age groups. Log fires in winter. Food served lunchtimes and evenings Mon–Fri and all day Sat–Sun. Children welcome. Car park. Situated in Uppermill village, turn into New Street and continue to Church Road. Pub will be found near the church.

OPEN *12–11pm (10.30pm Sun).*

WHALLEY RANGE
The Hillary Step
199 Upper Chorlton Road, Whalley Range, Manchester M16 0BH
☎ *(0161) 881 1978* Rob Goater

Freehouse serving four ales from mainly local breweries including Phoenix, Bazens', Copper Dragon, Thwaites and Millstone.

A converted terrace shop, licenced since 2004. More of a bar than a pub, with no juke box. Cask Marque and Beautiful Beer accredited. Bar snacks such as olives, nuts, crisps and salamis and a cheeseboard. Outside seating area.

OPEN *4pm–close Mon–Fri; 12–close Sat–Sun.*

WIGAN
The Bowling Green
106 Wigan Lane, Swinley, Wigan WN1 2LF
☎ *(01942) 519871* Colin Pendlebury

Caledonian Deuchars IPA, Greene King Old Speckled Hen and an Adnams brew, plus four rotating guests, changed every few days.

D ating from 1803, with a traditional vault, open fires and a friendly atmosphere. No food. Games room. Beer garden. Function room. Occasional live music. Beer festival during August bank holiday.

OPEN *3–11pm Mon–Thurs; 3pm–1am Fri; noon–1am Sat; 12–11pm Sun.*

Moon Under Water
5–7 Market Place, Wigan WN1 1PE
☎ *(01942) 323437* Valerie Jary

JD Wetherspoon's pub serving Greene King Abbot, Marston's Pedigree, Cains Mild and Courage Directors plus six guest cask ales from local breweries such as Moorhouse's, Northern and George Wright and from other breweries around the UK.

V ery busy town-centre pub, with food available all day. Children are welcome to eat until 8pm. Two beer festivals per year, one at the end of April and one at the end of October. Disabled access and facilities.

OPEN *All day, every day.*

The Old Pear Tree
44 Frog Lane, Wigan WN1 1HG
☎ *(01942) 517623* Lynn Wilson

Three real ales from breweries such as Jennings, Marston's and Banks's, always changing.

R eputed to be the oldest dedicated pub in Wigan. Two bars, one main room and one games room/vault. Refurbished in February 2008, including a new kitchen. Food served every afternoon and evening, Sunday roasts available. Children welcome. Located two minutes' walk from the town centre.

OPEN *12–12.*

The Orwell
Wigan Pier, Wallgate, Wigan WN3 4EU
☎ *(01942) 323034* Robin Harston
www.wiganpier.co.uk

Freehouse with two real ales from micro-breweries whenever possible. Brews from Pictish, Archers, Ossett, Weetwood, Bradfield and Rosebridge may be featured, and all rotate.

T ourists' pub on the edge of town on the pier. A converted traditional Victorian cotton warehouse on the Leeds–Liverpool canal, with restaurant, snug, lounge and games room. Two large function rooms available for hire. Food available 12–2.30pm every day and Sunday carvery 1–6pm. Follow signs to Wigan Pier.

OPEN *Winter: 12–3pm and 5pm–close. Summer: 11.30am–close. Hours vary, so phone to check.*

The Tudor House Hotel

New Market Street, Wigan
☎ *(01942) 700296* Russell Miller

Freehouse with Moorhouse's Pendle Witches Brew among the beers always available plus up to four guests including Everards Tiger, Hop Back Summer Lightning, Wychwood Hobgoblin, O'Hanlon's Summer Gold and Phoenix Wobbly Bob.

Predominantly a student pub with open fires, a beer garden and accommodation. Food available at lunchtime and evenings. Children allowed during the day.

OPEN *All day, every day.*

The Victoria Hotel

438 Wilmslow Road, Withington, Manchester M20 3BW
☎ *(0161) 434 2600* Janice Oliver

Hydes Brewery tied house with Bitter, Mild and Jekylls Gold always on offer, plus seasonals and specials rotated on one other tap.

A Victorian building, trading as a pub since 1904. Two lounges, games room and beer garden. A friendly atmosphere where students mix with locals. No food. Monthly live music. Weekly quiz nights. Outside smoking area. Off the B5093 Wilmslow Road.

OPEN *11.30am–11pm Mon–Sat; 12–10.30pm Sun.*

THE BREWERIES

BRIMSTAGE BREWING COMPANY LTD
Home Farm, Brimstage Lane, Brimstage, Wirral CH63 6LY
☎ *(0151) 342 1181*
www.brimstagebrewery.com

 TRAPPER'S HAT BITTER 3.8% ABV
RHODE ISLAND RED 4.0% ABV
Plus seasonals and specials.

CAMBRINUS CRAFT BREWERY
Home Farm, Knowsley Park, Prescot L34 4AQ
☎ *(0151) 546 2226*

HERALD 3.8% ABV
A light refreshing summer ale.
YARDSTICK 4.0% ABV
A coloured, malty best mild.
DELIVERANCE 4.2% ABV
A hoppy, dry bitter with a moreish aftertaste.
ENDURANCE 4.5% ABV
An IPA-style beer, smooth, hoppy and oaky.
Plus seasonals and specials.

GEORGE WRIGHT BREWING COMPANY
11 Diamond Business Park, Sandwash Close, Rainford Industrial Estate, Rainford, St Helens WA11 8LU
☎ *(01744) 886686*

DRUNKEN DUCK 3.9% ABV
Citrus overtones.
WOUNDED GOOSE 3.9% ABV
Straw colour.
LONGBOAT 3.9% ABV
Sweet berries flavour.
PIPE DREAM 4.3% ABV
Lingering malty dryness, hints of grapefruit.
IPA 4.5% ABV
Straw colour, spicy.
KING'S SHILLIN' 4.5% ABV
Gold colour.
CHEEKY PHEASANT 4.7% ABV
Gold, fruity, malty.
BLUE MOON 4.9 ABV
Clean, crisp, hoppy.
Plus seasonal and occasional brews.

HIGSON'S BREWERY
Unit 21, Brunswick Business Centre, Brunswick Business Park, Liverpool L34BD
☎ *(0151) 228 2309*

 HIGSON'S BITTER 4.1% ABV
PORTER 5.0% ABV
STINGO 8.0% ABV

ROBERT CAIN BREWERY LTD
The Robert Cain Brewery, Stanhope Street, Liverpool L8 5XJ
☎ *(0151) 709 8734*
www.cainsbeers.com

DARK MILD 3.2% ABV
IPA 3.5% ABV
CAINS FINEST BITTER 4.0% ABV
CAINS FA 5.0% ABV
Plus seasonal and occasional brews.

SOUTHPORT BREWERY
Unit 3, Southport Enterprise Centre, Russell Road, Southport PR9 7RF
☎ *07748 387652*

 SANDGROUNDER BITTER 3.8% ABV
BEST BITTER CAROUSEL 4.0% ABV
NATTERJACK 4.3% ABV
OLD SHRIMPER 5.5% ABV
Winter only.
GOLDEN SANDS 4.0% ABV

WAPPING BEERS
The Baltic Fleet, 33A Wapping, Liverpool L1 8DQ
☎ *(0151) 709 3116*
www.wappingbeers.com

 CONNOISSEUR MARK'S 3.6% ABV
WAPPING BITTER 3.6% ABV
BALTIC GOLD 3.9% ABV
STOUT 5.0% ABV
CONNOISSEUR AURORA 5.1% ABV
CONNOISSEUR STRANGE FRUIT 6.2% ABV
Plus occasionals and seasonals including:
BOW SPRIT 3.6% ABV
SUMMER ALE 4.2% ABV

THE PUBS

BARNSTON
The Fox & Hounds
Barnston Village, Wirral CH61 1BW
☎ *(0151) 648 7685* Ralph Leech
www.the-fox-hounds.co.uk

 A freehouse serving six real ales: Webster's Bitter, Theakston Best and Old Peculier, plus three guests, changed every week. Examples include Brimstage Trappers Hat, Woodlands Oak Beauty and Spitting Feathers Thirst Quencher. Also 60 whiskies, five lagers and 12 wines by the glass.

Situated in the conservation area of Barnston, the present pub dates from circa 1911 and retains its original character. An extensive seasonal menu including bar snacks, daily specials, pies and fish of the day, is served 12–2pm (2.30pm Sun). Outside drinking area with spectacular container flower displays in summer. On the A551 Barnston road.

OPEN 11am–11pm Mon–Sat; 12–10.30pm Sun.

BEBINGTON
Traveller's Rest Hotel
169 Mount Road, Higher Bebington, Wirral CH63 8PJ
☎ *(0151) 608 2988* Annie Irving

Seven real ales including Greene King Abbot, Timothy Taylor Landlord, Shepherd Neame Spitfire and Wychwood Hobgoblin plus a guest from an independent berwery that changes every week.

A traditional street-corner village pub a few miles south of Birkenhead on the Wirral. Perhaps 300 years old, with one bar and open fires, bordering fields with a view of Wales. Food available at lunchtime (not Sun). Children aged 10 and over welcome. Two minutes from M53 J4, handy for Tranmere Rovers supporters.

OPEN 12–11pm Mon–Thurs and Sun; 12–12 Fri–Sat.

The Crown & Cushion

60 Market Street, Birkenhead L41 5BT
☎ *(0151) 647 8870* Martin Freel

Cains Bitter or Black Sheep Bitter available on a weekly-rotating basis.

A traditional town-centre two-bar community pub now over 100 years old. Free sandwiches available daily. All-day happy hours. Children allowed until 7pm. Close to the town hall and Mersey ferries, two minutes from Hamilton Square station.

OPEN *All day, every day.*

The Crown Hotel

128 Conway Street, Birkenhead L41 6JE
☎ *(0151) 650 2035* Martin Freel

Six cask ales, with regulars being Cains Traditional Bitter and Mild.

Typical old alehouse. Bar food available. Parking, darts/meeting room, beer garden. Children allowed. Head for Birkenhead town centre, not far from the Birkenhead tunnel (Europa Park).

OPEN *11am–midnight Mon–Sat; 12–11.30pm Sun.*

The Dispensary

20 Chester Street, Birkenhead CH41 5DQ
☎ *(0151) 649 8259* Brenda Adams
www.cainsbeers.com

Cains tied house, with Traditional Bitter and Dark Mild plus a selection of seasonal and special ales.

A modern, refurbished building with raised glass ceiling. Formerly a chemist, hence the name. Used to be known as The Chester Arms. Food served 12–7pm. Beer garden. Children welcome.

OPEN *All day, every day.*

The Old Colonial

167 Bridge Street, Birkenhead CH41 1AY
☎ *(0151) 650 1110* Tricia McGrann

Cains Traditional Bitter, Mild and Doctor Duncan's IPA plus seasonal brews usually available.

Friendly, traditional pub with a family atmosphere. Cask Marque award winner. Food served 12–2pm every day. Live entertainment. Car park. Children welcome.

OPEN *12–12 Sun–Thurs; noon–1am Fri–Sat.*

The Stork Hotel

41 Price Street, Birkenhead, Wirral CH41 6JN
☎ *(0151) 647 7506* Karen Murphy

Admiral Taverns pub serving four rotating guest beers.

Built in 1840 with an original oak island bar, news room, original mosaic floor and leaded stained glass windows, decorated with William Morris designs. Happy hour 4–7pm daily. Food served 12–2pm and 4.30–6.30pm Mon–Fri; 2–6pm Sun. Large beer garden with large heated smoking area. Private room for hire. Located two minutes' walk from Conway Park railway station.

OPEN *11.30am–11.30pm.*

Dibbinsdale Inn

Dibbinsdale Road, Bromborough, Wirral CH63 0HJ
☎ *(0151) 334 5171*
Andrew Leather and Sharon Whitfield

Freehouse with up to five real ales, always including brews from Thwaites.

Friendly country inn built in 1835. Food available 12–9.30pm. B&B in 13 en-suite rooms. Car park. Close to Wirral Country Park.

OPEN *9am–1am.*

Freshfield Hotel

Massams Lane, Formby L37 7BF
☎ *(01704) 874871*
Greg Byrne and Julie Evans (managers)

Moorhouse's Black Cat Mild, Black Sheep Bitter, Timothy Taylor Landlord and Castle Eden Ale are among the brews usually available, plus six constantly changing guest beers, wherever possible ordered by customer request.

A traditional pub with polished wooden floor and log fire. Beer garden and separate music/conference room at rear. Food served 12–2pm Mon–Fri and 12–4pm Sat–Sun. Car park. No children.

OPEN *12–11pm (10.30pm Sun).*

Irby Mill

Mill Lane, Greasby, Wirral CH49 3NT
☎ *(0151) 604 0194* Suzanne Downward

A Scottish Newcastle tied house. Charles Wells Bombardier, Theakston Old Peculier, Greene King Old Speckled Hen and Abbot plus a Cains ale. Three or four guests each month including Hydes Trojan Horse, Caledonian Chocolate Drop and Bateman Hooker.

An old pub, part of which is listed. Food served 12–3pm and 5–9pm Mon–Fri; all day Sat; 1–4pm Sun. Children welcome until 7pm. Large garden and car park.

OPEN *11am–11pm.*

Shippons Inn

84 Thingwall Road, Irby, Wirral CH61 3UA
☎ *(0151) 648 0449* S Thompson and S Arnold

Thwaites Original, Lancaster Bomber and Phoenix Wobbly Bob plus a weekly-changing guest brew.

Ten years old, a rustic one-bar pub with beams and stone floor in the middle of the village. Food available 12–2.30pm daily. No children. Beer garden and car park.

OPEN *All day, every day.*

LIVERPOOL

The Augustus John

Alsop Buildings, University of Liverpool, Brownlow Hill, Liverpool L3 5TX
☎ (0151) 794 5507 Joe Highdale

A freehouse owned by the University of Liverpool. Greene King Abbot plus four guests, changed on a rotational basis. Guests include Oakham JHB, Phoenix Wobbly Bob, Cains IPA and Exmoor Gold. Also traditional scrumpy.

Named after the painter, the pub was opened in 1969 by his son, Caspar. Popular with students and the general public alike. Big-screen TV. Juke box, pool table and dart board. Annual beer festival every February. Situated at the top of Brownlow Hill, next to Blackwells bookshop.

OPEN *11am–11pm Mon–Thurs and Sat; 11am–midnight Fri.*

The Baltic Fleet

33A Wapping, Liverpool L1 8DQ
☎ (0151) 709 3116 Kevin Yates

The only brewpub in Liverpool, home of Wapping Beers, with seven hand pumps serving four home-brewed ales, a cider and two guests, changed very frequently, from micro and regional brewers. A mild is usually on the menu.

Town pub in a 150-year-old painted Victorian building near the Albert Dock and featuring beams and a fireplaces. A network of tunnels, reputedly haunted, leads from the cellar to the docks. Food served 12–2pm daily; brunches 11am–4pm Sat; Sunday lunches 12–4pm. Free weekly quiz night, monthly Laurel and Hardy film show. Parties catered for. Free room hire.

OPEN *12–11pm Mon–Fri; 11am–11pm Sat; 12–10.30pm Sun. Open from 11am every day in summer.*

The Blackburne Arms Hotel

24 Catharine Street, Liverpool L8 7NL
☎ (0151) 707 1249 Ivan Jenkins

Timothy Taylor Landlord, Caledonian Deuchars IPA, Black Sheep Bitter and a Jennings ale plus two weekly-changing guests.

A traditional pub with contemporary décor, dating from 1930. Gastropub food served 12–8.45pm Mon–Sat; 12–6pm Sun. Attached to a seven-bedroom boutique hotel, adjacent to the Anglican and Catholic cathedrals and the Georgian quarter of the city.

OPEN *12–12 Sun–Thurs; noon–1am Fri–Sat.*

The Brewery Tap

Stanhope Street, Liverpool L8 5XJ
☎ (0151) 709 2129 Roy Walker

 Tied to the Robert Cain brewery, so Cains Bitter, Dark Mild, 2008 and Formidable Ale (FA) always available, plus a couple of seasonal and special brews such as Sundowner and Doctor Duncan's IPA.

Built in 1887 and refurbished in January 2004, but with the original character retained. One bar, food available at lunchtimes. Children allowed if eating. Large car park opposite. Brewery tours by arrangement. Close to Albert Docks.

OPEN *All day, every day.*

The Cambridge

Mulberry Street, Liverpool L7 7EE
☎ (0151) 708 7150 Lorraine Loates

Burtonwood Bitter and Top Hat plus one ever-changing guest.

One of the few traditional pubs in the area, this has a friendly atmosphere and is popular with students and lecturers. Food available 11.30am–2pm Mon–Fri. No children. Outside drinking area.

OPEN *11.30am–11pm (10.30pm Sun).*

The Cambridge Pub

28 Picton Road, Liverpool L15 4LH
☎ (0151) 280 5126 Joan Adali

Freehouse with Chester's Mild among the brews always available, plus two twice-monthly changing guests.

A modern pub with music. No food. No children.

OPEN *All day, every day.*

Ye Cracke

13 Rice Street, Liverpool L1 9BB
☎ (0151) 709 4171 Michael Jones

Oak Best, Phoenix Wobbly Bob, a Cains brew and Timothy Taylor Landlord always available, plus two guests from independent and micro-breweries whenever possible. Examples include Cottage, Weetwood, Wye Valley and Hanby.

A traditional local with beer garden. Food available until 6pm. Children allowed in the pub until 6pm. Located in a back street off Hope Street.

OPEN *All day, every day.*

Dr Duncan's

St John's House, 1 St John's Lane, Liverpool L1 1HF
☎ (0151) 709 5100 Chris Mossop
www.cains.co.uk

Cains pub with six brewery ales, including Cains Finest, IPA, Formidable Ale, Dark Mild and 2008 (a special ale celebrating Liverpool's year as Capital of Culture), plus one Cains guest ale changed every two months.

City-centre pub in a traditional listed building with an ornate and ever-popular tiled room dating from the turn of the last century. Frequented by both students and real ale enthusiasts. Food served throughout the pub 12–3pm, plus curry night on Monday that includes a free pint of beer! Children allowed up to 3pm. Located behind St George's Hall, opposite St John's Gardens.

OPEN *11.30am–11pm Mon–Sat; 12–10.30pm Sun.*

Everyman Bistro

5–9 Hope Street, Liverpool L1 9BH
☎ *(0151) 708 9545* Joe Power (bar manager);
Alan Crowe (general manager)
www.everyman.co.uk

Freehouse with a Cains beer always available, plus a constantly changing range of guests, usually including Timothy Taylor Landlord, Marston's Pedigree, Black Sheep Bitter or a beer from Castle Eden.

A lively pub with a bohemian atmosphere, situated between the cathedrals. Popular with an eclectic mix of people. Food always available – menu, with meat and vegetarian options, changes twice daily (choices can be limited outside main lunchtime and evening periods). More of a pub than a bistro after 8pm. Children allowed until 9pm.

OPEN *Bistro: 12–12 Mon–Wed; noon–1am Thurs; noon–2am Fri–Sat (closed Sun). Foyer Café Bar: 10am–2pm Mon–Fri.*

Lion Tavern

67 Moorfields, Liverpool L2 2BP
☎ *(0151) 236 1734* John O'Dowd
www.liontavern.co.uk

Punch Taverns tied house with Caledonian Deuchars IPA and JW Lees Bitter always available, plus five daily-changing guests. One real cider.

Grade II listed pub built in 1841 with public bar and two lounges. The current impressively restored interior dates from 1914 and includes ornate glass and tiles. Food served 12–3pm daily with bar snacks available at other times. Car parks nearby. Also stocks 80 malt whiskies. Located in Liverpool city centre near Moorfields underground station.

OPEN *11am–11pm Mon–Sat; 12–10.30pm Sun.*

The Philharmonic

36 Hope St, Liverpool L1 9BX
☎ *(0151) 709 1163*

Up to ten real ales, almost certainly including something from Cains brewery.

Built at the end of the 19th century, a remarkable city-centre pub with hugely ornate interior and a first-floor restaurant. Tiles, chandeliers, marble, wood panelling, stained glass and ironwork. Grade II listed. Food available 12–3pm and 6.30–8.30pm. Perhaps the finest Gents of any pub in Britain?

OPEN *12–11pm (10.30pm Sun).*

The Ship & Mitre

133 Dale Street, Liverpool L2 2JH
☎ *(0151) 236 0859* Brian Corrin
www.shipandmitre.co.uk

Thirteen real ales, with Hydes and Thwaites often featured, together with brews from numerous micro-breweries (800 beers per year), plus two ciders.

Town-centre pub, popular with students and council staff, with newly refurbished art deco function room. Four-times winner of CAMRA Merseyside Pub of the Year. Good value food served 12–2pm and 5–9pm Mon–Sat. The pub has a starred entry in the *Good Pub Food Guide*. Pay and display car park opposite. Children not allowed. Near the Mersey tunnel entrance, five minutes' walk from Lime Street station and Moorfields station.

OPEN *11am–11pm Mon–Wed; 11am–midnight Thurs–Sat; 12–11pm Sun.*

The Swan Inn

86 Wood Street, Liverpool L1 4DQ
☎ *(0151) 709 5281* Clive Briggs

Freehouse serving Marston's Pedigree, Phoenix Wobbly Bob and a Cains brew plus three constantly changing guests from breweries such as Hanby Ales, Durham, Cottage, Wye Valley (Dorothy Goodbody's) or Belhaven.

A traditional backstreet pub with wooden floors. Food served in separate dining area. No children. Located off Berry Street at the back of Bold Street.

OPEN *All day, every day.*

Thomas Rigby's

23–25 Dale Street, Liverpool L2 2EZ
☎ *(0151) 236 3269* Fiona Watkin

Okells tied house offering three Okells ales and five guest ales. Also large range of continental beers.

One of Liverpool's oldest pubs, dating from 1726. Public bar, parlour, quiet rear room. Food served 11.30am–7.45pm. Sky Sports and UK racing shown. Setanta Sports. Large outside courtyard.

OPEN *11.30am–11pm.*

Clarence Hotel

89 Albion Street, New Brighton CH45 9JQ
☎ *(0151) 639 3860* Les Hayes

Enterprise Inns pub serving Caledonian Deuchars IPA and Draught Bass plus up to two guests from local brewers. Cask Marque awarded.

Friendly, suburban pub with bar, lounge and dining area. Food served Thurs–Sat lunchtimes and evenings and Sun lunchtimes only. Beer garden with smoking shelter. Children welcome up to 8.30pm. Annual beer festival held in July. Five minutes' walk from New Brighton station.

OPEN *11.30am–11pm Mon–Thurs; 11.30am–midnight Fri–Sat; 12–11pm Sun.*

RABY
The Wheatsheaf Inn
Raby Mere Road, Raby, Wirral CH63 4JH
☎ (0151) 336 3538 TW Charlesworth

 Thwaites Original, Greene King Old Speckled Hen, Charles Wells Bombardier, Black Sheep Bitter, Brimstage Brewery Trappers Hat permanently available, plus two guests, changed on completion of every firkin. Also one cider.

A black-and-white thatched freehouse with one bar, three rooms including inglenook fireplace, and a separate restaurant. Food served every lunchtime and evening (except Mon evening). Children welcome. Two beer gardens. Bistro patio area. Outdoor smoking area. Large car park. Set in quiet, country hamlet, within easy reach of Chester and Liverpool. Off the B5151 at Willaston.

11am–11pm Mon–Sat; 12–10.30pm Sun.

RAINHILL
The Manor Farm
Mill Lane, Rainhill, Prescot L35 6NE
☎ (0151) 430 0335 Noel and Lesley Berrill

Marston's pub serving Smooth and Pedigree, plus beers from the Mansfield and Jennings range, and many more.

A 17th-century farmhouse converted into a pub 30 years ago. Food served all day from 12, plus evening menu 6–9pm. Booking advisable for upstairs restaurant. Small functions catered for. Large patio area and beer garden with children's play area.

All day, every day.

ST HELENS
Beechams Bar
Water Street, St Helens WA10 1PZ
☎ (01744) 623420 Beverley Duffy

A well-established freehouse. Five traditional beers, with Beechams Crystal Wheat a regular fixture, plus three seasonals and one other guest, changed weekly.

Listed 19th-century pub built by Thomas Beecham, who had images of his family carved into the brickwork. Food available 11.30am–1.30pm Tues–Fri term-time only, with ready-made sandwiches available Mon–Fri all year round. Coffee and cakes from 10.30am Mon–Fri. Nearby public car park. No children. The town has twice-yearly European markets. Handy for the Glass Museum. Located under Beechams clock tower.

10.30am–11pm Mon–Fri; 12–11pm Sat; closed Sun and bank holidays.

The Turks Head
49–51 Morley Street, St Helens WA10 2DQ
☎ (01744) 751289 Amanda Roue

 Freehouse serving up to ten real ales, all on a guest basis, usually changed daily. Many micro-breweries are featured. Also real cider and perry.

Built in the 1870s in the Tudor style, with a turret. Lounge, bar and pool room with beer garden. Sandwiches available; curry night 6–9pm on Tues. Three beer festivals each year: Easter, Hallowe'en and Christmas. Live blues and jazz music. Five minutes' walk from the town centre. CAMRA's regional Pub of the Year 2008.

2–11.30pm Mon–Thurs; 2pm–12.30am Fri; noon–12.30am Sat; 12–11.30pm Sun. No entry after 11pm.

SOUTHPORT
Barons Bar
The Scarisbrick Hotel, 239 Lord Street, Southport PR8 1NZ
☎ (01704) 543000 George Sourbutts
www.baronsbar.com

Freehouse serving a wide variety of up to eight real ales, including Flag & Turret, the house brew, Moorhouse's Pride of Pendle, plus five guests, changed daily, with the main emphasis on local beers and those from other smaller breweries around the UK.

Refurbished, but retaining a baronial look and feel! The hotel's other facilities can also be enjoyed. Barmcakes and sandwiches available 12–2.45pm. Two annual beer festivals, in May and November. Outside seating in summer. Children allowed in the family room until 6pm. Conference and banqueting facilities. On the main shopping street in the town centre.

11am–11pm Mon–Thurs; 11am–11.45pm Fri–Sat; 12–11pm Sun.

Sir Henry Segrave
93 Lord Street, Southport PR8 1RH
☎ (01704) 530217 Donna Pagett

Wetherspoon's pub. Regular guest beers served on two pumps include Cotleigh Osprey, Hop Back Summer Lightning and brews from Burton Bridge, Hook Norton, Everards and Banks and Taylor.

An old-fashioned, quiet, drinkers' pub. Food available.

All day, every day.

WALLASEY

The Cheshire Cheese

2 Wallasey Village, Wallasey CH44 2DH
☎ *(0151) 630 3641* Ken Robinson

Trust Inns tenancy with five real ales, namely Theakston Best Bitter and Mild, plus three weekly guests from breweries such as Brimstage, Spitting Feathers, Beartown, Robinson's, Hydes, Jennings and Copper Dragon, to name but a few.

The oldest licence in Wallasey, there has been a pub on this site since the Middle Ages. William of Orange is said to have stayed here on his way to the Battle of the Boyne. Separate lounge and bar area, large beer garden. Food served 12.30–7pm (not Thurs). Beer festivals held twice a year (April and Sept). Regular hog roasts. Many awards, including local CAMRA Pub of the Year 2007. Close to Wallasey Village railway station.

OPEN *11am–11pm Sun–Thurs; 11am–midnight Fri–Sat.*

WAVERTREE

The Willow Bank

329 Smithdown Road, Wavertree, Liverpool L15 3JA
☎ *(0151) 733 5782* Paula Culvin

Eight real ales, with Greene King IPA and two Tetley's brews as permanent fixtures, and the five guests rotated daily.

A friendly two-bar pub with a good mix of students and regulars. Built in the 1800s and originally part of a dairy. Food available 12–7pm Mon–Fri and 12–6pm Sat–Sun. Beer garden with outside plasma screen. Covered, heated smoking area. Quiz every Wed. Live music. Beer festivals held at Easter, Hallowe'en and Christmas. Car park. Children welcome 12–6pm. Opposite Asda.

OPEN *12–12 Sun–Tues; noon–12.30am Wed–Thurs; noon–1am Fri–Sat.*

THE BREWERIES

BLACKFRIARS BREWERY LTD
Unit 4, Queens Road, Great Yarmouth NR30 3HT
☎ *(01493) 850578*

YARMOUTH BITTER 3.8% ABV
SYGNUS BITTERGOLD 4.0% ABV
OLD HABIT 5.6% ABV
Plus seasonals and specials.

BLUE MOON BREWERY
The Cock Inn, Watton Road, Barford NR6 4AS
☎ *(01603) 757646*

EASY LIFE 3.8% ABV
DARKSIDE 4.0% ABV
SEA OF TRANQUILITY 4.2% ABV
MOONDANCE 4.7% ABV
HINGHAM HIGH 5.2% ABV
MILK OF AMNESIA 5.2% ABV
LIQUOR MORTIS 7.5% ABV
TOTAL ECLIPSE 7.5% ABV

BULL BOX BREWERY
c/o 1 Brickyard Cottage, Fordham, Downham Market PE38 0LW
☎ *07920 163116*

BITTER 4.0% ABV
MID-LIFE CRISIS 4.5% ABV
KERB CRAWLER 5.2% ABV
Plus seasonals and specials.

CHALK HILL BREWERY
Rosary Road, Thorpe Hamlet, Norwich NR1 4DA
☎ *(01603) 4770778*

BREWERY TAP 3.6% ABV
CHB 4.2% ABV
DREADNOUGHT 4.9% ABV
FLINTKNAPPERS' 5.0% ABV
OLD TACKLE 5.6% ABV
Plus occasionals and seasonals.

FAT CAT BREWING COMPANY
The Cider Shed, 98–100 Lawson Road, Norwich NR3 4LF
☎ *(01603) 788508*

FAT CAT 3.8% ABV
ALLEY CAT 4.2% ABV
BLACK CAT 4.6% ABV
TOP CAT 4.7% ABV
Plus seasonals and specials.

FOX BREWERY
Fox & Hounds, 22 Station Road, Heacham, Kings Lynn PE31 7EX
☎ *(01485) 570345*
www.foxbrewery.co.uk

BRANTHILL BEST 3.8% ABV
DROP OF REAL NORFOLK 3.8% ABV
HEACHAM GOLD 3.9% ABV
NINA'S MILD 3.9% ABV
LJB 4.0% ABV
RED ADMIRAL 4.2% ABV
CERBERUS STOUT 4.5% ABV
BRANTHILL NORFOLK NECTAR 4.9% ABV
PEDDARS SWAY 5.0% ABV
IPA 5.2% ABV
PUNT GUN 5.9% ABV
Plus occasionals and seasonals.

FRONT STREET BREWERY
The Chequers Inn, Front Street, Binham, Fakenham NR21 0AL
☎ *(01328) 830297*
www.binhamchequers.co.uk

BINHAM CHEER 3.9% ABV
CALLUM'S ALE 4.3% ABV
UNITY STRONG 5.0% ABV
Plus seasonals and specials.

HUMPTY DUMPTY BREWING CO.
Church Road, Reedham NR13 3TZ
☎ *(01493) 701818*
www.humptydumptybrewery.co.uk

SWALLOWTAIL 4.0% ABV
HUMPTY DUMPTY ALE 4.1% ABV
THE KING JOHN 4.5% ABV
CHELTENHAM FLYER 4.6% ABV
RAILWAY SLEEPER 5.0% ABV
GOLDEN GORSE 5.4% ABV
HUMPTY DUMPTY PORTER 5.4% ABV
Plus occasionals and seasonals.

THE ICENI BREWERY
Foulden Road, Ickburgh, Mundford IP26 5HB
☎ *(01842) 878922*
www.icenibrewery.co.uk

HONEY MILD 3.6% ABV
Black and charged with honey.
THETFORD FOREST MILD 3.6% ABV
Traditional mild.
BOADICEA CHARIOT ALE 3.8% ABV
Amber colour and moreish.
ELVEDEN FOREST GOLD 3.9% ABV
Golden and delicately finished.
CELTIC QUEEN 4.0% ABV
Gold and refreshing.
FINE SOFT DAY 4.0% ABV
Maple syrup and hops give bittersweet flavour.
MUNDFORD PRIDE 4.0% ABV
Full flavoured with a slight sweetness.
PRIDE OF NORFOLK 4.0% ABV
Red golden colour and malty.
RED, WHITE AND BLUEBERRY 4.0% ABV
Full-bodied bitter with blueberry flavour.
SWAFFHAM PRIDE 4.0% ABV
Refreshing and lightly fruity.
CRANBERRY WHEAT 4.1% ABV
Dry, light ale.
GOOD NIGHT OUT 4.1% ABV
Amber colour, full-bodied flavoured with half a bottle per firkin.
SNOWDROP 4.1% ABV
Crisp spring ale made with American hops.
BRENDAN'S CELTIC STOUT 4.2% ABV
Dry and dark.
FEN TIGER 4.2% ABV
Malty with coriander.
ON TARGET 4.2% ABV
Amber and hoppy.
THOMAS PAINE PORTER 4.2% ABV
Dry Irish-style stout.
HONEY STOUT 4.3% ABV
Dry, balanced and black.
DEIRDRE OF THE SORROWS 4.4% ABV
Amber and complex.
PORTED PORTER 4.4% ABV
A bottle of port added to each cask.
ROISIN DUBH 4.4% ABV
Dark with sweet flavour.
WOOLLY MAMMOTH 4.4% ABV
Straw coloured.

IT'S A GRAND DAY 4.5% ABV
Golden, refreshing with a hint of ginger.
NORFOLK GOLD 5.0% ABV
Crisp but smooth.
NORFOLK WINTER LIGHTNING 5.0% ABV
Straw-coloured, smooth, easy drinker.
RASPBERRY WHEAT 5.0% ABV
American-style summer fruity ale.
SWAFFHAM GOLD 5.0% ABV
Gold with fine aftertaste.
MEN OF NORFOLK 6.2% ABV
Rich flavour and dark.
Plus seasonal and occasional brews.

NORFOLK COTTAGE BREWERY
22 The Green, North Burlingham, Norwich
NR13 3DJ
☎ *(01603) 3270520*

 BEST 4.1% ABV

REEPHAM BREWERY
Unit 1, Collers Way, Reepham, Norwich
NR10 4SW
☎ *(01603) 871091*

GRANARY BITTER 3.5% ABV
RAPIER PALE ALE 4.2% ABV
VELVET SWEET STOUT 4.5% ABV
ST AGNES 4.6% ABV
TYNE BROWN 4.6% ABV

SPECTRUM BREWERY
Unit 11, Wellington Road, Tharston, Norwich
NR15 2PE
☎ *07949 254383*
www.spectrumbrewery.co.uk

LIGHT FANTASTIC 3.7% ABV
DARK FANTASTIC 3.8% ABV
BEZANTS 4.0% ABV
42 4.2% ABV
BLACK BUFFLE 4.5% ABV
XXXX 4.6% ABV
WIZZARD 4.9% ABV
OLD STOATWOBBLER 6.0% ABV
TRIP HAZARD 6.5% ABV
Plus seasonal beers.

TINDALL ALE BREWERY
Toad Lane, Thwaite, Bungay NR35 2EQ
☎ *(01508) 483844*

 IPA 3.6% ABV
BEST BITTER 3.7% ABV
Smooth hop taste.
MILD 3.7% ABV
Dark mild – very moreish.
LIBERATOR 3.8% ABV
ALLTIME 4.0% ABV
DITCHINGHAM DAM 4.2% ABV
Dark ale with a subtle hint of ginger.
SEETHING PINT 4.3% ABV
NORWICH DRAGON 4.6% ABV
Occasionals and seasonals:
SUMMER LOVING 3.6% ABV
FUGGLED UP 3.7% ABV
AUTUMN BREW 4.0% ABV
LOVER'S ALE 4.0% ABV
MUNDHAM MILD 4.0%
XMAS CHEERS 4.0% ABV
NORFOLK 'N' GOOD 4.6% ABV
HONEY DO 5.0% ABV

TIPPLES BREWERY
Unit 6, Damgate Lane Industrial Estate, Acle
NR13 3DJ
☎ *(01493) 741007*
www.tipplesbrewery.com

LONGSHORE 3.6% ABV
Pale amber, malt flavour.
GINGER 3.8% ABV
Ginger flavour.
THE HANGED MONK 3.8% ABV
Sweet mild.
REDHEAD 4.2% ABV
Nutty bitter.
BATTLE BEST BITTER 4.3% ABV
Caramel finish.
TOPPER 4.5% ABV
Rich stout.
MOONROCKET 5.0% ABV
Hoppy pale ale with citrus finish.
JACK'S REVENGE 5.8% ABV
Malty.
Plus seasonals.

UNCLE STUART'S BREWERY
Antoma, Pack Lane, Lingwood, Norwich
NR13 4PD
☎ *(01603) 211833*

PACK LANE 4.0% ABV
CHURCH VIEW 4.7% ABV
BUCKENHAM WOODS 5.6% ABV
Plus occasionals and seasonals including:
CHRISTMAS ALE 7.0% ABV

WAGTAIL BREWERY
New Barn Farm, Old Buckenham, Attleborough
NR17 1PF
☎ *(01953) 887133*
www.wagtailbrewery.com

BEST BITTER 4.0% ABV
GOLDEN ALE 4.0% ABV
ENGLISH ALE 4.3% ABV
IRISH ALE 4.5% ABV
RUBY ALE 4.5% ABV
STOUT 4.5% ABV
Plus seasonals and specials.

WAVENEY BREWING COMPANY
Queen's Head, Station Road, Earsham, Bungay
NR35 2TS
☎ *(01986) 892623*

EAST COAST MILD 3.8% ABV
LIGHTWEIGHT 3.9% ABV
GREAT WHITE HOPE 4.8% ABV
Plus seasonals and specials.

THE WHY NOT BREWERY
17 Cavalier Close, Thorpe, St Andrew, Norwich
NR7 0TE
☎ *(01603) 300786*
www.thewhynotbrewery.co.uk

WALLY'S REVENGE 4.0% ABV
CAVALIER RED 4.7% ABV
CHOCOLATE NUTTER 5.5% ABV

WINTER'S BREWERY

8 Keelan Close, Norwich NR6 6QZ
☎ *(01603) 787820*
www.wintersbrewery.com

 MILD 3.6% ABV
BITTER 3.8% ABV
GOLDEN 4.1% ABV
REVENGE 4.7% ABV
Yellow, with hops throughout; sweet aftertaste.
STORM FORCE 5.3% ABV
Blend of sweetness and malt.
TEMPEST 6.2% ABV

WISSEY VALLEY BREWERY

The Clover Club, Low Road, Wretton PE33 9QN
☎ *(01366) 500767*

 **CAP 'N GRUMPY'S WILD WIDOW MILD
3.6% ABV**
Gentle chocolate and vanilla flavours in this
lightly-hopped classic.
Plus occasionals and seasonals.

WOLF BREWERY LTD

*Rookery Farm, Silver Street, Besthope, Attleborough
NR17 2LD*
☎ *(01953) 457775*
www.wolfbrewery.com

CAVELL ALE 3.7% ABV
Sweet blackcurrant flavour.
GOLDEN JACKAL 3.7% ABV
Golden ale.
LAVENDER HONEY 3.7% ABV
Delicate honey flavour.
WOLF IN SHEEP'S CLOTHING 3.7% ABV
Mild with malty finish.
WOLF ALE 3.9% ABV
Copper colour, lots of bite.
COYOTE BITTER 4.3% ABV
Straw coloured pale ale, moreish.
STRAW DOG 4.5% ABV
Pale, slightly sweet wheat beer.
WOLF WHISTLE 4.7% ABV
Malty with citrus hints.
GRANNY WOULDN'T LIKE IT!!! 4.8% ABV
Malty with sweet finish.
WOILD MOILD 4.8% ABV
Dark and fruity.
TIMBER WOLF 5.8% ABV
Dark and malty.
Plus seasonal and special brews including:
LUPINE 4.5% ABV
WERWOLF 4.5% ABV
PRAIRIE 5.0% ABV

WOODFORDE'S NORFOLK ALES

*Broadland Brewery, Woodbastwick, Norwich
NR13 6SW*
☎ *(01603) 720353*
www.woodfordes.co.uk

 MARDLER'S 3.5% ABV
Nut brown with roast malt chocolate
notes.
WHERRY BEST BITTER 3.8% ABV
Citrus flavour, floral aroma.
GREAT EASTERN ALE 4.3% ABV
Golden with malt flavour.
NORFOLK NOG 4.6% ABV
Roast treacle flavour.
ADMIRAL'S RESERVE 5.0 % ABV
Nutty almond flavour.
HEADCRACKER 7.0% ABV
Orange and peaches aroma, slightly sweet.
Occasionals:
NELSON'S REVENGE 4.5% ABV
Citrus, dried fruit flavours.
NORFOLK NIP 8.5% ABV
Mahogany colour, liquorice flavour.
Plus seasonals.

YETMAN'S BREWERY

*c/o Yetman's Restaurant, 37 Norwich Road, Holt
NR25 6SA*
☎ *07774 809016*
www.yetmans.net

 YELLOW BEER 3.6% ABV
Citrus edge.
RED BEER 3.8% ABV
Fruity bitterness.
ORANGE BEER 4.2% ABV
Hoppy.
GREEN BEER 4.8% ABV
Dark and sweet.

THE PUBS

ATTLEBOROUGH

The Griffin Hotel

Attleborough NR17 2AH
☎ *(01953) 452149* Richard Ashbourne

Wolf Best and Coyote plus Greene King
Abbot plus two hand pumps serving
guest ales from a range of small breweries.

A 16th-century freehouse in the centre of
town. Beams, log fires, dining area,
accommodation. Food available at lunchtime
and evenings. Children allowed.

OPEN *10.30am–3.30pm and 5.30–11pm Mon–
Thurs; 11am–11pm Fri–Sat; 10.30am–
3.30pm and 5.30–10.30pm Sun.*

BARFORD

The Cock Inn

Watton Road, Barford NR9 4AS
☎ *(01603) 757646 Peter Turner*

 Home of the Blue Moon Brewery, with the home-brewed Hingham, Darkside and Easy Life and either Moondance or Milk of Amnesia plus seasonals and specials.

Two hundred years old with rustic character and lots of nooks and crannies. Two bars, separate dining areas and a beer garden with bowling green and petanque pitch. Food available lunchtimes and evenings. Children allowed at lunchtime only. Situated four miles west of Norwich on the B1108.

OPEN *12–2.30pm and 6–11pm Tues–Sat; 12–3pm and 7–10.30pm Sun.*

BINHAM

The Chequers Inn

Front Street, Binham NR21 0AL
☎ *(01328) 830297 Mr and Mrs Chroscicki*
www.binhamchequers.co.uk

 Home of the Front Street Brewery. Between three and five real ales always available, including Front Street ales and guests.

A 17th-century former Guildhall with single bar, large garden and car park. Food served every lunchtime and evening. Children welcome. Occasional beer festivals. Close to Binham Priory, Walsingham and the north Norfolk coast.

OPEN *11.30am–2.30pm and 6–11pm Mon–Sat (11.30pm Fri–Sat); 12–2.30pm and 7–11pm Sun.*

BLAKENEY

The Kings Arms

Westgate Street, Blakeney, Nr Holt NR25 7NQ
☎ *(01263) 740341*
Howard, Marjorie and Nicholas Davies
www.blakeneykingsarms.co.uk

 Five real ales on offer at this freehouse. Examples include Woodforde's Wherry, Sundew and Nelson's Revenge, Marston's Pedigree, Adnams Bitter, Regatta, Fisherman, Tally Ho and Broadside, Greene King Old Speckled Hen and Theakston Best.

The building dates back to 1500. The pub has two bars and six adjoining rooms, most of them long and thin. Food served 12–9.30pm (9pm Sun). Seven B&B rooms. Substantial garden, car park. Accompanied children and dogs welcome. Just off the west side of Blakeney Quay.

OPEN *11am–11pm Mon–Sat; 12–10.30pm Sun.*

BLICKLING

The Buckinghamshire Arms

Blickling, Nr Aylsham NR11 6NF
☎ *(01263) 732133 Pip Wilkinson*
www.buck-arms.co.uk

 Freehouse with Woodforde's Wherry plus Adnams and guest brews.

An olde-English, food-oriented coaching inn at the gates of Blickling Hall. One large bar, snug, log fires and beer garden.

Food available at lunchtimes and evenings (not Sun or Mon evening) Mon–Fri and all day at weekends during summer season, in the pub and dining room. En-suite accommodation, with four-poster beds. Overlooking the National Trust property of Blickling Hall.

OPEN *11.30am–3pm every day; 6.30–11pm Mon–Fri; 6–11pm Sat; 7–10.30pm Sun.*

BRANCASTER STAITHE

The White Horse

Brancaster Staithe PE31 8BY
☎ *(01485) 210262*
Clifford Nye and Kevin Nobes
www.whitehorsebrancaster.co.uk

 Genuine freehouse with up to four ales. Woodforde's Wherry, Adnams Bitter and Fuller's London Pride are regular features.

Situated near stunning tidal marshland with panoramic views to Scolt Head island and sandy beaches beyond, this is a traditional local pub (within a hotel) which retains strong local ties. The ancestors of the fishermen who drink in the bar today pictured on the walls. Food served in the conservatory restaurant, with locally caught fish often available. Outdoor area. Children and dogs welcome. Large car park. New sunken garden and alfresco eating area. On the A149 coast road, between Hunstanton and Wells-next-the-Sea.

OPEN *11am–11pm Mon–Sat; 12–10.30pm Sun.*

BRANDON CREEK

The Ship

Brandon Creek, Downham Market PE38 0PP
☎ *(01353) 676228*
Malcolm and Michelle Whiting

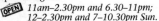 Something from Adnams and Courage plus two guests changed on a weekly basis.

A 17th-century pub situated by the River Ouse with easy river and road access. Quality food available 12–2.30pm and 6–9pm (reservations recommended). Children welcome. Large car park. On the A10.

OPEN *12–3pm and 6–11pm Mon–Fri; 12–11pm Sat; 12–10.30pm Sun. Longer weekday hours in summer.*

BRISTON

The John H Stracey

West End, Briston, Melton Constable NR24 2JA
☎ *(01263) 860891 Mr RE Fox*

Freehouse with Ruddles County a permanent feature, plus one guest, perhaps Woodforde's Wherry, Greene King Old Speckled Hen or Triumph or something from Reepham, changed every week.

Country pub, built in 1565, with 46-seat restaurant, fires, beams and oak furniture. Garden and car park. One twin and two double rooms available for bed and breakfast. Well-behaved children welcome. On the B1354 (Fakenham to Aylsham) in Briston. Special nights.

OPEN *11am–2.30pm and 6.30–11pm; 12–2.30pm and 7–10.30pm Sun.*

BURNHAM THORPE
The Lord Nelson
Walsingham Road, Burnham Thorpe,
King's Lynn PE31 8HL
☎ *(01328) 738241* Simon Alper
www.nelsonslocal.co.uk

 Greene King house with Abbot and IPA and Woodforde's Wherry plus one guest, changed every month or two.

The original 'Lord Nelson' pub – Lord Nelson used to eat and drink here! Built in 1637, the pub is well known for a unique rum-based drink, Nelson's Blood, and its companion, Lady Hamilton's Nip. It features stone floors, original oak settles and log fires. Traditional pub games. No bar, just a serving hatch! Large beer garden with children's play area. Food available at lunchtimes and evenings (not Sunday evening) with the emphasis on local produce (won a Norfolk Restaurant of the Year award in 2004). Barbecues in summer. Celebrations for Trafalgar Night (Oct), Nelson's birthday (Sept) and Lady Hamilton's birthday (April). Live music every Thurs. Victory barn available for functions. Children and dogs welcome.

OPEN *12–3pm and 5–11pm Tues–Sat; 12–10.30pm Sun; closed Mon except school and bank holidays; open 12–11pm in summer holidays.*

BURSTON
The Crown
Crown Green, Burston, Nr Diss IP22 5TW
☎ *(01379) 741257*
J Piers-Hall, and S and B Kembery

 Beers from Adnams, Woodforde's and Earl Soham are among the four always on offer at this freehouse, and there is also a weekly-changing guest.

A 16th-century brick village pub at the heart of the community, with two bars, a restaurant seating 20, and open fires. Food served 12–2pm and 6.30–9pm Mon–Sat and 12–3.30pm Sun. Beer garden. Children and dogs welcome. Car park. Two miles north of Diss, two miles off the A140.

OPEN *12–11pm (10.30pm Sun).*

BUXTON
The Old Crown
Crown Road, Buxton NR10 5EN
☎ *(01603) 279958* Tony and Alison Burnham

 Freehouse serving Woodforde's Wherry and Adnams Bitter. Occasionally an extra guest.

A 17th-century dairy farm converted into a pub by the Coltishall Brewery in the 18th century. Friendly and welcoming atmosphere with darts and pool room. Bar snacks, pub lunches, Sunday roasts and à la carte restaurant food served 12–2pm and 6–9pm Tues–Sat; 12–3pm Sun. Children welcome. Walkers welcome. Beer garden. Situated on the B1354 between Aylsham and Coltishall.

OPEN *All day, every day.*

CANTLEY
The Cock Tavern
Manor Road, Cantley NR13 3JQ
☎ *(01493) 700893* Mike and Susan Enright

 Five real ales, including beers from Tindall Ales and Elgood's, plus two guests, changed weekly.

Country pub not far from Norwich with many separate areas, a beamed ceiling and two open fires. Bar food is available at lunchtimes and evenings. Car park, garden, children's room, plus pond and sheep. Turn right off the A47 (Norwich to Yarmouth road) near Acle, then signposted Cantley. Approx four miles from the turn.

OPEN *11am–3pm and 6–11pm Mon–Sat; 12–3pm and 6–11pm Sun.*

CASTLE ACRE
The Ostrich Inn
Stocks Green, Castle Acre, Kings Lynn PE32 2AE
☎ *(01760) 755398* Felicity Atherton
www.ostrichinn.com

 Greene King tied house with three brewery ales plus one guest changed every three months.

Sixteenth-century coaching inn with traditional bar, comfortable lounge and separate restaurant. Al fresco eating area, private meeting room. Accommodation. Food served 12–9pm Mon–Sun. Large car park, beside the village green. Off the A1065 Swaffham to Fakenham road.

OPEN *12–11pm Sun–Thurs; 12–12 Fri–Sat.*

CHEDGRAVE
The White Horse
5 Norwich Road, Chedgrave, Norwich NR14 6ND
☎ *(01508) 520250* Chris Kennedy

 Punch Taverns pub serving Timothy Taylor Landlord, Caledonian Deuchars IPA, Black Sheep Bitter, Adnams Broadside and one different guest each week.

Traditional village local, converted from three cottages in 1836. Large real fire; 'Norfolk twister' in bar. Wood panelling throughout. Bar food and fine dining in the Garden Gallery restaurant served daily. Children welcome. Dog friendly (free biscuits and water). Beer garden and bowling green. Car park. Two beer festivals each year: St George's Day and Remembrance Sunday weekends. Monthly jazz nights and quiz nights. Situated one mile from the A146.

OPEN *12–3pm and 6–11pm. All day Sat–Sun during summer.*

COLTISHALL

The Red Lion

77 Church Street, Coltishall NR12 7DW
☎ *(01603) 737402* Peter and Melanie Lamb

 Tied to Enterprise Inns, with Adnams Bitter and Weaselpis, the house beer brewed by Shepherd Neame, plus a rotating guest.

Olde-worlde, 350-year-old pub full of nooks and crannies, with oak beams and log fires. Two bars and two restaurants. Food served 12–2pm Mon–Fri and all day Sat–Sun and bank holidays. Large car park, beer garden and indoor children's play area. Opposite the church in the heart of the village.

OPEN *11am–3pm and 5–11pm Mon–Fri; 11am–11pm Sat and bank holidays; 12– 10.30pm Sun.*

COLTON

The Ugly Bug Inn

High House Farm Lane, Colton, Norwich NR9 5DG
☎ *(01603) 880794*
John and Alison Lainchbury
www.uglybuginn.co.uk

 Freehouse with three real ales, including Beeston Worth the Wait plus regularly changing guests from Crouch Vale, Wolf, Elgood's and Oakham.

Exquisite converted barn with restaurant, grounds and lake in three acres. The intimate restaurant has an outstanding reputation for imaginative home-cooked food, served 12–2pm and 7–9pm Mon–Sat and 12–3.30pm Sun, with both traditional pub and à la carte meals available. Patio dining in summer. Private room for hire. Games room, large car park, beer garden, cosy accommodation. Children and dogs welcome. Fishing and golf nearby. Just off the A47, two minutes from Norforlk Showground.

OPEN *12–2.30pm and 5–11pm Mon–Sat; 12– 3pm and 7–10.30pm Sun.*

DEREHAM

The George Hotel

Swaffham Road, Dereham NR19 2AZ
☎ *(01362) 696801* Elaine Shaw
www.lottiesrestaurant.co.uk

 Freehouse with six real ales, usually from Adnams, Woodforde's and Beeston.

An 18th-century coaching inn with wood-panelled bar and restaurant. Outside heated area for smokers. Food served 12–2pm and 6–9.30pm. Accommodation. Beer garden. Licensed for civil weddings. Off the A47 Old Swaffham Road.

OPEN *7am–midnight. Licensed hours: 11am– 11pm (midnight Fri–Sat).*

DOWNHAM MARKET

The Crown Hotel

Bridge Street, Downham Market PE38 9DH
☎ *(01366) 382322*
Richard Williams and Clive Hughes

 Freehouse serving Greene King IPA and Abbot, and something from Adnams plus two guests from the likes of Woodforde's, Oldershaw, Elgood's, Iceni, Wolf, Tring and Tom Wood.

Olde-worlde pub dating from the 1600s, with open fires. One bar and two restaurants. Food available at lunchtimes and evenings. Accommodation. Function room. Car park. Children welcome. In the centre of Downham Market, just off the High Street.

OPEN *10am–11pm Mon–Sat; 12–10.30pm Sun.*

The Old White Bell

20 Lipgate Street, Southery, Downham Market PE38 0NA
☎ *(01366) 377057*
Nicola Thomas and Peter Smith
www.oldwhitebell.co.uk

Freehouse with City of Cambridge IPA plus two guests such as Gale's HSB or Nethergate Barfly.

Dating from the 19th century, this is a large country local with bar, pool room and separate restaurant. Food served 12– 2.30pm and 6–8.30pm. Children allowed until 9pm. Large beer garden. Large car park. Just off the A10 between Ely and King's Lynn.

OPEN *3pm–close Tues–Thurs; 12–close Fri–Mon. Hours vary in summer.*

EARSHAM

The Queen's Head

Station Road, Earsham NR35 2TS
☎ *(01986) 892623* John Hamps

Home of The Waveney Brewing Company, with Lightweight and East Coast Mild permanently available. Plus two guests.

Small village local, circa 1684. Bar with beamed ceilings, tiled floor, real fire; games room and dining room. Food served 12–2pm Wed–Sun. Large beer garden. Car park. Located off the A143, one mile from Bungay.

OPEN *12–3pm and 5–11pm Mon–Thurs; 12–11pm Fri–Sat; 12–10.30pm Sun.*

EAST RUNTON

The White Horse

High Street, East Runton, Nr Cromer NR27 9NX
☎ *(01263) 519530* Kevin and Anita Meagan

 Adnams Bitter and Greene King Abbot plus one or two guests, changed weekly.

A ward-winning village family pub, built in 1845. Cask Marque accredited. Food served 12–2.30pm and 7–9pm every day in the low season and 12–3pm and 5–9pm through the summer. Roasts on Sunday. Two bars, 40-seat restaurant, function room, garden and terrace, car park. Live music through the summer. Children and dogs welcome.

OPEN *12–11pm.*

ELSING

The Mermaid Inn

Church Street, Elsing, Dereham NR20 3EA
☎ *(01362) 637640*
Helen Higgins and Kevin Wills

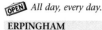 Genuine, freehold freehouse. Three regular real ales: Wolf Jackal, Woodforde's Wherry and Adnams Broadside, plus one rotating feature guest beer, changed weekly in winter, twice weekly in summer.

C harming 17th-century village pub with a growing reputation for good, locally sourced food. Public bar and pool area, separate dining and function room. Log fire in winter, two gardens in summer, one displaying tropical plants. Steak night Tues; burger night Fri; special quiz and pool nights. Ten minutes from the North Tuddenham turn off of the A47, between Norwich and Dereham.

OPEN *All day, every day.*

ERPINGHAM

The Spread Eagle

Eagle Road, Erpingham, Norwich NR11 7QA
☎ *(01263) 761591* Billie Carder

Four real ales: Woodforde's Wherry and Adnams Best plus two guests, changed monthly, perhaps Greene King Fireside, Adnams Broadside or Woodforde's Nelson's Revenge.

A traditional village pub with real fires and comfortable bar and lounge. New restaurant due to open spring 2008. Front and back courtyards, beer garden. Live music once a month. Food available 12–2.30pm and 7–9.30pm. Families and well-behaved dogs welcome. En-suite accommodation.

OPEN *11am–3pm and 6.30–11pm Mon–Sat; 12–4pm and 7–10.30pm Sun.*

FAKENHAM

The Bull

41 Bridge Street, Fakenham NR21 9AG
☎ *(01328) 853410*
Vince Stewart and Ian Harper
www.thefakenhambull.co.uk

Freehouse serving Woodforde's Wherry and Black Dog Mild plus three rotating guests, changed every few days.

A town pub. Food served 11.30am–3pm plus steak nights on Wed evening.

Children welcome. Beer terrace. Accommodation. Close to Norfolk coastal bird watching area and Burford steam museum.

OPEN *9am–close.*

FOULDEN

The White Hart Inn

7 White Hart Street, Foulden, Thetford IP26 5AW
☎ *(01366) 328638*

 The second of Buffy's tied houses, with Bitter, Norwegian Blue and one other beer on offer.

V illage pub with three letting rooms, conservatory, 8-foot pool table, woodburner and cosy dining area. Food available 12–2.30pm 6–9pm Wed–Fri; 12–9.30pm Sat–Sun. Beer garden and car parking. Children and dogs welcome. Two miles from Oxburgh Hall (National Trust). Off the A134 (Thetford to Kings Lynn), three miles from Mundford.

OPEN *5.30–11.30pm Mon–Tues; 12–11.30pm Wed–Sun.*

GAYTON

The Crown Inn

Lynn Road, Gayton, Kings Lynn PE32 1PA
☎ *(01553) 636252* Felicity Atherton
www.gaytoncrown.co.uk

Greene King tied house, with four Greene King ales always on offer, plus one guest.

A traditional country village pub since 1652, although the building dates from the 12th century. Refurbished ensuite accommodation. Three small bars and one large restaurant. Food served 12–9pm Sun–Thurs; 12–9.30pm Fri and Sat. Visit our website for further details. Beer garden. Front patio. Large car park. On the B1145 from Kings Lynn.

OPEN *12–11pm Sun–Thurs; 12–12 Fri–Sat.*

GELDESTON

The Locks Inn

Locks Lane, Geldeston NR34 0HW
☎ *(01508) 518414*
www.geldestonlocks.co.uk

Owned by the Green Jack Brewery with Canary, Orange Wheat, Grasshopper and Gone Fishing available, plus seasonal and occasional brews and guests.

O n the banks (Norfolk side) of the River Waveney, near Beccles and Bungay, you can arrive by boat on the Big Dog Ferry. Built in the 14th century, modernised in the 15th and licensed since the 17th. Food served 12–2.30pm and 6–8.30pm (except Sun and bank holiday evenings). Curry nights (Fri), live music nights (Thurs and weekends). Real fires, real games. Huge riverside garden. Function/dining room.

OPEN *All day, every day from noon in summer. Winter hours may be shorter and the pub is closed on Mon and Tues.*

GORLESTON

The Albion

87 Lowestoft Road, Gorleston NR31 6SH
☎ *(01493) 661035* Jonathan Beales

Punch Taverns pub with four permanent real ales and two weekly-changing guests. Regular beers include Greene King IPA, Caledonian Deuchars IPA, Timothy Taylor Landlord, Black Sheep Bitter and Shepherd Neame Spitfire.

A community pub with two bars and a great mix of people. No food. Sky Sports shown on big-screen TV. Two outside smoking areas. Theme evenings held.

OPEN *All day, every day.*

The Cliff Hotel

Gorleston NR31 6DH
☎ *(01493) 662179* Vaughan Cutter

Fuller's London Pride, Greene King IPA, Woodforde's Wherry and Marston's Pedigree usually available.

Hotel with two bars and two restaurants overlooking Gorleston beach and harbour. Food served 12–2.30pm and 7–9.30pm every day. Children welcome in gardens or hotel only, not in the bars. Two car parks.

OPEN *11am–11pm.*

The Short Blue

47 High Street, Gorleston, Great Yarmouth NR31 6RR
☎ *(01493) 602192* Kevin Duffield

Greene King IPA and Adnams Best Bitter plus one regularly changing guest ale. Whenever possible, guest ales are from a local brewery such as Woodforde's.

Dating from 1693, this traditional olde-worlde pub houses carved wood, stained glass and wooden barrels. No juke box or pool table. Food available 12–2pm Mon–Sun and 6–10.30pm Fri. Riverside garden with covered patio, children allowed in the garden only. Roadside parking in Riverside Road.

OPEN *11am–11pm (10.30pm Sun).*

GREAT BIRCHAM

The King's Head

Lynn Road, Great Bircham PE31 6RJ
☎ *(01485) 578265* Davy Gallagher
www.the-kings-head-bircham.co.uk

Fuller's London Pride, Woodforde's Wherry and Adnams Bitter are among the four real ales at this freehouse, with the fourth one a fortnightly guest such as Beartown Grizzly Bear or Fuller's Chiswick.

Hotel with restaurant, private dining facilities and conference facilities, which prides itself on being a breath of fresh air in rural Norfolk. Modern contemporary bar, beer garden and small children's play area. Food served 12–2pm and 7–9pm. Head towards Fakenham from King's Lynn (A148), turn left on the B1153.

OPEN *11am–11pm Mon–Sat; 12–10.30pm Sun.*

GREAT CRESSINGHAM

The Olde Windmill Inn

Water End, Great Cressingham, Watton IP25 6NN
☎ *(01760) 756232* Caroline and Michael Halls

Greene King IPA and Adnams Best Bitter and Broadside plus two guests, changed regularly, normally one local beer and one from elsewhere in the UK.

Olde-worlde country pub dating from 1650, with five acres of park land and paddocks, three bars, five family rooms, games room and conservatory. Food is served 12–2pm and 5.30–10pm Mon–Sat, and 5.30–10pm Sun. There is an extensive bar menu. Children are welcome in the family rooms, the beer garden and the play area, and the pub has high chairs and a children's menu. Conferences, meetings and private parties are a speciality. Car parks front and back (80 cars). Just off the A1065 Swaffham–Brandon road, or the B1108 Watton–Brandon road.

OPEN *11.30am–3pm and 5–11pm Mon–Fri; 11.30am–11pm Sat–Sun.*

GREAT YARMOUTH

The Gallon Pot

1–2 Market Place, Great Yarmouth NR30 1NB
☎ *(01493) 842230*

Enterprise Inns house with Woodforde's Wherry, Fuller's London Pride, Adnams Bitter and Greene King Old Speckled Hen always available.

Two floors, one with a children's area. Food served 11am–10pm. Located in the town centre, by the market place.

OPEN *10am–11pm Mon–Sat; 12–10pm Sun.*

The Mariner's Tavern

69 Howard Street South, Great Yarmouth NR30 1LN
☎ *(01493) 332299* Shaun Underdown
www.themarinersalehouse.co.uk

Freehouse with eight hand pumps serving Greene King Abbot, Bateman XXXB and The Mariners Shipwrecked. The five guests, changed every couple of days, might include Green Jack Orange Wheat, Humpty Dumpty Golden Gorse, Woodforde's Norfolk Nog and Elgood's Golden Newt. Continental beers (35+) also served, plus a range of hand-pulled draught and bottled ciders.

Traditional, friendly, family-run alehouse in the centre of town, with car park and beer garden. Two bars, one with real ales and continental beers, the other a cider lounge. Real open fire. Food served 12–2.30pm. A two-minute walk from the market place.

OPEN *11am–11pm Mon–Thurs; 11am–12.30am Fri–Sat; 12–11pm Sun.*

The Red Herring

24–5 Havelock Road, Great Yarmouth NR30 3HQ
☎ *(01493) 853384* Wendy and Dave Woolford

Freehouse serving Greene King IPA and Abbot plus up to four guest ales from local and national breweries. Old Rosie cask cider also available.

Old-fashioned, country-style pub in a town location. Entertainment on Saturday nights, plus darts and pool. No food. No children. Havelock Road is off St Peter's Road which runs off the sea front.

 12–4pm and 7–11pm Mon–Fri; 11am–4pm and 7–11pm Sat; 12–4pm and 7–10.30pm Sun during quiet season, but mostly open all day through the summer.

St John's Head

58 North Quay, Great Yarmouth NR30 1JB
☎ *(01493) 843443* Barry Austin

 Freehouse with Elgood's Cambridge plus three ever-changing guests such as Blackfriar's Mitre Gold, Nethergate Dirty Dick and St Peter's Golden Ale. Also a real cider, Addlestons Cloudy Cider, on hand pump.

Listed pub dating from the 17th century. Single bar. Outside drinking area and heated smoking shelter. Snacks available at lunchtimes. Big-screen TV for football. Car park. Off the A47 close to Vauxhall railway station.

 12–12. Hours sometimes extended until 2am Sun–Thurs; 3am Fri–Sat.

GRESSENHALL
The Swan

The Green, Gressenhall, Dereham NR20 4DU
☎ *(01632) 860340* DV Walker

Adnams Bitter and Broadside, Greene King IPA and Charles Wells Bombardier always available.

Family-oriented country pub with L-shaped bar, small restaurant, beer garden and small car park. Food available 12–2pm and 6.30–9pm Tues–Sun. Three miles from Dereham.

 12–2.30pm and 6–11pm.

HAPPISBURGH
Hill House

Happisburgh NR12 0PW
☎ *(01692) 650004* Dr and Mrs EC Stockton

Freehouse offering six ales, usually two from Greene King, one from Buffy's and three guests, changed around twice a week.

A16th-century coastal village coaching inn known for its Sherlock Holmes connection. Exposed beams, open fire, restaurant and large garden. Bar and restaurant food served 12–2.30pm and 7–9.30pm (9pm Sun). Two en-suite rooms (one with disabled facilities), and two rooms that share a bathroom. Car park. Large garden. Summer solstice beer festival with at least 70 real ales, ciders and perries, and live music throughout the five days (Thurs–Mon). On the coast road, 20 miles north of Great Yarmouth, 14 miles south of Cromer.

 Winter: 12–3pm and 7–11pm Mon–Wed; 12–11.30pm Thurs–Sun. Summer: 12–11.30pm.

HEACHAM
Fox & Hounds

22 Station Road, Heacham PE31 7EX
☎ *(01485) 570345* Mark Bristow
www.foxbrewery.com

Six real ales, four of these from the on-site Fox Brewery. Two guests are rotated every couple of days.

One-room friendly local pub dating from around 1928, home of the award-winning Fox Brewery. Food served 12–2pm and 6–9pm. Three beer festivals a year (Easter, July and August bank holiday). Beer garden. Local CAMRA Pub of the Year 2008. Turn left at Norfolk Lavender, and the pub is opposite the fire station.

12–11pm (10.30pm Sun).

HILBOROUGH
The Swan

Brandon Road, Hilborough, Thetford IP26 5BW
☎ *(01760) 756380* Sally and Paul Figura

Freehouse serving Greene King IPA and two guest brews, changed twice a week.

An 18th-century pub with a new extension, featuring one bar, restaurant and function room. Food available 12–3pm and 6–9pm Mon–Fri and 12–9pm Sun. Seven en-suite letting rooms, beer garden, function room. Large car park. Beer festival in September. Close to Thetford Forest, Oxborough Hall, Iceni Village, and the towns of Thetford and Swaffham. On the main road between Swaffham and Mundford.

11am–close.

HINGHAM
The White Hart Hotel

3 Market Place, Hingham, Norwich NR9 4AF
☎ *(01953) 850214* Jane and Calvin Black

Woodforde's Wherry and Norfolk Nog plus two guests.

The only pub in Hingham, this is a family-oriented pub and restaurant with beer garden and accommodation. Food available at lunchtimes and evenings. Children allowed.

12–11pm Mon–Sat; 12–5pm and 7–10.30pm Sun.

HOCKERING
Victoria

The Street, Hockering NR20 3HL
☎ *(01603) 880507* Barry and Carol Surman

Freehouse with Elgood's Black Dog Mild plus three constantly changing guests, which could be from anywhere in the UK.

Victorian roadside pub in small village. Bar meals served evenings and weekends. Darts, quizzes, live music. Beer garden and car park. Families welcome. Off the A47 between Dereham and Norwich, four miles from Dinosaur World and ten miles from Norwich.

6–11pm Mon–Wed; 12–3pm and 6–11pm Thurs–Sat; 12–3pm and 7–10.30pm Sun.

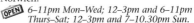

HOCKWOLD

The Red Lion

Main Street, Hockwold IP26 4NB
☎ *(01842) 828875* Mrs Miles

 Greene King IPA and Adnams Bitter, plus a rotating guest. A beer festival is held each August bank holiday.

Village pub and restaurant (curry night Mon, carvery Weds). Children allowed. Pop quiz on Sun.

OPEN *12–2.30pm and 6–11pm Sun–Fri; 12–11pm Sat.*

HOLKHAM

Victoria

Holkham NR23 1RG
☎ *(01328) 711008*
www.holkham.co.uk/victoria

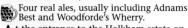 Four real ales, usually including Adnams Best and Woodforde's Wherry.

At the entrance to the Holkham estate on the A149 between Wells and Hunstanton, an upmarket hotel and restaurant built in 1837 with drinking areas that maintain the feel of a friendly local. Good food (often sourced from the estate) served at lunchtimes and evenings. Plenty of outside seating. Barbecues in summer. Directly opposite is a drive leading down to Holkham beach and the salt marshes.

OPEN *11am–11pm.*

INGHAM

The Swan Inn

Mill Road, Ingham NR12 9AB
☎ *(01692) 581099*
Heather Owen and Tim Ridley
www.theinghamswan.com

 Woodforde's pub with Wherry, Nelson's Revenge, Sundew, Norfolk Nog and Mardler's Mild.

Wonderful 14th-century inn with fireplaces and beams. Hearty English food served 12–2pm and 6–9pm every day. Patio, car park. Five cosy en-suite rooms. On the B1151, a mile from Stalham.

OPEN *12–3pm and 6–11pm Mon–Sat; 12–10.30pm Sun. Open all day in summer.*

KENNINGHALL

The Red Lion

East Church Street, Kenninghall, Diss NR16 2EP
☎ *(01953) 887849* Mandy and Bruce Berry

Freehouse offering Greene King IPA and Abbot, Woodforde's Wherry and Mardler's Mild plus one guest, perhaps from Wolf.

One-bar village pub with beams, open fires, bare stone floors and floorboards. A listed building with a snug, one of only two snugs in the area. Bar snacks and restaurant food available at lunchtimes and evenings every day. Rear patio garden. Beer garden. Children allowed, but not in the bar area. Bed and breakfast accommodation available.

OPEN *12–3pm and 6.30–11pm Mon–Thurs; 12–11pm Fri–Sat; 12–10.30pm Sun.*

KING'S LYNN

Live and Let Live

18 Windsor Road, Kings Lynn PE30 5PL
☎ *(01553) 764990* Rosina Woods

A freehouse with four real ales and two real ciders. No permanent ales – the constantly changing selection may include Blackfriar's Mild or Yarmouth Best, Highgate Irish Whisky Ale, Elgood's Black Dog or Wolf or Webster's Best.

Backstreet, traditional locals' local. A little on the quirky side, they hold a Christmas party every summer! No food. Live bands.

OPEN *12–10.30pm Mon; 11.30am–10.30pm Tues and Sun; 11.30am–11.30pm Wed–Thurs; 11.30am–midnight Fri–Sat.*

Stuart House Hotel

35 Goodwins Road, King's Lynn PE30 5QX
☎ *(01553) 772169* David Armes
www.stuarthousehotel.co.uk

Adnams Best Bitter and Broadside plus Woodforde's Wherry and Greene King IPA. One guest beer is also served, such as Timothy Taylor Landlord, Fuller's London Pride, Woodforde's Nelson's Revenge or Oakham JHB.

Family-run hotel, quietly situated within its own grounds in the centre of King's Lynn. Cosy bar with a real fire in winter and doors that open on to the garden in summer. Regular entertainment. Bar menu and à la carte restaurant. Food served 7–9.30pm daily. Car park. Well-behaved children welcome until 8.30pm. Pets' corner in garden. Music and events throughout the year – check website for details. Beer Festival held in grounds at the end of July.

OPEN *6–11pm (10.30pm Sun).*

LARLING

The Angel Inn

Larling, Norwich NR16 2OU
☎ *(01953) 717963* Andrew Stammers

Freehouse with Adnams Bitter and four guest beers, perhaps from Iceni, Woodforde's, Wolf, Mauldons or Orkney, changed after every firkin.

A 400-year-old former coaching inn in the same family for three generations. Quarry-tiled, beamed public bar, real fire and local atmosphere. Two dining rooms. Food served 12–9.30pm Sun–Thurs, 12–10pm Fri–Sat. Car park. En-suite accommodation plus camping and caravanning. Children welcome in the lounge and picnic area. Small, fenced play area outside. Annual beer festival in August. Ideal for quiet outdoor pursuits and handy for Banham Zoo, Snetterton Race Circuit and Sunday Market. Off the A11, within 20 miles of Norwich and Bury St Edmunds.

OPEN *All day, every day.*

LITTLE DUNHAM
The Black Swan
The Street, Little Dunham, Nr Swaffham,
King's Lynn PE32 2DG
☎ *(01760) 722200*

Freehouse with three real ales. Greene King IPA and Abbot plus a guest changed after every barrel.

Built in 1640 as a private house, once owned by William Nelson, the uncle of Horatio. A pub since around 1815, it has one bar, log fires, restaurant and patio beer garden with tables for dining. Food available 12–2.30pm and 6.30–9pm Tues–Sun. Children welcome. Large car park. Located a mile and three quarters off the A47, signposted 'Dunhams'.

OPEN *12–3.30pm Tues–Fri; 6.30–11pm Mon–Fri; noon–12.30am Sat; 12–11pm Sun.*

LYNFORD
Lynford Hall
Lynford, Thetford IP26 5HW
☎ *(01842) 878351 Peter Scopes*

Woodforde's Wherry, St Peter's Ale and an Iceni brew always available.

Public bar located within Lynford Hall, a stately home and tourist attraction open to the public. Separate restaurant and beer garden. Food available. Children allowed.

OPEN *11am–11pm.*

MUNDFORD
The Crown Hotel
Crown Street, Mundford, Nr Thetford IP26 5HQ
☎ *(01362) 878233 Barry Walker*
www.the-crown-hotel.co.uk

Four real ales, usually including Woodforde's Norfolk Wherry, Marston's Pedigree, Courage Directors and Greene King IPA. Guests are changed weekly.

Dating from 1652, a whitewashed, beamed freehouse that has been used as a magistrates' court, a doctor's surgery and a hunting lodge. Two bars, open fires in winter. Bar and restaurant food available 12–3pm and 7–10pm. Pool and darts, car park, beer garden, function room, 30 en-suite bedrooms. Children allowed. Close to Thetford Forest, on the village green.

OPEN *11am–2am.*

NORTH ELMHAM
The Railway Freehouse
20 Station Road, North Elmham, Dereham
NR20 5HH
☎ *(01362) 668300 Colin and Julie Smith*
www.tracks-at-the-railway.co.uk

Four or five constantly changing real ales at this freehouse. Beers from Norfolk, Suffolk, Lincolnshire and Cambridgeshire are often featured, with the emphasis on medium-sized breweries and micro-breweries such as Elgood's Wolf, Spectrum, Buffy's, Nethergate and many more!

Flint-built pub dating from 1861 which has been in the Smith family for 50 years. Open fire surrounded by comfy chairs, small dining room and larger public area with pool table. Food served 11.30am–1.30pm and 6–8.30pm. Beer garden and patio/dining area. Annual beer festival August bank holiday. Rough camping available behind the pub at no cost. Separate music venue, with live music most weekends both here and in the bar area of the pub. The venue can also be hired for functions. Follow the signs for Holt on the B1110, at Elmham follow B1145 signposted Reepham. The pub is 250 metres east of the level crossing.

OPEN *All day, every day (except Christmas Day evening).*

NORTHWOLD
The Crown Inn
High Street, Northwold, Thetford IP26 5LA
☎ *(01366) 727317 Gary and Kym Widdicks*

Freehouse with four constantly changing real ales. Local breweries are favoured, in particular Adnams, Woodforde's and occasionally Iceni.

Village pub with log fires and beer garden. Bar snacks and à la carte food served 12–2.30pm and 6.30–9.30pm Wed–Sun (no food Mon–Tues).

OPEN *12–3pm and 6–11pm Mon–Thurs; 12–11pm Fri–Sat; 12–10.30pm Sun.*

NORWICH
Alexandra Tavern
16 Stafford Street, Norwich NR2 3BB
☎ *(01603) 627772 James Little*

Freehouse with Chalk Hill Best and Tap plus three guests changed every fortnight.

Traditional local with log fires in winter. Bar snacks always available, and bar meals are served 12.30–7pm. Children allowed until 7pm. Just off Earlham Road on the way to the university.

OPEN *10.30am–11pm Mon–Wed; 10.30am–midnight Thurs–Sat; 12–11pm Sun.*

The Beehive
30 Leopold Road, Norwich
☎ *(01603) 451628 Alexandra Kerridge*
www.beehivepubnorwich.co.uk

Freehouse with up to eight real ales. Beers from breweries such as Wolf, Hop Back, Burton Bridge, Fuller's, Greene King and Crouch Vale are regularly featured.

Licensed since 1892, this traditional pub has one bar, one lounge, function room and beer garden. No food. Quiz night every Wed. BBQs in summer. Children welcome. Annual beer festival.

OPEN *5–11.30pm Mon–Thurs; 5pm–12.30am Fri; noon–12.30am Sat; 12–3pm and 7–11.30pm Sun.*

Coach & Horses

82 Thorpe Road, Norwich NR1 1BA
☎ *(01603) 477077* Bob Cameron

Six real ales, all from the Chalk Hill Brewery, which is on the same site. Real cider also available.

A 200-year-old traditional pub with an open fire and wooden floors. Wide range of food 12–9pm Mon–Sat, 11am–8pm Sundays. Well-behaved children welcome. Close to Norwich Station and football ground.

OPEN *11am–midnight Sun–Thurs; 11am–1am Fri–Sat.*

The Eaton Cottage

75 Mount Pleasant, Norwich NR2 2DQ
☎ *(01603) 453048* Philip Birchall

Up to seven real ales, changing all the time but including brews from Wolf and a house ale called Eaton Cottage Bitter.

M id-Victorian corner pub, refurbished in 2005 and offering all Sky Sports plus live music on Thursday and occasional Saturdays. Small rolls available all day. Suntrap garden, function room. New outside smoking areas. Children welcome (under close supervision) until 5pm. Five minutes from the city centre.

OPEN *12–11pm Sun–Thurs; 12–12 Fri–Sat.*

The Fat Cat

49 West End Street, Norwich NR2 4NA
☎ *(01603) 624364* Colin and Marge Keatley

Up to 25 beers available at any one time. Regulars include Timothy Taylor Landlord, Hop Back Summer Lightning and Oakham Bishop's Farewell plus a guest list that now runs into thousands. Belgian beers (four on draught, plus bottles) also stocked.

T raditional Victorian pub decorated with breweriana and pub signs. Filled rolls available at lunchtime. Street parking. CAMRA National Pub of the Year 2005.

OPEN *12–11pm Mon–Thurs; 11am–11pm Fri–Sat; 12–10.30pm Sun.*

The Freemasons Arms

27 Hall Road, Norwich NR1 3HQ
☎ *(01603) 623768* Kezia Brett

Freehouse with up to eight real ales, including Oakham JHB, Winter's Golden, Greene King Abbot, Elgood's Black Dog and Adnams Broadside. The three guests are changed fortnightly, and might include Iceni Fine Soft Day, Adnams Bitter, Oyster Stout or Tally Ho, Cambridge Boathouse Bitter or Elgood's North Brink Porter.

A pub since the 1850s, traditional in design but refurbished with a contemporary theme. Formerly called The Billy Bluelight. It is close to the city centre, and has darts, a snug, Sky Sports and a friendly atmosphere. No food is served, but customers are welcome to bring their own (plates, cutlery and condiments are provided). Beer garden with heaters, occasional live music. Children welcome until 6pm. Located just down from the junction of Kings and Hall Roads.

OPEN *11am–11pm Mon–Thurs; 11am– midnight Fri–Sat; 12–10.30pm Sun.*

The Jubilee

26 St Leonards Road, Norwich NR11 4BL
☎ *(01603) 618734* Tim and Kate Wood

Freehouse with Fuller's London Pride, Greene King IPA, Woodforde's Wherry and Nelson's Revenge plus Hop Back Summer Lightning and guest ales.

A traditional freehouse offering a warm welcome and a great atmosphere, with two bars, beer garden, conservatory and two pool tables. Sky Sports. Food available all day. Children allowed until 7pm. Comfortable outdoor smoking areas. Five minutes from the train station and football ground, and ten minutes from the city centre.

OPEN *All day, every day.*

The Kings Arms

22 Hall Road, Norwich NR1 3HQ
☎ *(01603) 766361*
Richard Roberts and Michaela Fry

Former freehouse now owned by Bateman, with 13 real ales from Bateman, Adnams, Wolf plus many more regional and micro-breweries across the UK. Five of the beers are regulars, and the eight guests are changed daily but always include a mild and stout or porter. Belgian ales and fruit beers also served.

O ne-bar traditional alehouse, with no music and no machines, just good beer and good company! Cask Marque accredited. Bar food served at lunchtimes every day. Bring your takeaways in the evening. Courtyard beer garden and conservatory. Disabled facilities. Quiz night last Wednesday of the month. Quarterly beer festivals. All major sporting events shown live. Just off Inner Ring Road, near Sainsbury's.

OPEN *11am–11pm Mon–Thurs; 11am– midnight Fri–Sat; 12–10.30pm Sun.*

The King's Head

42 Magdalen Street, Norwich NR3 1JE
☎ *(01603) 620468*
Jonathan Smith and Roland Coomber

Genuine freehouse with up to 12 real ales, mainly from Norfolk micro-breweries and always including a mild. Also serves a large selection of Belgian and continental beers.

D ating from 1316, but renovated in 2005 in a Victorian style, this pub is a keg-free zone! Very traditional, with two bars, bar billiards and no music or machines. A selection of filled rolls and pork pies available. Well-behaved children and pets welcome. No television. On the north city inner ring road, 20 minutes walk from the station. Local CAMRA Pub of the Year 2006 and 2008.

OPEN *12–12 (11pm Sun).*

The Mustard Pot

101 Thorpe Road, Norwich NR1 1TR
☎ *(01603) 432393* Jason Bates

Adnams house serving Best, Broadside and Extra plus Regatta when in season. A range of guest ales such as Charles Wells Summer Solstice or Fuller's London Pride is also served.

A drinkers' pub with a beer garden and food available at lunchtimes and evenings. No children. Pool table, sport on TV.

OPEN *All day, every day.*

The Nelson

22 Nelson Street, Norwich NR2 4DR
☎ *(01603) 626362*

Six real ales, probably including Woodforde's Wherry and Caledonian Deuchars IPA.

Friendly, community local with two drinking areas. Food served at lunchtimes and evenings. Quiz (Sun) and live music nights. Large beer garden and car park. Sky Sports TV. Function room. Occasional beer festivals.

OPEN *12–11pm (10.30pm Sun).*

The Reindeer Ale House

10 Dereham Road, Norwich NR2 4AY
☎ *(01603) 762223* Paul Leech

Elgood's tied house with Cambridge Blue, Black Dog Mild, Greyhound and Golden Newt permanently on offer, plus Timothy Taylor Landlord and up to four other guests.

Once known as the best real ale pub in Norwich, and still retaining an excellent range of cask beers. Bar and separate restaurant; food served 12–2pm and 6–9pm Mon–Thurs; 12–10pm Fri–Sat; 12–4pm Sun. Children welcome. Decked beer garden and seating area. Small car park. Close to Norwich city centre.

OPEN *11am–11pm Mon–Thurs; 11am–midnight Fri–Sat; 12–11pm Sun.*

The Ribs of Beef

24 Wensum Street, Norwich NR3 1HY
☎ *(01603) 619517*
Roger and Anthea Cawdron, Paula Eaglen
www.ribsofbeef.co.uk

Genuine freehouse serving nine cask ales. Woodforde's Wherry, Courage Best and Adnams Bitter and a mild (usually Elgood's Black Dog) are permanently available. The five guests, changed frequently, might include beers from Oakham, Hop Back, Fuller's and Timothy Taylor.

Dating back to 1743 and brewing its own beer until 1818, a popular local situated near the river with a private jetty. Food available 12–3pm Mon–Fri and 12–5pm Sat–Sun. Large-screen TV. Children's room. Families welcome. Wherry Room for hire. Two minutes from the cathedral, five from the city centre. On the Fye Bridge, 200 yards on the left from Tombland roundabout.

OPEN *11am–midnight Mon–Thurs; 11am–1am Fri; 10.30am–1am Sat; 12–12 Sun.*

Rosary Tavern

95 Rosary Road, Norwich NR1 4BX
☎ *(01603) 666287* Tim and Michelle

At least seven real ales. Adnams Best and Black Sheep Best are on permanently plus five constantly changing guests. Also sells real Norfolk cider and 30 whiskies.

A traditional pub with a friendly atmosphere. Food available 12–2pm and 6–9pm Mon–Fri, 12.30–3.30pm Sun. Car park, beer garden and function room. Easy to find, near the yacht and railway station, and the football ground.

OPEN *11.30am–11pm Mon–Sat; 12–10.30pm Sun.*

St Andrew's Tavern

4 St Andrews Street, Norwich NR2 4AF
☎ *(01603) 614858*
Jenny Watt and Alan Allred

Adnams house serving up to 16 cask ales, including the full range of Adnams brews. Always an interesting choice of constantly changing guest beers from around the country.

Friendly, traditional pub, close to the city centre. Bar food available at lunchtimes (12–2pm). In the evenings, order your choice of takeaway and eat in the pub. Terrace garden with barbecue. Cellar bar available for parties, functions and meetings. Children not allowed. At the junction of Duke Street and St John Maddermarket opposite St Andrew's car park.

OPEN *12–11pm Mon–Sat; 12–5pm Sun.*

Seamus O'Rourke's

92 Pottergate, Norwich NR2 1DZ
☎ *(01603) 626627* Phil Adams

Freehouse serving Adnams Best and O'Rourke's Revenge (house beer) plus up to eight guests including Charles Wells Bombardier, Wolf Coyote, Iceni Fine Soft Day or a Burton Bridge beer.

Irish sports-themed pub with open fires and food available at lunchtime. No children.

OPEN *All day, every day (except Christmas Day 12–3.30pm).*

The Steam Packet

39 Crown Road, Norwich NR1 3DT
☎ *(01603) 441545* Nick Howlett
www.myspace.com/the_steampacket

Adnams-owned pub with Bitter and Broadside plus three guests on tap, as well as bottled beers. Good selection of wines, and one of the largest choices of whisky in the city.

Victorian pub with a modern twist, with a relaxed atmosphere and friendly staff. Serves home-cooked food, and ground coffee from local suppliers. Quiz nights and live acoustic music. Close to the castle and Cathedral, and a short walk from the train station, football ground and city centre. Situated off Rose Lane, next to Anglia TV.

OPEN *12–12 Mon–Sat.*

The Trafford Arms

61 Grove Road, Norwich NR1 3RL
☎ *(01603) 628466* Chris and Glynis Higgins
www.traffordarms.co.uk

 Genuine freehouse serving Adnams Bitter and Woodforde's Wherry plus seven rotating guest ales. There is always a cask mild on offer, and usually a porter or stout. Many classic ales are featured, such as Caledonian Deuchars IPA, Fuller's London Pride, Oakham JHB, Haviestoun Bitter and Twisted, Crouch Vale Brewer's Gold, Timothy Taylor Landlord, plus many more throughout the year.

Welcoming community pub appealing to all age groups. No juke box, just a cacophony of chatting voices. CAMRA Norfolk and Norwich Pub of the Year 2005. Cask Marque accredited. Food served 12–2.30pm and 6–8.30pm Mon–Fri, 12–3pm and 6–8pm Sat, 12–3pm Sun. Limited parking. No children's licence, but no upper age limit! Annual Valentine beer festival in February. Situated very close to Sainsbury's on Queens Road, just a ten-minute walk from the city centre.

OPEN *11am–11pm Mon–Sat; 12–10.30pm Sun.*

The York Tavern

1 Leicester Street, Norwich NR2 2AS
☎ *(01603) 620918* Andrew Bolton

 Woodforde's Wherry and Adnams Broadside plus a guest such as Wolf Golden Jackal.

Friendly, London-style pub with open fires, restaurant and beer garden. Food available 12–5pm Sat–Sun; curry and a pint 6–9pm Wed. Pool room, upstairs Sky Sports bar, no TV in main bar. Children allowed in the restaurant only. First-floor function room. Close to the city centre.

OPEN *12–11pm.*

The Royal Oak

44 The Street, Poringland, Norwich NR14 7JT
☎ *(01508) 493734* Nick and Deira Perry

 Freehouse with 10 real ales. Elwood's Black Dog, Woodforde's Wherry and Caledonian Deuchars IPA are permanent fixtures, plus seven others, constantly rotated. Over 3,000 beers served in the last two years. CAMRA Norfolk Pub of the Year 2007.

A pub since 1890, this is a large, community-focused, open-plan village pub, with lounge seating area, pool room and darts room. No food. No TV or juke box. Large car park. Large beer garden. Quiz night Sun, crib night Tues. Monthly live music. Two annual beer festivals. On the main Norwich to Bungay road, on a main Norwich bus route.

OPEN *12–3pm and 5–11pm Mon–Thurs; 12–2pm and 5–11pm Fri–Sun.*

The King's Head

The Street, Pulham St Mary IP21 4RD
☎ *(01379) 676318* Graham Scott

 Brews from Adnams always available plus two guests including beers from Harvest Moon, Jennings, Woodforde's and smaller local breweries.

Built in the 1600s, this pub has an old oak timber frame with exposed beams and inglenook fireplaces. Quiz nights alternate Thursdays. Off the A140, on the B1134 near Harleston.

OPEN *5–11pm Mon–Fri; 3–11pm Sat; 3–10.30pm Sun.*

The Railway Tavern

17 The Havaker, Reedham NR13 3HG
☎ *(01493) 700340*
James Lunn and Christina Felix

 Adnams ales always available plus many guest beers, including those from Iceni and the local Humpty Dumpty brewery plus other small local operations. Beer festivals held in April and September.

Listed Victorian railway hotel freehouse. Two bars. No fruit machines. Bar and restaurant food is available 12–3pm and 6–9pm on weekdays, all day at weekends. Car park, garden and children's room. Three bedrooms available in separate stable block. Take the A47 south of Acle, then six miles on the B1140. By rail from Norwich, Great Yarmouth or Lowestoft.

OPEN *11.30am–11pm.*

The Crown

Ollands Road, Reepham, Norwich NR10 4EJ
☎ *(01603) 870964* Mr Good

Greene King Old Speckled Hen and IPA among the beers always available.

Village pub with dining area and beer garden. Food available at lunchtimes and evenings. B&B available. Children allowed.

OPEN *12–3pm and 7–11pm Mon; 7–11pm Tues–Fri; 12–5pm and 7–11pm Sat; 12–5pm and 7–10.30pm Sun.*

The Kings Arms

Market Place, Reepham, Norwich NR10 4JJ
☎ *(01603) 870345* Peter Salisbury

Genuine freehouse with five permanent real ales, namely Woodforde's Wherry, Adnams Best, Elgood's Cambridge, Greene King Abbot and Timothy Taylor Landlord. There is also one rotating guest.

A late-17th-century family-owned village community pub with two bars, beams, brickwork, open fires and a restaurant area, courtyard and garden. Food served every day. Jazz in courtyard on Sundays in summer. Children welcome, plus dogs with well-behaved owners. No music inside. Car park. On the B1145 from Aylsham.

OPEN *11.30am–3pm and 5.30–11pm; 12–3pm and 7–10.30pm Sun.*

The Old Brewery House Hotel

Market Place, Reepham, Norwich NR10 4JJ
☎ *(01603) 870881* David Hurst
www.oxfordhotelsandinns.com/ourhotels/
oldbreweryhouse

Freehouse with four real ales available.
Greene King IPA, Abbot and Old Speckled
Hen are regulars plus a rotating guest.

Olde-worlde hotel with a locals' bar,
beams, log fires, restaurant, beer garden
and 23 en-suite bedrooms. Food available 12–
2pm and 6.30–9.30pm Mon–Sat, 12–2.15pm
and 7–9pm Sun. Children allowed. Ten miles
west of Norwich.

OPEN *11am–11pm.*

The Gin Trap Inn

6 High Street, Ringstead, Nr Hunstanton
PE36 5JU
☎ *(01485) 525264* Steve and Cindy Knowles
www.gintrapinn.co.uk

Freehouse with Woodforde's Wherry and
an Adnams ale plus guests.

A 350-year-old traditional English country
freehouse. Dining area, large beer garden
and three en-suite bedrooms. Food available
12–2pm and 6–9pm. Children and dogs
welcome. Plenty of parking. Ring for
directions.

OPEN *11am–2.30pm and 6–11pm Mon–Thurs;*
all day Fri–Sun. Open all day, every day
in summer.

The Windham Arms

15 Wyndham Street, Sheringham NR26 8BA
☎ *(01263) 822609* Spyros and Peta Garnavos

Beers from Wolf and Woodforde's always
available, plus a wide selection of weekly
changing guest ales served on three hand
pumps (never the same beer twice).

Large pub with restaurant, function room
and beer garden. Food available at
lunchtimes and evenings. Children and well-
behaved dogs allowed. Beer festivals in
summer.

OPEN *All day, every day.*

The Red Lion

44 Wells Road, Stiffkey, Wells-next-the-Sea
NR23 1AJ
☎ *(01328) 830552* Stephen Franklin
www.stiffkey.com

Freehouse with Woodforde's Wherry and
Nelson's Revenge among the beers always
available plus at least one guest, changed
every quarter.

Old, rustic pub dating from 1680, with two
bars, tiled floor, four log fires and beer
garden. Views of the river valley from the bar,
and a fabulous marsh and beach just 5/10mins
walk. Good food available at lunchtimes and
evenings (12–2.30pm and 6–9pm) and all day
Sunday. Children and dogs welcome.
Accommodation in ten en-suite bedrooms.
Camp site nearby. Outside seating. On the
A149 coast road, two miles east of Wells.

OPEN *11am–11pm.*

The Heron

Station Road, Stowbridge, King's Lynn PE34 3PP
☎ *(01366) 384147* Andrew and Julie Hyde

Freehouse with six real ales. Greene King
Old Speckled Hen, Adnams Best and
brews from Archers and Tom Wood are
regularly featured. Three are changed every
fortnight.

Riverside pub and restaurant built in 1935,
with two bars and a great atmosphere.
Full menu served Tues–Sun, plus steak nights
Wed and Thurs. Beer garden, large car parks,
landing stage for boats. Children welcome.
Annual raft race in June or July. On the A10
to Kings Lynn, signposted from Stowbridge.

OPEN *12–late Tues–Sun.*

The Angel

66 Greengate, Swanton Morley, Norwich
NR20 4LX
☎ *(01362) 637407*
Avril Evans and Peter Groves

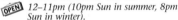Freehouse serving Wolf Golden Jackal
and Mighty Oak Oscar Wilde plus three
rotating guests changed every few days.

Country village pub dating from 1609 with
log fires, original beams, beer garden and
dining room. Bowling green, pool room.
Food available 12–8pm Mon–Sat, 12–4pm
Sun. Car park. Children welcome. Take the
B1147 from Dereham to Bawdeswell.

OPEN *12–11pm (10pm Sun in summer, 8pm*
Sun in winter).

Darby's Freehouse

1 Elsing Road, Swanton Morley, Dereham
NR20 4JU
☎ *(01362) 637647*
John Carrick and Louise Battle

A genuine freehouse serving eight real
ales. Adnams Best and Broadside,
Woodforde's Wherry, Badger Tanglefoot and
Greene King Abbot are permanent features,
plus three guests changed every two days.

Genuine, family-owned and -run freehouse
converted from two derelict farm
cottages. Traditional English food available
12–2.15pm and 6.30–9.45pm Mon–Fri, all
day Sat–Sun. Attached to a nearby farmhouse
that offers accommodation and camping. Car
park, garden and children's room and
playground. Take the B1147 from Dereham
to Bawdeswell, turn right on to Elsing Road
at Swanton Morley.

OPEN *11.30am–3pm and 6–11pm Mon–Fri;*
11am–11pm Sat; 12–10.30pm Sun.

THORNHAM

The Lifeboat Inn

Ship Lane, Thornham, Hunstanton PE36 6LT
☎ *(01485) 512236* Leon Mace
www.maypolehotels.com/lifeboatinn

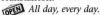 Genuine freehouse with Adnams, Greene King and Woodforde's ales plus a couple of guest beers, mainly from small independents.

A 16th-century smugglers' alehouse and hotel on the north Norfolk coast with wood beams, hanging paraffin lamps and open fires overlooking salt marshes. Bar and restaurant food available 12–2.30pm and 6.30–9.30pm. Car park, garden and accommodation. Children and pets welcome. Turn first left when entering the village from Hunstanton.

(OPEN) *All day, every day.*

TIBENHAM

The Greyhound

The Street, Tibenham NR16 1PZ
☎ *(01379) 677676* David and Colleen Hughes
www.thetibenhamgreyhound.co.uk

 Adnams Bitter and Broadside and Fuller's London Pride plus a guest, which might be Timothy Taylor Landlord, Shepherd Neame Spitfire, Early Bird or Late Red, Young's Bitter or Elgood's Greyhound.

B uilt in 1731, a quintessential village pub with oak beams and log fire. The public bar has a dart board, the lounge bar has low beams and a wood fire. Two beer gardens, children's play area and paddock. Outside heated smoking shelter. Large car park. Traditional pub food served 6.30–8.30pm Mon and Wed–Fri, all day Sat–Sun. Camping and caravanning facilities.

(OPEN) *6.30pm–close Mon–Fri; 12–close Sat–Sun.*

TOFT MONKS

Toft Lion

Toft Monks, Nr Beccles NR34 0EP
☎ *(01502) 677702* Jan and Giles Mortimer

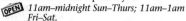 Adnams Bitter and a real cask mild plus an ever-changing selection of guest ales from local and nationwide breweries. Various cask strengths are available, and seasonal ales are featured.

A pub since 1650, this has always been the hub of the community. Good old-fashioned pub with the emphasis on fine ales, served in a convivial atmosphere complete with log fires. En-suite B&B accommodation is available in a double or family room, as you may decide you don't want to go home!

(OPEN) *5.30–11pm Mon–Fri; 12–3pm and 5.30–11pm Sat; 12–7.30pm Sun.*

TRUNCH

The Crown Inn

Front Street, Trunch, Nr North Walsham NR28 0AH
☎ *(01263) 722341* Phil Whitaker
www.trunchcrown.co.uk

A Bateman Brewery tied house. XB, Dark Mild and Valiant plus Greene King IPA. Two guests, changed each week, from any independent brewery in England.

O ne bar, one small restaurant and a beer terrace. Food served 12–2.30pm and 6.30–9pm Wed–Sat; 12–4pm Sun. Children and dogs welcome. Car park. Monthly quiz nights. Annual beer festival held in August.

(OPEN) *12–3pm and 5.30–11pm Mon–Thurs; 12–11pm Fri–Sun.*

UPTON

The White Horse

17 Chapel Road, Upton, Norwich
☎ *(01493) 750696* Raymond Norman

Freehouse with up to four beers. Greene King IPA and Adnams Best are regularly featured, with other favourites including Adnams Broadside, Shepherd Neame Spitfire and Thwaites Lancaster Bomber.

D ating from the 19th century, full of character with two inglenook fireplaces, a snug and a main bar with two further rooms. Food available 12–3pm and 6.30–9pm, with fish and chips served all day Friday. Children and dogs welcome. Conservatory. Beer garden. Live music most Saturday evenings. Taxi service available for parties. Ten minutes' walk from Upton Dyke.

(OPEN) *11am–midnight Sun–Thurs; 11am–1am Fri–Sat.*

WALSINGHAM

The Bull Inn

Common Place, Shire Hall Plain, Walsingham NR22 6BP
☎ *(01328) 820333* Philip Horan

Ridleys Tolly Original and Marston's Pedigree among the beers always available.

A 600-year-old olde-worlde pub with open fires, restaurant, beer garden and accommodation. Food available lunchtimes and evenings. Children allowed.

(OPEN) *11am–3pm and 6–11pm Mon–Sat; 12–3pm and 7–10.30pm Sun.*

WARHAM

The Three Horseshoes

Bridge Street, Warham, Nr Wells-next-the-Sea NR23 1NL
☎ *(01328) 710547* Iain Salmon
www.warham.biz

Woodforde's Wherry and Greene King IPA plus a guest from a small local independent brewery.

T raditional 18th-century cottage pub in the centre of the village, with three rooms, gas lighting, stone floors, old furniture and open fires. There is even a fruit machine dating from 1936. Listed in CAMRA's National Inventory of Pub Interiors. Freshly cooked traditional English food available 12–2.30pm and 6–8.30pm Mon–Sat; 12–3pm and 6–8.30pm Sun. Car park, large garden, courtyard, function room and accommodation next door. From Wells take the A149, then the B1105 on the right, and follow the signs.

 11.30am–2.30pm (3pm Sun) and 6–11pm.

WELLS-NEXT-THE-SEA
The Golden Fleece
The Quay, Wells-next-the-Sea NR23 1AH
☎ *(01328) 710650* Stephen Franklin
www.goldenfleecepub.co.uk

Freehouse serving Fuller's London Pride, Greene King Abbot and two guest brews rotated on a monthly basis.

Overlooking the quay and out to the beach, this three-storey, 400-year-old pub claims to have some of the best views in Norfolk. Food served at lunchtimes and evenings June–Sept. Pool table, juke box. Beer garden. Children welcome. On the A149.

 11am–11pm.

WEST BECKHAM
The Wheatsheaf
Church Road, West Beckham, Holt NR25 6NX
☎ *(01263) 822110* Daniel Mercer
www.wheatsheaf.ukpub.net

Woodforde's Wherry and Nelson's Revenge and Greene King IPA plus two constantly changing guest ales are always on offer at this freehouse.

Flint and brick farmhouse, converted into a pub. Wooden beams, flint interior and two open log fires. Central bar and three dining areas. Homemade food served 12–2pm and 6.30–9pm (Sun lunchtimes only). Families welcome. Large beer garden with children's play area. Two large car parks and disabled parking spaces. Covered patio. Private room for hire. Turn off the A148 near Sheringham Park.

 11.30am–3pm and 6.30–11pm Mon–Sat; 11.30am–3pm and 7–10.30pm Sun.

WEST RUDHAM
The Duke's Head
Lynn Road, West Rudham, King's Lynn PE31 8RW
☎ *(01485) 528810* MF Tham

Freehouse with Adnams Bitter and Shepherd Neame Spitfire always available.

A 15th-century coaching inn. Food-oriented with separate dining area and food available 12–2pm and 5.30–10.30pm. Car park, children welcome. Two miles from Houghton Hall, five miles from Sandringham. On the A148.

12–2pm and 5.30–10.30pm.

WEST SOMERTON
The Lion
West Somerton, Great Yarmouth NR29 4DP
☎ *(01493) 393289* Tony and Tracy Wilkins

Freehouse with Greene King IPA and Blackfriars Yarmouth Bitter plus two guest beers, often Greene King Morland Original and another local beer.

Traditional country pub close to the Norfolk Broads and the coast. Food served 12–2.30pm and 5–9pm. Families and dogs welcome. En-suite B&B accommodation. Car park, outdoor seating area.

11.30am–3.30pm and 6–11pm Mon–Sat; 12–3.30pm and 6–10.30pm Sun.

WHINBURGH
The Mustard Pot
Dereham Road, Whinburgh, Dereham NR19 1AA
☎ *(01362) 692179* Melanie and Michael

Freehouse with Wolf Golden Jackal plus two guest ales changed every week such as RCH Pitchfork, St Austell Tribute, Rudgate Battleaxe and Black Country Pig on the Wall.

An old village pub with low-beamed ceiling, open fireplace and beer garden. Proper homemade food available 12–2pm and 6.30–8.45pm Tues–Sat and 12–2pm Sun. Children warmly welcomed. On the B1135 three miles from Dereham.

12–3pm and 6.30–11.30pm Tues–Sat; 12–4pm Sun. Closed Sun evening and all day Mon.

WICKLEWOOD
The Cherry Tree
116 High Street, Wicklewood NR18 9QA
☎ *(01953) 606962*
Julie Savory and Roger Abrahams
www.buffys.co.uk

A Buffy's tied house with four Buffy's ales always available.

Built in the 1850s, a very traditional real ale lovers' pub. Proper pub grub (pigs a speciality!) served 12–2.30pm and 6.30pm–close Mon–Fri; all day Sat; 12–5pm Sun. No fancy food, machines or pool table. Children and dogs welcome. Beer garden with children's play area and smokers' patio. Just off the B1135 between Wymondham and Hingham.

12–2.30pm and 6–11pm Mon–Thurs; 12–12 Fri–Sat; 12–11pm Sun.

WINTERTON-ON-SEA
Fisherman's Return

The Lane, Winterton-on-Sea NR29 4BN
☎ *(01493) 393305 Darrin Winter*
www.fishermans-return.com

 Freehouse serving up to six real ales including Woodforde's Wherry and Norfolk Nog, Adnams Bitter and Broadside plus two seasonal guests.

A 300-year-old brick and flint village pub. Food served daily 12–2pm and 6–9pm. Three en-suite B&B rooms available. Function room and family room available. Garden with children's play equipment. Located off the B1149, eight miles north of Great Yarmouth.

OPEN *11am–2.30pm and 6–10.30pm Mon–Fri; 11am–11pm Sat; 11.30am–10.30pm Sun.*

WIVETON
The Wiveton Bell

Blakeney Road, Wiveton, Holt NR25 7TL
☎ *(01263) 740101 John Olsen*
www.wivetonbell.co.uk

 Freehouse with Woodforde's Wherry and Nelson's Revenge plus a weekly guest during the summer, perhaps from the local Yetmans brewery.

A traditional, beamed village pub with conservatory restaurant. Beer garden. Adjoining cottage to let. Food available at lunchtimes and evenings. Well-behaved children and dogs welcome.

OPEN *Summer: 12–2.30pm and 6.30–11pm. Winter opening hours vary – closed Sun evening and all day Mon.*

WOODBASTWICK
The Fur & Feather Inn

Slad Lane, Woodbastwick, Norwich NR13 6HQ
☎ *(01603) 720003 Tim Ridley*
www.thefurandfeatherinn.co.uk

 Woodforde's Brewery tap serving the full range of Woodforde's ales on gravity.

T hatched country pub situated in the heart of the Norfolk Broads. Building sympathetically converted from two cottages. Food served 12–2pm and 6–9pm. Well-behaved children welcome. Sorry, no dogs. Large beer garden. Car park. Follow the brown signs to Woodforde's Brewery.

OPEN *11.30am–3pm and 6–10.30pm Mon–Tues; 11.30am–3pm and 6–11pm Wed–Sat; 12–10.30pm Sun.*

WRENINGHAM
Bird in Hand

Church Road, Wreningham NR16 1BJ
☎ *(01508) 489438*
Colin McIntyre and Vivienne McIntyre

 Freehouse with Woodforde's Wherry and an Adnams brew always available.

O lde-worlde one-bar pub, around 150 years old, with woodburners, restaurant and beer garden. Food available at lunchtimes and evenings. Well-behaved children welcome. Private room available, car park. On the B1113 seven miles south of Norwich.

OPEN *11.30am–3pm and 6–11pm Mon–Sat; 12–3pm and 7–10.30pm Sun.*

WYMONDHAM
The Feathers

13 Town Green, Wymondham NR18 0PN
☎ *(01953) 605675 Eddie Aldous*

 Freehouse serving Greene King Abbot, Adnams Bitter, Marston's Pedigree and Elgood's Feather Tickler, plus two constantly-changing guests.

A town-centre pub dating from 1867. No pool table, juke box or TV. Food served daily. Beer garden. Car park.

OPEN *11am–3pm and 7–11pm Mon–Thurs; 11am–3pm and 6pm–12 Fri; 11am–3pm and 7–11.30pm Sat; 12–3pm and 7–10.30pm Sun.*

The Railway

Station Road, Wymondham NR18 0JY
☎ *(01953) 605262*
www.therailwaypub.com

 Freehouse serving four real ales, perhaps including Adnams Bitter and Broadside, Green Jack Canary and a guest from an independent brewery such as Wolf or Elgood's.

R efurbished traditional alehouse close to the railway station. Two large bars plus courtyard and beer garden with children's play area. Food served 12–2.30pm and 5–9.30pm Mon–Fri, 12–3pm and 6–9.30pm Sat and 12–5pm and 7–9pm Sun. Regular special themed events.

OPEN *All day, every day.*

THE BREWERIES

DIGFIELD ALES
North Lodge Farm, Thurning Road, Barnwell, Peterborough PE8 5RJ
☎ *(01832) 293295*

 BARNWELL BITTER AND TWISTED 3.9% ABV
BARNWELL BITTER 4.0% ABV
MARCH HARE 4.7% ABV

FROG ISLAND BREWERY
The Maltings, Westbridge, St James Road, Northampton NN5 5HS
☎ *(01604) 587772*
www.frogislandbrewery.co.uk

BEST BITTER 3.8% ABV
Golden, quenching and well hopped. Malty finish.
SHOEMAKER 4.2% ABV
Malty with delicate hoppiness and bitter finish.
NATTERJACK 4.8% ABV
Sweet and malty, pale and dangerously drinkable.
FIRE-BELLIED TOAD 5.0% ABV
Pale gold, single hop award winner.
CROAK AND STAGGER 5.6% ABV
Dark and spicy.
Plus seasonal ales.

GREAT OAKLEY BREWERY
Bridge Farm, 11, Brooke Road, Great Oakley, Nr Corby NN18 8HG
☎ *(01536) 744888*
www.greatoakleybrewery.co.uk

WOT'S OCCURRING 3.9% ABV
Bittersweet and golden.
HARPERS 4.3% ABV
Malty and chocolatey.
GOBBLE 4.5% ABV
Straw colour, hoppy.
TAIL SHAKER 5.0% ABV
Golden and floral.

HOGGLEYS BREWERY
c/o 30 Mill Lane, Kislingbury NN7 4BD
☎ *(01604) 831762*
www.hoggleys.co.uk

KISLINGBURY BITTER 4.0% ABV
MILL LANE MILD 4.0% ABV
NORTHAMPTONSHIRE BITTER 4.0% ABV
SOLSTICE STOUT 5.0% ABV

NOBBY'S BREWERY
3 Pagent Court, Kettering NN15 6GR
☎ *(01536) 521868*
www.nobbysbrewery.co.uk

ALEXANDRA'S BEST 3.8% ABV
Crisp clean hop finish.
NOBBY'S BEST 3.8% ABV
Well balanced and hoppy.
MONSTER MASH 4.3% ABV
Light gold, crisp and spicy.
WILD WEST ALE 4.6% ABV
Mahogany coloured and full bodied.
LANDLORD'S OWN 5.0% ABV
Golden colour, medium bodied with fruit tones.
Plus occasionals and seasonals including:
DARK SPELL 4.0% ABV
Deep red, biscuity flavour.
WET SPELL 4.2% ABV
Hoppy and floral with dry finish.

POTBELLY BREWERY
25–31 Durban Road, Kettering NN16 0JA
☎ *(01536) 410818*
www.potbelly-brewery.co.uk

BEST 3.5% ABV
STREAKY 3.6% ABV
AISLING 4.0% ABV
SEATON 4.3% ABV
BEIJING BLACK 4.4% ABV
MADE IN ENGLAND 4.4% ABV
PIGS DO FLY 4.4% ABV
INNER DAZE 4.6% ABV
REDWING 4.8% ABV
BLACK SUN 5.0% ABV
GROUNDHOG 5.0% ABV
OLD SPOT 5.5% ABV
SUNNY DAZE 5.5% ABV
EASTFIELD IPA 7.0% ABV

ROCKINGHAM ALES
c/o 25 Wansford Road, Elton, Peterborough PE8 6RZ
☎ *(01832) 280722*
www.rockinghamales.co.uk

FOREST GOLD 3.9% ABV
HOP DEVIL 3.9% ABV
A1 AMBER ALE 4.0% ABV
SAXON CROSS 4.1% ABV
FRUITS OF THE FOREST 4.5% ABV
DARK FOREST 5.0% ABV
Plus seasonals and occasionals.
This micro-brewery has brewed more than 40 ales, but production is limited and there is often a waiting list.

THE PUBS

ARTHINGWORTH

The Bull's Head

Kelmarsh Road, Arthingworth, Market Harborough LE16 8JZ
☎ *(01858) 525637* Kevin Hopcraft
www.thebullsheadonline.co.uk

 Thwaites Original and Lancaster Bomber plus four guests.

A traditional, rural freehouse. Log fires, darts, Northamptonshire skittles and cards. Heated garden patio. Food served in a separate restaurant 12–2.30pm and 6–9pm Mon–Sat; 12–8pm Sun. Children welcome. ETB 3-diamond accommodation. Annual August bank holiday beer festival. One and a half miles from the A14 J2.

OPEN *12–3pm and 6–11pm Mon–Sat; 12–10.30pm Sun.*

ASHTON

The Chequered Skipper

Ashton, Oundle, Peterborough PE8 5LD
☎ *(01832) 273494* Ian and Colin Campbell

Oakham JHB plus three weekly-changing guests from breweries such as Newby Wyke, Timothy Taylor, Crouch Vale, Rockingham and many more.

Thatched freehouse and restaurant in a Rothschild estate village with modern minimalist interior, with stunning village green front drinking area and rear beer garden. Food available at lunchtimes and evenings. Events include beer festivals with live music, the World Conker Championships and Morris dancing – phone for details. Children allowed. A mile out of Oundle, just off the A605.

OPEN *11.30am–3pm and 6–11pm Mon–Fri; 11am–11pm Sat; 12–10.30pm Sun.*

BARNWELL

The Montagu Arms

Barnwell, Oundle, Peterborough PE8 5PH
☎ *(01832) 273726* Ian Simmons

Genuine freehouse with Fuller's London Pride, Adnams Broadside and Oakham JHB plus two guest beers (about 200 per year).

Country inn built in 1601 and retaining many original features. Heavily beamed bar area and more modern restaurant. Food served 12–2.30pm and 7–10pm daily. Free children's facilities include log swings and activity centre. Car park. Just past bridge.

OPEN *12–3pm and 6–11.30pm Mon–Fri; 12–11.30pm Sat; 12–10.30pm Sun.*

BRACKLEY

The Greyhound Inn

Milton Malsor, Brackley, Northampton NN7 3AP
☎ *(01604) 858449* Mr and Mrs Rush

 At least six beers, with Greene King Old Speckled Hen among them.

A 15th-century inn, cosy atmosphere with real fires. Large beer garden. Food available. Children allowed. Situated on the main road into the village.

OPEN *All day, every day.*

BUGBROOKE

The Wharf Inn

Cornhill Lane, Bugbrooke, Northampton NN7 3QB
☎ *(01604) 832585*

Freehouse with Frog Island Best Bitter and Greene King IPA plus a weekly-rotating guest.

Canalside pub/restaurant with modern exterior and traditional interior, featuring an old red phonebox! There is a balcony for eating, a garden lawned to the canal and a boules area, venue for the Frog Island Boules Competition. Live music on Fri nights and jazz on Sun lunchtimes. Food served at lunchtimes and evenings (all day in summer). Well-behaved children allowed, if eating. Private room available for hire. Situated on the outskirts of the village, heading out towards the A5.

OPEN *12–3pm and 5.30–11pm in winter; 12–11pm in summer.*

BULWICK

The Queen's Head

Main Street, Bulwick NN17 3DX
☎ *(01780) 450272* GMA Smith

Freehouse with four real ales. Shepherd Neame Spitfire usually on offer, plus three guests from breweries such as Rockingham, Newby Wyke, Whim and Crouch Vale.

With parts of the building dating from the 13th century, this pub has a traditional atmosphere with open fires, flagstone floors and beamed ceilings. Les Routiers Real Ale Pub of the Year award 2007 and Peterborough CAMRA Gold award 2006. Food available Tues–Sun lunchtimes and Tues–Sat evenings. Pretty outdoor patio in rural setting with sightings of red kites overhead. Car park. Just off the A43 between Stamford and Corby.

OPEN *All day Tues–Sun; closed Mon.*

CORBY

Knight's Lodge

Towerhill Road, Corby NN18 0TH
☎ *(01536) 742602* Fred Hope

Everards house with Tiger, Beacon and Old Original. Two other guests including, perhaps, Greene King Old Speckled Hen, Wadworth Farmers Glory or Perfick, Nethergate Old Growler, Everards Equinox, Charles Wells Fargo or Wood Shropshire Lad.

A traditional 17th-century inn linked to Rockingham Castle by a network of tunnels. Food available in dining area Fri–Sun. Garden. Children allowed in the dining area if eating, and in the garden.

OPEN *12–3pm and 6–11pm Mon–Thurs; 12–4pm and 6–11pm Fri–Sat; 12–3.30pm and 6–10.30pm Sun.*

DESBOROUGH
The George
79 High Street, Desborough NN14 2NB
☎ *(01536) 760271*
Philip Coe and Susan Pugsley

Tied to Everards, serving Beacon and Tiger. There is also a guest, changed every two weeks.

Drinkers' pub in the town centre, with two bars. Food available 12–2pm. Pool, darts, skittles. Patio, car park, en-suite letting rooms. Children allowed.

OPEN *11am–midnight Sun–Thurs; 11am–1am Fri–Sat.*

EASTCOTE
The Eastcote Arms
6 Gayton Road, Eastcote, Towcester NN12 8NG
☎ *(01327) 830731* John and Wendy Hadley

Fuller's London Pride, Adnams Bitter and Greene King IPA plus one guest, constantly changing. An annual beer festival takes place over the Whitsun bank holiday.

A 330-year-old freehouse with dining area and beer garden. Food served at lunchtimes and Thurs–Sat evenings. Children allowed in the dining area only. Ring for directions.

OPEN *6–11pm Mon; 12–2.30pm and 6–11pm Tues–Sat; 12–3pm and 7–10.30pm Sun.*

FINEDON
The Bell Inn
Bell Hill, Finedon, Nr Wellingborough NN9 5ND
☎ *(01933) 680332* Dennis Willmott

Freehouse serving Fuller's London Pride and Greene King IPA plus one guest.

An ancient pub, reputed to date from 1042. Food served at lunchtimes and evenings in dining area. Children allowed if accompanied by an adult for meals only.

OPEN *11.30am–3pm and 5.30–11pm Mon–Sat; 12–3pm and 7–10.30pm Sun.*

FOTHERINGHAY
The Falcon Inn
Fotheringhay, Oundle, Peterborough PE8 5HZ
☎ *(01832) 226254* Dee Chambers
www.thefalcon-inn.co.uk

Freehouse with three real ales, including beers from Digfield and a range of guests.

Pub and restaurant in a beautiful historic village. Mary Queen of Scots was held and executed at Fotheringhay Castle. Food served 12–2.15pm and 6.15–9.15pm Mon–Sat; 12–3pm and 6.15–8.30pm Sun. Wonderful church nearby with lots of royal connections. Handy for some wonderful walks.

OPEN *12–11pm.*

GAYTON
Eykyn Arms
20 High Street, Gayton, Northampton NN7 3HD
☎ *(01604) 858361* Tracy Hughes

Freehouse with Greene King IPA plus two guest beers available.

Dating from 1766, a traditional freehouse with accommodation and two bars. Food available at lunchtimes and evenings (not Tues). Car park. Children welcome, but no special facilities.

OPEN *11.30am–3pm (closed Tues lunch) and 7–11pm Mon–Fri; 12–11pm Sat–Sun.*

GEDDINGTON
The Star Inn
2 Bridge Street, Geddington, Kettering NN14 1AD
☎ *(01536) 742386* Alister Robertson
www.star-inn-geddington.com

Freehouse with four real ales, with Greene King IPA a permanent fixture, plus weekly-changing brews from local breweries such as Nobby's and Digfield.

A traditional pub steeped in history set in the heart of Geddington, opposite the Queen Eleanor cross and near the memorial to US fighter pilots. Good range of food, from freshly filled baguettes to pheasant and game dishes, served 12–2.30pm and 6–9.45pm Mon–Sat, 12–3pm Sun. Main bar, snug, gallery featuring work by local artists, and restaurant. Car park, children's menu. Located off the A43 between Kettering and Corby.

OPEN *12–3pm and 6–11pm Mon–Sat; 12–10.30pm Sun and bank holidays.*

GREAT BRINGTON
The Fox & Hounds
Althorp Coaching Inn, Great Brington, Northampton NN7 4JA
☎ *(01604) 770651* Jacqui Ellard

Freehouse with nine real ales. Greene King IPA, Old Speckled Hen and Abbot and Fuller's London Pride are permanent fixtures, and the five guests, changed every barrel, might be beers such as Bateman Valiant, Tring Colley's Dog, Potbelly Pigs Do Fly and Yarmouth Blackfriars.

A 16th-century coaching inn with open fires, low beams and flagstone floors. There are fresh flowers all around the pub, and outside there is a very pretty courtyard and a walled garden. Bar and à la carte meals served 12–2.30pm and 6.30–9.30pm Mon–Sat, and 12–3pm and 6.30–8.30pm Sun. Children, walkers and horses welcome. Nearby attractions include Althorp House and Holdenby House. Take the A428 from Northampton past Althorp House, then take the first left turn before railway bridge.

OPEN *11am–11pm Mon–Sat; 12–10.30pm Sun.*

GREAT HOUGHTON

The Old Cherry Tree

8 Cherry Tree Lane, Great Houghton,
Northampton NN4 7AT
☎ *(01604) 761399* Mark and Vicky Ashby
www.theoldcherrytree.co.uk

 Wells and Young's house serving Charles Wells Eagle IPA and Young's Bitter plus one rotating guest changed weekly, such as Courage Directors, Old Hooky or Wadworths 6X.

A 500-year-old thatched pub and restaurant and one large bar area, separate restaurant, beer garden and heated patio. Popular with walkers and families. Food served 12–2.30pm every day and 6.30–9pm Tues–Sat. Children welcome. Located off the A428 from Northampton to Bedford. Turn right into the village, then first left.

OPEN *11am–3pm and 5.30–11pm Mon–Sat; 12–7pm Sun.*

GRENDON

The Half Moon

42 Main Road, Grendon
☎ *(01933) 665532* Anthony and Michelle Pool

 Charles Wells Eagle IPA, Courage Directors and one guest beer changed frequently.

A 300-year-old thatched pub with low ceilings and original beams. Beer garden. Freshly prepared food served lunchtimes and evenings Mon–Sat and Sun lunchtimes. Car park. Children welcome.

OPEN *12–3pm and 6–11pm Mon–Thurs; 12–11.45pm Fri–Sat; 12–10.30pm Sun.*

GRETTON

The Hatton Arms

Arnhill Road, Gretton NN17 3DN
☎ *(01536) 770268* Carl Butler
www.thehattonarms.com

 Freehouse serving Marston's Pedigree and Great Oakley Wot's Occurring plus one weekly-changing guest, often from small and/or local breweries.

Thatched, stone-built pub, the oldest part of which dates from the 13th century. Beamed bar and lounge with stone flags and open fires, full of character. Restaurant and terrace to the rear with views over Welland Valley. Freshly prepared, locally sourced food served 12–2pm and 6–9pm. Children welcome, with high chair and children's menu available. Small car park. Small function room. Annual beer festival, plus participation in Welland Valley Beer Festival. Located in the town centre, off the high street.

OPEN *Closed Mon; 12–2pm and 6–11pm Tues–Sat (5pm Fri); 12–10.30pm Sun.*

HIGHAM FERRERS

The Green Dragon

4 College Street, Higham Ferrers, Rushden
NN10 8DZ
☎ *(01933) 312088* Nic Stocks

Freehouse with Hop Back Summer Lightning and Greene King Abbot often available plus up to four guests from a wide selection, usually from small local breweries.

An 18th-century coaching inn with open fires, restaurant, beer garden, accommodation. Food served 12–2pm Mon–Tues, 12–2pm and 6–9.30pm Wed–Sat, 12–5pm Sun. Children allowed. Beer festivals over Whitsun and August bank holidays.

OPEN *12–11.30pm Mon–Thurs; 12–12 Fri–Sat; 12–10.30pm Sun*

The Griffin Inn

High Street, Higham Ferrers, Rushden
NN10 8BW
☎ *(01933) 312612*
Ray, Lynn and Justin Gilbert

Charles Wells Eagle, Greene King Abbot and Everards Tiger plus two guests, changed every week (eight new beers per month).

Lovely 17th-century freehouse, family-owned since 1990, with leather Chesterfields and inglenook fireplaces. Conservatory and piano bar. Newly refurbished patio and car park for up to 20 cars. Fine à la carte dining, with up to ten fresh fish dishes daily plus a good range of steaks and chicken; food served 11.30am–3pm and 5.30–11pm, plus carvery all day on Sundays. Children allowed in the restaurant only. Just off the A45.

OPEN *11.30am–3pm and 5.30–11pm Mon–Sat; all day Sun.*

HOLCOT

The White Swan Inn

Main Street, Holcot, Northampton NN6 9SP
☎ *(01604) 781263* Peter Stubbins (licensee), Samantha Drage Rogers (manager)

Freehouse with Black Sheep Best and Bateman XB plus one or two guests rotated weekly.

A pub in a thatched country cottage with bar and 40-seater restaurant. Snacks and à la carte food served 12–2pm and 6–9pm Mon–Sat and 12–6pm Sun. Beer garden. Regular events, newsletter available. Beer festival during Holcot Steam Fair. In the main street of the village.

OPEN *12–2pm and 5.30pm–close Mon–Fri; all day Sat–Sun.*

KETTERING

The Alexandra Arms

39 Victoria Street, Kettering NN16 0BU
☎ *(01536) 522730* Ivan Thornley ('Nip')

 Freehouse with up to ten real ales. One house beer, Nobby's, is brewed on the premises and is always on offer, but the rest of the selection changes constantly, all from independent breweries around the UK.

Built in 1901, this pub was local CAMRA Pub of the Year 2005 and 2006, and East Midlands runner-up 2006. No food. Beer garden. Just outside the town centre, about 15 minutes from the railway station.

OPEN *2–11.30pm Mon–Thurs; 12–12 Fri–Sat; 12–11pm Sun.*

The Park House

Kettering Venture Park, Kettering NN15 6XE
☎ *(01536) 523377* Rachael Early
www.pathfinderpubs.co.uk

Banks's Bitter and Marston's Pedigree always available.

A bar downstairs and a restaurant upstairs, with a relaxed family atmosphere throughout. Although the pub is modern, it is traditional in character. Food served 12–9pm. Large patio area, disabled parking and access. Families welcome. Large car park. Party bookings welcome. Near Tesco and Wicksteed Park. Off the A14 junction 9 towards the town centre, go right at the second roundabout.

OPEN *11.30am–11pm Mon–Sat; 12–9pm Sun.*

Sawyers

44 Montagu Street, Kettering NN16 8RU
☎ *(01536) 484800* Lianne Erskine
www.myspace.com/sawyersvenuecouk

Freehouse and brewery tap for the Potbelly Brewery. Up to six real ales, including beers from the Potbelly range, Caledonian Deuchars IPA and Wychwood Hobgoblin, plus guests such as Oakham Bishop's Farewell, Hop Back Summer Lightning, beers from Newby Wyke and others. Also Potbelly bottled beer, a traditional perry/scrumpy on hand pump and a large selection of continental bottled beers.

O ne of the oldest pubs in Kettering. No food. Live music six nights a week, ranging from punk to blues to rock to acoustic evenings. Weekend opening hours subject to change depending on the artists playing – call venue for details. Car park. Beer garden.

OPEN *Closed Mon; 4–11pm Tues–Wed; 4–7pm and 8–11pm Thurs; 4–7pm and 8pm–12 Fri; 2pm–12 Fri–Sat; 2–11.30pm Sun.*

KINGS SUTTON

The Butchers Arms

10 Whittall Street, Kings Sutton, Banbury OX17 3RD
☎ *(01295) 810898* Alan Newman

Tied to Hook Norton, with Hooky Bitter, Hooky Dark, Hooky Gold (Old Hooky in summer) and between one and three guests every month, such as beers from Fuller's, Everards, Greene King, Marston's, Wadworth, St Austell, Wells and Young's and Shepherd Neame.

A ctually in Northamptonshire, despite the postal address. Set in an ancient village near the River Cherwell and the Oxford Canal. Local brick building with oak beams and real fires. A patio area in front and a beer garden behind. Good food served at lunchtimes and evenings.

OPEN *11am–3pm and 6pm–12 Mon–Sat; 12–4pm and 7–11pm Sun.*

LITCHBOROUGH

The Old Red Lion

Banbury Road, Litchborough, Towcester NN12 8HF
☎ *(01327) 830250* Mr and Mrs O'Shey

Banks's Bitter and a Marston's ale always available.

S mall, 300-year-old pub with log fires and beer garden. Food available Tues–Sat, lunchtimes and evenings. Children allowed.

OPEN *11.30am–2.30pm and 6.30–11pm Mon–Sat; 12–3pm and 7–10.30pm Sun.*

LITTLE BRINGTON

Ye Olde Saracen's Head

Little Brington, Northampton NN7 4HS
☎ *(01604) 770640* Richard Williams

Fuller's London Pride, Timothy Taylor Landlord and Greene King IPA plus one changing guest.

T he only pub in Little Brington. Open fires and refurbished garden. Food available in two dining areas. Children allowed throughout. En-suite accommodation. Function room available for private hire.

OPEN *12–2.30pm and 6–11pm Mon–Fri; 12–11pm Sat–Sun.*

LITTLE HARROWDEN

The Lamb Inn

Orlingbury Road, Little Harrowden, Wellingborough NN9 5BH
☎ *(01933) 673300* Thomas Adam Coley

Wells and Young's house with Charles Wells Eagle and Bombardier plus one constantly changing guest, perhaps Highgate Davenports Bitter, Young's Special or Adnams Bitter.

T raditional 17th-century Northampton inn. Skittles table. Live entertainment. Beer garden. Food is available in separate dining area 12–2.30pm and 6.30–9.30pm daily. Senior citizens' lunch Mon–Thurs, £6.50 for two courses. Theme nights, curry nights, steak and wine nights and accoustic nights. Quiz night every other Sun at 8pm. Function room for up to 16 people available. Children welcome.

OPEN *12–3pm and 5.30–11pm Mon–Fri; 12–11pm Sat; 12–10.30pm Sun.*

MARSTON ST LAWRENCE

Marston Inn

Merestone, Marston St Lawrence, Banbury OX17 2DB
☎ *(01295) 711906* Carole and Nigel Davis
www.marstoninn.co.uk

Tied to Hook Norton with Hooky Bitter and a monthly-changing guest ale.

A 15th-century roses-round-the-door village pub in a building once taken over by Cromwell. Converted from three cottages, with one bar, snug, lounge and dining area. Dining throughout. Food served 12–2pm daily and 6–9pm Mon–Sat. Traditional pub games. Children welcome.

OPEN *12–3pm and 6.30–11pm Mon–Sat (until late Fri–Sat); 12–3pm and 7–11pm Sun.*

MEARS ASHBY

The Griffin's Head

28 Wilby Road, Mears Ashby, Northampton NN6 0DX
☎ *(01604) 812945* Peter Stubbins

Four to six real ales, with Black Sheep Best, Timothy Taylor Landlord, Greene King IPA and plus three guests changed weekly. Examples of guests include Great Oakley Wagtail, Adnams Best and beers from Cottage.

Stone-built pub with two rooms and open log fire. Home-cooked food served 12–2pm and 6–9pm Mon–Sat; traditional Sunday lunch 12–4pm. Events, large car park. At the A43 Holcot roundabout head towards Sywell, then Mears Ashby. The pub is in the centre of the village.

OPEN *12–3pm and 5pm–close Mon–Fri; 11am–close Sat–Sun.*

MILTON KEYNES

The Navigation Inn

Thrupp Wharf, Castlethorpe Road, Cosgrove, Milton Keynes MK19 7BE
☎ *(01908) 543156* Duncan Cameron
www.navigationinn.net

Greene King IPA, Abbot or Olde Trip plus two guests, changed every month or two, which might include beers like Batemans XXXB or St Austell Tribute.

A 200-year-old canalside pub with a decent menu, and food to match! Log fires in winter. Food served 12–2.30pm and 6–9pm Mon–Fri; all day until 9pm Sat–Sun. Busy canalside garden and terrace in summer. Children and pets are welcome, as are boaters. Recently listed in *Sunday Telegraph* as one of top ten waterside pubs in UK. Just off the A508 Northampton–Milton Keynes road.

OPEN *12–3pm and 5.30–11pm Mon–Fri; 12–11pm Sat–Sun.*

NASEBY

Royal Oak

Church Street, Naseby NN6 6DA
☎ *07985 408240* Elaine Kiggs

Five real ales from various local breweries including Potbelly, Oakley, Grainstore, Oakham and Newby Wyke.

Traditional pub near the site of the Battle of Naseby, with a copper-topped bar supported by an oak tree. Beer garden with a lovely view. Games room with table skittles. Children welcome. Annual St George's beer festival in April. No food.

OPEN *4.30pm–12 Mon–Fri; 3pm–12 Sat; 12–7pm Sun.*

NORTHAMPTON

The Lamplighter

66 Overstone Road, Northampton NN1 3JS
☎ *(01604) 631125* Nigel North

Enterprise Inns house with up to four hand pumps serving a range of ales from micro- and regional breweries. Selection changes every few days.

Victorian corner terrace, traditionally decorated, with one bar and a soft-furnished area. Food served 5–8.30pm Mon–

Thurs; 12–8pm Sat; 12–4pm Sun. Traditional pub games. No children. Wed and Fri: quiz nights. Paved rear courtyard. Located in the Upper Mounts, five minutes' walk from the bus station and town centre.

OPEN *5–11pm Mon–Fri; 12–11pm Sat; 12–4pm Sun.*

The Malt Shovel Tavern

121 Bridge Street, Northampton NN1 1QF
☎ *(01604) 234212*
www.maltshoveltavern.com

Award-winning freehouse, now the brewery tap for the Great Oakley brewery. Regular ales include Great Oakley Wot's Occurring and Harpers, Frog Island Natterjack and Fuller's London Pride. Up to eight constantly changing guests come from micro-breweries around the country.

A traditional pub with beer garden. Food served Mon–Sat lunchtimes 12–2.30pm. Children allowed in the garden only. CAMRA East Midlands Pub of the Year 2004. Located opposite the Carlsberg Brewery, ten minutes from the railway station and M1 J15.

OPEN *11.30am–3pm and 5–11pm Mon–Sat; 12–3pm and 7–10.30pm Sun.*

Moon On The Square

6 The Parade, Market Place, Northampton NN1 2EE
☎ *(01604) 634062*
Andrew Hodgson and Maria Fox

Marston's Pedigree, Burton Ale, Greene King Abbot Ale and Shepherd Neame Spitfire plus Courage Directors, Theakston Best and at least two guest beers from a wide selection supplied by the excellent East-West Ales.

Large city-centre pub with one bar, conservatory, disabled access and no music or games tables. Food served all day, every day. Children welcome for meals. Two annual beer festivals (April/May and Sept/Oct).

OPEN *10am–11pm (10.30pm Sun).*

The Old Black Lion

Black Lion Hill, Northampton NN1 1SW
☎ *(01604) 639472* Mr Wilkinson

Frog Island Natterjack is among the beers always served, with other Frog Island beers featured as guests.

Very old building on the outside of the town centre, near the station. Refurbished interior, with one bar, function room and patio. Food available. Children allowed.

OPEN *11am–11pm Mon–Sat; 12–10.30pm Sun.*

The Queen Adelaide

50 Manor Road, Kingsthorpe, Northampton NN2 6QJ
☎ *(01604) 714524* Paul Barton
www.queenadelaide.com

Tied to Enterprise Inns, with seven real ales. Adnams Bitter and Copper Dragon Golden Pippin are the permanent beers, and the four daily-changing guests might be from Potbelly, Great Oakley, Nobby's, Hoggleys, Bateman or Vale.

Claims to be Northampton's best-kept secret, this traditional village pub is tucked away but well worth finding! Food served 12–2pm Mon–Sat and 7–9pm Mon–Thurs. Extensive gardens and ample car parking.

OPEN *11.15am–11pm Mon–Sat; 12–10.30pm Sun.*

The White Elephant
Kingsley Park Terrace, Northampton NN2 7HG
☎ *(01604) 711202* Darren Greenfield

Tied to the Spirit Group, with five real ales. Greene King IPA permanently available, plus four monthly-changing guests.

One-bar operation, dating from 1865. Food served 12–10.30pm. Live music every Sun. Tues: quiz night.

OPEN *11am–11pm Mon–Sat; 12–10.30pm Sun.*

The Queen's Arms
11 Isham Road, Orlingbury NN14 1JD
☎ *(01933) 768258* Steven Draper

Five real ales, Adnams Bitter and Greene King Abbot, the rest changing weekly. Examples include Fuller's London Pride, Greene King Old Speckled Hen, Wychwood Hobgoblin and Brains SA.

A traditional country pub with restaurant and beer garden. Food served at lunchtimes and evenings. Car park. Children welcome.

OPEN *6–11pm Mon; 12–3pm and 6–11pm Tues–Fri; all day Sat–Sun.*

The Chequers
Chequer's Lane, Ravensthorpe NN6 8ER
☎ *(01604) 770379* Gordon Walker

Freehouse with five hand pumps, serving beers from Greene King, Jennings, Bateman plus local guests.

Cosy village pub serving traditional English fare. Restaurant and bar food served lunchtimes and evenings. Beer garden and children's play area – children welcome.

OPEN *12–3pm and 6–11pm Mon–Fri; all day Sat; 12–3pm and 7–10.30pm Sun.*

The Samuel Pepys
Slipton Lane, Slipton, Nr Kettering NN14 3AR
☎ *(01832) 731739* Frazer Williams
www.thesamuelpepys.net

A freehouse. Oakham JHB and Potbelly Aisling plus three guest ales changed once a week, such as Great Oakley Wot's Occurring.

A country pub and restaurant, named after the famous diarist. Extensive menu available 12–3pm and 7–9.30pm (all day Sun). Wedding receptions.

OPEN *12–3pm and 7–11pm Mon–Fri; all day Sat–Sun and bank holidays.*

The Shuckburgh Arms
Main Street, Southwick, Nr Oundle, Peterborough PE8 5BL
☎ *(01832) 274007* Celia Sanders

Genuine freehouse with Fuller's London Pride plus two guests changed once or twice a week.

Family-run 15th-century stone and thatch pub with oak beams, open log fire, lots of history and a warm welcome. One bar, one family room. Food served 12–2pm and 6–9pm Tues–Sat, 12–5pm Sun. Large secure garden, children's play equipment, large rear patio for alfresco dining. Large car park. Campers can be accommodated in secure garden area. Situated three miles east of Oundle, within easy driving distance of Fotheringhay, Stamford Burghley and Peterborough.

OPEN *12–2pm and 6–11pm Tues–Sat; 12–10.30pm Sun.*

The Boat Inn
Stoke Bruerne, Nr Towcester NN12 7SB
☎ *(01604) 862428*
Andrew and Nicholas Woodward
www.boatinn.co.uk

Freehouse with Banks's Bitter, Marston's Bitter, Pedigree and Empire, Frog Island Best Bitter, and Adnams Bitter as the permanent beers. Two guests are rotated every month.

Canalside pub, run by the same family since 1877. The original part of building has a thatched roof, stone floors and open fires. Bar food available 10am–2pm and 6–9pm Mon–Thurs, and all day Fri–Sun. Meals served 12–2pm and 7–9pm (6.30–8.30pm Sun) in the 80-seater restaurant. There is also an extension with lounge bar, bistro and cocktail bar. A 40-seater passenger narrowboat is available for hire for party trips all year. Live music at least once a month and cabarets at Christmas in restaurant. Children allowed. Opposite the canal museum, approximately six minutes from M1 junction 15.

OPEN *9.30am–11pm (10.30pm Sun). Closed 3–6pm Mon–Thurs in winter. Open all day, every day in main season.*

The Vane Arms
Main Street, Sudborough NN14 3BX
☎ *(01832) 730033* Graeme Walker

Tied to Everards, with Tiger and Beacon plus one guest, changed weekly.

A centuries-old listed village inn. Good reputation for food, with bar and restaurant meals available lunchtimes and evenings. Car park, games room. Children allowed. Two letting rooms. Just off the A6116 between Thrapston and Corby.

OPEN *12–3pm and 6–11pm (midnight Fri).*

SULGRAVE

The Star Inn

Manor Road, Sulgrave OX17 2SA
☎ *(01295) 760389*
Mr and Mrs R Jameson King

 Hook Norton Hooky Bitter and Old Hooky plus a monthly guest ale.

Idyllic 17th-century country inn on the Northants/Oxon borders. Flagstone bar and large inglenook fireplace, plus separate dining room and snug. Vine-covered terrace and benches in the garden. Food served 12–2pm and 6–8.30pm Mon–Fri; 12–2.30pm and 6–9pm Sat; 12–2.30pm and 6.30–8.30pm Sun. Car park. Children welcome in restaurant and garden. Three en-suite B&B rooms. Follow brown signs for Sulgrave Manor.

OPEN *12–2.30pm and 6–11pm Mon–Fri; 12–3pm and 6–11pm Sat; 12–3pm and 6.30–10.30pm Sun.*

TOWCESTER

The Plough Inn

96 Watling Street, Towcester NN12 6BT
☎ *(01327) 350738* Robert 'Bob' Goode

Tied to Wells and Young's, with Charles Wells Eagle and Bombardier, Adnams Broadside and Young's Bitter always available.

Cosy, 400-year-old, award-winning pub which has been in the same hands for many years. Two bars, handmade furniture. Good food served 12–2pm and 5.30–10pm Mon–Sat, 12–2.30pm and 6.30–9.30pm Sun. Egon Ronay recommended. Car park. Children's eating area, large patio garden with award-winning flower displays (regular Towcester in Bloom winner, plus the prize for food and flowers awarded across the whole brewery chain). In the market square.

OPEN *11am–3pm and 5.30–11.30pm Mon–Thurs; all day Fri–Sat.*

WALGRAVE

The Royal Oak

Zion Hill, Walgrave NN6 9PN
☎ *(01604) 781248* John Grimes

Adnams Best and Greene King Abbot plus three guests from breweries such as Archers, Hoggleys and Shepherd Neame.

Typical village pub, approximately 150 years old. Two bars, private room for hire, beer garden with children's play area. Food served 12–2pm and 5.30–9.15pm (except Sun evening). Car park. Annual beer festival. Off the A43 between Kettering and Northampton.

OPEN *12–2.45pm and 5.30–11pm.*

WELLINGBOROUGH

The Coach & Horses

17 Oxford Street, Wellingborough NN8 4HY
☎ *(01933) 441848*
Graham and Pamela Burgess

Ten real ales, including Fuller's ESB, Wychwood Hobgoblin, Adnams Bitter, St Austell Tribute and Jennings Cumberland. The five weekly guests might be from breweries such as Potbelly, Great Oakley, Potton, Grainstore, Oakham, Frog Island or Hoggleys.

A pub that prides itself on its real ale and friendly atmosphere. No juke box, no pool table, no alco-pops! Good food served lunchtimes and evenings. Large beer garden, heated smoking shed. Over-18s only. Just off the town centre behind Morrisons.

OPEN *12–11pm (6pm Sun).*

The Locomotive

111 Finedon Road, Wellingborough NN8 4AL
☎ *(01933) 276600* Steven Elliott

Freehouse with nine real ales, all served on a guest basis and changed constantly.

Built in the late 19th century as a Quaker house, this is a traditional two-room, one-bar pub with beer garden, games room, skittles, pool, darts and other pub games. Food served 12–2pm. Dogs welcome. Children allowed in the garden only. Car park. Themed beer festival every bank holiday weekend, including August 'pirates' weekend and Hallowe'en. Monthly quiz night; weekly meat raffle. On the outskirts of Wellingborough, 20 minutes' walk from the station.

OPEN *11am–11pm Mon–Sat; 12–11pm Sun.*

Red Well

16 Silver Street, Wellingborough NN14 1PA
☎ *(01933) 440845*
Steve Frost and Tina Garner

Freehouse with five guest ales. Regulars include Hop Back Summer Lightning, Nethergate Old Growler, Greene King Old Speckled Hen, Cotleigh Osprey and Adnams Regatta. Beer festivals held three times a year.

A new-age pub, no music, no games. Disabled access, garden. Food available all day, every day. Children allowed in the garden only.

OPEN *All day, every day.*

WESTON-BY-WELLAND
The Wheel & Compass
Valley Road, Weston-by-Welland, Nr Market Harborough LE16 8HZ
☎ *(01858) 565864* David Woolman

 Freehouse serving Marston's Pedigree, Bathams Bitter and Greene King Abbot plus two guests, changing every other day.

A 17th-century pub with beamed ceilings and two real fires. New restaurant extension, in which food is served every lunchtimes and evening, and all day Sat–Sun. Children welcome, away from the bar area. Beer garden. Large car park. Annual beer festival in September. Located four miles from Market Harborough.

OPEN *Lunchtime and evening Mon–Fri; all day Sat–Sun.*

WESTON FAVELL
The Bold Dragoon
48 High Street, Weston Favell NN3 3JW
☎ *(01604) 401221* Phillip Gidley

 Churchill Taverns pub with Greene King IPA and Abbot, Fuller's London Pride, Black Sheep Bitter and Timothy Taylor Landlord plus three weekly-changing guests.

B uilt in the 1930s with a public bar, lounge bar and now a conservatory restaurant. Food served 12–2.30pm and 6–9pm Mon–Sat; 12–3pm Sun. Small beer garden with patio terrace. Wheelchair access and disabled toilets. Car park.

OPEN *11.30am–11.30pm Mon–Sat; 12–10.30pm Sun.*

WOODFORD
The Dukes Arms
High Street, Woodford, Nr Kettering NN14 4HE
☎ *(01832) 732224* Mr and Mrs Keith Wilson

 Fuller's London Pride, Greene King Old Speckled Hen, Banks's Best Bitter and Shepherd Neame Spitfire.

D elightful setting for the oldest pub in the village which prides itself on good real ale and down-to-earth food. Garden and restaurant. Food served lunchtimes and evenings. Children welcome, but no special facilities. Car park.

OPEN *12–2.30pm and 7–11pm (10.30pm Sun).*

WOODNEWTON
The White Swan Inn
22 Main Street, Woodnewton, Peterborough PE8 5EB
☎ *(01780) 470381* Steve and Tracy Anker

 Tied to Punch Taverns, with four real ales. Greene King IPA and Old Speckled Hen, Black Sheep Bitter and Adnams Bitter are regularly served, with the beers rotated quarterly.

F riendly village pub with children's play area. Food served lunchtimes and evenings (not Mon lunch), plus breakfast at weekends 9–11am, and cream teas in summer. Children and dogs welcome. Car park. Beer garden. Darts and petanque. Close to quaint market town. North of Oundle, off the A605 at Warmington, follow sings to Fotheringhay and continue.

OPEN *6pm–12 Mon; 12–3pm and 6pm–12 Tues–Fri; 12–12 Sat–Sun.*

YARWELL
The Angel Inn
59 Main Street, Yarwell, Nr Peterborough PE8 6PR
☎ *(01780) 782582* Nick Lander
www.angelinn.wordpress.com

 Up to three real ales including Brewsters Hophead.

A 17th-century village pub with two bars and a games room. The back bar has a motorbike racing theme. Limited snack food. Weekly live music or karaoke (Sats). Quiz alternate Sundays. Darts, pool, football table, quiz and fuit machines. Children and dogs welcome. Car parking is unrestricted on the street outside. One mile from the A1/A47 junction.

OPEN *Closed Mon; 12–3pm Tues–Sun; 7–11pm Tues–Thurs; 7pm–12 Fri–Sun.*

THE BREWERIES

ALLENDALE BREWERY
*Allendale Brewery Co. Ltd, Allendale, Hexham
NE47 9EQ*
☎ *(01434) 618686*
www.allendalebrewco.co.uk

ALLENDALE BEST BITTER 3.8% ABV
Slightly spicy aroma.
BLACK GROUSE BITTER 4.0% ABV
Coffee and chocolate hints.
GOLDEN PLOVER 4.0% ABV
Blonde, clean taste.
CURLEW'S RETURN 4.2% ABV
Citrus, floral hop character.

BAREFOOT BREWERY
*Unit 7, The Whitehouse Farm Centre,
Stannington, Morpeth NE61 6AW*
☎ *(01670) 789988*

BAREFOOT 3.8% ABV
MELLOW YELLOW 3.8% ABV
BLACK FOOT 4.2% ABV
FIRST FOOT 4.2% ABV
SOLE BEER 4.2% ABV
MILK OF AMNESIA 4.5% ABV
SB 5.0% ABV

HEXHAMSHIRE BREWERY
Leafields, Ordley, Hexham NE46 1SX
☎ *(01434) 606577*

DEVIL'S ELBOW 3.6% ABV
SHIRE BITTER 3.8% ABV
DEVIL'S WATER 4.2% ABV
WHAPWEASEL 4.8% ABV
OLD HUMBUG 5.5% ABV

HIGH HOUSE FARM BREWERY
High House Farm, Matfen NE20 0RG
☎ *(01661) 886192*
www.highhousefarmbrewery.co.uk

AULD HEMP 3.8% ABV
Amber colour, malty aroma.
NEL'S BEST 4.2% ABV
Gold and full bodied.
MATFEN MAGIC 4.8% ABV
Brown ale with blackberry aroma.
Plus seasonals and specials including:
SUNDANCER 3.6% ABV
Golden colour, biscuit finish.
RED SHEP 4.0% ABV
Copper colour, hint of spice, fruity flavour.
BLACK MOSS 4.3% ABV
Dark porter with chocolate finish.
NETTLE ALE 4.5% ABV
Grassy taste, made from farm-grown nettles.

THE NORTHUMBERLAND BREWERY LTD
*Accessory House, Barrington Road, Bedlington
NE22 7AR*
☎ *(01670) 822112*
www.northumberlandbrewery.co.uk

CASTLES 3.8% ABV
Gold, with lingering hops.
HOLY ISLAND ALE 3.8% ABV
Hoppy finish.
LUNATICK 3.8% ABV
Light and hoppy.
PIT PONY 3.8% ABV
Amber, floral aftertaste.
GOLDEN LAB 3.9% ABV
Fruity.
TYNEMOUTH TIPPLE 3.9% ABV
Grapefruit hints.
BYKER BITTER 4.0% ABV
Lingering hoppiness.
COUNTY 4.0% ABV
Amber fruit and hop finish.
DARK 4.0% ABV
Fruity bitter.
HIGHWAY ROBBERY 4.0% ABV
Light and fruity.
KITTY BREWSTER 4.0% ABV
LOCAL HERO 4.0% ABV
STRAWBERRY BLONDE 4.0% ABV
Pale ale.
BLYTH SPIRIT 4.1% ABV
CUNNING CUCUMBER 4.1% ABV
FOG ON THE TYNE 4.1% ABV
ASHINGTON ALE 4.2% ABV
BEDLINGTON TERRIER 4.2% ABV
G.N.C. 4.2% ABV
GRUESOME GRAPE 4.3% ABV
LEGENDS OF THE TYNE 4.3% ABV
MAIN SEAM 4.3% ABV
ORIGINAL 4.3% ABV
BEST 4.5% ABV
IPA 4.5% ABV
SHEEPDOG 4.7% ABV
MCCRORY'S IRISH STOUT 4.8% ABV
BOMAR 5.0% ABV
GATESHEAD GOLD 5.0% ABV
PREMIUM 5.0% ABV
WHITLEY WOBBLER 5.0% ABV
Plus seasonals and occasionals.

WYLAM BREWERY LIMITED
South Houghton Farm, Heddon-on-the-Wall
NE15 0EZ
☎ *(01661) 853377*
www.wylambrew.co.uk

HEDONIST 3.8% ABV
Four types of grain are used with
Bramling X and Cascade hops. A fine session
bitter.

WYLAM BITTER 3.8% ABV
A refreshing lighter version of the 4.4 Rocket
using similar ingredients but producing a beer
with its own distinctive character.

GOLD TANKARD 4.0% ABV
Made with all gold ingredients: pale malt,
golden naked oats, First Gold hops with a
Willamette hop finish. Refreshing, with a hint of
grapefruit.

HOPPIN MAD (WAS HOUBLON NOUVEAU)
4.2% ABV
Uses 2002 vacuum-packed hops as the Houblon
was so popular.

WYLAM MAGIC 4.2% ABV
A quenching ale made with Amarillo hops and
pale malt. Pale gold with a hint of elderflower in
the nose. Citrus and spice on the palate with a
good bitter finish.

WHISTLE STOP 4.4% ABV
Coppery coloured, slightly maltier with a hop
character provided by Challenger and Bramling
X hops.

BOHEMIA CZECH RECIPE PILSNER BEER 4.6% ABV
Deep gold in colour with layered malt and hops
and a fruity finish.

LANDLORD'S CHOICE 4.6% ABV
A complex ale full of interesting flavours and
aromas using Styrian Goldings, Fuggles and
Hersbrucker hops.

WYLAM HAUGH 4.6% ABV
A dark, satisfying porter which is smooth, full of
character and complex. There are hints of chocolate, liquorice and malt. Made with roast, crystal
and pale malts, Wye Target and Goldings hops.

SILVER GHOST 5.0% ABV
Pale and smoothly satisfying, it is made with
pale malts, Bramling and Fuggles hops.
Plus seasonals and specials.

THE PUBS

ACOMB

The Miners Arms
Main Street, Acomb, Hexham NE46 4PW
☎ *(01434) 603909*
Lynn Crozier and Campbell Donald
www.theminersacomb.com

Freehouse with beers from Yates, Wylam,
Mordue and Black Sheep usually
available, plus one weekend guest, usually a
unique or national quality ale.

A welcoming and cosy village pub from
1746 with an open fire. A traditional pub
menu of home cooked foods and vegetarian
options offers great dining with a good
selection of wines. Outside seating to front,
and a pleasant beer garden offer the perfect
places to relax during the fine weather, but
the open fire provides warmth in winter.
Families will feel welcomed. Food served
Tues-Sat. Booking advised for Sunday lunch.

OPEN *Open weekday evenings and all day
weekends.*

ALLENDALE

The King's Head Hotel
Market Place, Allendale, Hexham NE47 9BD
☎ *(01434) 683681* Peter Wood

Freehouse with Jennings Cumberland
Ale, Banks's Original and Marston's
Pedigree. One beer rotates every six to eight
weeks.

Cosy former coaching inn dating from
around 1776, with two bars, fires and a
function room. No music or games.
Homemade food served from 12. Children
and dogs welcome. Accommodation in four
en-suite rooms. Great walking country.
Located in the centre of the village.

OPEN *All day, every day.*

ALNWICK

The John Bull Inn
12 Howick Street, Alnwick NE66 1UY
☎ *(01665) 602055* David 'Gus' Odlin
www.john-bull-inn.co.uk

Freehouse offering three or four ever-
changing guest beers from micro-
breweries nationwide, but with an emphasis
on locals such as Hadrian and Border, Wylam,
Mordue and Jarrow. More than 600 different
ales served in four years. At least 120 single-
malt whiskies and over 40 Belgian beers also
stocked.

Old-fashioned backstreet boozer, purpose-
built as a pub in 1832, with walled beer
garden. A non-food pub with no music, TV
or games machines. North Northumberland
CAMRA Pub of the Year 2007. Beer festivals
in July (phone for further details). Difficult to
find – ring for directions, or ask at Tourist
Information.

OPEN *7–11pm Mon–Fri; 12–3pm and 7–11pm
Sat; 12–3pm and 7–10.30pm Sun.*

ASHINGTON

The Black Diamond
29 Southview, Ashington NE63 0SF
☎ *(01670) 851500* Paul Gray

Two constantly changing guest ales, with
local breweries featured whenever
possible.

Town-centre pub with lounge/diner and
public bar. Pool, darts, gaming machines.
Separate à la carte restaurant open Tues–Sat
evenings and Sun lunch. Four letting rooms.
Children allowed. Car park.

OPEN *11am–11pm Mon–Sat; 12–10.30pm Sun.*

Bubbles Wine Bar
58a Station Road, Ashington NE63 9UJ
☎ *(01670) 850800* David Langdown
www.bubblesbar.co.uk

Freehouse with three pumps serving a
range of real ales. Too many to list; all
breweries stocked as and when available.

A town-centre pub for all ages. One bar,
back-yard area, entertainment and discos.
Food served at lunchtimes and evenings.
There is a nightclub on the premises, open
Fri and Sat nights. Children allowed.

OPEN *10am–11pm Mon–Wed; 10am–midnight
Thurs; 10am–2am Fri–Sat;
7am–12.30am Sun.*

BEDLINGTON

The Northumberland Arms

112 Front Street East, Bedlington NE22 5AE
☎ *(01670) 822754* Mary Morris

Three regularly changing guest beers served, such as Timothy Taylor Landlord, Fuller's ESB or London Pride, Charles Wells Bombardier, Shepherd Neame Spitfire or Bishop's Finger, Black Sheep Bitter or Special and Bateman XXXB.

Typical family community pub that has been serving real ale since 1859. Food served 11.30am–2.30pm Wed–Sat. Private room for hire.

OPEN *7–11pm Mon–Tues; 11am–11pm Wed–Sat; 12–10.30pm Sun.*

BERWICK-UPON-TWEED

Barrels Ale House

Bridge Street, Berwick-upon-Tweed TD15 1ES
☎ *(01289) 308013* Ben and Ollie Bennett
www.thebarrels.co.uk

Freehouse with five real ales, including Shepherd Neame Spitfire, Stewart Pentland IPA, Timothy Taylor Landlord and two constantly changing guests. A wide range of international lagers and malt whiskies is also available.

A traditional two-bar pub, a renowned live music venue, with one upstairs bar, one basement bar and outside smoking area. CAMRA North Northumberland Pub of the Year 2008. On the banks of the River Tweed.

OPEN *All day, every day (until 1am Fri–Sat).*

The Pilot Inn

31 Lows Green, Berwick-upon-Tweed TD15 1LZ
☎ *(01289) 304214* Debbie Dixon

Freehouse with Caledonian Deuchars IPA and a Hadrian and Border ale plus one guest.

Dating from 1916, with three rooms including a small snug and lounge. Food served in the summertime (March–October) 12–3pm including Sunday lunch. No pool tables, juke box or fruit machines. Tues: guitar night; Thurs: folk and fiddlers; Sat: live music. Beer garden. Accommodation. Quoits outside in summer. Located 200 yards from the railway station.

OPEN *12–12 Sun–Fri; 11am–midnight Sat.*

BLYTH

The Joiners Arms

Coomassie Road, Blyth
☎ *(01670) 352852* Ann Holland

Northumberland Secret Kingdom plus a guest beer.

Small, friendly, one-bar pub with entertainment on Thursday, Saturday and Sunday evenings. Seating area at side of pub. Sandwiches and toasties available. Car park. Children welcome.

OPEN *12–11pm (10.30pm Sun).*

CRAMLINGTON

The Plough

Middle Farm Buildings, Cramlington NE23 9DN
☎ *(01670) 737633* Roy Apps

Four real ales. Theakston XB is a regular fixture, but the other three rotate from a varied range up to twice a week with an emphasis on local brews.

Two-bar village freehouse in old farm buildings with dining area and two beer gardens. Food served every lunchtime (11.30am–2pm), including traditional Sunday roasts. Well-behaved children welcome. Two function rooms. Big-screen TV in bar. Car park. Opposite the church.

OPEN *11am–3pm and 6–11pm Mon–Wed; all day Thurs–Sun.*

FEATHERSTONE

The Wallace Arms

Rowfoot, Featherstone, Nr Haltwhistle NE49 0JF
☎ *(01434) 321872* Tom Goundry

Jennings Cumberland, Greene King Abbot and IPA are the permanent beers here, plus a guest which changes every couple of weeks.

Country pub rebuilt in 1850 with large beer garden, adjacent to the South Tyne Trail, with one bar, snug and pool room. Two dining areas. Food served 12–2.30pm and 6–9pm every day. Children and dogs welcome. Car park. Two miles from Hadrian's Wall and two miles south of Haltwhistle.

OPEN *12–3pm and 5.30pm–12 Mon–Fri; 12–12 Sat–Sun.*

GREAT WHITTINGTON

The Queens Head Inn

Great Whittington, Newcastle upon Tyne NE19 2HP
☎ *(01434) 672267* Ron and Gill Jackman

Nel's Best and Red Shep, both from the local High House Brewery, are regularly featured. One of them is changed every so often.

A 15th-century coaching inn which incorporates a restaurant. Comfortable bar with warming open fires. Food served 12–2pm and 6–9pm Mon–Sat, and 12–8pm Sun. Beer garden for summer months. Well-behaved children welcome. Nearby attractions include Alnwick Gardens, historic Corbridge and Hexham, and Roman wall and forts. Situated four miles north of Corbridge, off the Military Road (B6318) towards Newcastle.

OPEN *12–3pm and 5.30–11pm Mon–Fri; 12–11pm Sat; 12–10.30pm Sun.*

HALTWHISTLE

The Black Bull

Market Square, Haltwhistle NE49 0BL
☎ (01434) 320463 DJ Hutton

Six real ales from a wide range, with four of these changed every few days.

A small, quiet 16th-century freehouse down a cobbled lane from the market place, with one main bar, low ceiling, beams and a real fire. Dining room (seats 20). Food available 7–9pm Mon and 12–9pm Tues–Sun in summer; 12–2pm and 6–9pm Tues–Sat in winter. Outside seating. Less than two miles from Hadrian's Wall in good walking country.

OPEN 7–11pm Mon; 12–11pm Tues–Sat; 12–10.30pm Sun. Winter hours may vary.

HEDLEY ON THE HILL

The Feathers Inn

Hedley on the Hill, Stocksfield NE43 7SW
☎ (01661) 843607
Rhian Cradock and Helen Greer
www.thefeathers.net

Mordue Workie Ticket is always available, plus three guests from local breweries, such as Hadrian Gladiator, High House Auld Hemp, Big Lamp Bitter and Wylam Magic. Orkney Red MacGregor is also popular. The beers are changed very regularly, sometimes daily.

Old coaching inn, full of character, with oak beams, fires in each of the three rooms, and stone walls. Good-quality, interesting home-cooked food, including excellent puddings and vegetarian dishes, and using produce from local suppliers, served 12–2pm Tues–Sun and 6–8pm Tues–Sat. Picnic tables on the village green. Children welcome. An annual beer festival is held over Easter, with approximately 20 ales served from the barrel, plus a barrel race on Easter Monday across the hills from Stocksfield. The pub can be hired during weekdays. Village signposted from New Ridley, OS ref 078592.

OPEN 6–11pm Mon; 11am–11pm Tues–Sat; 11am–10.30pm Sun.

HEXHAM

The Dipton Mill Inn

Dipton Mill Road, Hexham NE46 1YA
☎ (01434) 606577 Geoff Brooker

Genuine freehouse not far from the Hexhamshire brewery, so Hexhamshire beers such as Devil's Elbow, Shire Bitter, Devil's Water, Whapweasel and Old Humbug usually available.

Formerly a farmhouse, this is an old-fashioned country pub with real fires. No music or games. One bar, beer garden, disabled access. Food served 12–2pm and 6.30–8.30pm Mon–Sat, 12–2.30pm Sun. Children allowed. Two miles south of Hexham.

OPEN 12–2.30pm and 6–11pm Mon–Sat; 12–3pm Sun.

The Tap & Spile

Battle Hill, Hexham NE46 1BA
☎ (01434) 602039 Sandra Calff

Black Sheep Best Bitter and Caledonian Deuchars IPA plus four guests, changed when the cask is empty, such as Timothy Taylor Landlord, Jennings Cumberland Ale, Everards Tiger and Durham Whitegold, and beers from Exmoor, Greene King, Wylam, High House and others too numerous to mention!

Community pub in a listed building dating from 1862 – there has always been a public bar on the premises. Traditional town-centre, one-bar pub with two rooms, including a lounge where children are allowed. Pub food and snacks served 12–2pm Mon–Sat. Monthly traditional music night and other live events. Easy access to the Lake District, Border Country, Northumberland countryside and coast, Newcastle and Roman sites. Situated on the main road, on the corner of the race course.

OPEN 11am–midnight Sun–Thurs; 11am–1am Fri–Sat.

HIGH HORTON

The Three Horseshoes

Hathery Lane, High Horton, Blyth NE24 4HF
☎ (01670) 822410 Ian Trinder
www.threehorseshoes.co.uk

Tetley Bitter and Greene King Abbot are the permanent beers at this freehouse. Plus five guests (usually 10–15 different ones each week) which might include Greene King Old Speckled Hen, Adnams Broadside, Bateman XXXB, Charles Wells Bombardier or Northumberland Secret Kingdom.

An 18th-century coaching inn on the outskirts of town, with beamed ceiling, open-plan bar, conservatory, restaurant area and two beer gardens. Food available 12–2.30pm Mon–Sat, 12–9pm Sun. Gaming machines. Children allowed. Car park. The pub is a large white building overlooking the B189.

OPEN 11am–11pm Mon–Sat; 12–10.30pm Sun.

HORSLEY

The Lion and the Lamb

Horsley, Newcastle-upon-Tyne NE15 0NS
☎ (01661) 852952 Anthony Milne

Enterprise Inns pub with five or six real ales. Greene King IPA, Black Sheep Bitter, Castle Eden Ale and Cumberland Ale are regular features, plus guests from local brewers.

Built in 1718 as a farmhouse and converted to a pub in 1744. Now a gastropub, with one bar, a separate restaurant area and a lounge/TV area. Food served 12–2.30pm and 6–9.30pm Mon–Sat; 12–3pm and 7–9pm Sun. Children's play area. Two outdoor patios and beer garden. Car park. Just off the A69.

OPEN 12–12.

LONGFRAMLINGTON

The Anglers Arms

Weldon Bridge, Longframlington, Morpeth NE65 8AX
☎ *(01665) 570655* John Young
www.anglersarms.com

 Freehouse offering a selection of four guest ales, e.g. Landlord, Black Sheep, Theakstons, Spitfire etc. Ales selection changed every couple of days.

A 17th-century country inn with restaurant, beams and fireplaces. Food is available 12–9.30pm Mon-Sat and 12–10pm Sun. Garden, car park, seven letting rooms. Children allowed. Just off the A697 on Rothbury Rd.

OPEN *11am–11pm Mon-Sat. 12–10.30pm Sun.*

LOW NEWTON

The Ship Inn

Newton Square, Low Newton, Nr Alnwick NE66 3EL
☎ *(01665) 576262* Christine Forsyth

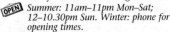 Now producing its own beer, including Sandcastles at Dawn, Dolly Day Dream and Ship Hot Ale, plus guests changed daily from local breweries including Wylam, Northumberland, Durham and Isle of Skye.

U nspoilt 18th-century seaside village pub in a unique and breathtaking setting. Imaginative bar food at lunchtime, evening menu including varied vegetarian food, fresh local seafood and lobster, and meat from local farms. Booking is advisable for food. Outside tables located on the village green, 20 yards from the beach. Live music occasionally. Children and dogs welcome.

OPEN *Summer: 11am–11pm Mon–Sat; 12–10.30pm Sun. Winter: phone for opening times.*

MORPETH

Tap & Spile

Manchester Street, Morpeth NE61 1BH
☎ *(01670) 513894* Margo Boyle

Eight beers, from breweries such as Black Sheep, Hadrian & Border, Caledonian, Bateman, Everard, Wylam, High House, Hambleton and Mordue, rotated several times a week.

A friendly, old-fashioned, locals' pub with a wide variety of customers. Bar and separate lounge. No electricity! No food except on special occasions. Well-behaved children allowed in the lounge only. Lounge available for private hire. Going north through the town, turn right at the traffic lights.

OPEN *12–2.30pm and 4.30–11pm Mon–Thurs; 12–11pm Fri–Sat; 12–10.30pm Sun.*

NEWBIGGIN BY THE SEA

The Queen's Head

7 High Street, Newbiggin by the Sea NE64 6AT
☎ *(01670) 817293* David Stringer

Freehouse serving up to three constantly changing real ales, served on a guest basis.

R e-built in 1907 with many original characteristics including a public bar, lounge bar and snug. A strongly local and regulars' pub, in a seaside location, serving the fishing and ex-mining trade. No food. Well-behaved children allowed in lounge and snug.

OPEN *9.45am–midnight.*

SEAHOUSES

The Olde Ship Hotel

Main Street, Seahouses NE68 7RD
☎ *(01665) 720200* David G Swan
www.seahouses.co.uk

Freehouse with seven or eight constantly rotating guest ales, which could include Black Sheep Bitter, Draught Bass, Greene King Old Speckled Hen, Courage Directors and brews from Hadrian.

O riginally a farm dating back to 1745, this building was licensed as a pub in 1812 and has been under its current family ownership since 1910. Maritime themed throughout. Food served 12–2pm and 7–8.30pm. Eighteen en-suite bedrooms available mid Jan–mid Dec. Private function room, beer garden overlooking the busy harbour. Limited parking. Close to wonderful beaches and local boat trips. Located 22 miles south of Berwick and 14 miles north of Alnwick.

OPEN *11am–11pm Mon–Sat; 12–11pm Sun.*

SHOTLEY BRIDGE

The Manor House Inn

Carterway Heads, Shotley Bridge, Nr Consett DH8 9LX
☎ *(01207) 255268*

Tied to Enterprise, with four real ales: Theakston Best, Charles Wells Bombardier, Courage Directors and a weekly-changing guest brew. Plus at least 70 malt whiskies.

C onverted 1760s farmhouse, with open log fires in winter. Stunning views over the Derwent Valley. Bar and restaurant food available 12–9.30pm (until 9pm Sun). Large car park, garden, accommodation (four bedrooms). Farm shop sells home-produced and other local produce. Children and dogs welcome. On the A68 south of Coxbridge.

OPEN *11am–11pm Mon–Sat; 12–10.30pm Sun.*

TWEEDMOUTH

The Angel Inn
11 Brewery Bank, Tweedmouth
☎ *(01289) 303030* Pauline Huntley

Freehouse with Camerons Creamy Bitter a permanent feature, plus a guest ale, changed weekly.

Apub with a laid-back, friendly atmosphere. No food. Children and pets welcome. Beer garden, car park. Close to the A1, Berwick Rangers football club and local attractions in Berwick town centre.

OPEN *5.30–11pm Mon–Thurs; 5–11pm Fri; 12–11pm Fri–Sat; 12–10.30pm Sun.*

WYLAM

The Boat House
Station Road, Wylam NE41 8HR
☎ *(01661) 853431*
Mark and Norman Weatherburn

A constantly changing selection of 12 real ales. Wylam Gold Tankard plus 11 guests, changed daily. Two ciders also served.

Warm, friendly pub, formerly a ferryman's cottage, on the south bank of the Tyne. Northumberland CAMRA Pub of the Year 2001, 2003, 2004, 2006, 2007 and 2008! Unspoilt bar with real fire. Soup and sandwiches available every day, plus meals 12–4pm Sat–Sun. Two beer gardens, car park. Children welcome in the lounge only until 9pm. On the A69 to Wylam. Close to the railway stations, with regular trains from Newcastle.

OPEN *11am–11pm Mon–Sat; 12–10.30pm*

THE BREWERIES

ALCAZAR BREWING CO.
(A division of Sherwood Forest Brewing Company Limited)
Church Street, Old Basford, Nottingham NG6 0GA
☎ *(0115) 978 2282*
www.alcazarbrewery.co.uk

Flagship beers:
ALCAZAR ALE 4.0% ABV
NEW DAWN 4.5% ABV
FOXTALE ALE 4.9% ABV
VIXEN'S VICE 5.2% ABV
WINDJAMMER IPA 6.0% ABV
BOMBAY CASTLE IPA 6.5% ABV
Occasionals and seasonals including:
BLACK FOX 3.9% ABV
NOTTINGHAM NOG 4.2% ABV
MAPLE MAGIC WINTER ALE 5.5% ABV
BOMBAY CASTLE IPA 6.5% ABV

CASTLE ROCK BREWERY
Queensbridge Road, The Meadows, Nottingham NG2 1NB
☎ *(0115) 985 1615*

BLACK GOLD 3.5% ABV
A dark mild ale with a slight bitterness but without undue sweetness.
NOTTINGHAM GOLD 3.5% ABV
A golden beer with a distinct hop character derived from 100% Goldings hops.
HARVEST PALE 3.8% ABV
A pale ale which is well balanced with a pleasant bitterness derived from American hops.
HEMLOCK BITTER 4.0% ABV
The 'superstar' of quaffing ales. Mid strength, full flavoured with fruity notes and a hop finish.
ELSIE MO 4.7% ABV
A blonde and beautiful malt beer, light in colour and refreshing on the palate.
Plus seasonals and occasionals including:
SNOWHITE 4.2% ABV
A refreshing single malt beer with a distinctive hop character. Very pale in colour.
NOTTINGHAM DARK STOUT 4.5% ABV
A dark, heavy, well-hopped traditional stout (November–March).
Plus special brews and a 'wildlife' selection of 12 brews, each named after a different wildlife species for each different month of the year.

CAYTHORPE BREWERY
Trentham Cottage, Boat Lane, Hoveringham NG14 7JP
☎ *(0115) 966 4376*

COCKER BECK 3.7% ABV
DOVER BECK BITTER 4.0% ABV
OLD NOTTINGHAM EXTRA PALE ALE 4.2% ABV
STOUT FELLOW 4.2% ABV
Plus seasonal and occasional brews.

FELLOWS, MORTON & CLAYTON BREWHOUSE COMPANY
54 Canal Street, Nottingham NG1 7EH
☎ *(0115) 950 6795*
www.fellowsmortonandclayton.co.uk

SAMUEL FELLOWS BITTER 3.8% ABV
MATTHEW CLAYTON'S ORIGINAL STRONG BREW 4.4% ABV
POST HASTE BITTER 4.5% ABV
Plus seasonal brews.

FULL MASH BREWERY
17 Lower Park Street, Stapleford NG9 8EN
☎ *(0115) 949 9262*

OUIJA 3.7% ABV
SÉANCE 4.0% ABV
SPIRITUALIST 4.3% ABV
APPARITION 4.5% ABV
Plus occasionals.

HOLLAND BREWERY
5 Browns Flat, Kimberley, Nottingham NG16 2JU
☎ *(0115) 938 2685*

GOLDEN BLONDE 4.0% ABV
LIP SMACKER 4.0% ABV
CLOGHOPPER 4.2% ABV
DOUBLE DUTCH 4.5% ABV
MAD JACK STOUT 4.5% ABV
Seasonals and occasionals including:
CHOCOLATE CLOG MILD 3.8% ABV
GLAMOUR PUSS 4.2% ABV
HOLLY HOP GOLD 4.7% ABV
DUTCH COURAGE 5.0% ABV

MAGPIE BREWERY
4 Ashling Court, Iremonger Road, Nottingham NG2 3JA
☎ *(0115) 961 1556*
www.magpiebrewery.com

FLEDGLING BITTER 3.8% ABV
Spicy orange nose.
TWO4JOY 4.2% ABV
Malt and fruit flavours.
EARLY BIRD 4.3% ABV
Hoppy with hint of lime.
THIEVING ROGUE 4.5% ABV
Grassy.
FULL FLIGHT 4.8% ABV
Biscuity, malt nose.

MALLARD BREWERY
15 Hartington Avenue, Carlton, Nottingham NG4 3NR
☎ *(0115) 952 1289*
www.mallard-brewery.co.uk

DUCK 'N' DIVE 3.7% ABV
Light and single hopped.
WADDLERS MILD 3.7% ABV
Ruby mild with fruity finish.
BEST BITTER 4.0% ABV
Dry with hoppy nose.
FEATHERLIGHT 4.1% ABV
Floral and hoppy.
DUCKLING 4.2% ABV
Clean, with honey notes.
SPITTIN' FEATHERS 4.4% ABV
Hints of toffee and coffee.
DRAKE 4.5% ABV
Robust bitter.
OWD DUCK 4.8% ABV
Ruby bitter, smooth, with smoky notes.
FRIAR DUCK 5.0% ABV
Pale, malty, with taste of blackcurrant.
Seasonals and occasionals:
DUCK DOWN STOUT 4.6% ABV
Black and fruity.
D.A. 5.8% ABV
Complex winter ale.
QUISMAS QUACKER 6.0% ABV
Dark, smoky, coffee-flavoured Christmas ale.

MAYPOLE BREWERY

North Laithes Farm, Wellow Road, Eakring
NG22 0AN
☎ *07971 277598*
www.maypolebrewery.co.uk

MAYFLY 3.8% ABV
BXA 4.0% ABV
MAYFAIR 4.1% ABV
MAYBEE 4.3% ABV
MAE WEST 4.6% ABV
WELLOW GOLD 4.6% ABV
Occasional brews including:
MAYDAY MILD 3.5% ABV
COCKCAFER 4.1% ABV
FLANAGAN'S STOUT 4.4% ABV
MAJOR OAK 4.4% ABV
GHOST TRAIN 4.7% ABV
MAYHEM 5.0% ABV

MILESTONE BREWING CO.

Great North Road, Cromwell, Newark NG23 6JE
☎ *(01636) 822255*
www.milestonebrewery.co.uk

HOPTIMISM 3.6% ABV
LION'S PRIDE 3.8% ABV
NORTH ROCK 4.0% ABV
SHINE ON 4.0% ABV
LOXLEY 4.2% ABV
BLACK PEARL IRISH STOUT 4.3% ABV
CRUSADER 4.4% ABV
RICH RUBY 4.5% ABV
DELIVERANCE 4.6% ABV
IPA 4.8% ABV
OLDE HOME WRECKER 4.9% ABV
RASPBERRY WHEAT BEER 5.6% ABV

NOTTINGHAM BREWERY

Plough Inn, 17 St Peter's Street, Radford,
Nottingham NG7 3EN
☎ *(0115) 942 2649*
www.nottinghambrewery.com

ROCK BITTER 3.8% ABV
ROCK MILD 3.8% ABV
LEGEND 4.0% ABV
EXTRA PALE ALE 4.2% ABV
COCK AND HOOP 4.3% ABV
DREADNOUGHT 4.5% ABV
BULLION 4.7% ABV
SOOTY OATMEAL STOUT 4.8% ABV
NOTTINGHAM SUPREME 5.2% ABV
Plus specials.

SPRINGHEAD FINE ALES LTD

Unit 3, Sutton Workshops, Old Great North
Road, Sutton on Trent, Newark NG23 6QS
☎ *(01636) 821000*
www.springhead.co.uk

PURITAN'S PORTER 4.0% ABV
SPRINGHEAD BITTER 4.0% ABV
CHARLIE'S ANGEL 4.5% ABV
THE LEVELLER 4.8% ABV
ROARING MEG 5.5% ABV
Seasonals:
SURRENDER 1646 3.6% ABV
ROUNDHEAD'S GOLD 4.2% ABV
RUPERT'S RUIN 4.2% ABV
GOODRICH CASTLE 4.4% ABV
OLIVER'S ARMY 4.4% ABV
SWEET LIPS 4.6% ABV
NEWARK CASTLE BROWN 5.0% ABV
CROMWELL'S HAT 6.0% ABV

THE PUBS

BASFORD

The Horse & Groom

462 Radford Road, Basford NG7 7EA
☎ *(0115) 970 3777 David Took*
www.horseandgroombasford.com

Part of the Bartsch Inns chain of pubs.
Fuller's London Pride and Caledonian
Deuchars IPA plus a local brew which changes
three times weekly. Seven guest pumps serve
over 400 real ales each year, such as Brains
SA, Gale's HSB, Nottingham Legend and
Bradfield Farmer's Blond.

The former Shipstone's Brewery tap,
decorated with brewery artefacts and
pictures. Food available 12.30–3pm Mon–Sat
and 12.30–4pm Sun. No food evenings
except for curry nights Tues (5–9pm). Annual
beer festival, plus 10 mini beer festivals each
year. Function room. Street parking. CAMRA
Pub of Excellence award 2007. Located two
miles north of the city centre, on the
Shipstone Street or Wilkinson Street tram
stops.

OPEN *11am–11pm Mon–Thurs; 11am–*
11.30pm Fri–Sat; 12–11pm Sun.

BARNBY IN THE WILLOWS

The Willow Tree

Front Street, Barnby in the Willows, Newark
NG24 2SA
☎ *(01636) 629003*
Kathryn Whittaker and Brett Handley
www.thewillowtreeinn.co.uk

Freehouse with two real ales available
from a wide range of regional breweries.

An 18th-century Grade II listed village inn
with quaint interior and low beams. Cosy
log fires and candlelit tables in winter. There
is a beautiful floral courtyard, ideal for early-
evening drinks in summer. Good food served
from 7pm Mon–Sat and lunchtimes Sat–Sun.
Traditional Sunday lunches available. Quiz
night on Sundays. Four miles from Newark.

OPEN *7–11pm Mon–Fri; 12–3pm and 7–11pm*
Sat; 12–3pm and 7–10.30pm Sun.

BEESTON

The Victoria Hotel

85 Dovecote Lane, Beeston, Nr Nottingham
NG9 1JG
☎ *(0115) 925 4049*
Neil Kelso and Graham Smith
www.victoriabeeston.co.uk

Genuine freehouse with 12 changing real ales, with beers from Castle Rock, Everards and Bateman permanently featured. The nine guests are changed every couple of days, and will always include one from a local micro-brewery, one mild and a stout or porter.

A ward-winning Victorian railway pub with high ceilings. Bar and restaurant food is available 12–8.45pm Mon–Tues; 12–9.30pm Wed–Sat; 12–7.45pm Sun. There is also a brunch menu 10.30am–noon Mon–Sat. The restaurant menu includes a wide vegetarian range. Car park, garden. Accompanied children allowed in the restaurant and garden until 8pm only. Beer festivals at Easter and the end of July. Frequent brewery nights featuring micro-breweries. Off Queens Road, behind Beeston railway station. Local CAMRA Pub of the Year 2005.

OPEN *10.30am–11pm Mon–Sat; 12–11pm Sun.*

BINGHAM

The Horse & Plough

25 Long Acre, Bingham, Nottingham NG13 8AF
☎ *(01949) 839313* Craig Anderson
www.horseandploughbingham.com

Part of the Bartsch Inns chain of pubs. Charles Wells Bombardier and Caledonian Deuchars IPA. Four guest pumps serve over 400 real ales each year, such as Thwaites Lancaster Bomber, Oakham JHB and Orkney Red MacGregor.

C onverted 17th-century chapel with a separate restaurant on the first floor. A traditional atmosphere with no machines, juke box or pool table – a comfortable, friendly local. Food served 12–2.30pm (bar); 7–9.45pm (restaurant) Mon–Sat; 12–3pm Sun (bar and restaurant). Council car parks nearby. CAMRA Regional Pub of the Year 2007. Cask Marque accredited. Situated on the main road through the village, on the left after the traffic lights.

OPEN *11am–11pm Mon–Thurs; 11am–11.30pm Fri–Sat; 12–11pm Sun.*

CARLTON ON TRENT

The Great Northern Inn

Ossington Road, Carlton on Trent, Newark
NG23 6NT
☎ *(01636) 821348*
Mark Priestly and Glynis Ray

Freehouse with four pumps. Hardy's Kimberley Bitter and Olde Trip plus a mild and rotating guest.

A family-oriented pub with two bars, family room, restaurant, outside playground and large car park. Food served 12–2.30pm and 5.30–8.30pm Mon–Fri, all day Sat and 12–4pm Sun (carvery), including a children's menu. Located 100 yards from the A1, with easy return access to the A1.

OPEN *All day every day.*

CARRINGTON

The Gladstone

45 Loscoe Road, Carrington NG5 2AW
☎ *(0115) 912 9994* Chris Hackett

Timothy Taylor Landlord, Fuller's London Pride, Greene King Abbot, Caledonian Deuchars IPA and Castle Rock Harvest Pale. One pump serving up to three different guests each week, for example, Slaters Top Totty or Queen Bee, Nottingham EPA, Charles Wells Bombardier or Kelham Pale Rider.

V ictorian character pub with bar and separate lounge. Covered beer garden. Beer festivals held. Folk club and function room. No food.

OPEN *5–11pm Mon–Wed; 5–11.30pm Thurs; 3–11.30pm Fri; 12–11.30pm Sat; 12–11pm Sun.*

CAYTHORPE

The Black Horse

29 Main Street, Caythorpe, Nottingham
NG14 7ED
☎ *(0115) 966 3520* Sharron Andrews

Freehouse and brewpub with four real ales. A home-brewed beer from Caythorpe, Greene King Abbot and Black Sheep Bitter are permanent features, and there is also one guest.

V illage pub with coal fires, two beamed bar areas, garden and large car park. Freshly prepared food served 12–1.45pm Tues–Sat and 7–8.30pm Tues–Thurs (booking necessary). Good location for walkers and cyclists. No children, no music.

OPEN *12–3pm and 5.30–11pm Tues–Sat (from 6pm Sat); 12–5pm and 8–10.30pm Sun. Closed on Monday except bank holidays.*

COLSTON BASSETT

The Martins Arms Inn

School Lane, Colston Bassett NG12 3FD
☎ *(01949) 81361* Lynne Strafford Bryan and Salvatore Inguanta

Seven beers, with regulars including Timothy Taylor Landlord, Greene King Abbot and IPA, Black Sheep Bitter, Adnams Bitter, Woodforde's Wherry and Marston's Pedigree. Two of the beers are changed regularly.

T his award-winning village freehouse was built in 1700 as a farmhouse set in 100 acres owned by the local squire. Now set in one acre with original stables surrounded by National Trust parkland. Antique furniture, prints, old beams, Jacobean fireplace and bar. Private room, snug, dining room. Bar and restaurant food available 12–2pm and 6–10pm (except Sunday evening). Beer garden with 80 seats, car park for 35 cars. Children welcome, dogs welcome in garden. Accommodation. Handy for Belvoir Castle and Langar Wild Flower Farm, and a good walk to Colston's medieval church. On the A46 Newark to Leicester road.

OPEN *12–3pm and 6–11pm (7–10.30pm Sun).*

DAYBROOK
The Vale Hotel
Mansfield Road, Daybrook, Woodthorpe NG5 3GG
☎ *(0115) 926 8864* Martin and Patrick Byrne

 Punch Taverns tied house serving Black Sheep Bitter, Caledonian Deuchars IPA and Adnams Broadside plus two guests from breweries such as Jennings or Brains.

A1930s Grade II listed building with original home brewery décor. Food served 12–8pm Mon–Sat; 12–5pm Sun. Children welcome in designated areas. Front beer garden. Car park. Function room. Summer beer festivals. Situated on the main ring road into Nottingham.

OPEN *12–close.*

DUNHAM ON TRENT
The Bridge Inn
Main Street, Dunham on Trent, Newark NG22 0TY
☎ *(01777) 228385* Gordon and Lucy Cairns

Freehouse with three pumps serving Hardys & Hansons Olde Trip and a couple of guest ales, with local breweries featured when possible.

Atraditional 200-year-old village pub with two bars, restaurant and beer garden. Disabled access. Food available 12–2pm and 5–8.30pm Mon–Sat, 12–3pm Sun. No children. Live music. On the A56 beside the River Trent and Lincolnshire border.

OPEN *12–2pm and 5–11pm Mon–Fri; all day Sat–Sun.*

EDINGLEY
The Old Reindeer
Main Street, Edingley, Nr Newark NG22 8BE
☎ *(01623) 882253* Rob and Gina Joseph
www.oldreindeer.co.uk

A Marston's tied house. Pedigree and Jennings Bitter plus a variety of monthly-changing guests such as Black Sheep Bitter or Wychwood Hobgoblin.

Village pub with open fire and warm sense of the past. Rear beer garden and front raised patio area. Food – including a carvery and self-proclaimed great fish and chips! – served in a separate dining room.

OPEN *11.30am–11.30pm.*

EPPERSTONE
Cross Keys
Main Street, Epperstone NG14 6AD
☎ *(0115) 966 3033* Alan Thompson

A Greene King tied house serving IPA, Old Speckled Hen and Hardys & Hansons Olde Trip plus one monthly-changing guest. Cask Marque accredited.

Old coaching inn with two bars, open fire, comfy sofas and welcoming atmosphere. Recently refurbished. Homemade food served 12–2pm and 6–9pm Tues–Sat; 12–4pm Sun. Children welcome, trampoline in the garden. Beer garden. Car park. Off the A6097 between Nottingham and Southwell.

OPEN *6–11.30pm Mon (closed Mon lunch); 11.30am–3pm and 6–11.30pm Tues–Sat; all day Sun.*

GRANBY
Marquis of Granby
Dragon Street, Granby NG13 9PN
☎ *(01949) 859517* S McArdel
www.themarquisofgranby.co.uk

Five real ales, namely Brewsters Hophead and Marquis plus three guests, changed three times a week, from a varied range. Beers from Great Oakley often served.

Freehouse with bar, lounge and private rooms. Food served 6–8pm Thurs; 12–2.30pm and 6–8pm Fri–Sun. Children welcome. Handy for Belvoir Castle.

OPEN *5.30pm–12 Mon–Thurs; 12–12 Fri–Sun.*

HOVERINGHAM
The Marquis of Granby
Main Street, Hoveringham NG14 7JR
☎ *(0115) 966 3080* Paul and Kim Simpson

Freehouse serving five real ales, changed regularly. The two fixed beers are from Bateman and Bass, and the three guests rotate every month.

Refurbished country pub with public bar, dining room, original beams and fireplaces, a public house since 1840. Country views. Lunch and evening menu plus à la carte served 12–2.30pm and 6–9.30pm Wed–Sat, and 12–4pm Sun. Beer garden, patio, accommodation, car park. Disabled access and facilities. Handy for Hoveringham Show. Off the A612 Lowdham to Southwell road.

OPEN *4–11pm Mon–Tues; 12–2.30pm and 4–11pm Wed–Fri; 12–11pm Sat–Sun.*

The Reindeer Inn
Main Street, Hoveringham NG14 7JR
☎ *(0115) 966 3629* Steve Taylor
www.thereindeerinn.com

A freehouse. Calthorpe Stout Fellow, Castle Rock Harvest Pale and Black Sheep Bitter plus one guest, changed twice-weekly. Brews from across the UK such as Woodforde's Wherry, Oakham JHB, York Brewery Yorkshire Terrier and Caledonian Deuchars IPA have featured.

Atraditional pub, over 100 years old. One bar, separate restaurant and beer garden on a cricket pitch! A mix of modern and traditional food served lunchtimes Wed–Sun and evenings Tues–Sat. Children welcome, dogs welcome in the bar. Car park. Functions catered for.

OPEN *5pm–close Mon–Tues; 12–2.30pm and 5pm–close Wed–Fri; 12–close Sat–Sun.*

The Nelson & Railway

Station Road, Kimberley NG16 2NR
☎ *(0115) 938 2177* Harry and Mick Burton
www.nelsonandrailway.co.uk

Three real ales, including Hardys & Hansons Kimberley Best and Olde Trip. Also an interesting guest from a range changed once a month.

Opposite the Hardys & Hansons brewery. A Victorian, family-run village pub with dining area. Cask Marque accredited. Bar food available 12–2.30pm and 5.30–9pm Mon–Fri, 12–9pm Sat and 12–6pm Sun. Car park, garden, skittle alley and games. Accommodation. Children welcome in dining area for meals. One mile north of M1 junction 26.

OPEN *11am–midnight Mon–Sat; 12–11pm Sun.*

Il Rosso

180 Nottingham Road, Mansfield NG18 4AF
☎ *(01623) 623031* Lee Everett

Three real ales, changed every few days. Fuller's London Pride, Black Sheep Bitter, Timothy Taylor Landlord, Greene King Abbot Ale and Old Speckled Hen and Hook Norton Old Hooky regularly feature.

Taken over by the current landlord in 2002, this is a modern, spacious bar and restaurant, with a varied age range in the clientele creating a lively yet comfortable atmosphere. Big-screen for all major sporting events. Food served 11am–11pm Mon–Sat; 12–10.30pm Sun (claims to serve the best Sunday lunch in the area). The restaurant has facilities for babies and young children. Huge car park. On the A60 on the outskirts of Mansfield.

OPEN *9am–late.*

The Star

Warsop Road, Mansfield, Woodhouse NG19 9LE
☎ *(01623) 403110* Angela Kerr

Four real ales, often including Highgate Lone Wolf, Mordue Radgie Gadgie, Springhead Roaring Meg and Goff's Jouster. Beers rotated on a 12-week rotation system.

A 17th-century pub with two bars, dart board and pool table. Food served 12–2pm and 5.30–8pm Mon–Sat; 12–3pm Sun. Beer garden. Car park. Children welcome. On the crossroads between Portland Street and New Mill Lane.

OPEN *12–3pm and 5.30–11pm Mon–Fri; 12–3pm and 5.30pm–12 Sat; 12–12 Sun.*

The Duke of Cambridge

548 Woodborough Road, Mapperley NG3 5FH
☎ *(0115) 962 3083* Mark and Carol Symonds

Three real ales, including Charles Wells Bombardier and Caledonian Deuchars IPA and a guest changed every few days, too many to give examples.

Traditional one-room community pub. Bar snacks available 12–2pm Mon–Sat. Function room available for hire. Outside patio/decking area. Children welcome until 5pm. Music quiz Sun 9pm, general knowledge quiz Mon 9pm. Jazz band last Sunday of month 2–5pm. Large car park. A mile from Nottingham city centre heading towards Woodborough.

OPEN *12–12 (11pm Tues and Sun).*

The Lion Inn

Mosley Street, New Basford, Nottingham NG7 7FG
☎ *(0115) 970 3506* Theresa Singleton

Ten real ales are on offer at this Bateman tenancy, usually including three Bateman ales, plus guests such as Charles Wells Bombardier, Kelham Island Pale Rider, Castle Rock Elsie Mo, Everards Tiger, Bateman XXXB and beers from Nottingham and Mallard. Other seasonal celebration beers on bank holidays, at Christmas and Easter etc.

A traditional pub with wooden floorboards, open fires, beer garden and play area. A broad clientele. Live bands on Fri and Sat nights, plus jazz at Sun lunchtimes. Quiz on Mon, open mic on Thurs. An extensive menu served at lunchtimes and evenings (lunchtimes only on Sunday). Regular music and beer festivals. Ska music night on first Sunday of every month. Children allowed.

OPEN *All day, every day.*

The Castle

5 Castlegate, Newark NG24 1AZ
☎ *(01636) 640733*
Heidi and Tony Yale (Managers)

Six pumps of regularly changing guest beers featuring Sharps, Black Sheep, Brains Rev James, local brewer Oldershaws and many more.

A relatively new pub with a warm and friendly atmosphere, in the historic town of Newark. Live music five nights a week, featuring jazz, blues and acoustic. Real ale, real music, real people. Reborn as Newark's premier real ale and live music venue. Simple food such as freshly made rolls and pork pies available.

OPEN *11am–11pm Sun–Thurs; 11am–midnight Fri–Sat.*

The Old Malt Shovel

25 North Gate, Newark NG24 1HD
☎ *(01636) 702036* Tim Purslow

Timothy Taylor Landlord, Adnams Broadside, Everards Tiger and Caledonian Deuchars IPA plus one or two guest beers. These may be from Brewsters, Cains, Black Sheep, York, Rudgate, Glentworth, Hop Back, Cottage, Shepherd Neame, Oakham, Exmoor, Badger or many, many other independent breweries from around the UK.

Popular, 400-year-old pub situated 200 yards from the River Trent with lovely walks nearby. Home-cooked food available 12–2.30pm and 5.30–9.30pm Mon–Sat and 12–4pm Sun, both as bar meals and in a continental-style restaurant. Beer garden. Monthly meetings of the RAT (Real Ale Tasting) Society held in pub. Children welcome in the restaurant. Located midway between North Gate and Castle stations.

 11.30am–3pm and 5.30–11pm Mon–Tues; 11.30am–11pm Wed–Sat; 12–10.30pm Sun.

NOTTINGHAM

The Bell Inn

18 Angel Row, Market Square, Nottingham NG1 6HL
☎ *(0115) 947 5241* Brian Rigby
www.thebell-inn.com

 A typical selection of beers would be Greene King IPA, Abbot, XX Mild and Old Speckled Hen, plus Nottingham EPA, Oakham JHB, Castle Rock Hemlock, Banks and Taylor Edwin Taylor Stout and Burton Bridge Golden Delicious.

A traditional 15th-century coaching inn that traces its origins back to 1276 with the arrival of a group of Carmelite friars. It now comprises two medieval buildings masked by a Georgian-style frontage, and is located in the old Market Square of this historic city. The pub features architraves following the design of the original 15th-century building, and sits above a network of sandstone caves. Nottingham CAMRA Pub of the Year 2006, Heritage Award 2003 and Pub of Excellence Award 2005. Cellar tours are conducted Tues and Thurs 7.30pm for those wishing to learn more about this fascinating pub and the sandstone beer cellars below (booking via website). Live music from resident jazz bands The Footwarmers, the Omega and the JJ Quintet, Sunday afternoons and Mon, Tues and Sun evenings.

 10am–close Mon–Sat; 11am–close Sun.

The Bunkers Hill Inn

36–8 Hockley, Nottingham NG1 1FP
☎ *(0115) 910 0114*
Vanessa Frearson and John Rogers

 Six real ales. Oakham JHB is generally one of them, plus a mild. Others might include Abbeydale Moonshine, Bateman XB and Kelham Island Pale Rider but the range changes every week.

Drinkers' pub on the outskirts of town, previously a Barclays bank. Two bars, function room and snug (the former bank safe). Food is available at lunchtimes and evenings. Quiz nights, curry nights, open mic nights and live music. Quiet children allowed. Situated next to the ice arena.

 12–12 (1am Fri–Sat).

Cast

Nottingham Playhouse, Wellington Circus, Nottingham NG1 5AN
☎ *(0115) 852 3898* Dennis Janisse

 Three real ales, including Legend and EPA from Nottingham Brewery.

Grade II listed building with brasserie-style restaurant and lounge bar. Freshly cooked food available 12–10pm, with a range of different menu options, including tapas in the lounge bar and an à la carte menu in the evenings. Outdoor drinking and dining area in the plaza, where customers can appreciate Anish Kapoor's Sky Mirror sculpture.

Children welcome all day. Private room available for hire. Attached to Nottingham Playhouse and Nottingham Albert Hall.

 11am–11pm Mon–Thurs; 11am–midnight Fri–Sat; 12–10.30pm Sun (deli open 8am–8pm).

The Cock & Hoop

25–7 High Pavement, Lacemarket, Nottingham NG1 1HE
☎ *(0115) 852 3231* Katherine Abbiss
www.cockandhoop.co.uk

 Freehouse serving Fuller's London Pride, Caledonian Deuchars IPA, Timothy Taylor Landlord and a home brew: Cock and Hoop by Nottingham brewery, plus one rotating guest.

A gastropub and alehouse, the only pub in Nottingham to be featured in the Michelin guide. Part of Lacemarket Hotel which offers function rooms, cocktail bar, restaurant and accommodation. Food served 12–10pm. Children and dogs welcome.

 12–11pm Sun–Wed; 12–12 Thurs; noon–1am Fri–Sat.

Fellows, Morton & Clayton

54 Canal Street, Nottingham NG1 7EH
☎ *(0115) 950 6795* Les Howard
www.fellowsmortonandclayton.co.uk

 Home of the Fellows, Morton and Clayton Brewhouse Company, with Fellows Bitter and Claytons Bitter among the seven real ales usually available, plus beers such as Timothy Taylor Landlord, Caledonian Deuchars IPA, Fuller's London Pride, Mallard Duckling and Black Sheep Best Bitter.

Traditional pub with brewhouse upstairs, converted from a warehouse in the late 1970s. Large conservatory, large outside decking area, separate restaurant and function room. Three plasma screens. Food served 11am–9pm Mon–Fri; 10am–9pm Sat; 10am–6pm Sun. Next to the canal, and close to Nottingham Castle and city centre. From Nottingham station, turn right, and the pub is on the left on the main road.

 11am–11pm Mon–Thurs; 11am–1am Fri; 10am–1am Sat; 10am–10.30pm Sun.

The Forest Tavern

257 Mansfield Road, Nottingham NG1 3FT
☎ *(0115) 947 5650*
Martin Meyer and Alex Young

 Castle Rock Harvest Pale and Greene King Abbot plus two guests, usually from Oakham or Castle Rock breweries. The largest range of continental bottled beers in Nottingham plus three Belgian brews on tap.

Continental-style late-licence pub with a live music venue (The Maze) behind it. Folk, country, Americana and blues nights during the week, funk and rock at weekends. Food served until half an hour before closing. No children.

 12–12 Mon–Thurs; noon–2am Fri–Sat; 12–11.30pm Sun.

The Globe

152 London Road, Nottingham, NG2 3BQ
☎ *(0115) 986 6881* Cassandra Jackson
www.theglobenottingham.com

 Nottingham Brewery Legend and Extra Pale Ale (EPA), plus four guests every week including Magpie Brewery beers and something from Oldershaws, Archers, Bradfield, Milestone and other micro-breweries.

Part of a local chain of freehouse pubs, with a light atmosphere. Close to cricket, football and rugby grounds. Sporting fixtures frequently shown on several large screens. Function room available. Cosy alcove with a dart board. Cold snacks only available on match days. Situated on main bus route from West Bridgford and Clifton into town.

OPEN *11.30am–11pm Mon–Sat; 12–10.30pm Sun.*

The Golden Fleece

105 Mansfield Road, Nottingham NG1 3FN
☎ *(0115) 947 2843*
Kathryn Pyer, Richard Scott and James Busby
www.myspace.com/goldenfleecenottingham

Four real ales, Caledonian Deuchars IPA and Everards Tiger plus two exceptional guest ales from the finest cask selection.

Refurbished city-centre pub that retains its 19th-century character. There is a 40-foot cellar with a glass trap-door visible from the pub. Freshly prepared food using local produce served 12–8.30pm Mon–Sat and 12–6pm Sun (booking advisable Sun). Beer garden and smoking area. Children welcome. Open mic on Mon, quiz on Wed, live bands Thurs, various DJs and entertainment Fri and Sat, reggae roasts Sun afternoon. Close to town centre.

OPEN *12–12.*

Lincolnshire Poacher

161–3 Mansfield Road, Nottingham NG1 3FR
☎ *(0115) 941 1584* Karen Williams
www.castlerockbrewery.co.uk

 Freehouse with 14 real ales, always featuring Castle Rock Harvest Pale and Screech Owl, plus ten guests, including a mild and a stout or porter and a beer from Batemans. Beers from Kelham Island, Thornbridge, Brewdog, Crouch Vale, Oldershaws, Newby Wyke and Everard are often on offer, and the guests are changed every day or two. Part of the LoCale scheme (always have a beer on that was brewed within a 20-mile radius of the pub). Regular 'meet the brewer' nights, and trips out to visit local breweries.

A traditional alehouse. No juke box, no games machines, just plenty of conversation. Nottingham CAMRA Pub of the Year 2007 and 8. Food available 12–8pm Mon–Fri and 12–5pm Sat–Sun – outside these times, ask and they will do their best to provide something. Enclosed and heated outside area, conservatory. Private room for hire (maximum capacity 40). Children allowed at the management's discretion. Live music Sunday nights. Just north of the city centre on the A60.

OPEN *11am–11pm Mon–Wed; 11am–midnight Thurs–Fri; 10am–midnight Sat; 12–11pm Sun.*

Ye Olde Trip to Jerusalem

Brewhouse Yard, Castle Road, Nottingham NG1 6AD
☎ *(0115) 947 3171* Karen Ratcliffe
www.triptojerusalem.com

Hardys & Hansons tied house with Kimberley Mild, Bitter and Olde Trip plus Marston's Pedigree. Other seasonal Kimberley ales available as guests.

A three-bar pub built inside raw sandstone caves in the Castle Rock, a contender for Britain's oldest inn (1189). Two bars, two courtyards, five rooms. No music or juke box. Food served 12–6pm daily with a snack menu also on Sun–Thurs evenings. Children welcome until 7pm. Beer garden, beer festivals, function room for hire

OPEN *11am–11pm Mon–Sat; 12–10.30pm Sun.*

The Plough Inn

17 St Peter's Street, Radford, Nottingham NG7 3EN
☎ *(0115) 942 2649*
Peter Darby and Dave Williams
www.nottinghambrewery.com

Home of the Nottingham Brewery, with Rock Bitter, Mild, Legend, Bullion and EPA brewed on the premises and always available. Up to five rotating guests, either own brews or guests from micro-breweries.

Dating from 1792 but rebuilt, this is a traditional pub with two bars, a dining area and real fires. The brewery was relaunched in autumn 2001. Good food available lunchtimes and evenings including Sunday roasts and curries on Tuesdays. Well-behaved children allowed. Beer garden. Car park. Live music on Thursday nights. Located off Ilkeston Road going out of Nottingham.

OPEN *12–3pm and 5–11pm Mon–Wed; 12–11pm Thurs–Sat; 12–10.30pm Sun.*

Sir John Borlase Warren

Ilkeston Road, Canning Circus, Nottingham NG7 3DG
☎ *(0115) 947 4247* Graham Shaw

An Everards tied house serving Tiger and Sunchaser plus Timothy Taylor Landlord and Greene King IPA plus two regularly changing guests. Beers have included Castle Rock Harvest Pale, St Austell Tribute and Okells IPA.

Named after the famous naval captain and philanthropist (1753–1822) who was born locally. Food served 12–4pm and 5–9pm Mon–Thurs; 12–4pm and 5–7pm Fri; 12–5pm Sat; 12–9pm Sun. Beer garden winner of Nottingham In Bloom award. On-street, metered parking. Ten minutes from Nottingham city centre on frequent bus route.

OPEN *12–11.30pm Mon–Thurs; 12–12 Fri–Sat; 12–11pm Sun.*

Stratford Haven

2 Stratford Road, West Bridgeford, Nottingham NG2 6BA
☎ *(0115) 982 5981* Natasha Averre
www.castlerockbrewery.co.uk

Part of Castle Rock, serving Castle Rock Harvest Pale, Batemans XB and XXXB, Everards Tiger plus Castle Rock guests. There is always a mild, and other guests could be from Kelham Island, Archers, Everards, York, Exmoor, Phoenix or Shepherd Neame.

 Focused on traditional real ales and popular with students and business-people alike. Food served 12–8pm including two roasts on Sundays. Curry night on Mondays. Monthly live music. Located near Nottingham Forest FC and Trent Bridge cricket ground.

OPEN *10.30am–11pm Mon–Wed; 10.30am–midnight Thurs–Fri; 12–11pm Sun.*

The Vat & Fiddle

Queensbridge Road, Nottingham NG2 1NB
☎ *(0115) 985 0611* Neil Trafford

 The full range of Castle Rock ales brewed and served on the premises. Plus guest ales such as Archers Golden, Newby Wyke Bear Island or Everards Tiger also available. Micro-breweries favoured.

An old-fashioned alehouse, situated on the edge of Nottingham, near the railway station. Food served 12–3pm daily, plus Mon–Sat 6–8pm. Children allowed if eating.

OPEN *All day, every day.*

The Horse Chestnut

Main Road, Radcliffe on Trent NG12 2BE
☎ *(0115) 933 1994* Jonathan Thomas
www.horsechestnutradcliffeontrent.com

 Part of the Bartsch Inns chain of pubs. Castle Rock Harvest Pale, Fuller's London Pride and Bateman XB plus five guests, changed up to six times a week. Over 250 guests each year, such as Magpie Early Bird, Rudgate Ruby, Kelham Island Pale Rider and Oldershaw Newtons Drop.

Fully re-fitted in 2006 and a finalist in the pub design of the year 2007. Unique, quiet room with books and leather armchairs. Food served 12–3pm and 5–9pm Mon–Sat; 12–4pm Sun. Private oak-pannelled meeting/dining room. Car park. Annual beer festival, plus mini beer festivals quarterly. Beer garden and terrace.

OPEN *11am–11pm Mon–Thurs; 11am–11.30pm Fri–Sat; 12–11pm Sun.*

The Royal Oak

Main Road, Radcliffe on Trent NG12 2FD
☎ *(0115) 933 3798*
Mark Upton, Diane Upton and Luke Taylor

Five or six brews, usually including Marston's Pedigree, Timothy Taylor Landlord, Greene King Old Speckled Hen, Bass and Everards Tiger. Also various guest beers throughout the year and up to four ciders.

A traditional-style 18th-century pub in the village centre. Cosy lounge and extended public bar, which includes pool table and large-screen TV. Food served lunchtimes and evening on Wed and Thurs and at lunchtimes on Fri–Sun. Large, private car park. Children welcome until 8pm.

OPEN *11am–11pm Mon–Sat; 12–10.30pm Sun.*

Market Hotel

West Carr Road, Ordsall, Nr Retford DN22 7SN
☎ *(01777) 703278* Graham Brunt

 Up to eight real ales. Shepherd Neame Spitfire, Jennings Sneck Lifter and Thwaites Bitter are regular features plus four ever-changing guest ales generally from local brewers.

Family-run traditionally decorated pub. Bar food available 12–2pm and 6–9.30pm (not Sun). Large car park, conservatory restaurant, large banqueting suite. Children welcome. Beer festival in September. Located two minutes through the subway from the railway station.

OPEN *11am–3pm and 6–11pm Mon–Fri; all day Sat; 12–4pm and 7–10.30pm Sun.*

Three Crowns

23 Easthorpe Street, Ruddington NG11 6LB
☎ *(0115) 921 3226* Ben Chapman
www.ruddingtonbeer.co.uk

 Freehouse with five or six real ales, including Nottingham Rock Bitter and Rock Mild plus three or four weekly guests. Church End, Cottage, Newby Wyke, Springhead, Oldershaws, Magpie and Mallard are among the breweries featured.

Clean, modern pub offering relaxed, convivial surroundings. No juke box or big screens. Food available Tues–Sat: bar snacks lunch and early evening; full international and Thai menu evenings only, in restaurant. Functions, meetings and special meals can be accommodated 10am–5pm daily. Bi-annual beer festivals.

OPEN *12–3pm and 5–11pm Mon–Fri; 12–11pm Sat; 12–10.30pm Sun.*

White Horse Inn

60 Church Street, Ruddington NG11 6HD
☎ *(0115) 984 4550* Lindsey Flint
www.whitehorse-inn.co.uk

Black Sheep Bitter, Charles Wells Bombardier and a Nottingham Brewery Ale (normally EPA) are regulars. Two guests are also available from local micro-breweries and nationals, such as Batemans, Adnams, Sharp's, Brains and Everards.

Traditional village pub concentrating on cask ales, with a large garden area that's a sun trap in summer. Hot food and rolls available weekday lunchtimes. Co-host of the Ruddington Beer Festival every May. CAMRA Pub of Excellence. An adult pub, so children not encouraged. Large car park, facilities for private hire. Church Street is near the village green, and there are regular buses from Nottingham.

OPEN *12–11pm (10.30pm Sun).*

UPPER BROUGHTON

The Golden Fleece

Main Road, Upper Broughton LE14 3BG
☎ *(01664) 822262*
Adrian and Rebecca Butcher

Freehouse serving Belvoir Beaver plus two guests, changed weekly.

A 19th-century traditional one-bar country pub situated on the edge of the Vale of Belvoir. Large beer garden and children's play area, plus 'Henry's Farm'. Food served 12–3pm and 5–9.30pm Mon–Thurs; 12–9.30pm Fri–Sun. Large car park. On the A606 towards Melton, just off the A46.

OPEN *12–3pm and 4–11pm Mon–Thurs; 12–11pm Fri–Sat; 12–10pm Sun.*

UPTON

Cross Keys

Main Street, Upton, Nr Newark NG23 5SY
☎ *(01636) 813269* E Tuckwood

Three real ales, with two rotating weekly. Black Sheep Bitter, Timothy Taylor Landlord, Charles Wells Bombardier and Caledonian Deuchars IPA are among the beers regularly served.

A 17th-century listed freehouse and restaurant. One bar, open fires, beams and brasses. The former dovecote has been converted into a restaurant, the tap room has carved pews from Newark parish church. Homemade food, including local beef, available 12–2.30pm and 6–9pm Mon–Sat, plus carvery Sun from 12.30pm. Car park, garden, children's area, private room for hire. Live music on last Friday of the month. Close to clock museum.

OPEN *12–2.30pm and 6–11pm.*

WATNALL

The Queen's Head

40 Main Road, Watnall NG16 6HT
☎ *(0115) 938 6774* Mick Popple

An Everards Brewery owned house serving Tiger and Original plus Adnams Broadside, Charles Wells Bombardier and Greene King Old Speckled Hen. One guest, changed every two–three days, such as Castle Rock Elsie Mo, Greene King Abbot, Bateman XXXB, Brains SA Gold or Holden's Golden Glow.

H istorical pub, approximately 300 years old. One main bar which consists of lounge/diner/bar/snug. Food served 12–2pm and 6–8pm Mon–Thurs; 12–2.30pm and 5.30–8pm Fri; 12–4pm Sat; 12–3pm Sun (roasts only). Children welcome. Beer garden with swings and slide. Car park.

OPEN *12–12.*

The Royal Oak

25 Main Road, Watnall NG16 1HS
☎ *(0115) 938 3110* Linda Wood

Greene King tied house serving Abbot, Old Speckled Hen and Hardys & Hansons Bitter and Olde Trip.

S mall village pub, built around 1890. Upstairs lounge, function room, pool room. No food. Darts and dominoes. Outside seating area at front and rear patio. Winner of Pubs In Bloom competition. Located near M1 J26.

OPEN *12–12.*

WELLOW

The Olde Red Lion

Eakring Road, Wellow, Nr Ollerton NG22 0EG
☎ *(01623) 861000* Michelle Bartle

Freehouse with Charles Wells Bombardier and Olde Lion's Ale from the local Maypole brewery. One guest, changed weekly, might be Caledonian Deuchars IPA, Black Sheep Best, Oakham JHB or Inferno, or a Tom Woods brew.

A 400-year-old country village pub. No music or games. Three bars, restaurant and beer garden front and back. Food available 12–2.30pm and 5–9pm Mon–Sat (lunchtimes and evening menus); 12–4pm Sun (roast dinner menu). Children welcome. Large car park. There is a permanent maypole opposite the pub! Good walks nearby – walking parties welcome. Just off the A617, three miles from Ollerton towards Newark.

OPEN *12–11pm (10.30pm Sun).*

WEST BRIDGFORD

The Southbank Bar

1 Bridgford House, Pavilion Road, Trent Bridge, West Bridgford NG2 5GJ
☎ *(0115) 945 5341* Tom Holodynsky
www.southbankbar.com

Freehouse with Caledonian Deuchars IPA, Fuller's London Pride and ESB, Mallard Duck 'n' Dive and Nottingham Rock Bitter, although the range does change. No 'guests' as such.

O ne of Nottingham's top music venues and sports bar, with eleven high-definition 42-inch plasma screens, two big screens and the ability to show three live sporting events at any time. Live music (free entry) Thurs–Mon. Food served 11am–9pm (from 10am weekends). Heated raised outdoor terrace. Close to Nottingham Forest FC and Trent Bridge cricket ground, 15 minutes' walk from city centre.

OPEN *11am–midnight Mon–Thurs (11pm Tues); 11am–1am Fri; 10am–1am Sat; 10am–midnight Sun.*

WORKSOP

Mallard

Worksop Railway Station, Station Approach, Worksop S81 7AG
☎ *(01909) 530757* Sarah Cadman

No permanent beers here, just two regularly changing guests from micro- and small breweries.

G rade II listed building, part of Worksop Station. Occasional beer festivals are held in the cellar bar. Car park. Sandwiches and snacks available. No children.

OPEN *5–11pm Mon–Thurs; 2–11pm Fri; 12–11pm Sat; 12–4pm Sun (closed Sun evening).*

THE BREWERIES

APPLEFORD BREWERY COMPANY LTD

Iron Bridge House, St Peter's Court, Appleford-on-Thames OX14 4YA
☎ *(01235) 848055*
www.applefordbrewery.co.uk

 RIVER CROSSING 3.6% ABV
POWER STATION 4.2% ABV
Plus seasonals.

THE BRAKSPEAR BREWING COMPANY

Wychwood Brewery, Eagle Maltings, The Crofts, Witney OX28 4DP
☎ *(01993) 890800*
www.brakspear-beers.co.uk

BRAKSPEAR BITTER 3.4% ABV
Bittersweet with fruity finish, amber colour.
BRAKSPEAR SPECIAL 4.3% ABV
Golden red, dry hop, slightly sweet.
Plus a range of seasonal beers.

BURFORD BREWERY

Downs Road, Witney OX28 0SY
☎ *(01993) 703333*

 ALE 4.3% ABV
BEST BITTER 4.3% ABV

BUTLERS BREWERY CO. LTD

The Brewery, Wittles Farm, Mapledurham RG4 7UP
☎ *(0118) 972 3201*
www.butlersbrewery.co.uk

 BOB (BUTLER'S OXFORDSHIRE BITTER) 3.6% ABV
Pale with hop aroma.

CHILTERN VALLEY WINERY AND BREWERY

Old Luxters Vineyard, Hambleden, Henley-on-Thames RG9 6JW
☎ *(01491) 638330*
www.chilternvalley.co.uk/brewery.html

BITTER 4.0% ABV
SPECIAL 4.5% ABV
DARK ROAST 5.0% ABV
GOLD 5.0% ABV
Beers are only available from the brewery.

THE HOOK NORTON BREWERY CO. LTD

Brewery Lane, Hook Norton OX15 5NY
☎ *(01608) 737210 or 730384*
www.hooknortonbrewery.co.uk

HOOKY DARK 3.2% ABV
Chestnut colour, roast malt flavour.
HOOKY BITTER 3.6% ABV
Golden, malty, easy drinker.
HOOKY GOLD 4.1% ABV
Pale and crisp.
OLD HOOKY 4.6% ABV
Fruity balanced beer.
Plus seasonal ales including:
303AD 4.0% ABV
DOUBLE STOUT 4.8% ABV
HAYMAKER 5.0% ABV
FLAGSHIP 5.3% ABV
TWELVE DAYS 5.5% ABV

THE LODDON BREWERY

Dunsden Green Farm, Church Lane, Dunsden RG4 9QD
☎ *(0118) 948 1111*
www.loddonbrewery.co.uk

HOPPIT CLASSIC BITTER 3.5% ABV
Malty body, quite bitter.
DRAGONFLY 4.0% ABV
Refreshing and clean tasting.
HULLABALOO 4.2% ABV
Copper colour, dry, nutty herb flavour.
FERRYMAN'S GOLD 4.4% ABV
Golden and zesty.
BAMBOOZLE 4.8% ABV
Pale, malty body.
Plus seasonal and occasional brews including:
FLIGHT OF FANCY 4.2% ABV
KITE MILD 4.2% ABV
RUSSET 4.5% ABV
HOCUS POCUS 4.6% ABV
FORBURY LION IPA 5.5% ABV

LOVIBONDS BREWERY LTD

Lovibonds, Henley-on-Thames
☎ *07761 543987*
www.lovibonds.com

HENLEY BITTER 3.4% ABV
HENLEY GOLD 4.6% ABV
HENLEY DARK 4.8% ABV

THE OLD BOG BREWERY

Masons Arms, 2 Quarry School Place, Headington OX3 8LH
☎ *(01865) 764579*
www.masonsquarry.co.uk

BEST BITTER 4.0% ABV
QUARRY GOLD 4.1% ABV
QUARRY CRACKER 4.8% ABV
WHEAT BEER 5.1% ABV
QUARRY W-RECKED 5.5% ABV
Plus seasonals and specials.

THE WHITE HORSE BREWERY CO. LTD

3 Ware Road, White Horse Business Park, Stanford-in-the-Vale SN7 8NY
☎ *(01367) 718700*
www.whitehorsebrewery.com

BITTER 3.7% ABV
VILLAGE IDIOT 4.1% ABV
DRAGON HILL 4.2% ABV
FLIBBERTIGIBBERT 4.3% ABV
WAYLAND SMITHY 4.4% ABV
BLACK HORSE PORTER 5.0% ABV
Plus seasonals including:
CHRISTMAS ALE 4.8% ABV

THE WYCHWOOD BREWERY CO. LTD

The Eagle Maltings, The Crofts, Witney OX28 4DP
☎ *(01993) 890800*
www.wychwood.co.uk

GOLIATH ALE 4.2% ABV
FIDDLER'S ELBOW 4.5% ABV
CIRCLE MASTER 4.7% ABV
BLACK WYCH 5.0% ABV
HOBGOBLIN 5.2% ABV
Plus seasonals and specials.

THE PUBS

ABINGDON

The Old Anchor Inn

1 Saint Helen's Wharf, Abingdon OX14 5EN
☎ *(01235) 521726* Linda and Mike Gillen

 Greene King tied house with Morland Original, Abbot Ale and IPA plus seasonal Greene King beers or a guest beer from breweries such as Caledonian may also be available.

Refurbished 18th-century building housing one bar and a snug with a stone floor known as The Cabin. Separate wood-panelled dining room. Street parking. Situated on the Thames, 400 yards from the centre of town beside almshouses built in 1447.

OPEN *12–3pm and 6–11pm Mon–Sat; 12–10.30pm Sun.*

ADDERBURY

The Bell Inn

High Street, Adderbury, Banbury OX17 3LS
☎ *(01295) 810338* John and Trisha Bellinger
www.the-bell.com

A Hook Norton tied house serving four Hook Norton Ales, a selection of 'Cocked Ales' and guest ales occasionally, such as Marston's Pedigree, Adnams Regatta and Brains SA.

An 18th-century Inn located in the heart of a beautiful village close to an historic church, with two letting rooms. Full of character with oak pannelling, beams and inglenook fireplace. No machines, pool table or juke box. Secluded garden. Food available 12–2pm and 7–9pm (except Sun evening). Children, dogs and walkers welcome. Regular folk nights and quiz. Local CAMRA Pub of the Year 2008, Publican Food and Drink Award 'Cask Ale Pub of the Year' finalists 2008, Cask Marque accredited.

OPEN *12–2.30pm and 6–11pm Mon–Thurs; 12–2.30pm and 6pm–12 Fri–Sat; 12–3pm and 7–11pm Sun.*

ASTON

The Flower Pot Hotel

Ferry Lane, Aston, Henley-on-Thames RG9 3DG
☎ *(01491) 574721* AR Read and PM Thatcher

Four real ales, including Brakspear Mild, Bitter and Special, plus guests.

Built around 1890, the Flower Pot retains its Victorian character. Situated in pleasant countryside close to the river and half a mile from Hambledon Lock. Large garden. Food served 12–2pm and 6.30–9pm. Children welcome. Car park.

OPEN *11am–3pm and 6–11pm (6–10.30 Sun).*

BAMPTON

The Morris Clown

High Street, Bampton OX18 2JW
☎ *(01993) 850217* Steven Mace

Freehouse serving Brakspear Bitter and Adnams Bitter plus one rotating guest. Four or five guests each week.

Old coaching inn with one bar and a huge open fire. Proud not to serve food. Families welcome. Beer garden. Bar billiards. Car park. Morris dancing and folk festival May spring bank holiday. Off the A420 between Swindon and Oxford.

OPEN *5pm–close Mon–Fri; 12–11pm Sat–Sun.*

The Romany Inn

Bridge Street, Bampton OX18 2HA
☎ *(01993) 850237* Trevor Johnson

Archers Village plus guest beers from breweries such as Cottage, Hook Norton, Moles, Wells and Young's or Hardys & Hansons.

A 17th-century Grade II listed pub with Saxon arches in the cellar. Bar and restaurant food is available at lunchtimes and evenings. Car park, garden, picnic tables and children's play area. Accommodation. Bampton is situated on the A4095 Witney to Faringdon road. The pub is in the centre of the village.

OPEN *11am–11pm Mon–Sat; 12–10.30pm Sun.*

BANBURY

The Dun Cow

West End, Hornton, Banbury OX15 6DA
☎ *(01295) 670524*
Gwyneth and Martin Gelling

Freehouse serving three or four real ales: Hook Norton Best and Charles Wells Bombardier plus up to two guests.

A 400-year-old traditional thatched pub with original flagstone floors and inglenook fireplace with log fires. Food served 7–9pm Mon–Fri; 12–2.30pm and 7–9pm Sat–Sun. Canine and equine friendly. Beer garden. Car park. Small function room. Two beer festivals each year: Feb and July. North Oxfordshire Cider and Perry Pub of the Year 2007. Medieval banquets a speciality. Opposite a children's playground. Located six miles north-west of Banbury.

OPEN *6–11pm Mon–Fri; 12–11pm Sat; 12–10.30pm Sun.*

Ye Olde Reindeer Inn

47 Parsons St, Banbury OX16 5NA
☎ *(01295) 264031* Tony Puddifoot

Four Hook Norton ales plus a monthly guest.

Located in the town centre, the building dates from 1570 and Oliver Cromwell is said to have held court here during the Civil War. This lovely character pub has two bars, beams and wooden floors, and a courtyard at the back. It is famous for its Globe Room. Food served 11am–2.30pm. In the town centre, with large sign hanging across the street!

OPEN *All day, every day.*

BLOXHAM
The Red Lion Inn
High Street, Bloxham, Banbury OX15 4LX
☎ *(01295) 720352* Neil Wingfield
www.redlionbloxham.co.uk

Fuller's tied house with London Pride, ESB and Discovery always available.

Two-bar local village pub with a large beer garden including stream. Homemade food is served 11am–3pm Mon–Thurs and all day Fri–Sun, and special dietary needs are catered for. Family-oriented, with child-friendly beer garden and play area. Function area available. Large car park. On the Banbury–Chipping Norton road.

OPEN *11am–3pm and 5pm to close Mon–Thurs; 11am to close Fri–Sun.*

BODICOTE
The Plough Inn
Goose Lane, Bodicote, Banbury OX15 4BZ
☎ *(01295) 262327* Peter Eaton

Tied to Wadworth, with Henry's IPA, 6X, JCB, Bishop's Tipple and a seasonal guest on offer.

Village pub with separate bar and lounge/dining room, refurbished and re-opened by Wadworth in March 2006. Early Tudor building, with open fires and beams. Food available 12–2pm and 6.30–9pm Tues–Sat, and 12–2pm Sun. Small enclosed courtyard garden with outside dining available.

OPEN *5.30pm–close Mon; 12–3pm and 5.30pm–close Tues–Fri; 11.30am–close Sat; 12–close Sun.*

BRIGHTWELL-CUM-SOTWELL
The Red Lion
The Street, Brightwell-cum-Sotwell OX10 0RT
☎ *(01491) 837373* Sue Robson

Four real ales, including West Berkshire Good Old Boy and Loddon Hoppit, plus guests from the village's Appleford brewery, Vale and more.

Built in 1540, a thatched freehouse with tables at the front and in the courtyard. One bar, garden and restaurant area. Delicious home-cooked food using locally sourced produce where possible served lunchtimes. Children welcome. Car park. Off the main Wallingford to Didcot road.

OPEN *11am–3pm and 6–11pm Mon–Sat; 12–3pm and 7–10.30pm Sun.*

BROUGHTON
The Saye & Sele Arms
Main Road, Broughton, Nr Banbury OX15 5ED
☎ *(01295) 263348* Danny McGeehan
www.sayeandselearms.co.uk

Adnams Bitter plus three constantly changing guests such as Black Sheep Bitter, Fuller's London Pride and Brakspear Bitter.

Immaculate 16th-century pub with a friendly welcome, a comfortable spot for an excellent meal. The cosy restaurant and bar have beams decked with colourful water jugs and horse brasses. Cask Marque accredited. The emphasis is very much on food, and the extensive menu has something for everyone, including those with dietary needs. Food served 12–2pm and 7–9.30pm Mon–Sat; 12–3pm Sun. Danny's famous wholesome 'proper pies' are always on the menu, and his homemade desserts are not to be missed – especially the bread and butter pudding! Sunday lunches are very popular, and booking is recommended. The garden is an ideal spot for outside dining in summer. Car park. Located three miles from Banbury Cross, handy for visits to Broughton Castle, home of Lord and Lady Saye and Sele.

OPEN *11.30am–2.30pm and 7–11pm Mon–Sat; 12–5pm Sun.*

BURFORD
The Lamb Inn
Sheep Street, Burford OX18 4LR
☎ *(01993) 823155* Andrew Swan
www.cotswold-inns-hotels.co.uk/lamb

Hook Norton Hooky Bitter and Wadworth 6X usually on offer.

A traditional 15th-century Cotswold inn with stone-flagged floor and log fire. Tranquil walled courtyard garden with a profusion of cottage-garden flowers. The restaurant has two rosettes. Food available 12–2.30pm and 6.30–9pm (until 9.30pm Fri–Sat), with cold sandwiches served 12–9pm. Three star accommodation. Descending Burford High Street, take the first turning on the left – the pub is the last building on the right.

OPEN *11am–11pm.*

The Royal Oak
26 Witney Street, Burford OX18 4SN
☎ *(01993) 823278* Gary Duffy

Wadworth tied house with 6X and Henry's IPA plus occasional seasonal Wadworth ales.

Two-bar pub decorated with over 1,000 mugs and jugs hanging in the bars. Food served 12–2pm and 7–9pm daily. Bar billiards. Car park. Beer garden. Accommodation. Convenient for the Cotswold Wildlife Park. Just off the main high street in Burford.

OPEN *11am–3pm and 7–11pm Sun–Fri (closed Tues lunch); 11am–11pm Sat.*

CAULCOTT

Horse and Groom

Lower Heyford Road, Caulcott, Nr Bicester
OX25 4ND
☎ *(01869) 343257*
Jerome Prigent and Anne Gallacher

Freehouse with Hook Norton plus three constantly rotating guest ales.

A 16th-century thatched pub with old-fashioned décor including old beams, brasses and settees. One bar and one small dining room. Full of character and friendly locals. Freshly prepared food served 12–2pm and 7–9pm Mon–Sat, 12–2pm Sun. Beer garden. Ample parking in layby opposite pub. Occasional beer festivals. Children over age of 10 allowed in garden and dining room. Dogs allowed in garden. Near Blenheim Palace and Bicester shopping centre. From Bicester, head towards Middleton Stoney, go over the crossroads and continue for two miles; the pub is on the left.

OPEN *12–3pm and 6–11pm Mon–Sat; 12–3pm and 7–10.30pm Sun.*

CHADLINGTON

The Tite Inn

Mill End, Chadlington, Chipping Norton
OX7 3NY
☎ *(01608) 676475*
www.titeinn.com

Six real ales always on offer. Sharp's Doom Bar and Rasmbury Bitter plus four guest beers, changed weekly. A draught cider and a draught perry are also on offer.

A 16th-century Cotswold stone pub with superb views, named CAMRA North Oxfordshire Pub of the Year 2005. Bar and restaurant food available 12–2.30pm and 7–9pm. Car park, garden and garden room. Children welcome. Chadlington is just over two miles south of Chipping Norton off the A361.

OPEN *Closed Mon (except bank holidays); 12–2.30pm and 6.30–11pm (10.30pm Sun).*

CHARLBURY

Ye Olde Three Horseshoes Inn

Sheep Street, Charlebury OX7 3RR
☎ *(01608) 810780* Barry Dodman-Edwards

The home of the Charlbury Brewing Company with one own brew: Wizard Ale always available, plus two others in winter, five others in summer. Range of beers changes weekly.

A 17th-century stone-built pub with exposed joists and rafters and inglenook fireplaces. Food served during the summer months. Children welcome. Beer garden. Convenient for Woodstock, Blenheim Palace and Oxford.

OPEN *7–11.30pm Mon–Thurs; 5pm–close Fri; 12–close Sat–Sun. (Licensed until 2.30am.)*

The Rose & Crown

Market Street, Charlbury, Chipping Norton
OX7 3PL
☎ *(01608) 810103* Tom Page

Young's PA plus six guest beers (400 per year), changed every two or three days.

Popular two-bar Victorian pub with courtyard, located in the town centre. No food. Beer garden. Children and walkers welcome. Close to the Oxfordshire Way.

OPEN *12–12 Sun–Thur; noon–1am Fri; 11am–1am Sat.*

CHECKENDON

The Black Horse

Checkendon, Reading RG8 0TE
☎ *(01491) 680418* M and MA Morgan

Freehouse always offering ales from West Berkshire and Butler's. Beers served straight from the barrel.

Country pub, approximately 350 years old and run by the same family for over 100 years. Three rooms. Beer garden. Baguettes available at lunchtimes only. Well-behaved children welcome. Car park.

OPEN *12–2pm and 7–11pm.*

CHILDREY

The Hatchet

High Street, Childrey, Nr Wantage OX12 9UF
☎ *(01235) 751213* Ian James Shaw

Five real ales, from breweries such as Skinner's, St Austell, Woodforde's, Harviestoun, White Horse and Ramsbury.

Welcoming one-bar, beamed village pub. Food served 12–2pm daily. Car park. Garden play area for children. On the B4507 out of Wantage.

OPEN *12–2.30pm and 7–11pm (10.30pm Sun).*

CHINNOR

The Gardeners Arms

3 High Street, Chinnor OX39 4DL
☎ *(01844) 353468* Ian Whayman

Enterprise Inns pub with four real ales. Greene King IPA, Loddon Ferryman's Gold, Hook Norton Old Hooky plus a guest such as Theakston XB or a seasonal ale from Tring, Cottage, Loddon, Hook Norton or another SIBA brewery.

A pub in a 400-year-old building featuring low ceilings, large inglenook fireplace with comfy seating area, real fire. Two bars, one with TV and dart board. Food served 12–2pm and 7–9pm (except Sun evenings). Beer garden and large decked area. Children's play area. Car park. Take J6 of the M40 for three miles on the B4009 towards Princes Risborough.

OPEN *12–2pm and 5–11pm Mon–Fri (midnight Fri); all day Sat–Sun.*

CHIPPING NORTON

The Bell Inn

56 West Street, Chipping Norton OX7 5ER
☎ *(01608) 642521* Jan Blackburn

Greene King IPA usually available, plus a guest ale.

Community local in an old stone building, with beams and a wooden floor. Two bars (sports bar and lounge), pool, darts. Food available daily from a limited menu. Children allowed in the garden only. Car park. On the road from Churchill to Bledington. Accommodation available.

OPEN *10.30am–11pm Mon–Sat; 12–10.30pm Sun.*

Stones

Market Place, Chipping Norton OX7 5NH
☎ *(01608) 644466* Brian Galbraith

Freehouse with Greene King IPA plus guest beers from breweries such as Arkells, Archers and Wizard.

Town pub in a listed stone building, with modern interior and traditional values! Annual beer festival (phone for details). Food is available, plus a good selection of coffees. The pub's terrace overlooks the market place. Car parking available. Children allowed.

OPEN *10am–midnight Mon–Thurs; 10am–2am Fri–Sat; 10am–11.30pm Sun.*

CLIFTON

The Duke of Cumberland's Head

Clifton OX15 0PE
☎ *(01869) 338534* Marcus Bond

Hook Norton Hooky Bitter plus four or five guest ales from breweries such as Adnams, Caledonian, Black Sheep or Jennings.

Built in the late 1600s, this thatched Oxfordshire village pub serves bar and restaurant food. Car park, attractive gardens, accommodation. Children allowed.

OPEN *12–2.30pm (not Mon) and 6.30– 10.30pm (11pm Fri–Sat).*

COWLEY

The Original Swan

Oxford Road, Cowley OX4 2LF
☎ *(01865) 778888*
Don Critten and Audrey Bryant

Tied to Arkells, with 3B and Kingsdown always on offer.

Community pub in a building dating from 1902, with two bars, function room and patio. Food available 12–2pm. Discos and occasional live music. B&B. Outdoor seating. Car park. Two and a half miles from Oxford town centre.

OPEN *12–11pm Sun–Wed; 12–12 Thurs–Sat.*

CROWELL

The Shepherd's Crook

The Green, Crowell, Chinnor OX9 4RR
☎ *(01844) 351431* Mr Scowen

Hook Norton Hooky Bitter, Batham Best, Timothy Taylor Landlord and a seasonal ale from Loddon usually available, plus one other guest ale.

A quiet, one-bar country pub, no music or games. Beer garden. Food served 12– 2.30pm and 7–9.30pm. Fish is a speciality. Bookings taken. Children allowed.

OPEN *11.30am–3pm and 5–11pm Mon–Fri; 11am–11pm Sat; 12–10pm Sun.*

EAST HENDRED

The Eyston Arms

High Street, East Hendred, Wantage OX12 8JY
☎ *(01235) 833320*
George Dailey and Daisy Barton
www.eystonarms.co.uk

Genuine freehouse serving Wadworth 6X and Adnams Bitter.

Traditional, beamed village pub, part of which dates from the 17th century. Log fire in winter. Outside terraces at front and back, car park. Good English food with lots of fresh fish available 12–2.30pm and 6.30– 10pm. Children welcome until 7pm. Just off the A417 between Wantage and Rowstock.

OPEN *11am–close.*

EYNSHAM

The Talbot Inn

Oxford Road, Eynsham OX21 4BT
☎ *(01865) 881348* Trevor Johnson

Arkells pub with 2B and 3B plus one seasonal Arkells ale such as Moonlight.

Family-run country pub in an 18th-century Cotswold stone building, with one bar and a dining area. Bar food and an à la carte menu available 12–2pm and 6–9pm, with the emphasis on fresh local produce and fish. Lawn area with seating, plus outdoor decking over the river. Ten letting rooms. Children welcome. Car park. Five miles from Oxford, 250 yards from the Thames.

OPEN *All day, every day.*

FARINGDON
The Bell

Market Place, Faringdon SN7 7HP
☎ *(01367) 240534*
www.bellhotelfaringdon.com

Wadworth 6X and Henrys IPA plus a seasonal Wadworth ale such as Bishop's Tipple.

A 17th-century coaching inn with many original features, a unique mural in the bar, log fires in winter and a welcoming atmosphere. Food served lunchtimes and evenings Mon–Sat and all day Sun. Eight en-suite bedrooms, car park, courtyard, beer garden. Room/restaurant for hire. Children welcome. Handy for local racecourses and Cotswolds attractions. In the market place in the centre of Faringdon, on the A420.

OPEN *11am–close Mon–Sat; 12–close Sun.*

FERNHAM
The Woodman Inn and Restaurant

Fernham, Nr Faringdon SN7 7NX
☎ *(01367) 820643* Steven Whiting
www.thewoodmaninn.net

Freehouse serving a range of six guest real ales, all served from the cask. Regular features include White Horse Bitter, Village Idiot and Wayland Smithy, Greene King IPA and Abbot, Wadworth 6X, Wychwood Hobgoblin, and ales from Brakspear, Timothy Taylor, Hop Back, Moles and Butts.

A 17th-century pub in the Vale of the White Horse. Open log fire, low-beamed ceilings, medieval banqueting hall, lots of character. Food served 12–2pm and 6.30–9pm. Children welcome. Beer garden at front and rear. Car park. Function room. Annual beer festival in September. Off the A420.

OPEN *All day, every day.*

FEWCOTT
The White Lion

Fritwell Road, Fewcott, Nr Bicester OX27 7NZ
☎ *(01869) 346639* Paul and Carol King

Genuine freehouse with four weekly-rotating real ales sourced from all over the country.

Cotswold stone, country village community pub dating from 1749. Large beer garden. No food (only bar snacks). Car park. Children welcome. Sky television, pool room. Letting room available, ensuite with kitchenette. M40 junction 10.

OPEN *7pm–close Mon–Thurs; 5.30pm–close Fri; noon–close Sat; 12–6.30pm Sun.*

FIFIELD
Merrymouth Inn

Stow Road, Fifield OX7 6HR
☎ *(01993) 831652* William Prince
www.merrymouthinn.co.uk

Freehouse with three rotating real ales from Hook Norton, West Yorkshire and Loddon.

An old-style, 13th-century, one-bar inn and restaurant with garden. Accommodation in nine letting rooms. Food available 12–2.30pm and 6–9.30pm. Large car park. Children welcome. On the A424 between Burford and Stow-on-the-Wold.

OPEN *11am–3pm and 6–11pm Mon–Sat; 12–3pm and 7–10.30pm Sun.*

FRITWELL
The Kings Head

92 East Street, Fritwell, Bicester OX27 7QF
☎ *(01869) 346738* Gregor Stevenson
www.thekingsheadfritwell.co.uk

Enterprise Inns pub serving Hook Norton Hooky Bitter plus three guests, all served by gravity.

Set in a village location and dating from the 17th century, and first licensed in 1800. One bar, separate dining room. Food served Tues–Sat lunchtimes and evenings and Sun lunchtime. Children welcome. Beer garden. Car park. Annual bottled beer festival. Situated close to M40 J10, 15 minutes from Silverstone, 10 minutes from Bicester shopping village.

OPEN *3–11pm Mon; 12–12 Tues–Sat; 12–9pm Sun.*

FYFIELD
The White Hart

Main Road, Fyfield, Abingdon OX13 5LW
☎ *(01865) 390585* Kay and Mark Chandler
www.whitehart-fyfield.com

Freehouse with up to five real ales. Ales change when a barrel finishes and might include Hook Norton Hooky Bitter, Loddon Hullabaloo, Sharps Doombar, White Horse Village Idiot and a variety of beers from other independent breweries, both local and from further afield.

Unique and historic 15th-century former Chantry House built in 1442 to house priests and almsmen. Great hall with flagstone floors and 30-foot beamed ceiling, minstrels' gallery and several charming side rooms. Cosy bar with large inglenook fireplace and low beamed ceiling. Food served 12–2.30pm and 6–9.30pm Tues–Sat and 12–4pm Sun, with the emphasis on seasonal local produce, freshly cooked. Everything is homemade – even the bread and pasta! Large patio terrace and lawned beer garden. Large car park. Annual beer festivals at May Day and August bank holidays, with more than 12 real ales, jazz and hog roasts. Plenty of local attractions, including Millets Farm Centre, Ashmolean Museum, Oxford and the Cotswolds. Fyfield is just off the A420 Oxford to Swindon road, about seven miles south of Oxford.

OPEN *12–3pm and 5.30–11pm Tues–Fri; 12–11pm Sat; 12–10.30pm Sun.*

GREAT TEW

The Falkland Arms

Great Tew, Nr Chipping Norton OX7 4DB
☎ *(01608) 683653* Paula and James Meredith
www.falklandarms.org.uk

 Up to seven beers available from hand pumps at any one time from a range of about 350 per year. Owned by Wadworth, so Henry's IPA, 6X and JCB all favoured. Guests come from smaller brewers and some regionals, and are changed whenever the barrel runs out (sometimes within hours!). Also a selection of country wines and draught cider.

A 16th-century Oxfordshire village inn with a vast inglenook fireplace, smooth flagstone floor, high-backed settles, oak beams and panelling and sparkling brasses. Bar food served 12–2pm daily. Evening food served in a small dining room 7–8pm Mon–Sat, booking essential. Beer garden to the rear of the pub with picturesque view over the Great Tew Estate. Live folk music every Sunday evening. Five double en-suite rooms (two with four poster bed). Clay pipes and snuff for sale, in keeping with the picture of a traditional English country inn. Beer festival first weekend in July. Off the A361, between Banbury and Chipping Norton.

 11.30am–2.30pm and 6–11pm Mon–Fri; 11.30am–3pm and 6–11pm Sat; 12–3pm and 7–10.30pm Sun. Open all day Sat–Sun in summer.

GROVE

The Volunteer Inn

Station Road, Grove OX12 0DH
☎ *(01235) 769557* Kevin and Carol Nichol

Hook Norton tied house serving Old Hooky, Hooky Bitter, Hooky Gold and Hooky Dark 303 plus seasonals and specials. A traditional local pub. No food. Beer garden. Car park.

11am–midnight.

HENLEY-ON-THAMES

Bird in Hand

61 Greys Road, Henley-on-Thames RG9 1SB
☎ *(01491) 575775* Graham Steward

Freehouse with Hook Norton Mild, Brakspear Bitter and Fuller's London Pride plus guests on two hand pumps, for example beers from Butts, Vale and Cottage breweries.

Old-fashioned one-bar pub. No music, fruit machines or pool table, not even a till! Large garden. Food served at lunchtimes only.

11.30am–2.30pm and 5–11pm Mon–Fri; 11am–11pm Sat; 12–10.30pm Sun.

The Horse & Groom

40 New Street, Henley-on-Thames RG9 2BT
☎ *(01491) 575719* Peter and Linda Powell

Greene King house serving IPA and Abbot plus one guest.

A 200-year-old, traditional, family-run pub in the town centre, close to the river. Three bars and large, award-winning garden.

Homemade food served daily 12–9pm. Accommodation, beer garden, Sky Sports, children welcome. Close to the town centre, 500 metres from the River Thames. The landlords are enthusiastic supporters of Wasps rugby club.

 11.30am–11.30pm Mon–Thurs; 11.30am–midnight Fri–Sat; 12–10.30pm Sun.

HIGHMOOR

The Dog & Duck

Highmoor, Nettlebed, Henley-on-Thames RG9 5DL
☎ *(01491) 641261* John Donohue

Brakspear tenancy with Brakspear Bitter and Oxford Gold plus two monthly guests such as Wychwood Hobgoblin or Owzat, or Brakspear Hooray Henley.

Traditional 17th-century country pub with friendly atmosphere, welcoming to strangers and regulars alike. Excellent homemade food and puddings served 12–2pm and 6.30–9pm. Traditional and non-traditional pub games available on every table, with musical instruments for use by people who can play. Live bands Friday nights. Large car park, beer garden. Plans to hold festivals in summer. Children welcome. Between Sonning Common and Nettlebed.

11.30am–3pm and 6–11pm.

HOOK NORTON

Pear Tree Inn

Scotland End, Hook Norton OX15 5NU
☎ *(01608) 737482* Ian Miller

The brewery tap for Hook Norton, so five beers from the brewery always on offer, including a seasonal ale changed every two months.

An 18th-century inn at the end of the brewery lane, with one large room, open fires and friendly service. Attracts mainly local trade, but is also a haven for Hooky fans and brewery visitors. Food served 12–2.15pm and 6.30–9.15pm Mon–Sat and 12–2.30pm Sun. Children welcome. Large garden with play area. Accommodation. Large beer festival in July.

 11.30am–1.30am Mon–Sat; 12–12 Sun.

MIDDLETON CHENEY

The New Inn

45 Main Road, Middleton Cheney, Banbury OX17 2ND
☎ *(01295) 710399* Paul and Trish Randell

Punch Taverns pub with Fuller's London Pride, Adnams Broadside and a Hook Norton ale plus two weekly-changing guests.

A 17th-century coaching inn in a village location. Homemade food served every lunchtimes and evening, except Sun evening. Live music Fri. Annual beer festival. Beer garden with children's play area, families and dogs welcome. Car park. Function room. Located two miles east of Banbury, off the A422.

 12–3pm and 5pm–close Mon–Thurs; 12–3pm and 5pm–1am Fri; noon–1am Sat; 12–12 Sun.

MINSTER LOVELL

Mill & Old Swan

Minster Lovell, Witney OX29 0RN
☎ *(01993) 774441*
Amy Gorden and Marrianne Long

Three Hook Norton beers, including Hooky Bitter, Old Hooky, and a seasonal beer, which changes monthly.

Traditional stone-built pub situated in the picturesque Windrush valley. Several drinking areas and a restaurant divide up this 600-year-old pub with flagstone floors, exposed beams and log fires in winter.

OPEN *11am–11pm Mon–Sat; 12–10.30pm Sun.*

MURCOTT

The Nut Tree Inn

Murcott, Kidlington OX5 2RE
☎ *(01865) 331253* Mike and Imogen North

Hook Norton Hooky Bitter is among the three real ales usually available, with beers such as Oxfordshire Marshmellow and Bateman XB also served. Two of the three are changed every couple of weeks.

Picturesque 14th-century thatched pub opposite the village pond, featuring low beams and wood-burning stoves. Noted for its good traditional food, served 12–2.30pm and 6.30–9pm Tues–Sat and 12–2.30pm Sun. Beer garden, large car park. Aunt Sally on Wednesdays. Children welcome. The pub has its own pigs! Private parties up to 24 people can be catered for. Fifteen minutes from junction 9 of the M40 and A34.

OPEN *12–2.30pm and 6.30–11pm Tues–Sat; 12–4pm Sun.*

NORTH LEIGH

The Woodman Inn

New Yatt Road, North Leigh, Witney OX29 6TT
☎ *(01993) 881790* John and Leanda Birch

Wadworth 6X and either Brakspear Bitter or Hook Norton Hook Bitter plus one or two weekly guest beers from breweries such as Wells and Young's, Everards, Exmoor, St Austell or local micro-breweries.

Community pub in good walking and cycling countryside. Food served 12–2pm and 6–9pm Mon–Sat, and 12–4pm Sun. The West Oxfordshire beer festival takes place here twice a year, at Easter and August bank holiday. Large garden. Families and dogs welcome. Aunty Sally and traditional pub games, plus regular events. Look out for the well in the pub! Located off the A4095 Witney to Woodstock road.

OPEN *12–11pm.*

NORTH MORETON

Bear at Home

High Street, North Moreton OX11 9AT
☎ *(01235) 811311* Tim Haworth
www.bear-at-home.co.uk

Freehouse serving Timothy Taylor Landlord and its own 'Bear Beer' plus two guests such as Loddon Hoppit or White Horse Bitter.

A 500-year-old country pub, full of character, in an attractive English village location, overlooking a cricket pitch. Food

served 12–2.30pm and 6–9pm. Children and dogs welcome. Pub games such as darts and boules and Aunt Sally. Function room. Beer garden. Car park.

OPEN *12–3pm and 6–11pm (extended opening Fri–Sat).*

OXFORD

The Eagle Tavern

28 Magdalen Road, Oxford OX4 1RB
☎ *(01865) 204842* Mr and Mrs Tom Quinn

Arkells 2B and 3B are the permanent beers at this Arkells house.

Refurbished pub in an old building on the outskirts of town, with one bar and garden. Bar snacks available. Occasional live music. Children allowed if kept under control.

OPEN *11.30am–3pm and 7–11pm (10.30pm Sun).*

Folly Bridge Inn

38 Abingdon Road, Oxford OX1 4PD
☎ *(01865) 790106* Roger and Margaret Carter

Wadworth house serving Bishop's Tipple, 6X, IPA and seasonal guest beers.

Traditional English pub by the river on the edge of the city centre. Disabled access, outside patio, darts, TV and games. Food served 11am–3pm and 6–9pm Mon–Sat, 12–3pm Sun. Children allowed.

OPEN *11am–midnight Mon–Sat; 12–12 Sun.*

The Gardeners Arms

39 Plantation Road, Oxford OX2 6JE
☎ *(01865) 559814* Paul Silcock

Tied to Marston's, with Jennings Bitter among the four real ales, with the three guests changed monthly. Examples include Jennings 1828, Adnams Broadside and Camerons Castle Eden Ale.

A 200-year-old pub with a function room and turfed beer garden. The menu is 100% vegetarian, and food is available 5–9pm Mon–Tues; 12–2.30pm and 5–9pm Wed–Sat; 12–6pm Sun. Children welcome. Quiz on Sunday nights. Off the Woodstock road.

OPEN *5pm–12 Mon–Tues; 12–2.30pm and 5pm–12 Wed–Sat; 12–11pm Sun.*

Kings Arms

40 Holywell Street, Oxford OX1 3SP
☎ *(01865) 242369* Ali Dunn
www.youngs.com

Wells and Young's tied house, serving the brewery's ales plus a range of guests.

Large, imposing city-centre pub with five contrasting rooms, standing on the site of an Augustinian friars' religious house. Food served 11.30am–9.30pm. Children welcome. Outside area. Private room available. Situated opposite the Bodleian Library.

OPEN *10.30am–midnight.*

The Lamb & Flag

12 St Giles, Oxford OX1 3JS
☎ *(01865) 515787* Noel Quigley

Freehouse with seven real ales: Palmers Lamb & Flag and IPA, Skinner's Betty

Stogs, Shepherd Neame Spitfire and Theakston Old Peculier, and two rotating guests from breweries such as Cottage, Vale, Eccleshall, Sharp's, Three Castles, White Horse, Burford and many more.

Student pub dating from 1615 with two bars. Food served 12–3pm (children allowed during these times). No TV, no games machines, no music – this is a pub for conversation. Situated in the city centre, off the A40.

 11am–11pm.

The Masons Arms

2 Quarry School Place, Headington, Oxford OX3 8LH
☎ *(01865) 764579* C Meeson
www.masonsquarry.co.uk

 Five real ales. Hook Norton Old Hooky, Brakspear Oxford Gold, West Berkshire Good Old Boy and an Old Bog beer (brewed on the premises), plus a guest changed four times a week. Guests come from small and large breweries across the country.

Local freehouse with one bar, the home of Oxford's oldest brewery (Old Bog). Large garden with decking area, function room for 120 people. No food. Headington beer festival held here every September. Quiz night every Saturday. Car park.

 5–11pm Mon–Fri; 11am–11pm Sat; 12–4pm and 7–10.30pm Sun.

Turf Tavern

4 Bath Place, Oxford OX1 3SU
☎ *(01865) 243235*
Edwina Dear – interim manager
www.theturftavern.co.uk

 Eleven pumps serve a range of real ales, including Greene King beers and guests changed daily.

One of the oldest pubs in Oxford, this is a country-style pub in the city centre. Two bars plus outside alehouse. Three patios kept warm in winter by coal-fired braziers. Traditional food available 12–7.30pm. Children allowed.

 11am–11pm Mon–Sat; 12–10.30pm Sun.

The White Horse

52 Broad Street, Oxford OX1 3BB
☎ *(01865) 204801*
Des and Jacqueline Paphitis, Fellow MBII
www.whitehorseoxford.co.uk

 Leased from M&B, with four to six real ales including White Horse Wayland Smithy, Brakspear Oxford Gold, Timothy Taylor Landlord and St Austell Tribute. Wychwood Hobgoblin is one of the two regular guests, and the other varies.

Step back in time with this small, cosy, one-bar pub with friendly staff, frequented by a wide range of customers. Good food served 11.30am–9pm every day. No music, bright lights or machines.

 11am–midnight every day.

The Crown Hill

Pishill, Henley-on-Thames RG9 6HH
☎ *(01491) 638364* Jeremy Cafon
www.crownpishill.co.uk

 Brakspear Bitter plus one or two guests, changed every week or two, such as Scattor Rock Teign Valley Tipple or beers from West Berkshire or Marlow.

A 15th-century freehouse with three log fires, two bars, beer garden, dining room and function room. Food served 12–2.30pm and 7–9.30pm Mon–Sat; 12–3pm and 7–9pm Sun. Large car park. Cottage for B&B. One mile from the historic country house of Stonor Park. On the B480 between Henley-on-Thames and Watlington.

 11.30am–2.30pm and 6–11pm Mon–Sat; 12–3pm and 7–10.30pm Sun.

The Royal Oak

High Street, Ramsden OX7 3AU
☎ *(01993) 868213* Jon Oldham

 Three real ales, and all rotate weekly. Beers from Hook Norton, Wye Valley, Wells and Young's, Butts and White Horse are regular features.

A 17th-century former coaching inn situated in a small, charming Cotswold village. One bar with log fires plus separate restaurant. English and French cuisine served 12–2pm and 7–10.30pm. Car park and sunny patio. Four double bedrooms in separate cottages. On the B4022, three miles north of Witney.

 11.30am–3pm and 6.30–11pm Mon–Sat; 12–3pm and 7–10.30pm Sun.

The Rose & Crown

Featherbow Lane, Ratley, Banbury OX15 6DS
☎ *(01295) 678148* Mary and Laura Houguez

 Freehouse usually offering Charles Wells Eagle IPA and Bombardier and three other beers such as Greene King Old Speckled Hen and Abbot Ale, plus a beer from another independent brewery.

Small, traditional pub, reputedly dating from 1098. Food served 12–2pm and 7–9.30pm (not Sun or Mon evening). Children are welcome, but no special facilities. The pub is on the MacMillan Way, so walkers are also welcome. Bed and breakfast available (two rooms). Car park. Ratley is a small, picturesque village off the A422 Stratford Road, and the pub is at the far end of the village.

 12–2.30pm (not Mon) and 7–11pm (6.30–11pm Fri–Sat); 12–3pm and 7–10.30pm Sun.

The Shaven Crown

High Street, Shipton-Under-Wychwood OX7 6BA
☎ *(01993) 830330* Philip Mehrtens
www.theshavencrown.co.uk

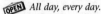 Freehouse serving Hooky Bitter plus two weekly-changing guests from breweries such as Wychwood, Archers, Cottage and Arkells.

This 700-year-old inn is one of the ten oldest in England. One bar and one restaurant with lots of outdoor space. Food served 12–2pm and 6–9.30pm Mon–Fri, 12–9.30pm Sat, 12–9pm Sun. Eight rooms for B&B. Beer garden. Car parking for 15 cars. Private room for hire. Located on the A361 between Burford and Chipping Norton.

OPEN *All day, every day.*

SHRIVENHAM

The Prince of Wales

High Street, Shrivenham SN6 8AF
☎ *(01793) 782268* Jane and Mike Binyon
www.powshrivenham.co.uk

 Wadworth tied house serving four Wadworth ales plus a monthly-changing guest from another independent brewery. Ales served straight from the cask.

Country village pub dating from the 17th century, with low ceilings, log fires, oak beams and no horsebrasses! Homemade food served 12–2.30pm and 6.30–9pm every day except Sun evening. Beer garden with BBQ. Car park. Private room for hire. Wi-Fi hotspot. Annual beer festival May spring bank holiday. Weekly quiz night. BBQs every bank holiday Mon lunchtime. Regular live music, trips to beer festivals and brewery tours. Located off the A420.

OPEN *12–3pm and 6–11pm (closed Sun evening).*

SHUTFORD

The George & Dragon

Church Lane, Shutford, Banbury OX15 6PG
☎ *(01295) 780320* Paul Stanley
www.thegeorgeandragon.com

 Freehouse with three constantly changing real ales, including beers from Hook Norton, Adnams and many other breweries.

Grade II listed country pub with open fire in winter, beer garden in summer. Food available in an informal restaurant 6.30–9pm Tues–Sat and 12–2.30pm Sun. To find Shutford, take the Shipston on Stour road from Banbury.

OPEN *12–2.30pm and 6–11pm Mon–Sat; 12–10.30pm Sun (closed Mondays except bank holidays).*

SKIRMETT

The Frog

Skirmett RG9 6TG
☎ *(01491) 638996*
Jim Crowe and Noelle Greene
www.thefrogatskirmett.co.uk

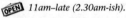 Freehouse serving Rebellion IPA and Adnams Bitter plus a guest such as Sharp's Doom Bar.

A 350-year-old brick and flint pub situated in the Hambledon Valley, popular with walkers. Food served 12–2.30pm and 6.30–9.30pm. Children welcome. Beer garden. Accommodation. Car park. Function room.

OPEN *11am–3pm and 6–11pm.*

SOUTH HINKSEY

The General Elliot

Manor Road, South Hinksey, Oxford OX1 5AS
☎ *(01865) 739369* John Wescendorp
www.generalelliot.co.uk

Four real ales always available. All guest ales, and could be from any micro-brewery. CAMRA Pub of the Year 2007.

Approximately 200 years old, in a pretty, country village a 20-minute walk from Oxford city centre. Food served 11am–8.30pm Mon–Sat; 11am–6.30pm Sun. Dogs and children welcome. Large beer garden with children's play frame. Large car park. Regular beer and music festivals. Located off the A34.

OPEN *11am–late (2.30am-ish).*

SOUTH MORETON

The Crown Inn

High Street, South Moreton, Didcot OX11 9AG
☎ *(01235) 812262* Simon and Veronica Dallas
www.crown-southmoreton.co.uk

 Wadworth pub with IPA, 6X and a guest from another brewery, changed weekly.

Traditional country village pub, Victorian with extended restaurant areas. Bar and restaurant food available 12–2.15pm and 6.30–9pm. Two car parks, two beer gardens, separate dining area for private bookings (seats 30). Excellent quiz night every Monday at 8pm sharp! Children welcome. The village is signposted from both Didcot and Wallingford.

OPEN *12–3pm and 6–11pm Mon–Sat (midnight Fri–Sat); 12–3pm and 7–10.30pm Sun.*

SPARSHOLT

The Star Inn

Watery Lane, Sparsholt, Wantage OX12 9PL
☎ *(01235) 751539*
Lee Morgen and Carena Lewis

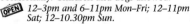 Punch Taverns pub selling up to four ales from breweries such as Adnams, Timothy Taylor, Wells and Young's and Black Sheep.

A 400-year-old country inn with beams and fireplaces. Food is available, and there is a 30-seater dining room. Eight en-suite letting rooms, converted barn, live music occasionally. Children and dogs allowed.

OPEN *12–3pm and 6–11pm Mon–Fri; 12–11pm Sat; 12–10.30pm Sun.*

STOKE LYNE

The Peyton Arms

Stoke Lyne, Bicester OX27 8SD
☎ *(01869) 345285*
Mick and Jean Weston

Hook Norton pub with Mild, Hooky Bitter and Old Hooky usually available.

Friendly, unspoilt pub situated in a small village. Two bars and a games room. All beers are gravity dispensed. Large garden. Rolls and pies available Fri, Sat and Sun lunchtimes only. Traditional games such as shove ha'penny, Aunt Sally, puzzles and pool. Car park. Children and dogs welcome.

OPEN *12–3pm and 6–11pm (5–11pm Fri); 12–11pm Sat; 12–10.30pm Sun.*

SWACLIFFE

The Stag's Head

The Green, Swacliffe OX15 5EJ
☎ *(01295) 780232* Steve Kingsford

Adnams Bitter plus two weekly-changing guests.

Unspoilt 500-year-old thatched village pub. No fruit machines. Food served 12–2pm and 7–9pm Tues–Sat; 12–3pm Sun. Children and dogs welcome. Terraced gardens. One accommodation room. Near Broughton Castle, in beautiful walking and cycling country. On the B4035.

OPEN *Closed Mon; 12–2.30pm and 6–11pm Tues–Sat; 12–4pm Sun.*

THAME

The Abingdon Arms

21 Cornmarket, Thame OX9 2BL
☎ *(01844) 260332* W Bonner

Wadworth 6X, Hook Norton Hooky Bitter and Fuller's London Pride plus two guest beers which may include Vale Wychert Ale or Notley Ale, Hampshire Lionheart or Fuller's ESB.

A 16th-century coaching inn which was extensively rebuilt after a fire in 1991, with log fires and Sky TV in separate area. Food served lunchtimes and evenings Mon–Fri and all day Sat–Sun. Children welcome, with nappy-changing facilities and high chairs provided, plus play equipment and sand pit. Car park.

OPEN *11am–11pm (10.30pm Sun).*

The Falcon

1 Thame Park Road, Thame OX9 3JA
☎ *(01844) 212118*
Christine Harris and Paula Dimmock
www.hook-norton.co.uk

A Hook Norton tied house serving Hooky Bitter plus a seasonal Hook Norton ale. One guest each month, such as St Austell Tribute, Greene King Abbot or Ruddles Ale.

Family-friendly local. Food served 12–2pm Mon–Fri; 6–9pm Tues, Thurs, Fri; 12–3pm Sun (roasts). Outside seating area. Situated on the B4012 on the south side of Thame.

OPEN *12–11pm (10.30pm Sun).*

The Swan Hotel

9 Upper High Street, Thame OX9 3ER
☎ *(01844) 261211* Jamie and Haydn Foskett
www.swanhotelthame.com

Fuller's London Pride and Hook Norton Hooky Bitter plus two guest beers, changed every week or two.

A 16th-century coaching inn situated in the heart of Thame and retaining many original features. Medieval restaurant with original Tudor painted ceiling, oak-beamed bar, log fire, comfortable Chesterfields and seven en-suite bedrooms. Food served in the Thai restaurant 12–3pm and 6–10.30pm Mon–Sat, plus traditional roast dinner 12–4pm Sun. Large, free public car park close by. Families welcome. Party bookings for restaurant are a speciality.

OPEN *11am–11pm Mon–Wed; 11am–midnight Thurs; 11am–1am Fri–Sat; 12–11pm Sun.*

WANTAGE

The Royal Oak Inn

Newbury Street, Wantage OX12 8DF
☎ *(01235) 763129* Paul Hexter

Principal outlet for real ales from the West Berkshire Brewery, including Dr Hexter's Wedding Ale, Healer or Maggs Mild, and Wadworth 6X always available, plus up to six guest ales from independent breweries.

Fair deals and no frills at this genuine freehouse. Navy paraphernalia decorates the bar. All beers served straight from the cask. No food.

OPEN *5.30–11pm Mon–Fri; 12–2.30pm and 7–11pm Sat; 12–2pm and 7–10.30pm Sun.*

WEST HANNEY

The Lamb Inn

West Hanney OX12 0LA
☎ *(01235) 868917* Ryan Mullins

Freehouse with Wadworth 6X plus two guests from independent breweries.

A traditional freehouse with one bar, split into two, children's play area and garden. No juke box, but live music once a week. Annual beer festival on August bank holiday. Food served at lunchtimes and evenings. Children allowed in the back room and garden.

OPEN *11am–11pm (3–11pm Mon); 12–10.30pm Sun.*

WITNEY

House of Windsor

31 West End, Witney OX28 1NQ
☎ *(01993) 704277* Terry McHugh

St Austell Tinners plus guests from breweries such as Vale, Rebellion, Burford and Hook Norton.

No machines, no pool or darts in this friendly pub. Coal fire in winter. Large beer garden. Children allowed. Off the A40 and straight across two mini-roundabouts.

OPEN *6–11pm Mon–Thurs; 6pm–midnight Fri; 12–3pm and 6pm–midnight Sat; 12–10.30pm Sun.*

The New Inn

111 Corn Street, Witney OX28 6AU
☎ *(01993) 703807* Martin Cornish

 A Punch Taverns pub serving six or seven real ales, including brews from Brakspear, Black Sheep, Jennings, Timothy Taylor and Wychwood, plus two guests.

A 200-year-old pub with one bar, fairly traditional in attitude with a focus on beer and conversation. No food. No fruit machines or background music, but televised sport for discerning drinkers and live music most Saturdays. Car park. Drinking courtyard with smoking area. Beer festivals. Aunt Sally played extensively in summer, crib in winter. The last pub on the left on the way out of town.

OPEN *12–12 Mon–Thurs; noon–1am Fri–Sat; 12–11.30pm Sun.*

The Highwayman

Exlade Street, Woodcote RG8 0UE
☎ *(01491) 682020* Mrs Murphy

Freehouse serving Fuller's London Pride, plus up to two guest beers, usually from Loddon or Butlers – the local Woodcote brewery.

R ambling 17th-century country inn with two-roomed bar, beams and open fire. Bar and restaurant food available at lunchtimes and evenings. Car park, garden, accommodation. Children allowed in restaurant. Signposted from the A4074 Reading to Wallingford Road.

OPEN *11am–3pm and 6–11pm Mon–Sat; 12–3pm and 7–10.30pm Sun.*

THE BREWERIES

ALL NATIONS
20 Coalport Road, Madeley, Telford TF7 5DP
☎ *(01952) 585747*

COALPORT DODGER 3.5% ABV
DABLEY ALE 3.8%ABV
DABLEY GOLD 5.0% ABV
Plus seasonals.

CORVEDALE BREWERY
The Sun Inn, Corfton, Craven Arms SY7 9DF
☎ *(01584) 861 239*

KATIE'S PRIDE 4.3% ABV
NORMAN'S PRIDE 4.3% ABV
NORMAN'S SECRET HOP 4.3% ABV
NORMAN'S DARK AND DELICIOUS 4.6% ABV

THE DOLPHIN BREWERY LTD
Dolphin Inn, 48 St Michael's Street, Shrewsbury SY1 2EL
☎ *(01743) 350419*

BEST BITTER 4.0% ABV
GOLD 4.3% ABV
PORTER 4.6% ABV
BREW 5.0% ABV
Plus seasonal brews.

HANBY ALES LTD
The New Brewery, Aston Park Industrial Estate, Wem SY4 5SD
☎ *(01939) 232432*
www.hanbyales.co.uk

PURE GOLD 3.7% ABV
DRAWWELL BITTER 3.9% ABV
ALL SEASONS 4.2% ABV
RAINBOW CHASER 4.3% ABV
WEM SPECIAL 4.4%ABV
CASCADE BITTER 4.5%ABV
GOLDEN HONEY 4.5% ABV
Premium beers:
HANBY'S PREMIUM 4.6% ABV
TAVERNERS ALE 5.3% ABV
Specials:
BLACK MAGIC MILD 4.0% ABV
SHROPSHIRE STOUT 4.4% ABV
SCORPIO PORTER 4.5% ABV
CHERRY BOMB 6.0% ABV
JOYBRINGER 6.0% ABV
NUTCRACKER 6.0% ABV

LION'S TALE BREWERY
The Red Lion Hotel, High Street, Cheswardine, Market Drayton TF9 2RS
☎ *(01630) 661234*

LION BRU 4.0% ABV
Plus seasonals.

LUDLOW BREWING COMPANY
Kingsley Garage, 105 Corve Street, Ludlow SY8 1DJ
☎ *(01584) 873291*
www.theludlowbrewingcompany.co.uk

GOLD 4.2% ABV
BOILING WELL 4.7% ABV

THE SALOPIAN BREWING COMPANY LTD
The Brewery, 67 Mytton Oak Road, Shrewsbury SY3 8UQ
☎ *(01743) 248414*
www.salopianbrewery.co.uk

SHROPSHIRE GOLD 3.8% ABV
Copper colour, fruity.
ABBEY GATES 4.3% ABV
Floral bitter.
HOP TWISTER 4.5% ABV
Pronounced hop flavour.
LEMON DREAM 4.5% ABV
Wheat beer, citrusy.
GOLDEN THREAD 5.0% ABV
Bittersweet, vinous aroma.

SIX BELLS BREWERY
The Six Bells, Church Street, Bishops Castle SY9 5AA
☎ *(01588) 638390*
www.bishops-castle.co.uk/sixbells/brewery.htm

BIG NEV'S 3.8% ABV
Pale, moderately hopped.
MARATHON 4.0% ABV
Malty, ruby coloured.
CLOUD NINE 4.2% ABV
Pale, citrus finish.
Plus seasonals including:
SPRING FORWARD 4.6% ABV
BREW 101 4.8% ABV
CASTLE RUIN 4.8% ABV
FESTIVAL RALE 5.2% ABV
OLD RECUMBENT 5.2% ABV
7 BELLS 5.5% ABV

THE WOOD BREWERY LTD
Wistantow, Craven Arms SY7 8DG
☎ *(01588) 672523*
www.woodbrewery.co.uk

QUAFF 3.7% ABV
Pale, light, clean finish.
CRAVEN ALE 3.8% ABV
Hop aroma.
WOOD'S PARISH 4.0% ABV
Light coloured, hoppy.
WOOD'S SPECIAL 4.2% ABV
Fruity and hoppy.
POT 'O' GOLD 4.4% ABV
Smooth.
SHROPSHIRE LAD 4.5% ABV
WOOD'S WONDERFUL 4.8% ABV
Plus seasonal brews including:
SUMMER THAT 3.9% ABV
SATURNALIA 4.2% ABV
WOODCUTTER 4.2% ABV
GET KNOTTED 4.7% ABV
HOPPING MAD 4.7% ABV
CHRISTMAS CRACKER 6.0% ABV

THE PUBS

ASTON ON CLUN

The Kangaroo Inn

Clun Road, Aston on Clun SY7 8EW
☎ *(01588) 660263* Michelle Harding
http://kangarooinn.co.uk

 Freehouse with Charles Wells Bombardier, Ludlow Best and Wye Valley HPA are the regular beers, plus one guest, changed at least weekly.

Prettily situated olde-worlde pub built in the early 1700s with scenic views. Friendly atmosphere, cosy fires, daily newspapers. Food available 12–3pm Wed–Sun and 7–9pm Wed–Sat. Regular quizzes and live music. Large, well-manicured beer garden, separate dining area, large car park, games rooms. Broadplace and internet hotspot. Pub's own beer festival at August bank holiday, Clun Valley beer festival first weekend in October. Children allowed. Two miles from Craven Arms, off the A49, on B4368.

OPEN *6–11pm Mon–Tues; 12–3pm and 6–11pm Wed–Thurs; 2-11pm Fri; 12–11pm Sat–Sun.*

ATCHAM

The Mytton & Mermaid Hotel

Atcham, Shrewsbury
☎ *(01743) 761220* Daniel and Ann Ditella
www.myttonandmermaid.co.uk

Freehouse with Wood Shropshire Lad, Salopian Shropshire Gold and Hanby All Seasons a typical selection of the three beers available. One is rotated every six months.

Country house hotel bar in a Grade II listed building dating from 1735, on the banks of the River Severn. Steeped in history, it features oak floorboards and a large open fireplace. Restaurant and bar food, including seasonal dishes and featuring local produce, served at lunch and dinner every day. Children welcome. Car parks, lawns. Accommodation. Close to National Trust Property Attingham Park. Two miles south-east of Shrewsbury town, on the B4380.

OPEN *11am–11pm (10.30pm Sun).*

BISHOPS CASTLE

The Six Bells

Church Street, Bishops Castle SY9 5AA
☎ *(01588) 638930* Neville Richards

Home of The Six Bells Brewery. Four home brews are always available: Big Nev's, Cloud Nine, Goldings BB and DA, plus monthly specials.

Grade II listed building dating mainly from the 18th century, tastefully renovated and restored with original fireplaces, stone and timberwork. Food available 12–1.45pm and 6–8.45pm Tues–Sat, and 12–1.45pm Sun. No music or games, but live music nights. Children allowed. Patio. Brewery tours available. An annual beer festival takes place on the second weekend in July, with over 60 beers in six pubs and two breweries.

OPEN *5–11pm Mon; 12–2.30pm and 5–11pm Tues–Fri; all day Sat; 12–3pm and 7–10.30pm Sun.*

The Three Tuns Inn

Salop Street, Bishops Castle SY9 5BW
☎ *(01588) 638797* Tim and Cath Curtis-Evans

Freehouse with five real ales usually available, with beers from the adjoining Three Tuns brewery always on offer. These include XXX, Cleric's Cure, Axis, Three 8 and Castle Steamer, and the selection will often include seasonal brews.

A genuine old-fashioned pub dating from 1642, with real fires, three bars, dining area, courtyard, garden and function room. No fruit machines or music in the pub; live music events in the function bar. Food available 12–3pm and 7–9pm Mon–Sat; 12–3pm Sun. Annual beer festival second weekend in July. Dogs welcome. Perfect base for ramblers. At the top of the hill in picturesque Bishops Castle.

OPEN *12–11pm (10.30pm Sun).*

BOULDON

The Tally Ho Inn

Bouldon, Nr Craven Arms SY7 9DP
☎ *(01584) 841362* JG Woodward

 A selection of real ales always available on one or two hand pumps, featuring a wide variety of independent breweries.

Traditional one-bar village pub with garden. Bar snacks available on weekday evenings and at weekends 12–3pm and from 7pm. Children allowed.

OPEN *7–11pm Mon; closed Tues–Wed; 7–11pm Thurs–Fri; 12–3pm and 7–11pm Sat; 12–3pm and 7–10.30pm Sun.*

BRIDGNORTH

The Bear Inn

Northgate, Bridgnorth WV16 4ET
☎ *(01746) 763250* G Corns

Timothy Taylor Landlord, Greene King Old Speckled Hen and Abbot and Caledonian Deuchars IPA permanently available, plus three daily changing guests from any independent brewery.

A two-bar town pub with large beer garden. Food available 12–9pm. Accommodation. Weekly live music. Children welcome. Through Northgate, off High Street.

OPEN *11am–late Mon–Fri; 10.30am–late Sat; 12–late Sun.*

The Railwayman's Arms

Severn Valley Railway, The Railway Station, Bridgnorth WV16 5DT
☎ *(01746) 764361* Mary Boot

Batham Bitter and Hobsons Best Bitter are always on offer, together with a mild. Three guests, constantly changing, are also served, from breweries such as Hobsons, Holden's, Olde Swan, Burton Bridge, Wye Valley, Cannon Royall, RCH, Stonehenge, Berrow, Cottage, Eccleshall and many, many more from all over the country. Hobsons bottle-conditioned brews also sold, plus a selection of bottled Belgian beers.

The bar is on Platform One of the Severn Valley Railway's northern terminus and is housed in part of the original station building which dates back to the days of the Great Western Railway. The older part of the bar is the original licensed refreshment room. Sandwiches and local pork pies served at weekends and every day from May to September. Accompanied children welcome until 9pm in the back room only. Car park.

 11.30am–4pm and 6–11pm Mon–Fri; 11am–11pm Sat; 12–10.30pm Sun.

The Swan Inn Hotel and Restaurant

Knowle Sands, Bridgnorth WV16 5JL
☎ *(01746) 763424* Kevin Cooper

 Freehouse offering three guest beers (two changed per fortnight), with Wood Shropshire Lad a regular favourite. Others might come from Hanby Ales or Salopian Brewery.

A 16th-century inn on the outskirts of Bridgenorth, with one bar and log-burning stoves. Completely refurbished and with views of the Severn valley. Food available 12–2pm and 6–9.30pm. Conservatory, library room, seven letting rooms, beer garden with wishing well. Children welcome. Occasional live music, barbecues in summer. Car park. Two minutes out of town on the B4555.

 12–3pm and 6–11pm Mon–Fri; 11am–11pm Sat; 12–10.30pm Sun.

BURWARTON

The Boyne Arms

Burwarton, Bridgnorth WV16 6QH
☎ *(01746) 787216* Jamie and Nere Yardley
www.theboynearms.co.uk

 A freehouse. Timothy Taylor Landlord, Hobson's Town Crier and Bridgnorth Best. One weekly-changing guest, for example, Ludlow Gold, Wood Shropshire Lad and Wye Valley HPA.

Georgian coaching house on the Boyne estate. Three bars (one out-building) plus a restaurant, large beer garden and children's adventure playground. Food, from fresh local produce, available Monday morning to Sunday evening. Pool, table football, quiz, golf and fruit machines. Car park. Situated between Ludlow and Bridgnorth.

 11.30am–3pm and 6–11pm Mon–Fri; 11am–11pm Sat–Sun.

CARDINGTON

The Royal Oak

Cardington, Church Stretton SY6 7JZ
☎ *(01694) 771266*
Steve Oldham and Eira Williams
www.at-the-oak.com

Wye Valley Butty Bach and Hobsons Best always available, plus two guests such as Wood Parish and Six Bells Goldings Best Bitter.

Dating from around the 15th century, this traditional freehouse in a conservation village nestles in lovely countryside close to the South Shropshire hills, and offers a friendly welcome to strangers and locals alike. It is reputed to be the oldest continuously licensed pub in Shropshire, and features a low-beamed bar with roaring log fire in winter, cauldron, black kettle and

pewter jugs in the vast inglenook fireplace, and red and green tapestry seats. Good-value homemade food is served 12–2pm and 7–9pm Tues–Sat, 12–2pm Sun and bank holiday Mon, including bar snacks, full menu and Sunday roasts. Famous for its 'Fidget Pie', a Shropshire recipe of gammon, apples and cider that was once sampled here by Prince Edward! No music, TV or games machines. Darts and dominoes. Floral beer patio to front of pub. Car park. Children welcome. Dogs allowed outside food sessions. Around four miles north-east of Church Stretton; follow signs to Cardington from A49 at Leebotwood, or from B4371 at Wall or Longville.

 Closed Mon (open 12–3.30pm bank holiday Mon); 12–2.30pm and 7pm–12 Tues–Thurs; 12–2.30pm and 7pm–1am Fri–Sat; 12–3.30pm and 7pm–12 Sun.

CHETWYND ASTON

The Fox

Pave Lane, Chetwynd Aston, Newport TF10 9LQ
☎ *(01952) 815940* Sam Cornwall Jones
www.fox-newport.co.uk

Owned by the Brunning and Price company with up to six real ales available, three of these changed weekly. The selection might include Timothy Taylor Landlord, Batham Best, Wood Shropshire Lad, Thwaites Original, Holden's Mild and Phoenix Arizon.

Lovely big Edwardian-style pub with a mix of nooky private corners and sunny spacious rooms, all wrapped around a busy central bar. The largest vaulted room leads out onto a large south-facing terrace with good views. Food served 12–10pm (9.30pm Sun). Children welcome until 7pm. Large beer garden, large car park. Off the A41 near Lilleshall Sports Centre.

 12–11pm (10.30pm Sun).

CHURCH ASTON

The Last Inn

Wellington Road, Church Aston, Newport TF10 9EJ
☎ *(01952) 820469* Sheila J Austin

Everards Tiger and Original, Hobsons Best Bitter, Bank's Bitter and Original, and one Salopian ale always available plus two guests which could be Hobsons Town Crier, Marston's Pedigree, Everards Lazy Daze or an ale from Timothy Taylor, Slaters, Cottage, Worfield or Wood.

A busy 19th-century country pub with a large conservatory and patio/terrace overlooking the Wrekin and Shropshire countryside. Food available 12–2.30pm and 6–9.30pm Mon–Thurs; 12–2.30pm and 6–10pm Fri–Sat; 12–9.30pm Sun. Large car park. Under 10s welcome in the conservatory and garden up to 8pm.

 12–11pm (10.30pm Sun).

CLEOBURY MORTIMER
The King's Arms Hotel
6 Church Street, Cleobury Mortimer DY14 8BS
☎ *(01299) 271954* John Dolphin

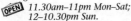 Hobsons Town Crier, Mild and Best are permanently available, plus one guest beer changed weekly, such as Black Sheep Bitter, Caledonian Deuchars IPA, Greene King IPA

A Punch Tavern, part owned by Hobsons Brewery. Recently refurbished village pub in a 17th-century coaching inn, with beams, fires and comfortable leather sofas. Home-cooked, locally sourced snacks from 10am–3pm. Four en-suite bed and breakfast letting rooms.

OPEN *11.30am–11pm Mon–Sat;*
12–10.30pm Sun.

CLUN
The White Horse Inn
The Square, Clun SY7 8JA
☎ *(01588) 640305* Jack Limond
www.whi-clun.co.uk

 Up to seven real ales available. Three Tuns XXX, Salopian Shropshire Gold, Wye Valley Butty Bach, Hobsons Best and Mild usually on offer, plus constantly changing guest beers and real cider and perry. Cask Marque award winner.

S et in the beautiful Clun Valley, in the historic and peaceful town of Clun, close to the castle. Homemade meals served in the cosy bar, dining room and garden, 12–2pm and 6–8.30pm daily. Four en-suite letting rooms (English Tourist Board three diamonds). Children welcome, but no special facilities. Beer festival held on the last weekend in May and the first weekend in October.

OPEN *11am–midnight Mon–Sat; 12–12 Sun.*

COALBROOKDALE
The Coalbrookdale Inn
12 Wellington Road, Coalbrookdale, Telford TF8 7DX
☎ *(01952) 433953* Dawn Wood
www.coalbrookdaleinn.co.uk

Up to seven real ales available. These might include Hobsons Town Crier, Wye Valley HPA, Holden's Golden Glow and John Roberts XXX or other ales from micro-breweries, both local and across the country. The menu changes every day or two.

A traditional, award-winning village pub and restaurant built in 1831 with no fruit machines, pool table or juke box. One bar and a small patio area. Food served 12–2.30pm and 6–9pm Tues–Sat, 12–2.30pm Sun. Small beer garden and car park. Children welcome. On the main road out of Ironbridge.

OPEN *All day, every day.*

CRAVEN ARMS
The Stokesay Castle Inn
School Road, Craven Arms SY7 9PE
☎ *(01588) 672304* Steve Pitchford

An Enterprise Inns pub, with three or four guest ales on offer, including beers such as Greene King Old Speckled Hen, Timothy Taylor Landlord and Wadworth 6X.

H otel inn dating from 1894 on the outskirts of Craven Arms village, with oak-panelled restaurant and oak-beamed bar with fireplace. Food served 12–2.30pm and 7–9pm daily, including traditional Sunday roasts. Twelve en-suite rooms. Pool, darts, dominoes. Garden, car park for 36 cars. Children allowed, plus pets by arrangement. From Ludlow, take the first turning right as you enter Craven Arms village. From Shrewsbury, take the last turning on the left in the village. Next to the Secret Hills Discovery Centre (signposted).

OPEN *11am–11pm (10.30pm Sun).*

The Sun Inn
Corfton, Craven Arms SY7 9DF
☎ *(01584) 861503*
Norman, Teresa and Katie Pearce

Home of the Corvedale Brewery, with Norman's Pride, Katie's Pride, Farmer Ray's (brewed from locally grown hops) and Dark and Delicious usually available, plus two guests from micro-breweries such as Cottage and Hanby. Finalists in the Society of Independent Brewers Association (SIBA) National Beer Festival four years running.

F riendly country brewpub with two bars, a quiet lounge and a dining area. Food available 12–2pm and 6–9pm Mon–Sat, 12–3pm and 7–9pm Sun. Exceptionally good disabled facilities, which have been commended by the Heart of England Tourist Board 'Tourism for All' and British Gas's 'Open to All' award, and have made the pub a National Winner of The Ease of Access Award. Children's certificate. Situated on the B4368.

OPEN *12–2.30pm and 6–11pm Mon–Sat;*
12–3pm and 7–10.30pm Sun.

DORRINGTON
The Fox Inn
Great Ryton, Dorrington, Nr Shrewsbury SY5 7LS
☎ *(01743) 718499* Sue and John Owen
www.shropshirepublichouses.co.uk

Freehouse with three or four real ales from breweries such as Hobsons, Salopian, Stonehouse and Jennings.

V illage freehouse, refurbished in 2007, with separate restaurant, in a tiny hamlet just outside Condover. Lunch menu, weekly changing evening menu and specials board available 12–2.30pm (except Mon) and 7–9pm; traditional Sunday lunch and specials served 12–2.30pm. Large beer terrace with one of the best views in Shropshire. No juke box or fruit machines. Children welcome. Large car park. Beer festival every summer, quiz nights every other Wednesday.

OPEN *12–2.30pm and 7–11pm Mon–Fri;*
12–3.30pm and 7–11pm Sat; 12–3.30pm
and 7–10.30pm Sun.

ELLERDINE HEATH
The Royal Oak (The Tiddly)
Ellerdine Heath, Telford TF6 6RL
☎ *(01939) 250300* Barry Colin Malone

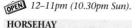 Hobsons Bitter, Salopian Shropshire Gold and Wye Valley Hereford Pale Ale usually available, plus a guest from any small independent brewery rotated twice a week. Weetwood and Archers beers make regular appearances.

Lovely one-bar country pub in a quiet backwater, yet only a short distance from Telford. Food served during the week 12–2pm and 5–9pm (not Tues). Children's play area. Cider festival on last Saturday in July. Car park. Located halfway between the A53 and A442.

OPEN *12–11pm (10.30pm Sun).*

HORSEHAY
The Station Inn
Station Road, Horsehay, Telford TF4 2NJ
☎ *(01952) 503006* Peter and Tracey Halliday

 A freehouse. St Austell Tribute and Wood Parish. Two guests, changed at least weekly, such as Salopian Abbey Gates, Hobson's Town Crier, Wye Valley Butty Bach, Six Bells Big Nev, Three Tuns XXX, Ludlow Gold, Wood Shropshire Lad, Holden's Golden and Cotleigh Barn Ale, amongst many others.

A traditional family-run pub, dating from 1860, with a quarry-tiled floor in the bar area. Chatty and happy atmosphere. Homemade food (including steak nights and a sausage board) available in a separate dining area 6–9pm Tues–Thurs; 12–3pm and 6–9.30pm Fri–Sat; 12–8.30pm Sun. Beer garden. Car park. Function room. Children welcome. Beer festivals held spring and December. Also an annual cider festival. Located 200 yards from the Telford Steam Railway.

OPEN *6pm–12 Tues–Thurs; noon–1am Fri–Sat; 12–11pm Sun.*

IRONBRIDGE
The Golden Ball Inn
1 New Bridge Road, Ironbridge, Telford TF8 7BA
☎ *(01952) 432179* Matthew Rowland

 Hook Norton Old Hooky and Everards Tiger always available, plus three guests from local independent breweries, changed at least twice a week.

Dating from 1728, this pub in a village setting has one large bar, a separate restaurant, courtyard and garden. Well-behaved children allowed (no play area). Four en-suite letting rooms. Car parking. Tucked away, off Madley Road.

OPEN *12–11pm (10.30pm Sun).*

It's All About Me Wine Bar & Dining
29 High Street, Ironbridge, Telford TF8 7AD
☎ *(01952) 432716*
Candida and Adrian Woolcott

Freehouse with three real ales, changed weekly. Examples include Shepherd Neame Bishop's Finger, Greene King IPA and Thwaites Lancaster Bomber.

A modern wine bar in a listed building in the heart of the World Heritage Site of the Ironbridge Gorge. Upstairs restaurant plus downstairs bar and exquisite sun terrace with bridge views. Bar and evening restaurant food served 12–2.30pm and 6–9pm. Children and dogs welcome. Private parties and weddings catered for. Live music most Fridays. Outside smoking area. Keeping the bridge on your right, walk around 100 yards along and the bar is the pink building on the right.

OPEN *11am–1am Tues–Sat; 11am–midnight Sun. Closed Mon.*

Ye Olde Robin Hood Inn
33 Waterloo Street, Ironbridge, Telford TF8 7HQ
☎ *(01952) 433100* Finbarr O'Shaughnessy
www.yeolderobinhood.com

Holden's Golden Glow plus two to three weekly-changing guests, such as Salopian Golden Thread, Bradfield Farmers Pale Ale and Maypole Platinum Blonde.

A traditional 17th-century inn tied to Holden's Brewery, with two bars and no juke boxes or slot machines. Large car park. Outdoor seating area next to the River Severn. Child and biker friendly. Traditional 'pub grub' served 12–3pm and 6–9pm (not on Mondays).

OPEN *11am–midnight.*

LITTLE STRETTON
The Ragleth Inn
Ludlow Road, Little Stretton, Church Stretton SY6 6RB
☎ *(01694) 722711* Chris and Wendy Davis
www.theraglethinn.co.uk

Freehouse offering three real ales in winter, five in summer. Regulars include Hobsons Best, Wood Quaff Ale, Theakston Old Peculier, Greene King Ruddles County and Courage Directors, with the selection changed every couple of weeks.

Classic country inn dating back to 1663 with restored old beams and brick walls, and log burners at both ends of the pub. Food served 12–2.15pm and 6.30–9.30pm. Separate dining room overlooking the gardens. Very large beer garden and new patio, both with plenty of benches. Children's play area. In the centre of a small village off the A49 at the base of the Stretton Hills, 12 miles from Shrewsbury. Good walking and picnic area.

OPEN *12–2.30pm and 6pm–close; open all day Sat–Sun Easter–end of Sept.*

LOWTOWN

Black Horse

4 Bridge Street, Lowtown, Bridgnorth
☎ *(01746) 762415*

Two pumps always serve Banks's beers, and seven guest ales, changed daily, might include something from Hobsons, Wood, Holden's, Wychwood or Brakspear.

A 250-year-old village pub in a listed building on the banks of the River Severn. Food available. Two bars plus lounge and courtyard, and seating by the river. Live music once a month. Beer festival once a year in summer (call for details). Seven letting rooms. Children allowed. Car park,

OPEN *6–11pm Mon–Fri; 12–11pm Sat; 12–10.30pm Sun.*

LUDLOW

The Church Inn

Buttercross, Ludlow SY8 1AW
☎ *(01584) 872174* G Wilson Lloyd

A freehouse serving up to eight real ales. Wye Valley Eastgate, Ludlow Gold and Boiling Well and Hobson's Town Crier and Mild. Two guests, which are changed every few days.

Standing on an ancient site which goes back at least 700 years, and known in past centuries as The Cross Keys. Bar and restaurant food served 12–2.30pm and 6.30–9pm Mon–Fri; 12–3.30pm and 6.30–9pm Sat; 12–3pm and 6.30–8.30pm Sun. Function room. Accommodation.

OPEN *11am–11pm Mon–Thurs; 11am–midnight Fri–Sat; 12–11pm Sun.*

MADELEY

All Nations Inn

20 Coalport Road, Madeley, Telford TF7 5DP
☎ *(01952) 585747* Jim Birtwhistle

Dabley Ale, Dabley Gold and Coalport Dodger, all brewed on the premises, plus a guest, changed every few days, such as Wye Valley Dorothy Goodbody's Stout, Hobsons Old Henry and beers from small/micro-breweries.

Unspoilt, historic pub that has been brewing since 1831, and has been owned by three families during this period. It was one of only four brewpubs that remained in existence during the 1970s, and has a real fire and a relaxed, friendly atmosphere. No juke box, pool table or fruit machine. Six Nations Rugby shown on a TV mounted on two beer barrels in the corner of the bar. Large outdoor seating area with attractive views overlooking Blist Hill Victorian Town open-air museum. Good-quality rolls and pork pies from local suppliers served every session. Small functions catered for. Popular quiz night on Mondays. Regular live blues, folk and jazz sessions in summer. B&B and camping. Follow signs to Blist Hill (Ironbridge Gorge Museum), the pub is located opposite the museum entrance on the old road which runs above Legges Way.

OPEN *12–12.*

MUCH WENLOCK

The George & Dragon

2 High Street, Much Wenlock TF13 6AA
☎ *(01952) 727312*

Greene King Abbot and IPA, Hobsons Town Crier, Timothy Taylor Landlord and a guest on the fifth pump that is rotated weekly.

Small country town pub, first mentioned in records in 1496, but possibly used by monks since the 11th century. Food is available 12–2pm and 6–9pm daily, and there is a restaurant area (no restaurant service on Wed and Sun evenings). The pub participates in Shropshire Beer Week Festival. Children allowed. Public car park.

OPEN *All day, every day.*

MUNSLOW

The Crown Country Inn

Munslow, Nr Craven Arms SY7 9ET
☎ *(01584) 841205* Richard and Jane Arnold
www.crowncountryinn.co.uk

Six real ales including Holden's Black Country and Golden Glow, Three Tuns Clerics Cure and XXX are the favourites.

Grade II listed Tudor inn set in an Area of Outstanding Natural Beauty. Winner of 'Deliciously Shropshire' Best Restaurant two years running, with food prepared by a Masterchef of Great Britain served 12–2pm and 7–9pm (not Mon all day and Sun evening). Car park. Children welcome. Beer garden, room for hire, accommodation. Situated on the B4368 between Aston Munslow and Beambridge.

OPEN *12–2.30pm and 7–11pm (closed Sun evening and all day Mon).*

OAKENGATES

Crown Inn

Market Street, Oakengates, Telford TF2 6EA
☎ *(01952) 610888* John Ellis
www.crown.oakengates.com

Freehouse with Hobson's Twisted Spire and Best Bitter plus up to ten ever-changing brews and hand-pulled cider. So far, some 10,000 ales have been served! Hundreds of micro-breweries and regionals featured. Wood, Wem, Hook Norton, Weetwood, Everards, Wye Valley, Slaters and Beowulf are just a few of the regulars. Milds and stouts/porters are usually available. Foreign beers, fruit wines and single malt whiskies also on offer.

A homely oasis of a traditional town-centre pub with three indoor drinking areas and a sun–trap courtyard. The Morning Advertiser's Cask Ale Pub of the Year 2008 and Freehouse of the Year 2007 for East and West Midlands. Cask Marque award held. Landlords dating back to 1835 are listed. No food, except for private parties. Telford Acoustic Club meets on Weds, quality live music on Thurs. Well-behaved children and animals welcome. Off Oakengates inner ring road, next to Oakengates bus station. Oakengates rail station nearby. Car park. Beer festivals held twice a year on the first weekends in May and October, now featuring 34 cooled hand pumps specialising in up to 60 new beers.

 12–11pm daily.

OLDWOODS
Fox Inn

21 Church Street, Oswestry SY11 2SU
☎ *(01691) 679669*
Amanda Woof and Jon Edwards

Jennings Lakeland Bitter and Dark Mild plus three weekly changing guests from a large range, including Fiddlers Elbow and Hook Norton 303AD.

An olde-worlde Marston's pub, with a large four-room interior and a courtyard with a stage. Regular music and an outside smoking area. Serves homemade scotch eggs. Food served 12–2.30pm Tues–Sun and 6.30pm–8.30pm Tues–Sat.

6pm–12 Mon; 11.30am–3pm and 6pm–12 Sun and Tues–Thurs; 11.30am–1am Fri–Sat.

The Romping Cat

Old Woods, Nr Bomere Heath, Shrewsbury SY4 3AX
☎ *(01939) 290273* Robin Beddoes

Freehouse with six real ales, four of which are locally sourced.

Traditional 150-year-old rural pub with one beamed bar, a slate floor, real fire, no machines or music. Large car park, beer garden and patio. No food. No children. Car park. Six miles outside Shrewsbury.

4–11pm Mon–Fri; 11am–11pm Sat–Sun.

PONTESBURY
The Horseshoes Inn

Minsterley Road, Pontesbury, Shrewsbury SY5 0QJ
☎ *(01743) 790278* Derek Brookes

Freehouse with three real ales that could well include brews from Archers, Wye Valley, Cottage and Six Bells. Two of the beers are changed every few days.

A100-year-old rural pub with one bar and a small dining room. Food available 11.30am–2pm and 6.30–9pm. Children welcome until 9pm. Beer garden, car park. On the B488 Shrewsbury–Bishops Castle road.

11.30am–3pm and 6–11pm.

PORT HILL
The Boathouse Inn

New Street, Port Hill, Shrewsbury SY3 8JQ
☎ *(01743) 362965*

Six guest ales, regularly rotated (15 different ones a week in summer). Examples include regular favourite Marston's Pedigree, Salopian Golden Thread, Greene King Abbot and Old Speckled Hen.

Pub on the outskirts of Shrewsbury dating from before the 17th century, with beams and fireplaces. Food available. Two bars, garden, car park. Children allowed in certain areas.

11am–11pm Mon–Sat; 12–10.30pm Sun.

RATLINGHOPE
The Horseshoe Inn

(also known as The Bridge)
Bridges, Nr Ratlinghope SY5 0ST
☎ *(01588) 650260*
Maureen and Bob Macauley

Freehouse with Adnams Bitter and Timothy Taylor Landlord plus a guest from a local brewery.

A400-year-old countryside pub in an isolated beauty spot in the South Shropshire hills. Home-cooked food available 12–2.45pm and 6–8.45pm Mon–Fri; 12–8.45pm Sat, 12–4pm Sun. Separate dining area. Supervised children allowed. Beer garden with tables and seating. Large car park. Phone for directions.

4–11pm Mon; 12–11pm Tues–Sat; 12–10.30pm Sun.

SHIFNAL
Oddfellows Wine Bar

Market Place, Shifnal TF11 9AV
☎ *(01952) 461517* Matt Jones
www.odleyinns.co.uk

Freehouse with four ales, perhaps including Salopian Shropshire Gold, Wye Valley HPA and two guests, changed every barrel, from breweries such as Holden's, Batham, Three Tuns, Ludlow or Slaters.

Former coaching inn that was rebuilt after a fire in 1901, with a single room broken up by partial walls. Open-plan bar, open fires, outside seating, nice bedrooms. Food served 12–2.30pm and 6–9.30pm Mon–Sat, and all day Sun. Car park. Right in the centre of Shifnal.

12–12.

The White Hart

High Street, Shifnal TF11 8BH
☎ *(01952) 461161* Andy Koczy

A genuine freehouse serving seven real ales. The five permanently available are Exmoor Gold, Wye Valley Hereford Pale Ale, Holden's Best and Mild and Adnams Broadside. The other two pumps serve guest ales, changing constantly.

Two-roomed black and white timbered coaching inn dating from 1595, with a mature clientele. Local CAMRA Pub of the Year 2004, 2005, 2006 and 2007. Cask Marque accredited. Food available 12–2pm Mon–Sat. Patio is strictly for adults only, but children are welcome in the garden. Close to Ironbridge gorge. Off the M54, junction 4.

12–11pm.

SHREWSBURY

The Abbey

83 Monkmoor Road, Shrewsbury SY2 5AZ
☎ *(01743) 36788* Gary Bellingham

 A Mitchells & Butlers Ember Inn with nine real ales. M&B Mild and Brew XI, Fuller's London Pride and six constantly rotating guests such as Durham White Bullet, Sharp's Eden, Kelham Island Pale Rider, Wood Shropshire Lass, Saltaire Cascade and Coach House Innkeeper's Special Reserve. Over 400 ales per year, mostly from smaller breweries.

Adult-oriented pub with large open-plan lounge bar that has both open and secluded seating. No bar games – this is a talking pub. Large car park and beer garden. Food served 12–9pm every day. No under-14s, and over-14s only when dining. Bi-weekly charity quiz nights and regular beer festivals. Tasting notes, tasters and advice provided. Follow signs to the police station, the pub is halfway up the hill on the left.

OPEN *11.30am–11pm Mon–Thurs; 11.30am–midnight Fri–Sat; 12–11pm Sun. Later openings for special occasions and events.*

The Dolphin Inn

48 St Michael's Street, Shrewsbury SY1 2EZ
☎ *(01743) 350419* Nigel Morton

Home of the Dolphin Brewery, with Dolphin Best Bitter and guest beers from other breweries, including Exmoor and Titanic. Cask cider also served.

Brewpub dedicated to real ales. No lager or beers from national breweries. Traditional décor, wide-ranging, friendly clientele. Coffee available. No food. No children.

OPEN *5–11pm only.*

The Peacock Inn

42 Wenlock Road, Shrewsbury SY2 6JS
☎ *(01743) 355215* C Roberts

Marston's ales are a speciality here, with Pedigree and Owd Roger always available, plus seasonal brews and other guests such as Banks's Mild on one hand pump.

Pub/restaurant with one bar, beer garden, disabled access. Food available at lunchtimes and evenings in separate dining area. Children allowed.

OPEN *11.30am–3pm and 6–11pm (10.30pm Sun).*

The Salopian Bar

Smithfield Road, Shrewsbury SY1 1PW
☎ *(01743) 351505* Oliver Parry
www.thesalopianbar.co.uk

Freehouse with Oakham Bishop's Farewell, Dark Star Hophead, Stonehouse Station Bitter and Sarah Hugher Dark Ruby. The two guests, changed twice a week, might be Salopian Oracle, Batham's Bitter, Castle Rock Harvest Pale Ale or Crouch Vale Brewers Gold. Wide selection of ciders and perries. Two cider festivals held annually, in July and September.

Modern, comfortable pub with attractive, subtle décor, featuring a display of paintings by local artists. Fresh homemade cobs and locally sourced pork pies served daily. Live acoustic music every Friday. Shrewsbury and West Shropshire CAMRA Pub of the Year. A two-minute walk from bus station, three-minute walk from train station.

OPEN *Closed Mon; 12–11pm Tues–Thurs; 12–12 Fri–Sat; 12–11pm Sun.*

The Three Fishes

Fish Street, Shrewsbury SY1 1UR
☎ *(01743) 344793* David Moss

 Five or six real ales. Timothy Taylor Landlord, Sharp's Doom Bar and Hobsons Mild are permanent fixtures, plus local beers from breweries such as Stonehouse, Ludlow or Thornbridge. Guests are changed as they run out – sometimes several times a day!

A black and white pub dating from 1640 on a cobbled street in the heart of medieval Shrewsbury. Single room with central servery. Food available 12–2.15pm and 6–8.30pm (not Sun evening). No under 14s. Just off the High Street.

OPEN *11.30am–3pm and 5–11pm Mon–Thurs; 11.30am–11.30pm Fri–Sat; 12–4pm and 7–10.30pm Sun.*

Woodman Inn

32 Coton Hill, Shrewsbury SY1 2DZ
☎ *(01743) 351007* Robin Beddoes

Freehouse with six real ales always on tap, including Weetwood Oasthouse Gold, Hobsons Best Bitter, Shepherd Neame Spitfire and three constantly changing guests such as Millstone Tiger Rut, Bath Barnstormer, Oakham White Dwarf and beers from Salopian. The guests are sourced from all over the country.

Established in 1850 and rebuilt after a fire in 1925, the only pub in Shrewsbury that has two log fires in the lounge and one in the bar. The lounge is oak-panelled, the bar is very traditional, with four darts and four domino teams. No juke box, fruit machines or Sky TV. Traditional rolls available. Beer garden. Children welcome until 7pm. Ten-minute walk from the historic town centre and the train station.

OPEN *4–11pm Mon–Fri (doors close, but licensed until 2am); all day Sat–Sun.*

UPPER FARMCOTE

The Lion O'Morfe

Upper Farmcote WV15 5PS
☎ *(01746) 710678* Dave Chantler

 Freehouse offering six guest beers, usually changed every three days, with Wood Shropshire Lad and beers from Wye Valley, Shepherd Neame, Worfield, Greene King and Banks's regularly featured.

Country pub built in the 19th century. Freshly cooked food is available, including a good vegetarian selection, and there is a private, intimate dining room. Two bars, beer garden and car park. Live music weekly. Pool. Children allowed.

OPEN *12–2.30pm (closed Mon lunch) and 7–11pm Mon–Fri; hours vary on Sat/Sun.*

WELLINGTON

The Cock Hotel

148 Holyhead Road, Wellington, Telford TF1 2DL
☎ *(01952) 244954* Peter Arden

Freehouse with eight real ales, which might include Hobsons Town Crier, Enville White and occasionally Heaven's Gate, a house brew produced for the hotel by the Salopian Brewery.

A traditional pub with two bars. No food. No children.

OPEN *4–11pm Mon–Wed; 12–11pm Thurs–Sat; 12–4pm and 7–10.30pm Sun.*

WISTANSTOW

The Plough Inn

Wistanstow, Craven Arms SY7 8DG
☎ *(01588) 673251* Richard Sys

Owned by the Wood Brewery, serving three to five of their beers, including Shropshire Lad, Parish and Pot o' Gold, plus seasonal Wood ales.

The brewery tap for Wood, dating back to 1782. Traditional locals' country pub with two bars and a games room. Food is prepared on the premises using local produce where possible, and is available 12–2pm and 6.30–9pm every day. Situated one mile north of Craven Arms, just off the A49.

OPEN *12–2.30pm and 5pm–12 (10.30pm Sun).*

WORFIELD

The Dog Inn and Davenports Arms

Main Street, Worfield WV15 5LF
☎ *(01746) 716020*

Charles Wells Bombardier, Marston's Pedigree and Highgate Mild are among the permanent beers. An occasional guest is also served, with the emphasis on local breweries such as Hobsons, Wood and Hanby.

A 17th-century village pub with beams and log burner. Award-winning food served lunchtimes and evenings, often featuring fish and local produce. Patio, car park. Occasional live music. Children allowed. Follow signs to Worfield from Bridgenorth Road – the pub is in the village.

OPEN *12–2.30pm and 7–11pm Mon–Sat; 12–3pm and 7–10pm Sun.*

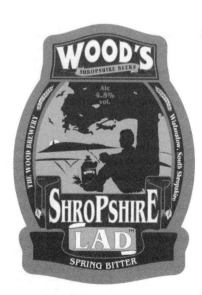

THE BREWERIES

ABBEY ALES LTD

The Abbey Brewery, Camden Row, Bath BA1 5LB
☎ *(01225) 444437*
www.abbeyales.co.uk

MILD 4.0% ABV
Slightly sweet, dark.
BELLRINGER 4.2% ABV
Golden, hoppy, dry finish, award winner.
CHORISTER 4.5% ABV
Brown and malty.
BATH STAR 4.6% ABV
Amber, strong hoppy taste.
RESURRECTION 4.6% ABV
Easter beer.
STEEPLE JACK 4.7% ABV
SALVATION 4.8% ABV
TWELFTH NIGHT 5.0% ABV
Christmas brew.
WHITE FRIAR 5.0% ABV
Seasonal.
Occasional:
BLACK FRIAR 5.3% ABV
Stout.

BERROW BREWERY

Coast Road, Berrow, Burnham-on-Sea TA8 2QU
☎ *(01278) 751345*

BBBB/4BS 4.0% ABV
PORTER 4.6% ABV
Mellow and fruity.
TOPSY TURVY 6.0% ABV
Golden, fruity and refreshing.
Seasonals:
CARNIVALE 4.5% ABV
Available late Oct–mid Nov.
CHRISTMAS ALE 4.8% ABV
Available Dec–Jan.

BLINDMANS BREWERY LTD

Talbot Farm, Leighton, Nr Frome, Somerset
BA11 4PN
☎ *(01749) 880038*
www.blindmansbrewery.co.uk

BUFF 3.6% ABV
A light brown smooth session beer.
GOLDEN SPRING 4.0% ABV
Straw colour, award winner.
ECLIPSE 4.2% ABV
A porter full of chocolate flavours and subtle bitterness.
MINE BEER 4.2% ABV
Robust, rich and malty.
ICARUS 4.5% ABV
Rich, with plenty of fruit.
SIBERIA 4.7% ABV
Traditional mid-brown full-bodied ale.
Plus specials.

BUTCOMBE BREWERY LTD

Cox's Green, Wrington, Bristol BS40 5PA
☎ *(01934) 863963*
www.butcombe.com

BITTER 4.0% ABV
BLOND 4.3% ABV
GOLD 4.7% ABV
BRUNEL 5.0% ABV

COTLEIGH BREWERY

Ford Road, Wiveliscombe, Taunton TA4 2RE
☎ *(01984) 624086*
www.cotleighbrewery.co.uk

HARRIER LITE 3.5% ABV
Slightly sweet, floral aroma, hoppy finish.
TAWNY BITTER 3.8% ABV
Well-hopped, balanced bitter.
25TH ANNIVERSARY ALE 4.0% ABV
Golden, fresh and fruity.
GOLDEN SEAHAWK 4.2% ABV
Malty with background of honey.
BARN OWL BITTER 4.5% ABV
Smooth, refreshing and hoppy.
BUZZARD DARK ALE 4.8% ABV
Deep copper ale, nutty flavour.
Plus occasional and seasonal brews.

COTTAGE BREWING CO.

High Street, West Lydford TA11 7DQ
☎ *(01963) 240551*

SOUTHERN BITTER 3.7% ABV
SOMERSET AND DORSET ALE 4.4% ABV
GOLDEN ARROW 4.5% ABV
GOLDRUSH 5.0% ABV
NORMAN'S CONQUEST 5.0% ABV
Plus seasonals and specials.

DUNKERY ALES LTD

The Brewery, Edgcott Farm, Exford TA24 7QG
☎ *(01643) 831115*
www.dunkeryales.co.uk

DUNKERY ALE 4.0% ABV

EXMOOR ALES LTD

The Brewery, Golden Hill, Wiveliscombe,
Taunton TA4 2NY
☎ *(01984) 623798*
www.exmoorales.co.uk

ALE 3.8% ABV
Smooth and full flavoured, with malt throughout.
FOX 4.2% ABV
Easy drinking and flavour packed.
GOLD 4.5% ABV
Initially sweet, with a hoppy finish.
HART 4.8% ABV
Malty, with balancing hoppiness.
STAG 5.2% ABV
Well balanced with lingering finish.
Seasonals:
HOUND DOG 4.0% ABV
Mar–May.
WILD CAT 4.4% ABV
Sept–Nov.
EXMAS 5.0% ABV
Nov–Dec.
BEAST 6.6% ABV
Oct–April.

GLASTONBURY ALES

Unit 10, Wessex Park, Somerton Business Park,
Somerton TA11 6SB
☎ *(01458) 272244*

MYSTERY TOR 3.8% ABV
LADY OF THE LAKE 4.2% ABV
HEDGE MONKEY 4.6% ABV
GOLDEN CHALICE 4.8% ABV
Plus seasonal and occasional brews.

JUWARDS BREWERY
Unit 14 Tonedale Business Park, Wellington TA21 0AW

BISHOPS SPECIAL MILD 3.8% ABV
BITTER 3.9% ABV
BISHOPS SOMERSET ALE 4.0% ABV
JUWARDS 4.0% ABV
AMBER 4.1% ABV
PREMIUM 4.3% ABV

KEYNSHAM BREWING COMPANY LTD
Brookleaze, Stockwood Vale, Keynsham, Bristol BS31 2AL
☎ *(0117) 986 7889*
www.keynshambrewery.co.uk

PIXASH 4.1% ABV
CHEW BITTER 4.3% ABV
SOMERDALE GOLDEN 4.5% ABV
STOCKWOOD STOUT 5.0% ABV

MATTHEWS BREWING COMPANY LTD
Unit 7 Tinsbury Workshop Estate, Hayeswood Road, Tinsbury, Bath BA2 0HQ
☎ *(01761) 472242*
www.matthewsbrewing.co.uk

BRASSKNOCKER 3.8% ABV
BOB WALL 4.2% ABV
Plus seasonals and monthly specials.

MILK STREET BREWERY
25 Milk Street, Frome BA11 3DB
☎ *(01373) 467766*
www.milkstreet.5u.com

GULP! 3.5% ABV
Sugary, hazelnut flavour.
FUNKY MONKEY 4.0% ABV
Blonde summer beer with citrusy lemon character.
MERMAID 4.1% ABV
Rich hop character, hint of passion fruit.
NICK'S 4.4% ABV
Malty bitter with hints of chocolate.
BISON 4.5% ABV
Complex fruity flavour, copper colour.
ZIG ZAG STOUT 4.5% ABV
Ruby colour, roast malt flavour. November–March.
BEER 5.0% ABV
Golden yellow, lime notes.
ELDER FIZZ 5.0% ABV
Elderflower edge to balanced hop flavour.
Plus seasonal and occasional ales.

MOOR BEER COMPANY
Whitley Farm, Ashcott TA7 9QW
☎ *(01458) 210050*
www.moorbeer.co.uk

REVIVAL 3.8% ABV
Light colour, hoppy bitter.
MILLY'S 3.9% ABV
Dark with roasted barley finish.
Plus seasonals and a monthly special including:
AVALON SPRINGTIME 4.0% ABV
MERLINS MAGIC 4.3% ABV
PORTED PEAT PORTER 4.5% ABV
CONFIDENCE 4.6% ABV
SOMERLAND GOLD 5.0% ABV
OLD FREDDY WALKER 7.3% ABV

NEWMANS BREWERY
107 Wemberham Lane, Yatton BS49 4BP
☎ *(01934) 830638*
www.newmansbrewery.com

WOLVERS ALE 4.1% ABV
Robust hoppy flavour.
MENDIP MAMMOTH 4.3% ABV
Fresh alpine taste, fruit aroma.
BITE IPA 4.6% ABV
Spicy hop finish.
Plus seasonals and specials including:
RED STAG BITTER 3.6% ABV
Dry bitter, fruity and slightly spicy.
CAVE BEAR STOUT 4.0% ABV
Irish stout with residual sweetness.

THE ODCOMBE BREWERY
41 Lower Odcombe, Yeovil BA22 8TX
☎ *(01935) 862591*

ODCOMBE NO.1 4.0% ABV
ODCOMBE SPRING 4.1% ABV

RCH BREWERY
West Hewish, Nr Weston-super-Mare BS24 6RR
☎ *(01934) 834447*
www.rchbrewery.com

HEWISH IPA 3.6% ABV
Citrus tones, floral aroma, light brown.
PG STEAM 3.9% ABV
Floral hop aroma, bittersweet taste.
PITCHFORK 4.3% ABV
Slightly sweet and fruity.
OLD SLUG PORTER 4.5% ABV
Dark, chocolatey, coffee and black cherry flavours.
EAST STREET CREAM 5.0% ABV
Malty, hoppy fruit bitter.
DOUBLEHEADER 5.3% ABV
Golden hoppy beer.
FIREBOX 6.0% ABV
Cherry fruit flavour, dry bitter finish.

STOWEY BREWERY
25 Castle Street, Nether Stowey TA5 1LN
☎ *(01278) 732228*

NETHER ENDING 4.2% ABV

Plus seasonals and specials.

YEOVIL ALES LTD
Unit 5, Bofors Park, Lufton Trading Estate, Lufton, Yeovil BA22 8YH
☎ *(01935) 414888*
www.yeovilales.com

SUMMERSET 4.1% ABV

THE PUBS

ASHCOTT

Ring o'Bells

High Street, Ashcott, Bridgwater TA7 9PZ
☎ *(01458) 210232*
John and Elaine Foreman and John Sharman
www.ringobells.com

Genuine freehouse with three hand pumps serving a range of constantly changing real ales. The local Moor Beer Company in Ashcott is regularly supported, plus Glastonbury Ales and smaller independents and micros.

Medium-sized village pub with parts dating back to the mid-18th century. Three bars, dining area and beer garden. Large function room and skittle alley. Food available 12–2pm and 7–10pm daily. Children allowed. Off the A39.

OPEN *12–2.30pm and 7–11pm (10.30pm Sun).*

AXBRIDGE

The Crown Inn

St Mary's Street, Axbridge BS26 2BN
☎ *(01934) 732518*
A K Kamel and Linda Bishop

A freehouse. Sharp's Doom Bar and Crown Inn Glory (house ale) and Cheddar Potholer. Plans to stock guest ales from summer 2008.

Under new ownership since December 2007, although there has been a Crown Inn on this site since around 1500. Originally three cottages but over time linked into one. Two bars. Homemade food from local produce served 5–9pm Mon–Fri; all day Sat–Sun. Pool, darts, table skittles and skittle alley. Children and dogs welcome, with children's menu available. Street parking. Close to Cheddar Gorge and caves and Wookey Hole.

OPEN *5pm–12 Mon–Thurs; 5pm–2am Fri; noon–2am Sat; 12–12 Sun.*

The Lamb Hotel

The Square, Axbridge BS26 2AP
☎ *(01934) 732253* Alan Currie

Butcombe Bitter and Gold and Bath Gem plus a guest beer rotated weekly.

Family pub built in 1480, set in a historic medieval square. Opposite beautiful medieval building, formerly a hunting lodge, now a museum. One curiosity is the bar that has bottles of wine set in concrete underneath it. Food available 12–2.30pm and 6.30–9pm (except Sun evening). Children welcome in the dining area. Function room for up to 70. Parking in market square. Small garden. Skittle alley and table skittles.

OPEN *11.30am–3pm and 6–11pm Mon–Wed; 11.30am–11pm Thurs–Sun.*

BABCARY

The Red Lion Inn

Main Street, Babcary TA11 7ED
☎ *(01458) 223230* Charles Garrard

Teignworthy Springtide and Otter Bright are the two regular beers at this freehouse, and the weekly guest might be something like Bath Gem.

A locals' bar in a thatched building dating from 1650, dimly lit and featuring open fire, low ceilings, flagstones, woodburner, sofa and large wooden tables. Lounge and 50-seater restaurant. Boules. Food served 12–2.30pm and 7–10pm. Large car park, large garden. Children's area. Half a mile from the A37, four miles from the A303.

OPEN *12–3pm and 6pm–12.*

BARRINGTON

The Royal Oak

Barrington, Nr Ilminster TA19 0JB
☎ *(01460) 53455*

Leased from Punch Taverns with three real ales available. Butcombe brews and Bass are regulars plus a weekly-rotating guest.

A 16th-century Grade II listed building. Food served 12–2.30pm and 7–9.30pm every day. Car park, garden, skittle alley and function room for larger parties. Follow the National Trust signs for Barrington Court.

OPEN *12–3pm and 6–11pm Mon–Fri; open all day Sat–Sun.*

BARTON ST DAVID

The Barton Inn

Barton St David, Somerton TA11 6BZ
☎ *(01458) 850451* Damon Brooke
www.barton-inn.co.uk

A freehouse with two ales, changing daily. Among the breweries featured are many locals such as Glastonbury Ales, Otter, Bath, Cheddar, Hop Back, Downton, Cotleigh, Church End and Teignworthy.

A 1920s brick-built village watering hole. Simply furnished with a real fire. Tasty, simple food served lunchtimes and evenings. Children and dogs welcome. Skittle alley and function room. Live music and events. Annual beer festival. Situated between Somerton and Glastonbury.

OPEN *12–2pm and 4.30–11pm Mon–Fri; 12–11pm Sat–Sun.*

BATH–CITY

The Bell

103 Walcot Street, Bath BA1 5BW
☎ *(01225) 460426* Ian Wood (landlord)/
Jamie Matthews (manager)
www.walcotstreet.com

Abbey Bellringer, Bath Gem, Butcombe Blond, Stonehenge Danish Dynamite, Hop Back Summer Lightning, RCH Pitchfork and Otter Ale plus two guests that change every four or five days.

There has been a pub on this site for at least 400 years. Bohemian in character, with a clientele of all ages and classes. Live rootsy music Mon and Wed nights, and Sun lunchtimes (see website for band listings).

Vegetarian and vegan rolls available daily, plus organic and Fairtrade coffee and tea. Delightful beer garden and back room for (supervised) children. Dogs welcome on a lead. Free Wi-Fi throughout. Local CAMRA Pub of the Year in 2004. Home to the world's smallest launderette. Half a mile due north of Bath Abbey – just ask!

OPEN *11.30am–11pm Mon–Sat; 12–10.30pm Sun.*

The Hobgoblin

47 St James' Parade, Bath BA8 1UZ
☎ *(01225) 460785* John Whinnerah

Freehouse specialising in Wychwood ales, so Hobgoblin and Fiddler's Elbow always available plus four guests.

Lively town pub with a student clientele. Two bars. Food available at lunchtime. No children. Pool room, quarterly beer festivals. Two minutes from the train and bus stations.

OPEN *All day, every day.*

Hop Pole

7 Albion Buildings, Bath BA1 3AR
☎ *(01225) 446327* Tim Wilkins (manager)
www.bathales.co.uk

Bath Ales pub offering four Bath brews plus one guest, changed weekly.

A 17th-century pub with a friendly atmosphere, traditional décor and a fantastic garden. Food served 6.30–9pm Mon; 12-2pm and 6.30-9pm Tues–Sat; 12–3pm Sun. The 32-seater restaurant. Booking is preferred at weekends. Private functions are also catered for. New chef with amazing menu, changing weekly. On Upper Bristol Road, opposite Queen Vic Park.

OPEN *12–11pm Sun–Thurs; 12–12 Fri–Sat.*

King William

36 Thomas Street, Bath BA1 5NN
☎ *(01225) 428096* Mr and Mrs JC Digney
www.kingwilliampub.com

Freehouse with four rotating real ales, all from small breweries in the South West, and all changing weekly.

Small corner pub over three floors, including snug in cellar and two dining rooms on the first floor. A pub since 1827. Food served 12–2.30pm every lunchtime, 6.30–10pm Mon–Sat for bar snacks, and 6.30–10pm for dinner on Wednesdays. Private dining room available Sun, Mon and Tues night, plus Mon–Fri lunchtimes. Well-behaved children welcome for lunch. On the corner of Thomas Street and the A4 London Road, just ten minutes' walk from the centre of Bath.

OPEN *12–2.30pm and 5pm–12 Mon–Fri; 12–12 Sat; 12–11pm Sun.*

Ye Old Farmhouse

1 Lansdown Road, Bath BA1 5EE
☎ *(01225) 316162*
Matthew Warburton and Morley Coulson

Wadworth 6X, JCB, Farmhouse Ale and Henry's IPA are permanent fixtures, and a Wadworth seasonal guest is also served.

Refurbished in late 2006, this is a classic jazz pub, lively and atmospheric, with one bar, back service area and two roaring log fires. Food made from freshly sourced produce served 12–2.30pm (3pm Sun) daily, 5.30–9.30pm Mon–Thurs, 5.30–10pm Fri–Sat and 7–9pm Sun. Booking is recommended. Regular jazz and blues on Tues and Sun evenings. Outside smoking facilities. Children welcome. Beer garden in spring/summer. Close to the attractions of Bath. Halfway up the Lansdown Hill, ten minutes' walk uphill from the city centre.

OPEN *11.30am–2.30pm and 5.30pm–12 Mon–Sat; 12–4pm and 7pm–12 Sun.*

The Old Green Tree

12 Green Street, Bath BA1 2JZ
☎ *(01225) 448259*
Nick Luke and Tim Bethune

Only stocks draught beer from micro-breweries within a 100-mile radius. Six or seven beers available including RCH Pitchfork and Wickwar Brand Oak Bitter. Others rotated regularly including brews from Abbey, Hidden, Otter, Stonehenge and Blindmans. Also real cider.

A small oak-lined city-centre real ale institution. Built during the 18th century and a pub for almost 250 years. Traditional, with no recorded music or machines. Food available, including specials, at lunchtimes (12–3pm). Three rooms. On a small street in city centre between Milsom Street and the post office. No children.

OPEN *11am–11pm Mon–Sat; 12–10.30pm Sun.*

The Pig & Fiddle

2 Saracen Street, Bath BA1 5BR
☎ *(01225) 460868*
Jenny Brown and Fran Haley

Freehouse with Abbey Bellringer and four guests from local breweries within a 40-mile radius, changed every three months.

Opened in the late 1980s, a busy town-centre pub but with relaxed atmosphere. Bar food available 11am–7pm Mon–Fri, 11am–6pm Sat and 12–6pm Sun. Beer garden. Big screen with all sports shown. Children and dogs welcome in garden. Opposite the Hilton Hotel.

OPEN *11am–11pm Mon–Sat; 12–10.30pm Sun.*

The Royal Oak

Lower Bristol Road, Bath BA2 3BW
☎ *(01225) 481409* John Whinnerah
www.theroyaloak-bath.co.uk

 Freehouse with ten ales, all daily-changing rotating guests from micro-breweries.

A real ale specialist pub in an early 19th-century building with two bars and open fires. CAMRA Pub of the Year 2007. Garden, car park. Beer and music festivals held three times a year. Children welcome. Weekly Irish session and fortnightly music nights Sat and Sun. Located five minutes from Oldfield Park station. On the number 5 bus route from the town centre.

OPEN *12–12.*

The Salamander

John Street, Bath BA1 2JL
☎ *(01225) 428889* Rob Kinsella

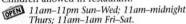 Bath Ales house serving Bath Gem, SPA and Barnstormer plus three guest beers, perhaps something like Butcombe Gold or an ale from one of the smaller breweries.

G rade II listed building dating from around 1730 which opened as a coffee bar in 1957. Taken over by Bath Ales in 2001, revamped and refurbished but with some original features retained. Food is available. Children allowed in restaurant.

OPEN *11am–11pm Sun–Wed; 11am–midnight Thurs; 11am–1am Fri–Sat.*

Star Inn

23 The Vineyards, Bath BA1 5NA
☎ *(01225) 425072*
Alan Morgan and Paul Waters
www.star-inn-bath.co.uk

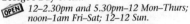 Abbey Bellringer and Bass served from the jug plus three rotating guests, changed daily.

T imeless local built around 1760 with a friendly atmosphere within the wonderful old interior. One bar with four small rooms including 'death row', where the old folk sit. The pub was built by a local coffin maker and is actually coffin-shaped. Freshly prepared rolls only. Traditional games such as shove ha'penny. Regular beer festivals, plus annual Cornish festival in July, and St George's Day event.

OPEN *12–2.30pm and 5.30pm–12 Mon–Thurs; noon–1am Fri–Sat; 12–12 Sun.*

Volunteer Rifleman Arms

3 New Bond Street Place, Bath BA1 1BH
☎ *(01225) 425210* Paul Alvis

 Freehouse serving Abbey Bellringer, Mole's Molecatcher and Exmoor Gold as permanents, plus guests such as Timothy Taylor Landlord and beers from Otter, Abbey and Cheddar.

C osy little pub tucked away down a backstreet shopping alley, could be described as a little bit of Amsterdam in the centre of Bath. One bar. Food every session.

OPEN *11am–11pm Mon–Thurs; 11am–2am Fri–Sat; 12–10.30pm Sun.*

BATH–BATHWICK

The Pulteney Arms

37 Daniel Street, Bathwick, Bath BA2 6ND
☎ *(01225) 463923* Ash McMorris
www.pulteneyarms.co.uk

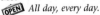 Butcombe Bitter, Young's Bitter, Wadworth 6X, Fuller's London Pride and Bath Gem plus a sixth beer, rotated every six weeks.

O ld-fashioned local with gas lighting around the bar and gas fires, a sporting institution with strong links to rugby and hockey in Bath. It was built as a house in 1759 and converted to a pub in 1792 by the then Walcot Brewery. There is a restaurant upstairs, and homemade food is served Wed–Sun lunchtimes and every evening, with the pub's own sausages a speciality. Darts, dominoes and cribbage. Outside sun-trap. Well-behaved children welcome until 7pm. Situated around the corner of Great Pulteney Street, near the Holburne Museum.

OPEN *5–11pm Mon–Tues; 12–3pm and 5–11pm Wed–Fri; all day Sat–Sun.*

BATH–LOWER WESTON

Dolphin Inn

103 Locksbrook Road, Lower Weston, Bath BA1 3EN
☎ *(01225) 445048*
Gareth Leakey and Samantha Humphries

Marston's Pedigree, Flowers Original (brewed by Badger), Wadworth 6X and Butcombe Bitter are usually available.

A friendly and busy community pub, located by the riverside and on the Bath–Bristol cycleway. Food served all day. Children welcome. A range of different areas, including a purpose-built one for smoking. Car park and garden. Darts, skittle alley, function room.

OPEN *11am–11pm Mon–Thurs; 11am–midnight Fri–Sat; 11am–11.30pm Sun.*

BAWDRIP

The Knowle Inn

115 Bath Road, Bawdrip, Nr Bridgwater TA7 8PN
☎ *(01278) 683330* PD Mathews

Bitters from Otter and Butcombe, Newmans Wolver Ale, Cotleigh Barn Owl and Cottage Champflower are regular features, plus guests. Cask Marque accredited.

A 16th-century coaching inn created from three farm cottages, close to the site of the Battle of Sedgemoor. Food is served lunchtimes and evenings, and the restaurant specialises in fish and grills. Children welcome. Large well-kept beer garden and car park. Darts. Roadside pub just north of Bridgwater on the A39, off junction 23 of the M5.

OPEN *All day, every day.*

BLAGDON

New Inn

Church Street, Blagdon BS40 7SB
☎ *(01761) 462475* Roger and Jackie Owen

 Wadworth Henry's IPA, 6X, JCB and Bishops Tipple always available, plus occasional guest beers.

Welcoming country pub in a 17th-century cider house, with beams, log fires, and fantastic views of Blagdon Lake from the beer garden. Two bar areas. Food served 12–2pm and 7–9pm every day. Children over 10 welcome. Wassail in January. Cheddar Gorge and Weston-super-Mare nearby. Turn down by the school, opposite St Andrew's Church.

OPEN *11am–3pm and 6–11pm.*

Queen Adelaide

High Street, Blagdon BS40 7RA
☎ *(01761) 462573* Andrew McKendrick
www.queen-adelaide.com

Butcombe Bitter plus one rotating guest, changed every four to six weeks.

Traditional one-bar country village pub in a Grade II listed building. Food served 12–2pm and 6–9.30pm Mon–Fri all year round; Nov–Easter: 12–2pm and 6–9.30pm Sat, 12–6pm Sun; Easter–Oct: 12–9.30pm Sat, 12–9pm Sun. Beer garden with views. Car park. Dogs welcome. In Mendip Area of Outstanding Natural Beauty, close to Cheddar, Wookey Hole, Wells, Bath and Bristol. On the A368 at the western end of Blagdon, between Bath and Weston-super-Mare.

OPEN *12–2.30pm and 6–11pm Mon–Sat (open 12–11pm Sat in summer); 12–10.30pm Sun.*

BLEADON

The Queen's Arms

Celtic Way, Bleadon, Nr Weston-super-Mare BS24 0NF
☎ *(01934) 812080* Daniel Pardoe

Butcombe pub serving Bitter, Blond and Gold plus a couple of guests, which may include Palmers IPA and Ringwood Old Thumper.

A 16th-century freehouse with flagstone floors and settles, specialising in good food and real ales served straight from the barrel. A good stop for refreshment on the Mendip Walk. Food served daily lunchtimes and evening, except Sunday evening in the winter when the pub holds a very popular quiz night. Skittle alley also available.

OPEN *11.30am–2.30pm and 5.30–11pm Mon–Fri; 11.30am–11pm Sat; 12–10.30pm Sun.*

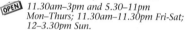

BRIDGWATER

Annie's Bar

North Street, Bridgwater TA6 3PW
☎ *(01278) 433053* Mr Truman

Freehouse serving Butcombe Bitter and St Austell Tribute plus one weekly-changing guest, such as a beer from Teignworthy, Stonehenge or Cottage.

Country pub on the outskirts of town in an old, traditional building with beams and fireplaces. Back bar and front bar. Food available (back bar for dining). Garden. Children allowed until 7.30pm.

OPEN *5–11.30pm Mon–Sat; 12–3pm and 6–10.30pm Sun.*

The Fountain Inn

1 West Quay, Bridgwater TA6 3HL
☎ *(01278) 424115* Paul and Emma Gover
www.alefountain.com

Owned by Wadworth, with up to eight real ales. Wadworth beers are heavily featured, plus Butcombe Bitter and other guests changed weekly.

A traditional 400-year-old one-bar country pub overlooking the River Parrott in the town centre. Background music and occasional live bands. Freshly prepared food available at lunchtimes only. Euchre and darts teams. En-suite rooms available. Home to Bridgwater carnival. Convenient for Glastonbury, Longleat, Cheddar, Minehead and other attractions. Just off the M5.

OPEN *11.30am–3pm and 5.30–11pm Mon–Thurs; 11.30am–11.30pm Fri-Sat; 12–3.30pm Sun.*

The Horse & Jockey

1 Durleigh Road, Bridgwater TA6 7HU
☎ *(01278) 424283* Ron Chedgey

Beers from Exmoor and Teignworthy are always on offer. Four guests, often changed daily, might include Timothy Taylor Landlord or something from Shepherd Neame.

Out-of-town, traditional pub in a coaching house dating from 1770. Extended to make the dining area bigger. Two function rooms. No children.

OPEN *2–11pm.*

BROADWAY

The Bell Inn

Broadway, Nr Ilminster TA19 9RG
☎ *(01460) 52343* Andrew and Fiona Atkins
www.bellinnbroadway.co.uk

Wells and Young's tied house serving Young's Bitter and Special and Charles Wells Bombardier.

Traditional country inn with flagstone floor, open fires and feature well! Lounge bar, restaurant and function room. Food served 12–2pm every day plus 6.30–9.30pm Tues–Sat. Six en-suite twin bedrooms with full English breakfast. Attractive patio. Conference facilities, skittle alley, car park. Just off the A358 Taunton road.

OPEN *11am–3pm and 5pm–12 Mon–Sat; 12–3pm and 7–11pm Sun.*

BUCKLAND DINHAM

The Bell Inn

High Street, Buckland Dinham, Nr Frome BA11 2QT
☎ *(01373) 462956* Jeremy Westcott
www.bellatbuckland.co.uk

Enterprise Inns leased pub serving Wychwood's Hobgoblin, Butcombe Best and London pride plus one rotating guest changed twice weekly.

This 16th-century village pub in the countryside has two bars, a restaurant, cinema and three resident ghosts. Award-winning food served Wed–Sun lunchtimes and Mon–Sun evenings. Large car park. Annual beer and music festivals, a cider festival, and a cider and tobacco festival. Barn with bar and screen for hire. Beer gardens with BBQ facilities. Children and dogs welcome. Showground available for displays and fetes. Licensed for civil wedding ceremonies. And - Pet Weddings!! Located south of Bath between Frome and Radstock.

OPEN *12–3pm and 6pm–12.*

BURNHAM ON SEA

The Royal Clarence Hotel

31 The Esplanade, Burnham on Sea TA8 1BQ
☎ *(01278) 783138*
Graham and Joanne Townley

RCH and Butcombe beers plus one other guest, changed throughout the year.

An old coaching hotel. Bar food available. Conference facilities. Accommodation. Parking. Children allowed. Take M5 junction 22, then make for the sea front. The hotel is on the sea front.

OPEN *11am–11pm Mon–Sat; 12–10.30pm Sun.*

CANNINGTON

Malt Shovel Inn

Blackmoor Lane, Bradley Green, Cannington TA5 2NE
☎ *(01278) 653432* Tracy Twine

Freehouse serving Butcombe Bitter, Exmoor Fox and one guest ale, changed every barrel.

Old country pub with beamed ceilings and log fires. Extensive menu of freshly prepared food, including children's meals, served 12–2pm and 7–9pm; there is a carvery on Sundays. Beer garden, small function room, car park. Dogs on leads and children are welcome. Just off the A39 at Cannington.

OPEN *11.30am–2.30pm and 6.30–11pm.*

Rose & Crown

30 High Street, Cannington TA5 2HF
☎ *(01278) 653190* Jack Phippen

Punch Taverns tied pub serving Greene King Abbot and IPA, Courage Directors and Caledonian Deuchars IPA plus one weekly-changing guest.

Said to have been built in 1638, this one-bar pub is filled with lots of old and interesting artefacts including over 130 clocks and watches. Comfortable and friendly atmosphere with log burner. Large award-winning beer garden with BBQ facilities. Car park. Two beer festivals held each summer. Near to Quantock Hills and Exmoor, with the West Country coastline easily accessible. Located on the A39 between Minehead and Bridgwater.

OPEN *12–12.*

CHARD

The Bell & Crown Inn

Combe Street, Chard TA20 1JP
☎ *(01460) 62470* Michael Hood

Otter Bitter is a permanent fixture, plus four guests, usually from West Country breweries, or seasonal and celebration ales.

Quiet, old-fashioned pub with gas lights. No music. Beer garden. Food available Tues–Sun lunchtime. Children allowed.

OPEN *12–2.30pm (closed Mon lunchtime) and 7–11pm Mon–Fri; 12–3pm and 7–11pm Sat–Sun (10.30pm Sun).*

CHELYNCH

Poacher's Pocket

Chelynch, Shepton Mallet BA4 4PY
☎ *(01749) 880220* Stephanie and Ken Turner

Freehouse serving Cotleigh Tawny, Butcombe Bitter and Wadworth 6X and generally a guest beer.

A traditional village pub with various different rooms off the one bar; has been licensed since the 17th century. Food every session. Children and dogs allowed if well-behaved. Skittle alley and shove ha'penny. Folk club once a month. Beer festival on last weekend of September and cider festival during May bank holiday. Car park and garden.

OPEN *12–3pm and 6–11pm.*

CHEW MAGNA

The Bear & Swan

13 South Parade, Chew Magna BS40 8SL
☎ *(01275) 331100* Nigel Pushman
www.bearandswan.co.uk

Butcombe Bitter plus Courage Best and a guest such as Bath Ales Gem.

Pub and restaurant with accommodation at the centre of the village. Food served 12–2pm and 7–9.45pm (not Sun evenings). No children's facilities. Car park.

OPEN *11am–11pm Mon–Sat; 12–6pm Sun.*

CHILCOMPTON
The Somerset Wagon

Broadway, Chilcompton, Radstock, Bath BA3 4JW
☎ *(01761) 232732* Adrian and Kate Brixey
www.thesomersetwagon.co.uk

 Wadworth pub offering 6X and IPA plus Butcombe Bitter. A seasonal guest is also served.

A 200-year old quintessential Somerset pub with connections to the railway industry and with part of building once used as a smithy. Olde-worlde character with one bar and beams. Food served 12–3.30pm and 6.30–9.30pm (7–9pm Sun evening). Child-friendly. Front and back beer garden, large car park. Regular music on Sunday. Near to Wells, Bath, Cheddar, Longleat and Bristol. On the B3139 between Wells and Bath.

OPEN *12–3.30pm and 5–11.30pm (opens at 6pm at weekends).*

CHISELBOROUGH
The Cat Head Inn

Cat Street, Chiselborough, Stoke sub Hamdon TA14 6TT
☎ *(01935) 881231* Avril and Duncan Gordon
www.thecatheadinn.co.uk

 Enterprise Inns pub usually offering three real ales, with Otter Best, Butcombe Bitter, Sharp's Doom Bar and St Austell Tribute among the favourites.

Q uiet, clean creeper-clad village local with flagstone floors and logs fires, converted from a farmhouse in the 1897. Food served 12–3pm and 7–9.30pm daily. Large, award-winning beer garden, skittle alley and children's play area. Close to Montecute House and Barrington House and Gardens. Just off the A303, take the A356 to Crewkerne.

OPEN *12–3pm and 6–11pm.*

CHURCHILL
The Crown Inn

Skinners Lane, The Batch, Churchill, Nr Bristol BS25 5PP
☎ *(01934) 852995* Tim Rogers

Beers from RCH, Palmers, St Austell, Butcombe, Cotleigh, Bass and Cheddar are among the nine real ales always available, and two weekly guests are also served.

A 16th-century coaching inn with two bars, five small rooms, flagstone floors and two real fires. Food made and prepared to order with fresh local produce when practical, 12–2.30pm. Children welcome. Extensive beer gardens surrounding the pub. In the foothills of the Mendip Hills, near Churchill Ski Slopes and Riding Centre and ten minutes' south of Bristol airport.

OPEN *11am–11pm (midnight Sat–Sun).*

CLEVEDON
The Old Inn

9 Walton Road, Clevedon BS21 6AE
☎ *(01275) 340440* Lesley Butler
www.theoldinnclevedon.co.uk

 Courage Best plus three rotating guests, changed twice weekly.

T his one-bar pub is approximately 200 years old. Breakfast served 7–10.30am Mon–Sun. Lunch served 12–2.30pm Mon–Fri and Sun, all day Sat. B&B available. Beer garden with children's play area. Located off the M5.

OPEN *7am–11pm.*

COMBE HAY
The Wheatsheaf

Combe Hay, Nr Bath BA2 7EG
☎ *(01225) 833504*
Sean Walker and Jaki Hathway

Freehouse with Greene King Old Speckled Hen as a regular and two guest beers changing weekly. One beer will come from a Bath brewery.

A ttractive gastropub in a pretty village just south of Bath. Log fires in the winter and barbecues during summer weekends. Food served 11am–2.30pm and 6–9.30pm Mon–Sat, 12–4pm and 6–9pm Sun. Large and pleasant garden. Children and dogs welcome. Car park. Accommodation.

OPEN *Winter: 11am–3pm and 6–11pm Mon–Thurs; all day Fri–Sun. Open all day every day from Easter to 30 September.*

COMPTON MARTIN
Ring O' Bells

Compton Martin BS40 6JE
☎ *(01761) 221284* Roger Owen

 Freehouse serving a range of real ales, including Butcombe Bitter, Blond and Gold, plus a rotating guest such as Fuller's London Pride.

A quiet yet busy typical English pub with low ceilings and wooden beams, popular for food. Two bars and a restaurant room with food served at every session. Large car park and garden. Children welcome in family room. Darts and shove ha'penny.

OPEN *11.30am–2.30pm and 6.30–11pm Mon–Fri; 11.30am–3pm and 6.30–11pm Sat; 12–3pm and 6.30–10.30pm Sun.*

CONGRESBURY
The Plough Inn

High Street, Congresbury BS49 5JA
☎ *(01934) 877402* Gary and Charlotte Polledri

Freehouse with six real ales. Butcombe Best plus five guests from RCH, St Austell, Otter, Cheddar and many more small breweries.

A 200-year-old alehouse with two small serveries and rooms with flagstoned floors. Food lunchtimes and evenings (not Fri or Sun evening). Car park, large garden. Charity quiz night is Sunday.

OPEN *11.30am–2.30pm and 4.30–11pm Mon–Sat; 12–3pm and 7–11pm Sun.*

CORTON DENHAM

The Queen's Arms

Corton Denham DT9 4LR
☎ *(01963) 220317 Rupert Reeves*
www.thequeensarms.com

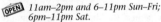 A freehouse. Butcombe Bitter, moor Revival, Timothy Taylor Landlord. Two guests, changing twice weekly, including Cheddar Ales Potholer, Bath Ales Wild Hare, Adnams Tally Ho, Harveys Sussex, Fuller's Golden Pride and Yeovil Ales Summerset. 55 classic bottled beers from around the world.

Country pub dating from the late 18th century, tucked away in a sleepy village on the Somerset/Dorset border. Bar, bustling dining room and garden terrace, plus function room. Children welcome, with a large basket of toys provided. Food, including an innovative children's menu, served 12–3pm and 6–10pm. Accommodation in modern stylish bedrooms. Summer hog roasts, cider events and beer tastings. From A303 Chapel Cross exit, go through South Cadbury and follow signs to Corton Denham, the pub is at the end of the village.

(OPEN) *11am–3pm and 6–11pm Mon–Fri; 11am–11pm Sat–Sun.*

CREWKERNE

The Old Stagecoach Inn

Station Road, Crewkerne TA18 8AL
☎ *(01460) 72972 Anton, Jordi and Delores*
www.stagecoach-inn.co.uk

Freehouse with something from Glastonbury Ales or another West Country brewer always available plus two weekly-changing guests and a range of Belgian beers.

Built in 1880 as a posting house, this one-bar pub has been under its present licensee since 2000. Food served 11am–2pm and 6.30–9.30pm Sun–Fri, 6–10pm Sat. Fusion kitchen featuring food cooked in Belgian beers. Children welcome. Special Belgian weekends held by appointment. Located on the A356 next door to Crewkerne station. Accommodation.

(OPEN) *11am–2pm and 6–11pm Sun–Fri; 6pm–11pm Sat.*

CROSCOMBE

The George Inn

Croscombe, Nr Wells BA5 3QH
☎ *(01749) 342306 Peter Graham*
www.thegeorgeinn.co.uk

A family-run freehouse. Blindmans King George the Thirst and Cheddar Ales' Gorgeous George are brewed exclusively for the pub. Butcombe Bitter and also one or two West Country regularly changing guest ales. Breweries featured include Berrow, Box Steam, Cheddar, Cottage, RCH, Taunton, Palmers, Milk Street, Matthews, Moor, Glastonbury, Cotleigh and Sharp's.

Stone-built 17th-century village pub with log fire, heated all-weather patio, beer garden, children's games and play area, skittle alley and family room. Restaurant, public bar and B&B. Food served 12–2pm and 7–9pm. Dogs welcome. Disabled access.

Two beer festivals each year. On the A371 between Wells and Shepton Mallet.

(OPEN) *12–2.30pm and 7–11.30pm (from 6pm Fri).*

CROSS

The New Inn

Old Coach Road, Cross BS26 2EE
☎ *(01934) 732455*
Steven Gard and Emma Britton

Four real ales, always including one from Otter Brewery, plus rotating guests including Exmoor Stag, Cheddar Ales Potholer, RCH Double Header and Dorset's JD 1742.

Sixteenth-century coaching inn tied to Enterprise Inns. Large beer garden with panoramic views across the Mendips. Family friendly with a children's play area. Two beer festivals each year. Traditional homemade food served 12–9pm Mon–Sat and 12–8pm Sun. Located ten minutes from J23 northbound on A38 at Cheddar turning.

(OPEN) *12–11pm.*

CULMHEAD

The Holman Clavel Inn

Culmhead, Taunton TA3 7EA
☎ *(01823) 421432 Cara Lawrence*

 Freehouse serving Butcombe Bitter and Gold plus four guests per week, including beers such as Sharp's Doom Bar, Cheddar Potholer, Milk Street Funky Monkey and Greene King Old Speckled Hen.

A 14th-century rural inn with oak beams and real fires. Very traditional, with no juke box or fruit machines. Beer garden, parking front and back. Food available 12–2.30pm and 7–9.30pm. Children, dogs and horses welcome. From Taunton follow signs to cafe at the top of the hill. Turn left and the pub is 100 yards along on the right-hand side.

(OPEN) *12–12 Mon–Sat; 12–4pm and 7–11pm Sun.*

DINNINGTON

Dinnington Docks

Lower Street, Dinnington, Nr Hinton St George TA17 8SX
☎ *(01460) 52397 Hilary Hardisty*

Freehouse offering Wadworth 6X and Butcombe Bitter plus two or three guests normally from small local breweries.

Friendly village local formerly known as the Rose & Crown. A 17th-century building containing a selection of pictures, signs and memorabilia relating to its rail and maritime past. Reasonably priced food available every session. Children welcome. Play equipment in the garden. Car park and skittle alley. Haircuts in the pub on last Tues night of the month.

(OPEN) *11.30am–3.30pm and 6–11pm.*

EAST HARPTREE

Castle of Comfort Inn

East Harptree, Bristol BS40 6DD
☎ *(01761) 221321* Steve and Wendy Crook

Freehouse serving Butcombe Best plus two or three other real ales, changing weekly.

Pleasant country pub located in the middle of nowhere on the top of the Mendips. On the B3134. Food served 12–2.30pm and 6.30–9.30pm. Children welcome. Garden with play equipment plus decking area for sunny days. Car park. Traditional pub games.

OPEN *12–3pm and 6–11pm.*

EAST LYNG

Rose & Crown

East Lyng, Taunton TA3 5AU
☎ *(01823) 698235* Derek Mason

Freehouse serving Butcombe Bitter and Gold plus Palmers 200.

A respectable grown-ups' pub with classic lounge furniture – a good place to take mum! Food every session. Accommodation, garden, car park and skittle alley. On the A361 between Glastonbury and Taunton.

OPEN *11am–2.30pm and 6.30–11pm Mon–Sat; 12–3pm and 7–10.30pm Sun.*

EVERCREECH

The Bell Inn

Bruton Road, Evercreech BA4 6HY
☎ *(01749) 830287* Lee Carlton

Freehouse serving three real ales, with Butcombe Bitter, Sharp's Doom Bar and Blindmans Creech Ale regularly featured.

A 16th-century coaching inn, now a warm, welcoming, traditional village pub with a large bar and restaurant area. Opposite the village church that has apparently the most perfect spire in the country. Accommodation. Food, including homemade specials, 12–9pm Mon–Sat and 12–6pm Sun (including roasts). Beer garden, function room, skittle alley, pool, darts. Car park. Children and families welcome. Close to Royal Bath and West Showground. Near Shepton Mallet – follow signs for Evercreech from the A371.

OPEN *11am–midnight Mon–Sat; 12–11pm Sun.*

EXFORD

Exmoor White Horse Inn

Exford, Exmoor TA24 7PY
☎ *01643 831229* Peter and Linda Hendrie
www.exmoor-whitehorse.co.uk

Freehouse with four real ales. Beers from Exmoor and Dunkery are regularly featured, and one of the beers is changed every four weeks. Over 100 malt whiskies also available.

A 16th-century coaching inn in the heart of the Exmoor National Park, nestling by the pretty River Exe in the village of Exford. Oak-beamed bars and log fires. Three-star accommodation in 28 en-suite rooms. Food using local produce served 12–2.30pm every day, with cold food available all day. Private function suite for conferences, weddings and other events. Riverside beer garden. Children's licence. Exmoor Food Festival held in October. Handy for Exmoor Safaris.

OPEN *8am–11pm.*

FARLEIGH HUNGERFORD

Hungerford Arms

Farleigh Hungerford, Nr Bath BA3 6RX
☎ *(01225) 752411*
Hamish and Emma Curwen-Reed

Freehouse offering four real ales, all rotated weekly, from breweries such as Otter, Milk Street, Hidden and Palmers.

A 17th-century pub and restaurant with stone floors, open fires and a brilliant atmosphere. Large garden and patio with views of the whole valley and the castle. Long, characterful bar, restaurant and lounge. Food served 12–2.30pm and 6.15–9.30pm. Children and dogs more than welcome. Ample car parking.

OPEN *Summer: 10.30am–11pm.*
Winter: 11am–3pm and 6–11pm.

FAULKLAND

Tucker's Grave Inn

Faulkland, Nr Radstock BA3 5FX
☎ *(01373) 834230* Ivan and Glenda Swift

Butcombe Bitter served straight from the cask.

Really traditional rural pub – basic but with plenty of friendly rustic charm. Edward Tucker was buried here in 1747. No food. Skittle alley and shove ha'penny. Two car parks, beer garden.

OPEN *11.30am–3pm and 6–11pm Mon–Sat; 12–3pm and 7–10.30pm Sun.*

FROME

The Griffin

25 Milk Street, Frome BA11 3DB
☎ *(01373) 467766* Rik Lyall

The Milk Street Brewery tap, with four beers from the range available during the week and a fifth added for the weekend.

There has been a pub on the site for 400 years. It is now a busy single-bar community pub for real ale lovers, where customers are assured a warm welcome. No food. No children. Car parking, beer garden in summer.

OPEN *5–11pm (10.30pm Sun).*

The Horse & Groom

East Woodlands, Frome BA11 5LY
☎ *(01373) 462802*
Rick Squire and Kathy Barrett
www.horseandgroom.care4free.net

 Four real ales usually available, perhaps including Timothy Taylor Landlord, Branscombe Vale Branoc, Butcombe Bitter and Blindmans Mine Beer. The guests change on demand.

A 17th-century, two-bar country freehouse with log fires, flagstone floors, restaurant, conservatory and beer garden. Restaurant and bar food available at lunchtimes (Tues–Sun) and evenings (Mon–Sun). Children allowed in the restaurant, lounge and garden only. A mile from Longleat.

OPEN *6.30–11pm Mon; 11.30am–2.30pm and 6.30–11pm Tues–Sat; 12–3pm and 7–10.30pm Sun.*

GLASTONBURY

Who'd A Thought It

17 Northload Street, Glastonbury BA6 9JJ
☎ *(01458) 834460* Martin and Maureen Beech

 Tied to the Palmers brewery, regularly serving IPA and 200, and occasionally others such as Tally Ho! and Dorset Gold.

A real curiosity of a pub, full of bric-à-brac, old features and loads of character – there's an old red telephone kiosk in the corner, a bike attached to the ceiling and award-winning loos. Strong emphasis on homemade food served lunchtimes and evenings. Car park and patio. Children allowed.

OPEN *Summer: 11am–11pm Mon–Sat; 12–10.30pm Sun. Winter: 11am–2.30pm and 5.30–11pm Mon–Sat; 12–2.30pm and 5.30–10.30pm Sun.*

HALSE

The New Inn

Halse, Nr Taunton TA4 3AF
☎ *(01823) 432352* Jason Sinclair
www.newinnhalse.com

Home of the Taunton Brewing Company, which commenced brewing in late 2006, so all their brews served.

Independent 17th-century country freehouse. Home-cooked food every session. Many pub games including skittle alley, pool and darts. Well-behaved children and dogs welcome. Garden and car park. Accommodation in eight rooms. On walking routes, and close to West Somerset Railway.

OPEN *12–2.30pm and 6.30–11pm Mon–Fri; all day Sat–Sun.*

HARDINGTON MOOR

The Royal Oak Inn (Sonnys)

Moor Lane, Hardington Moor, Yeovil BA22 9NW
☎ *(01935) 862354* Martin and Debbie Hooper

Freehouse with three real ales, including Otter Bitter and two or three guests from breweries such as Yeovil, Butcombe, Sharp's, Cotleigh and Glastonbury.

Traditional country pub with separate dining room, games room, skittle alley and outdoor seating. Food served lunchtimes (not Mon) and evenings (not Sun). Children and pets welcome. Large car park. Motorcycle-friendly. Beer festival in May. Handy for many local attractions. Just off the A38 (Crewkerne Road) – turn left at the Yeovil Court Hotel.

OPEN *12–2.30pm and 7–11pm (10.30pm Sun). Closed Monday lunchtime.*

HENSTRIDGE

The Bird in Hand

2 Ash Walk, Henstridge, Templecombe BA8 0QD
☎ *(01963) 362255* M Williams

Freehouse serving Wadworth 6X plus two rotating guests changed every two to three days.

A 16th-century typical village inn retaining its original features including beams. Food served 12–2pm Mon–Sat. Beer garden. Skittle alley available for hire and private functions. Car park.

OPEN *11am–2.30pm and 5.30–11pm Mon–Fri; 11am–midnight Sat; 12–3pm and 7–10.30pm Sun.*

HILLCOMMON

The Royal Oak

Hillcommon, Taunton TA4 1DS
☎ *(01823) 400295* Richard Bolwell
www.royaloak-taunton.co.uk

 Freehouse with four real ales from micro-breweries in the South West such as Cotleigh, Teignworthy, Hop Back and Taunton.

Surrounded by beautiful countryside, this delightful village pub is an old coaching inn with timber ceiling beams, wood panelling and open fires. Food served 12–2.30pm and 6.30–9.30pm Mon–Sat, 12–2.30pm Sun including a £3.95 carvery. Walled courtyard garden. Car park. Function room available (holds up to 60). Annual beer festival. Children welcome. Near Oake golf course, Hestercombe house & gardens and Taunton racecourse. Located on the B3227 from Taunton to Wiveliscombe.

OPEN *12–3pm and 6–11.30pm Mon–Sat; 12–4pm and 6–11pm Sun.*

HINTON BLEWITT

Ring O'Bells

Hinton Blewitt, Nr Bristol BS39 5AN
☎ *(01761) 452239* Carla McCardle
www.butcombe.com

 Two Butcombe beers plus guests, rotated every couple of days.

Traditional 200-year-old country pub at the top of the Chew Valley, with one bar, roaring log fire and wonderful views. Small restaurant area known as the 'Snug'. Traditional English fayre served 12–2pm and 6–9pm. Lovely beer garden and boules piste. Children welcome. Handy for fishing at Chew Valley Lake, caving on Mendips, and fabulous walking and cycling routes. Situated between Bristol and Bath, just off the Wells Road.

OPEN *Mon-Thurs 12–3pm and 5–11pm; Fri-Sat 12-12; Sun 12-11pm.*

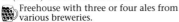

HOLCOMBE ROGUS
The Prince of Wales Inn
Holcombe Rogus, Wellington TA21 0PN
☎ *(01823) 672070* David Heard

 Freehouse with three or four ales from various breweries.

This refurbished pub with an olde-worlde feel dates back to the 17th century and has a restaurant and open fires. Food served 12–2pm and 6–9.30pm. Beer garden, skittle alley. Outdoor functions catered for. Large car park. Children welcome. Regular beer festivals.

OPEN *6–11pm Mon; 12–2pm and 6–11pm Tues–Fri; all day Sat–Sun.*

HORSINGTON
The Half Moon Inn
Horsington, Templecombe BA8 0EF
☎ *(01963) 370140*
Andrew and Philippa Tarling
www.horsington.co.uk

Freehouse serving Wadworth 6X plus four or five guests, rotating all the time but with two brews usually from micros and two from regionals.

Community country pub that tries to present a traditional front – a pretty exterior, pleasant interior, real fires and a friendly atmosphere. Stone-built in the 18th century. One large open-plan bar and separate restaurant. Accommodation. Darts and skittle alley. Food every session except Sunday evenings (book at weekends). Car park and large beer garden. Disabled access.

OPEN *12–2.30pm and 6–11pm Mon Fri; 12–3pm and 6–11pm Sat; 12–5pm Sun.*

HUISH EPISCOPI
The Rose & Crown (Eli's Inn)
Huish Episcopi, Langport TA10 9QT
☎ *(01458) 250494* Eileen Pittard and family

Genuine freehouse serving Teignworthy Reel Ale plus three guests, with examples including Hop Back Summer Lightning, Glastonbury Mystery Tor, Branscombe Vale Summa That and beers from Butcombe, plus many others. These are rotated weekly.

Built in 1640, a traditional country pub with thatched roof and gothic windows, in the same family for over 140 years (four generations). There is no bar – customers are served from the stone-flagged cellar, with lots of smaller adjoining rooms and a large room with pool, darts and skittle alley. Home-cooked food, using local produce whenever possible, available lunchtimes and evenings until 7.30pm. Large outside play area, beer garden. Children welcome. Wheelchair access. Pleasant riverside walks. Handy for swimming pool, garden centre and sports facilities. The nearby church is noted for its fine tower. Close to Somerset Wetlands, Muchelney Abbey and local potteries. On the A372 Langport to Long Sutton road, 300 yards from St Mary's Church in Huish Episcopi, towards Long Sutton.

OPEN *11.30am–2.30pm and 5.30–11pm Mon–Thurs; 11.30am–11pm Fri–Sat; 12–10.30pm Sun.*

KELSTON
The Old Crown
Bath Road, Kelston, Nr Bath
☎ *(01225) 423032*
Rebecca Swift and Stuart Roper
www.butcombe.com

 Butcombe Bitter, Blond, Gold and Brunel IPA, Bath Ales Gem, Wadworth 6X and Bass always available, with one of the beers rotating.

Traditional old-English pub with open fire, original flagstones and great atmosphere. Food every lunchtime and every evening except Sun. Car park and beer garden. Three en-suite rooms. Children and dogs welcome. On A43 Bitton to Bath road, three miles outside Bath.

OPEN *11am–11pm Mon–Sat; 12–10.30pm Sun.*

KINGSBURY EPISCOPI
The Wyndham Arms
Folly Road, Kingsbury Episcopi, Nr Martock TA12 6AT
☎ *(01935) 823239* Rob Rigby
www.wyndhamarms.com

Freehouse with four real ales on offer: Butcombe Bitter, Yeovil Summerset, Glastonbury Lady of the Lake and a weekly guest such as Otter Ale.

Lovely, listed, 16th-century country pub, comfortable, friendly and laid back, with mullion windows, sandstone walls and original flagstones, plus roaring open fires at each end. Superb home-cooked food and snacks available 12–2pm and 7–9pm Mon–Sat; traditional Sunday roasts 12–7pm. Large garden and excellent outside smoking and eating area. Skittle alley, large function room (up to 80 people). Well-behaved children and dogs welcome. On the River Parrett Trail and close to Thorney Lakes, Muchelney Abbey and local potteries. From the A303 follow the signs to Kingsbury Episcopi.

OPEN *12–4pm and 6.30pm–1am Mon–Thurs; noon–1am Fri–Sun.*

LANGFORD BUDVILLE
Martlet Inn
Langford Budville, Wellington TA21 0QZ
☎ *(01823) 400262* Vic and Paulette Bigg

Freehouse with Exmoor Ale and Gold and Budville Bitter from Master's Brewery in Wellington plus at least one guest per week from Cotleigh, Taunton or O'Hanlon's. Local cider from Sheppy's also on offer.

Village inn with beams, flagstones and inglenook fireplaces. Two bars, two separate dining areas, function room, award-winning gardens. Food available 12–2pm and 7–9.30pm Tues–Sun. Large and luxurious four-star B&B suites available. Large car park. A wonderful and convenient location from which to explore Somerset and Devon. Just off the B3187, a mile and a half north of Wellington (ten minutes from junction 26 of the M5).

OPEN *12–3pm and 7–11pm Tues–Sun (closed Monday except bank holidays).*

LANGLEY MARSH

The Three Horseshoes

Langley Marsh, Wiveliscombe TA4 2UL
☎ *(01984) 623763* Mark and Julie Fewlass

Exmoor Ale and Cotleigh 25 are permanent features. Guests usually include Otter bitter and Palmers IPA or Tribute.

A 17th-century traditional local pub providing excellent home-cooked food and a variety of real ales. Featured in numerous good pub guides. Spacious beer garden, families welcome. Two-bedroom barn conversion holiday accommodation. On the edge of Exmoor, in an ideal location for exploring the whole of the West Country. Follow the B3227 to Wiveliscombe, then follow signs to Langley Marsh.

OPEN *12–2.30pm and 7–11pm Tues–Sat; 12–2.30pm Sun.*

LANGPORT

The Black Swan

North Street, Langport
☎ *(01458) 250355* David and Anita Smith

Butcombe Gold is always available, and Fuller's London Pride alternates with other brews such as Otter.

Characterful inn with restaurant, skittle alley and beer garden. Food served 12–2pm and 7–9.30pm every day except Tuesday. Car park. Children welcome.

OPEN *11am–2.30pm and 6–11pm Mon–Thur; all day Fri–Sun.*

LEIGH COMMON

Hunters Lodge Inn

Leigh Common, Wincanton BA9 8LD
☎ *(01747) 840439* Mr Bent

Freehouse offering Butcombe Gold, Greene King Abbot and Fuller's London Pride.

Country pub with bars, dining area and beer garden. Food available at lunchtimes and evenings. Children allowed.

OPEN *11am–3pm and 6–11pm (10.30pm Sun).*

LIMPLEY STOKE

Hop Pole

Woods Hill, Limpley Stoke, Nr Bath BA2 7FS
☎ *(01225) 723134* Steve and Pauline Goddard

Freehouse always serving Butcombe Bitter, Marston's Pedigree and Courage Best, plus one rotating guest ale, changed weekly.

A typical old-English village pub characterised by the dried hops hanging from the beams and the wood panelling. Food served 12–2pm and 6.30–9pm (7–9pm Sun). Car parking. Children welcome. Large garden overlooking the valley.

OPEN *11am–2.30pm and 6–11pm Mon–Sat; 12–3pm and 7–10.30pm Sun.*

LOWER ODCOMBE

Mason's Arms

41 Lower Odcombe, Odcombe, Yeovil BA22 8TX
☎ *(01935) 862591* Paula Tennyson
www.masonsarmsodcombe.co.uk

Home of Odcombe Ales. The micro-brewery produces two regular ales, No. 1 and Spring, plus three seasonal ales, Odcombe Roly Poly, Winters Tail and Odcombe Half Jack. Three own brews usually on offer, with an occasional guest if they can't brew enough to keep up with demand!

Lovely village pub, the oldest building in the village, and the only survivor of the three original pubs. Gaining a reputation for good food, so it is advisable to book in the evening. Beer garden. Well-behaved children and dogs welcome. Camping and caravanning. Accommodation. Car park.

OPEN *12–3pm and 6pm–12.*

LUXBOROUGH

Royal Oak of Luxborough

Exmoor National Park, Luxborough, Nr Dunster TA23 0SH
☎ *(01984) 640319* James Waller
www.theroyaloakinnluxborough.co.uk

Freehouse serving Quantock Brewery beers, featuring Quantock Ale and White Hind.

A 15th-century country inn with two bars and three restaurants, with flagstones and open fire. No music or mobile phones. Food served 12–2pm and 7–9pm. Selection of baguettes, and cream teas in summer, served 2–5pm Sat–Sun. Car park and beer garden. Children over the age of 10 allowed, under-10's welcome at lunchtime. Dogs welcome. Accommodation in 11 letting rooms. Directly on the Coleridge Way walking route. Off the A396, four miles south of Dunster.

OPEN *12–2.30pm and 6–11pm Mon–Fri, all day Sat–Sun.*

MARTOCK

The Nag's Head

East Street, Martock TA12 6NF
☎ *(01935) 823432* Dawn and Steve

Beers from Badger plus others from various local breweries, changed every week or two.

A 200-year-old local village pub, formerly a cider house. Two bars (lounge and public), large beer garden and sun deck. Skittle alley, darts, pool. Large car park. Well known locally for its good homemade food, available 12–2pm Tues–Sun, 6–8pm Mon–Tues and 6–9pm Wed–Sat (no food Sun evening or Mon lunch). Families welcome. Near the village centre, by the post office.

OPEN *6–11.30pm Mon; 12–3pm and 6–11.30pm Tues–Thurs; all day Fri–Sun. Open bank holiday Mondays.*

The White Hart

East Street, Martock TA12 6JQ
☎ *(01935) 822005* Peter Halkyard
www.whiteharthotelmartock.co.uk

 Freehouse with Weymouth DBC plus two weekly-changing guests from breweries such as Sharp's and Otter.

Coaching inn dating from 1735, with one bar and a skittle alley. Fresh food 12–2pm and 6–9pm Tues–Sat; 12–2pm Sun. Children and dogs welcome. Car park. Ten en-suite rooms available. One mile from A303, four miles from Yeovil.

OPEN *5.30–11pm Mon; 12–3pm and 5.30–11.30pm Tues–Sat; 12–3pm Sun.*

MIDDLEZOY

George Inn

42 Main Road, Middlezoy, Nr Taunton TA7 0NN
☎ *(01823) 698215* Graeme and Candice Bell

 Genuine freehouse serving Butcombe Bitter as a permanent and three guests, perhaps a brew from Hop Back, Cottage or Otter, Sharp's, Slaters or Church End.

Lovely 16th-century village inn in the middle of the Somerset Levels. Stone floors, wooden beams and open fire. Characterful and atmospheric. Food every session except Sun and Mon evenings. Two bars. Children welcome by day. Beer terrace. Car park. Function room, skittle alley and darts. Easter beer festival. A mile from the junction of the A361 and A372.

OPEN *Closed Mon lunch; 12–2.30pm Tues–Fri; 12–3pm Sat–Sun; 7–11pm every day (10.30pm Sun).*

MIDSOMER NORTON

The White Hart

The Island, Midsomer Norton BA3 2HQ
☎ *(01761) 412957* Malcolm Curtis

 Bass and Butcombe Bitter usually available.

Interesting Victorian pub in the centre of town. Lots of different rooms including a skittle alley with full length mural. Food served at lunchtimes only – renowned for its ham, egg and chips. Tiny patio. Well-behaved children welcome. Twelve miles from Britsol, six from Bath.

OPEN *All day, every day.*

MINEHEAD

The Queen's Head Hotel

Holloway Street, Minehead TA24 5NR
☎ *(01643) 702940* C D A Seers

 Otter Ale, Exmoor Gold and St Austell Tribute. A selection of guest ales vary according to availability.

A 17th-century freehouse with pool, darts and skittles available. Juke box. Two beer festivals each year. Food served 12–2pm and 6.30–8.30pm.

OPEN *12–3pm and 5.30–11pm Sun–Fri (midnight Wed and Fri); all day Sat.*

MOORLINCH

The Ring of Bells

Pit Hill Lane, Moorlinch, Nr Bridgwater TA7 9BT
☎ *(01458) 210358*
Clive Davies and Patricia Gill

 Freehouse serving at least three real ales, all on a rotating basis, changing daily.

Pleasant, friendly and surprisingly spacious typical community village rural inn dating from the 1800s, with open fire, lounge, public bar and restaurant. Food served 12–2pm Tues–Sun and 6–9pm Tues–Sat (no food Sun evening or Mon). Beer garden, skittle alley, darts and pool. Car park. Children welcome. Near Clarks Village. Off the A39 between Street and Bridgwater, or off the A361 Old Taunton Road near Greinton.

OPEN *5pm–close Mon; 12–2.30pm and 5pm–close Tues–Fri; 12–close Sat–Sun.*

NAILSEA

The Blue Flame Inn

West End, Nailsea BS48 4DE
☎ *(01275) 856910* Mick Davidson

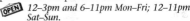 Fuller's London Pride, RCH East Street Cream, Bath Gem and something from Butcombe would be a typical selection, with two of the beers rotated regularly.

Charming, 200-year-old real country pub between Nailsea and Clevedon, popular with locals, joggers, riders and walkers. Three rooms and a bar, all with real character. Furnished with mismatched tables and chairs, as far as you can get from high-street theme pubs. Large garden with swings, covered drinking area and a barbecue. Children allowed everywhere except the public bar. Car park. No food.

OPEN *12–3pm and 6–11pm Mon–Fri; 12–11pm Sat–Sun.*

NETTLEBRIDGE

Nettlebridge Inn

Nettlebridge, Nr Oakhill
☎ *(01749) 841360* Rob and Angie Piner

Butcombe Gold and Bass regularly available.

Two-bar pub with nice walks nearby. Food from a substantial menu served 12–1.45pm and 6–9pm Mon–Sat, 12–8pm Sun; lunchtimes special is £5 for three courses. Car park for 70 cars (may need to ask inside to park). Children welcome. Six en-suite rooms for bed and breakfast. On the A367.

OPEN *12–3pm and 6–10.30pm Mon–Sat (11pm Sat); 12–10pm Sun.*

NORTH CURRY
The Bird in Hand
1 Queen Square, North Curry, Taunton TA3 6LT
☎ *(01823) 490248* James Mogg

Freehouse with Otter Bitter plus one or two constantly changing guests.

One-bar country pub with log fires and patio, located in attractive village. Food is available during all opening hours in both the bar and the pretty à la carte restaurant. Children allowed.

OPEN *12–3pm and 7–11pm Mon–Fri; 12–4pm and 7–11pm Sat; 12–3pm and 7–10.30pm Sun.*

NORTON ST PHILIP
Fleur de Lys
High Street, Norton St Philip, Nr Bath BA2 7LQ
☎ *(01373) 834333* Simon Shannon

A Wadworth house with 6X and IPA, plus Butcombe Bitter.

An old building and an old-style pub that prides itself on its food. Two bars and a restaurant above. Darts and skittles. Children welcome in one bar. Food served lunchtimes and evening seven days a week. Parking.

OPEN *11am–3pm and 5–11pm Mon–Fri; all day Sat; 12–4pm and 7–10.30pm Sun.*

NORTON SUB HAMDON
Lord Nelson
Rectory Lane, Norton sub Hamdon TA14 6SP
☎ *(01935) 881473*
Richard and Elaine Morrisey

Wadworth tied house serving 6X and Henry's IPA plus a seasonal guest.

Traditional village pub with a contemporary modern feel and a welcoming atmosphere. Home-cooked food using local produce served 12–2pm and 7–9pm every day. Skittle alley available for hire. Outside seating areas at front and back of pub. Close to Ham Hill and Montacute House. Signposted off the A303 to Taunton.

OPEN *12–2pm and 6.30–11pm Mon–Thurs; all day Fri–Sun.*

OAKHILL
Oakhill Inn
Fosse Road, Oakhill BA3 5HU
☎ *(01749) 840442*
Charlie and Amanda Digney
www.theoakhillinn.com

Three or four real ales - Butcombe Bitter on a permanent pump, plus two or three guests changed weekly, sourced from West Country breweries. Examples include Yeovil Ales' Summerset, Otter Ale, Stonehenge Spire Ale, Glastonbury Ales' Lady of the Lake and Bristol Beer Factory Red. Seasonals and specials may also appear.

Two-bar local dating from the 18th century, situated in the centre of the village. Families and dogs welcome. Open log fire in winter. Freshly cooked food using locally sourced ingredients served 12–3pm and 6–9pm Mon–Sat, 12–4pm Sun. Three miles north of Shepton Mallet on the A367.

OPEN *12–3pm and 5–11pm Mon–Fri (midnight Fri); 12–12 Sat; 12–11pm Sun.*

PITMINSTER
The Queen's Arms
Pitminster, Nr Taunton TA3 7AZ
☎ *(01823) 421529*
Deborah Turner and David Henderson
www.queensarms-taunton.co.uk

Leased from Enterprise, serving Otter Ale and Exmoor Ale plus one guest beer that changes every fortnight, such as Taunton Castle, Fuller's London Pride or Butcombe Blond.

Stone-built village pub, with country furniture, oak and slate floors and log fires. Food-oriented, with a daily changing menu using fresh local produce including fresh fish. Food served 12–2pm and 7–9pm. Runner-up in *Somerset Life's* Dining Pub of the Year 2007. Private function rooms for hire and refurbished skittle alley. Patio garden with parasols and heaters. Well-behaved children and dogs allowed. Car park. Follow the signs for Corfe from Taunton and turn right in Corfe – pub is three-quarters of a mile along on the left.

OPEN *Closed Mon; 12–3pm and 6–11pm Tues–Sat; 12–4pm Sun.*

PITNEY
The Halfway House
Pitney Hill, Nr Langport TA10 9AB
☎ *(01458) 252513* J Litchfield

Up to ten beers available, including brews from Teignworthy, Butcombe, Branscombe and Hop Back, plus other small West Country breweries.

A very popular real ale pub, 300 years old with flagstone floors and log fires. No music or games machines. Home-cooked food is available lunchtimes and evenings (not Sun). Car park and garden. Well-behaved children and dogs allowed. CAMRA Somerset Pub of the Year 2001, 2003 and 2008 and the winner of many other regional and national awards. On the main road between Somerton and Langport (B3153).

OPEN *11.30am–3pm and 5.30–11pm Mon–Sat; 12–3pm and 7–11pm Sun.*

PORLOCK WEIR
The Ship Inn
Porlock Weir, Nr Minehead TA24 8PB
☎ *(01643) 862753* H Allen
www.theanchorhotelandshipinn.co.uk

A freehouse. Exmoor Ale, Cotleigh Tawny and Otter Ale plus one guest, changed each month, such as Taunton Ale.

A 16th-century inn, overlooking the harbour. One main bar and outside seating area. Food served 12–2.30pm and 6.30–9pm. Children welcome. Street parking at the front.

OPEN *11am–11pm.*

PORTISHEAD

Windmill Inn

58 Nore Road, Portishead BS20 6JZ
☎ *(01275) 843677* J S Churchill

Freehouse with Courage, Bass, Butcombe RCH plus two guests, changed two to three times a week.

Originally built in 1832, the building had a golf pavilion added to it in 1908 before becoming a pub. It was refurbished and altered in 2000 and serves food 12–9.30pm Sun–Thurs and 12–10pm Fri–Sat. Large outdoor seating area overlooking the Channel and Bath bridges. Car park. Annual Easter beer festival. Located on the coastal road out of Portishead, off J19 of the M5.

OPEN *11am–11pm (10.30pm Sun).*

PRIDDY

Hunters Lodge Inn

Eastwater, Priddy, Near Wells BA5 3AR
☎ *(01749) 672275* Roger Dors

A freehouse. Butcombe Bitter and Blindmans Mine Beer. One or two guests changed twice a week. Range includes Cheddar Ales Potholer and ales from Glastonbury, Matthews and Bath Ales.

A rural pub, approximately 250 years old. Food served all day, every day. Garden. Car park. Situated close to Wookey Hole and Cheddar caves, and Wells Cathedral. A mile and a half east of Priddy.

OPEN *11.30am–2.30pm and 6.30–11pm Mon–Sat; 12–2pm and 7–11pm Sun.*

Queen Victoria Inn

Pelting Drove, Priddy, Nr Wells BA5 3BA
☎ *(01749) 676385* Alex Douglas
www.queenvictoria-butcombe.com

Owned by Butcombe, so offering Traditional and Gold, plus weekly guests including beers from Hidden and Bath.

Rural pub in the Mendip Hills dating from 1852 with a pleasant atmosphere, real fires and low wooden ceiling. Children and dogs welcome. Home-cooked food served 12–2pm and 7–9pm weekdays and 12–9pm Sat–Sun. Children's menu available. Car park, courtyard, beer garden and children's play area. Bar billiards and shove ha'penny. Close to Cheddar Gorge and Caves, and Wookey Hole. Signposted from the village green.

OPEN *12–3pm and 6–11pm Mon–Fri; 12–11.30pm Sat–Sun. Open 12–11pm every day in summer.*

RIMPTON

White Post Inn

Rimpton Hill, Rimpton, Yeovil BA22 8AR
☎ *(01935) 851218*
Graham and Colleen Brown

Freehouse serving St Austell Tinners and Dartmoor and Charles Wells Bombardier, plus a weekly guest such as another St Austell beer.

An 18th-centruy pub, recently completely refurbished from roof to foundations. One main bar with pool table and a 30-cover restaurant, with food served all day, every day. Live music at weekends. Huge car park. Accommodation in three modern en-suite 4-star rooms. Three miles north-west of Sherborne on the Marston Magner road, one mile south-east of Marston Magner.

OPEN *11am–11pm.*

RODE

The Bell Inn

13 Frome Road, Rode BA3 6PW
☎ *(01373) 830356* Richard Vestey

Freehouse with Butcombe Bitter, Courage Best and three other beers regularly available, perhaps something from Sharp's and Bristol Beer Factory.

Food-oriented country village pub with fresh fish always on offer. Two bars, real fires, dining area and family beer garden. Food available 12–2pm and 6.30–9pm. Children welcome. On the A361 between Trowbridge and Frome.

OPEN *11am–3pm and 6–11pm (10.30pm Sun).*

Cross Keys

20 High Street, Rode, Frome BA11 6NZ
☎ *(01373) 830900* Mike and Jane Baker

Butcombe brewery tied house serving Butcombe Bitter plus two guests, changed frequently, often including beers from other local breweries such as Hidden, Glastonbury or Milk Street. Cask Marque recognition.

A historical pub with a contemporary feel that re-opened in 2003 following a ten-year closure. Two bars and separate restaurant. Food served lunchtimes and evenings Mon–Sun. Beer garden with new patio. Children and pets welcome. Function room and beer festivals planned. Close to Longleat. Located in the centre of Rode village, just along from the green.

OPEN *11.30am–3pm and 6–11.30pm Mon–Fri; all day Sat–Sun.*

ROWBERROW

Swan Inn

Rowberrow, Winscombe BS25 1QL
☎ *(01934) 852371*

Butcombe Bitter, Blond and Gold always on offer.

Gimmick-free country pub that lets the customers create the atmosphere. Two spacious bars. Parking and garden areas. Food available lunchtimes and evening seven days a week. No children under 14. Just off the A38.

OPEN *12–3pm and 6–11pm Mon–Sat; 12–3pm and 7–10.30pm Sun.*

Sportsman's Inn

Sandyway, Exmoor EX36 3LU
☎ *(01643) 831109*

 Freehouse serving beers from Exmoor and St Austell plus others.

Isolated but cosy pub on the edge of Exmoor between North Molton and Withypool. Curiosities include a well in the middle of the bar. Popular with walkers and riders because of its location. Food available. Car park. Pool. Accommodation. Children allowed in restaurant.

OPEN *7–11pm Mon–Sat; 12–3pm and 7–11pm Sun. Open lunchtimes on a seasonal basis.*

Duke of York

North Street, Shepton Beauchamp TA19 0LW
☎ *(01460) 240314 Paul Rowlands*

Freehouse serving Teignworthy Reel Ale, Otter Ale, St Austell Proper Job plus a monthly-changing guest.

This 16th-century pub has exposed beams and open fires, and an open-plan bar area. Separate dining area, though many people prefer to stay in the bar area to eat. Food served lunchtimes and evenings Tues–Sun. Beer garden. Car park. Separate restaurant which can be used for private functions. Skittle alley. Five en-suite letting rooms. Well-behaved children and dogs welcome. Close to Barrington Court and on cycle paths and popular walking routes.

OPEN *6–11pm Mon (closed lunchtimes);12–3pm and 6.30–11pm Tues–Fri; 12–12 Sat; 12–11pm Sun.*

The Apple Tree

Shoscombe, Nr Bath BA2 8LF
☎ *(01761) 432263 Mark Bryan*

Greene King IPA, Exmoor Stag and Matthews Bob Wall are regulars, and a couple of other real ales are also served.

Quiet and friendly rural pub set in the heart of the village. Food every session from Wed lunchtimes to Sun lunchtime. Children welcome. Car park and garden.

OPEN *7–11pm Mon–Tues; 12–3pm and 7–11pm Wed–Fri; all day Sat–Sun.*

The Shurton Inn

Shurton, Bridgwater TA5 1QE
☎ *(01278) 732695 Jeffrey Bryant*

Freehouse with Exmoor Ale and Sharp's Doom Bar plus two guest ales, changed regularly, from breweries such as Hop Back, Cotleigh and Teignworthy.

A 300-year-old traditional country pub with a friendly atmosphere. Food served lunchtimes and evenings. Accommodation in four en-suite rooms. Beer garden, conservatory, skittle alley and restaurant. Beer festivals in summer (20 barrels) and February (12 barrels). Children welcome. Great walks, sea fishing, fly fishing and golf are all available locally, and the Minehead Railway is nearby.

OPEN *12–3pm and 6–11pm (from 7pm Sun).*

Brewers Arms

18 St James Street, South Petherton TA13 5BW
☎ *(01460) 241887 Duncan Webb*

Freehouse with Otter Bitter as a permanent and three constantly changing guest beers.

Busy, popular 17th-century former coaching inn in a pleasant town. One community bar and a separate restaurant in the old bakehouse. Beer festivals held last bank holiday in May and August bank holiday. Food every session, 12–2.15pm and 6–9pm. Courtyard and beer garden. Children welcome. Darts and skittle alley. Accommodation in three en-suite rooms. Half a mile from the A303.

OPEN *11.30am–2.30pm and 6–11pm Mon–Sat (open till 12 Fri–Sat); all day Sun.*

Sparkford Inn

High Street, Sparkford BA22 7JH
☎ *(01963) 440218 Paul Clayton*

Three real ales, changing frequently. Brews from Butcombe and Castle Eden are regulars.

A 15th-century coaching inn that is quite large yet retains a cosy olde-worlde atmosphere with two bars, window seats and interesting furnishing. Food served every session. Children welcome. Accommodation in ten en-suite bedrooms. Car park and small garden. Just off the A303.

OPEN *11am–3pm and 5.30–11pm.*

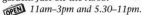

STANTON WICK

The Carpenters Arms

Stanton Wick, Nr Pensford BS39 4BX
☎ *(01761) 490202 Simon Pledge*
www.the-carpenters-arms.co.uk

 Freehouse offering Butcombe Bitter, Courage Best and Wadworth 6X plus the occasional guest.

Quaint, traditional, 300-year-old pub with restaurant, situated just off the A368. Converted from a row of miners' cottages. Cosy window seat by large fire. Disabled access. Food available in the bar and restaurant at lunchtimes and evenings every day. Accommodation (12 en-suite bedrooms). Large patio, car park. Children's menu.

OPEN *11am–11pm Mon–Sat; 12–10.30pm Sun.*

TAUNTON

The Eagle Tavern

South Street, Taunton TA1 3AF
☎ *(01823) 275713 Phil Steele and Jo Porter*

Otter Bitter plus one guest, maybe Timothy Taylor Landlord, Fuller's London Pride or something from Exmoor.

Country-style pub in the town, with wooden floors and open fire. Beer garden. Food available whenever open. Children not allowed.

OPEN *5–11pm Mon–Thur; all day Fri–Sun.*

The Hankridge Arms

Hankridge Way, Taunton TA1 2LR
☎ *(01823) 444405 Shelley Chase*

Badger Gold and Tanglefoot are permanents, plus one guest beer.

Grade II listed 16th-century building bizarrely located in a modern retail park. Handy after a visit to Sainsburys or B&Q. Large fireplace, stone floors and wooden beams. Food all day. Small garden. Car park.

OPEN *All day, every day.*

Perkin Warbeck

22 East Street, Taunton TA1 3LP
☎ *(01823) 335830 Ian and Leanne Borsing*

Wetherspoon's pub serving Shepherd Neame Spitfire and Greene King Abbot Ale plus up to three regularly changing regional guest ales, often including something from Butcombe.

Two-bar town-centre pub with patio. Food available all day, every day. Children allowed for dining until 5pm.

OPEN *All day, every day.*

TRUDOXHILL

The White Hart

Trudoxhill, Nr Frome BA11 2DT
☎ *(01373) 836324 Graeme Barry*

Shepherd Neame Spitfire and White Gold (brewed especially for the pub) plus two weekly guest beers from local breweries.

A 16th-century country pub. One bar, restaurant and garden. Food available 12–2.30pm and 5.30–9pm Mon–Sat; 12–4pm and 5.30–9pm Sun. Children allowed.

OPEN *All day, every day.*

WANSTROW

The Pub at Wanstrow

Station Road, Wanstrow, Shepton Mallet BA4 4SZ
☎ *(01749) 850455 Paul and Daria Stevens*

 Genuine freehouse serving something from Blindmans, Hop Back GFB and Bass plus two other ales, which could be from anywhere!

A very friendly little village local with a strong emphasis on the beer. Food every session except Monday and Sunday night. Two bars, dining area. Car park and small garden. Bar billiards, darts and skittle alley. On the A359.

OPEN *6.30–11pm Mon; 12–2.30pm and 6–11pm Tues–Fri; 12–3pm and 6–11pm Sat; 12–3pm and 7–11pm Sun.*

WATCHET

The Star Inn

Mill Lane, Watchet TA23 0BZ
☎ *(01984) 631367 Ross Nuttycombe*

An Enterprise Inns pub. Cotleigh Tawny, Ringwood Fortyniner, Otter Ale and Bitter and a Butcombe brew plus three guests, from in and around Somerset, changed every two or three days. Beers have included Bath Ales Gem, Stonehenge Pigswill, RCH Pitchfork and Firebox, Hop Back Summer Lightning and Hook Norton Old Hooky.

Traditional surroundings and a pretty beer garden in summer. Home-cooked food served 12–2.30pm and 6.30–9pm. Locally sourced meats for Sunday roasts. From the harbour, turn left for 300 yards, then left again.

OPEN *12–3pm and 6.30–11.30pm (later at weekends).*

WEDMORE

The New Inn

Combe Batch, Wedmore BS28 4DU
☎ *(01934) 712099 Angela Sayer*

Freehouse always serving a Butcombe brew plus a guest ale such as Fuller's London Pride, changing twice a week.

A popular little local, 300 years old with interesting corners in the two rooms. Food served 6–8.30pm daily and 12–2pm Tues–Sun. Beer garden and small car park. Pool, darts and skittle alley. Children welcome.

OPEN *6–11pm Mon; 12–3pm and 6–11pm Tues–Fri; all day Sat–Sun.*

WELLINGTON

The Cottage Inn

Champford Lane, Wellington TA21 8BH
☎ *(01823) 664650 Nobby and Penny Clarke*

Sharp's Doom Bar and O'Hanlon's Royal Oak plus two guests.

Town pub with a village feel, with two bars, skittle alley and patio garden for 50 people. Food served 12–2pm daily except Sunday. Children welcome, but no special facilities. Car park. In Wellington town centre, go past cinema and take the second turning on the left.

OPEN *11am–3pm and 6–11pm Mon–Fri; Sat 12–11pm and Sun 12-10.30pm.*

WELLOW

The Fox & Badger

Railway Lane, Wellow BA2 8QG
☎ *(01225) 832293* Eric and Susanne Hobbs
www.foxandbadger.co.uk

Three beers on offer: London Pride, Sharps Doombar, Butcombe. Traditional ciders also served.

Grade II 16th-century rural village pub set in picturesque countryside, with open log fires and flagstone floors. Public bar, lounge bar, dining room, conservatory, courtyard and skittle alley. Food served lunchtimes and evening Tues–Sat, plus Sun lunch, including children's menu. Skittle alley and dining room are available for hire. Children and dogs welcome. Situated in beautiful walking country, near to Wellow Trekking Centre. On the A367, 15 minutes out of Bath.

OPEN *11am–3pm and 6–11pm Sun–Thurs; all day Fri–Sat.*

WELLS

The City Arms

69 High Street, Wells BA5 2AG
☎ *(01749) 673916* Penny Lee

Freehouse with Sharp's Doom Bar, Greene King Old Speckled Hen, IPA and Abbot, Butcombe Gold plus two rotating guests, changed monthly.

Formerly the city jail, dating back to the 16th century, this traditional pub retains its original features with beams and is oozing with character. Food served 9am–9.30pm. The Shackles Restaurant at the pub was refurbished in 2008. Courtyard and terrace for alfresco dining. Families and children most welcome. Nearby attractions include Wells Cathedral, Bishops Palace, Wookey Hole Caves, Clark's retail village and the Cheddar caves and gorge. From the lower end of the High Street go right at the fork into Broad Street. The pub is on the corner of Queen Street, near St Cuthbert's Church.

OPEN *All day, every day.*

The Crown at Wells and Anton's Bistrot

Market Place, Wells BA5 2RP
☎ *(01749) 673457* Adrian Lawrence
www.crownatwells.co.uk

Freehouse with Butcombe Bitter, Sharp's Doom Bar and The Crown's Finest Cask Ale, also by Sharp's.

A 15th-century coaching inn overlooked by Wells Cathedral and a stone's throw from the Bishop's Palace. The Penn Bar is named after William Penn, who preached from an upper window in 1695. More recently, the exterior appeared as The Crown in the film *Hot Fuzz!* Bar and bistro food served every lunchtime and early evening, including vegetarian dishes and children's portions. Fifteen affordable, en-suite bedrooms. Friendly service in relaxed surroundings. Follow signs for Hotels and Deliveries.

OPEN *10am–11pm (midnight at weekends).*

The Fountain Inn

1 St Thomas Street, Wells BA5 2UU
☎ *(01749) 672317* Adrian and Sarah Lawrence
www.fountaininn.co.uk

Butcombe Bitter and Courage Best always available.

Award-winning 16th-century gastropub serving great food and fine wine for over 26 years. Bar and restaurant food served at lunchtimes and evenings daily, with menus changed frequently. Private function room. Car park. Child- and vegetarian-friendly. Follow signs for The Horringtons, 50 yards from Wells Cathedral. The pub is at the junction of St Thomas Street, Tor Street and St Andrew Street.

OPEN *11am–2pm and 6–11pm.*

WEST CRANMORE

The Strode Arms

West Cranmore, Shepton Mallet BA4 4QJ
☎ *(01749) 880450* Tim Gould
www.fromeonline.co.uk/thestrodearms

Wadworth 6X, Bishops Tipple and Henry's IPA plus the brewery's seasonal brews.

Unpretentious two-bar country pub overlooking the village duck pond. Food served every lunchtime and Mon–Sat evenings. Children allowed in the restaurant and over 16s in the bar. Car park, patio and beer garden. Off the A361 near the East Somerset Railway.

OPEN *11.30am–2.30pm and 6–11pm Mon–Sat; 12–3pm and 7–10.30 Sun.*

WEST HUNTSPILL

Royal Artillery Arms

2 Alstone Lane, West Huntspill TA9 3DR
☎ *(01278) 783553* Ray Sparls

A freehouse. RCH Double Header and Palmer's IPA. Plus six guests, changed daily, including Skinner's Betty Stogs, Hop Back Summer Lightning and Otter Head.

One-bar pub in a village location. Wood-burning stove. Beer garden. Car park. Food served daily 12–9pm. Skittle alley. Regular themed nights. Children's play area. Annual beer festival on Aug bank holiday. Located on the A38 main road.

OPEN *12–11pm.*

WESTON-SUPER-MARE

Off The Rails

Pub on the Station, Railway Station, Weston-super-Mare BS23 1XY
☎ *(01934) 415109* Mr Hicks

RCH Bitter plus two guests, changed weekly – Sharp's Doom Bar is popular.

Traditional pub in a building dating from 1880, with one bar and buffet in the railway station. Food available in the buffet area. Children allowed in the buffet area.

OPEN *7am for papers and coffee, then 10am–11pm.*

The Raglan Arms

42–4 Upper Church Road, Weston-super-Mare BS23 9WE
☎ *(01934) 626116* Fredderick

Freehouse with real ale on six pumps from local breweries such as Cotleigh, Exmoor, Hidden, Sharp's, O'Hanlon's and Blindmans, to name but a few. Real ciders also served.

Named after Lord Raglan during the Crimean War, the building dates back to the mid 1700s. Two bars, one a sports bar and one a traditional pub bar/lounge. No food. Live music including acoustic folk, jazz and blues.

OPEN *Every day.*

The Regency

22–4 Lower Church Road, Weston-super-Mare BS23 2AG
☎ *(01934) 633406* Mark Short

Freehouse serving Butcombe Bitter, Bass, Flowers IPA (brewed by Badger) and Courage Best plus one rotating guest.

Comfortable pub with pool room, skittle alley and beer yard. Good food available at lunchtimes, 12–3pm. Children allowed in the pool room. Situated opposite Weston College.

OPEN *9.45am–11.30pm Mon–Thurs; 9.45am–midnight Fri–Sat; 10.45am–10.30pm Sun.*

The Woolpack Inn

Shepherds Way, St Georges, Weston-super-Mare BS22 7XE
☎ *(01934) 521670*
Steve Beasley and Rose Cunningham

Butcombe pub with Bitter and Gold plus Fuller's London Pride and two guests, changed monthly, often including beers from Bath Ales.

Village freehouse, over 200 years old and recently renovated, run by award-winning licensees. Food served 11am–9pm, with a particularly impressive carvery. Families welcome Large car park. Off M5, junction 21, filter left to St Georges.

OPEN *11am–11pm.*

WILLITON

The Forester's Arms Hotel

Long Street, Williton, Taunton TA20 3PX
☎ *(01984) 632508* K Watts

Freehouse with Cotleigh Tawny plus three or four others.

A two-bar village pub with dining area, beer garden, accommodation. Pool room and darts. Food served at lunchtimes and evenings. Children allowed in the daytime.

OPEN *All day, every day.*

WINCANTON

The Bear Inn

12 Market Place, Wincanton BA9 9LP
☎ *(01963) 32581* Ian Wainwright

Freehouse with Greene King Abbot, Ringwood Best and Charles Wells Bombardier plus an occasional guest.

Old coaching inn with original beams and log fires in winter. Food available every lunchtimes and Mon–Sat evenings. Accommodation in seven letting rooms. Children welcome. Large car park, function room. In the town centre, handy for the racecourse. Coaches welcome

OPEN *11am–11pm Mon–Sat; 12–10.30pm Sun.*

The Unicorn Inn

Bayford, Wincanton BA9 9NL
☎ *(01963) 32324* Jon Waite
www.theunicorninnbayford.com

Freehouse with four real ales. Butcombe Bitter and Shepherd Neame Spitfire permanent features, plus two rotating guests.

A 210-year-old inn with one bar comprising three distinct areas. Home-cooked food served at all times except Sun evening and Mon lunch. Fish a speciality. Car park. Accommodation. Situated in a 15-mile radius of Longleat, Bath and the West Showground, Stourhead. One mile east of Wincanton on the old A303.

OPEN *12–3pm Tues–Sun; 7–11pm Mon–Sat.*

WINDMILL HILL

The Square & Compass

Windmill Hill, Nr Ilminster TA19 9NX
☎ *(01823) 480647* Chris Slow
www.squareandcompasspub.com

Exmoor Ale plus two or three guests.

Traditional country pub with comfortable and friendly atmosphere, specialising in very good pub food. Large covered patio area at front, and large gardens. Separate barn venue with bar and four real ale hand pumps, catering for functions up to 200. Off the A358 to Taunton.

OPEN *12–3pm and 6.30–11pm Mon–Sat; 12–3pm and 7–11pm Sun.*

WINSFORD

Royal Oak Inn

Winsford, Exmoor National Park TA24 7JE
☎ *(01643) 851455* Ed and Kirsty Hoskins
www.royaloakexmoor.co.uk

An Enterprise Inns house offering Exmoor Ale, Gold and Stag.

A 12th-century farmhouse and dairy with contemporary comforts. The pub offers relaxation, inspiring food and wine, local ales and exceptional service. Two menus (bar and restaurant), with food served 12–2.30pm and 7–9.30pm. Beer garden with BBQ. Children and dogs welcome in the bar. Eight en-suite rooms. Large car park. Off the A396 Tiverton–Minehead road.

OPEN *11.30am–3pm and 6–11.30pm.*

WIVELISCOMBE

The Bear Inn

10 North Street, Wiveliscombe TA4 2JY
☎ *(01984) 623537* A and H Harvey

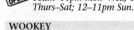 Freehouse with Cotleigh Tawny, Exmoor Gold and Sharp's Doom Bar plus a guest ale changed when it runs out, usually four times a week.

A 17th-century coaching inn with a large, well-laid-out beer garden and patio area. A real local pub with real food and a real welcoming atmosphere. Somerset CAMRA Pub of the Year 2007. Food served 12–2.30pm 6–9pm every day, with takeaway pizzas also available 6–9pm. Accommodation in five letting bedrooms. Children's play equipment, large car park. Disabled access and toilet. Dogs on leads welcome. Pool and darts. On the B3227, turn right in the centre of town.

OPEN *11am–11pm Mon–Wed; 11am–midnight Thurs–Sat; 12–11pm Sun.*

WOOKEY

The Burcott Inn

Wookey Road, Wookey, Nr Wells BA5 1NJ
☎ *(01749) 673874* Ian and Anne Stead

 Three cask-conditioned ales available. RCH Pitchfork, Teignworthy Old Moggie and Hop Back Summer Lightning are regulars. Guests (around 40 per year) might include Cotleigh Snowy, Branscombe Vale BVB, Otter Ale and Cheddar Potholer.

Three-hundred-year-old stone traditional pub with real beer, real fires and real homemade food. Two bars in one large room plus separate restaurant. Food available every session except Sun and Mon evening. Children welcome in games room, garden and restaurant. Parking and large garden. Traditional games such as darts, cribbage and shove ha'penny. En-suite accommodation available in converted stables. Two miles from Wells.

OPEN *11.30am–2.30pm and 6–11pm Mon–Fri; 12–3pm and 6–11pm Sat; 12–3pm and 7–10.30pm Sun.*

WOOKEY HOLE

Wookey Hole Inn

Wookey Hole, Nr Wells BA5 1BP
☎ *(01749) 676677*
Michael Davey and Richard Davey
www.wookeyholeinn.com

 Four real ales at this freehouse, with the selection changing constantly.

From the outside this looks like an ordinary pub, from the inside it has a very different and modern feel. Converted in 2000 and open-plan, it has one big bar and eating area, plus a Spanish bar for private functions and weekend use. CAMRA Bristol/Bath Pub of the Year 2003. Modern British food served 12–2.30pm and 7–9.30pm Mon–Sat and 12–3pm Sun. Accommodation in five en-suite rooms. Live modern jazz 1–3pm Sun. Large sculpture garden. Cider festival in October, art festival in September. Just across the road from the Wookey Hole caves.

OPEN *12–11pm Mon–Sat; 12–6pm Sun.*

WRANTAGE

The Canal Inn

Wrantage, Nr Taunton TA3 6DF
☎ *(01823) 480210* Clare Paul
www.thecanalinn.com

 Freehouse serving Ditch Water, a house beer especially brewed by Blackdown Brewery, something from Glastonbury Ales and at least two more West Country beers, perhaps from Otter, O'Hanlon's or Newmans. Also 12 different Belgian beers, three of them on draught. Draught cider.

Friendly and pleasant country pub with resident house parrot (called Bird!). Closed and then reopened in 2003 following a local campaign. Food, sourced locally, every session except Sun night and Mon lunchtime. Children welcome. Large beer garden with resident ducks and chickens. Skittle alley. Quiz and theme nights. Car park. Beer festival in July. CAMRA's Somerset Pub of the Year 2005. On the A372.

OPEN *5–11pm Mon; 12–2pm and 5–11pm Tues–Fri; 12–2pm and 7–11pm Sat; 12–3.30pm and 7–10.30pm Sun.*

YEOVIL

The Armoury

1 The Park, Yeovil BA20 1DY
☎ *(01935) 471047*
Yvonne and Martin Kojecki

 Wadworth tied house, with 6X, Henry's IPA and a Butcombe brew plus one guest ale such as Adnams Broadside.

A traditional real ale house with one large L-shaped bar plus eating area. Function room, patio and skittle alley, big-screen TVs. Food available 12–2.30pm and 5.30–8pm Mon–Fri, 12–2.30pm Sun. Children welcome when dining. At the top of the town.

OPEN *12–2.30pm and 5.30–11pm Mon–Thurs.*

THE BREWERIES

BLACK HOLE BREWERY LTD
Unit 63 Imex Business Park, Shobnall Road,
Burton upon Trent DE14 2AU
☎ *(01283) 534060*

BLACK HOLE BITTER 3.8% ABV
COSMIC 4.2% ABV
RED DWARF 4.4% ABV
SUPER NOVA 4.8% ABV
NO ESCAPE 5.2% ABV

BLYTHE BREWERY
Blythe House Farm, Lichfield Road, Hamstall
Ridware, Rugeley WS15 3QQ
☎ *07773 747724*
www.blythebrewery.co.uk

BLYTHE BITTER 4.0% ABV
Amber, fruity taste.
CHASE BITTER 4.4% ABV
Tawny, with hops and sweetness.
STAFFY 4.4% ABV
Golden, citrus flavour, grapefruit aftertaste.
PALMER'S POISON 4.5% ABV
Caramel, malty flavour.
OLD HORNY 4.6% ABV
Dark and full bodied.
Plus seasonals.

BURTON BRIDGE BREWERY LTD
Bridge Street, Burton upon Trent DE14 1SY
☎ *(01283) 510573*
www.burtonbridgebrewery.co.uk

GOLDEN DELICIOUS 3.8% ABV
XL BITTER 4.0% ABV
XL MILD 4.0% ABV
BRIDGE BITTER 4.2% ABV
DAMSON PORTER 4.5% ABV
PORTER 4.5% ABV
BRAMBLE STOUT 5.0% ABV
DAM DOG 5.0% ABV
STAIRWAY TO HEAVEN 5.0% ABV
TOP DOG STOUT 5.0% ABV
THOMAS SYKES OLD ALE 10.0% ABV
Plus seasonals.

THE ECCLESHALL BREWING CO. LTD
St Albans Road Industrial Estate, Stafford
ST16 3DR
☎ *(01785) 257976*
www.thegeorgeinn.freeserve.co.uk

MONKEY MAGIC 3.4%
Occasional. A dark mild.
BITTER 3.6% ABV
Golden amber colour, hoppy with a hint of
bitterness.
ORIGINAL 4.0% ABV
A distinctive amber beer, smooth and creamy.
TOP TOTTY 4.0% ABV
A light straw-coloured, fruit-flavoured beer.
PREMIUM 4.4% ABV
Strong, light and creamy. Slightly darker in
appearance with a dry texture.
SHINING KNIGHT 4.5% ABV
Oak coloured, smooth and creamy with a hoppy
finish.
SUPREME 4.7% ABV
Light golden colour, fresh and fruity with a
hoppy aroma.

KINVER BREWERY
Unit 2, Fairfield Drive, Kinver, Stourbridge
DY7 6EW
☎ *07715 842679*
www.kinverbrewery.co.uk

KINVER EDGE 4.2% ABV
CAVEMAN 5.0% ABV
OVER THE EDGE 7.6% ABV
A winter warmer for Christmas.

MARSTON, THOMPSON & EVERSHED PLC
The Brewery, PO Box 26, Shobnall Road,
Burton upon Trent DE14 2BW
☎ *(01283) 531131*

BITTER 4.0% ABV
Well-balanced, easy-drinking brew.
PEDIGREE BITTER 4.5% ABV
Smooth and rounded.
OLD EMPIRE IPA 5.7% ABV
Plus occasionals.

OLD COTTAGE BEER COMPANY
Unit 3, Brian Eccleshall Yard, Eccleshall Business
Park, Hawkins Lane, Burton upon Trent
DE14 1PT
☎ *(01283) 511615*

OAK ALE 4.0% ABV
STOUT 4.7% ABV
PASTICHE 5.2% ABV
HALCYON DAZE 5.3% ABV

PEAKSTONES ROCK BREWERY
Peakstones Farm, Cheadle Road, Alton, Stoke-on-
Trent ST10 4DH
☎ *(01538) 750974*

NEMESIS 3.8% ABV
OBLIVION 5.5% ABV

QUARTZ BREWING LTD
Archers Business Park, Alrevas Road, Kings
Bromley DE13 7HW
☎ *(01543) 473965*
www.quartzbrewing.co.uk

QUARTZ BLONDE 3.8 % ABV
QUARTZ CRYSTAL 4.2% ABV
QUARTZ EXTRA BLONDE 4.4% ABV

SHUGBOROUGH BREWERY
Shugborough Estate, Shugborough ST17 0XB
☎ *(01889) 881388*

Mainly one-off brews.

STAFFORDSHIRE BREWERY LTD
Unit 11 & 12 Churnet Court, Churnetside Business Park, Cheddleton, Leek ST13 7EF
☎ *(01538) 361919*

STAFFORDSHIRE GOLD 3.8% ABV
DUV'D ALE 4.0% ABV
DANEBRIDGE IPA 4.1% ABV
STAFFORDSHIRE BITTER 4.2% ABV
BLACK GROUSE 4.4% ABV
HEN CLOUD 4.5% ABV
ST EDWARDS ALE 4.7% ABV
RUDYARDS RUBY ALE 4.8% ABV
LECKENBRAU 5.0% ABV
STRAWBERRY SUNSET 5.0% ABV
DOUBLE SUNSET 5.2% ABV
LEEK ABBEY ALE 5.5% ABV
ROCHBERG BLONDE 5.8% ABV
CHEDDLETON STEAMER 6.0% ABV
TITTESWORTH TIPPLE WHEAT BEER 6.5% ABV

THE TITANIC BREWERY
Unit 5, Callender Place, Lingard Street, Burslem, Stoke-on-Trent ST6 1JL
☎ *(01782) 823447*
www.titanicbrewery.co.uk

BEST BITTER 3.5% ABV
Amber, gold and malty.
MILD 3.5% ABV
Rounded sweetness.
STEERAGE 3.5% ABV
Amber, hoppy and fruity.
LIFEBOAT 4.0% ABV
Dry, with caramel character.
ANCHOR 4.1% ABV
Gold and fruity.
ICEBERG 4.1% ABV
Zesty wheat beer.
STOUT 4.5% ABV
Dark, strong roast flavour.
WHITE STAR 4.8% ABV
Hoppy and fresh.
CAPTAIN SMITH'S 5.2% ABV
Sweet roast malt flavour.

TOWER BREWERY
The Old Water Tower, Walsitch Maltings, Glensyl Way, Burton upon Trent DE14 1LX
☎ *(01283) 530695*

MILD 4.0% ABV
TOWER BITTER 4.2% ABV
MALTY TOWERS 4.4% ABV
TOWER PALE ALE 4.8% ABV
TOWER OF STRENGTH 7.6% ABV
Plus occasionals.

TOWN HOUSE BREWERY
2 Town House Studios, Town House Farm, Alsager Road, Audley ST7 8JQ
☎ *07976 209437*

AUDLEY BITTER 3.8% ABV
FLOWERDEW 4.0% ABV
AUDLEY GOLD 4.5% ABV
ARMSTRONG ALE 4.8% ABV
DARK HOUSE 4.8% ABV
Plus seasonals and occasionals.

THE PUBS

ABBOTS BROMLEY

The Crown Inn
Market Place, Abbots Bromley, Nr Rugeley WS15 3BS
☎ *(01283) 840227* David Cowell
www.crowninnabbotsbromley.co.uk

Leased from Enterprise Inns, with Marston's Pedigree and two guests such as Caldeonian Deuchars IPA, Banks's Original, Everards Tiger or Greene King Ruddles Best.

Traditional village pub, part of which was an 18th-century coaching inn, sympathetically refurbished internally. Food served 12–2.30pm and 6–9pm Mon–Sat; 12–7pm Sun; children's menu available. Lounge and separate bar with Sky Sports and pool. Separate dining area. Six letting rooms, beer garden and large car park. Situated in the middle of Abbots Bromley, so once you've found the village, you've found the pub!

OPEN 12–3pm and 5pm–12 Mon–Thurs; noon–1am Fri–Sat; 12–11.30pm Sun.

ALSAGERS BANK

The Gresley Arms
High Street, Alsagers Bank ST7 8BQ
☎ *(01782) 720297* Linda Smith

Punch pub with six real ales. Black Sheep Bitter and Greene King Abbot are regulars, and the four guests, changed weekly, are from breweries such as Titanic, Brains, and others.

A 220-year-old country village pub that claims to have the best views in the county – it is high up, and nine counties can be seen, plus the Welsh mountains. One central bar, lounge and function room, dining room, garden. Food is served 12–8.30pm, with Black Rock Grills a speciality. Live music. Children allowed. Car park for 30 cars. Three miles from Newcastle under Lyme (look for signs for Alsagers Bank, not Alsagers).

OPEN 12–11pm (10.30pm Sun).

BIGNALL END

The Plough
Ravens Lane, Bignall End, Stoke-on-Trent CH39 4HP
☎ *(01782) 720469* Paul Holt

Banks's Bitter plus an ever-changing range of guest ales served on four hand pumps, usually from small, local breweries.

A traditional roadside pub. Food available lunchtimes and evenings. Children allowed if eating. Car park. Beer garden.

OPEN 12–3.30pm and 7–11pm Mon–Thurs; 12–11pm Fri–Sat; 12–10.30pm Sun.

The Swan Inn

58 Chapel Street, Bignall End, Stoke-on-Trent ST7 8QD
☎ *(01782) 720622* Carl Smith

 Part of the Dorbiere chain of pubs. Eight traditional beers: Bass plus seven guests, and four traditional ciders.

A traditional two-room pub with tiled floor in the bar suitable for workers, walkers and dogs. Comfortable lounge which serves home-cooked pub food 6–9pm Thurs–Mon. Children welcome. Beer garden with heated smoking shelter. Beer festival each August. CAMRA awards: Potteries Pub of the Year 2007, 2008, Staffordshire County Pub of the Year 2008, Potteries Cider Pub of the Year 2008.

OPEN *12–11pm.*

BLYTHE BRIDGE

The Black Cock

393 Uttoxeter Road, Blythe Bridge ST11 9NT
☎ *(01782) 392388*

Freehouse with six ales. These could include Charles Wells Bombardier, Greene King Abbot or Old Speckled Hen, Wadworth 6X, Shepherd Neame Spitfire or beers from Adnams and Black Sheep.

One-bar pub dating back 150 years with a very intimate atmosphere. Food served 12–2.30pm and 5.30pm onwards. Children welcome. Beer garden. Car park. Close to Alton Towers, Derbyshire dales, Trentham gardens and Royal Doulton.

OPEN *12–11pm Mon–Sat; 12–2.30pm and 7–10.30pm Sun.*

BREWOOD

Bridge Inn

22 High Green, Brewood ST19 9BD
☎ *(01902) 851999*
Kevin and Vivienne Sparrow

Marston's leased pub serving Jennings Cocker Hoop and Dark Mild plus three rotating guests from a large variety of brewers, changed twice weekly.

A traditional public bar with wooden floors and open fires. Comfortable lounge and separate 36-cover dining room. Traditional pub food and homemade dishes served 12–2.30pm Tues–Sun and 6–8.30pm Tues–Sat. Canalside patio with wooden narrowboat. Outside drinking area. Large car park. Dogs welcome. Adjacent moorings on Shropshire Union canal. Located by bridge 14 of the canal, 300 yards from the village centre.

OPEN *12–11pm (10.30pm Sun).*

The Swan Hotel

15 Market Place, Brewood ST19 9BS
☎ *(01902) 850330* Ann Leathordalz

Freehouse with up to five real ales, including three guests.

Dating from the 14th century with lots of character and an open-plan layout. Run by a self-proclaimed witch and favoured by the Brewood phantom. No food. Skittle alley. Large car park. Situated in Brewood square.

OPEN *11.45am–11.30pm.*

BURTON UPON TRENT

The Alfred

Derby Street, Burton upon Trent DE14 2LD
☎ *(01283) 562178* Glyn and Helen Holland

Burton Bridge Brewery tenancy serving Bridge Bitter, Golden Delicious, Festival Ale, Burton Porter and Stairway to Heaven Bitter plus guests, changed every few weeks.

Two-bar town pub, refurbished in late 2006, with bar, lounge and snug. Food served 12–2pm Mon, 12–2pm and 5–8pm Tues–Sat, 12–4pm Sun. Beer garden, large car park. Regular live entertainment weekends. On the outskirts of the town centre, five minutes' walk from the railway station.

OPEN *11.30am–3pm and 5–11pm Mon–Thurs; 11am–midnight Fri–Sat; 11am–11pm Sun.*

Burton Bridge Inn

Bridge Street, Burton upon Trent DE14 1SY
☎ *(01283) 536596* Kevin McDonald

Home of the Burton Bridge Brewery serving Bridge Bitter, Porter and Festival Ale. Seasonal ales, such as Summer Ale or Gold Medal Ale and other guests rotated on two pumps including beers from Timothy Taylor and York.

Brewpub with two rooms and a central bar. One room features oak panelling, a quarry-tiled floor and a feature fireplace. Dining area, patio. Food served lunchtimes. Children allowed.

OPEN *11.30am–2.15pm and 5–11pm.*

Coopers Tavern

43 Cross Street, Burton upon Trent DE14 1EG
☎ *(01283) 532551*

Freehouse with up to eight real ales. Plus real cider.

Once the Bass Brewery tap, a small, friendly, Victorian Grade II listed pub with food served at lunchtime. Occasional live music.

OPEN *12–2.30pm and 5–11pm Mon–Sat; 12–2.30pm and 7–10.30pm Sun.*

The Devonshire Arms

86 Station Street, Burton upon Trent DE14 1BT
☎ *(01283) 562392* Joseph Stout

Burton Bridge house serving Stairway to Heaven, Bridge Bitter, Golden Delicious and Porter plus a frequently changing guest.

Friendly Grade II listed pub dating from the 19th century, on the outskirts of Burton. Public and lounge bars decorated with photographs from 1860. Food available 11.30am–2.15pm and 5.30–8pm Mon–Thurs and 11.30am–8pm Fri–Sat. Also Sunday lunchtimes for traditional roasts. Children welcome. Patio. Beer festivals held twice a year. Two minutes from the station.

OPEN *11.30am–2.30pm and 5.30–11pm Mon–Thurs; 11am–11pm Fri–Sat; 12–3pm and 7–10.30pm Sun.*

The Old Cottage Tavern

36 Byrkley Street, Burton upon Trent DE14 2EG
☎ *(01283) 511615* Maurice Towner

 Cottage Halcyon Daze, Oak and Stout. Plus three guests, changed every three days, such as Vale Grumpling Premium, Hanby Golden Honey and Nutbrook Squirrel Bitter.

A traditional 19th-century corner pub, warm and welcoming. Central bar, cosy snug, restaurant serving traditional food 12–2pm and 6.30–9pm Mon–Sat; 12–3pm Sun. Garden. Function room. Skittles. Accommodation. Located off Derby Street, behind the town hall.

OPEN *12–11pm.*

The Roebuck

101 Station Street, Burton upon Trent DE14 1BT
☎ *(01283) 568660* Jon Walker

Marston's Pedigree, Adnams Broadside, Bateman XXXB and Shepherd Neame Spitfire plus a couple of guests that rotate on a weekly basis.

Friendly, fringe-of-town pub with one open-plan room, small patio, accommodation. Bar food, including Staffordshire oatcakes, 12–2.30pm and on theme nights from 6.30pm. Weekly quiz. No children. Three letting rooms. Next to the railway station.

OPEN *11am–11pm Mon–Sat; 12–10.30pm Sun.*

CHASETOWN

Uxbridge Arms

Church Street, Chasetown WS7 3QL
☎ *(01543) 674453* Tim Jones

Freehouse with five constantly rotating guest ales, changed daily. Three keg ciders and one regularly changing scrumpy on handpull. Over 80 single malts also available, as well as over 20 fruit wines.

This 200-year-old pub has a bar, lounge and restaurant. Small beer garden. Car park. Food served all day Mon–Sat, lunchtimes on Sun. Located midway between Cannock and Lichfield, just off the A5 and M6 toll.

OPEN *12–3pm and 5.30pm–12 Mon–Thurs; noon–1am Fri–Sat; 12–12 Sun.*

CHESLYN HAY

The Woodman Inn

Woodman Lane, Cheslyn Hay WS6 7ES
☎ *(01922) 413686*

Three guest beers on offer, usually Greene King Abbot and IPA and Theakston XB.

Village pub dating from the 1870s, with beamed ceiling in the lounge. Having been extended, it has a conservatory, two bars, a dining area and a garden. Frequent entertainment such as quiz nights and bingo. Food served all opening hours Mon–Sat, plus 12–3.30pm Sun for traditional roast. Car park. Children allowed. Can be difficult to find, as it is in a cul-de-sac, so call for directions.

OPEN *12–11pm.*

CODSALL

Codsall Station

Chapel Lane, Codsall WV8 2EH
☎ *(01902) 847061* Peter Williamson

Holden's brews such as Black Country Bitter, Golden Glow and Special plus ever-changing guests.

Welcoming pub in converted station buildings, sympathetically restored with railwayana and a cosy atmosphere. The patio overlooks the railway line. Regular local CAMRA award-winning pub. Food served 12–2pm daily and 6–8pm Sat–Sun. Annual beer festival in September. Car park. Two miles off the A41 – look for the railway station.

OPEN *11.30am–2.30pm and 5–11pm Mon–Fri; all day Sat–Sun.*

DOSTHILL

The Fox

105 High Street, Dosthill, Tamworth B77 1LQ
☎ *(01827) 280847* Peter Southwick

Greene King Abbot, Hobgoblin and Banks Bitter are among the four beers always available, plus one guest changed every couple of weeks. Cask Marque accredited.

A 17th-century coaching inn on the outskirts of Tamworth, with bar, lounge and wine/cocktail lounge. Curries and Pizza available all opening times. Extensive garden and decked area. Children welcome in lounge only until 9pm. Large car park at side of pub. On the main road out of Tamworth.

OPEN *6–11pm Mon; 4–11pm Tues–Thurs; 12–12pm Fri–Sun.*

ECCLESHALL

The George Hotel

Castle Street, Eccleshall ST21 6DF
☎ *(01785) 850300* Gerard and Moyra Slater

Six real ales from Slaters always available.

Opened in March 1995 by Gerard and Moyra Slater. The beer is brewed by their son, Andrew, at a 30-barrel plant in Stafford. The George is a 16th-century coaching inn with olde-worlde beams, log fires, real ales and malt whisky. Bar and restaurant food available. Annual beer festival at Easter. Car park. Accommodation. Children and dogs welcome.

OPEN *All day, every day (except Christmas Day).*

ENVILLE

The Cat Inn

Bridgenorth Road, Enville, Stourbridge DY7 5HA
☎ *(01384) 872209* Guy and Michelle Ayres
www.theenvillecat.co.uk

Freehouse with Enville Ale from the nearby brewery plus occasionals and seasonals from the range and four rotating guests changed at the end of every barrel. These might well include a couple of other local brews, plus offerings from independents across the country.

A 16th-century village inn with three bar areas, beams and fireplaces. Traditional and cosy. Food is available 12–2.30pm and 7–9.30pm (not Mon). Pool room, darts, garden, car park. Children allowed. Good walking and cycling.

OPEN *12–3pm and 7–11pm Mon–Tues; 12–3pm and 6.30–11pm Wed–Sat; 12–6pm Sun.*

ETRURIA
The Old Plough
147 Etruria Road, Stoke-on-Trent ST1 5NS
☎ *(01782) 269445* Rob and Jane Ward

 Robinson's tied house serving a rotating selection of Robinson's ales including Dark Mild. Robinson's Old Tom Strong Ale is also featured from November to March.

Country-style 200-year-old pub with a collection of valve radios, old TVs, gramophones, telephones, bottled beers and local pictures, plus a preserved classic bus. Originally two cottages, then a greengrocers. Well known locally for good food, which is available 12–2pm and 6.30–9pm Mon–Sat (from 6pm Sat). Small beer garden, car park. Children welcome if dining. From the A500 take the A53 for Leek, follow signs for Hanley (town centre), and the pub is on the right opposite Allied Carpets.

OPEN *12–2.30pm and 6.30–11pm Mon–Sat; closed Sun and bank holidays.*

FAZELEY
The Plough & Harrow
Atherstone Street, Fazeley B78 3RF
☎ *(01827) 289596* Emma Jeffries
www.theploughfazeley.com

 Two brews, probably Adnams Broadside and Bass, plus a guest changed frequently.

A 300-year-old two-bar village pub, first licensed in 1801, with beer garden and en-suite accommodation. Tiani's Italian restaurant open all day. Car park. Close to Drayton Manor Park, Belfry, Tamworth Castle and the Snowdome.

OPEN *11.30am–3pm and 5.30–11pm Mon–Thurs; all day Fri–Sun.*

GNOSALL
Royal Oak
Newport Road, Gnosall ST20 0BL
☎ *(01785) 822362*
Alexandra Timmins and Greg Williams

Punch Taverns pub serving Highgate Mild, Greene King Abbot and IPA plus three continually rotating guest beers changed every two or three days.

Approximately 200 years old, this traditional pub retains its original features with timber beams and open fires. A friendly locals' bar with popular restaurant. Food served 12–3pm and 6–9pm Mon–Sat (excluding Tues) and 12–6pm Sun. Large beer garden with skittle alley. Function room. Large car park. Two annual beer festivals to raise money for charity. Located on the A518 between Newport and Stafford.

OPEN *12–12.*

GREAT CHATWELL
The Red Lion Inn
Great Chatwell, Nr Newport TF10 9BJ
☎ *(01952) 691366* Paula Smith

 Everards Beacon Bitter and Tiger plus three guest beers, perhaps from Wells and Young's, Robinson's, Wood, Hook Norton, Mansfield, Shepherd Neame, Eccleshall, Lichfield and many others.

Traditional, ivy-clad pub, attracting a mixed clientele. Car park. Children's play area with animals and birds.

OPEN *12–11pm Sun–Thurs; 12–12 Fri–Sat.*

HARRISEAHEAD
The Royal Oak
42 High Street, Harriseahead, Stoke-on-Trent ST7 4JT
☎ *(01782) 513362*
Stephen and Diane Gallimore

Genuine freehouse with Fuller's London Pride, Courage Directors, John Smiths Bitter, Samuel Smith's Bitter plus three rotating guest ales, changed every few days, from breweries such as Oakham, Whim, Thornbridge, Townhouse and Pictish. Belgian Leffe and German Erdinger are available, plus a wide selection of Belgian bottled beers.

Locals' village pub that became an inn in 1857 and was fully licensed in 1889. Bar, lounge and open fires in winter. Room available for small functions and meetings. Snacks and sandwiches served. Beer garden, car park. Children and dogs welcome. Small annual beer festival in October/November. On the Tunstall to Congleton road.

OPEN *7–11pm Mon–Thurs; 5pm–12 Fri–Sat; 12–3pm and 7–10.30pm Sun.*

IPSTONES
The Linden Tree
47 Froghall Road, Ipstones, Stoke-on-Trent ST10 2NA
☎ *(01538) 266370* Graham Roberts
www.thelindentree.co.uk

Freehouse with Timothy Taylor Landlord plus two guest ales.

Country pub with separate 50-seater restaurant. Beer garden. Food at lunchtimes and evenings. Children allowed.

OPEN *12–3pm and 6–11pm (10.30pm Sun).*

KIDSGROVE

The Blue Bell

*25 Hardingswood, Kidsgrove, Stoke-on-Trent
ST7 1EG*
☎ *(01782) 774052* Dave and Kay Washbrook
www.bluebellkidsgrove.co.uk

 Genuine privately owned freehouse serving six frequently changing beers (over 2,500 in ten years) from small and micro-breweries, including beers from Acorn, Archers, Beowulf, Burton Bridge, Castle Rock, Crouch Vale, Millstone, Oakham, Sharp's, Thornbridge, Titanic, Townhouse, Whim and many more. Real cider and also quality Belgian and German bottled beers.

Smallish, four-room, out-of-town pub just north of the Potteries, on an island at the junction of the Trent & Mersey and Macclesfield Canals. Winner of numerous CAMRA awards 1999–2008. No juke box, no pool, no fruit machines. Outside drinking area to the front and garden to the rear. Basic snacks at weekends. Dog-friendly, well-behaved children welcome. Impromptu folk music Sunday evenings. Car park. Five minutes' walk from Kidsgrove Station along canal towpath.

OPEN *7.30–11pm Tues–Fri; 1–4pm and 7–11pm Sat; 12–10.30pm Sun; closed Mon except bank holidays.*

KINVER

The Plough & Harrow

High Street, Kinver DY7 6HD
☎ *(01384) 872659* Mrs Shirley

 Four pumps serve bitter and three serve mild, with Batham Bitter and Mild always on offer.

Traditional village pub, over 100 years old, with L-shaped lounge and small patio area. Food is available from a limited menu. Live music Thursday evenings. Car park. Well-behaved children allowed. Four miles from Stourbridge.

OPEN *6–11pm Mon–Thurs; 5–11pm Fri; 11am–11pm Sat; 12–10.30pm Sun.*

LEEK

The Bull's Head

35 St Edward Street, Leek ST13 5DS
☎ *(01538) 370269* Vicki

 Freehouse featuring beers from the Leek Brewing Company, two or three at a time, plus occasional guests.

Long, thin pub, with a lively atmosphere at weekends, quieter during the week. Pool table and darts at one end, pin-ball machine at the other. Ample street parking. Children and dogs welcome.

OPEN *5–11pm Mon–Tues, Thurs; 12–11pm Weds and Fri; all day Sat–Sun.*

Den Engel

23 St Edward Street, Leek ST13 5DR
☎ *(01538) 373751* Geoff and Hilary Turner

 Belgian bar and freehouse featuring four constantly changing real ales from small, independent and micro-breweries. These could change up to three times a week. Plus 11 Belgian beers available on draught and more than 120 in bottles.

An attractive, bow-fronted building dating from 1697. Bar food served Wed–Sun plus a separate restaurant serving food Wed–Sat. Floodlit courtyard with patio heaters. Ample street parking. Children and dogs welcome. Close to the market square.

OPEN *5–11pm Mon–Tues; 11am–11pm Wed–Sat; 12–10.30pm Sun.*

The Swan Hotel

2 St Edward Street, Leek ST13 5DS
☎ *(01538) 382081* David and Julie Ellerton

 Three or four rotating guests on offer. Wadworth 6X, Wychwood Hobgoblin and Robinson's Frederics are regular features, plus seasonal specials.

Four-bar town-style pub in moorlands, with an additional bar called JD's attached, which is a young person's modern themed sports bar. Food served at lunchtimes and evenings. Children allowed. Function room. Bridal suite.

OPEN *11am–3pm and 7–11.30pm.*

The Wilkes Head

16 St Edward Street, Leek ST13 5DA
☎ *(01538) 383616*

 The Whim Ales flagship pub serving Hartington Bitter and IPA, Magic Mushroom Mild, and Whim Arbor Light plus an ever-changing range of guest ales from around the country. Seasonal ales such as Whim Black Christmas and Old Isaak stocked when available.

An award-winning town pub, famous for its ales. Small and cosy with large beer garden. Children and dogs welcome.

OPEN *All day, every day.*

LICHFIELD

The Acorn Inn

16–18 Tamworth Street, Lichfield WS13 6JJ
☎ *(01543) 263400* Sian Elwell

A JD Wetherspoon's pub. Greene King Abbot, Marston's Pedigree and Burton Bitter plus up to six guests, perhaps including Greene King IPA, Springhead Roaring Meg, Bateman XXXB or Purity Pure Gold.

Town-centre pub opened in 1998, but in the traditional style with one main bar. Full menu available all day. Children welcome until 8pm. Two beer festivals each year. Special club food nights including steak, curry and Sunday roasts.

OPEN *9am–midnight Sun–Thurs; 9am–1am Fri–Sat.*

The Crown

12–14 Tamworth Street, Lichfield WS13 6JJ
☎ *(01543) 258925* Eleanor Owen

Three Greene King ales usually available, such as IPA, Abbot, Old Speckled Hen or Ruddles County.

One-bar pub offering friendly service and a good atmsposhere. Sky Sports. Food served 11am–7pm Mon–Fri, 11am–5pm Sat and 12–5pm Sun. Children not allowed. In Lichfield town centre, not far from Stowe Pool, Lichfield Cathedral and Dr Johnson Museum.

OPEN *11am–11pm Mon–Thurs; 11am–midnight Fri–Sat; 12–10.30pm Sun.*

Duke of Wellington

Birmingham Road, Lichfield WS14 9BJ
☎ *(01543) 263261*
Tracey Bradley and Susan Carter

Marston's Pedigree, Black Sheep Best and Fuller's London Pride. Two guest pumps, serving beers such as Holden's Golden Glow, Church End Cuthberts, Chasewater Beowulf and Wye Valley HPA.

A traditonal pub serving food 12–3pm Thurs–Sat. Large beer garden with patio and heated smoking area. Sky TV on three screens. Car park. Plans for a bowling green in 2009. Left from the railway station.

OPEN *4pm–close Mon–Wed; 12–close Thurs–Sun.*

The Queen's Head

Queen Street, Lichfield WS13 6QD
☎ *(01543) 410932* Roy Harvey

Adnams Best, Timothy Taylor Landlord and Marston's Pedigree plus two guests, rotated weekly, including beers from all over the British Isles.

Small backstreet pub. No music, small TV, one games machine. Bar food available at lunchtime (12–2.30pm), but the pub is really famous for its selection of cheeses, of which up to 20 different ones are available all day.

OPEN *All day Mon–Sat; 12–3pm and 7–10.30pm Sun.*

LONGDON

Swan With Two Necks

40 Brook End, Longdon, Rugeley WS15 4PN
☎ *(01543) 490251* David Dangerfield

Punch Taverns pub with four daily-changing ales always available.

Approximately 200 years old with beer garden and car park. Food served 12–2pm and 7–9pm Mon–Sat, all day Sun. Located off the A51.

OPEN *12–3pm and 6–11pm Mon–Fri; 12–11pm Sat–Sun.*

ONCOTE

The Jervis Arms

Oncote, Leek ST13 7RU
☎ *(01538) 304206* Peter Hill

Freehouse with Titanic Iceberg, Sharp's Doom Bar and Wadworth 6X plus three constantly rotating guests (up to nine per week during summer). Examples of breweries featured include Messrs. Maguire, Peakstones Rock, O'Hanlons, Coastal, Tower, Storm and College Green.

Built in approximately 1679, this one-bar pub has two beer gardens, one with a river running through it. Food served 12–2pm and 7–9pm Mon–Sat, and 12–9pm Sun. Large car park for 60 vehicles – camper vans and caravanettes welcome for overnight stays. Main beer festival is at start of May, with around 30 real ales and ciders from lesser-known micros across the UK and Ireland.

OPEN *12–3pm and 5pm–12.30am Mon–Fri; 12–3pm and 6pm–12.30am Sat; 12–12 Sun.*

PENKHULL

The Greyhound Inn

Manor Court Street, Penkhull, Stoke-on-Trent ST4 5DW
☎ *(01782) 848978* Pamela Rowlands
www.thegreyhoundinn.co.uk

Punch Taverns pub with Greene King Old Speckled Hen and Abbot, Wadworth 6X and Timothy Taylor Landlord plus one weekly-changing guest.

Tudor-built with many rooms, beamed ceilings, open fires and a cosy, community atmosphere. Food served 12–2pm Mon; 12–2pm and 5.30–8.30pm Tues–Sat; 12–3pm Sun. Beer garden. Games room. Mon: quiz night; Tues: open and balti; Wed: live music. Car park. One mile from centre of Stoke-on-Trent, five minutes from J15 M6.

OPEN *11am–11pm Mon–Wed; 11am–11.30pm Thurs; 11am–midnight Fri–Sat; 12–11pm Sun.*

PENKRIDGE

The Star Inn

Market Place, Penkridge, Stafford ST19 5DJ
☎ *(01785) 712513* Jayne and Terry Dunning

Banks's Original and Bitter plus guests from breweries such as Mansfield, Marston's or Jennings, changed every few days.

Olde-worlde pub set in a scenic village. Food 12–4pm. Beer garden. Car park. Children welcome until 9pm.

OPEN *12–11pm Sun–Wed; 12–11.30pm Thurs; 12–12 Fri–Sat.*

SILVERDALE

The Bush

199 High Street, Silverdale, Newcastle under Lyme ST5 6JZ
☎ *(01782) 713096* Christine Yates-Dutton

 A Scottish and Newcastle pub. Charles Wells Bombardier. Five regularly changing guests such as Abbeydale Moonshine and Absolution, Beartown Kodiak Gold and Titanic Iceberg.

A friendly family local with one bar and a lounge. Food served in a separate dining room 12–2pm and 6–9pm Mon–Thurs; 12–2pm and 6–7pm Fri; all day Sat–Sun. Beer garden with smoking hut and children's adventure play area. Car park. Private room.

OPEN *12–11pm Mon–Thurs; 12–12 Fri–Sat; 12–10.30pm Sun.*

STAFFORD

The Green Man

Milwich, Stafford ST18 0EG
☎ *(01889) 505310* Rodney Webb
www.greenmanmilwich.com

Freehouse with Adnams Best, Charles Wells Bombardier and Draught Bass plus one or two weekly-changing guests.

Licensed since 1792, this is a traditional real ale pub listed in the CAMRA *Good Beer Guide* continuously since 1994. List of all previous landlords displayed in the bar. Real fire. No food. Beer garden. Beer festivals held three times a year. Children welcome. Ample car parking. Pub games. On the B5027 Stone–Uttoxeter Road.

OPEN *5–11pm Mon–Wed; 12–2pm and 5–11pm Thurs–Fri; 12–11pm Sat–Sun (10.30pm Sun).*

The Greyhound

12 County Road, Stafford ST16 2PU
☎ *(01785) 222432* B Tideswell

Genuine freehouse serving up to eight real ales that change constantly, many of which are sourced from local brewers.

Located opposite the prison, a pub since the 1830s, thriving again after recent closure. Two rooms, plus outside smoking area. No food.

OPEN *4–11.30pm Mon–Thurs; 2pm–12 Fri; 12–12 Sat; 12–11pm Sun.*

Spittal Brook Inn

106 Lichfield Road, Stafford ST17 4LP
☎ *(01785) 245268* Pete Turner

Marston's Pedigree, Everards Tiger, Jennings Cumberland, Fuller's London Pride and Black Sheep Bitter plus one regularly rotating guest. Also Addlestones cask cider.

Dating from 1834, with two bars, this is a pub for beer and conversation. No juke box, TV or pool table. Coal fires in winter, beer garden in summer, smoking shelter with heating and TV. Folk music and quiz nights. Traditional pub food served every lunchtime and six evenings. Children and dogs

welcome. Car park. En-suite accommodation. Convenient for Alton Towers.

OPEN *12–3pm and 5–11pm Mon–Fri; 12–11pm Sat; 12–4pm and 7–10.30pm Sun.*

Tap & Spile

59 Peel Terrace, Stafford ST16 3HE
☎ *(01785) 223563*
Jon and Vicky Thwaites-Davis

Eight real ales are on offer, with two fixed, the rest rotated every week.

A traditional pub, over 100 years old, with one large bar and three other rooms. No food. No children. Log burner and open fires in two of the bars. Beer garden, darts, pool. Dogs welcome. Close to Stafford Rangers football ground, one mile from the town centre, just off Sandon Road.

OPEN *11am–close.*

STANLEY

The Travellers Rest

Stanley Village, Stoke on Trent ST9 9LX
☎ *(01782) 502580* S Bowers and T B Botham

Freehouse with Marston's Pedigree and Burton Bitter plus four rotating guests.

This two-bar village pub also has a 70-seat restaurant. Food served 12–2pm and 6.30–9.30pm Mon–Sat, 12–2.30pm and 7–9.30pm Sun. Car park. Beer garden. Children over the age of 10 welcome.

OPEN *12–3pm and 6–11pm Mon–Sat; 12–3pm and 7–10.30pm Sun.*

STOKE-ON-TRENT

The Bull's Head

14 St Johns Square, Burslem, Stoke-on-Trent ST6 3AJ
☎ *(01782) 834153* Bob Crumpton
www.titanicbrewery.co.uk

The original Titanic Brewery pub serving Steerage, Anchor, Iceberg and White Star plus between three and five guest and seasonal ales. Thatcher's Cheddar Valley cider also available.

This town-centre pub has an island bar and a quiet lounge area with an open fire. Conservatory leading to outdoor area with smoking shelter. Juke box, table skittles and bar billiards. Themed beer weekends at least once a month. Located in the centre of Burslem.

OPEN *3–11pm Sun–Tues; 3–11.30pm Wed–Thurs; 12–12 Fri–Sat. Open from noon April–September.*

The Potter

432 King Street, Fenton, Stoke-on-Trent ST4 3DB
☎ *07968 520147* Alan and Lisa Hope

Freehouse with Thwaites Lancaster Bomber plus ales from Coach House and Greene King. Also three weekly-changing guest ales.

A real-ale-focused pub also serving bar meals. Children welcome. Beer garden. Located in the village of Fenton.

OPEN *12–11pm.*

The Tontine Alehouse

20 Tontine Street, Hanley, Stoke-on-Trent ST1 1AQ
☎ *(01782) 263890* Becky Smith

 Marston's Pedigree plus four weekly-changing guest ales from independent breweries all over the country.

One-bar, city-centre pub with beer garden. Food served at lunchtime only. Children allowed, if eating.

OPEN *All day Mon–Sat; closed Sun.*

STONE

The Pheasant Inn

Old Road, Stone ST15 8HS
☎ *(01785) 818894* John Kerr

 Leased from Enterprise Inns, with three or four real ales including Marston's Pedigree and Banks's Original. Guests change weekly, and might be St Austell Tribute, Black Sheep Best, Greene King Abbot, Shepherd Neame Bishops Finger or Thwaites Bicentenary Ale. Range of bottled beers also served.

A traditional street-corner pub set between the town's shops and the canal and open countryside, with a history that has so far been traced back to 1790. Cask Marque accredited. Darts and traditional pub games. Food always available – if there's something in particular you fancy, just phone ahead and ask! Children welcome.

OPEN *3pm–close Mon–Thurs; 12–close Fri–Sun. Closing time is when the last person leaves!*

The Star Inn

Stafford Road, Stone ST15 8QW
☎ *(01785) 813096* Matthew Lowe

 Banks's Bitter and Marston's Pedigree plus two guests, such as Jennings Cumberland Ale.

Edge-of-town pub situated by the canal with access to the towpath. Two bars, garden and patio. Food available all day. Children allowed.

OPEN *All day, every day.*

The Swan Inn

18 Stafford Street, Stone ST15 8QW
☎ *(01785) 815570* Geoff Blundell
www.myspace.com/swaninnstone

 Freehouse with three Joules Ales plus seven rotating guests from independent or micro-breweries, changed every two to three days.

This former warehouse was used during the construction of the Trent and Mersey canal in 1771 before becoming a pub in 1851. A Grade II listed building with one main L-shaped bar split into three areas with two real fires. Light snacks available all day. Beer garden. Annual eight-day beer festival held in the second week of July. Live music held Mon, Weds, Thurs, Sat, each week. Over-18s only. Close to the canal. Quiz nights held on Tues. Free Sunday lunch buffet 12.30pm, free pint quiz 6-7pm Fri. Stafford Street forms the lower part of the Stonebypass (A520).

OPEN *11am–midnight Mon–Wed; 11am–1am Thurs–Sat; 12–11pm Sun.*

TAMWORTH

Sir Robert Peel

13–15 Lower Gungate, Tamworth B79 2BA
☎ *(01827) 300910*

 Two constantly changing real ales sourced from various independent and micro-breweries including Church End, Beowulf, Oakham, Wye Valley, Blythe, Wood, Oldershaw and York.

An Enterprise Inn alehouse in a listed building with lots of character. Live music. Can be quite lively at weekends. Dogs welcome. Located in the town centre, half a mile from the railway station.

OPEN *12–12 Fri–Mon; 5pm–12 Tues–Thurs.*

WHISTON

The Swan Inn

Whiston, Nr Penkridge ST19 5QH
☎ *(01785) 716200* Jim Davies

 Holden's Mild, Bitter and Golden Glow plus one or two guest, mostly from smaller breweries such as Titanic, Church End, Wood, Hanby, Jennings and Slaters.

Set in six acres in a rural location, this extended pub has a traditional bar, open fireplaces, a dining room and a beer garden with children's play area. Food available Tues–Sat lunch and Mon–Sat evenings, all day Sun. Children allowed. One letting room. Car park. Situated two miles off the main road – find Whiston and you find the pub!

OPEN *6–11pm Mon (closed Mon lunch); 12–3pm and 6–11pm Tues–Sat; all day Sun.*

WRINEHILL

The Crown Inn

Den Lane, Wrinehill, Nr Crewe CW3 9BT
☎ *(01270) 820472*
Mark Condliffe and Charles Davenhill

 A freehouse. Marston's Pedigree and Burton Bitter, Jennings Sneck Lifter and Cumberland Ale, and Brakspeare Organic Gold, plus one varying guest, invariably from the Townhouse Brewery.

A country pub, approximately 300 years old, with oak beams, real fire and summertime floral displays. Single room with single bar. Traditional pub food available. Outside patio. Car park.

OPEN *12–3pm and 6–11pm every day. (Closed Christmas Day evening, Boxing Day, New Years Day evening.)*

The Hand & Trumpet

Main Road, Wrinehill, Crewe CW3 9BJ
☎ *(01270) 820048* John Unsworth
www.handandtrumpet-wrinehill.co.uk

Timothy Taylor Landlord, Caledonian Deuchars IPA and Thwaites Original plus three guests, such as Sharp's Cornish Coaster, Derby Thrillingly Blonde, Wood Shropshire Lad and Slaters Top Totty. Guests changed every few days.

Refurbished in February 2006 and has a cosy atmosphere with rugs, open fires and a library. Home-cooked food served 12–10pm Mon–Sat; 12–9.30pm Sun. Children welcome until 7pm. Large beer garden with decking area and pond. Car park.

OPEN *12–11pm (10.30pm Sun).*

YOXALL

The Golden Cup

Main Street, Yoxall, Nr Burton-on-Trent DE13 8NQ
☎ *(01543) 472295*
Gregory and Rachael Turner

Freehouse with Marston's Pedigree plus a constantly rotating guest.

A 200-year old family-run former coaching inn with olde-worlde charm. Lounge and separate restaurant. Food served 12–2pm and 6.30–9.30pm daily. Accommodation available (five double en-suite rooms, one twin en-suite room and two en-suite penthouses). Large award-winning beer garden with children's play area. Car park and overnight caravan facilities. Nearby attractions include Alton Towers and Hoar Cross health spa. Located on the A515 between Lichfield and Sudbury.

OPEN *12–3pm and 5pm–close Mon–Fri; all day Sat–Sun.*

THE BREWERIES

ADNAMS PLC

Sole Bay Brewery, East Green, Southwold IP18 6JW
☎ *(01502) 727200*
www.beerfromthecoast.co.uk or
www.adnams.co.uk

 BITTER 3.7% ABV
Clean and well hopped, with fruity flavours.
EXPLORER 4.3% ABV
Strong citrus flavour.
BROADSIDE 4.7% ABV
Powerful malty brew with balancing hoppiness.
Seasonals including:
OYSTER STOUT 4.3% ABV
February–March.
REGATTA 4.3% ABV
June–August
BARLEY MOW 5.0% ABV
Autumn.
MAYDAY 5.0% ABV
April–May.
TALLY HO FROM 7.0% ABV VARIABLE
December. Gravity decided on brew day.
Plus other seasonal brews.

BARTRAMS BREWERY

Rougham Estate, Ipswich Road, Rougham, Bury St Edmunds IP30 9LZ
☎ *(01449) 737655*
www.bartramsbrewery.co.uk

MARLD 3.4% ABV
Spicy and hoppy, with smoky hints.
PREMIER BITTER 3.7% ABV
Dry and hoppy.
LITTLE GREEN MAN 3.8% ABV
Golden, with a hint of coriander.
ROUGHAM READY 3.8% ABV
Refreshing bitter.
RED QUEEN IPA 3.9% ABV
Chocolatey, malty style.
GREEN MAN 4.0% ABV
Golden bitter with citrus tang.
GROZET 4.0% ABV
Gooseberry flavours.
HEADWAY 4.0% ABV
Charity fund-raiser for Headway organisation.
PIERROT 4.0% ABV
Golden and malty.
THE CAT'S WHISKERS 4.0% ABV
Golden with added lemons and ginger.
BEE'S KNEES 4.2% ABV
Amber with floral tones.
CATHERINE BARTRAM'S IPA 4.3% ABV
Hoppy dryness in the aftertaste.
JESTER QUICK ONE 4.4% ABV
Red bitter, sweet.
BELTANE BRACES 4.5% ABV
Dark and rich.
COAL PORTER 4.5% ABV
Ruby colour with complex hoppy flavour.
STINGO 4.5% ABV
Light honey fruity flavour.
BEER ELSIE BUB 4.8% ABV
Strong honey flavour.
CAPTAIN BILL BARTRAM'S BEST BITTER 4.8% ABV
Traditional hoppy and malty.
CAPTAIN'S CHERRY STOUT 4.8% ABV
Chocolate and cherry flavour.
CAPTAIN'S DAMSON STOUT 4.8% ABV
Smoke tones, with a hint of tartness.
CAPTAIN'S STOUT 4.8% ABV
Malty, with biscuit hints.

DARKSIDE 5.0%
Complex fruity flavour.
SUFFOLK & STRONG 5.0% ABV
Smooth and malty easy drinker.
SEPTEMBER ALE 7.0% ABV
Organic fruity barley wine.
MOTHER IN LAW'S TONGUE TIED 9.0% ABV
Complex full-bodied barley wine, brewed twice a year.
Plus occasionals and seasonals.

BRANDON BREWERY

76 High Street, Brandon IP27 AOU
☎ *(01824) 878496*

BRECKLAND GOLD 3.8% ABV
BRANDON BITTER 4.0% ABV
SAXON GOLD 4.0% ABV
MOLLY'S SECRET 4.1% ABV
NORFOLK POACHER 4.1% ABV
ROYAL GINGER 4.1% ABV
GUNFLINT 4.2% ABV
WEE DROP OF MISCHIEF 4.2% ABV
RUSTY BUCKET 4.4% ABV
SLIPPERY JACK 4.5% ABV
NAPPER TANDY 4.8% ABV

COX & HOLBROOK

Manor Farm, Brettenham Road, Buxhall, Stowmarket IP14 3DY
☎ *(01449) 736323*

CROWN DARK MILD 3.2% ABV
SHELLEY DARK 3.5% ABV
OLD MILL BITTER 3.8% ABV
BEYTON BITTER 3.9% ABV
GAFC BRIDGE ROAD BITTER 4.0% ABV
RATTLESDEN BEST BITTER 4.0% ABV
REMUS 4.5% ABV
GOODCOCK'S WINNER 5.0% ABV
STORMWATCH 5.0% ABV
STOWMARKET PORTER 5.0% ABV
EAST ANGLIAN PALE ALE 6.0% ABV
Plus seasonals and specials.

EARL SOHAM BREWERY

The Old Forge, The Street, Earl Soham, Woodbridge IP13 7RT
☎ *(01728) 684097*
www.earlsohambrewery.co.uk

GANNET MILD 3.3% ABV
Dark and lightly sweet.
VICTORIA BITTER 3.6% ABV
Light and hoppy.
ALBERT ALE 4.4% ABV
Hop character with a hint of sweetness.
Seasonals:
EDWARD ALE 4.0% ABV
Summer only.
SIR ROGER'S PORTER 4.0% ABV
Winter only.
EMPRESS OF INDIA 4.7% ABV
JOLABRUGG 5.0% ABV
Christmas ale.
Plus specials.

ELVEDEN ALES

The Courtyard, Elveden Estate, Elveden, Thetford IP24 3TA
☎ *(01842) 878922*

FOREST GOLD 3.9% ABV
STOUT 5.0% ABV
ALE 5.2% ABV

GREEN DRAGON BREWERY
29 Broad Street, Bungay NR35 1EF
☎ *(01986) 892681*

CHAUCER ALE 3.8% ABV
GOLD 4.4% ABV
BRIDGE STREET BITTER 4.5%ABV
STRONG MILD 5.0% ABV

GREEN JACK BREWERY
29 St Peter's Street, Lowestoft NR32 1QA
☎ *(01502) 582711*
www.bikeways.freeserve.co.uk/greenjack.htm

CANARY 3.8% ABV
ORANGE WHEAT BEER 4.2% ABV
GRASS HOPPER 4.6% ABV
GONE FISHING 5.5% ABV
Seasonals including:
HONEY BUNNY 4.0% ABV
SUMMER DREAM 4.2% ABV
GOLDEN SICKLE 4.8% ABV
RIPPER 8.5% ABV

GREENE KING PLC
Westgate Brewery, Bury St Edmunds IP33 1QT
☎ *(01284) 763222*
www.greeneking.co.uk

GREENE KING XX MILD 3.0% ABV
GREENE KING IPA 3.6% ABV
RUDDLES BEST 3.7% ABV
MORLAND ORIGINAL 4.0% ABV
RUDDLES COUNTY 4.3% ABV
ABBOT ALE 5.0% ABV
OLD SPECKLED HEN 5.2% ABV
Plus specials and occasionals.

KINGS HEAD BREWERY CO.
132 High Street, Bildeston IP7 7ED
☎ *(01449) 741434*
www.bildestonkingshead.co.uk

NSB 2.8% ABV
Low-alcohol beer.
BEST BITTER 3.8% ABV
BLONDIE 4.0% ABV
FIRST GOLD 4.3% ABV
APACHE 4.5% ABV
CROWDIE 5.0% ABV
DARK VADER 5.4% ABV

MAULDONS BREWERY
13 Churchfield Road, Sudbury CO10 2YA
☎ *(01787) 311055*
www.mauldons.co.uk

MICAWBER'S MILD 3.5% ABV
Dark roasted barley tones.
MAULDONS BITTER 3.6% ABV
Floral nose and wheaty.
MOLE TRAP 3.8% ABV
Crisp bitterness, malty finish.
SUFFOLK PRIDE 4.8% ABV
Light, dry fruity finish.
BLACK ADDER 5.3% ABV
Stout. Roast nut aroma.
WHITE ADDER 5.3% ABV
Gold, strong, fruity.
Plus seasonals.

NETHERGATE BREWERY CO. LTD
Growler Brewery, Pentlow, Sudbury CO10 7JJ
☎ *(01787) 283220*
www.nethergate.co.uk

IPA 3.5% ABV
Clean hop flavour.
PRIORY MILD 3.5% ABV
Dark, slightly bitter mild.
UMBEL ALE 3.8% ABV
Distinctive hoppy and coriander flavours.
Champion speciality Beer of Great Britain.
THREE POINT NINE 3.9% ABV
Amber-coloured bitter.
SUFFOLK COUNTY BEST BITTER 4.0% ABV
Malty and bitter.
AUGUSTINIAN ALE 4.5% ABV
Smooth with hints of malt.
OLD GROWLER 5.0% ABV
Soft, chocolate malt flavours. Platinum medal
and best porter and stout, World Championship,
Chicago 2004. Champion Winter ale of Great
Britain, 1997 and 2003.
UMBEL MAGNA 5.0% ABV
Porter with coriander.
Plus monthly seasonal brews.

OLD CANNON BREWERY LTD
86 Cannon Street, Bury St Edmunds IP33 IJR
☎ *(01284) 768769*

OLD CANNON BEST BITTER 3.8% ABV
GUNNER'S DAUGHTER 5.5% ABV
Plus a regularly changing seasonal ale.

OLD CHIMNEYS BREWERY
*Hopton End Farm, Church Road, Market
Weston, Diss IP22 2NX*
☎ *(01359) 221013*

MILITARY MILD 3.4% ABV
GREAT RAFT BITTER 4.2% ABV
POLECAT PORTER 4.2% ABV
BLACK RAT STOUT 4.4% ABV
GOOD KING HENRY 9.0% ABV
Plus seasonal and occasional brews.

OULTON ALES LTD
*Unit 2, Harbour Road Industrial Estate,
Lowestoft NR32 3LZ*
☎ *(01502) 587905*
www.oultonales.co.uk

OULTON BITTER 3.5% ABV
BEE-DAZZLED 4.0% ABV
NAUTILUS 4.2% ABV
EXCELSIOR 4.5% ABV
GONE FISHING 5.0% ABV

ST PETER'S BREWERY CO. LTD
*St Peter's Hall, St Peter, South Elmham, Bungay
NR35 1NQ*
☎ *(01986) 782322*
www.stpetersbrewery.co.uk

BEST BITTER 3.7% ABV
ORGANIC BEST BITTER 4.1% ABV
ORGANIC ALE 4.5% ABV
GOLDEN ALE 4.7% ABV
GRAPEFRUIT 4.7% ABV
Refreshing citrus fruit flavour.
LEMON AND GINGER 4.7% ABV

THE PUBS

ALDEBURGH
The Mill Inn
Market Cross Place, Aldeburgh IP15 5BJ
☎ *(01728) 452563* Dennis and Sue Peel

 Tied to Adnams, serving Bitter, Broadside and Explorer plus seasonal Adnams guests, usually Regatta in summer and Fisherman in winter.

An inn dating from the 1600s, with many historical photographs. The lifeboat crew and fishermen meet here. Restaurant meals and bar snacks served 12–2pm and 6–9pm. Four letting rooms, all with sea views. On the sea front, just 50 metres from the beach.

OPEN *11am–3pm and 6–11pm Mon–Thurs; 11am–11pm Fri–Sun.*

BARHAM
The Sorrel Horse
Old Norwich Road, Barham IP6 0PG
☎ *(01473) 830327* Matthew Smith
www.sorrelhorse.co.uk

 Adnams Bitter and Shepherd Neame Spitfire always available. One guest, changed every six months, might be something from Adnams.

Country pub in a building dating from the 15th century, with one large bar, beams and open fireplaces. Food is available, and there is a dining area. Garden, eight letting rooms. Very occasional live music. Children's play area. Large car park. Situated opposite the Health Farm. Food served 12–2pm and 6.30–10pm daily.

OPEN *11am–3pm and 5–11.30pm Mon–Fri; 11am–11.30pm Sat; 12–10.30pm Sun.*

BILDESTON
The Kings Head Hotel
132 High Street, Bildeston, Ipswich IP7 7ED
☎ *(01449) 741434/741719*
James Kevin Harrison

 The Kings Head Brewery is located on the same premises, although run as a separate concern. However, Kings Head Best Bitter, First Gold, Billy and Old Chimneys Mild regularly available, plus a guest beer often from Old Chimneys, Iceni, Buffy's, Wolf, Mighty Oak, Mauldons or Nethergate.

A 15th-century timber-framed building with original wattle and daub, situated in a small village. Food served 12–3pm and 7–9.30pm daily. Car park. Children welcome. Accommodation and holiday flat available.

OPEN *11am–3pm and 5–11pm Mon–Fri; 11am–11pm Sat; 12–10.30pm Sun.*

BOXFORD
White Hart Inn
Broad Street, Boxford CO10 5DX
☎ *(01787) 211071* Peter Cay

 Greene King IPA plus three constantly rotating guest beers, changed after every firkin.

A 16th-century riverside village pub with gardens, separate pool room and log fires in winter. Entertainment and free quiz night every Sunday. Food served 12–2.30pm and 6–8.30pm. The pub is famous as the British birthplace of the 'Wall of Death'. Beer garden by the river. Families welcome.

OPEN *12–3pm and 6–11.30pm Mon–Fri; 11.30am–12.30am Sat; 11.30am–11.30pm Sun.*

BRANDON
The White Horse
White Horse Street, Brandon IP27 0LB
☎ *(01842) 815767* David Marsh

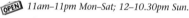 Ridleys Tolly Original, Greene King IPA and Iceni Fine Soft Day plus a variable number of guests, perhaps from Iceni, Mauldons, Wolf, Nethergate, Old Chimneys or Greene King.

Friendly, family-run freehouse with sporting bias, supporting several darts teams and a successful football team. No food. Car park. Well-behaved children welcome until 8pm. From London Road (by industrial estate), turn into Crown Street. Take the second of two close left turns into White Horse Street.

OPEN *11am–11pm Mon–Sat; 12–10.30pm Sun.*

BROME
The Cornwallis Country Hotel and Restaurant
Brome, Eye IP23 8AJ
☎ *(01379) 870326* Peter Bartlett

St Peter's Organic Best and Adnams Bitter plus a guest such as Greene King IPA changed every couple of months.

Former Dower House built in 1561, heavily timbered with a well in the bar. Set in 20 acres of gardens with fine yew topiary, water gardens and ducks. Bar and restaurant food served 12–2pm and 6–9pm. Children welcome. Sixteen bedrooms and function rooms for private hire. Car parking. From the A140, take the B1077 towards Eye.

OPEN *7am–11pm (10.30pm Sun).*

BUNGAY
The Chequers Inn
23 Bridge Street, Bungay NR35 1HD
☎ *(01986) 893579* Geoff Bryan

Freehouse with Adnams Best and Fuller's London Pride plus a range of guests.

A 17th-century, two-bar traditional town alehouse with log fire, large beer garden and patio. Home-cooked traditional pub grub served 12–2pm daily. Large play area for children. Large beer garden with separate smoking area. Outside bar facilities – festivals catered for.

OPEN *All day, every day.*

The Green Dragon

29 Broad Street, Bungay NR35 1EE
☎ *(01986) 892681* William and Rob Pickard

 Adnams Best is always available and the four beers from the Green Dragon range are brewed and served on the premises.

The pub was bought in 1991 from Brent Walker by William and Rob Pickard. The three-barrel brewery was built and the pub refurbished. Due to increased demand, a second brewery was then built and the capacity expanded to eight barrels. The Green Dragon is a popular pub with a friendly atmosphere. Bar food is available at lunchtime and evenings. Car park, garden, children's room.

OPEN *11am–3pm and 5–11pm Mon–Thurs; 11am–11pm Fri–Sat; 12–3pm and 7–10.30pm Sun.*

BURY ST EDMUNDS

The Old Cannon Brewery

86 Cannon Street, Bury St Edmonds IP33 1JP
☎ *(01284) 768769* Richard Eyton-Jones

 The full range of Old Cannon Brewery beers are brewed on the premises and are permanently available in the pub. Also featuring Adnams Bitter and at least one other guest beer, usually from local Suffolk or Norfolk independents.

Previously a Victorian brewhouse (brewing stopped in 1917). Now half restaurant, half bar, with unique stainless steel brewery sited in the bar. Production began again in 2000, with brewing on Mondays, when the pub is closed at lunchtime. Food available every other lunchtime and every evening except Sun and Mon. No children under 14. B&B accommodation. Situated parallel to Northgate Street, off the A14 and five minutes from station. Car park.

OPEN *12–3pm every day except Mon; 5–11pm Mon–Sat; 7–10.30pm Sun.*

The Queen's Head

39 Churchgate Street, Bury St Edmonds IP33 1RG
☎ *(01284) 761554*
Jan Rutherford and Mark Nicholson

 A true freehouse with Adnams Bitter, Nethergate IPA and Greene King IPA plus one or two guests from breweries such as St Peter's, Archers and Elgood's.

Totally refurbished in 2005, this popular town-centre pub has a mixed clientele during the day and a younger crowd in the evenings. One big bar with dining area plus conservatory and games room. An extensive menu plus daily specials is available 11am–9pm. Children welcome everywhere apart from the central bar area. Heated and lit beer garden. Opposite the Norman Tower, up from the cathedral.

OPEN *11am–11pm Mon–Wed; 11am–midnight Thurs; 11am–12.10am Fri–Sat; 12–11pm Sun.*

The Rose & Crown

48 Whiting Street, Bury St Edmunds IP33 1NP
☎ *(01284) 755934* Tony and Liz Fayers

 Greene King XX Dark Mild, IPA and Abbot are permanently served, plus one rotating guest.

Original street-corner local in the same street as the Greene King Brewery and in the same family for 30 years. Two bars and off sales. Food served 12–2pm Mon–Sat.

OPEN *11.30am–11pm Mon–Fri; 11.30am–3pm and 7–11pm Sat; 12–2.30pm and 7–10.30pm Sun.*

CARLTON COLVILLE

The Bell Inn

82 The Street, Carlton Colville, Lowestoft NR33 8JR
☎ *(01502) 582873* Pauline Rusby

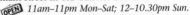 Oulton Bitter, Nautilus, Gone Fishing and Sunrise plus seasonal specials from Oulton Ales and guest breweries, all served straight from the barrel.

Village pub dating back to the 1700s, with restaurant, original flagstone floor and open fires. Food available lunchtimes (for traditional meals) and evenings (for à la carte). Children are allowed, and there are baby-changing facilities. Disabled access and toilet. Large car park, beer garden. On the main street in old Carlton Colville.

OPEN *11am–11pm Mon–Sat; 12–10.30pm Sun.*

COWLINGE

The Three Tuns

Queen Street, Cowlinge, Newmarket CB8 9QP
☎ *(01440) 821847* Chris and Sue Smith
www.threetunspub.com

 Freehouse with three real ales, including Adnams Bitter and one or two weekly guests from all over the UK. The aim is not to repeat guest beers.

A 17th-century pub at the hub of the local community, where lively conversation is on offer and all are welcome. One main bar, two large inglenook fireplaces, roaring fires in winter. Snug and two small restaurant areas. Traditional and contemporary food served 12–2.30pm and 6–9.30pm Wed–Sun. Beer garden and smoking patio. Just off the A143 between Newmarket, Haverhill and Bury St Edmunds.

OPEN *12–2.30pm and 5–11pm Wed–Fri; 12–12 Sat–Sun.*

EARL SOHAM

The Victoria

Earl Soham, Woodbridge IP13 7RL
☎ *(01728) 685758* Paul Hooper
www.earlsohambrewery.co.uk

Home to the Earl Soham Brewery, serving Victoria, Albert and Sir Roger's Porter plus occasional guests.

Traditional pub with tiled floors, wooden décor and interesting pictures of Queen Victoria. No frills, just two bars, good beer, food and conversation. Food served 11.30am–2.30pm and 6.30–10pm. Car park. Children welcome. Beer garden. CAMRA Suffolk Pub of the Year 2005. On the A1120.

OPEN *11.30am–3pm and 5.30–11pm Mon–Sat; 12–3pm and 7–10.30pm Sun.*

EAST BERGHOLT

The Red Lion

The Street, East Bergholt CO7 6TB
☎ *(01206) 298332* Rick and Dawn Brogan

Tied to Ridleys, with IPA and Old Bob the permanent beers.

Village country pub, 300–400 years old, with three fireplaces. Two bars – one with restaurant/family room attached. Live music in garden occasionally on bank holidays. Car park, family en-suite letting room. Children allowed in family eating area. Centrally located in the village, close to Flatford Mill.

OPEN *11am–3pm and 6–11pm Mon–Fri; 11am–11pm Sat; 12–10.30pm Sun.*

EDWARDSTONE

The White Horse Inn

Mill Green, Edwardstone, Sudbury CO10 5PX
☎ *(01787) 211211* Tom Norton (Manager)
www.edwardstonewhitehorse.co.uk

Freehouse with organic eco-friendly micro-brewery – Mill Green – in production. Always on offer: Mill Green Loveleys Fair, Mawkin Mild and Bull's Cross Bitter, plus Adnams Bitter and Crouch Vale Brewers Gold. Two rotating beers, one from Mill Green range, and one guest, e.g. Dark Star Hophead or Kings Head Landlady. Stillage behind bar enables beer to be served on gravity direct from cask.

A two-bar village pub with wind-generated turbines in the grounds in an effort to be environmentally friendly, wood burner feeding central heating, solar panels for hot water. Log fires in winter. Beer garden. Caravan and camping club on site for five caravans. There are two self-catering cottages in the pub grounds, available for holiday lets. Food available 6.30–9pm Tues–Sun. Three beer festivals a year: Dark Ale Day (May Day bank holiday), Music and Beer festival (August bank holiday) and Winter and Old Ale festival (February). Children allowed.

OPEN *5pm–close Mon–Fri; all day Sat–Sun.*

FELIXSTOWE

The Half Moon

303 High Street, Walton, Felixstowe
☎ *(01394) 216009* Patrick Wroe

Adnams tied house, so Adnams beers always available, plus two guests, such as Fuller's London Pride or Everards Tiger.

Old-fashioned, friendly alehouse. No food, no fruit machine, no music. Darts, cribbage, backgammon. Garden, children's play area, car park.

OPEN *12–2.30pm and 5–11pm Mon–Fri; 12–11pm Sat; 12–3pm and 7–10.30pm Sun.*

FRAMLINGHAM

The Station Hotel

Station Road, Framlingham IP13 9EE
☎ *(01728) 723455* Michael Jones
www.thestationhotel.net

Four real ales, three from Earl Soham Brewery and one weekly-changing rotating guest.

Destination pub with a warm bistro feel. Scrubbed floors and tables with woodburner and log fire in winter. Pub games. Food, including seafood, available 12–2pm and 7–9pm Mon–Fri, 12–2pm and 7–9.30pm Sat–Sun (booking advisable). Beer garden. Snug available for parties. Popular with shooting parties. Beer festival held in June or July. Located off the A12 between Woodbride and Saxmundham.

OPEN *12–2.30pm and 5–11pm Mon–Sat; 12–2.30pm and 7–10.30pm Sun.*

FRAMSDEN

The Dobermann

The Street, Framsden IP14 6HG
☎ *(01473) 890461* Sue Frankland

Adnams Best and Broadside plus guests such as Mauldons Moletrap.

A 400-year-old, traditional thatched and beamed Suffolk village pub. Extensive menu of bar food available. Car park, garden, accommodation. No children. Easy to find off B1077.

OPEN *12–3pm and 7–11pm; closed Mon except bank holidays, and Sunday evenings.*

FRECKENHAM

The Golden Boar Inn

The Street, Freckenham, Bury St Edmunds
IP28 8HZ
☎ *(01638) 723000* Vaggy Spyrou
www.goldenboar.co.uk

 Freehouse with four pumps serving Adnams Best, Timothy Taylor Landlord, Fuller's London Pride and Greene King IPA.

The only pub in Freckenham, this is a restored old-style country village pub dating from the 16th century with timber frames, old brickwork and fireplaces. Two bars and two separate dining areas, plus an acre of lawned gardens with children's area. Food times 12–2pm and 6.30–9pm Mon–Sat and 12–3pm Sun. Modern European à la carte menu served lunchtimes and evenings; traditional bar menu served lunchtimes and Mon–Thurs evenings; traditional three-course roast served Sundays. En-suite accommodation (singles and twins).

OPEN *12–11pm Mon–Sat; all day Sun.*

GISLINGHAM

The Six Bells

High Street, Gislingham, Eye IP23 8JD
☎ *(01379) 783349* Barry and Michelle

Freehouse with Adnams Bitter, Greene King IPA and Woodforde's Wherry plus a guest, changing every week.

A traditional 1850s village pub and restaurant with beer garden and function room. Pool and darts. Food available Wed–Sun. Monthly events such as quizzes, pool competitions, jam sessions, ride outs, curry nights, fresh fish and chips nights and karaoke. Bikers, hikers and children welcome. Disabled facilities. Situated close to Thornham Walks. Near Eye, between Stowmarket and Diss.

OPEN *7–11pm Mon–Tues; 12–3pm and 7–11pm Wed–Sat; all day Sun.*

GREAT CORNARD

The Five Bells

63 Bures Road, Great Cornard CO10 0HU
☎ *(01787) 379016* Wendy Hedley

Leased from Greene King with IPA, Old Speckled Hen, Abbot and Mild always available.

This dog- and child-friendly community locals' pub has two bars, patios at the front and back, beer garden and heated smokers' area. Car park. Games including petanque, darts, dominoes, crib, billiards, pool, chess and backgammon. Plans to start serving pub food during 2008. Functions catered for. Live music alternate Friday nights. Follow the B1115 out of Sudbury towards Bures, the pub is located next to St Andrew's Church.

OPEN *All day, every day.*

GREAT WENHAM

The Queen's Head

Great Wenham
☎ *(01473) 310590* M Harris

Freehouse with Adnams Best and Greene King IPA and Abbot plus one guest, perhaps from Mauldons, Crouch Vale, Woodforde's, Bateman or Fuller's.

Early-Victorian red-brick cottage-style pub in a pleasant rural location, catering for a mixed clientele (mainly aged over 25). English and Indian food is served 12–2pm and 7–9pm (not Sun evenings or Mondays), and booking is advisable. Children allowed at lunchtimes only, and not in the bar (advisable to phone in advance). Car park.

OPEN *12–2.30pm and 6.30–11pm Mon–Sat; 12–2.30pm and 7–10.30pm Sun.*

HASKETON

The Turk's Head Inn

Low Road, Hasketon, Woodbridge IP13 6JG
☎ *(01394) 382584* Kirsty Lambert

Ales from Greene King and Adnams always on offer, plus guest beers.

Country village pub with huge log fires and low beams, decorated with brewery memorabilia and antiques. Food available at lunchtimes and evenings, ranging from light snacks to a full menu. Children's menu. No food on Mondays. Beer garden and patio. Camping and caravanning in three acres of meadow. Children welcome.

OPEN *6–11pm Mon (closed Mon lunchtime); 12–3pm and 6–11pm Tues–Sat; 12–4pm and 7–10.30pm Sun.*

HAWKEDON

The Queen's Head

Rede Road, Hawkedon, Bury St Edmunds IP29 4NN
☎ *(01284) 789218* S Chapman

A freehouse. Adnams Bitter and Woodforde's Wherry plus four guests, changed weekly. Breweries such as Black Sheep, Nethergate, Timothy Taylor, Wolf, Cannon and Wells and Young's. Also traditional cider and perry.

An award-winning 15th-century pub, nestled off the beaten track. Unique character and charm with low timbered ceilings, flagstone floors, scrubbed pine tables and inglenook fireplaces. West Suffolk CAMRA Pub of the Year 2006. Locally sourced British food with the accent on game, fish and meat (rated UKTV Local Food Hero) served 6–9pm Wed–Thurs; 12–2.30pm and 6–9pm Fri–Sun.

OPEN *5pm–close Mon–Thurs; all day from 12 Fri–Sun.*

IPSWICH

The Cricketers

51 Crown Street, Ipswich IP1 3JA
☎ *(01473) 225910* Nicola Harney

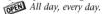 Wetherspoon's pub. Shepherd Neame Spitfire is among the beers available, plus three guests such as Hop Back Summer Lightning and a range of bottled beers.

Town-centre pub with two beer gardens. Food available all day. Children allowed up to 6pm if eating.

OPEN *All day, every day.*

The Dove Street Inn

76 St Helens Street, Ipswich IP4 2LA
☎ *(01473) 211270*
Adrian Smith and Karen Beaumont
www.dovestreetinn.co.uk

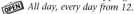 A huge rotating range of real ales, many from East Anglian brewers such as Adnams, Woodforde's, Mauldons, Crouch Vale etc, but others from further afield. Beers are changed as often as hourly during a busy session!

A single-bar three-roomed pub dating from the 17th century. Hot and cold bar snacks served all day, every day. Beer garden, disabled facilities. Three beer festivals take place each year in May, August and November. Dogs on leads welcome. Five minutes' walk from the Regent Theatre, at the end of the main shopping street.

OPEN *All day, every day from 12.*

The Fat Cat

288 Spring Road, Ipswich IP4 5NL
☎ *(01473) 726524* John Keatley
www.fatcatipswich.co.uk

 Freehouse with 16–20 real ales served straight from the barrel and rotating all the time. Woodforde's Wherry and Adnams brews are regular features.

A spit-and-sawdust pub with wooden floor, no music or machines, but 96-year-old tin pub sign. One bar, beer garden. Frequent CAMRA Suffolk Pub of the Year. Rolls available at lunchtime. Well-behaved children and dogs allowed. On the outskirts of town.

OPEN *All day, every day.*

The Steamboat

78 New Cut West, Ipswich IP2 8HW
☎ *(01473) 601902* Val Bint

A Ridleys tenancy serving IPA and Rumpus, plus one rotating guest from Ridleys, such as Old Bob.

Riverside pub (formerly the Steamboat ticket office), 100 years old with live music at night. Large beer garden and riverside views. Function room. The pub is available for private hire.

OPEN *12–11pm (10.30pm Sun).*

KERSEY

The Bell

The Street, Kersey IP7 6DY
☎ *(01473) 823229* Paul Denton

 Three or four beers always available plus brews from a guest list including Shepherd Neame Spitfire, Fuller's London Pride, Adnams Bitter and Greene King Abbot.

Built in 1380, a timber-framed Tudor-style property with log fires and cobbles. Bar and restaurant food available at lunchtimes and evenings. Car park, garden, private dining room. Children allowed. Signposted from Hadleigh.

OPEN *11am–3pm and 6.30–11pm Mon–Sat; 12–3pm and 7–10.30pm Sun.*

LAVENHAM

The Angel Hotel

Market Place, Lavenham CO10 9QZ
☎ *(01787) 247388*
Roy Whitworth and John Barry

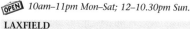 Adnams Bitter and Broadside plus Greene King IPA and Nethergate Suffolk County. The selection changes every six months, but always features Suffolk ales.

Family-run inn in the centre of Lavenham, first licensed in 1420 and winner of national awards for accommodation and food. Food served 12–2.15pm and 6.45–9.15pm every day. Bookings advisable for weekends. Garden and terrace, car park. Free Wi-Fi access. Eight en-suite bedrooms. Situated in one of England's finest medieval villages.

OPEN *10am–11pm Mon–Sat; 12–10.30pm Sun.*

LAXFIELD

The King's Head Inn

Gorams Mill Lane, Laxfield, Woodbridge IP13 8DW
☎ *(01986) 798395*

 Adnams house with all beers served straight from the barrel in the tap room. Adnams Best, Broadside and Explorer always available plus Adnams seasonal ales and Woodforde's Wherry.

Known locally as The Low House, this is a well-preserved 600-year-old country village pub. Tiled floors, real fires, wooden settles and tables. Food served 12–2pm and 7–9pm daily (not Sun in winter). Beer garden with children's play area. Live music in a marquee on the lawn during the summer. Separate dining room and card room. Children allowed in specified areas. Accommodation.

OPEN *12–3pm and 6–11pm Mon–Sat; 12–4pm and 7–10.30pm Sun (ring for confirmation).*

LIDGATE

The Star

The Street, Lidgate, Newmarket CB8 9PP
☎ *(01638) 500275* Teresa and Anthony Axon

 Greene King house with IPA, Abbot and Ruddles County.

Cask ale and Catalan cuisine at this 16th-century inn on the B1063, between Newmarket and Bury St Edmunds. Spanish food served every lunchtime and evenings except Sun. Outside seating, beer garden and car park. Children and dogs welcome at luchtimes only. Paella cooked outside on summer weekends.

OPEN *12–3pm and 6–11pm Mon–Sat; 12–3pm and 7–10.30pm Sun.*

LOWESTOFT

The Crown Hotel

High Street, Lowestoft NR32 1HR
☎ *(01502) 534808* C Simpson

Two real ales, one of which is changed monthly, with Greene King Abbot, IPA and Old Speckled Hen regularly featured.

An old coaching inn dating from the 1800s, with two bars and a function room. Food available 12–3pm every day. Large-screen TVs. Quizzes, karaoke and music at night. Car park.

OPEN *11am–midnight.*

The Oak Tavern

73 Crown Street West, Lowestoft NR32 1SQ
☎ *(01502) 537246* Debbie Fenn

Adnams Bitter and Greene King Abbot Ale plus two guest beers, perhaps from Woodforde's, Buffy's, Wolf, Elgood's or Bateman breweries.

Friendly community pub, specialising in real ale and Belgian beers, with a separate pool and darts area, plus Sky Sports widescreen TV. Five minutes from Lowestoft college. Car park. No food. No children.

OPEN *10.30am–11pm.*

Sun Rise Inn

6 Corton Road, Lowestoft NR32 4PL
☎ *(01502) 564616* Danny and Linda Smith

Greene King IPA, Abbot and Old Speckled Hen always available.

Small, friendly hotel with cosy beamed bar, carvery, steakhouse restaurant and 12 en-suite rooms. Food served 12–3pm and 6–9pm Mon–Sat, plus 12–3pm Sun, carvery. Car park. Children welcome, but no special facilities. Located off the A12 between Lowestoft and Great Yarmouth. On corner at the turn-off to Corton.

OPEN *11am–11pm Mon–Sat; 12–10.30pm Sun.*

The Triangle Tavern

29 St Peter's Street, Lowestoft NR32 1QA
☎ *(01502) 582711* Jockey Wilson
www.triangletavern.co.uk

Home of the Green Jack Brewery, so five or six of the brewery's ales always available plus two constantly changing guests. Real cider also served.

Pub in the High Street next to the Triangle Market Place, with cosy front bar and lively back bar. No food (customers are welcome to bring their own). Live music Thurs–Fri nights. Beer festivals held Easter, summer and Christmas. Parking. Brewery tours by arrangement.

OPEN *All day, every day.*

The Welcome

182 London Road North, Lowestoft NR32 1HB
☎ *(01502) 585500* David and Susan Carter

Freehouse with three real ales, including Adnams Bitter and Broadside and a weekly guest, perhaps from Wells and Young's, Greene King or another brewery.

A very old one-bar local with strong naval and fishing connections and a friendly atmosphere. It features photos from the Beach Village and the 1953 floods (the landlady was born in 1953 in the Beach Village). No food. Beer/smoking garden. Live music every Friday night and monthly karaoke on a Sunday. Large screen for sports. Children welcome until 7pm. Opposite TSB at the top of town.

OPEN *All day, every day (open till 1am at weekends).*

MARKET WESTON

The Mill Inn

Bury Road, Market Weston, Nr Diss IP22 2PD
☎ *(01359) 221018* Lesley Leacy

Five real ales, with brews from Old Chimneys, Greene King and Adnams regularly featured, plus a guest, changed weekly.

Village pub in an early-Victorian former mill house, with comfortable bar and dining area featuring open fires most of the time. Varied, homemade food available 12–2pm and 7–9.30pm every day except Monday. Beer garden, patio, stand-alone dining area for up to 16. Children welcome (preferably over 7 years). Occasional beer festivals and barbecues. Car park. On the B1111 Garboldisham–Stanton road.

OPEN *11am–3pm (not Mon) and 5–11pm Mon–Sat; 12–3pm and 7–10.30pm Sun.*

OULTON

The Blue Boar

28 Oulton Street, Oulton, Lowestoft NR32 3BB
☎ *(01502) 572160* Stewart Battrick

At least two real ales always available but from a constantly changing selection of brews and breweries.

Old village inn with two bars (public and lounge), games room, function room, large beer garden, patio and barbecue area. Food served 12–2.45pm. Children welcome in games room and garden area. Car park. On the main road between Great Yarmouth and Oulton Broad.

OPEN *All day, every day.*

PIN MILL
The Butt & Oyster
Pin Mill, Chelmondiston, Ipswich IP9 1JW
☎ *(01473) 780764* Steve and Louise Loman

Greene King IPA straight from the barrel plus Adnams Broadside and Bitter. One guest, changed occasionally.

A 16th-century inn with one bar and riverside seating area. Food served 12–2.30pm and 6.30–9.30pm Mon–Fri, and 12–9.30pm Sat–Sun. Children allowed.

OPEN *11am–11pm Mon–Sat; 12–10.30pm Sun.*

RATTLESDEN
The Five Bells
High Street, Rattlesden IP30 0RA
☎ *(01449) 737373* Deborah Caley

A freehouse. Three ales on at all times, all guests, changing daily. Beers from Wolf, Crouch Vale, Cox & Holbrook, Bateman, Cottage, Elgood's, Springhead, Everards, Brains, Cotleigh and many many more.

A 17th-century brick and timber building with open fire, one large bar and a games room with Sky Sports. The clientèle ranges from age 16 to 86 and crosses all walks of life. Toasted sandwiches available. Large garden. Pool table, darts and cribbage. Well-behaved children welcome. Live music twice a month.

OPEN *Noon–12.30am (11.30pm Sun).*

RENDHAM
The White Horse
Bruisyard Road, Rendham IP17 2AF
☎ *(01728) 663497* Paul and Lisa Boswell
www.whitehorserendham.co.uk

Genuine freehouse with four or five real ales. Earl Soham Victoria Bitter, Timothy Taylor Landlord and Mauldons Suffolk Pride are permanent features, plus two guests, changed every three to four weeks.

Grade II listed building dating from the 15th century, this is a traditional village pub with open-plan bar separated by a large chimney breast with an open fire one side and a log burner the other. A relaxed atmosphere provides an ideal environment to mix with the locals, enjoy the excellent menu or relish a good pint with the papers. Food served 12–2pm and from 6.30pm daily. Beer garden. Car park. Boules pitch and traditional pub games. Annual beer festival Aug bank holiday. On the B1119, opposite the church.

OPEN *12–2.30pm and 6–11pm Mon–Sat; 12–3pm and 7–11pm Sun.*

ST PETER SOUTH ELMHAM
St Peter's Hall
St Peter South Elmham, Bungay NR35 1NQ
☎ *(01986) 782288*
www.stpetershallsuffolk.co.uk

Home of the St Peter's Brewery since 1996, with the full range of real ales available.

Bar and restaurant in a building that dates from 1280. Three inside drinking areas, but the focus is on the food served at lunchtimes and evenings. The brewery is located across the courtyard. Tours available at weekends. Follow signs from the A144 or B1062.

OPEN *11am–3pm and 6–11pm Mon–Fri; 11am–11pm Sat; 12–2.30pm Sun.*

SNAPE
The Crown Inn
Bridge Road, Snape, Saxmundham IP17 1SL
☎ *(01728) 688324* Garry Cook

Adnams pub with Best Bitter, Broadside and Explorer. Seasonal brews are also served.

A 15th-century roadside inn not far from Snape Maltings. Attractive, open, brick-floored bar area with wooden settles plus separate dining room. Beer garden. Food served 12–2.30pm (until 3pm Sat–Sun) and 6–9.30pm; menu uses locally sourced seasonal produce and home-reared meat from animals on-site. Car park for 40 cars. Children welcome. Close to the town of Aldeburgh and the village of Orford, with its medieval castle. Also handy for sailing, golfing, bird-watching and walking. From the A12 going north from Woodbridge, take the A1094 to Snape.

OPEN *12–3pm and 6–11pm.*

The Golden Key
Priory Road, Snape, Saxmundham IP17 1SG
☎ *(01728) 688510* Nick Attfield

Adnams pub serving Bitter, Broadside and Explorer cask beers. Adnams seasonal beers offered when available: Old, Oyster Stout, Extrra, Regatta, Yuletide, Tally Ho and East Green. Also Adnams Spindrift, a kegged beer, and bottled beers Adnams Lighthouse, Gun, Broadside and Innovation. From Greenwich Meantime Brewery, bottled Wheat Beer and Raspberry Grand Cru.

Relaxed cottage-style dining pub dating from the 1500s, tucked away from the main road through the village. Large roaring fires in winter and a sunny front terrace for warmer times. Food served 12–2pm (until 2.30pm Sun) and 6.30–9pm (from 7pm Sun). As a small pub with a small cellar, we find that having a wide range of bottled beers, together with a beer list and suggested food matches, is the best way to promote beer drinking.

OPEN *12–3pm (until 4pm Sat–Sun) and 6–11pm (from 7pm Sun).*

The Dukes Head

Slugs Lane, Somerleyton, Lowestoft NR32 5QR
☎ *(01502) 730281* Hugh Crossley
www.somerleyton.co.uk

 Freehouse with between two and six real ales on offer. Adnams Bitter and Greene King IPA permanent fixtures, plus other guests from Norfolk, Suffolk and Essex breweries.

A 17th-century coaching inn, extended in the Victorian period. Two bars, one public and one with a restaurant focusing on locally sourced produce. Food served 12–3pm and 6–10pm daily, may be different in winter. Family-friendly policy with swings and climbing frame in the large beer garden. Annual beer festival. Private function room available. Just off the B1074.

OPEN *Winter: 11am–3pm and 5.30–close Mon–Fri; all day Sat–Sun. Summer: all day, every day.*

Harbour Inn

Blackshore, Southwold IP18 6TA
☎ *(01502) 722381* Colin and Katie Fraser

 Adnams house with Bitter, Broadside, Explorer and a seasonal ale available.

R iverside destination inn on an old working fishing harbour. Dating from before 1600, the pub is in an idyllic and romantic setting with spectacular views. Food served 12–2.30pm and 6–9pm. Beer garden, private room for hire, car park. Well-behaved children and dogs welcome. At the end of York Road.

OPEN *11am–11pm Mon–Sat; 12–10.30pm Sun.*

The Lord Nelson

East Street, Southwold IP18 6EJ
☎ *(01502) 722079*
David and Gemma Sanchez and John Illston

 Adnams Best Bitter, Broadside and Explorer on offer, plus a seasonal Adnams ale such as Mayday, Tally Ho or Oyster Stout.

F ormer coaching inn dating from the 1700s, a smugglers' pub close to Southwold cliffs. One bar, snug, family room. Enclosed garden at the rear. Homemade food using locally sourced produce served 12–2pm and 7–9pm. Children and dogs welcome. Voted one of Britain's Top Ten Pubs (*Good Pub Guide 2008*), and *Coast* magazine's Coastal Pub of the Year. On the Suffolk Sunrise Coast, in the character town of Southwold, with Adnams Brewery nearby. Just off the market place.

OPEN *10.30am–11pm Mon–Sat; 12–10.30pm Sun.*

The Royal William

53 Union Street, Stowmarket IP14 1HP
☎ *(01449) 674553* Patrick Murphy

A tied house with three to five ales, such as St Austell Tribute, Courage Best, Theakston and Young's Bitter.

T his traditional backstreet public house serves gravity-fed ale direct from the barrel. Bar snacks served 12–3pm and 6–9pm. Small enclosed beer garden. Occasional themed nights featuring, for example, morris dancing and local acoustic musicians. Five-minute walk from station; turn right out of the station, left into Stowpland Street and the second right is Union Street.

OPEN *All day, every day.*

The Stag Tavern

44–6 Bury Street, Stowmarket IP14 1HF
☎ *(01449) 613980* Phil Rudland

Three real ales on at any time, including beers from Greene King and Ansells, plus a weekly guest.

A traditional drinker's pub just outside the town centre, with two bars, traditional pub games and pool table. Community Pub of the Year 2008. Food available 12–2pm daily. Private room for up to 12. Well-behaved children welcome.

OPEN *11am–11pm Mon–Wed; 11am–midnight Thurs; 11am–1am Fri–Sat; 12–12 Sun.*

The Moon & Mushroom Inn

High Road, Swilland, Ipswich IP6 9LR
☎ *(01473) 785320* Elizabeth Gavin

Freehouse with up to eight real ales. Crouch Vale Brewers Gold, Woodforde's Wherry and Nelson's Revenge, Buffy's Hopleaf and Norwich Terrier, Nethergate Suffolk County and Wolf Golden Jackal are permanent features, plus a guest, which changes each month.

A 14th-century coaching inn, beamed and full of character. One main bar with two log fires, quarry tile floors and church pews. Dining room decorated with paintings. Food served 12–2pm Mon; 12-2pm and 6.30–8.45pm Tues–Sat; 12–2.30pm Sun. Two large patios full of vines and flowers, with heaters and retractable awnings. Small shingle rose garden with seating, parasols and heating. Seven miles from Ipswich – head for Witnesham and follow signs for Swilland.

OPEN *6–11pm Mon; 11.30am–2.30pm and 6–11pm Tues–Sat; 12–2.30pm and 7–10.30pm Sun.*

THEBERTON
The Lion Inn
Theberton, Nr Leiston IP16 4RU
☎ *(01728) 830185*
Caroline and Michael Jeffery

Freehouse with three or four real ales. Woodforde's Wherry and Adnams Bitter permanents, plus up to two guests from various breweries.

Approximately 300 years old and a listed building, this pub serves food 12–2.30pm and 6–9.30pm daily, with fresh fish a Friday speciality. Car park. Children welcome, children's menu available. Beer garden. Two miles from the beach.

OPEN *12–3pm daily; 6–11pm Mon–Thurs; 6pm–12 Sat; 7–10.30pm Sun.*

THURSTON
The Fox & Hounds
Barton Road, Thurston IP31 3QT
☎ *(01359) 232228* Mandy and Bernie Ruffles
www.thurstonfoxandhounds.co.uk

Freehouse serving ales from Greene King and Adnams plus four rotating guests changed every firkin.

Built around 1800, this Victorian building consists of two bars and a dining area. A good all-round village pub and winner of West Sussex Pub of the Year 2007. Home-cooked food available 12–2pm Tues–Sun, 7–8.30pm Tues–Sat. Two air-conditioned, en-suite guest rooms available for B&B. Beer garden. Car park. Pool table. Located 200 metres from the railway station in the village of Thurston, four and a half miles from Bury St Edmunds.

OPEN *12–2.30pm and 5–11pm Mon–Thurs; 12–12 Fri–Sat; 12–10.30pm Sun.*

WALBERSWICK
The Anchor
Main Street, Walberswick IP18 6UA
☎ *(01502 722112)* Mark and Sophie Dorber
www.anchoratwalberswick.com

Adnams house with Bitter, Broadside and a seasonal brew available.

Refurbished and now run by the couple behind the White Horse in Parsons Green, West London. Bright and airy, with lots of new wood panelling. Good food served 12–3pm and 6–9pm. Real fires. Children welcome. Accommodation in eight bedrooms. Close to the coastal path with easy access to the beach and across the river to Southwold. Food and drink festivals.

OPEN *11am–4pm (12–4pm Sun) and 6–11pm.*

Bell
Ferry Road, Walberswick IP18 6TN
☎ *(01502) 723109* Sue Ireland Cutting
www.bellinn-walberswick.co.uk

Adnams-owned with up to five of the brewery's ales including Bitter, Broadside and Explorer.

Fine location, very close to the beach and with a huge garden. Flagstones, oak beams, wood-burning stoves. Good food served 12–2pm and 7–9pm, and for longer periods at weekends and other busy times. Accommodation in six bedrooms. Children and dog friendly.

OPEN *11am–11pm Mon–Thurs; 11am–midnight Fri–Sat;12–10.30pm Sun.*

WALDRINGFIELD
Maybush
The Quay, Cliff Road, Waldringfield IP12 4QL
☎ *(01473) 736215* Steve and Louise Lomas

Adnams Best, Broadside and a seasonal brew available plus Greene King IPA.

On the banks of the River Debden with a boatyard (and boat trips) next door. Large bar with eating area and plenty of outside space in the terraced beer garden. Food served all day, every day. Children welcome.

OPEN *11am–11pm Mon–Sat; 12–11pm Sun.*

WOODBRIDGE
The Cherry Tree Inn
73 Cumberland Street, Woodbridge IP12 4AG
☎ *(01394) 384627* Mr and Mrs Ford
www.thecherrytreepub.co.uk

An Adnams tied house serving Bitter, Broadside and other seasonal Adnams ales. Also Nethergate Priory Mild along with regularly changing guest ales. Always eight cask ales available.

A traditional 17th-century inn with large garden, terrace and children's play area. Homemade food served all day every day. Car park. Four-star accommodation housed in a converted barn. Well-known locally for beer festivals. Situated close to the river on the main road to Woodbridge travelling from Ipswich.

OPEN *7.30am–11pm.*

THE BREWERIES

HOGS BACK BREWERY

Manor Farm, The Street, Tongham GU10 1DE
☎ *(01252) 783000*
www.hogsback.co.uk

HBB 3.7% ABV
Citrus flavour, long aromatic, hoppy finish.
TRADITIONAL ENGLISH ALE 4.2% ABV
Smooth, well-balanced flavours.
HOP GARDEN GOLD 4.6% ABV
Refreshing with good fruity hoppiness.
Seasonals:
SPRING CALL 4.0% ABV
SUMMER THIS 4.2% ABV
AUTUMN SEER 4.8% ABV
Available from Sept–Oct.
RIP SNORTER 5.0% ABV
Available from Nov–Jan.
Christmas Ales:
ADVENT ALE 4.4% ABV
OTT 6.0% ABV
SANTA'S WOBBLE 7.5% ABV
Plus special and commemorative ales.

LEITH HILL BREWERY

The Plough Inn, Coldharbour Lane, Nr Dorking RH5 6HD
☎ *(01306) 711793*
www.ploughinn.com

HOPPILY EVER AFTER 3.6% ABV
CROOKED FURROW 4.0% ABV
Hoppy, light bitter.
TALLYWHACKER 4.8% ABV
Beer with strong roast barley flavour.

PILGRIM ALES

The Old Brewery, 11c West Street, Reigate RH2 9BL
☎ *(01737) 222651*
www.pilgrim.co.uk

SURREY BITTER 3.7% ABV
Hoppy, with a good mixture of flavours.
PORTER 4.0% ABV
Dark with roast malt flavour.
PROGRESS BEST BITTER 4.0% ABV
Red and malty.
EXCALIBUR 4.5% ABV
CRUSADER PREMIUM BITTER 4.9% ABV
Gold, with hops and malt flavour.
TALISMAN 5.0% ABV
Plus seasonal brews.

SURREY HILLS BREWERY

Old Scotland Farm, Staple Lane, Shere, Guildford GU5 9TE
☎ *(01483) 212812*
www.surreyhills.co.uk

RANMORE ALE 3.8% ABV
SHERE DROP 4.2% ABV
Plus seasonals and specials including:
GILT COMPLEX 4.6% ABV (SUMMER)
ALBURY 4.6% ABV (WINTER)

THE PUBS

ALBURY

William IV

Little London, Albury, Nr Guildford GU5 9DG
☎ *(01483) 202685* G Madge

Freehouse serving Surrey Hills Shere Drop and Ranmore Ale, Hogs Back TEA and HBB plus a guest, changed two to three times a year. Draft scrumpy regularly available.

Dating back to the 16th century, this pub is in the heart of the Surrey Hills, an Area of Outstanding Natural Beauty. Two small bars and a large dining area that seats 40. No music and no game machines. There is a new kitchen, and food is served 12–2pm Mon–Sun, 7–9pm Mon–Sat. Beer garden. Car park. Children allowed but not encouraged. Dogs allowed in bar. Great location for walking, riding and fishing. Located just off the A25 between Guildford and Dorking.

OPEN *11am–3pm and 5.30–11pm Mon–Sat; 12–3pm and 7–11pm Sun.*

ASH

The Dover Arms

31 Guildford Road, Ash GU12 6BQ
☎ *(01252) 326025* Errol George Faulkner

Ringwood Best usually available, often also with Marston's Pedigree and Charles Wells Bombardier and guest beers rotated frequently from a range of micro-breweries.

Rural village pub with football game, pool and darts. Food served 12–2pm and 7–9pm daily. Large car park and garden. Children and pets welcome.

OPEN *11.30am–2.30pm and 6–11pm (10.30pm Sun).*

BAGSHOT

The Foresters Arms

173 London Road, Bagshot GU19 5DH
☎ *(01276) 472038* Peter and Gill

Up to seven real ales changed frequently, but probably including Timothy Taylor Landlord and Mild, Hogs Back TEA, Shepherd Neame Spitfire, Fuller's London Pride plus guests.

Traditional pub on the A30 with a growing real ale reputation. Food served at lunchtime. Skittle alley available for private functions. Quiz nights. Outside seating and smoking area.

OPEN *12–2.30pm and 5–11pm Mon–Sat; 12–3pm and 7–11pm Sun.*

BLETCHINGLEY
William IV

Little Common Lane, Bletchingley, Redhill
RH1 4QF
☎ *(01883) 743278* Sue and Rob Saunders

 Fuller's London Pride, Adnams Best, Harveys Sussex and Greene King Ruddles Best usually available.

An unspoilt, cosy Victorian country pub on the edge of the village. Two small bars, dining room and large beer garden. Family-run by a mother and son. Food available at lunchtimes and evenings (not Sun evening in winter). Children allowed in dining room and garden only. Off the A25 between Godstone and Redhill.

OPEN *12–3pm and 6–11pm Mon–Sat; 12–10.30pm Sun in summer, 12–4pm and 7–10.30pm in winter.*

BOUNDSTONE
The Bat & Ball Freehouse

15 Bat and Ball Lane, Boundstone, Farnham
GU10 4SA
☎ *(01252) 792108* Kevin and Sally Macready
www.thebatandball.co.uk

 Young's Bitter, Hogs Back TEA Itchen Valley Brewery, Harveys Sussex plus three guests from local and national micro-breweries, including Triple FFF, Hidden Brewery, Downton, Ballard's, Arundel.

A relaxed, rural freehouse with restaurant-quality food. Over 150 years old and renovated in 2003 with a family area and garden with covered patio. Barbecues. Beer festival on the second weekend in June. Food available 12–2.15pm and 7–9.30pm Mon–Sat; 12–3pm and 6–8.30pm Sun. Children allowed. Good walking country. Bat & Ball Lane is off Upper Bourne Lane via Sandrock Hill Road.

OPEN *11am–11pm Mon–Sat; 12–10.30pm Sun.*

BRAMLEY
Jolly Farmer Inn

Bramley, Guildford GU5 0HB
☎ *(01483) 893355*
Chris and Steven Hardstone
www.jollyfarmer.co.uk

 Freehouse with Badger First Gold and Hogs Back HBB plus six weekly-changing guests from numerous micro-breweries around the country.

This 16th-century former coaching inn has been family-owned for many years. No machines or games, just good beer, food and ambience. Food served 12–2.30pm and 6–10pm Mon–Sat, 12–2.30pm and 7–9.30pm Sun. Accommodation available. Two attractive beer patios. Car park. Well-behaved children welcome. Located in the Surrey Hills area, close to Heathrow and Gatwick airports. Exit the M25 at junction 10, take the Guildford exit off the A3 and take the A281 to Horsham.

OPEN *11am–11pm Mon–Sat; 12–11pm Sun.*

CARSHALTON
The Racehorse

17 West Street, Carshalton SM5 2PT
☎ *(020) 8647 6818* Julian Norton
www.racehorseinns.co.uk

 Freehouse with four real ales with Greene King IPA and Courage Best the permanent fixtures, and beers from Broughton, 1648, Hampshire, Loddon, Moorhouse's White Star, Westerham, Grand Union, Tring, Daleside and Hepworth, to name but a few, rotated every couple of days.

Two-bar food-oriented pub/restaurant, with beer garden. Bar food and full à la carte menu served lunchtimes and evenings Mon–Sat and Sunday lunch. Live music, theme nights. Car park at rear. Two minutes from Carshalton railway station.

OPEN *11am–11pm Mon–Sat; 12–10.30pm Sun.*

CHERTSEY
The Royal Marine

Lyne Lane, Chertsey KT16 0AN
☎ *(01932) 873900* Patrick Davey

 Four hand pumps for real ale. Ales are constantly rotated and changing. Quite often (virtually every week) a reasonably priced 'Landlords Special' is featured. Recent ales include: Sharps Doom Bar, Waylands Addlestone Ale (local micro-brewery), Hogs Back TEA, Robinsons Unicorn, plus numerous others.

Small, traditional country pub dating from the mid-19th century. One bar, lots of character. Children welcome. Beer garden. Car park. Local events hosted throughout the year, including village fête, hog roasts, curry nights and St George's Day celebration. Food served 12–2pm Mon–Sat; 6.30–9pm Tues–Fri; 12–2.30pm Sun. Sat 'Eat in Pub, Takeaway Evening': pub kitchen is closed, and selections from take-away menus from variety of local outlets can be ordered and delivered to eat in pub.

OPEN *12–2.30pm Mon–Sat, 12–3pm Sun; 5.30–11pm Mon–Fri; 6.30–11pm Sat. Closed Sun evenings.*

CHURT
The Crossways Inn

Churt, Nr Farnham GU10 2JE
☎ *(01428) 714323* Paul and Teresa Ewens

 Freehouse with Hop Back Crop Circle, Ringwood Fortyniner and Courage Best plus four guests. At least ten different beers are served every week, with more from micro-breweries than not. Four real ciders also on offer.

Friendly local country pub with two bars. Food available 12–2pm Mon–Sat. Well-behaved children over 10 allowed. Beer garden, car park. Beer festival in July featuring more than 40 beers. Between Farnham and Hindhead on the A287.

OPEN *11am–3.30pm and 5–11pm Mon–Thurs; all day Fri–Sat; 12–4pm and 7–10.30pm Sun.*

The Griffin

58 Common Road, Claygate, Esher KT10 0HW
☎ *(01372) 463799*
Tom and Marian Harrington

 Freehouse with Fuller's London Pride plus two constantly changing guests. Micro-breweries and smaller independents favoured.

A traditional two-bar village pub with log fires, beer garden and disabled access. Saloon bar with open fire, no machines or music. Public bar with 60" plasma screen, darts and music. Food available 12–2.30pm Mon–Fri, 12–3pm Sat, 12–6pm Sun, plus 6.30–9.30pm Wed–Sat. Large car park, children allowed. Short walk from Claygate Station, on the K3 bus route.

OPEN *11am–midnight.*

The Swan

Hare Lane, Claygate KT10 9BS
☎ *(01372) 462582* Timothy Kitch

Freehouse with Fuller's London Pride a permanent feature, plus three guest beers, perhaps Greene King IPA or something from Brakspear or Adnams.

Country pub in a building dating from 1804, with beams, Victorian ceiling, 20-foot bar, large garden and a field for use during festivals. Food is available, and there is a Thai restaurant. Annual beer festival in August, usually at the bank holiday (80 beers over four days). Superior en-suite accommodation. Children allowed.

OPEN *11am–11pm Mon–Sat; 12–10.30pm Sun.*

The Plough Inn

Coldharbour Lane, Coldharbour, Nr Dorking RH5 6HD
☎ *(01306) 711793* Anna and Richard Abrehart
www.ploughinn.com

Six real ales and a real cider always available. Three beers are brewed on the premises under the name of The Leith Hill Brewery. Also Ringwood Old Thumper and Shepherd Neame Spitfire, plus one guest changed every two months. Seasonal, special and topical beers, plus farm cider on hand pump, are also on offer.

A traditional family-run 17th-century pub in a beautiful rural Area of Outstanding Natural Beauty. Allegedly the highest freehouse in south-east England. Bar and restaurant food served 12–2.30pm and 6.30–9.30pm (9pm Sun). Car parking, beer garden. Children allowed. High-quality en-suite accommodation. Just over three miles south-west of Dorking.

OPEN *11.30am–11pm Sun-Thurs; 11.30am–1am Fri-Sat.*

Claret Free House

5 Bingham Corner, Lower Addiscombe Road, Croydon CR0 7AA
☎ *(020) 8656 7452* Mike Callaghan

Palmers IPA and Shepherd Neame Spitfire plus four regularly changing guests (32 different brews each month).

Small, friendly and comfortable community pub. No food. No children. Adjacent to the Tramlink station.

OPEN *11.30am–11pm Mon–Sat; 12–10.30pm Sun.*

The George

17 George Street, Croydon CR0 1LA
☎ *(020) 8649 9077*
Caroline Williams and Simon Pitcher

Ridleys Old Bob, Fuller's London Pride, Timothy Taylor Landlord, Shepherd Neame Spitfire and Greene King Abbot are among the beers usually available, plus three or four regularly changing guests.

Wetherspoon's pub in the town centre, next to the George Street Tramlink stop, converted from a furniture store. Two bars. Food served until 10pm.

OPEN *10am–11pm.*

The Spread Eagle

39–41 Katherine Street, Croydon CR0 1NX
☎ *(020) 8781 1134* Robin and Janet Butler

Typically five Fuller's and Gale's brews plus one guest, changed monthly.

A town-centre Fuller's Ale & Pie pub in a converted NatWest bank, built in 1893 and boasting chandeliers and other impressive features. Two upstairs function rooms with private bar. Food served 12–3pm and 5–9pm Mon–Fri, 12–9pm Sat and 12–6pm Sun. Outside smoking area. Less than ten minutes' walk from Croydon East station: head towards the town hall, and the pub is just behind the Queen Victoria monument, on the corner of the High Street and Katharine Street.

OPEN *11am–11pm Mon–Thurs; 11am–midnight Fri–Sat; 12–10.30pm Sun.*

The King's Arms

45 West Street, Dorking RH4 1BU
☎ *(01306) 883361* Stuart Yeatman

Fuller's London Pride and Greene King IPA plus two guests changing every week from micro-breweries and independents – the smaller and more unusual, the better!

Country-style pub in a town location, this is the oldest building in Dorking. More than 500 years old with oak beams, inglenook fireplace, restaurant and courtyard garden. Food available lunchtimes and evenings. Children allowed.

OPEN *11am–11pm (10.30pm Sun).*

The King's Head
*Pitland Street, Holmbury St Mary, Dorking
RH5 6NP*
☎ *(01306) 730282*

Freehouse with Greene King IPA, Surrey Hills Shere Drop and King Horsham Best plus one guest.

Dating from 1835, this pub has a welcoming atmosphere, with log fire and oak beams. Locally sourced food served 12–2pm and 6–9pm Tues–Sat; 12–2.30pm Sun, with local seasonal game and fish specials. Beer festivals at spring and summer bank holiday weekends. Dogs, cyclists and walkers welcome. Beer garden.

OPEN *4–11pm Mon; 12–11pm Tues–Sat;
12–10.30pm Sun.*

The Crown
38 High Street, Egham TW20 9DP
☎ *(01784) 432608* Linda Bowman

Fuller's London Pride, Greene King Abbot, Adnams Bitter and Broadside plus a weekly guest ale.

Country-style pub, part of the Barracuda chain, with beer gardens front and back, car park and pool table. Beer festivals twice a year. Food available until 9pm Monday to Saturday and 5pm on Sundays.

OPEN *11.30am–11pm Mon–Sat;
12–10.30pm Sun.*

The Beehive
*34 Middle Hill, Englefield Green, Nr Egham
TW20 0JQ*
☎ *(01784) 431621* Ian and Ann MacDonald

Fuller's London Pride and Discovery and Gale's HSB, with one of the beers rotated monthly.

A small country pub, over 100 years old, with one bar, real log fire in winter and beer garden. Real homemade food available 12–2.30pm and 6–8.30pm, including roasts on Sundays. Wed night curry or steak with free pint of beer or small glass of wine. Quiz night Tues with cash prizes and booby prize. Children welcome. Handy for Thorpe Park, Legoland, Windsor and Virginia Water. Just off the A30 between Ferrari's and Royal Holloway College.

OPEN *12–3pm and 5.30–11pm Mon–Thurs;
12–11pm Fri–11pm Sun.*

Happy Man
12 Harvest Road, Englefield Green TW2 0QS
☎ *(01784) 433265* David Lacey

A Pubs 'n' Bars pub with Hop Back Summer Lightning plus three rotating guests changed as often as possible.

Built in the mid- to late-Victorian era, this traditional warm pub has both a public and lounge bar. Food served 12–8.30pm Mon–Sun. Beer garden. Children welcome until 8.30pm. Darts. Located off the A30 between Egham and Sunningdale, near Royal Holloway University.

OPEN *12–11.30pm Mon–Thurs; 12–12 Fri–Sat;
12–10.30pm Sun.*

The Famous Green Man
71 High Street, Ewell Village KT17 1RX
☎ *(020) 8393 9719* John Kerwood
www.famousgreenman.com

An Enterprise Inns pub. Charles Wells Bombardier, Shepherd Neame Spitfire, Adnams Best and Young's Bitter plus at least one guest, changed weekly. Guest ales have included Black Sheep Bitter, Adnams Broadside, Hogs Back TEA, Caledonian Deuchars IPA, Timothy Taylor Landlord and Harveys Sussex.

An 80-year-old pub with three bars and a separate restaurant. Lots of character and a friendly atmosphere. Food served 12–9pm. Beer garden. Function room. Car park. Close to Chessington World of Adventure.

OPEN *12–11pm.*

The Ball & Wicket
104 Upper Hale Road, Farnham GU9 0PB
☎ *(01252) 735278* Gary Wallace

There is a small micro-brewery, Farnham Brewery, at the back of the pub, so four of their own ales are always available, namely Bishop Sumner, William Cobbett, Mike Hawthorne and a seasonal ale.

Friendly, 200-year-old freehouse with a single bar, open fire and a warm atmosphere. Huge refurbishment planned for 2008, including new dining area. Food will be available 12–2pm and 6–9pm Mon–Sat and 12–2pm Sun. Occasional live music, quiz nights every other Sunday, darts. Children allowed until evening. Car park. Plans for luxury B&B by 2009. Opposite the cricket green, two miles out of Farnham on the Odiham Road.

OPEN *12–11pm Sun–Thurs; 12–12 Fri–Sat.*

The Mulberry
Station Hill, Farnham GU9 8AD
☎ *(01252) 726673* Steve Driver
www.mulberryfarnham.co.uk

Greene King pub with two of the brewery's beers always on offer, plus a guest changed every two months.

A 200-year-old pub with one bar and a large garden. Food served all day. Car park. Nine en-suite rooms. Private room for hire. Music festivals held. Handy for Bird World and Farnham Castle. Located next to Farnham Station.

OPEN *All day, every day.*

The Shepherd & Flock

Moor Park Lane, Farnham GU9 9JB
☎ *(01252) 716675* Stephen Hill

Freehouse with Hogs Back TEA and Ringwood Old Thumper plus five guests, such as Hop Back Summer Lightning, or Arundel, Triple FFF, Itchen Valley or Welton's brews.

Situated on the outskirts of town, on Europe's biggest inhabited roundabout! A well-known local meeting place, close to the North Downs. Old building with one bar and 50-seater dining room. Food available lunchtimes and evenings. Beer garden. Children allowed in the dining room only.

OPEN *All permitted hours.*

GODALMING

The Anchor Inn

110 Ockford Road, Godalming GU7 1RG
☎ *(01483) 417085* Rob and Caroline Kemp
www.anchorinngodalming.741.com

Shepherd Neame Spitfire always available, plus three rotating guest ales changed once a week.

Rebuilt in 1911 after a fire, this pub has one large bar and a new restaurant area that was added in December 2006. Food served 11am–3pm Mon–Sat and 12–4pm Sun. Large decked terrace garden seating 200 people, new children's play area, giant chess board. Darts and bar billiards. Function room for hire. Live music. From the A3 at Milford, head to Godalming on the Portsmouth road, the pub is on the left-hand side.

OPEN *11am–midnight Mon–Thurs; 11am–1am Fri–Sat; 12–11pm Sun.*

The Star

17 Church Street, Godalming GU7 1EL
☎ *(01483) 417717* Ian Thomson, Andrew Mounsey, Paulina Zuk
www.thestargodalming.co.uk

A Greene King tied house. Three or four permanents, plus two or three Greene King seasonals and specials. Five selected micro-brewery beers also offered, and about three brewery guests, often Hardy and Hanson Olde Trip and Best Bitter. At least 6 scrumpy/real ciders and/or perries at any time, ever-changing, and about 48 bottled ciders, and English Cider Brandy. Maybe home-brewed cider soon. Easter and Hallowe'en Beer Festivals, Special Christmas Selection in December. Summer Hog Roasts. Sunday quiz nights. Occasional live entertainment. Information on website.

Housed in a 400-year-old building, this has been a pub for about 175 years. Small, with one bar and a function room and beer garden. Food served 12–2.30pm. Covered and heated smoking area. Close to the station. No dogs and very few children!

OPEN *11am–midnight Sun–Thurs; 11am–1am Fri–Sat.*

GUILDFORD

The George Abbot

7–11 High Street, Guildford GU2 4AB
☎ *(01483) 456890* Shaun Harris

Owned by Greene King, with IPA, Abbot and Old Speckled Hen available plus guests such as Hogs Back TEA changing every two weeks.

Drinkers' town pub in a traditional building, with beams, fireplaces and a friendly atmosphere. Food available 12–9pm Mon–Thurs, 12–7pm Fri–Sun. Fruit and quiz machines, plus Sky and Setanta Sports and four plasma screens. Children allowed. Quiz night Thurs. At the bottom of the High Street, near the river.

OPEN *12–11pm Mon–Thurs; 12–12 Fri–Sat; 12–10.30pm Sun.*

KINGSTON-UPON-THAMES

The Canbury Arms,

49 Canbury Park Road, Kingston-upon-Thames KT2 6LQ
☎ *(020) 8255 9129* Michael Pearson
www.thecanburyarms.com

Five real ales, including Timothy Taylor Landlord, Gale's HSB and Harveys Sussex, plus two monthly guests such as Sharp's Doom Bar or Twickenham Naked Ladies.

The pub has contemporary decor, but maintains original features from the 1800s. Traditional menu served 12–3pm and 5–10pm. Children welcome 9am–7pm. Live music. Car parking. Area available for private hire. Behind Kingston bus station, five minutes from the train station.

OPEN *9am–11pm.*

The Fighting Cocks

56 London Road, Kingston-upon-Thames KT2 6QA
☎ *(020) 8546 5174* Natalie Salt

Wadworth 6X among the brews always available plus two guests, such as Marston's Pedigree.

A town pub with wooden floors and panelled walls. Two bars and courtyard. No food. Children allowed.

OPEN *11am–11pm.*

The Kelly Arms

2 Glenthorne Road, Kingston-upon-Thames KT1 2UB
☎ *(020) 8541 4340* Kevin Mayhew

Young's PA and Sharp's Doom Bar, with plans to increase the number of real ales to four.

Backstreet community pub with a friendly atmosphere. One big bar. Darts, board games, daily quiz, plus quiz and bingo nights. Kitchen undergoing refurbishment – plans to serve food in future. Children welcome. Off Villers Road, less than a mile from Surbiton and Kingston stations.

OPEN *10am–11pm Mon–Thurs; 10am–midnight Fri–Sat; 12–11pm Sun.*

The Willoughby Arms

Willoughby Road, Kingston-upon-Thames KT2 6LN
☎ *(020) 8546 4236* Rick Robinson
www.thewilloughbyarms.com

 Timothy Taylor Landlord, Fuller's London Pride, Charles Wells Bombardier and something from Twickenham plus ever-changing guest beers. HQ of the Kingston branch of the Society of Preservation of Beers from the Wood (meet on first Wed of the month, when all cask ales are £2 per pint for full and temporary members alike). Beer festivals held on St George's Day and Hallowe'en (check website for details).

Refurbished Victorian corner local. No food except barbecues on summer Sundays (weather permitting). Children welcome in the large garden. Emphasis on sports viewing, with Sky TV, 80-seater sports viewing lounge, three large screens, four TVs and a sheltered outside plasma screen for smokers. Huge display of genuine signed sporting memorabilia. Website features further sports-related details. There is no juke box, but there is live music every Friday night with resident guitarist, plus different live music acts every Saturday night. Open mic night upstairs on second and last Friday of the month, and free quiz on Sunday evenings.

[OPEN] *10.30am–midnight Mon–Sat; 12–12 Sun.*

KNAPHILL
The Garibaldi

134 High Street, Knaphill GU21 2QH
☎ *(01483) 473374*
Darryn Crout and Debbie Harlow

 Three real ales usually on offer, with Greene King IPA and Wadworth 6X the regular beers, plus one guest, such as Greene King Old Speckled Hen, changed every two weeks.

One-bar 'pub for the village' with rustic character. Homemade traditional English food served 12–9.30pm Mon–Sat and 12–9pm Sun. Beer garden and BBQ. Children welcome until 8pm. Quiz night Sunday. Car park. New outside smoking area for al fresco dining. On the crossroads of Knaphill High Street and Chobham Road.

[OPEN] *12–11pm Mon–Thurs; 12–12 Fri–Sat; 12–10.30pm Sun.*

MICKLEHAM
King William IV

4 Byttom Hill, Mickleham, Nr Dorking RH5 6EL
☎ *(01372) 372590* Ian Duke
www.king-williamiv.com

 Four real ales including Adnams Bitter, Badger Best and Hogs Back TEA plus a guest such as Sharp's Doom Bar rotated every few months.

Family-run freehouse dating from 1790 perched on a hillside on the edge of the North Downs, in the same hands since 1991. Hillside alehouse originally for workers on Lord Beaverbrook's estate. Named Best Dining Pub in Surrey for 2006 – good food is served at lunchtimes and evenings. Two bars and attractive beer garden with views over the Mole Valley. Car park at the bottom of the hill. Can get crowded. Just off the A24 north of Dorking. Good walking country.

[OPEN] *11.30am–3pm Mon; 11.30am–3pm and 6.30–11pm Tues–Sat; 12–5pm Sun.*

NEWCHAPEL
The Blacksmith's Head

Newchapel Road, Newchapel, Lingfield RH7 6LE
☎ *(01342) 833697* Alex Duarte and Salie Deies
www.theblacksmithshead.co.uk

A freehouse. Fuller's London Pride and Harveys Sussex Best. Two guests, changed twice weekly, such as Fuller's Red Fox or Black Sheep Bitter.

Purpose-built in 1924 and offering an extensive à la carte menu as well as Spanish tapas and bar meals 12–2.30pm and 6–10pm. Children welcome. Large beer garden. AA 4-star rated B&B. Located off the A22 Eastbourne Road, towards Lingfield.

[OPEN] *12–3pm and 6–11pm Mon–Fri; 12–11pm Sat; 12–4pm Sun.*

NEWDIGATE
The Surrey Oaks

Parkgate Road, Newdigate, Dorking RH5 5DZ
☎ *(01306) 631200* Ken Proctor
www.surreyoaks.co.uk

Harveys Sussex and Surrey Hills Ranmore Ale plus three constantly changing guests from micro-breweries. Check the website for details.

Timber-beamed country pub, original parts of which date back to 1570. Two small bars, one with a magnificent inglenook fireplace and stone-flagged floors. Games room and restaurant. Surrey and Sussex CAMRA Pub of the Year 2006. Food served every lunchtimes and Tues–Sat evenings. Large car park. Children's play area and boules pitch in garden. Two beer festivals every year, at late May and August bank holidays. Situated one mile from Newdigate village on the Charlwood road.

[OPEN] *11.30am–2.30pm and 5.30–11pm Mon–Fri; 11.30am–3pm and 6–11pm Sat; 12–10.30pm Sun.*

NORTH CHEAM
The Nonsuch Inn

552–6 London Road, North Cheam SM3 9AA
☎ *(020) 8644 1808* Craig Pretorius

Five real ales, including Ringwood Fortyniner, Greene King Abbot and Marston's Pedigree, plus four or five guests changed every few days, from breweries such as Hogs Back, King, Twickenham and various micro-breweries.

One large bar and a dining area. Food available all day until 11pm. Disabled facilities. Well-behaved children allowed until 9pm (subject to certain rules – call for details).

[OPEN] *All day, every day (until 12 Sun–Thurs and until 1am Fri–Sat).*

OXTED

Royal Oak Inn

Caterfield Lane, Staffhurst Wood, Oxted RH8 0RR
☎ *(01883) 722207* Julian Mitchell

Genuine freehouse with five ales, which could be from Adnams, Harveys, Larkins or Horsham, including three guests rotated every six weeks.

Originally three cottages, this pub is composed of different sized rooms on different levels. Homemade pies and desserts prepared using locally farmed produce and fresh fish dishes served Mon–Sat and Sun lunchtimes (full range of food available from lobsters and steaks to cheese sandwiches). Large garden with splendid views of three counties. Large car park. Children and dogs welcome. Darts, crib and cricket teams. À la carte restaurant. Vintage port and stilton club. Located four miles from Lingfield racecourse and close to Chartwell, home of Winston Churchill.

OPEN *11am–11pm Mon–Sat; 12–10.30pm Sun.*

PURLEY

Foxley Hatch

8–9 Russell Hill Road, Purley CR8 2LE
☎ *(020) 8763 9307* Andy Rimmer

Wetherspoon's pub serving Shepherd Neame Spitfire and Greene King Abbot plus two guest beers from around the country. Three or four festivals are also held each year offering up to 20 beers at a time.

Friendly locals' pub free of music and television. Easy access for the disabled. Food served all day, every day. No children.

OPEN *11am–11pm Mon–Sat; 12–10.30pm Sun.*

PUTTENHAM

The Good Intent

62 The Street, Puttenham, Guildford GU3 1AR
☎ *(01483) 810387* Julain and Rachel Dance
www.thegoodintent-puttenham.co.uk

Enterprise Inns pub with six real ales. Timothy Taylor Landlord, Ringwood Best and Courage Best are the regular beers, and three guests are changed every week or two.

A typical village pub with low beams dating from around 1850, in an Area of Outstanding Natural Beauty on the North Downs Way. Two bars and dining room. No music. Food available 12–2pm every day plus evenings Tues–Sat, including fish and chips to eat in or take away every Wednesday night. Large garden, car park. Dogs and children welcome. Bi-annual beer festival. Excellent location for walkers and cyclists. Between Farnham and Guildford off the A31.

OPEN *11am–2.30pm and 6–11pm Mon–Fri; all day Sat–Sun.*

REDHILL

Garland

5 Brighton Road, Redhill RH1 6PP
☎ *(01737) 760377* Bill Thomson-Elliott

Harveys tied pub serving four regular fixtures plus between two and six seasonal guests.

This locals' real-ale-focused pub dates back to 1865. One bar. Food served lunchtimes Mon–Fri. Beer garden, car park. Private room available. Children welcome in certain areas. CAMRA Surrey Pub of the Year 2002. Located off the A23, just south of the town centre.

OPEN *11am–close Mon–Sat; 12–3pm and 7–10.30pm Sun.*

The Hatch

44 Hatchlands Road, Redhill RH1 6AT
☎ *(01737) 773387*
Shelley Bulled and Jeff Sykes

Shepherd Neame house with Spitfire and Kent's Best plus guests such as Bishop's Finger and seasonal beers Original Porter, Late Red, Early Bird and Whitstable Bay. Special ales from micro-breweries also served.

A newly decorated town pub with horseshoe-shaped bar and pool and darts room. Safe smoking area at rear, patio at front. New food menu served 12–3pm Sun–Fri. Families welcome. Near the A25 between Redhill and Reigate.

OPEN *12–12.*

RICHMOND

The Triple Crown

15 Kew Foot Road, Richmond TW9 2SS
☎ *(020) 8940 3805*

Fuller's London Pride and Timothy Taylor Landlord. Four guest beers are also served, from a list running into several hundreds.

Traditional, one-bar house. Food served 12–2.30pm. Children welcome.

OPEN *11am–11pm Mon–Sat; 12–10.30pm Sun.*

SEND

The New Inn

Send Road, Nr Guildford GU23 7EN
☎ *(01483) 762736* Tony Lilley

A Punch Taverns pub. Adnams Bitter, Fuller's London Pride, Greene King Abbot and Ringwood Best. Plus one guest ale, changed at least weekly. Guests include Hidden Brewery Hidden Potential, WJ King's Mother In Law and Cottage Vulcan.

Olde-worlde character pub, documented as being the source of the saying 'have a stiff drink' on account of its origins as an 18th century hospital and morgue! Food served 12–2pm 6.30–9pm Mon–Fri; 12–2.30pm and 6.30–9.30pm Sat–Sun. Child and dog friendly. Beer garden overlooking the river. Car park. Located just off the A3.

OPEN *11am–11pm Mon–Fri; 12–10.30pm Sun.*

SHAMLEY GREEN
The Bricklayer's Arms
The Green, Shamley Green, Guildford GU5 0UA
☎ *(01483) 898377* Carl and Paula

Shepherd Neame Spitfire, Young's Bitter and Fuller's London Pride plus a couple of guests such as Hogs Back TEA, Sharp's Doom Bar or Eden. There is also a comprehensive wine list.

Situated on the green, 150 years old, this pub has been sympathetically refurbished. One bar, eating area, real fires. Wide and varied menu. Large patio areas and beer garden surrounding an ornamental Koi carp pond. Regular barbecues, weather permitting. Families welcome.

OPEN *11.30am–11pm Mon–Sat;*
12–10.30pm Sun.

Red Lion Inn
The Green, Shamley Green GU5 0UB
☎ *(01485) 892202* Debbie Ersser
www.theredlion.uk.com

Three real ales, perhaps including Shepheard Neame Spitfire, Wadworth 6X, Young's Bitter, Greene King IPA or Abbot and Black Sheep Bitter.

Leased from Punch Taverns, a friendly village alehouse and restaurant. Outside seating to the front and rear, with views over the cricket ground. Parking. Food available 12–2.30pm and 6.30–9.30pm on weekdays, 12–3pm and 6.30–9.30pm Sat–Sun. On the B2128, Guildford to Cranleigh road.

OPEN *11.30am–11pm Mon–Sat;*
12–10.30pm Sun.

SHEPPERTON
The Barley Mow
67 Watersplash Road, Shepperton TW17 0EE
☎ *(01932) 225326* John Keary

A freehouse with up to five real ales available. Hogs Back TEA and Hop Back Summer Lightning, plus a different guest each day. Guests could include WJ King's Mother In Law, Twickenham Naked Lady or Stonehenge Surprise.

Built in 1853 as an ale-led backstreet pub with character. Mixed clientele of locals, regulars and students. Food served 12–3pm Mon–Sat. Darts and bar billiards. Live music nights: Wed: jazz; Fri: R&B; Sat: rock 'n' roll. Car park. Smoking area.

OPEN *12–11pm (10.30pm Sun).*

SHOTTERMILL
The Mill Tavern
Liphook Road, Shottermill, Haslemere GU27 3QE
☎ *(01428) 643183* Lee Forbes
www.themilltavern.net

Punch Taverns tied pub with five ales, which could include Fuller's London Pride, Greene King IPA, Charles Wells Bombadier and Sharp's Doom Bar plus three weekly-changing guests.

A 500-year-old country pub with family room and restaurant. Food served 12–2.30pm and 7–9.30pm Mon–Sun. Large beer garden with children's play area. Function room available. Children welcome. Large car park. Located near Shottermill Ponds.

OPEN *12–close.*

SURBITON
Coronation Hall
St Mark's Hill, Surbiton, Kingston KT6 4TB
☎ *(020) 8390 6164* Michael Wilkinson

Wetherspoon's pub with 12 real ales. Shepherd Neame Spitfire, Courage Best, Marston's Pedigree and Greene King Abbot, plus eight guests, changing constantly, from a range of around 100 ales. Three draught ciders also served.

Opened in 1911 as a cinema, reopened as a pub in 1997. Large bar area, family facilities. Food available 9am–11pm. Beer festivals twice a year. Opposite Surbiton train station.

OPEN *9am–midnight.*

The Lamb Inn
73 Brighton Road, Surbiton KT6 5NF
☎ *(020) 8390 9229* Ian Stewart

Greene King IPA and Young's Special plus one guest, changed every two or three days. A good choice of regional ales is offered, from the Isle of Wight to the Isle of Man.

A true old-fashioned community locals' pub. Darts, bar games and a friendly welcoming atmosphere. Large beer garden with grassed area for children. Bar food available every lunchtime. Children allowed in the garden only. From J10 of M25, take left turn towards Kingston; eventually you come to Brighton Road.

OPEN *11am–11pm Mon–Sat; 12–10.30pm Sun.*

WARLINGHAM
The Good Companions
Limpsfield Road, Warlingham, Croydon CR6 9RH
☎ *(020) 8657 6655*
Mark and Debbie Henderson
www.thegoodcompanionspub.co.uk

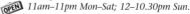Enterprise Inns tied pub with three ales usually available, including two monthly-changing guests.

Community pub with beer garden, car park and private room. Children welcome. Located three miles inside the M25, just south of Croydon.

OPEN *All day, every day.*

WEST BYFLEET
The Plough Inn
104 High Road, West Byfleet KT14 7QT
☎ *(01932) 353257* Carol Wells

Freehouse with nine pumps serving ever-changing brews, all from independents.

A traditional two-bar village pub with beams and two log fires. Cask Marque accredited. Beer garden, conservatory, car park. Food available 12–2pm Mon–Fri, plus roasts on Sunday 12–4pm. Monthly trivia quiz in winter. Children allowed in conservatory until 7pm.

OPEN *11am–3pm and 5–11pm (10.30pm Sun).*

WEST CLANDON
The Onslow Arms
The Street, West Clandon, Guildford GU4 7TE
☎ *(01483) 222447* Jill Morgan

 Hogs Back TEA, Courage Best and Directors plus two regularly changing guests such as Greene King Old Speckled Hen, Fuller's London Pride, St Austell Tribute, Ringwood Fortyniner, Adnams Explorer and Weltons St Georges.

Well-known 16th-century coaching inn with excellent French and English food available at lunchtimes and evenings (all day Sun) in a restaurant and a rotisserie. Large car park, disabled access. Garden and patio with arbours. Function rooms. Helipad. Children allowed. Just off the A3.
OPEN *All day, every day.*

WEYBRIDGE
The Prince of Wales
11 Cross Road, Oatlands, Weybridge KT13 9NX
☎ *(01932) 852082* Brian Ford
www.princeofwalesweybridge.co.uk

 Five real ales, usually Fuller's Chiswick, London Pride and ESB, Adnams Bitter and Young's Bitter.

A family-owned and -run local dating from 1854, with log fire in winter and a warm, friendly atmosphere. Cask Marque accredited. Big screen for sports, quiz nights once a fortnight. Fresh food cooked to order served 12–2.30pm every day and 7–9pm Mon–Sat. Live music every Thursday and Sunday evening. Restaurant available for private hire. On Anderson Road, off Oatlands Drive.
OPEN *All day, every day.*

WINDLESHAM
The Half Moon
Church Road, Windlesham GU20 6BN
☎ *(01276) 473329* CR Sturt

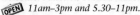 Freehouse with eight or nine ales from breweries such as Fuller's, Sharp's, Hop Back, Hogs Back, Theakston, Ringwood and Timothy Taylor.

True family-owned freehouse with two main bars and a 70-seat restaurant. Large family beer garden. Food served 12–3pm and 6–9pm Mon–Sat, 12–3pm Sun. Children's play area. Large car park. Dogs and children welcome. Function room available.
OPEN *11am–3pm and 5.30–11pm.*

WOKING
The Sovereigns
Guildford Road, Woking GU22 7QQ
☎ *(01483) 751426* Iain Bowman

 An Ember Inns pub. Caledonian Deuchars IPA and Adnams Broadside. Four guests, from any UK brewery, but Scottish ales especially favoured by the Scottish landlord. Examples have included Bath Ales Gem, Cairngorm Wildcat, Orkney Red MacGregor and Wickwar Long John Silver.

One bar, with food served 12–9pm. Two beer festivals each year in spring and autumn. Outdoor heated patios. CAMRA Surrey and Hampshire Pub of the Year 2007.
OPEN *12–11pm Sun–Thurs; 12–12 Fri–Sat.*

Wetherspoon's
51 Chertsey Road, Woking GU21 5AJ
☎ *(01483) 722818* Gary Hollis

Hogs Back TEA, Greene King Abbot and IPA and Courage Directors plus four guest ales rotated every few days.

A one-bar traditional town pub with no music or TV. Front drinking terrace, disabled access and toilets. Food available all day (9am–11pm). Children welcome for Sunday lunch. In the town centre, five minutes' walk from the station.
OPEN *All day, every day.*

WOODSTREET VILLAGE
The Royal Oak
89 Oak Hill, Woodstreet Village, Guildford GU3 3DA
☎ *(01483) 235137* Tony Oliver

Award-winning freehouse with Surrey Hills Sheer Drop plus five constantly changing guests, always including a mild. Hop Back Summer Lightning and Ringwood Best Bitter are just two examples from a huge range. Real cider always available.

Good old-fashioned village pub dating from the 1930s. One bar, beer garden. Food available Mon–Sat lunchtimes (12–2.15pm). Over-14s only allowed. Off the A323.
OPEN *11am–3pm and 5–11pm Mon–Fri; 11am–3.30pm and 5–11pm Sat; 12–3.30pm and 7–10.30pm Sun.*

WRECCLESHAM
The Sandrock
Sandrock Hill Road, Wrecclesham, Farnham GU10 4NS
☎ *(01252) 715865*
R Mifsud and C Haime

Eight real ale hand pumps to choose from, including beers from Black Country regulars such as Batham, Enville, Holden's and Sarah Hughes, plus a constantly changing selection of guest beers from an ever-increasing range of independent breweries.

Friendly, welcoming freehouse in a pleasant rural setting, though in easy reach of Farnham town centre and road and rail links. Extensive lunch and evening menus offer dishes from around the world, with something to suit all tastes. Food served 12–2.30pm and 6.30–9.30pm Mon–Sat, with traditional Sunday lunch available 12–4pm. Real log fire in the colder months, enclosed patio garden, annual beer festival. Dogs on a lead welcome. Along Farnham bypass towards Alton, left at roundabout onto the A325, left into School Hill, straight across at staggered crossroads into Sandrock Hill Road.
OPEN *12–11pm (10.30pm Sun).*

THE BREWERIES

1648 BREWING CO. LTD

Mill Lane, East Hoathly, Lewes, East Sussex BN8 6QB
☎ *(01825) 840830*
www.1648brewing.co.uk

1648 ORIGINAL 3.9% ABV
SIGNATURE 4.4% ABV
SAINT GEORGE 4.5% ABV
Seasonals:
ARMISTICE ALE 4.2% ABV
Available October–November.
LAMMAS ALE 4.2% ABV
August.
THREE THREADS 4.3% ABV
Available March–May.
BEE HEAD 4.6% ABV
Available May–September.
GINGER 4.7% ABV
November–March.
WINTER WARRANT 4.8% ABV
Available October–March.

ARUNDEL BREWERY

Unit C7 Ford Airfield Industrial Estate, Arundel, West Sussex BN18 0HY
☎ *(01903) 733111*

SUSSEX MILD 3.7% ABV
Slightly sweet, dark and hoppy.
CASTLE 3.8% ABV
Well-balanced and malty with some fruitiness.
SUSSEX GOLD 4.2% ABV
Hoppy with citrus finish.
ARUNDEL SPECIAL BITTER 4.5% ABV
Hoppy, bittersweet finish.
STRONGHOLD 4.7% ABV
Rounded and full flavoured.
OLD KNUCKER 5.5% ABV
Malty with coffee finish.
Plus a wide range of seasonals including:
HAIRY MARY 3.7% ABV
WELLY WEATHER 4.1% ABV
LAZY WILLIE 4.5% ABV
BLACK BEASTIE 4.9% ABV

CUSTOM BEERS LTD

Little Burchetts Farm, Isaac's Lane, Haywards Heath RH16 4RZ
☎ *(01273) 504988*

GOLDINGS PALE ALE 3.7% ABV
SMOOTH MILD 3.9% ABV
CASCADE SPECIAL 4.5% ABV
CHINOOK 4.7% ABV
DARK ROAST PORTER 5.5% ABV
Plus seasonals and specials.

DARK STAR BREWING CO. LTD

Moonhill Farm, Burgess Hill Road, Ansty, Haywards Heath RH17 5AH
☎ *(01444) 412311*
www.darkstarbrewing.co.uk

HOPHEAD 3.8% ABV
BEST BITTER 4.0% ABV
OLD ALE 4.0% ABV
ESPRESSO 4.2% ABV
DARK STAR 5.0% ABV
FESTIVAL 5.0% ABV
Plus seasonals and specials including:
MELTDOWN 4.8% ABV
Available spring–summer only.
SUNBURST 4.8% ABV
Available spring–summer only.
CRITICAL MASS 7.8% ABV
Winter only.

FILO BREWERY

14–15 High Street, Hastings TN34 3EY
☎ *(01424) 425079*
www.thefilo.co.uk

CROFTER'S BEST BITTER 4.0% ABV
FILO GOLD 4.3% ABV
GINGER TOM 4.4% ABV
CARDINAL SUSSEX PORTER 4.6% ABV

GRIBBLE BREWERY

The Gribble Inn, Gribble Lane, Oving, Nr Chichester PO20 6BP
☎ *(01243) 786893*
www.gribblebrewery.co.uk

GRIBBLE ALE 4.1% ABV
Hoppy bitter.
REG'S TIPPLE 5.0% ABV
Nutty flavour.
PORTERHOUSE 5.1% ABV
Malt flavour with a hint of liquorice.
PLUCKING PHEASANT 5.2% ABV
Light, dry-hopped beer.
PIGS EAR 5.8% ABV
Ruby coloured and robust.
WINTER WOBBLER 7.2% ABV
November–February.

HAMMERPOT BREWERY LTD

Unit 30, The Vinery, Poling BN18 9PY
☎ *(01903) 883338*
www.hammerpot-brewery.co.uk

VINERY MILD 3.2% ABV
METEOR 3.8 % ABV
RED HUNTER 4.2% ABV
WOODCOTE BITTER 4.5% ABV
MADGWICK GOLD 5.0% ABV
Plus seasonals and specials.

HARVEY & SONS (LEWES) LTD

The Bridge Wharf Brewery, 6 Cliffe High Street, Lewes, East Sussex BN7 2AH
☎ *(01273) 480209*
www.harveys.org.uk

SUSSEX XX MILD 3.0% ABV
Dark in colour, soft and sweet.
SUSSEX PALE ALE 3.5% ABV
SUSSEX BEST BITTER 4.0% ABV
ARMADA ALE 4.5% ABV
Golden and hoppy, with dryness in the aftertaste.
Plus seasonal brews.

HEPWORTH AND CO. BREWERS LTD

*Chipman House, Nightingale Road, Horsham
RH12 2NW*
☎ *(01403) 269696*
www.thebeerstation.co.uk

SUSSEX 3.6% ABV
PULLMAN 4.2% ABV
IRONHORSE 4.8% ABV
BLONDE 5.0% ABV

KEMPTOWN BREWERY CO. LTD

*Hand in Hand, 33 Upper St James's Street,
Brighton BN2 1JN*
☎ *(01273) 693070*

BLACK MOGGY 3.6% ABV
BEST BITTER 4.0% ABV
YE OLDE TROUT 4.5% ABV
STAGGERING IN THE DARK 5.0% ABV
Plus seasonals and specials.

RECTORY ALES

*Streat Hill Farm Outbuilding, Streat Hill, Streat,
Hassocks BN6 8RP*
☎ *(01273) 890570*

RECTOR'S BITTER 4.0% ABV
RECTOR'S BEST BITTER 4.3% ABV
RECTOR'S STRONG ALE 5.0% ABV
Plus seasonals and specials.

ROTHER VALLEY BREWING CO.

*Gate Court Farm, Station Road, Northiam, Rye
TN31 6QT*
☎ *(01797) 252922*

SPILED MILD 3.8% ABV
LEVEL BEST 4.0% ABV
HOPPER'S ALE 4.2% ABV
BOADICEA 4.6% ABV
Plus seasonal and occasional brews.

WJ KING & CO.

*3–5 Jubilee Estate, Foundry Lane, Horsham
RH13 5UE*
☎ *(01403) 272102*
www.kingfamilybrewers.co.uk

HORSHAM BEST BITTER 3.8% ABV
SPRING ALE 4.1% ABV
FOOL'S GOLD 4.5% ABV
RED RIVER ALE 4.8% ABV
DRAGON'S TALE 5.1% ABV
KINGS IPA 5.5% ABV
Plus three specials each month.

WELTONS BREWERY

*Unit 24 Vincent Works, Vincent Lane, Dorking
RH14 3HQ*
☎ *(01306) 888655*
www.weltons.co.uk

DORKING'S PRIDE 2.8% ABV
NORTH DOWNS BITTER 3.8% ABV
OLD COCKY 4.3% ABV
TOWER POWER 5.0% ABV
Plus special brews.

WHITE BREWING CO.

*The 1066 Country Brewery, Pebsham Farm Ind.
Est., Pebsham Lane, Bexhill-on-Sea TN40 2RZ*
☎ *(01424) 731066*

1066 COUNTRY ALE 4.0% ABV
DARK MILD 4.0% ABV
Plus seasonals.

THE PUBS

ALFRISTON

The Sussex Ox

Milton Street, Alfriston, East Sussex BN26 5RL
☎ *(01323) 870840* David Pritchard
www.thesussexox.co.uk

 Freehouse with Harveys Best usually
available, and an organic perry, plus two
other ales from Dark Star Brewery, and other
Sussex breweries.

Built in the late 1800s as a butchers and
slaughterhouse, this traditional pub
features scrubbed pine tables, log-burner and
cosy bar. Food served 12–2pm and 6–9pm.
Large landscaped beer garden with decked
eating area. Large car park. Panoramic views
of the South Downs. Separate dining room
seats up to 40. Located just off the A27
between Polegate and Alfriston.

OPEN *11.30am–3pm and 6–11pm Mon–Sat;
12–3pm and 6–10.30pm Sun.*

AMBERLEY

The Sportsman's Inn

*Crossgates, Amberley, Arundel, West Sussex
BN18 9NR*
☎ *(01798) 831787* Paul and Amanda Mahon
www.amberleysportsman.co.uk

Freehouse with four real ales. Young's
Bitter, Fuller's London Pride, Harveys
Best, Shepherd Neame Spitfire and Greene
King IPA are likely candidates, although the
selection changes every two weeks.

An edge-of-village pub with panoramic
views over Pulborough Wildbrooks
Reserve. Three bars, patio area, dining area in
conservatory. Good food served 12–2pm and
6.30–9pm. En-suite bed and breakfast
available. Well-behaved children and dogs
welcome. Car park. Good walking country.

OPEN *11am–3pm and 6–11pm Mon–Sat;
12–3pm and 7–10.30pm Sun.*

ARLINGTON

The Old Oak Inn

*Cane Heath, Arlington, Nr Hailsham, East
Sussex BN26 6SJ*
☎ *(01323) 482072* Brendan Slattery

Freehouse with up to four real ales from
breweries such as Harveys, Badger, King,
Wells and Young's and Adnams. One or two
guests are also served, changed weekly.

Situated between the South Downs and
Michelham Priory, an 18th-century
country freehouse that has been extensively
refurbished, with log fires, oak-beamed bar
and restaurant, beer garden and barbecue.
Food served 12–2.30pm and 6.30–9.30pm
Mon–Fri and all day Sat–Sun. Large car park,
beer garden, small play area. Children
welcome. Off the A22.

OPEN *11am–11pm.*

ARUNDEL
The King's Arms
*36 Tarrant Street, Arundel, West Sussex
BN18 9DN*
☎ *(01903) 882312* Charlie Malcomson

Freehouse always serving Fuller's London Pride and Young's Special plus two guests (one changed every fortnight) such as Hop Back Summer Lightning, Hogs Back TEA, Sharp's Doom Bar and Grand Union Gold, to name but a few.

A proper traditional pub dating from 1625 with two bars, one of which has a juke box, fruit machines and darts. No food. Patio and tables at the front. Covered smokers' area on patio. Children must be accompanied at all times. Dogs welcome. From the town square follow Tarrant Street, and the pub is 300 yards along.

OPEN *11am–11pm Mon–Sat; 12–10.30pm Sun.*

Ship & Anchor
*Station Road, Ford, Arundel, West Sussex
BN18 0BJ*
☎ *(01243) 551747* Arthur Cole

Up to eight real ales, generally including Ringwood Fortyniner and something from Goddards. Guests might include Greene King Abbot, IPA, Morlands Original, Ringwood Old Thumper and Goddards brews.

Family-run country freehouse built in the 1640s next to the River Arun. Traditional feel, with wooden beams and a wood-burning stove with sofas either side. Large forecourt with tables outside. Darts and cribbage. Walkers, cyclists and bikers welcome. Occasional live music on a Saturday. Annual beer festival in September. Food served 12–9pm March to October; 12–3pm and 6–9pm November to February. Campsite and marina part of the same family business. At Arundel, take unclassified road south for two miles, signposted to Ford. The pub is set back from the road, on the left after the level crossing.

OPEN *11am–11pm Mon–Sat; 12–10.30pm Sun.*

Swan Hotel
27–9 High Street, Arundel, West Sussex BN18 9AG
☎ *(01903) 882314*
Jim Dobbin and Stacey Reynolds
www.fullersinn.co.uk

Fuller's pub featuring Gale's HSB, plus Fuller's London Pride and a guest, changed every few weeks. Examples of guests include Wychwood Hobgoblin, St Austell Tribute and Tinners, Brains Reverend James, Castle Rock Nottingham Gold and beers from Adnams, Brakspear, Hook Norton, Butcombe and Oakham.

Dating from 1759, this one-bar hotel with restaurant area is a very popular meeting place for non-residents, locals and tourists. Situated in the heart of Arundel, close to the castle and river. Freshly prepared food served 12–9pm every day in summer, 12–3pm and 6–9pm in winter. Pay and display car park

behind the hotel. Fifteen en-suite rooms. Children allowed.

OPEN *11am–11pm Mon–Sat; 12–10.30pm Sun.*

ASHURST
The Fountain Inn
Ashurst, Nr Steyning, West Sussex BN44 3AP
☎ *(01403) 710219* Craig Gillet

Harveys Sussex Best, Gale's HSB and Fuller's London Pride plus guests from local breweries.

Unspoilt 16th-century inn with low beams, a flagstone floor and large inglenook fireplace. Picturesque cottage garden and large duck pond. No machines or music. Skittle alley and function room. Bar and restaurant food served every lunchtime and Mon–Sat evenings. Large car park. Children under 10 not allowed inside the pub. Located on the B2135 north of Steyning.

OPEN *11.30am–11pm Mon–Sat; 12–10.30pm Sun.*

BALCOMBE
The Cowdray
London Road, Balcombe, Haywards Heath, West Sussex RH17 6QD
☎ *(01444) 811280* Andy and Alex Owen
www.thecowdray.co.uk

Greene King tenancy serving Morland Original, IPA and a seasonal guest ales, which might be Abbot Ale, Hook Norton Old Hooky or a Greene King seasonal beer such as Hare Raiser or Bonkers Conkers.

One-bar Victorian pub with a bar and dining room. Large fenced garden refurbished in 2008. Large car park for 60 cars. Fresh, locally sourced food served 12–2.30pm and 6–9.30pm (extended times at weekends), with children's portions available. From Crawley/M23 follow signs to Balcombe.

OPEN *11.30am–3pm and 5.30–11pm Mon–Fri; 11.30am–11pm Sat and Sun (open Sunday evenings from April–October).*

BATTLE
The Squirrel Inn
North Trade Road, Battle, East Sussex TN33 9LJ
☎ *(01424) 772717* RG and C Coundley

Harveys ales plus several guests (200 per year) including Rother Valley Level Best and brews from Fuller's and Mansfield. New and seasonal beers ordered as and when available.

An 18th-century old drover's pub in beautiful countryside surrounded by fields. Family-run freehouse. Unspoilt public bar with log fires. Restaurant (suitable for functions and weddings). Two large beer gardens, ample parking, purpose-built children's room. Families welcome. Located just outside Battle on the A271.

OPEN *11.30am–3pm and 6–11pm Mon–Thurs; 11.30am–11pm Fri–Sat; 12–10.30pm Sun.*

BECKLEY

The Rose & Crown

Northiam Road, Beckley, Nr Rye, East Sussex
TN31 6SE
☎ *(01797) 252161* Alice Holland

 Harveys Best, Fuller's ESB and Timothy
Taylor Landlord plus two constantly
changing guests from independent breweries
such as Archers, Cottage and Rother Valley.

A 16th-century coaching inn on a site
which has been occupied by a pub since
the 12th century. Dining area, large garden,
petanque. Food available 12–2.30pm and
7–9.30pm Mon–Sat, and 12–3pm Sun. Well-
behaved children welcome. Just outside Rye.

OPEN *11.30am–12.30am Mon–Sat;*
12–11.30pm Sun.

BERWICK VILLAGE

The Cricketers Arms

Berwick Village, Nr Polegate, East Sussex
BN26 6SP
☎ *(01323) 870469* Peter Brown
www.cricketersberwick.co.uk

Harveys tied house with Best Bitter and
two seasonal brews, served straight from
the cask.

Three-roomed, cottage-style country pub
with stone floors, two open fires and
picturesque gardens. Situated near the South
Downs Way and very popular with walkers
and cyclists. Food served 12–2.15pm and
6.30–9pm Mon–Fri, all day Sat–Sun. Car park.
Children welcome in designated room.
Located west of Drusillas roundabout;
signposted to Berwick church. Off the A27
Lewes to Polegate road.

OPEN *11am–3pm and 6–11pm Mon–Thurs;*
11am–11pm Fri–Sat; 12–10.30pm Sun.

BEXHILL-ON-SEA

The Rose & Crown

Turkey Road, Bexhill-on-Sea, East Sussex
TN39 5HH
☎ *(01424) 214625* Charles Newman
www.hungryhorse.co.uk

Greene King Abbot and IPA, with
Harveys Sussex Best a regularly featured
guest.

One bar, dining area, big-screen sports,
darts, bar billiards and Bexhill in Bloom-
winning beer garden. 'Hungry Horse' menu
includes big plate specials and bar snacks.
Food is served 12–10pm Mon–Sat and 12–
9.30pm Sun. Disabled toilets. Under-14s
allowed until 9pm in designated area only.
Car park.

OPEN *All day, every day.*

BOGNOR REGIS

Old Barn

42 Felpham Road, Bognor Regis, West Sussex
PO22 7DF
☎ *(01243) 821564* Brian Griffith

Ringwood Best Bitter, Shepherd Neame
Master Brew and Hop Back Summer
Lightning plus one or two guest beers
perhaps from Hop Back, Fuller's, Ringwood,
Greene King and others.

Thatched, converted barn on the edge of
the village behind Butlin's. Pool, darts and
Sky TV. Popular with all ages, locals and
Butlin's staff, etc. Food available 11am–7pm.
Small car park. Well-behaved children
welcome.

OPEN *11am–11pm Mon–Sat; 12–10.30pm Sun.*

BRIGHTON

The Basketmakers Arms

12 Gloucester Road, Brighton, East Sussex
BN1 4AD
☎ *(01273) 689006* Peter Dowd
www.thebasketmakersarms.co.uk

A Fuller's tied house. London Pride, ESB
and Discovery plus Gale's HSB and Butser
and Adnams Bitter. One guest, changed
fortnightly, from a large list including Brains,
Everards, Otley, Ossett and Hook Norton.

A traditional local dating from the 1850s.
Two rooms, wooden floors, collection of
memorabilia. Extensive menu from locally
sourced produce, especially local seafood
(self-proclaimed legendary burgers!) available
12–8.30pm Mon–Thurs; 12–7pm Fri; 12–6pm
Sat; 12–5pm Sun.

OPEN *12–11pm Sun–Thurs; 12–12 Fri–Sat.*

The Cobbler's Thumb

10 New England Road, Brighton, East Sussex
BN1 4GG
☎ *(01273) 605636*
Geoff Eagle and Nicci Wessing

Freehouse serving Harveys Best Bitter
plus two guests rotating every couple of
months. These might come from Harveys,
Timothy Taylor, Charles Wells, Hop Back or
Badger.

Locals' pub with an Australian theme and
speciality drinks. Heated 'outback' beer
garden, pool table (free
12–7pm every day), Sky TV, pub games.
Occasional music and DJ on Thurs, pool
league and competition. Food available
12–4pm Mon–Fri. Cool dogs welcome.

OPEN *11am–11pm Mon–Sat; 12–10.30pm Sun.*

The Eddy

67 Upper Gloucester Road, Brighton, East Sussex
BN1 3LQ
☎ *(01273) 329540* J Capeling and R Dowell

Freehouse with Harveys Sussex Best Bitter
and HSB always available.

A lively local bar, cosy during the day and
on Sundays, and lively at weekends.
Good music, stylish decor, wooden floors and
quarry-tiled back nook. Food served 6–9pm
Mon–Fri, 1–5pm Sat, 12–6pm Sun, including
vegetarian options. Sky TV and Premiership
Plus. Children welcome during the day, dogs
welcome. Near Brighton train station.

OPEN *3pm–12.30pm Sun–Thurs; noon–1.30am*
Fri–Sat.

The Evening Star

55–6 Surrey Street, Brighton, East Sussex BN1 3PB
☎ *(01273) 328931* Matt and Karen Wickham
www.eveningstarbrighton.co.uk

 The home of the Dark Star Brewing Company, though the brewery is no longer on the same site as the pub. Seven real ales always available, including beers from Dark Star and a rotating guest list. Two real ciders and Belgian beers on draught also served plus eight bottled German and ten bottled Belgian brews.

Specialist real-ale house with wooden floors. Rolls available 12–3pm Mon–Sat. Children not allowed. Just 150 yards from railway station.

OPEN *12–11pm Sun–Thurs; 12–12 Fri; 11.30am–midnight Sat.*

Hand In Hand

33 Upper St James's Street, Brighton, East Sussex BN2 1JN
☎ *(01273) 699595* Chris Neale

Home of the Kemptown Brewery serving at least two Kemptown brews plus a couple of guests such as Badger Best and Tanglefoot.

Cosy, street-corner pub, probably the smallest tower brewery in England. No food. No children. A hundred yards from the seafront.

OPEN *12–11pm (10.30pm Sun).*

The Lion & Lobster

24 Sillwood Street, Brighton, East Sussex BN1 2PS
☎ *(01273) 327299* Gary Whelan

Genuine freehouse with five real ales (200 per year). Something from Harveys is always available, and the other beer changes constantly, with local micro-breweries often featured.

A traditional, Irish family-run pub with roof terrace, gallery and a great atmosphere. All ages welcome. Bar and restaurant food available 12–3pm Mon–Thurs and 12–10pm Fri–Sun. Live music weekly, including jazz and Irish music on Thurs and Sun. Bed and breakfast accommodation. Located 200 yards from the seafront, in between the Bedford Hotel and Norfolk Hotel, just off Western Road.

OPEN *11am–1am Sun–Thurs; 11am–2am Fri–Sat.*

The Sussex Yeoman

7 Guildford Road, Brighton, East Sussex BN1 3LU
☎ *(01273) 327985* Rosie Dunton

 Greene King IPA and Abbot plus a Harveys ale. Also occasional seasonal guests.

Trendy pub decorated in orange and blue with a young clientele (25–40) and a relaxed atmosphere. Games nights feature board games, or a pop quiz on Wednesday evenings. Bar snacks and fuller menu available until 9.30pm. No children.

OPEN *12–close.*

BURPHAM

The George & Dragon

Burpham, Nr Arundel, West Sussex BN18 9RR
☎ *(01903) 883131* James Rose and Kate Holle

 Three real ales: Harveys Best, King Horsham Best and something from Dark Star are usually on the menu.

Located in a small village two miles from Arundel off the main track, with some of the best views of the Arun valley. Excellent walking all around. Bar and restaurant food available 12–2pm and 7–9.30pm (restaurant evenings and Sunday lunch only). Car park. Children over 12 allowed.

OPEN *11am–2.30pm and 6–11pm Mon–Sat; 12–3pm and 7–10.30pm Sun.*

BYWORTH

The Black Horse Inn

Byworth, Nr Petworth, West Sussex GU28 0HL
☎ *(01798) 342424*
Mark and Penelope Robinson

Freehouse with Fuller's London Pride plus three rotating guests from breweries such as Sharp's, Arundel, Wells and Young's, Flowers and Timothy Taylor.

Part of the old tanneries, this building dates back to the 16th century. Two bars (one up, one down) and separate dining area and separate games room. Large beer garden facing the South Downs, with virgin spring running through it. Bleached scrubbed tables, open fires, wooden floors. Food served 11.30am–9pm Mon–Thurs, 11.30am–9.30pm Fri–Sat, 12–8.30pm Sun. Function room with bar free to hire. Children and pets welcome. Car park. Quiz and race machines. Located in the village of Byworth, two miles from Petworth, an antique market town, on the A283. Ten minutes from Pulborough train station.

OPEN *11.30am–11pm Mon–Sat; 12–10.30pm Sun.*

CHARLTON

The Fox Goes Free

Charlton, Nr Goodwood, West Sussex PO18 0HU
☎ *(01243) 811461* Kristian Brown
www.thefoxgoesfree.com

 Freehouse with Arundel's Fox Goes Free and Ballard's Best always available, plus a local guest ale which changes fortnightly.

Situated in the picturesque Sussex countryside, this superb 400-year-old flint freehouse with wood-burning fires and beamed ceilings offers fine food, drink, accommodation and large gardens. Food served 12–2.30pm and 6.30–10pm Mon–Fri, 12–10pm Sat–Sun. Accommodation available in three double rooms and two twins. Car park. Children welcome. Near Goodwood racecourse. Garden overlooks the South Downs. Situated off the A286.

OPEN *11am–11.30pm Mon–Sat; 12–11pm Sun.*

CHICHESTER
Four Chestnuts
234 Oving Road, Chichester, West Sussex PO19 7EJ
☎ *(01243) 779974* Julia Boyle

 Punch Taverns pub with Arundel Gold and Oakleaf Hole Hearted plus one or two guests, changed weekly. Examples include Goddards Fuggle Dee Dum, Triple FFF Moondance and Hogs Back Hop Garden Gold.

An early 20th-century former coaching house with one bar and outside drinking area, this is a popular community pub. Food served 12–2pm and 6–8.30pm Tues–Fri; 12–4pm and 6.30–8.30pm Sat; 12–3pm Sun. Private room and skittle alley available for hire. Pool, darts. Beer festival held last weekend of February. Car park. Children welcome until 7pm. Located on the outskirts of Chichester, 20 minutes' walk from the train station, on the main route for the ring road.

OPEN *12–11pm Mon–Thurs; 12–12 Fri–Sat; 12–10.30pm Sun.*

COMPTON
The Coach & Horses
Compton, Nr Chichester, West Sussex PO18 9HA
☎ *(01705) 631228* David Butler

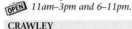 Fuller's ESB, Triple FFF Moondance and Dark Star Hophead are among the regular beers, plus one rotating guest beer.

Situated on the Sussex Downs, a coaching inn with two bars and a restaurant (closed Sun evening and Mon). One bar was built in 1640 and features oak beams and an open log fire. The main bar was added in 1840 and has early Victorian pine panels and two open fires. Food served 12–2pm and 6.30–9pm Mon–Sat, 12–2.30pm and 7–9pm Sun. Car park in the square. Dogs and children welcome. Good walking. On the B2146 South Harting to Emsworth road.

OPEN *11am–3pm and 6–11pm.*

CRAWLEY
The Swan Inn
Horsham Road, West Green, Crawley, West Sussex RH11 7AY
☎ *(01293) 527447* Robert Brindley

Fuller's London Pride and Flowers IPA (brewed by Badger) plus four other guest ales changed every other day.

A very traditional local dating from 1850, with two bars, pool room, friendly staff and locals of all ages. Cask Marque accredited. Live music Friday and Saturday nights. Internet-linked juke box/fruit machine/It box. Beer garden. Children welcome. Between the town centre and the hospital, just behind Asda.

OPEN *12–11pm Sun–Thurs; noon–1am Fri–Sat.*

CROWBOROUGH
The Wheatsheaf
Mount Pleasant, Crowborough, East Sussex TN6 2NF
☎ *(01892) 663756* Ted and Maggie Hirst
www.wheatsheafcrowborough.co.uk

Harveys tied pub with Harveys Best, Sussex Mild, Hadlow Bitter, Armada Ale (plus Old Ale Sept–April), and two rotating guests from the Harveys range of special brews, changed monthly.

Dating back to 1750, this cosy, wood-panelled traditional three-bar pub with open fires is set in a quiet location on the edge of town. Cask Marque accredited. Food served lunchtimes Mon–Sat and evenings Tues–Thurs. Beer garden with marquee for hire. Car park. B&B accommodation available. Cribbage, petanque, occasional live music. Thriving golf society. Beer festivals held late May bank holiday and in October. Near the railway station and close to Ashdown Forest and numerous National Trust properties.

OPEN *12–11pm (10.30pm Sun).*

CROWHURST
The Plough Inn
Chaple Hill, Crowhurst, Nr Battle, East Sussex TN33 9AW
☎ *(01424) 830310* John and Brenda Saunders

 Freehouse with Harveys Best and Armada, Rother Level Best and White 1066 plus seasonal guests from Harveys.

A country pub set in 1066 countryside with superb walks. One large bar. Good pub grub served 12–2pm Mon–Sun, 6.30–9pm Thurs–Sat. Beer garden. Private room available Sun–Wed. Large car park. Children and dogs welcome. Darts, pool. Boules, shovepenny. Located between Battle and Hastings.

OPEN *11.30am–2.30pm and 6–11pm Mon–Fri; 11am–11pm Sat; 12–4pm and 6–10.30pm Sun.*

DANEHILL
The Coach & Horses
School Lane, Danehill, Nr Haywards Heath, East Sussex RH17 7JF
☎ *(01825) 740369* Ian Philpots
www.coachandhorses.danehill.biz

Harveys Best plus weekly-changing guests, and seasonals and traditional ciders, often from local breweries such as Dark Star, Hammerpot, WJ King and Hepworths.

Two-bar freehouse dating from 1847, with traditional coach house bar, and restaurant in converted stables. Michelin Bib Gourmand award for five years in a row, with food served every lunchtime, and evenings except Sunday. Large beer garden with views of the Downs. Adults-only rear sun terrace. Secure children's play area. Off the A275 at Danehill.

OPEN *12–3pm and 6–11pm Mon–Fri; all day Sat–Sun.*

EAST ASHLING

The Horse & Groom

East Ashling, Chichester, West Sussex PO18 9AX
☎ *(01243) 575339 Michael Martell*
www.thehorseandgroomchichester.co.uk

 Freehouse with Hop Back Summer Lightning, Dark Star Hophead, Harveys Hadlow and Young's Bitter permanently available, occasional guest on separate pump.

A 17th-century inn with flagstone floor, one main bar with range and one small bar with open fire. Bar snacks and full restaurant menu available, with food served 12–2.15pm and 6.30–9.15pm Mon–Sat; 12–2.30pm Sun. Children welcome. Large beer garden. Car park. Function room available. Accommodation in 11 en-suite rooms. On the B2178, Funtington Road.

OPEN *11am–3pm and 6–11pm Mon–Sat; 12–6pm Sun (closed Sun evening).*

EASTBOURNE

The Lamb Inn

36 High Street, Old Town, Eastbourne, East Sussex BN21 1HH
☎ *(01323) 720545 Steve Hume (licensee), Chris Walker (manager)*

 Tied to Harveys Brewery, with five Harveys beers always available, including seasonal brews.

O ld-style, three-bar pub dating from 1180, with seating at the side. Food available 10am–2.30pm and 5.30–9pm Mon–Thurs; all day Fri–Sun. Function room available for hire, for dinners, parties, meetings etc. Plans for accommodation from summer 2008. Children allowed.

OPEN *10.30am–11pm Sun–Thurs; 10.30am–midnight Fri–Sat.*

The Windsor Tavern

165–7 Langney Road, Eastbourne, East Sussex BN22 8AH
☎ *(01323) 726206 Steve and Debbie Leach*

Leased from Enterprise Inns, with Adnams Bitter always available.

O ld-fashioned, traditional community pub, big on all sports, especially football and horse racing. Pub games, including darts, pool and regular cribbage competitions. Rolls available every day. Walled beer garden with large decked area. Comfortable heated outside smoking area. Close to the town centre and sea front.

OPEN *10.30am–11pm.*

EAST GRINSTEAD

The Ship Inn

Ship Street, East Grinstead, West Sussex RH19 4RG
☎ *(01342) 312089 Chris Phelps*

Owned by Wells and Young's, always serving Young's Bitter and Special plus a Young's guest such as St George.

A traditional English pub with two bars and a huge beer garden with decking, trees, plants and fish pond. Homemade food

available 11am–10pm. Two en-suite rooms with Sky TV. Car park. Situated at the top of the High Street.

OPEN *10.30am–11pm (midnight Thurs–Sat).*

EAST HOATHLY

The King's Head

1 High Street, East Hoathly, Lewes, East Sussex BN8 6DR
☎ *(01825) 840238 Robert Wallace*

 Home of the 1648 Brewing Company with one regular beer and seasonal ales from the brewery available. Harveys Best plus occasional guests from other micro-breweries also feature.

A 17th-century former coaching inn, now a freehouse and micro-brewery set in a conservation village. Character bar, restaurant, function room, enclosed garden. Home-cooked food served 12–2.30pm and 6.30–9pm. Children and dogs welcome. Off the A22.

OPEN *11am–11pm Mon–Sat; 12–4pm and 7–10.30pm Sun.*

FELPHAM

The Fox Inn

Waterloo Road, Felpham, Bognor Regis, West Sussex PO22 7EN
☎ *(01243) 865308 Andy and Alison Hirons*
www.thefoxfelpham.co.uk

An Enterprise Inns pub. Young's Bitter, Harveys Sussex Best and Fuller's London Pride plus three guests, changed every two–six months. Guest beers may include Gale's HSB, Fuller's ESB, Timothy Taylor Landlord and an ale from Gribble.

T he pub dates back to 1780 and has connections with William Blake. Two oak-pannelled bars (one child-friendly), decorated with old photographs of the village. Food served 12–2.30pm and 6–9pm. Beer garden with smoking areas. Car park. CAMRA Sussex Winner for Food and Drink 2007/08.

OPEN *11.30am–11pm Mon–Sat; 12–10.30pm Sun.*

FERNHURST

The King's Arms

Midhurst Road, Fernhurst, West Sussex GU27 3HA
☎ *(01428) 652005 Annabel and Michael Hirst*

 Freehouse with up to five real ales, perhaps including Ringwood Best and Hogs Back TEA plus Horsham Best and Timothy Taylor Best.

I n Sussex, but with a Surrey postcode. A 17th-century Grade II listed former farmhouse with oak beams and fireplaces. An L-shaped bar with servery to dining area, plus hay barn for live bands, weddings etc. Surrounded by farmland – customers may come by horse or helicopter. Food available 12–2.30pm and 7–9.30pm (not Sun). Children allowed until 7pm, over-14s thereafter. On the A286, a mile south of Fernhurst.

OPEN *11.30am–3pm and 5–11pm Mon–Fri; 11.30am–3pm and 6.30–11pm Sat; 12–3pm only Sun.*

FIRLE

The Ram Inn

The Street, Firle, Nr Lewes, East Sussex BN8 6NS
☎ *(01273) 858222* Hayley Bayes

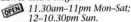 Harveys Best Bitter plus another of the brewery's ales and a regularly changing guest beer perhaps from Otter or Ringwood breweries.

Simple and unspoilt 16th-century coaching inn, situated in attractive village at the foot of the Downs. Three bars – main bar, snug and courtroom (which was the original court for the area), plus private dining room. Log fires during the winter months and large enclosed garden including play area. Food served 12–3pm and 6.30–9.30pm Mon–Fri, 12–4.30pm and 6.30–9.30pm Sat–Sun. Car park. Children welcome. Near Charleston and Firle Place. Just off the A27 between Lewes and Polegate.

OPEN *11.30am–11pm Mon–Sat; 12–10.30pm Sun.*

FISHBOURNE

The Bull's Head

99 Fishbourne Road, Fishbourne, Nr Chichester, West Sussex PO19 3JP
☎ *(01243) 839895* Roger and Julie Pocock

 The five permanent ales are Gale's HSB, plus Fuller's London Pride, ESB, Chiswick and Discovery. There is also an occasional guest.

Converted 17th-century farmhouse with a country atmosphere, just one mile from the city centre. Bar and restaurant food available every lunchtime, and evenings except Sunday. Car park and patio. On the A259.

OPEN *11am–3pm and 5.30–11pm Mon–Fri; 11am–11pm Sat; 12–10.30pm Sun.*

FLETCHING

The Griffin Inn

Fletching, Nr Uckfield, East Sussex TN22 3SS
☎ *(01825) 722890* James Pullan
www.thegriffininn.co.uk

 Freehouse with three beers from Sussex breweries, Harveys, King and Hepworth, always on offer.

A 16th-century, Grade II listed two-bar coaching inn situated in an unspoilt village. Run by the Pullan family for more than 20 years. Real fires and wood panelling. Two acres of gardens with lovely views towards Sheffield Park, plus terrace for outside dining. Restaurant and bar food served every lunchtime and evening. Car park. Children welcome. Accommodation in 13 en-suite rooms, including five next door in Griffin House. Nearby attractions include Sheffield Park Gardens (National Trust), Bluebell Railway and Glyndebourne Opera.

OPEN *12–11pm.*

FRANT

Abergavenny Arms Hotel

Frant Road, Frant, Nr Tunbridge Wells, East Sussex TN3 9DB
☎ *(01892) 750233*
Paul Vallis and Paula Schofield

 Four real ales, including Fuller's London Pride, Harveys Sussex Best and Greene King Abbot, plus a guest changed every week.

Built in the 1430s, a large, two-bar country inn with restaurant. The lounge bar was used as a courtroom in the 18th century, with cells in the cellar. Bar and restaurant food available at lunchtimes and evenings every day, and all day Sunday. Fresh fish a speciality. Three letting rooms (one family suite of two rooms, and one double en-suite). Car park, garden. Children allowed. Easy to find, on the A267 south of Tunbridge Wells.

OPEN *All day, every day.*

GRAFFHAM

The Foresters Arms

Graffham, Petworth, West Sussex GU28 0QA
☎ *(01798) 867202*
Nicholas Bell and Serena Aykroyd
www.foresters-arms.com

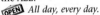 Four real ales in summer, two or three in winter, including a wide range of beers from King, Ballard's, Goddards, Ringwood and Itchen Valley, plus many guests from other breweries.

Heavily beamed 17th-century inn with one bar, large inglenook fireplace and large garden, situated at the foot of the South Downs. Food served 12–2pm and 7–9pm Tues–Sun. Car park. Children are permitted in certain areas of the bar and restaurant, but there are no special facilities. En-suite accommodation.

OPEN *11am–3pm and 6–11pm Tues–Sun (closed all day Mon).*

HAILSHAM

The Bricklayers Arms

1 Ersham Road, Hailsham, East Sussex BN27 3LA
☎ *(01323) 841587* C Walker

Brews from Wells and Young's and Harveys plus a guest ale, changed every month.

More than 100 years old, a traditional two-bar pub with fishing, football and chess clubs, darts, pool and bar billiards. Real food available in the bar until 8pm. Interesting beer garden. Children allowed in the garden only. Live music and beer festivals. Five miles from Eastbourne, off the A22.

OPEN *All day, every day.*

HALFWAY BRIDGE

Halfway Bridge Inn

Halfway Bridge, Lodsworth, Nr Petworth,
West Sussex GU28 9BP
☎ *(01798) 861281* Paul and Sue Carter

Skinner's Betty Stogs, Sharp's Doom Bar, local brewery Langham's Halfway to Heaven are regularly featured, with one of the beers changed monthly. Also local cider.

Built in 1710 on the A272 halfway between Midhurst and Petworth, an authentic staging post on the Dover to Winchester road. Four rooms around a central serving area, with inglenook fireplace and dining areas. Food served 12–2.30pm and 6.30–9.15pm (until 8.30pm Sun). Car park, walled patio, large beer garden, traditional games. Children welcome. Luxury accommodation (two doubles and four suites) available in the converted stable behind the pub.

OPEN *11am–11pm Mon–Sat; 12–10.30pm Sun.*

HALNAKER

The Anglesey Arms at Halnaker

Stane Street, Halnaker, Chichester, West Sussex
PO18 0NQ
☎ *(01243) 773474* Roger Jackson
www.angleseyarms.co.uk

Punch Taverns pub with four ales, which could include Young's Bitter, Adnams Bitter and Hop Back Summer Lightning.

A pub from the day it was built, this Georgian building is situated in the old Roman area. Separate dining room. Open fires, floorboard and flagstones. Food served, much of it organic, lunchtimes and evenings. Large country beer garden with boules and orchard. BBQ facilities. Large car park. Well-behaved children and dogs welcome. On the Goodwood Estate, close to Boxgrove Priory and Fontwell racecourse. Situated on the A285 Chichester to Petworth road, three miles east of Chichester.

OPEN *11am–3pm and 5.30–11pm Mon–Fri;*
11am–11pm Sat; 12–10.30pm Sun.

HASTINGS

The Carlisle

Pelham Street, Hastings, East Sussex TN34 1PE
☎ *(01424) 420193* Mike Ford

Freehouse serving brews from various local breweries, including Arundel and White, plus seasonal guests.

Bikers' pub but with a mixed clientele. Rock music, bar games. Large function room. Outside seating on concrete mushrooms. Children allowed until 7pm.

OPEN *All day, every day.*

First In Last Out

14–15 High Street, Hastings, East Sussex
TN34 3EY
☎ *(01424) 425079* Mr Bigg
www.thefilo.co.uk

Four beers brewed on the premises, with two always available. Two guest ales such as Hop Back Rye and Coriander, but always changing. Smaller breweries favoured and normally their stronger brews. Occasional beer festivals.

Definitely a real ale house, known locally as FILO, refurbished, with lots of character and charisma. No pool or machines. The food was mentioned in *The Guardian* Good Food supplement, and is available 12–3pm Tues–Sat. Quiz night on first Sunday of each month, plus regular live music events. Regular beer festivals held. Covered outside area with protection from inclement weather! Children allowed during the daytime only.

OPEN *All day, every day.*

The White Rock Hotel

1–10 White Rock, Hastings, East Sussex TN34 1JU
☎ *(01424) 422240*
Laurence Bell and Catherine Parr
www.thewhiterockhotel.com

A freehouse offering four constantly changing real ales. Only Sussex beers served, including Dark Star, Harveys, Kings, Hepworth and Rother Valley.

Completely refurbished, upmarket, seafront café bar with large terraces. Part of the Quality Hotel which has also been refurbished and has its own car park for overnight guests only. Food served 7am–10pm. Situated opposite the pier, on the seafront.

OPEN *7am–11.30pm.*

HAYWARDS HEATH

The Star

1 The Broadway, Haywards Heath, West Sussex
RH16 3AQ
☎ *(01444) 413267* Jason Flexen

Up to 12 beers. Brakspear Bitter, Wadworth 6X, Harveys Sussex and Marston's Pedigree plus guests including Timothy Taylor Landlord and Hop Back Summer Lightning. Monthly '4 for 3' offers on selected ales. Micro beer festival in April (25 ales) and two-week festival in October (50 ales and ciders).

Large, refurbished real ale house in the town centre. Food served all day, every day. Car park and outside seating. Part of the Hogshead pub group.

OPEN *11am–11pm Mon–Sat; normal hours Sun.*

HEATHFIELD

The Prince of Wales

Station Road, Heathfield, East Sussex TN21 8DR
☎ *(01435) 862919* Bryan and Steph Bayley

Three real ales on offer, always including Harveys Best, plus two rotating guests, changed fortnightly.

A freehouse partly dating back to the early 19th century, when it was used as a drovers' stop-over alehouse. An open fire creates a warm atmosphere in the two bars, restaurant and conservatory. Restaurant open 12–2.30pm and 6–9pm Mon–Sat and 12–6pm Sun. Well-behaved children. Car park.

OPEN *12–11pm.*

HERSTMONCEUX

The Brewer's Arms

Gardner Street, Herstmonceux, East Sussex
BN27 4LB
☎ *(01323) 832226 Ian and Julie Hanks*
www.thebrewersarms.co.uk

 Greene King pub with IPA plus two other beers, changed every quarter.

An Elizabethan village pub dating from 1580. Cask Marque accredited. Food available 12–2pm and 6.30–9pm. Two bars and a restaurant area. Child-friendly, with baby-changing facilities, and dog-friendly. Disabled facilities. Garden with swings and toys. Covered decking with heaters and lighting. On the A271.

OPEN *12–2.30pm and 6–11pm Mon–Sat; 12–3pm and 6–10.30pm Sun. (12–3pm and 6–11pm bank hols except Christmas and Boxing Day.)*

HORSHAM

The Black Jug

31 North Street, Horsham, West Sussex RH12 1RJ
☎ *(01403) 732254*
www.blackjug-horsham.co.uk

S&N tied pub with Harveys Sussex and Greene King IPA plus three rotating guests changed every few days.

Dating back to the Victorian period, this pub retains its original features with wooden panelling and wooden floors. Food served 12–10pm Mon–Sat, 12–9.30pm Sun. Parking available nearby. Children over the age of 10 welcome during the day. Well-behaved dogs allowed in the bar. Located between Horsham town centre and the train station.

OPEN *12–11pm Mon–Thurs; 12–12 Fri–Sat; 12–10.30pm Sun.*

The Foresters Arms

43 St Leonards Road, Horsham, West Sussex
RH13 6EH
☎ *(01403) 254458 Joe Paine*

Three real ales, namely Young's Bitter, Harveys Sussex Best and Charles Wells Bombardier.

Old-English pub with Sussex flagstones, oak beams and inglenook fireplace. One large bar and a separate 18-seater restaurant. Homemade pub food served 12–2.30pm and 6.30–9pm Tues–Sun. Large garden and patio area with rustic seating and boules court.

OPEN *6–11pm Mon; 12–3pm and 6–11pm Tues–Thurs; 12–11.30pm Fri–Sat; 12–10.30pm Sun.*

The Malt Shovel

15 Springfield Road, Horsham, West Sussex
RH12 2PG
☎ *(01403) 254543 Lyn Williams*
www.maltshovel.com

 Enterprise Inns pub with Brakspear Bitter, Harveys Sussex Bitter and Timothy Taylor Landlord, plus six frequently changing guests such as Wychwood Hobgoblin, Hepworth Iron Horse and Prospect, Gale's HSB and Fuller's London Pride.

A traditional pub with floorboards, open fire, one bar, patio and car park. Food served 12–2.30pm. Beer festival every October, featuring 100 beers over five weeks. The pub is renowned for its live music at weekends.

OPEN *All day, every day.*

HORSTED KEYNES

The Green Man

The Green, Horsted Keynes, West Sussex
RH17 7AS
☎ *(01825) 790656 Peter Tracey*

The permanent beers here include Greene King IPA, Morland Original and Old Speckled Hen, and the guest beer is changed every six to eight weeks.

One-bar traditional village pub set on the village green, with large inglenook open fire and relaxed atmosphere created by conversation, not loud music and fruit machines! Food served 12–2.15pm daily, 6–9.15m Tues–Fri and 6.30–9.30pm Sat. There is a large beer garden, close to the Bluebell Railway. No under-5s allowed; ages 5–14 allowed in dining area; no under-14s allowed in the bar. Between Adringly and Lindfield.

OPEN *12–3pm and 5.30–11pm Sun–Fri; all day Sat (plus all day Sun in summer).*

HOVE

The Farm Tavern

13 Farm Road, Hove, East Sussex
☎ *(01273) 325902*

Greene King IPA, Abbot Ale and Old Speckled Hen plus a guest or seasonal Greene King ale. Regional finalist in Greene King Excellence Awards 2005.

Hidden little gem of a pub, chilled at lunchtimes, funky and fun in the evenings. Friendly and cosy, with upstairs room where families are welcome. Homemade food and bar snacks served 12–3pm and 5–9pm Mon–Fri, 12–6pm Sat and 12.30–9pm Sun. Open mic Sun evening, quiz Mon, magician Tues. Upstairs room has its own bar and is available for private hire. Just off Western Road, halfway between Brighton and Hove town centres.

OPEN *12–12 (1am Fri–Sat).*

Freemasons

38–9 Western Road, Hove, East Sussex
BN3 1AF
☎ *(01273) 732043 Stephen Simpson*

 Greene King IPA and Harveys Sussex plus a guest such as Adnams Broadside.

A 150-year-old bar/restaurant with cocktail bar upstairs. Cask Marque approved. Outside seating. Disabled access and toilets. Food available 12–3pm and 6–9pm daily, all day at weekends. Traditional roasts on Sun lunchtimes. Children allowed until 5pm. On the main shopping street.

OPEN *12–12 (1am Fri–Sat).*

ICKLESHAM
The Queen's Head
Parsonage Lane, Icklesham, Winchelsea,
East Sussex TN36 4BL
☎ *(01424) 814552*
Ian Mitchell and Lee Norcott
www.queenshead.com

 Freehouse with five real ales from an ever-changing selection, with a range of national and local breweries used.

A Jacobean pub dating from 1632. Farm implements on ceiling, boules pitch, function room, beer garden overlooking Rye. Food available at lunchtimes and evenings, all day at weekends. Live music most Sundays 4–6pm. Hop festival, mini beer festival in September. Under-12s allowed until 8.30pm. Car park. Situated off the A259.

OPEN *11am–11pm Mon–Sat; 12–10.30pm Sun.*

ISFIELD
The Laughing Fish
Station Road, Isfield, Nr Uckfield, East Sussex
TN22 5XB
☎ *(01825) 750349* Linda and Andy Brooks
www.laughingfishonline.co.uk

Tied to Greene King with IPA and two other ales (more in summer).

R ural village pub built in the 1880s with two bars and real fires, offering genuine homemade food 12–2.30pm and 6–9pm (except Sun evening). Sandwiches and light snacks also available. Families welcome. Separate dining area, garden, patio and children's play area. Large car park. Situated just off the A26 between Uckfield and Lewes, next door to the Lavender Line Railway HQ at Isfield Station.

OPEN *11.30am–11pm.*

ITCHENOR
The Ship Inn
The Street, Itchenor, Chichester PO20 7AH
☎ *(01243) 512284* Silas Woolley
www.theshipinn.biz

Freehouse with Itchen Valley Godfathers, WJ King Horsham Best Bitter, Ballard's Best Bitter and Ringwood Fortyniner.

A 1930s pub on the edge of Chichester harbour with oak panelling and nautical paraphernalia. One main bar and restaurant serving fresh local fish. Food (including traditional pub food, only better!) served 12–2.30pm and 6.30–9.30pm Mon–Sat, 12–4pm Sun. Accommodation available. Beer patio. Car park. Dogs welcome, children tolerated! A proper pub. Located six miles south of Chichester, just off the A286.

OPEN *11am–11pm Mon–Sat; 12–10.30pm Sun.*

LANCING
The Crabtree Inn
140 Crabtree Lane, Lancing, West Sussex
BN15 9NQ
☎ *(01903) 755514* Philip G Houghton

 Fuller's London Pride plus three weekly-changing guest beers, which could include Timothy Taylor Landlord, Meteor from Hammerpot Brewery (local). All real ales sourced locally, from the many small brewers within 40-mile radius. Recent guests have included Undercliff Experience, Red Hunter, Langham Hip Hop and Nuptual Ale.

T his art-deco-style pub dates back to 1931, with a Spitfire room, restaurant and bar with aeronautical theme. Separate games room with pool and music. Central snug area with chesterfields. Homemade bar food and grills served Tues–Sat, Thai buffet Wed–Sat evenings, full carvery on Sundays in the spitfire room. Huge beer garden. Children welcome (children's outdoor assault course). Function room available. Car park. One mile from Shoreham airport, half a mile from the sea at the foot of the South Downs. Located on the south coast between Worthing and Shore-by-Sea, just south of the A27.

OPEN *12–11.30pm.*

LEWES
The Black Horse Inn
55 Western Road, Lewes, East Sussex BN7 1RS
☎ *(01273) 473653* J Bowell

Four ales from the Greene King range plus two guest ales, changed frequently.

B uilt in 1805 as a hotel, this is an unspoilt, traditional two-bar pub situated on the main road through Lewes. Varied menu served lunchtimes Mon–Sat, with roasts served Sun lunch. No TV. Bar billiards, darts, cribbage, toad in the hole. Courtyard garden. Folk music and quiz nights. B&B. Dogs welcome. Western Road follows on from the High Street.

OPEN *11am–2.30pm and 5.30–11pm Mon–Fri;*
11am–3pm and 6–11pm Sat; 12–5pm
Sun (closed Sun evening).

The Brewer's Arms
91 High Street, Lewes, East Sussex BN7 1XN
☎ *(01273) 475524* Kevin and Joan Griffin
www.brewersarmslewes.co.uk

 Freehouse with Harveys Best plus up to four real ales, constantly rotating. Biddenden real cider is also served.

T here has been a pub on this site since 1540. Family-run, in a central location near the castle. Well-equipped, with two bars and a beer garden. Front bar has no piped music. Back bar has pool, darts, toad-in-the-hole, juke box and big-screen TV. Food, including homemade specials, available every day until early evening. Dogs welcome if on a lead.

OPEN *10am–11pm Mon–Sat; 12–10.30pm Sun.*

The Elephant & Castle

White Hill, Lewes, East Sussex BN2 2DJ
☎ *(01273) 473797* Huw and Dec

 Enterprise Inns leased house with Harveys Best, Wychwood Hobgoblin plus one guest. The guest rotates on an ad hoc basis.

Built in 1838 as a coaching inn. One bar with three drinking areas and two function rooms. Floor boards and tiles, old furniture and eclectic decoration. Meeting place for the neighbourhood Bonfire Society. Food available 12–2.30pm Mon–Fri; 5–8pm Tues–Thurs; 12–5pm Sat–Sun. Pool and darts played, plus sport on TV. Just off the high street.

OPEN *11.30am–11pm Mon–Thurs; 11.30am–midnight Fri–Sat; 12–11pm Sun.*

The Gardener's Arms

46 Cliffe High Street, Lewes, East Sussex BN7 2AN
☎ *(01273) 474808* Andy Fitzgerald

 A constantly changing range of six real ales from independent breweries across the UK. Harveys Best is a regular feature, but the five others are changed every nine gallons, and more than 2,000 different brews have been served in the past seven years.

Small traditional two-bar street-corner pub opposite Harveys Brewery, sympathetically restored after the floods in 2000. Locally made pies and pasties available during all opening hours. Dogs welcome. In the town centre, but also handy for walking on the Downs.

OPEN *11am–11pm Mon–Sat; 12–10.30pm Sun.*

Snowdrop Inn

119 South Street, Lewes, East Sussex BN7 2BU
☎ *(01273) 471018* Hugh

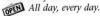 Harveys Best and Adnams Broadside are regulars, plus a monthly guest such as a Black Sheep beer.

At the bottom of town, a thriving, friendly, child-friendly local with wooden floors, function/dining room, gardens and bars on two levels. Pool table. Outside yard. Live music. Good food (100% vegetarian) available 12–3pm and 5–9pm Mon–Thurs and all day Fri–Sun.

OPEN *All day, every day.*

LINDFIELD

The Stand Up Inn

47 High Street, Lindfield, West Sussex RH16 2HN
☎ *(01444) 482995*
Laura Espinosa and Daisy Parsons
www.darkstarbrewing.co.uk

 Dark Star tied house serving Best and Hophead plus four regularly changing guests.

Country village real ale pub serving hot pasties and fresh-filled rolls, quality ciders plus a variety of bottled Belgian and German beers. Sun-trap patio garden. Dogs welcome. Dart board, billiards and chess table. Regular quiz nights and live music. Pasties and fresh filled rolls available – there are plans to expand the menu to serve good, simple pub food. Families welcome. Car park within 20 yards. Beer festivals held three or four times a year. Located within a mile of Haywards Heath station.

OPEN *11.30am–midnight Mon–Thurs; 11.30am–12.30am Fri–Sat; 12–12 Sun.*

LITLINGTON

The Plough & Harrow

Litlington, Nr Alfriston, East Sussex BN26 5RE
☎ *(01323) 870632* Paul Woolven and Pat Low

 Harveys Sussex Best, Badger Tanglefoot and Greene King Old Speckled Hen plus guests from a range of independent breweries.

A 17th-century freehouse with oak beams, two bars and a busy restaurant. Bar and restaurant food (organic and local) available. Car park and garden. Children and dogs allowed. Three miles south of the A27, two miles from the nearest village (Alfriston).

OPEN *12–3pm and 5.30–11pm Mon–Fri; all day Sat–Sun.*

MAPLEHURST

The White Horse Inn

Park Lane, Maplehurst, Nr Horsham, West Sussex RH13 6LL
☎ *(01403) 891208* Simon Johnson

 Genuine freehouse serving Weltons Pride and Joy and Harveys Best plus a couple of guests, changed in rotation, up to 200 a year with small breweries favoured.

Traditional, 200-year-old three-bar pub in the middle of a Sussex hamlet. No juke box, machines or piped music. Conservatory leading to large garden with good views and a children's play area. Sussex and Surrey CAMRA Pub of the Year 2007. Food served 12–2pm and 6–9pm Tues–Sun. Situated less than two miles north of the A272 and south of the A281, five miles from Horsham. Good walking country.

OPEN *12–2.30pm (3pm Sun) and 6–11.30pm Sun–Thurs; 12–2.30pm and 6pm–12.30am Fri–Sat. Evening last order times may vary.*

MIDHURST

The Crown Inn

Edinburgh Square, Midhurst, West Sussex GU29 9NL
☎ *(01730) 813462* L Williams and R Cox

 Fuller's London Pride and Badger Tanglefoot plus up to five constantly changing real ales from independent brewers from across the UK. Gravity and hand pump served.

A 16th-century freehouse with wooden floors and open fires. Three bar areas including pool and games room and 50-inch plasma TV in main bar. Courtyard. Behind and below the church in the old part of town.

OPEN *11am–11pm Mon–Sat; 12–10.30pm Sun.*

NUTBOURNE

The Rising Sun

The Street, Nutbourne, Pulborough, West Sussex RH20 2HE
☎ *(01798) 812191* Regan Howard

 Freehouse serving Fuller's London Pride, Greene King Abbot and King and Barnes Sussex Ale plus a minimum of two guests such as Harveys Sussex and Hogs Back TEA, or something from an independent such as Cottage.

A 400-year-old pub with Victorian frontage in walking country. Two bars, wooden floors, dining area, mixed clientele and very friendly landlord! Food served at lunchtimes and evenings. Children allowed.

OPEN *11am–3pm and 6–11pm (10.30pm Sun).*

NUTHURST

The Black Horse Inn

Nuthurst Street, Nuthurst, West Sussex RH13 6LH
☎ *(01403) 891272* Clive Henwood
www.theblackhorseinn.com

 Harveys Sussex, Fuller's London Pride, King Horsham Best and Timothy Taylor Landlord plus guests on up to three pumps, which always include a regional ale and are changed at least twice a week.

A 17th-century freehouse with front terrace and stream-side rear beer garden. Lots of original features including a spitroast inglenook fireplace, exposed wattle and daub walls, two bars, one with a Horsham stone floor, a snug and a restaurant. Private room for hire. Food, including daily specials, available 12–2.30pm and 6–9.30pm through the week and all day until 9.30pm on Sat and 8.30pm on Sun. Children welcome with menu provided. Dogs also welcome. Outside bars catered for. Beer festivals on bank holidays. Car park and outside bar. Good for local walks. Located four miles south of Horsham.

OPEN *12–3pm and 6–11pm Mon–Fri; 12–11pm Sat and bank holidays; 12–10.30pm Sun.*

OLD HEATHFIELD

The Star Inn

Church Street, Old Heathfield, East Sussex TN21 9AH
☎ *(01435) 863570* Fiona Airey

 Harveys Best plus two weekly changing guests.

A freehouse built in 1348, licensed in 1388. Original beams and open fires. Famous gardens and views. Bar and restaurant food served 12–2.15pm and 6–9pm Mon–Thurs; 12–2.15pm and 6–9.30pm Fri–Sat; 12–3pm Sun. Car park and garden. Children allowed. At the dead end of a road to the rear of Old Heathfield church.

OPEN *11am–3pm and 5.30–11pm; 11am–11pm Sat; 12–10.30pm Sun.*

OVING

The Gribble Inn

Oving, Nr Chichester, West Sussex PO20 6BP
☎ *(01243) 786893* David and Linda Stone

 Badger Best and Tanglefoot plus seasonal brews and Gribble Ales available. Also a couple of guests.

Picturesque red-brick 16th-century inn now owned by Hall & Woodhouse and no longer home to the (still nearby and now fully independent) Gribble Brewery, although the pub still serves the brewery's beers. A traditional country pub, serving good, wholesome home-cooked food at both lunchtimes and evenings, seven days a week. Car park, large attractive garden, children's room, skittle alley.

OPEN *11am–3pm and 5–11pm Mon–Fri; 11am–11pm Sat; 12–10.30pm Sun.*

PORTSLADE

The Stanley Arms

47 Wolseley Road, Portslade, East Sussex BN41 1SS
☎ *(01273) 430234* Stephen Bennett
www.thestanley.com

 Five hand pumps offer 30 different beers every week from various micro-breweries across the country. As one beer finishes, a different one starts.

Two-bar traditional 19th-century freehouse with attractive garden. CAMRA South Downs Pub of the Year 2007 and runner-up in 2006. Selection of snacks (pies, olives, pasties, Scotch eggs) always available. Beer garden. Three beer festivals a year, in Feb, June and Sept. Live music once a month, quiz Wed and Sun. Football, cricket and cribbage teams. Situated 400 yards north of Fishersgate station.

OPEN *4–11pm Mon; 3–11pm Tues–Fri; 12–11pm Sat; 12–10.30pm Sun.*

ROBERTSBRIDGE

The Seven Stars Inn

High Street, Robertsbridge, East Sussex TN32 5AJ
☎ *(01580) 880333* Mark Fox and Lisa Conn

 Harveys Best Bitter and Old Ale plus Harveys seasonal brews.

Claims to be Britain's oldest haunted pub, dating from the 14th century. Homemade food available, including freshly prepared pizzas, 12–2.30pm and 6–9pm Mon–Sat. Sunday carvery 12.30–3.30pm. One bar, dining area, car park and beer garden. In the centre of Robertsbridge.

OPEN *12–11pm.*

RUDGWICK

Thurlow Arms

Baynards, Rudgwick, Nr Horsham, West Sussex RH12 3AD
☎ *(01403) 822459* Mr Gibbs

Fuller's London Pride, Hogs Back TEA, Ringwood Best Bitter, Badger Tanglefoot and Dorset Best regularly available.

Large Victorian pub situated on the South Downs Way, with railway memorabilia relating to the closure of Baynards station in 1965. Games room with darts and pool, restaurant, dining rooms and large garden. Food served 12–2pm and 6.15–9.30pm Mon–Fri, 12–2.15pm and 6.15–9.30pm Sat, and 12–2.30pm and 7–9pm Sun. Large car park. Children's play castle and menu.

OPEN *11am–3pm and 6–11pm Mon–Sat; 12–10.30pm Sun.*

RUSPER

The Lamb Inn

Lambs Green, Rusper, Nr Horsham, West Sussex RH12 4RG
☎ *(01293) 871336*
Ben Bokor-Ingram and Chris Durnin

A freehouse. WJ King Horsham Best plus three guests, changed constantly. Beers featured may include Dark Star Original, 1648 Signature, Hepworth Iron Horse, Weltons Old Harry, Hogs Back TEA and Hampshire Hare. Only beers from small independent brewers are sold.

Dating back to 1867 with flagstone floors, wooden beams and a double-sided open fire. Homemade food, from locally sourced produce, served 12–2pm and 7–9.30pm Mon–Sat; 12–9pm Sun. Children and dogs welcome. No fruit machines, pool table or juke box. Private room for functions. Five miles from Horsham between Rusper and Faygate, ten minutes from Gatwick.

OPEN *11.30am–3pm and 5.30–11pm Mon–Fri; 11.30am–11pm Sat; 12–10.30pm Sun.*

The Royal Oak

Friday Street, Rusper, West Sussex RH12 4QA
☎ *(01293) 871393* Sara Blunden

A freehouse. Surrey Hills Ranmore, Dark Star Best, Oakleaf I Can't Believe It's Not Bitter plus one mild. Three guests changed approximately twice a week.

A small country pub with beer garden and dining area. Real fires at both ends of the pub to create a cosy atmosphere. Friendly locals. Home-cooked food served every day except Sun and Mon evening. Turn off the A24 at Clarks Green and turn right into Friday Street.

OPEN *11am–3pm and 5–11pm Mon–Fri; 11am–11pm Sat; 12–9pm Sun.*

RUSTINGTON

The Fletcher Arms

Station Road, Rustington, West Sussex BN16 3AF
☎ *(01903) 784858* Mr and Mrs Baden

Harveys Best, Shepherd Neame Spitfire, Greene King Old Speckled Hen and Ringwood Best plus a daily-changing guest beer perhaps from King, Wolf, Ballard's, Wild, Timothy Taylor, Hogs Back, Fuller's, Ringwood, or many others from around the country.

Large, friendly, 1920s pub, winner of many awards including Cask Marque. Live entertainment, public and saloon bar and olde-worlde barn. Food available 11.30am–2.30pm and 6–9pm Mon–Sat, 12–2.30pm Sun. Large car park. Large garden with swings and bouncy castle.

OPEN *All day, every day.*

RYE

The Inkerman Arms

Harbour Road, Rye Harbour, Rye, East Sussex TN31 7TQ
☎ *(01797) 222464* Ken and Marlene Bowman

Freehouse with Greene King IPA and something from Harveys plus a guest changed weekly.

A 19th-century pub with one bar, a designated area for dining and a beer garden with boules piste. Food served 12–2.20pm and 7–9.20pm daily except Sun evening and all day Mon. Car park. Close to historic Rye town, harbour and wildlife reserve.

OPEN *12–3pm and 7–11pm Tues–Sat; 12–4pm Sun.*

The Ypres Castle Inn

Gun Garden, Rye, East Sussex TN31 7HH
☎ *(01797) 223248* Ian Fenn
www.yprescastleinn.co.uk

Freehouse serving Harveys Bitter, Adnams Broadside, Fuller's London Pride and Timothy Taylor Landlord plus guests from South West brewers such as Exmoor, Cotleigh and RCH changed every couple of weeks.

Traditional weatherboarded one-bar pub and restaurant dating from the 17th century. No juke box or gaming machines. Safe pub garden (the only one in Rye) with lovely river views. Live music Fridays. Food using local produce available at lunchtimes and evenings (except Sunday evening) – reservations recommended. At least ten wines available by the glass. Children welcome. Behind the parish church.

OPEN *11am–11pm Mon–Fri; 11am–late Sat; 12–9pm Sun.*

ST LEONARDS ON SEA

The Dripping Spring
34 Tower Road, St Leonards on Sea, East Sussex RN37 6JE
☎ *(01424) 434055*

Seven real ales, with at least four rotating guests changed daily.

A small two-bar public house with attractive courtyard to the rear. Sussex CAMRA Pub of the Year 1999, 2000, 2001 and 2003, National CAMRA Pub of the Year runner-up 2001. Beer festivals. Bar food (rolls) available 11am–6pm. Car parking. Situated in a side street off the A21.

OPEN *11am–11pm Mon–Sat; 12–10.30pm Sun.*

SEAFORD

The Wellington
Steyne Road, Seaford, East Sussex BN25 1HT
☎ *(01323) 890032 Mr Shaw*

Fuller's London Pride, Greene King IPA, Abbot and Harveys Best Bitter plus one guest from an independent or micro-brewery, changing daily.

Community pub with two bars and a function room. Parking nearby. Food available at lunchtime only. Children allowed.

OPEN *All day, every day.*

The White Lion
74 Claremont Road, Seaford, East Sussex
☎ *(01323) 892473 John Treacy*
www.whitelionhotelseaford.co.uk

Harveys Sussex Best Bitter and Fuller's London Pride plus a guest such as Shepherd Neame Spitfire, rotated monthly.

Friendly, small, family-run hotel by the seafront. Two bars and large conservatory. Food served 12–2.30pm and 6–9pm. Car park. Children welcome. En-suite accommodation. Private room for hire.

OPEN *11am–11pm.*

SEDLESCOMBE

The Queen's Head
The Green, Sedlescombe, Battle, East Sussex TN33 0QA
☎ *(01424) 870228 Samantha Fisher*

Charles Wells Bombardier plus Rother Valley Level Best and Flowers Original (brewed by Badger).

A country pub with beams and brasses, on the village green. Beer garden, car park. Food served 12–2.30pm, including fish and chips, jacket potatoes, baguettes and sandwiches. Traditional Sunday lunch in separate restaurant. Children welcome. Pool table.

OPEN *10am–11pm Mon–Sat; 12–10.30pm Sun.*

SELSY

The Seal
6 Hillfield Road, Selsy, West Sussex PO20 0JX
☎ *(01243) 602461*
www.the-seal.com

Hop Back Summer Lightning, Dark Star Hophead, Green King Old Speckled Hen, Young's Bitter, and up to four constantly changing guests, such as Harveys Sussex, Arundel Best or Oakleaf Hole Hearted.

Traditional family-run community pub. Function room available. Car park, patio and live music. Traditional food served lunchtime and evenings, and throughout the day at weekends and in the summer. West Sussex CAMRA Pub of the Year 2008.

OPEN *10.30am–11.30pm.*

SHOREHAM

The Duke of Wellington
368 Brighton Road, Shoreham-by-Sea, West Sussex BN43 6RE
☎ *(01273) 389818 Roy Chuter*

A Dark Star Brewery tied house. Hophead plus others from the Dark Star range, plus one rotating guest. Over 300 guests served in two years. All guests come from small independent brewers, perhaps Hopdaemon, Custom Ales, Red Squirrel and Triple FFF.

Built in the 1920s on the site of a former pub, by the former Kemp Town Brewery. Twenty-two original stained glass windows from the Kemp Town era remain, along with other livery. Single L-shaped bar. Well-behaved children welcome until 7.30pm. Bar billiards. Live music weekly. Three beer festivals held each year: May: UK; July/Aug: Belgian; Feb/Mar: German. No food. Five minutes' walk from Shoreham-by-Sea railway station, five miles west of Brighton on the main coast road.

OPEN *12–11pm Sun–Thurs; noon–1am Fri–Sat.*

The Lazy Toad
88 High Street, Shoreham-by-Sea, West Sussex BN43 5DB
☎ *(01273) 441622 Mr Cederberg*

Greene King Abbot, Badger Tanglefoot, Shepherd Neame Spitfire and Gale's Festival Mild among the beers always available plus up to three guests.

A small, friendly freehouse with one big bar. Food served only at lunchtime. Children over 14 allowed.

OPEN *All day, every day.*

The Red Lion
Old Shoreham Road, Shoreham-by-Sea, West Sussex BN43 5TE
☎ *(01243) 453171 Natalie Parker*
www.theredlionshoreham.co.uk

Harveys Best Bitter and four or five guest beers, perhaps from King, Hop Back, Hogs Back, Ringwood, Dark Star, Arundel, Fuller's, Cottage or more. The fastest-selling beers are changed every couple of days. Annual Easter beer festival features 50–60 beers, live music and barbecue.

Widely considered to be Shoreham's premier country pub, this 16th-century coaching house has low beams, inglenook and secluded beer garden. Good atmosphere, full of tales and history. Food served 12–2.30pm and 6–9pm Mon–Fri (until 9.30pm Fri), 12–9.30pm Sat and 12–8pm Sun. There are themed food nights Mon–Thurs, with specialities and offers available. Children welcome. The car park is situated some distance from the pub: pass the pub on your left, turn left at mini-roundabout then first left again. Follow the road to church and the car park is opposite.

OPEN *11.30am–11pm Mon–Sat; 12–10.30pm Sun.*

SHOTTERMILL

The Mill Tavern

Liphook Road, Shottermill, Haslemere, West Sussex GU27 3QE
☎ *(01428) 643183* Lee Forbes
www.themilltavern.net

 Punch Taverns tied pub with five ales, which could include Fuller's London Pride, Greene King IPA, Charles Wells Bombadier and Sharp's Doom Bar plus three weekly-changing guests.

A 500-year-old country pub with family room and restaurant. Food served 12–2.30pm and 7–9.30pm Mon–Sun. Large beer garden with children's play area. Function room available. Children welcome. Large car park. Located near Shottermill Ponds.

OPEN *12–close.*

SOUTHWICK

The Romans

Manor Hall Road, Southwick, East Sussex BN42 4NG
☎ *(01273) 592147* Chris Pobjoy
www.theromanspub.com

 Punch Taverns pub with three real ales always available. At least 24 different ales served every month.

A 1938 Charrington house, featuring original oak panelling. Two bars, one public, one lounge. Food served all day, every day. Large beer garden. Billiards room. Dog and child friendly. Car park. Function room. Two beer festivals held every year. Off the A27.

OPEN *12–11pm Mon–Thurs; 12–12 Fri; 11am–midnight Sat; 12–10.30pm Sun.*

STOUGHTON

The Hare & Hounds

Stoughton, West Sussex
☎ *(023) 9263 1433* Graham Minto

Itchen Valley Hampshire Rose, Ballard's Golden Bine, Timothy Taylor Landlord, Badger Tanglefoot and Flowerpots Bitter plus guests, changed every couple of months.

More than 300 years old, a traditional flint-built village public bar nestling in the Sussex Downs. Bar and restaurant food available at lunchtime and evenings. Car park and garden. Children welcome. Signposted at Walderton off the B2146.

OPEN *11am–3pm and 6–11pm Mon–Thurs; all day Fri–Sun. Open all day, every day Jun–Oct.*

TARRING

The Vine Inn

High Street, Tarring, Worthing, West Sussex BN14 7NN
☎ *(01903) 202891*
Stephen and Deborah Benson

Badger Dorset Best, Champion Ale and Tanglefoot, King and Barnes Sussex,

Ringwood True Glory, Hop Back Summer Lightning and Gribble Inn Fursty Ferret always available, plus guests.

Old-fashioned pub in a listed building dating from 1645. Cask Marque accredited. One bar. Live entertainment on Mondays plus a quiz every Thursday. Enormous garden and courtyard, car park. Food available 12–2.30pm and 5.30–8pm Mon–Fri and 12–2.30pm Sat–Sun. Children and dogs welcome.

OPEN *12–3pm and 6–11pm Mon–Thurs; 11am–11pm Fri–Sat; 12–10.30pm Sun.*

THAKEHAM

The White Lion Inn

The Street, Thakeham Village, West Sussex RH20 3EP
☎ *(01798) 813141* Adrian Browne

 Freehouse with Caledonian Deuchars IPA, Harveys Sussex Best and Hogs Back TEA plus one regularly changing guest. Examples include Timothy Taylor Landlord, Wychwood Dirty Tackle, Adnams Broadside, King Horsham Best plus beers from Cottage.

Traditional pub in a Grade II listed building in the centre of a picturesque village. Food, which is freshly prepared in an open-plan kitchen, served 12–2.30pm and 7–9pm (9.30pm Fri–Sat), 12–4pm Sun.

OPEN *11am–3pm and 5.30–11pm Mon–Sat; 12–10.30pm Sun.*

TICEHURST

The Bull Inn

Three Leg Cross, Nr Ticehurst, East Sussex TN5 7HH
☎ *(01580) 200586*
William Orr and Angie Perrie
www.thebullinn.co.uk

 Freehouse with three real ales, including Harveys Sussex Best plus two guests changed monthly, often local beers such as King Horsham Best Bittter, White 1066 Country Bitter and Rother Valley Level Best. Examples of others include Timothy Taylor Landlord, Gale's HSB and Greene King Old Speckled Hen.

A 13th-century beamed pub close to the Bewl Water reservoir, an ideal base for walkers and cyclists. Food served 12–2.30pm (until 3pm Sat) and 6.30–9pm Mon–Sat; 12–8pm Sun, with traditional home-cooked carvery and main menu. Two beer gardens, children's play area. B&B. Quiz night every third Wed in the month. Private party bookings. Spectacular bonfire parties. Dogs welcome. Coming into Ticehurst from the north on the B2099, turn left beside corner house called Tollgate just before village.

OPEN *12–11pm Mon–Sat; 12–10.30pm Sun.*

UCKFIELD

The Alma Arms

Framfield Road, Uckfield, East Sussex TN22 5AJ
☎ *(01825) 762232*
Phil Tucker and Jim Mahoney

Harveys house serving Mild, IPA, Best Bitter and Old, plus seasonal guests. Thatcher's cider also available.

Traditional local, refurbished in period style, with an elegant saloon bar, an atmospheric public bar and resident ghosts! Cask Marque award. Food served 12.30–2.30pm (not Tues) and 6–8pm Wed–Sat (until 9pm Fri); traditional home-cooked Sunday lunches. Beer garden, function room for hire, large car park. Theme nights, quiz night Thursday, guest chefs, regular live jazz. With the railway station on the left, head up the hill to the traffic lights near the police station, then turn left.

 *12–2.30pm and 5–11pm Mon–Wed; 11am–3pm and 5–11pm Thurs–Sat; 12–4pm and 6–10.30pm Sun.*

The Peacock Inn

Shortbridge, Piltdown, Uckfield, East Sussex TN22 3XA
☎ *(01825) 762463* Matthew Arnold

Harveys Best Bitter, Fuller's London Pride and Greene King Abbot are permanent features here.

Grade II listed 16th-century freehouse and restaurant. Food is served 12–2.30pm and 6–9.30pm, and there is a children's menu. Beer garden. Car park. Close to Bluebell Railway and Lavender Line, and 17 miles from Brighton. Off the main A272 Haywards Heath to Lewes road.

 11am–3pm and 6–11pm.

WARNHAM

The Sussex Oak at Warnham

2 Church Street, Warnham, West Sussex RH12 3SQ
☎ *(01403) 265028* Peter Nottage
www.thesussexoak.co.uk

An Enterprise Inns pub. Adnams Best, Fuller's London Pride, Young's Bitter, Timothy Taylor Landlord and two guest beers from local micro-breweries. King Old Ale or Clark's Westgate Gold are previously featured examples.

A 16th-century pub with flagstone floors and inglenook fireplace, set in beautiful walking countryside. Separate restaurant. Food served lunchtimes and evenings Mon–Fri; all day Sat–Sun. Large beer garden with outdoor smoking area. Car park. Beer festivals held on bank holiday weekends. Situated north of Horsham, off the A24.

 11am–11pm.

WARTLING

The Lamb Inn

Wartling, Nr Herstmonceux, East Sussex BN27 1RY
☎ *(01323) 832116* Robert Farncombe

Harveys Sussex Bitter plus two other real ales, rotating quarterly. King and Gribble are examples of breweries featured.

Refurbished 16th-century pub specialising in fine ales and homemade food. Food available lunchtimes and evenings in the bar and in a separate restaurant; four fresh fish dishes are a daily speciality. Children allowed. Situated one mile from Hertmonceux Castle.

 11am–3pm and 6–11pm.

WEST ASHLING

The Richmond Arms

Mill Road, West Ashling, West Sussex PO18 8EA
☎ *(01243) 575730*
Tomas and Milena Macourek
www.richmondarms.net

Greene King pub with Abbot, Old Speckled Hen and IPA, plus one or two guest ales changed weekly, such as Hook Norton Old Hooky, Bath Gem, or Greene King Ale Fresco, Chariots or Morland Tanner's Jack.

Comfortable and cosy Victorian pub with open fires, separate restaurant and skittle alley. Patio at the front. Traditional home-cooked bar and à la carte meals available at 12–2.30pm and 6–9pm Mon–Fri; 12–9pm Sat–Sun; Sunday carvery; Czech specialities also available. Well-behaved children allowed. Functions catered for. Situated one mile from Funtington and three miles from Chichester.

 11am–2.30pm and 6–11pm Mon–Fri; 11am–11pm Sat–Sun.

WEST CHILTINGTON

The Five Bells

Smock Alley, West Chiltington, West Sussex RH20 2QX
☎ *(01798) 812143* Mr Edwards

Five beers from an ever-changing range, sometimes served straight from the wood. Favoured brewers include Ballard's, Adnams, Bateman, Black Sheep, Brakspear, Bunces, Flowerpots, Exmoor, Fuller's, Harveys, Hogs Back, Hook Norton, Jennings, Rebellion, Palmers, St Austell, Shepherd Neame, Smiles, Samuel Smith, Timothy Taylor and Wells and Young's.

An attractive Edwardian-style version of a Sussex farmhouse. Bar and restaurant food available at lunchtime and evenings. Car park, conservatory and beer garden. Well-behaved children allowed. Accommodation available in five en-suite rooms. Ask for directions.

 12–3pm and 6–11pm.

WHITEMANS GREEN

The Ship

Whitemans Green, Cuckfield, West Sussex RH17 5BY
☎ *(01444) 413219* Bill Parke

A freehouse. A Harveys ale, plus up to three guests from breweries such as WJ King, Goddards, Fuller's and Greene King.

Old coaching house dating back to 1690 situated near the coast and the Bluebell Railway. One bar, food served 12–2.30pm and 6–9pm. Car park. No children allowed. Accommodation.

 12–2.30pm and 5.30–11pm (closed Wed lunch).

WILMINGTON

The Giant's Rest

The Street, Wilmington, Polegate, East Sussex
BN26 5SQ
☎ *(01323) 870207*
Adrian and Rebecca Hillman
www.giantsrest.co.uk

 Freehouse with Harveys Best, Timothy Taylor Landlord and Hop Back Summer Lightning always available.

An attractive pub set in Wilmington village within the South Downs and near 'the long man of Wilmington' chalk figure. One bar with simple pine tables and chairs. Each table has a different wooden game on it. Food served 12–3pm and 6.30–9pm Mon–Fri, 12–9pm Sat & Sun. Two B&B rooms available. Beer garden at front and rear. Car park. Well-behaved children welcome. Close to Drusilla's Zoo. Located just off the A27 between Polegate and Berwick.

OPEN *11.30am–3pm and 6–11pm Mon–Fri; 11.30am–11pm Sat; 12–10.30pm Sun.*

WORTHING

The George & Dragon

1 High Street, Tarring Village, Worthing, West Sussex BN14 7NN
☎ *(01903) 202497* Gary Cox
www.cox-inns.co.uk

 An Enterprise Inns pub. Five ales permanently available, including Directors, plus one guest, changed every two or three days. Guests, from regional and micro-breweries, have included St Austell Tribute, Timothy Taylor Landlord and beers from Dark Star.

One of the oldest pubs in Worthing, with fires, beams and no music! One big bar, darts area and restaurant. Large beer garden and patio areas with smoking areas. Children welcome. Food served 12–2pm Mon–Fri; 12–2.30pm Sat; 12–3pm Sun. Car park. Functions catered for.

OPEN *11am–11pm Mon–Fri; 11am–midnight Fri–Sat; 12–10.30pm Sun.*

The Richard Cobden

2 Cobden Road, Worthing, West Sussex BN11 4BD
☎ *(01903) 236856* Valerie and Erika Davies
www.therichardcobden.co.uk

 Greene King IPA and Abbot plus two other real ales including Young's Special always available. The guest changes every couple of days.

A traditional Victorian alehouse built in 1868, friendly and full of character. Genuine home-cooked food served 12–2pm Tues–Sat. Award-winning courtyard garden. Beer and wine festivals in summer. Children welcome in the garden. Traditional pub games.

OPEN *11am–3pm and 5.30–11pm Mon–Thurs; all day Fri–Sat; 12–4pm and 7–10.30pm Sun.*

Selden Arms

41 Lyndhurst Road, Worthing, West Sussex BN11 2DB
☎ *(01903) 523361*
Bob McKenna and Michele Preston

 Six real ales, usually including Ringwood Fortyniner, something from Dark Star and regularly rotating guests from smaller, independent breweries. A stout or mild is generally among them. Also real cider and bottled Belgian beers.

Genuine freehouse and the local CAMRA Pub of the Year several times in recent years. Popular community local with real fires, good food available at lunchtime (notably the sizeable sandwiches). Live music, outside seating. Beer festival in January. Children welcome by day. Close to Worthing hospital.

OPEN *All day, every day.*

YAPTON

The Lamb Inn

Bilsham Road, Yapton, Arundel, West Sussex BN18 0JN
☎ *(01243) 551232* Justin Whayman

Punch Taverns pub with Greene King Old Speckled Hen and Harveys Sussex Best Bitter.

Traditional beamed pub with a 200-year-old front and later additions to the rest of the building, and featuring brick and wood floors and real open fire. Food served 12–3pm Tues–Sun, and 6–9pm Tues–Sat. An old courtyard has been covered to provide a comfortable outside smoking area. Restaurant seats 44. Free Wi-Fi for customers, pool table. Large family beer garden and car park. Families and children welcome. Off the A259 towards Yapton.

OPEN *12–11pm Mon–Thurs; 12–12 Fri–Sat; 12–10.30pm Sun.*

The Maypole Inn

Maypole Lane, Yapton, Arundel, West Sussex BN18 0DP
☎ *(01243) 551417* Alan Wingate

Freehouse with six real ales on offer. King Horsham Best, Arundel Mild and Skinner's Betty Stogs are always available, plus three guests, changed daily.

Country pub with public and lounge bars, log fires, skittle alley, patio garden. Bar snacks available at lunchtime and Sunday roasts. Children allowed in the public bar only until 8.30pm. Beer festival in October.

OPEN *11.30am–close Mon–Sat; 12–close Sun.*

THE BREWERIES

BIG LAMP BREWERS
Big Lamp Brewery, Grange Road, Newburn,
Newcastle upon Tyne NE15 8NL
☎ *(0191) 267 1689*
www.keelmanslodge.co.uk

 BITTER 3.9% ABV
DOUBLE M MILLENNIUM ALE 4.3% ABV
SUMMERHILL STOUT 4.4% ABV
PRINCE BISHOP ALE 4.8% ABV
Plus occasionals including:
SUNNY DAZE 3.6% ABV
EMBERS 5.5% ABV
KEELMAN BROWN 5.7% ABV
OLD GENIE 7.4% ABV
BLACKOUT 11.0% ABV

BULL LANE BREWING COMPANY
The Clarendon, 143 High Street East, Sunderland
SR1 2BL
☎ *(0191) 510 3200*
www.bull-lane-brewing.co.uk

 BLACK BARREL 3.8% ABV
RYHOPE TUG 3.9% ABV
NOWTSA MATTA 4.0% ABV
JACK'S FLAG 4.7% ABV
Plus seasonals and specials.

DARWIN BREWERY
63 Back Tatham St, Sunderland SR1 2QE
☎ *(0191) 514 4746*
www.darwinbrewery.com

EVOLUTION ALE 4.0% ABV
Clean, dry, hoppy.
GHOST ALE 4.1% ABV
Balanced fruity flavour.
PENSHAWS 4.1% ABV
Light tan colour, malty flavour.
CAULDRON SNOUT 5.6% ABV
Winter beer, rich and hoppy, peaty finish.
KILLER BEE 6.0% ABV
Gold with honey sweetness.
Plus a range of specialist beers.

HADRIAN & BORDER BREWERY
Unit 10, Hawick Crescent Industrial Estate,
Newcastle upon Tyne NE6 1AS
☎ *(0191) 276 5302*

 VALLUM BITTER 3.6% ABV
Rich, golden bitter.
GLADIATOR 3.8% ABV
A rich, dark ruby-coloured session bitter.
FARNE ISLAND 4.0% ABV
Amber-coloured, blended malt and hops.
FLOTSAM 4.0% ABV
Dark golden-coloured.
LEGION ALE 4.2% ABV
Malt flavour.
REIVER'S IPA 4.4% ABV
Award-winning bitter with citrus throughout.
CENTURION BITTER 4.5% ABV
Award-winning, pale-coloured, hoppy bitter,
fruity and quenching.
Plus seasonals and specials.

JARROW BREWERY COMPANY
The Robin Hood, Primrose Hill, Jarrow NE32 5UB
☎ *(0191) 483 6792*

JARROW BITTER 3.8% ABV
RIVET CATCHER 4.0% ABV
JOBLING'S SWINGING GIBBET 4.1% ABV
WESTOE CROWN 4.2% ABV
WESTOE NETTY SPECIAL 4.3% ABV
RED ELLEN 4.4% ABV
VENERABLE BEAD 4.5% ABV
MCCONNELL'S IRISH STOUT 4.6% ABV
WESTOE IPA 4.6% ABV
OLD CORNELIUS 4.8% ABV
Plus seasonals and specials.

MORDUE BREWERY
D1/D2, Narvik Way, Tyne Tunnel Trading
Estate, North Shields NE29 7XJ
☎ *(0191) 296 1879*
www.morduebrewery.com

FIVE BRIDGE BITTER 3.8% ABV
Fruity and amber coloured.
GEORDIE PRIDE 4.2% ABV
Hoppy bitter.
WORKIE TICKET 4.5% ABV
Complex malt and hop balance.
RADGIE GADGIE 4.8% ABV
Long, lingering finish.
INDIA PALE ALE 5.1% ABV
Dry bitter.
Plus seasonals and specials.

THE PUBS

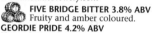

BYKER

The Cumberland Arms
Off Byker Bank, The Ouseburn, Byker,
Newcastle upon Tyne NE6 1LD
☎ *(0191) 265 6151* The Hodson family
www.thecumberlandarms.co.uk

Freehouse with a house ale rotating
between Wylam Rapper and Jarrow JB,
plus three constantly changing guests from
breweries such as Allendale, Big Lamp, Bull
Lane, Consett, Derwent, Durham, Hadrian &
Border, Hexhamshire, High House Farm,
Mordue, Northumberland, Old Bear, Rudgate,
Wentworth and Wear Valley. Beers usually
available by both pump and gravity straight
from the cask.

Established in 1832, this CAMRA award-
winning pub (National Inventory of Pub
Interiors and Cider Pub of the Year for the
North-East 2007) is 15 minutes' walk from
the city centre, overlooking the lush green
Ouseburn Valley with its preserved industrial
buildings and a section of Hadrian's Wall.
Food served all day (limited menu after
9pm). Real open fires for the colder nights,
plus south-facing beer garden with real-ale-
themed smoking shelters for summer
evenings. Four B&B rooms. Free live music
sessions, pub quiz. Fully 'teched-out' venue
(capacity 100) for hire, hosting a variety of
band nights, comedy, poetry and more.
Leaving Newcastle centre, over Byker Bridge,
at the major roundabout turn right (Byker
Bank) and second right (cul-de-sac).

3–11pm Mon–Fri (midnight Wed and
Fri); 12.30pm–12 Sat; 12.30–11pm Sun.

The Free Trade Inn

*St Lawrence Road, Byker, Newcastle upon Tyne
NE6 1AP*
☎ *(0191) 265 5764* Richard Turner

Mordue Workie Ticket and a Mordue seasonal ale plus four guest beers, from local breweries such as Hadrian & Border, Wylam or Cropton.

Town pub with a lovely view of the River Tyne. Two beer gardens, one bar. Sandwiches available. Children allowed during the daytime and early evening only.

OPEN *11am–11pm (10.30pm Sun).*

CRAWCROOK

The Rising Sun Inn

Bank Top, Ryton, Crawcrook NE40 4EE
☎ *(0191) 413 3316* Pauline Baxter

Up to five real ales from a mixture of local and national independent brewers, including two or three guests.

Old coaching inn, extended over the years. Food served 12–9pm Mon–Sat and 12–7pm Sun. Children welcome. Beer garden. Car park. South of Gateshead, between Blaydon and Prudhoe.

OPEN *11.30am–11pm Mon–Thurs; 11.30am–midnight Fri–Sat; 12–11pm Sun.*

FELLING

The Old Fox

13 Carlisle Street, Felling, Gateshead NE10 0HQ
☎ *(0191) 454 1038* Mark Horn

Freehouse with eight real ales: Camerons Strong Arm and Castle Eden Ale plus six guests, constantly changing, such as St Austell Tribute, Wychwood Hobgoblin, Fuller's London Pride, O'Hanlon's Firefly and Everards Tiger.

Traditional real ale pub, with real fire and beer garden. No food. Regular beer festivals. Car park to rear. Children welcome until 7pm. Regular buskers' nights Mon and Thurs. Close to Felling Metro station. Easy access to the coast and central Newcastle.

OPEN *11am–11pm Mon–Thurs; 11am–midnight Fri–Sat; 12–11pm Sun.*

The Wheatsheaf

26 Carlisle Street, Felling, Gateshead NE10 0HQ
☎ *(0191) 420 0659* Jim Storey

A range of Big Lamp beers such as Bitter, Prince Bishop, Premium Ale, Sandgates or Keelman Bitter always available.

Old-fashioned community pub with one bar tied to the Big Lamp brewery. Sandwiches and pies available. Children allowed until 7pm.

OPEN *12–11pm (10.30pm Sun).*

GATESHEAD

The Borough Arms

82 Bensham Road, Gateshead Ne8 1PS
☎ *(0191) 478 1323* Peter Arnold

Enterprise Inns pub with Charles Wells Bombardier and Wylam's Gold Tankard plus three guests, usually from local micro-breweries.

A traditional pub, approximately 300 years old. Open-plan bar and lounge. No food. Beer garden. Car park. Children allowed in the garden only. Live music fortnightly. Five minutes from Tyne Bridge, next to Gateshead Metro interchange.

OPEN *12–3.30pm and 6–11.30pm Mon–Thurs; 12–12 Fri–Sat; 12–11.30pm Sun.*

GOSFORTH

Gosforth Hotel

High Street, Gosforth
☎ *(0191) 285 6617* Yvonne Goulden

Eight real ales, including Charles Wells Bombardier, Fuller's London Pride, Marston's Pedigree, Black Sheep Bitter, Timothy Taylor Landlord, Bass, Tetley and Mordue Workie Ticket. Plus one rotating guest beer.

Busy two-bar pub with a friendly atmosphere. Bar food available 12–7pm Mon–Fri, 12–5pm Sat and 12–3pm Sun. Car parking opposite pub. No children.

OPEN *12–11pm (10.30pm Sun).*

JARROW

The Robin Hood Inn

Primrose Hill, Jarrow NE32 5UB
☎ *(0191) 428 5454* Jess and Alison McConnell
www.jarrowbrewery.co.uk

Five Jarrow ales plus an ever-changing guest list.

Dating back to 1824, this former coaching inn housed the multi-award winning Jarrow Brewery operation from its inauguration in 2002 until 2008 when all brewing was transferred to The Maltings in South Shields. Public bar, restaurant and conservatory overlooking the river, and a very popular Beer and Music Hall which replaced the brewing space. The pub has won many awards, including CAMRA Best Pub in Britain 2006. Close to the Bede's World monastery attraction and situated a six-minute walk from Fellgate railway station.

OPEN *12–11pm Sun–Thurs, 12–11.30pm Fri–Sat.*

JESMOND

The Archer

*Archibold Terrace, Jesmond,
Newcastle upon Tyne NE2 1DB*
☎ *(0191) 281 3010* Richard Norris

Black Sheep Bitter and Caledonian Deuchars IPA always available.

Formerly known as Legendary Yorkshire Heroes and with fewer real ales than before. But a lively refurbished pub within an office complex. Bar food available on weekday lunchtimes. Four pool tables, big-screen sports, live bands Thurs and Sat. Children allowed at lunchtimes only. Five minutes out of Newcastle centre, five minutes from Jesmond Metro.

OPEN *11am–11pm Mon–Sat; 12–10.30pm Sun.*

LOW FELL

The Ale Taster

*706 Durham Road, Low Fell, Gateshead
NE9 6JA*
☎ *(0191) 487 0770* Lawrence Gill

Mordue Workie Ticket and Radgie Gadgie plus up to six guests such as Timothy Taylor Landlord or Badger Tanglefoot. Beer festivals held in May and September, serving 30 extra beers.

An old coaching inn with beams and wooden floors, in the town centre. One bar, snug area, large courtyard with play area. Food available until 6pm. Children allowed.

OPEN *11am–11pm Mon–Sat; 12–10.30pm Sun.*

NEWBURN

The Keelman

*Grange Road, Newburn, Newcastle upon Tyne
NE15 8NL*
☎ *(0191) 267 1689* Lee Goulding

Owned by Big Lamp Brewery, with Bitter, Prince Bishop Ale, Premium, Summerhill Stout and other brews regularly available.

Superb conversion of 19th-century water board building into a traditional family pub. Situated next to the leisure centre in Newburn Country Park, on the River Tyne. Food served daily 12–9pm. Car park, beer garden with children's play area. Accommodation.

OPEN *11am–11pm Mon–Sat; 12–10.30pm Sun.*

NEWCASTLE UPON TYNE

The Bodega

*125 Westgate Road, Newcastle upon Tyne
NE1 4AG*
☎ *(0191) 221 1552* Ben Rea

Mordue Workie Ticket, Geordie Pride and Durham Magus plus two guests from breweries such as Hadrian & Border, Shepherd Neame, Black Sheep and Ridleys, changed every three days.

A traditional real ale pub on the outskirts of the town centre. One bar, food available 11am–2.30pm Mon–Sat and 12–2.30pm Sun. No children.

OPEN *11am–11pm Mon–Sat; 12–10.30pm Sun.*

The Bridge Hotel

Castlegart, Newcastle upon Tyne NE1 1RQ
☎ *(0191) 232 6400* Christine Cromarty

Freehouse with Black Sheep Bitter and Mordue Workie Ticket, plus three constantly changing guest beers, perhaps Hadrian & Border Gladiator, Castle Eden Nimmo's 4X, Hexhamshire Whapweasel, or something from Caledonian, Everards, Ridleys or Adnams.

A 100-year-old town-centre real ale pub with a function room, terrace and garden overlooking the Tyne Bridge and the quayside. Food available at lunchtimes (12–2pm and 12–3pm Sun). Live music in function room, folk club Monday night, jazz on Tuesdays. No children. Situated opposite the castle and above the quayside.

OPEN *11.30am–11pm Mon–Sat;
12–10.30pm Sun.*

The Cluny

36 Lime Street, Newcastle upon Tyne NE1 2PQ
☎ *(0191) 230 4474* Julian Ive
www.theheadofsteam.co.uk

Genuine freehouse, with up to seven real ales on offer, mostly from local independents, such as Wylam, Mordue, Durham and Hadrian & Border.

Operating since November 2003, part of the Head of Steam group of freehouses. Food served 11.30am–9pm daily. Children welcome until 7pm. Function room. Regular beer festivals held. Just outside central Newcastle, in the Ouseburn Valley.

OPEN *11.30am–11pm Mon–Thurs; 11.30am–
midnight Fri–Sat; 12–10.30pm Sun.*

The Cooperage

*32 The Close, Quayside, Newcastle-upon-Tyne
NE1 3RF*
☎ *(0191) 233 2940* Leon Gingell

An Enterprise Inns pub. Five real ales, changed daily, such as Hop Back Summer Lightning and High House Maften Magic. A mixture of national and local breweries.

Built in 1535, this pub is a National Trust Grade I listed, timber-framed and stone building, with lots of character. Three stories, three bars plus two function rooms and a live music venue/nightclub. Food served 9am–3pm Mon–Fri; 2–9pm Sat. Off-street parking. Situated on Newcastle quayside, under High Level Bridge.

OPEN *9am–3am (when nightclub open) Mon–
Fri; 2pm–3am Sat; closed Sun.*

Crown Posada

31 The Side, Newcastle upon Tyne NE1 3JE
☎ *(0191) 232 1269* Derek Raisbeck

Freehouse owned by the Sir John Fitzgerald group. Six real ales always available. Timothy Taylor Landlord, Hadrian Gladiator and Jarrow Bitter permanent, plus three guests.

Steeped in history, with stained glass windows and pre-Raphaelite ceilings, and dating from the 18th century. One snug, one bar. No food. Located beneath the Tyne Bridge, next to the river.

OPEN *11am–11pm Mon–Sat; 7pm–10.30pm
Sun.*

The Head of Steam

2 Neville Street, Newcastle upon Tyne NE1 5EN
☎ *(0191) 230 4236* Steve Caulker
www.theheadofsteam.co.uk

Freehouse with up to four real ales from breweries such as Black Sheep, Sam Smith, Wylam, Mordue and Hadrian & Border, plus a variety of bottled real ales including beers from Timothy Taylor and Allendale.

A two-bar pub in a great location opposite the train station. The downstairs bar is a live music venue at night with a capacity of 90. No children.

OPEN *Noon–1am (midnight Sun).*

The Hotspur

Haymarket, Newcastle upon Tyne
☎ *(0191) 232 4352* Richard Steel

Leased from Punch by the creator of the Tap & Spile chain. Eight real ales including Greene King Ruddles County, Timothy Taylor Landlord, Black Sheep Bitter and Charles Wells Bombardier plus four guests changed daily, such as Caledonian Deuchars IPA.

Very busy traditional alehouse, refurbished in 2008 to restore the building's great architectural features. The pub offers a friendly welcome and attracts discerning ale drinkers from all walks of life, including students and young professionals. Toasted sandwiches available all day. Beer alley with smoking solution and big-screen TV for sports enthusiasts. Located opposite Haymarket Bus Station.

OPEN *11am–11pm Sun–Thurs; 11am–midnight Fri–Sat.*

Newcastle Arms

57 St Andrews Street, NE1 5ES
☎ *(0191) 260249* Neil Amos
www.newcastlearms.co.uk

Caledonian Deuchars IPA plus five daily-changing guests, sourced from all over the country and perhaps including Thornbridge Jaipur IPA, Highland Orkney Best and Brewdog Paradox.

A Trust inn, built in 1903. One room with original curved windows and mosaics. Annual beer festivals in February and June. Tyneside and Northumberland CAMRA Pub of the Year 2006, 2007 and 2008. Located next to Chinatown, between St James's Park and The Gate. Gets very busy on match days.

OPEN *11am–11pm Mon–Sat; 12–10.30pm Sun.*

The Tut & Shive

52 Clayton Street West, Newcastle upon Tyne NE1 4EX
☎ *(0191) 261 6998*

A Castle Eden ale and Black Sheep Bitter always available.

Friendly, relaxed city-centre pub with a mixed clientele, from students to OAPs! Weekly promotional discounts on draught and bottles. No food. Live music up to five nights a week, plus pool knockouts every Sunday. No children. Two minutes from the Central Station.

OPEN *11am–11pm (12–11pm in summer) Mon–Sat; 12–10.30pm Sun.*

The Three Horseshoes

Washington Road, North Hylton, Sunderland SR5 3HZ
☎ *(0191) 536 4183* Frank Nicol

Four real ales. Greene King Old Speckled Hen and Caledonian Deuchars IPA plus two rotating guests. Annual beer festival held at the end of July.

A traditional 200-year-old country pub with two bars (public and lounge), separate dining area, open fire, pool, darts etc. Food available 12–2.30pm daily and 6–9.30pm

(not Sun). Children allowed. Follow signs for Air Museum, by Nissan entrance. B&B accommodation.

OPEN *11am–11pm Mon–Sat; 12–10.30pm Sun.*

The Garricks Head

Saville Street, North Shields NE30 1NT
☎ *(0191) 296 2064* Ken Liddell/Janice Duffin

Genuine freehouse with four pumps all serving weekly-changing real ales, such as Greene King Old Speckled Hen, Charles Wells Bombardier, Marston's Pedigree, Young's Special and Hartleys XB.

Traditional Victorian town pub with one bar, upstairs function room and restaurant. Food available throughout the day. Children welcome in the restaurant only. Live music, karaoke and quiz nights.

OPEN *11am–11pm Mon–Thurs; 11am–midnight Fri–Sat; 12–10.30pm Sun.*

The Magnesia Bank

1 Camden Street, North Shields NE30 1NH
☎ *(0191) 257 4831*
Richard, Dee and Kate Slade
www.magnesiabank.com

The brewery tap for Mordue, so Workie Ticket, Geordie Pride, Radgie Gadgie and seasonals are regularly featured, as is Durham Magus, plus five guest ales. The selection changes daily and comes from regional and micro-brewers around the country.

A true freehouse, family-owned and winner of the *Morning Advertiser*'s Freehouse of Britain 2001 and a *Publican* food award in 2004. Good range of food, specialising in fresh fish and local lamb and beef, available 12–9.45pm Mon–Sat and 11.30am–8.45pm Sun. Live music three nights a week. Children allowed until 9pm. Function suite available for hire, four beer festivals held annually. No juke box or games machines. The pub also has its own flock of lambs. Situated close to North Shields fish quay, opposite the Beacon Centre shoppers' car park.

OPEN *11am–midnight Mon–Fri; 10am–midnight Sat; 11am–11.30pm Sun.*

The Porthole

11 New Quay, North Shields NE29 6LQ
☎ *(0191) 257 6645* Michael Read

Directors, Bass. Guests include Durham Magus, Jarrow Rivet Catcher, Northumberland Pit Pony, Consett, Steeltown, High House, Nell's Best and many more.

Traditional, nautical-themed pub of tremendous character next to the Tyne ferry, renowned for its live daytime jazz sessions (Tues, Wed and Fri starts 1pm) and live music (Wed, Fri, Sat and Sun starts 9pm). Bar and separate lounge. Food served until 9pm. Children allowed until 8pm in lounge, dogs welcome. Smoking shelter, free barbeque use, outside seating. Car park.

OPEN *11am–midnight Mon–Thurs; 11am–1am Fri–Sat; 12–12 Sun.*

Shiremoor House Farm

Middle Engine Lane, North Shields NE29 8DZ
☎ *(0191) 257 6302* Bill Kerridge

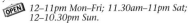 Freehouse with Mordue Workie Ticket plus up to five guests such as Moorhouse's Pendle Witches Brew, Jennings Cumberland, Timothy Taylor Landlord or Durham Brewery's Celtic. Beers changed two or three times a week.

Converted farmhouse with two bars, stone floors and separate restaurant. Food available 12–10pm daily. Children allowed.

 11am–11pm (10.30pm Sun).

The Tap & Spile

184 Tynemouth Road, North Shields NE30 1EG
☎ *(0191) 257 2523* J O'Keefe

A selection of up to eight real ales from a large and varied list. Beers from the Durham brewery usually feature.

A real ale bar with a friendly atmosphere. Bar food served at lunchtime Tues–Sat. Parking. Opposite the magistrates court in North Shields. Beer festivals held four times a year.

12–11pm Mon–Fri; 11.30am–11pm Sat; 12–10.30pm Sun.

RYTON

Ye Olde Cross

Barmoor Lane, Old Ryton Village, Gateshead NE40 3QP
☎ *(0191) 413 4689*

Tied to Enterprise Inns, with Charles Wells Bombardier plus two guests changed every week, such as Caledonian Deuchars IPA, Wylam Gold Tankard or Summer Magic, or Black Sheep Bitter.

Over 100 years old, and retaining an olde-worlde charm, this is a family-oriented pub where children are welcome. There is a secret garden to the rear and a beer garden at the front. Traditional homemade food served 4–8pm Thurs–Fri; 12–8pm Sat; 12–4pm Sun. Upstairs function room. Beer festival held in May. Turn right from Ryton Main Street into the village.

4–11pm Mon–Fri; 12–12 Sat; 12–11pm Sun.

SOUTH SHIELDS

The Dolly Peel

137 Commercial Road, South Shields NE33 1SQ
☎ *(0191) 427 1441*

Timothy Taylor Landlord and Black Sheep Bitter plus guest ales from breweries throughout the UK.

Traditional suburban pub with outside seating. Named after an 18th-century smuggler – details on request! No juke box, pool table, darts or bandits, just good conversation and excellent beer in pleasant surroundings. Sandwiches available.

11am–11pm Mon–Sat; 12–10.30pm Sun.

Holborn Rose & Crown

Hill Street, South Shields NE33 1RN
☎ *(0191) 455 2379* Bob Overton

Two real ales usually served, often from Marston's, Bateman, Fuller's, Black Sheep or Mordue breweries.

One-roomed traditional freehouse with beer garden, opposite the old middle docks. Toasted sandwiches available. Children welcome during daytime only.

11am–11pm Mon–Sat; 12–10.30pm Sun.

The Maltings

9 Claypath Lane, South Shields NE33 4PG
☎ *(0191) 427 7147*
Jess and Alison McConnell
www.jarrowbrewery.co.uk

Six permanent Jarrow Brewery ales and four seasonals brewed on the premises, plus an ever-changing list of guest ales from around the country.

All Jarrow's brewing operation takes place on the ground floor of this former dairy, while the first floor pub, accessible from a grand staircase of brewery memorabilia, has the décor and atmosphere of a Victorian gentlemen's club. Bar lunches served daily. Live acoustic entertainment Fri-Sat. Quiz nights Wed, Sun. Located opposite the town hall.

12–11pm Sun–Thurs; 12–11.30pm Fri–Sat.

The Riverside

3 Mill Dam, South Shields NE33 1EQ
☎ *(0191) 444 2328* Paul Hedley

Six real ales, including Timothy Taylor Landlord and Black Sheep Special plus two guest beers from micro-breweries around the UK and one cask cider.

Smallish, well-decorated pub offering a friendly welcome. Background music, very busy at weekends, with a clientele mostly over 30. On the B1302, close to ferry landing, market place and customs house.

12–12.

The Steamboat

Milldam, South Shields NE33 1EQ
☎ *(0191) 454 0134* Joe Mooney

A Punch Taverns pub. Caledonian Deuchars IPA, Charles Wells Bombardier and Wychwood Hobgoblin, plus three guests, changed twice-weekly. Guest ales may include Bath Ales Barnstormer, Elgood's Old Wagg, Shepherd Neame Bishops Finger, Titanic Stout and Mauldons White and Black Adder.

A traditional 200-year-old sea-farer's pub, located near the river Tyne. There is a smuggler's tunnel and a resident ghost called Captain Jack. Hot and cold snacks available all day. Children and pets welcome. Two beer festivals each year in spring and autumn.

12–11pm Mon–Wed; 12–12 Thurs–Sat; 12–11.30pm Sun.

SUNDERLAND

Fitzgeralds

10–12 Green Terrace, Sunderland SR1 3PZ
☎ *(0191) 567 0852* Mat Alldis

A constantly changing selection of nine real ales from all over Britain. Beers from Durham and Rooster's are regularly featured, and all the ales are changed daily.

One of Sunderland's most popular bars, this traditional, high-quality city-centre alehouse has two bars and attracts a mature, discerning clientele. Food is available until 3pm every day. Popular on match days, both pre- and post-match. Sky TV (three screens). Beer garden. In the middle of an 'evening economy area'.

OPEN *11am–11pm Mon–Thurs; 11am–midnight Fri–Sat; 12–10.30pm Sun.*

The King's Arms

1 Hanover Place, Deptford, Sunderland SR4 6BU
☎ *(0191) 567 9804* Lucie Young

Freehouse with up to nine real ales including Timothy Taylor Landlord. All guests come from micro- and independent brewers and are constantly changing. Also one cask cider.

Built circa 1830 and of historical interest. One bar and a marquee. Toasted sandwiches available all day, every day. Beer garden. Live music in summer. CAMRA's North East Pub of the Year 2006, 2007 and 2008. Close to the river.

OPEN *11am–11pm Mon–Thurs; 11am–midnight Fri–Sat; 12–10.30pm Sun.*

SUNNISIDE

The Potter's Wheel

Sun Street, Sunniside, Newcastle upon Tyne NE16 5EE
☎ *(0191) 488 6255* Richard Steel

Five hand pumps serve Caledonian Deuchars IPA plus four guests, changed every week.

Welcoming community pub with bar, lounge, dining area and beer terrace. A 'Britain in Bloom' winner for seven consecutive years. Food served 12–10pm Mon–Sat and 12–6pm Sun. Live music Sunday evenings. Children's certificate. Car park. Two minutes from Tanfield Railway and ten minutes from Beamish Museum.

OPEN *11am–11pm Mon–Thurs; 11am–midnight Fri–Sat; 12–10.30pm Sun.*

TYNEMOUTH

The Cumberland Arms

17 Front Street, Tynemouth NE30 4DX
☎ *(0191) 257 1820* David Irving
www.cumberlandarms.co.uk

Jennings Cumberland, Theakston Best Bitter, Courage Directors and up to six rotating guests.

Friendly, local traditional pub with one bar and one lounge. Cask Marque accredited. Food served in separate restaurant 12–8pm

Mon–Thurs and 12–5pm Fri–Sun. Children welcome in restaurant area. Big-screen plasma TV for sport. Two minutes from Tynemouth Metro station.

OPEN *12–11pm (10.30pm Sun).*

Tynemouth Lodge Hotel

Tynemouth Road, Tynemouth NE30 4AA
☎ *(0191) 257 7565* Hugh Price
www.tynemouthlodgehotel.co.uk

Freehouse with Caledonian Deuchars IPA and Belhaven 80/- plus one guest, changed up to three times a week.

Unspoilt, Georgian, one-room bar built in 1799. No TV, music, pub games or hot food. Cold pies available. No children, except in the garden. Beer garden. Car park. Five minutes from Tynemouth Metro station.

OPEN *11am–11pm Mon–Sat; 12–10.30pm Sun.*

WARDLEY

The Green

White Mare Pool, Wardley, Gateshead NE10 8YB
☎ *(0191) 495 0171* Deborah Mackay

Freehouse with six guest ales. Timothy Taylor Landlord, Jennings Cumberland, Big Lamp Bitter, Black Sheep Special and Oakham American Blonde are some of the regular features.

A traditional village pub with one bar and one lounge. Patio and restaurant. Disabled facilities. Food available all day, every day. Children allowed in the lounge if eating.

OPEN *11.30am–11pm Mon–Sat; 12–10.30pm Sun.*

WASHINGTON

The Courtyard

Arts Centre Washington, Biddick Lane, Fatfield, Washington NE38 8AB
☎ *(0191) 417 0445* Martin Thompson

Freehouse serving Timothy Taylor Landlord plus six constantly rotating guests all from micro-breweries. Real cider and perry also available.

A converted farm building, this pub is located within a council-run arts centre and features an open-plan café/bar with a light, airy feel and plenty of character. Separate bar in function room. Outside patio area in courtyard. Local arts and crafts on sale. Food served 11.30am–2.30pm daily. Beer garden. Disabled access. Car park. Oversized lined pint glasses, Cask Marque accredited.

OPEN *11am–11pm Mon–Thurs; 11am–midnight Fri–Sat; 12–11pm Sun.*

The Sandpiper

Easby Road, Biddick, Washington NE38 7NN
☎ *(0191) 416 0038* Gill Cardy

Owned by Greene King, with five beers on offer. Abbot and Old Speckled Hen, Caledonian Deuchars IPA, Black Sheep Bitter and Timothy Taylor Landlord would be a typical selection, and two of the beers are changed every four to six weeks.

Locals' village community pub with bar, lounge and a friendly atmosphere. Food available 12–7.30pm Mon–Fri, 12–3.30pm Sat and 12–2.30pm Sun. Children welcome until 7.30pm. Balcony with seating. Car park.

OPEN *12–11pm Mon–Thurs; 11am–11pm Fri–Sat; 12–10.30pm Sun.*

The Steps

47–49a Spout Lane, Washington NE38 7HP
☎ *(0191) 415 0733* Gary McLelland

Up to four real ales changed every two to three days, from a variety of breweries based mainly in the North East.

A real village pub with real ale and real people. One-room lounge bar. Food served daily 12–2.30pm with roasts on Sun, plus themed food nights (fish and feather, 6–8pm Tues; steak 4–8pm Thurs). Quiz nights on Wed and Sun. Bar games and darts. Big-screen Sky Sports and occasional live music.

OPEN *12–11pm (10.30pm Sun).*

WEST BOLDON

The Black Horse

Rectory Bank, West Boldon NE36 0QQ
☎ *(0191) 536 1814* Sarah Reid

Darwin Black Horse and Black Sheep Bitter plus one monthly-changing guest.

Traditional village pub dating from the 17th century. Food served all day, every day, except Sun evening. Beer garden. Car park. Just off the A19, next to St Nicholas church.

OPEN *11am–11pm Mon–Sat; 12–10.30pm Sun.*

WESTMOOR

George Stephenson Inn

Great Lime Road, Westmoor, Newcastle upon Tyne NE12 0NJ
☎ *(0191) 268 1073* Richard Costello

Four real ales, including two constantly changing guests, one of them usually from a local micro-brewery.

Community beer-drinker's pub with lounge, bar and garden. Adult clientele, no games, live music every Wednesday, Thursday and Saturday. No food. No children.

OPEN *12–11pm (10.30pm Sun).*

WHITLEY BAY

The Briar Dene

71 The Links, Whitley Bay NE26 1UE
☎ *(0191) 252 0926* Susan Gibson

Eight different real ales available at any one time, always changing and often something new – every day is a beer festival!

Award-winning seafront pub with one bar, family room and lounge. Good food available 12–2.30pm and 6–8.45pm. Large car park.

OPEN *11am–11pm Mon–Sat; 12–10.30pm Sun.*

The Fat Ox

278 Whitley Road, Whitley Bay NE26 2TG
☎ *(0191) 251 3852* JP Cowings

Eight monthly-changing real ales, including favourites such as Marston's Pedigree, Black Sheep Bitter and Greene King Old Speckled Hen, plus beers from a wide range of breweries around the UK.

A traditional one-bar town-centre pub with a small beer garden. Live bands on Friday and Saturday nights, big-screen TV. No food. No children. Disabled facilities. In the centre of Whitley Bay.

OPEN *12–11pm Mon–Fri; 11am–11pm Sat; 12–10.30pm Sun.*

Ye Olde Fat Ox

Holywell Village, Whitley Bay NE25 0LJ
☎ *(0191) 237 0964* Carol Forster

Punch Taverns house serving three or four real ales, all changed weekly. Regulars include Caledonian Deuchars IPA, Greene King Old Speckled Hen, Ruddles County and brews from Black Sheep.

Old-fashioned pub with character. One bar, supplying three separate areas. Bar snacks served 12–8pm. Large, well-planted beer garden facing the local dean and fields. Children welcome. Well-behaved dogs on leads allowed. Situated on the main road in the centre of the village.

OPEN *12–11pm Sun–Thurs; noon–12.30am Fri–Sat.*

THE BREWERIES

ATOMIC BREWERY
*c/o Sounds Expensive, 12 Regent Street, Rugby
CV21 2QF*
☎ (01788) 542170
www.atomicbrewery.com

ATOMIC STRIKE 3.7% ABV
ATOMIC FUSION 4.1% ABV
ATOMIC BOMB 5.2% ABV
Plus seasonals and specials.

CHURCH END BREWERY LTD
109 Ridge Lane, Nuneaton CV10 0RD
☎ (01827) 713080
www.churchendbrewery.co.uk

CUTHBERTS 3.8% ABV
WHAT THE FOX'S HAT 4.2% ABV
WITHOUT A BIX 4.2% ABV
POOH BEER 4.3% ABV
VICAR'S RUIN 4.4% ABV
STOUT COFFIN 4.6% ABV
Plus an extensive range of seasonal ales including:
POACHER'S POCKET 3.5% ABV
GOAT'S MILK 3.8% ABV
GRAVE DIGGERS 3.8% ABV
SHAKES BEER 4.0% ABV
HOPGUN 4.1% ABV
EXCOMMUNICATED 5.0% ABV
FALLEN ANGEL 5.0% ABV
HOLY BONES 5.0% ABV
INDIA GREEN ALE 5.0% ABV
IPA 5.0% ABV
YUL BRYNNER'S 5.2% ABV
OLD PAL 5.5% ABV

PURITY BREWING COMPANY
*The Brewery, Upper Spernall Farm, Off Spernall
Lane, Great Alne BA9 6JF*
☎ (01789) 488007
www.puritybrewing.com

PURE GOLD 3.8% ABV
PURE UBU 4.5% ABV

RUGBY BREWING COMPANY
Unit 2–6 Upton Road, Rugby CV22 7DL
☎ 0845 0091626

1823 3.5% ABV
TWICKERS 3.7% ABV
VICTORIOUS 4.2% ABV
WEBB ELLIS 3.8% ABV
NO.8 5.0% ABV
Plus seasonals and specials.

SLAUGHTERHOUSE BREWERY
Bridge Street, Warwick CV34 5PD
☎ (01926) 490986
www.slaughterhousebrewery.com

SADDLEBACK BEST BITTER 3.8% ABV
SOW WESTER 4.2% ABV
HOG GOBLIN 4.6% ABV
HOG TOBERFEST 5.0% ABV
WILD BOAR 5.2%ABV
Plus seasonals and specials.

TUNNEL BREWERY
*Lord Nelson Inn, Birmingham Road, Ansley,
Nuneaton CV10 9PQ*
☎ (024) 7639 6450
www.tunnelbrewery.co.uk

LATE OTT BITTER 4.0% ABV
TRADE WINDS IPA 4.6% ABV
SWEET PARISH ALE 4.7% ABV
NELSON'S COLUMN 5.2% ABV
Plus seasonals and occasionals.

WARWICKSHIRE BEER CO. LTD
*Cubbington Brewery, Queen Street, Cubbington,
Leamington Spa CV32 7NA*
☎ (01926) 450747
www.warwickshirebeer.co.uk

SHAKESPEAR COUNTY 3.4% ABV
BEST BITTER 3.9% ABV
LADY GODIVA 4.2% ABV
FALSTAFF 4.4% ABV
GOLDEN BEAR 4.9% ABV
XMAS BARE 4.9% ABV
Christmas brew.
KING MAKER 5.5% ABV

WIZARD ALES
*The Hops, Whichford, Shipstone-on-Stour
CV36 5PE*
☎ (01608) 684355
www.wizardales.co.uk

APPRENTICE 3.6% ABV
BLACK MAGIC 4.0% ABV
ONE FOR THE TOAD 4.0% ABV
MOTHER IN LAW 4.2% ABV
SORCERER 4.3% ABV
WHITE WITCH 4.5% ABV
BULLFROG 4.8% ABV
DRUID'S FLUID 5.0% ABV
BAH HUMBUG 5.8% ABV

THE PUBS

ALCESTER

Lord Nelson
69 Priory Road, Alcester B49 5EA
☎ (01789) 762632 Dennis and Brenda Stubbs

Greene King IPA and Charles Wells
Bombardier are the permanent beers,
plus one other real ale, varying weekly.

Parts of this pub date back 600 years. There
is a mature beer garden, a bar with darts
and bar billiards and a restaurant area. Food
is available 7–9am (booking essential for
breakfasts), 12–2pm Fri–Sun and 7–9pm
Mon–Sat, with roasts on Sundays. Car park.
Children welcome. Accommodation.

 6–11pm Mon–Thurs (closed Mon–Thurs
lunch except for special occasions);
12–3pm and 6–11pm Fri–Sat;
12–3pm and 7–10.30pm Sun.

The Three Tuns
34 High Street, Alcester B49 5AB
☎ *(01789) 762626* P Burdett

 Hobsons Best and Goff's Jouster plus six guest ales from independent breweries, with Greene King and Salopian brews making regular appearances.

A 16th-century public house with open-plan bar, converted back from a wine bar. Beer festivals are held every three months.

OPEN *12–11pm (10.30pm Sun).*

ARMSCOTE
The Fox & Goose
Armscote, Nr Stratford-upon-Avon CV37 8DD
☎ *(01608) 682293* Paul Stevens
www.foxandgoose.co.uk

Genuine freehouse always serving two real ales, such as Shepherd Neame Spitfire or Hook Norton Old Hooky, plus one rotating guest.

B usy, privately owned inn, formerly two cottages and a blacksmith's forge, totally refurbished in a very distinctive style. The bar features an open fire, flagstone floors, squishy velvet cushions and plenty of reading matter. Scrumptious, creative menu created from fresh produce served 12–2.30pm and 7–9pm. The garden has a large grassy area, a decked space and 20 seats for dining under the vines and enjoying lovely country views. Accommodation in four delightfully eccentric luxury en-suite rooms named after Cluedo characters! George Fox, founder of the Quakers, once visited the village, and the Fosse Way Roman road (now the A429) is only a mile away.

OPEN *12–3pm and 6–11.30pm.*

ASHBY ST LEDGERS
The Olde Coach House Inn
Ashby St Ledgers, Nr Rugby CV23 8UN
☎ *(01788) 890349*
Pete and Christine Ballinger

Everards Old Original plus six guest ales (200 per year) including Hop Back Summer Lightning, Hook Norton Haymaker, Frog Island Natterjack, Adnams Broadside and beers from Timothy Taylor.

A n olde-English converted farmhouse in the middle of a historic village. Lots of family tables and small intimate nooks and crannies. Large secure garden for children. Plenty of parking space. Bar and restaurant food available 12–3pm and 6–9.30pm. Car park. Accommodation. Three miles from M1 junction 18, close to M6 and M40 and adjacent to A5. Daventry three miles to the south, Rugby four miles to the north.

OPEN *12–11pm (10.30pm Sun).*

ASHORNE
The Cottage Tavern
Ashorne, Warwick CV35 9DR
☎ *(01926) 65140* Chris Goudie

Freehouse with three ales from breweries such as Archers, Crouch Vale and Stonehenge, changed every two days.

A long-established, one-bar real country pub. Food served Thurs–Sun. Beer patio.

OPEN *5–11pm Mon; 12–3pm and 7–11pm Tues–Fri; 12–11pm Sat; 12–10.30pm Sun.*

ATHERSTONE
Horse & Jockey
Coleshill Road, Bentley, Atherstone CV9 2HL
☎ *(01827) 715236* George and Julie Woods

Freehouse with draught Bass plus two to three weekly-changing guests.

A pproximately 200 years old, this pub is owned by the Merevale estate and features two bars and a snug. Food served 12–2pm and 5.30–9pm Tues–Sat; 12–4pm Sun. Beer garden. Children welcome. Quiz every Sunday night. Private room and marquee available for hire. Beer and music festival held at beginning of May. Located just outside of Atherstone.

OPEN *12–3pm and 5.30–11pm Tues–Fri; all day Sat–Sun.*

BADDESLEY
The Red Lion Inn
Baddesley, Ensor CV9 2BT
☎ *(01827) 718186* David Baillie Bell

Six real ales including Everards Tiger and Marston's Pedigree. Three guests, such as Titanic Iceberg, Morgan's Scrumptious and Milestow Home Wrecker.

V ictorian bar, 350 years old, created at the front of two much older cottages. Comfortable ambience and fires in winter. An adults' pub. No food. No music.

OPEN *7–11pm Mon–Thurs; 4–11pm Fri; 12–3pm Sat–Sun.*

BEDWORTH
The White Swan
All Saints Square, Bedworth
☎ *(024) 7631 2164* Paul Holden

Charles Wells Eagle IPA and Bombardier plus one guest beer such as Greene King Old Speckled Hen, Badger Tanglefoot or Adnams Broadside.

C entral pub, catering for a mixed clientele of all ages. Food served 12–2pm daily. Car parks close by. Children welcome at lunchtime.

OPEN *11am–11pm (10.30pm Sun).*

BISHOPS TACHBROOK
The Leopard
Oakley Wood Road, Bishops Tachbrook,
Nr Leamington Spa CV33 9RN
☎ *(01926) 426466* Ian Richardson

Hook Norton Hooky Bitter, Timothy Taylor Landlord and Greene King Abbot plus one changing guest.

Country pub and restaurant in an old A-frame building dating back to 1066. Garden. Food available. Children allowed. Car park.

OPEN *12–3pm and 6–11pm Mon–Fri; 12–11pm Sat; 12–10.30pm Sun.*

CHAPEL END
The Salutation Inn
Chancery Lane, Chapel End, Nuneaton CV10 0PB
☎ *(024) 7632 9360* Mark Stringer

Jennings Cumberland plus one guest, changed weekly.

Very old out-of-town pub, formerly a coaching inn. Quiet and welcoming. Food served 12–2.30pm and 5–8.30pm Mon–Fri; 12–7pm Sat and 12–3pm Sun. Live entertainment at weekends. Children welcome. Car park and outside seating. Darts and bar billiards.

OPEN *12–11pm (10.30pm Sun).*

CHURCH LAWFORD
Old Smithy
Green Lane, Church Lawford, Nr Rugby CU23 9EF
☎ *(024) 7654 2333* Yvonne and David Atkins
www.king-henrys-taverns.co.uk

Three or four real ales, rotated on a regular basis.

Traditional freehouse situated on the village green. Food-oriented, with meals served all day, every day. Car park. Beer garden and children's play area.

OPEN *All day, every day.*

COUGHTON
The Throckmorton Arms
Coughton, Alcester B49 5HX
☎ *(01789) 766366*
Adrian and Nigel Staley (owners),Tom Jack and Antoinette Webb (managers)

One of two freehouses under the Proper Job Pub Company Ltd serving St Austell Tribute and Hook Norton Hooky plus two weekly-changing guests from breweries such as Cottage and Wye Valley.

Set in the Warwickshire countryside, an ideally located inn for those seeking a relaxing break. Separate restaurant with à la carte menu. Traditional log fire in main bar, comfortable lounge area. Outdoor patio dining. Ten en-suite letting rooms. Food served 12–2.15pm and 6.30–9pm Mon–Fri, 12–2.15pm and 6.30–9.30pm Sat–Sun. Car park. Near Warwick and Stratford-upon-Avon. Located opposite the National Trust property Coughton Court on the A435 between Alcester and Studley.

OPEN *All day, every day.*

EDGEHILL
The Castle Inn
Edgehill, Nr Banbury OX15 6DJ
☎ *(01295) 670255* Mr Tony Sheen
www.thecastle-edgehill.com

Hook Norton pub with four or five real ales on offer.

An unusual inn on the summit of Edgehill near the civil war battle site. Built in the 18th century to commemorate the centenary of the battle, it is a copy of Guy's Tower at Warwick Castle. Two bars plus balcony overlooking the battlefield and large garden. Food served 12–2pm and 6.30–9pm. Car park. Original en-suite bedrooms. Ideal for exploring Banbury, Stratford, Warwick, Leamington Spa, Oxford and the Cotswolds, plus paths for walking and bridleways for horseriding.

OPEN *12–2.30pm and 6pm–12; extended opening hours in summer – please call for details.*

GREAT WOLFORD
The Fox & Hounds Inn
Great Wolford, Nr Shipston-on-Stour CV36 5NQ
☎ *(01608) 674220* Gillian Tarbox
www.thefoxandhoundsinn.com

Hook Norton Hooky Bitter, Purity Pure UBU and something from Cottage would be a typical selection, with one of the three beers on offer changed weekly.

An unspoilt 16th-century Cotswold village inn with stone-flagged floors, log fires, hops, faded hunting pictures – and an infamous pub sign! Seasonal, local produce served 12–2pm and 7–9pm Tues–Sat and 12–2.30pm Sun. Car park, beer terrace, and three charming en-suite B&B rooms. Children welcome. Between the A3400 and A44 south of Shipston-on-Stour, 30 minutes from Stratford and Warwick.

OPEN *12–3pm and 6pm–12 Tues–Sat; 12–3pm and 7–11.30pm Sun; closed Mon.*

HAMPTON LUCY
The Boars Head
Church Street, Hampton Lucy CV35 8BE
☎ *(01789) 840533* Susan Maindonald (owner), Paul Kearney (manager)

Five real ales, including local and national brews. Four of the beers are rotated on a daily basis.

Traditional English pub next to an impressive village church, with great atmosphere. Food served 12–2pm and 6–9pm Mon–Thurs; 12–2.30pm and 6–9.30pm Fri–Sat and 12–3pm Sun. Beer garden, car park. From junction 14 of the M40, follow the signs to Charlcote.

OPEN *12–3pm and 6–11pm Mon–Sat; 12–10.30pm Sun.*

HARTSHILL
The Anchor Inn
Mancetter Road, Hartshill, Nuneaton CV1 0RT
☎ *(024) 7639 8839* Mark Wade

 Everards pub serving Tiger and Original plus four guests changed weekly.

Pleasant rural pub dating from around the construction of the Coventry Canal in 1790 and offering moorings. Close to bridge 29. Large garden, bar and restaurant, summer garden bar and function room. Varied menu available throughout the week 12–2pm (not Mon) and 6.30–9pm, plus traditional carvery served Fri–Sat evenings and Sun lunch (12–5pm). Children welcome in the bar until 9pm. Off the A5.

OPEN *6–11pm Mon; 12–2.30pm and 6–11pm Tues Fri–Sat; 12–10.30pm Sun.*

HENLEY-IN-ARDEN
The White Swan Hotel
100 High Street, Henley-in-Arden B95 5BY
☎ *(01564) 792623* Nigel May

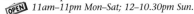 One guest, changed weekly, might be Everards Beacon, Bateman XB, Greene King Old Speckled Hen, Wadworth 6X or a seasonal or celebration ale.

Situated in the centre of the smallest market town in England, this black and white coaching inn dates from 1352. Food available. One bar, restaurant, garden, ten letting rooms. Jazz on Wednesdays. Children allowed. Car park.

OPEN *11am–11pm Mon–Sat; 12–10.30pm Sun.*

ILMINGTON
The Howard Arms
Lower Green, Ilmington CV36 4LT
☎ *(01608) 682226* Martin Devereux
www.howardarms.com

Purity Pure Gold and Hook Norton Old Hooky are near permanent fixtures at this freehouse, which also offers one guest, changed regularly, such as Goff's Tournament and Jouster, North Cotswold Brewery's Pig Brook, Blue Bear Kempsford's Roar Spirit, and Warwickshire Beer Company's Lady Godiva and Darling Buds.

A 16th-century stone-built pub with log fire and a cosy atmosphere, nestling beside the village green. Award-winning seasonal food with frequently changing menus and daily specials served 12–2.30pm and 6.30–9.30pm seven days a week. Garden and terrace, car parking. Seven en-suite double bedrooms, and one en-suite twin. Children welcome. Eight miles south of Stratford-on-Avon off the A3400.

OPEN *11am–11pm Mon–Sat; 12-10.30pm Sun.*

KENILWORTH
The Old Bakery
12 High Street, Kenilworth CV8 1LZ
☎ *(01926) 864111* Alan Blackburn
www.theoldbakeryhotel.co.uk

Freehouse serving Hook Norton Hooky Bitter and St Austell Tribute plus two daily-changing guests which could be from local breweries such as Church End, Cottage, Hobsons or Purity, or from various national breweries.

This building has been part of Kenilworth's picturesque High Street for nearly 400 years. Comfortable oak-beamed main bar and smaller snug. No fruit machines, juke box, piped music or TV screens. Homemade bar snacks available. Fourteen luxurious en-suite rooms available for B&B, each with telephone, TV and tea- and coffee-making facilities. Outdoor seating area. Free Wi-Fi. Children welcome in early evening. Nearby attractions include Kenilworth Castle, Warwick Castle, Stratford-upon-Avon, Hatton Country Park and various canals for narrowboating.

OPEN *5.30–11pm Mon–Thurs; 5–11pm Fri–Sat; 12–2pm and 7–10.30pm Sun.*

The Virgins & Castle
7 High Street, Kenilworth CV8 1LY
☎ *(01926) 853737* Laurie Howe

 Everards Tiger, Beacon, Original and Sunchaser, Fuller's London Pride and Charles Wells Bombadier plus two weekly-changing guests.

Reputed to be the oldest pub in Kenilworth, this was built in 1563 and has been used as a pub/inn since 1777. Retains the original snug and has two bars. English, Filipino and Japanese food served 12–3.30pm and 6–9.30pm daily. Private courtyard garden. Short walk to Kenilworth Castle, situated adjacent to the Abbey Fields park.

OPEN *11am–11pm Mon–Sat; 12–10.30pm Sun.*

The Wyandotte Inn
Park Road, Kenilworth CV8 2GF
☎ *(01926) 863219* Mrs Jaeger

Banks's Bitter plus Marston's Bitter and Pedigree regularly available.

Street-corner local with split-level single room and coal fire in winter. Beer garden. Pool table. Musical events every week. Food served 5–9pm Tues–Fri, all day Sat–Sun. Car park. Children welcome.

OPEN *5–11pm Mon–Fri; 10am–11pm Sat–Sun and major holidays.*

LEAMINGTON SPA
Benjamin Satchwell
112–14 The Parade, Leamington Spa CV32 4AQ
☎ *(01926) 883733* Andy Tompkins

Hop Back Summer Lightning, Greene King Abbot and Shepherd Neame Spitfire are among the permanent beers at this 12–pump pub. The six guests, changed every two days, might include Wyre Piddle Piddle in the Wind, Castle Eden Nimmo's 4X or something from Mordue.

Traditional open-plan Wetherspoon's town pub, holding beer festivals throughout the year (call for details). Food available. No children.

OPEN *11am–11pm Mon–Sat; 12–10.30pm Sun.*

LONG LAWFORD
The Sheaf & Sickle
Coventry Road, Long Lawford, Rugby CV23 9DT
☎ (01788) 544622
Roger Singh and Ruth Clarkson

Two real ales available from a range of breweries.

An old village coaching inn with saloon, lounge and à la carte restaurant. Beer garden, private room for hire. Food available during all opening hours. Children welcome. Beer festivals held and parties catered for.

OPEN *12–2.30pm and 6–11pm Mon–Fri; all day Sat–Sun.*

NAPTON
The Bridge
Daventry Road, Napton CV47 8NQ
☎ (01926) 812466 Hugo and Quintin Gilbert
www.thebridgeatnapton.co.uk

Punch Taverns pub serving three constantly rotating guests, with Wadworth 6X and beers from Black Sheep and Greene King often available.

Situated on the banks of the Oxford Canal, this pub offers a range of traditional home-cooked meals, cask ales and friendly service. Two bars and separate restaurant. Food served lunchtimes and evenings Tues–Sun. Large beer garden. Large car park. Beer festival held in July. Children and dogs welcome. Near Warwick Castle and Silverstone. Located on the A425 between Daventry and Southam.

OPEN *12–3pm and 6–11pm Tues–Sun.*

NUNEATON
The Crown Inn
10 Bond Street, Nuneaton CV11 4BX
☎ (024) 7637 3343 Julian Harkins
www.thecrownnuneaton.com

A freehouse. Oakham JHB, plus over 500 different guests served each year, from breweries such as Bays, Wychwood, Brampton, Shardlow, Potbelly, York, Milk Street, Isle of Skye, Westons and Church End.

Dating from 1901 with open fires, beer garden, function room and car park. Food available all day every day. Winner of CAMRA Best Ale House Coventry and Nuneaton 2008. Summer BBQs. Beer festivals in June and December. Live music Sat. Tues all ales £1.65. Located adjacent to the railway and bus station in the town centre.

OPEN *12–11pm Sun–Thurs; 12–12 Fri–Sat.*

RIDGE LANE
The Brewery Tap
109 Ridge Lane, Ridge Lane, Nuneaton CV10 0RD
☎ (01827) 713080 Ian Wood

Home of the Church End Brewery with eight beers, all own-brewed, including one permanent mild and seven rotating bitters, changed as soon as they run out, plus the occasional stout and porter.

A modern, clean pub for beer lovers, opened in 2002 as the brewery tap, with two comfortable bars and a meadow-style garden. No music, no TV. Brewery tours are available. No food. Large car park. No children. Two miles from Atherstone, in the centre of Ridge Lane village.

OPEN *6–11pm Thurs; 12–11pm Fri–Sat; 12–10.30pm Sun (closed Mon–Weds).*

RUGBY
The Alexandra Arms
72 James Street, Rugby CV21 2SL
☎ (01788) 578660 Julian Hardy
www.alexandraarms.co.uk

The pub has its own brewery, and features one ale brewed on site. Greene King Abbot and Fuller's London Pride also available, plus two rotating guests from a wide range of small breweries.

Award-winning genuine freehouse built in 1863 with bar billiards, table skittles and pool. Traditional lounge bar. No music or machines. Garden. Food available 12–2.30pm and 5–7pm. No children. Situated near the main post office. An annual beer festival is held on the second weekend of July.

OPEN *11.30am–11pm Mon–Thurs; 11.30am–midnight Fri; 11.30am–11.30pm Sat; 12–11pm Sun.*

The Merchants Inn
5–7 Little Church Street, Rugby CV21 3AN
☎ (01788) 571119 Scott Whyment
www.merchantsinn.co.uk

Freehouse with two house beers: B&T Shefford and Everards Tiger, plus seven rotating guests. Up to 30 beers served every week. Also a range of Belgian beers.

Historical, well-established pub serving a huge selection of real ales and good food. One of the UK's biggest collectors of breweriana. CAMRA Pub of the Year for Rugby 2005 and for Warwickshire 2003 and 2007. Food served 12–2.30pm Mon–Sat; 12–5pm Sun. Two beer festivals every year. Private room for hire. Next to Rugby school.

OPEN *12–12 Mon–Thurs; noon–1am Fri–Sat; 12–11pm Sun.*

The Three Horseshoes Hotel
Sheep Street, Rugby CV21 3BX
☎ (01788) 544585 Stephen Jones

Greene King Abbot is among the beers always available, plus one or two guest beers, changed weekly, from an extensive list.

Central refurbished 17th-century inn with open fires and beamed restaurant. Food available 12–2pm and 6–9.30pm Mon–Sat and 12–4pm Sun. Parking available nearby. Children welcome. Accommodation.

OPEN *11am–11pm Mon–Sat; 12–10.30pm Sun.*

The Victoria Inn
1 Lower Hillmorton Road, Rugby CV21 3ST
☎ (01788) 544374 Colin White

Genuine freehouse serving Cottage Champflower plus up to three guests rotated every couple of days.

A locals' pub, 125 years old, just outside the town centre. Two bars, original mirrors in both rooms. Disabled access. Food available at lunchtime only Mon–Fri. Jazz, Irish and Blues bands. No children.

 12–2.30pm and 6–11pm Mon–Thurs; 12–2.30pm and 5.30–11pm Fri; all day Sat; 12–4pm and 7–10.30pm Sun.

SHIPSTON-ON-STOUR

The Coach & Horses

16 New Street, Shipston-on-Stour CV36 4EM
☎ *(01608) 661335* Bob Payne

Hook Norton Hooky Bitter plus three guests from a long list including Hook Norton Haymaker, Wye Valley Brew 69, Dorothy Goodbody's Summertime Ale and Bateman XXXB and XB.

A 250-year-old village pub in the Cotswolds serving bar and restaurant food at lunchtimes and evenings. Car park, garden, accommodation. On the A3400 Birmingham to Oxford road, on the Oxford side of town.

 11am–11pm (10.30pm Sun).

SHUSTOKE

The Griffin Inn

Church Road, Shustoke B46 2LB
☎ *(01675) 481567* Michael Pugh

Ten real ales. Marston's Pedigree, Hook Norton Old Hooky, RCH Pitchfork, Hanson's Mild, Everards Tiger and Theakston Old Peculier always available, plus four guest ales rotated daily.

L arge country freehouse with oak beams and open fires set in large grounds. The Griffin Brewery now re-opened, with a very pretty wooden clad 2.5 barrel plant, producing 'Ere It Is 4.5%, Black Magic Woman 4.7%, and Firkin Slurcher 4.7%. Bar food is available at lunchtime (except Sunday) 12–2pm. Car park, garden. Children allowed in the conservatory and grounds. Named in The Top Ten British Country Pubs. Take the B4114 from Coleshill.

 12–2.30pm and 7–11pm Mon–Sat; 12–3pm and 7–10.30pm Sun.

STRATFORD-UPON-AVON

The Queen's Head

53 Ely Street, Stratford-upon-Avon CV37 6LN
☎ *(01789) 204914* Martyn Jones

Adnams Best, Charles Wells Bombadier and Bass plus a guest changed regularly.

A n 18th-century coaching inn that claims to be Stratford's best kept secret. Food available at lunchtimes only. One bar, beer garden, real fire, sport, live music once a month, five B&B rooms. Children allowed until 7pm only. Close to the river and theatre.

 11.30am–11pm Mon–Thurs; 11am–1am Fri–Sat; 12–11pm Sun.

STRETTON-ON-FOSSE

Plough Inn

Stretton-on-Fosse GL56 9QX
☎ *(01608) 661053* HM Sinclair, SM Sinclair and JP Gireme

Freehouse with Hook Norton Hooky Bitter and Purity Pure Gold plus two weekly-changing guests.

T his stone-built village pub is family-run. The building originally dates back to the 17th century with a salt box built into the wall. Open fire that operates as a spit fire on Sundays. One bar and one lounge. Traditional home-cooked food prepared fresh to order by the pub's own popular French chef; served 12–2pm every day, 7–9pm Mon–Sat. Car park. Beer garden. Children's play area opposite. Monthly quiz nights and folk sessions. Ten miles from Stratford-upon-Avon. Located on the A429 between Moreton-in-Marsh and Shipston-on-Stour.

 12–2.30pm and 6–11pm Mon–Sat; 12–2.30pm and 7–10.30pm Sun (varies on bank holidays).

STUDLEY

The Little Lark

108 Alcester Road, Studley B80 7NP
☎ *(01527) 853105* Mark Roskell

Adnams Best Bitter and Timothy Taylor Landlord, Ansells Mild plus one guest, changed regularly. Traditional cider also served.

A n interesting selection of printing paraphernalia is a feature in this real ale house. Food available lunchtimes and evenings every day. On the main A435 at the southern end of Studley.

 12–3pm and 6–11pm Sun–Fri; 12–11pm Sat.

ULLENHALL

The Winged Spur

Main Street, Ullenhall, Henley-in-Arden B95 5PA
☎ *(01564) 792005*
www.thewingedspur.com

Enterprise Inns pub, with four real ales always on offer. All served on a guest basis, and constantly changing.

O ne-bar, olde-worlde, traditional, with four real fires in winter. Home-cooked food including fresh fish served 12–2.30pm and 7–9.30pm Mon–Sat (9pm Sun). Well-behaved children welcome. Disabled facilities. Beer garden and patio. Smoking facilities with log fire. Car park. Access from J3A of M42.

 12–late. Last admittance 11pm.

WARWICK

The Old Fourpenny Shop Hotel

27–9 Crompton Street, Warwick CV34 6HJ
☎ *(01926) 491360* Jan Richard Siddle

Six guest beers, with RCH Pitchfork always available, the rest changing daily. Beers from Greene King, Church End, Abbey, Eccleshall, Litchfield, Burton Bridge, Bateman and Timothy Taylor are often featured.

P opular real ale house with restaurant. Food served 12–2pm and 7–10pm daily. Car park. Children over 10 years old welcome. Accommodation available, with 11 refurbished bedrooms. By the entrance to Warwick racecourse.

 12–2.30pm and 5.30–11pm Mon–Thurs; 12–11pm Fri; 12–3pm and 5.30–11pm Sat; 12–3pm and 5.30–10.30pm Sun.

The Simple Simon

105 Emscote Road, Warwick CV34 5QY
☎ *(01926) 400333* Dave Talbot

 Enterprise Inns pub serving Charles Wells Bombardier, Greene King Old Speckled Hen and Caledonian Deuchars IPA plus various guests from Slaughterhouse Brewery including Saddleback Bitter, Hob Goblin and Wild Boar. All ales are rotated, with the pub featuring around six each week.

A traditional pub with two bars, one of which specialises in live music and the other a lounge/restaurant. Food served lunchtime and early evening. Children and dogs welcome. Live music events held several times a week, as well as themed nights. Room hire available. Near to Grand Union Canal, on the main road between Leamington Spa and Warwick.

OPEN *12–12.*

The Norman Knight

Whichford, Shipston-on-Stour CV36 5PE
☎ *(01608) 684621* Julian Taylor

 Freehouse serving Hook Norton Hooky Bitter plus a couple of guests, changed every few weeks, such as Wye Valley HPA and Warwickshire Beer Co Best.

Brick-built, single-bar pub dating from around 1900, with a beer garden on the village green. Food served lunchtimes Tues–Sun and evenings Tues–Sat. Darts, Aunt Sally. Children and dogs welcome. Caravan site at rear.

OPEN *Closed Mon; 12.30-2.30pm and 7–11pm Tues–Thurs; 12–2.30pm and 6–11pm Fri–Sat; 12–3pm Sun.*

THE BREWERIES

DANIEL BATHAM & SON LTD

*The Delph Brewery, Delph Road, Brierley Hill
DY5 2TN*
☎ *(01384) 77229*
www.bathams.co.uk

MILD ALE 3.5% ABV
Fruity finish.
BEST BITTER 4.5% ABV
Dry and hoppy.
XXX 6.5% ABV
Malty fruit taste. Christmas ale.

THE BEOWULF BREWING CO.

*Unit 3–4, Chasewater Country, Park Pool Road,
Brownhills, Walsall WS8 7NL*
☎ *(01543) 454067*

BEORMA 3.9% ABV
NOBLE BITTER 4.0% ABV
WIGLAF 4.3% ABV
Gold coloured, with hops and malt.
CHASEWATER 4.4% ABV
DARK RAVEN 4.5% ABV
SWORDSMAN 4.5% ABV
Pale, refreshing and fruity.
DRAGONSMOKE STOUT 4.7% ABV
FINNS HALL PORTER 4.7% ABV
HEROES BITTER 4.7% ABV
Golden and hoppy with some sweetness.
MERCIAN SHINE 5.0% ABV
Light in colour, with hoppiness, and dry in the
aftertaste.
Plus seasonal brews.

BLACK COUNTRY ALES

*c/o Old Bulls Head, 1 Redhall Road,
Lower Gornal, Dudley DY3 2NU*
☎ *(01384) 231616*

BFG (BRADLEY'S FINEST GOLDEN) 4.2%
FIRESIDE BITTER 4.2%
PIG ON THE WALL 4.3%

ENVILLE ALES

*Enville Brewery, Cox Green, Enville, Hollies
Lane, Stourbridge DY7 5LG*
☎ *(01384) 873728*
www.envilleales.com

CHAINMAKER MILD 3.6% ABV
Underlying sweetness.
NAILMAKER 4.0% ABV
Hoppy with dry finish.
CZECHMATE SAAZ 4.2% ABV
Light and fruity.
ENVILLE WHITE 4.2% ABV
Straw colour, hop aroma.
ANNIVERSARY ALE 4.5% ABV
Golden, citrus nose.
ENVILLE ALE 4.5% ABV
Yellow, fruity bitter.
GARGOYLE 4.5% ABV
Smokey flavour.
OLD PORTER 4.5% ABV
Dark and fruity.
SLAYED 4.5% ABV
Hints of spice.
GINGER BEER 4.6% ABV
Ginger flavour.
PHOENIX IPA 4.8% ABV
Pale Indian-style beer.
GOTHIC ALE 5.2% ABV
Black beer, hints of honey.

MAN EATER 5.6% ABV
Malt flavour with undertones of fruit.
WOMANIZER 5.6% ABV
Slight flavour of damson gin.
MAIDEN'S RUIN 6.0% ABV
Christmas ale, rich and warming.
Plus special brews.

HIGHGATE BREWERY LTD

Sandymount Road, Walsall WS1 3AP
☎ *(01922) 644453*
www.highgatebrewery.com

HIGHGATE MILD 3.4% ABV
Liquorice, roast malt flavours,
bittersweet.
HIGHGATE SPECIAL BITTER 3.8% ABV
Citrus tones, slightly dry.
DAVENPORTS ORIGINAL 4.0% ABV
Copper colour, bitter finish.
Plus a range of special and seasonal brews.

HOLDEN'S BREWERY

*Hopden Brewery, George Street, Woodsetton,
Dudley DY1 4LW*
☎ *(01902) 880051*
www.holdensbrewery.co.uk

BLACK COUNTRY MILD 3.7% ABV
Nutty biscuit notes.
BLACK COUNTRY BITTER 3.9% ABV
Straw colour, medium body, malt finish.
GOLDEN GLOW 4.4% ABV
Gentle sweetness, almost citrus-like.
FOGGER 4.5% ABV
Gold, fruity aroma, malty taste.
SPECIAL BITTER 5.1% ABV
Robust malt flavour.
Plus specials and monthly seasonals including:
FLO JANGLES 4.2% ABV
Blonde, sweet, fruity.
FREDDIE FEBRIO 4.5% ABV
Zesty hop aroma, bitter edge.
CHRISTMAS BLASTER 4.8% ABV
Malty aftertaste.

OLDE SWAN BREWERY

89 Halesowen Road, Netherton, Dudley DY2 9PY
☎ *(01384) 253075*

OLD SWAN ORIGINAL 3.5% ABV
DARK SWAN (MILD) 4.2% ABV
OLD SWAN ENTIRE 4.4% ABV
BUMBLEHOLE 5.2% ABV
BLACK WIDOW 6.7% ABV
Winter only.
Plus seasonals.

RAINBOW BREWERY

*73 Birmingham Road, Allesley Village, Coventry
CV5 9GT*
☎ *(024) 7640 2888*

PIDDLEBROOK 3.8% ABV

SARAH HUGHES BREWERY

129 Bilston Street, Sedgley, Dudley DY3 1JE
☎ *(01902) 883380*

PALE AMBER 4.0% ABV
SEDGLEY SURPRISE 5.0% ABV
ORIGINAL DARK RUBY MILD 6.0% ABV
SNOWFLAKE 8.0% ABV
Occasional.

TOLL END
c/o Waggon and Horses, 131 Toll End Road,
Tipton DY4 0ET
☎ *(0121) 502 6453*

LOST CITY 4.0% ABV
DARBY GINGER 4.2% ABV
WILLIE PERRY 4.3% ABV
UPPER CUT 4.5% ABV
PA (PHOEBE'S ALE) 4.7%
BLACK BRIDGE 5.0%
COAL OLE 5.1% ABV
Plus special and seasonal brews.

WINDSOR CASTLE BREWERY LTD
7 Stourbridge Road, Stourbridge, Lye DY9 7DG
☎ *(01384) 895230*
www.windsorcastlebrewery.com

GREEN MAN 4.0% ABV
Pale lager style.
MILD 4.0% ABV
WORCESTER SORCERER 4.3% ABV
Pale with a hint of mint.
1900 ORIGINAL BITTER 4.5% ABV
Slightly dry.
THIN ICE 4.5% ABV
Spiced orange tang.
SADLER'S IPA 4.8% ABV
Refreshing and hoppy.
Plus seasonals and monthly beers.

THE WOLVERHAMPTON & DUDLEY BREWERIES PLC
Marston's Beer Company, Marston's House,
Wolverhampton WV1 4JT
☎ *(01902) 711811*
www.wdb.co.uk

BANKS'S ORIGINAL 3.5% ABV
BANKS'S BITTER 3.8% ABV
MANSFIELD CASK DARK MILD 3.5% ABV
MANSFIELD DARK SMOOTH ALE 3.5% ABV
MANSFIELD CASK ALE 3.9% ABV
MANSFIELD ORIGINAL BITTER ALE 3.9% ABV
MANSFIELD SMOOTH CREAMY 3.9% ABV

MARSTON'S SMOOTH 3.6% ABV
MARSTON'S BURTON BITTER 3.8% ABV
MARSTON'S OYSTER STOUT 4.5% ABV
MARSTON'S PEDIGREE 4.5% ABV
MARSTON'S RESOLUTION 4.7% ABV
OLD EMPIRE 5.7% ABV

JENNINGS DARK MILD 3.1% ABV
JENNINGS BITTER 3.5% ABV
JENNINGS OLD SMOOTHY 3.5% ABV
JENNINGS CUMBERLAND ALE 4.0% ABV
JENNINGS CUMBERLAND CREAM 4.0% ABV
JENNINGS CRAG RAT 4.3% ABV
JENNINGS GOLDEN HOST 4.3% ABV
JENNINGS RED BREAST 4.5% ABV
JENNINGS COCKER HOOP 4.6% ABV
SNECK LIFTER 5.1% ABV
LA'AL COCKLE WARMER 6.5% ABV
Plus seasonals and specials.

THE PUBS

ALBRIGHTON
The Harp Hotel
High Street, Albrighton, Nr Wolverhampton
WV7 3JF
☎ *(01902) 374381* Donna Pibworth

Freehouse with four guests changed daily, from breweries such as Slaters and Holden's.

This 100-year-old two-bar pub is host to international jazz Sun–Tues. Pool table, darts. No hot food, but cobs available daily. Beer garden. Children welcome. Beer festivals held in May and Octobr. Close to RAF Cosford. Located off junction 3 of the M54.
OPEN *12–12.*

ALLESLEY
Rainbow Inn
73 Birmingham Road, Allesley Village, Coventry
CV5 9GT
☎ *(024) 7640 2888* Jon Grote

Piddlebrook brewed and served on the premises plus Greene King IPA and Abbot and a guest beer changed every week.

Brewing started in October 1994 providing ale only for the pub and a few beer festivals. Production at the two-barrel plant takes place fortnightly. The pub dates from 1680 and is full of character (and characters!). Public bar and lounge, plus two patio areas with marquee. Bar and restaurant food, including homemade dishes, served 12–2.30pm and 6–9pm Mon–Fri and 12–3pm Sat–Sun. Small car park. Lounge bar available for private functions. Occasional live music. Just off the main A45, next to the Allesley Hotel.
OPEN *11am–11pm Sun–Tues; 11am–11.30pm Wed–Thurs; 11am–midnight Fri–Sat.*

AMBLECOTE
The Maverick Drinking House
1 High Street, Amblecote, Stourbridge DY8 4BX
☎ *(01384) 824099* Mark Boxley

Jennings Cumberland Ale plus three guests from around the country rotated daily (up to 12 guests a week).

A two-bar community pub dating from the 1850s, with traditional decor and an American/Mexican/Old West theme. Musicians' jam nights Wednesdays, rock 'n' blues Fridays, acoustic Saturdays. No food. Large-screen TV in separate room. Beer garden plus covered and heated smoking area. Charity events held. Children welcome. Real ale festival in October. Close to the canal and the Merryhill Shopping Centre. On the junction of the A49 and the A461.
OPEN *12–12 Mon–Tues and Thurs; noon–1am Wed and Fri–Sat; 12–11pm Sun.*

The Robin Hood Inn

*196 Collis Street, Amblecote, Stourbridge
DY8 4EQ*
☎ *(01384) 821120* B Jeavons

Batham Bitter, Enville Ale and Ginger, plus four ever-changing guests (160 per year) from breweries such as Holden's, Loddon, Kelham Island, Exmoor, Blackwater, Salopian, Cotleigh, RCH, Skinner's, Greene King, Thornbridge, Oakham, Acorn, Leeds, Ossett and Wenworth, to name but a few.

Family-run, cosy Black Country freehouse. Good beer garden. Bar and restaurant food available 12–2pm and 6–10pm Mon–Sat; 12–4pm Sun. Parking. Lively quiz on first Tues of the month. Children allowed in the pub when eating. Accommodation. Handy for the canal network. On the A4102.

OPEN *12–3pm and 6–11pm Mon–Thurs; 12–12 Fri–Sat; 12–11pm Sun.*

The Swan

10 Brettell Lane, Amblecote, Stourbridge
☎ *(01384) 76932* G Cook

Three weekly-changing guest beers, from breweries such as Salopian, Oakham, Wylam, Ossett, Olde Swan, Hop Back, Milk Street, Cotleigh, Okells, Outlaw, Blackwater, and others.

A traditional town pub with comfortable lounge, bar, darts and juke box. Beer garden. No food. No children.

OPEN *12–2.30pm and 7–11pm Mon–Fri; 12–11pm Sat; 12–3pm and 7–10.30pm Sun.*

BALLINGHAM
The British Oak

Ballingham, Stirchley B30 2XS
☎ *(0121) 458 1758* Anthony Madden

Punch Taverns tied house with M&B Mild and a traditional cider plus four rotating guests changed at least three times a week.

Built in 1926 and a listed building, this five-room pub has been restored to its original state with oak wooden panels, an art deco-style restaurant and traditional bar and is well known for its interior. Food served 12–2pm and 5–9pm Mon–Fri (5–9.30pm Sat), 12–4pm Sun. BBQs on Fri and Sat. Bowling green and club. Large beer garden with terrace area and outdoor kitchen for all year round spitroasts and BBQs. Family-friendly. Comedy club held every other month.

OPEN *11am–11pm Mon–Thurs; 11am–1am Fri–Sat; 12–11pm Sun.*

BARSTON
The Bull's Head

Barston Lane, Barston, Solihull B92 0JV
☎ *(01675) 442830* Martin Bradley

Four real ales, with something from Adnams, Hook Norton and Black Sheep usually on offer, plus one or two guest beers, changed every couple of weeks.

Unspoilt traditional country pub dating from 1490 and with a priest hole used in Oliver Cromwell's time. Log fires in both bars in winter, pleasant gardens. No machines.

Food served 12–2pm and 7–9pm Mon–Sat, 12–3pm Sun. In a conservation area, ten minutes from the Solihull junction of the M42.

OPEN *11am–2.30pm and 5–11pm Mon–Fri; 11am–11pm Sat; 12–10.30pm Sun.*

BERKSWELL
The Bear Inn

Spencer's Lane, Berkswell, Coventry CV7 7BB
☎ *(01676) 533202* Stephen Gamble

Two fixed ales and two guests, changed fortnightly, which might include Marston's Pedigree or Warwickshire Lady Godiva.

A two-bar Chef & Brewer pub in a village location, in a 15th-century building. Food is available all day, every day, and there is a separate dining area. Garden, car park. Children allowed.

OPEN *11am–11pm Mon–Sat; 12–10.30pm Sun.*

BILSTON
The Olde White Rose

20 Lichfield Street, Bilston WV14 0AG
☎ *(01902) 498339* John Denston

Twelve real ale pumps serve the crème de la crème from Shepherd Neame, Hop Back and all the other popular independent and micro-breweries; the list is endless!

Situated in the heart of the Black Country, this is a lounge-style pub, extended to include upstairs restaurant and downstairs bierkeller. Food available every day until 9pm. Children allowed, with designated play area outside. Beer garden. Easily accessible on the Snowhill–Wolverhampton Metro (tram) although be careful not to confuse it with The White Rose in the same town.

OPEN *12–11pm Mon–Sat; 12–4pm and 7–10.30pm Sun.*

Trumpet

58 High Street, Bilston WV14 0EP
☎ *(01902) 493723* Ann Smith
www.trumpetjazz.org

Holden's Special, Black Country Bitter, Mild and Golden Glow plus one guest every week from any one of a range of breweries. Jennings, Hanby Ales, Mauldons, Salopian, Burton Bridge, Cotleigh and many others have been featured.

A live jazz pub that has been entertaining nightly for at least 40 years. Music also played at lunchtime on Sundays. No food at present. Beer garden. Children allowed in the garden only. Car park. At the top end of the High Street.

OPEN *11am–3pm and 7.30–11pm Mon–Sat; 12–3pm and 7–10.30pm Sun.*

BIRMINGHAM

The Anchor

308 Bradford Street, Birmingham B5 6ET
☎ *(0121) 622 4516* Gerry Keane

Freehouse with a constantly changing menu of real ales. At least seven during the week and up to 13 at weekends. Favourite breweries include Church End, Rooster's, Beowulf and Hobsons. Three major beer festivals held each year (March, May and October), plus themed weekends, e.g. Burns' Night, St Patrick's Day and an organic festival in June/July.

Situated close to the city centre, a well-preserved three-bar pub in a Grade II listed building with a red terracotta exterior and stained glass and decorative tiling within. A decorative screen divides the main bar into two. Large-screen and plasma TV showing live sports. ATM on-site. Birmingham CAMRA Pub of the Year 2008 and four times previously. Food available at lunchtime and early evenings. Supervised children allowed in the pub until 9pm. Within walking distance of the Bullring shopping centre.

OPEN *11am–midnight Mon–Tues; 11am–1am Wed–Sat; noon–1am Sun.*

Bartons Arms

144 High Street, Aston, Birmingham B6 4UP
☎ *(0121) 333 5988* Stuart Wright

Oakham Ales pub serving Oakham JHB, White Dwarf and Bishop's Farewell plus five rotating guests, including one mild, from various micro-breweries.

This Grade II listed pub was built in 1901, and has many impressive features, including decorative tiles, snob screens and a feature staircase leading to the board and function rooms. Thai cuisine served 12–2.30pm and 5.30–10pm Mon–Sat and 12–8pm Sun. The board and function rooms are available for social and corporate events. Children welcome. Car parking. Beer festivals with at least 30 real ales held February and September. On the A34, and Birmingham–Walsall bus routes.

OPEN *12–11pm Mon–Fri; 11am–11pm Sat; 12–10.30pm Sun. Extended hours available for functions and special occasions.*

The City Tavern

38 Bishopsgate Street, Birmingham B15 1EJ
☎ *(0121) 643 8467* Christopher Nicholls

Formerly owned by the Highgate Brewery and still serving Dark Mild, Special Bitter, Saddlers Best, plus at least one guest changed regularly.

Formerly known as The Bulls Head, this Victorian pub has been completely refurbished and its original features restored. Food is available 12–3pm Mon–Fri and there is a function room upstairs on the first floor. Located just off Broad Street in the city centre.

OPEN *12–11pm (10.30pm Sun).*

Figure of Eight

236–9 Broad Street, Birmingham B1 2HG
☎ *(0121) 633 0917* Tom Taylor

Enville Ale and Wadworth 6X from a range of up to 12 real ales. Others are served on a guest basis, and may include beers from breweries such as Enville, Springhead, Wyre Piddle, Timothy Taylor, Hop Back, Hook Norton, Shepherd Neame and Greene King.

Busy JD Wetherspoon's freehouse, popular with all ages, serving the largest number of real ales in the area. Food available 10am–10pm Mon–Sat and 12–9.30pm Sun. No children.

OPEN *10am–11pm Mon–Sat; 12–10.30pm Sun.*

The Old Fox

54 Hurst Street, Birmingham B5 4TD
☎ *(0121) 622 5080* Pat Murray

Marston's Pedigree, Greene King Old Speckled Hen, St Austell Tribute and Everards Tiger plus four guests, changed twice-weekly, such as Wychwood The Dog's Bollocks or Trash and Tackle.

An 18th-century town freehouse with stained-glass windows, situated in a modern area near the Hippodrome. Food available 12–7.30pm. Outside seating. No children.

OPEN *11.30am–11pm Mon–Thurs; 11am–2am Fri–Sat; 11.30am–11pm Sun.*

The Old Joint Stock

4 Temple Row West, Birmingham B2 5NY
☎ *(0121) 200 1892* Alison Turner

Fuller's London Pride, Chiswick and ESB plus the brewery's seasonal ales and one-off specials. There might also be a guest from Beowulf.

A Fuller's Ale and Pie House. Large pub in traditional style, balcony area, club room and function room for hire. Food served 12–9pm Mon–Sat. Patio area. No children. Beer festivals held four times a year. Close to the Bullring shopping centre.

OPEN *11am–11pm Mon–Sat; closed Sun and bank holidays.*

The Pavilion

229 Alcester Road South, Kings Heath, Birmingham B14 6DT
☎ *(0121) 441 3286* Danielle Johnson

Banks's Original and Bitter plus Marston's Pedigree regularly available.

Friendly one-bar community local with a friendly, welcoming atmosphere. No Sky Sports! Food served 12–2.30pm and 5.30–9.30pm Mon–Thurs, 12–9.30pm Fri–Sat, 12–8pm Sun. Large car park. Children welcome until 9.30pm. Near to Birmingham city centre and Edgbaston cricket ground.

OPEN *12–11pm Sun–Wed; 12–11.30pm Thurs; 12–12 Fri–Sat.*

Pennyblacks

132–4 Wharfside Street, The Mailbox,
Birmigham B1 1RP
☎ *(0121) 632 1460* Susie Brown
www.penny-blacks.com

 Cropthorne Inns pub with St Austell Tribute, Wye Valley Butty Bach, Hook Norton Hooky Bitter and various brews from Church End plus two weekly-changing guests from breweries such as Enville, Scattor Rock, Black Country Ale, Purity and Malvern Hills.

This contemporary-looking bar with slate and wooden floors opened in 2005 and has a long brass bar. Beautiful canalside view down the Gas Street basin. Diverse mix of clientele. Very busy at weekends. Traditional English food with a twist available 10am–1pm for breakfast and 12–10pm Mon–Sun. No under-18s. Host-tutored wine-tasting sessions (prior booking required). Canal barge bus can be caught directly outside. Located at the back of The Mailbox, on canalside level.

OPEN *10am–11pm Mon–Thurs; 10am–midnight Fri–Sat; 10am–10.30pm Sun.*

The Wellington

37 Bennetts Hill, Birmingham B2 5SN
☎ *(0121) 200 3115* Nigel Barker
www.thewellingtonrealale.co.uk

 Freehouse with up to 15 real ales. Black Country Bradley's Finest Golden, Fireside and Pig on the Wall, and Wye Valley HPA are permanent fixtures, and 8 of the 12 guests are changed every day. Three rotating traditional ciders also served.

One-roomed specialist real ale pub converted from a café bar in 2004. No fruit machines, no music. No food, but customers are encouraged to bring their own, and plates and cutlery are provided. Beer festivals held four times a year. Five minutes from New Street and Snow Hill stations.

OPEN *10am–midnight.*

BLOXWICH

The Royal Exchange

24 Stafford Road, Bloxwich, Walsall WS3 3NL
☎ *(01922) 494256* Mr Beattie

Highgate Mild and Bitter are the permanent beers here, and four weekly-changing guests might be something from Batham, Bateman or Lichfield.

Community local in Grade II listed building, formerly a coaching inn. Four bars, garden area. Live music Wednesdays and Saturdays. Beer festivals held over August Bank Holiday and Easter (call to confirm). No food. Well-behaved children allowed. Car park.

OPEN *12–11pm (10.30pm Sun).*

Sir Robert Peel

104 Bell Lane, Bloxwich WS3 2JS
☎ *(01922) 470921* Paul Allen

 Charles Wells Bombadier plus one rotating guest changed every few days.

This 150-year-old pub has one main bar with pool, darts and crib teams. Two restaurants. Function room. Outside beer terrace. Large car park. Food served 12–3pm and 6–9pm Mon–Sat, 12–4pm Sun.

OPEN *12–12.*

BRIERLEY HILL

The Bull & Bladder

10 Delph Road, Brierley Hill DY5 2TN
☎ *(01384) 78293* Mr Wood

Batham Mild, Best and XXX.

Also known as The Vine, this is the brewery tap for Batham, which is situated behind. A multi-roomed pub with open fires. Bar food available at lunchtime. Car park, garden, children's room.

OPEN *12–11pm Mon–Sat; 12–4pm and 7–10.30pm Sun.*

COSELEY

Spread Eagle

Birmingham New Road, Coseley, Wolverhampton WV14 9PR
☎ *(01902) 663564* David Mark Ralph

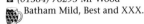 Banks's Original plus a changing range of guest ales.

Separate public bar and lounge. The lounge is comfortably furnished, with live entertainment Mon, Wed and Fri evenings. The public bar has pub games and Sky TV. Bar snacks and restaurant food available 12–3pm and 6–9pm Mon–Sat, 12–3pm Sun. Children welcome and children's menu available. Beer garden with children's play area. Large car park. Functions catered for. Located on the main A4123 Wolverhampton to Birmingham road, approximately three miles from Wolverhampton city centre.

OPEN *12–11pm Mon–Sat (10.30pm Sun).*

COVENTRY

The Beer Engine

35 Far Gosford Street, Coventry CV1 5DW
☎ *(024) 7627 0015* Ian McAllister

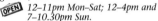 Enterprise Inns tied house with Black Sheep plus five constantly rotating guest ales, changed daily.

On a main road just outside the city centre, this friendly local is situated in a mixed working class/student area. One bar, long room, real fire. Regular live bands; busy rock nights held on Saturdays. No food during the week but customers welcome to bring their own. Sunday roasts served 12–3pm. Beer festivals held in May and October. Beer garden. Near many restaurants and takeaways. Conveniently located for Coventry university and the city centre. Leave the ringroad at junction 3 and take the third exit off the roundabout.

OPEN *Noon–2am (last entry midnight).*

The Nursery Tavern

38–9 Lord Street, Chapelfields, Coventry CV5 8DA
☎ *(024) 7667 4530* St John Berisford

Leased from Enterprise Inns, with seven real ales. Theakston Mild, Charles Wells Bombardier, John Smiths and Courage Best are fixtures, plus three rotating guests changed every couple of days.

A small, 150-year-old, village-style pub in a town location. Beams, wooden floors, one bar, three rooms. Bar snacks available 12–2pm Mon–Sat, 12.30–4pm Sun. Children allowed in the back room and garden. Summer and winter beer festivals.

OPEN *12–11.30pm Mon–Thurs; 11am–midnight Fri–Sat; 12–11pm Sun.*

The Old Windmill Inn

22–3 Spon Street, Coventry CV1 3BA
☎ *(024) 7625 2183* Robin Addey

Up to seven real ales. Timothy Taylor Landlord, Greene King Old Speckled Hen, Caledonian Deuchars IPA, Wychwood Hobgoblin and Theakston Old Peculier are permanent fixtures with two guests changed regularly.

Grade II listed Tudor building situated in the city centre. The oldest pub in Coventry with beams, flagstone floors, an old range in one bar, snug rooms and inglenook fireplaces. Food available 12–2.30pm. Children welcome. Private room for hire. Quiz and poker nights, beer and cider festivals. Student discount available.

OPEN *11am–11pm Mon–Thurs; 11am–midnight Fri–Sat; 12–12 Sun.*

Whitefriars Olde Ale House

114–15 Gosford Street, Coventry CV1 5DL
☎ *(024) 7625 1655* Matthew Young

Freehouse with six guest ales from a variety of breweries.

A 13th-century townhouse set within the grounds of Whitefriars monastery, thought to have been a medieval lodging house. One of the oldest buildings in the Coventry area. Food served 12–2.30pm Mon–Fri, 12–3.30pm Sun. Beer garden which plays host to annual beer festivals during May and August. Occasional live bands at weekends. Upstairs function room suitable for buffets, meetings, etc. Children welcome. Situated by Coventry University.

OPEN *12–12 Sun–Thurs; noon–1am Fri–Sat.*

CRADLEY HEATH

The Waterfall

132 Waterfall Lane, Cradley Heath B64 6RG
☎ *(0121) 561 3499* Marie Ann Smith

Ten beers, including Holden's Golden Glow, Special and Black Country Bitter and Batham Bitter. The six guests are rotated whenever the firkin runs out, and come from breweries such as Kelham Island, Abbeydale, RCH and Sarah Hughes, plus many others.

A traditional Black Country pub, over 100 years old. The beer garden has a raised decking area, waterfall and panoramic views. Food available 12–2pm and 6–8.30pm Mon–Fri, 12–8.30pm Sat and 12–4pm Sun. Up the hill from Old Hill Station.

OPEN *12–3pm and 5–11pm Mon–Thurs; 12–12 Fri–Sat; 12–10.30pm Sun.*

DUDLEY

Little Barrel

68 High Street, Dudley DY1 1PY
☎ *(07989) 814610* Paul and Kathy Jones

Up to four guests plus one hand-pulled cider. Local breweries such as Olde Swan (Ma Pardoe's) and Hop Back are supported.

A small, traditional town pub with wooden floors. One bar, dining area. No food. Children welcome until 9pm. Seasonal beer festivals.

OPEN *10am–11pm (10.30pm Sun).*

The Park Inn

George Street, Woodsetton, Dudley DY1 4LW
☎ *(01902) 661279* A Walford

Four Holden's beers plus one monthly-changing guest from Holden's.

Traditional pub with open fire and wooden floors. Large bar area and two other rooms. Beer garden, large conservatory. Food served 12–3pm and 6–9pm Mon–Sat; 1–4pm for Sun lunch. Two car parks. Children welcome.

OPEN *12–11pm (10.30pm Sun).*

HALESOWEN

Edward VII

88 Stourbridge Road, Halesowen B63 3UP
☎ *(0121) 550 4493* Patrick Villa

Banks's Bitter plus one guest, changing every three weeks. Beers might include Everards Tiger, Enville White or Marston's Bitter.

Beautiful, well-thought-out, comfortable pub/restaurant with two bars and outside seating. Food served every lunchtime and Tues–Sat evenings. Children allowed. Located on the A458, next to Halesowen Town Football Club.

OPEN *12–3pm and 5–11pm Mon–Thurs; 11am–11pm Fri–Sat; 12–10.30pm Sun.*

Hawne Tavern

76 Attwood Street, Halesowen B63 3UG
☎ *(0121) 602 2601* Raymond Weaver

A freehouse serving nine real ales. Batham Bitter, Banks's Bitter, Red Lion White Lion, Bank Top Mild. Five guests, changed when they run out, from breweries such as Archers, Holden's, Titanic, Malvern Hills, Black Sheep, Enville, Ossett, Abbeydale and Wood.

Small, traditional pub, approximately 130 years old, with a friendly Black Country welcome. Small selection of bar snacks available 5–8.30pm Mon–Fri; sandwiches 12–2.30pm and bar snacks 5–7pm Sat. No food Sun. Children and dogs welcome. From the Stourbridge road, turn left into Short Street and the pub is straight ahead.

OPEN *4.30–11pm Mon–Fri; 12–11pm Sat and bank holidays; 12–10.30pm Sun.*

The Waggon & Horses

21 Stourbridge Road, Halesowen B63 3TU
☎ *(0121) 550 4989* Bob Dummons

Freehouse with 14 real ales: Batham Bitter, Nottingham EPA, Holden's Golden Glow, Oakham White Dwarf, Bank Top Mild, Red Lion White Lion and a stout or porter, plus seven guests, changed after every cask, from breweries such as Thornbridge, Prospect, Naylors, Acorn, Pictish, Abbeydale, Purity, Teme Valley, Exmoor and Cotleigh, to name but a few. Four Belgian beers and two German beers on draught.

A classic West Midlands Victorian boozer. Bar food available 12–6.30pm. On the A458, and the number 9 bus route between Birmingham and Stourbridge.

OPEN *12–11.30pm Sun–Thurs; noon–12.30am Fri–Sat.*

HARBORNE

The White Horse

2 York Street, Harborne, Birmingham B17 0HG
☎ *(0121) 427 6023* Colin Raymond Marlow
www.whitehorseharborne.homestead.com/home.html

Spirit Group pub with seven to nine ales, all changed daily. Could include ales from Hydes, Greene King, Everards, Theakston or Wadworth.

This traditional backstreet boozer has two rooms. Mostly bare floorboards with carpet in the snug. Large plasma screen with Sky Sports and Premier Plus. Has been a pub for around 160 years. Food served 12–6pm Mon–Fri, 12–3pm Sun. Nearby attractions include Cadbury World, Sea World, Botanical Gardens and Bullring Shopping Centre. Situated ten minutes from Birmingham city centre, off Harborne High Street next to the clock tower.

OPEN *12–11pm Sun–Mon; 11am–11.30pm Tues–Thurs; 11am–midnight Fri–Sat.*

HIGHGATE

The Lamp Tavern

157 Barford Street, Highgate, Birmingham B5 6AH
☎ *(0121) 622 2599* Eddie Fitzpatrick

Freehouse with Stanway Stanney Bitter, Everards Tiger, Marston's Pedigree and Church End Grave Digger plus one guest pump serving beers such as Shepherd Neame Bishop's Finger or Church End What the Fox's Hat.

A small, friendly village pub situated near the town. Bar snacks available at lunchtime. No children.

OPEN *All day Mon–Sat; 12–3pm and 8–10.30pm Sun.*

HOCKLEY

Black Eagle

16 Factory Road, Hockley, Birmingham B18 5JU
☎ *(0121) 523 4008* Tony Lewis

Marston's Pedigree, Timothy Taylor Landlord and something from Beowulf plus two guest beers, perhaps from Wye Valley, Church End or Burton Bridge.

Popular award-winning pub with two small front lounges, a large back lounge, snug and restaurant. Original Victorian back bar. Beer garden. Well known locally for good food. Bar meals 12.15–2.30pm and 5.30–9.30pm, restaurant 7–10.30pm. No food on Sunday evenings. Children welcome to eat. Annual beer festival each July. Five minutes by Metro to Soho Benson from Snow Hill.

OPEN *11.30am–2.30pm and 5.30–11pm Mon–Fri; 11.30am–11pm Sat; 12–4pm Sun.*

KNOWLE

The Vaults

High Street, Knowle, Solihull B93 0JU
☎ *(01564) 773656* Nick Worrall

Freehouse with six ales, including Caledonian Deuchars IPA, Adnams Explorer and Tetley Bitter plus two guests changed every couple of days, from breweries such as Cottage, Wychwood, Smiles, Oakham and many more.

Traditional pub just off the High Street. Food served 12–2pm Mon–Sat. Ample parking. Regular beer festivals, fly-fishing trips. Annual pickled onion competition (quality rather than quantity!).

OPEN *12–2.30pm and 5–11.30pm Mon–Thurs; all day Fri–Sun.*

LOWER GORNAL

The Fountain Inn

8 Temple Street, Lower Gornal DY3 2PE
☎ *(01384) 24277* Alan Davis

Genuine freehouse with nine real ales. Enville Ale, RCH Pitchfork, Hook Norton Old Hooky and Greene King Abbot are regular fixtures plus five rotating guests. Three Belgian beers on draught and two real ciders also served.

A comfortable Victorian freehouse with a warm and pleasant atmosphere. One room with a central bar. Restaurant at the rear with 60 covers; food served 12–2.30pm and 6–9pm Mon–Thurs, 12–9pm Fri–Sat and 12–5pm Sun. Parking, garden. Children allowed in the restaurant area which was once the brewhouse. CAMRA West Midlands Pub of the Year 2003. Two miles from Dudley.

OPEN *12–11pm (10.30pm Sun).*

NETHERTON

The Olde Swan

89 Halesowen Road, Netherton, Dudley DY2 9PY
☎ *(01384) 253075* Tim Newey

 A revitalised brewpub, home of the Olde Swan Brewery (formerly known as Ma Pardoe's) with only home brews available, four or five at any one time: Olde Swan Original, Dark Swan, Entire and Bumblebee plus a monthly-changing occasional or celebration ale.

One of the original four brewpubs dating from the 1970s, this is a Victorian tower brewery plus a pub, unchanged since 1863, including original mirrored back bar and enamel plate ceiling. Separate bar, lounges and function room. A quiet, real ale drinkers' pub with no juke boxes, games machines or music. Food available 12–2pm and 6–9pm Mon–Sat, and 12–3pm Sun. Courtyard seating. Strictly over-14s only. Brewery tours by arrangement.

OPEN *11am–11pm Mon–Sat; 12–4pm and 7–10.30pm Sun.*

OLDBURY

The Waggon & Horses

17A Church Street, Oldbury B69 3AD
☎ *(0121) 552 5467* Andrew Gale

 Brains Reverend James, Enville White and Oakham JHB plus three guests, rotated every week.

Victorian Grade II listed building with tiled walls, copper ceiling and original brewery windows. Two rooms. Bar food available 12–2.30pm Mon–Sat and 5.30–8pm Tues–Fri. Car parking. Children welcome when eating. Function room with capacity for 40 people. At the corner of Market Street and Church Street in Oldbury town centre, next to the library, opposite the council offices.

OPEN *12–11pm Mon–Thurs; 12–12 Fri–Sat; 12–10.30pm Sun.*

PELSALL

The Sloan Inn

Wolverhampton Road, Pelsall, Walsall WS3 4AD
☎ *(01922) 694696* Catherine Yeats

Highgate Dark Mild and Saddlers Celebrated Best Bitter are always on offer.

The oldest pub in Pelsall, with a homely atmosphere. Food is available 12–2.30pm and 6–9pm Tues–Sat and 12–2.30pm Sun. Children allowed. Car park.

OPEN *11am–11pm Mon–Sat; 12–10.30pm Sun.*

SEDGLEY

The Beacon Hotel

129 Bilston Street, Sedgley, Dudley DY3 1JE
☎ *(01902) 883380* John Hughes

 Traditional Victorian brewery tap offering three home-brewed ales from Sarah Hughes: Dark Ruby, Sedgley Surprise Bitter and Pale Amber, plus three guest beers such as Thornbridge Jaipur, Hop Back Summer Lightning and Oakham Bishop's Farewell.

The three-storey Victorian brewery at the rear of the pub houses the Sarah Hughes Brewery, which was restored and reopened in 1987 after a 30-year closure. John Hughes, grandson of Sarah Hughes, discovered his grandmother's recipe for Dark Ruby Mild, and the brewery now supplies around 500 outlets and beer festivals. Brewery tours are available, but booking is essential. The pub has recently been refurbished, but retains its original Victorian charm. Ham and cheese and onion cobs available Mon–Sat. Children's room, plus beer garden with play area. Off the A4123.

OPEN *12–2.30pm and 5.30–11pm Mon–Fri; 12–3pm and 6–11pm Sat; 12–3pm and 7–10.30pm Sun.*

Mount Pleasant

144 High Street, Sedgley DY3 1RH
☎ *07950 195652*
Trevor Farmer and Lynn Armstrong

A freehouse. Eight real ales on offer. RCH Stumpy plus seven guests sourced from local micro-breweries and changed frequently.

An olde-worlde pub with real open fires, also know as The Stump. 'Cobs' available. Situated between Wolverhampton and Dudley.

OPEN *7–11pm Mon–Tues; 6.30–11pm Wed–Sat; 12–3pm and 7–10.30pm Sun.*

SHELFIELD

The Four Crosses Inn

1 Green Lane, Shelfield, Walsall WS4 1RN
☎ *(01922) 682518* Patrick J Cahill

Freehouse with Highgate Dark and Davenports plus two rotating guests changed at least twice a week from various micro-breweries around the country, including Stonehenge, Hanby and Wye Valley.

A traditional two-bar pub that dates from the 1930s, though there has been a pub on the site since the early 18th century. Open-plan kitchen, with food served 5–10.30pm Mon–Fri and all day Sat–Sun. Everything is cooked on a barbecue, from steaks and chicken skewers to traditional North Indian curries. Beer garden.

OPEN *All day, every day.*

SOLIHULL
The Harvester
Tanhouse Farm Road, Solihull B92 9EY
☎ *(0121) 742 0770*
Dawn Bickerton and Philip Jones
www.harvesterlife.com

Leased from Enterprise Inns, serving Greene King Abbot and John Smiths plus three guests which rotate weekly.

A traditional community pub with darts and pool in one bar, plus lounge/restaurant and huge beer garden. Big plasma TV in lounge. Food served all day except Saturdays. Lounge room available for hire. Bouncy castle, climbing frame, swings, tree house and five-a-side football pitch (fully enclosed).

OPEN *Noon–1.30am Sun–Thurs; noon–2.30am Fri–Sat.*

STOURBRIDGE
Hogshead
21–6 Foster Street, Stourbridge DY8 1EL
☎ *(01384) 371040* David Collins

Fourteen beers including ten guest ales. Examples include Enville White, Fuller's London Pride, Timothy Taylor Landlord, Marston's Pedigree, Wadworth 6X or something from Black Sheep, Brakspear or many others.

Hogshead original design, town-centre pub with ten beers on long front bar and four gravity-dispensed beers on back bar. Background music during the day, livelier in the evenings. Air-conditioned. Food available all day. Children welcome in designated areas until 8pm. Situated in pedestrian precinct.

OPEN *12–11pm (10.30pm Sun).*

The Windsor Castle Inn
7 Stourbridge Road, Lye Cross, Stourbridge DY9 7DG
☎ *(01384) 897809* John Sadler
www.windsorcastlebrewery.com

A freehouse and home of the Windsor Castle Brewery. The full range of Windsor Castle ales: Thin Ice, Worcester Sorcerer, Jack's Ale, Sadler's Mild, Mudcity Stout, Green Man, IPA and Sadler's Monthly Special on offer.

Opened in May 2006 in an old printer's buildings with the brewery at the back. Original decor, a mix of old and new. Full menu, including baked beer bread, beer-baked ham, special recipe beer sausages, beer-battered fish, plus grills, fish and salads from fresh local produce, whenever possible. Food served 12–3pm and 6–9pm Mon–Fri (10pm Sat); 12–4pm Sun.

OPEN *11am–11pm.*

TIPTON
The Port 'n' Ale
178 Horseley Heath, Great Bridge, Tipton DY4 7DS
☎ *(0121) 557 7249* Kevin Taylor

Freehouse with Greene King Abbot, RCH Pitchfork, Moorhouse's Pendle Witches and Badger Tanglefoot plus two guest pumps regularly serving RCH beers or something like Burton Bridge Summer Ale or Cotleigh Barn Ale.

A Victorian pub situated out of town. Bar, lounge and beer garden. Basic food served, including fish and chips and sandwiches. Children allowed in the garden only. Just down the road from Dudley Port railway station.

OPEN *12–3pm and 5–11pm Mon–Fri; 12–11pm Sat; 12–4.30pm and 7–10.30pm Sun.*

The Rising Sun
116 Horseley Road, Tipton DY4 7NH
☎ *(0121) 530 2308* Nicola Jane Skidmore

Eight real ales, with Oakham JHB and Banks's Traditional the permanent fixtures. Two of the remaining beers are changed every day, with favourite breweries including Church End, Stonehenge, Batham, Thornbridge, Red Lion and Ossett.

Very traditional lounge which boasts a newly refurbished bar and real fires. TV for sports. No food. Large beer garden. Private functions catered for. Close to Owen Street rail and Metro station.

OPEN *12-11pm every day.*

The Waggon & Horses
Toll End Road, Ocker Hill, Tipton DY4 0ET
☎ *(0121) 502 6453* Keith Darby

Freehouse with eight ever-changing real ales on offer, including beers from the pub's own micro-brewery.

Built around 1860, with one bar, one lounge and a conservatory. No food, except for barbecues in summer. Beer garden. Easy driving distance from Dudley Zoo, the Black Country Museum and Sandwell Valley. Ten minutes from M6 junction 9 – follow A461 through Wednesbury, pub is 200 yards on left from Ocker Hill island. Close to Wednesbury Central Metro station.

OPEN *5–11pm Mon–Thurs; 12–11pm Fri–Sat; 12–4pm and 7–10.30pm Sun.*

UPPER GORNAL
Britannia Inn
109 Kent Street, Upper Gornal DY3 1UX
☎ *(01902) 883253*

Batham tied house with Mild, Bitter and XXX usually available.

Main lounge bar, TV room and tap room. Real fires and outside seating. Loads of character. On the A459 Dudley to Sedgley road.

OPEN *12–3pm and 7–11pm Mon–Fri; 12–11pm Sat; 12–4pm and 7–10.30pm Sun.*

Jolly Crispin

25 Clarence Street, Upper Gornal DY3 1UL
☎ *(01902) 672220* Robin Carey
www.thejollycrispin.co.uk

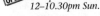 Genuine freehouse with up to nine real ales. Crispy Nail, brewed for the pub by Titanic, is always on offer, and the eight guests (from a range of 20 per week) are changed on a daily basis.

Character 18th-century pub split into two rooms served by one central bar. Sandwiches only available, plus buffets by request, and cook-your-own barbecues on summer weekends. Beer garden, large car park. Local CAMRA Pub of the Year 2005 and 2007, Black Country Tourism Pub of the Year finalist 2007, Dudley & South Staffs Pub of the Year 2007 and West Midlands County Pub of the Year 2007. No children under 14. Coaches by appointment. Five minutes from Dudley Castle. On the main Dudley–Sedgeley road – the 558 bus stops outside!

OPEN *4–11pm Mon–Thurs; 12–11pm Fri–Sat; 12–10.30pm Sun.*

WALSALL

The Rising Sun

90 Ablewell Street, Walsall WS1 2EU
☎ *(01922) 626575* Reg Turner

 A Highgate pub with Mild and Saddlers Celebrated Best Bitter the permanent beers. One guest beer, changed as consumption demands, could be Highgate Fox's Nob or Old Ale, or any one of the Wyre Piddle brews.

Traditional pub in an old building with cobbles outside, on the edge of the town centre. Excellent atmosphere. Food available. Rock-music-oriented at weekends – popular with bikers. Two bars, dining area, massive garden, frequent live music, disco Tues, Fri and Sat – call for details.

OPEN *12–11pm Mon–Wed; noon–1am Thurs–Sat; 12–10.30pm Sun.*

Tap & Spile

5 John Street, Walsall WS2 8AF
☎ *07772 408387* Trevor Vas

 Seven or eight real ales, with Theakston Best, Caledonian Deuchars IPA, Greene King Abbot, Wychwood Hobgoblin, Fuller's London Pride, Blythe Chase and something from Hook Norton and Enville a typical selection. Five of the beers are rotated weekly.

Small, traditional backstreet pub with friendly staff and great atmosphere, also known as 'The Pretty Bricks'. Two bars and function room. Food served 12–2.30pm and 6.30–9pm Mon–Sat and 12–6pm Sun. Children welcome. Quiz night on Wednesday. Beer garden. Leaving Walsall towards Bloxwich, go down Stafford Street and turn right into John Street after the magistrate's court.

OPEN *12–3pm and 5.30–11pm Mon–Thurs; 12–11.30pm Fri–Sat; 12–3pm and 6–10.30pm Sun.*

The Wharf 10 Café Bar

10 Wolverhampton Street, Walsall WS2 8LS
☎ *(01922) 613100* Lee Dyble

 Highgate Saddlers Best Bitter and Davenport's Smooth Pour Bitter plus a fortnightly guest such as Highgate Old Ale or Davenport's IPA, or Marston's Pedigree.

Town-centre bar with modern interior and a patio, located next to the art gallery, offering dining during the day and music at night. Food available 11am–4pm. Children allowed until 5pm. Car park. Outside dining in summer by the canal, live bands every weekend, jazz night Thurs, salsa Wed. Follow signs for the art gallery.

OPEN *11am–11pm Mon–Thurs; 11am–2am Fri–Sat; 12–11pm Sun.*

The White Lion

150 Sandwell Street, Walsall WS1 3EQ
☎ *(01922) 628542* Colin Joesbury

 Part tied to Admiral Taverns. Adnams Bitter, Greene King IPA and Kinver Half Centurion, Hobsons Bitter and Highgate Mild. One guest, changed every two or three days, from breweries such as Batham, Burton Bridge, Gadds and Shardlow. Old ales and porters available in winter.

A Victorian boozer. Bar, lounge and live music room. Food served 12–3pm and 5–9pm, every day. Live music Tues, Thurs and Sun. Beer garden. Beer festivals in summer and autumn. Located half a mile outside Walsall town centre.

OPEN *12–11pm Sun–Thurs; 12–12 Fri–Sat.*

WEATHEROAK

The Coach and Horses

Weatheroak, Alvechurch B48 7EA
☎ *(01564) 823386* Philip Meads
www.coachandhorsesinn.co.uk

 Former home to the Weatheroak Brewery, which is now based in Alvechurch. Brewing continues under the Weatheroak Hill naming, with Icknield Ale and Weatheroak Hill Bitter among the beers available in the pub. Guests beers change daily and come from breweries including Woods, Hook Norton, Hobsons, Malvern Hills and Purity.

Country pub set in four acres, eight miles south of Birmingham. Traditional bar, lounge and separate 70-seater restaurant. Food served 12–2pm (2.30pm Sun) and 6–9.30pm (not Sun). Large beer garden, festivals and hog roasts. Two miles off junction 3 of the M42, near Kings Norton golf course.

OPEN *11.30am–11pm Mon–Sat; 12–10.30pm Sun.*

WEDNESBURY

The Forge

Franchise Street, Wednesbury WS10 9RG
☎ *(0121) 526 2777* Paul Pugh

 Owned by Highgate, with Highgate Mild Ale a permanent fixture. One seasonal guest is also served.

Two-bar community pub, purpose-built in 1935 by Highgate Brewery. No food. Live music Fri, Sat and Sun. Children allowed. Car park. Situated behind IKEA.

OPEN *12–2pm and 5–11pm Mon–Thurs; 11am–11pm Fri–Sun.*

The Old Blue Ball

19 Hall End, Wednesbury WS10 9GD
☎ *(0121) 556 0197* Jonathan Bradley

Six real ales. Everards Old Original and Timothy Taylor Landlord are permanent fixtures, and the four rotating beers are from a range including Young's Special, Fuller's London Pride and Discovery, Black Sheep Bitter, Adnams Broadside, Brains Reverend James, Wadworth 6X, Greene King Ruddles County and Abbot and Hardys & Hansons Olde Trip.

Small, friendly, family pub dating back to 1800, with one small bar, one small lounge, one family lounge and plenty of history. Beer garden with two children's climbing frames. Sandwiches served every day, plus pork and stuffing sandwiches Fri–Sat. Barbecues in summer, bonfires in winter. From Wednesbury town, look for two churches on a hill. Follow this road and turn right.

OPEN *12–3pm and 5–11pm Mon–Thurs; 12–11pm Fri; 12–4.30pm and 7–11pm Sat; 12–3.30pm and 7–11pm Sun.*

WEDNESFIELD

The Pyle Cock Inn

Rookery Street, Wednesfield, Wolverhampton WV11 1UN
☎ *(01902) 732125* Tony Pugh

A tied house with ales from Marston's, Jennings and Banks's plus two rotating guests.

Dating back to the early 19th century this pub has a public bar, snug plus lounge. Patio areas at front and side of the pub. Heated smoking area. Bar snacks served lunchtimes Mon–Sat. Car park. Children welcome until 8pm. Close to Bentley Bridge shopping centre and leisure centre.

OPEN *10.30am–11pm (open later Fri–Sat).*

WEST BROMWICH

The Old Crown

56 Sandwell Road, West Bromwich B70 8TG
☎ *(0121) 525 4600*

Freehouse with four hand pumps serving an ever-changing selection of ales such as Timothy Taylor Landlord, Archers Golden, Kelham Island Pale and Easy Rider plus Oakham, Enville, Wye Valley, Bathams, St

Austell and Burton Bridge ales. RCH Pitchfork and Olde Swan Entire are other favourites.

Open-plan town pub dating from 1837. Food is available 12–2pm Mon–Sat and 6–9pm Thurs–Sat. Children allowed until 9pm. Off the high street.

OPEN *12–4pm and 5–11.30pm Mon–Thurs; 12–11pm Fri–Sat; 12–4pm and 7–10.30pm Sun.*

The Vine

152 Roebuck Street, West Bromwich B70 6RD
☎ *(0121) 553 2866* Suki Patel
www.thevine.co.uk

 Freehouse with one or two real ales. Breweries featured include Batham, Sharps, Blue Bear, Warwickshire Beer Company and Burton Bridge, and the selection changes once or twice a day.

A traditional two-bar pub with beams and gardens. Small on the outside, but Tardis-like within. Food available at 12–2pm and 5–10.30pm Mon–Fri, 1–10.30pm Sat–Sun. Barbecues and curries are specialities. Children welcome. Sky TV. Close to West Bromwich Albion football ground. Situated out of town near M5 junction 1, off Birmingham Road.

OPEN *11.30am–2.30pm and 5–11pm Mon–Thurs; 11.30am–11pm Fri; 12–11pm Sat; 12–10.30pm Sun.*

Wheatsheaf

379 High Street, Carters Green, West Bromwich B70 9QW
☎ *(0121) 553 2441* Jill Britton

Black Country Bitter, Golden Glow and a monthly special guest ale.

A two-bar pub; one light, airy traditional bar with large front window and the second in a relaxing lounge at the rear of the building. Food served at lunchtimes. Beer garden.

OPEN *11am–11.30pm Sun–Thurs; 11am–midnight Fri–Sat.*

WILLENHALL

The Falcon Inn

Gomer Street West, Willenhall WV13 2NR
☎ *(01902) 633378* Mick Taylor

Genuine freehouse with up to eight real ales. RCH Pitchfork, Oakham JHB, Pardoe's Mild and Greene King Abbot are regulars, plus four guest beers, occasionally including a stout or a porter. All beers are hand-pulled and served in oversized glasses. Range of malt whiskies also on offer.

A 1930s traditional backstreet pub near the town centre, run by the same family for almost 25 years. Walsall CAMRA Pub of the Year 2005, 2006 and 2008. Two rooms – bar and lounge – with no price difference! Bar snacks (pies, cobs and pasties) available all day. Beer garden with smoking area. Plenty of on-street parking. Children welcome until 9pm.

OPEN *12–11pm (10.30pm Sun).*

WOLLASTON

The Princess

115–17 Bridgenorth Road, Wollaston,
Stourbridge DY8 3NX
☎ *(01384) 443687* Dave Tibbetts

Leased from Enterprise Inns, with Charles Wells Bombardier, Greene King Abbot Ale, Enville Ale and Theakston Mild available, plus a quarterly-changing guest beer.

Single bar with wooden floor, quarry tiles and an interesting selection of mirrors and artefacts. Food served lunchtimes only. Car park. Children welcome, but no special facilities.

OPEN *11am–11pm Mon–Sat; 12–10.30pm Sun.*

The Unicorn

145 Bridgnorth Road, Wollaston, Stourbridge
☎ *(01384) 394823* C John Freeman

Batham Bitter and Mild.

Small pub with three rooms and a traditional, cosy, olde-worlde atmosphere. No music. Lovely beer garden. Rolls available at lunchtime. Public car park to the rear. Children welcome until 9pm in the garden and in a specified area of the pub.

OPEN *12–11pm Mon–Sat; 12–4pm and 7–10.30pm Sun.*

WOLVERHAMPTON

Chindit

113 Merridale Road, Wolverhampton
☎ *(01902) 425582* John Ralph Smith
www.thechindit.co.uk

Four real ales, including Caledonian Deuchars IPA, Wye Valley HPA and Enville Ale plus a guest such as Oakham JHB, White Dwarf or Bishop's Farewell, Hop Back Summer Lightning, or a local brew.

Cosy, two-roomed pub named after a Second World War regiment – the only pub in the world so named. Cask Marque accredited. Live music on Friday evenings. Annual beer festival with over 30 different beers over the May bank holiday. Located one mile from city centre, on the west side of Wolverhampton, on the 543 and 513 bus routes.

OPEN *2–11pm Mon–Fri; 12–12 Sat–Sun.*

Great Western

Sun Street, Wolverhampton WV10 0DJ
☎ *(01902) 351090* Jamie Atkins

Batham pub with six real ales. Batham Bitter, Holden's Golden Glow, Bitter and Special are regularly on offer, plus guests weekly.

Friendly, 150-year-old pub with railway memorabilia. Food sometimes available. Beer garden, car park. Children welcome at lunchtimes if dining. Situated two minutes' walk from railway station.

OPEN *Opening hours under review – call pub for details.*

Moon Under Water

53–5 Lichfield Street, Wolverhampton WV1 1EQ
☎ *(01902) 422447* Paul and Anne Ward

Greene King Abbot and IPA, Banks's Original, Enville Ale and Marston's Pedigree, plus five guests, changed every other day. Examples include Sadler's IPA, Wood Shropshire Lad, Marston's Old Empire, Highgate Old Ale and Theakston Old Peculier.

A one-bar Wetherspoon's pub in the city centre, frequented by locals and shoppers, with a young crowd in the evenings at weekends. Food available 9am–11pm. Children welcome for meals until 9pm.

OPEN *9am–midnight Sun–Thurs; 9am–1am Fri–Sat.*

The Newhampton

Riches Street, Wolverhampton WV6 0DW
☎ *(01902) 745773* Bill Kendrick

Seven ales, including Timothy Taylor Landlord, Caledonian Deuchars IPA, Theakston Old Peculier, Courage Best and Directors and Greene King Abbot, plus a daily-changing guest beer.

Traditional community pub, with bowling green, extensive beer garden and patio area, function room and children's play area. Homemade food served 12–9pm Mon–Sat and 12–4pm Sun. Function room available for private hire, and buffets can be supplied. Folk bands every other Saturday. Just over a mile from the town centre – just off the A41 (Tettenhall Road) or Newhampton Road.

OPEN *11am–11pm Mon–Thurs; 11am–midnight Fri–Sat; 12–11pm Sun.*

The Posada

48 Lichfield Street, Wolverhampton WV1 1DG
☎ *(07960 940243)* Chris Millard

A tied house serving Greene King Abbot Ale and Timothy Taylor Landlord plus three rotating guests. Guest ale list means that the pub has a choice of 30 ales which change every six to eight weeks.

This 132-year old traditional real ale pub retains its original bar, fireplace and 'snob screen'. Expansion completed summer 2007. Beer garden. Children welcome. Located in city centre, just off the main High Street.

OPEN *12–11pm Mon–Wed; 12–12 Thurs; noon–1am Fri–Sat.*

Tap & Spile

35 Princess Street, Wolverhampton WV1 1HD
☎ *(01902) 713319* Michael Stokes

Banks's Bitter and Mild are the permanent beers, plus up to six guest ales which could be from any brewery around the UK.

A locals' town pub with wooden floors, open fire, one main bar and snug rooms. Food available 12–4pm. Beer garden. Children allowed until 7pm.

OPEN *10am–11pm Mon–Sat; 12–10.30pm Sun.*

THE BREWERIES

ARKELLS BREWERY LTD
*Kingsdown Brewery, Hyde Road, Swindon
SN2 7RU*
☎ *(01793) 823026*
www.arkells.com

 2B 3.2% ABV
Light and quenching with good bitter
hoppiness.
SMOOTH 3.6% ABV
Silky texture.
3B 4.0% ABV
Amber, balanced and hoppy.
MOONLIGHT 4.5% ABV
Gold, toasty aroma.
KINGSDOWN ALE 5.0% ABV
Smooth, rounded and flavour-packed.
Plus seasonal brews.

BOX STEAM BREWERY LTD
*Unit 2, Oaks Farm, Rode Hill, Colerne,
Chippenham SN14 8AR*
☎ *(01225) 858383*
www.boxsteambrewery.com

REV. AWDRY'S ALE 3.8% ABV
Light straw colour, hoppy aftertaste.
TUNNEL VISION 4.2% ABV
Clean taste, slightly dry.
BLIND HOUSE 4.6% ABV
Dark, hoppy, hints of red wine.

THE HIDDEN BREWERY LIMITED
Wylye Road, Dinton, Salisbury SP3 5EU
☎ *(01722) 716440*
www.thehiddenbrewery.co.uk

PINT 3.8% ABV
Refreshing and tangy.
OLD SARUM 4.1% ABV
Floral notes and spiciness.
QUEST 4.2% ABV
Amber and fruity.
Plus seasonal brews including:
HIDDEN STRENGTH 3.4% ABV
HIDDEN POTENTIAL 4.2% ABV
HIDDEN SPRING 4.5% ABV
HIDDEN DEPTHS 4.6% ABV
HIDDEN FANTASY 4.6% ABV
HIDDEN TREASURE 4.8% ABV
HIDDEN PLEASURE 4.9% ABV

HOBDEN'S WESSEX BREWERY
*Farm Cottage, Norton Ferris, Warminster
BA12 7HT*
☎ *(01985) 844532*

NAUGHTY FERRET 3.5% ABV
TRUTH DECAY 3.9% ABV
CROCKERTON CLASSIC 4.1% ABV
KILMINGTON BEST 4.2% ABV
MERRY MINK 4.2% ABV
OLD DEVERILL VALLEY PALE 4.2% ABV
DEVERILL'S ADVOCAAT 4.5% ABV
WARMINSTER WARRIOR 4.5% ABV
WYLYE WARMER 6.0% ABV
RUSSIAN STOAT 9.0% ABV
Plus seasonals and specials.

THE HOP BACK BREWERY PLC
*Unit 22–4, Batten Road Industrial Estate,
Downton, Salisbury SP5 3HU*
☎ *(01725) 510986*
www.hopback.co.uk

GFB 3.5% ABV
Smooth and full flavoured for gravity.
ODYSSEY BEST BITTER 4.0% ABV
Full bodied with coffee notes.
CROP CIRCLE 4.2% ABV
Pale with wonderful thirst-quenching properties.
ENTIRE STOUT 4.5% ABV
Powerful roast maltiness.
SUMMER LIGHTNING 5.0% ABV
Superb, pale and quenching with good
hoppiness.

KEYSTONE BREWERY
*The Old Carpenter's Workshop, Berwick Street,
Leonard, Salisbury SP3 5SN*
☎ *(01747) 820426*
www.keystonebrewery.co.uk

BEDROCK 3.6% ABV
GOLD SPICE 4.0% ABV
GOLD STANDARD 4.0% ABV
LARGE ONE 4.2% ABV
CORNERSTONE 4.8% ABV

MOLE'S BREWERY
5 Merlin Way, Bowerhill, Melksham SN12 6TJ
☎ *(01225) 704734*
www.molesbrewery.com

TAP 3.5% ABV
Malty with clean, balancing bitterness.
BEST 4.0% ABV
Golden with quenching, hoppy finish.
LANDLORD'S CHOICE 4.5% ABV
Darker, with hops, fruit and malt.
MOLENNIUM 4.5% ABV
Fruit, caramel and malty overtones.
RUCKING MOLE 4.5% ABV
Chestnut colour, fruity palate, smooth, bitter
finish.
MOLECATCHER 5.0% ABV
Seasonals:
BARLEYMOLE 4.2% ABV
Pale, hoppy brew with malty finish.
MOLEGRIP 4.3% ABV
Rounded, balanced autumn ale.
HOLY MOLEY 4.7% ABV
Good malt flavour with hop balance.

THE RAMSBURY BREWERY
*Stockclose Farm, Mildenhall, Marlborough
SN8 2NN*
☎ *(01672) 541407*

BITTER 3.6% ABV
KENNET VALLEY ALE 4.0% ABV
FLINTKNAPPER 4.2% ABV
GOLD 4.5% ABV

STONEHENGE ALES LTD (BUNCES BREWERY)
The Old Mill, Mill Road, Hetheravon, Salisbury SP4 9QB
☎ *(01980) 670631*
www.stonehengeales.co.uk

SPIRE ALE 3.8% ABV
Hoppy bitter.
PIGSWILL 4.0% ABV
Mellow and hoppy.
HEEL STONE 4.3% ABV
Quenching fruity flavour.
GREAT BUSTARD 4.8% ABV
Amber red and fruity.
DANISH DYNAMITE 5.0% ABV
Golden and far too easy to drink!
Plus seasonal brews.

WADWORTH & CO. LTD
Northgate Brewery, 41–5 Northgate Street, Devizes SN10 1JW
☎ *(01380) 723361*
www.wadworth.co.uk

HENRY'S ORIGINAL IPA 3.6% ABV
Well balanced and smooth, biscuity, with malt throughout.
HENRY'S SMOOTH 3.6% ABV
Creamy taste.
6X 4.3% ABV
Rich, with malt flavours.
6X PREMIUM 4.3% ABV
Copper colour, more intense flavour than 6X.
JCB 4.7% ABV
Unique palate with chewy bite.
BISHOP'S TIPPLE 5.5% ABV
Golden, hoppy, with hint of spice.
Seasonals:
SUMMERSAULT 4.0% ABV
Quenching, lager-style beer. Summer only.
MALT 'N' HOPS 4.5% ABV
Sweet and nutty. September.
OLD TIMER 5.8% ABV
Ripe fruit and hop aromas. December.

WESTBURY ALES
Horse & Groom, Alfred Street, Westbury BA13 3DY
☎ *07771 976865*
www.westburyales.com

AMBER DAZE 4.1% ABV
Classically hoppy and malty.
EARLY DAZE 4.1% ABV
Crisp citrus flavour.
PALE STORM 4.3% ABV
Malt and balanced fruity, tawny colour.
BITHAM BLONDE 4.5% ABV
Malty and hop tastes.
MIDNIGHT MASH 5.0% ABV
Fruity with a hint of sweetness.
Occasionals:
DARK HORSE 3.7% ABV
FAITH, HOP AND CHARITY 3.7% ABV
PS2 4.0% ABV
HOLLY DAZE 4.2% ABV

THE PUBS

ABBEY MEADS

The Jovial Monk
Highdown Way, St Andrews Ridge, Abbey Meads, Swindon SN25 4YD
☎ *(01793) 728636* Oliver Cleary

Arkells tied house with 2B and 3B plus seasonal Arkells beers such as James' Real Ale.

A community pub built in 2000, with one bar, games room and separate 60-cover restaurant. Food available every day. Children welcome. Car park, beer garden, conservatory. Function room for up to 60 people available free of charge. On the A419 directly behind the Motorola building.

OPEN *10am–1am Mon–Sat; 11am–midnight Sun.*

ALDBOURNE

Crown Hotel
The Square, Aldbourne, Marlborough SN8 2DU
☎ *(01672) 540214*
Ian and Jane Clarkson-Cowles
www.crownataldbourne.co.uk

Freehouse with ales from Fuller's and Brakspear plus two guests, changed weekly.

This 17th-century coaching house has two bars and open fires. Four letting rooms available. Food served 11am–2.30pm and 6–9.30pm Mon–Sun. Beer garden. Conference room and private party room. Beer festivals. Near Silbury Hill, Avebury Circle, the White Horse and Stonehenge. Situated on the B4192, ten minutes from either junction 14 or 15 of the M4.

OPEN *11am–3pm and 6–11pm.*

AVEBURY

The Red Lion
High Street, Avebury SN8 1RF
☎ *(01672) 539266* Richard Bounds

Greene King Old Speckled Hen, Marston's Pedigree and Flowers IPA (brewed by Badger) generally available.

A large pub handy for the stones. There's an air of efficiency in the variety of different rooms. Supposedly one of Wiltshire's most haunted pubs. Accommodation. Food all day. Car park and patio area.

OPEN *11am–11pm Mon–Sat; 12–10.30pm Sun.*

AXFORD

The Red Lion Inn

Axford, Nr Marlborough SN8 2HA
☎ *(01672) 520271* N Molyneux
www.redlionaxford.com

Freehouse with Ramsbury Ale sold, and various guest beers added.

Restaurant and pub in a brick and flint building dating back 350 years, with low beams, inglenook fireplace and views of the River Kennet and valley. Lawned garden with garden furniture to the rear, plus sunny patio for outside dining. Food served 12–2pm and 7–9pm (9.30pm Sat). Large car park. Four miles east of Marlborough between Mildenhall and Ramsbury.

OPEN *12–2.30pm and 6.30–11pm (closed Sun evening).*

BERWICK ST JAMES

The Boot Inn

Berwick St James SP3 4TN
☎ *(01722) 790243* Kathie Duval

Wadworth tenancy serving Henry's IPA and 6X plus a guest ale, changed every month.

Attractive, traditional 16th-century village pub with one bar and two areas for eating and drinking. Food served lunchtimes Tues–Sun. Garden, car park. Children and dogs welcome. Nearby attractions include Stonehenge, Salisbury Cathedral and Wilton House. Between the A303 and the A36.

OPEN *6–11pm Mon; 12–3pm and 6–11pm Tues–Sat; 12–3pm Sun.*

BERWICK ST JOHN

The Talbot Inn

The Cross, Berwick St John, Nr Shaftsbury SP7 0HA
☎ *(01747) 828222* Peter Hawkins

Freehouse with Wadworth 6X, Ringwood Best and Bass plus a guest, rotated every two weeks, which might be Ringwood Fortyniner or a locally sourced brew.

Typical country inn about 400 years old with low beams and an inglenook fire. In the Chalke Valley below Cranbourne Chase just off the A30. Food served 12–2pm and 6.30–9pm Tues–Sat, 12–2pm Sun. Beer garden, car park. Children and dogs welcome. Five miles east of Shaftesbury.

OPEN *12–2.30pm and 6.30–11pm Tues–Sat; 12–4pm Sun (closed Sun evening and all day Mon).*

BOWDEN HILL

The Bell Inn

The Wharf, Bowden Hill, Lacock, Chippenham SN15 2PJ
☎ *(01249) 730308*
Alan and Heather Shepherd

Freehouse with five hand pumps serving Wadworth 6X plus a selection of real ales of varying strengths from local breweries, including smaller and micro-breweries. Farmhouse cider also available.

Traditional rural pub built in converted canal cottages on the edge of a National Trust village. One bar, dining area, beer garden, children's play area. Two boules pistes. Food available every session and all day on Saturday and Sunday. Children allowed.

OPEN *11.30am–2.30pm and 5–11pm Mon–Fri; all day Sat–Sun.*

The Rising Sun

32 Bowden Hill, Lacock, Nr Chippenham SN15 2PP
☎ *(01249) 730363* Paul and Denise Rogers

Five beers, including Mole's Tap, Best, Molecatcher, Rucking Mole and Black Rat, plus occasional seasonals.

Cotswold stone pub with flagstone floors and open fires. Bar food available at lunchtimes and evenings (not Sun evening or Mon lunchtime), roasts served on Sun. Car park, garden. Live music Wed evenings plus alternate Sun from 3pm. Children and dogs allowed. Turn into village, then go up Bowden Hill.

OPEN *12–3pm and 6–11pm Mon–Sat; all day Sun.*

BOX HILL

The Quarrymans Arms

Box Hill, Corsham SN13 8HN
☎ *(01225) 743569* John Arundel
www.quarrymans-arms.co.uk

Genuine freehouse with Wadworth 6X, Mole's Best Bitter and Butcombe Bitter plus two local guest ales, changed every week. Guest ale weeks from around Britain.

A 300-year-old former miners' pub, tucked away in the Wiltshire countryside, high above the Colerne Valley. Popular with potholers, cavers, walkers and cyclists. Food served 11am–3pm and 6–10pm, including up to ten fish dishes each day. Beer garden with great views over the Box Valley. Car park. Children and dogs welcome. Free wi-fi available throughout pub. Lots of nearby attractions. Very difficult to find, so ring for directions. En-suite accommodation.

OPEN *Every day and evening (except Christmas Day, which is lunchtime only).*

BRADFORD-ON-AVON

Bunch of Grapes

14 Silver Street, Bradford-on-Avon BA15 1JY
☎ *(01225) 863877* Mark Vicary

Six real ales, including Young's Bitter and Special and St Austell Tribute, plus monthly and seasonal guest beers.

A 17th-century, traditional town-centre pub that is supposedly haunted. Dark wood, one bar, open fire. Food available 12–2pm and 7–9.30pm (until 9pm Sunday). Sunday carvery. Dining area can be used for private functions. Regular theme nights (e.g. tapas). Dogs welcome. Just outside the centre of town.

OPEN *11am–11pm Mon–Thurs; 11am–midnight Fri–Sat; 12–11pm Sun.*

BRATTON

The Duke at Bratton

Bratton, Nr Westbury BA13 4RW
☎ *(01380) 830242* Ian and Marion Overend

 Mole's Best plus a rotating guest such as Holy Moley.

Originally three 1730s cottages, now an award-winning (including the best Sunday roast in Britain) community village pub close to the Westbury White Horse three miles east of the town. Two bars, beams. Food available. Well-behaved children welcome. Garden and car park. Four bedrooms.

OPEN *11.30am–2pm and 7–11pm Mon–Sat; 12–2pm and 7–10.30pm Sun.*

BROAD CHALKE

The Queens Head Inn

1 North Street, Broad Chalke, Nr Salisbury SP5 5EN
☎ *(01722) 780344* Mike Craggs

Freehouse serving Greene King IPA, Old Speckled Hen and Ruddles County plus Wadworth 6X and a guest, which may be Greene King Morland Original.

A popular 15th-century country local offering food and accommodation as well as the good range of beers. Patio. Large car park. Well-behaved children welcome. Darts.

OPEN *11am–3pm and 6–11.30pm.*

BROKERSWOOD

The Kicking Donkey

Brokerswood, Westbury BA13 4EG
☎ *(01373) 823250* Nicky Millard
www.kickingdonkey.net

Freehouse always serving Sharp's Doom Bar and IPA, Wadworth 6X and Butcombe Bitter.

Snug country inn dating from 1800, with two bars, a restaurant and a relaxing, friendly atmosphere. Excellent à la carte and snack menu served 12–2.30pm and 6.30–9.30pm. Children's play area and garden. Dog-friendly. Car park. Just off the A36 to Brokerswood.

OPEN *6–11.30pm Mon (closed Mon lunch); 12–3pm and 6–11.30pm Tues–Sun.*

BROUGHTON GIFFORD

The Bell on the Common

Broughton Gifford, Nr Melksham SN12 8LX
☎ *(01225) 782309* Anthony Stanley

 Wadworth pub offering 6X and Henry's IPA.

Popular country pub built in the 1700s on the edge of a 27-acre common. Two bars and a 34-cover restaurant, with food served 12–2.30pm and 6–9pm every day. Large beer garden, boules piste. Small room on the first floor available for private hire. Parking on the edge of the common. Leave Melksham on the B3107 towards Bradford-on-Avon, turn right after half a mile to Broughton Gifford, and the pub is one mile along the road.

OPEN *11am–11pm.*

BUSHTON

The Trotting Horse

Bushton, Nr Wootton Bassett, Swindon SN4 7PX
☎ *(01793) 731338* Richard and Jenny Nickolls

Freehouse with Archers Village and Wadworth 6X as permanent ales, plus one monthly-changing guest.

A friendly and traditional village pub. Food served Sat and Sun lunch, Tues–Sat evenings. Beer garden and large car park. Games including bar billiards and darts. Function room.

OPEN *5–11pm Mon–Fri; 12–2.30pm and 6.30–11pm Sat; 12–2.30pm and 7–10.30pm Sun.*

CASTLE COMBE

The White Hart

Market Place, Castle Combe, Chippenham SN14 7HS
☎ *(01249) 782295*
Peter Dixon and Sally Merrick

 Wadworth pub offering 6X, Henry's IPA and a guest changed every week.

Dating back over 600 years, and set in the heart of the pretty village of Castle Combe. Two bars, restaurant and terraced beer garden. Food served 12–2.30pm and 6–9pm. Children welcome.

OPEN *11am–11pm.*

CHARLTON

The Horse & Groom

The Street, Charlton, Malmesbury SN16 9DL
☎ *(01666) 823904* Nicola King

Archers Village and Wadworth 6X plus a guest such as Uley Old Spot, Smiles Best, Abbey Bellringer or Ridleys Spectacular.

A traditional country village pub with beams, fires and wooden floors. Two bars, beer garden, accommodation. Food served at lunchtimes and evenings in a separate dining area. Well-behaved children allowed.

OPEN *12–3pm and 7–11pm Mon–Fri; all day Sat–Sun in the summer.*

CHIPPENHAM
Four Seasons
6 Market Place, Chippenham SN15 3HD
☎ *(01249) 444668* Christopher Mills

Leased from Fuller's, with London Pride and Gale's HSB served, plus a guest from Gale's, changed weekly.

Traditional tavern in the centre of town, catering for all groups. All major sporting events shown. Good pub grub available 12–3pm every day. Chippenham Folk Festival in May and Eddie Cochran Festival in September.

 11am–11pm Mon–Wed; 11am–1am Thurs; 11am–2am Fri–Sat; 12–12 Sun.

Pheasant Inn
Bath Road, Chippenham SN14 OAE
☎ *(01249) 444083*
Kate Partridge and Richard Bennett

Wadworth 6X, Horizon and IPA always available, with guests such as Bishop's Tipple, Old Father Time, JCB or St George and the Dragon.

Large edge-of-town pub offering restaurant food 12–2.30pm and 6.30–9pm (no food Sun evenings). Function room, skittle alley, pool, large-screen TV. Beer garden, car park. Children welcome. Near Lacock Abbey and Bowood House.

11.30am–11pm Sun–Thurs; 11.30am–midnight Fri–Sat.

CHRISTIAN MALFORD
Mermaid Inn
Main Road, Christian Malford, Nr Chippenham SN15 4BE
☎ *(01249) 720313* John Gregory

Wadworth 6X and a Young's brew always available.

Friendly food-led destination pub with good beer and wine. One bar. Food every session. Children welcome. Car park. Garden. Darts and pool.

11.30am–11pm Mon–Sat; 12–10.30pm Sun.

The Rising Sun
Station Road, Christian Malford, Nr Chippenham SN15 4BL
☎ *(01249) 721571* Simon and Sue Woodhead

Freehouse offering Archers Village as a permanent plus a couple of guests that may include Badger Best or Molc's Rucking Mole.

Pleasant, friendly country pub. Food every session except Monday lunchtime. Children welcome. Garden and car park.

12–2pm and 6.30–11pm Mon–Sat; 12–2pm and 7–10.30pm Sun.

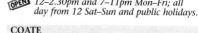

CLYFFE PYPARD
The Goddard Arms
Wood Street, Clyffe Pypard, Swindon SN4 7PY
☎ *(01793) 731386*
Raymond and Libby Orchard

Freehouse serving Wadworth 6X plus at least two guest beers from local breweries including Archers, Hidden, Wickwar, Cottage, Hampshire and Hop Back.

Homely village local, one of the oldest pubs in Wiltshire, with two bars, pool, darts, and art. Beer garden, patio and outside smoking area. Food available every session. Annual dog show and old vehicle show. Youth Hostel with 14 bunks in converted skittle alley. From M4 junction 16 take Wootton Bassett road, turn left at black and white building on stilts. After a mile and a half follow signs to Clyffe Pypard.

12–2.30pm and 7–11pm Mon–Fri; all day from 12 Sat–Sun and public holidays.

COATE
The Sun Inn
Marlborough Road, Coate, Swindon SN3 6AA
☎ *(01793) 523292* Rob Thorley

Arkells tied house with 2B and 3B permanently available plus occasionals and seasonals.

A country pub with family areas (including children's play area) and large beer garden. Food available. Quiz night Monday.

11am–2.30pm and 6–11pm.

COMPTON BASSETT
The White Horse Inn
Compton Bassett, Calne SN11 8RG
☎ *(01249) 813118* Mr and Mrs Adams

Freehouse with Greene King Old Speckled Hen, Wadworth 6X and two weekly guests.

Popular and friendly country pub, restaurant and B&B offering a warm welcome. Excellent reputation for food, all made on premises from local produce. Good wine and whisky lists. Children allowed in the restaurant. Large car park. Skittle alley for hire.

Seasonal opening hours – please call for details.

CORSHAM
The Two Pigs
38 Pickwick, Corsham SN13 0HY
☎ *(01249) 712515* Dickie and Ann Doyle

Stonehenge Pigswill plus three guests (200 per year), including beers from many local breweries. Guest ales rotating constantly, two in ABV range 4.1–4.6% and one at 5%+ ABV.

A traditional wood-panelled pub with stone floors. No food. Parking nearby. Covered courtyard. No children. Live blues music on Monday. On the A4 between Chippenham and Bath.

7–11pm Mon–Sat; 12–2.30pm and 7–10.30pm Sun.

CORSLEY

The Cross Keys

Lyes Green, Corsley, Nr Warminster BA12 7PB
☎ *(01373) 832406*
Fraser Carruth and Wayne Carnegie

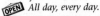 Wadworth house offering Henry's IPA, 6X and seasonal ale plus a rotating guest.

Homely and comfortable village pub. Food available. No children under 14 allowed. Car park and beer garden. Skittle alley and bar games.

OPEN *12–3pm and 6.30–11pm (10.30pm Sun).*

The White Hart

Lane End, Corsley, Nr Warminster BA12 7PH
☎ *(01373) 832805* AG Rimmer

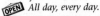 Butcombe Bitter and Sharp's Doom Bar plus one constantly changing guest.

Welcoming, traditional pub with good mix of clientele and comprehensive menu. Food served lunchtimes and evenings. Car park. Children's room, menu and high chairs.

OPEN *11.30am–close (depends on custom); 6–11pm Mon–Sat; 12–3pm and 7–10.30pm Sun.*

CORSTON

The Radnor Arms

Corston, Nr Malmesbury SN16 0HD
☎ *(01666) 823389* Eamonn Paul Kemp

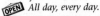 Freehouse offering Young's Bitter and two weekly rotating guests. Also traditional cider.

A traditional village inn dating from the 18th century, serving good food and proper beer. Food 12–3pm and 6.30–9pm daily (you must book on Sun evenings). Ongoing internal renovations will be near completion in 2009. Children and dogs welcome. Car park, beer garden, darts, skittle alley. Beer festivals and hog roasts. Plans for a brewery. On the A429.

OPEN *All day, every day.*

CORTON

The Dove Inn

Corton, Nr Warminster BA12 0SZ
☎ *(01985) 850109*
Michael and Beverley Wilson
www.thedove.co.uk

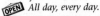 Three or four real ales, with Hop Back GFB, Butcombe Bitter, Shepherd Neame Spitfire and Young's IPA often served. A couple of the beers are rotated regularly.

Tastefully refurbished, traditional pub tucked away in a beautiful and tranquil village close to the River Wylye. Food served 12–2pm and 7–9pm every day. Separate restaurant area, beer garden and barbecue. Private rooms available. Car park. Children and animals welcome. Four en-suite double bedrooms, one en-suite double suite for families. Plenty of local attractions, including Longleat, Stonehenge, Salisbury and Bath.

OPEN *12–2.30pm and 6–11pm Mon–Sat; 12–3pm and 7–10.30pm Sun.*

CRICKLADE

The Red Lion

74 High Street, Cricklade SN6 6DD
☎ *(01793) 750776* Jim Mitchell
www.theredlioncricklade.co.uk

 Freehouse offering nine real ales. The four permanent beers are Mole's Best, Wadworth 6X, Ramsbury Gold and Sharp's Doom Bar, and the five guests are changed at least weekly.

There's a homely, characterful, open-spaced feel to this 16th-century inn with a large garden. No juke box, no pool table, no gaming machines. Food served 12–2pm and 7–9pm Tues–Sat and carvery on Sun 12–3pm. B&B in five well-appointed bedrooms. Just off the A419 between Swindon and Cirencester.

OPEN *12–11pm Mon–Thurs; 12–12 Fri–Sat; 12–10.30pm Sun.*

The White Hart Hotel

High Street, Cricklade SN6 6AA
☎ *(01793) 750206* Tom McAuliffe
www.arkells.com

 Arkells tied house with 3B and Kingsdown plus a guest.

An olde-worlde hotel built in 1628, with one bar, beer terrace and lots of history. Food available 12–2pm and 6.15–9.15pm. Accommodation in 14 en-suite rooms. Children welcome. Car park, conference facilities. Pool and darts nights. Local attractions include water park, and Cricklade Wild West Town Festival in June. On the A419 between Cirencester and Swindon.

OPEN *10.30am–11pm Mon–Sat; 11.20am–10.30pm Sun.*

CROCKERTON

Bath Arms

Clay Street, Crockerton, Warminster BA12 8AJ
☎ *(01985) 212262* Dean Carr
www.batharmscrockerton.co.uk

 Freehouse with three or four ales always available.

Grade II listed building dating back to the 1700s. With one main bar, this is a quality local pub serving great food, lunchtimes and evenings Mon–Sun. Two letting rooms available. Beer garden. Regular beer festivals and wine-tasting nights. Located off the A350 towards Shearwater.

OPEN *11am–3pm and 6pm–1am (last entry 11pm) Mon–Sat; 12–10.30pm Sun.*

DAUNTSEY LOCK

The Peterborough Arms

Dauntsey Lock, Nr Lyneham SN15 4HD
☎ *(01249) 890409* Philip Glover

 Freehouse serving Wadworth 6X, JCB and Henry's IPA plus a couple of guests.

A two-bar, traditional country roadside pub with oak beams, fires and antique decorations. Large beer garden. Bar and restaurant menus. Children welcome in restaurant area. Pets welcome. Ample parking. Accommodation. Jazz and other themed nights.

OPEN *12–3pm and 6–11pm Mon–Fri; all day Sat–Sun.*

DERRY HILL
Lansdowne Arms
Church Road, Derry Hill, Nr Calne SN11 9NS
☎ *(01249) 812422*
Annabel Terry and Patrick Young
www.wadworth.co.uk

 Wadworth 6X, JCB, Henry's IPA and Horizon, plus guests, changed every couple of months, such as Wychwood Hobgoblin and Charles Wells Bombardier.

Imposing 19th-century coaching inn with beautiful views across the Avon valley and close to Bowood House. Excellent homemade food from locally sourced produce. Hot food: 12–2pm and 6–9pm Mon–Sat; 12–3pm and 6–7.30pm Sun. Baguettes and ploughman's: 12–2.30pm Mon–Fri; 12–6pm Sat–Sun. Large garden. Car park. Children and dogs welcome.

OPEN *11am–3pm and 6–11pm Mon–Fri (midnight Fri); 11am–11pm Sat; 12–10.30pm Sun.*

DEVIZES
The British Lion
9 Estcourt Street, Devizes SN10 1LQ
☎ *(01380) 720665* Michael Dearing

 The only landlord-owned freehouse in the town, with four real ales available and constantly changing. The pub likes to support the West Country micro-breweries as much as it can, plus regional breweries and those from other parts of the country. The selection always includes a range of beer strengths and types, including stouts, porters and milds. One or two real ciders also available.

A popular single-bar character freehouse. Car park and large, sunny garden at the rear. No food. On the main Swindon (A361) road, opposite The Green.

OPEN *11am–11pm Mon–Thurs; 11am–midnight Fri–Sat; 12–11pm Sun. Open later on occasions.*

The Cavalier
Eastleigh Road, Devizes SN10 3EG
☎ *(01380) 723285* Sadie Honeywell

Wadworth pub offering Henry's IPA and 6X plus seasonals.

Warm welcoming local on an estate. Food. Roast on Sun but no food Sun evening. Children welcome until 8.30pm. Car park and garden. Games include shove ha'penny, darts and pool.

OPEN *11am–11pm.*

The Hare & Hounds
Hare and Hounds Street, Devizes SN10 1LZ
☎ *(01380) 723231* Janet Davies

Wadworth 6X and Henry's IPA plus seasonals.

A village pub atmosphere in the middle of the town. A public bar and a small lounge. Food at lunchtime only. Children allowed. Small car park. Garden.

OPEN *11am–2.30pm and 7–11pm Mon–Fri; 11am–3pm and 7–11pm Sat; 12–3pm and 7–10.30 Sun.*

The Queen's Head
Dunkirk Hill, Devizes SN10 2BG
☎ *(01380) 723726* Ian and David

Mole's pub serving Tap and Best.

Friendly edge-of-town local proud of its food, which is served every session. Children welcome. Beer garden. Car park. Skittle alley.

OPEN *12–3pm and 6–11pm.*

Southgate Inn
Potterne Road, Devizes SN10 5BY
☎ *(01380) 722872* Eduardo Cohen Bonniffini
www.southgateinn.co.uk

Four real ales, with Hop Back Summer Lightning one of the regulars. One of the beers changes every week. Also serves 15 Belgian beers, as well as the bottled Southgate Special, which is brewed in the USA and has an ABV of 14.5%.

Traditional upmarket English pub with a warm welcome and lots of nooks and crannies. Food served at lunchtimes. Operates as a private members' club from midnight to 4am Fri–Sat. Beer garden and small car park. Function room for hire. No under-21s. Easter beer festival. On the A360 Salisbury road out of town.

OPEN *Every day from 12.*

EAST KNOYLE
The Fox & Hounds
The Green, East Knoyle, Salisbury SP3 6BN
☎ *(01747) 830573* Murray Seator
www.foxandhounds-eastknoyle.co.uk

Freehouse offering five real ales, including Butcombe Bitter, Wadworth 6X, Young's Bitter, Palmers 200 and other local brews from Wessex, Keystone, Hidden and Dorset breweries. Two of the beers are changed every couple of weeks.

A thatched country pub with three eating and drinking areas, all refurbished in traditional style – flagstones, wooden flooring, rustic furniture, inglenook fireplace and wood-burning stove. The beams date back to the 16th century. Food available 12–2.30pm and 6.30–9pm. Beautiful views over Blackmore Vale. Large green in front, plus sheltered patio. Dogs and children welcome in all areas. East Knoyle is the birthplace of Sir Christopher Wren. Handy for Longleat Safari Park, Stourhead House and Gardens and Bison Farm. On Wise Lane, a mile and a half off the A303 or A350.

OPEN *12–3pm and 6–11pm (10.30pm Sun).*

EASTERTON
The Royal Oak
11 High Street, Easterton SN10 4PE
☎ *(01380) 812343* Wayne and Jane Nicholas

 Wadworth pub selling 6X, Henry's IPA and one guest beer.

There's a relaxed atmosphere to this 17th-century thatched inn. Various different rooms. Food. Small garden at the front. Car park. Children welcome. Accommodation.

OPEN *12–2.30pm and 5.30–11pm Mon–Sat; 12–10.30pm Sun.*

EASTON ROYAL

Bruce Arms

Easton Royal, Nr Pewsey SN9 5LR
☎ *(01672) 810216* WJ and JA Butler
www.brucearms.co.uk

 Wadworth 6X and Henry's IPA plus a guest beer.

Popular, traditional pub with many original features, situated on the B3087. Only cheese and onion rolls/sandwiches served lunchtimes and evenings. Car park. Children welcome in lounge, skittle alley or pool room.

OPEN *12–2.30pm and 6–11pm Mon–Sat; 12–2.30pm and 7–10.30pm Sun.*

EBBESBOURNE WAKE

The Horseshoe Inn

Ebbesbourne Wake SP5 5JF
☎ *(01722) 780474* Anthony CT Bath

 Ringwood Best, Otter Best, Bowman Swift One and Ringwood Old Thumper always available.

A traditional country pub in its original state, with the walls hung with old tools of a bygone age. Parts of the building date back to the 14th century. Food available 12–2pm and 7–9pm (no food Sunday night or all day Monday). Two rooms for B&B (no children). Children's play area. Well-behaved children allowed in the pub. Car park. Large beer garden. Situated in the beautiful Chalke Valley, just off the A30, close to Cranborne Chase, nine miles from Shaftsbury and ten miles from Salisbury.

OPEN *6.30–11pm Mon; 12–3pm and 6.30–11pm Tues–Sat; 12–3pm Sun.*

ENFORD

The Swan

Longstreet, Enford, Nr Pewsey SN9 6DD
☎ *(01980) 670338* Paul and Clare Jackson

 A good choice of real ales, changing regularly but usually including brews from Stonehenge (Heelstone) and other Wiltshire and West Country breweries plus Wychwood Hobgoblin. The emphasis is on local micro-breweries.

Old thatched and beamed pub with open fires. Bar food available at lunchtimes and evenings. Home-cooked food with local produce. Car park, garden, restaurant. Easy to find, close to Stonehenge. On the A345 between Amesbury and Pewsey.

OPEN *12–3pm and 7–11pm Mon–Sat; 12–4pm and 7–10.30pm Sun.*

FONTHILL GIFFORD

Beckford Arms

Fonthill Gifford, Tisbury SP3 6PX
☎ *(01747) 870385*
Alan Swan and Karen Costello
www.the-beckford.co.uk

Freehouse serving four real ales, with beers such as Hop Back Summer Lightning, Keystone Large One and brews from Hidden often featured, and rotated regularly.

Georgian inn dating from the 1700s and famous for its association with William Beckford (1760–1844). Food served 12–2.30pm and 7–9.30pm. Beautifully furnished interior and wonderful beer garden. Eight en-suite rooms (five double and three single). Children and well-behaved dogs welcome. Car park for 30 cars. Nearby attractions include Stonehenge, Avebury, Stourhead Gardens, Longleat, Salisbury Cathedral and Wardour Castle. Two miles off the A303.

OPEN *12–11pm (10.30pm Sun).*

FORD

The White Hart

Ford, Nr Chippenham SN14 8RP
☎ *(01249) 782213* Jane Leigh

 Wadworth 6X, Flowers IPA (brewed by Badger) and Adnams Bitter are permanent with one guest beer.

Old coaching inn off the A420 on the edge of a river. One main bar, restaurant and lounge. Bar food available at lunchtime. Restaurant open at lunchtimes and evenings. Car parks, river terrace, accommodation. Well-behaved children allowed.

OPEN *All day, every day.*

FOVANT

Pembroke Arms

Shaftesbury Road, Fovant, Nr Salisbury SP3 5JH
☎ *(01722) 714201* Janine Trevett

Freehouse serving three real ales, including Wadworth 6X and Ringwood Best.

An old country coaching inn decorated with military memorabilia. The village is also famous for its military badges, carved out of the chalk hillside. Restaurant/lounge and a public area. Food every session except Mon evening – Thurs is steak night. Children's certificate. Darts and crib. Garden and car park. Accommodation.

OPEN *11am–3pm and 6–11pm.*

FOXHAM

The Foxham Inn

Foxham, Nr Chippenham SN15 4NQ
☎ *(01249) 740665* Neil and Sarah Cooper
www.thefoxhaminn.co.uk

Freehouse offering Bath Ales Gem and Wadworth 6X on a permanent basis and one rotating guest changed every week.

Traditional village inn – small, cosy, very clean and tidy. One main bar and a dining area. Food served 12–2pm and 7–9.30pm, with game a speciality. Car park, beer garden. Children and dogs welcome.

OPEN *12–2.30pm and 7–11pm.*

GREAT WISHFORD
Royal Oak Inn
Langford Road, Great Wishford, Nr Salisbury SP2 0PD
☎ *(01722) 790079* Paul Firmin

Freehouse serving three or four different real ales, constantly changing, but local breweries such as Hop Back, Keystone and Flowerpots are favoured.

Friendly, welcoming 17th-century inn serving good food at lunchtimes and evenings daily. Log fires, oak-panelled bar, no machines. Car park and garden. No children in the bar. Five miles west of Salisbury in beautiful countryside.

OPEN *11.30am–2.30pm and 6–11pm Mon–Sat (closed all day Tues); 12–3pm and 7–10.30pm Sun.*

GRITTLETON
Neeld Arms
The Street, Grittleton SN14 6AP
☎ *(01249) 782470* Charlie and Boo West
www.neeldarms.co.uk

A freehouse. Wadworth 6X and Henry's IPA. Two guests, changed monthly, such as Sharp's Doom Bar, St Austell Tribute or a Butcombe ale.

A 17th-century inn serving real ales and home-cooked food. A classic drinkers' pub. Food served 12–2pm and 6.30–10pm. Accommodation.

OPEN *12–3pm and 5.30pm–12.*

HAMPTWORTH
The Cuckoo Inn
Hamptworth Road, Hamptworth, Nr Salisbury SP5 2DU
☎ *(01794) 390302* Tim Bacon

Wadworth 6X, Ringwood Best, Flowerpots Bitter, Hop Back Summer Lightning and GFB plus up to six guest beers in the summer from a long list including brews from Bunces, Adnams, Ringwood, Hampshire, Shepherd Neame and Cottage breweries.

A 300-year-old thatched pub in the New Forest. Bar food available at lunchtime. Car park, garden, play area, petanque area. Just off the A36 near Hamptworth golf course.

OPEN *11.30am–2.30pm and 5.30–11pm Mon–Fri; all day Sat, Sun and Bank Holidays.*

HEDDINGTON
The Ivy Inn
Stockley Road, Heddington, Calne SN11 0PL
☎ *(01380) 850276* Andrew Burner

Wadworth pub selling Henry's IPA and 6X plus sometimes a seasonal.

Picturesque thatched country pub, wooden beams, open fire, perhaps Bob Dylan as background music, with gravity-fed ales. One bar. Food every session. Children welcome. Car park, garden and darts.

OPEN *6.30–11pm Mon; 12–3pm and 6.30–11pm Tues–Sat; 12–5pm and 7–10.30pm Sun.*

HIGHWORTH
The Plough Inn
Lechlade Road, Highworth, Swindon SN6 7HF
☎ *(01793) 762224* Tina Muskett

Arkells tied house with 2B and Moonlight permanently available.

Locals' country pub. Separate lounge, bar and pool room. Live music some Saturdays. Children allowed. Beer garden. Accommodation. Parking available.

OPEN *5–11pm Mon–Fri (closed lunchtimes); 11am–11pm Sat; 12–10.30pm Sun.*

HILMARTON
The Duke Hotel
Hilmarton, Nr Calne SN11 8SD
☎ *(01249) 760634* Angela Ramirez

Arkells house with 2B and 3B permanently available plus an Arkells seasonal ale.

Old-style pub with bar food available, 6–9pm Tues–Sat and 12–2pm Sun. Children allowed. Large beer garden with children's play area. Quiz nights twice a month. Located on the main road between RAF Lyneham and Calne.

OPEN *12–3pm and 6–11pm Mon–Sat; 12–8pm Sun.*

HOLT
Tollgate Inn
Ham Green, Holt, Nr Bradford-on-Avon BA14 6PX
☎ *(01225) 782326*
Alex Venables and Alison Ward-Baptiste
www.tollgateholt.co.uk

Freehouse with eight real ales, with a constantly changing selection of local beers, changed weekly.

A 16th-century inn, previously a weaving shed and Baptist chapel, with restaurant for 30 upstairs and buttery for 22 downstairs. Food using local produce served lunchtimes Tues–Sun and evenings Tues–Sat. The pub's mature gardens overlook the Westbury White Horse. Four en-suite double letting rooms. Car park for 40. Garden, patio. Children allowed at lunchtimes. No dogs. Close to The Courts and Great Chalfield (both National Trust gardens) and to Lacock village. On the B3107 between Melksham and Bradford-on-Avon.

OPEN *11am–3pm and 5.30–11.30pm Tues–Sat; 11am–3pm Sun (closed Sun evening and all day Mon).*

IDMISTON

The Earl of Normanton

Tidworth Road, Idmiston, Salisbury SP4 0AG
☎ *(01980) 610251* Alan and Nicola Howe
www.earlofnormanton.co.uk

 Freehouse serving Flowerpots Bitter and Hop Back Summer Lightning plus three weekly-changing guest ales from breweries such as Butcombe, Triple FFF, Palmers, Bowman, Fuller's, Butts and many more.

Village pub close to Stonehenge, with horseshoe-shaped bar and good atmosphere. Excellent pub food served 12–2pm and 6–9pm Mon–Sat, and 12–2pm Sun. Patio and raised garden with great views. Two en-suite bedrooms available for B&B. Quiz every Sunday at 8.30pm. On the A338 between Porton and Allington, six miles north of Salisbury.

OPEN *12–2.30pm and 6–11pm Mon–Sat; 12–3pm and 7.45–10.30pm Sun.*

KILMINGTON

Red Lion Inn

Kilmington, Warminster BA12 6RP
☎ *(01985) 844263* Christopher Gibbs

 Genuine freehouse serving Butts Jester, Wessex Kilmington Best and Butcombe Bitter plus one rotating guest ale changed every few days.

Originally a farm on the Hoare estate, this unspoilt 15th-century character country pub features beams, settle and two log fires in winter. Food served 12–1.50pm. Darts, shove ha'penny and cribbage. Large beer garden. Children welcome until 8pm. Car park. Close to Longleat Safari Park and National Trust Stourhead House and Gardens. The hill behind the pub is used for walking, riding and remote-controlled gliding. On the B3092, three miles north of Mere (A303).

OPEN *11.30am–2.30pm and 6.30–11pm Mon–Sat; 12–3pm and 7–11pm Sun. Open later if enough demand.*

KINGTON ST MICHAEL

The Jolly Huntsman

80 Kington St Michael, Chippenham SN14 6JB
☎ *(01249) 750305* Simon and Helen Curtis
www.kingtonstmichael.com

 Four or five real ales, with beers from Wadworth, Greene King, Keystone, Stonehenge, Hidden, Bath and Moles Brewery regularly featured. Two or three of these are rotated after every barrel. Rotating guest scrumpy cider.

Lively village pub with seasonal open fire, lots of character and a warm welcome. Traditional home-cooked fare, with full main menu and daily specials served 11.30am–2pm and 6.30–9.30pm Mon–Sat; 12–2pm and 7–9pm Sun. Quality en-suite B&B accommodation, all rooms with wireless broadband. Dogs and children welcome. Car

park. In the heart of the Cotswolds, near to Castle Combe, Bath and Stonehenge. M4 junction 17, follow signs to Chippenham, then turn right into the village at the traffic lights.

OPEN *11.30am–2.30pm and 6–11pm Mon–Sat (midnight Fri–Sat); 12–3pm and 7–10.30pm Sun.*

LACOCK

The George Inn

4 West Street, Lacock, Nr Chippenham SN15 2LH
☎ *(01249) 730263* J Glass

 Wadworth 6X, JCB and Henry's IPA always available.

A very old inn that has been licensed continuously since 1361, with two bars, two restaurants, a large patio and a large garden with play area. The beautiful National Trust village is a popular location for film shooting. Coffee available at 9am every morning. Food served 12–2pm and 6–9pm. Children welcome. Local attractions include Lacock Abbey, a tithe barn, and a beautiful church where Laura Parker-Bowles was married in 2006. Off the A350 about three miles from Chippenham and three miles from Melksham.

OPEN *9am (for coffee)–2.30pm and 5–11pm Mon–Thurs; all day Fri–Sun. Open all day Wed–Sun in summer.*

LANGLEY BURRELL

Langley Tap

41 The Common, Langley Burrell, Chippenham SN15 4LQ
☎ *(01249) 652707* Peter Dixon

 Wadworth pub serving 6X, Henry's IPA and seasonals plus an occasional guest.

Known previously as the Brewery Arms it has now returned to its original title. This is a traditional village pub providing real ales and good food at reasonable prices. Meals every session. Children allowed in eating area. Function room. Car park and garden.

OPEN *11.30am–3pm and 6.30–11pm Mon–Sat; 12–3pm and 7–10pm Sun.*

LITTLE CHEVERELL

The Owl

Low Road, Little Cheverell, Devizes SN10 4JS
☎ *(01380) 812263*
Paul Green and Jamie Carter

Freehouse serving Wadworth 6X plus three constantly changing guests from independent breweries such as Hop Back, Ringwood or Uley.

A country pub with beams and a wood-burning stove. One bar, separate dining area. Large streamside beer garden. Food available at lunchtime and evenings. Children allowed. Accommodation.

OPEN *11am–3pm and 6.30–11pm Mon–Sat; 12–4pm and 7–10.30pm Sun. Open all day in the summer.*

LOWER CHICKSGROVE
The Compasses Inn
Lower Chicksgrove, Tisbury, Salisbury SP3 6NB
☎ *(01722) 714318* Alan Stoneham
www.thecompassesinn.com

Freehouse with Hidden Quest, Keystone Large One, Wadworth 6X and Bass a typical selection of the four beers on offer, with two of them rotated every week.

Genuine 14th-century thatched pub in a tiny rural hamlet set in wonderful countryside, with two beer gardens boasting lovely views. The unspoilt interior features flagstone floors and farming implements on the walls, while small booths and settles enhance the original character. Food available lunchtimes and evenings every day. Children and dogs welcome. Four en-suite guest rooms, plus small detached cottage (AA four stars). Close to Stonehenge, Longleat and Wilton House, and within one hour of the Jurassic Dorset coast. A mile and a half west of Fovant on the A30, turn right to Chicksgrove, and after half a mile turn left into Lagpond Lane. The inn is a mile along on the left. Off the A30.

OPEN *12–3pm and 6–11pm (10.30pm Sun).*

MALMESBURY
The Smoking Dog
62 High Street, Malmesbury SN16 9AT
☎ *(01666) 825823* Martin Bridge

Archers Best and Brains Reverend James plus three guests rotated twice a week.

A traditional small-town Cotswold stone pub with log fires, beams and oak floors. Occasional live music. Food available in the bar and restaurant 12–2.30pm and 6.30–9.30pm. Famous for annual beer and sausage festival held at spring bank holiday weekend, with up to 35 different real ales on offer. Large beer garden. Children and dogs welcome.

OPEN *12–11pm Mon–Thurs; 12–12 Fri–Sat; 12–10.30pm Sun.*

The Three Cups Inn
90 The Triangle, Malmesbury SN16 0AH
☎ *(01666) 823278* Lee Goodship

Three real ales from a constantly rotating range, including something from breweries such as Sharp's, Wickwar and Wychwood. A selection board is available to allow drinkers to choose their favourites for the following week.

Traditional town pub with lively bar and quieter lounge. Food. Pool, darts and skittle alley.

OPEN *12–12.*

MARKET LAVINGTON
The Green Dragon
26–8 High Street, Market Lavington SN10 4AG
☎ *(01380) 813235* Steve Wragg
www.greendragonlavington.co.uk

Wadworth 6X, Henry's IPA and between one and three changing guest beers.

A 17th-century coaching inn and now a friendly village local with a grand exterior and a casual interior. Food served at lunchtimes and evenings every day. Children welcome. Accommodation. Games include boules, skittles, pool and darts. Garden and car park. The village is on the edge of Salisbury Plain between Stonehenge and Avebury, and is an ideal central location for exploring Salisbury, Bath and Longleat. Accommodation available.

OPEN *12–3pm and 5.30pm–12 Mon–Thur; 12–12 Fri–Sun and bank holidays.*

MARLBOROUGH
The Bear Hotel
1 High Street, Marlborough SN8 1AA
☎ *(01672) 515047* Andrew and Victoria Hall

Arkells 3B permanently available plus Arkells seasonal guests.

A 200-year-old brick-built town-centre pub designed in the style of a galleon. Food available every day – famous locally for fish and chips. Beer garden. Occasional live music. Children allowed. Function room for medieval banquets. Situated opposite the Town Hall.

OPEN *11am–11pm Mon–Sat; 12–10.30pm Sun.*

MARSTON MEYSEY
The Old Spotted Cow
Marston Meysey SN6 6LQ
☎ *(01285) 810264* Anna Langley-Poole
www.theoldspottedcow.co.uk

Freehouse serving at least three real ales, all of which rotate regularly. Sharp's Doom Bar and Ramsbury Popham's Pride are often featured, while Fuller's London Pride is also a frequent guest. Real cider and an extensive wine list.

Popular 19th-century country inn at the edge of a beautiful village. Large, yet intimate, with oak floors, exposed beams and log fires. Food served lunchtimes and evenings every day (except Sun evening). Separate room for private functions. Car park. Large, safe children's play area and attractive beer garden.

OPEN *12–3pm and 6–11pm Tues–Fri; 12–11pm Sat; 12–10.30pm Sun.*

NETHERHAMPTON
Victoria & Albert
Netherhampton, Nr Salisbury SP2 8PU
☎ *(01722) 743174*
Peter Martin and Maggie Scott

 Genuine freehouse with a constantly changing selection of four real ales with the emphasis on smaller and local microbreweries. Plus real cider.

Built in 1540, thatched and set in a small hamlet with low beams and open fires. Food at lunchtimes and evenings. Children and dogs welcome. Large beer garden and covered, heated patio. Local CAMRA Pub of the Year 2005 and 2007. B&B available.

OPEN *11am–3pm and 5.30–11pm Mon–Sat; 12–3pm and 7–10.30pm Sun.*

NEWTON TONY
The Malet Arms
Newton Tony, Salisbury, SP4 0HF
☎ *(01980) 629279* Noel Cardew

 Four rotating real ales. Ramsbury, Stonehenge, Palmers, Archers, Hop Back, Wadworth, Crouch Vale and Fuller's breweries all feature.

A 300-year-old freehouse with a main bar, snug bar and a dining room. Walled garden, aviary and paddock. Car park. No background music or games. Food served 12–2.30pm and 6.30–10pm. Four miles from A303 on A338 towards Salisbury.

OPEN *11am–3pm and 6–11pm Mon–Sat; 12–3pm and 7–10.30pm Sun.*

NORTH WROUGHTON
The Check Inn
Woodland View, North Wroughton, Nr Swindon SN4 9AA
☎ *(01793) 845584* Doug Watkins
www.checkinn.co.uk

 Genuine freehouse with ten hand pumps serving a constantly changing range of beers from around the UK and Eire. All guests are changed daily and are on continual rotation.

Award-winning country pub in an urban setting. Traditional pub games and log fires create a warm atmosphere in the single bar and separate restaurant/lounge areas. Fresh home-cooked food served lunchtimes and evenings. AA-recommended accommodation, boules, picturesque beer garden. Family- and dog-friendly. Traditional pub games and barbecue. Beer festivals. Car park. From the A361 Swindon–Devizes road, take immediate first right after the dual carriageway over the M4.

OPEN *11.30am–3.30pm and 6pm–12 Mon–Thurs; 11.30am–1am Fri–Sun.*

OAKSEY
The Wheatsheaf at Oaksey
Malmesbury, Oaksey SN16 9JB
☎ *(01666) 577348* Tony Robson-Burrell
www.thecompletechef.co.uk

 A freehouse. Hook Norton Hooky Bitter and Wickwar Cotswold Way or BOB. One guest, changed weekly, such as Bath Ales Gem, English Rose or Longbarrow.

A 16th-century village inn with bar, restaurant and small beer garden. Awarded many stars and rosettes in pub and restaurant guides, including two AA rosettes for food. Food served 12–2pm and 6.30–9pm Tues–Sat; 12–2.30pm Sun. No food Sun evening or Mon. Children and dogs welcome. Turn off the A417 at Kemble Airfield, pub two miles further on.

OPEN *6pm–close Mon (closed Mon lunch); 11.30am–2.30pm and 6pm–close Tues–Sat; 12–close Sun.*

OGBOURNE ST GEORGE
The Inn With The Well
Marlborough Road, Ogbourne St George, Nr Marlborough SN8 1SQ
☎ *(01672) 841445* Megan and Michael Shaw
www.theinnwiththewell.co.uk

Freehouse with Wadworth 6X plus three weekly-changing guest beers.

Built in 1654, this traditional pub has a bar and restaurant which features the well and has been known as the village local for over 300 years. Food served 12–2pm and 6.30–9.30pm daily in the summer, 12–2pm and 7–9pm daily in winter. Car park for 15 cars. Six en-suite bedrooms available for letting. Heated beer patio. Beer festivals held regularly.

OPEN *12–2.30pm and 4–11pm Mon–Sat; 12–2.30pm and 6–9.30pm Sun.*

PEWSEY
The Cooper's Arms
37–9 Ball Road, Pewsey SN9 5BL
☎ *(01672) 562495*
Sally and John Holmes and Val Norton

Freehouse with Wadworth 6X and Fuller's London Pride plus two guests, changed every day or two, from small and local breweries including Butts, Hop Back, Cottage, Slaters, Archers, Ballard's, Ringwood, Stonehenge, Mole's and many more.

A 17th-century thatched country pub in a picturesque area overlooking Pewsey Downs. Log fires, wooden floors, beams. Food served on Sunday lunchtime only. Large beer garden. Live music every Friday. Children allowed. Self-catering accommodation.

OPEN *6–11pm Mon–Thurs; 5–11pm Fri; 12–11pm Sat; 12–10.30pm Sun.*

The Crown Inn
60 Wilcot Road, Pewsey SN9 5EL
☎ *(01672) 562653* John Wall
www.thecrownpewsey.co.uk

A freehouse. Wadworth 6X plus four guest ales, changed every barrel. Vale Ale Knights Porter, Three Castles Stoned and Cottage DBS are examples of guests previously on offer.

Two-bar pub, 120 years old, with games room and beer garden. No food. Live music. Two beer festivals each year. Three minutes' walk from the station.

OPEN *12–12.*

PURTON
The Angel
High Street, Purton SN5 4AB
☎ *(01793) 770248*
Mark and Shani Humphries

Arkells tied house with 2B and 3B plus Arkells seasonal guests such as Summer Ale and Noel.

Village pub dating from 1704 with lounge, main bar, beams and open fireplaces. Food available 12–2.30pm and 6–9pm Mon–Sat; 12–3pm and 6–9pm Sun. Children and families welcome. Beer garden. Large car park. Private function room for hire. Live music. Handy for the local carnival (May), Swindon and Cricklade Railway, and exploring the Cotswolds. Four miles from Swindon.

9am–midnight Sun–Thurs; 9am–2am Fri–Sat (at discretion of licensees).

QUEMERFORD
The Talbot Inn
Quemerford, Calne SN11 0AR
☎ *(01249) 812198* Sharon Godwin

Wadworth 6X is regularly available, plus one rotating guest.

A small pub with a reputation for good food and real ales. One bar, wooden floors, beams, large beer garden and car park. Conservatory dining area. Food available at lunchtime and evenings. Children allowed in the conservatory and garden only.

12–11pm Sun–Thurs; 12–12 Fri–Sat.

ROWDE
The George & Dragon
High Street, Rowde, Devizes SN10 2PN
☎ *(01380) 723053* Philip Hale, Michelle Hale and Christopher Day
www.thegeorgeanddragonrowde.co.uk

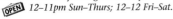Freehouse with Butcombe Bitter and a rotating guest ale such as Fuller's London Pride, Wessex Kilmington Best, Ringwood Fortyniner or something from Sharp's or Mole's.

A 14th-century inn with beams, wooden floors, antique rugs and open fires. One bar, 35-seater restaurant and garden. Food available 12–3pm and 7–10pm Mon–Sat, plus 12–4pm Sun. Car park. Children and dogs welcome in bar. Three AA four-star B&B rooms. Close to Bowood House, Stonehenge and Avebury. Take the A342 out of Devizes towards Chippenham.

12–3pm (4pm Sat) and 7–11pm Mon–Sat; 12–4pm Sun.

SALISBURY
The Deacon Arms
118 Fisherton Street, Salisbury SP2 7QT
☎ *(01722) 504723* Frank Keay

Freehouse with Hop Back GFB and Summer Lightning and Mole's Best plus occasionals.

Community pub with two bars, wooden floors, open fires in winter and air conditioning in summer. Accommodation. No food. Children allowed.

5–11pm Mon–Fri; 12–11pm Sat; 12–10.30pm Sun.

Devizes Inn
53–5 Devizes Road, Salisbury SP2 7LQ
☎ *(01722) 327842* Brian Corrigan

Ringwood Best and Hop Back GFB plus one other real ale, often Hop Back Summer Lightning, but constantly varying.

Locals' town pub near the railway station. En-suite accommodation. No food. Car park. Children welcome.

4–11pm Mon–Thurs; 2–11pm Fri; 12–11pm Sat; 12–10.30pm Sun.

The Duck Inn
Duck Lane, Laverstock, Salisbury SP1 1PU
☎ *(01722) 327678* Debbie and Malcolm Purvis and Laura Hayman

Four Hop Back ales on offer, namely Summer Lightning, GFB, Odyssey and Crop Circle.

Over 100 years old, the pub once housed the village post office. Three areas, two of which can be joined. The front of the pub seats 60, and the duck pond area at the rear seats 40. Traditional pub food available 12–2pm and 6–9pm Tues–Sat; 12–3pm Sun; smaller portions available. Patio, beer garden. Two car parks, and a bus stop at the end of the lane.

12–12 Sun–Wed (closed Sun evening and Mon evening); 11am–midnight Thurs–Fri; noon–2am Sat.

Rai D'Or
69 Brown Street, Salisbury SP1 2AS
☎ *(01722) 327137*
www.raidor.co.uk

Freehouse with two real ales, both constantly rotated, from breweries such as Downton, Stonehenge, Keystone, Bowman and Butts.

Traditional tavern dating from 1292, with wooden floors, panelled benches and open fires. Food is a major feature, with Thai meals served every session. Dogs on leads and children welcome. South Wiltshire CAMRA Pub of the Year 2008. Pub will open during the day and on Sundays for booked groups. In the historic city centre, five minutes' walk from the Cathedral, behind the White Hart Hotel next to the Brown Street public car park.

5–11pm Mon–Sat. Closed Sun except for booked groups.

Tom Brown's
225 Wilton Road, Salisbury SP2 7JY
☎ *(01722) 335918* Geoff Price

Goldfinch Brewery tied house with a range of Goldfinch beers rotated on three pumps and always available: Tom Brown's Best, Flashman's Clout, Midnight Blinder and Midnight Sun.

A basic one-bar town pub for real ale drinkers. No food. No children.

6–11pm Mon–Fri; 12–3pm and 6–11pm Sat; 12–3pm and 6–10.30pm Sun.

The Village Freehouse

33 Wilton Road, Salisbury SP2 7EF
☎ *(01722) 329707* Joe Morris

 Freehouse with Downton Quadhop and Timothy Taylor Landlord plus guest beers selected by the local drinkers. There is a permanent dark mild pump.

Popular street-corner pub on the A36 close to the station and featuring displays of railway memorabilia. Limited food (rolls). Regular local CAMRA Pub of the Year.

OPEN *3–11pm Mon; 12–11pm Tues–Sat; 12–10.30pm Sun.*

The Wig & Quill

1 New Street, Salisbury SP1 2PH
☎ *(01722) 335665* Patricia Trinder

Wadworth tenancy with Henry's IPA, 6X and JCB plus Bishop's Tipple and a guest ale rotated weekly.

A traditional English pub in the city centre but with a warm and welcoming atmosphere that resembles a village local. One bar serving three separate areas, open fires, beams and secluded courtyard beer garden. Food served at lunchtime and evening. Children welcome. Close to the cathedral.

OPEN *10am–12.30am Sun–Weds; 10am–2.30am Thurs–Sat.*

SANDY LANE

The George Inn

Sandy Lane, Nr Chippenham SN15 2PX
☎ *(01380) 850403* Mark and Karen Jenkins

A Wadworth pub selling 6X and Henry's IPA, plus seasonals.

Traditional village pub with a quiet atmosphere and an emphasis on food (served lunchtime and evening). Children welcome. Car park and garden.

OPEN *12–3.30pm and 7–11pm Mon–Fri; 12–3pm and 6.30–11pm Sat–Sun.*

SHAW

The Golden Fleece

Folly Lane, Shaw, Nr Melksham SN12 8HB
☎ *(01225) 702050* Luke Bate

Fuller's London Pride, Wadworth 6X and Mole's Best are permanent features.

Classic country pub with beams and low ceilings. Restaurant with food served 12–2pm and 7–9pm. Garden at rear. Car park. On the A365 Bath–Melksham road.

OPEN *12–2.30pm and 6–11pm Mon–Sat; 12–2.30pm and 7–11pm Sun.*

SHREWTON

The George at Shrewton

London Road, Shrewton, Salisbury SP3 4DH
☎ *(01980) 620341* Rob Rigby

Freehouse with Courage Best and brews from Sharp's and Archers on offer, plus a guest from Hampshire or Holden's, changed weekly.

Remote 16th-century country pub with traditional beams, open fires, one main bar, large covered patio area, beer garden, skittle alley and a 26-seater restaurant.

Refurbished in 2005. Food available 12–2pm and 7–9pm (not Tues). Children allowed. Beer festival held every August bank holiday.

OPEN *12–2pm and 6pm–12 (2am Thurs–Sat); all day Sat–Sun in summer, regular hours in winter.*

SOUTH MARSTON

The Carriers Arms

Highworth Road, South Marston, Nr Swindon
☎ *(01793) 822051* Liz and Jim Sansum

 Wadworth 6X is a permanent fixture, plus one guest.

Traditional, village-centre, two-bar pub with separate dining area and patio. Car park. Children welcome when eating, but no special facilities.

OPEN *12–2.30pm and 6.30–11pm Mon–Sat; 12–3pm and 7–10.30pm Sun.*

STAPLEFORD

The Pelican Inn

Warminster Road, Stapleford, Nr Salisbury SP3 4LT
☎ *(01722) 792643* Deborah and Laurie Scott

Beers from Banks's and Jennings plus guests rotating every month.

Roadside pub with one long bar. Food served 12–2pm (2.30pm Sun) and 6–9pm daily, with two-for-one offers on main courses Mon–Fri. Five en-suite letting rooms. Beer garden, bouncy castle. Children welcome. On the A36 Salisbury–Warminster road.

OPEN *11am–11.30pm Mon–Sat; 12–10.30pm Sun.*

STRATTON ST MARGARET

The Rat Trap

Highworth Road, Stratton St Margaret SN3 4QS
☎ *(01793) 823282*
Mark and Claire Richardson

 Arkells tied house with 2B and 3B permanently available plus occasional Arkells seasonal guests.

A traditional village two-bar pub with garden. Food available. Pool and darts. Occasional live music. Children allowed. Car park.

OPEN *12–3pm and 5–11pm Mon–Fri; all day Sat–Sun.*

The Wheatsheaf

Ermin Street, Stratton St Margaret SN3 4NH
☎ *(01793) 823149* Alun Rossiter

 Arkells 2B and 3B are always on offer, and the one guest is often an Arkells beer.

Small, cosy, clean pub with patio and garden. Rolls served 12–2pm Mon–Fri. Children allowed until 7pm (no special facilities). Car park.

OPEN *11.30am–2.30pm and 5–11pm Mon–Thur; 11am–11pm Fri–Sat; 12–10.30pm Sun.*

SWINDON

The Famous Ale House

146 Redclife Street, Swindon SN2 2BY
☎ *(01793) 522503* Josie McAlly

 Wadworth 6X, Greene King Old Speckled Hen, Courage Directors and one guest ale.

Victorian, olde-worlde locals' community pub decorated with football memorabilia. Pool room. Large open-plan bar, restaurant and garden. Food served 12–3pm and 6–9pm Mon–Fri, 12–4pm Sat and Sun. Large car park, wheelchair access. Children allowed in the restaurant and garden. Regular charity events.

OPEN *12–11pm (10.30pm Sun).*

The Glue Pot Inn

5 Emlyn Square, Swindon SN1 5BP
☎ *(01793) 523935* Michael Pomery

 Tied to the Hop Back brewery, with Crop Circle, Summer Lightning and GFB, plus Mole's Best regularly available, with two to four rotating guests.

Town pub in the centre of Swindon, located by the old railway museum. One small bar, patio. Bar snacks available at lunchtime only. No children.

OPEN *All day, every day.*

The Savoy

38 Regent Street, Swindon SN1 1JL
☎ *(01793) 533970*
Paul Pearson and Nicole Calver
www.jdwetherspoon.co.uk

 Wetherspoon's pub. Greene King Abbot, Shepherd Neame Spitfire and Marston's Pedigree are among the beers always available, plus four or five guests, with beers from Archers and Ramsbury often featured.

A one-bar town-centre pub in traditional style. No music. Games machines. Food served 9am–11pm, with special offers available. Children welcome until 7pm when dining. Beer festivals twice a year, with over 50 ales. At the top of town, near the tourist office.

OPEN *9am–midnight Sun–Thurs; 9am–1am Fri–Sat.*

The Wheatsheaf

32 Newport Street, Old Town, Swindon SN1 3DP
☎ *(01793) 523188* Jim Bowd

 Wadworth house with Henry's IPA, 6X and Horizon always on offer, plus seasonal brews and weekly-changing guest ales.

Unspoilt 19th-century traditional town pub with intimate Victorian 'snug' bar, spacious stable bar with pool table and darts, and attractive courtyard with smoking shelter. Bar menu available Wed–Sat, plus regular themed food evenings. Well-behaved children welcome until 7.30pm.

OPEN *12–2.30pm and 5–11pm Mon–Thurs; all day Fri–Sun.*

The White Hart

Oxford Road, Swindon SN3 4JD
☎ *(01793) 822272* Derek Rowlands

 Arkells house with 2B and 3B plus Summer Ale, Noel or other Arkells seasonals on a guest basis.

Situated on the outskirts of Swindon Town, off the A419, this is a three-bar pub with separate restaurant plus function room and skittle alley. Big-screen TV. Children allowed in the restaurant only, plus play area outside.

OPEN *11am–3pm and 5–11pm Mon–Fri; all day Sat–Sun.*

TISBURY

The Boot Inn

High Street, Tisbury, Nr Salisbury SP3 6PS
☎ *(01747) 870363* RF Turner

 Three real ales, always changing, but with beers from Marston's regularly featured.

A 17th-century stone-built traditional village pub with one bar and a number of small rooms. Bar food every day except Sunday evening and Tuesday. Beer garden, small car park. Public bar not suitable for children. Convenient for Stonehenge, Salisbury, Shaftsbury, Longleat, Stourhead and Wardour Castle.

OPEN *12–3pm and 7–11pm Mon–Sat; 12–3.30pm Sun (closed Sun evening).*

UPPER CHUTE

The Cross Keys Inn

Upper Chute, Andover SP11 9ER
☎ *(01264) 230295* George Humphrey
www.upperchute.com

 A freehouse. Fuller's London Pride and Discovery and Gale's Butser plus one weekly-changing guest. Guests have included Sharp's Doom Bar, Hop Back Crop Circle, Bowman Swift One and Stonehenge Pigswill.

Country pub on an old drovers' road, first cited as a pub in 1715. Two bars and a separate restaurant. Food served 12–2pm and 6–9pm (except Sun evenings). Large gardens front and back. Accommodation. Car parking. Annual beer festival third weekend in August. Excellent walking, riding and cycling opportunities. Located six miles north-west of Andover.

OPEN *11am–2.30pm and 5–11pm Mon–Fri; 11am–midnight Sat; 12–11pm Sun.*

UPTON LOVELL

Prince Leopold

Upton Lovell, Nr Warminster BA12 0JP
☎ *(01985) 850460*
Graham and Pamela Waldron-Bradley
www.princeleopoldinn.co.uk

 Ringwood Best Bitter and a twice-monthly changing guest beer.

Single-bar freehouse, with garden, pleasantly situated by the River Wylye. En-suite accommodation. Food served 12–3pm and 7–9.30pm daily, with a good reputation locally. Restaurant. Car park. Children welcome.

OPEN *12–3pm and 7–11pm.*

WANBOROUGH
The Black Horse Inn
Wanborough, Swindon SN4 0DQ
☎ *(01793) 790305* Chris Deacon
www.black-horse-inn.com

 Arkells house with 2B, 3B and JRA plus seasonal guests.

Old converted farmhouse set in the hills of the White Horse, with views across three counties. Food available 12–2pm and 6–9pm. Large car park, private room and marquee for hire. Children welcome. Located on the Bishopston Road out of Wanborough.

OPEN *12–3pm and 6pm–12 Mon–Sat; all day Sun.*

The Brewers Arms
High Street, Wanborough SN4 0AE
☎ *(01793) 790707* Darryl Dinwiddy

Arkells house with 2B and 3B plus an Arkells seasonal ale.

Family pub with conservatory, dining area, and large garden featuring a children's play area. Food available lunchtimes and evenings including Sunday roasts. Children welcome.

OPEN *11.30am–2.30pm and 5–11pm Mon–Fri; all day Sat–Sun.*

WARMINSTER
The Fox & Hounds
6 Deverill Road, Warminster BA12 9QP
☎ *(01985) 216711* Christopher Pitcher

Freehouse with Ringwood Best and Warminster Warrior plus one rotating guest, changed every two days. Three ciders also available.

Atypical locals' real ale and cider pub with beer garden and car park. Pool, darts, crib. New skittle alley planned for end of 2008. No food. Children welcome.

OPEN *11am–11pm (later at weekends).*

The George Inn
Longbridge Deverill, Warminster BA12 7DG
☎ *(01985) 840396* Laurie Creighton
www.thegeorgeinnlongbridgedeverill.co.uk

Hobden's Wessex Deverill Advocate and Best Bitter plus Wadworth 6X and a guest.

Lively 17th-century coaching inn in a picturesque village, set in two acres of garden on the banks of the River Wylye and offering a warm welcome. Food served 12–3pm and 6–9.30pm Mon–Wed, 12–9.30pm Thurs–Sat and 12–9pm Sun. Oak-beamed bar and two restaurants. Accommodation in 11 luxurious en-suite rooms. Weddings, private parties and conferences for up to 120 guests. Located on the main A350, six miles from Longleat.

OPEN *11am–11pm (10.30pm Sun).*

Rose & Crown
57 East Street, Warminster BA12 9BZ
☎ *(01985) 214964* Emma Kidd

 Punch Taverns pub with Charles Wells Bombardier, Shepherd Neame Spitfire and Black Sheep Bitter plus three guests changed every few days, which could include Greene King Old Speckled Hen or Wychwood Hobgoblin.

Quirky 18th-century pub with one main brick-fronted, slate-topped bar, open fireplace and other original features. Sports room with plasma screen. Friendly staff and the ghost of a previous landlady! No food. Attractive beer garden. Children and dogs welcome. Live music held two or three times a month. Near to Longleat and Center Parcs, a quarter of a mile from the market place on the Salisbury Road.

OPEN *4–11pm Mon–Thurs; 12–12 Fri–Sat; 11.30am–10.30pm Sun.*

WHITLEY
The Pear Tree Inn
Top Lane, Whitley SN12 8QX
☎ *((01225) 709131* Martin and Debbie Still

Up to six real ales rotated regularly but likely to include Wadworth 6X and Henry's IPA, Mole's Best, Stonehenge Pigswill and something from the Hidden brewery.

Former farmhouse with front bar, restaurant, garden room, terrace and gardens. Flagstones, wooden beams and log fire. Food served at lunchtime (12–2.30pm, 3pm Sun) and evenings (6.30–9.30 or 10pm, 7–9pm Sun). Comfortable accommodation.

OPEN *12–11pm.*

WILTON
The Bear Inn
12 West Street, Wilton SP2 0DF
☎ *(01722) 742398* Julian Cheeseright

 Badger First Gold and Tanglefoot always served.

Asmall, homely local dating from around 1750, with one bar, pool room, beams and a coal fire. Food available lunchtimes and evenings. Large walled garden. Free car park nearby. Local attractions include Wilton Carpet Factory and Shopping Village, Wilton House, Italian-style church and antique shops. Just 150 metres from Market Square car park.

OPEN *11am–2.30pm and 4.30pm–12 Sun–Thurs; 11am–2.30pm and 6pm–1am Fri–Sat.*

WOOTTON BASSETT

The Five Bells

Wood Street, Wootton Bassett, Swindon SN4 7BD
☎ *(01793) 849422* Simon Cole

Punch house with Black Sheep Bitter and Fuller's London Pride plus three weekly-changing guests, at least one of which is from a local brewer.

A 300-year-old thatched inn with two bars, open fires and snug. Food served 12–2.30pm Mon–Sun and Wed evening which is a themed night. Children welcome. Beer festival held first weekend in August. Car park. Take junction 16 off the M4 and follow the signs for Wootton Bassett; take the first right after the town hall on stilts.

OPEN *12–3pm and 5pm–12 Mon–Thurs; noon–1am Fri–Sun.*

Sally Pussey's Inn

Swindon Road, Wootton Bassett, Swindon SN4 8ET
☎ *(01793) 852430*
Michael Randall and Norah Thomas

Arkells tied house with three real ale pumps, and with 2B and 3B permanently available and a seasonal Arkells brew (Kingsdown, Noel, JRA or Summer Ale).

Pub/restaurant dating from the 19th century, with an open, contemporary style. Food available 9.30am–11am (breakfast) and full menu until 9.30pm Mon–Sat, 12–8.30pm Sun, with carvery Friday and Saturday evenings and all day Sunday. Beer garden, private conference rooms. Close to steam museum and outlet village. Off junction 16 of the M4, 800 yards on the right.

OPEN *8am–11pm Mon–Sat; 12–10pm Sun.*

WROUGHTON

The Carter's Rest

High Street, Wroughton SN4 9JU
☎ *(01793) 812288*
Kevin and Caroline MacDivitt
www.cartersrest.co.uk

Ten real ales, including Box Steam Carters Rest Alternative Porter (exclusive); Cotswold Spring Codrington Royal and Old English Rose, Hop Back Crop Circle and Sharp's Doom Bar, plus four regular changing guest ales. Traditional ciders.

Friendly village pub with separate bar and lounge. The first mention of an inn on this site is in the Parish Register in 1671. It was rebuilt in 1912/13, when it took on its classic Victorian appearance, with large gables and high ceilings. No food. Regional runner-up (out of 550 pubs!) in Punch Shine Awards 2008. Swindon and N Wilts Pub of the Year 2009. Cask Marque accredited. Patio and smoking areas. Premiership football, rugby etc on large plasma TV in bar. Children and dogs welcome. Car park. Live music nights. Quiz nights Thursdays. Poker league Tues 8pm. Christmas beer festival. Three miles south of Swindon on the A361.

OPEN *5–11pm Mon–Thurs; 5pm–1am Fri; noon–1am Sat; 12–11pm Sun.*

THE BREWERIES

BRANDY CASK BREWERY
25 Bridge Street, Pershore WR10 1AJ
☎ *(01386) 552602*

WHISTLING JOE 3.6% ABV
BRANDY SNAPPER 4.0% ABV
JOHN BAKER'S ORIGINAL 4.8% ABV

CANNON ROYALL BREWERY LTD
The Fruiterer's Arms, Uphampton, Ombersley, Droitwich WR9 0JW
☎ *(01905) 621161*
www.cannonroyall.co.uk

FRUITERER'S MILD 3.7% ABV
Dark and malty with chocolate notes.
KINGS SHILLING 3.8% ABV
Hoppy and bitter.
ARROWHEAD BITTER 3.9% ABV
Clean dry aftertaste.
MUZZLELOADER 4.2% ABV
Fruity, dry bitter.
ARROWHEAD EXTRA 4.3% ABV
Hop aroma, slightly sweet.
Plus special and seasonal brews.

EVESHAM BREWERY
SM Murphy Assoc Ltd, The Blue Maze, 17 Oat Street, Evesham WR11 4PJ
☎ *(01386) 443462*

ASSUM ALE 3.8% ABV
ASSUM GOLD 5.2% ABV
Plus seasonals and specials.

HOBSONS BREWERY & CO.
Newhouse Farm, Tenbury Road, Cleobury Mortimer DY14 8RD
☎ *(01299) 270837*
www.hobsonsbrewery.co.uk

MILD 3.2% ABV
Dark and chocolatey.
BEST BITTER 3.8% ABV
Excellent, hoppy session bitter.
TOWN CRIER 4.5% ABV
Smooth, mellow sweetness with balancing hops.
OLD HENRY 5.2% ABV
Darker, smooth and flavoursome.

MALVERN HILLS BREWERY LTD
15 West Malvern Road, Great Malvern WR14 4ND
☎ *(01684) 560165*
www.malvernhillsbrewery.co.uk

RED EARL 3.7% ABV
MOEL BRYN 3.9% ABV
NIGHTINGALE 4.0% ABV
WORCESTERSHIRE WHYM 4.2% ABV
PRESSNIT 4.3% ABV
BLACK PEAR 4.4% ABV
WOBBLE 4.5% ABV
PHOEBE 4.7% ABV
DOCTOR GULLY'S WINTER ALE 5.2% ABV

ST GEORGE'S BREWING CO. LTD
The Old Bakehouse, Bush Lane, Callow End, Worcester WR2 4TF
☎ *(01905) 831316*

MAIDEN'S SAVIOUR 3.7% ABV
FORTITUDE 3.9% ABV
PARAGON STEAM BITTER 4.0% ABV
WAR DRUM 4.1% ABV
ST GEORGE IS CROSS 4.2% ABV
PREMIUM BITTER 4.3% ABV
Award-winning beer made with English hops.
WORCESTER PALE ALE 4.3% ABV
NIMROD 4.5% ABV
A smoky taste and sharp hopping make for a pronounced character for this traditional ale.
Plus occasional beers.

TEME VALLEY BREWERY
The Talbot Inn, Bromyard Road, Knightwick, Worcester WR6 5PH
☎ *(01886) 821235*

T'OTHER 3.5% ABV
Pale, gentle bitter.
THIS 3.7% ABV
Light and hoppy.
THAT 4.1% ABV
Chestnut and malty.
Plus seasonal beers.

WEATHEROAK BREWERY LTD
25 Withybed, Alvechurch, Birmingham B48 7NX
☎ *(0121) 445 4411*
www.weatheroakales.co.uk

LIGHT OAK 3.6% ABV
WEATHEROAK ALE 4.1% ABV
REDWOOD 4.7% ABV
KEYSTONE HOPS 5.0% ABV

WYRE PIDDLE BREWERY
Highgrove Farm, Pinvin, Pershore WR10 2LF
☎ *(01905) 841853*

PIDDLE IN THE HOLE 3.9% ABV
PIDDLE IN THE WIND 4.2% ABV
PIDDLE IN THE DARK 4.5% ABV
PIDDLE IN THE SNOW 5.2% ABV
Plus occasional and seasonal brews including:
PIDDLE IN PARADISE 4.3% ABV
PIDDLE IN THE PUDDLES 4.3% ABV
PIDDLE IN THE POT 4.8% ABV

THE PUBS

ABBERLEY

The Manor Arms

Abberley Village WR6 6BN
☎ *(01299) 896507* Peter Vant

Leased from Enterprise Inns with Timothy Taylor Landlord, Fuller's London Pride, Wye Valley HPA and Bitter and Hobsons Mild plus a monthly guest such as Greene King Old Speckled Hen, Malvern Hills Black Pear or Hobsons Town Crier.

This 16th-century Grade II listed building has been a coaching inn, a court house and a manor house before becoming a pub. One main bar, one lounge bar, a 50-seat restaurant and a smaller 16-seat restaurant. Food served 6–9pm Mon, 12–2.30pm and 6–9pm Tues–Sat, 12–3pm Sun. Ten letting rooms available. Beer garden with wonderful views. Patio with marquee. Car park. Follow the brown tourist signs off the main Worcester–Tenbury road (A443).

OPEN *6pm–12 Mon; 12–3pm and 6pm–12 Tues–Thurs and Sun; 12–3pm and 6pm–12.30am Fri–Sat.*

BADSEY

Round of Gras

47 Bretforton Road, Badsey WR11 7XQ
☎ *(01386) 830206* Graham Brown
www.roundofgras.co.uk

Freehouse with Uley Pig's Ear and Flowers IPA (brewed by Badger) plus two guests from micro-breweries, changed twice weekly.

A pub famous for its asparagus! Food served 11.30am–2pm and 5.30–9pm Mon–Sat, 12–8pm Sun. Beer garden. Games room. Restaurant.

OPEN *11am–11pm.*

BEWDLEY

The Mug House Inn and Angry Chef Restaurant

12 Severnside North, Bewdley DY12 2EE
☎ *(01299) 402543* Drew Clifford
www.mughousebewdley.co.uk

A Punch Taverns pub. Wye Valley HPA, Bewdley Brewery Old School and Timothy Taylor Landlord plus one guest, such as RCH Doubleheader, Titanic Captain Smith's and Kinver Half Centurion.

A 17th-century inn with bar and restaurant (one AA rosette) and accommodation (AA four star highly recommended). Riverside views and outdoor tables with patio garden and heated glass atrium. Food served 12–2.30pm and 6.30–9pm. Annual beer festival each May bank holiday.

OPEN *12–11pm.*

The Plough Inn

Far Forest, Bewdley DY14 9TE
☎ *(01299) 266237* Mr and Mrs Giles
www.nostalgiainns.co.uk

A range of Wye Valley and Wood ales rotated plus two guests, changed two or three times a week. Local micro-breweries such as Enville, Holden's, Purity, Sadler's and Eccleshall are supported.

Steeped in history with a 350-year-old locals' bar with open log fire. Homemade food, including carvery, 12–2pm and 6–9pm Mon–Sat; 12–8pm Sun. Beer garden. Follow signs from Bewdley to Cleobury on the A4117.

OPEN *12–12.*

The Woodcolliers Arms

76 Welch Gate, Bewdley DY12 2AU
☎ *(01299) 400589* Anna Coleman
www.woodcolliers.co.uk

Four or five weekly changing guest ales, from a huge range of independent breweries, such as Hobsons, Holden's, Wye Valley, Ludlow, Three Tuns, Sadler's, Hook Norton, Caledonian, Teme Valley, Salopian, Wyre Piddle and St Georges.

Grade II listed building, dating from at least 1780, in a conservation area. Snug, saloon and lounge. Olde-worlde style, with beams decorated with a wide collection of historic items. Russian food a speciality, served Mon–Fri evenings and all day Sat–Sun. Outside patio. Parking. Accommodation single, twin and 3 doubles (three star AA and Visit Britain rated).

OPEN *Summer: noon–12.30am (including drinking-up time). Winter: 5pm–12 (including drinking-up time).*

BIRLINGHAM

The Swan Inn

Church Street, Birlingham, Nr Pershore WR10 3AQ
☎ *(01386) 750485*
Nicholas and Imogen Carson
www.theswaninn.co.uk

A freehouse. Wye Valley Best plus two guests, changed every other day. Over 300 different ales served each year, mostly from micro-breweries such as Ossett, Kelham Island, Holden's and Cottage.

Black-and-white thatched building dating back nearly 500 years. A typical village pub, serving home-cooked food 12–2.30pm and 6.30–8.30pm (not Sun evening). South-facing beer garden which hosts two beer festivals each year (May and September). Children and dogs welcome. Both the landlord and landlady speak Japanese! Situated south of Pershore, on the A4104.

OPEN *12–3pm and 6.30–11pm.*

BIRTSMORTON

The Farmer's Arms

Birts Street, Birtsmorton, Malvern WR13 6AP
☎ *(01684) 833308* J and J Moore

 Hook Norton Hooky Bitter and Old Hooky plus one guest from breweries such as Wye Valley, Cottage or Cannon Royall.

A traditional two-bar country village freehouse with beer garden. Beams and open fire. Food available at lunchtime and evenings in a separate dining area at one end of the bar. Children allowed. Garden with play area.

OPEN *11am–4pm and 6–11pm Mon–Sat; 12–4pm and 7–10.30pm Sun.*

BRETFORTON

The Fleece Inn

The Cross, Bretforton WR11 5JE
☎ *(01386) 831173* Nigel Smith
www.thefleeceinn.co.uk

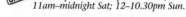 Hook Norton Hooky Bitter, Purity Pure UBU and Uley Pig's Ear plus three guests, often rotated every few days.

Quintessentially English pub, owned by the National Trust and set in an idyllic Cotswold village. Food served 12–2.30pm (4pm Sun) and 6.30–9pm. Large orchard beer garden. Children welcome. B&B room available. Home of the Vale of Evesham Asparagus Festival! Ten minutes from Evesham towards Chipping Campden.

OPEN *11am–3pm and 6–11pm Mon–Fri; 11am–midnight Sat; 12–10.30pm Sun.*

BROADWAY

The Crown & Trumpet Inn

Church Street, Broadway WR12 7AE
☎ *(01386) 853202* Andrew Scott

 Timothy Taylor Landord plus a seasonal ale from the Stanway Brewery and a guest such as Stroud Tom Long.

A 17th-century village inn built from Cotswold stone. Seasonal and homemade dishes cooked on the premises are available 12–2.15pm and 6–9.15pm Mon–Fri; 12–3.30pm and 6–9.15pm Sat–Sun; food served all day Sat–Sun in summer. Awards: Shakespeare's Branch of CAMRA's Worcestershire Pub of the Year 2008-09 and Cask Marque accreditation. Landlord celebrates his 25th year there this year. Beer garden in front of pub. Accommodation in one family room, three double rooms and one twin room (all en-suite with TV and tea/coffee-making facilities). Well-behaved children allowed. Live music. Car park. Five miles from Evesham, eight miles from Chipping Campden. In the village of Broadway, just round from the main green.

OPEN *11am–2.30pm and 5–11pm Mon–Thurs; 11am–11.30pm Fri–Sat; 11am–11pm Sun.*

BROMSGROVE

The Hop Pole Inn

78 Birmingham Road, Bromsgrove B61 0DF
☎ *(01527) 870100* Jeff Kay
www.hop-pole.com

Leased from Punch Taverns, with Worfield OBJ plus three rotating guests, changed weekly.

This 200-year-old community locals' pub also serves as a live music venue. Single lounge bar. Snacks, gourmet sandwiches, burgers, chips etc served 12–2.30pm Thurs–Sat. Magnificent beer garden. Located on the main road into Bromsgrove.

OPEN *4–11pm Mon–Wed; 12–12 Thurs–Sun.*

The Red Lion

73 High Street, Bromsgrove B61 8AQ
☎ *07825 271905* Richard and Mini Scott
www.redlionbromsgrove.co.uk

A Marston's tied house. Marston's ales plus Banks's Bitter and Original and Jenning Dark Mild, plus four guests. The list of guests may include any Jennings ale, Brains St David's Ale, Everards Pitch Black, Thwaites Double Century, Adnams Broadside or Rooster's Wild Mule.

Licensed as a pub in 1863. A one-room bar plus outside patio with covered area. Extensive menu, much of it homemade, served 11am–2pm Mon–Fri; 5–8pm Mon–Thurs; 3.30–6pm Fri–Sat. Speciality nights such as cheese tasting and chocolate fountain! Regular beer festivals. Located on the pedestrianised High Street.

OPEN *10.30am–11pm Mon–Wed; 10.30am–11.30pm Thurs; 10.30am–midnight Fri–Sat.*

CASTLEMORTON

The Plume of Feathers

Gloucester Road, Castlemorton WR13 6JB
☎ *(01684) 833554* Emma Harvey

Hobsons Best Bitter, a Batham brew and Greene King Old Speckled Hen or Abbot plus two guests, which may well come from breweries such as Spinning Dog, Cottage, Wood and Slater's.

A traditional, unspoilt 16th-century pub with oak beams in the bar and an open fire in winter. Set in idyllic surroundings looking across Castlemorton Common to the Malvern hills. Food available all day, every day. Car park. Children allowed with play area in the garden. On the main Malvern–Gloucester road, on the edge of Castlemorton Common.

OPEN *12–11pm (10.30pm Sun).*

CLAINES

The Mug House
Claines Lane, Claines WR3 7RN
☎ *(01905) 456649* Judith Allen

 Marston's leased pub with Marston's Original and Bitter plus two rotating guests changed monthly.

This 900-year-old building is the only pub in the country situated on consecrated ground. Main bar, lounge, snug, open fires. No music and no gaming machines. Food served 12–2pm Mon–Sat, 12–2.30pm Sun. Three award-winning beer gardens, with jazz events held outdoors once a month during summer. Children welcome, also very dog-friendly. Exit the M5 at junction 6, taking the A449 to Kidderminster and take the first exit off the roundabout to Claines. Located behind St John's Baptist Church.

OPEN *12–2.30pm and 5–11pm Mon–Fri; 12–11pm Sat–Sun.*

DROITWICH

Hadley Bowling Green Inn
Hadley Heath, Hadley, Droitwich WR9 0AR
☎ *(01905) 620294* Simone Pascolutti
www.hadleybowlinggreen.com

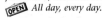 Freehouse with five real ales: Banks's Bitter, Jennings Cumberland Ale and something from Enville, plus two guests changed weekly, such as Enville Ginger Beer or Black Sheep Bitter.

A refurbished country inn set in the heart of Worcestershire. Food served 12–9.30pm every day. Fourteen en-suite rooms, gardens and one of the oldest bowling greens in the country. Children welcome. Off the M5, junction 6, on A449 north.

OPEN *All day, every day.*

DROITWICH SPA

The Hop Pole
40 Friar Street, Droitwich Spa WR9 8ED
☎ *(01905) 770155* Timothy John Radley
www.thehoppoleatdroitwich.co.uk

Freehouse with Wye Valley HPA and Butty Bach, Malvern Hills Black Pear and Purity Pure Gold always available, plus one monthly-changing guest.

Known as the fourth oldest building in Droitwich, this pub has been converted and extended from a row of cottages that date back to the 1700s. Beer garden with swimming pool. Annual beer festival. Food served 12–2pm Mon–Sun. Parties catered for. Children welcome until 6pm. Located in the town centre; from the A38 turn in to the high street and turn right onto Friar Street – the pub is right at the end.

OPEN *12–11pm.*

EVESHAM

The Green Dragon
17 Oat Street, Evesham WR11 4PJ
☎ *(01386) 443462*

Home of the Evesham Brewery. Two Asum brews produced and sold, 'Asum' being the local pronunciation of 'Evesham'. Other guest ales also offered.

The brewery is housed in the old bottle store. A Grade II listed pub with a cosy lounge. Bar and restaurant food is served at lunchtimes and evenings. Car park, garden, large function room. Children allowed.

OPEN *11am–11pm Mon–Thur; 11pm–1am Fri–Sat.*

The Queens Head
Iron Cross, Evesham WR11 5SH
☎ *(01386) 871012* Emma Wendon

Greene King IPA, Timothy Taylor Landlord, Wychwood Hobgoblin, Fuller's London Pride and Hook Norton Hooky Bitter plus one guest.

Rural pub on B4088 Evesham to Alcester road opposite Salford Priors. Food served all day. Children welcome. Car park.

OPEN *All day, every day.*

FERNHILL HEATH

Halfway House
Droitwich Road, Fernhill Heath WR3 8RA
☎ *(01905) 451489* Harry and Norma West

Banks's Original, Marston's Bitter and Pedigree plus one monthly-changing guest.

A genuine old-fashioned pub with public bar and lounge. Under the same landlord for 12 years with a mostly local clientele. Large beer garden with a new patio. Food available 12–2pm and 6–8.30pm Mon–Sat. Car park. Children allowed. Located on the A38 between Droitwich and Worcester.

OPEN *11am–3.30pm and 6pm–12.*

HANLEY BROADHEATH

The Fox Inn
Hanley Broadheath, Tenbury Wells WR15 8QS
☎ *(01886) 853189* James Lawson
www.foxinn-broadheath.co.uk

Batham Best Bitter and Hobsons Best Bitter plus two rotating guest ales, changed every few days.

Set in lovely countryside, part of this black and white beamed, family-run pub dates from the 16th century. The cosy Phannipa restaurant specialises in authentic Thai cuisine, and serves food 6.30–10pm Thurs–Sat; Thai quick snacks served 12–6pm Fri–Sun. Games room, large car park and children's play area in beer garden. Children welcome. Situated on the B4204 Tenbury Wells to Worcester road.

OPEN *4–11.30pm Mon–Wed; 4pm–12 Thurs; 4pm–1am Sat–Sun; 12–11pm Sun.*

HANLEY CASTLE

The Three Kings

Church End, Hanley Castle WR8 0BL
☎ *(01684) 592686* Sheila Roberts

 Hobsons and Butcombe brews plus three guest beers (more than 200 per year) perhaps from Archers, Beowulf, Burton Bridge, Cannon Royall, Goff's, Malvern Hills, St George's, Scattor Rock, Titanic or Weatheroak, to name but a few.

Award-winning, traditional 15th-century freehouse that has been in the same family for over 90 years. Bar food available at lunchtimes and evenings. Parking, garden, children's room. Accommodation, live music. A beer festival is held in November. Just off the B4211 Upton-upon-Severn to Malvern road. Take the third turn on the left from Upton.

OPEN *11am–3pm and 7–11pm Mon–Sat; 12–3pm and 7–10.30pm Sun.*

KEMPSEY

Walter de Cantelupe Inn

Main Road, Kempsey WR5 3NA
☎ *(01905) 820572* Martin Lloyd-Morris
www.walterdecantelupeinn.com

 Freehouse with four real ales. Timothy Taylor Landlord, Cannon Royall Kings Shillings and Hobsons Best are regulars, plus one guest from a wide range which changes every week.

Village pub dating from the early 1700s with wooden beams and stone floors. One bar, dining area and walled garden. Under the same owner/manager since 1991. Food available Tues–Sun lunchtimes and evenings, also bank holiday Mondays. Children allowed during the day. Quality en-suite accommodation, car park. Four miles south of Worcester city centre.

OPEN *12–2.30pm and 6–11pm Tues–Sat; 12–3pm and 7–10.30pm Sun. Also open bank holiday Mondays.*

KIDDERMINSTER

The Boar's Head

39 Worcester Street, Kidderminster DY10 1EA
☎ *(01562) 862450* Andy Hipkiss

 Banks's Bitter and Original, Camerons Strongarm and Marston's Pedigree plus three guests such as Fuller's London Pride, Cains Formidable and Brewery Bitter or a selection from Bateman.

A two-bar town-centre pub with stone floors, beamed ceilings and wood-burning stoves. Small beer garden and all-weather bricked courtyard covered with a glass pyramid. Live bands on Thurs and Sun nights. Food available Mon–Sat 12–3pm. Children allowed in the courtyard only.

OPEN *12–11pm Mon–Sat; 12–3pm and 7–10.30pm Sun.*

The King & Castle

Severn Valley Railway Station, Comberton Hill, Kidderminster
☎ *(01562) 747505* Rosemarie Hyde

Freehouse with five real ales. Batham Best and Wyre Piddle Royal Piddle (house brew) are usually available, and the three rotating guests, changed four times a week, are from breweries such as Enville, Hobsons, Three Tuns, Burton Bridge, Everards, Cannon Royall, Titanic and Wye Valley.

The pub is a copy of the Victorian railway refreshment rooms, decorated in the 1930s, GWR-style, with covered outside platform. Breakfast served 10am–noon, lunch noon–2pm (2.30pm weekends), plus 6–8pm Fri–Sat, 6–9pm. Function room available. Museum and shop on site. Car park and garden. Children allowed until 9pm. Located next to Kidderminster railway station – follow signs to Severn Valley Railway.

OPEN *11am–3pm and 5–11pm Mon–Fri; 11am–11pm Sat; 12–10.30pm Sun.*

The Red Man

92 Blackwell Street, Kidderminster DY10 2DZ
☎ *(01562) 67555* Richard Burgess

 Greene King Old Speckled Hen and Abbot, Black Sheep Best Bitter, Adnams Broadside and Timothy Taylor Landlord are always on offer. Guests, changed three or four times a week, might include Stonehenge Sign of Spring, brews from Berrow, or seasonal ales such as Smiles Old Tosser (for a week around Pancake Day, with pancakes on the menu!).

Country pub in the town, in a 1930s building, with a focus on traditional ale, traditional fayre and traditional values. Claims to be the only pub of this name in the country. Food available 12–7pm every day. A base for local clog dancers on Mondays in winter. Conservatory, 'tardis' garden, darts, two pool tables, pinball. Children allowed in the conservatory and garden only. Car park.

OPEN *11.30am–11pm Mon–Wed; 11.30am–1am Thurs–Sat; 12–10.30pm Sun.*

KNIGHTWICK

The Talbot

Knightwick, Worcester, WR6 5PH
☎ *(01886) 821235* Annie Clift
www.the-talbot.co.uk

Home of the Teme Valley Brewery, so with This, That, T'Other and a range of seasonal ales usually available, plus Hobsons Best Bitter.

Attractive, 500-year-old country inn standing by the River Teme, well known locally for its home-produced food. Food available lunch and dinner every day. Accommodations. Car park. Children welcome. Private room available for hire. Riverside garden. Green Hop Beer Festival. Past winner of CAMRA South Worcestershire Pub of the Year. The cathedral cities of Worcester and Hereford are nearby, and there are plenty of country walks in the area. Teme Valley Market on the second Sunday of every month. Just off the A44 on the B4197.

OPEN *11am–11pm Mon–Sat; 12–10.30pm Sun.*

MALVERN

The Foley Bar

Foley Arms Hotel, 14 Worcester Road, Malvern WR14 4QS
☎ *(01684) 573397* Nigel Thomas
www.foleyarmshotel.com

 Charles Wells Bombardier and Bass plus one or two guests, such as Malvern Hills Black Pear and Blue Bear White Bear.

Friendly, cosy, locals' pub situated in the historic Foley Arms Hotel, with a sun terrace that overlooks the Severn Valley. Full bar menu available 12–2pm and 6–9pm and all day Sat. Car park. Children welcome. Situated in middle of Malvern on the A449.

OPEN *12–2.30pm and 5–11pm Mon–Fri; 12–11pm Sat; 12–3pm and 7–10.30pm Sun.*

The Nag's Head

Bank Street, Malvern WR14 2JG
☎ *(01684) 574373* Duncan Ironmonger

 Freehouse with 15 real ales from a range of national and local breweries including their own, St George's. Nine of these are changed daily.

Originally three cottages, parts of this pub date back to around 1740. Two bars, two open fires, various nooks and crannies, old furniture and a K6 telephone box. Food served 12–2pm and 6.30–8.30pm Mon–Sun. Two beer gardens. Heated patio with giant umbrellas. Annual beer festival on St George's Day. Close to Malvern Hills, half a mile from Malvern town centre.

OPEN *11am–11pm.*

MONKWOOD GREEN

The Fox Inn

Monkwood Green, Nr Hallow WR2 6NX
☎ *(01886) 889123* David Lewis

 Freehouse serving Cannon Royall Arrowhead and Muzzleloader and Wye Valley Hereford Pale Ale, with the occasional guest. Also serves Barker's Best cider and perry.

Old-fashioned single-bar country pub which has remained unchanged for 25 years. Set in rural area with the Malvern Hills in view. Food available only by prior arrangement (for parties, functions, etc). Small beer garden. Skittle alley. Well-behaved dogs and children welcome. Located near Monkwood nature reserve, five miles north-west of Worcester.

OPEN *5–11pm Mon–Thurs; 12.30–2.30pm and 5–11pm Fri; 12–11pm Sat and bank holidays; 12–10.30pm Sun.*

OFFENHAM

The Bridge Inn and Ferry

Offenham, Evesham WR11 8QZ
☎ *(01386) 446565* Rob and Sue Morris
www.bridge-inn.co.uk

 Something from Wye Valley, plus two guest ales from various independent breweries, changed weekly.

A 300-year-old historic, typical English country pub in a riverside setting on the banks of the River Avon opposite the site of the 1265 Battle of Evesham. Food served 12–2.30pm and 6–9.30pm. Beer garden, car park. Private room for hire. Children welcome. Beer festivals held. Follow signs to Offenham, then brown tourist signs for the riverside pub.

OPEN *Winter: 12–11pm Sun–Thurs; noon–2am Fri–Sat. Summer: 11am–11pm Sun–Thurs; 11am–2am Fri–Sat.*

OMBERSLEY

The Crown & Sandy's Hotel

Main Road, Ombersley, Worcester WR9 0EW
☎ *(01905) 620252* Richard and Rachel Everton
www.crownandsandys.co.uk

 Freehouse with five real ales. Marston's Pedigree and Burton Bitter, Greene King Ruddles Best and County, Wood Shropshire Lad and Windsor Sadlers Thin Ice are regular favourites, and two of the beers rotate every week.

Refurbished 17th-century freehouse with large bar and three busy restaurants. Food served 12–2.30pm and 6–10pm Mon–Sat and 12–9pm Sun. Outside patio and gardens. Luxury en-suite accommodation. Car park. Children welcome. Off junction 6 of the M5, on the A499 to Kidderminster.

OPEN *11am–3pm and 5–11pm Mon–Fri; 12–12 Sat; 12–10.30pm Sun.*

PENSAX

The Bell

Pensax, Abberley WR6 6AE
☎ *(01299) 896677* John and Trudy Greaves

 Genuine freehouse with at least five real ales. Brews from Hobsons are always on offer, but beers from Timothy Taylor, Cannon Royall, Holdens and Wood are also regulars. Also local ciders. Beers are changed as soon as they run out (in some cases, after only two hours!).

Award-winning, friendly, rural freehouse built in 1883 with various traditional drinking areas and dining room. Large garden, superb views, three real fires in winter. West Midlands CAMRA Pub of the Year 2008. Beer festival held at the end of June. Seasonal home-cooked bar and restaurant food served 12–2pm (not Mon) and 6–9pm on weekdays and 12–3pm Sun. Families welcome. Camping available across the road. Located on the B4202 Great Witley to Cleobury Mortimer road, between Abberley and Clows Top.

OPEN *5–11pm Mon (closed Mon lunchtimes except bank holidays); 12–2.30pm and 5–11pm Tues–Sat; 12–10.30pm Sun.*

PERSHORE
The Brandy Cask
25 Bridge Street, Pershore WR10 1AJ
☎ *(01386) 552602* Spencer Cooper

 Small craft brewery supplying its own pub with three beers all year round, with occasional out-sales to beer festivals, etc. Plus two guest beers, always changing, from small independent breweries.

Town-centre freehouse dating from the mid-1700s with lounge bar and restaurant. Food is served at lunchtimes (12–2pm) and evenings (7–9pm). Large riverside garden. On the B4084 main road through the town.

OPEN *11.30am–2.30pm and 7–11pm Mon–Wed; 11.30am–2.30pm and 7–11.30pm Thurs–Fri; 11.30am–3pm and 7–11.30pm Sat; 12–3pm and 7–11pm Sun.*

SHATTERFORD
The Red Lion Inn
Bridgnorth Road, Shatterford, Nr Kidderminster DY12 1SU
☎ *(01299) 861221* Richard Tweedie

 Banks's Mild and Bitter plus Batham Bitter usually available. Two guest beers are also served, often from Wood, Wye Valley, Marston's and Cannon Royall breweries.

Truly rural pub, well known locally for its food. Food every lunchtime and evening, including traditional Sunday roasts. Two car parks: one in Worcestershire, the other in Shropshire! Children welcome, with special children's menu available.

OPEN *11.30am–2.30pm and 6.30–11pm Mon–Sat; 12–3pm and 7–10.30pm Sun.*

STOKE PRIOR
The Gate Hangs Well
Woodgate Road, Stoke Prior, Nr Bromsgrove B60 4HG
☎ *(01527) 821957* Neil and Helen McMahon

 At least four real ales, perhaps including Banks's Bitter, Black Sheep Special and a wide range of other guest brews often from local breweries.

Award-winning, open-plan freehouse, set in the Worcestershire countryside. Log fires, conservatory, pool table, garden. Good food served 12–2.30pm and 6–9pm Mon–Sat, 12–4pm Sun.

OPEN *12–3pm and 5–11pm Mon–Fri; 12–11pm Sat–Sun.*

STOURPORT-ON-SEVERN
The Rising Sun
50 Lombard Street, Stourport-on-Severn DY13 8DU
☎ *(01299) 822530* Robert Hallard

Banks's Mild and Bitter and two guest beers always available.

A 200-year-old canalside pub. One bar, small dining area and patio. Food available at lunchtimes (12–2pm) and evenings (6.30–9pm), 12–4pm Sun. Children allowed in the dining room and patio only.

OPEN *All day, every day.*

The Wheatsheaf
39 High Street, Stourport-on-Severn DY13 8BS
☎ *(01299) 822613* M Webb

 Banks's Mild, Bitter and Hanson's Bitter usually available.

Games-orientated house in the town centre, with relaxing lounge and cosy bar. Food served 10.30am–3pm Mon–Sat and 12–2pm Sun. Children welcome until 9.30pm. Car park.

OPEN *10.30am–11pm.*

TENBURY WELLS
The Ship Inn
Teme Street, Tenbury Wells WR15 8AE
☎ *(01584) 810269* Michael Hoar

Freehouse with Hobsons Best plus a guest beer that changes every week and could come from any brewery in the country.

A 17th-century market-town pub that has been under the same ownership since 1984. The pub has daily deliveries of fresh fish and is renowned for its food, which is served at lunchtimes and evenings every day; there are two separate restaurants. Recommended in two good-food guides. Pretty beer garden, accommodation, private room for hire. Children allowed. On the main street, opposite Barclays bank.

OPEN *11am–3pm and 7–11pm (10.30pm Sun).*

UPHAMPTON
The Fruiterer's Arms
Uphampton, Ombersley WR9 0JW
☎ *(01905) 620305/620527* EJ May

 Cannon Royall brews produced and served on the premises plus a guest beer.

Brewing began in this converted cider house in July 1993 and the maximum output is now 16 barrels per week. The pub has two bars and a log fire in winter, and has been in the same family since around 1850. No food. Car park. No children. Off the A449.

OPEN *12.30–3pm and 7pm–12. Open all day Sat–Sun in summer.*

WORCESTER

The Dragon Inn

51 The Tything, Worcester WR1 1JT
☎ *(01905) 25845* SM Payne
www.thedragoninn.com

A true ale-lovers' paradise. Up to six ales, a stout and a real cider available year-round. They source their own ales and ciders, and regulars include brews from Beowulf, Church End, Otter, Stonehenge, Teme Valley, Millstone, Salamander and Cannon Royall, to mention just a few.

Late-Georgian, Grade II listed alehouse with L-shaped bar and outside patio area for warm summer days. Food served 12–2pm Mon–Sat. Well-behaved children welcome. Situated a three-minute walk from Foregate Street Station, away from the city centre. No parking.

OPEN *12–3.30pm and 4.30–11pm Mon–Fri; 12–11pm Sat; 1–4pm and 7–10.30pm Sun.*

The Plough

23 Fish Street, Worcester WR1 2HN
☎ *(01905) 21381*
Matt Vernon and Kate Brookes

Six real ales available plus draught cider and perry.

Re-opened in March 2006 after a fight with potential developers, a classic 300-year-old city-centre freehouse. Pub grub served 12pm–5.30pm. Head down Deansway from the cathedral towards Worcester Bridge.

OPEN *All day, every day.*

The Postal Order

18 Foregate Street, Worcester WR1 1DN
☎ *(01905) 22373* Roger Beesley

Marston's Pedigree, Greene King Abbot Ale and Teme Valley always available, plus five guest ales changed daily.

An open-plan JD Wetherspoon's house converted from the old post office, a popular alehouse with one bar and a welcoming atmosphere. Food available 9am–noon for breakfasts, 9am–11pm for full menu. Grill night Tues, curry club Thurs, roasts Sun. Disabled access and facilities. Children's licence 9am–8.30pm for diners. By the train station, opposite the Odeon cinema.

OPEN *9am–midnight (1am Fri–Sat).*

The Saracen's Head

4 The Tything, Worcester WR1 1HD
☎ *(01905) 24165* Steven Robert Kitchener

A freehouse serving seven real ales. Marston's Pedigree, Caledonian Deuchars IPA and Greene King Old Speckled Hen. Four weekly-changing guests, from breweries such as Malvern Hills, Titanic and Cannon Royal.

Dating from 1706, the pub has two bars (public and lounge) and a function room. There is a heated, covered courtyard for smokers, complete with outdoor TV. Darts team, skittle alley with skittles team. Occasional charity quiz nights. Located on the A38, at the top of Castle Street.

OPEN *12–11.30pm Sun–Thurs; 12–12 Fri–Sat.*

The Swan With Two Nicks

28 New Street, Worcester WR1 2DP
☎ *(01905) 28190* Colin Griffin
www.theswanwithtwonicks.co.uk

Freehouse with four constantly rotating guest ales such as Malvern Hills Black Pear, Whittington's Cats Whiskers, RCH Pitchfork, Wye Valley Butty Bach and brews from Timothy Taylor and Hobsons. Scrumpy ciders and perries, plus over 30 malt whiskies and a selection of rums.

Grade II listed pub dating from 1550, with three bars. One is traditional, one a retro cocktail bar and the other hosts live music events and serves a good selection of wines. Home-cooked food served 12–5pm Mon–Sun. Beer patio. Disabled access. Children welcome at lunchtime. Guide dogs only. Located in the town centre, next to King Charles House.

OPEN *11am–midnight Mon–Thurs; 11am–3am Fri–Sat; 12–11pm Sun.*

WYNDS POINT

Malvern Hills Hotel

Jubilee Drive, Wynds Point, Malvern WR13 6DW
☎ *(01684) 540690* Matthew Cooke
www.malvernhillshotel.co.uk

Wye Valley and Malvern Hills brews plus two guest beers, which change every week.

High on the western slopes of the Malverns at British Camp with 'one of the goodliest vistas in England', offering walks with breathtaking views. Warm, traditional oak-panelled lounge bar with sun terrace. Bar food and separate restaurant food available 12–2.15pm Mon–Fri, 12–9pm Sat and 12–8pm Sun. Car park. Children welcome but no special facilities. Situated on the A449 at British Camp hill fort (also known as the Herefordshire Beacon) midway between Malvern and Ledbury.

OPEN *10am–11pm Mon–Sat; 12–10.30pm Sun.*

THE BREWERIES

ABBEY BELLS BREWERY
5 Main Road, Hirst Courtney, Selby,
North Yorkshire YO8 8QP
☎ *07940 726658*
www.abbeybells.co.uk

MONDAY'S CHILD 3.7% ABV
Fruity, banana notes.
HOPPY DAZE 4.1% ABV
Lemon nose, toffee overtones.
CORDELIA'S GIFT 4.3% ABV
Dark Dandelion and Burdock flavour with
aftertaste of nuts.
SANTA'S STOCKING FILLER 4.5% ABV
Caramel and malt flavours.
GREASE 4.6% ABV
Smells of honey, tastes of liquorice.
1911 CELEBRATION ALE 4.8% ABV
Malty, claret colour.
THE AMBER NECK TIE 5.0% ABV
Vanilla and biscuit tones.
ORIGINAL BITTER 5.1% ABV
Dark with whiskey nose.
BLACK SATIN 6.2% ABV
Sweet stout.

ABBEYDALE BREWERY
Unit 8, Aizlewood Road, Sheffield,
South Yorkshire S8 0YX
☎ *(0114) 281 2712*
www.abbeydalebrewery.co.uk

MATINS 3.6% ABV
Straw colour, herby aroma.
BRIMSTONE 3.9% ABV
Russet colour, spicy flavours, especially cloves.
BEST BITTER 4.0% ABV
Smooth and malty with good hoppiness.
MOONSHINE 4.3% ABV
Fruity easy quaffer.
DEVOTION 4.4% ABV
Pale beer, lychee flavours.
RESURRECTION 4.6% ABV
Golden brown, floral aromas, fruity flavour.
ABSOLUTION 5.3% ABV
Golden, smooth and refreshing.
BLACK MASS 6.66% ABV
Stout, with good hoppiness.
LAST RITES 11.0% ABV
Smooth toffee sweetness.
Plus special brews and the Dr Moreton Cure-all
range.

ACORN BREWERY
Unit 11–12, Mitchells Enterprise Centre,
Bradberry Balk Lane, Wombwell, Barnsley, South
Yorkshire S73 8HR
☎ *(01226) 270734*
www.acornbrewery.net

ACORN BARNSLEY BITTER 3.8% ABV
Brewed using original Barnsley yeast
strains. Chestnut in colour, having a well-
rounded rich flavour with a lasting bitter finish.
BARNSLEY GOLD 4.3% ABV
Award-winning golden beer – good bitterness
level, with a fresh citrus and hop aroma.
OLD MOOR PORTER 4.4% ABV
SIBA Champion Porter of Great Britain 2004.
Full-bodied Victorian Porter with hints of
liquorice. Initial bitterness gives way to a
smooth mellow finish.
Plus seasonal and special brews including:
FORESTER 4.1% ABV
SUMMER PALE 4.1% ABV

HARVESTER 4.5% ABV
WINTER ALE 4.5% ABV
THE FIRST NOEL 4.8% ABV

ANGLO-DUTCH BREWERY
Unit 12 Savile Bridge Mills, Mill Street East,
Dewsbury, West Yorkshire WF12 6QQ
☎ *(01924) 457772*
www.anglo-dutch-brewery.co.uk

BEST BITTER 3.8% ABV
IMPERIAL PINT 4.0% ABV
KLETSWATER 4.0% ABV
SPIKE'S ON T'WAY 4.2% ABV
GHOST ON THE RIM 4.5% ABV
AT T'GHOUL AND GHOST 5.2% ABV
TABATHA THE KNACKERED 6.0% ABV
Plus seasonal and occasional brews.

THE BLACK SHEEP BREWERY PLC
Wellgarth, Crosshills, Masham, Ripon, North
Yorkshire HG4 4EN
☎ *(01765) 689227*
www.blacksheep.co.uk

BEST BITTER 3.8% ABV
Golden, well hopped and dry.
EMMERDALE 4.2% ABV
Dry, bitter finish.
BLACK SHEEP ALE 4.4% ABV
Fruity aroma, bitter finish.
RIGGWELTER 5.7% ABV
Hints of coffee and banana.

BRISCOE'S BREWERY
16 Ash Grove, Otley, West Yorkshire LS21 3EL
☎ *(01943) 466515*

BURNSALL CLASSIC BITTER 4.0% ABV
CHEVIN CHASER 4.3% ABV
DALEBOTTOM DARK MILD 4.3% ABV
BADGER STONE BITTER 4.4% ABV
OTLEY GOLD 4.6% ABV
Plus seasonals and occasionals including:
3 PEAKS ALE 4.5% ABV
VICTORIAN VELVET 4.9% ABV

BROWN COW BREWERY
Brown Cow Road, Barlow, Selby, North Yorkshire
YO8 8EH
☎ *(01757) 618947*
www.browncowbrewery.co.uk

MISTLE MILD 3.7% ABV
Dry and malty.
HOW NOW 4.5% ABV
Pale, fruity and single hopped.
WOLFHOUND 4.5% ABV
Straw coloured, full and rounded palate of malt
and traditional English hops.
Plus seasonals and specials.

CAPTAIN COOK BREWERY LTD
1 West End, Stokesley, Middlesbrough,
North Yorkshire TS9 5BL
☎ *(01642) 710263*
www.thecaptaincookbrewery.co.uk

SUNSET 4.0% ABV
Smooth and light.
MIDSHIPS 4.1% ABV
Smooth with toffee and vanilla hints.
SLIPWAY 4.2% ABV
Light and hoppy, malt aftertaste.
BLACK PORTER 4.4% ABV
Dark, slightly sweet, roast barley.

CONCERTINA BREWERY

9a Dolcliffe Road, Mexborough, South Yorkshire
S64 9AZ
☎ *(01709) 580841*

CLUB BITTER 3.9% ABV
OLD DARK ATTIC 3.9% ABV
ONE-EYED JACK 4.0% ABV
BENGAL TIGER 4.5% ABV
DICTATORS 4.7% ABV

COPPER DRAGON SKIPTON BREWERY LTD

Snaygill Industrial Estate, Keighley Road,
Skipton, North Yorkshire BD23 2QR
☎ *(01756) 702130*
www.copperdragon.uk.com

BLACK GOLD 3.7% ABV
Roasted malt flavour.
BEST BITTER 3.8% ABV
Malty flavour.
GOLDEN PIPPIN 3.9% ABV
Blonde, citrus fruit flavour.
SCOTTS 1816 4.1% ABV
Hoppy and rounded.
CHALLENGER IPA 4.4% ABV
Fruity with hoppy undertones.

CROPTON BREWERY

Woolcroft, Cropton, Nr Pickering, North
Yorkshire YO18 8HH
☎ *(01751) 417330*
www.croptonbrewery.co.uk

ENDEAVOUR ALE 3.6% ABV
KING BILLY 3.6% ABV
TWO PINTS 4.0% ABV
HONEY GOLD 4.2% ABV
SCORSEBY STOUT 4.2% ABV
UNCLE SAM'S 4.4% ABV
RUDOLPH'S REVENGE 4.6% ABV
YORKSHIRE MOORS 4.6% ABV
MONKMAN'S SLAUGHTER BITTER 6.0% ABV

DALESIDE BREWERY

Camwal Road, Starbeck, Harrogate,
North Yorkshire HG1 4PT
☎ *(01423) 880022*
www.dalesidebrewery.com

BITTER 3.7% ABV
Light bitter, amber colour.
BLONDE 3.9% ABV
Citrus sherbert.
PRIDE OF ENGLAND 4.0% ABV
Floral aroma.
OLD LEGOVER 4.1% ABV
Nutty, fruity taste.
SPECIAL BITTER 4.1% ABV
Malty sweetness.
ST GEORGE'S ALE 4.6% ABV
Crisp palate, hop aroma.
MONKEY WRENCH 5.4% ABV
Fruity, malty, sweet.

EASTWOOD & SANDERS BREWERY (FINE ALES) LTD

The Brewery, Unit 3–5 Heathfield Ind. Est.,
Heathfield Street, Elland, West Yorkshire
HX5 9AE
☎ *(01422) 377677*
www.eandsbrewery.co.uk

FIRST LIGHT 3.5% ABV
A light Yorkshire ale with delicate hop
flavours balanced by underlying malt sweetness.
BARGEE 3.8% ABV
A full-flavoured bitter made with four different
malts and hops from England and America.
ELLAND BEST BITTER 4.0% ABV
A dry and aromatic beer made with Maris Otter
pale malt and using hops from England and
America.
BEYOND THE PALE 4.2% ABV
A pale, golden bitter with a touch of Amber
Malt. Pronounced floral hop aroma from the
inclusion of North American Cascade hops and a
long, dry hoppy finish.
NETTLETHRASHER 4.4% ABV
A deep copper-coloured traditional strong ale,
brewed using six different malts with English
and American hops.
GOLDRUSH 4.6% ABV
Floral, herby and spicy.
IPA 6.5% ABV
Pale amber with malty sweetness.
1872 PORTER 6.5% ABV
Bittersweet and malty.
Plus seasonal brews.

FERNANDES BREWERY

The Old Malthouse, 5 Avison Yard, Kirkgate,
Wakefield, West Yorkshire WF1 1UA
☎ *(01924) 291709*
www.fernandes-brewery.gowyld.com

BOYS BITTER 3.2% ABV
Lingering citrus aftertaste.
SHAKESPEARE SB 3.5% ABV
Cigar brown bitter.
BEST BITTER 3.8% ABV
Refreshing and hoppy.
LONESOME PINE 3.8% ABV
Pine aroma, lemon notes.
MALT SHOVEL MILD 3.8% ABV
Dark and chocolatey.
DOWN IN ONE 4.3% ABV
Copper-coloured hoppy bitter.
HAMPTON CAUGHT BITTER 4.3% ABV
Gold and sweet.
TO BE JOYFUL 4.3% ABV
Fruity bitter.
GREEN BULLET 4.5% ABV
Light, bittersweet aftertaste.
WAKEFIELD PRIDE 4.5% ABV
Light and clean tasting.
CASCADE 5.0% ABV
Pale, citrus notes and hoppy.
DOUBLE SIX 6.0% ABV
Roast malt and chocolate flavours.
EMPRESS OF INDIA 6.0% ABV
Easy drinker with dry finish.
MOODIES MILD 6.0% ABV
Dry and malty.

FROG AND PARROT BREWHOUSE

64 Division Street, Sheffield, South Yorkshire
S1 4GF
☎ *(0114) 272 1280*

ROGER AND OUT 12.5% ABV

GARTON BREWERY

Station House, Station Road, Garton-on-the-Wold, Driffield, North Yorkshire YO25 3EX
☎ *(01377) 252340*

 OLD BUFFER 4.5% ABV
WOLDSMAN BITTER 4.5% ABV
Very light, straw-coloured bitter.
STUNNED MULLET BITTER 5.0% ABV
Very deep red bitter.
LIQUID LOBOTOMY STOUT 8.0% ABV
Heavy-duty stout.
Plus seasonals and specials.

GLENTWORTH BREWERY

Glentworth House, Crossfield Lane, Skellow, Doncaster, South Yorkshire DN6 8PL
☎ *(01302) 725555*

LIGHTYEAR 3.9% ABV
NORTH STAR 4.3% ABV
PERLE 4.4% ABV
DIZZY BLONDE 4.5% ABV
WHISPERS 4.5% ABV
ICE AND FIRE 5.0% ABV
Plus seasonals including:
TEARDROPS 4.3% ABV
SUN GOD 4.4% ABV

GOLCAR BREWERY

Swallow Lane, Golcar, Huddersfield, West Yorkshire HD7 4NB
☎ *(01484) 644241*

GOLCAR DARK MILD 3.2% ABV
GOLCAR BITTER 3.8% ABV
PENNINE GOLD 3.8% ABV
WEAVERS DELIGHT 4.2% ABV
Plus specials.

GOOSE EYE BREWERY

Ingrow Bridge, South Street, Keighley, West Yorkshire BD21 5AX
☎ *(01535) 605807*
www.goose-eye-brewery.co.uk

BARMPOT 3.8% ABV
Golden and hoppy.
BRONTE BITTER 4.0% ABV
Malty and well balanced.
NO EYE DEER 4.0% ABV
Fruity aftertaste.
WHARFEDALE BITTER 4.5% ABV
Light but hoppy.
POMMIE'S REVENGE 5.2% ABV
Straw coloured, soft and smooth.
Plus occasional brews.

H B CLARK & CO. (SUCCESSORS) LTD

Westgate Brewery, 136 Westgate, Wakefield, West Yorkshire WF2 9SW
☎ *(01924) 373328*
www.hbclark.co.uk

 CLASSIC BLONDE 3.9% ABV
Pale, hoppy citrus flavour.
NO ANGEL 4.0% ABV
Bitter with clean hop flavours.
WESTGATE BRUNETTE 4.2% ABV
Light colour, fruity.
RAM'S REVENGE 4.6% ABV
Full-bodied ruby ale with roast barley and malt.
Plus seasonal brews.

HALIFAX STEAM BREWING CO. LTD

The Conclave, Southedge Works, Hipperholme, Halifax, West Yorkshire HX3 8EF
☎ *(01484) 715074*

MORNING GLORY 3.8% ABV
JAMAICA GINGER 4.0% ABV
LILLY FOG 4.0% ABV
PICKLE HUT IMPOSTER 4.0% ABV
BANTAM LIGHT 4.1% ABV
JOKER 4.1% ABV
TOKYO JOE 4.5% ABV
GOLDEN RAIN 4.6% ABV
COCK O' T'NORTH 4.9% ABV
Plus seasonals.

KELHAM ISLAND BREWERY

23 Alma Street, Sheffield, South Yorkshire S3 8SA
☎ *(0114) 249 4804*
www.kelhambrewery.co.uk

KELHAM ISLAND GOLD 3.8% ABV
Light golden ale with hops throughout.
KI BITTER 3.8% ABV
Straw-coloured thirst-quencher.
EASY RIDER 4.3% ABV
Hoppy pale ale.
PALE RIDER 5.2% ABV
Flavoured with American hops.
Plus seasonals.

LINFIT BREWERY

Sair Inn, Lane Top, Linthwaite, Huddersfield, West Yorkshire HD7 5SG
☎ *(01484) 842370*

DARK MILD 3.0% ABV
BITTER 3.7% ABV
GOLD MEDAL 4.2% ABV
SPECIAL 4.3% ABV
AUTUMN GOLD 4.7% ABV
ENGLISH GUINEAS STOUT 5.3% ABV
OLD ELI 5.3% ABV
LEADBOILER 6.6% ABV
ENOCH'S HAMMER 8.0% ABV
Plus seasonals.

LITTON ALE BREWERY

Queen's Arms, Litton, Skipton, North Yorkshire BD23 5QJ
☎ *(01756) 770208*
www.yorkshirenet.co.uk/stayat/queensarms/littonale.htm

LITTON ALE 3.8%ABV
POTTS BECK 4.2% ABV

THE MOORCOCK BREWING CO.

Hawes Rural Workshop Estate, Brunt Acres Road, Hawes, Leyburn, North Yorkshire DL8 3UZ
☎ *(01969) 666188*
www.moorcockinn.co.uk

GARSDALE MILD 3.2% ABV
HAIL ALE 3.8% ABV
OAKLEY PALE ALE 3.8% ABV
MESCANS PORTER 4.3% ABV
1888 BLONDE 5.0% ABV

NAYLOR'S BREWERY

Unit 1, Midland Mills, Station Road, Cross Hills,
Keighley West Yorkshire BD20 7RN
☎ *(01535) 637451*
www.naylorsbrewery.co.uk

SPARKEY'S MONDAY NIGHT 3.4% ABV
Dark colour, malty taste.
MOTHER'S BEST 3.9% ABV
Amber, strong bitterness, citrus fruit.
STONEY'S TRIPPEL S 4.5% ABV
Very hoppy.
Plus seasonals and specials.

NICK STAFFORD HAMBLETON ALES

Unit 2a Barker Business Park, Melmerby Green
Lane, Melmerby, Ripon, North Yorkshire HG4 5NB
☎ *(01765) 640108*
www.hambletonales.co.uk

BITTER 3.6% ABV
Full flavour, mid-brown, moreish.
GOLDFIELD 4.2% ABV
Gold with clean aftertaste.
STALLION 4.2% ABV
Malty, nutty character, bitter.
STUD 4.3% ABV
Straw coloured, hoppy aroma.
NIGHTMARE 5.0% ABV
Stout, creamy and malty brew.

NORTH YORKSHIRE BREWING CO.

Pinchinthorpe Hall, Pinchinthorpe, Guisborough,
North Yorkshire TS14 8HG
☎ *(01287) 630200*
www.nybrewery.com

BEST BITTER 3.6% ABV
Pale, hoppy.
BORO BEST 4.0% ABV
Malty aroma, mid-brown, full bodied.
FOOL'S GOLD 4.6% ABV
Pale, with hops throughout.
FLYING HERBERT 4.7% ABV
Malty fruit taste, dry.
Speciality brews:
PRIOR'S ALE 3.6% ABV
Hoppy.
ARCHBISHOP LEE'S RUBY ALE 4.0% ABV
Maltiness predominant.
GOLDEN ALE 4.6% ABV
Powerful hoppiness.
LORD LEES 4.7% ABV
Smooth, full-flavoured malt.
Special monthly beers:
GOLDEN GINSENG 3.6% ABV
Golden-coloured, hoppy beer, made with
ginseng.
CRYSTAL TIPS 4.0% ABV
Full-bodied crystal malt flavoured beer, ruby
colour.
LOVE MUSCLE 4.0% ABV
Golden ale, crisp.
HONEY BUNNY 4.2% ABV
A pale ale Easter drink, hints of honey.
MAYHEM 4.3% ABV
Hoppy, clean taste.
XMAS HERBERT 4.4% ABV
Malty, fruity, dry finish.
CEREAL KILLER 4.5% ABV
Wheat beer, hoppy nose.
BLOND 4.6% ABV
Golden bitter.
WHITE LADY 4.7% ABV
Hoppy, strong pale-coloured ale.
DIZZY DICK 4.8% ABV
A strong, smooth, dark ale, hoppy.

ROCKET FUEL 5.0% ABV
A strong, golden ale.
Cosmic beers:
COSMIC GLOW 4.8% ABV
Full-flavoured malty bitter.
NORTHERN STAR 4.8% ABV
Golden and well balanced.
SOUTHERN CROSS 4.8% ABV
Hoppy, golden ale.
SHOOTING STAR 4.8% ABV
Dark and smooth.
All beers are organic.

OAKWELL BREWERY

Unit 11, Pontefract Road, Barnsley,
South Yorkshire S71 1EZ
☎ *(01226) 296161*

BARNSLEY BITTER 3.8% ABV
OLD TOM MILD 3.8% ABV

OLD BEAR BREWERY

Unit 4B Atlas Works, Pitt Street, Keighley,
West Yorkshire BD21 4YL
☎ *(01535) 601222*
www.oldbearbrewery.com

BRUIN 3.5% ABV
ESTIVATER 3.8% ABV
OLD BEAR ORIGINAL 3.9% ABV
BLACK MARI'A 4.2% ABV
OLD BEAR HONEY POT 4.4% ABV
GOLDILOCKS 4.5% ABV
OLD BEAR HIBERNATOR 5.0% ABV

OLD MILL BREWERY

Mill Street, Snaith, East Yorkshire
DN14 9HU
☎ *(01405) 861813*

TRADITIONAL MILD 3.4% ABV
Nutty, chocolatey.
TRADITIONAL BITTER 3.9% ABV
Malty palate, delicate fruits flavour.
OLD CURIOSITY SHOP 4.5% ABV
Lightly hopped, mellow.
BULLION 4.7% ABV
Roasted malts flavour.
Plus seasonal and occasional brews including:
SPRINGS ETERNAL 4.0% ABV
CUPID'S KISS 4.2% ABV
BLACKJACK 5.0% ABV

OSSETT BREWING COMPANY

Low Mill Road, Ossett, West Yorkshire WF5 8ND
☎ *(01924) 261333*
www.ossett-brewery.co.uk

PALE GOLD 3.8% ABV
Floral, spicy.
BLACK BULL BITTER 3.9% ABV
Refreshing and dark.
SILVER KING 4.3% ABV
Citrus fruits flavours.
FINE FETTLE 4.8% ABV
Clean, fruity.
EXCELSIOR 5.2% ABV
Hoppy, toffee flavour, floral aroma.
Plus seasonals and specials including:
ELIZABETH ROSE 4.0% ABV
Bittersweet.
MAYPOLE 4.2% ABV
Floral, hop aroma.
SNOWDROP 4.2% ABV
Fruity and spice flavours.
TREACLE STOUT 5.0% ABV
Chocolate and liquorice flavours.

RIVERHEAD BREWERY
2 Peel Street, Marsden, Huddersfield,
West Yorkshire HD7 6BR
☎ *(01484) 841270*

SPARTH MILD 3.6% ABV
BUTTERLY BITTER 3.8% ABV
DEERHILL PORTER 4.0% ABV
CUPWITH LIGHT BITTER 4.2% ABV
BLACKMOSS STOUT 4.3% ABV
MARCH HAIGH SPECIAL 4.6% ABV
REDBROOK PREMIUM BITTER 5.5% ABV
Plus special brews.

ROOSTER'S BREWERY
Unit 3, Grimbald Park, Wetherby Road,
Knaresborough, North Yorkshire HG5 8LJ
☎ *(01423) 865959*
www.roosters.co.uk

SPECIAL 3.9% ABV
Pale, with citrus-fruit freshness.
LEGHORN 4.3% ABV
Aromatic and floral.
WHITE ROSE 4.3% ABV
Pale, with some hoppy bitterness.
YANKEE 4.3% ABV
Pale, soft and fruity.
YPA – YORKSHIRE PALE ALE 4.3% ABV
Gold, raspberry aroma, medium bitterness.
CREAM 4.7% ABV
Smooth and soft, with fruit flavours.
ROOSTER'S 4.7% ABV
Golden brown, sweet and fruity.
Plus occasional and seasonal brews including:
MAYFLOWER 3.7% ABV
SILVER LINING 4.3% ABV
OYSTER STOUT 4.7% ABV
NECTAR 5.0% ABV
Pale, soft, bitter beer. Christmas.
Additional brews produced under the Outlaw
Brewing Co. label.

RUDGATE BREWERY LTD
2 Centre Park, Marston Moor Business Park,
Rudgate, Tockwith, York, North Yorkshire
YO26 7QF
☎ *(01423) 358382*
www.rudgate-beers.co.uk

VIKING 3.8% ABV
Award-winning bitter.
BATTLEAXE 4.2% ABV
A robust premium bitter.
RUBY MILD 4.4% ABV
A dark premium mild.
SPECIAL 4.5% ABV
A hoppy pale ale.
WELL BLATHERED 5.0% ABV
A premium golden ale.
Plus monthly brews.

SALAMANDER BREWING CO.
22 Harry Street, Bradford, West Yorkshire BD4 9PH
☎ *(01274) 652323*

OLD AMOS 3.8% ABV
SALAMANDROID 3.8% ABV
MUDPUPPY 4.2% ABV
HELLBENDER 4.8% ABV
PORTER 4.8% ABV
HAMMER AND TONG 5.0% ABV
THOR 5.0% ABV
DARK DESTROYER 5.8% ABV
Plus a wide range of seasonals and specials.

SALTAIRE BREWERY
6 County Works, Dockfield Road, Shipley,
West Yorkshire BD17 7AR
☎ *(01274) 594959*
www.saltairebrewery.co.uk

FUGGLES 3.8% ABV
Fruity aroma.
GOLDINGS 4.2% ABV
Citrus fruity flavour.
XB 4.3% ABV
Slight butterscotch flavour.
CASCADE PALE ALE 4.8% ABV
Floral aromas.
CHALLENGER SPECIAL 5.2% ABV
Copper colour, hop fruitiness.

SAMUEL SMITH OLD BREWERY
High Street, Tadcaster, North Yorkshire LS24 9SB
☎ *(01937) 832225*

OLD BREWERY BITTER 4.0% ABV
Rounded and flavoursome.

T AND R THEAKSTON LTD
The Brewery, Wellgarth, Masham, Ripon,
North Yorkshire HG4 4YD
☎ *(01765) 680000*
www.theakstons.co.uk

TRADITIONAL MILD 3.5% ABV
Malty, dark.
BEST BITTER 3.8% ABV
Clean, golden, citrus hints.
BLACK BULL BITTER 3.9% ABV
Fruity, crisp, dry.
XB 4.5% ABV
Bittersweet.
OLD PECULIER 5.6% ABV
Malty.
Plus seasonals and specials.

TIMOTHY TAYLOR & CO. LTD
Knowle Spring Brewery, Keighley, West Yorkshire
BD21 1AW
☎ *(01535) 603139*
www.timothy-taylor.co.uk

DARK MILD 3.5% ABV
Mellow and malty with balancing
hoppiness.
GOLDEN BEST 3.5% ABV
Balanced, crisp and hoppy.
BEST BITTER 4.0% ABV
Refreshing, hoppy and bitter.
LANDLORD 4.3% ABV
Distinctive combination of malt, hops and fruit.
RAM TAM 4.3% ABV
Landlord with added caramel.

TIGERTOPS BREWERY
22 Oakes Street, Flanshaw, Wakefield,
West Yorkshire WF2 9LN
☎ *(01924) 897728*

Constantly changing range of beers with an
emphasis on Belgian beer styles.

AXEMAN'S BLOCK 3.6% ABV
DARK WHEAT MILD 3.6% ABV
CHARLES TOWN BEST 4.1% ABV
BLANCHE DE NEWLAND 4.5% ABV
Belgian style wheat beer.
BIG GINGER 6.0% ABV
Plus seasonals and specials.

WENSLEYDALE BREWERY
Manor Farm, Bellerby, Leyburn, North Yorkshire DL8 5QH
☎ *(01969) 625250*
www.wensleydalebrewery.com

LIDSTONES ROWLEY MILD 3.2% ABV
Award-winning, full-flavoured beer with chocolate and toffee aromas.
FORESTERS SESSION BITTER 3.7% ABV
A well-balanced hoppy session beer.
SEMER WATER 4.1% ABV
Caramel and citrus hints.
GAMEKEEPER 4.3% ABV
Very moreish and highly drinkable best bitter.
AYSGARTH FALLS 4.4% ABV
Wheat beer.
BLACK DUB STOUT 4.4% ABV
A black beer with chocolate throughout.
POACHER 5.0% ABV
Light and quenching, with strong citrus notes.
HARDRAW FORCE 5.6% ABV
Malty molasses flavour.
WENSLEYDALE PORTER 6.6% ABV
Chocolatey and raisin flavour.
WENSLEYDALE BARLEY WINE 8.5% ABV
Powerful and flavoursome.

WENTWORTH BREWERY LIMITED
The Powerhouse, Gun Park Works, Wentworth, Rotherham, South Yorkshire S62 7TF
☎ *(01226) 747070*
www.wentworth-brewery.co.uk

NEEDLES EYE 3.5% ABV
Traditional Yorkshire light ale.
WPA 4.0% ABV
Pale-coloured, hoppy, with citrus overtones.
EARLY FRUITS 4.1% ABV
BEST BITTER 4.3% ABV
Mid-brown beer with both hoppy and malty character, a proper traditional beer with citrus notes.
BUMBLE BEE 4.3% ABV
BLACK ZAC 4.6% ABV
A wonderfully flavoursome ale.
OATMEAL STOUT 4.8% ABV
Black, rich, with plenty of roast, malt and coffee.
RAMPANT GRYPHON 6.2% ABV
A lightly coloured and pleasingly strong ale.
Plus seasonals and specials.

WHALEBONE BREWERY
The Whalebone, 163 Wincolnlee, Hull, East Yorkshire HU2 0PA
☎ *(01482) 327980*

DIANA MILD 3.6% ABV
NECK OIL 3.9% ABV
Plus seasonals.

WHARFEDALE BREWERY LTD
Coonlands Laithe, Rylstone, Skipton, North Yorkshire BD23 6LY
☎ *(01756) 730555*
www.follyale.com

FOLLY ALE 3.8% ABV
Award-winning ale. Traditional full-bodied malty bitter.
EXECUTIONER 4.5% ABV
Mahogany colour, complex, roasted malt flavour.
FOLLY GOLD 5.0% ABV
Straw colour, citrus overtones.

WOLD TOP BREWERY
Hunmanby Grange, Wold Newton, Driffield, North Yorkshire YO25 3HS
☎ *(01723) 892222*
www.woldtopbrewery.co.uk

WOLD TOP BITTER 3.7% ABV
FALLING STONE 4.2% ABV
MARS MAGIC 4.6% ABV
WOLD GOLD 4.8% ABV

YORK BREWERY
12 Toft Green, Micklegate, York, North Yorkshire YO1 1JT
☎ *(01904) 621162*
www.yorkbrew.co.uk

GUZZLER 3.6% ABV
Crisp and refreshing.
STONEWALL 3.8% ABV
Malty with hoppy finish.
YORKSHIRE TERRIER 4.2% ABV
Gold coloured with good bitter finish.
CENTURION'S GHOST ALE 5.4% ABV
Roasted malt taste.
Seasonals including:
PEACHES AND CREAM 3.9% ABV
DECADE 4.1% ABV
Light and hoppy. (May)
WILD WHEAT 4.1% ABV
Crisp and dry. (August and September)
BLACK BESS STOUT 4.2% ABV
YULETIDE ALE 4.8% ABV
YORK IPA 5.0% ABV
Balanced tawny ale with pleasant finish. (October–November)
YORK SPA 5.5% ABV

YORKSHIRE DALES BREWING COMPANY LTD
Seata Barn, Elm Hill, Main Street, Askrigg, Leyburn, North Yorkshire DL8 3HG
☎ *07818 035592*

HERRIOT COUNTRY ALE 4.0% ABV
GUNNER'S GOLD 4.4% ABV
NAPPER SCAR 4.8% ABV
WHERNSIDE 5.2% ABV
Plus seasonals and specials.

YORKSHIRE

THE PUBS

APPLETREEWICK

The Craven Arms
Appletreewick, Nr Skipton, North Yorkshire BD23 6DA
☎ *(01756) 720270*
Ashley and Hayley Crampton

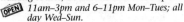 Freehouse with Timothy Taylor Golden Best, Tetley Bitter and two rotating guest beers changed monthly from breweries such as Saltaire.

A traditional Yorkshire Dales pub with Cruck Barn function room/restaurant (open weekends). Food served 12–2pm (until 2.30pm Fri–Sun) and 6.30–9pm (until 8.30pm Sun). Beer garden. Car park. Dogs and children welcome. Located on lots of walking routes, 10 miles outside of Skipton.

OPEN *11am–3pm and 6–11pm Mon–Tues; all day Wed–Sun.*

AUCKLEY

The Eagle & Child
24 Main Street, Auckley, Doncaster, South Yorkshire DN9 3HS
☎ *(01302) 770406* Barry Lax
www.eagleauckley.co.uk

 An Enterprise Inns pub. Black Sheep Bitter and Theakston XB. Two twice-weekly changing guests, from a variety of independent breweries.

An inn was first recorded on the site in 1510 and the historic character is maintained in today's country village pub. Two bars, restaurant and lounge. Food available lunchtimes and evenings Mon–Thurs and all day Fri–Sun. Large, outside decked area and children's play area. Car park. Children welcome.

OPEN *11.30am–3pm and 5.30–11pm Mon–Thurs; 11.30am–11.30pm Fri–Sat; 12–11pm.*

BAILDON

The Junction
1 Baildon Road, Baildon, West Yorkshire BD17 6AB
☎ *(01274) 582009* Bill and Chris Arnold

Freehouse serving seven real ales including Fuller's ESB, Dark Star Hophead, Tetley Bitter and somehing from Saltaire and Timothy Taylor plus two rotating guests from predominantly local breweries. Plus two real ciders.

Traditional pub with lots of character and pub memorabilia. CAMRA local Pub of the Year 2006 and 2007. Lounge, games room, public bar area. Food served 12–2pm daily. Heated outdoor decking area for smokers. Annual beer festival. Children and dogs welcome. Near local canal and river. Ten minutes from Shipley station. Small car park. Right on the junction of Baildon Road and Otley Road.

OPEN *12–12 Sun–Thurs; noon–1am Fri–Sat.*

BARKISLAND

The Fleece Inn
Ripponden Bank, Barkisland, Halifax, West Yorkshire
☎ *(01422) 822598*
Stewart Taylor and Clare Ward

 Black Sheep Best, Timothy Taylor Landlord and something from Theakston plus three guests, changed regularly.

Country pub with a warm welcome. Beamed ceilings and open fires. Beer garden with impressive views across the Calder valley and Ryburn valley. Food available 12–2.30pm and 6–9pm Mon–Sat, 12–7pm Sun. Live music every Thursday. Children allowed, with play areas outside and inside. Four en-suite rooms, ample parking.

OPEN *12–11pm.*

BARNSLEY

The Cherry Tree
High Hoyland, Barnsley, South Yorkshire S75 4BE
☎ *(01226) 382541* Kenneth Horbury

Five real ales, with Elland Best and Nettlethrasher plus Black Sheep Bitter among the regulars.

Country pub with central bar and beautiful views. Food available 12–2pm and 6–9pm Mon–Sat and 12–8pm Sun. Children welcome. Outside seating. Car park.

OPEN *12–3pm and 5.30pm–12 Mon–Fri; 12–12 Sat–Sun.*

The Gatehouse
35 Eldon Street, Barnsley, South Yorkshire S70 2JJ
☎ *(01226) 282394*

Acorn Barnsley Bitter. Four guests, constantly rotating, including Clark's Ram Revenge, Copper Dragon 1816, Hanby Taverners and Marston's Pedigree.

A large, town-centre bar. Two beer festivals each year, each showcasing new micro-brewers and new beers from established independents. No food. No garden.

OPEN *11am–11pm; closed Sun.*

Miller's Inn
Dearne Hall Road, Low Barugh, Barnsley, South Yorkshire S75 1LX
☎ *(01226) 382888* Wayne Stephenson

Marston's house with three real ales usually available, with Jennings Bitter and Sneck Lifter among the regulars.

A 200-year-old, family-friendly, waterside village pub with two bars, beer garden (overlooking the River Dearne) and children's play area. Pool, darts, TV. Food available 12–2pm and 5–8pm Mon–Sat, and 12–5pm Sun. Accommodation. Large car park. Off junction 38 of the M1.

OPEN *12–3pm and 5pm–close.*

BATTYEFORD
Airedale Heifer

53 Stocksbank Road, Battyeford, Mirfield, West Yorkshire WF14 9QB
☎ *(01924) 493547* Melvin Charles

 Eastwood & Sanders Bargee plus occasional seasonal guests.

Old village pub with food available 12–3pm Tues–Sun. Beer garden. Children allowed. Car park. Live music once a month and odd events throughout the year – call for details.

OPEN *3–11pm Mon; 12–11pm Tues–Sat; 12–10.30pm Sun.*

BECK HOLE
Birch Hall Inn

Beck Hole, Goathland, Whitby, North Yorkshire YO22 5LE
☎ *(01947) 896245* Glenys Crampton
www.beckhole.info

 Genuine freehouse with Black Sheep Best Bitter and two or three guests, rotated often and with local brewers strongly favoured.

Licensed since the early 19th century, this pub has been run by the same landlords for more than 20 years and offers a memorable step back in time. Much favoured by locals, it has two small bars crammed with memorabilia and separated by a shop which offers produce you thought had died out long ago. Pies and sandwiches available whenever the pub is open. Children allowed in the smaller bar; dogs anywhere. Split-level garden with splendid views over the village. Limited parking, but popular walking country, so travel on foot. Two miles west of A169.

OPEN *Winter: 11am–3pm Mon; closed Tues Nov–March; 11am–3pm and 7.30–11pm Wed–Sun. Summer (May Day Bank Holiday to end of August): 11am–11pm every day.*

BELTON
Crown Inn

Church Lane, Churchtown, Belton DN9 1PA
☎ *(01427) 872834* H Burkinshaw

 Freehouse with four ales, including two rotating guests changed every three weeks.

A traditional pub with beer garden and car park. Located at the back of the church.

OPEN *4–11pm Mon–Sun.*

BEVERLEY
Green Dragon

51 Saturday Market, Beverley HU17 8AA
☎ *(01482) 889801* Alan Clarke

 Mitchells & Butlers pub with Greene King IPA and Charles Wells Bombardier among the seven beers on offer. The five constantly rotating guests will be from breweries such as Cropton, Rudgate, Abbeydale, Wold Top, Leeds and Wentworth – mainly Yorkshire micro-breweries.

Historic inn that has been called the Green Dragon since 1765. This Tudor-fronted building has an entrance down a side passage and a bar that is 30 feet long! Food available 11am–9pm. Beer garden with heaters. Two quizzes each week (Tues and Wed). Near Beverley Cathedral, racecourse and Westwood events.

OPEN *11am–11pm Mon–Wed; 11am–midnight Thurs–Sat; 12–11.30pm Sun.*

BINGLEY
Myrtle Grove

141 Main Street, Bingley BD16 1AJ
☎ *(01274) 568637* Adam Johnson

 Wetherspoon's pub with six or seven real ales. Theakston Old Peculier, Greene King Abbot Ale and Marston's Pedigree are permanent fixtures, plus several rotating guests changed daily from breweries such as Saltaire, Ossett or Wharfdale.

Glass-fronted pub with an airy feel. Food served 9am–11pm daily.

OPEN *9am–midnight.*

BRADFORD
The Beehive Inn

583 Halifax Road, Bradford, West Yorkshire BD6 2DU
☎ *(01274) 678550* Kevin Guthrie

 At least two guest ales, one from a local brewery such as Salamander, Ossett, Eastwood & Sanders or Daleside. The other guest will be from the Cask Marque seasonal range.

One-bar locals' pub, with bar snacks available all day. Bradford CAMRA Pub of the Season Spring 2003. Children allowed.

OPEN *11am–11pm (10.30pm Sun).*

The Castle Hotel

20 Grattan Road, Bradford, West Yorkshire BD1 2LU
☎ *(01274) 393166* James Duncan

 Mansfield Riding and Riding Mild plus seven guest beers (200 per year) from brewers such as Goose Eye, Brains, Moorhouse's, Marston's, Wadworth, Shepherd Neame and many more.

A pub built like a castle in 1898. Bar food is served at lunchtime from Monday to Thursday and until 7.30pm on Friday and Saturday. Parking at weekends and evenings. Children not allowed. Located in the city centre.

OPEN *11.30am–11pm Mon–Sat; closed Sun.*

The Corn Dolly

*110 Bolton Road, Bradford, West Yorkshire
BD1 4DE*
☎ *(01274) 720219* Neil Dunkin

 Genuine freehouse with eight real ales. Brews from Moorhouse's, Black Sheep, Everards, Timothy Taylor and four ever-changing guest beers from independents all over the country, including breweries such as Durham, Ossett, Coach House and Exmoor.

A freehouse with a friendly atmosphere. Frequent Bradford CAMRA Pub of the Year. Food is available at lunchtimes Mon–Fri; buffets also catered for. Beer garden and car park. Situated just off the city centre (Forster Square).

OPEN *11.30am–11pm Mon–Sat; 12–10.30pm Sun.*

The Fighting Cock

*21–3 Preston Street, Bradford, West Yorkshire
BD7 1JE*
☎ *(01274) 726907* Sue Turner

 Twelve beers always on offer. Timothy Taylor Landlord, Best and Golden Best, Theakston Old Peculier, Greene King Abbot and brews from Copper Dragon and Red Lion Ales are regulars, and the five guests are changed every couple of days.

F riendly, back-to-basics, open-plan alehouse dating from the early 1900s, with open fire and cosmopolitan atmosphere. Bar food available 12–2.30pm Mon–Sat. Go left onto Thornton Road from the former cinema in the city centre, then left again at the second set of traffic lights.

OPEN *11.30am–11pm Mon–Sat; 12–10.30pm Sun.*

Haigy's Bar

*31 Lumb Lane, Bradford, West Yorkshire
BD8 7QU*
☎ *(01274) 731644* David and Yvonne Haigh

 Genuine freehouse with up to six real ales, changed as often as daily. Beers from Ossett, Oakham and Newby Wyke are regulars.

E dge-of-city-centre pub with homely decor. The outside is painted in Bradford City colours. Games, pool, disco at weekends. One bar, three rooms. Disabled access, small beer garden. Limited food served afternoons. Room available for private hire. Children allowed in the afternoons only. Yorkshire Day Festival held. Handy for local tourist attractions, including National Media Museum.

OPEN *5pm–2am Mon–Fri; noon–4am Sat; 2–11pm Sun.*

The New Beehive Inn

*171 Westgate, Bradford, West Yorkshire
BD1 3AA*
☎ *(01274) 721784* William Wagstaff

 Six beers, from breweries such as Kelham Island, Salamander, Ossett, Phoenix and Mordue, with the selection changing daily. Listed on CAMRA's National Inventory.

C lassic Edwardian inn, barely altered over the years, with unique gas lighting. Six

separate drinking rooms. Bar food available 12–2pm and 6–8pm. Accommodation (16 bedrooms). Beer garden, function room. Situated on the outskirts of the city centre on the B6144. There is a beer festival in June.

OPEN *All day Mon–Sat; 6–11pm Sun.*

Sir Titus Salt

*Windsor Baths, Morley Street, Bradford,
West Yorkshire BD7 1AQ*
☎ *(01274) 732853* Andrew Mathery (manager)
www.jdwetherspoon.co.uk

 JD Wetherspoon's pub with Greene King Abbot, Marston's Pedigree and beers from Theakston, Springhead and Saltaire plus a selection of guests from breweries such as Hook Norton, Highgate, Rooster's and Banks & Taylor.

L arge open pub which used to be a swimming pool! Food available 9am–11pm every day. Children allowed. Small beer garden. Two or three beer festivals every year. Near the Alhambra Theatre, the National Media Museum and the University.

OPEN *9am–midnight (1am Fri–Sat).*

The Malt Shovel

*Main Road, Brearton, Harrogate, North Yorkshire
HG3 3BX*
☎ *(01423) 862929* J and H Stewart

 Five beers always available – up to 100 guests per year. Daleside Bitter, Black Sheep Bitter and Timothy Taylor Landlord are permanent fixtures, and the two guests are changed weekly.

A 16th-century beamed village freehouse, with an oak-panelled bar and open fires in winter. Local home-cooked food, with specials board, available 12–2pm and 7–9pm Tues–Sat, 12–2pm Sun. Car park, beer garden. Credit cards accepted. Children and dogs welcome. Off the B6165, six miles from Harrogate.

OPEN *Closed on Mondays; 12–3pm and 6.45–11pm Tues–Sat; 12–3pm and 7–10.30pm Sun.*

The Old Ship Inn

*90 St John's Street, Bridlington, East Yorkshire
YO16 7JS*
☎ *(01262) 670466* Audrey Green

 Four real ales, with Caledonian Deuchars IPA, Timothy Taylor Landlord, Black Sheep Bitter and Greene King IPA often featured. Two of the beers are changed every three days.

A 125-year-old town pub with two bars and a well-frequented beer garden. Food served 12–2pm (12–3pm for Sunday lunches in summer); 5–7.15pm Tues–Thurs and 5–8pm Fri–Sat. Children are allowed, and there is a family room. Pool, darts, Tues quiz night, Sat live music. In an old town with antique shops, art galleries and a priory church. At the north end of Bridlington, on the road towards Scarborough.

OPEN *11.30am–11.30pm Mon–Fri; 11am–midnight Sat; 12–11pm Sun.*

BRIGHOUSE
The Crown
6 Lightcliffe Road, Brighouse, West Yorkshire HD6 2DR
☎ *(01484) 715436* Colin and Anne Brown

 An Enterprise Inns pub. Milestone Black Pearl and Springham Roaring Meg plus two guests, such as Abbeydale Moonshine, Grindleton Ribble Gold, Ossett Silver King and Moorhouse's Pride of Pendle to name a few.

A two-bar pub. Pool table, decked outdoor seating area. Piano sing-a-long on Sat evenings, Sunday quiz nights with free supper. Live entertainment once a month. Car park. No food.

OPEN *11am–11.30pm Mon–Thurs; 11am–midnight Fri–Sat; 12–11pm Sun.*

The Red Rooster
123 Elland Road, Brighouse, West Yorkshire HD6 2QR
☎ *(01484) 713737* Eddie and Claire

 Freehouse with Timothy Taylor Landlord and Ram Tam, Copper Dragon Golden Pippin, Moorhouse's Blond Witch and Kelham Island Easy Rider plus four rotating guests.

Traditional real ale house with stone floors. No juke box, pool table, dart boards or TV – strictly for conversation and good beers! Large open bar with some dividing walls. Curry night Thursdays. Beer garden. Car park. Dogs and well-behaved children welcome. Annual 'Septoverfest' (end Sept/beginning Oct). Annual charity week mid-August. Live blues/jazz event last Sunday of the month. Exit the M62 at junction 25 and follow signs for Elland; pub is on sharp turn just before turn-off to Southowram.

OPEN *3–11pm Mon–Thurs; 12–11pm Fri–Sat; 12–10.30pm Sun.*

BROMPTON
The Crown Inn
Station Road, Brompton, Northallerton, North Yorkshire DL6 2RE
☎ *(01609) 772547* Mrs Addington

 Two guest ales such as Marston's Pedigree in addition to the two regular brews.

A traditional country inn with one bar, coal fires and a small garden. No food. Children allowed.

OPEN *12–3pm and 7–11pm Mon–Thurs; all day Fri–Sun.*

BURLEY
The Fox & Newt
9 Burley Street, Burley, Leeds, West Yorkshire LS3 1LD
☎ *(01132) 432612* Roy Cadman

A wide range of guest ales always available. Regulars include Young's Special, Greene King Abbot, Timothy Taylor Landlord, Wadworth 6X, Marston's Pedigree, Fuller's London Pride and Caledonian 80/-. The beers are changed weekly.

Old-style pub with a wooden floor. Food available at lunchtime only in a separate dining area. Children allowed for lunches only.

OPEN *All day, every day.*

BURN
The Wheatsheaf Inn
Main Road, Burn, Selby, North Yorkshire YO8 8LJ
☎ *(01757) 270614* Andrew Howdall
www.thewheatsheafburn.co.uk

 A freehouse. Timothy Taylor Best, John Smiths Cask. Four guest pumps, always including a dark ale, turning 12–15 ales per week. Guests may include Brown Cow Celestrial Light, York Guzzler, Copper Dragon Golden Pippin, Leeds Pale and Rudgate Ruby Mild.

Over 100 years old, a mock-Tudor, friendly village pub, renowned locally for ever-changing guest ales. One open-plan bar with beer gardens to side and rear. Traditional pub food served 12–2pm daily; 6.30–8.30pm Thurs–Sat. Parking. Games room. Beer festivals.

OPEN *12–12.*

CARLTON-IN-CLEVELAND
The Blackwell Ox
Main Street, Carlton-in-Cleveland, Nr Stokesley, North Yorkshire TS9 7DJ
☎ *(01642) 712287* Jeff Burton
www.theblackwellox.co.uk

 A freehouse. Black Sheep Bitter plus two guests, changed two or three times a week. Breweries featured include Hambleton, York, Rudgate, Copper Dragon, Shepherd Neame and Thwaites.

Large, rural pub, over 100 years old. One bar, separate function room. Authentic Thai food served alongside traditional pub fayre 12–2pm and 5.30–10pm. Two beer gardens and adventure playground. Large car park. Situated three miles south of Stokesley, off the A172.

OPEN *11.30am–11.30pm.*

CARLTON MINIOTT
The Dog & Gun
Carlton Road, Carlton Miniott, Thirsk, North Yorkshire YO7 4NJ
☎ *(01845) 522150* Nigel and Dawn
www.thedogandgun.co.uk

 Theakston Bitter plus two or three guest ales, changed weekly. Guests may include Saltaire Cascade, Wensleydale Poacher, North Yorkshire Bitter or Rooster's Cream.

A one-bar pub with separate conservatory and restaurant. A traditional feel with wood burner and oak beams, and a warm welcome. The emphasis is on local food and beer. Food served 12–2pm and 6–9.30pm Tues–Sat; 12–2pm and 6–8.30pm Sun. Children welcome. Outside drinking/eating areas at the front and back. Car park.

OPEN *12–3pm and 6pm–12 Tues–Fri; all day Sat–Sun.*

CAWOOD

The Ferry Inn

2 King Street, Cawood, Selby, North Yorkshire
YO8 3TL
☎ *(01757) 268515*
Keith and Gemma Bellwood
www.theferryinn.com

Caledonian Deuchars IPA, Timothy Taylor Landlord and Theakston Best plus two guests, such as Fuller's London Pride and Daleside Pride of England.

A 16th-century village inn with stone floor, beams, real fires, outside decking and large beer garden overlooking the River Ouse and Cawood's 19th-century swing bridge. Private functions can be catered for. Excellent food prepared by the French chef available every day from Easter to October; no food Mon, Tues and Wed lunch during winter months (phone to check). Separate dining area. Children and dogs welcome. En-suite accommodation available. Next to Cawood Bridge, the only river crossing between York and Selby.

OPEN *12–11pm Sun–Wed; 12–12 Thurs–Sat.*

CHAPEL HADDLESEY

The Jug Inn

Chapel Haddlesey, Selby, North Yorkshire
☎ *(01757) 270307* Paul King

A Brown Cow brew is usually available, plus three guest beers, often from Glentworth, Rudgate, Barnsley, Cropton, Eccleshall, Goose Eye, Kelham Island or Tigertops.

W elcoming village pub with beamed ceilings and open coal fires. Food served 6–9pm daily. South-facing beer garden next to river. Car park.

OPEN *5.30–11pm Tues–Fri; 12–11pm Sat; 12–10.30pm Sun. Closed all day Mon.*

CHAPEL-LE-DALE

The Hill Inn

Chapel-le-Dale, Ingleton, North Yorkshire
LA6 3AR
☎ *(015242) 41246* Sabena Martin
www.oldhillinn.co.uk

Freehouse serving Black Sheep Best and Special, Dent Aviator, Theakston Best and Timothy Taylor Landlord.

A ncient family-run inn with lots of character, with part dating back to 1615 and the other part to 1835. Nestling between Ingleborough and Whernside, and close to the White Scar Caves and the Ribblehead Viaduct. Pub features a pulled and blown sugar display. Delicious home-cooked food available (phone to check times and book), with puddings a speciality! Well-behaved children allowed. Two lovely en-suite letting rooms. Car park.

OPEN *Opening times vary, depending on the season and level of custom. It is advisable to ring ahead and check.*

CHAPELTOWN

The Commercial Inn

107 Station Road, Chapeltown, Sheffield,
South Yorkshire S35 2XF
☎ *(0114) 246 9066* Paul Menzies

Wentworth Imperial, Bumble Beer, WPA and Oatmeal Stout plus four guest ales changed continually from a range of independent breweries. Continental lagers, Belgian fruit beer and real cider also served.

T raditional town pub dating from 1887 with one central bar serving a lounge, games room and snug. Homemade food available 12–2.30pm and 6–9pm; 12–3pm Sun. Hot roast pork sandwiches at 10pm every Sat. Beer garden, function room, car park. Beer festivals on the last weekends of May and November. Not far from the railway station, just off M1 junction 35.

OPEN *12–3pm and 5.30–11pm Mon–Thurs; 12–11pm Fri–Sat; 12–10.30pm Sun.*

CLAPHAM

New Inn

Clapham, Nr Settle, North Yorkshire LA2 8HH
☎ *(01524) 251203* Martin Brook
www.newinnclapham.co.uk

Four real ales, rotated weekly, from breweries such as Copper Dragon, Black Sheep and Timothy Taylor.

A 17th-century former coaching inn with 18 en-suite bedrooms. Typical village pub with darts, pool, dominoes and quiz teams. Food served 12–2pm and 6.30–8.30pm. Beer garden, riverside seating. Car park. Separate restaurant. Children welcome. Located in the village of Clapham, just off the A65 Leeds–Kendal road, six miles north of Settle.

OPEN *8am–11pm.*

CLECKHEATON

The Marsh Hotel

28 Bradford Road, Cleckheaton,
West Yorkshire BD19 5BJ
☎ *(01274) 872104* Neil and Karen Barker

An Old Mill Brewery tied house serving all the Old Mill range: Bitter, Mild and Bullion, plus seasonal ales such as Springs Eternal, Blackjack, Summer Sunshine and Autumn Breeze on a guest basis.

W edge-shaped pub, full of character, with one bar, a pool room, darts and TV for Sky Sports. No food. Outdoor covered area and beer garden. Car park.

OPEN *1pm–11pm Mon–Thurs; noon–1am Fri–Sat; 12–11pm Sun.*

CRAY

The White Lion

Cray, Nr Skipton, North Yorkshire BD23 5JB
☎ *(01756) 760262* Kevin Roe
www.whitelioncray.com

Freehouse with four or five real ales. Copper Dragon Golden Pippin and Scotts 1816 plus Timothy Taylor Golden Best is the usual line-up.

Formerly a drovers' hostelry dating from the 17th century, this is a peaceful pub in the Yorkshire Dales. Situated in a popular walking Area of Outstanding Natural Beauty. Food available 12–2pm and 5.45–8.30pm daily, tea and coffee available all day. Outside seating in a beer garden, and also beside the cascading Cray Gill. Superior accommodation (with special offers available). Children welcome, baby listening service available to residents. Directions available from Grassington National Park centre, 20 minutes north of Skipton.

OPEN *10am–11pm.*

CRAYKE

The Durham Ox

Westway, Crayke, Nr Easingwold, York, North Yorkshire YO61 4TE
☎ *(01347) 821506*
Michael Ibbotson and Zoe Slagle
www.thedurhamox.com

Freehouse with John Smith's, Theakston Best and Timothy Taylor Landlord plus one or two rotating guests changed weekly, which could include Greene King IPA or Black Sheep.

Situated in the historic village of Crayke with fantastic views over the Vale of York, this is a delightful country pub with well-kept local ales. Oak-panelled bar, enormous inglenook fireplace. Private dining room available for hire. Food served 12–2.30pm and 6–9.30pm Mon–Fri, 12–2.30pm and 6–10pm Sat, 12–3pm and 6–8.30pm Sun. Cosy cottage bedrooms available for B&B. Large car park. Children allowed on the proviso that they do not disturb others. Situated in the Howardian Hills, an Area of Outstanding Natural Beauty, within easy reach of historic city of York and market towns Helmsley, Castle Howard and Beningbrough Hall. From York take the A19 to Easingwold. Drive through the market place and follow signs to Crayke. Turn left up the hill and the pub is on the right-hand side.

OPEN *All day, every day.*

CROPTON

The New Inn

Cropton, Nr Pickering, North Yorkshire YO18 8HH
☎ *(01751) 417330* Philip Lee
www.croptonbrewery.com

Home of the Cropton Brewery, with Honey Gold, Endeavour, Two Pints and Monkman's Slaughter plus a regularly changing guest beer.

Cropton Brewery was established in 1984 in the basement of the New Inn in this tiny moorland village. It owes its existence to the deep-seated local fear that, one day, the harsh moors winter weather would prevent the beer wagon from getting through. The brewery's reputation has since spread and, as demand exceeded capacity, a new purpose-built brewery was constructed in an adjacent quarry. Home-cooked bar and restaurant food is served daily 12–2pm and 6–9pm. Car park, garden, children's room, accommodation. Brewery tours available. Large beer festival held every November. Off the A170 between Pickering and Kirbymoorside.

OPEN *11am–11pm Mon–Sat; 12–10.30pm Sun.*

DELPH

Royal Oak Inn

Broad Lane Heights, Delph, Saddleworth, West Yorkshire OL3 5TX
☎ *(01457) 874460* Michael and Sheila Fancy

Freehouse serving Moorhouse's Black Cat Mild plus four guest ales, often including Fuller's London Pride or brews from Black Sheep or Millstone.

Built in 1767 this is an unspoilt pub with low beams, open fires and dining area. Situated in a remote setting off the Delph–Denshaw road, with good views over Saddleworth Moor. Food available Fri–Sat only. Children allowed.

OPEN *7–11pm Mon–Fri (closed lunchtime); 12–3pm and 7–11pm Sat–Sun.*

DENBY DALE

The White Hart

380 Wakefield Road, Denby Dale, Huddersfield, West Yorkshire HD8 8RT
☎ *(01484) 862357* Donna M Brayshaw

Timothy Taylor Landlord, Black Sheep Bitter and Tetley's available.

Friendly, village-centre pub with an open fire in winter. Beer garden and Tuesday night quiz with free buffet. Heated smoking area. Sky Sports on big screens and plasma TV (including pay-per-view). Friday night disco. Car park. Children welcome.

OPEN *12–11pm Sun–Thurs; 12–12 Fri–Sat.*

DEWSBURY

The Leggers Inn

Stable Buildings, Mill Street East, Dewsbury, West Yorkshire WF12 9BD
☎ *(01924) 502846*
Mark Wallace and John Smithson

Up to seven real ales. Everards Tiger plus rotating guests that are likely to include a pale ale from Rooster's.

Situated in an old hay loft in a canal boatyard: pub upstairs, brewery downstairs. Basic food: pies and peas plus sandwiches served all day, every day. Live music most Thursdays. Outside seating. Children allowed. Situated past Carlton Cards in Mill Street East, to the right. Can be hard to find so phone for directions.

OPEN *11am–11pm Mon–Sat; 12–10.30pm Sun.*

West Riding Licensed Refreshment Rooms

Dewsbury Railway Station, Wellington Road, Dewsbury, West Yorkshire WF13 1HF
☎ *(01924) 459193*
Michael Field and Sarah Barnes
www.imissedthetrain.com

Genuine freehouse serving Black Sheep Bitter and Timothy Taylor Landlord plus up to six guests, including something from the local Anglo-Dutch brewery.

Situated in the railway station and doubling as a waiting room, this is a real ale pub with one central bar, wooden floors and beer garden. CAMRA Regional Pub of the Year 2006, and finalists in the Nationals. Live music throughout the year. Food available 12–3pm Mon–Fri, plus Tuesday nights (pies), Wednesday nights (curries) and Thursday nights (steaks); all-day breakfasts 10–4pm Sat. Children allowed until 5pm unless travelling by train. Two beer festivals a year, one in June and one in December. On Trans-Pennine route – four trains an hour in each direction.

OPEN *12–11pm Mon; 11am–11pm Tues–Wed; 11am–midnight Thurs–Fri; 10am–midnight Sat; 11am–11pm Sun.*

DISHFORTH

The Crown Inn

Main Street, Dishforth, North Yorkshire YO7 3JU
☎ *(01845) 577398*
Dan Ripley and Hayley Fisher

Up to four real ales available at this freehouse, with beers from Timothy Taylor, Ossett, Wold Top and Daleside among the regular features. One or two guests are changed every week.

Small, country pub with large beer garden, pool room, dining room, and a friendly welcome. Food available 5–9pm Tues–Fri, 12–9pm Sat and 12–4pm Sun. Children welcome. Car park. Coach parties welcome (advance notice required for food). On the junction of the A1M and the A168.

OPEN *All day, every day from 12.*

DONCASTER

The Corner Pin

St Sepulchre Gate West, Doncaster, South YorkshireDN1 3AH
☎ *(01302) 323159*
Lee Plant (aka the wrestler "The Donny Bull")

John Smith's Cask, plus two or three guests changed every two to three weeks, including Ossett Silver King, Wychwood Hobgoblin, Wentworth Oatmeal Stout, Copper Dragon Golden Pippin, York Guzzler and Kelham Island Easy Rider.

A traditional pub with a beer garden to the rear. Children welcome. Sunday lunch served 12.30–2.30pm, with hot and cold sandwiches available the rest of the time. CAMRA Pub of the Season in spring 2008 and local Pub of the Year 2008. Located round the corner from the main rail station, with the racecourse and Doncaster Rovers ground two miles away.

OPEN *12–12 (or later).*

The Salutation

14 South Parade, Doncaster, South Yorkshire DN1 2DR
☎ *(01302) 340705* Gayle Bee

A renowned real ale pub with at least two popular guests from breweries such as Wells and Young's, Greene King and Adnams.

A 300-year-old coaching inn with strong connections with Doncaster Racecourse. A one-roomed bar with lots of cosy corners and a real fire in winter. Food available every day – Sunday lunch a speciality. Sunny beer garden and large function room. Coach parties welcome (by appointment).

OPEN *All day, every day.*

Tut 'n' Shive

6 West Laithe Gate, Doncaster, South Yorkshire DN1 1SF
☎ *(01302) 360300* Nick Coster

Greene King pub with IPA, Abbot Ale, Old Speckled Hen and Black Sheep Best plus three constantly changing guest ales.

This small, one-room alehouse in the centre of Doncaster is also a popular music venue and shows all Sky Sports football games. Food served 12–6pm daily (everything on the menu is £2.95 or under). Located adjacent to Frenchgate shopping centre, 200 yards from the railway and bus stations. Cask Marque accredited.

OPEN *11am–11pm Mon–Thurs; 11am–1am Fri–Sat; 12–12 Sun.*

DRIFFIELD

The Bell In Driffield

46 Market Place, Driffield, East Yorkshire YO25 6AN
☎ *(01377) 256661* George Riggs
www.bw-bellhotel.co.uk

Two or three real ales during the week with an extra one at weekends from a range of local brews, often including something from Wold Top, Hambleton or Daleside. Plus about 300 malt whiskies.

Characterful and friendly early-18th-century coaching inn retaining many original features and run by the same owners for the past 30 years. Food served 12–1.30pm and 7–9.30pm daily. Accommodation. Car park. Disabled access. In the town centre.

OPEN *All day, every day.*

The Foundry

7 Market Walk, Driffield, East Yorkshire YO25 6BW
☎ *(01377) 240343* John Alvey

Freehouse with five ales, all constantly rotating guests which change every few days. Could include Camerons Strong Arm or Timothy Taylor Landlord.

Dating back to the 1800s, this was a foundry until the 1960s, remaining derelict until it was restored as the award-winning pub it is today. On three storeys, with a daytime restaurant on two floors, it then reverts to a pub on the ground floor in the evenings. Food served 11am–4pm Mon–Sat, 12–3pm Sun. Private room for hire. Large car park. Children welcome with adults until 9pm. Functions and outdoor events catered for. Annual beer festival at the end of April with ten ales. On the Cross Hill car park in the middle of town. This pub had closed, we hope temprarily, as we went to press.

 Closed Mon; 10am–11pm Tues–Sun (alcohol served from 11am).

EASINGWOLD
The George Hotel
Market Place, Easingwold, York, North Yorkshire YO61 3AD
☎ *(01347) 821698* Michael Riley
www.the-george-hotel.co.uk

A freehouse. Black Sheep Best Bitter and Moorhouse's Pride of Pendle plus one guest. Guest ales from throughout Yorkshire offered, especially from the micro-breweries.

A coaching inn, overlooking a cobbled market place. Food served 12–2pm and 6–9pm. Outside tables. Car park. Meeting facilities. Accommodation. Conveniently located for York, the Dales, the moors and the coast.

 11am–11pm.

EAST WITTON
The Cover Bridge Inn
East Witton, Leyburn, North Yorkshire DL8 4SQ
☎ *(01969) 623250* Nick and Anne Harrington
www.thecoverbridgeinn.co.uk

Freehouse with Theakston Best and Old Peculier, Black Sheep Best Bitter, John Smith's Cask and Timothy Taylor Landlord plus three rotating guests.

D ating back to 1674, this former coaching inn has three letting rooms, a small bar and lounge, open fires and lots of atmosphere. Food served 12–2pm and 6–9pm. Beer garden. Car park. Children welcome. Close to Middleham Castle and Jervaux Abbey. Seven miles from Masham, home of Theakston and Black Sheep breweries. On the A6108 Leyburn to Masham road.

 11am–midnight Mon–Sat; 12–11.30pm Sun.

ELLAND
Barge & Barrel
10–20 Park Road, Elland, West Yorkshire HA5 9HB
☎ *(01422) 373623* Mark Dalton

Eleven real ales. Eastwood & Sanders Bargee, John Eastwood Best Bitter and Gold Award, Black Sheep Bitter, Shepherd Neame Spitfire, Phoenix Wobbly Bob and Rooster's Yankee are permanently served, plus four rotating guests, changed as often as they sell out!

C analside pub, just outside the small town. Food available every day except Monday lunchtimes. Children allowed up to 8pm. Waterside garden. Two beer festivals a year, at spring bank holiday and the end of October. Live music occasionally. Curry night Sunday 7–9pm, quiz night Wednesday from 7.30pm. Car park.

 12–12 Sun–Thurs; noon–1am Fri–Sat.

The Market Hotel
2–4 Wentworth Road, Elsecar, Barnsley, South Yorkshire S74 8EP
☎ *(01226) 742240* David Wright

A freehouse. Wentworth Old Pale Ale plus four guests, changed every two–three days. Guest breweries include Titanic, Oldershaw, Acorn, Leeds, Wold Top, Cottage and Brampton.

T wo bars including a pool/function room. Large beer garden. Children welcome. No food.

 12–11.30pm.

ELSLACK
The Tempest Arms
Elslack, Nr Skipton, North Yorkshire
☎ *(01282) 842450* Veronica Clarkson
www.tempestarms.co.uk

Freehouse with six real ales, namely Timothy Taylor Landlord and Best Bitter, Black Sheep Bitter, Copper Dragon Best Bitter, and something from Theakston and Moorhouse's.

B eautiful, cosy, traditional pub dating from 1890, in a building from 1690. Situated in glorious countryside. One bar, log fires, quality furnishings. Bar and restaurant food served 12–2.30pm Mon–Sat and 12–7.30pm Sun, plus 6–9pm Mon–Thurs and 6–9.30pm Fri–Sat. Large function room for up to 100 guests, private dining room and 21 luxury bedrooms. Children welcome. Large car park. Close to Skipton, on the A56.

 11am–11pm Mon–Sat; 12–10.30pm Sun.

EMBSAY
The Elm Tree Inn
5 Elm Tree Square, Embsay, Skipton, North Yorkshire BD23 6RB
☎ *(01756) 790717* Karen Hodgson

Goose Eye No Eye Deer and Charles Wells Bombardier plus three guests such as Fuller's London Pride, Black Sheep Bitter, Timothy Taylor Landlord, Caledonian Deuchars IPA or something from Greene King.

A traditional country inn in the village square, dating from 1780-ish and serving meals every lunchtime 12–2pm, plus 6–8pm Mon–Tues, 5.30–9pm Wed–Sat, 5.30–7.30pm Sun. Outside seating. Two en-suite accommodation rooms. Car park. Local CAMRA Pub of the Season 2007.

 11.30am–3pm and 5.30–11pm Mon–Sat; 12–3pm and 7–10.30pm Sun.

FLAXTON

The Blacksmiths Arms

Flaxton, York, North Yorkshire YO60 7RJ
☎ *(01904) 468210* Lorraine and Andy Ritchie

 Genuine freehouse with Black Sheep Bitter, Timothy Taylor Landlord and York Guzzler regularly available.

A 250-year-old country pub with separate dining area serving home-cooked food Tues–Sat evening, lunchtime and evening Sun. The cellar used to be the village mortuary, so the beer is always cold! Car park. Children welcome. Six minutes from the centre of York.

(OPEN) *7–11pm Tues–Sat (closed Mon); 12–3pm Sun.*

FLOUCH

The Dog & Partridge

Bord Hill, Flouch, Sheffield, South Yorkshire S36 4HH
☎ *(01226) 763173* Stephen and Audrey Marsh
www.dogandpartridgeinn.co.uk

Four real ales, including Timothy Taylor Landlord, Acorn Barnsley Bitter and Black Sheep Bitter plus guests.

Isolated family-run inn in an Elizabethan building on the edge of the Peak District National Park with stunning moorland views. Licensed since 1740. Good food served at lunchtimes and evenings. Live entertainment. Families welcome. Beer garden and four-star accommodation. Licensed for civil weddings. Local CAMRA Pub of the Year 2006. Off the A628 Woodenhead Pass.

(OPEN) *All day, every day.*

GIGGLESWICK

Hart's Head Hotel

Belle Hill, Giggleswick, Settle, North Yorkshire BD24 0BA
☎ *(01729) 822086* Trevor Reynolds
www.hartsheadinn.co.uk

Freehouse with six ales always on offer, four of them rotating guests.

This 18th-century country inn is family-owned and -operated. Food served daily lunchtimes and evenings (not Thurs lunchtime). Ten en-suite letting rooms available. Beer garden. Full-size snooker table. A great base from which to explore the Yorkshire Dales, good walking and cycling location. Within an hour of Harrogate, Leeds, Lancaster and the Lake District. Located half a mile west of Settle on the B6480.

(OPEN) *12–2.30pm and 5.30–11pm Mon–Fri; 12–11pm Sat–Sun. (Closed Tues and Thurs lunchtimes, except during school holidays.)*

GOODMANHAM

The Goodmanham Arms

Main Street, Goodmanham, East Yorkshire YO43 3JA
☎ *(01430) 873849*
Roberta Pickard and Stuart Bell
www.goodmanham-arms.co.uk

Black Sheep Bitter and Theakston Bitter plus one guest, rotated weekly.

A freehold country pub on the Wold's Way along distance footpath. Real fires, friendly local clientele and walkers welcome. Bar food available 12–3pm Sun. Beer garden. Children and dogs welcome.

(OPEN) *5pm–close Mon–Fri; 12–close Sat–Sun and bank holidays.*

GOOLE

The Macintosh Arms

13 Aire Street, Goole, East Yorkshire DN14 5QW
☎ *(01405) 763850* Mel Lockwood

 Freehouse with Tetley Bitter, Dark Mild, Imperial and Burton Ale plus one rotating guest changed twice weekly.

Part of this 19th-century pub was used as a magistrate's court during the last century. Now a Grade II listed building, it is a three-bar pub. No food. Outdoor seating. Annual beer festival in February. Home of the Goole & district motorcycle club, 'The Wobbly Goolies and We'. Live music events on the last Friday of each month. Karaoke Sunday evenings. Situated just outside the town centre, near the docks.

(OPEN) *10.30am–midnight Sun–Mon; 10.30am–1am Tues–Thurs; 10.30am–2am Fri–Sat.*

GRINTON

The Bridge Inn

Grinton, Richmond, North Yorkshire DL11 6HH
☎ *(01748) 884224* Andrew Atkin
www.bridgeinn-grinton.co.uk

Marston's tied house with Jennings Cumberland Ale and Cocker Hoop plus two guest ales, changed several times each week.

A 17th-century coaching inn with great fresh, local food, a friendly atmosphere, cosy bar, games room and separate restaurant. Food served 12–9pm daily. Accommodation available. Beer garden. Car park. Beer festivals held. Well-behaved children welcome. Regular live music events. Nestled in the Yorkshire Dales near Reeth. Just off the A6108.

(OPEN) *12–12 Sun–Wed; noon–1am Thurs–Sat.*

GUISBOROUGH

The Tap & Spile

11 Westgate, Guisborough, North Yorkshire TS14 6BG
☎ *(01287) 632983* Don Davies-Evans

Seven real ales from breweries all over the country. Caledonian Deuchars IPA, Timothy Taylor Landlord and Durham Magus rotate on one pump, and the other beers are changed every few days.

Plenty of olde-worlde charm, a beamed ceiling and snug. Beer garden with smoking area. Bar food available at lunchtime. Parking. Children allowed. Situated on the main street in Guisborough.

(OPEN) *11.30am–1am Mon–Thurs; 11.30am–2am Fri–Sat; noon–12.30am Sun.*

GUISELEY
Coopers
*4–6 Otley Road, Guiseley, West Yorkshire
LS20 8AH*
☎ *(01943) 878835*
www.markettowntaverns.co.uk

Copper Dragon Golden Pippin and beers from Timothy Taylor and Black Sheep, plus five constantly changing guest ales.

Converted from a Co-op store in 2005, a light, airy bar and dining area. Upstairs function room available for hire. Food served at lunchtimes and evenings Mon–Sat and 12–6pm Sun. Small outside terrace. Live music nights. On the main A65.

OPEN *12–11pm.*

GUNNERSIDE
The Kings Head
Gunnerside, North Yorkshire DL11 6LD
☎ *(01748) 886261*
Steve Stewart and Sam Mealing
www.kingsheadgunnerside.co.uk

Black Sheep Bitter and John Smith's Cask on offer, plus at least one guest every month in winter, two changed weekly in summer. Guests might be from breweries such as Rudgate, Copper Dragon, Bradfield and Daleside.

Traditional Dales walkers' pub dating from 1752, with stone walls and open fire. Food served 12–3pm and 6–9pm every day (except Mondays in winter) – booking is advisable for parties over six people. Children and dogs welcome.

OPEN *12–11pm (closed on Monday in winter).*

HALIFAX
The George
66 Rochdale Road, Kings Cross, Halifax, West Yorkshire HX2 7HA
☎ *07773 614598* Selwyn Cheetham

Freehouse with two ales from Timothy Taylor plus four rotating guests changed by the barrel.

Dating back to the 1800s, previously called The Wellington, this is a traditional, one-bar pub. No food. Beer garden. Car park. Dogs and children welcome. Located on the A58 Halifax to Sowerby Bridge Road.

OPEN *6–11pm Mon–Thurs; 12–12 Fri–Sat; 12–11pm Sun.*

The Royal Oak
1 Clare Road, Halifax, West Yorkshire HX1 2HX
☎ *(01422) 353661* Chris Dalton

Timothy Taylor Landlord plus five guests, changed every fortnight.

A traditional town pub in a listed building, formerly a Tap and Spile, with one bar and a dining area. Food available at lunchtime only. No children.

OPEN *All day, every day.*

The Three Pigeons
1 Sunfold, South Parade, Halifax, West Yorkshire HX1 2LX
☎ *(01422) 347001* Christine Winterbottom

Award-winning, family-run pub owned by the Ossett Brewery since 2005. Eight ales with four from Ossett plus others from Durham, Rooster's, Abbeydale and Pictish. The guests are changed daily, and real cider is also available.

Unique, unspoilt 1930s art deco pub just a few minutes' walk from the railway station. Real fires, one octagonal bar and lobby plus three parlour rooms. On CAMRA's National Inventory of Pub Interiors and winner of CAMRA/English Heritage Conservation Award 2007. Patio at front. Accoustic music, occasional curry nights and pie nights, quiz. Near Piece Hall, Dean Clough Mills, local theatres and Shay football ground.

OPEN *3pm–12 Mon–Wed; 12–12 Thurs; noon–12.30am Sat; 12–11pm Sun.*

HARLEY
The Horseshoe
9 Harley Road, Harley, Rotherham, South Yorkshire S62 7UD
☎ *(01226) 742204* Robert Uff

Wentworth WPA. Two guests, changed every three days. Guests may include Moonshine Bumble Beer, Black Sheep Strata or Fog on the Tyne.

A refurbished country pub with one central bar. Children welcome up to 8.30pm. Food served 5–8pm Mon, Wed–Fri and 12–3pm Sun. Patio garden. Located off the main Barnsley–Sheffield road, one mile from Wentworth.

OPEN *4–11pm Mon–Fri; 1–11pm Sat; 12–10.30pm Sun.*

HAROME
The Star
Harome, Nr Helmsley, North Yorkshire YO62 5JE
☎ *(01439) 770397* Andrew and Jacquie Pern
www.thestaratharome.co.uk

Black Sheep Special plus two guests, often from Cropton, Hambleton or Skipton, changed weekly.

Traditional, 14th-century thatched freehouse and Michelin-starred restaurant. One bar and a separate restaurant plus a large beer garden. Food available Tues–Sat 11.30am–2pm and 6.30–9.30pm, plus 12–6pm on Sundays. Private dining room and coffee loft. Children welcome. Two miles south of the A170.

OPEN *7.30–11pm Mon; 11.30am–3pm and 6.30–11pm Tues–Sat; 12–10.30pm Sun.*

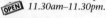

HARROGATE
Old Bell Tavern

6 Royal Parade, Harrogate, North Yorkshire HG1 2SZ
☎ *(01423) 507930* Andrew Bates
www.markettowntaverns.co.uk

A Timothy Taylor brew, Theakston Best, Black Sheep Bitter plus something from Rooster's and a mild always available. Regularly changing guests also served, plus Erdinger WeissBier (a Belgian ale) and a range of Belgian, German and world bottled beers.

Period town-centre bar. Food available every day in the bar and in an upstairs dining room/brasserie every day except Sunday. Children over 14 allowed in the brasserie only. Situated close to the Pump Room Museum and Valley Gardens.

OPEN *12–11pm (10.30pm Sun).*

The Tap & Spile

Tower Street, Harrogate, North Yorkshire HG1 5AB
☎ *(01423) 526785* Roger Palmer
www.tapandspile.net

Enterprise Inns house with eight real ales including Rooster's Yankee and Theakston Old Peculier and six guests changed every couple of days. Examples include Leeds Pale Ale, Goose Eye Chinook Blonde, York Guzzler, Outlaw Wild Mule and many more!

A traditional two-bar pub situated just off the town centre. Stone walls and half-carpet in lounge; tiled floor and half-carpet in public bar. Fireplace. No food. Patio at front. Beer garden with lighting at rear of pub available for smokers. Children welcome.

OPEN *All day, every day.*

The Winter Gardens

Parliament Street, Harrogate, North Yorkshire HG1 2RR
☎ *(01423) 877010* Andrew Robson
www.jdwetherspoon.co.uk

Wetherspoon's pub with Greene King Abbot, Marston's Pedigree and a local brew such as Rooster's YPA plus five constantly rotating guests from local breweries such as Daleside, Wharfdale, York and Ossett.

Open since 2002, this pub is set in a Grade I listed historical site of interest, covering 8,000 square feet. One bar. Food served 9am–11pm Mon–Sun. Beer garden. Regular beer festivals, largest ones held in April and October. Curry nights Thurs, grill nights Tues. Conference facilities.

OPEN *9am–midnight (1am Fri–Sat).*

HAWES
The Fountain Hotel

Market Place, Hawes, North Yorkshire DL8 3RD
☎ *(01969) 667206* Angus McCarthy
www.fountainhawes.co.uk

A genuine freehouse for 20 years, with five real ales available. Black Sheep Riggwelter, Bitter and Ale and Theakston BB. One monthly-changing guest, such as Dent Dale Bitter, Wensleydale Ale and beers from Copper Dragon.

Built in the 17th century and recently refurbished in a country style. One bar. Food served 12–2.30pm and 6.30–8.30pm. Children welcome. Pool table. Accommodation. Car park.

OPEN *11.30am–11.30pm.*

HAWORTH
The Fleece Inn

Main Street, Haworth, Nr Keighley, West Yorkshire BD22 8DA
☎ *(01535) 642172* Nick Hindle
www.timothy-taylor.co.uk/fleeceinn

Timothy Taylor Landlord, Golden Best, Best Bitter, Dark Mild and Ram Tam are always on offer.

A 150-year-old pub featuring recently converted roof terrace with stunning views over Haworth. Cask Marque accredited. Beautiful Beer Gold Award and Platinum Award (only pub in Yorkshire). Seven luxury en-suite rooms – four-star tourist board grade. Food available 12–9pm Mon–Fri and 10am–4pm Sat–Sun. Well-behaved children welcome. On Haworth's cobbled Main Street.

OPEN *12–11.30pm Mon–Sat; 10am–10.30pm Sun.*

HEADINGLEY
Arcadia Ale & Wine Bar

34 Arndale Centre, Otley Road, Headingley, Leeds, West Yorkshire LS6 2UE
☎ *(0113) 274 5599* Rhian Aitken
www.markettowntaverns.co.uk

Eight real ales available including Timothy Taylor Landlord and Black Sheep Bitter plus a pump dedicated to Elland Brewery beers and five guests, rotated constantly. German beers, Belgian fruit beers and lagers on draught, plus extensive range of bottled beers.

Converted from a Lloyds Bank in 2004, a modern bar with mezzanine area (available for bookings) and a contemporary continental feel. Snacks, sharing plates, sandwiches and bar meals served 12–2pm and 6–8pm Mon–Fri, 12–7pm Sat, and lunches from 1pm on Sun. No children. Dogs welcome. On the main road (A660) through Headingley.

OPEN *12–11pm.*

HEBDEN BRIDGE
The Fox & Goose

9 Heptonstall Road, Hebden Bridge, West Yorkshire HX7 6AZ
☎ *(01422) 842649* Simon and Julia Trapp
www.foxale.co.uk

Margery's Tiddlywink, the house beer, is brewed by Millstone, and is suitable for vegans (no isinglass finings). It is named after the owner of an illegal alehouse said to have been on this site in the early 1300s. Four rotating guest pumps with a selection of real ales, mostly from local breweries, including one dark. Wide selection of continental bottled beers plus draught and bottled ciders.

Small, friendly, family-owned and -run freehouse. The eclectic mix of customers and the absence of both a juke box and games machines encourage lively conversation! Bar billiards. No food. Yorkshire CAMRA Pub of the Year Runner-up 2006; Halifax and Calderdale CAMRA Pub of the Year 2004 and 2006. Beer festivals Whitsun bank holiday weekend and third weekend in November. Regular folk music sessions – see website for details. New hillside beer garden with stunning views across the valley. Wi-Fi access. Well-behaved dogs welcome. Children must be on a lead.

OPEN *5pm–12 Mon; noon–midnight Tues–Sat; noon–11.30pm Sun.*

Moyles Hotel

6–10 New Road, Hebden Bridge, West Yorkshire HX7 8AD
☎ *(01422) 845272* Martin Carpenter
www.moyles.com

 Freehouse serving Pictish Brewers Gold and four rotating guests, changed weekly. Examples include Phoenix White Monk and Arizona, Sarah Hughes Dark Ruby, Fuller's London Pride, B&T Edwin Taylor's and Crouch Vale Brewers Gold.

A family-run hotel, bar and restaurant, refurbished to a very high standard. Local CAMRA Pub of the Season 2008. Twelve bedrooms available, each decorated in a unique fusion of contemporary design and the building's original Victorian structure. Modern state-of-the-art bar. Food served 12–3pm and 6–10pm. Restaurant renowned for using fresh, locally sourced ingredients. Annual arts festival. Near Brontë parsonage in Haworth and country walks. Centrally located opposite the marina, on the main A646 Burnley road from Halifax to Todmorden.

OPEN *12–11pm.*

The Stubbing Wharf

King Street, Hebden Bridge, West Yorkshire HX7 6LU
☎ *(01422) 844107* Matthew Browne
www.stubbingwharf.com

Timothy Taylor Landlord, Black Sheep Bitter and Copper Dragon Golden Pippin are the permanent beers here, and the four guests, from breweries such as Sarah Hughes and Phoenix, are rotated every few days.

Situated on the edge of Hebden Bridge, this pub dates back to 1800 when the canal was built. Food served 12–2.45pm and 5.30–9pm Mon–Fri, 12–9pm Sat and 12–8pm Sun. Lots of seating outside in covered courtyard, plus towpath seating. Well-behaved children and dogs welcome. Annual cider festival. Just off the A646 towards Todmorden.

OPEN *12–11pm (midnight Fri).*

The Golden Lion Inn

Main Street, Helperby, York, North Yorkshire YO61 2NT
☎ *(01423) 360870*
Denise Oddy and Paul Lindley

Freehouse with four real ales, from breweries such as Rooster's, Copper Dragon, Black Sheep, Brakspear, Everards and more. Three beers rotate every week in summer, every two weeks in winter.

Traditional village country inn with stone floor and two log fires, offering a warm welcome for all, including families. Bar meals with a varied selection of choices available 12–9pm Mon–Sat, with Sunday lunch (12–3pm) attracting diners from far and wide! Regular quiz nights, pool and darts. Live bands Sunday teatime 6–8pm. Parties catered for, and coaches welcome by appointment. Situated five miles from the A1M through Boroughbridge, 15 miles north of York.

OPEN *12–12 (1am weekends).*

The Angel

Hetton, Nr Skipton, North Yorkshire BD23 6LT
☎ *(01756) 730263*
www.angelhetton.co.uk

Yorkshire beers from Black Sheep, Timothy Taylor and Wharfedale breweries usually available.

Once a crofter's cottage, now a multi-award-winning inn and restaurant below Cracoe Fell in the Yorkshire Dales. Five hundred years old in parts, with plenty of real fires and oak beams. Food available at lunchtimes and evenings. Accommodation.

OPEN *Summer: 12–3pm and 6–11pm Mon–Sat; 12–3pm and 6–10pm Sun. Winter: 12–2.30pm and 6–10.30pm Mon–Fri; 12–2.30pm and 6–11pm Sat; 12–3pm and 6–10pm Sun.*

The Farmer's Arms

2–4 Liphill Bank Road, Holmfirth, West Yorkshire HD9 2LR
☎ *(01484) 683713* Grahame and Sue Nutt

Tetley Cask, Tetley Dark Mild, Bombardier, Greene King IPA, Adnams Bitter and Timothy Taylor Landlord plus a constantly changing guest.

A traditional country village pub with the emphasis on quality real ale and food to complement it. Cask Marque accredited. Food served 5–8.30pm Mon–Sat, and 12–2pm Fri, 12–2.30pm Sat, 12–7pm Sun. Children welcome until 9pm. Private room available. Outside drinking area. Car park. From Compo's Café take the second on the right.

OPEN *5pm–12 Mon–Thurs; 12–12 Fri–Sun.*

Hervey's Wine Bar

Norridge Bottom, Holmfirth, West Yorkshire HD9 7BB
☎ *(01484) 686925* Hazel and Jon Shaw
www.herveys.co.uk

Freehouse with three ales, which could include Copper Dragon Golden Pippin, Best, Scotts 1816 and Black Sheep Best Bitter. Weston's Old Rosie cider also available on pump.

In the style of a wine bar, this small building is decorated in a continental style. Located in the town centre opposite the bus station. Bar snacks available 12–3pm and 6–9.30pm daily. Cask Marque accredited.

OPEN *Closed Mon (except bank holidays); 4pm–12.30am Tues–Fri; 2pm–12.30am Sat–Sun (winter); 11am–12.30am Mon–Fri (summer).*

The Rose & Crown (The Nook)

*7 Victoria Square, Holmfirth, West Yorkshire
HD9 1DN*
☎ *(01484) 683960*
Ian Roberts and Sheila Sutton
www.thenookholmfirth.co.uk

Seven or eight real ales, including
Timothy Taylor Best and Landlord, plus
regularly rotating guest beers. Plans to start a
micro-brewery in 2009.

Unique traditional alehouse dating from
the 1750s, family-run for over 40 years.
Food served 12–9pm Sun–Thurs and 12–7pm
Fri–Sat. Two bars plus a garden, plus outdoor
heated smoking area. Live music on last
Saturday of the month. Annual beer festival
over the August bank holiday weekend, with
more than 40 real ales.

OPEN *11.30am–midnight Mon–Sat;
12–12 Sun.*

HORBURY

Boon's

*6 Queen Street, Horbury, Wakefield,
West Yorkshire WF4 6LP*
☎ *(01924) 280442* John Bladen

Timothy Taylor Landlord and Clark's
Bitter, with up to four guests often from
Adnams, Orkney, Shepherd Neame or
Wychwood.

Traditional, single-bar olde-worlde pub
with patio and beer garden. Established as
a pub circa 1710, it retains an open fire,
beams and flagged floor. Walls with sporting
pictures. Children in beer garden and patio
only.

OPEN *11am–3pm and 5–11pm Mon–Thurs;
11am–11pm Fri–Sat; 12–10.30pm Sun.*

The King's Arms

*27 New Street, Horbury, Wakefield,
West Yorkshire WF4 6NB*
☎ *(01924) 264329* Mike Davidson

Marston's house with Pedigree, Bitter and
others available, plus one guest pump
regularly featuring a Banks's ale.

A one-bar village pub with wooden floors in
bar area. Pool and games area.
Conservatory, dining area, garden. Food
available 5–7pm. Children allowed.

OPEN *3–11pm Mon–Thurs; 12–11pm Fri–Sat;
12–4pm and 7–10.30pm Sun.*

HORSFORTH

Town Street Tavern

*16–18 Town Street, Horsforth, Leeds,
West Yorkshire LS18 4RJ*
☎ *(0113) 281 9996*
Lucy Gaunt and Garth Kirsten-Landman
www.markettowntaverns.co.uk

Eight real ales. Leeds Pale Ale, Black
Sheep Bitter, Timothy Taylor Best Bitter
and a Copper Dragon beer always available,
plus four constantly changing guests. Over 30
bottled German, Belgian and world beers.

A light, airy bar, traditional but with a
continental feel. Small, pretty beer
garden. Upstairs brasserie dining room
available for private hire. Food available
every day. Children over 14 welcome with an

adult. Dogs welcome, and a dog menu is
available!

OPEN *12–11pm.*

HOWDEN

Barnes Wallis Inn

*Station Road, North Howden, Nr Goole,
East Yorkshire DN14 7LF*
☎ *(01430) 430639* Kieron Lockwood
www.barneswallisinn.com

Genuine freehouse with four real ales
including Timothy Taylor Landlord, plus
guests, changed daily, from breweries such as
Salamander, Hambleton, Hop Back, Goose
Eye, Theakston and Black Sheep.

Traditional, one-room real ale house with
dining area and a permanent exhibition
of Barnes Wallis (and other) prints. Large
main garden and small sheltered one.
Barbecue. Food available 5–9pm Tues–Fri; 12–
9pm Sat; 12–8pm Sun. Large car park.
Children welcome, but no special facilities.
Four beer festivals every year, one in each
season. Situated directly outside Howden
railway station, once mile north of the town.

OPEN *5–11pm Mon–Fri; 12–12 Sat; 12–11pm
Sun.*

HUDDERSFIELD

The Grove

*2 Spring Grove Street, Huddersfield,
West Yorkshire HD1 4BD*
☎ *(01484) 430113* Ian Hayes
www.groveinn.co.uk

A genuine freehouse serving up to 18 ales
at any one time. Timothy Taylor
Landlord and Golden Best, College Green
Molly's Chocolate Stout, Durham Magus,
Empire Grove Grog, Marble Ginger,
Thornbridge Jaipur IPA, Fullers ESB (Oct–
Mar), Fullers London Pride (Apr–Sep). Plus up
to 10 guests from a huge variety of
independent breweries. Also large selection
(up to 260) of British and continental bottled
beers, and 10 genuine draught World Beers.

A two-bar, two-room corner pub dating
from circa 1860. A traditional pub
atmosphere with no TV, music, machines or
pool table. Unusual selection of quality bar
snacks. Traditional Irish music session Thurs
evenings. Children welcome in lounge bar.
Beer garden.

OPEN *12–11pm Sun–Weds; 12–12 Thu–Sat.*

Rat & Ratchet

*40 Chapel Hill, Huddersfield, West Yorkshire
HD1 3EB*
☎ *(01484) 542400* Sam Birkhead

Tied to Ossett Brewery, with 12 ales, four
from Ossett plus eight ever-changing
guests. There is always a mild and a porter or
stout. Two or three real ciders also served.

Traditional Victorian one-bar pub, formerly
The Grey Horse. Huddersfield CAMRA Pub
of the Year 2006, Mild Pub of the Year 2007
and Yorkshire Cider Pub of the Year Silver
Medalist 2008. Beer garden. Food served 12–
2pm Wed–Sat. Mild May festival, plus beer
festival in September. Car park. On the A616.

OPEN *3pm–12 Mon–Tues; 12–12 Wed–Thurs;
noon–12.30am Fri–Sat; 12–11pm Sun.*

The Star Inn

7 Albert Street, Folly Hall, Lockwood, Huddersfield, West Yorkshire HD1 3PJ
☎ *(01484) 545443* Sam Watt
www.thestarinn.info

Freehouse serving Timothy Taylor Landlord and Best plus Pictish Brewers Gold and a huge range of rotating guests including milds, stouts and porters from breweries near and far. Up to seven real ales at any one time. Regular beer festivals.

Award-winning backstreet ale house recently renovated and reopened. Real fires and beer garden. No food. Off the A616 half a mile from Huddersfield town centre.

Closed Mon; 5–11pm Tues–Fri; 12–11pm Sat; 12–10.30pm Sun.

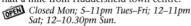

HULL

Falcon

60 Falkland Road, Hull, East Yorkshire HU9 5HA
☎ *(01482) 713721/713724*
Keith French and Michaela Thurston

Freehouse with JW Lees permanently available, plus three constantly rotating guests.

Two-bar pub with a friendly, welcoming atmosphere. No food. Beer garden. Children welcome. Near Hull Kingston Rovers. From Hedon Road, turn on to Marfleet Lane.

11am–midnight Mon; 11am–11.30pm Tues–Thurs; 11am–midnight Fri–Sat; 11am–11.30pm Sun.

The Gardeners Arms

35 Cottingham Road, Hull, East Yorkshire HU5 2PP
☎ *(01482) 342396* Steve Bark

A Mitchells & Butlers tied house. Black Sheep Best plus guests from Bateman, Cropton, Rudgate and Anglo-Dutch – all local and regional micro-breweries. Also one real cider.

Original front bar in an alehouse style, plus large rear bar/lounge, comfortably furnished. Food served 12–8pm. Several pool tables and TVs showing live sports in both bars. Large beer garden. Large car park. Winner of CAMRA Hull Pub of the Year 2004. Located near the university, on a main bus route.

12–11.30pm Sun–Mon; 11am–midnight Tues–Sat.

Minerva Hotel

Nelson Street, Hull, East Yorkshire HU1 1XE
☎ *(01482) 326909* Adam Brailsford

Four guest beers usually available, changed every three or four days.

Traditional, 19th-century pub built on the banks of the River Humber in 1831 and packed with maritime memorabilia. One bar, four main rooms, plus nooks and possibly the smallest snug in Britain which seats three. Outside seating. Home-cooked food served 12–8.30pm Sat–Wed; 12–3pm and 5–8.30pm Thurs–Fri (2-for-1 offer 3–8.30pm Mon–Wed). Children welcome if dining. Private room for hire, with buffets supplied at £3.50 a head. Parking available. Situated on Nelson Street, facing the river and Victoria pier. Ideal if visiting 'The Deep'.

11am–11pm Mon–Sat; 12–10.30pm Sun.

Ye Olde Black Boy

150 High Street, Hull, East Yorkshire HU1 1PS
☎ *(01482) 326516* Alan Murphy

Up to six guest beers available, from breweries such as Caledonian, Hop Back, Titanic, JW Lees, Hydes, Robinson's, Arundel, Fuller's and Harviestoun. Hoegaarden and real cider also served.

Historic 14th-century Grade II listed real ale pub in the centre of Hull. Cask Marque accredited. Local CAMRA Pub of the Season summer 2002. Light snacks and sandwiches available 12–3pm. Upstairs function room available for meetings and small private parties (up to 30 people). Situated on the old High Street, next to the river, on the fish trail and only five minutes' walk from 'The Deep'.

12–11pm (10.30pm Sun).

Springbank Tavern

29 Spring Bank, Hull, East Yorkshire HU3 1AS
☎ *(01482) 581879* Belinda Beaumont

Banks's Original plus two guest beers which could be something like Bateman XXXB or Brakspear Special.

A one-room alehouse with traditional games (darts, dominoes and pool). Students and locals provide mixed clientele. Background music, but no juke box. Bar food available 12–2pm daily (12–6pm Sunday). Beer garden. Street parking, disabled facilities. Children allowed in the bar for meals. Just off the city centre.

11am–11pm Mon–Sat; 12–10.30pm Sun.

The Wellington Inn

55 Russel Street, Hull, East Yorkshire HU2 9AB
☎ *(01482) 329 486* Richard and Janette Gant
www.thewellington-hull.co.uk

Tetley Bitter, plus up to six guests at any one time, rotating through 50–70 per month. Featured breweries include Yorkshire Dales, Wold Top, Abbeydale, Saltaire, Rudgate, Springhead and York.

A refurbished freehouse, built in 1861. Friendly atmosphere. Car park. Beer garden. No food served, but customers are welcome to bring their own sandwiches! Located just off Free Town Way, five minutes from the bus and train stations.

4–11pm Mon–Thurs; 12–12 Sat–Sun; 12–11pm Sun.

Whalebone

165 Wincolmlee, Kingston Upon Hull, Hull, East Yorkshire HU2 0PA
☎ *(01482) 226648* Alex Craig

 Freehouse brewing its own mild and bitter, with ales from Copper Dragon and Timothy Taylor also served, plus a weekly rotating guest.

This building dates back to 1793 but was rebuilt in 1903. Two rooms, open fires and dartboard. No bandits. Snacks available all day, Located by the River Hull, just north of the old town.

OPEN *11am–midnight.*

IDLE

Symposium

7 Albion Road, Idle, Bradford, West Yorkshire BD10 9PY
☎ *(01274) 616587* Karen Ball
www.markettowntaverns.co.uk

Copper Dragon Golden Pippin plus five constantly changing guests. Also a guest Belgian ale, often Erdinger WeissBier, and a range of over 30 bottled Belgian, German and world beers.

A traditional ale and wine bar. Restaurant-quality food available every day. Sun terrace available for alfresco drinking and dining. Children allowed at the landlord's discretion. Situated in the centre of Idle village, close to the Green.

OPEN *5.30–11pm Mon–Tues; 12–2.30pm and 5.30–11pm Wed–Thurs; 12–11pm Fri–Sat; 12–10.30pm Sun.*

ILKLEY

Bar t'at

7 Cunliffe Road, Ilkley, West Yorkshire LS29 9DZ
☎ *(01943) 608888* Stella Mallinson
www.markettowntaverns.co.uk

Timothy Taylor Landlord, Copper Dragon Golden Pippin, Black Sheep Best and a mild, stout or porter, plus four guests, changed weekly, from over 30 different breweries. Erdinger WeissBier and Belgian fruit beers are on tap, and a selection of continental and world bottled beers and wines is also served.

Traditional real ale pub over two floors. No music, no juke box, no games machines. Food available lunchtimes 12–2pm and 6–9pm Mon–Sat (9.15pm Fri–Sat); 12–6.30pm Sun. Under-14s allowed when dining, until 9pm. Dogs welcome. Heated patio outside for smokers. Adjacent to large public car park. Very close to Ilkley Moor.

OPEN *12–11pm.*

INGLETON

The Wheatsheaf Inn

22 High Street, Ingleton, North Yorkshire LA6 3AD
☎ *(01524) 241275*
www.wheatsheaf-ingleton.co.uk

 A Cains pub with Finest Bitter, IPA and FA plus a monthly craft beer.

Olde-worlde one-bar country pub with dining room and large beer garden. Disabled access. Accommodation. Food available 12–2.30pm and 6–9pm daily (plus 12–9pm Sat–Sun in summer). Children welcome. Good walking country. Off the A65.

OPEN *12–11pm.*

KEIGHLEY

The Boltmaker's Arms

117 East Parade, Keighley, West Yorkshire BD21 5HX
☎ *(01535) 661936* Phil Booth
www.boltmakers.co.uk

Tied to Timothy Taylor with Landlord, Best Bitter, Golden Best, Ram Tam and Dark Mild plus one rotating guest ale, changed at least once a week.

Small, traditional, one-room pub full of warmth, character and charm. Has served as a pub since around 1850 and features a collection of music memorabilia. Very friendly and welcoming, with open fires in winter. Cask Marque accredited, CAMRA award-winning. Small beer garden. Weekly quiz night on Tues. Fortnightly live music. Just 300 yards from the steam railway, three miles from Haworth and Brontë country. Located off the A6035 through Keighley.

OPEN *11am–11pm Mon; 11am–midnight Tues–Sat; 12–11pm Sun.*

The Cricketers Arms

23 Coney Lane, Keighley, West Yorkshire BD21 5JE
☎ *(01535) 669912* John Mitchell
www.cricketersarmskeighley.co.uk

Moorhouse's Premier Bitter plus up to six guests every day.

Situated close to the Keighley Worth Valley railway. A two-bar pub with beer garden and smoking area. Beer festival every April.

OPEN *11.30am–11pm Mon–Thurs; 11.30am–midnight Fri–Sat; 12–11pm Sun.*

The Old White Bear

6 Keighley Road, Crosshills, Keighley, West Yorkshire BD20 7RN
☎ *(01535) 632115* Neil and Mark Pickles

Wide selection of Naylor's Pinnacle ales ranging from Best Bitter to Blonde to Porter.

The pub was built in 1735 and retains the original beams taken from an old ship. Brewing began in the old stables here in 1993. The current owners took over in 2006. Bar and restaurant food available at lunchtimes and evenings. Car park, small garden. Children welcome.

OPEN *All day, every day.*

KIRBY HILL

The Shoulder of Mutton

Kirby Hill, Nr Richmond, North Yorkshire DL11 7JH
☎ *(01748) 822772*
Michael Yates and Toni Bennett
www.shoulderofmutton.net

Freehouse with Daleside Best and Black Sheep Best plus two rotating guests, changed weekly.

A 200-year-old ivy-clad building with one bar and separate restaurant. No juke box, pool table or fruit machines. Food served 7–

9pm Wed–Fri, 12–2pm and 7–9pm Sat–Sun (no food Mon–Tues). Accommodation available. Car park.

 OPEN *6–11pm Mon–Fri; 12–3pm and 6–11pm Sat; 12–3pm and 6–10.30pm Sun.*

KIRKBYMOORSIDE

The George & Dragon Hotel

17 Market Place, Kirkbymoorside, North Yorkshire YO62 6AA
☎ *(01751) 433334* David and Alison Nicholas
www.georgeanddragon.net

Black Sheep Ale, something from Copper Dragon and a rotating guest beer are among the brews on offer.

Hospitable, olde-worlde bar, restaurant and bistro, with blazing log fire in the winter and delightful covered and heated outside seating areas. Completely refurbished, but retaining its character. York CAMRA Best Town Pub 2007/8. Food served lunchtimes and evenings every day, including Sunday lunches, and all day Easter–October. Blackboard specials are always available, plus à la carte menu in the evening.

OPEN *10am–11pm Mon–Sat; 12–10.30pm Sun.*

The King's Head Hotel

5 High Market Place, Kirkbymoorside, North Yorkshire YO62 6AT
☎ *(01751) 431340* Simon Morrissey
www.kingsheadkirkbymoorside.co.uk

A Marston's Brewery house serving Jennings Cumberland, Bitter and Cocker Hoop. Two or three guests each week, such as St Austell Tribute, York Guzzler and perhaps something from Copper Dragon.

A 16th-century coaching inn with public bar, à la carte restaurant and conservatory. Rear terrace and walled garden. Food served 11.45am–2pm and 6–9pm Mon–Sat; 12–6pm Sun. Accommodation.

OPEN *10am–11pm.*

KNARESBOROUGH

Blind Jacks

19 Market Place, Knaresborough, North Yorkshire HG5 8AL
☎ *(01423) 869148*
Paul and Debbie Holden-Ridgway
www.villagebrewer.co.uk

Up to nine real ales. Village Brewer's White Boar (the house beer) and Black Sheep Bitter are always on offer, plus a constantly changing range of six or seven guest ales from independent brewers. Four continental beers on tap.

A 17th-century listed building, beamed with wooden floors, panelled walls and lots of mirrors. Two cosy upstairs snugs. No food. No children. Parking nearby. Dogs allowed.

OPEN *5.30–11pm Mon; 4–11pm Tues–Thurs; 12–11pm Fri–Sat; 12–10.30pm Sun.*

George & Dragon

9 Briggate, Knaresborough, North Yorkshire HG5 8BQ
☎ *(01423) 863973* Steve Foulis

Freehouse with Rooster's and Daleside plus two rotating guests from Yorkshire

micro-breweries such as Elland, Ossett, Anglo-Dutch, Yorkshire Dales, Wold Top, York.

A bright and comfortable town pub with an open-plan interior and large central bar. Popular with all ages. B&B accommodation available. Car park. Pool table, dart board, dominoes. Well-behaved dogs welcome. Close to the market square, just off the Knaresborough high street.

OPEN *5–11pm Mon–Thurs; 5pm–12 Fri; 12–12 Sat–Sun.*

The Mitre

4 Station Road, Knaresborough, North Yorkshire HG5 9AA
☎ *(01423) 868948* Diane Lockerbie
www.themitreinn.co.uk

A freehouse. Always one ale from Thwaites Wainwright, Black Sheep, Rooster's, Copper Dragon and Timothy Taylor available. Plus three guests, changed weekly, from micro-breweries across the north of England.

Built in 1922 and comprehensively refurbished in 2007. Two separate bar areas plus separate dining room, brasserie restaurant and function room. Food served lunchtimes and evenings Mon–Sat; 12–5pm Sun. Beer patio. Children and dogs welcome. Accommodation. Adjacent to railway station.

OPEN *12–11pm.*

LANGDALE END

Moorcock Inn

Langdale End, Scarborough, North Yorkshire YO12 0BN
☎ *(01723) 882268* Susan Mathewson

Two brews on offer, usually one from Wold Top or Slaters, plus a guest, rotated weekly. Selection of bottled beers also available.

Dating from 1640, an unspoilt, two-bar country pub with hatch servery. No music or machines. Food served Thurs–Sun evenings and Sat–Sun lunch in the winter, more often in summer. Well-behaved children welcome until 9pm. Situated at the Scarborough end of Forrest Drive.

OPEN *Hours may vary – ring first to be sure.*

LEAVENING

The Jolly Farmers Inn

Main Street, Leavening, Nr Malton, North Yorkshire YO17 9SA
☎ *(01653) 658276* Richard and Sarah Smith

Freehouse with Timothy Taylor Landlord, Tetleys and Black Sheep Bitter plus two rotating guests changed every few days.

This 300-year-old traditional country alehouse is a busy village locals' pub. Cosy bar, lounge, snug, family/games room and dining room. Food served Wed–Sat evenings, Sat–Sun lunchtimes. Beer garden. Children welcome. Car parking. First beer festival held Aug 2007. Located near the beautiful Yorkshire Wolds, 14 miles east of York and 6 miles south of Malton.

OPEN *Every evening; all day Sat–Sun.*

LEEDS

The Cross Keys

107 Water Lane, Holbeck Urban Village, Leeds, West Yorkshire LS11 5WD
☎ *(0113) 243 3711*
www.the-crosskeys.com

A freehouse with Rooster's always available. Up to six guests, such as Abbeydale Black Mass or ales from Daleside or Saltaire.

Gastropub situated a few minutes' walk from Leeds City station. A 200-year-old inn with roaring fires, brick walls, wooden beamed ceilings and spiral staircase. Traditional British pub food served lunchtimes and evenings. Outdoor courtyard.

OPEN *12–11pm (10.30pm Sun).*

The Duck & Drake

43 Kirkgate, Leeds, West Yorkshire LS2 7DR
☎ *(0113) 246 5806*

Timothy Taylor Landlord plus six guests (300 per year) from breweries including Jennings, Clark's, Exmoor, Rooster's and Pioneer. Also real cider.

Traditional alehouse with wooden floors, coal fires, bare boards and live bands. Bar food served at lunchtime. Get to Leeds market and ask for directions.

OPEN *All day, every day.*

The Eagle Tavern

North Street, Sheepscar, Leeds, West Yorkshire LS2 1AF
☎ *(0113) 245 7146* Max and Mandy Thomson

Samuel Smith tied house serving Old Brewery Bitter.

An 1826 Georgian building close to the city centre. Food available 12–8pm Mon–Sat, plus Sunday lunches 12–4pm. Parking. Ten minutes' walk out of the city centre. B&B accommodation. Children welcome.

OPEN *11.30am–11pm (10.30pm Sun).*

The Grove Inn

Back Row, Holbeck, Leeds, West Yorkshire LS11 5PL
☎ *(0113) 243 9254* Rachel Nicola Scordos

Enterprise Inns pub with up to eight real ales, with Caledonian Deuchars IPA and 80/-, Daleside Blonde and Moorhouse's Black Cat regularly featured, plus beers from local breweries. At least two of the guests are changed every day and a mild is always available. Real cider and continental beers on draught.

Award-winning corridor pub with separate tap and snug, and large concert room to the rear. Food served 12–2pm Mon–Fri and 1–3pm Sun (no food Sat). Side rooms for hire (free of charge). Live acoustic music most nights. Beer festival last weekend in Jan, outdoor blues festival third week of July. Only five minutes' walk due south of Leeds railway station.

OPEN *12–11pm Mon–Thurs; 12–12 Fri–Sat; 12–10.30pm Sun.*

The Midnight Bell

101 Water Lane, Leeds, West Yorkshire LS11 5QN
☎ *(0113) 244 5044*
www.midnightbell.co.uk

The first pub opened by the recently founded Leeds Brewery so serving the brewery's Best, Pale and Midnight Bell, plus seasonal brews and two guests.

Converted from offices in a Victorian building and opened in 2007. Open plan with distinct areas. Outside courtyard. Food available 12–3pm and 5–9pm (12–6pm Sun). Quiz nights on Thursdays.

OPEN *11.30am–11pm (midnight Fri–Sat).*

North Bar

24 New Briggate, Leeds, West Yorkshire LS17 8AW
☎ *(0113) 242 4540* Matt G Orecki
www.northbar.com

A freehouse serving a huge range of beer. Up to 15 British ales, including Rooster's Ale, a guest and a stout, porter or mild at all times. Over 100 guests served each year. Also 30–50 Belgian beers, 10–20 German beers, 20–30 World beers and 10–15 American beers.

An award-winning bar with an impressive selection of quality ales. One of the first bars in the country to serve a full range of Belgian and German beers. Food served 12–close. Supervised children allowed during the daytime.

OPEN *Noon–1am Mon–Tues; noon–2am Wed–Sat; 12–10.30pm Sun.*

The Old Vic

17 Whitecote Hill, Leeds, West Yorkshire LS13 3LB
☎ *(0113) 256 1207* P Willacy

Freehouse with Timothy Taylor Landlord, Black Sheep Bitter and something from Copper Dragon among the brews available, plus a monthly guest.

Three-room pub with open fire plus a function room. Food served 12–6pm Mon–Sat and 12–2.30pm Sun. Beer garden, large car park. Children welcome until 8pm. Disco on Friday, live entertainment Saturday, quiz night Thursday, karaoke. At the end of the town street, towards Rodley and Horsforth.

OPEN *12–11pm Mon–Thurs; 12–12 Fri–Sat; 12–10.30pm Sun.*

The Reliance

76–8 North Street, Leeds, West Yorkshire LS2 7PN
☎ *(0113) 295 6060* Joss Ainsworth
www.the-reliance.co.uk

Theakston Black Bull. Up to four different guests per week rotated on one pump. Breweries include Goose Eye, Phoenix, Rooster's, Mordue, Elland, Ossett, Kelham Island and Springhead.

Housed in an old glass workshop, this informal pub specialises in a selection of world beers, real ales and modern English food. Located across the flyover at the top of New Briggate.

OPEN *12–11pm Mon–Thurs; 12–12 Fri–Sat; 12–10.30pm Sun.*

The Stables

Otley Road, Leeds, West Yorkshire LS16 5PS
☎ *(0113) 230 6000*
www.weetwood.co.uk

A freehouse. Copper Dragon Golden Pippin and Challenger IPA, Black Sheep Bitter and Timothy Taylor Landlord. One pump dedicated to guest beers, changed every three or four days. Beers featured include Adnams Explorer, Fuller's London Pride, Jennings Cocker Hoop, Greene King Old Speckled Hen, Marston's Pedigree and brews from Wentworth Brewery.

Converted from the original stable block of the manor house, this pub retains many original features and is located in the cobbled courtyard. Traditional pub food served 12–9pm daily. Children welcome. Outdoor seating and games in summer months.

OPEN *12–11pm (10.30pm Sun).*

The Victoria

28 Great George Street, Leeds, West Yorkshire LS1 3DL
☎ *(0113) 245 1386* Carol Ann Coleman

A Mitchells & Butlers tied house. Timothy Taylor Landlord and Barnsley Bitter and Acorn. Four daily-changing guests, such as Everards Sly Fox, Otter Bright, Coach House Dick Turpin and a Bateman ale.

Built in 1865 with splendid Victorian features. One large bar, two other function/meeting rooms. Food served 10am–10pm. Children welcome. Live jazz Thurs. Located behind the town hall.

OPEN *10am–11pm Mon–Wed; 10am–midnight Thurs–Sat; closed Sun.*

Whitelocks

Turks Head Yard, Leeds, West Yorkshire LS1 6HB
☎ *(0113) 245 3950* Charlie Hudson
www.whitelocks.co.uk

Punch leased house with Caledonian Deuchars IPA, Theakston Best and Old Peculier and John Smith's Cask plus a wide range of constantly changing guests from breweries such as York, Daleside, Abbeydale, Copper Gragon, Greene King, Spitfire and Adnams.

Established in 1715, this traditional pub has a main luncheon bar, restaurant and second top bar which is open Wed–Sat. Food (with large variety of vegetarian options) served in the restaurant 12–2.30pm and 4–7pm daily, plus bar food 12–8pm. Large beer garden. Children welcome in restaurant and garden. Located in the town centre, down an alley between Carphone Warehouse and the Northern Rock Bank.

OPEN *11am–11pm Mon–Sat; 12–10.30pm Sun. Top bar 12–11pm Wed–Sat.*

LINTHWAITE

Sair Inn

Lane Top, Linthwaite, Huddersfield, West Yorkshire HD7 5SG
☎ *(01484) 842370* Ron Crabtree

Up to eight Linfit beers are brewed and served on the premises.

Home of the award-winning Linfit Brewery, which began production in

1982 for the Sair Inn. The pub is a traditional 18th-century alehouse. Outdoor seating with a lovely view, plus smoking area. Parking in road. Dogs welcome, children allowed in any of the rooms away from the bar. No food.

 5–11pm Mon–Fri; 12–11pm Sat and public holidays; 12–10.30pm Sun.

LIVERSEDGE

The Black Bull

37 Halifax Road, Liversedge, West Yorkshire WF15 6JR
☎ *(01924) 403779* Jamie Lawson

The first house owned by the Ossett Brewery, with Pale Gold, Black Bull Bitter, Excelsior and Timothy Taylor Landlord always available. Four rotating guests will include one mild.

A true, traditional ale house with two bars, beamed ceilings and real fires. Disabled access at the rear. No food. Children allowed in the afternoons only. Beer garden and car park. Accoustic live music every Tuesday. Situated out of town.

OPEN *12–3pm and 5–11pm Mon–Tues; 12–11pm Wed–Sat; 12–10.30pm Sun.*

The Cross Keys

283 Halifax Road, Liversedge, West Yorkshire WF15 6NE
☎ *(01274) 873294* GA and PG Stephenson

Marston's Pedigree and John Smith's Bitter usually available.

Open-plan, community-style 100-year-old pub, with two bars. Sky TV. Food served every day except Tues. Beer garden, large car park, children and walkers welcome.

OPEN *4–11.20pm Mon–Thurs; 12–11.50pm Fri–Sat; 12–10.50pm Sun.*

LONG PRESTON

Maypole Inn

Long Preston, Settle, Nr Skipton, North Yorkshire BD23 4PH
☎ *(01729) 840219* Robert Palmer
www.maypole.co.uk

Timothy Taylor Landlord and a Moorhouse's beer plus two rotating guests, changed weekly. Scrumpy cider also available.

A 17th-century inn in the Yorkshire Dales National Park, situated beside Maypole Green. Two bars with open fires in each. Outdoor seating available. Car park. Food served in dining room and bar 12–2pm and 6.30–9pm Mon–Fri, all day Sat–Sun and bank holidays. Accommodation available in six en-suite rooms. Beer garden. Children and dogs welcome. Local sporting activities catered for, including walking, pony-trekking, mountain-climbing, cycling, pot-holing, fishing and golf. An hour's drive from the Lake District. Located on the A65 between Skipton and Settle.

 11.30am–2.30pm and 6–11pm Mon–Thurs; all day Fri–Sun.

LONGWOOD
Dusty Miller
2 Giled Road, Longwood, Huddersfield,
West Yorkshire HD4
☎ *(01484) 651763* John Drummond

Black Sheep Special, Eastwood & Sanders Best and Timothy Taylor Landlord and Best plus a guest from Phoenix, Golden Hill or Brakspear.

A 17th-century village pub for real ale lovers – a drinkers' pub. No food. Children allowed. Patio.

OPEN *5–11pm Mon–Fri; 11am–11pm Sat; 12–10.30pm Sun.*

LUND
The Wellington Inn
19 The Green, Lund, Driffield, East Yorkshire
YO25 9TE
☎ *(01377) 217294* Russell and Sarah Jeffrey

Freehouse with Timothy Taylor Landlord, Black Sheep Best and Rooster's Yankee plus a weekly-changing guest ale, usually from local Yorkshire micro-breweries.

S mart two-bar country village pub with separate restaurant. Cask Marque accredited. York stone floors, three open log fires and small patio. Bar food available at lunchtimes (not Mon) and evenings (Tues–Sat). Restaurant open in the evenings.

OPEN *7–11pm Mon; 12–3pm and 7–11pm Tues–Sat (10.30pm Sun).*

MALHAM
The Lister Arms Hotel
Malham, Skipton, North Yorkshire BD23 4DB
☎ *(01729) 830330* Nick Frankgate
www.listerarms.co.uk

Freehouse serving Thwaites beers – Wainwrights, Lancaster Bomber, Thwaites Original, Nutty Black plus seasonal changes.

H istoric former coaching inn dating back to the 1600s, located by the village green. Retains original features such as oak beams and inglenook fireplaces. Takes its name from a previous owner, Thomas Lister, who was the first Lord of Ribblesdale in 1723. Food served 12–3pm and 6pm Mon-Sat; 12–8pm Sun. Outdoor seating. Car park. Accommodation available. Pet-friendly.

OPEN *Open all day.*

MALTON
The Kings Head
5 Market Place, Malton, North Yorkshire
YO17 7LP
☎ *(01653) 692289* Deborah Watts

One real ale always available, plus two constantly changing guests.

A refurbished modern pub with lounge bar, tap room and upstairs restaurant. À la carte menu and sandwiches available 12–3pm and 6–9pm daily. Live entertainment Fri, disco Sat. The pub is wheelchair-friendly, and children are welcome. Car park opposite pub.

OPEN *11am–midnight Mon–Sat; 12–10.30pm Sun.*

Suddaby's Crown Hotel
Wheelgate, Malton, North Yorkshire YO17 7HP
☎ *(01653) 692038* Neil Suddaby
www.suddabys.co.uk

Eight ales always on offer, from Suddaby's and other breweries. Four are rotated regularly, with seasonal brews sometimes available.

T he pub is a traditional inn, full of character and located in the town centre. It is popular with locals and visitors alike, and is famous for its regular beer festivals throughout the year. Sandwiches available Fri and Sat, with other bar snacks available Sat. Parking, children's room, accommodation.

OPEN *11am–11pm Mon–Sat; 12–10.30pm Sun.*

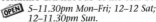

MANFIELD
The Crown Inn
Vicars Lane, Manfield, Nr Darlington, North
Yorkshire DL2 2RF
☎ *(01325) 374243* Peter and Karen Hynes
http://crowninn.villagebrewer.co.uk

Up to eight real ales including Village Brewer White Boar and a monthly special 4% beer, known as 'seasonable'. Plus guests changed sometimes daily, such as Daleside Old Legover, Timothy Taylor Landlord and Yorkshire Dales Butter Tubs.

A n 18th-century two-bar village inn with open fires and games room. Food served 5–9pm Mon–Fri, 12–9pm Sat and 12–4pm Sun. Beer garden, car park. Two beer festivals and one cider festival per year. Seven times Darlington CAMRA Country Pub of the Year, Yorkshire CAMRA Pub of the Year 2005.

OPEN *5–11.30pm Mon–Fri; 12–12 Sat; 12–11.30pm Sun.*

MARSDEN
Riverhead Brewery Tap
2 Peel Street, Marsden, Huddersfield,
West Yorkshire HD7 6BR
☎ *(01484) 841270* Philip Holdsworth

Home of the Riverhead Brewery with seven pumps selling only Riverhead ales (named after local reservoirs) brewed on the premises.

O pened in 1995, a real pub for drinking and chatting, with no juke box or bandit machines. View into the brewery from the pub to watch the brewing. No food. Beer garden. Two hundred yards from Marsden railway station.

OPEN *12–11pm Mon–Fri; 11am–11pm Sat; 12–10.30pm Sun.*

MASHAM
Black Sheep Brewery
Wellgarth, Masham, Ripon, North Yorkshire
HG4 4EN
☎ *(01765) 680100/680101* Paul Theakston
www.blacksheepbrewery.co.uk

Part of the brewery, this bistro serves all the ales brewed on-site (three on tap and five in bottles).

T his site has the brewery, visitors' centre, bistro and bar located together for a true ale experience. Food served 12–2.30pm Mon–Wed, 12–2.30pm and 6.30–9.30pm Thurs–

Sat, 12–3pm Sun. The bistro serves dishes prepared with locally sourced produce and Black Sheep beer. Wonderful views over the River Ure. Brewery tours available. Beer garden. Coach and car park. Children welcome.

 10.30am–5pm Mon–Wed; 11am–11pm Thurs–Sat; 11am–5pm Sun.

The White Bear
Masham, North Yorkshire HG4 4EN
☎ *(01765) 689319* Sue Thomas

 A Theakston-tied pub with Theakston Best, Black Bull, Old Peculier, XB, Mild and Caledonian Deuchars IPA plus one weekly-changing guest.

Approximately 60 years old, this pub has a tap room and a lounge/dining area. Food served 12–3pm and 6–9pm Mon–Sun. Annual beer festival in June held in marquee with over 35 cask ales. Car park. Beer patio. Children and dogs welcome. Parties catered for. Located on the edge of the Yorkshire Dales. Follow signs for Masham from the A1.

OPEN *All day, every day.*

MELMERBY
The George & Dragon Inn
Main Street, Melmerby, Nr Ripon,
North Yorkshire HG4 5HA
☎ *(01765) 640970*
Paul Grimshaw and Linda Nalias

Freehouse with four real ales. Hambleton Bitter, Timothy Taylor Golden Best and Marston Moor Matchlock Mild are regulars, and guests are changed every two or three months.

An 18th-century pub with real fires, no TV, games machines or juke box. Food available 6.30–9pm Fri–Sat; 12–2.30pm and 6–9pm Sun. Wednesday is quiz night. Children welcome. Car park. Three B&B rooms available. Near to Lightwater Valley and on the edge of the Yorkshire Dales.

OPEN *5pm–12 Mon–Fri; noon–1am Sat; 12–11pm Sun.*

MEXBOROUGH
The Falcon
12 Main Street, Mexborough, South Yorkshire S64 9DW
☎ *(01709) 513084* Desmond Smyth

Old Mill Bitter plus several seasonal, celebration or guest ales, changed frequently (as soon as they finish).

A traditional brewery tap room situated out of the town centre. Food served 11am–5pm Mon–Sat, with traditional Irish breakfasts and Irish stew available. No children.

OPEN *11am–11pm Mon–Sat; 12–3pm and 7–11pm Sun.*

MIDDLESBROUGH
Doctor Brown's
135 Corporation Road, Middlesbrough,
North Yorkshire TS1 2RR
☎ *(01642) 213213* Tony Linklater

At least four real ales, including brews from Black Sheep, Cropton, Jarrow, Hadrian & Border, Wylam, York, Rudgate, Dent and other locals. Plus guests such as Caledonian Deuchars IPA, Greene King Abbot, Marston's Pedigree and more.

Built in 1867, a traditional town-centre pub. Live music every Fri and Sat. Food available 12–2pm Sun–Fri. Outdoor café-style seating area. Disabled facilities, accompanied children for meals. Within easy reach of Middlesbrough centre and Riverside Stadium.

OPEN *All day, every day.*

The Isaac Wilson
61 Wilson Street, Middlesbrough,
North Yorkshire TS1 1SB
☎ *(01642) 247708* Vanessa Stewart

 Up to six guests usually on offer.

Town pub with food available 11am– 10pm daily. No music or TV. Disabled access. Children's licence until 9pm. Plasma screen for major sporting events.

OPEN *9am–midnight Sun–Thurs; 9am–1am Fri–Sat.*

MIRFIELD
Navigation Tavern
6 Station Road, Mirfield, West Yorkshire WF14 8NL
☎ *(01924) 492476* Kevin O'Donnell

A freehouse serving Theakston Mild, Best Bitter, Old Peculiar and XB plus a selection of seasonal guests.

Set beside the Calder and Hebble Navigation Canal. Games/function room with pool, darts and large-screen TV for Sky Sports. Food served 12–2.30pm and 6– 9.30pm Tues–Sat and 12–4pm Sun. Disabled facilities and access. Accommodation. Just 200 metres from Mirfield station.

OPEN *11.30am–11pm Mon–Sat; 12–10.30pm Sun.*

MYTHOLMROYD
The Shoulder of Mutton
36 New Road, Mytholmroyd, Halifax,
West Yorkshire HX7 5DZ
☎ *(01422) 883165* John Hartley

 An Enterprise Inns pub. Black Sheep Best, Copper Dragon Golden Pippin, Scotts 1816, Timothy Taylor Landlord and Greene King IPA. Plus guest beers from local breweries.

Riverside pub featuring a collection of memorabilia relating to The Cragg Vale Coiners, a notorious 18th-century gang of forgers. Food served 11.30am–2pm (except Tues) and 7–8.15pm Wed–Sun. Beer garden. Dogs welcome.

OPEN *11.30am–3pm Mon–Fri (closed Tues lunch); 7–11pm Mon–Fri; 11.30am–11pm Sat–Sun.*

NORTH DUFFIELD

The King's Arms

Main Street, North Duffield, Selby,
North Yorkshire YO8 5RG
☎ *(01757) 288492* Gail and Glen

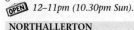 Freehouse with Black Sheep Bitter plus up to three guests, such as Timothy Taylor Landlord or ales from Greene King, Adnams or local independent brewers.

Village pub with one bar, beamed ceilings and inglenook fireplace. Bar food available, plus restaurant menu during evenings only. Children allowed. Beer garden.

OPEN *12–11pm (10.30pm Sun).*

NORTHALLERTON

Tithe Bar & Brasserie

2 Friarage Street, Northallerton, North Yorkshire
DL6 1DP
☎ *(01609) 778482* Louise Walker
www.markettowntaverns.co.uk

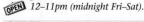 Timothy Taylor Landlord and a beer from Durham Brewery. The four regularly changing guests might come from Black Sheep, Hambleton, Moorhouse's, Salamander, Rudgate, Ossett, Wentworth, Phoenix, Rooster's, Daleside, Abbeydale, Elland or a range of other breweries. Plus Belgian, German and world bottled beers.

Built in the old tithe barn of Northallerton, this is a traditional real ale house. Food available 12–2.30pm and 6–7.30pm Mon–Sat and 12–3pm Sun in the bar. The restaurant is open 7–9.30pm Tues–Sat. Well-behaved children welcome. Bar games, occasional live music. At the northern end of town, just off the High Street.

OPEN *12–11pm (midnight Fri–Sat).*

OGDEN

The Causeway Foot Inn

13 Causeway Foot, Ogden, Halifax,
West Yorkshire HX2 8XX
☎ *(01422) 240273* Terry Kelly
www.thecausewayfootinn.co.uk

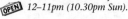 Six real ales, with regulars including Timothy Taylor Landlord, Black Sheep Ale and Bitter, and Goose Eye No Eye Deer. Two guests are rotated monthly.

An 18th-century coaching inn. No TV, no pool, no gambling machines. Cask Marque accredited, Black Sheep 'Flag Sheep' award. Freshly prepared food using traditional local produce served 6-9pm Wed–Fri; 12–3 and 6-9pm Sat; 12–7pm Sun. Dogs welcome. Dog walking club, Tues. The pub's large field is often used for bikers' weekends (no scooters), dog shows etc. Beer garden, car park. Adjacent to Ogden Water Country Park. On the main Keighley–Halifax road (A629).

OPEN *Closed Mon except bank holidays;*
6–11pm Tues, summer time only;
12–2.30pm and 5.30-11pm Wed–Fri;
12-11.30pm Sat; 12-7pm Sun.

OSSETT

The Brewer's Pride

Low Mill Road, Healey Road, Ossett,
West Yorkshire WF5 8ND
☎ *(01924) 273865* Sally Hastewell
www.brewers-pride.co.uk

Totally independent freehouse with nine real ales, including Rudgate Ruby Mild and Red Lion White Lion. The other beers are from a wide selection of micro-breweries. Phoenix, Rooster's, Oakham, Durham, Ossett, Goose Eye, Kelham Island and Red Lion are among the favourites. Beers range from 3.8% to at least 6% ABV, offering a choice of light, hoppy ales, medium-colour malty ones, rich, dark porters and stouts, and 'top of the shop' strong beers.

Traditional real ale house in a characterful old stone building in the old Healy Mills area. Wood and stone floors, open fires, one main bar, lounge and tap room. Beer garden. Food available 12–2pm Mon–Sat and themed Wednesday evenings 7–9.30pm. Dogs and children allowed. Live music in summer, and annual August bank holiday beer festival.

OPEN *12–11pm (10.30pm Sun).*

The Red Lion

73 Dewsbury Road, Ossett, West Yorkshire
WF5 9NQ
☎ *(01924) 273487* Brian and Tricia Battye

A brewpub, home of Red Lion Ales, with White Lion and at least one other home brew always available, plus one guest, changed weekly.

A traditional old English pub with low ceiling, beams, brasses, dining area, and outside seating between the brewery and the pub. Food available 12–2pm and 6–9pm Mon–Sat, with Sunday roasts available 12–4pm. Children allowed. Located off J40 of the M1, towards Dewsbury.

OPEN *12–11pm (10.30pm Sun).*

OTLEY

The Junction Inn

44 Bandgate, Otley, West Yorkshire LS21 1AD
☎ *(01943) 463233* Tony Grey

A Scottish and Newcastle tied house. Timothy Taylor Best and Landlord, Theakston Best and Old Peculier, Caledonian Deuchars IPA. Six guests, changed every one–two weeks. Examples include Fuller's London Pride, Sharp's Doom Bar, Wadworth 6X and Everards Pitch Black.

Traditional one-roomed pub with a tiled floor and open fire. Enclosed, heated and lit courtyard drinking area. Two beer festivals held each year. Tues: live music. Wed: quiz. No food. Situated equidistant from Leeds, Bradford and Harrogate.

OPEN *11am–11pm Mon–Thurs; 11am–*
midnight Fri–Sat; 12–10.30pm Sun.

OUTWOOD

The Kirklands Hotel

605 Leeds Road, Outwood, Wakefield,
West Yorkshire WF1 2LU
☎ *(01924) 826666* Gareth and Fiona Tate

Beers from the Old Mill Brewery always on offer, including a mild and a bitter, plus a guest, changed monthly.

Olde-worlde hotel built in 1850 with open bar featuring brick fireplaces and a library plus a restaurant. Food served 6–9pm Tues–Sat, 12–2pm Wed–Sat and 12–3pm Sun. Children welcome, but no special facilities. Car park. Private room for hire. Situated on main Wakefield to Leeds road, next door to the church in Outwood. Five letting rooms available.

OPEN *11.30am–11pm Mon–Thurs; 11.30am–midnight Fri–Sat; 12–11pm Sun.*

PICKHILL

Nags Head

Pickhill, Thirsk, North Yorkshire YO7 4JG
☎ *(01845) 567391* Edward Boynton
www.nagsheadpickhill.co.uk

Genuine freehouse, three or four real ales available and always including Black Sheep Bitter, Theakstons Black Bull and York Brewery Guzzler. Guest beers might be Deuchars IPA, Holmfirth IPA, Harviestoun Bitter and Twisted and a variety of Theakstons brews.

Former 17th-century coaching inn with well furnished rooms. Excellent food and ales. Monthly wine selection. Beer garden, putting green, quoits and boules. Food served 12–2pm and 6–9.30pm. 1 mile east of A1, 4 miles north of A1/A46 junction.

OPEN *11am–11pm.*

PONTEFRACT

The Counting House

Swales Yard, Pontefract, West Yorkshire WF8 1DG
☎ *(01977) 600388* Helen Clayworth

No permanent beers, just a changing range of up to eight ales from breweries such as Black Sheep, Jennings and Old Mill.

Town pub on two levels in a medieval building. Food available at lunchtime only. Children allowed.

OPEN *11am–3pm and 7–11pm (10.30pm Sun).*

Shoulder of Mutton

Main Street, Kirk Smeaton, Pontefract,
West Yorkshire WF8 3JY
☎ *(01977) 620 348* Gerald Tindal

Black Sheep Best Bitter plus one guest that changes every six weeks and might well be something from the Old Mill Brewery.

Village freehouse built in the 17th century. Two bars with open fires, a children's area and a beer garden with a smoking shelter. Large car park. Next to Brockdale Nature Reserve with good local walks. Just off A1 at the Wentbridge turn-off.

OPEN *5pm–12 Mon–Thurs (12–2pm in summer only); 12–12 Fri–Sun.*

POOL-IN-WHARFEDALE

The Hunter's Inn

Harrogate Road, Pool-in-Wharfedale, Nr Otley,
North Yorkshire LS21 2PS
☎ *(0113) 284 1090* Carrie Holt

Nine beers available, including Fuller's London Pride, Theakston Best, Ossett Silver King, Everards Tiger and Hook Norton Old Hooky, plus regularly changing guests.

Roadside diner dating from the 1960s, now a warm, friendly pub with plenty of character. No food. Children welcome until 9pm. Large car park, beer garden with country views. Beer festivals. Between Harrogate and Pool-in-Wharfedale.

OPEN *11am–11pm Mon–Sat; 12–10.30pm Sun.*

PUDSEY

The Commercial Hotel

48 Chapetown, Pudsey, West Yorkshire LS28 8BS
☎ *(0113) 257 7153* Michelle Farr

Freehouse serving a range of real ales.

A lively town pub with Friday evening disco, Saturday evening 60s and 70s music and live entertainment once a month. Free dripping and black pudding on the bar on Sundays. Patio. No children.

OPEN *All day, every day.*

QUARMBY

Field Head

219 Quarmby Road, Quarmby, West Yorkshire
HD3 4FB
☎ *(01484) 654581* John Timmins (landlord)/
Ivan Smith (manager)

Four real guest ales, including Jennings Cumberland and guest beers rotated weekly.

Community village pub built in 1920, with views across the Colne Valley. Separate tap room for darts, pool room in the conservatory. No food. Children welcome. Beer garden. Large car park.

OPEN *4–11pm Mon–Fri; 12–11pm Sat; 12–10.30pm Sun.*

RIPON

The Drovers Inn

Dallowgill, Ripon, North Yorkshire HG4 3RH
☎ *(01765) 658510* Steve Kemp

Freehouse serving Old Mill Bitter, Black Sheep Bitter and Hambleton Bitter.

A small, friendly, one-room pub on the edge of the moor. Food served 6.30–8.30pm Tues–Fri, 12–2.30pm and 6.30–8.30pm Sat–Sun. Outdoor seating. Car park. Close to Pateley Bridge and Masham.

OPEN *Closed Mon except bank holidays. Opening hours vary to suit the needs of the rural community.*

One Eyed Rat

*51 Allhallowgate, Ripon, North Yorkshire
HG4 1LQ*
☎ *(01765) 607704* David Hamby

Black Sheep Bitter plus five guests, constantly changing, which may be from Rooster's, Durham, Hambleton, Rudgate, Copper Dragon or any other independent brewery. No beers from national breweries served. A real freehouse.

Unspoilt, terraced pub, very popular. Superb beer garden. No music, no TV, but fine ales and good conversation. Children allowed in beer garden only. Regular summer barbecues. Beer festivals, monthly quiz, curry trips. Just off the market square in the centre of Ripon.

OPEN *5–11pm Mon–Thurs; 11am–11pm Fri–Sat; 12–10.30pm Sun (plus 11am–11pm bank holidays).*

RIPPONDEN

The Old Bridge Inn

*Priest Lane, Ripponden, Sowerby Bridge,
West Yorkshire HX6 4DF*
☎ *(01422) 822595*
Tim and Lindsay Eaton Walker

Genuine freehouse serving Timothy Taylor Golden Best, Best Bitter and Landlord plus three guest beers rotated weekly from breweries such as Oakham, Moorhouse's, Newby Wyke, Copper Dragon, Ossett, Saltaire and Howard Town.

Historic pub in lovely riverside setting. Open fires in winter and flowers in summer. Award-winning window boxes and hanging baskets all year round. Homemade food prepared on the premises served 12–2pm every day and 6.30–9.30pm Mon–Fri. Car park. Children welcome until 8.30pm.

OPEN *12–3pm and 5.30–11pm Mon–Fri; 12–11pm Sat; 12–10.30pm Sun.*

ROBIN HOOD'S BAY

The Victoria Hotel

*Station Road, Robin Hood's Bay, North Yorkshire
YO22 4RL*
☎ *(01947) 880205*
Paul Goodenough and Lydia Gibson
www.thevictoriahotel.info

Two brews from Camerons plus three frequently changing guests from a wide range of breweries.

Victorian pub built in 1897 with a large bar and scenic views of the bay. Food is available every session except Sunday evenings and Christmas and New Year. Ten en-suite letting bedrooms. Beer garden, patio area, car park for residents. In the middle of the village, at the top of the bank.

OPEN *Lunchtime and evenings Mon–Thurs; all day Fri–Sun. Hotel open mid-Jan–mid-Dec.*

ROTHERHAM

The Blue Coat

The Crofts, Rotherham, South Yorkshire S60 2DJ
☎ *(01709) 539500* Garry Carr
www.jdwetherspoon.co.uk

Wetherspoon's pub with nine real ales, including Marston's Pedigree, Greene King Abbot and IPA plus guests changed every couple of days from breweries such as Abbeydale, Kelham Island, Wentworth, Acorn, Milestone and Saltaire.

Former school now part of the Wetherspoon's chain, this pub continues to impress. Rotherham CAMRA Pub of the Year 2006, 2007 and 2008. Food served 9am–11pm. Monthly 'meet the brewer' nights. Children welcome.

OPEN *9am–midnight Sun–Thurs; 9am–1am Fri–Sat.*

The Waverley

*Brinsworth Road, Catcliffe, Rotherham,
South Yorkshire S60 5RW*
☎ *(01709) 360906* Ron Woodthorpe

Freehouse with four hand pumps serving a range of guest brews. Regular breweries supported include Glentworth, Slaters (Eccleshall), Banks's and Timothy Taylor.

A large suburban pub with separate lounge and children's room, garden and play area. Disabled access and toilets. Food available at lunchtimes and evenings. Children allowed in children's room only.

OPEN *12–4pm and 6–11.30pm Mon–Fri; all day Sat; 12–4pm and 7–10.30pm Sun.*

ROTHWELL

The Rosebud Inn

*Westfield Road, Rothwell, West Yorkshire
LS26 0SJ*
☎ *(0113) 393 4808* Nigel K Ball

Punch Taverns inn offering up to seven real ales. The selection varies, according to Punch's Finest Cask scheme, and is complemented by other guest ales.

Semi-rural, traditional local, over 100 years old. One lounge bar, one bar with real fire. Bar snacks available. Children welcome until 7pm. Large beer garden. Car park. Easy access to Leeds (10 minutes), near Carlton, just off the main Wakefield road.

OPEN *5pm–12 Mon–Fri; 12–12 Sat; 12–11pm Sun.*

SCARBOROUGH

Cellars

*35–7 Valley Road, Scarborough,
North Yorkshire YO11 2LX*
☎ *(01723) 367158* Brian Witty
www.scarborough-brialene.co.uk

Freehouse with Black Sheep Riggwelter and a Copper Dragon beer plus four regularly changing guests from breweries such as Durham, Archers, York, Rooster's, Anglo-Dutch and many others from all parts of the country.

A family-run basement real ale bar in the cellars of an elegant Victorian building. Restaurant and holiday apartments above.

Bar and restaurant food available 12–2pm and 5–9pm, including what is claimed to be the best Sunday lunch in town! Children welcome. Live music Thursdays and Saturdays, open mic night on Wednesdays. Patio, car park. Two beer festivals a year. On the main road to the seafront.

OPEN *Summer: 11am–11pm Mon–Sat; 12–10.30pm Sun. Winter: 4–11pm Mon–Tues; all day Wed–Sun.*

The Highlander Hotel
15–16 The Esplanade, Scarborough,
North Yorkshire YO11 2AF
☎ *(01723) 365627* Jim Hobbs

Five ales, including Black Sheep Bitter and Hancock's HB (brewed by Brains) plus guests changed every other night.

On the South Cliff Esplanade, a traditional pub with coal fire and real atmosphere. No gimmicks, just pleasant conversation. Beer garden, large function room available for hire. Food available 12–2pm every day and 5–7pm (except Tues). Tea room open 12–4pm. Six en-suite rooms. Hotel and restaurant open all year.

OPEN *11am–11pm.*

Indigo Alley
4 North Marine Road, Scarborough,
North Yorkshire YO12 7PD
☎ *(01723) 381900* Graham Forrest

Freehouse with six regularly changing guest beers, perhaps from Rooster's, Timothy Taylor, Kelham Island or Hambleton, but could be from anywhere in the UK (over 1,000 different ones in three years). Belgian beers such as Leffe (Brun and Blond) and Hoegaarden also stocked.

Wooden-floored, town-centre bar specialising in ever-changing guest beers and live music on Tues, Wed, Thurs and Sun evenings. No food. No children.

OPEN *3–11pm Mon–Fri; 1–11pm Sat; 1–10.30pm Sun. Extra hours Fri–Sun Jun–Sept.*

The North Riding Hotel
161–3 North Marine Road, Scarborough,
North Yorkshire YO12 7HU
☎ *(01723) 370004* Stuart and Karen Nielson

Tetley Bitter, Timothy Taylor Landlord and Caledonian Deuchars IPA plus at least three guest ales.

Taken over in August 2005 by the former landlord of The Cricketers, who is maintaining his reputation as a local real ale champion in the new venue. The first beer festival took place in October 2005 and they are repeated at least twice a year. Bar with large-screen TV, lounge and dining room. Food served at lunchtimes and evenings. Accommodation.

OPEN *From 12 every day.*

Old Scalby Mills Hotel
Scalby Mills Road, Scarborough,
North Yorkshire YO12 6RP
☎ *(01723) 500449* Keith Dufton

Five real ales. Wold Top North Bay Premium is made exclusively for the pub and Copper Dragon Black Gold is also a pemanent fixture, while the three guests, changed several times a week, come from a wide range of breweries.

A 17th-century converted watermill with the river at the side and the sea in front. Two bars with original stonework and beams, plus extensive outside seating areas. Food available 12–8pm. Children and dogs welcome. Situated near the Sea Life Centre.

OPEN *11am–4am.*

The Scholar
Somerset Terrace, Scarborough, North Yorkshire
☎ *(01723) 360084* John Bingham

Four real ales, including York Yorkshire Terrier, Charles Wells Bombardier and something from Durham or Daleside.

Hotel bar featuring a large drinking area with library bar and separate drinking area for those in the know! Home-cooked food served 12–2.30pm and 5.30–8.30pm. Regular jazz club. On the town side of the Bedford Hotel.

OPEN *12–3pm and 5.30–11pm Mon–Thurs; 12–11pm Fri–Sat; 12–10.30pm Sun.*

The Tap & Spile
94 Falsgrave Road, Scarborough, North Yorkshire
YO12 5AZ
☎ *(01723) 363837* IM Kilpatrick and V Office

Big Lamp Bitter, Everards Tiger, Timothy Taylor Landlord and Caledonian Deuchars IPA plus up to five guest beers and a real cider.

Lovely old coaching inn with low beams and old Yorkshire stone floor. Bar food available 11.30am–3pm Mon–Fri, 11.30am–4.30pm Sat, 12.30–3pm Sun. Car park, garden, children's room. Turn left out of the railway station, going towards the roundabout.

OPEN *11am–11pm.*

The Valley Bar
51 Valley Road, Scarborough, North Yorkshire
YO11 2LX
☎ *(01723) 372593* Linda and John Soden
www.valleybar.co.uk

Theakston Best and Wold Top Mars Magic are regularly featured, and there are eight guest ales, many from local micro-breweries. Eight real ciders and perries and 100 bottled Belgian beers.

Friendly, family-run pub in a Victorian villa. CAMRA National Cider and Perry Pub of the Year 2007 and local Town Pub of the Year 2007. Beer festivals every month in winter. Live music, quiz nights, occasional theatrical performances and large-screen TV. Pool and function room. Great value home-cooked food available most times of the day.

OPEN *11am–midnight.*

SELBY

The Albion Vaults

1 The Crescent, New Street, Selby,
North Yorkshire YO8 4PT
☎ (01757) 213817 Patrick Mellors

Old Mill Brewery tied house serving only Old Mill ales. Old Traditional and Bullion always available, plus either Old Curiosity, Springs Eternal or Nellie Dean.

Old dark-wood pub with brick fireplaces, taproom and lounge. Beer garden, disabled access. Food available at lunchtimes and evenings. Organises brewery tours of The Old Mill Brewery, which is four miles away, during October–April. Children allowed up to 7pm.

OPEN *12–11pm (10.30pm Sun).*

The Royal Oak

70 Ousegate, Selby, North Yorkshire YO8 4NJ
☎ (01757) 291163 Simon Compton

Three guest pumps with ales such as Timothy Taylor Landlord or Eccleshall Top Totty.

Real ale pub comprising a balance of the traditional and the modern: live music in a Grade II listed building with wooden floors and original beams. Beer garden. No food. Children allowed on Sunday afternoons only.

OPEN *12–11pm (10.30pm Sun).*

SHEFFIELD

The Bath Hotel

66–8 Victoria Street, Sheffield, South Yorkshire
S3 7QL
☎ (0114) 249 5151 CB Johnson

Freehouse with Moonshine, Barnsley Bitter and Imperial plus three weekly-changing guests.

A public house since 1908, this building originally dates back to 1863. Tap room and lounge bars. Food served lunchtimes Mon–Fri. Children welcome. Close to Sheffield university, botanical gardens and the cathedral, in the city centre.

OPEN *12–11pm Mon–Sat; 7–10.30pm Sun.*

The Broadfield

Abbeydale Road, Sheffield, South Yorkshire S7 1FR
☎ (0114) 255 0200
Hannah Creasy and Martin Bedford

Guests such as Greene King Old Speckled Hen, Wadworth 6X and brews from Kelham Island and Black Sheep. Only popular beers, such as Kelham Island Pale Rider, are repeated, and requests are encouraged!

A two-bar pub with snooker and pool room and beer garden. Just out of the city centre. Food available 12–7pm daily, plus Sunday breakfast at 11am. Children allowed if eating.

OPEN *11am–11pm Mon–Sat; 11am (for breakfast)–10.30pm Sun.*

The Coach & Horses

Sheffield Road, Dronfield, Sheffield,
South Yorkshire S18 2GD
☎ (01246) 413269 Catherine Mueller

A Thornbridge Brewery tied house serving a range of Thornbridge ales, which change weekly.

Owned by Sheffield Football Club with its own football pitch. Food served 12–2pm and 6–8.30pm. Beer patio. Car park.

OPEN *12–12.*

East House

19 Spital Hill, Sheffield, South Yorkshire S4 7LG
☎ (0114) 272 6916 Rita Fielding

Freehouse with Timothy Taylor Landlord and Abbeydale Moonshine among the beers always available, plus one guest such as Greene King Old Speckled Hen or Timothy Taylor Dark Mild or Golden Best.

Student pub situated conveniently close to the local curry houses! No food. Children allowed until 8pm.

OPEN *Closed during day; 6–11pm Mon–Sat; 7–10.30pm Sun.*

The Fat Cat

23 Alma Street, Sheffield, South Yorkshire
S3 8SA
☎ (0114) 249 4801
www.thefatcat.co.uk

Four beers from its own Kelham Island brewery and Timothy Taylor Landlord plus five alternating guests.

This olde-worlde pub is a Kelham Island Brewery tap, situated a short walk from the city centre. Voted UK Cask Ale Pub of the Year 2004 in the *Morning Advertiser*. No music, no fruit machines. Award-winning home-cooked food is served 12–8pm Mon–Sat and 12–3pm Sun, and always includes vegetarian and vegan dishes. Beer garden, open fires. Children- and animal-friendly. Privately owned and fiercely independent!

OPEN *12–12.*

The Frog & Parrot

Division Street, Sheffield, South Yorkshire S1 4GF
☎ (0114) 272 1280 Nick Simmonite

A brewpub with Roger and Out (formerly the Guinness Book of Records World's Strongest Beer!) always available in third-of-a pint measures, plus Timothy Taylor Landlord, Black Sheep Bitter and Greene King IPA. The two ever-changing guest ales will be from regional and micro-breweries around the country. Hoegaarden and the occasional cask-conditional lager also served.

Traditional, but light and airy, town pub in the heart of the cosmopolitan Devonshire Quarter. Good food served 12–8pm every day, and Freetrade coffee is always available. Located 100 yards from West Street Supertram stop.

OPEN *11am–11pm (10.30pm Sun).*

The Gardeners Rest

105 Neepsend Lane, Sheffield, South Yorkshire
S3 8AT
☎ *(0114) 272 4978* Pat Wilson

 Up to four beers on offer from the Sheffield Brewery (the pub is the brewery tap), plus Timothy Taylor Landlord, Golden Best, Dark Mild and Best Bitter, Wentworth Needle's Eye, WPA, Bradfield Blonde and Stout. The four guests are from breweries all over the UK. Draught continental beers also available, including a wheat beer and fruit beers.

A traditional backstreet pub with modern conservatory and beer garden on the river bank. No juke box but traditional pub games such as bar billiards. Disabled access and facilities. No food. Close to city centre and on bus and tram routes, but ring for directions if necessary.

OPEN *3–11pm Mon–Thurs; 12–11pm Fri–Sat; 12–10.30pm Sun.*

The Harlequin

108 Nursery Street, Sheffield, South Yorkshire
S3 8GG
☎ *(0114) 275 8195* Hannah Vessey
www.harlequin.dawnweb.co.uk

 A freehouse. Bradfield Farmer's Blonde plus four constantly changing guest ales. Guests may include Kelham Island Pale Rider, Thornbridge Jaipur or Abbeydale Brimstone.

The pub is around 200 years old and started life as a hotel before it was partly destroyed by flood in 1864. Flooded again in 2007, it overlooks the river and is near the canal and city centre. Food served 12–2pm. Two beer festivals each year and participates in the Philadelphia Beer and Blues Festival.

OPEN *11.30am–close.*

The Hillsborough Hotel

54–8 Langsett Road, Sheffield, South Yorkshire
S6 2UB
☎ *(0114) 232 2100* Wendy Douglas

Owned by Helen and Andrew Walker and home of the Crown Brewery, with eight pumps serving 40 different beers every week. Regular brews are Hillsborough Pale Ale, Stannington Stout and Loxley Gold.

Hotel with six en-suite rooms. Renamed in 1999, having been called the Hero and his Horse and then the Wellington. Quiet, traditional atmosphere with no juke box. Food served 12–7.30pm Mon–Sat and 12–3pm Sun. Quiz night on Tuesday, with free roast potatoes and the chance to win a gallon of beer! Folk night on Sunday. Regular beer festivals. Sun terrace and conservatory. On the Supertram route (Primrose View stop). Available for private functions.

OPEN *12–11pm Sun–Thurs; 12–12 Fri–Sat.*

Kelham Island Tavern

62 Russell Street, Sheffield,
South Yorkshire S3 8RW
☎ *(0114) 272 2482* Trevor Wraith
www.kelhamislandtavern.co.uk

Acorn Barnsley Bitter, Bradfield Farmer's Blonde and Pictish Brewers Gold usually available, plus up to 40 constantly changing guests each week spread over thirteen handpumps, Most brews come from micro-breweries and a mild and stout or porter always feature.

A traditional 19th-century freehouse with two rooms and an award-winning beer garden. Children welcome in the rear room and garden. Annual beer festival in mid-June. CAMRA Sheffield Pub of the Year 2004–2008 and regional CAMRA award 2004, 2007 and 2008, CAMRA National pub of the year 2008. Food served 12–3pm Mon–Sat. Follow north section of inner ring road (A61), signposted Kelham Island.

OPEN *12–11pm Mon–Thurs; 12–late Fri–Sun.*

The New Barrack Tavern

601 Penistone Road, Sheffield, South Yorkshire
S6 2GA
☎ *(0114) 234 9148*
Kevin and Stephanie Woods
www.tynemill.co.uk

Tynemill house with 11 ales regularly served, including Abbeydale Moonshine, Castle Rock Harvest Pale and Elsie Mo, Acorn Barnsley Bitter and seven guests, changed weekly.

Roadhouse-style pub built in the early 1930s, with a tap room and a main lounge with log fire. Food served 11am–3pm and 5–9pm Mon–Sat; 12–4pm (carvery) and 7–9pm Sun. There is a takeaway menu on Friday and Saturday evenings 10pm–12. Large beer garden. Live music Fri, Sat and some Sun. Room available for small private functions. Children welcome.

OPEN *11am–11pm Mon–Thurs; 11am–midnight Fri–Sat; 12–11pm Sun.*

The Old Grindstone

3 Crookes, Sheffield, South Yorkshire S10 1UA
☎ *(0114) 266 0322* Sarah Lyon

Six guest ales from breweries such as Greene King, Charles Wells, Timothy Taylor and Wadworth. The beers are changed every firkin.

One-bar local community pub with three log fires, built in 1845. Main part has a traditional feel, but has been extended at the back to make a sports area. Food available 12–8pm, with full carvery Wed–Sun. Two pool tables, a three-quarter snooker table, Sky Sports, large and small screens. Beer patio. Children welcome until 9pm. On the corner of Lydgate Lane and Crookes.

OPEN *12–11pm Sun–Thurs; 12–12 Fri–Sat.*

The Ranmoor Inn

330 Fulwood Road, Sheffield, South Yorkshire
S10 3GD
☎ *(0114) 230 1325*
Vanessa and Nigel Williams

An Enterprise Inns pub. Timothy Taylor Landlord, Abbeydale Moonshine, and Bradfield Farmer's Bitter and Farmers Blonde. Also one guest, from a local or Yorkshire micro brewer.

A 200-year-old stone building with adjoining stables and yard. One bar with comfortable traditional feel, with open fires and decorative cut-glass panels and windows. Outside drinking area in the stable yard. Food served 12–2pm Tues–Sat. Off the A57.

OPEN *11.30am–11pm.*

Sheaf View Hotel

25 Gleadless Road, Sheffield, South Yorkshire
S2 3AA
☎ *(0114) 249 6455* James Birkett

Bradfield Farmer's Blonde, Kelham Island Easy Rider and Wentworth WPA plus five constantly changing guest ales from around the country, always including a dark beer. Examples of guests include Whim Hartington IPA, Fenland Osier Cutter, Pictish Porter, Rooster's YPA, Williams Gold and O'Hanlon's Port Stout, to name but a few! Continental beers and scrumpy also available on draught, plus a wide range of imported bottled beers and around 60–70 malt whiskies.

A community pub with conservatory and beer garden. Outside covered smoking area. Children allowed in the garden only. Fresh homemade sandwiches Mon–Sat. Quiz night on Wed. Car park. Disabled access. Can be difficult to find so call for directions.

OPEN *12–11.30pm.*

The Wellington Inn

1 Henry Street, Infirmary Road, Sheffield,
South Yorkshire S3 7EQ
☎ *(0114) 249 2295*

Up to eight regularly changing guest beers, including a pale, hoppy bitter, a mild and a stout or porter. Beers are mainly from Glentworth, Pictish, Millstone, Salamander and Ossett, plus seasonal specials from all over the country. Also serve Thatcher's cider and around 15 Belgian bottled beers. There is a micro-brewery at the rear of the pub which brews on a small scale, mainly for festivals.

B uilt in 1842, a largely unspoilt street-corner local with two rooms. No music or fruit machines. On-street parking. Real fire in cold weather. Beer garden. Occasional beer-themed events held. Situated 100 yards from Shalesmoor Supertram stop. Adjacent to junction of A61 and B6079, one mile north of the city centre.

OPEN *12–3pm and 5–11pm Mon–Thurs;*
12–11pm Fri–Sat; 12–3.30pm and
7–10.30pm Sun.

Fanny's Ale & Cider House

63 Saltaire Road, Shipley, Nr Bradford,
West Yorkshire
☎ *(01274) 591419* S Marcus Lund

Timothy Taylor Golden Best and Landlord plus eight guest beers such as Fuller's London Pride, Timothy Taylor Ram Tam, Black Sheep Bitter, Glentworth Whispers, Daleside Monkey Wrench, Rooster's Yankee or Cream and many others.

O lde-worlde alehouse with wooden floorboards and open fire, full of brewery memorabilia. Gas lighting still used in the lounge bar. Extra seating area upstairs. Public car park nearby. Children welcome at lunchtimes only.

OPEN *5–11pm Mon; 11.30am–11pm Tues–Sat;*
12–10.30pm Sun.

The Old Tramshed

199 Bingley Road, Saltaire, Shipley,
West Yorkshire BD18 4DH
☎ *(01274) 582111* Oliver Bache

Eight real ales usually on offer at this freehouse, from a range of independent breweries. Six of the beers are rotated weekly.

C onverted tramshed with impressive glass entrance, balcony with seating, and outside tables. Food, ranging from bar snacks and business lunches to full à la carte menu, available all day Tues–Sat, with early bird offers 5–9pm (7pm Fri–Sat); Sunday lunch also served. Parking for 100 cars. Handy for exploring Saltaire village (a UN World Heritage Site). On the A650, on Saltaire roundabout.

OPEN *12–12.*

Cock & Bottle

30 Swadford Street, Skipton, North Yorkshire
BD23 1RD
☎ *(01756) 794734*
Erik and Lorraine Wilkinson
www.cockandbottle.co.uk

Enterprise Inns house with Tetley's Cask Bitter and three constantly changing guests from various brewers nationwide.

O ne-roomed, small town-centre pub dating back to 1685 with low ceilings and log fires. Food served 12–2.30pm and 5–9pm Mon–Sun. Beer garden and seating area. Children welcome. Opposite the main post office on Swadford Street, at the end of the High Street. Close to canal. Sightseeing tours and boat hire nearby.

OPEN *Closed Mon; 12–10.30pm Tues–Thurs*
(11pm Wed); 12–12 Fri; 11am–midnight
Sat; 12–10.30pm Sun.

The Narrow Boat

38 Victoria Street, Skipton, North Yorkshire
BD23 1JE
☎ *(01756) 797922* Tim and Sharron Hughes
www.markettowntaverns.co.uk

Eight real ales typically served, with Timothy Taylor Landlord, Black Sheep Bitter, Caledonian Deuchars IPA and two hand pumps dedicated to the local Copper Dragon brewery plus four regularly changing guests, from local breweries such as Goose Eye, Salamander, Durham and Daleside whenever possible. Also Erdinger WeissBier (a German wheat beer), a guest Belgian beer and a range of Belgian, German and world bottled beers.

A traditional ale and wine bar with mezzanine floor. The pub has been extended and offers a larger eating/drinking area and a private function room. No juke box, no games machines. Food available 12–2.30pm and 5.30–8pm Tues–Sat, plus 12–4pm Sun. Children allowed if dining. Well-behaved dogs welcome. Situated on a quiet cobbled street off the high street, close to the canal basin and train station.

OPEN *12–11pm.*

SNAITH
Brewers Arms

10 Pontefract Road, Snaith, Nr Goole, East Yorkshire DN14 9JS
☎ *(01405) 862404*

The brewery tap for the Old Mill Brewery with Old Mill Bitter, Old Curiosity, Bullion and seasonal and occasional brews.

I mpressive brewery tap offering good food at lunchtimes and evenings (all day at weekends) and en-suite accommodation.

OPEN *11.30am–3pm and 5–11pm Mon–Fri; 11.30am–11pm Sat; 12–10.30pm Sun.*

SOWERBY BRIDGE
The Moorcock Inn

Norland, Sowerby Bridge, West Yorkshire HX6 3RP
☎ *(01422) 832103 Mr Kitson*

Freehouse with Samuel Smith Old Brewery Bitter plus two guest ales including, perhaps, Coach House Innkeeper's Special Reserve or Phoenix Old Oak Bitter.

A one-bar country pub with wooden beams, restaurant and outside area. Food available at lunchtimes and evenings. Children allowed. Disabled access.

OPEN *12–3pm and 5.30–11pm (10.30pm Sun).*

The Moorings

Canal Basin, Sowerby Bridge, West Yorkshire HX6 2AG
☎ *(01422) 833940 Anthony Baker*
www.themooringspub.co.uk

Black Sheep Bitter and Special, Timothy Taylor Landlord and Greene King Ruddles County plus two constantly changing guests.

F riendly, medium-sized, traditional-style pub with good quality beers, food and service. Cask Marque approved. Beams, stone walls, wooden floors. Outside seating on canalside. Food available 12–2.30pm and 6–9pm Mon–Fri, 12–9pm Sat and 12–7pm Sun. Children allowed if dining. Car park. Large parties catered for. Two miles outside Halifax.

OPEN *12–11pm (10.30pm Sun).*

The Navigation Inn

Chapel Lane, Sowerby Bridge, West Yorkshire HX6 3LF
☎ *(01422) 831636 John and Nicola Goldsmith*

Timothy Taylor Landlord and Black Sheep Bitter are among the beers usually available, plus a guest, changed monthly.

C harming canalside pub with historic fireplace dating from before 1722. Two beer gardens, plus heated and lit smoking shelter. Pool, darts. Homemade food available 12–2.30pm and 5.30–8pm Mon–Sat and 12–6pm Sun and bank holidays. Car park. Just off the A58, two miles outside Halifax heading towards Rochdale.

OPEN *12–11pm.*

The Works

12 Hollins Mill Lane, Sowerby Bridge, West Yorkshire HX6 2QG
☎ *(01422) 834821 Sara-Jo Cooper*

Freehouse with three ales from Timothy Taylor plus six constantly rotating guest beers from micro-breweries across the country.

T his old engineering/joinery workshop is situated on the side of the canal. It was converted to a real ale house in 2005 and was awarded the CAMRA national award for 'Best Conversion' in 2007. Food (not your typical pub grub!) served 12–2.30pm and 5–8pm Mon–Fri, 12–5pm Sat, 10.30am–2.30pm Sunday brunch. Wed night is 'Gita's curry night'. Private room available for hire. Car park. Disabled facilities. Dogs welcome. Outside catering service available. Quiz night Tues, live acoustic music Thurs. Beer garden. No loud music – conversation friendly! Monday is host to 'Phoebe's Night', for young adults with learning difficulties. Located opposite the swimming baths.

OPEN *12–11pm Mon–Sat; 10.30am–10.30pm Sun.*

STAITHES
Captain Cook Inn

60 Staithes Lane, Staithes, Saltburn-by-the-Sea, North Yorkshire TS13 5AD
☎ *(01947) 840200*
www.captaincookinn.co.uk

Rudgate Viking and up to four guest brews from micro-breweries nationwide.

F ormerly the Station Hotel, set in the fishing village that was home to Captain Cook. Food served lunchtimes and evenings. There are three beer festivals every year, with 30 ales. The first, in April, commemorates St George; the one in July or August coincides with the village lifeboat celebrations; the third is at Hallowe'en, and is themed accordingly. Live music most weekends, with traditional jazz on last Saturday of each month. Children welcome. Garden and accommodation.

OPEN *11am–11pm.*

STAVELEY

The Royal Oak

Main Street, Staveley, Nr Knaresborough,
North Yorkshire HG5 9LD
☎ *(01423) 340267* Steve Wharton

 Black Sheep Bitter, Thwaites Bitter, Timothy Taylor Landlord and a Rudgate brew could well be the four real ales available. The two guests from small independent breweries change every week.

Typical country pub, cosy, friendly, with open fires and two bars. Bar and restaurant food available at lunchtimes and evenings Tues–Sat, and 12–8pm Sun (no food on Monday). Car park, garden, children's play area. Two miles from the A6055.

OPEN *12–3pm and 5–11pm Mon–Sat;*
12–10.30pm Sun.

STOKESLEY

The White Swan

1 West End, Stokesley, Middlesbrough,
North Yorkshire TS9 5BL
☎ *(01642) 710263* June Skipp

 A brewpub with the full range of Captain Cook Brewery beers always available. Also guests such as Everards Tiger and Shepherd Neame Spitfire.

An 18th-century market town pub with one bar, open fire, background music and traditional pub games. Brewery on premises, tours available. Annual cheese and ale festival (30 cheeses and 24 ales) on Easter weekend. Close to the North York Moors.

OPEN *11.30am–3pm and 5–11pm Mon–Thurs;*
11.30am–11pm Fri–Sat; 12–3pm and
7–10.30pm Sun.

SUTTON UPON DERWENT

St Vincent Arms

Main Street, Sutton upon Derwent, East Yorkshire
☎ *(01904) 608349* Simon Hopwood

Fuller's Chiswick, London Pride and ESB plus Timothy Taylor Landlord, Old Mill Bitter, York Yorkshire Terrier and Charles Wells Bombardier always available. One rotating guest changed every week.

About 200 years old, with white-washed walls. Two bars, four rooms, open fires. Bar and restaurant food available 12–2pm and 7–9.30pm. Car park, beer garden. Children allowed. On main road through village.

OPEN *11.30am–3pm and 6–11pm Mon–Sat;*
12–3pm and 7–10.30pm Sun.

THIXENDALE

Cross Keys Inn

Thixendale, Nr Malton, North Yorkshire YO17 9TG
☎ *(01377) 288272* Paddy Clooney and Mary and Steve Anstey

Freehouse with Tetley Bitter and Jennings Bitter plus one rotating guest.

One-bar pub situated in the heart of the Yorkshire Wolds. Food served 12–2pm and 6.30–9pm Mon–Fri; 12–2.30pm and 6.30–9pm Sat; 12–2.30pm and 7–9pm Sun. Accommodation available in three en-suite bedrooms. Beer garden. Children over the age of 14 welcome in the pub. Located 10 miles south-east of Malton, 12 miles west of Driffield. Dogs allowed in garden. Ideal location for exploring the Yorkshire Wolds. Nearby attractions include Sledmere House, Castle Howard and Burton Agnes.

OPEN *12–3pm and 6–11pm Mon–Fri; 12–4pm*
and 6–11pm Sat; 12–3pm and 7–
10.30pm Sun.

THORNE

Canal Tavern

South Parade, Thorne, Doncaster,
South Yorkshire DN8 5DZ
☎ *(01405) 813688* D and D Merrigton

 Freehouse with three guest ales changing weekly and not repeated if at all possible. Examples have included Thwaites Bloomin' Ale, Greene King Triumph and Marston's Pedigree.

Two-bar canalside country pub with dining area. Coal fires in winter, waterside beer garden. Food available at lunchtimes and evenings. Children allowed, if eating.

OPEN *All day, every day.*

THORNTON WATLASS

The Buck Inn

Thornton Watlass, Ripon, North Yorkshire
HG4 4AH
☎ *(01677) 422461* Mike Fox

 Five real ales, including Black Sheep and Theakston brews.

Traditional country pub overlooking the village cricket pitch. Open fire. Food available at lunchtimes and evenings. En-suite accommodation. Car park, beer garden, children's play area. Regular live jazz. Between Bedale and Masham, ten miles north of Ripon.

OPEN *All day, every day.*

THORNTON-IN-LONSDALE

The Marton Arms Hotel

Thornton-in-Lonsdale, Nr Ingleton,
North Yorkshire LA6 3PB
☎ *(01524) 241281* Graham Wright
www.martonarms.co.uk

 Freehouse with 15 real ales. The selection changes every week but Timothy Taylor Golden Best, Caledonian Deuchars IPA, Black Sheep Bitter, Theakston Best and a Dent brew are fixtures. A selection of over 300 malt whiskies also available.

A 17th-century coaching inn, now a Grade II listed country house hotel with 13 rooms. Patio and garden. Children allowed. Food served 12–2.30pm and 5.30–9pm Mon–Fri, all day Sat–Sun and bank holidays. Car parking. Handy for the Three Peaks in classic Yorkshire Dales country. Just off the A65.

OPEN *12–11pm (10.30pm Sun).*

THRESHFIELD

Old Hall Inn

Threshfield, Grassington, North Yorkshire BD23 5HB
☎ *(01756) 752441* H Walters
www.oldhallinnandcottages.co.uk

 Timothy Taylor Landlord, John Smiths Cask, Theakston's Best Bitter plus one guest, changed monthly.

Traditional Dales pub with dining room, patio and beer garden. Food served 12–3pm and 6–9pm Tues–Thurs; 12–3pm and 6–10pm Fri–Sat; 12–4pm Sun. Two restaurants, two car parks. Children and dogs welcome. Four en-suite double rooms, two cottages. On the main street of Threshfield.

OPEN *12–12.*

TOCKWITH

The Spotted Ox

Westfield Road, Tockwith, York, North Yorkshire YO26 7PY
☎ *(01423) 358387* Terry and Sue Fellows

 Freehouse with a selection of three real ales. Timothy Taylor Landlord is among the regulars, plus a weekly-changing guest.

Country pub with a snug and tap room. Food available at lunchtimes and evenings every day. Beer garden, car park. Forge for hire to the rear. Children allowed. Handy for Wetherby racecourse.

OPEN *Lunchtimes and evenings Mon–Wed; all day Thurs–Sat.*

TODMORDEN

The Masons Arms

1 Bacup Road, Todmorden, West Yorkshire OL14 7PN
☎ *(01706! 812180* Glyn Schofield
www.themasonsarms.biz

Copper Dragon house with five ales. Copper Dragon Best Bitter, Golden Pippin and Black Gold, plus Tetley's cask, are permanently featured. There is also a guest, changed weekly.

A traditional drinkers' freehouse dating from 1840, with beamed ceiling and real fire. Small selection of home-cooked food served 12–6pm every day. Children welcome. Small beer garden. Close to Rochdale Canal. At the junction of Bacup Road and Rochdale Road, next to the viaduct.

OPEN *12–close.*

UPPERTHONG

The Royal Oak

19 Towngate, Upperthong, Holmfirth, West Yorkshire HD9 3UX
☎ *(01484) 683450* Paul and Ann Bratt

Timothy Taylor Landlord plus a weekly guest, perhaps Caledonian Deuchars IPA.

A 200-year-old olde-worlde village pub with beamed ceiling and fireplaces. The walls are decorated with lots of plates and local scenes. Food available in the conservatory,
which seats 38, 5.30–8.30pm Tues–Sat and 12–4pm Sun. There is a chef's specials board, and an early bird offer 5.30–7.30pm. Children allowed. No dogs. Small car park. Call for directions.

OPEN *12–12 (11pm Sun).*

WAKEFIELD

Fernandes Brewery Tap

The Old Malt House, Kirkgate, Wakefield, West Yorkshire WF1 1UA
☎ *(01924) 369547* Maureen James

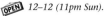 Two Fernandes brews plus six guests, changed daily.

Original old malt house built in 1922 by Louis Fernandes. The micro-brewery was opened in 1997 and the one-bar Brewery Tap on the upper floor two years later. Interesting decor incorporating old pub signs and pictures of brewers. Sandwiches served lunchtimes Fri–Sat. No children. Two public car parks nearby. Only 400 metres from Kirkgate station.

OPEN *11am–11pm.*

Harry's Bar

107B Westgate, Wakefield, West Yorkshire WF1 1EL
☎ *(01924) 373773* Ian Fisher

A freehouse serving seven real ales. Red Lion Chardonnayle, Ossett Silver King and Timothy Taylor Landlord. Four guests, changed twice a week, from brewers such as Leeds, Castle Rock, Red Lion, Anglo-Dutch, Elland, Crouch Vale and Copper Dragon.

One large bar with a real fire, relatively new, but still with plenty of character. A self-proclaimed real ale haven in the centre of Wakefield! Large heated smoking and patio area. Parking. No food. Located down an alleyway opposite Westgate railway station.

OPEN *5pm–close Mon–Sat; 12–12 Sun.*

Henry Boon's

130 Westgate, Wakefield, West Yorkshire WF2 9SR
☎ *(01924) 378126*
Barbera Cudworth and Russell Brennan

Part of the HB Clark's group of pubs. Timothy Taylor Landlord, Clark's Classic Blonde, Westgate Gold and a seasonal or special. Customers are consulted over the choice of guest, which may be a Clark's seasonal ale.

City-centre pub with a friendly local atmosphere and chatty bar staff. Decorated in an old style with classic wood and brass. Food served 9am–3pm Mon–Sat. Two function rooms. Located five minutes down the hill from Westgate railway station, opposite PC World.

OPEN *11am–11pm Mon–Thurs; 11am–midnight Fri; 11am–1am Sat; 12–10.30pm Sun.*

Kings Arms

Heath, Wakefield, West Yorkshire WF1 5SL
☎ *(01924) 377527* Alan Tate

 HB Clark pub serving Tetley, Timothy Taylor Landlord, Clark's Classic Blonde and a monthly-changing guest from Clark's.

Country pub with separate restaurant. Food served 12–2pm and 6–9.30pm Mon–Fri, 12–2.30pm and 6–9.30pm Sat, 12–8.30pm Sun. Caters for private parties and special occasions.

OPEN *All day, every day.*

The White Hart

77 Westgate End, Wakefield, West Yorkshire WF2 9RL
☎ *(01924) 375887* Alison Lund

 Two to four real ales rotated monthly, perhaps including Black Sheep Bitter and Greene King Old Speckled Hen.

Traditional alehouse with flagstone floors and real log fires in winter. All-year-round beer garden, which is covered and heated in winter. Sandwiches and pork pies served. Children welcome. Five minutes from the station.

OPEN *2–11.30pm Mon–Thurs; noon–1.30am Fri–Sat; 12–11.30pm Sun.*

WALSDEN

The Cross Keys Inn

649 Rochdale Road, Walsden, Todmorden, West Yorkshire OL14 6SX
☎ *(01706) 815185* Bayram Pallauus

 Timothy Taylor Landlord, Jennings Cumberland, Banks's Original and Boddingtons usually available.

Lively pub, set on the side of the Rochdale Canal. One bar with beer garden. Food served 12–2pm and 5–9pm Mon–Sat, 12–8pm Sun. Children welcome. Twelve miles from Rochdale.

OPEN *12–11pm (10.30pm Sun).*

WALTON

New Inn

144 Shay Lane, Walton, Wakefield, West Yorkshire WF2 6LA
☎ *(01924) 255447* Tommy Turtle
www.newinnwalton.co.uk

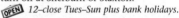 John Smith's, Timothy Taylor Landlord, Leeds Pale and Copper Dragon Best Bitter plus one rotating guest from local breweries, changed two to three times a week. Examples include beers from Ossett, Leeds, Clark's, Bowland, Old Bear and many more.

An 18th-century old village pub with one bar. Extremely friendly atmosphere with wide-ranging customer base. Food served Tues–Sun. Beer garden, car park. Live music and quiz nights. First beer and music festival held summer 2008. Folk music night every Weds. The only pub in Walton, three miles south of Wakefield.

OPEN *12–12.*

WATH-UPON-DEARNE

The Church House

Montgomery Square, Wath-Upon-Dearne, South Yorkshire S63 7RZ
☎ *(01709) 879518* Garry

 Wetherspoon's pub serving Marston's Pedigree and Greene King Abbot plus three rotating guests changed every few days, from national and local breweries, as well as those specific to Wetherspoon's.

A town-centre pub set in the pedestrian square over two floors. One main bar. Food served 9am–11pm. Two annual beer festivals. Beer garden. Car park. Children welcome to dine. Opposite the bus station.

OPEN *9am–midnight (1am Fri–Sat).*

WEAVERTHORPE

Star Country Inn

Weaverthorpe, Malton, North Yorkshire YO17 8EY
☎ *(01944) 738273* Benjamin Micallef

 Genuine freehouse with John Smith's Cask and a rotating beer from Theakston. Bottled beer from Wold Top is also served.

Traditional country inn, recently refurbished, with two bar areas and a dining room. Car park and beer garden at the rear. Food served 12–9pm Tues–Sat; 12–3pm and 6–9pm Sun. Family friendly. Accommodation. Four miles from the A64, turn off at Sherburn or Staxton.

OPEN *12–close Tues–Sun plus bank holidays.*

WENTWORTH

The George & Dragon

85 Main Street, Wentworth, Rotherham, South Yorkshire S62 7TN
☎ *(01226) 742440* Ian and Jayne Hodgson

Freehouse with seven real ales, with beers from Timothy Taylor, Wentworth, Abbeydale and Phoenix regularly featured. Guests are constantly rotated.

A 14th-century former court house, with two bars, real fires and stone floors. Breakfast served 10am, with other meals available 12–8.45pm. Private function room seating up to 28. Barbecue hire in summer. Large beer garden with children's play area. Two car parks. Ten minutes from junction 35/35A of the M1.

OPEN *10am–11pm Sun–Wed; 10am–midnight Thurs–Sat.*

WETHERBY

Muse Ale and Wine Bar

16 Bank Street, Wetherby, West Yorkshire LS22 6NQ
☎ *(01937) 580201* Richard Morgan
www.markettowntaverns.co.uk

A beer from Black Sheep and three guest real ales from various breweries.

Converted from a former restaurant in 2004, a stylish bar with a continental feel. Bar and brasserie menu served lunchtimes and evenings every day (except Sunday evening). Beer garden, small car park. Just north of the market square. Handy for Wetherby Racecourse.

OPEN *11am–11pm.*

WHITBY
The Station Inn
New Quay Road, Whitby, North Yorkshire YO21 1DH
☎ *(01947) 603937*
Colin Stonehouse and Andrew Waller

Tied to Enterprise Inns, with Timothy Taylor Golden Best and Copper Dragon IPA among the eight real ales usually available. Three guests are changed weekly.

Two-bar, three-roomed traditional town pub with wooden floors and beams, and relaxing, friendly atmosphere. Bar meals 12–3pm in summer. Children welcome in the family room until 8pm. Live music Wed and Fri, quiz on Thurs. Located in the town centre, opposite the railway station.
OPEN *10am–midnight (11.30pm Sun).*

WOMBWELL
Royal Oak Hotel
13 Burch Street, Wombwell, South Yorkshire
☎ *(01254) 883541* Helen Jones

Five real ales available from a long list including, perhaps, Bateman brews.

A 1920s-style town-centre pub. Bar food available at lunchtimes and evenings. Car park, accommodation. Children allowed at restricted times.
OPEN *11am–11pm Mon–Sat; 12–10.30pm Sun.*

WORTLEY
Wortley Arms Hotel
Halifax Road, Wortley, South Yorkshire S35 7DB
☎ *(0114) 288 8749* Andy Gabbitas

Timothy Taylor Landlord plus two beers from Wentworth and one from Black Sheep.

A classic 16th-century coaching inn with inglenook fireplace, upstairs restaurant and private dining room. Food served 12–2.30pm and 5–9pm Mon–Sat and 12–5pm Sun. Car park. Children welcome. Popular with walkers and cyclists on Trans-Pennine and Timberland trails. Off the Manchester road (Stocksbridge by-pass).
OPEN *11.30am–11pm Mon–Thurs; 11.30am–11.30pm Fri; 11.30am–midnight Sat; 12–10.30pm Sun.*

YORK
The Ackhorne
9 St Martins Lane, York, North Yorkshire YO1 6LN
☎ *(01904) 671421* Ron Cooper

Rooster's Special Bitter and Caledonian Deuchars IPA are the regular beers, plus three guest ales, changed twice weekly.

Tucked away down a cobbled alley at the bottom of Micklegate this is a one-bar town-centre local with small lounge area, and wood and Yorkshire flagstones in the bar. No music or TV, instead there are pub games and conversation! Heated patio to the rear. Food available 12–2pm and 5–7pm. Children welcome during the day. Dogs welcome. Located at the bottom of Micklegate, close to the junction with Rougier Street is St Martin's Church. The pub is on the cobbled lane next to the church.
OPEN *12–12.*

The Blue Bell
53 Fossgate, York, North Yorkshire YO1 9TF
☎ *(01904) 654904* Jim Hardie

Caledonian Deuchars IPA, Adnams Bitter, Jennings Cumberland, Highgate Lone Wolf, John Smith's Cask and Tetley Dark Mild are regularly featured, and two beers are rotated every week.

The smallest pub in York, with a perfectly preserved 1903 Edwardian interior. No juke box, TV or machines, just beer and chatter. Pie and peas plus hot and cold sandwiches served 12–2.30pm every day. Dogs welcome. No children, no groups of any description. Regular beer festival in November. In central York.
OPEN *11am–11pm Mon–Sat; 12–10.30pm Sun.*

Brigantes Bar & Brasserie
114 Micklegate, York, North Yorkshire YO1 6JX
☎ *(01904) 675355* Kevin Jones
www.markettowntaverns.co.uk

Eight real ales, from breweries such as Timothy Taylor, Black Sheep, Leeds and York, changed frequently.

Converted from a former restaurant, this freehouse is in a listed building, the birthplace of the inventor of the Hansom cab. Wooden floor in bar. Cask Marque accredited. No loud music. Home-cooked food served lunchtimes and evenings Mon–Sat and 12–4pm Sun. Upstairs function room available for hire. Children welcome for food. Near the city walls on a famous York street, five minutes' walk from the train station
OPEN *12–11pm.*

The Golden Ball
2 Cromwell Road, Bishophill, York, North Yorkshire YO1 6DU
☎ *(01904) 652211* Linda and Dave Foster
www.goldenball-york.co.uk

An Enterprise Inns tied house. Charles Wells Bombardier, Adnams Bitter, Everards Tiger, Marston's Pedigree and Caledonian Deuchars IPA. One guest, changed two or three times a week, which may include Oldershaw Regal Blonde, Great Newsome Sleck Dust, Shepherd Neame Spitfire, Copper Dragon Golden Pippin or York Guzzler.

Dating from the 1860s and refurbished in 1930, this pub has an original tiled bar front, four rooms and a snug. Bar billiards. Beer garden. No food. Situated within the city walks, five minutes' walk from the city centre. Turn left at the railway station, walk down Nunnery Lane and through Victoria bar to the end of the road.
OPEN *4–11.30pm Mon–Fri; 12–11.30pm Sat; 12–11pm Sun.*

Last Drop Inn

27 Colliergate, York, North Yorkshire
☎ *(01904) 621951* David Gardner
www.yorkbrew.co.uk

 York Brewery's first pub, serving Stonewall, Yorkshire Terrier, Centurion's Ghost, Bitter and a seasonal ale, plus one guest beer changed twice a week.

Opened in 2000, this small pub has a friendly atmosphere, with wooden floors and panelling. Bar area and lower lounge area. Food available 12–5pm. Situated in the historic heart of York near the top of The Shambles. No juke box, no TV, no children, no pool or darts. Beer garden. Live music twice a week.

OPEN *11am–11pm Mon–Thurs; 11am–midnight Fri–Sat; 12–10.30pm Sun.*

The Maltings

Tanners Moat, York, North Yorkshire YO1 16HU
☎ *(01904) 655387* Shaun Collinge
www.maltings.co.uk

Genuine freehouse with Black Sheep Bitter plus something from Rooster's and five guests changing daily (60 per month). Too many to mention but with an emphasis on small, independent brewers. Also Belgian bottled and draught beers, fruit wines and four traditional ciders.

Small city-centre freehouse, handy for all York's many attractions. The sign outside reads: 'If you like music, singing, swearing or crap beer, you are entering the wrong pub'. Pub grub served at lunchtime, 12–2pm on weekdays, 12–4pm at weekends. Situated on Lendal Bridge, close to the railway station.

OPEN *11am–11pm Mon–Sat; 12–10.30pm Sun.*

Rook & Gaskill

12 Lawrence Street, York, North Yorkshire YO10 3WP
☎ *(01904) 674067* Neil and Collette Trafford

York Yorkshire Terrier and Castle Rock Harvest Pale are regularly featured, plus up to ten guests, including a mild, stout or porter.

Locals' pub just outside the city walls, with wooden floor and panelling. No darts, no pool. Food available 12–2.30pm and 5–8pm Mon–Sat. Rook and Gaskill were the last two people to be hanged in York, for stealing sheep. Well-behaved children allowed in the conservatory. Occasional quiet background music at one end of the pub. Located outside the city walls, near the Barbican Centre.

OPEN *12–11pm Sun–Thurs; 12–12 Fri–Sat.*

Spread Eagle

98 Walmgate, York, North Yorkshire
☎ *(01904) 635868* Ralph Tomlinson

Three beers always available, including Marston's Pedigree and two guests, changed every week or two.

Victorian-style pub. Full menu available 12–6pm Mon–Fri, 12–5pm Sat and 12–4pm Sun. Live bands, quiz night, curry club. Beer garden available for smokers. Well-behaved children welcome till 7pm.

OPEN *10am–midnight Mon–Thurs; 10am–1am Fri–Sat; 11am–11pm Sun.*

The Tap & Spile

29 Monkgate, York, North Yorkshire YO31 7BP
☎ *(01904) 656158* Melanie Merry
www.tapandspileyork.co.uk

Five real ales, mainly from northern breweries. Four are changed several times a week.

A traditional pub built in 1897, formerly called The Black Horse. Food served 12–2.30pm Mon–Fri and 12–4pm Sat–Sun, plus evenings Easter–October. Tea and coffee available all day. TV, large beer garden, car park, small private room for hire. Barbecues, music, outdoor events. Close to York Minster, just outside the walls.

OPEN *12–11pm Sun–Wed; 12–12 Thurs–Sat.*

Three-Legged Mare

18 High Petergate, York, North Yorkshire YO1 7EN
☎ *(01904) 638246* Mandy Pegg

York Brewery pub offering Stonewall, Yorkshire Terrier and Centurion's Ghost plus seasonal brews and guests from Castle Rock and elsewhere.

Opened in 2001, a pub combining the traditional values of a local with a cosmopolitan bar atmosphere. No games machines, TV, juke box or children. For discerning drinkers only. Sunny conservatory and outside drinking area. Award-winning sandwiches served 12–3pm daily. Round the corner from the Minster.

OPEN *All day, every day.*

The Yorkshire Terrier

10 Stonegate, York, North Yorkshire YO1 8AS
☎ *(01904) 676722* Jan McDermont
www.yorkbrewery.co.uk

A York Brewery tied house serving Yorkshire Terrier, Stonewall, Guzzler and Centurion's Ghost. Also five guests from other breweries, such as Castle Rock Elsie Mo and Oldershaw Grantham Stout.

Situated behind the York Brewery gift shop, and the third pub to be tied to York. CAMRA Summer Pub of the Season 2007. Food served 12–4pm Mon–Sun; 6–9pm Mon–Thurs. Children welcome 11am–6pm. Function room. Free Wi-Fi access. Situated a stone's throw from York Minster, at the bottom of Stonegate.

OPEN *11am–11pm Sun–Thurs; 11am–midnight Fri–Sat.*

Thurso

Tongue

Wick

Stornoway

Ullapool

Dornoch

Gairloch

Invergordon

Cromarty

Lossiemouth

Fraserburgh

Forres

Banff

Peterhead

Nairn

Rothes

Keith

Portree

Strathcarron

Inverness

Dufftown

Huntly

Inverurie

HIGHLAND

Grantown on Spey

GRAMPIAN

Aberdeen

Kingussie

Ballater

Banchory

Arisaig

Fort William

Tobermory

Pitlochry

Montrose

Forfar

Arbroath

TAYSIDE

Crieff

Perth

Dundee

Inveraray

Callander

Auchterarder

FIFE

St Andrews

M18

Falkland

Lochgilphead

CENTRAL

Stirling

Kirkcaldy

Dumbarton

M9

Dunfermline

Dunbar

Greenock

Airdrie

M8

Edinburgh

Eyemouth

Rothesay

Largs

M8

Glasgow

LOTHIAN

Penicuik

Duns

Berwick upon Tweed

STRATHCLYDE

Peebles

Galashiels

Kelso

Irvine

Kilmarnock

M74

Campbeltown

Ayr

Cumnock

BORDERS

Jedburgh

Alnwick

Sanquhar

Moffat

Hawick

Ballycastle

Girvan

DUMFRIES & GALLOWAY

Langholm

NORTHUMBERLAND

RIM

Dumfries

Annan

Newcastle upon Tyne

Larne

Newton Stewart

Carlisle

TYNE & WEAR

Carrickfergus

Stranraer

Kirkcudbright

Dalbeattie

Whithorn

Maryport

M6

Sunderland

THE BREWERIES

ABERDEENSHIRE

HILLSIDE BREWERY
Hillside Corse, Lumphanan AB31 4RY
☎ *(01339) 883506*
www.hillsidecroft.eclipse.co.uk

MACBETH 4.2% ABV
Hoppy and citrus flavours.
BRUDE 4.3% ABV
Fruity.

ARGYLL

ATLAS BREWERY LTD
Lab Road, Kinlochleven PH50 4SG
☎ *(01855) 831111*
www.atlasbrewery.com

LATITUDE PALE ALE 3.6% ABV
Apricot fruitiness, crisp, slightly dry.
THREE SISTERS SCOTTISH ALE 4.2% ABV
Dark, citrus tones.
WAYFARER IPA 4.4% ABV
Orange marmalade taste, golden ale, slightly spicy.
EQUINOX 4.5% ABV
Honey sweetness, floral aroma.
BLIZZARD 4.7% ABV
Spicy, dry hoppy aftertaste.
TEMPEST 4.9% ABV
Wheat beer, zesty character with hint of banana.
NIMBUS STRONG PALE ALE 5.0% ABV
Pale, malty, sweet nuttiness.
Plus seasonals and specials.

FYNE ALES
Achadunan, Cairndow PA26 8BJ
☎ *(01499) 600120*
www.fyneales.com

PIPER'S GOLD 3.8% ABV
Golden with floral flavour.
MAVERICK 4.2% ABV
Dark and fruity.
VITAL SPARK 4.4% ABV
Hints of blackcurrant.
Plus seasonals including:
SOMERLED 4.0% ABV
Golden, bitter aftertaste.
HOLLYDAZE 5.0% ABV
Fruity hop flavour.
FYNE PORTER 4.5% ABV
Dark, malty.

ISLAY ALES COMPANY LTD
The Brewery, Islay House Square, Bridgend,
Isle of Islay PA44 7NZ
☎ *(01496) 810014*
www.islayales.com

FINLAGGAN ALE 3.7% ABV
Hoppy.
BLACK ROCK ALE 4.2% ABV
Dark, full body.
DUN HOGS HEAD ALE 4.4% ABV
Dry stout.
Plus seasonals including:
SALIGO ALE 4.4% ABV
ANGUS OG ALE 4.5% ABV
ARDNAVE ALE 4.6% ABV
NERABUS ALE 4.8% ABV

ISLE OF MULL BREWING COMPANY LTD
Ledaig, Tobermory, Isle of Mull PA75 6NR
☎ *(01688) 302821*

ISLAND PALE ALE 3.9% ABV
MCCAIG'S FOLLY 4.2% ABV
THE TERROR OF TOBERMORY 4.6% ABV
GALLEON GOLD 5.0% ABV

OYSTER BREWERY
Elenabeich Harbour, Isle of Seil, Oban PA34 4RQ
☎ *(01882) 300121*
www.oysterbrewery.com

EASD'ALE 3.8% ABV
THISTLE TICKLER 4.0% ABV
RED PEARL 4.4% ABV
OLD TOSSER 5.0% ABV

AYRSHIRE

WINDIE GOAT BREWERY
Failford Inn, Failford, Nr Maichline KA5 5TF
☎ *(01292) 540117*
www.failfordinn.co.uk

PEDEN'S COVE 3.5% ABV
PRIEST'S WHEEL 4.3% ABV

CAITHNESS

FAR NORTH BREWERY
Melvich Hotel, Melvich, Thurso, Caithness
KW14 7YJ
☎ *(01641) 531206*

REAL MACKAY 3.8% ABV
SPLIT STONE PALE ALE 4.2% ABV
FAST REACTOR 4.8 % ABV
EDGE OF DARKNESS 7.0% ABV

CLACKMANNANSHIRE

DEVON ALES
Mansfield Arms, 7 Main Street Suchie, Nr Alloa
FK10 3JR
☎ *(01259) 722020*
www.devonales.com

CHOPPER'S CHOICE 3.8% ABV
DEVON ORIGINAL 3.8% ABV
DEVON THICK BLACK 4.1% ABV
DEVON PRIDE 4.9% ABV

HARVIESTOUN BREWERY LTD
Hillfoots Business Village, Alva Industrial Estate,
Alva FK12 5DQ
☎ *(01259) 769100*
www.harviestoun-brewery.co.uk

BITTER AND TWISTED 3.8% ABV
Blond with clean citrus fruit flavours.
PTARMIGAN 80/- 4.5% ABV
Pale with Bavarian hops.
SCHIEHALLION 4.8% ABV
Plus seasonal and occasional brews.

WILLIAMS BROS BREWING COMPANY

Heather Ales Ltd, New Alloa Brewery, Eglinton, Kelliebank, Alloa FK10 1NT
☎ *(01259) 725511*

> **FRAOCH 4.1% ABV**
> **BLACK 4.2% ABV**
ROISIN TAYBERRY 4.2% ABV
GROZET 4.5% ABV
RED 4.5% ABV
Plus seasonals and specials.

EAST LOTHIAN

BELHAVEN BREWERY COMPANY

Spott Road, Dunbar EH42 1RS
☎ *(01368) 862734*
www.belhaven.co.uk

> **BEST 3.2% ABV**
> Honey coloured.
BEST EXTRA GOLD 3.2% ABV
80/- 4.2% ABV
Malty and nutty.
ST ANDREW'S ALE 4.6% ABV
Dry aftertaste.

FOWLER'S ALE

The Gothenburg, 227–9 High Street, Prestonpans EH32 9BE
☎ *(01875) 819922*

> **IPA 4.1% ABV**
> **PRESTONPANS 80/- 4.2% ABV**
GOTHENBURG PORTER 4.4% ABV

MCCOWANS BREWHOUSE

134 Dundee Street, Edinburgh EH11 1AF
☎ *(0131) 228 8198*

> **DOMNHUL BAN 3.8% ABV**
> **DOMNHUL 4.5% ABV**
DOMNHUL DUBH 4.5% ABV

STEWART BREWING LTD

Unit 5 42 Dryden Road, Bilson Glen Industrial Estate, Loanhead, Edinburgh EH20 9LZ
☎ *(0131) 440 2442*
www.stewartbrewing.co.uk

> **PENTLAND IPA 4.1% ABV**
> Slightly fruity.
COPPER CASCADE 4.2% ABV
Deep red, blackcurrant character.
EDINBURGH N0.3 4.3% ABV
Malty taste, deep colour.
EDINBURGH GOLD 4.8% ABV
Hop aroma, gold colour.
Plus seasonals.

FIFE

FYFE BREWING COMPANY

The Harbour Bar, 469 High Street, Kirkcaldy KY1 2SN
☎ *(01592) 646211*
www.fyfebrewery.co.uk

> **ROPE OF SAND 3.7% ABV**
> **GREENGO 3.8% ABV**
WEISS SQUAD 4.5% ABV
FYFE FYRE 4.8% ABV
JBS 5.0% ABV
Plus large range of seasonals and specials.

INVERNESS-SHIRE

CAIRNGORM BREWING COMPANY LTD

Dalfaber Industrial Estate, Aviemore PH22 1ST
☎ *(01479) 812222*
www.cairngormbrewery.com

> **STAG 4.1% ABV**
> Good hop character.
TRADE WINDS 4.3% ABV
Light gold, citrus fruit flavour, elderflower aroma.
BLACK GOLD 4.4% ABV
Rich dark roast barley hints.
NESSIE'S MONSTER MASH 4.4% ABV
Malty full-flavoured beer.
CAIRNGORM GOLD 4.5% ABV
Lager style, malt flavour.
SHEEPSHAGGER'S GOLD 4.5% ABV
Golden ale.
WILD CAT 5.1% ABV
Malt, fruit and hop flavour.
Plus seasonals including:
MILD MAY 3.7% ABV
WINTER FURRY 3.8% ABV
BARD'S ALE 4.4% ABV
BLESSED THISTLE 4.5% ABV
GLEN AMPLE 4.5% ABV
HORIZON 4.5% ABV
RED MOUNTAIN PORTER 4.5% ABV
MOUNTAIN DEW 4.6% ABV
WHITE LADY 4.7% ABV
WITCHES CAULDRON 4.9% ABV
HIGHLAND IPA 5.0%
SANTA'S SLEDGEHAMMER 5.6% ABV

CUILLIN BREWERY LTD

Sligachan, Isle of Skye IV47 8SW
☎ *(01478) 650204*
www.cuillinbrewery.co.uk

> **EAGLE ALE 3.8% ABV**
> **SKYE ALE 4.1% ABV**
PINNACLE 4.7% ABV
Plus specials.

THE ISLE OF SKYE BREWING COMPANY (LEANN AN EILEIN) LTD

The Pier, Uig, Portreee, Isle of Skye IV49 9XP
☎ *(01470) 54277*
www.skyebrewery.co.uk

> **YOUNG PRETENDER 4.0% ABV**
> Gold, lightly hopped, dry aftertaste.
RED CUILLIN 4.2% ABV
Slightly malty, fruit and hop finish.
HEBRIDEAN GOLD 4.3% ABV
Smooth, hoppy.
BLACK CUILLIN 4.5% ABV
Stout-like, hints of chocolate and honey.
BLAVEN 5.0% ABV
Golden, fruity.
Plus seasonals including:
BEN NEVIS ALE 4.1% ABV
WEDDING ALE 4.1% ABV
FOURSEASONS 4.2% ABV

KIRKCUDBRIGHTSHIRE

SULWATH BREWERIES LTD
The Brewery, 209 King Street, Castle Douglas DG7 1DT
☎ *(01556) 504525*
www.sulwathbrewers.co.uk

CUIL HILL 3.6% ABV
Pale amber, fresh malt and hop tastes.
BLACK GALLOWAY 4.4% ABV
Porter.
CRIFFEL ALE 4.6% ABV
Rounded malt and hop flavours with delicate bitterness.
GALLOWAY GOLD 5.0% ABV
Lager style.
KNOCKENDOCH 5.0% ABV
Deep roast malt flavour and hoppy aftertaste.
Plus occasional brews.

LANARKSHIRE

BROUGHTON ALES LTD
Broughton, Biggar ML12 6HQ
☎ *(01899) 830345*
www.broughtonales.co.uk

BROUGHTON SPECIAL BITTER 3.8% ABV
Light colour, bittersweet taste.
THE REIVER 3.8% ABV
Hoppy aroma.
CLIPPER IPA 4.2% ABV
Malt flavour with strong hop character.
MERLINS ALE 4.2% ABV
Golden and hoppy.
EXCISEMANS 80/- 4.6% ABV
Strong, malty brew.
OLD JOCK ALE 6.7% ABV
Full bodied, hoppy bitterness.

THE CLOCKWORK BEER COMPANY
1153–5 Cathcart Road, Glasgow G42 9HB
☎ *(0141) 649 0184*

AMBER IPA 3.8% ABV
GOLDEN ALE 4.2% ABV
CLOCK DUBH STOUT 4.5% ABV
HAZY DAYS SERIOUSLY GINGER 5.0% ABV
STRONG ALE 6.0% ABV
Plus seasonals and specials.

STRATHAVEN ALES
Craigmill, Strathaven ML10 6PB
☎ *(01357) 520419*
www.strathavenales.co.uk

CLYDESDALE IPA 3.8% ABV
DUCHESS ANNE 3.9% ABV
OLD MORTALITY 4.2% ABV
TRUMPETER 4.2% ABV
CLYDESDALE REAL ALE 4.5% ABV

MIDLOTHIAN

CALEDONIAN BREWING COMPANY
42 Slateford Road, Edinburgh EH11 1PH
☎ *(0131) 337 1286*
www.caledonian-brewery.co.uk

DEUCHARS IPA 3.8% ABV
Pale, well hopped.
80/- ALE 4.1% ABV
Golden award-winner.
CALEDONIAN XPA 4.3% ABV
Golden with bittersweet finish.
GOLDEN PROMISE 5.0% ABV
Light coloured, hoppy, organic.
Plus seasonals, including:
SANTA'S LITTLE HELPER 3.9% ABV
GREAT SCOTT 4.1% ABV
TOP BANANA 4.1% ABV
SIX NATIONS 4.2% ABV
TRY'D AND TESTED 4.2% ABV
NECTAR SUMMER ALE 4.3% ABV
REBUS 4.4% ABV
TRICK OR TREAT 4.6% ABV
MERMAN XXX 4.8% ABV

ORKNEY

HIGHLAND BREWING COMPANY LTD
Swannay Brewery, Swannay by Evie, Orkney KW17 2NP
☎ *(01856) 721700*
www.highlandbrewingcompany.co.uk

SCAPA PALE ALE 4.2% ABV
ST MAGNUS ALE 4.5% ABV
ORKNEY BLAST 6.0% ABV

THE ORKNEY BREWERY
Quoyloo, Sandwick, Orkney KW16 3LT
☎ *(01667) 404555*
www.orkneybrewery.co.uk

RAVEN ALE 3.8% ABV
Malt, hop, citrus fruit flavours and nuttiness.
DRAGONHEAD STOUT 4.0% ABV
Black, powerful roast maltiness with nutty flavours.
NORTHERN LIGHT 4.0% ABV
Mellow, malty with nut and hop finish.
DARK ISLAND 4.6% ABV
Smooth.
SKULLSPLITTER 8.5% ABV
Smooth, hoppy, dry finish.
Plus seasonals and specials. Parent company Sinclair Breweries Ltd also own Atlas Brewery.

PEEBLESSHIRE

TRAQUAIR HOUSE BREWERY
Traquair House, Innerleithen, EH44 0PW
☎ *(01896) 830323*
www.traquair.co.uk

TRAQUAIR ALE 7.2% ABV

Plus seasonals.

PERTHSHIRE

THE INVERALMOND BREWERY
1 Inveralmond Way , Inveralmond, Perth PH1 3UQ
☎ *(01738) 449448*
www.inveralmond-brewery.co.uk

INDEPENDENCE 3.8% ABV
Malt and hop tastes with some spiciness.
OSSIAN 4.1% ABV
Golden and hoppy.
THRAPPLEDOUSER 4.3% ABV
Deep golden, hoppy.
LIA FAIL 4.7% ABV
Smooth, dark, full flavour.

MOULIN BREWERY
Moulin Inn and Brewery, Pitlochry
☎ *(01796) 472196*
www.moulinhotel.co.uk

LIGHTALE 3.7% ABV
BRAVEHEART 4.0% ABV
ALE OF ATHOLL 4.5% ABV
OLD REMEDIAL 5.2% ABV

RENFREWSHIRE

HOUSTON BREWERY COMPANY
South Street, Houston PA6 7EN
☎ *(01505) 614528*
www.houston-brewing.co.uk

KILLELLAN 3.7% ABV
Golden, mellow, zesty finish.
BAROCHAN 4.1% ABV
Smooth ruby, roasted barley flavour.
ST PETER'S WELL 4.2% ABV
Fruity flavour.
TEXAS 4.5% ABV
Amber, full bodied.

KELBURN BREWING COMPANY LTD
10 Muriel Lane, Barrhead G78 1QB
☎ *(0141) 881 2138*
www.kelburnbrewery.com

GOLDI HOPS 3.8% ABV
Clean with lingering hoppy aftertaste.
RED SMIDDY 4.1% ABV
Smooth dry ale.
DARK MOOR 4.5% ABV
Fruity with a hint of liquorice.
CART BLANCHE 5.0% ABV
Robust and dry.
Plus seasonals including:
MISTY LAW 4.0% ABV
CA'CANNY 5.2% ABV

ROSS-SHIRE

BLACK ISLE BREWING COMPANY LTD
Old Allangrange, Munlochy IV8 8N2
☎ *(01463) 811871*
www.blackislebrewery.com

YELLOWHAMMER 4.0% ABV
RED KITE 4.5% ABV
Plus specials.

AN TEALLACH ALE COMPANY LTD
Camusnagaul, Dundonnell, Garve IV23 2QT
☎ *(01854) 633306*

BEEINN DEARG 3.8% ABV
ANTEALLACH ALE 4.2% ABV
CROFTER'S PALE ALE 4.2% ABV
BREWHOUSE SPECIAL 4.4% ABV
KILDONAN 4.4% ABV
Plus specials.

HEBRIDEAN BREWING COMPANY
18 Bells Road, Stornoway, Isle of Lewis, Western Isles HS1 2RA
☎ *(01851) 700123*
www.hebridean-brewery.co.uk

CELTIC BLACK 3.9% ABV
Caramel aftertaste.
CLANSMAN 3.9% ABV
Light golden bitter.
ISLANDER 4.8% ABV
Deep ruby, with powerful hops throughout.
BERSERKER EXPORT PALE ALE 7.5% ABV
Malty with intense hops.

SHETLAND

VALHALLA BREWERY
Shetland Refreshments Ltd, Baltasound, Unst, Shetland ZE2 9DX
☎ *(01957) 711658*
www.valhallabrewery.co.uk

WHITE WIFE 3.8% ABV
Golden, fruity aftertaste.
SIMMER DIM 4.0% ABV
Gold-coloured bitter.
AULD ROCK 4.5% ABV
Dark, malty.

STIRLINGSHIRE

BRIDGE OF ALLAN BREWERY
Queen's Lane, Bridge of Allan FK9 4NY
☎ *(01786) 834555*
www.bridgeofallan.co.uk

STIRLING BITTER 3.7% ABV
Full flavour, nutty aftertaste.
STIRLING BRIG 4.1% ABV
Rich, malty, slightly sweet.
BANNOCKBURN ALE 4.2% ABV
Light colour, moreish.
GLENCOE WILD OAT STOUT 4.5 % ABV
Creamy, toasted oatmeal flavour.
LOMOND GOLD 5.0% ABV
Hint of citrus.
Plus seasonals including:
ALEOWEEN PUMPKIN ALE 4.2% ABV
BRAMBLE ALE 4.2% ABV

EGLESBRECH BREWING COMPANY
Eglesbrech@Behind The Wall, 14 Melville Street, Falkirk FK1 1HZ
☎ *(01324) 633338*
www.behindthewall.co.uk

FALKIRK 400 3.8% ABV
ANTONINE ALE 3.9% ABV
TALL BLONDE 4.0% ABV
EAGLE'S BREATH SPECIAL ALE 4.1% ABV

STIRLING BREWERY
Traditional Scottish Ales Ltd, Unit 7c Bandeath Industrial Estate, Throsk, Stirling FK7 7NP
☎ (01786) 817000

COPPER 4.0% ABV
SILVER 4.5% ABV
GOLD 5.0% ABV
JUGS 7.0% ABV

TRYST BREWERY
Lorne Road, Larbert FK5 4AT
☎ (01324) 554000
www.trystbrewery.co.uk

BROCKVILLE DARK 3.8% ABV
BROCKVILLE PALE 3.8% ABV
FESTIVAL RED 4.0% ABV
BUCKLED WHEEL 4.2% ABV
CARRONADE IPA 4.2% ABV

THE PUBS

ABERDEENSHIRE

ABERDEEN

Archibald Simpson
5 Castle Street, Aberdeen AB11 5BZ
☎ (01224) 621365 Alec Beattie
www.jdwetherspoon.co.uk

 Six to eight real ales, changed weekly, and from anywhere across the UK, Europe and the world!

It's not difficult to imagine this Grade I listed building as it used to be: a Clydesdale Bank. Now a one-bar JD Wetherspoon freehouse situated on the corner of Union and King Streets. Food served 9am–11pm. Children welcome until 8pm. Beer festivals held twice a year.

OPEN *9am–midnight Mon–Thurs; 9am–1am Fri–Sat; 9am–11pm Sun.*

The Blue Lamp
121–3 Gallowgate, Aberdeen AB25 1BU
☎ (01224) 647472 Mr Brown

 Freehouse with Caledonian 80/– and Deuchars IPA plus up to five guest beers. Regulars include Isle of Skye Young Pretender and many others from small Scottish breweries.

A pub combining the traditional and the contemporary, with live entertainment at weekends. Two bars, one with an early 1960s feel, the other spacious. Small function room available to hire. Sandwiches only. No children.

OPEN *All day Mon–Sat; 12.30–3.30pm and 6.30–11pm Sun.*

Carriages Bar & Restaurant
The Brentwood Hotel, 101 Crown Street, Aberdeen AB11 6HH
☎ (01224) 595440/571593 Jim Byers
www.brentwood-hotel.co.uk

Ten real ales always on tap, including Caledonian Deuchars IPA and Black Sheep Ale among five permanents plus five guests, changing weekly, such as Marston's Pedigree, Wadworth 6X, Fuller's London Pride, Shepherd Neame Spitfire, Greene King

Abbot Ale, Orkney Dark Island or something from Aviemore, Isle of Skye, Houston or any other independent brewery. Different and unusual ales from independent breweries across the UK are constantly sourced. CAMRA Aberdeen City Pub of the Year 2003.

Carriages is a freehouse, part of the Brentwood Hotel, run by the director/licensee, who is a fount of local knowledge. It has a relaxed, informal atmosphere. A hot buffet lunch is served 12–2pm Mon–Fri; dinner in the restaurant 6–9.45pm Mon–Sun. Car park. Children welcome in lounge area and restaurant, when eating. Special children's menu available.

OPEN *12–2.30pm and 5pm–12 Mon–Sat; 6–11pm Sun.*

J & R Tennent
Aberdeen Airport, Dyce, Aberdeen
☎ (01224) 722331 J and R Tennent

 Two real ales regularly served, such as Caledonian IPA, 80/– or Marston's Pedigree.

Airport bar. Food served 8am–5pm. Children welcome.

OPEN *8am–9.45pm.*

Old Blackfriars
Castle Street, Aberdeen AB11 5BB
☎ (01224) 581922 Sharon Strange

 Belhaven-managed house with seven real ale pumps. Greene King IPA and Abbot, Inveralmond Ossian, Caledonian 80/– and either Belhaven 80/– or St Andrew's permanently available. The two guests are changed every few days.

Quaint and cosy pub set in the heart of the historic part of Aberdeen, and serving a dynamic menu made with local produce. Food available 11am–9pm Mon–Thurs, 11am–8pm Fri–Sat and 12.30–9pm Sun. Ceilidh band every couple of months.

OPEN *11am–midnight Mon–Sat; 12.30–11pm Sun.*

The Prince of Wales
7 St Nicholas Lane, Aberdeen AB10 1HF
☎ (01224) 640597 Steven Christie

 Freehouse with house ale from Inveralmond – Prince of Wales Ale – and Caledonian 80/– always on the menu. Four guest beers, changed weekly, may include Isle of Skye Red Cuillin and Young Pretender, Timothy Taylor Landlord or Orkney Dark Island, but ales from other independents also available as and when.

A classic city-centre Victorian bar. No music. Food available at lunchtime. Children allowed.

OPEN *All day, every day.*

GLENKINDIE
The Glenkindie Arms Hotel
Glenkindie AB33 8SX
☎ *(01975) 641288* Eddie Falk
www.theglenkindiearmshotel.com

 Sentinal Pale Ale (4.2%) is brewed in-house plus one guest, changed weekly, such as Kelburn Pivo Estivo or Inveralmond Thrappledouser. More home-brewed beers are expected to follow.

Historic drovers' inn, approximately 400 years old, now a freehouse and home of the single-barrel Old Foreigner Brewery since 2007. Small cosy bar, real fire. Food served 5–9pm Mon–Fri and 12–2pm and 5–9pm Sat–Sun. Located five miles from Mossat on the A97. Three en-suite bedrooms.

OPEN *5–11pm Mon–Thurs; 5pm–1am Fri; (closed weekday lunch); noon–12.45am Sat; 12.30–11pm Sun.*

METHLICK
The Gight House Hotel
Sunnybrae, Methlick, Ellon AB41 7BP
☎ *(01651) 806389* Les Ross

 Two real ale pumps serve a regularly changing range of beers, with Hook Norton Old Hooky, Timothy Taylor Landlord, Black Sheep Bitter and Marston's Pedigree all having featured often, plus Scottish brews such as Isle of Skye Red Cuillin.

Not only is the demon drink served in this former Free Kirk manse, there is a putting green on the lawn. Beamed lounge with open fires, restaurant, two conservatories, children's play area. Food served at lunchtimes and evenings Mon–Sat and all day Sun.

OPEN *12–2.30pm and 5pm–12 Mon–Fri; all day Sat–Sun.*

STONEHAVEN
The Marine Hotel
9–10 Shorehead, Stonehaven AB3 2JY
☎ *(01569) 762155* Phil Duncan

Timothy Taylor ales plus five guests (200 per year) perhaps from Orkney or Harviestoun breweries, plus a wide range of English ales.

The pub overlooks the harbour and has a large bar with a juke box. Bar and restaurant food served at lunchtime and evenings. Local seafood and game. Parking. Follow the signs to the harbour.

OPEN *9am–1am (midnight Sun).*

ANGUS

ARBROATH
Lochlands Bar
14–16 Lochland Street, Arbroath DD11 3AB
☎ *(01241) 437728* Stewart Baxter

A freehouse. Three beers, all stocked on a guest basis, although Caledonian Deuchars IPA is usually featured. Others come from a range of breweries such as Elgood's and Moorhouse's.

Community local, friendly and welcoming to all. Traditional, back-to-back lounge and bar, sports-oriented, with Live Sky football. Awarded Angus CAMRA Pub of the Year 2007. No food.

OPEN *11am–midnight.*

BROUGHTY FERRY
Fisherman's Tavern
10–16 Fort Street, Broughty Ferry, Dundee DD5 2AD
☎ *(01382) 775941* Rhys Martinson
www.fishermanstavern.co.uk

 Belhaven-managed house, with six real ales, changed after each firkin. Examples include Timothy Taylor Landlord, Fuller's London Pride, Harviestoun Bitter & Twisted, Greene King Old Speckled Hen and Ruddles County, and Belhaven St Andrew's, plus seasonal beers.

A 300-year-old listed building, formerly a fisherman's cottage. Winner of *Scottish Licence Trade News's* Best Poured Pint in Scotland award in 2001 and Wine by the Glass award 2002. Food available 12–3pm Mon–Sat, 12.30–3.30pm Sun, and 5–8pm every day. Live music Thursdays from 8pm. Also 11 en-suite rooms in hotel with walled garden. Annual beer festival at end of May, featuring 35 ales and 2 continental lagers, as a fundraiser for the local lifeboat. Children welcome. Situated by the lifeboat station at Broughty Ferry.

OPEN *11am–midnight Mon–Wed; 11am–1am Thurs–Sat; 12.30pm–12 Sun.*

CARNOUSTIE
The Stag's Head Inn
61 Dundee Street, Carnoustie DD7 7PN
☎ *(01241) 852265* Mr Duffy

Freehouse with real ale on four pumps. Guest ales, which change constantly, may include Timothy Taylor Landlord, Caledonian 80/- or Orkney Dark Island.

A locals' pub with two bars. Food served at lunchtimes and evenings in the summertime. Children only allowed in the pool table area.

OPEN *All day, every day.*

DUNDEE
Drouthy Neebors
142 Perth Road, Dundee DD1 4JW
☎ *(01382) 202187* Marc Fotheringham

Caledonian Deuchars IPA plus other guests regularly featured.

Traditional pub, refurbished, with a friendly, contemporary atmosphere. Good selection of food served 12–11pm Mon–Sat and 12.30–11pm Sun.

OPEN *All day, every day.*

Mickey Coyle's

21–3 Old Hawkhill, Dundee DD1 5EU
☎ *(01382) 225871* Andrew Knowles
www.mickeycoyles.com

Tied to Scottish & Newcastle, serving Caledonian Deuchars IPA and three guests, changed every couple of days, from a selection including Theakston, Harviestoun, Everards and Caledonian brews.

Traditional community pub on the north side of Dundee's main university, popular with both staff and students, and always offering a friendly welcome. Becoming well known for its range of rums and bourbons, as well as its great ales. Dundee CAMRA Pub of the Year for past four years. Food available 12–2.30pm and 5–8pm Mon–Thurs; 12–7.30pm Fri–Sun. Car park.

(OPEN) *11am–midnight.*

The Phoenix Bar

103 Nethergate, Dundee DD1 4DH
☎ *(01382) 200014* Alan Bannerman

Freehouse always offering Orkney Dark Island, Caledonian Deuchars IPA and Timothy Taylor Landlord.

A traditional, one-bar pub with TV and music. Food served lunchtimes and evenings. No children.

(OPEN) *All day, every day.*

Speedwell Bar

165–7 Perth Road, Dundee DD2 1AS
☎ *(01382) 667783* Jonathan Iain Stewart
www.speedwell-bar.co.uk

Freehouse with real ale on three pumps. Caledonian Deuchars IPA is permanent, and the two guests, changed daily, might be beers such as Adnams Broadside, Sam Smith's Old Brewery Bitter and Fuller's London Pride. Cask Marque accredited.

Truly stunning Edwardian pub, largely unchanged since it was built in 1903, and now rightly recognised as part of the city's architectural heritage. New landlord, has recently taken pub over from father. Known locally as Mennies. On the ground floor of a four-storey tenement building with one L-shaped bar and two rooms. An authentic Edwardian pub, so no kitchen, but drinks, coffees etc are available for those bringing in food from the bakery next door or other local takeaways. No children. Special weekend event in September, with cellar tours and complimentary refreshments. Ranked as no.68 of Britain's Best Loved Pubs, in 2009 (*Daily Telegraph*), only 4 others in Scotland.

(OPEN) *11am–midnight.*

Glen Clova Hotel

Glen Clova, By Kirriemuir DD8 4QS
☎ *(01575) 550350* June Coventry
www.clova.com

Freehouse with Caledonian Deuchars IPA and 80/– plus Houston Brewery's Texas and Peter's Well on tap.

Country hotel and climbers' bar with food served 12–8.30pm. Accommodation available in ten en-suite bedrooms and a 32-bed bunk house. Thirteen miles north of Kirriemuir.

(OPEN) *All day, every day.*

The Chance Inn

Main Street, Inverkeilor, Arbroath DD11 5RN
☎ *(01241) 830308* Mrs Lee

Freehouse offering three real ales, changed weekly.

Two bars, two recommended restaurants plus accommodation. Food served lunchtimes and evenings. Children allowed. Scottish Tourist Board 3 star rated, and Tayside CAMRA award-winner.

(OPEN) *12–3pm and 5pm–12 Tues–Fri; all day Sat–Sun.*

ARGYLL

The Village Inn

Shore Road, Arrochar G83 7AX
☎ *(01301) 702279* Jose Andrade
www.maclay.com/villageinn.html

A pub owned by Maclay Inns, serving a Fyne brew plus two guests, changed weekly.

A traditional inn, full of character and original features, built in 1827 on the shores of Loch Long. Food served all day up to 8.45pm (may change in winter). Children welcome in bar until 8pm. Large beer garden with spectacular views, car park, 14 bedrooms. A CAMRA Pub of the Year 2004. Just off the A82, two miles from Tarbet, and close to Loch Lomond.

(OPEN) *11am–midnight Sun–Thurs; 11am–1am Fri–Sat.*

The Coach House Inn

Main Road, Cardross G82 5JX
☎ *(01389) 841358* Mark Fennell
www.coachhousecardross.com

Caledonian Deuchars IPA and one weekly changing guest such as Shepherd Neame Spitfire, Black Sheep Bitter, Courage Directors or Marston's Pedigree.

Village inn tied to Admiral Taverns. Bar, pool room, lounge with a coal fire, dining conservatory and two beer gardens with a smoking area. Four en suite rooms available. Food served 12–9pm. Children welcome. Car park and good train service. Close to amenities of Loch Lomond. Cardross is between Dumbarton and Helensburgh on the A814.

(OPEN) *12–12 Mon–Wed; noon–1am Thurs–Sat; 12.30pm–midnight Sun.*

COVE
Knockderry House Hotel
Shore Road, Cove, Nr Helensburgh G84 0NX
☎ *(01436) 842283* Murdo MacLeod
www.knockderryhouse.co.uk

 Freehouse with real ale on four pumps, regularly featuring Greene King Abbot and Ruddles County and brews from Fyne Ales, Kelburn, Houston, Belhaven and Archers, rotated every few days.

A 14-bedroom hotel on the shores of Loch Long, in an old building extended in the Victorian period. Two bars, open fires and wood panelling. Breakfast, lunch and dinner available every day. Six moorings at the bottom of the garden. Private rooms for hire. Yachtspeople, children and dogs welcome!

OPEN *All day, every day.*

FURNACE
Furnace Inn
Furnace, Inverary PA32 8XN
☎ *(01499) 500200* John Mather

Freehouse with one or two real ales. There will usually be something from Fyne, and all beers rotate, often weekly.

Detached stone pub built in the 1700s, with bar and restaurant with open fire, and stone walls. Food served 12–3.30pm and 5–8.30pm. Children most welcome. Car park, beer garden. Good fishing, hill walking, mountain biking and diving. Seven miles north of Inverary on the A83.

OPEN *Summer: 12–12 every day. Winter: 4.30pm–12 Mon–Thurs; 4pm–1am Fri; 12–12 Sat–Sun.*

GLENCOE
Clachaig Inn
Glenco PH49 4HX
☎ *(01855) 811252* Guy and Ed Daynes
www.clachaig.com

Beers from Atlas such as Latitude and Three Sisters are regularly featured, together with ales from many other Scottish breweries. Up to eight real ales at any one time, more during regular festivals.

A pub and hotel, popular with hillwalkers who flock to Glencoe. Food available 12–9pm daily. Children allowed in the lounge bar. Beer garden. Accommodation.

OPEN *11am–11pm.*

INVERARY
The George Hotel
Main Street East, Inverary PA32 8TT
☎ *(01499) 302111* Donald Clark
www.thegeorgehotel.co.uk

Real ale on two pumps in this genuine freehouse. Guests are changed as they run out, with regulars including Caledonian Deuchars IPA and brews from Fyne Ales.

Built in 1770, an old-fashioned country house with two bars and a beamed restaurant, in the same family since 1860. Beer garden. Good food served 12–9pm.

Children and dogs welcome. Unusual bedrooms. Car park. Next to the jail in this conservation town on Loch Fyne.

OPEN *All day, every day (except Christmas Day).*

KILMICHAEL GLASSARY
The Horseshoe Inn
Kilmichael Glassary, Lochgilphead PA31 8QA
☎ *(01546) 606369* Iain Allison
www.horseshoeinn.biz

A freehouse. Caledonian Deuchars IPA and a Fyne ale in summer. Two Fyne ales in winter.

Old drovers' inn with bar, lounge bar, dining room and games room. Food served 5–9pm Mon–Fri; 12–9pm Sat–Sun. Beer garden. Accommodation. Situated in the historic village of Kilmartin Glen, three miles north of Lochgilphead, on the A816.

OPEN *5–11pm Mon–Thurs; 5pm–12 Fri; noon–1am Sat; 12–11pm Sun.*

KINLOCHLEVEN
The Tailrace Inn
Riverside Road, Kinlochleven PH50 4QH
☎ *(01855) 831777* Elizabeth Ferguson
www.tailraceinn.co.uk

A short walk from the Atlas Brewery, at least two of whose ales are on offer. These might include Nimbus and a seasonal ale, changed monthly, such as Blizzard.

Modern one-bar pub with beer garden. Food available 8am–9pm. Six en-suite bedrooms. Car park. Rooms for hire. Handy for Ice Factor activity centre, golf courses, climbing, walking and horseriding, and close to Fort William.

OPEN *8am–12.30am.*

LOCH ECK
The Coylet Inn
Loch Eck, Dunoon PA23 8SG
☎ *(01369) 840426* Sam Copson
www.coyletinn.co.uk

As good a place as any to sample Fyne Ales Highlander (4.8% ABV) – the Argyll-brewed beer is this 17th-century inn's top seller. Also two guest beers.

A 17th-century coaching inn on the shores of Loch Eck. Atmospheric bar with log fires and hotel with four rooms. Outside seating overlooking loch. Food available 12–2.30pm and 6–8.45pm. Popular with anglers (Loch Eck fishing permits available from the hotel) and orienteers. Children welcome. Close to Benmore Botanical Gardens.

OPEN *Open all day, every day in summer (closed Mon–Tues during Nov–Apr).*

PORT BANNATYNE, ISLE OF BUTE

The Russian Tavern at the Port Royal Hotel

37 Marine Road, Port Bannatyne, Isle of Bute PA20 0LW
☎ *(01700) 505073* Olga Crawford
www.butehotel.com

 Freehouse with three constantly rotating ales, which could include Kelburn Goldihops or Cart Blanche, Fyne Vital Spark or Highlander, plus Erdinger Wheat Beers. Selection of Russian bottled beers.

Built in 1811, this stone-front village inn built on the waterfront features Tsarist Russian cuisine as well as Russian beers, wines and vodkas. Food includes fresh fish caught in the bay, such as langoustines, crab, scallops and mussels. Food served in Les Routiers gastropub all day, every day. Five guest rooms available. Children welcome. Located next to Port Bannatyne yacht marina.

OPEN *All day, every day April–October (closed Tues). Closed Oct 20–Easter.*

TIGHNABRUAICH

The Kames Hotel

Kames, By Tighnabruaich PA21 2AF
☎ *(01700) 811489* Patrick Jenner, Philippa Elliott and Sheely Theaker
www.kames-hotel.com

 Freehouse with two ales from the local Fyne Ales brewery, namely Highlander plus a weekly guest. Over 50 malt whiskies.

Originally a drovers' pub, this is an Edwardian hotel by the sea on the Kyles of Bute, with three main bars, a restaurant overlooking the Kyles and ten recently renovated rooms. Good wholesome food served in either the bars or the restaurant 12–3pm and 6–9pm, with all produce being fresh and locally sourced. The beer garden also overlooks the Kyles and the Island of Bute. There are 17 moorings for boats, with some of the best sailing in Scotland in this area. From the M8 from Glasgow: either take the ferry from Gourock to Dunoon and follow the A8003 to Tighnabruaich; or cross the Erskine Bridge, drive round Loch Lomond, take the A83 over the mountain pass, the A815 to Dunoon, and the A8003 to Tighnabruaich. GPS co-ordinates on the website.

OPEN *12–12 Sun–Thurs; noon–1am Fri–Sat.*

AYRSHIRE

AYR

Burrowfields Café Bar

13 Beresford Terrace, Ayr KA7 2EU
☎ *(01292) 269152* Daniel Kelly

Real ale on three pumps in this freehouse. Regular guests, changed weekly, include brews from Caledonian, Clearwater, Greene King and Cains.

Live music once a week, TV and lounge bar. Food at lunchtimes and evenings. Children allowed at lunchtime.

OPEN *All day, every day.*

Geordie's Byre

103 Main Street, Ayr KA8 88U
☎ *(01292) 264325*

 Caledonian 80/- and Deuchars IPA plus three guest beers (450 per year) from Orkney (Skullsplitter) to Cornwall and Devon (Summerskill's Whistle Belly Vengeance).

Friendly freehouse managed by the owners. Decorated with memorabilia and Victoriana. No food. Children not allowed. Located 50 yards from the police headquarters on King Street.

OPEN *11am–11pm (midnight Thurs–Sat); 12.30–11pm Sun.*

Old Racecourse Hotel

2 Victoria Park, Ayr KA7 2TR
☎ *(01292) 262873* Mark Valentine

Freehouse with three or four ales, all rotating guests from various national and regional breweries.

A small, friendly hotel with great ales, wine and food. Food served 12–2.30pm and 5–9pm Mon–Fri, 12–9pm Sat–Sun. Seven letting rooms available. Beer garden. Private room available for hire. Children welcome. Located close to the old racecourse, a few minutes from the town centre.

OPEN *All day, every day.*

BRODICK, ISLE OF ARRAN

Catacol Bay Hotel

Catacol, Lochranza, Brodick, Isle of Arran KA27 8HN
☎ *(01770) 830231* Norman Bond
www.catacol.co.uk

 Freehouse with Arran Brewery ales always available.

Small, family-run hotel with lounge bar and pool room. Food available 12–10pm, plus Sunday buffet 12–4pm. Beer garden, car park. The pub has a children's certificate and outdoor play area. Outside catering and bars available. At the north end of the Isle of Arran.

OPEN *All day, every day (except Christmas Day).*

Ormidale Hotel

Brodick, Isle of Arran KA27 8BY
☎ *(01770) 302293* Tommy Gilmore
www.ormidale-hotel.co.uk

Freehouse with two Arran ales plus one weekly-changing guest.

A lively rural pub in a Victorian building with large conservatory extension and beer garden. Home-cooked bar meals served 12.30–2pm and 6–9pm daily. Seven en-suite letting rooms available. Children welcome. Regular weekend discos. Folk nights on Sundays, pop quiz on Tuesdays, informal general knowledge quiz Thursdays. Located on the first left past the Brodick church.

OPEN *12–2pm and 4.30pm–12 Mon–Fri (summer); 4.30pm–12 Mon–Fri (winter); 12–12 Sat–Sun (all year).*

DUNDONALD
The Old Castle Bar
29 Main Street, Dundonald, Kilmarnock KA2 9HH
☎ *(01563) 851112*
Terry Quinn and Derek Callaghan

Freehouse serving Fuller's London Pride and beers from the Houston range.

Three hundred years old, with three bars, a restaurant, function room and beer garden. There is a natural spring well in the bar. Food served at lunchtimes and evenings. Children allowed, live music, large-screen TV. Just off the B739, five miles from Kilmarnock.

OPEN *11am–midnight.*

FAILFORD
The Failford Inn
Failford, Mauchline KA5 5TF
☎ *(01292) 540117 Chris and Michelle Kelsall*
www.failfordinn.co.uk

Home of the Windie Goat Brewery, with two of the brewery's beers plus a weekly guest.

Village inn dating from the 18th century on the banks of the River Ayr and adjacent to the River Ayr Way walk. Restaurant, bar and lounge. Food served 12–2.30pm and 5–9pm Mon–Thurs (until 7.30pm Wed), 12–9pm Fri–Sat and 12.30–7.30pm Sun. Beer garden. Children and dogs welcome. Easter and Hallowe'en beer festivals. Over the road from the Highland Mary Burns monument. On the B743 Ayr to Mauchline road.

OPEN *12–12 Mon–Thurs; noon–12.30am Fri–Sat; 12.30pm–12 Sun.*

KILMARNOCK
The Hunting Lodge
14–16 Glencairn Square, Kilmarnock KA1 4AH
☎ *(01563) 322920 R Hughes*

Freehouse with four real ales, including Caledonian Deuchars IPA and guests rotated every two weeks.

Olde-worlde Georgian pub with three bars and a separate eating area. Food served 12–6pm. Children welcome. Close to Kilmarnock FC ground.

OPEN *11am–midnight Mon–Wed; 11am–1am Thurs–Sat; 12.30pm–12 Sun.*

LARGS
The Clachan Bar
14 Bath Street, Largs KA30 8BL
☎ *(01475) 672224 William Shekleton*
http://the-clachan.bebo.com

Tied to the Belhaven brewery. One real ale in winter, two in summer, such as Belhaven St Andrew's Ale.

A traditional one-bar pub. Breakfast served 8am–12, lunch 12–5pm, high tea 5–8pm. Children welcome until 9pm.

OPEN *8am–midnight Mon–Wed; 8am–1am Thurs–Sat; 12.30pm–12 Sun.*

TROON
Dan McKay's Bar
69 Portland Street, Troon KA10 6QU
☎ *(01292) 311079 Dan McKay*

Freehouse with Caledonian Deuchars IPA plus three guest ales, changed frequently, which might be another Scottish brew or Timothy Taylor Landlord, Wadworth 6X, Young's Special or Fuller's London Pride.

Traditional single-bar family-run establishment, leaning towards a café bar, with TV, live music and jazz. Food at lunchtime. Children allowed during the day. Beer garden. Occasional beer festivals. In the town centre.

OPEN *All day, every day.*

WHITING BAY, ISLE OF ARRAN
Eden Lodge Hotel
Whiting Bay, Isle of Arran KA27 8QH
☎ *(01770) 700357 Victoria McAllister*
www.edenlodgehotel.co.uk

A freehouse. Caledonian Deuchars IPA plus one guest, changed every few days. Orkney Dark Island and Isle of Skye brews are regulars.

A sandstone hotel built in 1903, situated on the seafront with a huge beer garden. Locally sourced food served 12.30–9pm. Children welcome. Winner of CAMRA Regional Pub of the Year 2007/08. Accommodation. Car park. Located eight miles from the Brodick ferry terminal.

OPEN *12–12.*

BANFFSHIRE

PORTSOY
The Shore Inn
The Old Harbour, Church Street, Portsoy AB45 2QR
☎ *(01261) 842831 Mr Heron*

Freehouse with Isle of Skye Red Cuillin among the brews always available. A guest, changed weekly, is also offered.

A traditional, 300-year-old pub, overlooking a 17th-century harbour. Separate restaurant. Food served at breakfast, lunch and dinner. Children allowed.

OPEN *Summer: all day, every day. Winter: 11am–2pm and 5pm–close Mon–Fri; all day Sat–Sun.*

TOMINTOUL

The Glenavon Hotel

1 The Square, Tomintoul, Ballindalloch AB37 9ET
☎ *(01807) 580218* Mark and Sheona Finnie
www.glenavon-hotel.co.uk

 Freehouse always offering something from the Cairngorm Brewery plus a monthly guest.

A family-run country hotel with restaurant, cosy bar, sofas and real fire. Food served 12–2pm and 6–8pm. Six bedrooms. The restaurant seats 44 and there is also a private room seating 12. Patio with covered area. Beer garden, pool, darts. Parking. Children allowed. On the A939 Grantown to Ballater Road

OPEN *All day, every day.*

BERWICKSHIRE

ALLANTON

The Allanton Inn

Allanton, Duns TD11 3JZ
☎ *(01890) 818260* PR Hunter
www.allantoninn.co.uk

 Genuine freehouse with one or two real ales, changing weekly. Inveralmond Ossian is a favourite.

P rivately owned 18th-century coaching inn with two restaurants, beer garden and seven luxury en-suite bedrooms. Good food served 12–1pm and 6.30–8pm every day (not Sunday evening). Taste of the Borders winner 2004, 2005, 2006 and 2007. Children not welcome. One mile from Chirnside.

OPEN *12–2pm and 6–11pm.*

AUCHENCROW

The Craw Inn

Auchencrow TD14 5LS
☎ *(018907) 61253* Trevor Wilson

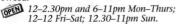 Two guest beers, varying on a regular basis – over 450 served in the last eight years (count the clips, which all go on display in the bar).

F amily-run, 18th-century, listed country inn in small, attractive Borders village. Borders CAMRA Pub of the Year 2008. Bar and restaurant food served 12–2pm (2.30pm Sun) and 6pm (7pm Sun)–9.30pm daily. Car park. Children welcome. En-suite accommodation. Off the A1, 14 miles north of Berwick-on-Tweed.

OPEN *12–2.30pm and 6–11pm Mon–Thurs; 12–12 Fri–Sat; 12.30–11pm Sun.*

BONCHESTER BRIDGE

Horse & Hound Hotel

Bonchester Bridge, Hawick TD9 8JN
☎ *(01450) 860645* Rebecca and Marie Hope

Weekly guest beers from breweries such as Maclay, Longstone, Bateman, Jennings, Caledonian, Belhaven or Holt.

A former coaching inn dating from 1704 with comfortable accommodation. Bar and restaurant food is available at lunchtimes and evenings. Car park. Children's certificate. Hawick is seven miles from Carter Bar on the England–Scotland border.

OPEN *11.30am–3pm and 6–11pm Mon–Fri; 11.30am–midnight Sat–Sun.*

EYEMOUTH

The Ship Hotel

Harbour Road, Eyemouth TD14 5HT
☎ *(01890) 750224* Lawrence Giacopazzi

Caledonian Deuchars IPA plus one guest, changed weekly.

L ocal fishermen's pub and family-run hotel near the harbour, with lounge bar featuring a coal fire, pool table, darts and live music at weekends. The Ship is a landmark in the village, and is mentioned repeatedly in the book *Children of the Sea* by Peter Aitchinson. Separate dining area serves food all day. Children allowed.

OPEN *All day, every day.*

GREENLAW

Cross Keys Inn

3 The Square, Greenlaw, Duns TD10 6UD
☎ *(01361) 10247* Mary O'Brian

Two real ales always available. Regulars including Timothy Taylor Landlord and Caledonian Deuchars IPA.

V ery old-fashioned freehouse with one bar and a restaurant area. Food lunchtimes and evenings. Children allowed.

OPEN *Closed daily between 2.30 and 5pm.*

PAXTON

The Cross Inn

Paxton TD15 1TE
☎ *(01289) 386267* Mike and Julie Ivison

Freehouse with two real ales that rotate weekly, all from local breweries.

A typical 17th-century village pub with a warm and friendly bar and separate dining room, where children are welcome. Food available 12–2pm and 5–9pm every day. Outside eating area. Car park. Children welcome. On the Borders Coast and Castles cycle route, close to Paxton House stately home. Follow the brown tourist signs.

OPEN *12–3pm and 5pm–12.*

CAITHNESS

MELVICH

Melvich Hotel

Melvich, Thurso KW14 7YJ
☎ *(01641) 531206* Peter Martin

Beers from the Far North range are always on offer.

Country hotel with two bars and a restaurant, overlooking the Pentland Firth to Orkney. Food served 6–8.15pm daily. Car park. Children welcome.

OPEN *All day, every day.*

CLACKMANNANSHIRE

ALVA

Cross Keys Inn

120 Stirling Street, Alva FK12 5EH
☎ *(01259) 760409* Moira Michie

Owned by Maclay Inns and serving three real ales with the emphasis on Scottish breweries. Maclay Kane's Amber (by Belhaven), Caledonian Deuchars IPA and something from Harviestoun are likely candidates.

A traditional pub with two bars. Popular with locals and visitors alike. Food at lunchtimes and evenings. Children allowed. On-street parking. B&B accommodation.

OPEN *All day, every day.*

DOLLAR

Castle Campbell Hotel

11 Bridge Street, Dollar FK14 7DE
☎ *(01259) 742519*
www.castle-campbell.co.uk

Freehouse with real ale on two pumps, Harviestoun Bitter & Twisted plus one guest changed at least weekly. Over 70 malts also available.

Built in 1822, a traditional Scottish country town hotel, with a great welcoming atmosphere. Bar and restaurant food served 12–2pm and 5.30–8.45pm. Children welcome. Nine bedrooms. Private room for hire, car park. An easy walk to Castle Campbell itself. In the centre of the village on the A91 between Stirling and St Andrews.

OPEN *All day, every day.*

The King's Seat

19 Bridge Street, Dollar FK14 7DE
☎ *(01259) 742515* Sharon McKnight

Harviestoun Bitter & Twisted plus three guest beers.

Village inn serving families (with a children's certificate). Bar and restaurant food available at lunchtimes and evenings. Parking. Dollar is on the main A91 road between Stirling and St Andrews.

OPEN *11am–midnight summer; 11am–11pm winter.*

The Lorne Tavern

17 Argyll Street, Dollar FK14 7AR
☎ *(01259) 743423* Jim Nelson

Freehouse with Harviestoun and Abbeydale brews always available. Two pumps, changed every four days, offer guests which include regulars from the Inveralmond brewery and the Maclay range.

A traditional local with separate restaurant. Children allowed in the dining room.

OPEN *All day, every day.*

POOL OF MUCKHART

The Inn at Muckhart

Pool of Muckhart, Muckhart FK14 7JN
☎ *(01259) 781324* Lorna Graham

Freehouse serving Devon Original, Pride and Thick Black plus others.

One-bar pub in a building dating from 1806, with beamed ceilings and log fires. Food available all day. Beer garden, car park, holiday cottages. Children welcome. On the A91 Stirling to St Andrews road.

OPEN *All day, every day.*

SAUCHIE

Mansfield Arms

7 Main Street, Sauchie, Nr Alloa FK10 3JR
☎ *(01259) 722020* Martin Gibson

The home of Devon Ales micro-brewery, with three beers brewed and served on the premises.

The four-barrel brewhouse was built from spare parts and discarded equipment and now produces cask ales in the English tradition. Brewing began in 1994. Food available all day. Car park, garden. Children allowed. Just north of Alloa.

OPEN *All day, every day.*

TILLICOULTRY

The Woolpack

1 Glassford Square, Tillicoultry FK13 6AH
☎ *(01259) 750332* D McGhee

Freehouse serving Harviestoun Ptarmigan 85/– and Orkney Dark Island plus a guest beer, changed every two days.

Built around 1700, a one-bar pub with restaurant and children's room. Food served all day. No children in the bar. Off the beaten track, no signposts. Head towards the Glen.

OPEN *·All day, every day.*

Brewed by **DEVON ALES** in Sauchie Alloa

DUMFRIESSHIRE

DALBEATTIE

The Pheasant Hotel

1 Maxwell Street, Dalbeattie DG5 4AH
☎ *(01556) 610345* Frances Thomson

Caledonian Deuchars IPA always available.

High-street community pub with TV and second-floor dining area. Food at lunchtimes and evenings (all day in summer). Children allowed. Friendly mix of local sport fans and out-of-town mountain bikers looking for a rare pint of real ale in Dalbeattie.

OPEN *All day, every day.*

DUMFRIES

Caven Arms

20 Buccleuch Street, Dumfries DG1 2AH
☎ *(01387) 252896* Gary Jeffries

Freehouse with Greene King Abbot Ale, Timothy Taylor Landlord, Caledonian Deuchars IPA and Phoenix Arizona plus four changing guests.

Warm and friendly pub known for having guest ales from all over the British Isles. Traditional home-cooked meals served 12–9pm Tues–Sun. Children over age of 14 welcome. Located next to the court.

OPEN *11am–11pm Tues; 11am–midnight Wed–Sat; 12.30–11pm Sun.*

Douglas Arms

Friars Vennel, Dumfries DG1 2RQ
☎ *(01387) 256002* A Whitefield

Broughton Greenmantle Ale, Merlin's Ale, The Ghillie, Black Douglas and Old Jock plus one guest beer (150 per year) to include Whim Magic Mushroom Mild and Hartington Bitter.

Old-style pub with a real coal fire. No food available. Situated in the town centre.

OPEN *11am–11pm Sun–Thurs; 11am–midnight Fri–Sat.*

The New Bazaar

38 Whitesands, Dumfries DG1 2RS
☎ *(01387) 268776* George Schneider

Freehouse with four real ales changed daily from a list of breweries including Belhaven, Bateman, Adnams, Titanic, Moorhouse's and Jennings.

A traditional Victorian public house consisting of public bar, lounge, family room and beer garden. The public bar has an old-fashioned gantry stocked with more than 200 malt and other whiskies. Lounge has real coal fire. Covered and heated beer garden/smoking area. Food available. Car park. Wheelchair access. The pub overlooks the River Nith.

OPEN *11am–11pm (midnight Fri–Sat).*

The Ship Inn

99 St Michael Street, Dumfries DG1 2PR
☎ *(01387) 255189* Keith Brown

Up to five real ales usually available. Brews from Greene King and Belhaven are regulars, and the guests are changed every three months.

Traditional pub with good conversation, good regulars and relaxed atmosphere. Lively, but with no loud music or other distractions. No food. No children. In St Michaels – follow signs for the hospital.

OPEN *All day, every day.*

Tam O'Shanter

117 Queensberry Street, Dumfries DG1 1BH
☎ *(01387) 254055* Kevin Hetterington

Caledonian Deuchars IPA and McEwans 80/- plus four guests, changed frequently, from a broad selection of brewers including Timothy Taylor, Jennings, Adnams, Orkney, Harviestoun, Fuller's and Greene King.

A traditional two-bar pub with upstairs restaurant and lounge. Food all day (not Sun). No TV or loud music. No children. Local CAMRA Pub of the Year 2003 and 2004.

OPEN *All day, every day from 11am.*

LANGHOLM

The Crown Hotel

High Street, Langholm DG13 0JH
☎ *(01387) 380247* A Barrie and B Bailey

Orkney brews always available in this freehouse, plus a guest beer changed weekly.

An 18th-century coaching house with five bars and a dining area. Food served. Children allowed.

OPEN *All day, every day.*

LOCKERBIE

Somerton House Hotel

35 Carlisle Road, Lockerbie DG11 2DR
☎ *(01576) 202583* Alex Arthur

Freehouse always offering Caledonian Deuchars IPA and Broughton Greenmantle. A guest is changed each week. Favourites include beers from Fuller's, Jennings and Caledonian breweries.

Hotel built in the 1880s with a separate dining area. Food served at lunchtime and evenings. Children allowed.

OPEN *All day, every day.*

MOFFAT

Black Bull Hotel

Churchgate, Moffat DG10 9EG
☎ *(01603) 220206* Jim Hughes
www.blackbullmoffat.co.uk

Freehouse serving Theakston Best Bitter and Caledonian Deuchars IPA.

An olde-worlde inn, circa 1568, full of history from Robert Burns to the Covenators to memorabilia from the Caledonian Railway. Two bars, one in hotel and one in railway bar. Food served 11am–2.15pm and 5–9.15pm Fri–Thurs, all day Sun. Accommodation available. Outside courtyard with covered bistro area and TVs. Children welcome. Exit the M74 at junction 15, take the A701 into town; the Black Bull is on the right.

OPEN *11am–11pm all year round.*

THORNHILL

Buccleuch & Queensberry Hotel

112 Drumlanrig Street, Thornhill DG3 5LU
☎ *(01848) 330215* Naomi Spencer
www.buccleuchhotel.co.uk

Freehouse with Caledonian 80/– plus one guest, changing every couple of days, perhaps Greene King Old Specked Hen or something from the local area.

Family-owned and -run coaching inn, built in 1714 for the Duke of Buccleuch. Traditional bar for shooters, fishers and locals, with log fires. Fresh food served 12–2.30pm and 5.30–9.30pm. Beer garden, function room (seats 60), private dining room, games room. Free car park. Children welcome. Fourteen en-suite rooms plus self-catering flat. At the centre of Thornhill Cross.

OPEN *11am–midnight (1am Fri–Sat).*

EAST LOTHIAN

BELHAVEN

The Mason's Arms

8 High Street, Belhaven, Dunbar EH42 1NP
☎ *(01368) 863700* Peter Sullivan

Freehouse with Belhaven 80/– or St Andrew's Ale usually available, or occasionally Sandy Hunter's Traditional Ale or something from Harviestoun.

Traditional country inn in a listed building, situated between West Barns and Dunbar. Bar, separate lounge and restaurant. Bar snacks served 12–2pm Mon–Tues, full bar menu 12–2pm and 6.30–9pm Wed–Sun. Children welcome until 9pm, with grass play area set within the beer garden. Next to Belhaven Brewery.

OPEN *12–3pm and 5–11pm Mon–Thurs; noon–1am Fri–Sat; 12–11pm Sun.*

EAST LINTON

The Drover's Inn

5 Bridge Street, East Linton EH40 3AG
☎ *(01620) 860298* Alison and John Burns

Freehouse with Adnams Broadside and Caledonian Deuchars IPA always on the menu. Two guests, changed most weeks, include regular choices such as Greene King Abbot, Fuller's London Pride or Orkney Red MacGregor.

Old-fashioned pub/restaurant with one bar, dining area and bistro. Live entertainment and folk bands monthly. Food at lunchtimes and evenings. Courtesy coach for parties of six or more operates within 25-mile radius. Children allowed.

OPEN *Summer: 11.30am–11pm Mon–Wed; 11.30am–1am Thurs–Sat; 12.30pm–12 Sun. Winter: times as above, except closed 2.30pm–5pm Mon–Sat.*

HADDINGTON

Waterside Bistro and Restaurant

1–5 Waterside, Nungate, Haddington EH41 4BE
☎ *(01620) 825674* James Findlay

Regular guests at this freehouse include Belhaven brews, Caledonian Deuchars IPA, Greene King Abbot and Timothy Taylor Landlord.

An old, restored cottage overlooking the River Tyne and the abbey. Separate dining area. Food at lunchtime and evenings. Children allowed.

OPEN *11am–2.30pm and 5–11pm.*

MUSSELBURGH

The Volunteer Arms (Staggs)

81 North High Street, Musselburgh EH21 6JE
☎ *(0131) 665 9654* Nigel Finlay

Freehouse with Caledonian Deuchars IPA plus guests, with 12 rotated each week.

Established in 1858 (so celebrated its 150th anniversary in 2008). A traditional inn with two bars, old Victorian wood panelling and stained glass. Former National CAMRA Pub of the Year, and named local Pub of the Year several years running. Beer garden. Annual beer festival on Remembrance Sunday. No food, but customers are welcome to bring their own. Sky TV. Car park. Located behind Brunton Theatre, known locally as Staggs.

OPEN *12.30–11pm Mon–Fri; 11.30am–midnight Sat; 1–11pm Sun.*

NORTH BERWICK

Nether Abbey Hotel

20 Dirleton Avenue, North Berwick EH39 4BQ
☎ *(01620) 892802* Stirling Stewart
www.netherabbey.co.uk

Freehouse with Caledonian Deuchars IPA plus three guests, changing all the time.

A hotel offering traditional values with a modern twist, and a warm, friendly atmosphere. Situated in a leafy Victorian avenue and run by the Stewart family for the last 40 years. One main bar. Food served 12–2.30pm and 6–9.30pm Mon–Thurs, 12–9.30pm Fri–Sun. Children welcome. There are 11 rooms, revamped in March 2007 to a very high standard. Beer garden, car park. Local attractions include the seabird centre. Five minutes from the train station.

OPEN *8am–11pm.*

PRESTONPANS

The Prestoungrange Gothenburg

227–9 High Street, Prestonpans EH32 9BE
☎ *(01875) 819922* Steven Cross
www.prestoungrange.org

Home of Fowler's Real Ales, with Gothenburg Porter, Prestonpans IPA and 80/– always available.

Remarkable 1908 building with two bars, function suite, micro-brewery and bistro. Profits over 5% are ploughed back into the local community. Food served 12–8.30pm (9pm Fri and Sat). Car park, beer festivals.

OPEN *12–close.*

FIFE

ABERDOUR

The Cedar Inn

20 Shore Road, Aberdour KY3 0TR
☎ *(01383) 860310* Richard Anthistle
www.cedarinn.co.uk

Four real ales, with Caledonian Deuchars IPA a permanent feature, plus three guests that rotate every week.

Friendly locals' pub, built in the mid-18th century, with two bars and a refurbished lounge bar. Food at lunchtimes and evenings. Children allowed. Beer garden. Ten en-suite bedrooms. Live music on Fridays. Golf available nearby. Close to the A921 and Aberdour railway station.

OPEN *All day, every day.*

ANSTRUTHER

Dreel Tavern

16 High Street, Anstruther KY10 3DL
☎ *(01333) 310727* Barry Scarsbrook

Freehouse with three real ales, changed at least once a week, including Tetley Bitter and ales from Scottish breweries.

A 16th-century coaching inn offering public bar, pool room, dining areas, plus a garden bar for summer days. Food available 12–2pm and 5.30–9pm (children's menu until 7pm).

OPEN *11am–midnight.*

CERES

Ceres Inn

The Cross, Ceres, Cupar KY15 5NE
☎ *(01334) 828305* Norma Stewart

Caledonian Deuchars IPA plus two other guest ales, often from Inveralmond and other Scottish breweries.

Olde-worlde pub built 1721, with good atmosphere, situated in the centre of Ceres (near St Andrews). Public bar. Restaurant bar. Food served 12–2.30pm and 5.30–9pm daily. Beer garden. Car park. Children allowed.

OPEN *12–11pm Mon–Tues; noon–1am Thurs–Fri; 12–12 Wed, Sat–Sun.*

EARLSFERRY

Golf Tavern (19th Hole)

Links Road, Earlsferry KY9 1AW
☎ *(01333) 330620* Gordon Davidson
www.golf-tavern.co.uk

Freehouse with Caledonian Deuchars IPA plus guests in summer, perhaps including Caledonian 80/- or Fuller's London Pride.

Traditional golfing pub featuring local memorabilia, renovated and extended in 2005, with bar, restaurant and games room. Food served all day until 9pm in summer; evenings and all day at weekends in winter. Children welcome. Located beside the fourth tee of Elie golf course.

OPEN *Summer: 11am–1am. Winter: 4pm–12.*

FREUCHIE

Albert Tavern

2 High Street, Freuchie KY15 7BG
☎ *(01337) 857192* Robbie Hunter

Freehouse regularly serving Belhaven 80/– plus up to three frequently changing guests from breweries across Scotland and further afield.

Two-bar, 18th-century village coaching inn with small upstairs restaurant bought in April 2000 by the current landlords, who were former regulars. Outside drinking area, children welcome. Some live entertainment. Food served at lunchtimes and evenings. CAMRA 2002 Scottish Pub of the Year.

OPEN *12–2pm and 5.30–11pm Mon–Thurs; noon–1am Fri–Sat; 12.30pm–12 Sun.*

KETTLEBRIDGE

Kettlebridge Inn

9 Cupar Road, Kettlebridge KY15 7QD
☎ *(01337) 830232* Paul and Sue Pinkney
www.ojila.co.uk

Freehouse with Belhaven St Andrew's always available.

A traditional village coaching inn in Fife golfing country on the A914 road to St Andrews. Open fires, lounge bar and restaurant. Mexican food available at 12–2pm and 6–9pm Tues–Sun. Street parking. Beer garden. Children welcome.

OPEN *Closed Mon; 12–12 Tues–Sun.*

KINGHORN

Auld Hoose

6–8 Nethergate, Kinghorn KY3 9SY
☎ *(01592) 891074* John Campbell

A freehouse. Fuller's London Pride and Caledonian Deuchars IPA. Plus one or two guests, changed weekly, from independents across the UK, such as Young's Special, Greene King Old Speckled Hen or Abbot, Shepherd Neame Spitfire or Marston's Pedigree.

A 100-year-old pub converted from original workers' houses; an old-style Scottish pub. Large bar area with pool table and darts board. Comfortable lounge bar. Sky Sports. Accommodation. No food. Off-street parking. Close to the beach and the coastal path.

OPEN *11am–midnight Mon–Sat; 12.30pm–12 Sun.*

KIRKCALDY

Betty Nicol's

297 High Street, Kirkcaldy KY1 1JL
☎ *(01592) 642083* Sandy Haxton

Freehouse with Caledonian Deuchars IPA always available.

Historic pub dating from 1726 in a listed building with unique features. One bar plus separate lounge for private functions. Bar food available Thurs–Sat, and snacks every day. Less than 200 metres from the harbour at the east end of the High Street.

OPEN *11am–11pm Mon–Thurs; 11am–midnight Fri–Sat; 12.30–10.30pm Sun.*

Harbour Bar

469 High Street, Kirkcaldy KY1 2SN
☎ *(01592) 264270*

Home of the Fyfe Brewing Company offering the full range of Fyfe beers. Also guests from Belhaven Brewery and elsewhere.

The brewery is located in an old sailworks behind and above the pub. Auld Alliance, the first brew, was launched in May 1995. The plant size is for two and a half barrels, with a ten-barrel per week restriction. The Harbour Bar is a traditional alehouse. Snacks are available at lunchtimes and evenings. Parking. Children not allowed.

OPEN *11am–2.30pm and 5pm–12 Mon–Wed; 11am–midnight Thurs–Sat; 12.30pm–12 Sun.*

LESLIE

Burns Tavern

184 High Street, Leslie, Glenrothes KY6 3DB
☎ *(01592) 741345* Archie McCormack

Timothy Taylor Landlord and Caledonian Deuchars IPA regularly served. Wide selection of ales from surrounding local breweries. Customers' requests are welcome.

Very friendly local Scottish pub. Functions catered for and folk club every Wednesday. Food available.

OPEN *All day, every day.*

PITLESSIE

The Village Inn

Cupar Road, Pitlessie, Cupar KY15 7SU
☎ *(01337) 830595* Randolph D Wallace
www.thevillageinnpitlessie.co.uk

Caledonian Deuchars IPA plus one constantly changing guest ale.

A 17th-century coaching inn with one main bar and separate function room with its own bar. Food served lunchtimes and evenings Mon–Sun. Beer garden. Car park. Children welcome. Near St Andrew's golf courses, Cairnie farm maze and the Fife coastline. Located on the A914 between Glenrothes and Cupar.

OPEN *11am–2.30pm and 5pm–12 Mon–Thurs; 11am–3pm and 5pm–1am Fri; 11am–1am Sat; 12–12 Sun.*

ST ANDREWS

Drouthy Neebors

209 South Street, St Andrews KY16 9EF
☎ *(01334) 479952* Mr Shug

Belhaven tied house with St Andrew's and 80/- plus four guest ales. Regular features include Orkney Dark Island and Raven Ale, plus Ridleys Rumpus.

A real mixed-bag clientele here: students, locals, tourists. Food available. Children allowed. Car parking.

OPEN *11am–midnight Mon–Thurs; 11am–1am Fri–Sat; 12.30pm–12 Sun.*

The Whey Pat Tavern

1 Bridge Street, St Andrews KY16 9EX
☎ *(01334) 477740* Andy Cunningham

Belhaven/Greene King pub serving Greene King IPA plus three rotating guests changed every two or three days.

A traditional bar firmly lodged in the heart of the community and managing to attract a large student clientele. The oldest licensed premises in the area of St Andrews. Food served 12–2pm Mon–Sun. Outdoor heated, secluded yard. Two beer festivals held in May and October to promote real ale. Cask Marque accredited. Located across the road from West Port, the old town port.

OPEN *11am–midnight Sun–Thurs; 11am–1am Fri–Sat.*

INVERNESS-SHIRE

AVIEMORE

Old Bridge Inn

Dalfaber Road, Aviemore PH22 1PU
☎ *(01479) 811137* Nigel Reid
www.oldbridgeinn.co.uk

Three rotating real ales at this freehouse. The menu changes weekly but could well include Caledonian 80/- and Deuchars IPA plus Gale's HSB.

Traditional Highland inn set in a rural location just off the 'Ski Road' (B970) and next to the River Spey. Separate dining area. Food is available 12–2pm and 6–9pm. Good-value, quality accommodation available in adjacent bunkhouse. Beer garden, car park. Children welcome. Smoking veranda.

OPEN *All day, every day.*

CARRBRIDGE

Cairn Hotel

Main Road, Carrbridge PH23 3AS
☎ *(01479) 841212* Andrew Kirk
www.cairnhotel.co.uk

Beers from Cairngorm, Black Isle, Isle of Skye, Atlas are regularly available plus perhaps something from An Teallach or Orkney.

Family-owned, traditional freehouse in ideal touring area. Situated in the centre of the village, well visited by locals and tourists alike. Food served 12–2.15pm and 6–8.30pm. Snacks and soup all day. Car park. Children's certificate. En-suite accommodation.

OPEN *11am–midnight Mon–Fri; 11am–1am Sat; 12–11pm Sun.*

DRUMNADROCHIT
Benleva Hotel

Drumnadrochit, Inverness IV63 6UH
☎ *(01456) 450080*
Allan and Stephen Crossland
www.benleva.co.uk

Freehouse with an Isle of Skye ale plus three constantly rotating guests, mainly from Highland breweries. One real cider also available.

A 400-year-old former manse with hanging tree at the front. One main bar and cosy lounge bar. Food prepared with fresh, local produce served early evening all year round and at lunchtimes during summer. Six en-suite letting rooms. Children and dogs welcome. Plenty of car parking. Home of the annual Loch Ness beer festival in September. Near Urquhart Castle. Located just off the main Fort William–Inverness road (A82).

OPEN *All day, every day (reduced hours in winter, phone for details).*

FORT WILLIAM
The Grog & Gruel

66 High Street, Fort William PH33 6AE
☎ *(01397) 705078* Guy and Ed Daynes
www.grogandgruel.co.uk

Up to eight ales on offer in regular rotation, including beers from the Atlas Brewery in Kinlochleven, Williams Bros. Brewing, and Isle of Skye Brewery. Seasonal and celebration ales, and occasional festivals.

A traditional town pub in an old building. Bar and restaurant food available. Children allowed daytimes only.

OPEN *12–12 Mon–Wed; noon–1am Thurs–Sat; 12–11pm Sun.*

INVERNESS
Blackfriars Highland Pub

93–5 Academy Street, Inverness IV1 1LU
☎ *(01463) 233881* Janette Scott

Five real ales, three of them Scottish, the other two English. All are changed monthly.

Single large bar with aged character, originally built in 1793 as a shop. In 1867 it became a Temperance Hotel, and between 1930 and 1960 was called the Abertarff Bar. Home-cooked Scottish fayre available 11am–9pm Mon–Sat and 12.30–8pm Sun. Beer festivals, regular entertainment such as ceilidhs, country nights and Scottish nights. Children welcome. Car parking available two minutes away. Close to shops, castle and River Ness, and two minutes from railway station.

OPEN *11am–midnight.*

The Castle Tavern

1 View Place, Inverness IV2 4SA
☎ *(01463) 718178* George Maclean
www.castletavern.net

Freehouse with their own brew, Flora Macdonalds, Cairngorm's Trade Winds and Atlas' Dark Island plus two daily-changing guests from breweries such as Adnams and Greene King.

This pub is focused on serving quality real ales and good food. Two bars. Food served all day every day until late evening. Large beer garden. Joint-hosting the Inverness Beer Festival with Clachnaharry Inn. Nearby attractions include Inverness Castle and Loch Ness. Located in Inverness city centre. CAMRA local Pub of the Year for 2008.

OPEN *11am–1am.*

Clachnaharry Inn

17–19 High Street, Clachnaharry Road, Inverness IV3 8RB
☎ *(01463) 239806* Charlotte Boyle

Freehouse offering up to ten real ales, plus their own village ale brewed by Skye.

Old coaching inn next to the railway and canal. Lounge and public bar. CAMRA Inverness Pub of the Year 2007 – they've won six times in the past eight years! The beer garden used to be a train platform. Co-host of the Inverness Beer Festival every September. Food served all day. Regular live entertainment. Children allowed in lounge only. A good starting point for historic tours around the town.

OPEN *All day, every day.*

The Heathmount Hotel

Kingsmills Road, Inverness IV2 3JU
☎ *(01463) 235877* Fiona Newton
www.heathmounthotel.com

Freehouse where Atlas Three Sisters and Latitude, Black Isles Red Kite and Isle of Skye Red Cuillin are rotated (three real ales on every night).

Victorian building given a contemporary revamp. Two bars, seven guest rooms. Food available all day. Children allowed. Five minutes' walk from city centre.

OPEN *All day, every day.*

Number 27

27 Castle Street, Inverness IV2 3DU
☎ *(01463) 241999* Grant Skinner

Freehouse serving two constantly changing real ales such as Caledonian Deuchars IPA and beers from Black Isle, An Teallach, Atlas, Cairngorm and Orkney.

Well-established city-centre bar and restaurant, situated below the castle at the top of the High Street. Food is served in the renowned restaurant 12–2.45pm and 5–9.30pm. Children welcome. Parking available nearby.

OPEN *11am–11pm (12.30am Fri–Sat); 12.30–11pm Sun.*

The Glen Hotel
Main Street, Newtonmore PH20 1DD
☎ *(01540) 673203* Chris and Kim Goodhill
www.theglenhotel.co.uk

 Freehouse with three constantly rotating guest ales from across Scotland.

A one-bar Edwardian village inn located within Cairngorms National Park. Open fires. Food served 12–2.30pm and 6–9pm Mon–Sun. Ten letting rooms available. Families welcome. Large car park. Outdoor beer terrace. Close to Cairngorm mountains and Loch Ness. Situated halfway between Perth and Inverness, just off the A9, easily found on the village's main street.

OPEN *All day, every day.*

SLIGACHAN, ISLE OF SKYE
The Sligachan Hotel
Sligachan, Isle of Skye IV47 8SW
☎ *(01478) 650204* Iain Campbell

Freehouse with five real ale pumps in the public bar. Beers from the pub's own Cuillin Brewery feature along with a range from Houston and Heather Ales. Also over 200 malt whiskies.

A 100-year-old building with a large public bar/restaurant. Pool tables, children's play areas and fresh local food.

OPEN *Easter–October and New Year only; 8am–close Mon–Sat; 11am–close Sun.*

WATERNISH, ISLE OF SKYE
Stein Inn
Waternish, Isle of Skye IV55 8GA
☎ *(01470) 592362*
Angus and Teresa McGhie
www.steininn.co.uk

Brews from the local Isle of Skye brewery including Red Cuillin and house beer Reeling Deck, plus guests and at least 90 malt whiskies.

Dating from 1790, this is the oldest pub on Skye. A lochside inn on the Waternish Peninsula with stunning views. Real fires, pool room, beer garden. Good food, including local seafood, served 12–4pm and 6–9.30pm in summer. Reduced hours in winter. Bed and breakfast or self-catering accommodation plus yacht moorings nearby. A great place to arrive by sea.

OPEN *11am–midnight (1am Fri, 12.30am Sat). Hours may vary in winter.*

KIRKCUDBRIGHTSHIRE

CASTLE DOUGLAS
The Royal Hotel
17 King Street, Castle Douglas DG7 1AA
☎ *(01556) 502040* Mrs Bennett

Freehouse with Orkney Dark Island and Caledonian Deuchars IPA.

Small, family-run hotel with two bars and a separate restaurant. Children allowed.

OPEN *All day, every day.*

GATEHOUSE OF FLEET
The Masonic Arms
10 Ann Street, Gatehouse of Fleet, Castle Douglas DG7 2HU
☎ *(01557) 814335*
Danielle Cipa and James Macintosh
www.themasonic-arms.co.uk

Freehouse with Caledonian Deuchars IPA, and specially brewed house ale The Masonic Boom.

Former masonic lodge, with three distinct areas. Food served 12–2pm and 6–9pm. The only pub in the area to be featured in Egon Ronay's *Guide to the Best Restaurants and Gastropubs* 2006.

OPEN *11.30am–2.30pm and 5.30–11.30pm.*

HAUGH OF URR
Laurie Arms Hotel
11–13 Main Street, Haugh of Urr, Castle Douglas DG7 3LA
☎ *(01556) 660246* Sandra Yates

Freehouse offering a selection of three Scottish and traditional English ales, all changed two or three times a week.

A friendly, local country pub with log fires, main bar, dining area and beer garden, plus a growing reputation for its excellent cuisine. Homemade food served in bar, dining room and beer garden 12–2pm and 5.30–9pm. Children welcome. Large car park. Between Dumfries and Castle Douglas off the A75.

OPEN *12–3pm and 5.30pm–12 Mon–Fri; 12–12 Sat–Sun.*

KIRKCUDBRIGHT
Selkirk Arms Hotel
High Street, Kirkcudbright DG6 4JG
☎ *(01557) 330402* Douglas McDavid
www.selkirkarmshotel.co.uk

Freehouse with Sulwath Criffel plus two guests, changed weekly, often including Theakston Old Peculier, Greene King Old Speckled Hen or Timothy Taylor Landlord. The pub's own real ale, The Grace, is brewed by Sulwath, and celebrates the fact that Robert Burns wrote 'The Selkirk Grace' in the hotel.

Georgian hotel with public and lounge bars and a bistro plus garden. Food at lunchtimes (12–2pm) and evenings (6–9.30pm). Children allowed. Beer festivals. Five miles off the A75.

OPEN *All day, every day.*

NEW GALLOWAY
The Cross Keys Hotel
High Street, New Galloway DG7 3RN
☎ *(01644) 420494*
Kevin Chisnall and Susan O'Hare
www.crosskeys-newgalloway.co.uk

Freehouse with two rotating guests, from breweries such as Houston.

Village hotel with a locals' bar in a beautiful part of Scotland. Food served Wed–Sun. Beer garden. Ten en-suite letting rooms. Located 13 miles from the A75 at the top of Loch Ken.

OPEN *All day, every day.*

LANARKSHIRE

AIRDRIE

The Cellar Bar

79 Stirling Street, Airdrie ML6 0AS
☎ *(01236) 764495* George Cairs

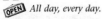Two guest ales always available from the local Belhaven brewery.

A traditional pub with a range of real ales and 369 malt whiskies. Food served 12–8pm daily. Car park. No children.

OPEN *11am–1am Mon–Sat; 12.30pm–12 Sun.*

BARRHEAD

Cross Stobs Inn

2–6 Grahamston Road, Barrhead G78 1NS
☎ *(0141) 881 1581*

Kelburn Brewery's Red Smiddy, Goldi Hops and Carte Blanche almost always available, plus guest beers.

Historical locals' pub.

OPEN *All day, every day.*

BIGGAR

The Crown Inn

109–11 High Street, Biggar ML12 6DL
☎ *(01899) 220116* Mr and Mrs Watkins
www.thecrownbiggar.co.uk

Freehouse offering real ale on two pumps, with the constantly changing selection ranging from Adnams Broadside to local ales such as those from Broughton. No two weeks are the same!

A 17th-century pub with two bars. Food served all day. Beer garden. Children allowed. Function room available.

OPEN *All day, every day.*

CASTLECARY

Castlecary House Hotel

Main Street, Castlecary, Cumbernauld G68 0HB
☎ *(01324) 840233* C McMillan
www.castlecaryhotel.com

Freehouse with two or three real ales, from breweries such as Caledonian, Moorhouse's, Mordue, Crouch Vale, Hobsons and Brains. All are rotated weekly.

Traditional, family-owned hotel with two lounge bars and friendly service. Beer garden, outside smoking area. Food served all day, every day. Children welcome. Accommodation (55 rooms). Private rooms for hire for weddings, meetings etc. Free car parking. Spring and autumn beer festivals. Live entertainment. Just off the A80, 15 minutes from Stirling and Falkirk.

OPEN *11am–11pm Mon–Wed; 11am–11.30pm Thurs–Sat; 12.30–11pm Sun.*

GLASGOW

Blackfriars

36 Bell Street, Glasgow G1 1LG
☎ *(0141) 552 5924* Jon McMillan
www.blackfriarsglasgow.com

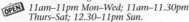A freehouse. Various Kelburn ales plus four guests from breweries such as Dark Star, Inveralmond, Stewart and Williams. Also an extensive collection of European bottled beer such as Weisse, Orval, Chimay and Leffe.

A city-centre pub. Food served 11am–8pm Mon–Sat; 12.30–8pm Sun. Winner of CAMRA Glasgow and West Scotland Pub of the Year 2006. Live entertainment most nights. Situated on the corner of Bell Street and Albion Street, just off Argyle Street.

OPEN *11am–midnight Mon–Thurs; 11am–3am Fri–Sat; 12.30pm–12 Sun.*

The Bon Accord

153 North Street, Glasgow
☎ *(0141) 248 4427*
Paul McDonagh (proprietor)

At least ten real ales (600 a year), including offerings from Kelburn, Atlas, Orkney, plus Marston's Pedigree and Caledonian Deuchars IPA. Regular festivals when over 20 brews are on.

The pub that led the reintroduction of real ale to Glasgow in the early 1970s. Remains one of the city's best – and best known – cask ale haunts. Cellar tours can be arranged for groups of 10–15, Mon–Thurs. Good value pub grub; quiz 8pm Wed night; live music 8.30pm Sat night. Home of Clan Pompey, the Scottish Portsmouth FC supporters club. Glasgow CAMRA Pub of the Year.

OPEN *12–11.45pm.*

The Counting House

2 St Vincent Place, Glasgow G1 2DH
☎ *(0141) 225 0160* Stuart Coxshall
www.jdwetherspoon.co.uk

This JD Wetherspoon house hosts a real ale festival in the spring, when there may be 50 brews on sale. The rest of the time, Caledonian 80/– and Deuchars IPA are among the eight beers always available. Guests change weekly.

Converted Bank of Scotland building with original fixtures and fittings, including the safe. Ninety tables. Food available all day (10am–10pm). Children allowed until 7pm, if eating. In the city centre.

OPEN *10am–midnight every day.*

Mulberry St

778 Pollokshaws Road, Strathbungo, Glasgow G42 2AE
☎ *(0141) 424 0858* Bernadetta Corvi
www.myspace.com/mulberryst

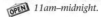Three beers, including Caledonian Deuchars IPA and Harviestoun Bitter & Twisted, plus one guest.

Café-style bar and bistro serving traditional and European dishes, a nice place to relax. Food served 12–late every day. Children welcome till 8pm. Outside seating for summer. Room for private functions. Situated beside Queen's Park railway station, not far from Shawlands Cross.

OPEN *11am–midnight.*

The State

148 Holland Street, Glasgow G2 4NG
☎ *(0141) 332 2159* Agnes Lyons

Caledonian Heritable pub with Caledonian 80/–, Houston Killellan, Stewarts Edinburgh No. 3 and Caledonian Deuchars IPA plus three constantly changing guest ales from breweries all over the UK.

Victorian-style pub with island bar and downstairs lounge. Interior includes original stained glass, dark wood and many pictures of Glasgow and acts from Kings Theatre. Food served 12–2pm Mon–Fri. Long-established and popular blues night on Tuesdays. Well-attended comedy club on Saturdays. Occasional acoustic events with artists from the USA and UK. Close to Kings Theatre and Charing Cross train station. Located between Bath Street and Sauchiehall Street.

 11am–midnight.

Station Bar

55 Port Dundas Road, Glasgow G4 0HF
☎ *(0141) 332 3117* Derek Watson (manager)
www.agreatpub.co.uk

A famous freehouse with Caledonian Deuchars IPA and Greene King Abbot plus two guests from around the country.

Steeped in tradition, this local has been licensed since 1850, and unlike many city-centre venues, has retained its name for many decades. Its clientele is an amazing mixture of locals, blue collar workers, professional customers and visitors from around the world. Breakfast from 8am Mon–Fri. Bar meals and snacks are available 12–3pm, and Sunday Lunches 12.30–5.30pm.

All day, every day.

Tap

1055 Sauchiehall Street, Glasgow G3 7UD
☎ *(0141) 339 0643* Gary Hamilton

Caledonian Deuchars IPA and 80/– usually served, with guest beers such as Heather Ale and Marston's Pedigree.

Traditional bar in a residential area catering mainly for student clientele. Specialising in jazz, with live music at weekends. A light-hearted and welcoming pub favoured by musicians and arty types. Food served 12–9pm. No children. Situated directly opposite Kelvingrove Art Gallery in West End.

12–11pm Sun–Thurs; 12–12 Fri–Sat.

Tennents Bar

191 Byres Road, Hillhead, Glasgow G12
☎ *(0141) 341 1024* Alison O'Conner

Up to 12 beers available from a guest list (100 per year) that may include Fuller's London Pride, Jennings Cumberland, Greene King Old Speckled Hen and Marston's Pedigree. Plus Scottish brews such as Arran Dark Island and Caledonian Deuchars IPA and 80/–.

A large public bar with a friendly atmosphere and no music. Bar food available lunchtimes and evenings. Adjacent to Glasgow University and Hillhead subway.

11am–11pm Mon–Thurs; 11am–midnight Fri–Sat; 12.30–11.30pm Sun.

The Three Judges

141 Dumbarton Road, Partick Cross, Glasgow G11 6PR
☎ *(0141) 337 3055* Angela Bradley

Eight real ales, from micro-breweries all over Britain. The beers are rotated on a daily basis, and a farmhouse cider is also served.

One-bar pub in a tenement building, near Byres Road in the west end of Glasgow. No food. Parking available. Beer festivals held in March (stouts, porters and milds) June (Scottish beers), plus a cider festival in October. Near Kelvin Hall underground.

 11am–11pm Sun–Thurs; 11am–midnight Fri–Sat.

HAMILTON

The George Bar

18 Campbell Street, Hamilton ML3 6AS
☎ *(01698) 424225* Lynn Adams
www.thegeorgebar.com

Belhaven pub with a Greene King ale usually among the three beers available, the rest rotating every few days.

A friendly, traditional-style, town-centre pub, a Cask Marque award winner. Main bar with small back room. Beer festivals twice a year. Food available 12–4pm. Children welcome. Outside area with licence. Can be tricky to find because of the one-way system! Ten minutes from the station.

All day, every day.

LANARK

Horse & Jockey

56 High Street, Lanark ML11 7ES
☎ *(01555) 664825* Ian Dick

Freehouse with one or two constantly rotating ales, from breweries such as Houston, Timothy Taylor, Harvieston, Strathaven and Northumberland.

Dating back to the 1730s, this pub takes its name from a racecourse once located in Lanark. A traditional Scottish bar with good hospitality. Live music on occasional weekends. Food served 11.30am–2.30pm Mon–Sat, Sat evening meals available from 5pm. Car park. Lounge bar available for private functions. Town-centre location.

11am–midnight Mon–Sat; 12.30pm–12 Sun.

STRATHAVEN

The Weavers

1/3 Green Street, Strathaven, ML10 6LT
☎ *07749 332914* Brendan Smith

The only pub in Strathaven selling brews from Strathaven Ales, plus two to three guests changed every few days, such as Greene King Abbot Ale, Fuller's London Pride, Bateman XXXB, Thwaites Lancaster Bomber and Charles Wells Bombardier.

Family-run freehouse, formerly the Crown Hotel. CAMRA Lanarkshire Pub of the Year 2006 and 2007. No televisions. No food.

11am–midnight Mon; 4.30pm–midnight Tues–Wed; 4.30pm–1am Thurs; 11am–1am Fri–Sat; 7pm–1am Sun.

MIDLOTHIAN

EDINBURGH

Barony Bar

81–5 Broughton Street, Edinburgh EH1 3RJ
☎ *(0131) 558 2874 Malcolm Binnie*

 Punch Taverns leased pub with Caledonian Deuchars IPA, Black Sheep Bitter, Caledonian 80/– and Young's Bitter plus three guests, changed twice weekly.

One-bar pub in a 200-year-old listed building just outside the city centre. Large mirrors, tile-work and gantry. Food served 11am–10pm daily. Disabled access. Beer festivals. Live music on Sundays. Located just off Princes Street.

OPEN *11am–midnight Mon–Thurs; 11am–1am Fri–Sat; 12.30–11.30pm Sun.*

The Blue Blazer

2 Spittal Street, Edinburgh EH3 9DX
☎ *(0131) 229 5030 James Nisbet*

A Scottish and Newcastle Pub Enterprises house, but free of tie for guest ales. Cairngorm Trade Winds, Stewart 80/–, Orkney Dark Island and Pentland IPA plus four guests, changed twice weekly. Mostly Scottish beers served from breweries such as An Teallach, Houston, Fyne, Orkney and Heather Ales. Also 70 rums, 15 gins, 20 bourbons, 50 malts and a selection of cocktails.

A traditional pub dating from 1889 in the west port area of the city centre. A two-room alehouse with a large selection of beer and spirits. A mixed clientele of actors, professionals, students, hospitality workers and musicians. Bar snacks (pies and sandwiches) available all day. Situated off Lothian road, on the corner of Bread Street and Spittal Street.

OPEN *11am–1am Mon–Sat; 12.30pm–1am Sun.*

The Bow Bar

80 West Bow, Edinburgh EH1 2HH
☎ *(0131) 226 7667 Helen McLoughlin*

Belhaven 80/–, Caledonian Deuchars IPA and Timothy Taylor Landlord plus five constantly changing guests, including a couple from Scotland and the rest from other independent breweries – from Orkney to Cornwall (550 each year).

Quite simply one of Edinburgh's – and Scotland's – finest bars. A well-loved and staunchly supported one-room freehouse offering an unparalleled selection of real ales and malt whiskies. No music. Beer festivals usually twice yearly, depending on pressure from the bar's regulars. Snacks at lunchtime, pork scratchings any time. No children but well-behaved dogs welcome. In the old town, five minutes from Waverley train station.

OPEN *12–11.30pm (11pm Sun).*

The Caley Sample Room

42–58 Angle Park Terrace, Edinburgh EH11 2JR
☎ *(0131) 337 7204*
www.thecaleysampleroom.co.uk

Caledonian Deuchars IPA and 80/– plus three guest beers and wines by the bottle or glass.

Restored and refurbished bar serving food from 12–9pm and drinks at other times.

OPEN *11.30am–midnight Mon–Thurs; 11.30am–1am Fri; 10am–1am Sat; 10am–11pm Sun.*

The Cambridge Bar

20 Young Street, Edinburgh EH2 4JB
☎ *(0131) 225 2120 Jon and Nicky Clemence*
www.thecambridgebar.co.uk

 Caledonian Deuchars IPA plus a guest, rotated every few weeks, perhaps from Stewart Brewing or Fyne Ales.

The Cambridge's friendly atmosphere has made it the base for a host of clubs and societies, from cavers to conservationists. Small, traditional pub on the ground floor and basement of a mews house off Charlotte Square. Gourmet burgers served 12–9pm.

OPEN *11am–11pm Mon–Wed; 11am–midnight Thurs; 11am–1am Fri–Sat; 12–11pm Sun.*

The Cask & Barrel

115 Broughton Street, Edinburgh EH1 3RZ
☎ *(0131) 556 3132 Patrick Mitchell*

Harviestoun Bitter & Twisted, Young's Special, Caledonian 80/– and Deuchars IPA are fixtures among an impressive daily line-up of ten real ales that includes four guests, changed once or twice a week. Large selection of continental bottled beers also on offer.

Popular horseshoe-style bar opened in 1992 and pulling in an eclectic bunch of customers. Food available 12–2pm. Outside seating from March–Oct. Disabled toilets and access. At the bottom of Broughton Street, half a mile from the city centre.

OPEN *11am–12.30am Mon–Wed; 11am–1am Thurs–Sat; 12.30pm–12.30am Sun.*

Cloisters Bar

26 Brougham Street, Edinburgh EH3 9JH
☎ *(0131) 221 9997 Barry Robertson*
www.cloistersbar.co.uk

 Freehouse with nine real ales. Caledonian Deuchars IPA, Timothy Taylor Landlord, Cairngorm Trade Winds and Stewart No. 3 are permanently featured, and the five guests are regularly rotated. There are also over 80 whiskies on offer, plus a good selection of international bottled beers.

Built in 1878 as a parsonage, this friendly, relaxed pub has a mixed clientele of students and real ale lovers. Meals are served 12–6pm every day. No children under 14. Wireless internet access. Board games and book exchange available. Two beer festivals a year.

OPEN *12–12 (1am Fri–Sat).*

The Cumberland Bar

1–3 Cumberland Street, Edinburgh EH3 6RT
☎ *(0131) 558 3134 Jo Douglas*
www.cumberlandbar.co.uk

Freehouse with eight real ales, including beers from Caledonian, Timothy Taylor, Greene King and Harviestoun, plus four guest ales, changed when they run out.

A traditional one-bar alehouse with rooms off for functions and gatherings. Food served every lunchtime and evening. Regular winter 'buy three get one free' beer festivals. Children allowed in part of the bar if under control. Beer garden and private meeting room. In the New Town.

OPEN *11am–1am Mon–Sat; 12.30pm–1am Sun.*

The Guildford Arms

1 West Register Street, Edinburgh EH2 2AA
☎ *(0131) 556 4312* Steve Jackson
www.guildfordarms.com

Deuchars IPA, Orkney Dark Island, Harviestoun Bitter & Twisted, Fyne Ales Avalanche and a rotating beer from Stewart plus five guest beers such as Wylam Rocket, Black Isle Yellow Hammer, Highland Brewing St Magnus, Taylors Best, Leeds Best, Isle of Skye Hebridean Gold, Hadrian and Borders Byker Jazz , to name but a few. As one beer goes off it is immediately replaced by a different one.

B eautiful Jacobean pub. Restaurant food available 12–2.30pm and 6–9.30pm Mon–Thurs; 12–3pm and 6–10pm Fri–Sat; 12.30–3pm and 6–9.30pm Sun. Edinburgh Fringe Festival Venue, 7–30 August. 7–19 August: Jazz Festival sponsored by Orkney and Atlas Brewery, 20-29 August Folk and Blues Festival sponsored by Caledonian Brewery. Additional brewery weekends and beer festivals throughout year. At the east end of Princes Street, behind Burger King.

OPEN *11am–11pm Mon–Thurs; 11am–midnight Fri–Sat; 12.30–11pm Sun.*

Halfway House

24 Fleshmarket Close, High Street, Edinburgh EH1 1BX
☎ *(0131) 225 7101* John Ward
www.halfwayhouse-edinburgh.com

Specialising in Scottish breweries, with four real ales available. Atlas, Fyne, Harviestoun, Houston, Inveralmond, Kelburn, Stewart, Isle of Skye, An Teallach and many others on offer at admirably low prices for cask beer in the Old Town. Look out for brewery 'showcase' weeks during the seven weeks of the Edinburgh Festival. Also a fine range of malt whiskies.

C AMRA Pub of the Year 2005 for Scotland and Northern Ireland. One of the smallest and friendliest pubs in the Old Town, hidden away between Waverley station and the Royal Mile and very close to both. Good-value homemade Scots fare including stovies, cullen skink, haggis. Food available all day, if it hasn't sold out! The pub was given a 'star' rating in the *Good Pub Food Guide*. Take the Old Town exit from Waverley station and up the steps opposite (50 metres).

OPEN *12–12 (later at weekends and during Festival).*

Homes Bar

102 Constitution Street, Leith, Edinburgh EH6 6AW
☎ *(0131) 553 7710* Patrick Fitzgerald

Freehouse with five real ales served on custom-made hand pumps. Guest beers a speciality.

T raditional one-room friendly bar, with interesting decor featuring antiques and memorabilia. Snacks served 12–3pm daily.

OPEN *All day, every day.*

Kay's Bar

39 Jamaica Street, Edinburgh EH3 6HF
☎ *(0131) 225 1858*
Dave MacKenzie and Fraser Gillespie

Caledonian Deuchars IPA plus five guests, changed daily. Sample beers include Young's Special, Belhaven 80/–, Fyne Gold, Exmoor Gold and Sharp's Doom Bar.

T he building started life in 1812 as a shop/workshop for a George Street wine merchant. It was converted into a bar in 1976 and is now a regulars' pub, full of local characters, not to mention the staff! Small bar, even smaller back room. Coal fire in winter. Food served 12–2.30pm. No children. Located north of Princes Street, in the New Town area.

OPEN *11am–midnight Mon–Thurs; 11am–1am Fri–Sat; 12.30–11pm Sun.*

Leslie's Bar

45 Ratcliffe Terrace, Edinburgh EH9 1SU
☎ *(0131) 667 5957* Gavin Blake
www.lesliesbar.com

Freehouse with real ale on six pumps. Caledonian 80/– and Deuchars IPA plus Timothy Taylor Landlord always available. Three guest beers also offered, which often include a Maclay, Atlas or Orkney brew.

U pmarket Victorian local unchanged in over 100 years, with ornate ceiling, old-fashioned gantry and open fire. Original stained glass and numbered serving hatches. Named after a legendary licensee who presided between 1902 and 1924. One bar. Pies and toasties only. No children. Beer and whisky festivals held twice-yearly. Two miles south of the city centre.

OPEN *11am–11pm Mon–Wed; 11am–11.30pm Thurs; 11am–12.30am Fri–Sat; 12.30–11.30pm Sun.*

Old Chain Pier

32 Trinity Crescent, Edinburgh EH5 3ED
☎ *(0131) 552 1233* Brian Donnelly

Caledonian Deuchars IPA, Black Sheep Best Bitter and Timothy Taylor Landlord are permanent fixtures plus one guest, changed weekly.

A pub in a listed building dating back to the 19th century, with sea views and original old chain pier mooring. Mixed clientele, both young and old. Separate conservatory and outside seating. Home-cooked food served 12–9pm. Children's certificate. Find the sea at Newhaven, and the pub is there!

OPEN *12–11pm (open 12.30pm Sun).*

Ossian's

185 Morrison Street, Edinburgh EH3 8DZ
☎ *(0131) 228 9149* Craig McGhee

Belhaven house with Caledonian Deuchars IPA and Inveralmond Ossian's Ale plus three rotating guest ales, changed every couple of days. A selection of malt whiskies is also served.

A traditional bar with a mixed clientele. One main bar and an upstairs gallery. Two plasma screens. Food served 10am–7pm daily. Live music. Private functions catered for. Close to the conference centre on the main road from Haymarket station.

OPEN *11am–1am.*

The Oxford Bar

8 Young Street, Edinburgh EH2 4JB
☎ *(0131) 539 7119* Harry Cullen
www.oxfordbar.com

Caledonian Deuchars IPA plus two guests, which might include Belhaven Best, Greene King IPA, Cairngorm Trade Winds or Houston Peter's Well.

Tucked away on a backstreet corner in the New Town, ten minutes from Princes Street, but well worth searching out. Known locally as The Ox, licensed since the late 19th century and retaining some original fixtures and fittings. One bar plus lounge with fireplace. Outside canopy installed for smokers. Snacks and pies available.

OPEN *11am–midnight Mon–Thurs; 11am–12.30am Fri–Sat; 12.30–11pm Sun.*

Royal Ettrick Hotel

13 Ettrick Road, Edinburgh EH10 5BJ
☎ *(0131) 228 6413* Steven Balsillie

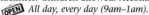Caledonian 80/– and Deuchars IPA plus guests from a wide range likely to include Timothy Taylor Landlord, Black Sheep Bitter, Harviestoun Bitter & Twisted, Marston's Pedigree or Bateman XB.

Part of a mansion and conservatory built in 1875 in the leafy suburbs. Bar and restaurant food available 12–9pm. Morning and afternoon teas also served. Car park, large beer garden, banqueting and conference facilities. Children allowed. Accommodation.

OPEN *All day, every day (9am–1am).*

Southsider

3–7 West Richmond Street, Edinburgh EH8 9EF
☎ *(0131) 667 2003* Kelly McSherry

Five real ales, often including Caledonian Deuchars IPA and 80/– plus something from Harviestoun. Three guests are rotated at least weekly and the emphasis is on smaller breweries.

Refurbished traditional bar, popular with students, locals and professionals alike. Extensive menu available 11am–7pm Mon–Sat and 12.30–7pm Sun. Live music Saturday, quiz night Wednesday. Pool and table football. Disabled access. Outside smoking area. Car park in the city centre.

OPEN *11am–midnight Mon–Wed; 11am–1am Thurs–Sat; 12.30pm–12 Sun.*

The Starbank Inn

64 Laverockbank Road, Edinburgh EH5 3BZ
☎ *(0131) 552 4141* TS Brown

Freehouse with eight real ales, with Belhaven 80/–, Caledonian Deuchars IPA, Sandy Hunter's Traditional Ale and Timothy Taylor Landlord the permanent fixtures. The four rotating guests are changed at least twice a week.

Traditional, old-fashioned pub with one bar, overlooking the River Forth. Food served 12–2.30pm and 6–9pm Mon–Fri, 12–9pm Sat and 12.30–9pm Sun. Children allowed. North Edinburgh, close to Newhaven village.

OPEN *11am–11pm Mon–Wed; 11am–midnight Thurs–Sat; 12.30–11pm Sun.*

The Steading

118–20 Biggar Road, Edinburgh EH10 7DU
☎ *(0131) 445 1128*
William Store and Claire Gibb

Freehouse with Caledonian Deuchars IPA, Timothy Taylor Landlord and Orkney and Atlas brews always available.

Country inn with two bars plus a separate dining area and two conservatories. Food served all day. Private functions, children allowed.

OPEN *10am–midnight Mon–Sat; 12.30–11pm Sun.*

Thomson's Bar

182–4 Morrison Street, Edinburgh EH3 8EB
☎ *(0131) 228 5700* Lee Thorburn
www.thomsonsbar.co.uk

Freehouse with seven or eight ales always on offer. Caledonian Deuchars IPA is a permanent fixture, plus six or seven constantly rotating guests, which could include XPA or Timothy Taylor Landlord.

Award-winning pub based on the designs of Glasgow architect Alexander Thomson. Pies served 12–2pm Mon–Sat. Outdoor tables and chairs. Within walking distance of Haymarket station, EICC, Lothian Road and Princes Street, and 15 minutes from Murryfield Rugby Stadium. Plans to hold beer festivals. Located at west end of town near Haymarket.

OPEN *12–11.30pm Mon–Wed; 12–12 Thurs; noon–1am Fri; 4–11.30pm Sun.*

MORAYSHIRE

CRAIGELLACHIE

Highlander Inn

10 Victoria Street, Craigellachie AB38 9SR
☎ *(01340) 881446* Duncan Elphick
www.whiskyinn.com

 A freehouse. Cairngorm Trade Winds, plus two constantly changing guest beers. Over 150 different independent ales already featured, and the list grows constantly. Also an award-winning whisky bar.

Located in the centre of the village, at the heart of Scotland's malt whisky trail. Food served 12–9.30pm. Children welcome. Private parties. Accommodation.

OPEN *12–11pm.*

ELGIN

The Muckle Cross

34 High Street, Elgin IV30 1BU
☎ *(01343) 559030* Gary Webster

 Wetherspoon's pub serving Greene King Abbot plus three constantly rotating guests from various Scottish breweries.

This building has been a JD Wetherspoon's site since 2001. Food served 9am–11pm Mon–Sun. Two annual JD Wetherspoon's festivals per year. Children welcome. Whisky trail. Forty miles from Loch Ness. Located on the High Street next to the council headquarters.

OPEN *9am–close (alcohol served from 11am Mon–Sat, 12.30pm Sun).*

Sunninghill Hotel

Hay Street, Elgin IV30 1NH
☎ *(01343) 547799* Donald Ross
www.sunninghillhotel.com

Freehouse offering three or four real ales. Timothy Taylor Landlord is usually available, and the guests are changed weekly.

Hotel lounge bar with meeting rooms, function room and conservatories. Food served 12–2pm and 5–8.30pm. Children welcome. Accommodation. Garden, car park.

OPEN *11am–2.30pm and 5–11pm Mon–Thurs (midnight Fri); 11am–midnight Sat; 12.30–11pm Sun.*

FINDHORN

Crown & Anchor Inn

Findhorn, Nr Forres IV36 3YF
☎ *(01309) 690243* Heather Burrell

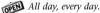 Freehouse serving at least four real ales and up to seven in summer. Regulars include Timothy Taylor Landlord, Fuller's ESB and Bateman brews.

Built in 1739, a pub offering bed and breakfast accommodation, live entertainment and a lounge area. Food at lunchtimes and evenings. Children allowed.

OPEN *All day, every day.*

Kimberley Inn

94 Findhorn, Nr Forres IV36 3YG
☎ *(01309) 690492* John Hessel

Freehouse with real ales changing regularly, including Timothy Taylor Landlord, Fuller's London Pride, Black Sheep Bitter and guest ales from Orkney, Black Isle and Aviemore.

Village seafood pub with log fires, views across the bay, outside seating and heating and a 'special' smoking area. Fresh seafood daily, including salmon, mussels, langoustines, and much more! Food served all day, every day throughout the year. Children welcome until 8pm.

OPEN *All day, every day.*

NAIRNSHIRE

NAIRN

The Invernairne Guest House

Thurlow Road, Nairn IV12 4EZ
☎ *(01667) 452039* Douglas Mitchell
www.invernairne.com

Cairngorm Trade Winds always available.

A 19th-century Italianate-style freehouse with wood-panelled bar and sea view (garden path leads to the beach). Full of character, with log fires and oak beams. Twelve bedrooms. No food. Beer garden.

OPEN *12–8.30pm every day Easter–Oct.*

ORKNEY

KIRKWALL

The Bothy Bar, Albert Hotel

Mounthoolie Lane, Kirkwall, Orkney KW15 1JZ
☎ *(01856) 876000* Dawn Flett
www.alberthotel.co.uk

Orkney Dark Island and The Red MacGregor plus a selection of guest beers and a wide selection of whiskies.

Popular traditional bar in the centre of town with open fires. Food served 12–2pm and 5–9.30pm. Famous for hosting 'tunes', impromptu Orcadian folk music sessions.

OPEN *All day, every day.*

STROMNESS

The Stromness Hotel

The Pier Head, Stromness, Orkney KW16 3AA
☎ *(01856) 850298* Leona Macleod
www.stromnesshotel.com

Freehouse with Orkney The Red MacGregor and Highland Scapa Special always available.

The largest three-star hotel in Orkney, with 42 bedrooms. Victorian architecture with harbour views, in the heart of the town. Open fires in both bars (not summer). Food served 12–2pm and 6–9pm in spring and summer; 6–9pm in autumn and winter; carvery on Sundays 12–2pm. Beer garden, car park. Beer festival late August. Children welcome. Private room hire. Close to World Heritage sites of Scara Brae, Maes Howe, Ring of Brodgar and Standing Stones of Stenness.

OPEN *All day, every day.*

PEEBLESSHIRE

INNERLEITHEN

Traquair Arms Hotel

Traquair Road, Innerleithen EH44 6PD
☎ *(01896) 830229* David and Jane Rogers
www.traquairarmshotel.co.uk

Freehouse with real ales on three pumps offering the local Traquair House Bear Ale on draught. Caledonian Deuchars IPA and 80/– also available.

Country-style pub built in the late 1800s, with two public bars and a restaurant. Food served 12–2pm and 5–9pm, and all day at weekends. Beer garden, large car park. Children welcome. Coffee/bistro bar. Fifteen bedrooms. Centrally located in Innerleithen.

OPEN *11am–11pm (midnight at weekends).*

PEEBLES

Green Tree Hotel

41 Eastgate, Peebles EH45 8AD
☎ *(01721) 720582* Mervyn Edge

Caledonian 80/– plus one or two guest beers such as Timothy Taylor Landlord or something from Broughton Ales.

Lively, traditional hotel bar. Food served 12–2.30pm and 5–8.30pm. Car park. Children welcome.

OPEN *11am–midnight.*

PERTHSHIRE

ABERNETHY

Cree's Inn

Main Street, Abernethy PH2 9LA
☎ *(01738) 850714* Brian Johnston
www.creesinn.co.uk

Freehouse offering six real ales, including Fuller's London Pride, Harviestoun Bitter & Twisted, Young's Bitter, Charles Wells Eagle IPA and Bass, plus six different guests each week, such as Greene King IPA and Black Sheep Bitter.

A one-bar listed pub with separate restaurant and long, L-shaped bar seating 60. Food served 12–2pm and 6–8.45pm. En-suite rooms. Turn off M90 at J9, follow signs for Newburgh and Cupar (A912).

OPEN *11am–2.30pm and 5.30–11pm Mon–Fri; all day Sat–Sun.*

BLAIR ATHOLL

The Bothy Bar

Atholl Arms Hotel, Old North Road, Blair Atholl PH18 5SG
☎ *(01796) 481205* Heather Reeves
www.athollarms.co.uk

The sister hotel to the Moulin Hotel, offering four Moulin Brewery ales, namely Braveheart, Old Remedial, Light and Ale of Atholl.

This 'bothy' (the word means a place of refuge and comfort) was rebuilt using beams and wood from the old hotel stables. Food served 12–9.30pm: good home cooked bar food with a specials board daily serving good Scottish Fare with a twist. Gardens and children's play area. Disabled access and facilities. Accommodation available in the adjoining 174-year-old Highland Hotel. By the gates of Blair Castle.

OPEN *All day, every day.*

BLAIRGOWRIE

Ericht Ale House

13 Wellmeadow, Blairgowrie PH10 6ND
☎ *(01250) 872469* Kenneth Fraser

Six real ales from a varying range, changed almost daily, including offerings from Inveralmond, Cairngorm, Atlas and Kelburn. Good Cider Guide listed.

Award-winning, 200-year-old town-centre freehouse. No food, bring your own! On the Cateran Trail, near the Miekelour Hedge.

OPEN *Opening times vary – call for details.*

The Stormont Arms

101 Perth Street, Blairgowrie PH10 6DT
☎ *(01250) 873142* Lewis Forbes Paterson

Three real ales, often from Caledonian, Inveralmond, Houston, Belhaven or Orkney. Occasionally also guests from England.

Traditional pub with lots of mirrors, favoured by sporting types. Two bars, plus extension to beer garden. No food. Car park. No facilities for children.

OPEN *11am–11pm Sun–Mon; 2pm–11pm Tues–Thurs; 11am–midnight Fri–Sat.*

DUNBLANE
The Dunblane Hotel
10 Stirling Road, Dunblane FK15 9EP
☎ *(01786) 822178* Tom McLean

A Punch Taverns inn. Greene King Abbot and Timothy Taylor Landlord. Two weekly-changing guests, such as Fyne Highlander, Houston Killellan and Inveralmond Ossian or Kelburn Dark Moor.

Overlooking the River Allan and more than 200 years old, this hotel features a public bar with Sky Sports and lounge bar with dining area. Food served 12–2.30pm and 5–8pm. Children welcome, with dedicated children's menu. Beer garden with heated, covered smoking terrace. Car park. Dog friendly. Meeting room. Accommodation. Situated close to Stirling Castle, the Wallace monument and Dunblane Cathedral, directly opposite the railway station.

OPEN *11am–midnight Sun–Thurs; 11am–1am Fri–Sat.*

The Tappit Hen
Kirk Street, Dunblane FK15 0AL
☎ *(01786) 825226* Helen McClymant

Two ales from Belhaven plus five guests, changed weekly.

Community bar with a warm, welcoming atmosphere, situated opposite the cathedral. Bar snacks available. No children.

OPEN *All day, every day.*

GLENDEVON
An Lochan
Tormaukin, Glendevon FK1Y 7JY
☎ *(01259) 781252* Roger McKie
www.anlochan.co.uk

Freehouse with ales from Inveralmond in Perth, Harviestoun in Alloa, and Ales in Auchtermuchty, as well as a lager from a micro brewery in Glasgow.

Dating back to 1710, this one-bar coaching inn has 14 beamed bedrooms available. Local food served 12–3pm and 5.30–9pm daily. Private room available. Located near Gleneagles Hotel.

OPEN *All day, every day.*

KILMAHOG
The Lade Inn
Kilmahog, Callander FK17 8HD
☎ *(01877) 330152* Frank Park
www.theladeinn.com

Freehouse with WayLade, LadeBack and LadeOut, brewed exclusively for them by Douglas Ross of Traditional Scottish Ales. (Guardian best Pub in the Loch Lomond & The Trossachs National Park.) The Trossachs Beer Festival runs for 10 days from 27th August to 5th September featuring Gust Local Real Ales. There was an on-site brewery; this is now a retail outlet selling over 120 different Scottish bottled beers.

Built as tea rooms in the 1930s and licensed in the 1960s, with a bar and restaurant. Scottish menu served 12–9pm Mon–Sat and 12.30–9pm Sun, ranging from hearty bar meals to gourmet dishes. Winner of the Forth Valley Good Food Award 2006 for Best Informal Eating Place. Children's menu (plus activities) available. Children welcome, dogs allowed in the bothy bar. Large, wildlife-friendly beer garden. (Featured in Times Top Ten Pub Gardens.) Informal sing-along ceilidhs on Friday and Saturday nights from 8.30pm. Special events are also held. At the foot of Ben Ledi Mountain, just off the junction of the A84 and A821.

OPEN *12–11pm Mon–Fri; 12pm–1am Sat; 12.30–10.30pm Sun.*

KINROSS
The Muirs Inn
49 Muirs, Kinross KY13 8AU
☎ *(01577) 862270* Gordon Westwood

A wide selection of Scottish ales from the eight-tap beer engine, including Belhaven 80/- and an array of ever-changing guests from the Harviestoun and Border breweries, among others. Also a rare range of Scottish malt whiskies.

A traditional Scottish country freehouse, featuring original stonework and fireplaces. Games room, courtyard, beer garden, car park. Bar food available all day, every day, plus chef's Scottish country carvery Wed–Fri evenings and all day Sat–Sun. Children allowed. En-suite accommodation with country-style ambience. M90 junction 6, then follow signs for the A922. At the T-junction, the inn is diagonally opposite to the right.

OPEN *All day, every day, from 12pm.*

KIRKMICHAEL
Strathardle Inn
Kirkmichael, Blairgowrie PH10 7NS
☎ *(01250) 881224* Tim Hancher
www.strathardleinn.co.uk

Freehouse with three constantly rotating guests from breweries such as Inveralmond, Houston, Orkney and Kelburn. Changed weekly.

Small, cosy, family-run hotel dating back to the 1700s when it was established as a drovers' inn. Bar and separate restaurant. Open fires, malts and real ales. Food served daily, 12–2pm for lunch, and 6–9pm for dinner. Beer garden. Lounge. Children and dogs welcome. Letting rooms available. Car park. Located between Pitlochry and Blairgowrie on the A924.

OPEN *12–2pm and 6–11pm, every day.*

MEIKLEOUR

Meikleour Hotel

Meikleour, Nr Blairgowrie PH2 6EB
☎ *(01250) 883206* Kia and Andrew Mathieson
www.meikleourhotel.co.uk

 Lure of Meikleour, brewed for the pub by Inveralmond, plus two guest beers, changed regularly.

Built in 1820 as a coaching inn, with lounge and public bar, traditionally furnished with roaring log fires in the winter. Food served 12.15–2.30pm and 6.30–9pm. Beer garden, car park, restaurant, letting rooms. The famous Meikleour Beech Hedge – the world's largest – is next door to the pub. On the A984 Couper Angus to Dunkeld road, which is off the A93 Perth to Blairgowrie.
OPEN *All day, every day (all year except 25–29 Dec).*

MOULIN

Original Moulin Inn

Moulin Hotel, 11–13 Kirkmichael Road, Moulin, By Pitlochry
☎ *(01796) 472196* Heather Reeves
www.moulinhotel.co.uk

 A Moulin Brewery tied house – the brewery is located on the same premises. The full range of Moulin ales (Braveheart; Ale of Athol; Old Remedial; Moulin Light Ale) normally available.

A 17th-century coaching inn situated in the village square, with open fires, beams and stone walls. Originally the traditional meeting house for the Parish. Extended in 1880 and again in 1970. Food served all day, every day. Car park. Children welcome away from the bar area.
OPEN *12–11pm Sun–Thurs; 12–11.45pm Fri–Sat.*

PERTH

The Cherrybank Inn

210 Glasgow Road, Perth PH2 0NA
☎ *(01738) 624349* Jack Findlay
www.cherrybankinn.co.uk

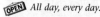 Five real ales usually available. Inveralmond Ossian and Independence. Three guests, changed weekly, mostly from Scottish brewers, such as Stewart 80/–, Caledonian Deuchars IPA, Fyne Pipers Gold, Kelburn Misty Law and Tryst Stars and Stripes.

Dating from 1761 and thought to be one of the oldest public houses in Perth, this former drovers' inn is on the western outskirts of the town. Public bar with two snugs and large lounge bar/restaurant. Food served 12–3pm daily; 7–9pm Mon–Thurs; 5–9pm Sat–Sun. Accommodation. Golf parties catered for and golf can be arranged. Car park and grounds.
OPEN *11am–11pm Mon–Thurs; 11am–midnight Fri–Sat; 12.30–11pm Sun.*

Greyfriars

15 South Street, Perth PH2 8PG
☎ *(01738) 633036* Pauline Marshall

 Freehouse with Friar's Tipple, the exclusive house ale brewed locally by Inveralmond Brewery. Guests include regular favourites Caledonian Deuchars IPA, St Austell Tribute and Greene King Old Speckled Hen.

Old-fashioned pub with stone walls and upstairs dining room. The clientele tends to be 25 and upwards. Homemade food at lunchtimes and Fri–Sat nights. Accompanied children welcome at lunchtimes.
OPEN *All day, every day.*

Lovat Hotel

90–2 Glasgow Road, Perth PH2 0LT
☎ *(01738) 636555* Graeme Gillon

 Freehouse with real ale on three pumps, one rotated each week. The nearby Inveralmond brewery suppplies Lia Fail, Ossian and others.

Large bistro/bar, offering food at lunchtimes and evenings. Children welcome. Accommodation. On the outskirts of Perth, a mile from Broxton roundabout.
OPEN *11am–2.30pm and 5–11pm.*

Scone Arms

Cross Street, Scone, Perth PH2 6LR
☎ *(01738) 551341* John and Robert

 Freehouse with ales from Perth's own Inveralmond Brewery, including Independence session beer and Ossian's Ale plus regular monthly guest brews.

Historic pub, built in 1807, with food served 12–9pm every day.
OPEN *All day, every day.*

STRATHTUMMEL

Loch Tummel Inn

Strathtummel, Nr Pitlochry PH16 5RP
☎ *(01882) 634272* Robert Gilmour

 Freehouse with Moulin Braveheart plus guest ales. Beers from Isle of Skye and Greene King are regular features.

A 200-year-old traditional coaching inn overlooking the loch, with two character bars, beer garden, restaurant, patio and sun terrace. Food served all day, every day, all year round. Six en-suite letting rooms with feature bathrooms. Dogs and children welcome. Car park. 'Visit Scotland' three-star inn. Annual beer festival. On the B8019 seven miles north of Pitlochry, just past the Queen's View.
OPEN *11am–11pm.*

RENFREWSHIRE

GOUROCK

Spinnaker Hotel

121 Albert Road, Gourock
☎ *(01475) 633107* Stewart McCartney
www.spinnakerhotel.co.uk

 Tied to Belhaven, with Belhaven 80/– regularly available, plus three guest beers, often Caledonian Deuchars IPA, Orkney Dark Island or Fuller's London Pride. Will endeavour to get the beers that customers request.

Small hotel, situated a quarter of a mile west of the town centre, with panoramic views over the River Clyde and Cowal

Peninsula. Food available all day, every day. Children welcome. Beer garden. Nine guest rooms.

 11am–midnight Mon–Wed; 11am–1am Thurs–Sat; 12.30pm–12.30am Sun.

HOUSTON
The Fox & Hounds
South Street, Houston, Johnstone PA6 7EN
☎ *(01505) 612991* Jonathan Wengel
www.foxandhoundshouston.co.uk

Freehouse and brewpub. Home of the Houston Brewing Company, so home brews such as Texas, Killellan, Warlock Stout and Crystal are always on the menu, plus two guests, one changed weekly and one monthly.

Traditional coaching inn with three bars and a separate restaurant area. Food served 12–10pm every day. Quiz every Tuesday, live music. Summer beer festivals. Follow A737 from Glasgow, then signs for Houston/Bridge of Weir.

 All day, every day.

INVERKIP
Inverkip Hotel
Main Street, Inverkip, Greenock PA16 0AS
☎ *(01475) 521478* AW Hardy

Caledonian Deuchars IPA always available.

Family-run old coaching inn with dining area and separate restaurant. TV in the public bar. Food at lunchtimes and evenings. Children allowed. Popular with boaties from Scotland's biggest marina over the road. Accommodation. Car park.

 All day, every day.

JOHNSTONE
Coanes
26 High Street, Johnstone PA5 8AH
☎ *(01505) 322925* Kirsty Brown

Leased from Scottish & Newcastle and always offering Caledonian 80/– and Deuchars IPA, plus five guests, changed weekly.

An olde-worlde pub with a bar and lounge. Bar food served every lunchtime, Wed and Thurs evenings, and all day Fri–Sun. Children welcome. A short walk from Johnstone train station.

 All day, every day.

LOCHWINNOCH
The Brown Bull
33 Main Street, Lochwinnoch PA12 4AH
☎ *(01505) 843250* Laura Hunt

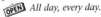Four real ales from a constantly changing range. More than 400 different brews are served each year.

Olde-worlde, welcoming one-bar pub built in 1809. Coal fire in winter. Food served 12.30–3pm and 5.30–8pm during the week, 12.30–8.30pm Sun. Children welcome until 8pm.

 All day, every day.

PAISLEY
Bull Inn
7 New Street, Paisley PA1 1XU
☎ *(0141) 849 0472* Craig MacFadyen

Owned by Maclay Inns, with Caledonian Deuchars IPA and something from Kelburn and Houston breweries plus at least one other rotating guest.

This traditional bar in the centre of town has been a pub since 1901. Small snug rooms. Live sport on TV. Food served 12–3pm Mon–Thurs and 12–5pm Fri–Sat. Children welcome during food service times. Situated in the town centre.

 11am–11pm Mon–Thurs; 11am–1am Fri–Sat; 12–11pm Sun.

Gabriels
33 Gauze Street, Paisley PA1 1EX
☎ *(0141) 887 8204* Jane McCall

Owned by Belhaven, with Caledonian Deuchars IPA and Harviestoun Bitter & Twisted always available. Guests change weekly.

An oval bar with traditional decor on the walls. Separate dining area and restaurant. Food all day. Children allowed.

 All day, every day.

The Wee Howff
53 High Street, Paisley PA1 2AE
☎ *(0141) 889 2095*

Caledonian Deuchars IPA plus a changing selection of guest beers all from finest cask.

Down-to-earth drinking bar in the centre of town, but something of a Paisley institution. A tune in honour of the Wee Howff, by piper John 'Stormy' Winter, has been recorded by Strathclyde Police Pipe Band.

 All day, every day.

ROSS-SHIRE

APPLECROSS
Applecross Inn
Shore Street, Applecross IV54 8LR
☎ *(01520) 744262* Judith Fish
www.applecross.uk.com

A freehouse. Isle of Skye Brewery's Red Cuillin and Young Pretender. Plus occasional guests, such as Hebridean Gold, Skye Light or Black Cuillin. Also a good selection of malts.

One welcoming bar with magnificent sea views across to Skye and cosy log fire in winter. Award-winning food, including fresh local seafood, served 12–9pm. Children welcome. Seaview accommodation and beer garden on the shore.

 11am–11.30pm (closed Christmas Day and New Year's Day).

FORTROSE

The Anderson

Union Street, Fortrose IV10 8TD
☎ *(01381) 620236* Jim Anderson
www.theanderson.co.uk

Freehouse with three constantly rotating ales from independent breweries across the UK. Also always stocks on tap: a strong Belgian ale, a fruit beer and a wheat beer. One real cider pump, 100 Belgian beers, 218 single-malt whiskies.

A 19th-century fire-lit coaching inn located in the town centre, with whisky bar, country public bar and separate restaurant. Local CAMRA Pub of the Year 2007 and 2008. Featured in *Sunday Herald's* Top 10 Restaurants in Scotland 2007 and 2008; Press and Journal's Top 10 Restaurants 2008, Scottish Chefs Awards Bronze Medal 2008, plus Ambassadeur Orval award 2008 and 2009. Food served every evening plus Sunday lunch. Nine en-suite letting rooms available. Beer garden. Car park. Regular beer, wine and whisky tastings. Children welcome (games provided). Many activities nearby including golf and dolphin/bird watching. Located 11 miles north of Inverness, off the A9.

OPEN *From 4pm Mon–Sat; from 12.30pm Sun.*

GAIRLOCH

The Old Inn

Flowerdale, Gairloch IV21 2BD
☎ *(01445) 712006* A Pearson
www.theoldinn.net

A selection of real ales always available, including An Teallach and Beinn Dearg from local brewers, The An Teallach Brewery, and Black Cuillin and Red Cuillin from Isle of Skye who also provide The Blind Piper of Gairloch, a special house brew. Caledonian Deuchars IPA, Marston's Pedigree and Greene King Abbot Ale are among the likely guests.

Three-hundred-year-old coaching inn at the foot of the Flowerdale Valley on the west coast, 90 minutes from Inverness. Spectacular views across the harbour to the islands. Good local food at lunchtimes and evenings, specialising in local seafood and game. Outside seating. Accommodation.

OPEN *11am–1am Mon–Fri; 11.30am–midnight Sat; 12–11.30pm Sun.*

LOCHCARRON

Rockvilla Hotel

Main Street, Lochcarron IV54 8YB
☎ *(01520) 722379* Peter Bartlett
www.rockvilla-hotel.co.uk

Freehouse with beers from the Isle of Skye, Atlas, Orkney and Cairngorm breweries, plus monthly guests such as Black Sheep Bitter and Tring Huck Me Buck.

Small, welcoming, family-run hotel on the north-west Highland coast with stunning views. Caters for a wide range of customers, including hill walkers, climbers, cyclists and motorcycle tourers. Food served until 9.30pm. All food homemade by chef proprietor Wendy and her team. Directly on the main street through Lochcarron.

OPEN *3–11pm. (Last orders 10.30pm)*

STORNOWAY, ISLE OF LEWIS

The Carlton Public and Lounge Bar

19 Francis Street, Stornoway, Isle of Lewis HS1 2ND
☎ *(01851) 701265*
Moray Weir and David Pearce

Freehouse with an ale from the Hebridean Brewing Co and one guest ale, changed every two to three weeks.

Formerly The Whaler's Rest, this typical island freehouse has a public bar and lounge bar. Live music every weekend. Food served in both bars, with special menu at weekends, 12–9pm Mon–Sat, 12.30–9pm Sun. Small car park. Only beer garden in town. Children welcome in the lounge bar. Lounge bar available for private functions. Close to local brewery and arts centre.

OPEN *11am–11pm Mon; 11am–1am Tues–Sat; 12.30–11pm Sun.*

ULLAPOOL

Morefield Motel

North Road, Ullapool IV26 2TQ
☎ *(01854) 612161* Anthony Oulton
www.morefieldmotel.co.uk

A freehouse. Three pumps, all stocked on a guest basis, and alternated between local micro-breweries. Favourite brewers include An Teallach, Isle of Skye, Cairngorm, Hebridean and Highland.

Relaxed lounge bar with beer garden and motel accommodation. Food served 12–2pm and 5.30–9pm. Private room available. Large car park. Annual beer festival in October. Situated near to the golf course, coastal walks and shops in Ullapool, on the main North Road.

OPEN *11am–2.30pm (from 12.30pm Sun) and 5–11pm.*

ROXBURGHSHIRE

DENHOLM

Auld Cross Keys Inn

Main Street, Denholm TD9 8NU
☎ *(01450) 870305* David Mackay Bennett
www.crosskeysdenholm.co.uk

Freehouse with one rotating guest ale.

A 200-year-old inn with traditional public bar, lounge bar, dining and function room. Open fires. Food served 12–2.30pm and 5.30–8.30pm daily. Sunday carvery. Children welcome. Car park, two en-suite rooms available. On the A698 between Hawick and Jedburgh.

OPEN *12–12.*

NEWCASTLETON

The Grapes Hotel

16 Douglas Square, Newcastleton TD9 0QD
☎ *(01387) 375245 Jim McDonald*

Up to eight pumps operating, with Caledonian Deuchars IPA among the beers always available. Guests are changed monthly.

A small hotel with restaurant. Food at lunchtimes and evenings. Children allowed until 8.30pm (residents later).

OPEN *All day, every day.*

SELKIRKSHIRE

GALASHIELS

Ladhope Inn

33 High Buckholmside, Galashiels TD1 2HR
☎ *(01896) 752446 Scott Paterson*

Freehouse with Caledonian Deuchars IPA permanently plus guests from Hadrian, Broughton, Inveralmond, Stewart Brewing and High House Farm.

A former coaching inn dating from 1792, situated on the main road, the first pub on the A7. Regular live music and theme nights, plus three plasma TVs. Children allowed.

OPEN *11am–1pm and 4–11pm (midnight Fri–Sun).*

ST MARY'S LOCH

Tibbie Shiels Inn

St Mary's Loch, Selkirk TD7 5LH
☎ *(01750) 42231 Jill Brown*
www.tibbieshielsinn.com

Freehouse offering Broughton Greenmantle IPA and Belhaven 80/–.

Remote 19th-century coaching inn beside the loch. Associations with Sir Walter Scott and James Hogg. Food served 12.30–8pm. Children welcome. Five en-suite bedrooms, car parking. On the A708.

OPEN *All day, every day (closed Sun evening and Mon–Wed from 1 November–Easter and over Christmas).*

SHETLAND

UNST

Baltasound Hotel

Baltasound, Unst, Shetland ZE2 9DS
☎ *(01957) 711334 Sharn Swan*
www.baltasound-hotel.shetland.co.uk

A freehouse serving the full range of Valhalla ales: Auld Rock, White Wife, Simmer Dim, Old Scatness, Sjolmet Stout and Island Bere.

Britain's most northerly hotel, situated on the island of Unst. Food served 12.30–2pm and 7–8.30pm. Children welcome. Car parking.

OPEN *12.30–2.30pm and 5–11pm Mon–Thurs; 12.30–2.30pm and 5pm–1am Fri; 11am–midnight Sat; 12.30–11pm Sun.*

STIRLINGSHIRE

BRIDGE OF ALLAN

The Queen's Hotel

24 Henderson Street, Bridge of Allan, Stirling FK9 4HD
☎ *(01786) 833268 Mr Ross*

Freehouse with Stirling Brig, Bitter, IPA and Dark Mild from the local Bridge of Allan Brewery plus seasonal specials.

Two-bar pub with restaurant and occasional live entertainment. Food at lunchtimes and evenings. Children allowed.

OPEN *All day, every day.*

FALKIRK

Behind The Wall Bar and Restaurant

14 Melville Street, Falkirk FK1 1HZ
☎ *(01324) 633338 Brian Flynn*
www.behindthewall.co.uk

Home of the Eglesbrech Brewing company, with eight real ales usually available. Two or three will be Eglesbrech beers, with another five or six rotated weekly.

A town-centre complex with three bars, restaurant, music venue and on-site brewery. Food served 11am–10pm. Car park opposite. Child-friendly. Live music Fri–Sat. Big-screen sports. Close to the Falkirk Wheel.

OPEN *11am–midnight Mon–Thurs; 11am–1am Fri–Sat; 12.30pm–12 Sun.*

Wheatsheaf Inn

16 Baxters Wynd, Falkirk FK1 1PF
☎ *(01324) 638282 Alexander Black*

Freehouse with four ales usually on offer, including Caledonian Deuchars IPA and guests changed every couple of days. Examples include Yates Bitter, Barngates Tag Lag or Westmorland Gold, Coniston Bluebird or XB, Timothy Taylor Landlord, Greene King Old Speckled Hen or Houston Killelan Bitter.

The oldest pub in Falkirk dating back to 1797, this is a traditional one-bar inn with private enclosed beer garden and private meeting room. Food served at lunchtimes. A mile from the Falkirk Wheel, 50 yards from Falkirk steeple through Wilson's Close.

OPEN *11am–11pm Mon–Thurs; 11am–1am Fri–Sat.*

STIRLING

The Birds & Bees

Easter Cornton Road, Causewayhead, Stirling FK9 5PB
☎ *(01786) 473663 R Henderson*

Freehouse with two or three real ales, changed weekly. Beers from Haviestoun, Everards, Marston's, Caledonian and Hydes are regularly featured.

A farm steading, dating back to 1850, with two bars and two private function suites. Food served 12–3pm and 5–10pm Mon–Fri and 12–10pm Sat–Sun. Two beer gardens, barbecue deck. Car park. Children's certificate. Around 500 metres from the Wallace Monument.

OPEN *11am–midnight Sun–Thurs; 11am–1am Fri–Sat.*

SUTHERLAND

BRORA

Sutherland Inn

Fountain Square, Brora KW9 6NX
☎ *(01408) 621209* Leon Sims
www.sutherlandinn.co.uk

Freehouse offering one regularly changing real ale, from the range of Isle of Skye beers or Scapa Special from the Highland Brewery.

An old coaching inn dating from 1850. Good quality food served. Collection of over 130 malt whiskies. Six en-suite rooms. Free Wi-Fi. Families welcome. Food served 12–3pm, 6–9pm. On A9, 60 miles north of Inverness.

OPEN *11am–midnight every day.*

LAIRG

Scourie Hotel

Scourie, Lairg IV27 4SX
☎ *(01971) 502396* Patrick and Judy Price
www.scourie-hotel.co.uk

Privately owned freehouse with up to three cask ales on handpump, two bottled real ales and two real ciders. A wide range of beers is rotated, including beers from Black Isle Brewery and Aviemore Brewery.

This 17th-century building has two bars, smoking shelter and outside seating. Twenty bedrooms, large car park, children's certificate. Fishing and walking nearby.

OPEN *11am–2.30pm, 5–11pm Mon–Sat; 12.30–2.30pm, 6–11pm Sun.*

WEST LOTHIAN

BALLOCH

Tullie Inn

Balloch Road, Balloch G83 8SW
☎ *(01389) 752052* Tony James

Owned by Maclay Inns, with Caledonian Deuchars IPA permanently featured, plus three guests, including beers such as Greene King Abbot, Old Speckled Hen, Fyne Highlander, Vital Spark and something from Theakston.

Large 19th-century inn with bar, restaurant and 12 en-suite bedrooms, on the banks of Loch Lomond. Old English in style with hanging baskets outside, very busy all year. Food served 12–9pm. Large beer garden. Children allowed until 8.30pm. Small car park, with additional parking nearby. Quiz on Thursday, disco party on Friday, cabaret/bands on Saturday, karaoke on Sunday. Next to the railway station.

OPEN *11am–11.45pm Mon–Thurs; 11am–12.45am Fri–Sat;12–11.45pm Sun.*

LINLITHGOW

The Four Marys

65–7 High Street, Linlithgow EH49 7ED
☎ *(01506) 842171* Evaleen and Ian Forrest

Greene King pub with six or seven real ales, including beers from Belhaven, Orkney, Greene King and Harviestoun. Guests are often changed daily.

Traditional pub with antique furniture and stone walls. *Sunday Mail* Pub of the Year 2002 plus Licensee of the Year 2005. The bar has masses of mementoes of Mary Queen of Scots, who was born at Linlithgow Palace. Food available 12–3pm and 5–9pm Mon–Fri and 12–9pm Sat–Sun. Outside smoking facilities with canopy, lights, heating, tables and chairs. Parking. Children allowed. Two real ale festivals held every year, with 20 real ales at each. Opposite the entrance to Linlithgow Palace.

OPEN *12–11pm Mon–Wed; noon–12.45am Thurs–Sat; 12.30–11pm Sun.*

West Port Hotel

18–20 West Port, Linlithgow EH49 7AZ
☎ *(01506) 847456* Ian Leask
www.maclay.com/westporthotel.html

Owned by Maclay Inns, with Caledonian Deuchars IPA always available and two other rotating real ales changed on a daily basis.

A 14-bedroom inn with lounge, bar and function room. Food served 8am–10pm with breakfast, afternoon tea, lunch and dinner. Car park, families welcome. Close to central Linlithglow and the palace.

OPEN *8am–late.*

MID-CALDER

Torpichen Arms

36 Bank Street, Mid-Calder, Livingston EH53 0AR
☎ *(01506) 880020* Helen Hill

Caledonian 80/– and Deuchars IPA always available, plus guests, changed weekly. Harviestoun, Nethergate, Robinson's and Cains breweries are regularly featured.

Old village pub with weekend entertainment. B&B. Lunches only. Children allowed until 8.30pm.

OPEN *All day, every day.*

SOUTH QUEENSFERRY

The Ferry Tap

36 High Street, South Queensferry, Nr Edinburgh EH30 9YL
☎ *(0131) 331 2000* Linda Gamble

Freehouse always offering Caledonian 80/– and Deuchars IPA plus two guests, changed weekly.

Old-fashioned 300-year-old real ale house with one bar and lounge, and a vaulted roof. Lunches and snacks served 11am–3pm. In South Queensferry village, between the Forth road and rail bridges.

OPEN *11am–11.30pm (12.30am weekends).*

UPHALL

Oatridge Hotel

24 East Main Street, Uphall EH52 5DA
☎ *(01506) 856465* Gordon MacGregor
www.theoatridgehotel.co.uk

 Punch Taverns pub serving Caledonian Deuchars IPA plus two weekly-changing guests.

An old coaching house dating back to 1805, this pub has been run by the same family since 1973. One public bar, one games room and separate restaurant. Food served 12–2pm and 6–9.30pm Mon–Fri, 12–9.30pm Sat, 12.30–9.30pm Sun. Beer garden. Seven letting rooms available. Children welcome. Car park. Take exit for Livingston from the M8 and follow signs for Uphall.

OPEN *All day, every day.*

WIGTOWNSHIRE

BLADNOCH

The Bladnoch Inn

Bladnoch, Wigtown DG8 9AB
☎ *(01988) 402200* Derek Hart

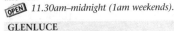 Greene King Abbot Ale and Flowers Original (brewed by Badger) plus weekly guest ales.

Two-hundred-year-old country inn and restaurant overlooking the river next to the Bladnoch distillery (guided tours). Food at lunchtimes and evenings. Children allowed.

OPEN *11.30am–midnight (1am weekends).*

GLENLUCE

Kelvin House Hotel

53 Main Street, Glenluce, Newton Stewart DG8 0PP
☎ *(01581) 300303* Jenny and Ray Dyer
www.kelvin-house.co.uk

Freehouse offering three real ales, one changed once or twice a week. Caledonian Deuchars IPA is always on the menu, with guests from a good selection that may include Timothy Taylor Landlord and Orkney Dark Island.

A hotel off the A75, with residents' lounge, public bar and restaurant. Food served at lunchtimes (12–2pm) and evenings (6–9.30pm). Six bedrooms. Children welcome.

OPEN *11am–3pm and 6–11.30pm.*

ISLE OF WHITHORN

Steampacket Inn

Harbour Row, Newton Stewart,
Isle of Whithorn DG8 8LL
☎ *(01988) 500334* Alisatair Scoular
www.steampacketinn.com

Timothy Taylor Landlord plus up to three guests, possibly soon a fourth, that might include Black Sheep and Wychwood, but also Scottish brews such as Houston, Strathaven, Sulwath, Kelburn, Atlas, Arran, Orkney and Caledonian. CAMRA area pub of the year.

Family-run harbourside inn with two bars, restaurant, conservatory and beer garden. Food served 12–2pm and 6.30–9pm. The name commemorates the steam ships which used to sail between the Isle of Whithorn and Liverpool. Children and dogs welcome. Seven rooms, five of them with harbour views.

OPEN *Summer: 11am–11pm. Winter: 11am– 2pm and 6–11pm Mon–Thurs; 11am– 11pm Fri–Sun.*

KIRKHOLM

The Blue Peter Hotel

23 Main Street, Kirkcolm, Nr Stranraer DG9 0NL
☎ *(01776) 853221* Ian and Ruth Murray

 Freehouse with a constantly-rotating range of real ales sold at less than £2 a pint when we went to press.

CAMRA's Pub of the Year for Scotland in 2008, a family-run hotel with lounge and public bars. Locally produced food served at lunchtimes and evenings. Accommodation. The area is popular with golfers, birdwatchers and anglers. Five miles north of Stranraer on the A718.

OPEN *All day, every day.*

NEWTON STEWART

The Creebridge House Hotel

Creebridge, Newton Stewart DG8 6NP
☎ *(01671) 402121* Mr and Mrs D Morby
www.creebridge.co.uk

Genuine freehouse with up to three real ales, all rotating, and changed when one is finished.

A country house hotel built in 1760, with one large bar, brasserie and restaurant. Award-winning food available 12–2pm and 6–8.45pm. Children's certificate. Beer garden, car park, function room for hire. Eighteen bedrooms.

OPEN *12–2.30pm and 6–11pm Sun–Thurs; 12– 2.30pm and 6.30pm–12 Fri–Sat.*

PORTPATRICK

Harbour House Hotel

53 Main Street, Portpatrick, Stranraer DG9 8JW
☎ *(01776) 810456* Julie Reynolds

Freehouse with Black Sheep Bitter plus two guests, changed monthly.

Seafront hotel originally used by the Admiralty in 1790 as a harbour HQ. Lounge bar, outside seating and bistro. Food available all day, every day in summer, and 12–2pm and 5–9pm in winter. Children welcome. Beer festivals. Accommodation.

OPEN *11am–11pm Sun–Wed; 11am–midnight Thurs–Sat.*

Whitehaven
CUMBRIA
Windermere ·
· Kendal
·Ramsey
Peel
stle
·Douglas
Morecambe· ·Lancaster
M6
LANCASHIRE
Blackpool· Burnley
Preston· H
Southport· M6
GREATER
MERSEYSIDE MANCHESTER
Holyhead Liverpool · Manchest
Llandudno· ·Colwyn Bay M53 M56
Denbigh· Flint CHESHIRE
Caernarvon CLWYD Chester M6
Wrexham· Crewe S
Portmadoc· ·Llangollen o
GWYNEDD ·Bala STAFFORD
Llanfyllin
Barmouth· ·Dolgellau Telford M6
·Towyn SHROPSHIRE
Newtown Wolverhampton·
Aberystwyth Birn
·Llanidloes · Ludlow
Aberayron POWYS Knighton HEREFORD
New Quay · &
Lampeter Kington WORCESTER
Cardigan · DYFED Hereford· W
Fishguard Llandovery Brecon Ross on Wye · M50
WEST Monmouth· Gl
Haverfordwest GLAMORGAN MID GWENT GLO
Pembroke M4 GLAMORGAN Stroud
Swansea ·Newport AVON
Porthcawl· SOUTH ·Cardiff
GLAMORGAN M5
·Bristol
·Weston ·Bath
Ilfracombe Minehead Super Mare
Barnstaple Warmi
Bideford· SOMERSET

THE BREWERIES

CLWYD

BRAGDY'R BRYN
*Unit 2 Vale Park, Colomendy Industrial Estate,
Denbigh LL16 5TA*
☎ *(01745) 812266*
www.bragdyrbryn.co.uk

BITTER 4.0% ABV
SPECIAL 4.5% ABV
HERALD 6.2% ABV
Plus specials.

JOLLY BREWER
1 College Street, Wrexham LL13 8LU
☎ *(01978) 261884*
www.jollybrewer.co.uk

BITTER 4.0% ABV
TAID'S FRAGRANT GARDEN 4.0% ABV
DIOD Y GYMRAEF 5.0% ABV
Y DDRAIG GOCH 5.0% ABV
STRANGE BREW 6.0% ABV
TAFFY'S TIPPLE 6.0% ABV

PLASSEY BREWERY
The Plassey, Eyton, Wrexham LL13 0SP
☎ *(01978) 781111*
www.plasseybrewery.co.uk

PLASSEY BITTER 4.0% ABV
Well hopped, straw colour, blackcurrant
fruitiness.
OFFA'S DYKE ALE 4.3% ABV
Light and refreshing.
FUSILIER 4.5% ABV
Full-bodied bitter with big malty flavour.
CWRW TUDNO 5.0% ABV
Malty, sweet, but dry aftertaste.
DRAGON'S BREATH 6.0% ABV
Fruity bitter.

CONWY

CONWY BREWERY LTD
*Unit 17 Conwy Morfa Business Park, Ffordd Sam
Pari, Conwy LL32 8HH*
☎ *(01492) 585287*
www.conwybrewery.co.uk

CASTLE BITTER 3.8% ABV
Malty session ale.
WELSH PRIDE 4.0% ABV
Hoppy bitter.
ARBENNIG SPECIAL 4.5% ABV
Mellow, roast caramel flavour.
HONEY FAYRE 4.5% ABV
Golden, crisp, bitter honey flavour.

GREAT ORME BREWERY
*The Great Orme Brewery, Nant-y-Cywarch, Glan
Conwy LL28 5PP*
☎ *(01492) 580548*
www.greatormebrewery.co.uk

ORME'S BEST 4.2% ABV
EXTRAVAGANZA 4.6% ABV
THREE FEATHERS 5.0% ABV

DYFED

BRAGDY CEREDIGION BREWERY
Bryn Hawk, New Quay, Ceredigion SA45 9SB
☎ *(01545) 561417*

YSBRYD O'R GOEDEN
(SPIRIT OF THE FOREST) 3.8% ABV
GWRACH DU (BLACK WITCH) 4.0% ABV
Porter.
Y DRAIG AUR (THE GOLD DRAGON) 4.2% ABV
Gold in colour and full flavoured.
BARCUD COCH (RED KITE) 4.3% ABV
Red in colour, with fruit flavours.
MERLIN 4.5% ABV
Organic ale.
MORWEN 5.0%

BRAGDY GWYNANT
Tynllidiart Arms, Capel Bangor, Aberystwyth
☎ *(01970) 880248*

CWRW GWYNANT 4.2% ABV

COLES FAMILY BREWERY
*White Hart Inn, Llanddarog, Carmarthen
SA32 8NT*
☎ *(01267) 275395*

NETTLE ALE 3.8% ABV
AMBER ALE 4.0% ABV
BEETROOT ALE 4.0% ABV
BLACK STAG 4.0% ABV
OATEN BARLEY STOUT 4.0% ABV
ROASTED BARLEY STOUT 4.0% ABV
Plus seasonals and specials.

FELINFOEL BREWERY CO. LTD
Farmers Row, Felinfoel, Llanelli SA14 8LB
☎ *(01554) 773357*
www.felinfoel-brewery.com

BEST BITTER 3.8% ABV
Hoppy flavour and aroma.
CAMBRIAN BITTER 3.9% ABV
Hoppy, malty aroma.
FELINFOEL STOUT 4.1% ABV
Roast barley tones.
DOUBLE DRAGON 4.2% ABV
Rich colour, hoppy.

THE FLOCK INN BREWERY
*Ty Mawr Country Hotel, Brechfa, Carmarthen
SA32 7RA*
☎ *(01267) 202332*

BOIS BAAACH 3.8% ABV
TUP OF THE MORNING 4.0% ABV
EWE-PHORIA 4.2% ABV
SHEAR DELIGHT 4.2% ABV
EWE-REEK-A 4.5% ABV

THE JACOBI BREWERY OF CAIO
Penlanwen, Plum Saint, Llanwrda SA19 8RR
☎ *(01558) 650605*
www.jacobibrewery.co.uk

LIGHT ALE 3.8% ABV
BITTER 4.0% ABV
ORIGINAL 4.4% ABV
DARK ALE 5.0% ABV
Plus seasonals.

NAGS HEAD BREWERY
Nag's Head Inn, Abercych, Boncath SA37 0HJ
☎ *(01239) 841200*

 OLD EMRYS 3.8% ABV

WM EVAN EVANS BREWERY
*The New Brewery, 1 Rhosmaen Street, Llandeilo
SA19 6LU*
☎ *(01588) 824455*
www.evan-evans.com

BEST BITTER 3.8% ABV
WELSH ALE 4.2% ABV
WARRIOR 4.4% ABV
Plus seasonals and specials.

FACER'S BREWERY
*Tan y Coed, Bryn Y Garreg, Mynydd y Ffling,
Sir y Fflint CH6 5QT*
☎ *07713 566370*

CLWYD GOLD 3.5% ABV
Biscuity palate, mid-range bitterness.
NORTHERN COUNTY 3.8% ABV
Light in colour with excellent lacing and a
creamy head, the fruity palate has a moreish hop
character with orange citrus the predominant
impression.
AB BITTER 3.9% ABV
Malty and golden.
SUNNY BITTER 4.2% ABV
Amber colour, malty and hoppy.
DAVE'S HOPPY BEER 4.3% ABV
Dry and hoppy.
SPLENDID 4.3% ABV
LANDSLIDE 4.9% ABV
Golden brown in colour with a gentle malt
introduction, the bitterness coming through
later, enhanced by additional notes including
resinous esters, full lemon and orange fruitiness
with a hint of cherry and strong mouth-feel.

GWENT

CWMBRAN BREWERY
*Gorse Cottage, Graig Road, Upper Cwmbran,
Cwmbran, Torfaen NP44 5AS*
☎ *(01633) 485233*
www.cwmbranbrewery.co.uk

DRAYMAN'S BITTER 3.5% ABV
DRAYMAN'S CHOICE 3.8% ABV
DRAYMAN'S GOLD 3.8% ABV
VC 3.8% ABV
BLACKCURRANT STOUT 4.0% ABV
DOUBLE HOP 4.0% ABV
CROW VALLEY BITTER 4.2% ABV
Bitter and hoppy.
CROW VALLEY STOUT 4.2% ABV
EASTER BUNNY 4.5% ABV
GOLDEN WHEAT 4.5% ABV
PINK PANTHER 4.5% ABV
FOUR SEASONS 4.8% ABV
Light, summer ale.
THE FULL MALTY 4.8% ABV
Malty cross between a bitter and mild.
SANTA'S TIPPLE 5.0% ABV
Plus seasonal brews.

KINGSTONE BREWERY
*Kinsons Farm, White Brook, Monmouth
NP25 4TX*
☎ *(01600) 860778*

3 CASTLES 3.8% ABV
CLASSIC 4.5% ABV
GATEHOUSE ALE 5.1% ABV
Plus seasonals and specials.

WARCOP COUNTRY ALES
*9 Neville Park, St Bride's Wentlodge, Newport
NP10 8SE*
☎ *(01633) 680058*
www.warcopales.com

PIT SHAFT 3.4% ABV
PITSIDE 3.7% ABV
Delicate and malty.
ARC 3.8% ABV
Light, hoppy session beer.
PIT PROP MILD 3.8% ABV
Dark mild.
BLACK AND AMBER 4.0% ABV
Pale ruby bitter.
CASNEWYDD 4.0% ABV
Light, quaffer.
DRILLERS 4.0% ABV
Yellow, with some hoppiness.
HILSTON PREMIER 4.0% ABV
Dry and refreshing.
STEELERS 4.2% ABV
Malt flavours.
RAIDERS 4.3% ABV
Powerful hoppiness.
ROLLERS 4.3% ABV
Pale ruby bitter.
ZEN 4.4% ABV
Golden, dry finish.
FURNACE 4.5% ABV
Malt, dry in the aftertaste.
REFUGE 4.5% ABV
Yellow, with hops throughout.
RIGGERS 4.5% ABV
Golden version of Furnace.
DOCKER'S 5.0% ABV
Full bodied, with fruit throughout.
DP DEEP PIT 5.0% ABV
Flavoursome ruby beer.
Plus seasonal and occasional ales.

WEBBS BREWERY
*Unit 12, Cwm Business Park, Cwm, Ebbw Vale
NP23 7TB*
☎ *(01495) 370026*
www.webbsbrewery.co.uk

HUNTSMAN 3.8% ABV
BLACK WIDOW 4.5% ABV
TARANTULA 4.6% ABV
ARACHNAPHOBIA 5.1% ABV

GWYNEDD

PURPLE MOOSE BREWERY
Madoc Street, Porthmadog LL49 9DB
☎ *(01766) 515571*
www.purplemoose.co.uk

CWRW ERYRI 3.6% ABV
CWRW MADOG 3.7% ABV
CWRW GLASLYN 4.2% ABV
Plus seasonals.

THE SNOWDONIA BREWERY
*Snowdonia Park Hotel, Beddgelert Road,
Waunfawr LL55 4AQ*
☎ *(01286) 6650409*
www.snowdonia-park.co.uk

WELSH HIGHLAND BITTER 5.0% ABV

Plus occasionals and specials.

MID GLAMORGAN

OTLEY BREWING COMPANY LTD
*Unit 42, Albion Industrial Estate, Cilfynydd
Road, Pontypridd CF37 4NX*
☎ *(01443) 480555*
www.otleybrewing.co.uk

DARK 0 3.8% ABV
01 4.0% ABV
C02 4.2% ABV
0BB 4.5% ABV
0G 5.4% ABV
08 8.0% ABV

RHYMNEY BREWERY
*Unit A2, Valley Enterprise Centre, Dowlais,
Merthyr Tydfil CF48 2SR*
☎ *(01685) 722253*
www.rhymneybreweryltd.com

1905 3.9% ABV
BEVANS BITTER 4.2% ABV
RHYMNEY BITTER 4.5% ABV

POWYS

BRECONSHIRE BREWERY
*CH Marlow Ltd, Ffrwdgrech Industrial Estate,
Brecon LD3 8LA*
☎ *(01874) 623731*
www.breconshirebrewery.com

BRECON COUNTY ALE 3.7% ABV
Award-winning traditional bitter, hoppy
and full flavoured.
GOLDEN VALLEY 4.2% ABV
Award-winning golden ale, refreshing with a
'soft' bitterness.
RED DRAGON 4.7% ABV
Classic red ale, smooth and easy-drinking.
RAMBLERS RUIN 5.0% ABV
Award-winning dark amber traditional strong
best bitter.
Seasonal:
WELSH PALE ALE 3.7% ABV
BRECKNOCK BEST 4.5% ABV
END OF THE ROAD 4.8% ABV
Plus occasionals.

SOUTH GLAMORGAN

S A BRAIN AND CO. LTD
*The Cardiff Brewery, Crawshay Street, Cardiff
CF10 1SP*
☎ *(029) 2040 2060*
www.sabrain.com

BRAINS DARK 3.5% ABV
Chocolate and nut flavours, dry finish.
BRAINS BITTER 3.7% ABV
Combination of malts, Brains' own yeast strain
and Fuggles and Goldings hops. Initial sweet
malt flavour with a dry, well-hopped finish.
BUCKLEY'S BEST BITTER 3.7% ABV
Light, with a pleasingly hop character. Well
balanced with nutty overtones.

BRAINS S.A. 4.2% ABV
A distinctly hoppy strong ale brewed to a recipe
combining the characteristics of pale and crystal
malts with the choicest traditional ale hop
varieties.
REVEREND JAMES 4.5% ABV
Full flavoured and warming, the Reverend James
is rich in palate, spicy and aromatic with a
deeply satisfying finish.
SA GOLD 4.7% ABV
Citrus aroma, hop flavour.
Plus seasonals including:
BREAD OF HEAVEN 4.0% ABV
ST DAVID'S ALE 4.1% ABV
MERLIN'S OAK 4.3% ABV
DRAGON'S ALE 4.4% ABV
CWRW SEREN 4.6% ABV

BULLMASTIFF BREWERY
14 Bessemer Close, Leckwith, Cardiff CF11 8DL
☎ *(029) 2066 5292*

WELSH GOLD 3.8% ABV
JACK THE LAD 4.1% ABV
THOROUGHBRED 4.5% ABV
WELSH BLACK DOUBLE STOUT 4.8% ABV
WELSH RED 4.8% ABV
BRINDLE 5.0% ABV
SON OF A BITCH 6.5% ABV
Seasonal:
SUMMER MOULT 4.3% ABV
MOGADOG 10.0% ABV

VALE OF GLAMORGAN BREWERY
Unit 84 Atlantic Trading Estate, Barry
☎ *(01446) 730757*
www.vogbrewery.co.uk

BITTER 4.1%

WEST GLAMORGAN

BRYNCELYN BREWERY
*Wern Fawr Inn, 47 Wern Road, Ystalyfera,
Swansea Valley SA9 2LX*
☎ *(01639) 843625*

BUDDY MARVELLOUS 4.0% ABV
OH BOY 4.5% ABV
Occasional and seasonal beers:
FEB 59 3.7% ABV
PEGGY'S BREW 4.0% ABV
BUDDY'S DELIGHT 4.2% ABV
CWRW CELYN 4.4% ABV
CHH 4.5% ABV
MAY B BABY 4.5% ABV
BUDDY CONFUSING 5.0% ABV
RAVE ON 5.0% ABV
THAT'LL BE THE SLEIGH 7.1% ABV

SWANSEA BREWING COMPANY
*Joiner's Arms, 50 Bishopston Road, Bishopston,
Swansea SA3 3EJ*
☎ *(01792) 290197*

DEEP SLADE DARK 4.0% ABV
BISHOPSWOOD BITTER 4.3% ABV
THREE CLIFFS GOLD 4.7% ABV
ORIGINAL WOOD 5.2% ABV
Plus seasonal and occasional brews.

TOMOS WATKIN ALES

Now brewed c/o The Hurns Brewing Company Phoenix Brewery, Unit 3 Century Park, Valley Way, Swansea Enterprise Park, Swansea SA6 8RP
☎ *(01792) 797300*
www.hurnsbeer.co.uk

WATKIN BB 4.0% ABV
Malty, with moderate bitter flavour and floral hoppiness.
CHWARAE TEG 4.1% ABV
Golden, malty, nutty.
MERLIN'S STOUT 4.2% ABV
Dark, with powerful liquorice flavour.
CWRW BRAF 4.5% ABV
Amber, gentle hoppiness.
WATKIN OSB (OLD STYLE BITTER) 4.5% ABV
Award-winning, malty with delicate hoppiness.
Plus seasonal ales including:
CWRW CERIDWEN 4.2% ABV
DEWI SAINT 4.2% ABV
OWAIN GLYNDWR 4.2% ABV

THE PUBS

CLWYD

ABERGELE

The Bull Hotel

Chapel Street, Abergele, Conwy LL22 7AW
☎ *(01745) 832115* Lindsay While

Lees GB Mild and JW Bitter regularly available.

Just outside Conwy town on the Llanrwst road, this family-run pub has a restaurant and music-free main bar. Food served Wed–Mon 11am–2pm and 6–8pm. Car park. Children welcome. Accommodation.
OPEN *All day, every day.*

BROUGHTON

The Spinning Wheel Tavern

The Old Warren, Broughton CH4 OEG
☎ *(01244) 531068* Mike Vernon

Guest beers regularly rotated, including Greene King IPA, Fuller's London Pride and Marston's Pedigree.

Family-run pub in a secluded spot well off the main road, with a popular restaurant.
OPEN *11.30am–3pm and 6–11pm Mon–Sat; all day Sun.*

BRYNFORD

The Llyn y Mawn Inn

Brynford Hill, Brynford CH8 8AD
☎ *(01352) 714367* Dewi and Annette Lewis

Freehouse serving up to six brews every week. Welsh ales are favoured, plus others from small breweries.

Typical Welsh longhouse with restaurant and gardens. Real fires, background music. Food available 12–3pm and 6.15–8.15pm weekdays; 12–9.30pm weekends. Booking is advisable for food. Well-behaved children allowed, but not in the bar. Adjacent to the A55 expressway and can be seen from there.
OPEN *12–3pm and 5.30–11pm Mon–Thurs; all day Fri–Sun. All day, every day in summer.*

BETWS-Y-COED

Pont-y-Pair Hotel

Holyhead Road, Betws-y-Coed LL24 OBN
☎ *(01690) 710407* Bethan Mathews

S A Brains and Greene King Abbot Ale usually available.

Small hotel situated in the heart of Snowdonia with lots of rural pursuits close by. Home-cooked food available day and night. Children welcome.
OPEN *11am–11pm Mon–Sat; 12–10.30pm Sun.*

BETWS-YN-RHOS

The Wheatsheaf Inn

Betws-yn-Rhos, Abergele LL22 8AW
☎ *(01492) 680218* Raymond Perry
www.thewheatsheafinn.org.uk

Purple Moose Madog's Ale, Spitting Feathers and Wychwood Hobgoblin are examples of the three real ales available.

Located in the Best Kept Village in Wales 2003, a former coaching inn with an olde-worlde atmosphere and lots of brass, first licensed in 1640. Locals' bar with pool plus lounge bar. Food every lunchtime and evening. Car park. Beer garden, smoking pavilion with heating and lighting. High chairs available. Function room, B&B accommodation. Village has bowling green, golf course, tennis and football. On the B5381.
OPEN *12–3pm and 6pm–12.*

CADOLE

Colomendy Arms

Gwernaffield Road, Cadole, Mold CH7 5LL
☎ *(01352) 810217* Elsie Butler

Five different guests on pumps. Shepherd Neame Master Brew plus other guest examples including Ridleys Prospect, Orkney The Red McGregor, Shepherd Neame Early Bird, Weetwood ales and a range of others.

Small, cosy, but extremely friendly pub with bar, small lounge and beer garden. Located in tiny village just off the main Mold to Ruthin road.
OPEN *7–11pm Mon–Wed; 6–11pm Thurs; 4–11pm Fri (closed weekday lunchtimes); 12–11pm Sat; 12–10.30pm Sun.*

CAERWYS

The Travellers Inn

Pen y Cefn, Caerwys, Mold CH7 5BL
☎ *(01352) 720251* Kevin Jones

Freehouse with Charles Wells Bombardier plus various other guests rotated on the two remaining pumps. One home brew: Roy Morgan's Original (3.8–3.9% ABV) usually on offer.

A family pub and restaurant with food available all day. Children allowed. Located on the A55.
OPEN *11am–11pm Mon–Sat; 12–10.30pm Sun.*

CILCAIN
The White Horse
The Square, Cilcain, Nr Mold CH7 5NN
☎ *(01352) 740142* Peter Jeory

Genuine freehouse with four hand pumps serving a wide range of beers. Banks's Bitter plus rotating guests perhaps from Caledonian, Brains, St Austell, Bateman, Jennings, Black Sheep and Everards breweries. The range changes every other day.

Small, cosy, mountainside village inn, several hundred years old, spread over four rooms with real fires and beams. No juke box or pool table. Food available 12–2pm and 7–9pm Mon–Sat; 12–3pm and 7–9pm Sun. No children. Outside seating, car park. Two miles off the Mold to Denbigh road.

OPEN *12–3pm and 6.30–11pm Mon–Fri; 12–11pm Sat; 12–10.30pm Sun.*

CLAWDD-NEWYDD
Glan Lyn Inn
Clawdd-Newydd, Ruthin LL15 2NA
☎ *(01824) 750754* Nigel Cooper

Real ales rotated regularly to include the likes of Wychwood Hobgoblin, Greene King Abbot Ale, Jennings Cumberland and others.

Old-style typical village pub. Food available 6–9pm Thurs–Fri; 4–9pm Sat; 12–4pm Sun.

OPEN *4.30–11pm Mon–Fri; 12–11pm Sat; 12–10.30pm Sun.*

COLWYN BAY
The Pen-y-Bryn Freehouse
Wentworth Avenue, Colwyn Heights, Colwyn Bay LL29 6DD
☎ *(01492) 533360* Graham Arathoon
www.penybryn-colwynbay.co.uk

Thwaites Original plus five guests changed twice weekly, perhaps including Great Orme Orme's Best, Timothy Taylor Landlord, Conwy Honey Fayre or something from Purple Moose.

A Brunning and Price freehouse with antique furniture, oak floors, a library area and real fires. Beer garden with views over the bay. Car park. Disabled facilities. Children welcome at lunchtime and until 7.30pm. Food served 12–9.30pm Mon–Sat and 12–9pm Sun. From Colwyn Bay go up Kings Road to the top of the hill and the pub is on the left.

OPEN *11.30–11pm Mon–Sat; 12–10.30pm Sun.*

Rhos Fynach
Rhos Promenade, Colwyn Bay LL28 4NG
☎ *(01492) 548185* Robert Skellie

Marston's Pedigree and Banks's Bitter plus guest ales rotate approximately every two weeks.

Historic pub central to Colwyn Bay, family friendly with spacious beer garden and restaurant. Also caters for weddings and parties. Food served 12–9pm.

OPEN *11am–11pm (10.30pm Sun).*

The White Lion Inn
Llanelian-yn-Rhos, Colwyn Bay, Conwy LL29 8YA
☎ *(01492) 515807* Simon Cole
www.whitelioninn.co.uk

Freehouse with three real ales, including Marston's Bitter and Pedigree and a weekly guest.

Stone-built Welsh country inn with slate floor, log fires and beams. Food available 12–2pm and 6–9pm. Beer garden, car park, jazz nights, children welcome. A mile outside Colwyn Bay (check website).

OPEN *11.30am–3pm and 6–11pm Tues–Sat (closed Mon); 12–4pm and 6–10.30pm Sun.*

CYMAU
Ye Olde Talbot Inn
Cymau Lane, Cymau, Nr Wrexham
☎ *(01978) 761410* WJ Mee

Hydes Anvil Bitter plus a changing seasonal beer every two months.

A traditional drinkers' pub. No food. Car park. Children welcome.

OPEN *7–11pm Mon–Fri; 12–4pm and 7–11pm Sat; 12–4pm and 7–10.30pm Sun.*

DENBIGH
The Eagle Inn
Back Row, Denbigh, Denbighshire LL16 3TE
☎ *(01745) 813203* Karen Williams

Freehouse serving three real ales, including Wadworth 6X, Marston's Pedigree and a guest.

A large pub with a snooker room, pool, darts etc. Quiz nights. Food available at lunchtime. Children allowed if eating.

OPEN *12–3pm and 6.30–11pm Mon–Fri; 11am–11pm Sat; 12–10.30pm Sun.*

FFRITH
The Poacher's Cottage
High Street, Ffrith, Wrexham LL11 5LH
☎ *(01978) 756465* David Griffiths

Greene King Old Speckled Hen and Charles Wells Bombardier plus one guest such as Thwaites Lancaster Bomber or Young's Bitter.

Busy country restaurant and old-style pub. Real food served lunchtimes and evenings Wed–Sun. Tuesday is curry and a pint night, plus quiz. Spacious car park.

OPEN *12–3pm and 6pm–12 Tues–Sat; all day–Sun.*

GLYN MYFYR
Crown Inn
Llanfihangel, Glyn Myfry LL21 9UL
☎ *(01490) 420209* Michael Morley

Two pumps in regular use with frequently rotating guests, which could be from Phoenix, Wye Valley, Weetwood and several smaller micro-breweries.

Winner of local CAMRA branch award for Best Pub of Year 2002 and North Wales, Merseyside and Cheshire regional winner for 2002. Bar meals available. Children welcome.

OPEN *7pm–close Tues–Fri; 12–close Sat–Sun.*

GORSEDD

The Druid Inn

Gorsedd, Holywell CH8 8QZ
☎ *(01352) 710944* Elizabeth Craig

Freehouse with three hand pumps serving a variety of real ales such as Charles Wells Bombardier, Caledonian Deuchars IPA and Greene King Old Speckled Hen. The range rotates every week.

A listed 12th-century longhouse with oak beams and log fires. The separate restaurant serves food every evening and Sunday lunchtime. Children allowed. Located off the A5026, two miles west of Holywell. Private functions catered for.

OPEN *All day, every day.*

GRESFORD

Pant yr Ochain

Old Wrexham Road, Gresford, Wrexham LL12 8TY
☎ *(01978) 853525* Lindsey Douglas
www.brunningandprice.co.uk

Locally brewed Plassey beers plus Timothy Taylor Landlord, Caledonian Deuchars IPA, Flowers Original (brewed by Badger) and two rotating guests.

L arge, 16th-century pub set in its own grounds with big garden and overlooking a lake. Several dining areas and food served all day, 12–9.30pm (9pm Sun). Attracts clientele from all around the locality and further afield.

OPEN *12–11pm (10.30pm Sun).*

GWERNAFFIELD

Miner's Arms

Church Lane, Gwernaffield CH7 5DT
☎ *(01352) 740803* P Hammersley

Camerons Bitter and rotating guests, including Banks's ales and Marston's Pedigree.

Q uiet rural pub in former mining village, catering mainly for local clientele. There is a lounge and bar with darts and pool table. Bar snacks available.

OPEN *All day, every day.*

HALKYN

Britannia Inn

Pentre Road, Halkyn CH8 8BS
☎ *(01352) 780272* Jim Price

JW Lees house with Traditional Bitter always available.

A traditional country pub overlooking the Dee and Mersey estuaries – you can see as far as Blackpool Tower! Two bars, a family area, games room with darts, dominoes and pool, and a homely conservatory which is used as the main dining area. Homemade food specialising in local produce available 12–2.30pm and 5.30–9pm Mon–Sat, plus 12–6pm Sun, when there is a set Sunday lunch menu, including traditional roasts. Children welcome, highchairs available. Small beer garden, outside seating area overlooking the estuary. Quiz on Sun nights, plus monthly live music. Disabled access and facilities. Car park.

OPEN *12–11.30pm (11pm Sun).*

HOLYWELL

Glan-yr-Afon Inn

Milwr, Holywell CH8 8HE
☎ *(01352) 710052* G Wallis

Five real ales at any one time, rotated weekly.

A 16th-century inn hidden away in the heart of Flintshire. Three bars, private function room, restaurant, two real fires. Homemade food served 12–2.30pm Mon–Sat and 12–4.30pm Sun, plus 6–9pm every evening. Beer garden, car park. Children and dogs welcome. Disabled access and facilities. Children's play area. En-suite accommodation.

OPEN *12–11pm (10.30pm Sun).*

LLANGOLLEN

The Corn Mill

Dee Lane, Llangollen LL20 8PN
☎ *(01978) 869555* Andrew Barker
www.brunningandprice.co.uk

Local Plassey beers plus three regularly rotating guests including Timothy Taylor Landlord.

T wo-bar rural riverside pub full of beams over three floors with watermill still turning behind the bar. Opened as a pub in June 2000. Bar and restaurant food available 12–9.30pm. Outside seating, no facilities for children, guide dogs only. In the town centre, just off the A5.

OPEN *12–11pm (10.30pm Sun).*

The Sun Inn

49 Regent Street, Llangollen LL20 8HN
☎ *(01978) 860233*
Alan Adams and Paul Lamb

Freehouse offering six real ales that could well include Salopian, Phoenix or Thwaites brews plus three guests rotated as and when. Four Belgian beers and two real ciders also available.

F riendly, lively, beer-drinkers' pub which gets very busy, with a good atmosphere and old-style decor. Take the A5 towards Llangollen. Live music four nights a week – open mic, Mon; jazz, Tues; rock, Thurs; blues/folk, Fri. Beer garden.

OPEN *Summer: 11am–11pm Mon–Sat; winter: 3–11pm Mon–Fri, 11am–11pm Sat; 12–10.30pm Sun all year round.*

LLOC

The Rock Inn

Lloc, Nr Holywell CH8 8RD
☎ *(01352) 710049* T Swift

Burtonwood Bitter and at least one guest bitter always available.

S mall, friendly, family-run two-bar pub with dining room. Large car park with picnic benches. Food available lunchtimes and evenings except Tues. Children welcome.

OPEN *12–11pm (10.30pm Sun).*

MELIDEN
Melyd Arms
23 Ffordd Talargoch, Meliden LL19 8LA
☎ *(01745) 852005* Frank Del-Pinto

Marston's Bitter plus rotating guests including Marston's Pedigree and Banks's ales.

Popular village-centre pub with split-level eating area, log fires, pleasant atmosphere.

OPEN *12–11pm (10.30pm Sun).*

NORTHOP
Stables Bar Restaurant
Soughton Hall Country House Hotel and Restaurant, Northop CH7 6AB
☎ *(01352) 840577* Annette Gallop
www.soughtonhall.co.uk

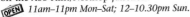

Freehouse serving real ales from Plassey and three monthly guests.

Converted stable block dating from 1714, with a bar in the stable, a restaurant in the hayloft and a large wine shop. Food is available 12–9.30pm, and gourmet evenings are held in the hotel. Accommodation, private room for hire in hotel. Beer garden. Large car park. Children welcome. Located off the A55 Flint/Northop junction.

OPEN *11am–11pm Mon–Sat; 12–10.30pm Sun.*

OLD COLWYN
The Red Lion
385 Abergele Road, Old Colwyn, Colwyn Bay, Conwy LL29 9PL
☎ *(01492) 515042* Geoff and Debby Hughes

Freehouse serving seven cask ales, with Marston's Burton Bitter plus six constantly rotating guests (18–20 a week), always including a mild.

A village pub on the main road with one traditional bar, one games room including Sky TV, one lounge and one rear lounge with real fire. Breweriana abounds throughout the pub. No food. Rear courtyard with covered smoking area including external heaters. Children allowed in courtyard (not in pub). Right in the middle of Old Colwyn.

OPEN *5–11pm Mon–Thurs; 4pm–12 Fri; 12–12 Sat; 12–11pm Sun.*

PONTBLYDDYN
New Inn
Corwen Road, Pontblyddyn, Nr Mold CH7 4HR
☎ *(01352) 771459* D Hunt

Three guests, changed weekly, including a full range such as Highgate, Brains and Weetwood ales.

Child-friendly pub with play area. Food available.

OPEN *12–close.*

RHEWL
The Drovers Arms
Rhewl, Ruthin LL15 2UD
☎ *(01824) 703163* A Given and A Nancarrow

Freehouse serving Fuller's London Pride and Young's Bitter.

A 300-year-old one-bar pub and an old meeting place for drovers. An English Civil War skirmish took place on the bridge outside the pub. Large garden with tables, barbecues in nice weather. Beer festivals, live music etc. Hot food available 12–2pm and 6–9pm, with sandwiches and snacks served from 2pm onwards. Well-behaved children allowed. Conservatory and children's safe play area in the beer garden. Bank holiday events such as music and treasure hunts. Good walks.

OPEN *12–2.30pm and 5–11.30pm Mon–Thurs; 12–2.30pm and 5pm–1am Fri; noon–1am Sat; 12–12 Sun.*

RHYL
Sussex
Sussex Street, Rhyl LL18 15G
☎ *(01745) 362910* Derek Smith

Very wide range of real ales on the pumps, constantly rotating to include guests such as Shepherd Neame Bishop's Finger, Hop Back Summer Lightning, Bateman XXXB and many others.

Designated family dining areas. Food served 9am–11pm. Children welcome.

OPEN *9am–midnight (1am Fri–Sat).*

ROSSETT
The Golden Grove
Llyndir Lane, Burton Green, Rossett
☎ *(01244) 570445* Dennis and Gail Ames
www.thegoldengrove.co.uk

Part-tied to Marston's, with four real ales including Marston's Burton Bitter and something from Jennings, plus guests such as Brains St David's, Adnams Broadside and Rooster's Wild Mule. Thatcher's draught cider also available.

Beautiful historic drovers' inn, off the beaten track, with ship's bar dated 1362. Authentic bar and snug with real fires. Friendly Winchester Suite restaurant seating 50 (wedding venue) plus James Clarke restaurant seating 45 (featuring the gravestone of James Clarke, dated 1740). Food served 12–9.30pm Tues–Sun. Caravan Club certified touring site. From Chester turn right at sign for Burton Green; from Wrexham turn left at sign for Llynd Hall.

OPEN *11am–11.30pm Tues–Sun.*

RUTHIN

Red Lion

Cyffylliog, Ruthin LL15 2DN
☎ *(01824) 710664* CF Kimberley Jones

JW Lees Bitter plus seasonal beers from the same brewery.

Friendly, family-run country pub with lots of character. Caters for everyone, including family meals and bed and breakfast. Food served 7–10pm Mon–Fri and 12–10pm Sat–Sun. Car park. Children welcome.

OPEN *7–11pm Mon–Fri; 12–11pm Sat–Sun.*

Three Pigeons Inn

Graigfechan, Ruthin LL15 2EU
☎ *(01824) 703178* Jim Thornley
www.threepigeonsruthin.co.uk

Freehouse with Hancock's HB (brewed by Brains) and Brains Reverend James plus a guest in summer.

A 17th-century drovers' pub in tranquil setting, with old beams, public bar, walkers' bar and lounge. Jugs of beer are served straight from the cellar. Food served Sat–Sun lunch and Wed–Sat evenings. Camp site and self-catering accommodation, function room, beer terrace and garden. Families, walkers and dogs welcome. Graigfechan is signposted off the Ruthin to Wrexham road.

OPEN *5.30–11pm Mon–Fri; 12–11pm Sat–Sun.*

ST ASAPH

The Kentigern Arms

High Street, St Asaph LL17 ORG
☎ *(01745) 584157* Mrs Redgrave

Freehouse offering Caledonian 80/– plus maybe another guest.

A 17th-century coaching inn with beams and open fires. A separate small room can be used for children or as a dining room. Four bedrooms. Food available. Children allowed.

OPEN *12–3pm and 7–11pm (10.30pm Sun).*

SYCHDYN

Glasfryn

Raikes Lane, Sychdyn, Nr Mold CH7 6LR
☎ *(01352) 750500* James Meakin
www.glasfryn-mold.co.uk

Freehouse with eight real ales. Flowers Original, Thwaites Bitter, Timothy Taylor Landlord, Purple Moose Snowdonia Ale and Facers Flintshire bitter are permanently on the pumps, and the guests, changed every few days, might include Sharp's Doom Bar, Weetwood Eastgate ale, Hawkeshead Lakeland Gold and Old Tuns brewery.

Originally built as a judge's residence to serve the nearby courts, this red-brick pub has an interesting mix of customers. One bar, four rooms, open fires and bookcases. There is a popular and often busy restaurant serving food 12–9.30pm (9pm Sun). Children welcome until 7pm, away from the bar. Dogs on a lead welcome, away from dining areas. Beer garden, car park. Near Flintshire County Hall and the County Courts, opposite Clwyd Theatr Cymru.

OPEN *11.30am–11pm Mon–Sat; 12–10.30pm Sun.*

TREUDDYN

Liver Inn

Rhydtalog, Treuddyn, Nr Mold CH7 4LF
☎ *(01824) 780878*
Jane Davies and Robert Ankers

Freehouse with an ever-changing selection of real ales, including local beers from small Welsh brewers and traditional ales such as Greene King Old Speckled Hen, Wychwood Hobgoblin and Brains Rev James.

Traditional country pub in beautiful surroundings on the edge of Llandegla Moors. Public bar, lounge, games room and small dining room. There is a separate lounge and restaurant with open fires. Bar and à la carte meals available lunchtimes and evenings. The restaurant is also available for private functions. Children welcome. Large car park, outside seating.

OPEN *12–2.30pm and 6–11pm Tues–Sat; 12–3.30pm and 7–10.30pm Sun.*

YSCEIFIOG

Fox Inn

Ysceifiog, Nr Holywell CH8 8NJ
☎ *(01352) 720241* Trevor Bradford

Three real ales. Brakspear Bitter is a regular and the constantly rotating guests could well feature something from a local micro-brewery.

Small, 17th-century, friendly, traditional village freehouse which features in CAMRA's National Inventory of Historic Pub Interiors. Public bar and lounge bar, both with open fires, plus additional rooms. Children welcome in the snug until 9pm. Outside seating. Local CAMRA branch Pub of the Year 2004. Close to Offa's Dyke path, with several circular walks around the village, through interesting woodland and open countryside. The village is located off the A55.

OPEN *6–11pm Mon–Fri (closed Wed); 2–11pm Sat–Sun.*

DYFED

ABERCYCH

The Nag's Head Inn

Abercych, Boncath SA37 0JH
☎ *(01239) 841200* Sam Jamieson

Freehouse and brewpub with Old Emrys brewed on the premises and always available, plus two guests, perhaps Greene King Abbot, Brains Reverend James, Wye Valley Butty Bach or something from the Ffos y Ffin brewery.

Friendly riverside pub with one bar, log fire and a large collection of beer bottles on display. Good pub food available 12–2pm and 6–9pm daily. Children's play area. Large car park. On the B4332 between Cenarth Falls and Boncath.

OPEN *12–3pm and 6–11.30pm (closed Mondays except bank holidays).*

ABERYSTWYTH

The Coopers Arms

Northgate Street, Aberystwyth, Ceredigion SY23 2JT
☎ *(01970) 624050* Geraint and Angela Evans
Felinfoel Brewery tied house serving Best, Double Dragon and Stout.

Friendly local with live music in bar and gigs in licensed upstairs function room. All rugby matches screened live. Parties catered for. Accommodation available. Private rooms for hire. At the bottom of the hill on the A487 into town.

OPEN *1pm–12 Sun–Wed; 1pm–1am Thurs–Sat.*

The Ship & Castle

1 High Street, Aberystwyth, Ceredigion SY23 1JG
☎ *07773 778785* Ian Blair
Freehouse serving five real ales. Wye Valley Hereford Pale Ale is regularly featured, and the other beers are changed twice a week. One real cider also served.

Built in 1760, the third oldest pub in Aberystwyth, with stone walls and timber floors. It has a reputation as the town's premier real ale pub. CAMRA Pub of the County 2007. One bar, no food. Beer festivals held in October and April. Musician nights on Wednesdays. At the top end of town, near the old castle.

OPEN *2pm–12.*

AMMANFORD

Ammanford Hotel

Wernoleu House, 31 Pontamann Road, Ammanford SA18 2HX
☎ *(01269) 592598* JP Kinch
Freehouse with five constantly rotating guests, changed daily or weekly.

Victorian mansion set in six acres. One bar and colonial pool room. Landscaped gardens. Six en-suite letting rooms. Plenty of parking. Food served evenings. Close to Brecon Beacons. Located off the Neath Road out of Ammanford.

OPEN *5.30–11pm Mon–Fri; 12–11pm Sat–Sun.*

CAPEL BANGOR

The Tynllidiart Arms

Capel Bangor, Nr Aberystwyth SY23 3LR
☎ *(01970) 880248*
Andrew Greenhouse and Margaret Phillips
Freehouse with Wye Valley Butty Bach, St Austell Tribute and Bragdy Gwynant Cwrw Gwynant (brewed on the premises) plus one or two constantly rotating guests such as Brains Reverend James or Greene King Old Speckled Hen.

Stylish pub dating back to 1688, the perfect environment for travellers and locals alike. Home to the world's smallest commercial brewery (officially listed in the *Guinness Book of Records!*). Food served both in bar and separate upstairs restaurant 12–2pm and 6.30–9pm (may vary at holiday times). Large bar area and separate restaurant seating 40, plus outdoor seating front and back. Sheltered and heated smoking area. Children welcome in all eating areas. Near to the Rheidol Valley visitors' centre and riding stables. Also close to butterfly farm, Nant Yr Arian red kite centre and outdoor activity park. Located on the A44, five miles east of Aberystwyth.

OPEN *11.30am–3pm and 5–11pm Mon–Thurs; 11.30am–midnight Fri–Sun.*

CWMANN

The Ram Inn

Cwmann, Lampeter SA48 8ES
☎ *(01570) 422556* Gary and Sian Pugh
Freehouse offering Archers Golden Bitter plus one or two guest beers changed frequently, from national and smaller breweries.

Old drover's pub one mile outside Lampeter on the Llandovery Road, dating from around 1560, with a dining room, bar and garden. Previous CAMRA Best Pub in Wales. Food available at lunchtime and evenings. Children allowed.

OPEN *All day, every day.*

DREFACH FELINDRE

Tafarn John Y Gwas

Drefach Felindre, Llandysul SA44 5XG
☎ *(01559) 370469* Mark Hann
www.johnygwas.co.uk
Freehouse with two or three weekly-changing guests, a mix of local and national breweries.

An 18th-century traditional village pub with one bar and dedicated restaurant. Separate, secluded snug area with open fire. Food served all day, every day. Small car park. Children and pets welcome. Beer garden. The only yellow building in the village!

OPEN *All day, every day.*

FELINFOEL

The Royal Oak

Felinfoel Road, Felinfoel, Llanelli SA14 8LA
☎ *(01554) 751140* M Cleland
Tied to the nearby Felinfoel Brewery, with two hand pumps serving the Felinfoel ales.

An old-fashioned local opposite the brewery, with food available lunchtimes and evenings. Children allowed.

OPEN *All day, every day.*

FISHGUARD

The Royal Oak

Market Square, Fishguard SA65 9HA
☎ *(01348) 873993* Dai Crowther
Brains Brewery leased pub serving Rev James plus two weekly-changing guests.

Over 300-years old, this pub is home to the signing of the last invasion of mainland Britain (1797). One main bar, two general bars and two separate restaurant areas with traditional oak beams. Food served 12–2pm and 6–9pm. Large beer garden with valley, mountain and sea views. Home of the Fishguard Folk Festival featuring 15 real ales in May.

OPEN *10am–12.30am (1.30am Fri–Sat).*

GOGINAN

The Druid Inn

High Street, Goginan, Nr Aberystwyth,
Ceredigion SY23 3NT
☎ *(01970) 880650* William John Howell

Genuine freehouse with three real ales: Banks's Bitter and Brains SA plus a guest changed every week or two.

The building dates back to 1719, when it was used by the local lead and silver mining community. One main bar, pool room and separate dining area. Food available 12–2.30pm and 6–9pm. Children welcome. B&B accommodation available. Beer garden, smoking area. Car parking. On the A44 seven miles from Aberystwyth.

OPEN *12–12 (1am Fri–Sat).*

HAVERFORDWEST

The Fishguard Arms

47 Old Bridge, Haverfordwest SA61 2EZ
☎ *(01437) 768123* Richard Carr

Brains leased house serving Rev James plus two rotating guests, changed twice weekly.

This 16th-century coaching inn is a listed building with one lounge bar and dining facilities. Food served daily 12–2.30pm and 6–9pm (Nov–Apr), 12–9pm (Apr–Nov). Separate restaurant. Letting rooms. Patio garden. Mini beer festivals held three times a year. Families welcome. Located at the foot of Haverfordwest Castle on the banks of the Clydau River.

OPEN *11am–1am Sun–Thurs;*
11am–2am Fri–Sat.

King's Arms Hotel

23 Dew Street, Haverfordwest
☎ *(01437) 763726* Chris Hudd

Six beers from a list of approximately 150 brews per year.

Old, beamed and flagstoned pub in the town, just past the library. Street parking, function room. No children.

OPEN *11am–3pm and 6–11pm Mon–Sat; 12–3pm and 7–10.30pm Sun.*

HEOL Y PLAS

Ye Olde Red Lion

Heol y Plas, Llannon, Llanelli SA14 6AA
☎ *(01269) 841276* Steven Ireland

Felinfoel Brewery tied house with two pumps serving Felinfoel ales.

A rural 16th-century pub with oak beams and log fires. Food every evening plus weekend lunchtimes. Children welcome.

OPEN *5–11pm Mon–Fri; 11am–11pm Sat; 12–10.30pm Sun.*

HERBRANDSTON

Taberna Inn

Herbrandston, Nr Milford Haven SA73 3TD
☎ *(01646) 693498* Brenda Absolon, Anna Absolon and Helen Jacob
http://taberna.mysite.freeserve.com

Freehouse with two or three real ales. A rolling beer festival! All are guests, popular ones brought back, unpopular ones are not restocked.

Traditional-style inn with something for everyone. Separate formal restaurant, Plaice to Meat, with maritime theme. Informal eating area with railway theme, Buffer Stop. The Durham Lounge is suitable for quiet conversation and the Aeron Bar for games and music. Open fires in winter. Food served lunchtimes and evenings (except Sunday evenings Oct–March, when there are charity quizzes) using local produce and fresh fish specials. B&B available. Beer garden. Private functions catered for. Car park. Children welcome. Located in the village of Herbrandston opposite the school on Dale Road, three miles from Milford Haven.

OPEN *12–close.*

HOREB

The Waunwyllt Inn

Horeb Road, Five Roads, Horeb, Llanelli SA15 5AQ
☎ *(01269) 860209* Martin Bartley

Freehouse with four pumps serving a constantly changing selection of real ales. Examples include Greene King Abbot and Old Speckled Hen, Ffos y Ffyn Dylan's Choice, and Evan Evans Cwrw and Cwrw Hâf. Two of the beers are changed monthly.

Very popular 17th-century country inn with log fire and leather suites. A former coach house in the quiet hamlet of Horeb, close to the Celtic Trail cycle route. One bar, restaurant, new courtyard for alfresco dining and new landscaped beer garden that is ramped for disabled access. Food is served during normal opening hours, with fresh local fish and local meats available, and vegetarian and other diets catered for. Five concrete hard standings for caravans, plus four-star accommodation. Restaurant available for private functions. Family-friendly. Beer festivals in summer. Plenty of local attractions within a few miles, including beaches, wildlife, gardens and leisure parks. Four miles north of Llanelli on the B4309, turn right at Five Roads onto Horeb Road for half a mile.

OPEN *11am–midnight (11pm Sun).*

LLANDDAROG

The White Hart Thatched Inn & Brewery

Llanddarog, Carmarthen SA32 8NT
☎ *(01267) 275395* Marcus and Cain Coles

Cwrw Blasus ('tasty beer'), Llanddarog Ale, Roasted Barley Stout and Golden Ale are examples of the four beers on offer, all from the Coles Family Brewery, and all brewed at The White Hart.

Beautiful rural village inn dating back to 1371, with open log fire, oak beams and ancient heavily carved furniture. The antiques create an olde-worlde atmosphere. Delicious home-cooked meals, using local produce where possible, are served during opening times. Children's play area, beer garden. Car park. Private room for meetings, parties, weddings and other events. Coaches by appointment only. On the way to West Wales, near the M4 corridor. Off the A48

near the National Botanic Garden of Wales.
 11.30am–3pm and 6.30–11pm Mon–Sat; 12–3pm and 7–10.30pm Sun.

LLANDEILO
The Castle Hotel
113 Rhosmaen Street, Llandeilo SA19 6EN
☎ *(01558) 823446* Simon Williams

Tomas Watkin tied house with award-winning ales such as Whoosh, Best, Old Style Bitter and Merlin's Stout. Other seasonal guests rotated on one hand pump.

Town-centre pub with two bars, five adjoining rooms, 65-seater restaurant and beer garden. Bar and restaurant food served lunchtimes and evenings. Children allowed. Easy, free parking.

 All day, every day.

LLANGOEDMOR
Penllwyndu Inn
Llangoedmor, Cardigan SA43 2LY
☎ *(01239) 682533* Ryan Williams

Freehouse with two or three ales, which could come from Cottage, Jacobs or Buckley's.

A pub until 1926 and then a private house which the current landlord rented during the 1970s. It reopened as a pub in 1986, and the aforementioned landlord took over in 2005. A one-bar inn with olde-worlde feel and slate floors. Food served 12–2pm and 6–9pm daily. Beer garden. Children welcome. Car park. Close to local breaks and the Pembrokeshire coastal path. Located on the B4570.

 12–12 (summer); 2pm–12 (winter).

LLANSAINT
The King's Arms
13 Maes yr Eglwys, Llansaint, Nr Kidwelly SA17 5JE
☎ *(01267) 267487* John and Debbie Morris

Freehouse serving three regularly changing real ales from a wide range of brewers.

An 18th-century pub with two bars and a restaurant. Food served lunchtimes and evenings. Log fire in season, beer garden, car park. Children allowed. Follow signs for Llansaint from Kidwelly – the pub nestles under the church tower. Accommodation available.

 12–2.30pm and 6.30–11pm (10.30pm Sun); closed all day Tues.

MYNYDD Y GARREG
The Prince of Wales
Heol Meinciau, Mynydd y Garreg, Kidwelly SA17 4RP
☎ *(01554) 890522* Gail and Richard Pickett

Freehouse with seven real ales from a list that includes brews from Wye Valley, Bullmastiff and various Welsh micro-breweries. Please phone ahead for details of beers currently on tap. Real cider also available Easter–Oct.

A 200-year-old cottage pub, in the same ownership since 1989, with a collection of cinema memorabilia and bric-à-brac. Bar and restaurant food available evenings. Car park and garden. No children. Take the Mynydd y Garreg turn from the Cydweli bypass, then just over a mile on the right.

 5–11pm Mon–Sat; closed all day Sun.

NARBETH
The Kirkland Arms
East Gate, St James Street, Narbeth SA67 7DB
☎ *(01834) 860423* Mr Edger

Felinfoel Brewery tied pub with guest beers rotated on one pump. These might include York Yorkshire Terrier, Swansea Bishopswood Bitter, Wadworth 6X and many others changed on a weekly basis.

Old, traditional pub with pool table, games machines and beer garden. Fresh rolls and sandwiches served every day. Children allowed.

 11am–11pm Mon–Sat; 12–10.30pm Sun.

NEWCASTLE EMLYN
The Bunch of Grapes
Bridge Street, Newcastle Emlyn SA38 9DU
☎ *(01239) 711185* Billy Brewer

Freehouse with Courage Directors plus two constantly rotating guests, changed two or three times a week.

Late 16th-century inn with oak beams and wooden and stone floors. One bar. Food served daily, every lunchtime and some evenings. Separate restaurant. Beer garden. Private room available for hire. Pool table. Located near the clock tower.

 All day, every day.

PEMBROKE
The Castle Inn
17 Main Street, Pembroke SA71 4JS
☎ *(01646) 682883* Nigel Temple

Freehouse usually serving Charles Wells Bombardier and Wadworth 6X plus one or two guests.

Very old pub with long and narrow stone walls and beams. No food. Children allowed.

 11am–11pm Mon–Sat; 12–10.30pm Sun.

The First & Last
London Road, Pembroke Dock SA72 6TX
☎ *(01646) 682687* Richard Maynard

Freehouse with Charles Wells Bombardier or Brains SA plus one other.

Local community pub with beer garden. Light lunches only served. Children allowed at lunchtime only.

 11am–11pm Mon–Sat; 12–10.30pm Sun.

PISGAH

The Halfway Inn

*Devil's Bridge Road, Pisgah, Aberystwyth
SY23 4NE*
☎ *(01970) 880631* David Roberts

Felifoel Double Dragon and Hancock's HB (brewed by Brains) plus one guest, changed several times during the summer.

Traditional olde-worlde hostelry 700 feet up with magnificent views of the Cambrian mountains and Rheidol Valley. Bar and restaurant food available 7–9pm (not Mon in winter), and 12.30–2pm in summer. Beer garden and large car park. Children welcome. B&B accommodation. Outside benches for eating. Free overnight camping for customers. Located halfway along the A4120 Aberystwyth to Devil's Bridge road. Note, this is not the Pisgah near Cardigan.

OPEN *12–2pm and 6.30–11pm (10.30pm Sun). Times may vary in winter.*

RHYDOWEN

The Alltyrodyn Arms

Rhydowen, Llandysul, Ceredigion SA44 4QB
☎ *(01545) 590319*
Russell Patterson and Chris Sheath

Genuine freehouse serving three or four constantly changing ales.

A 16th-century pub with open fires, a pool room and beer garden. Bar snacks available during the week, restaurant food at weekends. Regular folk music evenings. Children and dogs welcome. Functions catered for. Beer tastings organised. On the A475 between Lampeter and Newcastle Emlyn.

OPEN *12–11pm Tues–Sat; 12–4pm Sun (closed Mon).*

ST DOGMAELS

White Hart Inn

Finch Street, St Dogmaels, Cardigan SA43 3EA
☎ *(01239) 612099*
Lindsey and Ann Duckworth

Greene King IPA, Felinfoel Double Dragon and Brains Rev James, with a guest in summer, changed weekly, that might come from Brains or Breconshire Brewery.

Old-fashioned family-run pub, with a real fire and a cosy, friendly atmosphere. Pool, darts and bar games available. Beer garden and patio with a smoking area. Local beer festivals in summer. Separate restaurant. Food served 12.30–2pm and 7pm–9pm. From Cardigan head towards St Dogmaels, and the pub is on the right as you enter the village.

OPEN *11am–11pm (extensions during village events and in December).*

TREGARON

The Talbot Hotel

Main Square, Tregaron, Ceredigion SY25 6JL
☎ *(01974) 298208* Graham Williams

Freehouse with three hand pumps serving a range of real ales. Marston's Pedigree and Felinfoel Double Dragon are a couple of the favourites. One guest ale is also served, and this changes every week to ten days.

A 15th-century drovers' inn with two bars, open fires and a friendly atmosphere. Beer garden. Food served 12–2pm and 6.30–9.30pm every day. Ample parking. Children and dogs allowed. The pub is handy for walking, fishing, mountain biking and bird watching.

OPEN *All day, every day (all year round except Christmas Night).*

ABERGAVENNY

The Coliseum

Lion Street, Abergavenny NP7 5PE
☎ *(01873) 736960* Russell Sorrell
www.jdwetherspoon.co.uk

Wetherspoon's pub with Greene King Abbot Ale, Marston's Pedigree and Evan Evans Welsh plus two or three guest ales, changed daily, including beers such as Greene King Old Speckled Hen, Ringwood Fortyniner, Badger Tanglefoot, Marston's Old Empire and Shepherd Neame Bishops Finger.

Formerly a theatre, this has been a pub since 2001. It has one huge, long bar and is set in a large, open-plan listed building. Food served 9am–11pm daily (full menu, breakfast and children's menu). Family and disabled friendly. Balcony smoking area. Seasonal beer festivals held. Late license at weekends. Located in the centre of town.

OPEN *9am–midnight (1am Fri–Sat).*

BASSALEG

The Tredegar Arms

4 Caerphilly Road, Bassaleg, Newport NP10 8LB
☎ *(01633) 893247* Colin and Josie Dennis

Up to eight real ales from a range that changes every month. Regulars include Brains Bitter, Greene King Abbot, IPA, Ruddles County and Old Speckled Hen, Caledonian Deuchars IPA and Ridleys Rumpus.

Busy wayside inn built in 1750 on Lord Tredegar's estate, near junction 28 of the M4. Large beer garden, ample car parking. Food available 12–3pm and 6–9pm Mon–Sat; 12–3pm Sun. Children welcome.

OPEN *11am–11pm (12–10.30pm Sun).*

BETTWS NEWYDD

The Black Bear Inn

Bettws Newydd, Nr Usk NP15 1JN
☎ *(01873) 880701* Ruth and Michael Hewitt

Freehouse with two real ales, with brews from Wye Valley and Timothy Taylor regularly featured. The selection changes every two days.

A 16th-century one-bar country pub with roaring fire, fine restaurant, patio and beer garden. The only pub in the village, it has stone walls and quarry-tiled floors. Food available 12–3pm and 6–9pm, with local produce used. Accommodation (four en-suite bedrooms). Children welcome. Three miles outside Usk.

OPEN *12–3pm and 6pm–12 Mon–Fri; 12–12 Sat–Sun.*

BLAENAVON

Cambrian Inn

Llanover Road, Blaenavon, Torfaen NP4 9HR
☎ *(01495) 790327* Lesley and Ralph Harris

 Four pumps dedicated to real ale, two of which regularly serve Brains Bitter and Brains SA. Other beers favoured include Greene King Old Speckled Hen, and Brains Merlin's Oak and Reverend James.

Typical Welsh mining village pub. Darts, pool, cards, etc. No food. Street parking opposite the pub. Children allowed until 7pm in the games room.

OPEN *6–11pm Mon–Fri; 12–11pm Sat; 12–10.30pm Sun.*

CAERLEON

The Bell Inn

Bullmoor Road, Caerleon NP18 1QQ
☎ *(01633) 420613* Tony and Ceri Willicombe
www.thebellatcaerleon.co.uk

Enterprise Inns pub with three constantly rotating guest ales from various microbreweries, changed daily. Plus 20 real ciders.

Stone-built country pub circa 1600 with flagstones and inglenooks. Open-plan bar with dining area to one side. Food served evenings Mon–Sun and lunchtimes Wed–Sun (specialises in Welsh and Breton-influenced food). Beer garden and patio. Car park. Four annual beer and cider festivals. Children welcome. Extensive Roman remains nearby and links to Arthurian legends. Near Celtic Manor Resort and Ryder Cup. Five mins from J24 of the M4, 12 miles from Cardiff.

OPEN *6–11pm Mon–Tues; 12–3pm and 6–11pm Wed–Sun (often open all day Sat–Sun).*

CHEPSTOW

The Coach & Horses

Welsh Street, Chepstow NP6 5LN
☎ *(01291) 622626* Ian Meyrick

Brains tenanted pub, with the brewery's ales on four pumps and guest beers on two pumps with up to 12 guest beers per week from all over Britain. Always a good mix of milds, bitters, stouts and local ciders. The pub hosts Chepstow's Beer and Cider Festival, usually held in June or July, in which they hope to have about 50 ales and ciders.

A 17th-century traditional family pub with B&B accommodation (six rooms, two with ghosts) that mixes locals and tourists. Split-level bar with dining room. Locally sourced and home-made food available 12–2.30pm and 6–9pm Mon–Fri. Walled beer garden. Close to the historic Town Arch, Chepstow Castle, Offa's Dyke and the Wye Valley Walk.

OPEN *12–12pm, opens earlier on busy days.*

CLYTHA

Clytha Arms

Clytha, Nr Usk NP7 9BW
☎ *(01873) 840206* Andrew Canning
www.clytha-arms.com

Six real ales at this freehouse, with Hook Norton Hooky Bitter, Felinfoel Double Dragon and Rhymney Bitter among the regulars. Almost 400 different beers are featured every year.

Large old dower house with restaurant and traditional bar – a local country inn rather than a gastropub. Crib, cricket and boules teams. Bar and restaurant food available 12.30–2.15pm and 7–9.30pm (not Sun night or Mon lunch). Car park, large garden. Children welcome. Beer festival August bank holiday, plus Welsh cider festival in spring. Four guest bedrooms. Located on the old Abergavenny to Raglan road.

OPEN *12–3.30pm and 6pm–12 Mon–Thurs; all day Fri–Sun.*

CWMBRAN

The Bush

Craig Road, Cwmbran, Torfaen NP44 5AN
☎ *(01633) 483764* Robert Lewis

Beers from the nearby Cwmbran Brewery such as Crow Valley Bitter and Double Hop are always available here on at least two pumps.

Country pub in an 18th-century building, with one bar and garden. No food. Disco held every other Saturday. Car park. Children welcome. Call or ask for directions.

OPEN *12–3pm and 7–11pm Mon–Fri; all day Sat–Sun.*

The Queen Inn

Upper Cwmbran Road, Cwmbran, Torfaen NP44 5AX
☎ *(01633) 484252* Gareth Edwards

Two real ales, Wye Valley Butty Bach and either Charles Wells Bombardier or Shepherd Neame Spitfire (changes every few days).

Country inn on the edge of village in a 150-year-old stone building which is three cottages knocked into one. Food available 12–3pm and 6–9pm Tues–Sun. Restaurant, bar, lounge, new patio and garden with children's playground. Car park.

OPEN *12–11pm (10.30pm Sun).*

GOVILON

Bridgend Inn

Church Lane, Govilon, Nr Abergavenny NP7 9RP
☎ *(01873) 830177*
Judy and Rob Llewellyn-Feasey

 Adnams Bitter plus two guests such as Badger Tanglefoot and King & Barnes Sussex Bitter, although these could come from a wide selection of independent brewers.

A 16th-century pub with two bars, beams and outdoor patio area, less than two minutes' walk from the Monmouthshire–Brecon Canal towpath. Popular with visiting boaties, tourists and locals. Children welcome. Live music every Friday night. Bar meals available lunchtimes and evenings and all day at weekends.

OPEN *12–4pm and 7–11pm Mon–Fri; all day Sat–Sun.*

LLANDOGO

The Sloop Inn

Llandogo, Monmouth NP25 4TW
☎ *(01594) 530291* Peter Morse

 Freehouse with up to three real ales. Sharp's Doom Bar is a regular plus a guest rotated weekly. Local ales are often featured.

This 300-year-old pub has a dining room overlooking the river and a beer garden with swings for children. Set in a beautiful village location in the Wye Valley backing onto the river. Food available every lunchtime (12–3pm) and evening (6.30–10pm). Four en-suite bedrooms, large car park. Close to Tintern Abbey, on the A466.

OPEN *12–12 (11pm Sun).*

LLANISHEN

Carpenter's Arms

Llanishen, Nr Chepstow NP16 6QH
☎ *(01600) 860812* John Davies

Two pumps are dedicated to real ale at this country freehouse, with Wadworth 6X a permanent fixture. The guest will be a Kingstone brew such as Three Castles, Challenger, Classic or Kinson's Gold, and will be changed weekly.

The homely pub in the small village of Llanishen dates back to the 17th century and features beams, open fires, a lounge and a bar. You won't find a juke box or fruit machines here – just a good, old-fashioned pub welcome. Home-cooked food available lunchtimes and evenings. Beer garden, 20-seater reataurant. Car park. Children welcome.

OPEN *12–3pm and 6–11pm Tues–Thurs (closed all day Monday, and Tuesday lunch); 12–3pm and 5.10–11pm Fri–Sat; 12–3pm and 7–10.30pm Sun.*

LLANTHONY

Half Moon Inn

Llanthony, Abergavenny NP7 7NN
☎ *(01873) 890611* George Lawrence
www.halfmoon-llanthony.co.uk

Freehouse with Bullmastiff Son of a Bitch and Welsh Red plus one monthly-changing guest beer.

An attractive 16th-century inn which has remained virtually unchanged over the years. Set amidst the beautiful scenery of the Vale of Ewyas in the Black Mountains. Food served lunchtimes and evenings. B&B available. Beer garden. Private room available for hire. Children and dogs welcome. Near Offa's Dyke and Becconsway paths, next to Llanthony Abbey. Located on the B4423 at Llanthony, just off the A465.

OPEN *11.30am–3pm and 7–11pm Mon, Wed and Fri; closed Tues; 7–11pm Thurs; all day Sat–Sun.*

LLANVIHANGEL CRUCORNEY

Skirrid Mountain Inn

Llanvihangel Crucorney, Abergavenny NP7 8DH
☎ *(01873) 890258*
Daryl Hardy and Maria Appleton

 There are usually four real ales at this ancient, stone-walled pub. Marston's Pedigree and Wychwood Hobgoblin are regular features, plus one regularly changing guest ale.

Historic, 12th-century country inn, believed to be the oldest pub in Wales and situated in the beautiful Black Mountains. Food served all day, every day, except Sun and Mon evenings. Car park. Well-behaved children welcome, but no special facilities.

OPEN *11am–11pm Mon–Sat; 12–10.30pm Sun (closed mid-afternoon on winter weekdays).*

MONMOUTH

The Old Nag's Head

Granville Street, Monmouth NP25 3DR
☎ *(01600) 713782* Rhiannon Thomas

Two or three cask ales are served at this popular pub: Brains Bitter and Fuller's London Pride plus a guest, changed weekly.

This 400-year-old pub, an old toll gate for the town of Monmouth, is near to the River Wye and popular with local rowers as well as tourists. It has two bars, a pool room and a beer garden. Food is available, with curry night on Wednesday, plus Sunday lunches. Traditional Irish music Thursday evenings, with musicians welcome. Dogs on leads welcome.

OPEN *5–11pm Mon–Thurs; 5pm–12 Fri; 2pm–12 Sat; 12–11pm Sun.*

NEWPORT

The John Wallace Linton

Cambrian Retail Centre, Cambrian Road, Newport NP9 4AD
☎ *(01633) 251752* Paul McDonnell

JD Wetherspoon's pub with five hand pumps serving a wide range of real ales that change on a weekly basis.

Busy pub with a wide-ranging clientele, old and young. Particularly lively in the evenings. Food available all day. No children. Next to the railway station.

OPEN *10am–11pm Mon–Sat; 12–10.30pm Sun.*

St Julian Inn

Caerleon Road, Newport NP18 1QA
☎ *(01633) 243548*
Steve Williams and Mary Nelmes
www.stjulian.co.uk

Enterprise pub serving three or four real ales, often changed daily. Favourites include beers from Rhymney, Wells and Young's, Bath and Wye Valley.

Pretty 200-year-old coaching inn, with balcony and garden overlooking the River Usk. Skittle alley and bar games. Food available Mon–Sat lunchtimes and evenings. Ten-minute walk to historic Caerleon, Roman amphitheatre and baths, and museum. Head towards Caerleon from junction 25 of the M4 for one mile, and the pub is on the left-hand side overlooking the river.

 11.30am–11.30pm Mon–Wed; 11.30am–midnight Thurs–Sat; 12–11pm Sun.

PANTYGELLI

The Crown at Pantygelli

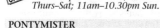

Old Hereford Road, Pantygelli,
Nr Abergavenny NP7 7HR
☎ (01873) 853314
Steve and Cherrie Chadwick
www.thecrownatpantygelli.com

Freehouse with Bass, Rhymney Bitter, Rhymney Best and Wye Valley Hereford Pale Ale plus occasional guests.

Dating back to the 15th century, this pub is situated in stunning scenery in the tiny hamlet of Pantygelli and retains its original features. Situated on lower slopes of the Sugar Loaf Mountain with breathtaking views of The Skirrid Mountain. Fresh flowers on every table and log fire in winter. Food served lunchtimes Tues–Sun and evenings Tues–Sat. Two outdoor terraces and large paddock. Large car park. Function areas available. Occasional beer festivals and fundraising activities. Children welcome. Close to pony-trekking centres, falconry centre, local craft centres and Brecon Beacons. Situated two miles outside market town of Abergavenny.

 6–11pm Mon; 12–2.30pm and 6–11pm Tues–Fri; 12–3pm and 6–11pm Sat; 12–3pm and 6–10.30pm Sun.

PENALLT

The Boat Inn

Lone Lane, Penallt, Monmouth NP25 4AJ
☎ (01600) 712615 Shaleen Goodman
www.theboatpenallt.co.uk

Freehouse with three real ales in winter, up to eight in summer, including Wye Valley Butty Bach and guests such as Greene King IPA and beers from Otley, Kingstone, Wye Valley, Spinning Dog, Severn Valley and Rhymney.

Small riverside inn on the England–Wales border built into the hillside, with stone floors and simple decor. Live music on Tuesday and Thursday evenings. Very cosy with no juke box or games machines. Bar food available 12–2.30pm every day and 7–9pm Mon–Sat. Car park on the other side of the river, terraced gardens with ponds. Children allowed. The car park is in Redbrook (Gloucestershire) on the A466, next to a football field. Follow the footpath over an old railway bridge across the Wye.

11am–11pm Mon–Wed; 11am–midnight Thurs–Sat; 11am–10.30pm Sun.

PONTYMISTER

The Commercial Inn

Commercial Street, Pontyminster NP11 6BA
☎ (01633) 612608 Steve and Terrie Jones
www.thecommercialpontymister.com

Hop Back Summer Lightning, with 8–10 regularly rotating guests from a large range from Brains, Wye Valley, Skinner's, Exe Valley, Brew Dog and more.

Community pub with an open-plan bar, lounge, several screens showing sports and a games area. Front patio area with a full canopy, fixed heaters and an outdoor TV. Won Gwent CAMRA Pub of the Year and Racing UK Regional Pub of the Year. Food served 11.30–3pm and 6–9.30 Mon–Thurs; 11.30–6pm Fri; 11.30–3pm Sat; 12–2.30pm Sun. Children welcome during food service hours. From junction 27 of the M4, follow signs to Risca.

11–11.30pm Mon–Thurs; 11am–midnight Fri–Sat; 12–11.30pm Sun.

RAGLAN

The Ship Inn

8 High Street, Raglan, Nr Usk NP15 2DY
☎ (01291) 690635 Jane Roper

Genuine freehouse regularly serving Greene King IPA plus two guests, regularly changed, usually from Wye Valley, Whittington's or Black Sheep.

A 16th-century olde-worlde coaching inn with beams, log fires and lots of character. There is a well in the cobbled forecourt. Restaurant, pool and darts room, digital juke box. Food served 12–3pm and 6–9pm. Children welcome. Parking available in High Street. CAMRA recommended for the past 15 years. Close to Raglan Castle. In the High Street, opposite the supermarket.

12–11pm Sun–Mon; 11.30am–11pm Tues–Sat.

RISCA

The Fox & Hounds

Park Road, Risca, Newport NP11 6PW
☎ (01633) 612937
Helene Lavender and Terry Wilmott

One real ale always available, with ales from all over the country featured.

Old-style traditional village pub in a stone building around 160 years old, attracting both local and passing trade. Snacks and light bites served 12–5pm. Pool, darts, Sky TV. Children welcome. Car park, beer garden. Opposite the park in Risca.

12–12.

SEBASTOPOL

The Open Hearth

Wern Road, Sebastopol, Pontypool NP4 5DR
☎ (01495) 763752 Hugh Jones

Up to nine real ales, seven of them guest beers which change frequently. Regular favourites include Greene King Abbot Ale, as well as beers from Shepherd Neame, Woodforde's, Thwaites, Hook Norton, Everards and Jennings.

A busy 19th-century pub on the Monmouthshire Brecon canal, with a reputation for good beer and food. Food available 12–2pm and 6.30–10pm every day in a separate restaurant. No juke box or pool table. Mixed clientele of all ages. Children welcome, with children's room provided. Large beer garden, beer festivals twice a year.

11.30am–11pm Mon–Sat; 12–10.30pm Sun.

SHIRENEWTON
The Carpenter's Arms
Shirenewton, Nr Chepstow
☎ *(01291) 641231* Gary Hayes

Tied to Punch, with Fuller's London Pride, Shepherd Neame Spitfire and Draught Bass, plus Brains Dark once a month.

Country inn crammed with antiques and memorabilia. Profusion of colour from the hanging baskets in summer months. Food served 12.30–2.30pm Mon–Sat and 6.30–9.30 Sat; 12–3pm Sun in summer, 12–5pm Sun in winter. Car park. Family room. Outside tables. Located on the B4235 Chepstow/Usk road, just outside the village.

OPEN *12–3pm and 5.30pm–close Mon–Fri; 12–close Sat–Sun.*

Tredegar Arms
Shirenewton, Nr Chepstow NP16 6RQ
☎ *(01291) 641274* Tracey Eastabrook

Three real ale pumps, with beers from Hook Norton and Brains plus a guest ale which changes regularly.

A pub since the mid-19th century although the building, which includes two bars and open fires, is considerably older. Situated in the centre of a picturesque Monouthshire village, a popular haunt for locals and occasional passing tourists. Food served lunchtimes and evenings. Children welcome. Outside patio area with seating and tables at the front of the pub.

OPEN *12–2.30pm and 6–11pm Mon–Fri; 12–11pm Sat; 12–4.30pm and 6–10.30pm Sun.*

TINTERN
The Moon & Sixpence
Monmouth Road, Tintern, Nr Chepstow NP16 5SG
☎ *(01291) 689284*
Dave Llewellyn and Sally Windley

Three real ales, including regular brews from Wye Valley.

Traditional country pub overlooking the River Wye, popular with tourists and locals alike. Main bar, five rooms, exposed beams. Riverside terrace, private room, parking. Traditional pub food, including specials, served. Children and dogs welcome. On the A466 between Chepstow and Monmouth.

OPEN *11.30am–midnight Mon–Thurs; 11.30am–1am Fri–Sat; 12–11pm Sun.*

The Wye Valley Hotel
Tintern, Nr Chepstow NP16 6SQ
☎ *(01291) 689441* Barry Cooke

Freehouse with Wye Valley Bitter and Butty Bach plus the occasional guest beer during the summer.

The original pub dates back to the 1820s, thought it was extended to become a small hotel in 1930. Located in Tintern, an Area of Outstanding Natural Beauty with its historic abbey. One main bar plus restaurant. Food served 12–2pm and 6–9pm Mon–Sun.

Nine guest bedrooms available. Outdoor drinking area. Car park. Children welcome. Dogs allowed in bar. Located on the A466 between Chepstow and Monmouth.

OPEN *All day, every day.*

TRELLECH
The Lion Inn
Trellech, Nr Monmouth NP25 4PA
☎ *(01600) 860322* Debbie Zsigo
www.lioninn.co.uk

An award-winning freehouse offering four real ales. Bath Ales SPA is usually on offer, plus something from Wye Valley, Archers and elsewhere.

Stone-fronted, Grade II listed, 16th-century typical country freehouse with open fire, no fruit machines or juke box. Favours traditional pub games such as bar billiards and bar skittles plus many social evenings. Food available every lunchtime and all evenings except Sunday. Well-behaved children and dogs allowed, but no dogs in the lounge. Accommodation. On the B4293 between Chepstow and Monmouth.

OPEN *12–3pm and 7–11pm Mon; 12–3pm and 6–11pm Tues–Fri (midnight Thurs–Fri); 12–12 Sat; 12–4.30pm Sun (closed Sunday evening).*

UPPER LLANOVER
The Goose & Cuckoo Inn
Upper Llanover, Abergavenny NP7 9ER
☎ *(01873) 880277*
Carol and Michael Langley
www.gooseandcuckoo.com

Freehouse with four pumps dedicated to real ale. One pump always serves Brains Reverend James and the others feature constantly changing guests from brewers such as Wadworth and Bullmastiff. Also an impressive 85 malt whiskies at the bar.

A small, isolated, picturesque country pub, 250 years old, with a log fire. The pub is family-orientated and has a collection of animals in the garden for youngsters. No juke box or games machines, but traditional games available including quoits, dominoes, cribbage and darts. Beer garden. Food available every lunchtime and evening. Accommodation. CAMRA local Pub of the Year 2004. Beer festivals in May and August. Off the A4042.

OPEN *Closed Mon; 11.30am–3pm and 7–11pm Tues–Thurs; all day Fri–Sun.*

USK
The Kings Head Hotel
18 Old Market Street, Usk NP15 1AL
☎ *(01291) 672963* Stephen Musto

Freehouse serving Fuller's London Pride and Timothy Taylor Landlord.

Built in 1590, a pub with en-suite accommodation. Famous open fireplace, function room and restaurant serving food at lunchtimes (12–2pm) and evenings (6–10pm). Children allowed.

OPEN *All day, every day.*

GWYNEDD

ANGLESEY

The Ship Inn
Red Wharf Bay, Anglesey LL75 8RJ
☎ (01248) 852568
www.shipinnredwharfbay.co.uk

Three real ales perhaps including Adnams Best, Black Sheep Bitter and Brains SA.

Set on the northeast coast of Anglesey and run by the same family for 40 years. Large waterside beer garden. Good food served at lunchtime and evenings seven days a week.

OPEN *11am–11pm (10.30pm Sun).*

BANGOR

Belle Vue
Holyhead Road, Bangor LL57 2EU
☎ (01248) 364439

Marston's Pedigree plus Flowers Original (brewed by Badger) and Bass and a rotating guest.

Spacious pub with lounge and public bars and beer garden at the rear. Lunchtime menu (12–2pm) of home-cooked food every day except Sat, including Sunday roasts. Children welcome at lunchtimes. In the centre of Upper Bangor.

OPEN *11am–close.*

The Castle
Glanrafon, off High Street, Bangor LL57 ILP
☎ (01248) 355866 Christopher Hughes

Part of the Laurel pub company with five hand pumps. Regular guests include Timothy Taylor Landord, Caledonian 80/–, Marston's Pedigree, Wadworth 6X, Brains SA, plus Hook Norton Old Hooky.

Roomy pub with a large open single floor, dark wood floors, background music. Wheelchair access. Food available 12–3pm. Children allowed until 4pm. Opposite the cathedral, close to the railway station.

OPEN *12–11pm Mon–Thurs; 12–12 Fri–Sat; 12–10.30pm Sun.*

Globe Inn
Albert Street, Bangor LL57 2EY
☎ (01248) 362095 Gerallt Williams

Two ales permanently on the pumps, one standard and one premium. Marston's Pedigree and Conwy Brewery's Castle Ale, plus a local guest beer.

Children welcome. Food available.

OPEN *11am–close.*

The Tap & Spile
Garth Road, Bangor LL57 2SW
☎ (01248) 370835
Dean and Elizabeth Ibbetson

Six rotating real ales from all over Britain. Greene King IPA, Abbot and Old Speckled Hen, Adnams Best and Broadside could well be among them, but local breweries such as Purple Moose, Conwy, Archers and George Wright are also featured.

An 18th-century seaman's inn opposite the pier, with split levels and accommodation in seven rooms. Local CAMRA Pub of the Year 2004 and 2006. Food served 12–2pm and 6–8pm Mon–Sat, 12–3pm Sun. Great views, children welcome, occasional beer festivals.

OPEN *12–11pm (10.30pm Sun).*

BLAENAU FFESTINIOG

Rhiw Goch Inn
Bron Aber, Transfynydd, Blaenau Ffestiniog LL41 4UY
☎ (01766) 540374 Janice Dodd

Ales changed either weekly or bi-weekly include Marston's Pedigree, Greene King IPA and a range of others.

Set on a Norwegian log cabin tourist site, which enables the proprietor to keep his selection of real ales going.

OPEN *12–11pm all year round (hours may be reduced in November).*

CAERNARFON

The Alexandra Hotel
North Road, Caernarfon LL55 1BA
☎ (01286) 672871 Ken Moulton

Whitbread tied house serving a range of guests. Regulars include Wadworth 6X, Flowers Original (brewed by Badger) and Draught Bass.

Tables outside. No food.

OPEN *5.30–11pm Mon–Fri; all day Sat; 11am–2pm and 5.30–11pm Sun.*

The Prince of Wales Hotel
Bangor Street, Caernarfon LL55 1AR
☎ (01286) 673367 Gareth Humphreys

Marston's Bitter is always on offer as are Welsh Highland Bitter and Haf, both from the Snowdonia Brewery. The one guest beer could be from any independent brewery.

Pub within a hotel in a townscape setting, half a mile from Caernarfon Castle and half a mile from the yacht marina. An ideal base for Snowdonia and the Irish ferries. Breakfast is served 7–9.30am, lunch 11.30am–2pm and dinner 6–8.30pm with the emphasis on home cooking. Children and dogs are welcome and the pub has designated family rooms. Car park.

OPEN *11am–11pm Mon–Sat; 12–10.30pm Sun.*

DULAS

Pilot Boat Inn
Dulas, Amlwch, Anglesey LL70 9EX
☎ (01248) 410205 Mark Williams

Frederic Robinson's tied house serving Unicorn Bitter.

Traditional country pub in an Area of Outstanding Natural Beauty. Popular with locals and tourists alike. One bar plus dining room. Food served 12–9pm daily. Car park. Children's menu and play area in the beer garden. Situated on the A5025.

OPEN *11.30am–11pm Mon–Sat; 12–10.30pm Sun.*

Gardd Fon Inn

1 Beach Road, Felinheli LL56 4RQ
☎ *(01248) 670359* William Hughes

The permanent beer is usually from Mansfield, and the one guest is changed fortnightly.

Friendly, family-run 200-year-old waterside village pub with small rooms, popular with locals, the sailing fraternity and walkers. Very popular bistro; food also available 12–2.15pm and 6–9pm, and all day Sunday. Children welcome. Beer garden overlooking the Menai Strait. Follow signposts to Caernarfon, then signs to Felinheli; the pub is situated down on the waterside.

OPEN *11am–midnight.*

The Queen Victoria

4 Church Walks, Llandudno LL30 2HD
☎ *(01492) 860952* Robert Watts

Tied to Banks's, with Banks's Bitter, Marston's Pedigree and Old Empire plus one guest, changed weekly.

Comfortable Victorian family-oriented pub with bar and lounge area downstairs and restaurant upstairs. Food is a speciality, and is served 12–9pm Mon–Sat and 12–8pm Sun. Small beer garden, private room for hire. Children and dogs welcome. Situated near the pier.

OPEN *11am–11pm Mon–Sat; 12–10.30pm Sun.*

Victoria Hotel

Telford Road, Menai Bridge, Anglesey LL59 5DR
☎ *(01248) 712309* Nicola Smeaton

Two or three ales, with beers from breweries such as Conwy and Brains regularly featured.

Family-run hotel dating from the 1820s, with three bars, a large function room with special licence, and lots of character. Food served 12–2.30pm and 6–9pm daily. Garden with spectacular views of the Menai Straits. Children welcome. Large car park. Seventeen en-suite bedrooms. In Telford Road, 100 yards from the Menai Suspension Bridge.

OPEN *11am–close Mon–Sat; 12–10.30pm Sun.*

Cliffs Inn

Beach Road, Morfa Nefyn LL53 6BY
☎ *(01758) 720356*
Lona Fitzpatrick and Peter Binch

Freehouse with two pumps usually serving one English and one Welsh ale, the Welsh brew usually from Brains.

A food-orientated pub with good beer. Outside patio, food available lunchtimes and evenings in a separate dining area. Children allowed.

OPEN *All day, every day.*

Giler Arms Hotel

Rhydlydan, Pentrefoelas, Nr Betws-y-Coed LL24 0LL
☎ *(01690) 770612* John and Sue Cowlishaw

Batham Mild and Bitter always available.

The hotel has a campsite, B&B, fishing lake and restaurant. Children welcome.

OPEN *12–2.30pm and 6.30pm–close Mon–Fri; all day Sat.*

Y Bedol

Penysarn, Anglesey LL69 9YR
☎ *(01407) 832590* Steven and Sheila Hughes

A selection of three Robinson's ales always available.

Warm, friendly pub with beer garden, pool room, karaoke and quiz nights and occasional local Welsh entertainment. Bar food available evenings. Children allowed. Credit cards accepted.

OPEN *12–11pm (10.30pm Sun).*

Ship Inn

Lombard Street, Porthmadog LL49 9AP
☎ *(01766) 512990* Patrick Hughes

Up to five real ales, with Brains SA, Greene King IPA and Old Speckled Hen and Banks's Bitter among the favourites, with guests changed monthly.

Popular two-roomed inn, full of character and with relaxed atmosphere, situated close to the harbour. Wine/cocktail bar upstairs. Food served 12–3pm and 5–9pm. Children welcome 12–3pm if dining. Parking at rear. Close to Ffestiniog Railway and Black Rock Sands, with easy access to Snowdonia. On the A487 in Porthmadog, opposite the playground in the town centre.

OPEN *12–11pm Sun–Wed; 12–12 Thurs–Sat.*

The Cwellyn Arms

Rhyd Ddu, Caernafon LL54 6TL
☎ *(01766) 890321* Graham Bamber
www.snowdoninn.co.uk,
www.cwellynarms.co.uk, www.cwellynarms.com

Freehouse serving nine real ales, 9 days a week, perhaps Conwy Welsh Pride, Cwrw Mel or Cwrw Bitter, or a Cottage beer such as Wheel Tappers, Deltic Diesel, Southern Bitter or Norman's Conquest.

A family-run traditional country inn and restaurant at the foot of Mount Snowdon. Two lounge areas, both with real log fires, creating a warm welcome and a relaxed, informal atmosphere. Excellent food, using fresh local ingredients where possible, served 11–9pm (until 10pm at weekends). Accommodation to suit all tastes, including camping in 26 acres (with campfires) leading to Cwellyn Lake, bunkhouse accommodation, suites, country cottage and farmhouse. At the foot of Mount Snowdon, on the Caernarfon–Beddgelert road (A4085).

OPEN *11am–11pm.*

TREFRIW
The Old Ship/Yr Hen Long
High Street, Trefriw LL27 0JH
☎ *(01492) 640013* Rhian Glyn Barlo
www.the-old-ship.co.uk

 Freehouse with Banks's Bitter and Marston's Pedigree plus two weekly-changing guests from local breweries.

Comfortable one-bar pub in the Conwy valley. No juke box or pool table. Log fire. Food served 12–2.30pm and 6–9pm Mon–Sun. Large beer garden and car park. Close to some of the best walking routes in North Wales. Children welcome with well-behaved adults!

OPEN *12–3pm and 6–11pm.*

TUDWEILIOG
Lion Hotel
Tudweiliog, Pwllheli LL53 8ND
☎ *(01758) 770244* Martin Lee

Freehouse with Purple Moose Cwrw Glaslyn and Eryri plus two guests.

Friendly, family-run village inn with a quiet lounge bar and tap room with pool, darts and juke box. Food served 12–2pm and 6–8.30pm (12–2.30pm and 5.30–9.30pm in summer). Four en-suite bedrooms available. Two separate dining rooms. Beer garden and small courtyard. Car park. A mile from the beaches, ideally located for horse-riding and walking. Located on the Llyn peninsula, on the B4417 Nefyn to Aberdaron road.

OPEN *12–2pm and 6–11pm (winter); 12–3pm and 6–11pm (autumn and spring); 11.30am–11pm (summer).*

WAUNFAWR
The Snowdonia Parc Brewpub and Campsite
Waunfawr, Caernafon LL55 4AQ
☎ *(01286) 650218* Carmen Pierce

A brewpub in which the owner brews Welsh Highland Gold. Marston's Bitter, Pedigree, Mild and a constantly rotating guest ale are also available.

A village pub in beautiful surroundings, with spacious main bar area, lounge, campsite, family room, children's play area and beer garden. Food available 11am–8.30pm daily. On the A4085 road from Caernarfon to Beddgelert. Steam trains from the Welsh Highland Railway stop at the pub on their way through Snowdonia.

OPEN *11am–11pm.*

MID GLAMORGAN

BLACKMILL
The Ogmore Junction Hotel
Blackmill, Bridgend CF35 6DR
☎ *(01656) 840371* Andrew Taylor

Two pumps including Greene King Old Speckled Hen and a guest beer from smaller brewers.

Country pub with beer garden and car park that backs on to the River Ogmore. Food available lunchtimes and evenings. Situated not far from the M4 on the main road to Ogmore Vale. A fortnightly sheep sale is held behind the pub from the end of July to the end of December.

OPEN *11am–11pm Mon–Sat; 12–10.30pm Sun.*

BRIDGEND
The Railway
Derwen Road, Bridgend CF31 1LH
☎ *(01656) 652266* Robert James

Two pumps serving Brains SA and Greene King Old Speckled Hen, plus a monthly guest.

Small, friendly, comfortable pub, originally The Railway Hotel, but more recently called The Pen y Bont Inn. Food available 11am–3pm Mon–Sat. Small function room for hire. Outside designated smoking area. Located at the bottom of Station Hill, which leads down from the railway station.

OPEN *11am–midnight Mon–Thurs; 11am–1.30am Fri–Sat; 12–12 Sun.*

LLANGYNWYD
The Old House Inn
Llangynwyd, Maesteg, Bridgend CF34 9SB
☎ *(01656) 733310* Richard David

Freehouse with Flowers Original Bitter (brewed by Badger) and something from Brains among the beers on offer, plus a guest changed monthly.

A traditional pub dating back to the 12th century, run by the same family since the mid-1960s. Claims to be the oldest pub in Wales, and the pub with the oldest surviving 'Mari Llwyd' (decorated horse skull that features in a New Year's Eve custom). Beautiful panoramic views overlooking wonderful countryside. Large children's play area. Follow signs from Sarn services.

OPEN *11am–midnight.*

MACHEN

The White Hart Inn

White Hart Lane, Machen, Caerphilly CF83 8QQ
☎ *(01633) 441005* Alan Carter

 A village freehouse, home of Carter's Brewery, offering four real ales, three guests changing frequently and one from the pub's own brewery. The range of beers comes from small and micro-breweries all around the UK.

Olde-worlde pub built in 1734 featuring oak panelling from an old ship (the captain's cabin came from the Empress of France). Food available at lunchtime and evenings. Play area and patio beer garden. Children allowed. Cottage accommodation available throughout the year. Five rooms. Please phone for availability. Located just off the main road (A448).

OPEN *11am–3pm and 6–11pm Mon–Sat; 12–10.30pm Sun; closed 3.30–6pm in winter.*

MWYNDY

The Barn

Cardiff Road, Mwyndy, Nr Llantrisant CF72 8PJ
☎ *(01443) 222333* Lyn Babbage
www.marstons.co.uk

 Marston's pub with four to six real ales. Examples of guests include Wychwood Hobgoblin, Jennings Snecklifter, Ringwood 49'er, Marston's Old Empire, as well as a range of beers from the following breweries - Marstons, Jennings, Wychwood, Ringwood, Banks's and Brakspear.

Trading as a pub since the 1980s, parts of this converted barn date back to the 15th century. There is a large enclosed beer garden (frequented daily by 5 local peacocks) and separate dining area as well as a traditional bar (no juke box) with large open fire. Food available 12–9.30pm Mon-Sat, and 12–6pm Sun. Large car park. From J34 of the M4 west, head for Llantrisant, turn right after second lights signposted Mwyndy Cross Industries.

OPEN *12–11pm (10.30pm Sun).*

OGMORE

The Pelican In Her Piety

Ogmore Village, Nr Bridgend CF32 0QP
☎ *(01656) 880049* Steve Fisher
www.pelicanpub.co.uk

Freehouse with six pumps with a selection that probably includes Fuller's London Pride, Wye Valley HPA, and Greene King Abbot and Old Speckled Hen.

Unusually named (it's from a local family's coat of arms), 17th-century country inn situated opposite Ogmore Castle on the river Ewenny, with welcoming bar and restaurant. Home-cooked food served 12–2.30pm and 6–9pm Mon-Sat and 12–8pm Sun. Child- and dog-friendly. Barn with pleasant views across the river. Near sanddunes that are a Site of Special Scientific Interest.

OPEN *11.30am–11pm.*

PORTHCAWL

The Prince of Wales Inn

Ton Kenfig, Nr Porthcawl, Bridgend CF33 4PR
☎ *(01656) 740356* Gareth and Julie Maund

Freehouse regularly serving beers from Welsh breweries such as Tomos Watkin, Felinfoel, Otley and Rhymney. Local Welsh cider from Gwynt yr Ddraig also available.

A 500-year-old pub in a Grade I listed building with historic building status, formerly used as the town hall and with the original courthouse upstairs (regular ghost sightings). Two open fires, a lounge and a function room (which was used as a Sunday School for 137 years, until 2000). Homemade bar meals available at lunchtimes and evenings Tues–Sat, plus Sunday lunch. Ample parking, children and dogs welcome. Overlooking Kenfig nature reserve and pool, one mile from an unspoilt beach. M4 junction 37, follow the brown tourist signs.

OPEN *11am–11pm (10.30pm Sun).*

RUDRY

Maenllwyd Inn

Rudry, Nr Caerphilly CF83 3EB
☎ *(029) 2088 2372* Alistair and Kellie Baker

Up to four real ales at this extremely busy country freehouse. Examples include beers from Wye Valley, Ridleys, Wells and Young's, Hydes, St Austell, Fuller's and Everards. The range changes twice a week.

A 16th-century grey stone farmhouse, now a village inn with beams, three open fires and one long bar on two levels. People drive from miles around for the food and atmosphere (food is served all day but no bookings). Car parks, beer garden, children and dogs welcome. Good walking and biking country from Cardiff to Caerphilly.

OPEN *12–11pm (10.30pm Sun).*

TONDU

Llynfi Arms

Maesteg Road, Tondu, Bridgend CF32 9DP
☎ *(01656) 720010* Neil Wisenden

One guest beer always available, changing every two weeks. This tends to be from smaller independents such as Cottage or Tomos Watkin.

The pub is close to Tondu railway station, and has two model trains running around the ceiling of the lounge bar. Food served 12–2pm and 7–9.30pm Wed–Sat and 12–2pm Sun. Booking advised Fri–Sun. Children welcome in the lounge bar at lunchtime.

OPEN *12–4pm and 6–11pm Mon–Thurs; 11am–11pm Fri–Sat; 12–10.30pm Sun.*

POWYS

ABERDEDW
The Seven Stars Inn
Aberdedw, Builth Wells LD2 3UW
☎ *(01982) 560494* Trisha and Ian Evans
www.7-stars.co.uk

 Freehouse with Brains Reverend James and a weekly-rotating guest such as Wood Shropshire Lad or Wadworth 6X.

Country pub with log fires, oak beams and a warm welcome. Food served in both the bar and the separate restaurant: 12–2pm and 6.30–9pm. Former CAMRA regional Pub of the Year. En-suite accommodation. Just off the B4567 at the end of the village.

OPEN *Every day.*

CRICKHOWELL
The Bear Hotel
High Street, Crickhowell NP8 1BW
☎ *(01873) 810408* Stephen Hindmarsh
www.bearhotel.co.uk

Freehouse with Brains Reverend James plus two guests.

A 15th-century coaching inn, now a hotel with extensive bar and lounge areas. Beer garden, 34 letting rooms. Bar food available every day, 12–2pm and 6–10pm. Restaurant open Tues–Sat evenings only. Dogs and children welcome.

OPEN *11am–3pm and 6–11pm.*

LLANBADARN FYNYDD
The New Inn
Llanbadarn Fynydd, Llandrindod Wells LD1 6YA
☎ *(01597) 840378* Robert Barton

Freehouse with two real ale pumps, changed at least monthly. Wood Shropshire Lad and brews from Eccleshall (Slaters) and Wye Valley are among those usually stocked.

A traditional ale and food house with log fires. Food available lunchtimes and evenings in a separate restaurant. Children allowed. Located on main A483 between Newton and Llandrindod Wells.

OPEN *10.30am–3pm and 5.30–11pm in summer; 12–2.30pm and 7–11pm in winter.*

LLANBEDR
The Red Lion Inn
Llanbedr, Crickhowell NP8 1SR
☎ *(01873) 810714* Marian Morgan

Freehouse with three real ales. Hancock's HB (brewed by Brains) plus something from Rhymney are regular features, and the guest might be a Wye Valley brew.

Quiet 300-year-old pub with beams and real fires. Car park, garden. Nearby campsite situated in a very beautiful spot in the Black Mountains. Home-cooked food served all opening times except Sunday evenings. Children welcome, but no dogs.

Boot-wash provided outside for walkers and up-to-date toilets are always open. Less than two miles from Crickhowell.

OPEN *7–11pm Tues; 2–5pm and 7–11pm Wed; 7–11pm Thurs–Fri; 1–11pm Sat; 12–10.30pm Sun.*

LLANFAIR CAEREINION
The Goat Hotel
High Street, Llanfair Caereinion SY21 0QS
☎ *(01938) 810428* Richard Arguement

Freehouse with Wood Quaff plus two guest ales, changed once or twice a week.

Dating back to the early 17th century, this one-bar inn has a lounge with log fires and leather sofas. Separate 30-seat restaurant and small games room. Outdoor patio area for eating and drinking. Food served 12–2.15pm and 7–9.15pm Mon–Sun. Accommodation available. Parking. Children welcome. Near Llanfair light railway and Offa's Dyke. Located just off the A458, nine miles west of Welshpool.

OPEN *11am–11pm Mon–Thurs; 11am–midnight Fri–Sat; 12–11pm Sun.*

LLANGORSE
The Castle Inn
Llangorse, Brecon LD3 7UB
☎ *(01874) 658225* Mr Williams

Freehouse with three pumps serving real ales, including Breconshire Golden Valley and guests such as Bateman XB, Greene King Old Speckled Hen and many more.

Olde-worlde village inn with a 27-seater restaurant. Food available at lunchtimes and evenings. Children allowed under supervision. Outside drinking area with good views.

OPEN *12–3pm and 6–11pm Mon–Fri; 11am–11pm Sat; 12–10.30pm Sun.*

LLANIDLOES
The Red Lion
8 Longbridge Street, Llanidloes SY18 6EE
☎ *(01686) 412270* Geoff and Eileen Hawkins

Freehouse serving Adnams Broadside and Hancock's HB (brewed by Brains) plus two guests, rotated monthly, perhaps Brains Rev James or something from Titanic.

Small, cosy, traditional hotel in the town centre, with genuine beams, old-fashioned fireplace and Chesterfield settees in the lounge bar. Games bar includes pool, darts and juke box. Big-screen TVs in both bars, with sport shown. Bar meals served 12–2pm and 5–9pm Mon–Sat; restaurant meals 7–9pm Mon–Sat; carvery roast 12–2pm Sun. Rear car park, rear patio area, disabled access. Monthly quiz nights for charity. Children welcome until 7pm. Eight en-suite rooms. Close to Clywedog Dam and local leisure facilities. In the centre of Wales, near Newtown and Aberystwyth.

OPEN *11am–midnight Sun–Thurs; 11am–1am Fri–Sat.*

LLANWRTYD WELLS

Neuadd Arms

The Square, Llanwrtyd Wells LD5 4RB
☎ *(01591) 610236* Lindsey Ketteringham
www.neuaddsrmshotel.co.uk

 Felinfoel Double Dragon and four guest
ales from Heart of Wales Brewery.

A 140-year-old family-run freehouse and
hotel in a listed building. Home of the
Heart of Wales Brewery. Two bars with log
fires, residents' lounge, games room,
restaurant and 21 en-suite rooms. Helps to
host the Mid-Wales 10-day beer festival every
November. Breakfast, lunch and evening
meals served. Located in the centre of
Britain's smallest town, on the A483 between
Builth Wells and Llandovery.

OPEN *All day, every day (11am–1pm Christmas Day).*

Stonecroft Inn

Dolecoed Road, Llanwrtyd Wells LD5 4RA
☎ *(01591) 610332/610327*
Pete and Jane Brown
www.stonecroft.co.uk

 Four regularly changing beers, perhaps
from Brains, Dunn Plowman, Wye Valley,
Breconshire or Evans Evans. One of the
venues for the Mid-Wales beer festival, held
in November.

W elcoming Victorian country pub
situated in the smallest town in Britain
and popular with cyclists and visitors. One
large bar with a real fire, plus large riverside
beer garden. Pool, darts, Sky TV. Bar food
served Fri–Sun lunchtime (12–3pm) and
every evening (6–9pm). Hot basket snacks at
other times. Car park. Children welcome.
Live music on Saturdays. Accommodation
available next door. Off the A483.

OPEN *5–11pm Mon–Thurs; 12–11pm Fri–Sat; 12–10.30pm Sun.*

MACHYNLLETH

The Wynnstay Arms Hotel

Maengwyn Street, Machynlleth SY20 8AE
☎ *(01654) 702941* Paul and Gareth Johns
www.wynnstay-hotel.com

 Freehouse with four real ales, including
Greene King IPA and Brains Reverend
James, plus two guests on rotation, such as
Wye Valley Butty Bach, and Welsh Pride from
the Conway Brewery.

A n 18th-century town house converted to
a coaching inn, with pizzeria at the rear.
Food served lunchtimes and evenings daily.
Three-star accommodation. Well-behaved
children welcome. In the town centre by the
clock, with car parking at the rear via Bank
Lane.

OPEN *12–2.30pm and 6–11pm.*

MONTGOMERY

The Dragon Hotel

1 Market Square, Montgomery SY15 6PA
☎ *(01686) 668359* Mark and Sue Michaels
www.dragonhotel.com

 Genuine freehouse serving three real ales.
Wood Special is a regular, plus a guest.

A 17th-century family-run coaching inn
with 20 letting rooms, a function room
and an indoor swimming pool. Food
available at lunchtimes (12–2pm) and
evenings (7–9pm). Traditional jazz on
Wednesday evenings. Children allowed.

OPEN *11am–11pm Mon–Sat; 12–10.30pm Sun.*

PENGENFFORDD

The Castle Inn

Pengenffordd, Talgarth, Brecon LD3 0EP
☎ *(01874) 711353* Heather Swann
www.thecastleinn.co.uk

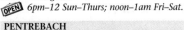 Freehouse with three pumps serving
alternating guest ales, changed weekly.
Wye Valley Butty Bach and Rhymney Bitter
are often featured, as are beers from Felinfoel
and Archers.

A former hill farm dating back to the 18th
century, in the heart of the Black
Mountains in the Brecon Beacons National
Park. With separate dining area. B&B, plus
bunkhouse and small camping site. Food
available every evening and weekend
lunchtimes in summer, with no food Mon
and Tues in winter. On the A479, four miles
south of Talgath.

OPEN *6pm–12 Sun–Thurs; noon–1am Fri–Sat.*

PENTREBACH

Shoemaker's Arms

Pentrebach, Sennybridge, Brecon LD3 8UB
☎ *(01874) 636508* Richard and Eileen Ingram

 Freehouse with Brains Rev James plus
one weekly-changing guest ale.

O ld country pub full of character set in
beautiful countryside. Open-plan bar.
Food served Mon evenings and all day Wed–
Sun (no food Tues). Beer garden. Children
welcome. Car park. Ideal location for
walking, cycling and fishing. From the A40
to Sennybridge, take the turning for
Pentrebach and follow signs to country pub.

OPEN *Lunchtimes Wed–Sun; evenings every day.*

RHAYADER

The Cornhill Inn

13 West Street, Rhayader LD6 5AB
☎ *(01597) 810029* Steve Lomax

Marston's pub with two real ales in
winter, four in summer. Jennings Cocker
Hoop and Sneck Lifter feature regularly, and
the guests, changed weekly or monthly,
might be Adnams Broadside, Titanic Iceberg
or Bateman Rosey Nosey.

B uilt in 1540, a pub with olde-worlde
character. Low beams, tiled floors and
open fires. Courtyard garden. Bar food
available 12–3pm and 6–8.30pm. Children
and dogs welcome. Accommodation (cottage
to let). On the road to Elan Valley.

OPEN *Noon–12.30am.*

Crown Inn

North Street, Rhayader LD6 5BT
☎ *(01597) 811099* John Leach
www.thecrownrhayader.co.uk

Brains tied house with Bitter and Reverend James plus rotating guests from Brains changed monthly.

Traditional 16th-century pub/hostelry with many photographs on display of the history of the area. Food served 12–2.15pm and 6–9.30pm Mon–Sun (all day Sat–Sun during summer). Families welcome. Three letting rooms available. Dining room available for groups and functions. Beer garden. Located in the centre of Rhayader.

OPEN *11.30am–11pm.*

TALYBONT-ON-USK

The Star Inn

Talybont-on-Usk, Brecon LD3 7YX
☎ *(01874) 676635* Ian and Anna Bell
www.starinntalybont.co.uk

Freehouse serving a constantly changing range of real ales on six pumps, including brews from Felinfoel, Brains, Breconshire and Wye Valley.

A 250-year-old riverside and canalside site, with lovely garden. Homemade food available 12–2pm and 6.30–9pm. Pool room, parking, garden. Live music (call for details), quiz nights on Tuesdays. Children welcome. En-suite accommodation. Less than a mile off the A40 between Brecon and Abergavenny (Brecon six miles, Abergavenny 14 miles).

OPEN *11am–3pm and 6.30–11pm Mon–Fri; all day Sat–Sun.*

SOUTH GLAMORGAN

ABERTHIN

The Farmer's Arms

Cowbridge Road, Aberthin, Cowbridge CF71 7HB
☎ *(01446) 773429* Michael Pugh

Wadworth 6X is always on offer plus one guest beer, which changes every week. Popular favourites include beers from local Cardiff brewer Bullmastiff and Cottage Brewing Company.

Victorian detached pub with a clean, modern interior. Central bar servery for two rooms. Comprehensive menu ranging from snacks to full à la carte served every lunchtime and evening, including traditional roasts on Sundays. Large outside decking area. Two car parks (front and rear). Disabled access and facilities. Children welcome. Five minutes from historic town of Cowbridge.

OPEN *12–3pm and 6–11pm Mon–Sat.*

Hare & Hounds

Aberthin, Cowbridge CF71 7LG
☎ *(01446) 774892* Nick Massey

Marston's tied pub with Marston's Pedigree and something from Banks's plus four guests changed every three to four weeks.

A 15th-century country pub with fine restaurant, patio, beer garden and a roaring fire in the old locals' bar. Food served 12–3pm and 6–9pm every day except Sun evening and Mon, with Welsh organic and local produce used where possible. Live music most Saturdays. Situated in the Vale of Glamorgan, popular for walking. Located one mile out of Cowbridge on the A4222.

OPEN *4pm–12 Mon; 12–12 Tues–Sun.*

CARDIFF

Cayo Arms

36 Cathedral Road, Cardiff CF11 9LL
☎ *(029) 2039 1910*
Nigel Sandford-Hill (manager)

Run by Celtic Inns, this busy pub has nine real ale pumps on the one bar serving Tomos Watkin ales including BB, OSB, Whoosh and Cwrw Haf. Brains beers such as Reverend James and SA make a regular appearance, and the guest is often from Bullmastiff, another local brewery.

Lively pub with a patio seating area at the front of this converted Victorian townhouse. Expect rugby fixtures to be shown on the screens inside (it's very busy on match days) and to hear Welsh spoken at the bar. Bed and breakfast accommodation available; food is served lunchtimes and evenings during the week and all day Saturday and Sunday.

OPEN *12–11pm (10.30pm Sun).*

Chapter Bar

Chapter Arts Centre, Market Road, Canton, Cardiff CF5 1QE
☎ *(029) 2031 1050* Dave Morgan (manager)
www.chapter.org

Four pumps serving Brains Rev James plus three ever-changing guest ales. Also three regular German weissbeers and pilsners. In addition, the bar is stocked with 250 bottled European beers, including Belgian Leffe and Duval and German ales and pilsners, and an impressive array of single malt whiskies.

Situated in a popular arts centre and cinema, this bar is buzzing with Cardiff's arty crowd on most evenings. Children are welcome. Nearby café in the centre (food 9am–9pm). Beer garden. Popular beer festivals in May and October. Five minutes from the city centre.

OPEN *5–11pm Mon–Thurs; 1pm–12.30am Fri–Sat; 4–10.30pm Sun.*

The Conway Inn

58 Conway Road, Pontcanna, Cardiff CF11 9NW
☎ *(029) 2023 2797*
Eddie and Gaynor Pritchard

Usually up to five real ales (sometimes more at weekends) including Greene King IPA and Abbot, Timothy Taylor Landlord, Adnams Broadside, Bass and Fuller's London Pride. Guest ales are ordered on a weekly basis.

This traditional, Victorian pub can be found on a quiet street corner in the leafy suburb of Pontcanna. It has a lounge, bar and outdoor tables and a strong, local following – thanks to its reputation for well-kept real ale. Live music each month. Food served 12–3pm Mon–Sat. Close to the rugby and cricket grounds.

OPEN *12–11pm (10.30pm Sun).*

The Gatekeeper

9–10 Westgate Street, Cardiff CF10 1DD
☎ *(029) 2064 6020* James Ace (manager)

Wetherspoon's pub serving two or three regular cask ales plus up to six guest beers. Regular ales include Brains SA, Arms Park and Dark, and guest beers come from a changing range of small breweries from all over the country.

Just across the road from the Millennium Stadium, this is a huge pub on two floors that is nearly always busy, especially on match days. Food served all day, every day until an hour before closing. Children allowed; baby-changing facilities and children's menu provided.

OPEN *10am–11pm Mon–Sat; 12–10.30pm Sun.*

Owain Glyndwr

St John's Street, Cardiff CF10 1XR
☎ *(029) 2022 1980* Ashley Inman

Four guests, regularly rotated, including beer from both local and national breweries such as Brains and Felinfoel.

Lively, modern city bar run by the same person as Tair Pluen next door. Freshly cooked, upmarket contemporary food served 12–9pm. Situated between the castle and the church.

OPEN *12–11pm (10.30pm Sun).*

Tair Pluen

Church Street, Cardiff CF10 1XR
☎ *(029) 2022 1980* Ashley Inman

Four guest ales, mainly from local breweries and micros, including Spinning Dog, Brecon and Bullmastiff.

Quiet, traditional local pub in the city (the name translates as Three Feathers), with a rustic feel and plenty of rugby memorabilia. Two TVs showing sport (especially rugby!). Traditional homemade Welsh food served 12–9pm every day. Outdoor smoking area with seating. Opposite St John's Church.

OPEN *12–11pm (10.30pm Sun).*

The Yard Bar & Kitchen

Old Brewery Quarter, St Mary Street, Cardiff CF10 1AD
☎ *(029) 2022 7577* Nick Newman (manager)
www.sabrain.com

Three real ales from Cardiff's own Brains brewery are always on offer here – Bitter, SA and Dark – plus one guest, changed monthly.

Large pub and bar created from the old brewery tap for the Brains brewery, The Albert, and part of the old brewery itself. The front half of the open-plan pub retains The Albert's traditional decor and cosy pub charm; the rear half sports flagstones and incorporates some of the industrial piping left behind when the brewery moved out. Food is served all day, every day from 10am to midnight. Children welcome until 7pm. The outdoor area is popular in the warmer months. Major 'destination' pub on Millennium Stadium event days.

OPEN *10am–1am or 2am (sometimes until 4am).*

COWBRIDGE

The Barley Mow

Craig Penllyn, Cowbridge CF71 1RT
☎ *(01446) 772558* Elia Pellegrotti

Freehouse serving two guest ales from brewers such as Cottage and Wye Valley.

An old Victorian village house with low ceilings and wooden beams, this is a popular pub both with locals and as a Sunday lunch venue. Food lunchtimes and evenings Wed–Sun. Small patio beer garden. Well-behaved children welcome.

OPEN *11am–11pm (10.30pm Sun).*

The Bear Hotel

63 High Street, Cowbridge CF71 7AF
☎ *(01446) 774814* Sian Bradley

Six real ales, including Brains Bitter and SA and Hancock's HB (brewed by Brains) plus three guests, changed every few days.

Part smart county hotel, part friendly local pub, the Bear Hotel's two bars are always busy with locals and residents. The building dates back to the 12th century, has open fires and two beer gardens. Children are welcome and bar food is served 12–2.30pm and 6–9.30pm; breakfast served through to 11pm. Large car park, excellent function facilities. Situated right on the main shopping street in Cowbridge where you'll find interesting individual shops and be hard pushed to find a single chain store.

OPEN *All day, every day.*

The Bush Inn

St Hilary, Cowbridge CF71 7OP
☎ *(01446) 772745* Phil Thomas
www.artizanleisure.com

Greene King Abbot and Hancock's HB (brewed by Brains) are among the regulars here, plus one guest, changed weekly.

This is a traditional 16th-century inn set in a beautiful village with two friendly locals' bars, a larger side bar with a warming inglenook fireplace and a restaurant in the back. Food is served 12–2.30pm and 6.30–9.30pm, with local produce used wherever possible. Children are welcome all day and there is a beer garden at the back of the pub. Situated just off the A48.

 11am–11pm.

The Vale of Glamorgan Inn

53 High Street, Cowbridge CF71 7AE
☎ *(01446) 772252* Alistair Sarjeant

Freehouse usually serving six real ales. Hancock's HB (brewed by Brains), Wye Valley HPA, Vale of Glamorgan No. 1 and Shepherd Neame Bishop's Finger are regulars; the guests will be from a wide range of independent breweries and will change every few days.

The building dates from the 18th century, and was originally the cottage used by the brewery at the back. A pub since the 1960s, it is now a friendly locals' inn, with one busy bar, a large beer garden and a real fire in winter. Children and dogs welcome. Food served 12–2.15pm Mon–Sat. Four en-suite bedrooms. Annual beer festival. In the centre of this popular market town. Off the A48 between Cardiff and Bridgend.

 11.30am–11pm Mon–Thurs; 11.30am–midnight Fri–Sat; 12–11pm Sun.

EAST ABERTHAW

The Blue Anchor Inn

East Aberthaw, Barry CF62 3DD
☎ *(01446) 750329* Jeremy Coleman
www.blueanchoraberthaw.com

Five real ales, including Wadworth 6X, Theakston Old Peculier, Wye Valley HPA, Brains Bitter and one rotating guest, changed twice a week.

This olde-worlde thatched Grade II listed smuggler's inn dates back to the 1380s. It has many small interconnecting rooms and an award-winning restaurant upstairs. Allegedly there is a tunnel from the pub down to the sea. Food served 12–2pm and 6–9.30pm Mon–Sat, and 12–2.30pm Sun. Two miles west of Cardiff airport.

 11am–11pm Mon–Sat; 12–10.30pm Sun.

GLAN-Y-LLYN

Fagin's Ale & Chop House

Cardiff Road, Glan-y-Llyn, Nr Taff's Well, Cardiff CF15 7QD
☎ *(02920) 811800*
Anne Wright and Simon Madley
www.faginsalehouse.co.uk

Genuine freehouse with RCH Pitchfork and '01' from the award-winning Otley Brewery at Pontypridd regularly on offer. Up to four gravity-fed ales at the back of the bar are sourced from small independent breweries, and change every couple of days. Gwynt y Ddraig Orchard Gold cider also on draught.

Warm, welcoming alehouse, popular with walkers, cyclists and locals alike, with flagstone flooring, real fire and wooden beams adorned with 'Wenglish' sayings. Food served 12–2.30pm and 6–9pm Mon–Sat; 12–

3pm Sun, either in the bar or in the 50-cover restaurant. Live music every Thursday and Saturday. Well-behaved dogs and children on a leash welcome. One mile from train station, two minutes from M4 junction 32.

 11am–midnight Mon–Thurs; 11am–1am Fri–Sat; 12–10.30pm Sun.

GWAELOD-Y-GARTH

Gwaelod-y-Garth Inn

Main Road, Gwaelod-y-Garth, Cardiff CF15 9HH
☎ *(02920) 810408*
Barbara Evans and Richard Angell

Freehouse serving regulars such as Wye Valley HPA, Crouch Vale Brewers Gold and Swansea's Three Cliffs Gold. Plus at least one guest changed on a weekly basis.

Friendly, award-winning freehouse, perched in the shadow of Garth Hill, at least 150 years old. A warm, local community-oriented pub and popular haunt for walkers. One big bar, three rooms, log fires, separate restaurant. Food available Wed–Sun. Beer garden overlooking the valley. Children and dogs welcome. Accommodation nearby. Car park. Beer patio with umbrellas and heating. Five minutes from M4 junction 32.

 12–11pm (10.30pm Sun).

LLANTWIT MAJOR

The Old Swan Inn

Church Street, Llantwit Major CF61 1SB
☎ *(01446) 792230* Sean Murphy
www.oldswaninn.com

Freehouse serving four real ales, all changing weekly.

Award-winning pub, over 600 years old, one of the oldest pubs in Llantwit Major. Food served 12–9.30pm. The pub has extensive gardens and is very family-oriented. Children are very welcome, and there are plans for a children's play area. Car park opposite. Two miles from the beach.

 12–11pm (10.30pm Sun).

LLYSWORNEY

The Carne Arms

Llysworney, Cowbridge CF71 7NQ
☎ *(01446) 773553* Matthew Foster

Wychwood Hobgoblin is among the beers always available, plus up to three guest ales such as Greene King IPA or Old Speckled Hen.

An old village pub popular with locals and passing tourists, with two bars, inglenook fireplaces and a covered, outdoor seating area. There is a large children's play area, and food (bar meals and à la carte menu) is served lunchtimes and evenings.

 12–2.30pm and 6–11pm Mon–Fri; 12–11pm Sat; 12–10.30pm Sun.

MARCROSS
Horseshoe Inn
Marcross, Llantwit Major CF61 1ZG
☎ *(01656) 890568* Beverly Chappell

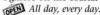 Freehouse with Evan Evans Cwrw, Shepherd Neame Spitfire, Tomos Watkin and Brecon County Ale plus four weekly-changing guests.

Victorian coaching inn with two bars and large garden, five minutes from Nash Point Lighthouse. Food served daily. Ideal location for many coastal walks. Children welcome. Located between Llantwit and Ogmore on the coastal road.

OPEN *All day, every day.*

MONKNASH
The Plough & Harrow
Monknash, Nr Llantwit Major CF71 7QQ
☎ *(01656) 890209* Gareth Davies
www.theploughmonknash.com

Up to eight real ales, perhaps including Wye Valley HPA and Butty Bach, Shepherd Neame Spitfire, Archers Golden, Skinner's Cornish Knocker, Brains Rev James and Tomas Watkin Cwrw Haf or Merlin Stout, plus many others. Six cask ciders and a selection of bottled beers also on offer.

This lively pub dates back to the 14th century and is situated next to the ruins of an old priory in the village of Monknash. Two bars, with huge log fires in the winter. Food served 12–2.30pm daily and 6–9pm Mon–Sat. Live music is a regular feature on Saturday nights. Large beer garden, with barbecues. Located only a short detour from the Glamorgan Heritage Coast footpath.

OPEN *12–11pm (10.30pm Sun).*

ROATH
The Albany Hotel
105 Donald Street, Roath, Cardiff CF24 4TL
☎ *(029) 2031 1075* Jeff and Cheryl Lane

Brains managed house with Brains Bitter, Dark, SA and SA Gold plus one rotating guest changed several times a week.

Former hotel/coaching inn dating from 1895, now a traditional street-corner local retaining much of its Victorian ambience. High-ceilinged, cosy lounge and livelier bar. Food served 12–2.30pm Mon–Sat. Beautiful 'secret' beer garden and covered, heated smoking area. Skittle alley and dartboard, subject to deposit. Sky Sports shown on large plasma screens. Wii sports available to play on bar big screen, for £20 returnable deposit. Free WiFi access. Tuesday is quiz night, Saturday features live singers, and occasionally karaoke, and there is a poker league on Sunday night. Accompanied children welcome before 9pm. Located a 20-minute walk from the city centre. From the five-point junction by the George pub, head along Albany Road, turn left between the Post Office and the former Woolworths, go past one crossroads, and the pub is on the next street corner.

OPEN *12–11.30pm Mon–Thurs; 12–12 Fri; 11am–midnight Sat; 12–11pm Sun (bar service stops half an hour prior to closing).*

ST BRIDES MAJOR
The Farmer's Arms
Wick Road, St Brides Major CF32 0SE
☎ *(01656) 880224/880329* Nigel Guy

Six cask pumps serving a regular selection, including beers such as Greene King Old Speckled Hen.

A 19th-century pub with patio garden overlooking the traditional village duck pond. Children welcome all day. Food served daily.

OPEN *12–3.30pm and 6–11pm (10.30pm Sun).*

SIGINGSTONE
The Victoria Inn
Sigingstone, Nr Cowbridge CF71 7LP
☎ *(01446) 773943* Eifion Watkins

Something from Tomos Watkin plus Hancock's HB (brewed by Brains) usually available at this village local, plus a seasonal guest ale.

Country inn well known for its food and attractive interior featuring antiques throughout. Parts of the building date back to 1300. Lunch and dinner served daily, including children's menu. Large car park. Two miles from the ancient market town of Cowbridge, with its specialist shops, and three miles from Llantwit Major beach.

OPEN *11.45am–3pm and 6–11pm Mon–Sat; 11.45am–3pm and 7–10.30pm Sun.*

WICK
The Lamb & Flag
Church Street, Wick, Cowbridge CF71 7QE
☎ *(01656) 890278* Tim Warrick

Two pumps dedicated to guest real ales such as Cottage Mallard Gold and local brew Bullmastiff Best Bitter.

Traditional 16th-century village pub (no juke box, no pool table) with mainly local clientele in the two bars and back lounge, but some tourists do drop in on their way to local beaches like Southerdown and Ogmore. Open fires in winter, outside seating in summer. Food available lunchtimes and evenings Mon–Fri, all day Sat–Sun.

OPEN *11.30am–3.30pm and 5.30pm–11pm Mon–Thurs; 11.30am–11pm Fri– Sun (10.30pm Sun).*

WEST GLAMORGAN

ABERCRAVE

The Copper Beech Inn

*133 Heol Tawe, Abercrave, Swansea Valley
SA9 1XS*
☎ *(01639) 730269* Helen Macadam

A family-run freehouse with two or three Welsh beers, changed once or twice a week.

Locals' pub, built in 1864 as a coal owner's house, and a pub since the 1960s. Large bar, function room and large beer garden. Children welcome. Bar and restaurant food served 12–3pm and 6–9pm. Accommodation. Close to Brecon Beacons National Park and show cave, and handy for riding and walking.

OPEN *11am–11.30pm.*

BISHOPSTON

The Joiners' Arms

*50 Bishopston Road, Bishopston, Swansea
SA3 3EJ*
☎ *(01792) 232658*
Ian, Kathleen and Phil Davies

Home of the Swansea Brewing Company. Eight pumps serving seven beers including all the home brews (Bishopswood Bitter, Three Cliffs Gold and Original Wood), plus Marston's Pedigree and a range of guests.

Traditional village pub with mixed clientele, no juke box. Food available at lunchtimes and evenings. Children allowed. Regular beer festivals held.

OPEN *11.30am–11pm Mon–Sat; 12–10.30pm Sun.*

CLYDACH

The Carpenter's Arms

High Street, Clydach, Nr Swansea SA6 5LN
☎ *(01792) 843333* Richie Saunders
www.carpentersarmsclydach.co.uk

Four or five real ales, mainly local brews, often from the Swansea Brewing Company, Bryncelyn Brewery, Wells and Young's, Tomos Watkin, Wye Valley and Marston's.

Stone-built village pub with two bars and a restaurant. *Morning Advertiser* HTV Pub of the Year 2006 and Best Cask Ale Pub of the Year for Wales 2006. Attracts mainly local clientele (a local cycle club holds regular meetings here) and runs four seasonal beer festivals a year. Meals using fresh produce available 12–2.30pm and 6–9.30pm every day except Mondays. Car park, beer garden with cover and patio heater. Private functions catered for. Just off route 43 of the National Cycle Network.

OPEN *11am–midnight Sun–Thurs; 11am–1am Fri–Sat.*

GOWER

The Greyhound Inn

Old Walls, Gower, Swansea SA3 1HA
☎ *(01792) 391027* Chris and Emily

Freehouse with a total of six real ales, always including Bass and Wadworth 6X.

An 18th-century pub, popular with walkers, locals and holidaymakers. Two bars and a function room. Homemade food available all day, including weekday lunchtime specials. Beer garden. Children welcome. Live folk music on Sunday nights.

OPEN *11am–11pm Mon–Sat; 12–10.30pm Sun.*

King's Head

Llangennith, Gower, Swansea SA3 1HU
☎ *(01792) 386212* Chris Stevens
www.kingsheadgower.co.uk

Freehouse serving at least three real ales, often more. Stalwarts include Wadworth 6X, as well as beers from local brewer Tomos Watkin including OSB and Brewery Bitter.

Situated in the centre of a picturesque Gower village, the pub comprises a row of three 17th-century buildings behind a splendid rough stone wall. It is a Mecca for daytrippers, campers and surfers from nearby beach, and recently appeared in *The Sunday Times* list of Top 10 Summer Pubs. Two bars, open fire and lots of character. Food served until 9.30pm daily, including curries and pies as well as a traditional menu. Luxurious en-suite bedrooms. Outside seating, ample parking. Children welcome. A mile from Rhossili beach, opposite the largest church on Gower. On North Gower Road, follow the B4295 to the end.

OPEN *11am–11pm Mon–Sat; 12–10.30pm Sun.*

MUMBLES

The Park Inn

52 Park Street, Mumbles, Swansea SA3 4DA
☎ *(01792) 366738* Richard Martin

There are five cask ales on offer at this traditional freehouse. These are rotated every three days, and could include anything from local ales to English beers such as RCH Pitchfork and Timothy Taylor Landlord, and Scottish brews from Caledonian.

Built in a 19th-century terraced house in the seaside village of Mumbles. One bar where locals mix with tourists, and there is a good range of ages. Dart room, dominoes, cards, puzzles and quiz machine. No food, no music. Free quiz night Thursday. Well-behaved children welcome. This pub takes part in the annual Mumbles Beer Festival over the August Bank Holiday weekend. Convenient for rambling on cliffs and other coastal paths.

OPEN *4–11.30pm Mon–Thurs; 12–11.30pm Fri–Sat; 12–11pm Sun.*

Borough Arms
New Henry Street, Neath SA11 1PH
☎ *(01639) 644902*

Four real ales from a constantly rotating range, some local, some from outside Wales.

A real ale oasis in the town, a traditional locals' local with one central bar. South Wales CAMRA Pub of the Year 2007.

OPEN *4–11pm Mon–Fri; 12–11pm Sat; 6–10.30pm Sun.*

The Pontardawe Inn
Herbert Street, Pontardawe, Swansea SA8 4ED
☎ *(01792) 830791* Hywel Roberts
www.pontardaweinn.co.uk

Marston's tied house with Pedigree and Banks's Original always on offer, plus a guest changed weekly.

A 17th-century coaching inn on the banks of the River Tawe, with central bar, concert bar area and snug. There is a restaurant seating 28, and food is served 12–2pm and 6–9pm Wed–Sat and 12–2.30pm Sun, with 'curry and a pint night' on Mondays. Beer festivals three times a year. Boules court. Large car park. Live music weekends, and traditional music on Wed evenings. Five minutes from junction 45 of the M4 – follow the A4067 (north).

OPEN *12–12.*

The Old White Horse Inn
12 High Street, Pontneddfechan SA11 5NP
☎ *(01639) 721219*
Darrel Millett and Lisa Richards

Freehouse with up to five ales from breweries such as Brains, Rhymney, Wye Valley and Scattor Rock.

A 400-year-old coaching house with bar and lounge area plus open fires in winter. Food served 12–3pm and 6–9pm Tues–Sat, 12–3pm Sun. Accommodation available. Beer garden. Families welcome. Games room. Beer festivals. Located at the start of 27 miles of waterfall walks.

OPEN *12–3pm and 6–9pm Tues–Fri; 12–close Sat–Sun (closed Mon).*

Plough & Harrow
59 Church Road, Llansamlet, Swansea SA7 9RL
☎ *(01792) 772263* Tracie Roberts

Tied to Marston's with Pedigree and a guest changed every couple of weeks, such as Jennings Sneck Lifter or Golden Host, Adnams Broadside or Greene King Old Speckled Hen.

F amily-run village pub with a friendly atmosphere on the outskirts of Swansea, mainly frequented by locals. One large bar, open fire and beer garden. Large car park. Children welcome. Food served 12–2pm daily and 6–9pm Tues–Sat. Disabled facilities, function room. Off M4 junction 44.

OPEN *12–10.30pm Sun–Mon; 12–11pm Tues–Fri; noon–1am Sat.*

The Potters Wheel
85–6 The Kingsway, Swansea SA1 5JE
☎ *(01792) 465113* Carl Jones

JD Wetherspoon's pub with up to ten real ales, including five regulars such as Greene King Abbot and Brains SA, plus at least three guests.

T own-centre pub on Swansea's main clubbing street. No music, games or pool. Food available all day. Children welcome.

OPEN *10am–11pm Mon–Sat; 12–10.30pm Sun.*

The Queens Hotel
Gloucester Place, Swansea SA1 1TY
☎ *(01792) 521531* Gary Owen

Four real ales, including Theakston Old Peculier, Theakston Best, Brains Buckley's Best plus one guest ale, often from the local Swansea Brewing Company.

V ictorian pub with original features in Swansea's Maritime Quarter. It is frequented by locals, tourists and journalists from the *South Wales Evening Post*. Photos of old ships decorate the walls. Food is available lunchtimes, when children are also welcome. Pavement tables outside.

OPEN *11am–11pm Mon–Sat; 12–10.30pm Sun.*

The Railway Inn
553 Gower Road, Upper Killay, Swansea SA2 7DS
☎ *(01792) 203946*
Adrian Martin and Rory Gowland

Freehouse with up to six cask ales. Three beers regularly come from the nearby Swansea Brewing Company, such as Original Wood or Deep Slade Dark. Two to three guests change regularly; favourites include Timothy Taylor Landlord.

D ating back to 1864, this pub was a house until the 1930s. It stands next to the ticket office and station master's house on the old Clyne railway line which ran down the valley into Swansea. The line is now a cycle track and the pub is a popular stop-off point for cyclists, as well as locals and trippers from the nearby Gower peninsula. One main bar, separate lounge bar, open fires in winter and a beer garden (two patios). Children welcome until 7pm.

OPEN *11am–11pm Mon–Sat; 12–10.30pm Sun.*

The Westbourne

1 Bryn-y-Mor Road, Swansea SA1 4JQ
☎ *(01792) 476637* Mark Lingwood

Four real ales, with Greene King Abbot and IPA, Felinfoel Double Dragon and Brains SA a typical selection. One of the beers is rotated every three months.

The Westbourne became a pub in 1912, and has been renovated to modern standards. It has one room and a heated outside terrace. Food served 12–6pm Mon–Sat and 12–4pm Sun. Children welcome until 8pm. Close to the town centre with its leisure facilities and tourist attractions. Located just off the sea front.

11am–11pm Mon–Tues; 11am–11.30pm Wed; 11am–midnight Thurs; 11am–12.30am Fri–Sat; 12–11pm Sun.

The Woodman Inn

Mumbles Road, Blackpill, Swansea SA3 5AS
☎ *(01792) 402700* Roland Jenkins

Two pumps regularly serving real ale, including one beer from Brains and one guest ale changing regularly.

Old pub on the main tourist route to Swansea's beaches, with low beams and old-fashioned charm, attracting regulars and tourists. Children welcome until 8pm.

11am–11pm Mon–Sat; 12–10.30pm Sun.

UPPER CWMTWRCH

The George IV Inn

Upper Cwmtwrch, Swansea Valley SA9 2XH
☎ *(01639) 830938* Roy and June King

Brains SA and Greene King Abbot are regular offerings plus one guest such as Adnams Broadside.

Friendly riverside rural pub and restaurant in a scenic valley in the foothills of West Wales' Black Mountains. Log fire, oak beams, antiques and plenty of olde-worlde atmosphere. Large beer garden and car park. Homemade food prepared in the open-plan kitchen and served during opening hours. Located just off the A4067 Brecon to Swansea road, not far from the famous Dan-yr-Ogof caves.

12–3pm and 6pm–11pm Mon–Sat; 12–3pm and 7pm–10.30pm Sun.

YSTALYFERA

Wern Fawr Inn

47 Wern Road, Ystalyfera, Swansea SA9 2LX
☎ *(01639) 843625* Will Hopton

The home of the Bryncelyn Brewery with a full range of own brews permanently available on three to four pumps. A tiny pub where all the home ales are named on a Buddy Holly theme and include Oh Boy, Peggy's Brew and 2003 CAMRA Welsh beer award winner, Buddy Marvellous.

A village pub dating back to the 1850s with two small bars. Background music is 1960s and 1970s. No food. Beer garden. Children allowed.

7–11pm Mon–Sat; 12–3.30pm and 7–10pm Sun.

You might think it wouldn't be too difficult to find bottle-conditioned beer in the high-street shops but, in fact, it's not that easy. The situation is little better in the supermarkets. On a recent visit to Sainsburys, amongst a range of about 30 English Ales, I found just four that were bottle-conditioned. While it is good to see the beer ranges in supermarkets increasing, they still have a long way to go in terms of their bottle-conditioned offerings.

So where can we go? Some micro-breweries run shops on their premises and there are also a handful of specialist off-licences around the country which cater for this growing market.

One such off-licence is The Beer Essentials in Horsham, West Sussex, where they keep over 150 different bottled beers in stock, over half of which are bottle-conditioned. Traditional independent off-licences are also beginning to offer more bottle-conditioned beers.

Real ale in a bottle, or bottle-conditioned beer, like cask ale, contains live yeast and fermentable sugars. A secondary fermentation takes place in the bottle, which develops the beer naturally and maintains its condition. Despite the almost hysterical passion for sell-by dates nowadays, these beers actually mature in the bottle and are likely to be in prime condition for some time. However, you should make your own decision as to whether your particular bottle is drinkable and will not cause you any upset.

Like cask beer, to allow enjoyment of the full complexity of flavour, bottle-conditioned beers should be between 13–15°C/55–59°F when drunk. The bottle should be allowed to stand for a sufficient period to allow the sediment to drop to the bottom, although while researching I found many of the beers had quite sticky sediment, making pouring relatively easy. That said, care should still be taken when pouring to prevent any of the sediment rising and clouding the beer. Bottle-conditioned beers should never be drunk straight from the bottle. Some less hoppy, continental beers can be drunk cloudy, but British bottle-conditioned beers generally should not.

The numbers beside the colours give an idea of the depth of colour on a scale of 1–20, with 1 being pale yellow and 20 being the darkest black.

ASCOT ALES ANASTASIA'S EXILE STOUT 5% ABV

Brewed by Ascot Ales Ltd, Unit 5, Compton Place Business Centre, Surrey Avenue, Camberley, Surrey GU15 3DX.
☎ (01276) 686696.
www.ascot-ales.co.uk
Colour: Black (20).
Head: Very little head.
Aroma: Subtle roasted malt.
Taste: Very dry heavily roasted malt flavour and a long dry finish.
Ease of Decanting: Seemed quite easy but as you cannot see through this beer it is difficult to check the clarity.
Opinion: Try this impressive dark beer with some stilton and biscuits.

ASCOT ALES POSH POOCH 4.2% ABV

Brewed by Ascot Ales Ltd, Unit 5, Compton Place Business Centre, Surrey Avenue, Camberley, Surrey GU15 3DX.
☎ (01276) 686696.
www.ascot-ales.co.uk
Colour: Light golden (5).
Head: Small white head which gradually disappeared.
Aroma: Intense fresh green hops.
Taste: Lots of crisp citrus hop flavour. Short dry finish.
Ease of Decanting: Extremely easy to pour.
Opinion: Great with cheddar cheese on toast.

B&T DRAGON SLAYER 4.5% ABV

Brewed by B&T Brewery Ltd, The Brewery, Shefford, Bedfordshire SG17 5DZ.
☎ (01462) 815080.
www.banksandtaylor.com
Colour: Golden-yellow (3).
Head: White dense large rocky head.
Aroma: A sweet malty aroma, most unexpected from such a pale beer.
Taste: Initial taste is a delicate yet sweet hop flavour that continues through to the end with a delicate hoppy aftertaste.
Ease of Decanting: Have two glasses ready. Not easy due to the large head, and pouring into one glass from start to finish could be difficult. Best to use the second glass, and watch out for swirls of yeast in the last quarter. Well worth the effort.

Opinion: A pale, delicate, thirst-quenching ale which would be a godsend after a hot curry.

B&T EDWIN TAYLOR'S EXTRA STOUT 4.5% ABV

Brewed by B&T Brewery Ltd, The Brewery, Shefford, Bedfordshire SG17 5DZ.
☎ (01462) 815080.
www.banksandtaylor.com
Colour: Black with ruby tints in the light (20).
Head: Pours with a small head with brown, dense bubbles.
Aroma: A very aromatic ale with earthy blackcurrant notes.
Taste: The theme of this B&T stout is definitely malt. The initial taste is smooth and malty, leading to hints of fruit, yet finishing with a subtle yet refreshing hoppy aftertaste.
Ease of Decanting: Quite easy as the head pours small and tight. Keep an eagle eye out for those yeast tendrils in the last quarter of the bottle – a steady hand wins the day.
Opinion: Very nice example of bottle-conditioned stout from a small brewery. Would be a very nice accompaniment to a roast dinner.

B&T SHEFFORD BITTER 3.8% ABV

Brewed by B&T Brewery Ltd, The Brewery, Shefford, Bedfordshire SG17 5DZ.
☎ (01462) 815080.
www.banksandtaylor.com
Colour: Amber (6).
Head: Smallish head, white with fine bubbles.
Aroma: A clean fresh nose with lots of hop.
Taste: Refreshing with a good hoppy bite and a long dry finish.
Ease of Decanting: A fairly easy pour.
Opinion: An excellent appetite sharpener or perfect with a bacon sandwich.

B&T SHEFFORD OLD DARK 5% ABV

Brewed by B&T Brewery Ltd, The Brewery, Shefford, Bedfordshire SG17 5DZ.
☎ (01462) 815080.
www.banksandtaylor.com
Colour: Dark Brown (15).
Head: Small brown head with dense bubbles.
Aroma: Malt and pronounced hop notes.
Taste: Luscious malt and lots of hop leading through to a tasty malty finish.

Ease of Decanting: Quite easy given the colour.
Opinion: Would go really well with steak pie, mash and peas.

B&T SHEFFORD OLD STRONG 5% ABV
Brewed by B&T Brewery Ltd, The Brewery, Shefford, Bedfordshire SG17 5DZ.
☎ *(01462) 815080.*
www.banksandtaylor.com
Colour: Reddish-brown (10).
Head: Large dense white head.
Aroma: Lots of rich fruit and malt with a hint of hops.
Taste: Rich fruit and malt flavours balance nicely with hops on the finish.
Ease of Decanting: Slightly tricky because of the head and the colour but I got there eventually.
Opinion: Great with a large plate of beef stew.

BALLARD'S BEST BITTER 4.2% ABV
Brewed by Ballard's Brewery Ltd, The Old Sawmill, Nyewood, Petersfield, Hampshire GU31 5HA.
☎ *(01730) 821301.*
www.ballardsbrewery.org.uk
Colour: Orange-brown (10).
Head: White, dense bubbles in a large head which keeps growing even after pouring has finished.
Aroma: Delicate toffee apple and caramel aroma.
Taste: Delicate caramel leading to hops on the side of the tongue, with caramel sweetness blending in to produce a slightly burnt, bitter aftertaste.
Ease of Decanting: Difficult. Due to the head growth I couldn't finish pouring it all into a pint glass, so it may need an hour or two in the fridge just to quieten it down a bit before opening. Worth the effort though.
Opinion: Nice beer with sirloin steak and chips.

BALLARD'S NYEWOOD GOLD 5.0% ABV
Brewed by Ballard's Brewery Ltd, The Old Sawmill, Nyewood, Petersfield, Hampshire GU31 5HA.
☎ *(01730) 821301.*
www.ballardsbrewery.org.uk
Colour: Amber-orange (6).
Head: White dense bubbles in a good head that did not need creating.
Aroma: Sweet and appley.
Taste: Fresh, frothy with apples slightly drying into a subtle cidery finish.
Ease of Decanting: Yeast clung to the base of the bottle. Pour carefully to control the head.
Opinion: An unusually cidery beer, very nice and well worth trying. Would go down well with roast pork and crackling.

BALLARD'S WASSAIL 6.0% ABV
Brewed by Ballard's Brewery Ltd, The Old Sawmill, Nyewood, Petersfield, Hampshire GU31 5HA.
☎ *(01730) 821301.*
www.ballardsbrewery.org.uk
Colour: Burgundy-brown (14).
Head: Brown, small head with dense bubbles.
Aroma: Malty with slight fruit notes.
Taste: Definite taste of molasses and malt, balanced with bitter fruits in the aftertaste.
Ease of Decanting: A nice easy-pouring ale with yeast that clings to the bottom of the bottle and a head that doesn't get too excited on pouring.
Opinion: A lovely beer with game pie.

BURTON BRIDGE BRAMBLE STOUT 5.0% ABV
Brewed by Burton Bridge Brewery, 24 Bridge Street, Burton upon Trent, Staffordshire DE14 1SY.
☎ *(01283) 510573.*
www.burtonbridgebrewery.co.uk
Colour: Black (20).
Head: Brown, dense, large head.
Aroma: Fruity, blackberry aromas.
Taste: Initial grainy fruit taste which explodes into blackberry sweetness, balanced by fruit bitterness in the aftertaste.
Ease of Decanting: Be careful with this one. Large-headed beer with yeast swirls in the last quarter of the bottle, but well worth the effort.
Opinion: Dark, fruity, interesting ale, good with a nice Stilton ploughman's.

BURTON BRIDGE BURTON PORTER 4.5% ABV
Brewed by Burton Bridge Brewery, 24 Bridge Street, Burton upon Trent, Staffordshire DE14 1SY.
☎ *(01283) 510573.*
www.burtonbridgebrewery.co.uk
Colour: Black with burgundy hints (20).
Head: Brown coloured with small, dense bubbles, stayed small and manageable.
Aroma: Slight vanilla aroma, sweet.
Taste: Fruity initial taste frothing on the tongue leading to vanilla pods and fruit cake, then a short bittersweet fruit aftertaste.
Ease of Decanting: Yeast clings to the base of the bottle and head stays small, so a nice easy pourer.
Opinion: Dark, frothy and easy to drink. Would go down a treat with O'Hagan's sausage and mash.

BUTTS GOLDEN BROWN 5.0% ABV
Brewed by Butts Brewery Ltd, Northfield Farm, Wantage Road, Great Shefford, Hungerford, Berkshire RG17 7BY.
☎ *(01488) 648133.*
www.buttsbrewery.com
Colour: Dark amber-chestnut (11).
Head: White, dense head with small bubbles, pours quite large and clings to side of glass.
Aroma: Slightly sulphuric with tar aromas.
Taste: Smooth initial impression leading to fruit with molasses, yet balanced in the aftertaste by bitter fruit and hops.
Ease of Decanting: Not an easy pour due to the large head, so you will possibly need two glasses and a steady hand. Well worth the effort.
Opinion: Would go down very nicely with a pork pie ploughman's.

CROPTON MONKMAN'S SLAUGHTER 6.0% ABV
Brewed by Cropton Brewery at The New Inn, Cropton, Near Pickering, North Yorkshire YO18 8HH.
☎ *(01751) 417330.*
www.croptonbrewery.co.uk
Colour: Dark brown (15).
Head: Tight, brown head.
Aroma: Rich, malty and faintly biscuity.
Taste: Complex and rich with a tasty, biscuity sweetness and a long finish.
Ease of Decanting: Quite easy to pour.
Opinion: Great after dinner with the cheese board.

CROPTON SCORESBY STOUT 4.2% ABV
Brewed by Cropton Brewery at The New Inn, Cropton, Near Pickering, North Yorkshire YO18 8HH.
☎ *(01751) 417330.*
www.croptonbrewery.co.uk
Colour: Black (20).
Head: Dark, inviting head.
Aroma: Roasted but not quite burnt.
Taste: Rich and roasted with a little hop to add balance.
Ease of Decanting: Some care required due to the colour of the beer, but worth the effort.
Opinion: Perfect with steak and mushroom pie and mash.

DOWNTON CHIMERA IPA 7% ABV
Brewed by Downton Brewery, Unit 11, Batten Road, Downton Business Centre, Downton, Wilts SP5 3HU.
☎ *(01722) 322890.*
Colour: Light golden (5).
Head: Small manageable head.
Aroma: Vinous and slightly citric.
Taste: Fresh fruit and malt. Hop flavour builds to a dry hoppy finish. Very easy-drinking for the strength.
Ease of Decanting: Very easy to pour. Yeast remained totally static.
Opinion: Perfect with Stilton and biscuits.

DOWNTON DARK DELIGHT 6% ABV
Brewed by Downton Brewery, Unit 11, Batten Road, Downton Business Centre, Downton, Wilts SP5 3HU.
☎ *(01722) 322890.*
Colour: Dark brown (15).
Head: Small tight white head.
Aroma: Roasted malt and subtle hops.
Taste: Roasted malt and subtle hop flavours and a long, dry, satisfying finish.
Ease of Decanting: Very easy to pour.
Opinion: Perfect with beef stew and dumplings.

DURHAM BENEDICTUS 8.4% ABV
Brewed by The Durham Brewery, Unit 5A, Bowburn North Industrial Estate, Bowburn, County Durham DH6 5PF.
☎ *(0191) 377 1991.*
www.durham-brewery.co.uk
Colour: Golden (6).
Head: Large white head with fine bubbles.
Aroma: Soft fruit.
Taste: A complex caramel and malt mixture with a long slightly bitter finish.
Ease of Decanting: Pour this carefully otherwise you could lose some beer because of the head.
Opinion: Savour slowly with some good strong cheese.

DURHAM EVENSONG 5% ABV
Brewed by The Durham Brewery, Unit 5A, Bowburn North Industrial Estate, Bowburn, County Durham DH6 5PF.
☎ *(0191) 377 1991.*
www.durham-brewery.co.uk
Colour: Deep ruby (14).
Head: Medium head with brown dense bubbles.
Aroma: Toffee and subtle hop notes.
Taste: Rich toffee sweetness with bitterness that builds through to the finish.
Ease of Decanting: A fairly easy pour with no overspill.
Opinion: A good accompaniment to a rich, warming beef casserole.

DURHAM TEMPTATION 10% ABV
Brewed by The Durham Brewery, Unit 5A, Bowburn North Industrial Estate, Bowburn, County Durham DH6 5PF.
☎ *(0191) 377 1991.*
www.durham-brewery.co.uk
Colour: Black (20).
Head: Small dark dense head.
Aroma: Very complex malty nose.
Taste: Robust coffee and liquorice flavours combined with smooth maltiness.
Ease of Decanting: Quite an easy pour despite the blackness of the beer.
Opinion: One to sip and share after a big meal.

FREEMINER SPECULATION 4.8% ABV
Brewed by Freeminer Brewery Ltd, Whimsey Road, Steam Mills, Cinderford, Royal Forest of Dean GL14 3JA.
☎ *(01594) 827989.*
www.freeminer.com
Colour: Reddish brown (12).
Head: Dense white head with small bubbles.
Aroma: Fresh hops and a hint of orange.
Taste: Tasty malt and bitter hops with a long, bitter, slightly citrus finish.
Ease of Decanting: Quite easy to pour.
Opinion: Perfect with spaghetti bolognese.

FREEMINER TRAFALGAR IPA 6.0% ABV
Brewed by Freeminer Brewery Ltd, Whimsey Road, Steam Mills, Cinderford, Royal Forest of Dean GL14 3JA.
☎ *(01594) 827989.*
www.freeminer.com
Colour: Golden (6).
Head: Very flat head with a few fine bubbles.
Aroma: Spirity malt.
Taste: Toffee and rich fruit. Spirity malt which gives way to bitterness in the finish.
Ease of Decanting: The flat head made this an easy beer to pour.
Opinion: The finishing touch to roast beef with all the trimmings.

FROG ISLAND CROAK & STAGGER 5.6% ABV
Brewed by Frog Island Brewery, The Maltings, Westbridge, St James Road, Northampton NN5 5HS.
☎ *(01604) 587772.*
www.frogislandbrewery.co.uk
Colour: Oak-burgundy (17).
Head: Small brown head that diminished quickly.
Aroma: Black treacle and molasses.
Taste: Initial acrid bakelite, tarry taste, warming and increasing in bitterness to floral grapefruit zinging the taste buds in a long aftertaste.
Ease of Decanting: Yeast stayed at the bottom and the head stayed small so an easy beer to pour.
Opinion: A robust beer which would complement a nice rabbit stew.

FROG ISLAND NATTERJACK 4.8% ABV
Brewed by Frog Island Brewery, The Maltings, Westbridge, St James Road, Northampton NN5 5HS.
☎ *(01604) 587772.*
www.frogislandbrewery.co.uk
Colour: Golden-yellow (3).
Head: Large dense white head.
Aroma: Malt, but with a slight peppery note.
Taste: Warming initially, then metallic-peppery taste with slight notes of plastic, the aftertaste is long and slightly rancid and furry on the sides of the tongue.
Ease of Decanting: Large head, but yeast stayed at the bottom of the bottle, so pour into an oversized glass.
Opinion: Drink at lunch with a pork pie ploughman's to clean the palate.

FULLER'S 1845 6.3% ABV
Brewed by Fuller, Smith & Turner PLC, Griffin Brewery, Chiswick Lane South, London W4 2QB.
☎ *(020) 8996 2000.*
www.fullers.co.uk
Colour: Oak-burgundy (17).
Head: Brown dense bubbles in a medium-sized head.
Aroma: Warming winter mulling spices with blackcurrant.
Taste: Initial frothy mouth-feel leading to a warming and pleasant grapefruit bitterness that increases in bitterness through to the aftertaste.
Ease of Decanting: A nice easy-to-pour beer with the yeast staying steadfastly at the bottom of the bottle.
Opinion: A distinctive beer which is one of the best-selling bottle-conditioned beers in the UK. Nice with the traditional London fayre of pie, mash and liquor.

HANBY RAINBOW CHASER 4.3% ABV
Brewed by Hanby Ales Ltd, New Brewery, Aston Park, Soulton Road, Wem, Shropshire SY4 5SD.
☎ *(01939) 232432.*
www.hanbyales.co.uk
Colour: Amber (7).
Head: White, small bubbles and controllable.
Aroma: Molasses and fruit cake.
Taste: Bitter honey like a dry mead, dry honey stays throughout finishing in a bitter flourish.
Ease of Decanting: Yeast clings to the bottom and the head stays small, so nice and easy.
Opinion: A nice thirst-quenching beer to be enjoyed on a hot summer's day with a honey-glazed ham baguette.

HOGS BACK A OVER T (AROMAS OVER TONGHAM) 9.0% ABV
Brewed by Hogs Back Brewery, Manor Farm, The Street, Tongham, Surrey GU10 1DE.
☎ *(01252) 783000.*
www.hogsback.co.uk
Colour: Oak-burgundy (17).
Head: Small creamy-coloured head with small bubbles.
Aroma: Sweet and alcoholic, like Christmas pudding.
Taste: Smooth thick caramel and molasses matures into liquorice then dries into thick caramel sweetness.
Ease of Decanting: Yeast stayed at the bottom of the bottle, the head was very small and the bottle was small which meant that it fit easily into my pint glass.
Opinion: A barley-wine style of beer, nice after dinner when appreciated like a fine port or brandy.

HOGS BACK BROOKLANDS GOLD STAR 4.5% ABV
Brewed by Hogs Back Brewery, Manor Farm, The Street, Tongham, Surrey GU10 1DE.
☎ *(01252) 783000.*
www.hogsback.co.uk
Colour: Brown (10).
Head: Small white head which rapidly disappeared.
Aroma: Fresh aromatic hops.
Taste: Appetite-sharpening peppery hops leading to a long fruity finish.
Ease of Decanting: Pretty easy to pour but watch out for the sediment.
Opinion: Great with pork pie and pickle.

HOGS BACK BSA (BURMA STAR ALE) 4.5% ABV
Brewed by Hogs Back Brewery, Manor Farm, The Street, Tongham, Surrey GU10 1DE.
☎ *(01252) 783000.*
www.hogsback.co.uk
Colour: Oak-burgundy (17).
Head: Stayed controllable, creamy white dense white bubbles.
Aroma: Subtle Ovaltine aroma, slightly fruity.
Taste: Subtle initial malt, fruit follows through, dries on the tongue, then bitter hops follow in a long aftertaste.
Ease of Decanting: Yeast stayed at the bottom of the bottle and the head can be created to whatever size is required.
Opinion: Nice beer with a cheese ploughman's.

HOGS BACK GARDENERS TIPPLE 4.2% ABV
Brewed by Hogs Back Brewery, Manor Farm, The Street, Tongham, Surrey GU10 1DE.
☎ *(01252) 783000.*
www.hogsback.co.uk
Colour: Dark amber (8).
Head: No head at all.
Aroma: Faint nose of appetising hops.
Taste: Appley freshness with clean bitterness and a short dry finish.
Ease of Decanting: Very easy due to lack of head.
Opinion: Excellent with a scotch egg and homemade pickles.

HOGS BACK OTT (OLD TONGHAM TASTY) 6.0% ABV
Brewed by Hogs Back Brewery, Manor Farm, The Street, Tongham, Surrey GU10 1DE.
☎ *(01252) 783000.*
www.hogsback.co.uk
Colour: Black with burgundy tints (20).
Head: Small head with brown, dense bubbles.
Aroma: Sweet liquorice aroma.
Taste: Frothy, strong liquorice flavour with hops drying on the tongue in a long aftertaste.
Ease of Decanting: Yeast clung to the base of the bottle and the head stayed small and controllable.
Opinion: Would go very nicely with liver and bacon.

HOGS BACK TEA (TRADITIONAL ENGLISH ALE) 4.2% ABV

Brewed by Hogs Back Brewery, Manor Farm, The Street, Tongham, Surrey GU10 1DE.
☎ (01252) 783000.
www.hogsback.co.uk
Colour: Orange-brown (10).
Head: Creamy-coloured small head which disappeared into the beer.
Aroma: Citrus zesty pear drops with a touch of blackcurrant.
Taste: Subtle and easy to drink with malt and subtle fruit flavours coming through then drying, then hops hit, then dry in the aftertaste.
Ease of Decanting: Yeast stayed at the bottom of the bottle and head stayed small, so nice and easy.
Opinion: An easy-to-drink bitter that would be a good thirst-quencher for a nice hot Indian curry.

HOGS BACK WOBBLE IN A BOTTLE 7.5% ABV

Brewed by Hogs Back Brewery, Manor Farm, The Street, Tongham, Surrey GU10 1DE.
☎ (01252) 783000.
www.hogsback.co.uk
Colour: Ruby-brown (13).
Head: Small head with small dense white bubbles.
Aroma: Citrus and slightly zesty.
Taste: Sweet caramel to start then develops into powerful bitter fruits leading to bitter lemon in a long drying aftertaste.
Ease of Decanting: Yeast clung to the bottom of the bottle and head stayed small, with the unusual 275 ml bottle, no problems to pour.
Opinion: A nice beer to sip and appreciate with roast pork and all the trimmings.

HOP BACK CROP CIRCLE 4.2% ABV

Brewed by Hop Back Brewery plc, Unit 22–24 Batten Road Industrial Estate, Downton, Salisbury, Wiltshire SP5 3HU.
☎ (01725) 510986.
www.hopback.co.uk
Colour: Straw (2).
Head: White dense small bubbles. Head stayed small and was controllable with care.
Aroma: Aroma of strong bitter lager hops with hints of elderflower.
Taste: Smooth and frothy with light berries changing to light fruit, turning slightly bitter in a short aftertaste.
Ease of Decanting: Yeast behaved impeccably and the head stayed small, though controlled with care, worth the effort.
Opinion: A light and refreshing thirst-quenching bitter, a godsend after a hot spicy curry.

HOP BACK SUMMER LIGHTNING 5.0% ABV

Brewed by Hop Back Brewery plc, Unit 22–24 Batten Road Industrial Estate, Downton, Salisbury, Wiltshire SP5 3HU.
☎ (01725) 510986.
www.hopback.co.uk
Colour: Pale straw (2).
Head: Small white head with small bubbles.
Aroma: Hard to describe, it reminded me of freshly mown hay.
Taste: Initial frothy sweetness dries to a fruit salad finish that dries with a slightly bitter aftertaste.
Ease of Decanting: Yeast swirls in the last quarter, so a steady hand is needed.
Opinion: A legendary beer, another good beer to enjoy with a good hot curry.

ICENI FINE SOFT DAY 4.0% ABV

Brewed by Iceni Brewery, 3 Foulden Road, Ickburgh, Mundford, Norfolk IP26 5HB.
☎ (01842) 878922.
www.icenibrewery.co.uk
Colour: Rich golden amber (8).
Head: White small bubble head that stayed controllable, sunk into beer.
Aroma: Damsons and unripe plums.
Taste: Smooth soft bitter fruits develop their bitterness then dry in a short bitter aftertaste.
Ease of Decanting: Easy to pour, yeast stayed at the bottom of the bottle.
Opinion: An easy-to-drink thirst-quencher that would cool the mouth after a fiery hot curry.

ICENI MEN OF NORFOLK 6.2% ABV

Brewed by Iceni Brewery, 3 Foulden Road, Ickburgh, Mundford, Norfolk IP26 5HB.
☎ (01842) 878922.
www.icenibrewery.co.uk
Colour: Black (20).
Head: A brown head with a mixture of small and large bubbles that was controllable by adjusting the height of the pour.
Aroma: Molasses and rich warm mince pie.
Taste: Blackcurrant and liquorice with bitter cherries coming through and drying on the back of the palate.
Ease of Decanting: A controllable head and yeast that stayed in the bottle, so an easy beer to pour.
Opinion: A nice robust ale that would go down nicely with steak and kidney pudding.

ICENI RED, WHITE AND BLUEBERRY 4.0% ABV

Brewed by Iceni Brewery, 3 Foulden Road, Ickburgh, Mundford, Norfolk IP26 5HB.
☎ (01842) 878922
www.icenibrewery.co.uk
Colour: Mid-brown (12).
Head: Small head with a mix of large and small white bubbles.
Aroma: Forest berries and fruits.
Taste: Thin initially, bitter and hoppy with delicate underlying fruit, hops zing on the taste buds then draw the juices in a long aftertaste.
Ease of Decanting: Yeast stayed where it should and the head stayed small, so nice and easy to pour.
Opinion: A nice easy-to-drink beer with a cheese ploughman's.

MAULDONS BLACK ADDER 5.3%

Brewed by Mauldons Ltd, The Black Adder Brewery, 13 Churchfield Road, Sudbury, Suffolk CO10 2YA.
☎ (01787) 311055.
www.mauldons.co.uk
Colour: Black (20).
Head: Small head with brown bubbles that disappeared into the beer.
Aroma: Rich fruity blackcurrant with hints of liquorice.
Taste: Smooth initially, then acrid charcoal and iron. Well conditioned, dry acrid creosote flavour dries in a long finish.
Ease of Decanting: Yeast clung to the base of the bottle and the head was small, so easy to pour.
Opinion: A strongly flavoured dark ale, would drink nicely with organic roast lamb with all the trimmings.

MAULDONS SUFFOLK PRIDE 4.8%

Brewed by Mauldons Ltd, The Black Adder Brewery, 13 Churchfield Road, Sudbury, Suffolk CO10 2YA.
☎ *(01787) 311055.*
www.mauldons.co.uk
Colour: Golden-orange (4).
Head: Small tight head with fine bubbles
Aroma: Fresh grassy hops.
Taste: Lots of fruit and tasty malt balanced by crisp hoppiness and a dry finish.
Ease of Decanting: An easy pour as the yeast stuck to the bottle.
Opinion: Try this refreshing yet full-bodied bitter with a Cheddar doorstep.

OAKLEAF EICHENBLATT BITTE 5.4% ABV

Brewed by Oakleaf Brewing Co. Ltd, 7 Mumby Road, Clarence Wharf Industrial Estate, Gosport, Hampshire PO12 1AJ.
☎ *(023) 9251 3222.*
www.oakleafbrewing.co.uk
Colour: Golden (8).
Head: Small white head with constant fine bubbles.
Aroma: Distinctive smoky nose with slightly earthy notes.
Taste: Refreshing wheat malt and peppery hops. Long dry smoky finish.
Ease of Decanting: Very easy to pour.
Opinion: Try this tasty wheat beer with some slices of smoked German sausage.

OAKLEAF HOLE HEARTED 4.7% ABV

Brewed by Oakleaf Brewing Co. Ltd, 7 Mumby Road, Clarence Wharf Industrial Estate, Gosport, Hampshire PO12 1AJ.
☎ *(023) 9251 3222.*
www.oakleafbrewing.co.uk
Colour: Light golden (6).
Head: Virtually no head.
Aroma: Flowery hops.
Taste: Fresh grapefruit flavour which is typical of American hop variety Cascade. Long, dry, hoppy finish.
Ease of Decanting: Very easy to pour.
Opinion: The perfect refresher with a creamy curry.

OAKLEAF I CAN'T BELIEVE IT'S NOT BITTER 4.9% ABV

Brewed by Oakleaf Brewing Co. Ltd, 7 Mumby Road, Clarence Wharf Industrial Estate, Gosport, Hampshire PO12 1AJ.
☎ *(023) 9251 3222.*
www.oakleafbrewing.co.uk
Colour: Light golden (6).
Head: Virtually no head.
Aroma: Very faint yeasty nose.
Taste: Clean, fresh and fruity with a short dry finish.
Ease of Decanting: Very easy to pour.
Opinion: Great with bacon quiche and salad.

ORGANIC BREWHOUSE LIZARD POINT 4.0% ABV

Brewed by The Organic Brewhouse, Cury Cross Lanes, Helston, Cornwall TR12 7AZ.
☎ *(01326) 241555.*
www.theorganicbrewhouse.com
Colour: Light golden brown (8).
Head: Large dense white head.
Aroma: Clean, fresh, zingy hops.
Taste: Tasty malt and appley fruit flavour with a long malt finish.
Ease of Decanting: Quite easy to pour.
Opinion: Perfect with a roast chicken salad.

ORGANIC BREWHOUSE SERPENTINE 4.5% ABV

Brewed by The Organic Brewhouse, Cury Cross Lanes, Helston, Cornwall TR12 7AZ.
☎ *(01326) 241555*
www.theorganicbrewhouse.com
Colour: Oak-burgundy (17).
Head: Small head with dense white bubbles.
Aroma: Glacé to bitter cherry with hot blackcurrant.
Taste: Marzipan and vanilla matures from sweetness to chocolate malt in the aftertaste, has a nice clean texture.
Ease of Decanting: Yeast stayed at the bottom of the bottle, the head stayed small, so nice and easy.
Opinion: Another of those fine beers that would go down nicely with a nice organic liver and bacon meal.

ORGANIC BREWHOUSE WOLF ROCK 5.0% ABV

Brewed by The Organic Brewhouse, Cury Cross Lanes, Helston, Cornwall TR12 7AZ.
☎ *(01326) 241555.*
www.theorganicbrewhouse.com
Colour: Ruby-brown (13).
Head: White small dense bubbled head.
Aroma: Sweet and fruity with pear drops coming through.
Taste: Smooth fruit initially leading through to pear-drop sweetness, then hop bitterness punching through and drying on the palate in a long bitter aftertaste.
Ease of Decanting: Unusually for bottle-conditioned beers, this comes in a clear bottle making it easy to see the yeast: there were swirls in the last quarter though the head was small, so an easy beer to pour.
Opinion: Organic bottle-conditioned beers are rare. Bottle-conditioning definitely improves organic beers as this was the best organic beer I have tasted and it would accompany cod and chips very nicely.

PITFIELD BREWERY ORGANIC PITFIELDS ECO WARRIOR 4.5% ABV

Brewed by Pitfield Brewery, Little Burchetts Farm, Isaacs Lane, Haywards Heath, West Sussex RH16 4RZ.
☎ *0845 8331492.*
www.pitfieldbeershop.co.uk
Colour: Rich golden amber (8).
Head: White dense bubbles in a small head.
Aroma: Pear drops, lemonade shandy, slightly lemony with a faint aroma of mushy bananas.
Taste: Sweet velvet taste of Caribbean fruit punch, then extreme fruit bitterness, sweet punch comes through near the end, then finishes with fresh fruity bitterness.
Ease of Decanting: Yeast stays at the bottom and the head is small, so nice and easy.
Opinion: An unusual beer that would go down nicely with coronation chicken.

PITFIELD BREWERY ORGANIC PITFIELD SHOREDITCH STOUT 4.0% ABV

Brewed by Pitfield Brewery, Little Burchetts Farm, Isaacs Lane, Haywards Heath, West Sussex RH16 4RZ.
☎ 0845 8331492.
www.pitfieldbeershop.co.uk
Colour: Black (20).
Head: Small head with brown small bubbles.
Aroma: Molasses and dark chocolate.
Taste: Bitter chocolate powder maturing to subtle bitter fruits in a short aftertaste.
Ease of Decanting: Yeast stayed at the bottom of the bottle and the head stayed small, so nice and easy to pour.
Opinion: A very clean-tasting stout, nice with a Melton Mowbray pork pie.

RCH FIREBOX 6.0% ABV

Brewed by RCH Brewery, West Hewish, Weston-super-Mare BS24 6RR.
☎ (01934) 834447.
www.rchbrewery.com
Colour: Ruby brown (13).
Head: Small tight head.
Aroma: Fresh hops and malt.
Taste: Lots of citrus fruit and bitter hops with a long, bitter, slightly roasted finish.
Ease of Decanting: Quite easy to pour.
Opinion: Perfect with steak and chips.

RCH OLD SLUG PORTER 4.5% ABV

Brewed by RCH Brewery, West Hewish, Weston-super-Mare, Somerset BS24 6RR.
☎ (01934) 834447.
www.rchbrewery.com
Colour: Rich burgundy (19).
Head: Medium head, light brown, dense small bubbles stayed throughout, clinging to the sides of the glass.
Aroma: Liquorice with toffee and blackcurrants.
Taste: Bitter fruits quickly lead to very slightly aniseed/liquorice and dark caramel, with sweetness slowly fading, giving a full mouth-feel.
Ease of Decanting: Yeast clung to the base of the bottle and head did not start feeding itself, so a nice easy-pouring ale.
Opinion: Fruity, yet well-balanced with a good finish. Nice beer with game pie or a good goulash.

RCH PITCHFORK 4.3% ABV

Brewed by RCH Brewery, West Hewish, Weston-super-Mare, Somerset BS24 6RR.
☎ (01934) 834447.
www.rchbrewery.com
Colour: Golden (10).
Head: Creamy dense head.
Aroma: Fresh fruit and malt.
Taste: Fresh fruity flavour which develops through to a lingering, bitter hop finish.
Ease of Decanting: Very easy to pour.
Opinion: Great with pasta in a mushroom sauce.

RINGWOOD FORTYNINER 4.9% ABV

Brewed by Ringwood Brewery Ltd, 138 Christchurch Road, Ringwood, Hampshire BH24 3AP.
☎ (01425) 471177.
www.ringwoodbrewery.co.uk
Colour: Orange-brown (10).
Head: Controllable white head with large and small bubbles.
Aroma: Faint aroma of fruity caramel.
Taste: Smooth initial taste, light fruit comes through and dries on the palate.
Ease of Decanting: Yeast stayed sticky and head was controllable, so an easy beer to decant.
Opinion: Surprisingly easy to drink for its strength, a nice beer with fish and chips.

RINGWOOD XXXX PORTER 4.7% ABV

Brewed by Ringwood Brewery Ltd, 138 Christchurch Road, Ringwood, Hampshire BH24 3AP.
☎ (01425) 471177.
www.ringwoodbrewery.co.uk
Colour: Black with deep burgundy hints in the light (20).
Head: Dense brown head which needs to be poured from height to create the desired head volume.
Aroma: Faint toffee and banana.
Taste: Creamy, light mouth-feel with sweet caramel and chocolate malt maturing into bitter hops developing long into the aftertaste.
Ease of Decanting: Nice easy-pouring ale with yeast that clings to the base of the bottle and a head that responds to what you like. For example, pour close to the glass for no head or pour from three inches for a large, rocky head – it's up to you.
Opinion: Lovely beer with a nice O'Hagan's sausage and mash.

SUTHWYK SKEW SUNSHINE ALE 4.6% ABV

Brewed by Suthwyk Ales, Offwell Farm, Southwick, Fareham, Hampshire PO17 6DX.
☎ (023) 9232 5252
www.suthwykales.com
Colour: Straw (2).
Head: White, dense bubbly large head.
Aroma: Slightly citrus with underlying forest fruit aromas.
Taste: Initial frothy mouth-feel gives way to a sweet malt taste with subtle fruit which matures on the roof of the mouth in a short aftertaste.
Ease of Decanting: Difficult unless kept in the fridge for an hour before pouring. Mine had a very large head and yeast swirls in the last quarter, so be careful. The taste is definitely worth the trouble.
Opinion: Lovely refreshing ale which would go down very well with a nice fresh baguette with ham off the bone and some English mustard.

TEIGNWORTHY BEACHCOMBER 4.5% ABV
(BOTTLE-CONDITIONED LAGER)
Brewed by Teignworthy Brewery, The Maltings, Teign Road, Newton Abbot, Devon TQ12 4AA.
☎ (01626) 332066.
www.teignworthybrewery.com
Colour: Amber (7).
Head: Stayed small, high pour to create the head, white dense bubbles.
Aroma: Fruit salad penny sweets.
Taste: Light bitter fruits maturing to delicate pears with bitter fruit drying the palate in a short aftertaste.
Ease of Decanting: Yeast clung to base of bottle and head controllable by height of pour, so nice and easy to pour.
Opinion: Unusually sweet for a lager but very tasty for it. Would drink nicely with fish and chips.

TEIGNWORTHY MALTSTERS ALE 4.5% ABV
Brewed by Teignworthy Brewery, The Maltings, Teign Road, Newton Abbot, Devon TQ12 4AA.
☎ (01626) 332066.
www.teignworthybrewery.com
Colour: Burgundy-brown (14).
Head: Small head with dense white bubbles.
Aroma: Pineapple with traces of zesty orange and kiwi fruit.
Taste: Bitter fruit developing to bitter cherry drying to a slightly burnt, long grapefruit aftertaste.
Ease of Decanting: Yeast clinging to the base of the bottle and the small head make this a nice easy beer to pour.
Opinion: Would accompany a nice game pie.

TITANIC CAPTAIN SMITH'S 5.2% ABV
Brewed by The Titanic Brewery, Unit 5 Callender Place, Lingard Street, Burslem, Stoke-on-Trent, Staffordshire ST6 1JL.
☎ (01782) 823447.
www.titanicbrewery.co.uk
Colour: Ruby-brown (13).
Head: White, large bubble head that disperses into the beer.
Aroma: Flowery and slightly acid hops.
Taste: Strong malt which continues though to a drying hoppy finish.
Ease of Decanting: Small head but tendrils to look out for in the last quarter require that all-important eagle eye.
Opinion: Nice beer to accompany beef cobbler.

TITANIC STOUT 4.5% ABV
Brewed by The Titanic Brewery, Unit 5 Callender Place, Lingard Street, Burslem, Stoke-on-Trent, Staffordshire ST6 1JL.
☎ (01782) 823447.
www.titanicbrewery.co.uk
Colour: Black with ruby hints in the light (20).
Head: Brown, dense bubbles in a medium-sized head.
Aroma: Dark chocolate and burnt caramel.
Taste: Initial chocolate malt and molasses maturing into bitter chocolate with full smooth mouth-feel, then hop bitterness maturing on the back of the tongue, balancing the chocolate in a long bitter aftertaste.
Ease of Decanting: A very easy pour.
Opinion: Strongly flavoured stout with long bitter aftertaste, a very nice accompaniment to a strong Cheddar ploughman's.

VALE BREWERY BLACK BEAUTY PORTER 4.3% ABV
Brewed by Vale Brewery Co. Ltd, Tramway Business Park, Ludgershall Road, Brill, Buckinghamshire HP18 9TY.
☎ (01844) 239237.
www.valebrewery.co.uk
Colour: Black (20).
Head: Small with dense brown bubbles that disappeared into the beer leaving a brown cream meniscus.
Aroma: Rich plum and autumn fruit.
Taste: Surprisingly light initial taste, delicate malt comes through with hops that dry to a blackberry bitter fruit taste, with residual sweetness countering the bitterness.
Ease of Decanting: Small head and yeast clinging to the base of the bottle making this nice and easy to pour.
Opinion: Lovely beer to drink with a beef hotpot.

VALE BREWERY BLACK SWAN DARK MILD 3.9% ABV
Brewed by Vale Brewery Co. Ltd, Tramway Business Park, Ludgershall Road, Brill, Buckinghamshire HP18 9TY.
☎ (01844) 239237.
www.valebrewery.co.uk
Colour: Dark brown to black (20).
Head: Brown head was created by pouring from height, stayed small.
Aroma: A subtle fruity with acetate tones.
Taste: Thin bitter taste initially, subtle aftertaste of drying chocolate malt.
Ease of Decanting: Yeast stayed at the bottom and the head needed creating, so no problems with this beer.
Opinion: Would go down nicely with steak and kidney pudding.

VALE BREWERY GRUMPLING ALE 4.6% ABV
Brewed by Vale Brewery Co. Ltd, Tramway Business Park, Ludgershall Road, Brill, Buckinghamshire HP18 9TY.
☎ (01844) 239237.
www.valebrewery.co.uk
Colour: Orange-brown (10).
Head: Small head with dense white bubbles.
Aroma: Subtle aroma of blackcurrant and pears.
Taste: Subtle initial flavour, smooth, slightly fruity blackberry malt, fruity bitterness zings on the sides of the tongue.
Ease of Decanting: A nice easy beer to pour, with the head staying small and the yeast staying at the bottom of the bottle.
Opinion: Goes down well with a cheese ploughman's and sweet pickle.

WELTONS OLD COCKY 4.3% ABV
Brewed by Weltons Brewery Ltd, 1 Mulberry Trading Estate, Foundry Lane, Horsham, West Sussex RH13 5PX.
☎ (01403) 251873.
www.weltonsbeer.com
Colour: Amber (6).
Head: Virtually no head.
Aroma: Fresh green fruit and hops.
Taste: Fresh hops and subdued malt with a long, delicate, dry finish.
Ease of Decanting: A relatively easy pour but some care is required to get a clear pint.
Opinion: Perfect with a cheese and onion doorstep.

WELTONS OLD HARRY 5.2% ABV
Brewed by Weltons Brewery Ltd, 1 Mulberry Trading Estate, Foundry Lane, Horsham, West Sussex RH13 5PX.
☎ *(01403) 251873.*
www.weltonsbeer.com
Colour: Chestnut (11).
Head: Small white head which gradually disappeared.
Aroma: Rich, malty fruit with hints of spirit.
Taste: Lots of tasty hops and rich malt leading to a complex, satisfying finish.
Ease of Decanting: Quite easy to pour.
Opinion: Great with beef stew and dumplings.

WELTONS PRIDE 'N' JOY 2.8% ABV
Brewed by Weltons Brewery Ltd, 1 Mulberry Trading Estate, Foundry Lane, Horsham, West Sussex RH13 5PX.
☎ *(01403) 251873.*
www.weltonsbeer.com
Colour: Golden (6).
Head: Small head which gradually disappeared.
Aroma: Subtle hops.
Taste: Fresh spicy hops and dry malt and a long dry finish.
Ease of Decanting: Very easy. Only a small amount of beer left in the bottle.
Opinion: Lots of flavour considering the low strength. Excellent with a light lunchtime snack.

WELTONS SUSSEX PRIDE 4% ABV
Brewed by Weltons Brewery Ltd, 1 Mulberry Trading Estate, Foundry Lane, Horsham, West Sussex RH13 5PX.
☎ *(01403) 251873.*
www.weltonsbeer.com
Colour: Brown (10).
Head: Dense white head.
Aroma: Rich malt and peppery hops.
Taste: Refreshing dry hops. Good malt balance and a clean dry finish.
Ease of Decanting: Some care is required as my bottle was a little bit explosive but it settled down after a few minutes.
Opinion: Perfect with a good ham sandwich.

WESTERHAM BRITISH BULLDOG 4.3% ABV
Brewed by Westerham Brewery Co, Grange Farm, Pootings Road, Crockham Hill, Edenbridge, Kent TN8 6SA.
☎ *(01732) 864427.*
www.westerhambrewery.co.uk
Colour: Dark amber (8).
Head: Small white head with fine bubbles.
Aroma: Faint nose of grassy hops.
Taste: Peppery, spicy hops balanced with subtle malt and a short hoppy finish.
Ease of Decanting: Quite easy beer to pour, although the yeast lifted a little.
Opinion: Would go nicely with gammon, egg and chips.

WICKWAR BOB 4.0% ABV
Brewed by Wickwar Brewery Co., The Old Brewery, Station Road, Wickwar, Gloucestershire GL12 8NB.
☎ *0870 7775671.*
www.wickwarbrewing.co.uk
Colour: Orange-brown (10).
Head: Small white head.
Aroma: Appetising malt.
Taste: Slightly dry fruit balanced with hops and a long, dry finish.
Ease of Decanting: Easy to pour.
Opinion: A perfect partner for a cheese doorstep.

WICKWAR MR PERRETTS TRADITIONAL STOUT 5.9% ABV
Brewed by Wickwar Brewery Co., The Old Brewery, Station Road, Wickwar, Gloucestershire GL12 8NB.
☎ *0870 7775671.*
www.wickwarbrewing.co.uk
Colour: Very dark brown (18).
Head: Dark dense head.
Aroma: Coffee and chocolate.
Taste: Bitter chocolate and dark tasty malt.
Ease of Decanting: Pour carefully due to colour.
Opinion: Great with Stilton and biscuits.

WOLF BREWERY GRANNY WOULDN'T LIKE IT 4.8% ABV
Brewed by The Wolf Brewery, 10 Maurice Gaymer Road, Attleborough, Norfolk NR17 2QZ.
☎ *(01953) 457775.*
www.wolf-brewery.ltd.uk
Colour: Rich burgundy (19).
Head: White, dense head that stayed small.
Aroma: Subtle sweet aroma of cinnamon.
Taste: Bitter fruits dry to rich malt leading to a bitter slightly metallic hop aftertaste.
Ease of Decanting: No problem decanting this beer, yeast stayed where you want it (at the bottom of the bottle) and the head stayed small.
Opinion: A nice thirst-quencher after a hot chilli con carne.

WOODFORDE'S NORFOLK NOG 4.6% ABV
Brewed by Woodforde's Norfolk Ales, Broadland Brewery, Slad Lane, Woodbastwick, Norwich NR13 6SW.
☎ *(01603) 720353.*
www.woodfordes.co.uk
Colour: Black with burgundy hints (20).
Head: Small head made of small dense brown bubbles.
Aroma: Caramel and molasses with black treacle.
Taste: Smooth mouth-feel initially, then bitter cherries come through, then dry to a slightly warming aftertaste.
Ease of Decanting: Easy-pouring beer, yeast staying at the bottom of the bottle.
Opinion: Would possibly complement a roast beef ploughman's.

WOODFORDE'S WHERRY 3.8% ABV
Brewed by Woodforde's Norfolk Ales, Broadland Brewery, Slad Lane, Woodbastwick, Norwich NR13 6SW.
☎ *(01603) 720353.*
www.woodfordes.co.uk
Colour: Rich golden amber (8).
Head: Small head made of dense white bubbles.
Aroma: Spice and fruits ranging from grapefruit to lemon.
Taste: Initial cream soda and vanilla, smooth and slightly prickly becoming slightly tart with subtle burnt toffee tempered by vanilla. The aftertaste is bitter and slightly cidery with bitter grapefruit drying and slightly furring the sides of the tongue.
Ease of Decanting: Yeast stayed at the bottom and the head stayed small, so no problems pouring this beer.
Opinion: A complex beer for its strength, a good thirst-quencher as well so would be a welcome alternative to lager after a hot Indian curry.

Please send us your experience of pubs featured in the guide and information on new pubs you feel are worthy of an entry. You can write, fax or e-mail.

Send the form to: The Real Ale Pub Guide, W. Foulsham & Co. Ltd,
The Oriel, Thames Valley Court, 183–187 Bath Road,
Slough, Berkshire SL1 4AA, England

Fax it to: 01753 535003

E-mail the details to: realale@foulsham.com

Pub name: _____   Already in   Yes ☐
Address: _____   the guide?   No ☐
_____

Comments: _____
_____
_____
_____

Your name: _____
Your address: _____
_____ Tel: _____

Pub name: _____   Already in   Yes ☐
Address: _____   the guide?   No ☐
_____

Comments: _____
_____
_____
_____

Your name: _____
Your address: _____
_____ Tel: _____

Pub name: _____
Address: _____   Already in   Yes ☐
_____ the guide?   No ☐

Comments: _____
_____
_____
_____

Your name: _____
Your address: _____
Tel:

QUESTIONNAIRE

Please send us your experience of pubs featured in the guide and information on new pubs you feel are worthy of an entry. You can write, fax or e-mail.

Send the form to: The Real Ale Pub Guide, W. Foulsham & Co. Ltd, The Oriel, Thames Valley Court, 183–187 Bath Road, Slough, Berkshire SL1 4AA, England

Fax it to: 01753 535003

E-mail the details to: realale@foulsham.com

Pub name: _____ Already in Yes ☐
Address: _____ the guide? No ☐

Comments: _____

_____

_____

_____

Your name: _____
Your address: _____

_____ Tel: _____

Pub name: _____ Already in Yes ☐
Address: _____ the guide? No ☐

Comments: _____

_____

_____

_____

Your name: _____
Your address: _____

_____ Tel: _____

Pub name: _____ Already in Yes ☐
Address: _____ the guide? No ☐

Comments: _____

_____

_____

_____

Your name: _____
Your address: _____

Tel: